Iron and Blood

Iron and Blood

*A Military History of the
German-Speaking Peoples
since 1500*

PETER H. WILSON

The Belknap Press of
Harvard University Press
Cambridge, Massachusetts
2023

Printed in the United States of America

First published in the United Kingdom by Allen Lane, an imprint of
Penguin Books, Penguin Random House, 2022

Set in 10.2/13.87 pt Sabon LT Std
Typeset by Jouve (UK), Milton Keynes

First Harvard University Press edition, 2023
Cataloging-in-Publication data is available from the Library of Congress
ISBN 978-0-674-98762-3

For Rosie

Contents

CONTENTS

PART IV
Nationalizing War

PART V
Democratizing War

List of Illustrations

20. Troops of the Austro-Hungary Railway and Telegraph Regiment, 1895. Painting by Oskar Brüch, 1895–6. Heeresgeschichtliches Museum – Militärhistorisches Institut, Vienna (Nr. 25322/2012). (Photo: copyright © Heeresgeschichtliches Museum, Vienna)

21. Austro-Hungarian dreadnoughts SMS *Prince Eugen, Szent Istvan, Tegetthoff*, and *Viribus Unitis*. Photograph, *c.* 1889–1918. Heeres-geschichtliches Museum – Militärhistorisches Institut, Vienna (Nr. 3535/2019). (Photo: copyright © Heeresgeschichtliches Museum, Vienna)

22. Škoda arms factory, Pilsen, showing 30.5 cm mortars awaiting delivery. Photograph, *c.* 1916–18. (Photo: Škoda Photo Collection, Státní Oblastní Archiv v Plzni, Pilsen (ref. SOAP / 02-78 / 2022-3))

23. Stormtroopers awaiting the signal to attack on the Western Front. Photograph, 1917. (Photo: Chronicle/Alamy)

24. Freikorps troops with a captured British tank, Berlin. Photograph, 1919. Collectie Spaarnestad / *Het Leven*, Nationaal Archief, The Hague. (Photo: Nationaal Archief / Spaarnestad Photo / Bridgeman Images)

25. A lieutenant and cycle messenger of the Tirolean Feldjäger, 1934. Lithograph from the series *Adjustireung und Ausrüstung des Österreichischen Bundesheeres*, 1918–38. Heeresgeschichtliches Museum – Militärhistorisches Institut, Vienna (Nr. 9876/2015). (Photo: copyright © Heeresgeschichtliches Museum, Vienna)

26. German Junkers Ju87 'Stuka' dive bombers over Poland. Photo-graph, 1939. (Photo: Scherl / Süddeutsche Zeitung Photo / Alamy)

27. German soldiers fire a MG34 machine gun from a window sill on the Russian front. Photograph, 1942. (Photo: Michael Cremin / Alamy)

28. German infantry and armoured vehicles entering a village on the Moscow front, Russia. Photograph, 1941. (Photo: Shawshots / Alamy)

29. Members of the German Wehrmacht's Free India Legion, during training for duties on the Atlantic Wall. Photograph, *c.* 1943. (Photo: Hulton Archive / Keystone / Stringer / Getty Images)

30. Russian auxiliary 'Hiwis' dig out a motorized column, Ukraine. Photograph, 1941. (Photo: akg-images)

31. Female Wehrmacht signals personnel in occupied France. Photograph, 1940. (Photo: Bundesarchiv, Koblenz (Bild 101I-768-0147-19))

List of Maps

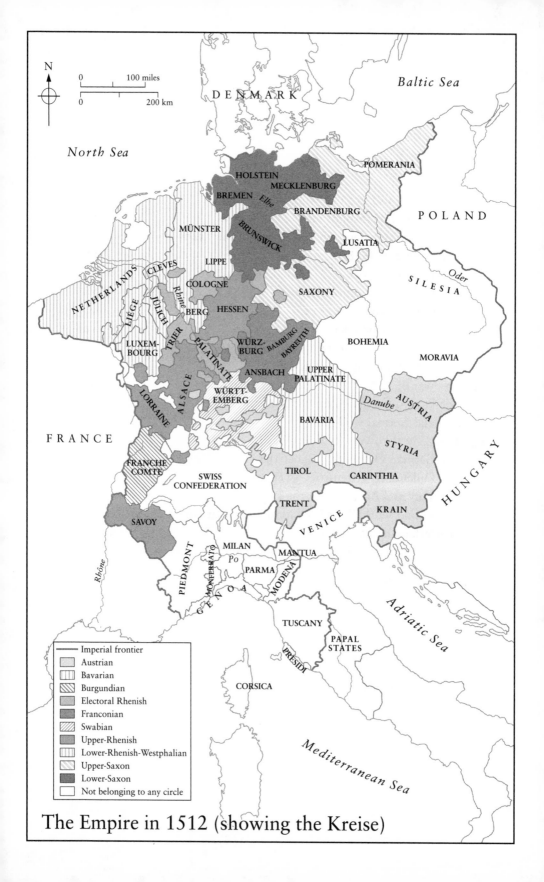

The Empire in 1512 (showing the Kreise)

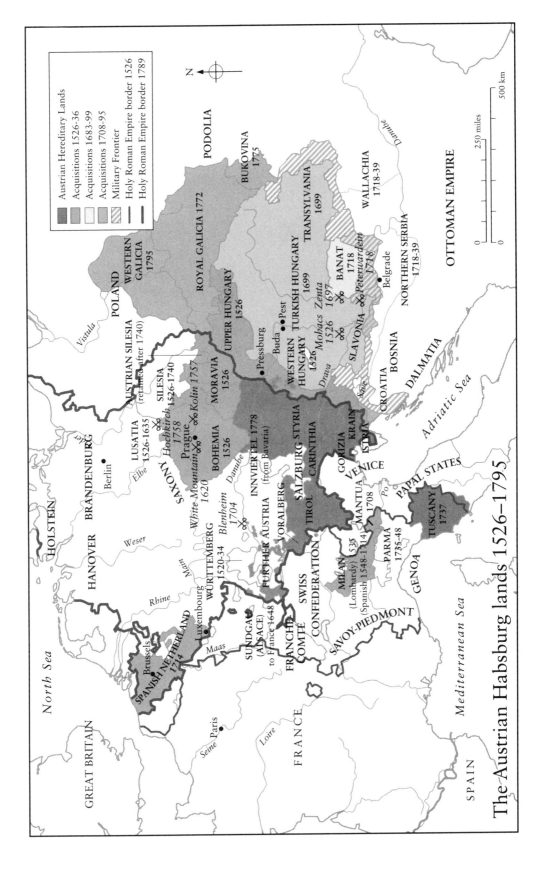

The Austrian Habsburg lands 1526–1795

Legend:
- Austrian Hereditary Lands
- Acquisitions 1526–36
- Acquisitions 1683–99
- Acquisitions 1708–95
- Military Frontier
- Holy Roman Empire border 1526
- Holy Roman Empire border 1789

N

500 km
250 miles
0

GREAT BRITAIN

North Sea

HOLSTEIN

HANOVER

BRANDENBURG
Berlin

POLAND

Vistula

Oder

Elbe

Weser

Main

Rhine

Seine

Paris

Loire

FRANCE

SUNDGAU (ALSACE)
to France 1648

FRANCHE COMTÉ

SWISS CONFEDERATION

SAVOY-PIEDMONT

GENOA

Mediterranean Sea

SPAIN

SPANISH NETHERLAND 1714
Brussels
Luxembourg
Maas

WÜRTTEMBERG 1520-34

Blenheim 1704

FURTHER AUSTRIA

VORALBERG

TIROL

MILAN (Lombardy) (Spanish 1548-1714) 1535

PARMA 1735-48

MANTUA 1708

Po

TUSCANY 1737

PAPAL STATES

VENICE

Adriatic Sea

LUSATIA 1526-1635

SAXONY

White Mountain 1620
Prague
Hochkirch 1758
Kolin 1757
BOHEMIA 1526

Silesia 1526-1740

AUSTRIAN SILESIA (retained after 1740)

MORAVIA 1526

Danube

INNVIERTEL 1778 (from Bavaria)

SALZBURG STYRIA

CARINTHIA

GORIZIA KRAIN ISTVA

CROATIA

BOSNIA

DALMATIA

WESTERN GALICIA 1795

ROYAL GALICIA 1772

PODOLIA

BUKOVINA 1775

UPPER HUNGARY 1526

Pressburg
Buda Pest

WESTERN HUNGARY 1526

Drava

Mohacs 1526

Drava

WESTERN HUNGARY 1526

TURKISH HUNGARY 1699

TRANSYLVANIA 1699

WALLACHIA 1718-39

Zenta 1697

BANAT 1718

Peterwardein 1718

SLAVONIA 1699

Save

Belgrade

NORTHERN SERBIA 1718-39

Danube

OTTOMAN EMPIRE

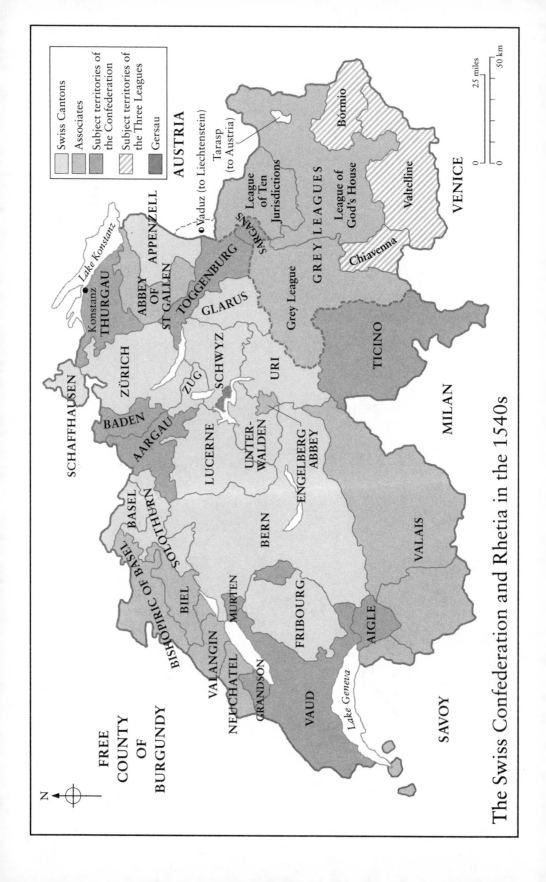

The Swiss Confederation and Rhetia in the 1540s

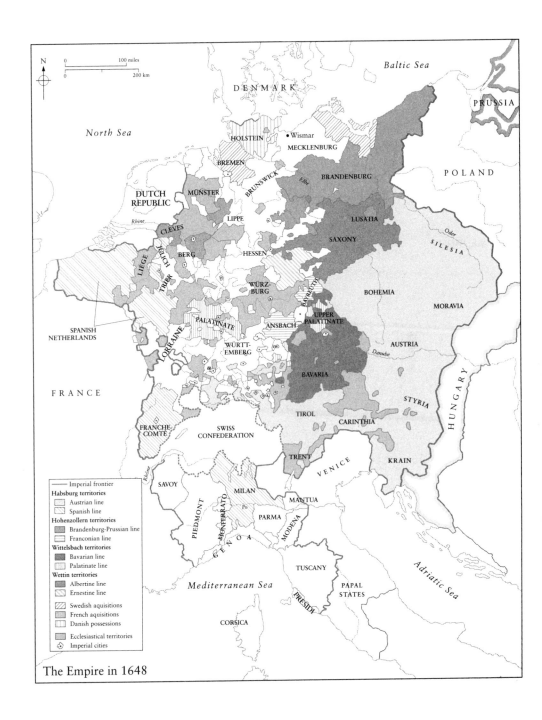

The Empire in 1648

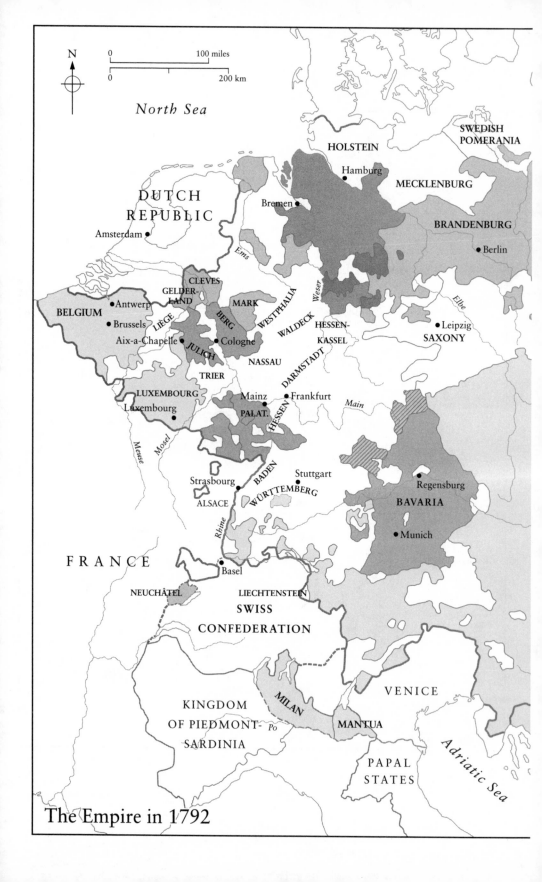

The Empire in 1792

Baltic Sea

PRUSSIA

	Habsburg
	Hohenzollern Franconian branch
	Wittelsbach Zweibrücken branch
	Hanover (Electoral branch)
	Brunswick (Ducal branch)
——	Boundary of the Empire
– –	Fief of the Empire
····	Boundary of extra-imperial possessions

POLISH-LITHUANIAN
COMMONWEALTH

Vistula

Oder

SILESIA

BOHEMIA

AUSTRIA

Danube

● Vienna

HUNGARY

Save

The End of the Empire in 1806

Map labels:

SWEDEN

Baltic Sea

KINGDOM OF DENMARK

North Sea

Swedish Pomerania

Holstein

Mecklenburg

KINGDOM OF HOLLAND

Olden-burg

P R U S S I A

Elbe

Vistula

Grand Duchy of Berg

Grand Duchy of Hessen

Electorate of Hessen-Kassel

Electorate of Saxony

Oder

Grand Duchy of Nassau

Saxon Duchies

Electorate of Würzburg

Bohemia

Austrian Silesia

Moldau

Moravia

AUSTRIAN EMPIRE

F R E N C H   E M P I R E

Rhine

Grand Duchy of Baden

① Kingdom of Württemberg

②

Kingdom of Bavaria

Hungary

Danube

③

HELVETIC REPUBLIC

Austria

Styria

Salzburg

Tirol

Carinthia

Drau

Krain

KINGDOM OF ITALY

Po

Adriatic Sea

Save

OTTOMAN EMPIRE

Mediterranean Sea

0   100 miles
0   200 km

	Principality of Aschaffenburg (Dalberg)
	Principality of Aremberg
	Counties of Salm-Salm + Salm Kyburg
	Principality of Isenburg-Birstein
	Confederation of the Rhine (July 1806)
	Imperial city territories
①	Pricipality of Von der Leyen
②	Principalities of Hohenzollern-Hechingen and Hohenzollern-Sigmaringen
③	Principality of Liechtenstein
—	Border of the Holy Roman Empire

The End of the Empire in 1806

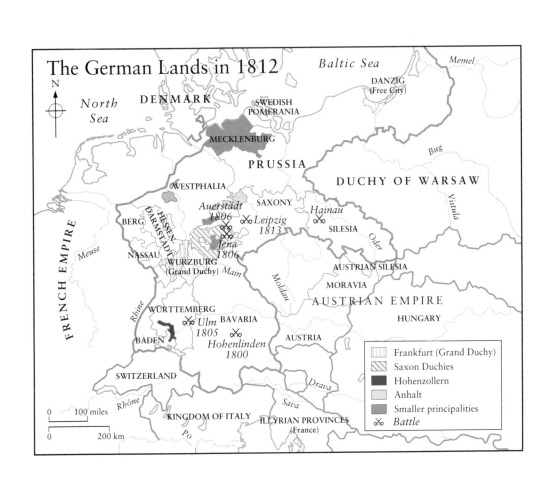

The German Lands in 1812

North Sea

Baltic Sea

Memel

DENMARK

SWEDISH POMERANIA

DANZIG (Free City)

MECKLENBURG

PRUSSIA

DUCHY OF WARSAW

Bug

WESTPHALIA

SAXONY

Auerstädt 1806

Hainau

Leipzig 1813

Vistula

SILESIA

Oder

FRENCH EMPIRE

BERG

HESSEN-DARMSTADT

NASSAU

Meuse

Jena 1806

WÜRZBURG (Grand Duchy)

Main

AUSTRIAN SILESIA

MORAVIA

Moldau

AUSTRIAN EMPIRE

WÜRTTEMBERG

BAVARIA

HUNGARY

Rhine

Ulm 1805

BADEN

Hohenlinden 1800

AUSTRIA

SWITZERLAND

Drava

Rhône

Sava

0   100 miles

0   200 km

KINGDOM OF ITALY

Po

ILLYRIAN PROVINCES (France)

Frankfurt (Grand Duchy)
Saxon Duchies
Hohenzollern
Anhalt
Smaller principalities
⚔ Battle

The German Confederation 1815–66

N

0   100 miles
0   200 km

DENMARK

MECKLENBURG-
STRELITZ

LITHUANIA

Memel

HOLSTEIN AND
LAUENBURG   Lübeck

NETHERLANDS

Hamburg

MECKLENBURG-
SCHWERIN

RUSSIAN EMPIRE

Vistula

Bremen

LIMBURG   OLDENBURG
(to the   HANOVER
confederation
1839)

Elbe

Berlin

PRUSSIA

CONGRESS
OF POLAND

LIPPE

BRUNSWICK

ANHALT

Oder

REPUBLIC OF CRACOW
(to AUSTRIA 1846)

BELGIUM

WALDECK

KURHESSEN

SAXONY

Moldau

GALICIA

NASSAU
Frankfurt

HESSEN-DARMSTADT

THURINGIAN
STATES

Main

BOHEMIA

to
Belgium
1839

PALATINE
(BAVARIA)

BAVARIA

LUXEMBOURG

WÜRTTEMBERG

AUSTRIAN EMPIRE

Danube

HUNGARY

FRANCE

BADEN

SWISS
CONFEDERATION

PIEDMONT

LOMBARDY
(to PIEDMONT
1859)

VENETO

ITALY

Prussian kingdom
German Confederation Frontier

MILITARY FRONTIER

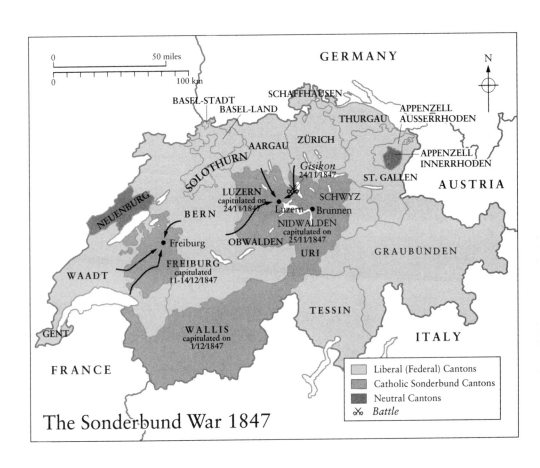

The Sonderbund War 1847

Legend:
- Liberal (Federal) Cantons
- Catholic Sonderbund Cantons
- Neutral Cantons
- ✄ Battle

Map labels:

0 — 50 miles
0 — 100 km

GERMANY

N

BASEL-STADT
BASEL-LAND
SCHAFFHAUSEN
AARGAU
THURGAU
APPENZELL AUSSERRHODEN
ZÜRICH
SOLOTHURN
APPENZELL INNERRHODEN
Gisikon 24/11/1847
ST. GALLEN
AUSTRIA
NEUENBURG
BERN
LUZERN capitulated on 24/11/1847
Luzern
SCHWYZ
Brunnen
NIDWALDEN capitulated on 25/11/1847
Freiburg
OBWALDEN
URI
GRAUBÜNDEN
WAADT
FREIBURG capitulated 11-14/12/1847
TESSIN
GENT
WALLIS capitulated on 1/12/1847
ITALY
FRANCE

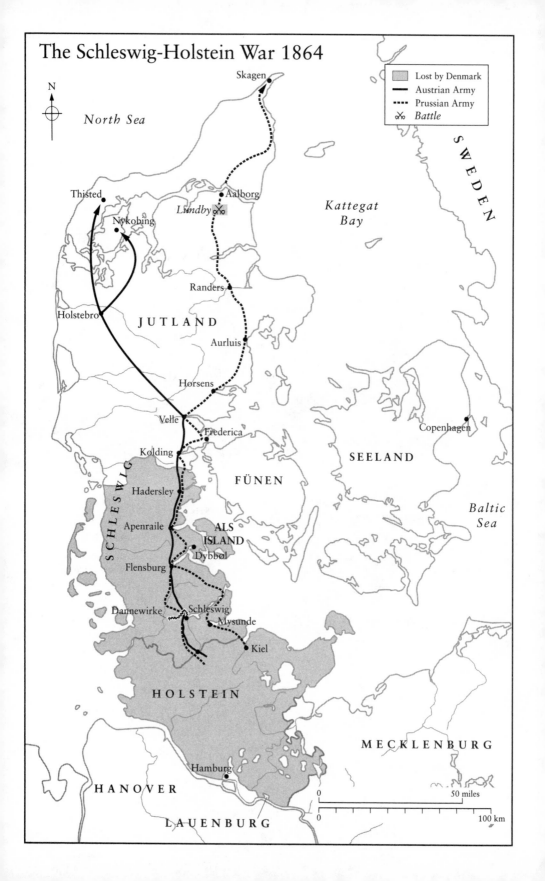

The Schleswig-Holstein War 1864

N

North Sea

Skagen

Kattegat Bay

S W E D E N

Thisted

Nykobing

Aalborg

Lundby ✂

Holstebro

J U T L A N D

Randers

Aurluis

Horsens

Velle

Frederica

Copenhagen

S E E L A N D

Kolding

F Ü N E N

Hadersley

Apenraile

ALS ISLAND

Dybbol

Baltic Sea

Flensburg

Dannewirke

Schleswig

Mysunde

Kiel

S C H L E S W I G

H O L S T E I N

M E C K L E N B U R G

Hamburg

H A N O V E R

L A U E N B U R G

	Lost by Denmark
	Austrian Army
	Prussian Army
✂	*Battle*

0   50 miles

0   100 km

The War of 1866

Legend:
- Prussia/Allies
- Austria/Allies
- Under Prussian administration 1865
- Under Austrian administration 1865
- H-D Hessen-Darmstadt
- H-K Hessen-Kassel
- ⚔ Battle
- ← Prussia/Allies Army
- ⇐ Austria/Allies Army

Labels on map:

SWEDEN
DENMARK
North Sea
SCHLESWIG
Kiel
HOLSTEIN
Lübeck
LAUENBURG
MECKLENBURG
EASTERN POMERANIA
Hamburg
Bremen
OLDENBURG
Elbe
Oder
Berlin
Hanover
Magdeburg
Langensalza
Gotha
WESTPHALIA
Kassel
Erfurt
SILESIA
Dresden
Gitschin
Breslau
Cologne
H-K
Weimar
Hühnerwasser
Sadowa
RHINELAND
H-D
Dermbach
Königgrätz
Frankfurt
Kissingen
Prague
Laufach-Aschaffenburg
Darmst
Rossbrunn
BOHEMIA
Tauber-Bischofsheim
Nuremberg
Nikolsburg
WÜRTTEMBERG
FRANCE
Stuttgart
BAVARIA
Rhine
Wien
Blumenau
BADEN
Munich
Vienna
Zurich
SWITZERLAND
TYROL
Badgastein
Drava
Sava
ROMANIA
VENETO
Versa
Verona
Trieste
Peschiera
Custoza
Venice
Po
Mantua
KINGDOM OF SERBS, CROATS AND SLOVENES
Legnago
Lissa
ITALY
Mediterranean Sea

0   100 miles
0   200 km

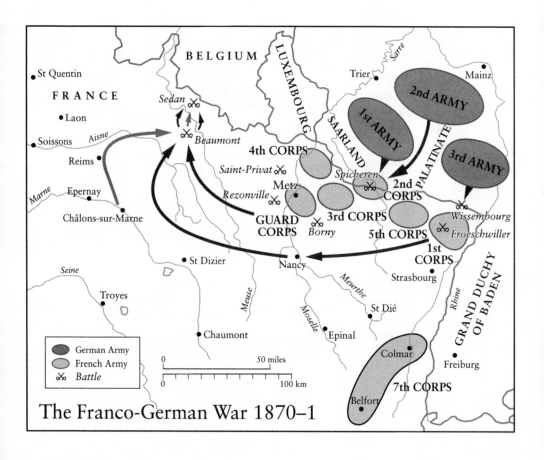

St Quentin

FRANCE

BELGIUM

LUXEMBOURG

Sarre

Trier

Mainz

Laon

Sedan

2nd ARMY

Soissons

Aisne

Beaumont

1st ARMY

Reims

4th CORPS

SAARLAND

3rd ARMY

Marne

Epernay

Saint-Privat

Spicheren

PALATINATE

Châlons-sur-Marne

Rezonville

Metz

2nd
CORPS

GUARD
CORPS

3rd CORPS

Wissembourg

Borny

5th CORPS

Froeschwiller

1st
CORPS

Seine

St Dizier

Nancy

Meurthe

Strasbourg

GRAND DUCHY
OF BADEN

Troyes

Meuse

St Dié

Rhine

Moselle

Epinal

Chaumont

Colmar

Freiburg

German Army

7th CORPS

French Army

Belfort

✗ Battle

0

50 miles

0

100 km

The Franco-German War 1870–1

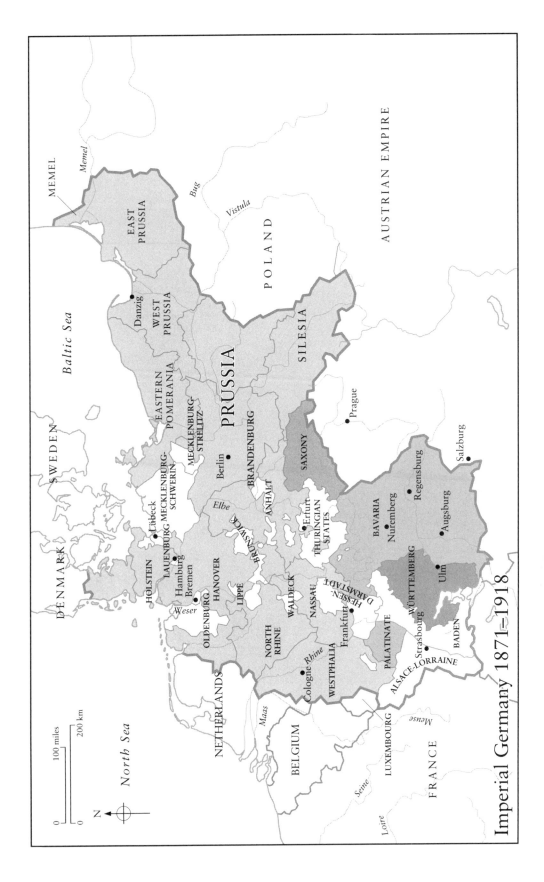

Imperial Germany 1871–1918

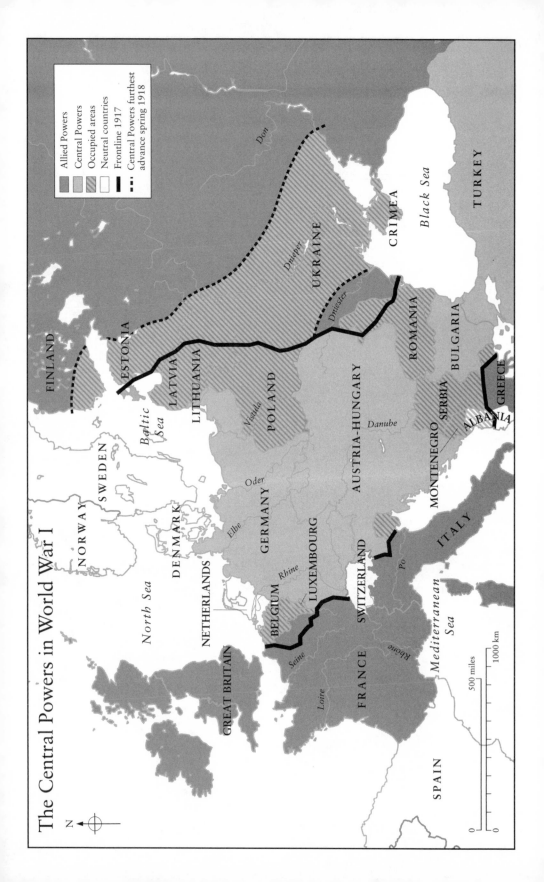

The Central Powers in World War I

N

Allied Powers
Central Powers
Occupied areas
Neutral countries
Frontline 1917
Central Powers furthest
advance spring 1918

FINLAND

Don

UKRAINE

Dnieper

CRIMEA

Black Sea

TURKEY

ESTONIA

LATVIA

LITHUANIA

Dniester

ROMANIA

BULGARIA

Baltic
Sea

Vistula

POLAND

AUSTRIA-HUNGARY

Danube

SERBIA

MONTENEGRO

GREECE

ALBANIA

SWEDEN

NORWAY

DENMARK

Oder

Elbe

GERMANY

LUXEMBOURG

SWITZERLAND

Po

ITALY

North Sea

Rhine

BELGIUM

NETHERLANDS

GREAT BRITAIN

Seine

FRANCE

Rhône

Mediterranean
Sea

Loire

500 miles

1000 km

SPAIN

0

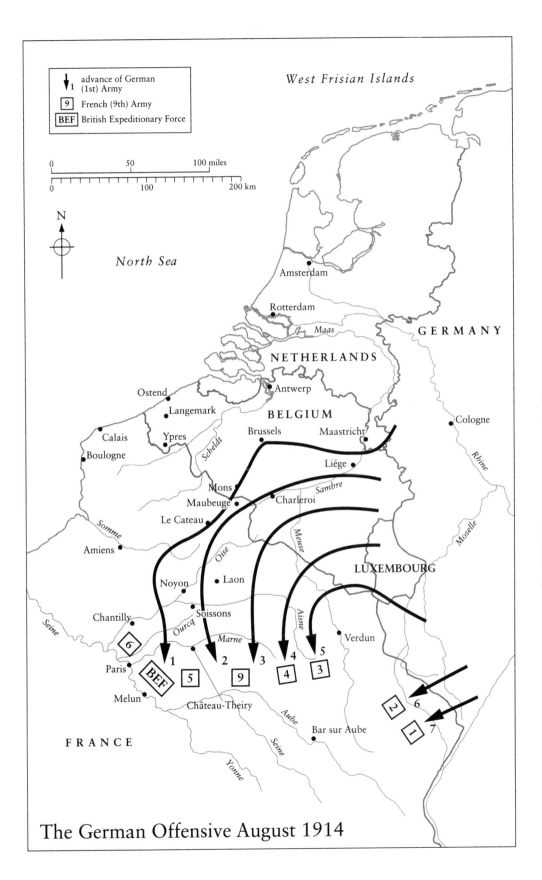

The German Offensive August 1914

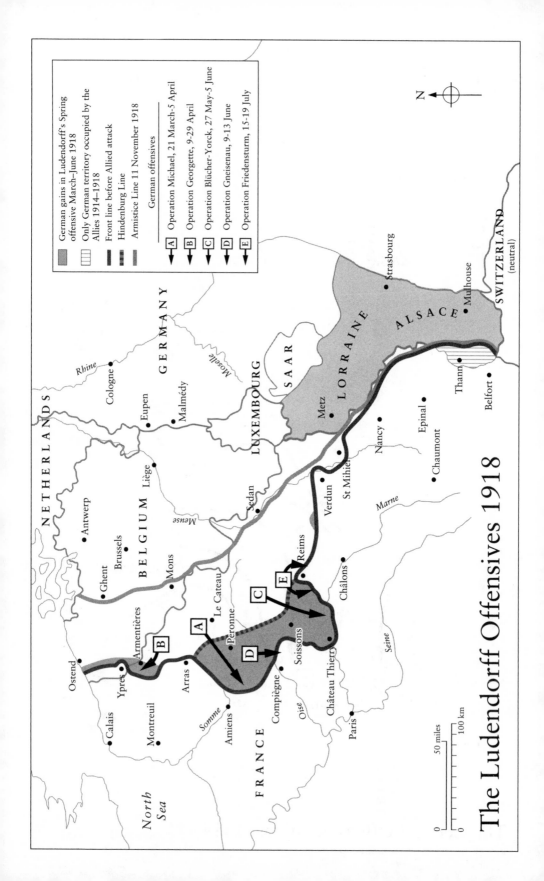

The Ludendorff Offensives 1918

German gains in Ludendorff's Spring
offensive March–June 1918

Only German territory occupied by the
Allies 1914–1918

Front line before Allied attack

Hindenburg Line

Armistice Line 11 November 1918

German offensives

A Operation Michael, 21 March–5 April

B Operation Georgette, 9–29 April

C Operation Blücher-Yorck, 27 May–5 June

D Operation Gneisenau, 9–13 June

E Operation Friedensturm, 15–19 July

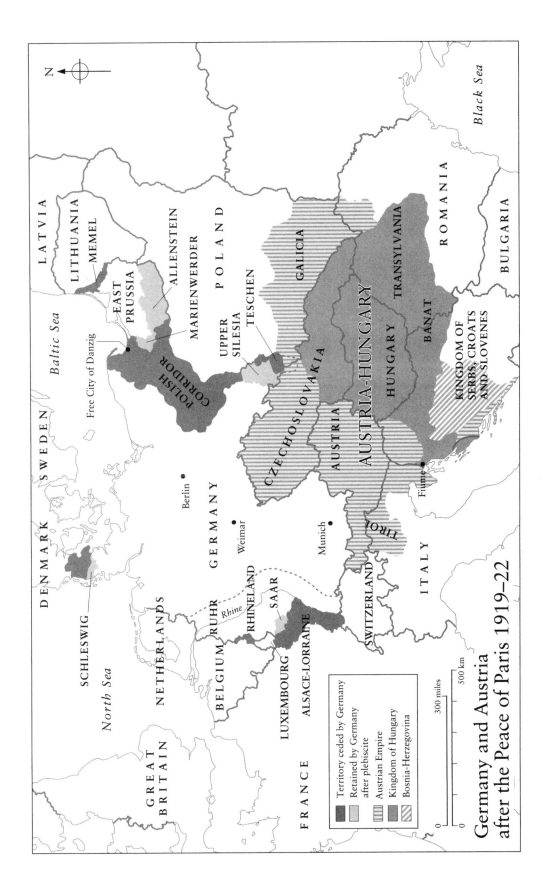

Germany and Austria
after the Peace of Paris 1919–22

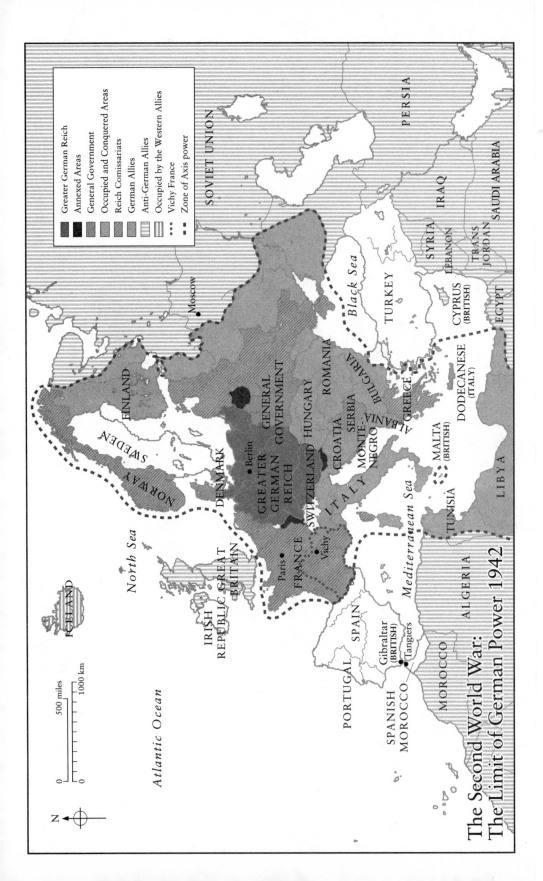

The Second World War:
The Limit of German Power 1942

Greater German Reich
Annexed Areas
General Government
Occupied and Conquered Areas
Reich Comissariats
German Allies
Anti-German Allies
Occupied by the Western Allies
Vichy France
Zone of Axis power

ICELAND

Atlantic Ocean

North Sea

IRISH REPUBLIC

GREAT BRITAIN

NORWAY

SWEDEN

FINLAND

DENMARK

Berlin

GREATER GERMAN REICH

GENERAL GOVERNMENT

SOVIET UNION

Moscow

Paris

FRANCE

Vichy

SWITZERLAND

HUNGARY

ITALY

CROATIA

SERBIA

MONTE-NEGRO

ROMANIA

BULGARIA

ALBANIA

GREECE

Black Sea

TURKEY

Mediterranean Sea

MALTA (BRITISH)

DODECANESE (ITALY)

CYPRUS (BRITISH)

SYRIA

LEBANON

TRANS JORDAN

IRAQ

PERSIA

SAUDI ARABIA

EGYPT

LIBYA

TUNISIA

ALGERIA

MOROCCO

SPANISH MOROCCO

Tangiers

Gibraltar (BRITISH)

SPAIN

PORTUGAL

N

500 miles

1000 km

0

0

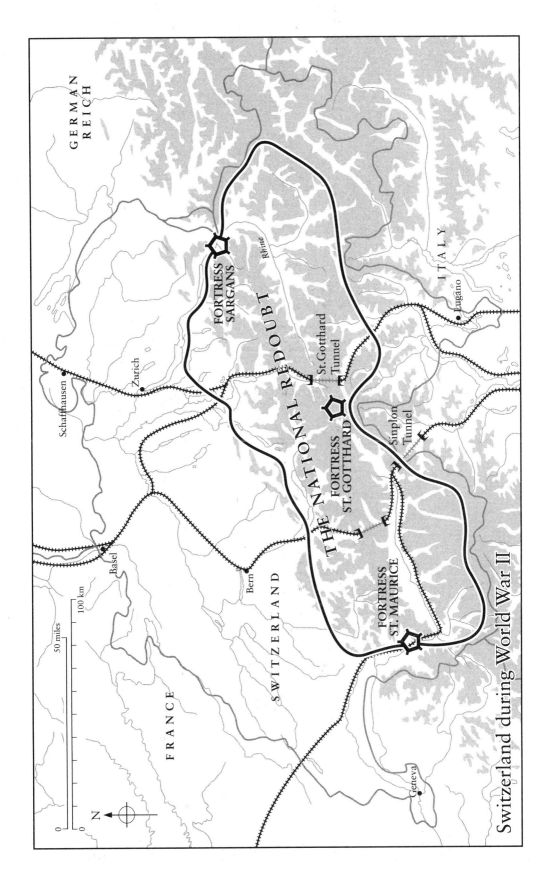

Switzerland during World War II

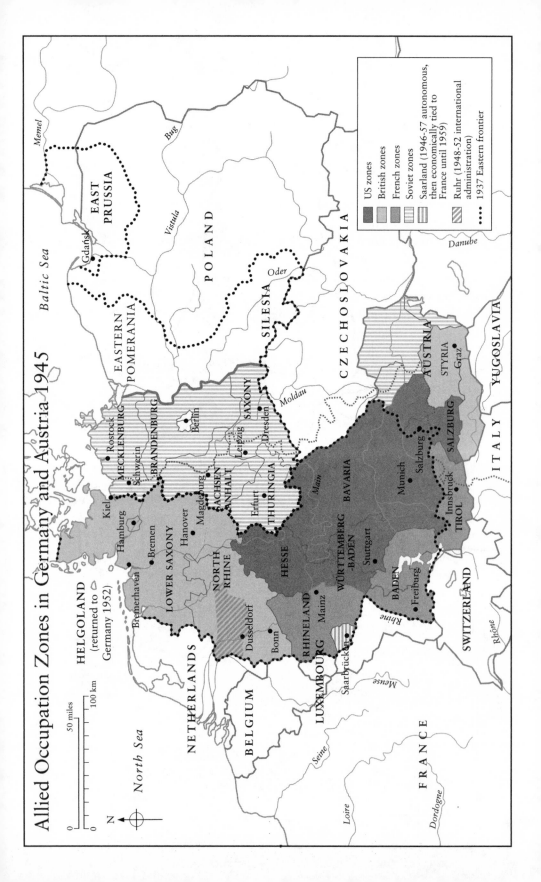

Allied Occupation Zones in Germany and Austria 1945

US zones
British zones
French zones
Soviet zones
Saarland (1946–57 autonomous, then economically tied to France until 1959)
Ruhr (1948–52 international administration)
1937 Eastern frontier

Baltic Sea

Memel

EAST PRUSSIA

Gdańsk

Bug

Vistula

POLAND

Oder

SILESIA

CZECHOSLOVAKIA

Danube

AUSTRIA

STYRIA

Graz

YUGOSLAVIA

EASTERN POMERANIA

Rostock

MECKLENBURG

Schwerin

BRANDENBURG

Berlin

Leipzig

Dresden

SAXONY

Moldau

SALZBURG

Salzburg

Munich

Innsbruck

TIROL

ITALY

Kiel

Hamburg

Bremen

Hanover

Magdeburg

ACHSEN NHALT

Erfurt

THURINGIA

Main

BAVARIA

HELGOLAND
(returned to Germany 1952)

Bremerhaven

LOWER SAXONY

NORTH RHINE

HESSE

WÜRTTEMBERG -BADEN

Stuttgart

BADEN

Freiburg

Rhine

SWITZERLAND

Düsseldorf

Bonn

RHINELAND

Mainz

Saarbrücken

Meuse

Rhône

NORTH Sea

NETHERLANDS

BELGIUM

LUXEMBOURG

Seine

FRANCE

Loire

Dordogne

50 miles
100 km

N

Note on Form

The terms 'German', 'Germany', and 'German lands' are used for convenience to denote the political space and its inhabitants as discussed in this book and are not intended to indicate that those places and peoples were necessarily German-speaking, nor that they would have identified themselves as 'German'. Place names and those of emperors, kings and other well-known historical figures are given in the form most commonly used in English-language writing. For east Central European locations, this tends to be the German version, while for some in the west it is usually the francophone one (e.g. Strasbourg rather than Straßburg). Royalty are generally identified by the anglicized form of their names, except where the German version has become established (e.g. Kaiser Wilhelm II). Otherwise, the modern German version is used. The term 'Empire' is used throughout for the Holy Roman Empire, distinguishing this from references to other empires, such as those of the Ottomans or Napoleonic France. Likewise, 'Estates' refers to corporate social groups, like the nobility and clergy, and to the assemblies of such groups, whereas 'estates' identifies land and property. Foreign terms are italicized and explained at first mention. Terms and their definitions can also be accessed using the index.

Currency is given in its historical form. For the first three centuries discussed here, there were two primary units of account: the north German silver taler (tlr) and the southern German and Austrian florin (fl). The nominal exchange rate was 1.5 fl to 1 tlr. Imperial Germany adopted the Mark (M) after 1871, valued (in 1873) at 3 tlr. Austria reformed its currency in 1858 when 100 new fl were worth 105 old fl. It replaced the florin with the *Krone* (crown), equal to 2 fl, in 1892. The First World War destabilized the German Mark, which was replaced by the *Reichsmark* (RM) in 1924; this was also introduced in Austria after its annexation in 1938. Germany's post-war division led to the adoption of the *Deutsche Mark* (DM) in Western Germany and the

Mark (M) in Eastern Germany. The DM was replaced by the Euro (€) in 2002. Switzerland lacked a standardized currency before the introduction of the franc in 1798, but even this only had a uniform value in all cantons after 1850.

Acknowledgements

This book is the culmination of my thinking on German military history across my career and is the kind of book I wished had been around when I started over three decades ago. The field has been transformed since the 1980s through critical reflections on warfare which place the study of conflict within its larger human context, as well as more recent efforts to reconnect that wider dimension with a discussion of how armed forces organize and conduct war. This book attempts to combine both approaches to provide a comprehensive account of the past five centuries. Such a venture would have been impossible without the efforts of several generations of scholars on whose work I have drawn. More immediately and personally, it has been my good fortune to have benefited from the advice of many generous colleagues. In particular, I would like to thank Rick Schneid and Jack Gill for sharing their research into German troop numbers during the Napoleonic Wars, as well as François Bugnion, Mary Sarotte, and Adam Storring, who kindly sent useful material or pointed me in the direction of books I had overlooked. Jan Tattenberg read extended sections of the draft and offered valuable comments and suggestions. Klára Andresová Skoupá provided great assistance with Czech-language literature. Simon Winder at Penguin enthusiastically supported the project from the start and offered innumerable insightful comments and suggestions on the entire work. I am also grateful to Kathleen McDermott and the staff at Harvard University Press for putting the book into production in the US, and to James Pullen at Wylie for support throughout. Cecilia Mackay and Danielle Nihill turned a wish-list of illustrations into reality, Richard Mason's punctilious copy-editing eliminated many potential errors and inconsistencies, and Ian Moores rendered my suggestions into beautifully clear maps. I am indebted to Rosie for her love, good humour and support, without which I doubt that I would have finished.

Peter Wilson, February 2022

List of Abbreviations

AA	anti-aircraft
ADB	*Allgemeine Deutsche Biographie*
AfD	Alternative für Deutschland (Alternative for Germany)
BEF	British Expeditionary Force
BND	Bundesnachrichten Dienst
CDU	Christian Democratic Union
CHF	Swiss franc
CSU	Christian Social Union
DDR	Deutsche Demokratische Republik (German Democratic Republic)
DM	Deutsche Mark
DWM	Deutsche Waffen- und Munitionsfabriken
EU	European Union
FDP	Frei Demokratische Partei (Free Democratic Party)
fl	florin
GDP	Gross domestic product
GNP	Gross national product
ICRC	International Committee of the Red Cross
ISAF	International Security Assistance Force
KPD	Kommunistische Partei Deutschlands (German Communist Party)
KVP	Kasernierte Volkspolizei (Barracked People's Police)
M	Mark (German currency)
NCO	non-commissioned officer
NDP	Nationaldemokratische Partei Deutschlands (National Democratic Party of Germany)
NVA	Nationale Volksarmee (National People's Army)
OEF	Operation Enduring Freedom
OHL	Oberste Heeresleitung (High Command)
OKW	Oberkommando der Wehrmacht (Armed Forces Supreme Command)

RLB	Reichsluftschutzbund (German Air Defence League)
RM	Reichsmark (German currency, 1924–48)
SA	Sturmabteilung (Stormtroopers)
SPD	Sozialdemokratische Partei Deutschlands (German Social Democratic Party)
SPG	self-propelled gun
STT	Stabilimento Tecnico Triestino
TF	Truppenführung (tactical manual, 1933–4)
tlr	taler
UN	United Nations
USSR	Union of Soviet Socialist Republics

Introduction

IRON AND BLOOD

'Not through speeches and majority decisions will the great questions of the day be decided – that was the great mistake of 1848 and 1849 – but by iron and blood [*Eisen und Blut*].'[1] These words come from Otto von Bismarck's famous address to the budget committee of the Prussian diet on 30 September 1862 as he sought to persuade the deputies to increase military spending. The final section was swiftly reversed as 'blood and iron' in contemporary and subsequent misquotation and became synonymous with German militarism, while Bismarck was known as the Iron Chancellor who advocated war as the only way to unify Germany. Closer inspection reveals this to be a caricature of a more complex and interesting story.

Bismarck's speech was carefully phrased to appeal to the deputies, most of whom were liberals favouring Germany's transformation into a national state governed by parliamentary democracy. He sought to remind the deputies of the realities of power; that Prussia's influence depended on sustaining its military capacity, not on providing ideological leadership. He was referring to the poem 'The Iron Cross' by Max von Schenkendorf, a volunteer in the 1813 War of Liberation against Napoleonic France, who wrote that 'only iron can save us, only blood can redeem us from the sins of heavy chains, from the pride of evil doers'.[2]

Like other poets from that era, Schenkendorf's works were later misappropriated by the Nazis to provide a cultural underpinning for their ideology. The poem's title refers to the new public service medal created by Prussia's king, Frederick William III, who had been pushed by liberal-minded officers into breaking his alliance with France. While careful to acknowledge the king's leadership, Schenkendorf's lyrics reference Prussia's Teutonic heritage, Christianity, and landscape. His other works are typical of the Romantic youthful idealism of his age and are sufficiently ambiguous to have been used by Christians, social democrats, and even modern advertisements for cars and clothes.

Bismarck's career was on the line. He had only been in office for a week and was required by Prussia's king to break the deadlock over the military budget. His reference to 1848–9 was a pointed attack on German liberals who had dominated the national parliament which met in Frankfurt at that time and yet had proved incapable of creating a unified state. His words failed to have their desired effect. The deputies rejected his call to increase military spending, plunging Prussia into a constitutional crisis from which it only escaped after fighting two successful wars in 1864 and 1866. Known as part of the 'Wars of German Unification', these conflicts partitioned the German Confederation by violently ejecting Austria and leaving a legacy that troubled central Europe for another century. Bismarck's speech had initially alarmed his political master, King Wilhelm I, who feared that he proposed settling Germany's problems by force. Although the king subsequently enjoyed his status as nominal leader of the victory over France in 1870–1, many Germans remained ambivalent about going to war.[3]

The speech and its reception exemplify the core argument of this book: that militarism has indeed been integral to the German past and has shaped how Germans have conducted wars, but that it was neither an end destination nor a single trajectory of development. The following intends to offer an accessible account of the military history of German-speaking Europe across the last five centuries within the wider story of developments in warfare, including on sea and in the air. It will highlight what made the German experience of war distinctive, as well as what it shared with that elsewhere in Europe and, where appropriate, with the rest of the world. Throughout, military history will be integrated with the wider political, social, economic, and cultural development of what are now Germany, Austria, and Switzerland.

A UNIQUE WAY OF WAR?

German military history is hugely popular and there is no shortage of books on Germany's wars, campaigns, generals, weapons, and militarism. Most of these works relate only to the period 1914–45, with the preceding fifty years of Imperial Germany coming a poor second. If treated at all, the period before the 1860s is usually reduced to the character of an introduction to the 'rise of Prussia', rather than an integral part of a much longer story. Most books are specialist studies, and are often highly technical, especially those covering weaponry, uniforms, and tactics. Many succeed superbly on their own terms, but a considerable number recycle well-worn interpretations and (often inaccurate) factual detail.

The preoccupation with the era of the two world wars has stunted debate and frozen German military history within an anachronistic and teleological framework originating in the later nineteenth century and crystallizing in the aftermath of 1945. This approach projects a myth of a specifically 'German' way of war, supposedly predetermined by that country's geopolitical situation in the heart of Europe which left it surrounded by hostile neighbours. Germans, it is widely believed, were somehow naturally predisposed to aggressive wars from fear of encirclement and from a desire to expand their 'living space'. This in turn supposedly fostered a uniquely authoritarian form of politics, because only a 'power state' could mobilize the resources necessary to develop and maintain the required 'first strike' capacity. Operationally, German wars had to be *Blitzkriege* (lightning wars) to win quick and decisive victories before their enemies could combine their superior numbers against them. German armed forces allegedly strove for technical proficiency and technological superiority to gain a comparative advantage over their more numerous foes. To achieve this, it is widely believed that the armed forces were entrusted to professionals operating largely beyond political control, all with fatal consequences for German society and wider European peace.[4]

This interpretation has become an almost unshakable orthodoxy, not least because German military institutions, like the General Staff, were widely emulated models from the 1870s. German developments have been used as yardsticks to measure the performance and efficiency of other countries' armed forces. Germany's example has profoundly influenced debates since the 1970s on whether there is (or should be) an American way of war. Dazzled by the illusion of the *Blitzkrieg*, the Bush administration in the 1990s promoted a hi-tech form of scientifically precise 'modern war' intended to secure a permanent advantage over opponents. The Chinese military, by contrast, has dropped its former admiration for German methods and now sees their failure in 1914 as a warning not to go to war with only an opening gambit rather than a strategic plan.[5]

More critical, left-leaning historians have done little to challenge this interpretation, because it reinforces widely held views about the supposed militarization and 'feudalization' of German society during the nineteenth century as preparing the ground for the First World War and, ultimately, Hitler and the Holocaust. Frequently, authors adopt a cultural explanation, rooting German militarism in Prussia's 'blood and soil' in an inversion of how nineteenth-century nationalists celebrated those same characteristics. Depending on perspective, Prussian aristocrats are variously subservient or independently minded, but always ruthless, while their soldiers are somehow 'natural' warriors – a controversial view which has recently been endorsed again from the political right as a potential source of inspiration for today's German armed forces.[6] The army supposedly remained an isolated, 'closed system', yet at the same time its martial ethos permeated the rest of society, warping its values.[7]

It is time to defrost German military history and to bring it in line with the way that the rest of the German past is being written about. Many decades of research have produced a far more nuanced and sophisticated view of German-speaking Europe. Much of this work has been explicitly comparative and questions whether German development can really be written as following a uniquely belligerent and authoritarian Special Path (*Sonderweg*) deviating from that of the rest of Europe.[8] If anything is 'special' then it is the fact that German development was characterized by military and political decentralization far longer than most other European countries. The customary links between political structures and military organization dissolve when we recognize that countries associated with liberal democracy, like Britain and France, established state monopolies of violence early on, while German development remained characterized by decentralized politics and collective security into the 1870s.

Above all, recent interest in global history and transnational developments raises valid questions about whether it is still appropriate to write 'national' military history. This is a particularly important issue for the German past, given modern Germany's very recent origins. There is no compelling reason why German military history should be framed by a political geography emerging only after 1866, any more than should German social, economic, religious, or cultural history. To that end, this book will cover the military history of those parts of central Europe that have been politically dominated by German-speakers throughout all or part of the timeframe, namely, roughly the area covered by modern Germany, Austria, and Switzerland.

The broad geographical approach will also address a major deficiency present in the few general military histories of Germany, all of which write German history teleologically as the rise and fall of Prussia.[9] Some works purport to trace even longer continuities from Arminius, who vanquished the ancient Roman legions, all the way to Hitler.[10] Most, however, truncate German history by starting only in the 1640s, which are commonly, if not accurately, identified as the decade of the 'birth' of the Prussian army. The entire German military past is read through the lens of Prussia's experience, while much of that experience is poorly understood because it is not set in its wider German and European context.

Institutional development is presented as the story of a single Prusso-German army, yet prior to its violent destruction of the German Confederation, Prussia only fought two wars (the Düsseldorf 'Cow War' of 1651 against the Palatinate, and its intervention in the Dutch Patriot Revolt of 1787) without the collaboration of at least one other German territory, and even in 1866, it was assisted by six small principalities. Far from being projected by a centralized state, military power remained decentralized for most of German history, with war-making being a collective activity through the Holy Roman Empire, and its more federal replacements of 1806–13 and 1815–66. Even the German Empire of 1871–1918 retained a contingent system with separate armies in Bavaria, Württemberg, and other states.

Perhaps more importantly, Prussia was not the leading 'German' military power until the later nineteenth century. Until then, the Austrian Habsburg monarchy always had a larger army and was still seen as a more desirable model by many, both within the German-speaking political world and elsewhere in Europe. As a proportion of population, more Swiss served as soldiers than did Prussians, yet it is 'Prussian militarism' that history generally remembers. By contrast, the military dimension to Swiss and especially Austrian history has been unduly neglected.[11] By freeing military history from anachronistic nationalist frameworks, we can explore these stories from fresh perspectives. The broader approach will reveal how ideas, practices, institutions, and technology transferred not only across German-speaking central Europe, but between that region and elsewhere in Europe and the world.

Only then can we determine how far there was a German way of war and what its broader historical significance may have been.

OUTLINE

The book combines chronology and theme. Chronology is important to the task of tracing long-term developments, while theme allows key aspects to be explored in greater depth. The chronology employed here is deliberately intended to disrupt the standard narrative based around Prussia's rise and then descent into two world wars. These conflicts are indeed important and will feature prominently, but the full picture only becomes apparent when the timeframe is extended not merely into the deeper past earlier than the 1640s, but also forward after 1945. The post-1990 reunified Germany has now existed for almost three times as long as the Third Reich, while the entire, largely peaceful era since 1945 is longer than that between 1870 and 1945. Yet, the military history of the Western Federal Republic, and its Eastern communist rival between 1949 and 1990, has yet to be integrated with that preceding the Second World War.

A major advantage of the longer view is that it allows a fuller appraisal of those events which appear as 'turning points' in German history, such as the Peace of Westphalia in 1648, the accession of Frederick the Great in 1740, Prussia's defeat to France at Jena in 1806, its victory over France at Sedan in 1870, a massive defeat in 1918 and the 'zero hour' of 1945, all of which are conventionally selected through a narrow focus on high politics. A key task will be to assess how far victories and defeats really 'made' German history, and thus to place war in the wider context of the German past.

Too often, existing accounts concentrate on successes, usually by emphasizing real or alleged greater aggressiveness or superior organization, especially the German General Staff and methods of command and control supposedly representing a unique 'genius for war'. While this approach has disappeared from most German-language scholarship, it remains deeply embedded in anglophone works, many of which are openly celebratory of Prusso-German methods.[12] There is a tendency for narratives to break off at the point when initial successes unravelled into costly wars of attrition ending in either stalemate (for example, Prussia in the Seven Years War) or total disaster (both world wars). Paying more attention to defeat reveals that the distinctiveness of Prusso-German methods between the mid-nineteenth and mid-twentieth centuries was an obsessive focus on how to achieve a quick victory, rather than what to do either with such a success or if it remained elusive.[13] Moreover, this approach generally stemmed from an anxiety that the country could not afford a long conflict, rather than a self-assured belief in the utility of force to achieve political goals. In fact, there was almost invariably a fatal disconnect between military planning and any wider national strategy leading to the neglect of other, possibly more fruitful, courses of action.

For this reason, the book's chronology is structured in five parts determined partly by the forms of military organization and practice which predominated during each century, as well as their relationship to social, economic, and political structures. Starting in the sixteenth century allows us to follow Germany, Austria, and Switzerland from their common origins in the Holy Roman Empire at a point when European warfare changed profoundly. Although medieval Europe was not short on conflict, wars were usually intermittent and localized. The later fifteenth century saw the emergence of mechanisms for mobilizing and directing resources in a more sustained and coordinated manner. Importantly for German history, this was not achieved by the creation of a single, national state, but through collective, multilateral structures. Autonomy, not centralization, remained the primary political characteristic into the twentieth century and re-emerged from the two world wars in modernized form as the federalism enshrined in the German, Austrian, and Swiss republics.

The institutional consolidation of the Empire accelerated between about 1480 and 1520, creating new mechanisms for raising men and money for war, as well as for resolving disputes between the multiple political authorities. All used a variation on a common three-tier mobilization system with a select levy of younger men, backed by two categories of reserves. Although much modified, this remained the way in which soldiers were recruited into the twentieth century. These structures, and the political culture they fostered, powerfully influenced subsequent developments, not least by sanctioning the existence of numerous 'warlords' (*Kriegsherren*) with legal possession of armed force.

At the other end of the book's timespan, we gain new perspectives on the two world wars if we view them as part of the broader sweep of the twentieth century, rather than as the supposedly inevitable outcome of botched attempts at unification under Imperial Germany between 1871 and 1914. A further major advantage of this structure is that it encompasses peace as well as war. To date, discussions of the 'German way of war' have focused almost exclusively on how war was conducted once hostilities were commenced, rather than the often-long periods of relative peace such as those in 1553–1618, 1815–48, 1871–1914, or 1945 to the present. The German states, including Prussia, were far from uniquely prepared for war. All European countries planned for future conflicts, and it is only when the German experience is properly contextualized that we can see how many of the claims for a uniquely militaristic past are exaggerated.

These arguments will be controversial, and it must be made clear from the outset that the book does not intend to whitewash German history or underestimate the destruction wrought by German forces, notably during the Second World War. As Federal President Joachim Gauck stated on 26 January 2015, 'There is no German identity without Auschwitz.'[14] Likewise, the comparative approach is intended to contextualize the German experience rather than relativize it through any kind of crude head count of victims – such as that criticized in the 1980s 'historians' dispute' over comparisons between Hitler, Stalin, and Pol Pot. Furthermore, the adjective 'German' is used for convenience to cover those parts of Europe which were within states ruled by German-speakers. The book explicitly rejects claims that Germans possess particular 'martial qualities' thanks to their relationship to their 'blood and soil'. In fact, 'German' military history makes no sense without including the experience of millions who spoke other languages. This is not only true for Switzerland and the Austrian Habsburg monarchy, but also for Prussia, which always had numerous Polish- and Lithuanian-speaking inhabitants.

Each of the book's five chronological parts is subdivided into three chapters to follow key themes across time while still providing a narrative. The opening chapter in each part deals chronologically with the relationship between war and politics, focusing on why wars were fought and how far German history was 'made on the battlefield'. Each part's middle chapter examines the exercise of command, planning, and intelligence, as well as how forces were recruited, organized, equipped, and trained. The final section of these chapters covers naval warfare with an additional section for that on the twentieth century (Chapter 14) discussing airpower. Each part's third chapter examines attitudes to war, soldiers' motivation, legal status, and their relationship to society, as well as the demographic and economic impacts of warfare.

PART I

Balancing War and Peace

I

Warlords

MILITARY POWER AND POLITICAL AUTHORITY

The Holy Roman Empire

The authority to use force was widely dispersed throughout late medieval Europe. To those writing in the nineteenth century, such authority appeared to lie with a dangerous jumble of robber barons and petty tyrants. Progress seemed to be represented by the emergence of powerful monarchs who consolidated states defined by a 'monopoly of legitimate violence'. Such figures include France's Louis XI, England's Henry VII, Hungary's Matthias Corvinus, and Spain's Ferdinand and Isabella, all of whom acceded to their thrones in the wake of prolonged civil wars and are associated with creating powerful 'new monarchies'. Nineteenth-century cartography marked this by showing these countries as solid blocks of colour, in contrast to the colourful patchwork of the Holy Roman Empire sprawling across the heart of Europe.

The differences were not as stark as the maps or grand narratives suggest, but the established view does point to the considerable diffusion of military power in the late medieval German lands where there were multiple warlords ranging from the emperor down to municipal councils. In German, the term *Kriegsherr* identifies a legitimate political authority wielding military power. It largely lacks the pejorative associations of its English counterpart 'warlord', which implies the personal use of military power to assert and exercise political authority. The presence of so many warlords was distinctive, but it was not necessarily a weakness. Instead, it represented a different way to conduct war, which

3

in turn reflected the Empire's character as a polity where power was dispersed and shared rather than monopolized centrally.

All late medieval European states encountered three forms of violence: the problems of enforcing the domestic peace, providing for external defence, and regulating the martial activities of their own subjects operating beyond the frontiers.[1] The peculiar character of German and Swiss political structures ensured these issues were handled differently from the western monarchies. France, Spain, and the Italian states were unusual in later fifteenth-century Europe in possessing permanent armies maintained in peacetime as well as war. The acquisition of such forces, together with the building of the institutions and tax systems required to maintain them, has been interpreted as a necessary step towards the modern state.[2]

In fact, there was considerable hostility to Christian rulers preparing for war during peace. War was considered a last resort, except against Ottomans and unbelievers. It was accepted that some inhabitants might be required to train and own weapons, but the expense of paying professional soldiers was expected to be exceptional. Provided forces could be raised when needed, it seemed both extravagant and an affront to God to remain armed in peacetime. The real difference between the Empire, and indeed also Switzerland, and many other European states, was not that they *failed* to develop permanent, centrally controlled forces, but that they *succeeded* in making the late medieval ideal work sufficiently well for their needs.

The Empire provided the political framework for German central Europe for three of the five centuries covered by this book, and the subsequent states of Austria, Switzerland, and Germany all sprang from it. It was 'Holy' thanks to its origins as the papacy's secular protector since 800, as well as the presence of Catholic ecclesiastical lords who were collectively known as the 'imperial church' and controlled around a seventh of its territory. It was 'Roman' through the claim that it was a direct continuation of ancient Imperial Rome, and it inherited that empire's pretensions to provide a pan-European order.[3]

Having expanded significantly eastwards in the high Middle Ages, the Empire contracted somewhat in the west and south after 1250, becoming more obviously 'German', though this was always defined more politically than either linguistically or culturally. The addition of the words 'of the German Nation' after Holy Roman Empire appeared in the late fifteenth century, but never became part of a formal title, and it was always accepted that many of the Empire's inhabitants spoke other languages. Other than some intellectuals, few found this problematic before the Empire ended in 1806.

It had never been a centralized kingdom, but instead evolved through several phases defined by differing relationships among its lordly elite. The distinction between hereditary and elective rule was blurred in many monarchies, and most European kingdoms suffered their share of instability and changes of dynasty. The elective character of the Empire's monarchy nonetheless grew more pronounced. After 1356, the franchise was restricted to seven princes, appropriately titled 'electors', while the number of potential candidates was generally even fewer and the provision of choosing a 'king of the Romans' enabled an incumbent emperor to secure recognition of his son as successor designate.

Imperial politics always contained both vertical relations of lord and vassal, and collective, horizontal associative elements. The two elements were not necessarily contradictory, and we should not oversimplify matters merely to a dualism between emperor and princes. Both were interdependent. The princes were not trying to reduce the emperor to a figurehead or escape imperial authority. Not only were their territories generally too small to make independent existence viable, but their own self-worth rested on their status as imperial princes, giving them rights and privileges within the much larger Empire. They might disagree violently with the emperor or their neighbours, but they did not contest the Empire's existence until just before its end. Moreover, the imperial legacy retained moral and legal authority well beyond its formal demise in 1806.

The emperor's power depended on circumstances and how well each ruler managed the varied challenges. The fifteenth century saw a consolidation of an internal hierarchy that became more rigid as it was recorded more precisely in constitutional documents which demarcated four levels of authority. The emperor was supreme overlord and the only European monarch with an imperial title. He shared key prerogatives with the principal lords and cities, which were distinguished by their 'immediate' status, meaning there was no intervening level of authority between them and the emperor. They collectively constituted the 'imperial Estates' (*Reichsstände*) entitled to meet in the *Reichstag* (imperial diet) when summoned by their overlord. The emperor was simultaneously monarch and an imperial Estate thanks to his own hereditary possessions. A new intermediary level was created in 1500–12 when most imperial Estates were incorporated regionally into ten *Kreise* (imperial Circles), establishing an additional arena to debate and coordinate policy and to raise troops and money for common action.[4]

While active at both the imperial and Kreis levels, the imperial Estates also collectively constituted the third 'territorial' level as rulers of the immediate imperial fiefs. Although usually labelled 'the princes', they were divided hierarchically into three status groups of electors, princes (who in fact also included counts and some lesser lords), and the cities governed by magistrates elected by their enfranchised burghers. The need to raise money and troops to counter common threats like the Hussite insurgency in Bohemia (1419–34) obliged the Reichstag to meet more regularly across the fifteenth century.

Those immediate vassals and cities that accepted these new responsibilities secured their status as imperial Estates by 1521, whereas those who were either unable or refused, slipped into the fourth political layer of mediate authorities. These included well over 50,000 noble families, numerous ecclesiastical institutions, and around 1,500 towns within the jurisdictions of the imperial Estates. In a process mirroring that at the imperial level, many of these lesser authorities secured representation in territorial or provincial Estates (*Landstände*), which debated how to meet common burdens, including the growing demands for troops and taxes from the Empire.

The Development of Collective Security

How the Empire apportioned these burdens proved a key factor in preserving this complex late medieval structure and ensuring it did not become a centralized monarchy. In an age when it was difficult to assess wealth, it seemed expedient to allocate fixed quotas to each imperial Estate and leave it up to them to find their own ways of raising what had been demanded. The quotas were recorded in 'matricular' lists, of which that from 1521 provided the benchmark for all subsequent calculations.[5] This apportioned 4,000 cavalry and 20,000 infantry among the imperial Estates to be provided either in kind or as cash set as equivalent to one month's wages of this force. Given the original intention of this force as the emperor's escort to Rome, the traditional location for imperial coronations, taxes raised using this system were known as 'Roman Months'.

The main drawback was that the quotas only approximated to each territory's actual potential and once fixed, it proved very hard to persuade anyone to accept revised levels – unless, of course, that meant a reduction! Nonetheless, the quota could be called up in fractions or multiples as required and the system suited the Empire's political culture and, moreover, it generally worked well enough.

Military authority was therefore fragmented rather than monopolized. The emperor and imperial Estates were all warlords, while the Empire and its Kreise could also act collectively in this capacity. From 1519, the emperor was obliged to consult the imperial Estates before making war in the Empire's name, but he could still do this in his own capacity using the resources of his own very extensive lands. The imperial Estates could also raise and maintain troops, while further legislation by 1555 empowered the Kreise to act on their own initiative to coordinate responses to immediate threats without first having to seek permission from the emperor or Reichstag.

Alliances offered an additional vehicle for military and security cooperation. Imperial Estates could combine for common purposes, but unlike their Polish or Hungarian counterparts, German lords lacked a constitutional right of resistance and, to be legal, any agreement between them had to be directed towards sustaining the Empire. The most important was the Swabian League, founded in 1488, which became a model for later alliances. Emperor Frederick III promoted the League to check the power of the Wittelsbach family in southern Germany, but it also served its stated purpose of sustaining the public peace, and its organization and practices contributed significantly to the development of imperial collective security.[6] The Kreise could also establish alliances, known since the seventeenth century as 'associations', which were formal defence pacts. The Habsburg lands were segregated into the Austrian and Burgundian Kreise, both of which consisted almost exclusively of the family's possessions with virtually no other members and they enabled the Habsburgs to use this structure as it suited them.

The internal use of force was curtailed by the perpetual public peace agreed at the Reichstag in 1495, which prohibited the imperial Estates from using force to settle their disputes. Similar legislation had been issued before, but this time it proved much more effective, because a new supreme court was established to adjudicate conflicts. The new judicial and institutional structures were not fully embedded when the

Reformation emerged as a permanent schism in western Christianity after 1517. Since his famous disputation with Luther in 1521, Emperor Charles V's policy was guided by his understanding of his imperial role to safeguard the secular order and he left the theological issues to the pope. Lutherans were targeted, not as heretics, but because they seized lands and revenues from the Catholic Church to fund the establishment of their own ecclesiastical structures. Thus, from the outset, the struggle was shaped by the rivalry among the imperial Estates over access to church resources, including the still substantial lands of the ecclesiastical princes. The princes and urban magistrates who embraced the new faith were swift to impose their authority on those who espoused it, and more grassroots movements, like those of the Anabaptists, were ruthlessly persecuted. This pushed religious conflicts upwards through the Empire's political levels to where theology mattered less than proving entitlement to exercise specific jurisdictions.

The 'Execution', or enforcement of court mandates, was entrusted to commissioners nominated by the emperor or Kreise. The ultimate sanction was the imperial ban that entailed the emperor declaring a malefactor an outlaw beyond the Empire's protection. Those enforcing these sanctions could expect recompense at the culprit's expense, giving the procedure real weight, though also adding potential political complications in its use. Understandably, the ban was employed sparingly and the usual response to violence was to escalate from formal warnings, through court injunctions, verdicts, and ultimately commissioning one or more imperial Estates to enforce the public peace. Negotiation remained an option at all stages, reflecting the general desire for peace and consensus that guided the Empire's political culture.

Despite these enforcement mechanisms, the Empire always suffered from the free-rider problem. Imperial Estates dodged common burdens by claiming, sometimes with good reason, that more immediate threats required them to retain their contingent. The Habsburgs regularly argued that their forces, regardless of where they were deployed, represented the contingents of the Austrian and Burgundian Kreise. Others complained they had been over-assessed, or given special exemptions, but few objected directly on political grounds and overall compliance generally compared well with the percentage of taxes collected in more centralized monarchies.[7]

It was left to the imperial Estates to devise how they raised the men and money demanded. Sixteenth-century authorities generally relied on vassalage to summon cavalry and non-combatant pioneers, with militia infantry recruited through other feudal obligations. Both forms were increasingly supplemented by paid professionals, some of whom were kept on retainer, but most were hired when needed through contractors. Each method had benefits and drawbacks and it was not a simple process of professionals replacing the feudal levy (see pp. 47–57).

Austria

Austria was already the pre-eminent power in the Empire by the mid-fifteenth century when the Habsburgs succeeded the Luxembourgs as the premier dynasty. Originally from Switzerland, the Habsburgs had ruled Austria since 1279, fashioning the unique, semi-regal status of 'archdukes' to elevate themselves above the other princes around 1358. Their extensive possessions were large enough to virtually guarantee continued re-election as emperor, but insufficient to sustain management of the Empire without the cooperation of the imperial Estates. The balance shifted significantly after the web of marriage alliances negotiated by Maximilian I bore fruit as the Habsburgs acquired Spain, Bohemia and a third of Hungary between 1516 and 1526.[8] These gains added to Maximilian's acquisition of most of Burgundy by 1493 and gave the Habsburgs over a third of the Empire as direct possessions, as well as even more land beyond imperial frontiers. The expansion of resources was more than offset by the accumulation of additional threats, which were heightened by France's recovery after a long period of internal and international wars, as well as a resumption of Ottoman Turkish expansion in the Balkans that triggered Hungary's collapse.

Keen to pursue a more prominent European role, the Habsburgs compromised within the Empire, accepting greater integration within the new institutions developing since the 1490s, in return for continued recognition of their imperial status and modest support for their activities outside the Empire, especially against the Ottomans. The new balance was formalized in the agreement between Charles V and the electors in 1519, which was renewed, with minor modifications, in all subsequent imperial elections. Charles's Spanish possessions were not integrated within the Empire (except those in Burgundy and Italy that were already part of it), leaving him free to use their resources as he pleased, but he was required to consult the electors and Reichstag if he wanted assistance from the imperial Estates.

The difficulties of managing this vast dynastic empire were immediately apparent in an age where political success still depended greatly on personal relations between a ruler and local elites. Recognizing he could not be everywhere at once, Charles devolved management of his dominions to his relations as viceroys. Austria was entrusted after 1521 to his younger brother Archduke Ferdinand, who increasingly substituted for his often-absent brother in managing the Empire.[9]

Germany

Austria, Burgundy, and Bohemia each qualified as only a single imperial Estate, despite being very large and each being subdivided into provinces. The 1521 register lists 402 imperial Estates, comprising 7 electors, 83 principalities, 226 counties, priories, and other lordships, and 86 cities. Additionally, there were around 1,500 knights' fiefs with the status of imperial immediacy. These figures are widely cited to convey the Empire as hopelessly fragmented. Many of the smaller entities had already disappeared during the sixteenth century as they were suppressed by higher lords who disputed their claims to autonomy or, in the case of around half of the 136 ecclesiastical Estates, were secularized by their neighbours, which included some Catholic lands like Austria. The overall number of political units was smaller still, because territories could be accumulated and held together by the same family.

It is thus more helpful to think in terms of family conglomerates, relatively few of which were of more than local significance. The most important after the Habsburgs were the Wittelsbachs, who held the Palatinate, Bavaria, Zweibrücken and various associated lands. Wittelsbach influence was undermined by their split into rival branches. The same affected the Saxon Wettins after 1485 as well as the Brandenburg Hohenzollerns, who came a distant fourth in the power ranking, even after 1618 when they inherited East Prussia, the former Teutonic Order land that had been secularized as a separate duchy outside the Empire under Polish overlordship in 1525. All four families, including the Habsburgs, had various junior branches who acted as a dynastic reserve, ready to inherit if the main line died out, but who could prove difficult to manage.

The Guelph (*Welf*) family in northern Germany was even more disparate, though the Hanoverian line would eventually rise to prominence at the end of the seventeenth century. The families ruling Hessen, Württemberg, Baden, and Nassau collectively occupied a sixth rank from which they would slowly climb as the hierarchy shifted in the eighteenth century when Austria and Prussia pulled ahead as distinct great powers, leaving Bavaria leading a pack of middling principalities, above a larger number of minor princes and counts, such as those of Sayn-Wittgenstein in the Rhineland whose various branches collectively ruled 467 square kilometres with just 16,000 subjects at the end of the eighteenth century.[10] Together, these middling and smaller principalities came to constitute a Third Germany alongside Austria and Prussia. From this discussion, it is apparent that those principalities that would survive the Empire's demise in 1806 and become independent states were already leading political players at the end of the middle ages. While the subtleties in the shifting relations between these princely families contribute to the richness of this period of German history, the broad underlying continuities are nonetheless striking.

Switzerland

Switzerland's gradual coalescence demonstrated the powerful potential of the associative element in imperial politics compensating for the country's lack of a common heritage. The French-speaking region originated in the old Carolingian kingdom of Burgundy, while the German areas had once been part of the duchy of Swabia. Linguistic divisions were complicated by the impact of geography and trade, which split Switzerland along north–south and east–west axes. However, there were few lords and most of these lived elsewhere, devolving local administration to village and town councils. The pressure of common tasks, such as maintaining roads and passes, pushed the villages to form incorporated valleys in the mountainous western and central areas. The other areas were organized in the more conventional late medieval pattern of rural lordships dependent on nobles or free towns.

Switzerland's origins are usually traced to the famous 'oath comradeship' (*Eidgenossenschaft*) between the three incorporated valleys of Uri, Schwyz and Unterwalden in 1291. This expanded to include other areas that collectively took its name, and the terms 'confederation' and 'canton' were only used officially after 1803. Each expansion was determined by specific circumstances and there was no overarching concept of what Switzerland was, or who should belong to it. The so-called 'war of liberation' against Habsburg overlordship in fact began as a local dispute over the rich abbey of Einsiedeln in 1315. The Habsburgs took their name from Habichtsburg castle in what is now Aargau and were the most powerful of the various absentee lords. They fought to uphold what they regarded as their lawful jurisdiction but were generally preoccupied with affairs elsewhere. The succession of Habsburg defeats at Morgarten (1315), Laupen (1339), Sempach (1386), and Näfels (1388) were only of regional significance and did not, contrary to the popular myth, establish an internationally recognized Swiss military reputation.

The Confederation was never democratic in the modern sense but remained true to its late medieval roots in communal governance exercised by councils elected by enfranchised property owners in a manner no different from many German towns and villages. While the mountainous 'Forest Cantons' of central Switzerland were both more rural and egalitarian, the others were dominated by their leading town where government became progressively more patrician and oligarchical as the victorious burghers appropriated the powers and trappings of the nobles they defeated. Most cantons acquired additional territory which they retained as dependencies whose inhabitants were denied equal rights. Many of these dependencies were seized during conflicts over the trade routes through the mountains. The Swiss conquered the Aargau and Thurgau from the Habsburgs, as well as making determined efforts after 1403 to take the fertile southern Alpine slopes from the duchy of Milan. Disputed jurisdictions in the Aargau and Thurgau contributed to the causes of several civil wars within the Confederation, and the two dependencies only secured full rights after 1798.

Violence remained endemic due to the constant friction between the cantons and the numerous inequalities within them.[11] Usually it was limited to cattle rustling and minor raiding, but it periodically erupted into more serious conflicts, notably the Old Zürich War (1436–50) over claims to the county of Toggenburg, which drew in France and the Habsburgs. It was now that Swiss military prowess caught wider attention, notably at the battle of St Jakob an der Birs on 26 August 1444 when a 1,500-strong Bernese force supposedly fought to the last man. Despite that defeat, Bern's ultimate victory over Zürich ensured it became the largest and most influential canton.

External interference encouraged the Swiss to join the conflicts stirred by the expansion of the duchy of Burgundy on the Upper Rhine during the 1460s. The unexpected Swiss victories of Murten, Grandson and Nancy 1476–7 ended Burgundy's expansion and firmly established their reputation as excellent infantrymen. The dispute over the rich Burgundian booty nearly caused a fresh civil war, but a rough equilibrium was achieved in 1481 when the rural cantons suspended their agitation among the dependent peasants of their urban neighbours in return for the latter abandoning plans for a more centralized confederation. By that point, the original three members of the Oath Comradeship had been joined by Zug and Luzern, both of which also counted as Forest Cantons, as well as Bern, Zürich, Glarus, Solothurn, and Fribourg. Each canton had two votes in the diet (*Tagsatzung*) that emerged after 1420 and met more regularly from 1471, but there was no capital, central government, or codified constitution. Neuchâtel, Valais, and St Gallen joined as associate members without equivalent rights or representation.

All the cantons originated as imperial towns or bailiwicks, and it was not inevitable that they should clash with the Empire. Nonetheless, the potential for conflict grew once the Habsburgs became the imperial dynasty, because disputes with them immediately entailed opposition to the Empire as a whole. Tensions escalated rapidly as the Swiss sought to dodge the common burdens by refusing to attend the Reichstag or pay the taxes agreed in 1495. Two years later, they allied with Rhetia, a network of three communal federations of which the Grisons (Grey League) was the most important, thereby pushing eastwards along the Alps and threatening the rich Habsburg province of the Tirol.

Cow Swiss and Sow Swabians

Meanwhile, Emperor Maximilian had emerged as the victor over France in the War of Burgundian Succession, triggered by the last duke's death at Nancy in 1477, and had acquired most of his lands, including the Franche Comté flanking Switzerland to the northwest. As head of the Swabian League, he was enforcing compliance with imperial policy among the small towns of southwest Germany, which the Swiss regarded as potential allies. Due to the new contest with France in Italy after

1494, Maximilian wanted to secure the Alpine passes and expected the Swiss, whom he regarded as his subjects, to permit transit.

Backed by the Swabian League, Maximilian attacked in January 1499, expanding the conflict three months later after the Swiss signed an alliance with France, complicating the war in Italy in which he, the French king and the Swiss were already belligerents. The Swiss won a string of small victories, notably at Dornach, but were unable to push across the Rhine into Swabia. Peace was agreed in Basel in September, with the Swiss securing exemption from the new common burdens, but their wider relationship to the Empire was left deliberately vague and they did not become a sovereign state.[12] The short war had been brutal with the protagonists calling each other 'Cow Swiss' and 'Sow Swabians' and taking no prisoners. Outsiders stressed mutual hatred and this was certainly displayed on sixteenth-century battlefields whenever Swiss and Germans clashed on opposing sides, but these differences should not be exaggerated. Trade, culture and religious ideas still flowed in both directions and men from both countries often served in the same units.

The city of Basel was compelled to abandon its neutrality and join the Confederation in 1501, as did Schaffhausen, giving the Swiss an outpost north of the Rhine. Appenzell on the Tirolean border joined as a thirteenth canton in 1513, but the prospect that other south German cities might 'turn Swiss' evaporated by the 1540s as the Empire increasingly appeared a better guarantor of civic autonomy than the fractious Confederation.[13]

THE PUBLIC PEACE AND FOREIGN SERVICE

Enforcing the Public Peace

The growth of Habsburg power greatly reduced the risk of internal conflict, since it became obvious that no other princely dynasty could challenge the family's leadership of the Empire. Their power was convincingly demonstrated in 1504–5 when Maximilian I intervened to support Bavaria against the Palatinate in the disputed Landshut succession. The Palatinate was defeated, losing its commanding influence in southwestern Germany, and allowing the Habsburgs to hold the balance between the rival Wittelsbach branches. Habsburg influence grew with the Swabian League's swift action against Duke Ulrich of Württemberg, who used the brief interregnum between Maximilian I's death and Charles V's election in 1519 to attack the imperial city of Reutlingen. Ulrich was defeated and driven into exile, demonstrating that the Empire's peace-enforcement mechanisms could operate effectively even without an emperor.

Both these conflicts involved relatively large forces but were brief and indicated the dangers of challenging imperial authority. Meanwhile, the territorial lords increasingly cooperated through the public peace framework to combat more local threats. Many of these problems were of their own making and culminated in the Knights' Revolt (1522–3) and the German Peasants' War (1524–6). Although later dismissed as 'robber barons', the knights were neither medieval reactionaries nor always particularly rapacious. The problems stemmed from the complexity of late medieval feudal relations, which led many to hold fiefs simultaneously from several princes. Banned from using force directly after 1495, some princes employed their knights to wage proxy wars with their neighbours over the numerous minor local disputes that bedevilled the Empire. These conflicts were pursued by invoking the traditional right of the feud in which a weaker party nominated a champion to secure redress. Meanwhile, some knights attempted to escape princely jurisdiction altogether by seeking immediacy under the emperor.[14]

These problems only became serious when the Palatine knight Franz von Sickingen used the opportunities presented by military contracting to pursue feuds on his own account on an unprecedented scale after 1515. Having attacked a variety of ever-more prestigious targets, he opened operations against the elector of Trier after 1522. This challenge to a member of the Empire's highest elite was a step too far; something Sickingen compounded by forming an alliance with other knights, which widened the conflict. Retribution was swift as the Swabian League was joined by other princes in assembling overwhelming forces that defeated him and his associates by 1523. In the longer term, tensions were defused by the knights' acceptance of collective burdens under special arrangements made directly with the emperor, which preserved their autonomy amid growing hostility from the princes.[15]

Collective peace enforcement also met the challenge of the Peasants' War, the bloodiest internal conflict in the Empire during the sixteenth century and Germany's last popular national revolt before 1848. The war

was a series of interconnected local and regional risings against lordly
exactions by those who felt disadvantaged by broader socio-economic
changes beyond their control. It was given a revolutionary character by
the peasants' interpretation of the new evangelical faith as legitimizing
demands for equality.[16]

The authorities were initially divided and mostly tried to negotiate,
only to renounce agreements once they felt sufficiently strong. Their
behaviour fuelled mutual suspicions, contributing to the violence, though
it is obvious that many in the Swabian League played up stories of peasant atrocities to legitimate their own brutal reprisals. Peasants formed
regional armies of up to 50,000 men, though these never operated in a
single body and all suffered continual fluctuations in strength as men
came and went depending on their domestic responsibilities and level of
commitment. Not all rural inhabitants backed the rising; many had to be
coerced and most cities closed their gates. Except for the Tiroleans, who
operated as guerrillas, the peasants lacked an alternative strategy if their
assembly in large numbers failed to overawe the authorities.

Representing the region first affected, the League took the lead in
organizing countermeasures, but its ability to act was impaired by the
reluctance of many of its civic members to support military action.[17] It
rarely fielded more than 7,000 men, though its cooperation with other
regional princely forces was much better than that among the peasants.
The princes distrusted much of their infantry, relying instead on superior artillery to demoralize the peasants, who then became vulnerable
to cavalry attack. Contemporaries accused the League of killing
100,000, and though that is probably an exaggeration, at least 20,700
Swabian peasants died in the six battles they lost, and casualties in
Franconia, Thuringia and Alsace were probably similar.

However, even the most ruthless of the authorities were concerned
not to cut off the hands that fed them, and the war was followed by a
range of local and imperial reforms. These confirmed the trend already
present since 1521 to restrict disputes over religion to the Empire's elite.
Ordinary folk were expected to believe whatever their local lords and
rulers considered God's true word. Religious animosities might still spill
over into rioting and other violence, but those in power refrained from
calls to holy war. The Empire's judicial framework was adjusted after
1526 to open access for subjects to the higher courts, enabling them to
appeal over their rulers' heads if they could prove they had been denied

justice. This 'juridified' conflict in the Empire, dampening its potential to explode violently, though that still occurred, especially in the smaller territories or if cases dragged on without resolution.[18]

Foreign Service

As violence was being curbed within the Empire, it was increasingly exported in the form of men who went to fight in wars elsewhere in Europe. This foreign service continued into the nineteenth century, with a legacy persisting today in the papacy's Swiss Guard. The Swiss are the most famous with an estimated 1 to 2 million men serving between 1450 and 1850, of whom at least 270,000 fought during the sixteenth century. The number from Germany was significantly higher. Men joined other armies individually or in units formed for that purpose or they served temporarily as hired auxiliaries.[19]

Interpretations of foreign service have diverged sharply. Many Swiss authors celebrated it as an expression of personal freedoms and the martial values of a hardy mountain folk. 'The Swiss soldier is the best soldier in the world,' declared the historian and infantry officer Paul de Vallière, whose book *Loyalty and Honour* presented the Swiss as heroic warriors who continued to serve dutifully even when they were not paid.[20] Others have noted that, almost from the outset, foreign service was condemned as 'human trafficking' (*Menschenhandel*) that corrupted the country morally and politically. German involvement has attracted equally polarized comments, though the overall balance of opinion has been much more critical, describing a traitorous 'soldier trade' (*Soldatenhandel*) that deepened and perpetuated the country's division into petty principalities (*Kleinstaaterei*), with only Prussia as an (allegedly) honourable exception.[21]

Foreign service fully emerged during the last third of the fifteenth century, though some Germans and Swiss had served in other armies before.[22] France first tried to secure the service of large numbers of Swiss in 1474, and after 1488 it had at least 5,000 who constituted up to 40 per cent of the infantry.[23] German infantry, known as *Landsknechts*, were found in similar numbers by the 1490s, including a contingent taken to Spain in 1506 to drill local troops, while others served France after 1510, either as substitutes for the Swiss or to supplement them.

No single factor explains this, and the conventional reference to overpopulation, already cited by contemporaries, oversimplifies a complex interaction between the demographic recovery from the Black Death and changes in inheritance practices, a commercializing economy, and broader political developments.[24] The seasonal character of warfare was another important influence, since those who served could expect to return home in the autumn, while it could suit the authorities to be rid of potentially troublesome young men. Those involved in authorizing and organizing recruitment hoped it would bring not just financial reward, but open other personal, political, and economic opportunities.

Central to the critique of foreign service is that it corrupted the Swiss and German professional soldiers, who degenerated 'into a merely opportunistic mercenary force', no longer serving 'national' interests.[25] The flow of recruits to enemies was a problem, but it is important not to interpret this through the lens of later nationalism. No early modern monarchy had a monopoly of violence, and it proved impossible to prevent subjects fighting for others, particularly as most rulers themselves relied heavily on foreigners. It could also be a convenient way to assist allies without becoming directly involved in their wars.

Thus, rather than prohibition, the authorities regulated service to profit from it and ensure it served their interests. The Swiss had already tried this from the later fourteenth century, but authorized expeditions were often accompanied by additional volunteers known as *Reisläufer*, who served without permission or pay in the expectation of booty. The frequency with which German mandates were reissued also indicates similar problems elsewhere in the Empire.[26] Nonetheless, regulation was not wholly ineffective. The general preference was to serve the emperor, since fighting for his enemies risked dishonour. Sebastian Vogelsberger and his subordinates were executed in 1548 for breaching an imperial ban on recruiting for France. Those entering foreign service without permission were liable to have their property confiscated. France was compelled to adjust how it presented itself in the Empire, posing as a champion of constitutional liberties to undercut imperial efforts to dissuade men from entering its service.

Wars in Italy

The Italian Wars opened with a French campaign to conquer the kingdom of Naples in 1494 and continued as a succession of conflicts until

1559.[27] A key reason for their prolonged, intermittent character was the fragility of the rival alliances of convenience among the belligerents, who included the emperor, the Swiss, Spain and England as well as Italian states. Coalitions came and went whenever one power's successes became too threatening for the others.

Most belligerents found it easier to raise than sustain armies, usually running out of money as autumn approached. It often proved difficult to exploit a victory or to hold on to conquered land. Small garrisons could be left in strategic towns, but the field army generally dispersed as men went home with their pay or booty. Forces had to be recruited again if another campaign was intended the following spring. Logistical failures were common, particularly in bad weather or underpopulated regions. At best, an army could cover 25 kilometres in a day, a speed not exceeded until the development of railways. Supply problems and uncertainty about enemy movements usually slowed the pace to less than half that. Given these constraints, it is unsurprising that sixteenth-century wars displayed a yawning gap between the ambitious plans of warlords and their actual achievements.

Spain had triumphed over France in Naples by 1503, though that did not stop the French trying again in 1527 and the 1550s. After 1499, the war increasingly focused on a struggle over the duchy of Milan where the once-powerful Sforza dynasty was losing its grip. Milan was the core of what was known as 'imperial Italy', which covered all of Lombardy eastwards to the Venetian border and south to Tuscany. Savoy, which controlled the western Alpine passes, counted as part of Italian politics, but formally belonged to the German kingdom and was the only Italian state to retain a seat in the Reichstag into the eighteenth century. Genoa belonged to imperial Italy, commanded the best access from the west by sea, and was consequently another key French target. Emperor Maximilian was determined to reassert imperial jurisdiction south of the Alps and unsurprisingly found himself usually opposed to France.

France could generally count on Venetian support, since that republic was surrounded to the north and east by Habsburg territory and was often at odds with the emperor, who repeatedly sought access across it to intervene in Italy. The papacy vacillated between neutrality and support for either the emperor or, more usually, France, which presented itself as a champion of Italian liberty against Habsburg imperial tyranny.

Maximilian had a relatively weak hand, as the Reichstag did not regard Italy as a common concern and rarely voted substantial support. Unlike France, he found it difficult to raise a large army by the start of each campaign and, instead, imperial forces often dissipated their effort by arriving piecemeal.

Contradictory alliances placed Swiss troops on opposite sides at the siege of Novara in the spring of 1500. Following mutual discussions, those serving the Sforza duke abandoned him to be captured by the French. Although the captain identified as responsible was executed on his return home, the episode fuelled the controversy in the Confederation on the morality of foreign service and contributed to the lasting impression of 'Swiss mercenaries'.[28] Meanwhile, the Swiss used the opportunity to seize two valleys on the southern side of the Alps from Milan, thereby signalling their presence as an active belligerent in northern Italy, as well as a troop provider.

That role became clearer when France decided it was cheaper to hire Landsknechts and did not renew its Swiss alliance in 1509. The Confederation now joined a new papal-led coalition dedicated to expelling the French from Milan. Although this also included Maximilian, Spain and England, the Swiss provided the backbone of the League's forces and their presence enabled both the Confederation and its Rhetian allies to expand their Alpine possessions at Milan's expense.

The Battle of Marignano and the 'Invention' of Swiss Neutrality, 1515

The run of success ended abruptly in 1515 when France's new king, Francis I, renewed claims to Milan and invaded with 38,500 men, including 23,000 Landsknechts.[29] Around half the cantons felt it was time to quit and agreed to sell most of the duchy back to the French. The others refused, and their 20,000 troops marched out of the capital to attack the French at Marignano on 13 September. The Landsknechts repulsed fierce attacks until nightfall. Unusually for early modern warfare, the battle was renewed the following day, but the arrival of Venetian reinforcements tipped the balance further against the Swiss, who were forced to retreat having lost over a third of their strength. Negotiations continued during further, inconclusive fighting, until all cantons and their associate members agreed an alliance with France on 26 November 1516, selling

Milan ostensibly in return for pay arrears from earlier service, as well as keeping most of their Alpine conquests.

The orderly retreat of the Swiss after Marignano was immortalized in the fresco by Ferdinand Hodler in the Weapons Room of the country's Historical Museum in 1900, showing the soldiers carrying their injured comrades, defeated but still defiant (see Fig. 1). Although Hodler's composition and style were controversial at the time, his interpretation perfectly encapsulated how the battle was remembered as a 'salutary defeat' that ended the era of expansion and inaugurated that of neutrality.[30] Central to this view is the belief that Switzerland's success in preserving its neutrality derives from the deterrence value of its own military prowess, rather than on the attitudes of its neighbours and potential enemies.[31]

In fact, there was no renunciation of further expansion. Geneva and Rottweil were accepted as allies, while both Bern and the allied republic of Valais conquered land from Savoy in 1536. The real explanation for the end to expansion is that there were no more easy pickings within reach, while existing disagreements over the wisdom of further conquests were complicated by the Reformation, which split the Confederation: Six Zwinglian cantons (Appenzell, Basel, Bern, Glarus, Schaffhausen, Zürich) faced seven who remained Catholic (Fribourg, Luzern, Schwyz, Solothurn, Unterwalden, Uri, Zug). Rhetia was predominantly Protestant but its subject lands in the Valtellina were Catholic, while the allied city of Geneva embraced Calvinism, which otherwise failed to find adherents in Switzerland.

Religion sharpened the long-standing territorial, economic and political rivalries, creating a complex geopolitical situation lasting until 1847. The main Protestant block of Bern and Basel split Fribourg and Solothurn from the five Forest Cantons. However, Protestant Appenzell and Glarus remained isolated enclaves to the east, while Zürich and Schaffhausen were separated from their natural allies by two corridors of dependent territories controlled by the Catholics. Tensions spilled over into war in 1529 and again in 1531. The latter conflict ended in a surprise defeat for the Protestants, who were caught unprepared by a Catholic counter-attack in which Zwingli was killed at the battle of Kappel.[32] Peace confirmed the stalemate in 1532, but the failure to resolve the ongoing tensions prompted the Catholics to form their own league in 1586, causing Appenzell's substantial Catholic minority to break away and exercise one of the two cantonal votes independently of the Protestants. A similar split followed in Glarus in 1655, indicating the intractability of the underlying problems.

More fundamentally, neutrality was something few sixteenth-century Swiss would have considered desirable. The prevailing idea of 'just war' held that only one side could be in the right and that Christians should aid the wronged party, or at least not assist its enemies. Only in the mid-eighteenth century did the practice of treating both sides equally become morally acceptable. Until then, 'sitting still' was considered tolerable, provided it was necessitated by self-preservation and that no action was taken to aid the unjust party.[33] With each canton generally favouring its own co-religionists in any conflict, sitting still often seemed the only way to prevent renewed civil war.

These considerations shaped the famous Franco-Swiss alliance of 1516, the Treaty of Perpetual Peace. Despite its name, this was not 'perpetual', nor did it preclude agreements with other powers. The treaty was already supplemented by another in 1521, which became the template of all further compacts. These were generally fixed for the lifetime of each French king plus around eight years into his successor's reign to allow for a renewal to be negotiated. There were gaps in 1597–1602 and 1651–3, while Zürich abstained between 1521 and 1614, and Bern did not cooperate from 1690 to 1752. All Protestant cantons refused to renew in 1723 until 1777, reducing the formal agreement meanwhile to just their Catholic neighbours.

The French alliance followed the late medieval practice of 'exceptions', permitting the Swiss to retain their Hereditary Accord with the Habsburgs agreed in 1511, which regulated relations with Austria until 1806.[34] The existence of such potentially conflicting alliances was addressed in the contracts agreed with France and other powers to supply troops. For example, Swiss regiments in French service were supposedly to be deployed only in defensive wars and were not to be sent across the Rhine to fight the emperor; a stipulation that several French monarchs ignored. The conventions also permitted the Swiss to recall their soldiers should they be themselves attacked, but this was impractical and was never invoked. France was formally an ally and promised military assistance – something that was also never called upon, because the first power to invade Switzerland was France in 1798!

The real glue behind the alliance were the pensions and economic concessions. France intermittently paid annual pensions to the cantonal elites after 1474 to have first call on Swiss troops. Austria, Spain, Savoy, and other powers did the same, but France trumped them all after 1521 with the relative scale and regularity of its payments. Each canton and Confederate ally received a fixed annual sum, but France disbursed other money through its permanent ambassador, based in Solothurn. These included direct payments to key families and educational bursaries for officers' sons. Despite interruptions and arrears, the regular payments were large enough to cover a substantial proportion of public expenditure, allowing most cantons to reduce taxation. Other payments were disbursed to the cantonal elites and their local clients, thereby consolidating the trend towards oligarchy, and causing innumerable squabbles over access to these handouts.[35] Meanwhile, France gave Swiss merchants privileged access to its markets and, crucially, guaranteed the supply of salt, the trade in which also became a lucrative source of income for cantonal elites. No other power could match the leverage that these measures bought France.

The alliances cemented the elite's grip on foreign service that persisted into the 1850s. 'Official regiments' were raised through formal contracts between the Confederation and another power. The cantonal authorities appointed the officers, subject to the hirer's approval. These posts were initially quite lucrative, and so were naturally reserved for the sons of elite families. During the first half of the sixteenth century, regiments still usually served for only one or two campaigns, but they became more permanent from the 1560s, meaning that additional recruits were sent out regularly to keep them up to strength. Although serving a foreign power, the units nominally 'belonged' to their canton. Further, 'non-recognized' regiments could be raised under 'particular capitulations' signed directly by their colonel-contractor and a foreign potentate. However, these still required approval from the cantonal authorities and were more risky enterprises, since the regiments could be returned or disbanded by the hirer without fear of disrupting a formal alliance.

THE WARS OF CHARLES V

Pavia and the Sack of Rome

The Italian Wars resumed in 1521 when Charles V, now ruling Spain and the Empire, sought to reverse the earlier outcome by invading Milan. His forces captured most of the duchy and repelled a counter-attack at the battle of Bicocca in April 1522 in which France's Swiss troops suffered heavy losses. Further French reverses culminated in Francis I's capture at the battle of Pavia in February 1525, which saw further bitter clashes between the Swiss and Landsknechts in imperial service (see Fig. 2).[36] Charles imposed heavy conditions on Francis, who immediately repudiated them once he had been released. The war resumed in 1526 when Pope Clement VII changed sides to oppose the growing imperial influence in Italy.

Unable to pay his army any longer, Charles encouraged it to march on Rome to demand money from the pope. Conscious that a strong Franco-Venetian relief army was hot on their tail, the imperial troops stormed the city on 6 May 1527, beginning the infamous sack that claimed up to 12,000 dead, including unarmed civilians, hospital patients and children slaughtered in a Vatican orphanage.[37] Pope Clement managed to escape into the papal fortress defended by his Swiss guards, whose heroic rearguard action subsequently became part of the positive variant of the Swiss mercenary myth. The sack was later interpreted as ending the Italian Renaissance, and while that is an exaggeration, it was certainly seared into Italian consciousness as a great national disaster.

The collapse of discipline was followed by an epidemic, temporarily impairing the imperial army's effectiveness, but it scored another convincing victory over the French at Landriano in June 1529. Francis made peace, effectively abandoning Italy to Charles who was now at the height of his power, being hailed as 'the emperor of the world' when he landed in Genoa that August.[38] Pope Clement had already made his own peace, absolving those responsible for the sack of Rome in return for recovering his lands and crowning Charles officially as emperor; the last imperial coronation conducted personally by a pope.

The Turkish Wars, 1521–33

Whereas Christian rulers were expected by moralists to live at peace, the infidel Turks were considered a mortal threat. Ottoman power had been growing, but remained contained by Hungary until 1521 when Belgrade, considered the gateway to Central Europe, fell to the new Sultan Suleiman. The Reichstag's decision to offer aid in 1522 involved the Empire in what would be a succession of 'Turkish Wars' lasting into the eighteenth century.

The two main protagonists were unevenly matched. The sultan ruled a true world empire straddling Asia, Africa, and southeastern Europe, but the war front in Hungary was over 1,000 kilometres from Istanbul. The Ottomans were often distracted by conflicts elsewhere, notably against Persia, and considered the emperor as simply one of many barbarian enemies. When they chose to attack, they usually arrived with large forces beyond Hungary's capacity to keep them fed for long.[39] Matters were very different for the Habsburgs. Hungary was their immediate neighbour, and its collapse brought the front line close to Vienna. They too faced other enemies, but the Ottomans posed an existential threat, while their alliance with Hungary's young King Louis II, who lacked a direct legitimate heir, added a powerful dynastic interest.

Louis's death at the disastrous battle of Mohács in August 1526 led to a succession dispute as the Habsburg Archduke Ferdinand's claim was challenged by John Zápolya, the leading landowner and governor of Transylvania who enjoyed majority support among the Hungarian nobility.[40] The ensuing struggle saw the Ottomans back Zápolya as Hungarian king, while Suleiman returned with another huge army in 1529, capturing Buda (the historic capital of Hungary), but failing to take Vienna after a six-week siege that autumn. Nonetheless, once the sultan departed, the Habsburgs were left with just a narrow strip of land immediately east of the imperial frontier amounting to only a third of Hungary.

The Turkish siege caused alarm throughout the Empire, where the Ottomans were now accepted as a general threat, rather than merely the Habsburgs' problem. Eastern defence became an unavoidable duty, whereas Charles's wars with Christian rulers in the west remained his private matter. The so-called Turkish Aid first voted in 1522 was renewed at a much higher rate, enabling Ferdinand to assert operational control over the disparate Hungarian and Croatian forces because he could now pay them.

Despite massing 100,000 men, he was unable to retake Buda in 1530. Suleiman returned two years later with a force reputed to be three times larger than the Habsburgs, intending to renew his siege of Vienna. The Protestant and Catholic factions in the Reichstag temporarily set aside their differences to agree further assistance. Contingents from the Empire totalled 36,000 or well over a third of the army assembled by Ferdinand, who was now joined by his imperial brother Charles.[41] Facing each other for the only time, both rulers decided against risking their prestige in a battle. Unable to winter in a denuded Hungary, Suleiman withdrew. Charles had the satisfaction of defeating the Ottoman rearguard but had run out of money and left to deal with other problems.

Both sides regarded peace as impossible for religious and ideological reasons, but the Habsburgs could no longer sustain war on this scale. Ferdinand agreed a truce in June 1533, recognizing the sultan as 'lord' and paying a humiliating annual tribute. The truce merely suspended major operations in Hungary and left both parties free to fight each other elsewhere. It was clear that a swift recovery of Hungary was now unlikely, and the Habsburgs expanded the Military Frontier they had established with Croatian assistance in 1522 to create a permanent militarized zone along the entire Hungarian border.

Renewed Italian and Turkish Wars

Charles V remained almost continually at war, but the conflicts of the mid-sixteenth century reached an unprecedented scale, fuelled by the resources deployed by all parties, and by the emperor's ambition to assert himself over all foes. War resumed in Italy following his sequestration of the duchy of Milan after the death of the last Sforza duke in November 1535. Francis I opposed this and exploited the emperor's departure on a crusading expedition to Ottoman Tunis to challenge the disappointing outcome of the previous war by invading Savoy, then an imperial ally. A Franco-Ottoman naval agreement linked this conflict to the ongoing struggles with the Turks. A large imperial invasion of Provence in 1536 failed to reverse this and France held much of Savoy until 1559.

Although the pope brokered a ten-year Franco-imperial truce in June

1538, Charles continued to anger Francis by enfeoffing his son, the future Philip II of Spain, with Milan in 1540. Francis renewed his Ottoman alliance the following year and declared war on the emperor in June 1542. The main flashpoints were in Luxembourg, Piedmont, and Perpignan; all key points of friction on Franco-Habsburg frontiers. As with Milan, Charles pursued dynastic objectives, seeking to expand Habsburg possessions. Amid the conflict with France, he settled matters with the duke of Cleves, who opposed his policies in the Netherlands. The duke swiftly capitulated after his principal towns had been stormed by a large imperial army in August 1543.[42]

Exceptionally, the Reichstag voted aid for the war against France in addition to fresh Turkish Aid in 1544. The imperial army was defeated at Ceresoles in April 1544, but the French were unable to exploit their victory due to a new alliance between Charles and Henry VIII of England. Another imperial army advanced up the Meuse into northeastern France in June, while an English expeditionary force reinforced by German troops captured Boulogne. Short of funds, Charles abandoned Henry VIII in a separate peace with France in September 1544, essentially restoring the truce from 1538.

Meanwhile, events had gone badly for the Habsburgs in the east where major operations had resumed in 1541 as Ferdinand renewed claims to all of Hungary following Zápolya's death. Despite mustering considerable forces, Ferdinand failed to reconquer the lost parts of Hungary. The Ottomans imposed their own rule on the central part of Hungary based at Buda, recognizing Zápolya's son as successor only in Transylvania, which now emerged more clearly as a separate principality. Ferdinand reluctantly accepted this tripartite division of Hungary in a new truce in 1547.

The Schmalkaldic War, 1546–7

The renewed Turkish war temporarily prolonged the tacit agreement between the Protestant and Catholic factions in the Reichstag, but this had frayed by 1545. War was not inevitable, but the actions of the leading Protestant princes made it more likely. Chief among these was Philipp, landgrave of Hessen, a compact and well-organized principality in central Germany. Dissatisfied with Saxony's political leadership of Germany's Protestants, he promoted an alliance to coordinate action at the Reichstag and to protect against suspected Catholic plotting. Once it became obvious that wider support depended on Saxony's inclusion, Philipp compromised and accepted Elector Johann Friedrich I as joint leader of the new group, which became known as the Schmalkaldic League after the Hessian town where it was formed in 1531.[43]

In common with the Swabian League and other early modern alliances, the new organization was an uneasy combination of ambitious but impecunious princes and wealthy but cautious cities. It was divided into a Hessian- and Saxon-led north and a largely urban south. The cities rightly complained at being over-assessed relative to their imperial tax quotas in the League's mobilization structure. As a purely Protestant body, the alliance was immediately controversial, not least because it claimed a higher loyalty to God, implying a right of resistance against the emperor that even Luther hesitated to endorse.

Political and confessional differences discouraged the Swabian League members from renewing their charter when it expired in 1534. Seizing this opportunity, Philipp of Hessen persuaded the Schmalkaldic League to back an attempt to restore his cousin Ulrich to the duchy of Württemberg. Outnumbered, Archduke Ferdinand's forces were defeated at Laufen in May and he accepted Ulrich's restoration in the Peace of Kaden a month later.[44] As many Schmalkaldic members privately acknowledged, Philipp's aggression breached the public peace, but he succeeded because he had more money and could recruit soldiers faster than the Habsburgs. Philipp had also masked his intentions by presenting his military preparations as directed against the Anabaptists, as well as relying on a network of professional officers kept on retainer who recruited small groups of soldiers covertly, able to be assembled quickly when needed.

The presence of seemingly 'masterless' bands of armed men added to the prevailing sense of anxiety in the Empire, especially as it was often difficult to distinguish between unemployed marauders, men being recruited illegally for France, or those raised legitimately by princes. Imperial mandates were issued against unemployed soldiers and illicit recruiting after 1444. These were tightened considerably after 1521, requiring all soldiers to carry passports and expanding the capacity of the Kreise to coordinate enforcement. The efficacy of these measures depended on the will to make them work, which unfortunately was undermined by mutual suspicion.[45] Rumours of soldiers lurking in woods or small villages fuelled fears among the imperial Estates that their enemies were conspiring against them, as Philipp had indeed already done when he attacked several Franconian bishoprics in 1528. He did so again in 1542 when he and the Saxon elector launched a 'preventative' invasion of Brunswick-Wolfenbüttel without consulting the other members of the Schmalkaldic League.

The occupation of Brunswick proved a costly millstone that Hessen and Saxony were considering surrendering to imperial sequestration when the displaced duke unsuccessfully attacked them in autumn 1545.[46] These actions stirred dissension in the League and prompted four princes to defect to Charles. The most important was Duke Moritz, head of the Albertine ducal Saxon line, who agreed to back the emperor in June 1546 in return for imperial toleration of his influence in the ecclesiastical principalities of Magdeburg and Halberstadt. The defections were important not only militarily but also because they substantiated Charles's claim that he was only restoring the public peace, not extirpating Protestantism. He was careful not to issue an imperial ban, since that would legitimate demands from those princes who assisted him to be rewarded with lands and titles to be taken from his enemies. Meanwhile, the recent peace with France and an armistice with the Ottomans created an opportunity for Charles to settle things in the Empire.

The Protestant Swiss rejected the League's request to recruit troops and closed their frontiers to both sides. Venice also refused to help, while England's Henry VIII, in his typically conceited fashion, only offered to help if the League made him its commander.[47] The League's division into northern and southern sections prevented it combining its full force, but it soon assembled over 50,000 men under Sebastian Schertlin, an experienced professional. Charles mustered only 34,000 men in Bavaria, which agreed to provide food, but otherwise refused to back him. Confidence grew within the League, which believed 'we have a lot of good troops and everyone is keen to fight'.[48]

Rather than attacking Charles directly, Schertlin struck south against the Tirol in early July to seize the Ehrenberg gorge and block Italian and papal reinforcements, who eventually reached the emperor after a wide detour. Another large body joined Charles from the Netherlands, having dodged a League force on the Middle Rhine. Both sides converged on Ingolstadt in Bavaria where the League briefly bombarded the imperial camp at the end of August. Skirmishes continued along the Danube into the autumn, but neither army was prepared to risk battle. Critically,

Habsburg-ruled Bohemia's numerous Protestant nobility largely failed to respond to the League's calls to revolt, freeing the Habsburgs from what might have been a serious distraction. Moritz launched a diversionary attack against electoral Saxony, which withdrew its forces, weakening the main army and allowing the imperialists to invade Württemberg, forcing it and the other southern members of the League to surrender.

Philipp ran out of money and was forced to disband much of his army, leaving just Johann Friedrich in the field. In January 1547 the Saxon elector expelled Moritz and relieved Leipzig, which had been besieged. Papal troops returned home that month, while the need to garrison south Germany further reduced the main imperial army to around 27,000. Money was now arriving from France and the north German members, emboldening Johann Friedrich to advance towards Bohemia in the hope of raising a revolt. Charles moved north through Franconia to join Moritz and invade Saxony. They caught the 21,000 Saxons unprepared and dispersed. The ensuing battle of Mühlberg on the Elbe on 24 April was a twelve-hour running fight culminating in the Saxon elector's capture. The emperor's victory was so comprehensive that it made no difference that the remaining northern League members defeated a separate imperial army at Drakensberg a month later.[49]

Despite his reluctance to reward his supporters, Charles was obliged to make an exception in Moritz's case. Johann Friedrich was imprisoned, and his lands and electoral title were transferred to Moritz on 4 June. This was the first adjustment to the Empire's electoral college since 1356 and set a dangerous precedent that was to cause the Habsburgs considerable trouble during the Thirty Years War. Moritz interceded for Philipp, who was his father-in-law. Charles spared Philipp a death sentence but nonetheless condemned him to fifteen years in prison. Most of the other members escaped relatively lightly, though the League was dissolved.

Charles was keen to capitalize on his victory to impose his own settlement to the Empire's problems, particularly as the deaths of both Francis I and Henry VIII in 1547 removed the likelihood of external intervention. The imperial Estates convened in Augsburg at what became known as the 'armoured Reichstag' thanks to Charles's heavy military presence. With the theologians still debating at the Council of Trent, Charles imposed his own religious 'Interim' settlement in May

1548; a compromise that pleased no one and alienated Moritz, who was charged with enforcing it in the defiant Lutheran city of Magdeburg, which eventually surrendered after a siege in 1550–1. Other measures enhanced the autonomy of the Habsburgs' Burgundian lands within the Empire and attempted to corral the leading princes into an alliance with Charles.[50]

The Princes' Revolt and Renewed War with France, 1551–9

Although this settlement scarcely changed the essentials of the imperial constitution, it was perceived as unwarranted and alarming following Charles's imprisonment of the Schmalkaldic leaders. Charles further alienated the German princes by suggesting that his son, the future Philip II of Spain, be his successor, instead of his brother Archduke Ferdinand, whom they preferred. Meanwhile, the emperor's costly attempt to take Parma depleted his resources. Moritz began conspiring with other disgruntled princes, who joined him in a loose alliance during 1551. Exploiting Charles's growing difficulties, the new French king, Henri II, reopened the Italian Wars by invading Piedmont in August before allying himself with Moritz's group in January 1552.[51] A large French army seized Metz, Toul and Verdun on the Empire's western frontier, and occupied parts of Alsace in April. Having recruited soldiers covertly with French money, Moritz declared his hand in March, launching the Princes' Revolt by striking southwards into Swabia.

Neither side really wanted to fight, but negotiations failed, and Moritz pressed onwards, trapping the outnumbered Habsburg forces in the Ehrenberg gorge, and forcing them to surrender in May. Meanwhile, Albrecht Alcibiades, Margrave of Brandenburg-Kulmbach, broke off to pursue his own 'Priests' War' against the bishops of Bamberg and Würzburg, as well as the rich city of Nuremberg, all of which he had already sought to conquer.

Archduke Ferdinand negotiated the Peace of Passau on 15 July 1552, releasing the two imprisoned princes, suspending the Interim, and accepting the secularization of Catholic church property to that date. In return, the princes switched sides and agreed to support Charles's campaign to recover Metz. The French garrison stoutly resisted through the winter, forcing the emperor to abandon the siege in the New Year, retire to Brussels and initiate what became a long process of partitioning Habsburg possessions between his son in Spain and brother in Austria, culminating in his own unprecedented abdication as emperor in 1556. The war in Italy and along the Netherlands frontier became Philip II's business as these areas were already assigned to his inheritance. The conflict outlasted Charles by a year, being successfully concluded by Philip in 1559 when France finally accepted Spanish hegemony in Italy. Spain's victory ended the Empire's security concerns to the south, but Philip's power led him to disregard the emperor's continuing formal rights in Italy when it suited him.[52]

Having temporarily joined the imperial army to avoid punishment, Albrecht Alcibiades resumed his attacks in Franconia but found his enemies had armed themselves meanwhile, forcing him to retreat northwards where he hoped to rally other disgruntled Protestant nobles and towns. Moritz caught him at Sievershausen in July 1553, defeating him in the bloodiest battle on German soil in the sixteenth century, but only at the cost of his own life. The margrave returned southwards, plundering his way back to Franconia, where he was defeated again at Schwarzach in 1554 and fled into exile.[53]

The events of 1546–54 demonstrated clear limits to imperial power, but also impressed upon the princes the dangers of partisan alliances and unilateral action. The desire for compromise was already indicated by the collective measures against the wayward margrave, which saw Catholic and Lutheran princes and cities collaborating to enforce a renewed imperial ban. Ferdinand skilfully capitalized on the growing desire for peace to broker the Treaty of Augsburg, which was ratified by the Reichstag meeting in that city in September 1555. Usually simply known as the Religious Peace, this in fact was a much wider settlement extending that agreed at Passau by allowing the secular princes to decide whether their subjects should be Catholic or Lutheran. The wording was deliberately ambiguous to allow adherents of both faiths to accept a common document. The vagaries would prove troublesome by the end of the century but, with some highly controversial exceptions, the imperial supreme courts managed to defuse most disputes and the Empire remained largely at peace for the next sixty-three years.[54]

In addition to a wide range of other measures, like currency reform, the Reichstag also enhanced internal security through the Imperial Executive Ordinance, which codified the rules governing the enforcement of the public peace. Further measures were put in place by 1570 strengthening coordination of police measures against covert recruitment and travelling soldiers. The defeats of the notable troublemakers Count Johann of Rietberg (1557) and Werner von Grumbach (1567), who attempted feuds in the manner of Franz von Sickingen, demonstrated the efficacy of collective action and generally deterred others from using force against their neighbours.[55]

PEACE AND SECURITY IN A CONFESSIONALIZED AGE

Western and Northern Security

The Empire's relative tranquillity stood in stark contrast to the problems of its neighbours. France descended into a series of violent civil wars known as the French Wars of Religion after 1562. Following several years of rioting and unrest, the Netherlands were also swept by war after 1568. Known as the Dutch Revolt, this was simultaneously a civil war in which most Catholics backed continued Spanish rule. Population displacement reinforced what effectively had become a permanent partition into a Spanish-controlled Catholic south, and a northern, largely Protestant, rebel republic. Meanwhile, Danish–Swedish rivalry in the Baltic drew the Hanseatic cities into the Northern Seven Years War of 1563–70.

All the belligerents in these conflicts sought troops and financial aid from their sympathizers in Germany. Around 25,000 Germans served in the opening stage of the Northern Seven Years War that was fought largely in Livonia (modern Latvia), which belonged to a branch of the Teutonic Order. The emperor rejected claims that Livonia was part of the Empire and helped mediate peace in 1570.[56]

The Dutch Revolt posed a greater risk, since the main route for Philip II to send reinforcements was along the Spanish Road by sea to Genoa, across the Swiss Alps and then down the Rhine. Even Catholic Swiss and Germans were uneasy about the constant passage of large bodies of armed men through their homelands, while their Protestant neighbours feared the Spanish might plunder or attack them.

Spain's last major recruiting drive in Germany had been in 1557 during the final phase of the Italian Wars. The Dutch Revolt broke out after the Habsburg partition, making Spanish access dependent on Austrian cooperation. Ferdinand I and his successor in 1564, Maximilian II, rejected Spain's interpretation of the Dutch Revolt as a breach of the public peace on the grounds that the Netherlands were formally part of the Burgundian Kreis and thus entitled to military assistance from the Empire. They refused direct military assistance and instead tried unsuccessfully to mediate. Nonetheless, they tolerated Spanish recruiting to maintain Philip II's goodwill. While it is unlikely that all the 94,000 men requested by 1578 were recruited, Germans nonetheless consistently formed a third of the infantry in the Army of Flanders between 1572 and 1607, always outnumbering the Spaniards and Italians, and sometimes even exceeding the locally recruited Walloons.[57]

The conflict strayed into Westphalia after 1583 when Spain backed the Bavarian candidate in a dispute over the strategic electorate of Cologne, which straddled the Lower Rhine. The conflict remained contained and Spanish forces withdrew in 1588 having achieved their objective. They returned a decade later in the infamous 'Spanish winter' when they sought billets and supplies, as well as to outflank the Dutch to the east. Although the Westphalians' military countermeasures were only partially effective, the Spanish again withdrew.[58]

Germans and Swiss formed around a third of French royal armies in the opening stages of the French Wars of Religion, while 107,600 Swiss had served on both sides by 1598.[59] The Protestant princes organized seven expeditions between 1562 and 1592 totalling 80,000 German and 20,000 Swiss to support the Huguenots.[60] To put this into perspective: the English expedition to the Netherlands in 1585 numbered only 7,000 effectives, while the three expeditions to assist the Huguenots totalled just 13,000.

The Bernese and Genevan councils rejected the Huguenots' appeal for aid as contradicting their treaties with France, and Bernese emissaries managed to persuade around 5,000 men enlisted with money supplied by Calvin to return home in 1562. However, it proved impossible to prevent men from joining the expeditions organized by the German princes, while after 1585 the Forest Cantons supplied troops to the French Catholic League and to Spain, both of which operated independently from the royal army in the ongoing civil war. The princely expeditions contravened imperial mandates against recruitment, but the only serious breach of the peace was the brief Strasbourg Bishops' War (1592) where a local dispute over an episcopal election was exacerbated by the final Protestant German expedition to France in support of the Huguenots. This saw even less fighting than the Cologne dispute and was settled by negotiation.

Eastern Security and the Long Turkish War

The Habsburgs were fortunate that the Ottomans renewed the 1547 truce, though they exploited the trouble in Germany to make a few additional gains on the Hungarian frontier between 1552 and 1554. The truce was renewed again in 1562, but Maximilian II used the opportunity of Suleiman's death four years later to launch a substantial attempt to reconquer Hungary. This failed, and he was forced to cede more border fortresses at a further renewal of the truce in 1568. The arrangement was extended three more times by 1590 in return for increased tribute from the Habsburgs. However, raids of up to 4,000 men were permitted, prolonging the sense of anxiety. The Reichstag accepted the arguments of Rudolf II, Maximilian's successor in 1576, that the Military Frontier served the common good and voted substantial tax grants that enabled its reorganization and maintenance.[61]

Having successfully concluded a long war against Persia in 1590, the Ottomans stepped up attacks on Croatia, using the Habsburgs' retaliation as an excuse to declare a breach of the truce and to open what became known as the Long Turkish War in 1593.[62] Rudolf saw his chance to fulfil his role as Christendom's champion and made ambitious plans to carry the war beyond a reconquest of Hungary. Money came from Spain and the pope, while alliances were sought with Russia and Persia.

The war followed what had now become a standard pattern determined by the geostrategic situation and the belligerents' fiscal-military constraints. Long preparations almost invariably delayed opening each campaign beyond the intended start date, leaving only a narrow window between July and November, when the onset of cold, wet weather made further major operations impossible, reducing activity to raiding and minor skirmishes until the following summer. The Habsburgs usually fielded around 50,000 men, or broadly similar to their opponents. The rump of Hungary provided around a fifth of the emperor's army, with most of the rest financed by the Empire and tax grants from the Habsburg provincial Estates. The Kreise organized additional contingents between 1594 and 1597 and from 1601 to 1605.

The war's duration forged the core of the Habsburg army into a permanent force. Already in 1592, units were retained in Hungary over the winter, rather than disbanding them or returning them to their home principality as had been the case in previous Turkish wars. This increased costs, but reduced preparation time and improved the capacity to wage successive campaigns. The numbers retained averaged around 10,000, but with higher peaks prior to planned major offensives. The field army was additional to the 20,000 garrison troops deployed along the Military Frontier since 1576, and though they were reduced considerably after 1607, they were never completely disbanded and gave the Habsburgs the first permanent army in the Empire.[63]

These forces were augmented by small numbers of papal and Tuscan troops, as well as Catholic volunteers from France following the pause in that country's internal strife after 1598. Other volunteers included Captain John Smith, the future founder of Virginia, who served briefly with the Styrian forces in 1601.[64] International involvement gave the war the character of a crusade, which was further sustained by the ideological mobilization of the Empire's inhabitants, who were summoned by the ringing of 'Turkish Bells' to regular days of penance and prayer at their parish churches.

The initially high expectations of success evaporated as the fighting ebbed and flowed across the long Hungarian frontier, with one side's gains in one sector generally offset by a defeat elsewhere. Rudolf overextended his front by launching a separate bid to conquer Transylvania, which drew in the Ottoman tributary states of Wallachia and Moldavia. Any chance of victory ended when much of Upper Hungary revolted against heavy-handed Habsburg policies in 1605.[65] Rudolf was determined to continue, especially after Persia finally declared war on the Ottomans in October 1603, but his younger brother Matthias saw the shah's intervention as an opportunity to make peace on better terms.[66]

A new truce was agreed at Zsitvatorok in November 1606 to last twenty years from the following January. The Turks kept two important fortresses they had captured, but otherwise confirmed the outcome of the previous war in 1568, except that the sultan now accepted the emperor as his equal and converted the annual Habsburg tribute of

30,000 ducats paid since 1547 into a one-off 'free gift' of 200,000 florins. This adjustment was of dubious benefit since it implied that the Habsburgs recognized the sultan as an emperor. Moreover, raids involving up to 6,000 men were not to be considered a breach of the terms, thereby providing potential for future conflict.

The war bankrupted the Habsburgs, who turned on each other in the Brothers' Quarrel that erupted into sporadic violence in 1608 and 1611, during which the rival archdukes made damaging political and religious concessions to the provincial Estates in return for financial and military support. Matthias eventually emerged as victor, effectively placing Rudolf under house arrest in his Prague palace for the last months of his life. Already crowned king of Bohemia, Matthias succeeded Rudolf as emperor in 1612 and managed to recover some of the influence lost in the Empire before the outbreak of the Thirty Years War in May 1618 presented him with an even greater challenge.[67]

The conflicts between the 1470s and 1530s determined the Empire's frontiers, which would, with some important but relatively small adjustments, last until its demise in 1806. The Habsburgs controlled over a third of the Empire as hereditary possessions, which underpinned their virtual monopoly over the imperial title. Their status, together with the acquisition of further land beyond imperial frontiers, confirmed them as Europe's leading family, despite the loss of two-thirds of Hungary to the Ottomans. The personal union of Spain with the Habsburgs' Austrian heartlands under Charles V had brought unprecedented resources, enabling the emperor to defeat France and exercise a dominance in Italy not seen for three centuries. Meanwhile, violence within the Empire was curbed, though the deepening religious divisions had added new anxieties.

Renewed warfare in the middle decades of the sixteenth century saw both the peak of Habsburg power and the limits to imperial authority. Having crushed the Schmalkaldic League, Charles overplayed his hand in 1548 when his efforts to impose tighter monarchical rule prompted a violent backlash that caught the Habsburgs off balance and widened the dualism between Spain and Austria already present since the emperor's partial devolution of authority to his brother in 1521. Charles completed that process, partitioning Habsburg possessions in 1556. Although Austria lost direct access to Spain's vast wealth, it could now concentrate on managing the Empire free of many of the wider problems that had confronted Charles. Ferdinand I brokered a compromise in 1555 that consolidated the trends since the fifteenth century, confirming the Empire as a mixed monarchy in which the emperor held the initiative, but shared the exercise of power with the imperial Estates. The settlement embedded the cities and other weaker elements within a common political system, ensuring that none joined the Swiss, who had already opted out of this process in 1499 while nonetheless remaining loosely associated with the Empire.

Partition of the Habsburg lands assisted Austria's efforts to keep the Empire out of the wars that ravaged western and northern Europe during the later sixteenth century. Although it proved impossible to prevent the continued outflow of German and Swiss soldiers, both the Empire and the Confederation managed to limit the domestic repercussions of this indirect involvement. Imperial collective security reorientated eastwards as the imperial Estates voted large, regular taxes to sustain the Habsburgs' Military Frontier against the Turks. Any chance that this might strengthen Habsburg imperial rule was wrecked by Rudolf II's political mistakes and the financial and political impact of the Long Turkish War. Although weakened, the Habsburgs had not lost control of the Empire and it was far from inevitable that a cataclysmic conflict would erupt after 1618.

2

Forming Armies

SUPREME FIELD CAPTAINS

Command and Control

The period 1470–1520 was one of rapid experimentation and innovation in warfare, warranting the label 'military revolution' more than the much longer epoch thereafter to which that term is normally applied.[1] Improvements in weapons created dilemmas over how best to use them, especially as new equipment and tactical thinking remained unproven. One victory was no guarantee of future successes, and it soon became clear that no single troop type or method was invincible. Warlords sought a 'comparative advantage' over their opponents through a building-block approach by assembling an army from a choice of differently armed and organized types of troops. Parts of Europe became associated with certain styles of fighting, with Germany and Switzerland initially best known for their disciplined infantry, as well as gunmakers and, later, effective pistol-armed cavalry.

Increasingly, the differences were more those of perceived reputation rather than actual organization, armament, or tactics. The pace of innovation slowed across the 1530s and 1540s as technological changes became evolutionary rather than revolutionary and the dissemination of weaponry and practice across Europe encouraged a gradual convergence of organization and practice to broadly common forms for infantry, cavalry, and artillery – the three branches of service. Meanwhile, the rapid growth in the scale of forces by the 1530s prompted efforts to train subjects as a cheaper alternative to hired professionals. Warfare remained intermittent, with forces raised only when needed, but some permanent infrastructure developed to facilitate this, notably through the establishment of arsenals, artillery parks, and new fortifications. Throughout, the Habsburgs were exceptional in creating a permanent army and supporting naval forces to confront the Ottomans.

Military command remained highly personalized, reflecting the nature of political authority in the sixteenth century, and blurring the boundary between function and entitlement. Those occupying positions of military or civil authority were office-holders, exercising jurisdictions and enjoying associated benefits, rather than officers commissioned by a higher power to perform a carefully circumscribed task. These characteristics derived from the much older relationship between office- and fief-holding, and enfeoffment was originally intended to provide the resources that would enable its beneficiary to perform the tasks required, most obviously in the case of vassals serving as knights. While fiefs had become hereditary, possession still had to be renewed at the death of each vassal and was dependent on performing homage and paying fees. Lord–vassal relations were reciprocal, with the former offering protection in return for the latter's subordination and service. Lords were expected to confirm the rights and privileges associated with the fief, while retaining powers to escheat it if the vassal failed to perform the expected duties.

Exercise of these rights and duties had become extremely complicated through the dispersal of authority within the Empire's multi-layered hierarchy. Vassals often held multiple fiefs from different lords, who could include ecclesiastical princes or imperial cities that had acquired territory. Jurisdictions were often separated by type, so that the exercise of judicial, fiscal, economic, religious, and military power over one area could be held by several different people or institutions. Vassals of one lord might themselves be lords over other, socially inferior vassals; most obviously in the distinction between those who enjoyed 'imperial immediacy' under the emperor as their overlord, but who exercised jurisdiction over territorial fiefs and offices. Finally, paid office-holders had proliferated since the eleventh century, but these were simply an additional element in this complex system, rather than representing a more modern phenomenon among supposedly antiquated feudal relics. Paid office-holders were also supported primarily 'from below', receiving cash from fees and materials such as firewood and wine from those for whom they performed functions, rather than being paid centrally from a treasury filled by taxes. While the latter practice was becoming more common in the fifteenth century, especially in the imperial cities, the differences between 'feudal' office-holders and 'modern' officers and officials had yet to emerge fully.[2]

Higher authorities did not have an entirely free choice as to who they appointed, because the hierarchical social and political order established firm expectations about who was appropriate to fill each rank. Things were never entirely rigid, and exceptions could generally be made, but appointments usually involved a trade-off between finding someone capable of fulfilling a role and managing competing groups and families with vested interests. Military command was traditionally associated with noble birth, and while the transformation of warfare across the later fifteenth and sixteenth centuries fostered new ideals of professional expertise, there was no bar on noblemen acquiring that. Some positions had become (or were even from the outset) essentially honorific, such as that of 'imperial standard bearer'.[3] Others were created in response to new requirements, but often without abolishing older offices whose holders might be too important to disturb. The reciprocity in lord–vassal relations was echoed throughout society where patron–client networks were fundamental to the functioning of the hierarchical order.[4]

Finally, the progressive 'territorialization' of power within the Empire from the fourteenth century demarcated the large jurisdictions more clearly and increased the importance of place. Territorial identities grew, especially with the emergence of the territorial and provincial Estates as representatives of the key social groups in dealing with their ruler. The Estates quickly insisted on restricting important appointments to locals, regarding outsiders as threatening their wealth and influence. The restrictions also worked in reverse since existing obligations to higher authorities often prevented taking service with another. The same applied to ordinary subjects, even in areas with the right of emigration such as much of southwest Germany, as taking up arms for another lord required prior permission. The exception in most cases was service for the emperor who, as supreme overlord, enjoyed a unique status.[5]

The personal character of office-holding was further reflected in the form of appointment. The shift to written culture during the late Middle Ages fuelled bureaucratization, with the names of vassals and office-holders recorded in registers, and new appointees agreeing a contract. These were generally termed a *Staat*; a word that also came to mean 'state' in the modern definition, but in this case combining aspects of an employment contract, household, and entourage. The document listed the expectations placed on both parties, including the functions to be performed and the emoluments and entitlements awarded. The latter still generally combined cash salaries with payments in kind, such as a set number of human and horse rations, as well as sometimes free accommodation. This renumeration package was intended not only to reward the office-holder, but also to enable him to perform his tasks, and thus assigned resources for his assistants, such as scribes, messengers, grooms, servants, or bodyguards, depending on the role.

Overall command rested with the warlord, who was not necessarily a person, since imperial cities also possessed military authority, as did the Empire collectively and associations of imperial Estates, such as the Swabian and Schmalkaldic Leagues. Likewise, the Swiss cantons assumed similar powers as they freed themselves from lordly jurisdiction in the later Middle Ages. Many rulers did exercise personal command, notably emperors Maximilian I and Charles V, as well as princes like Philipp of Hessen and Johann Friedrich I of Saxony. Doing so entailed personal and reputational risks. Elector Moritz of Saxony died of wounds received while commanding his troops at Sievershausen (1553), while both Rudolf II and his brother Matthias suffered criticism for their poor handling of the Long Turkish War. Departing on campaign also took a ruler away from the business of governing, which was becoming more complex and bureaucratic: Charles V signed over 100,000 documents during his reign. Thus, it was already common around 1500 to appoint someone else to lead troops in person and to exercise the ruler's delegated authority over them while on campaign.

The growth of imperial collective security across the fifteenth century saw challenges to the emperor's exclusive power to name commanders. The contingent system resulted in soldiers from each territory marching under officers appointed by their own warlord. While the imperial Estates accepted the emperor's authority should he command in person, they demanded a say in choosing any generals serving in his place, as well as the right to nominate experienced men to a war council to advise on operations. Both Maximilian I and Charles V conceded some role to the imperial Estates meeting in the Reichstag, but the commanders and councillors appointed this way only exercised authority over the collective forces, while the emperor still named the senior general. The Reichstag's role at this point was largely symbolic because the Habsburgs' vast possessions gave them the means to start and end wars as they chose, especially after 1519.

The Habsburgs usually appointed experienced Italian and Spanish generals for campaigns in Italy and Burgundy, with Germans more prominent among forces sent against the Turks. As it was common to keep soldiers recruited from different areas apart, Landsknechts sent to Italy were usually commanded by German captains, of whom Georg von Frundsberg was the most famous. The same applied to the Swiss in foreign service, who were led by men selected by the cantonal authorities.

The development of the Kreis structure by 1512 established an intermediary layer of political and military authority between the imperial Estates and the Empire as a whole. The position of regional colonel (*Kreisoberst*) assumed considerable significance as this role was filled in peacetime so that the individual would be ready to lead forces once mobilized. Generally, the leading princes of each region competed for the position, resulting in tensions among them and between the successful candidate and the other members acting collectively through the Kreis assembly. The appointment of other field commanders had eroded the colonel's role in several Kreise by the mid-seventeenth century, by which time the position of Kreis convenor, who summoned the assembly, had become much more important.[6]

The same issues affected leagues since these modelled their collective security on that of the Empire with each member naming the officers for their contingents and acting together to decide the overall commander and war council. Appointments worked relatively smoothly in the Swabian League, which enjoyed the Habsburgs' backing and where commanders, notably Truchseß von Waldburg, enjoyed reasonable relationships with the war councillors.[7] The Schmalkaldic League was split between a princely dominated north and a civic-led south, with Philipp of Hessen and Johann Friedrich leading in person, while the cities hired experienced captains.

The senior operational commander was known as *Feldherr* ('lord of the field'), a term that came to be more associated with 'generalship' as the qualities of a commander, rather than an actual rank. Since the function was frequently delegated, the senior officer was usually called Supreme Field Captain (*Oberster Feldhauptmann*) into the early seventeenth century, when it was displaced by the title of 'general'. Field marshal, a title used in the Middle Ages, reappeared during the early seventeenth century, but normally at that point as *Feldmarschallleutnant*, indicating a rank below that of overall general. Battle-size armies usually had separate generals of infantry, cavalry, and artillery, reflecting the trend away from the classic medieval tripartite division into advance guard, main battle and rearguard, and instead towards a more flexible combination of the three main arms.

Military Administration

Like the rest of early modern government, military administration grew out of the ruler's household.[8] Chancelleries, charged with record-keeping and correspondence, had emerged in the Middle Ages, followed by treasuries that received and disbursed funds and contracted loans. Separate bodies emerged to handle justice and ecclesiastical affairs, the latter expanding considerably following the Reformation. Policy was debated by an executive 'privy council', which generally included the heads of these other bodies, together with men selected for their experience or connections. These councils were primarily advisory, with the ruler retaining the final say. All those bodies included a mix of university-trained 'learned' men and noblemen, with the latter increasingly also educated. The territorial Estates usually insisted that only native subjects be appointed, but princes often ignored this. The Estates might criticize policy, but they could not formulate it; their task was to find the means to fund it and, increasingly, to promulgate laws agreed with the prince to regulate society and resolve its problems.

Administration was only partly centralized, since princes often ruled agglomerations of different territories and fiefs, each of which could have its own laws, taxes, and government, as was the case for Austria, Bohemia, Burgundy, and Hungary within the Habsburg monarchy. Rulers also maintained a court that combined the function of a house-hold serving their family's immediate needs with a representative role projecting an image of power and good governance to their subjects and peers among the other princely families and European monarchs.

The household continued to perform military functions into the late sixteenth century and, in some principalities, well beyond. The command and maintenance of castles, along with the artillery and weaponry stored in them, generally fell to the household because these remained princely residences into the seventeenth century. The household included

44

stables for horses used by the ruler for war and hunting, and for the movement of the court, which remained at least partly itinerant into the seventeenth century, when rulers settled in one place as their primary residence. Part of the household accompanied the ruler if he commanded in the field, including, usually, his personal chaplain and officials to maintain contact with his government.

The treasury handled funds for war, channelling these through a distinct 'war chest' (*Kriegskasse*), reflecting the pre-modern practice of separating finance according to its intended purpose. Similar distinct chests existed to fund the ruler's court, administration and, in Protestant areas after 1526, the Church. Further, secret personal 'purses' were often maintained as well to shield princely expenditure from the Estates' scrutiny. Meanwhile, the Estates maintained their own treasury, which primarily amortized princely debts. Each account had its own revenues and expenditure, and while money was switched between them, the system seriously impaired financial planning and there were no overall budgets until the administrative reforms around 1800.

The chancellery kept the register of vassals and those owing military obligations.[9] Maintenance of the militia rolls was devolved to the local authorities, who were empowered to muster the population periodically and check their weapons. Territories were subdivided for administrative and tax purposes into districts (*Ämter*) based around a market town and headed by a bailiff appointed by the prince, who usually commanded the area's militia if mobilized.

War Councils

The intermittent and temporary character of war removed the incentive to develop a permanent, specialized military administration. War among Christians was supposed to be exceptional and things were meant to return to 'normal' once it was over. There was no general staff to plan operations or prepare in peacetime for future conflicts. Field commanders were expected to manage with the assistance of their entourage, while each company had a scribe to maintain its roll of soldiers and pay records. A small staff of specialists would be appointed for each campaign. The quartermaster had combined responsibility for logistics, intelligence, movement and billeting, whereas these functions were usually handled separately elsewhere in Europe.[10] The provost marshal

(*Profoß*) oversaw the exercise of military justice, while separate 'masters' were appointed to look after pay, transportation, equipment and supply. The chain of reporting was often unclear, with all office-holders nominally servants of the warlord, but also usually directly subordinate to the field commander. The warlord usually sent commissioners to act as independent liaisons with the army and audit its administration.

Warlords were naturally concerned that their commanders took the right decisions and, in addition to providing written instructions, insisted they consult advisers. While in the field, these included the other senior generals in a large army, or at least unit commanders in a smaller force, and met on an ad hoc basis when needed, such as prior to battle to decide tactics. Separate war councils developed to advise the warlord, who now needed specialist, professional advice that was no longer obtainable from the more general membership of the privy council.

The Habsburgs' assumption of responsibility for Hungary's Military Frontier in 1526 confronted them with the Ottomans' enduring enmity and forced them to improvise a more permanent administration. Initially, they relied on their field commanders and staff, since these were men they had appointed in contrast to the Hungarian and Croatian nobles whose loyalty was not entirely secure. The failure to reconquer the rest of Hungary by the mid-1540s forced the Habsburgs to develop a more integrated system of defence, combining fortresses garrisoned by regular troops, border militias, a gunboat flotilla, and financial subsidies from their other provinces and the Empire. The Court War Council (*Hofkriegsrat*) was established in November 1556 to oversee this system and liaise with the other parts of the Habsburg administration.

Its remit included issuing contracts and commissions to officers, which became routine because of the permanence of border defence. Reflecting the belief that peace with the sultan was impossible, the Court War Council handled diplomatic relations with the Ottoman Empire into the eighteenth century and had its own translation department. However, it also developed a limited planning function to prepare for what was considered an inevitable resumption of conflict in the east. At this point, this was more concerned with preparing financial estimates to help secure funds from the Empire and Habsburg Estates, rather than strategic planning. Nonetheless, the Habsburgs' Court War Council was the first such permanent body in the Empire and became the model for other principalities, beginning with Bavaria (1583) and the Palatinate (1599).[11]

MILITIA AND 'MERCENARIES'

Vassals

Troops could be raised using vassals, militia, or paid professionals. Each had benefits and drawbacks and there was no simple trajectory from 'feudal' to 'modern' recruitment, since the authorities used whatever seemed to work best within their budget at any point. Vassals could be summoned as a 'fief levy' (*Lehensaufgebot*), using fief-holders' obligations to their lords. While all inhabitants were supposed to defend the territory, originally only immediate vassals could be required to serve beyond it under legislation codified in the thirteenth century. Medieval emperors had summoned the imperial vassals who in turn brought their retinues, but the decline of this system by the early fourteenth century eventually prompted the Empire to develop its contingent system from the 1420s.[12]

Princes still looked to their own vassals during the fifteenth century to pursue feuds with their neighbours and to meet the new obligations to the Empire. However, the fragmentation of most knights' fiefs through partition among family members eroded their capacity to sustain the cost of personal service. The development of full plate armour in the century after 1350 greatly increased the cost of equipment. A typical heavy cavalryman in 1300 wore a chainmail coat costing the equivalent of four cows, but his successor in 1515 appeared in a suit of 'Maximilian' armour consisting of 117 separate metal plates weighing 30–40 kilograms in total and worth twenty cows. The increased weight necessitated very large and expensive horses, which many knights were reluctant to risk in battle.[13]

In addition to the danger to themselves, knights were often busy with estate management and found personal service irksome. Their obligations to multiple princes could also discourage them from responding to a summons. The count of Württemberg had 400 vassals on his roll in 1480 but could only rely on 170 of them.[14] Many knights across the west and south had emancipated themselves from princely jurisdiction by securing 'imperial immediacy', often with the emperor's encouragement. Both Frederick III and Maximilian I promoted the Shield of St George association of Swabian knights, in the hope this would defend their lands and fight the Turks, but the imperial knights followed the trend of their territorial counterparts and preferred to commute personal service into cash taxes. Levies of vassals were summoned as late as 1647 by the Habsburgs, but the rout of the Saxon levy cavalry at the battle of Breitenfeld (1631) already signalled the real end of this service.[15]

There was no immediate transition to expensive 'mercenary' cavalry because warlords found other ways to compel men to fight. Members of their household and district officials were expected to serve as part of their contractual duties and in return for the accommodation, food, and salaries they received. Many of these were simultaneously fief-holders, thus blurring the boundaries with vassalage and preserving the fiction that this still functioned. Each nobleman came with three or four less-well-armed retainers, boosting overall numbers. In addition, princes began contracting 'servants outside the household' (*Diener vom Haus aus*), who were paid a retainer to appear with a set number of followers when summoned. Thus, by 1596 the now duke of Württemberg could call on 181 fief-holding vassals (54 of whom were commoners), 35 external servants with 96 men and 144 district officials liable to serve as heavy cavalry.[16]

Militia

Vassals could also be required to bring their tenants as unarmed entrenchment workers, but armed militia infantry were summoned through the population's obligation to maintain public order (*Gerichtsfolge*) and to defend the territory (*Landfolge*). These rules were codified in the thirteenth century and periodically revised, especially with the spread of written culture, which led to the detailed recording of the male population at parish level to identify who was liable to serve. This 'enrolling' served the interests of local elites, since it functioned to control young, unmarried men.[17]

Throughout the Empire and Switzerland all militia followed essentially the same method of a three-tier incremental mobilization that could be summoned according to the threat level.[18] The first contingent comprised young, unmarried men generally aged eighteen to thirty and was called *Auszug* in Switzerland, which roughly translates as 'expedition', indicating that this portion could be required to serve beyond cantonal boundaries. Elsewhere, it was called 'selection' (*Auswahl*) or levy (*Aufgebot*, or *Ausschuß*). The first contingent was rarely larger than a quarter of the total number enrolled, meaning that not all served and usually the required number were chosen by drawing lots. While physical fitness was always a criterion, the selection process allowed local leaders opportunities for favouritism or to settle scores. The second levy, usually called *Landwehr*, comprised older and married men and was primarily a reserve, while the third, called *Landsturm*, included the elderly, very young, and unfit, and was intended for home defence, but was rarely summoned.

The Swiss expected men to appear fully armed, and this was also the case in many German territories, but the growing importance of disciplined formations acting in unison encouraged the local authorities to provide weapons to ensure standardization. Territorial militias grouped men by district, combining those from smaller ones to achieve uniform-sized companies. The militias of imperial cities and large territorial towns were usually organized by parish and it was generally a requirement to own appropriate weapons to secure full burgher status. Civic militias were symbols of communal autonomy, and though they could serve in the field, those imperial cities with dependent territories, like Ulm and Nuremberg, usually relied on conscripting peasants to provide a significant proportion of their field forces.[19] Territorial militias were later adapted to draft conscripts into regular units, whereas civic militias were the inspiration for the future civic guards (*Bürgerwehren*). Thus, the German militia tradition had both authoritarian and liberal aspects, unlike those in Britain and North America where militia were regarded as a democratic alternative to a standing army.

The Swiss fought their fourteenth-century civil wars, and campaigns against the Habsburgs and Burgundians, using their militia. The first levy was mobilized under cantonal command during the first two decades of the Italian Wars, both when the Confederation made war on its own account, and when it served other powers for pay and political reward. Unauthorized volunteers (*Reisläufer*) usually accompanied the official cantonal contingents, making up to half of the total numbers. The shift to more stable relations with France after 1516 led to the formation of regiments created from volunteers serving for pay. The militia structure remained for home defence and was used to fight the 1529–31 civil war and later internal conflicts.

Subsequent mythologizing endowed the Swiss militia with a distinct ideological character as motivated citizens-in-arms. Militiamen did have greater say over officer appointments and served under commanders appointed by the cantonal authorities over which they had some influence through council elections. Things were more democratic in central Switzerland, but the situation in Bern and other cantons with dominant cities resembled that in Ulm and elsewhere in Germany where urban patricians exercised considerable control over dependent villages. A relatively high level of popular enthusiasm was sustained in the wars from the 1470s to 1510s, because the campaigns were generally brief, successful, and lucrative for participants. They also mainly affected younger men, for whom it was a rite of passage.

Prolonged or costly service was rarely popular, and this particularly affected the Swiss at home after the 1530s and the militias of the German territories. The obligation to provide weapons and drill on Sundays seemed onerous, particularly at a time when lords and town councils were demanding other kinds of labour service, to repair roads and dykes, and were imposing new or higher taxes. Territorial governments provided free gunpowder, beer and inducements, such as a pair of trousers offered for the best shot in Württemberg, but these were rarely sufficient to sustain enthusiasm for long. Professional officers were increasingly hired to improve training, but drill sessions often descended into boozy, boisterous behaviour that appeared to threaten public order.[20]

German and Habsburg territories seem to have relied on their militias to provide contingents to the Empire into the 1530s and in some cases beyond.[21] The higher legal and moral imperatives of these obligations overrode any local customs or laws preventing service beyond territorial boundaries. While never clearly specified, this established precedents which were used periodically until 1806 that allowed princes to conscript a select portion of the poorer, able-bodied population to fill out regular units serving at least nominally in the Empire's name. The fact that embodied militia were paid for their service blurred the distinction with hired soldiers. Militia turned out periodically to escort foreign soldiers transiting their land, but professional officers already doubted the efficacy of militia against disciplined troops. Two opposing views emerged by the 1560s, which were personified by Reinhard von Solms and Lazarus von Schwendi, both leading commanders and theorists. They agreed that militia were inferior to professionals, but whereas Solms felt militiamen made poor soldiers because they only thought of their families, Schwendi thought they would be motivated to defend their homes and that the select first levy could be improved through regular drilling.[22]

Schwendi hoped to combine the best of militia (cheaper, allegedly more motivated) with that of professionals (discipline and effectiveness). This vision would persist in reform debates into the nineteenth century, but first found practical implementation in Nassau after the late 1570s. The impetus for reform came from the concern that the Dutch Revolt would spill over the frontier into the Rhineland. The Nassau counts' close association with the Dutch rebel leadership led them to fear reprisals from Spanish troops on their way north to the main front. The main effort came after 1593 and in the following year the first general muster of the drilled Nassau militia impressed observers. The Nassau drill book was copied by most of the other Protestant territories, notably the Palatinate, which reorganized its first levy as six regiments totalling 15,000 in 1601. Beyond the references to ancient Greek and Roman examples, there was nothing new about these measures, which simply tried to ensure the existing first levy actually drilled properly. Austria, Bavaria, and other Catholic areas implemented similar reforms independently from the Protestants. All suffered the same fate: after a year or so of activity around a general muster, attendance at weekly drill sessions tailed off and the militia reverted to an organization more on paper than reality, until a new threat appeared to prompt reimplementation of the same reforms.[23]

Professionals

The most famous professional soldiers of sixteenth-century Europe were the Swiss and German pike-armed infantry, who are invariably called 'mercenaries' in modern histories.[24] The term is tricky to define and overloaded with ideological baggage. It originates in *merces*, the Latin for 'wages', leading to the critique that mercenaries 'offer themselves for hire like whores on market day'.[25] This charge had deep roots in Christian morality with the contrast between Christ, as the good shepherd, and the paid shepherd, who was unreliable because he was a *mercenarius* (hireling). The claim that mercenaries lacked loyalty because they served only for pay was made by influential writers, such as Machiavelli, who himself suffered at the hands of German troops, and Clausewitz, both of whom argued citizen soldiers were superior because they served a 'higher cause'.[26] This objection in turn determines the other two attributes supposedly defining 'mercenaries', that they are generally 'foreign' and their use is an 'expedient', either because indigenous troops are unavailable or inferior, or because governments wish to have troops who do not sympathize with rebellious subjects. In fact, the word 'soldier' has similar roots, deriving from *soldus*, the Latin for pay, and the German *Soelde* was used in the sixteenth century to denote a smallholder who had taken work on a neighbouring farm to support himself.

Paid men had long been used for war, but we need to dismiss the customary definition of 'mercenary' as a supposedly timeless phenomenon 'as old as war itself', and instead examine the specific context for the greater use of professional troops during the later fifteenth century. The underlying causes were a combination of rising wealth, growing population, and changes in weaponry and tactics. Germans had played a prominent role in the forces of the fourteenth-century professional captains operating in Italy (*condottieri*), with around 700 captains and 10,000 men serving in Italy between 1320 and 1360, notably Werner von Urslingen, whose 6,000-strong 'Great Company' formed in 1342 became the model followed by other entrepreneurs. These forces were predominantly heavy cavalry and their presence in Italy depended on a specific convergence of circumstances. They had disappeared by 1400, largely because professional troops were 'domesticated' as Italian commanders established more stable contractual relations with the cities that hired them.[27]

By contrast, the professionals of the later fifteenth and sixteenth centuries were primarily infantry. They emerged partly because the development of improved handguns and innovative use of long pikes made infantry more effective against the heavy cavalry that had long dominated the battlefield. However, as the Swiss case indicates, such infantry first became prominent as militias fighting to overthrow feudal lords or expand the power of their home town. The success of the new, disciplined mass-infantry formations opened professional soldiering to men who would otherwise have lacked the means to hire themselves out as warriors. Infantry weapons were cheap compared to the cost of equipping oneself as an armoured cavalryman, while foot soldiers were paid considerably less than knights. Moreover, effective infantry allowed warlords to tap into a far greater proportion of the population, especially as the existing militia systems provided the means to mobilize them. Meanwhile, the

reluctance of nobles and rich burghers to serve created additional opportunities to raise cash in lieu, which could be put to hiring the new
infantry.

Württemberg was already hiring Swiss in 1460 and paid pensions in
the 1500s to be sure of their services when needed.[28] Such retainers
(*Wartgeld*) were already common in the fifteenth century, though they
were usually paid to individuals, like the 'servants outside the household', and became common in the sixteenth century to secure the
services of experienced captains. German princes could no longer compete with France and Spain, who became the main employers of Swiss
after 1515, but small units of Swiss infantry continued to serve some
south German cities into the mid-sixteenth century.

Alongside Switzerland, Bohemia also already supplied professionals
from the 1440s, having gained fame during the Hussite Wars (1419–34)
as effective infantry armed with crossbows, handguns and protected by
parvises (large shields) and war wagons. The wars dislocated Bohemian
society and prompted poor men to hire themselves out as the light-
infantry component of Austrian, Hungarian, and other east-central
European armies. Their leaders came from the numerous minor nobles
with military experience and contacts, including with the robber bands
from which much of the manpower originated. Like their counterparts
in Hungary and Poland, Bohemian nobles claimed the right to fight for
others provided this did not harm their own kingdom, and they operated on their own account, forming 'little brotherhoods' (*Bratřici*) of up
to 1,000 men. Around 5,000 fought in the war in Prussia between
Poland and the Teutonic Order (1454–66), and 15,000–20,000 campaigned at any one time until the Habsburgs' acquisition of Bohemia in
1526 gave them a monopoly over their services.[29]

German infantry were hired by Burgundy and Lorraine after 1470,
but were initially less effective than the Swiss whom Louis XII hired to
reorganize his infantry after his defeat at Guinegate in August 1479.[30]
Although victorious in that action, Maximilian I found himself exposed
when his Flemish militia returned to their towns, and while he turned to
the Swiss, he found them expensive. Seeking a cheaper, more reliable
alternative, he appointed Swiss captains in 1482 to train German
recruits. By 1486, Konrad Gächuff from Thurgau boasted he had taught
the Swabians so well that each was worth two Swiss.[31] The new German
infantry were known as Landsknechts, but the origins of this term

remain obscure. It was primarily employed by Humanists discussing warfare, and by foreigners who called the Germans *lansquenets* or *lance-knights* to distinguish them from the similarly armed and often German-speaking Swiss.[32] Contemporary documents usually simply called them *Knechte* (servants), denoting their subordinate, hired status, while the collective term for soldiers and non-combatant camp followers was *Kriegsvolk* (war people) into the mid-seventeenth century when it was displaced by *Soldaten*.

Maximilian initially had two regiments, each of 3,000–4,000 men who included numerous Swiss volunteers serving without express cantonal permission. Swiss soldiers largely disappeared from Habsburg service after the 1499 war, but the rhetoric of enmity with the Germans cloaked efforts by cantonal authorities to assert control and ban volunteers. Likewise, there were very few 'free' companies of Landsknechts acting on their own account rather than directly contracted by a warlord like Maximilian. As in Switzerland and Bohemia, various small groups calling themselves *Vriheit* (freedom), *Böcke* (bucks) or *freie Knechte* engaged in cattle rustling and highway robbery, as well as joining campaigns if the opportunity arose. They represented a major public order problem into the 1550s but were not significant militarily.

There were several 'black bands', so called either on account of colouring their armour against rust or adopting signs of mourning after the death of their original commander. At least one of these was composed of Bohemians and was dispersed during the fighting between Austria and Hungary in the 1490s. Another was a unit of Italian light infantry and mounted arquebusiers under Giovanni de Medici in the 1520s. Only two were important autonomous Landsknecht units. One, also known as the *Magna Guarda* (Great Guard), probably originated in troops raised by Duke Albrecht of Saxony to fight the Hungarians in 1487, and subsequently served the emperor, before being turned loose in 1499. Hired the following year by Denmark when it numbered about 4,000 men, the Great Guard was destroyed by the Ditmarschen peasants at Hemmingstedt. The other unit denoted the main group of Landsknechts in French service between 1512 and 1525, who were independent only in the sense of being denounced as outlaws by the emperor.[33]

Contracting

Thus, the organizers of professional troops were rarely 'free agents' who formed units and then touted for business. Rather, contracting developed from the practice of keeping experienced captains on retainer, who were then instructed to raise troops when needed. Crucially, this method suited rulers' lack of means to maintain permanent armies, and the prevailing attitude that war should only be a last resort. Hiring professionals, therefore, did not 'contract out' a state function, because there was no expectation that states should be organizing for war in peacetime. Nor were contractors a barrier to state development as is often alleged, since they allowed rulers to wage war on an unprecedented scale.[34]

The crucial innovation was the emergence around 1500 of large-scale contractors who now raised the bulk of the forces, rather than small specialist units to supplement armies of vassal cavalry and militia infantry. In the Swiss case, the cantonal authorities assumed this role, either directly in agreements with France, the papacy, or other monarchies to provide units mobilized from the first militia levy, or licensing experienced captains to recruit men for foreign service. In Germany, contractors emerged from captains already on retainer who 'scaled-up' their operations by drawing on new credit networks to finance much larger forces. Access to credit proved decisive, since a major attraction of relying on contractors was that these, rather than the warlord, bore much of the risk.

Three innovations assisted this. Bankers developed 'units of account', or notional currencies theoretically tied to a fixed gold or silver value, that allowed them to convert payments between the Empire's real currencies of the florin in the south and the taler in the north. The emergence of exchange banks allowed business to be conducted safely *in banco* through transfer from one account holder to another, without having to send heavy barrels of coins on long, dangerous journeys. Meanwhile, bills of exchange developed as IOUs from merchants or governments endorsed by a signature on the reverse, allowing another person to use them as credit notes in long-distance payments. All three innovations had long antecedents, but combined as robust, reliable methods with the growing expansion and integration of European trade around 1500. The practice of discounting emerged by the later sixteenth century, allowing merchants to sell or redeem bills early against a reduction of their face value or remaining interest, which created a financial market in tradeable bonds. Courts of arbitration meanwhile developed in major commercial centres, providing a more reliable and peaceful means of resolving disputes than hiring armed men to pursue feuds, as in the later fifteenth century.[35]

Contracting remained controlled by warlords, and the Empire's problems stemmed not from military enterprisers acting on their own account, but from princes recruiting or holding men in readiness to pursue their own political or confessional ambitions into the 1550s. A warlord issued a contract (*Bestallungsbrief*) specifying the numbers and types of soldiers to be raised, pay arrangements, period of service and severance terms. These arrangements often remained retainers, activated only once the warlord required the troops. At that point, he issued a licence to recruit (*Werbepatent*), which specified which soldiers were to be sought and where they should be found.[36]

Units could be formed either by contracting captains directly to recruit each company or appointing a colonel (*Oberst*) who subcontracted this task. It was already common by 1510 to hire one primary contractor for each military arm. The Habsburgs contracted Franz von Sickingen for cavalry and Georg von Frundsberg for infantry to provide security during the 1519 imperial election. Sickingen's son, Hans, contracted to recruit 1,000 cavalry in collaboration with Christoph von Landenberg, who was to bring another 1,000, plus 4,000 infantry, in a joint contract with Henry VIII in 1544.[37] Artillery was not contracted, since warlords either used their own arsenals or, in the case of the emperor, summoned it from the imperial cities.

Recruits were often given a small allowance, called *Laufgeld* for infantry and *Anritt* for cavalry, to cover their expenses while they travelled to the designated *Musterplatz* where the unit would be embodied. Each man would receive a passport (*Laufzettel*) to allow him to travel unhindered and avoid falling foul of vagrancy laws. These arrangements never eliminated the liminal legal state prevailing until the men were formally mustered, sworn in, and passed fully under martial law, at which point they were also entitled to be paid. Local inhabitants feared disorder as recruits gathered at the muster site, while neighbouring governments could grow concerned if it was not clear who was recruiting or for what purpose. This explains the anxious rumours of *Vergardung*, or the unauthorized self-assembly of Landsknechts, during the era of heightened confessional tensions from the 1520s to 1550s.[38]

There were also considerable financial anxieties, as the whole operation ran on credit, from the money advanced by the warlord and main contractor to the food obtained on credit by recruits before the muster. Contracting thus required considerable personal wealth, or good credit. Sebastian Schertlin was only able to switch from working as the bishop of Konstanz's scribe to become captain in imperial service in 1518 by investing his wife's dowry and money from his two brothers-in-law.[39] Personal reputation was also crucial to establish trust and to secure the services of reliable men, both for the warlord and for the colonel using subcontractors. Landenberg received £9,266 in recruitment money, but never supplied the promised troops in 1544. Conversely, warlords often paid late and even in peacetime retainers were often a year in arrears. The huge monthly salaries offered to colonels of 800 to 1,000 fl, or fifty times that of ordinary soldiers, reflected the level of risk they carried.

PIKE AND SHOT

Army Size

Sixteenth-century armies could be large, but their size remains a matter of conjecture. Not only are there the usual problems of unreliable or missing documentation, but strengths fluctuated considerably even during a campaign that might last only six months. There were often important differences between the numbers of men raised and those sent into the field, particularly in the case of the Swabian and Schmalkaldic Leagues, which authorized quite substantial forces but whose members often retained a portion for home defence. Comparisons with population size are also difficult, as this cannot be determined with precision, though as a rough guide the Empire had around 21.1 million inhabitants in 1560 with a further 2.1 million in Habsburg Hungary. Even relatively modest numbers were hard to mobilize and sustain in an age without the ability to substitute machinery for missing labour, and when the logistical challenges of assembling large forces were even greater than in later centuries.

The Empire fielded over 35,000 soldiers against Burgundy in 1474–5, which gives some indication of its overall capacity at that point. Maximilian I usually struggled to field more than 14,000–16,000 men, but these were professionals, whereas princely armies were often swollen by additional militia of uncertain value. The emperor's opponent in the Landshut War of 1504, the elector Palatine, mustered 1,000 cavalry, 1,000 Swiss and 10,000–12,000 Bohemian professional infantry, and around 6,000 militia. Württemberg mobilized about 18,000 to oppose the Swabian League in 1519, but half of these were militia.[40] Militia still formed nearly a quarter of Philipp of Hessen's army in 1534 but they were now assigned to guard the baggage.

The Habsburgs' acquisition of new lands and resources between 1516 and 1526 enabled them to field much larger armies. In the summer of 1536 one imperial army of 4,500 cavalry, 25,000 infantry and thirty-six guns invaded northern France from the Netherlands, while another army of 10,000 horse and 40,000 foot marched into Provence. Similar forces were fielded against France in 1544, while during the Schmalkaldic War the army of Charles V peaked at 62,100. Habsburg forces for campaigns against the Ottomans fluctuated between 24,000 (1529) and 34,000 (1542), with the 90,000 deployed in 1532 being exceptional.[41]

The peak of imperial military power came in the summer of 1552 when Charles had 68,000 troops in Germany, 41,000 in the Netherlands and 24,000 in northern Italy to confront his various enemies. Of these, 14,000 cavalry and 64,000 infantry assembled before Metz at the end of the year, giving him the largest army he ever commanded, but he nonetheless failed to take the city.[42] The partition of the Habsburg monarchy prevented Charles's immediate successors from raising these numbers again, but the substantial assistance from the Empire nonetheless meant 83,600 were assembled for the 1566 campaign, while the now permanent garrisons of the Military Frontier averaged 22,000–27,000 between 1576 and 1593.[43]

Infantry

As the preceding figures indicate, infantry now formed the bulk of armies, compared with those of the Middle Ages dominated by cavalry. The reasons for this transformation are complex, but the rise of gunpowder weaponry was an important factor. Gunpowder manufacture is documented in central Europe from 1340, but experimentation continued into the 1420s to find the most effective balance between its three ingredients: saltpetre, sulphur and charcoal. This established different grades for artillery, handguns and priming powder to assist ignition. Early cannon were large 'wall breachers' (*Mauerbrecher*), and while handguns were being used by 1388, it took the development of improved casting techniques around 1450 to make these more effective. Gunpowder thus proved a disruptive technology, the ineffectiveness and uncertainty of which long deterred investment and development, and it was not until the 1470s that it exerted a transformative impact.[44]

By then, lighter, stronger gun barrels had produced the arquebus (*Hackenbüchse*) using a matchlock firing mechanism to depress a cock clasping a slow burning match to ignite the priming powder in the firing pan, which in turn sparked the main charge rammed down the muzzle to fire the lead ball. Since powder did the propelling, handguns did not require the same physical strength to fire as longbows or crossbows. Lighter metal also permitted longer barrels, increasing accuracy to 120m. The price meanwhile fell to between 2 and 3 fl, compared to 2 fl for a good sword and between 0.5 and 1 fl for a pike. These weapons were robust and 'soldier proof', being relatively simple to learn, and the rate of fire was already about two shots a minute under battlefield conditions by the 1520s when, given the close range and dense targets, the fatal hit ratio was around one per 90 rounds, compared to one for every 30,000 in the First World War.[45]

A second type of longarm gun appeared from the 1530s. Known as 'muskets', these were heavier at 7 kg and longer at around 1.5 to 1.8m, and consequently required a rest to steady them while aiming and firing; but with an increased range of up to 200m and, firing a heavier 57g ball, they were better able to penetrate armour. The two types coexisted, though arquebuses increasingly became restricted to mounted shot, whereas infantry carried muskets. These lightened by 1600 when a 45g ball became standard, and a further reduction in calibre, combined with other improvements, created lighter weapons by the 1630s that no longer required rests, but nonetheless achieved the same range. However, muzzle velocities did not increase between 1560 and the later nineteenth century.

The spread of more effective guns led to these becoming the main infantry missile weapon by 1507 when Maximilian formally abolished crossbows, around twenty years ahead of the French army. Whereas 9.5 per cent of the Württemberg militia had guns compared to 35 per cent with crossbows in 1480, crossbows were dropped in 1490 and nine years later 34.6 per cent carried arquebuses. The rapid adoption of fire-arms in Württemberg perhaps reflected its proximity to the Burgundian wars on the Upper Rhine, compared to the Upper Palatine militia that still had 35 per cent crossbows to 20.7 per cent guns in 1504. In both cases, the rest of the men were largely armed with halberds, spears and other shorter polearms.[46] The high proportion of shot in both cases reflected the predominance of light-infantry tactics at this point when foot soldiers primarily provided fire support to cavalry whose charge was expected to win the battle. If threatened by enemy cavalry, the skir-mishing missile troops would retire to the protection offered by their polearmed comrades who sheltered behind parvises or war wagons.

The famous victories of the Swiss over the Habsburg knights in the thirteenth- and fourteenth-century 'wars of independence' were based on defensive tactics and had nothing to do with their later fame as offen-sively orientated infantry. Each village was required to maintain stone and earth barriers along their boundaries. Small detachments would hold these in the valley floor to delay the advancing cavalry, who were strung out in a long column of march. The main Swiss force then sprang the ambush, rolling boulders down the hillside to cause confusion, before attacking with swords, spears and halberds.[47] The latter proved an ideal weapon for close combat against cavalry, since its hooked blade allowed the foot soldier to pull his opponent from his horse.

Swiss tactics changed as they shifted to offensives intended to conquer Habsburg territory and the rich Milanese uplands, as well as fight each other in the protracted civil war of 1436–50. One important innovation was the adoption of the 3m-long pike, prompted by the Swiss defeat in open country by Milanese cavalry at Arbedo in 1422. Initially intended for defence, the Swiss proved the effectiveness of pikes at St Jakob an der Birs in 1444, when they attacked a far superior French army and, though defeated, inflicted such losses that their enemy soon abandoned its invasion.[48]

The pike's adoption compelled the Swiss to work together since, unlike the halberd, it was not a weapon for individual combat and was only effective when used by a highly disciplined and motivated mass. They now formed up as a *Gewalthaufen*, literally 'power-crowd', or rectangu-lar block in close order with pikemen on all four sides enclosing a mass of halberdiers. Each block was three or four times as many men wide as deep. Its advance was screened by missile troops, whose fire would soften up the enemy before the main body surged forward. If threatened by cavalry, the skirmishers would retreat behind the block, or shelter underneath their comrades' levelled pikes. Experience by the 1460s prompted a reduction of the shot troops from a quarter to only a tenth of strength, whereas the ratio of pikes to halberds shifted from 1:4 to 1:3.[49]

The second innovation was to deploy three blocks in echelon, staggered one behind the other, usually with the lead unit on the right, often with a smaller fourth detachment as 'forlorn hope' (*Verlorene Haufen*) to spearhead the attack. While echoing the classic late medieval deployment in three 'battles', this practice shifted the weight entirely on to the infantry, who now operated in mutually supporting formations instead of being split to assist three groups of cavalry. Where cavalry were available, they had a purely supporting role as scouts or skirmishers. The Swiss relied on speed and shock, deliberately cultivating a fearsome reputation to intimidate their enemies into fleeing before contact. They also learned to spot when enemy artillery was about to fire, so they could throw themselves on the ground and let the shots pass harmlessly overhead. The aggressive tactics suited Swiss capacities, since the cantons lacked the resources to keep troops in the field for long and needed to bring each campaign to a swift, successful conclusion.

A series of spectacular victories over the Burgundians in the 1470s gave the Swiss a reputation for invincibility, while contemporaries were impressed by their hardiness and the loyalty they demonstrated when they refused to surrender their garrisons after their French paymasters pulled out of Italy in 1495–6. However, significant defeats at Cerignola (1503), Ravenna (1512) and Bicocca (1522) indicated they could be beaten by enemies occupying rough ground or defending entrenchments. The Swiss were also vulnerable to light cavalry, who could harass and disrupt their large block formations. It also became difficult to control their demands for more pay.[50]

The German Landsknechts already began diverging from the Swiss in the 1490s by substantially increasing the proportion of pikes relative to halberds and ensuring these were all 5m-long pikes. The Landsknechts also changed their handling of their pikes, so that when lowered for action, they gripped them closer to the butt end rather than nearer the middle. This made them harder to hold level for a sustained time as the weight became tremendous but ensured they projected further from the formation. There were now five ranks of pikemen followed by one or two of halberdiers, repeated throughout the block, which now narrowed to only twice as many men along its front as across its depth. Given that each man only occupied 50–75cm frontage, the formation was often more a square than column due to the larger gap between ranks to enable the men to move quickly and wield their weapons. The greater depth and proportion of pikes increased offensive power, while the longer pikes also protected the formation against enemy cavalry.

The retention of other weapons like halberds and two-handed swords stemmed from the problem of engaging similarly armed and organized opponents. The clash of two blocks could result either in a horrible, locked-together shoving match, or in a stand-off, where the opposing front ranks jabbed at each other's faces with levelled pikes. At this point, Landsknecht halberdiers and swordsmen would sortie, ducking under the pikes to slash at the enemy's legs or push his weapons away to expose him to fatal blows. All Landsknechts carried a 'cat gutter' (*Katzbalger*) sword with a short hilt and broad 50–55cm blade as an additional close-combat weapon. The imposing two-hander (*Bidenhänder*) sword had a blade of up to 170cm and featured prominently in contemporary engravings but was carried only by a small minority of men. Meanwhile, the cat gutter was increasingly replaced by the lighter but longer-bladed steel *Degen* carried for personal defence.[51]

However, the real innovation was to revive the proportion of shot, taking advantage of the improved arquebus around 1500 and the musket from about 1530. Already between one in eight and one in six Landsknechts carried an arquebus in the early sixteenth century. Nearly a third of the Austrian infantry at Laufen in 1534 were so armed, and the proportion increased steadily to a half by 1565, and to between that and over two-thirds by 1597, depending on the regiment. The proportion of those armed with halberds or two-handers had already dropped to under 15 per cent by the early sixteenth century and continued to decline slightly as these weapons became increasingly associated with being symbols of command carried by NCOs or men assigned to guarding the flag. The proportion of pikes among militia had risen to four-fifths by the early sixteenth century in imitation of Swiss tactics, and remained generally higher than among professionals thereafter, though it too declined relative to those with guns.

Rebalancing the pike to shot ratio offered more options for attack and defence. The shot could accompany the pike block as a 'hedge' (*Hecke*) on its flanks and front, fanning out when needed to provide covering fire. They could also be detached for traditional light-infantry roles or massed behind earthworks as at Bicocca to fire volleys at attackers. Various methods were developed to sustain steady fire by men moving to the front rank to shoot and then returning to the rear to reload. Deployment switched back to rectangular blocks wider than they were deep to bring more guns to bear and make it easier for those in the rear to move forward when firing. These tactics often remained more effective in theory than in practice, since they required superior discipline and control to stop men simply shooting into the air and hastening back to the rear to avoid being hit by incoming fire.

The renewed proportion of shot prompted a greater use of defensive armour among infantry. A full set of infantry armour (*Harnisch*), including a morion helmet (*Sturmhaube*), breast and backplate, neck (*gorget*), arm (*brassards*) and thigh (*tassettes*) protectors, cost 10–12 fl in the early sixteenth century, putting it beyond most soldiers' budget. Efforts to make it bulletproof against the heavier muskets pushed the weight of just a breastplate up to 8 kg by the 1550s, leading to the development of 'half armour' (*Halbharnisch* or *corselet*) protecting just the head and torso. Around 40 per cent of Landsknechts in French service in 1562 wore corselets, while the Swiss were also now much more heavily armoured.[52]

The effectiveness of the Swiss and Landsknecht tactics lay in the close cooperation between the differently armed soldiers within the same unit. Efforts were already being made in the fifteenth century to ensure that each militia contingent carried the appropriate mix of weapons. This practice ensured consistency regarding the size of the block, which, in the case of the Swiss, was initially determined less by military necessity than the strength of the cantonal contingents composing it. Contingents varied greatly in size, but 200 was considered the minimum to warrant its own *Fähnlein*, or 'little banner', distinct from the main flag of the block. The term Fähnlein persisted into the 1640s when it was displaced by *Compagnie*, a borrowing via France of the original term *com pani* from the fourteenth-century Italian *condottieri* units that 'shared bread' together.

The size of these subunits varied considerably, from the 170-man companies raised by Bavaria in 1504, to the 500 authorized by the

Reichstag in 1530. Company sizes seem to have been particularly large for troops sent as imperial contingents to campaign in Hungary, probably because of the high attrition rate, but it usually fluctuated between about 260 and 470 effectives, though 400 remained the desired theoretical strength into the mid-sixteenth century after which it fell to 300.[53] The gradual reduction in size improved command and control, because the number of officers in each company remained the same. Whereas blocks of up to 10,000 men had been deployed into the 1520s, thereafter both the Swiss and Landsknechts adopted ten company regiments as a general standard, with each forming a block of 3,000–4,000 men. This was sufficiently large to absorb casualties while maintaining momentum in attack, but the smaller size allowed the infantry to be subdivided into more blocks, increasing tactical flexibility. Under-strength units could still be combined with others to achieve the desired tactical strength.

The belligerents of the Italian Wars and other conflicts sought Swiss and Germans as their main battle infantry, hiring Italians and Spaniards in smaller numbers as light troops. Only where cost or unavailability prevented this did they train their own troops in the *allmayn* or German manner. Both Scotland and England adopted elements of heavy-infantry tactics, with the latter copying Landsknecht drum signals to transmit orders. France established permanent 'legions' in 1534, while Sweden eventually created 'a domestic budget army' using peasant conscripts drilled and armed like Landsknechts in 1544. Spain blended its own light-infantry tactics with those of heavy-pike infantry, eventually creating permanent regiments called tercios in 1537.[54]

Nonetheless, Swiss and Germans were still regarded as superior, or at least as possessing distinct qualities that warranted them being hired in separate regiments. Both continued to be regarded as steady under fire and determined in attack, and these two qualities were generally linked to the higher proportion of pikemen than among native troops, notably the French. Pikemen required courage, since they had to endure being shot at without being able to retaliate at a distance like missile troops, and at this point were often expected to provide their own armour. As it was easier to recruit shot than pikes, the proportion of the latter in French regiments declined from 50 per cent to 10 per cent between 1550 and 1590, leading the Huguenot commander François de la Noue to complain that 'arquebuses without pikes are arms and legs without a body'.[55] German and

Swiss regiments were employed by both sides in the French Wars of Religion to provide large pike-heavy blocks that could be flanked by the weaker local units, who were largely musketeers.

A higher proportion of musketeers was more desirable when campaigning against the Ottomans, and imperial regiments could consist of 75 per cent shot during the Long Turkish War. Usually outnumbered, imperial armies preferred to fight defensively, relying on superior firepower to halt Turkish attacks before counter-attacking themselves. Large pike blocks still featured prominently in the campaigns of the 1530s and 1540s, but primarily as a stable reserve around which other units could regroup, rather than as a strike force. Whereas war wagons and other mobile defences were abandoned when units were campaigning elsewhere, they remained essential equipment in Hungary, where they were used to protect lines of musketeers and artillery.[56]

Cavalry

If cavalry no longer dominated the battlefield, it nonetheless remained an important component in all armies. Its advantages lay in its greater speed and the psychological factor of the charge, since the sight of a dark mass of horses moving at speed and the thunder of multiple hooves could easily intimidate inexperienced, demoralized, or surprised enemies. German and especially Swiss armies were already infantry-heavy by the later fifteenth century, in contrast to those in France, Burgundy and Italy, where up to half were still mounted. The proportion of cavalry in these other armies declined to about one-sixth by the mid-sixteenth century, or roughly the level it had already reached in the Empire by 1500 where it remained constant to the end of the century. It could still vary in individual battles according to circumstances, and Sievershausen (1553) was notable for involving 13,500 cavalry to only 20,000 infantry.

In contrast to much of Europe, German cavalry were not organized around the 'lance', or a unit of one heavy cavalryman and up to eight more lightly armed retainers or servants, but instead were already recruited individually as *Einspänner* (literally 'one horse') into companies composed of men armed and equipped the same. In contingent forces, like the imperial army or that of the Swabian League, men were combined to form standard-sized companies of usually about 300 men.

What were known elsewhere as *gendarmes* (men-at-arms) were called *Riesige*, literally 'giants', who rode large horses 16 hands high, weighing up to 550 kg, which were taught to rear and strike an enemy's mount when prodded, or kick an enemy soldier with their hind legs (see Fig. 2). Training took place in fields with blazing fires and heaps of carrion to accustom the animal to the smell of battle. Riders needed not only to be able to handle their powerful mounts, but to handle their weapons while mounted. At this point, the heavy cavalryman's primary weapon was a long wooden lance held level while charging, plus a long sword for close combat. They also had to learn to draw their sword with their right hand alone, because, unlike foot soldiers who could use their left hand to steady the scabbard, they needed the left hand to hold the reins.

Heavy cavalry wore full plate armour into the 1540s that cost 16 fl. At this point, most heavy cavalrymen were expected to buy the armour themselves. Considering that a large warhorse cost 37 to 44 fl, this represented a substantial investment and was reflected in their monthly pay of 24 fl, or twice that of other cavalry. Efforts were made from the 1530s to lighten the equipment with the development of three-quarter 'riding armour' (*Trabharnisch*), which became standard by about 1550 and involved leather gloves and boots, replacing the earlier metal protection for these parts of the body.[57]

Cavalry advanced at a walk of about 125m per minute (7.5 kmh), compared to infantry in formation moving at around 75m, increasing to a trot of 14 kmh as they neared their target. The attack remained controlled, as cavalry speeded up to a gallop of 19 kmh only for the last 50m or so; a practice that remained unchanged since the late Middle Ages and was still recommended on the eve of the Thirty Years War some seventy years later.[58] It was possible to go faster, but that risked loss of formation and would tire the horses too quickly. The attack was made in a deep wedge pointing towards the enemy to pierce their line, in contrast to the French practice of charging *en haye*, or a long, thin line that brought more men to bear, but could become disordered when moving at speed. The wedge was replaced by a square block from 1530 and this became standard into the Thirty Years War era, though gradually thinning to a long rectangle, closer to French practice. Medium cavalry wore less armour and were initially primarily lancers armed with boar spears, but increasingly became the missile element of mounted troops. They emerged from the armed retainers of vassal cavalry, who were detached from the heavy cavalry into separate units during the late fifteenth century, possibly copying Italian practice. Medium cavalry appear to have initially formed only a small proportion, with only one mounted crossbowman for every nine lancers among the Swabian League cavalry in the 1522 campaign against the Franconian knights.[59] This indicates that crossbows persisted longer among cavalry than infantry, though by this date these too were being replaced by arquebuses, which were suspended while riding from a belt slung over the man's shoulder, hence the term *Bandolierreiter*. These weapons still required both hands to fire, forcing the rider to halt to do so. The Reichstag instructed that a tenth of cavalry in imperial contingents in 1530 and 1542 should be mounted arquebusiers.[60]

Firearms became increasingly important during the 1540s following the invention of the wheellock firing mechanism around 1515, which led to the development of pistols that could be fired singlehandedly while on the move. The wheellock worked better than the matchlock in wet weather, but was generally inaccurate over ten metres, and riders were advised not to pull the trigger until the barrel of their pistol was touching an opponent. Despite such drawbacks, these weapons could be deadly in close combat and virtually all the 350 noblemen killed at Sievershausen died of gunshot wounds, mostly from pistols.[61]

Pistols were also very effective when delivered en masse at a larger, stationary target, such as an infantry block. German cavalry pioneered the caracole, or 'snail' tactic, involving successive ranks riding forward, firing at close range, then peeling off either side and returning to the rear to reload. Large formations of around twenty files, six ranks deep, were used to achieve the sustained volume of fire. Although much derided by later commentators, the caracole allowed cavalry to damage infantry without needing to charge home, particularly as their speed and continued use of helmets, breast and backplates offered some protection against their enemies' musketry.

The practice of blackening their armour against rust led to the new pistoleers being known as *schwarze Reiter*. Brunswick became a major centre of pistol manufacture and its location close to the north German horse-breeding areas enabled units to be raised and equipped locally. Their lighter equipment meant that Reiters did not require large, expensive horses, increasing their attraction for warlords. Henry VIII had already hired some for the 1544 Boulogne campaign, surprising his

French opponents, who swiftly recruited their own, mustering 1,500 in 1555, rising to 8,000 by 1558 when they formed the bulk of their cavalry.[62] Their effectiveness was demonstrated at Dreux, the opening battle of the French Wars of Religion in 1562, where German Reiters in Huguenot service halted two large Swiss pike blocks and gradually wore them down, shooting into their flanks and killing their officers until both units disintegrated. The Huguenots' continued success in securing the services of Reiters forced the French Crown to expand its heavy cavalry and detach a major portion of it in futile efforts to prevent the Germans entering the country.

The development of improved, lighter arquebuses, known as carbines, saw the re-adoption of longer-barrelled and thus more accurate firearms by cavalry from the 1570s. Units so armed were known as carabineers or *Arquebus-Reiter* and had become the typical medium cavalry by 1600. Although their main weapon still required two hands to fire, mounted arquebusiers also carried two pistols in holsters either side of their saddle, as well as a sword for personal defence. The increased effectiveness of mounted firepower saw the now-dwindling numbers of heavy cavalry abandon their lances and re-equip themselves likewise with two pistols as well as their sword. The term 'cuirassier', already used briefly around 1498, now reappeared to designate this remodelled heavy cavalry. Both cuirassiers and arquebusiers performed essentially the same battlefield roles, but the former were regarded as more effective in attack, thanks to their better armour and heavier horses, yet more expensive to recruit and equip.[63]

Light cavalry emerged as an important element in Habsburg armies during the Italian Wars through the encounter with these types employed by Venice and other belligerents for scouting, raiding, and to harass and disrupt enemy formations in battle. They wore little or no armour, but often carried an asymmetrical shield and were armed with light lances, swords and, increasingly, pistols and carbines. They were generally recruited from across the Balkans and east-central Europe and were initially called 'Stradiots', and later known variously as hussars, Cossacks, or Croats. While each group had distinctive dress, they commonly wore brightly coloured long coats and tall fur hats, and their generally wild appearance added to their fearsome reputation; something they deliberately fostered through collecting the severed heads of captives and other brutal acts intended to inspire fear. The Habsburgs' acquisition of

Croatia and Hungary enabled them to recruit substantial numbers of hussars, not only to oppose the Turks but also for campaigning in the Empire. Charles V had 800 Hungarian hussars at the battle of Mühlberg (1547).[64] The low proportion of light cavalry reflected the strategic imperative of seeking a swift decision, rather than a prolonged attritional campaign of skirmishing, because of the cost of keeping armies in the field.

Artillery

Artillery emerged first as a significant factor in siege warfare, with its potency demonstrated in the successful capture and destruction of Tannenberg Castle, south of Darmstadt, in 1339.[65] Nonetheless, this did not immediately make all existing castles obsolete, especially as fortification techniques adapted. Moreover, given the weight of both gun and ammunition, artillery developed primarily as a defensive weapon placed in castles and cities. In contrast to western European monarchies where it became a royal monopoly, the production and possession of artillery in the Empire was driven mainly by the imperial cities; something that was encouraged by the close connection between gun- and bell-founding, as well as the production of gunpowder that was also urban based. Aachen had possessed heavy guns since 1345 and most cities had significant arsenals by 1400, well ahead of those owned by princes.[66]

The cities' prominence in developing artillery was an important factor sustaining their political influence at a point when power was slipping increasingly to the larger princely territories, which could field more men and were becoming better at raising taxes. Artillery had not yet proven its worth: Margrave Albrecht of Brandenburg-Kulmbach lost the battle of Giengen an der Brenz (1462) despite having more cannon. A single cannon made for Frankfurt in 1394 cost the equivalent of 442 cows.[67] Given the uncertainty and cost, princes were happy to let cities carry the risks, provided they loaned guns when needed in the regional conflicts of the fifteenth century. The imperial cities continued to supply a significant proportion of the emperor's artillery during the sixteenth century: six of the twenty guns with the force sent to Hungary in June 1542 came from Ulm.[68]

The dukes of Burgundy were famous for developing Europe's largest artillery train during the fifteenth century. Much of this fell into the hands of the Swiss, who had around 1,000 cannon in 1500. Although impressive, few of these could be used in the field and many were obsolete, brittle iron guns. Guns during the sixteenth century were increasingly made of bronze, which was lighter and stronger if much more expensive. Improved iron cannon appeared in the 1570s, which, while cheaper, were also heavier and mainly restricted to warships and fortresses. German gun-founders and artillerymen enjoyed a good reputation by the late fifteenth century and were important in cannon production in Hungary, Spain, and the Ottoman Empire.[69]

In addition to creating the Landsknechts, Maximilian I was at the forefront of developing artillery in the Empire, having been impressed by a parade of Burgundian cannon while still archduke. His acquisition of the Tirol in 1490 gave him both the wealth and the local metalworking expertise to establish centralized production at Innsbruck, where a new arsenal was completed between 1500 and 1505 and still stands today (see Fig. 3). Built around a courtyard, this multi-storey building became the model for all future arsenals with the heavier pieces stored outside and on the ground floor, and the lighter weaponry on the higher floors. Cannon were prestige items and their display in the new arsenal consciously symbolized imperial power and pretensions, as well as artillery's status as the only permanent element of armed force which, given the expense and time invested in assembling it, was kept in readiness, whereas soldiers could be raised relatively quickly when needed. Annual production of heavy guns in Innsbruck rose dramatically from 50 in 1500 to 385 in 1506, with that of arquebuses increasing from 500 in 1498 to over 4,100 by 1506.[70] The potency of Maximilian's artillery was demonstrated when he took the previously impregnable Kufstein in just three days during the Landshut War of 1503–5.

Another powerful influence behind centralizing production was to free dependency on too many different manufacturers and introduce standardized types that eased problems of ammunition supply and allowed more coherent and effective tactical use of cannon. Again, Maximilian proved an important innovator with his illustrated arsenal inventory of 1502 that categorized artillery into four basic types.[71] 'Large guns' (*Hauptbüchsen*) weighed up to 100cwt and required huge teams of horses to transport them and their equipment which, combined with their slow rate of fire, relegated them to siege work. Cannon (*Kartaunen*) had shorter barrels where the weight saved in length was invested in thickness, enabling them to withstand a greater powder charge and so fire their projectile with greater velocity, making them more useful in smashing castle walls than long-barrelled culverins (*Schlangen*, literally 'snakes'), which had the greater accuracy and range required in battle. The final category of *Haufnitzen* included a great variety of guns delivering a hail of shot as anti-personnel weapons, as well as mortars for indirect fire.

These categories illustrate the difficult trade-offs between desired characteristics, manufacturing capabilities and cost. Categorization was greatly refined through the invention around 1540 of the calibre system by Georg Hartmann, who used his local Nuremberg weights and measures to standardize guns according to the diameter of their bore. Given that guns were muzzleloaders and required windage, or gap difference in diameters between bore and shot, it became common to denote them by the weight of their cast-iron roundshot; the form of projectile replacing those laboriously made of stone around 1500. Hartmann's system spread throughout Europe and remained the standard method into the nineteenth century, though it was much modified by later artillerymen and ballistic theorists. While it had already become common in the mid-sixteenth century to standardize in rounded multiples from a 'two-pounder' (2pdr) upwards, guns were still known by names, with the smallest called a falconette, followed by a falcon, then culverins and cannons both as 'quarter', 'half' or 'full' depending on size. Contemporaries used these names inconsistently into the later seventeenth century when greater standardization reduced the types and calibres employed.

Cities continued to possess large numbers of guns into the seventeenth century. Strasbourg already had 158 of all types in 1475, rising to 32 large guns, 49 falconettes, 162 cannon and 1,069 wall guns and petards by 1545. That compared to the 239 guns of the pugnacious Philipp of Hessen.[72] These huge arsenals did not translate into large-scale deployment in battles. Cities and princes stored guns well beyond their useful lives, partly through reluctance to part with things that had been so expensive to acquire, but also keeping them as trophies and as a reserve of metal that could be reused. A significant proportion were retained for civic defence. The wooden gun carriages required constant maintenance and often proved too rotten to be used in the field. Guns also remained heavy, with a falconette typically weighing 7cwt and requiring three horses to pull it, while a half cannon weighed four tons and needed up to twenty-five horses and fifteen to twenty men. Considerable additional resources were thus required to include guns in an army, while their presence slowed movement and there was always the risk that they might be captured.

The Swabian League required its members to provide one 'field gun' (*Feldschlange*) for every 400 infantry and the ratio of three guns per 1,000 men seems to have been common for armies up to about 25,000 men, with a lower proportion for larger forces. During the Schmalkaldic War, Charles V deployed roughly one gun per 700 effectives. Unlike the other two military arms, artillery was not organized into companies. Instead, guns of various types were assembled with their associated equipment and ammunition into a 'train' for each campaign. There was usually one master gunner for every piece, along with a small number of craftsmen for maintenance. Gunners' assistants were generally drawn as needed from the infantry, while pioneers and transport personnel were usually conscripted from peasant militia.

Artillery generally engaged at no more than 1,000m, or well below the theoretical maximum range of the larger pieces. Rates of fire were slow, with eight rounds per hour considered standard for sieges where guns fired from fixed positions against a static target. After four hours' continuous firing it was customary to stop to let the barrel cool down to avoid the heat warping it. Although sixteenth-century cannon were greatly improved, risks remained: during the bombardment of Pest in October 1542, six of the forty imperial guns burst.[73] The Schmalkaldic League's 110 guns fired 3,800 shots during its cannonade of the imperial camp at Ingolstadt between 31 August and 3 September 1546, lasting from 7 a.m. to 4 p.m. each day. Charles V's thirty-two guns fired 1,100 shots in response, but his army lost two of their six large cannon and another six smaller ones to accidental explosions, in four cases due to overloading the powder charge. Around 500–600 imperial soldiers were killed or wounded on the first day, including an Italian shot at the emperor's side.[74]

In battle, guns were usually posted slightly forward of the main line and were placed well apart to allow space for their powder and ammunition. Once positioned, their large teams of horses were moved to the rear to avoid becoming a target or obscuring the view. The slow rate of fire reduced the chances of inflicting heavy losses on an advancing enemy, while gunners stood little chance of defending themselves in close combat and fled before contact. The cost of cannons and their symbolic value nonetheless ensured that fierce fights could develop, as at Marignano in 1515, where the Swiss and the Landsknechts fought for possession of the French gun line.

However, artillery was not necessarily immobile as demonstrated by the Hessian victory over the Austrian Habsburgs at Lauffen on 13 May 1534, which developed into a running fight along a valley. The larger Hessian army posted guns on a hill, forcing the Austrians to retire to a ridge from where their own artillery returned fire, inflicting some losses on the main body of Hessian infantry. The Austrians resumed their retreat but were cut off further down the valley by Hessian cavalry who outflanked them by riding ahead. The Austrians used artillery to blast their way clear, but the delay allowed the main Hessian force to catch up behind. A renewed artillery duel followed, before the Hessian infantry attacked, finally breaking Austrian resistance.[75] Similar flexibility was demonstrated in the fighting around Nordheim in October 1545 between Heinrich of Brunswick-Wolfenbüttel and the Hessians and Saxons who had occupied his duchy.[76]

These actions also indicate the evolution of tactics since the late fifteenth century, away from reliance on either traditional heavy cavalry or the new pike blocks as battle-winners, to a more choreographed coordination between the different military arms and between units. Infantry predominated, but it required cavalry and artillery in support. Commanders adapted formation sizes and deployment to suit the terrain and their objectives. Armies generally deployed the different blocks of horse and foot in a single line, with few or no reserves behind, hoping to outflank their opponents. Opposing units paired off in what could become individual fights, but close support from cavalry and artillery often tipped the balance, as at Ceresole (1544), where French gendarmes first drove off the opposing imperial cavalry and then joined units of Gascon and Swiss infantry to defeat the main block of imperial Landsknechts.[77]

Fortifications

The Empire is usually presented as a backwater in the history of early modern fortifications and siege warfare, which focus on developments in

Italy, France and the Netherlands.[78] In part, this reflects the historiographical convention that associates these regions, along with Spain, with the 'military revolution', while neglecting developments elsewhere. It also stems from the fact that the Empire largely escaped prolonged conflict, especially after 1554, and thus rulers lacked the urgency to invest in new or improved defences. This did not mean that fortifications were not valued, nor that the period was entirely devoid of innovation.

The years after 1450 were characterized by considerable experimentation as military architects responded to the improved potential of artillery in both attack and defence. The *trace italienne* of pointed rather than rounded bastions (angled projections from the walls) proved superior in creating interlocking fields of fire by 1500 and was adopted throughout Europe from the 1530s, though the expense and difficulty of building such works often meant they took years to construct. Solothurn, Zürich, Geneva and other Swiss towns modernized their defences in this manner after 1504, as did Kufstein (1518–22), Klagenfurt (1543–92) and Jülich (1549), often with the assistance of Italian architects. Entirely new works were expensive, because their construction entailed demolishing whatever was already in place, including suburbs, monasteries, and other buildings that might obscure the field of fire. Most imperial cities simply added bastions to their existing medieval walls. The Empire's numerous castles were generally on high hills unsuited for their conversion from defence in height to that in depth, though this did not prevent several princes investing large sums trying to do so.[79]

The main area of innovation was the development of the Military Frontier to provide permanent defence against the Ottomans following the Habsburgs' acquisition of Croatia and Hungary in 1526.[80] This entailed a division of financial and military labour, with Austria assuming primary responsibility for fortifications and regular garrisons, while the Hungarian and Croatian magnates modified their county forces and private armies to provide the light cavalry patrolling the frontier and launching retaliatory raids across it. Refugees were settled along the frontier to serve as border militia infantry in return for tax exemptions and other privileges. Those at the western end at Senj also manned small boats to defend the coast. Finally, the Empire voted financial and military aid through the Reichstag that subsidized the cost of the defences and provided additional manpower for major operations.

Whereas Habsburg officers had little knowledge of Hungary before

1521, two decades later they were more prepared to work with the local elite in creating a more coherent command structure. Meanwhile, the Hungarian magnates recognized that only the Habsburgs could provide the necessary coordination and finance, and relinquished direct personal control of many of the key forts. After 1546 the border was divided into captaincies under men appointed from Vienna and subdivided into sectors based around major fortresses with smaller stone and wooden palisade outposts in between. A new, higher tier of six general captaincies was established in 1560.

Following the failure of another major offensive from 1565 to 1568 to dislodge the Turks, the Habsburgs decided on Schwendi's advice to invest instead in further strengthening their defences. By 1576, these ran to a strip 1,000 km long and up to 50 km wide, protected by 123 forts and watchtowers held by 22,500 troops, or around a third more than twenty years previously. Responsibility was redistributed in 1578, with Austria and Hungary financing defences north of the Mur, while Inner Austria and Croatia maintained those to the south. Several new fortresses were built to plug gaps, while the trauma of the 1529 siege prompted the extensive refortification of Vienna from 1531 to 1567. The long period of construction indicates that fortifications remained works in progress, resumed as funds became available, or as new techniques or threats compelled further activity. Despite substantial additional funding from the Empire, the modernization programme was incomplete by the outbreak of the Long Turkish War in 1593, and the loss of Raab (Györ) the following year proved that even the best and most complete forts were not invulnerable, though it was retaken in 1598.

The Habsburgs' defences represented a far higher level of fortification than along the French or Netherlands borders. Although it cost them more to maintain their side than it did the Ottomans, who had the benefit of interior lines, the expense proved worthwhile. The Ottomans were forced to waste most of the 1566 campaign – the last by Suleiman the Magnificent – in unproductive sieges and turned their attention to softer targets until 1593. Rudolf II's decision to escalate the Long Turkish War proved ruinously expensive and destabilized the Habsburg monarchy, but the border defences nonetheless largely held.

COMMAND OF THE RIVERS

Navies in German History

Permanent naval forces were an important element in Habsburg border defences since all major operations followed the line of the Danube and its tributaries. This aspect is scarcely known outside specialist studies, as the focus on Prussia reinforces the impression of German warfare as primarily land-based prior to the late nineteenth century. In terms of surface fleets, the German powers were indeed latecomers, with Austria embarking on this slightly earlier and maintaining a lead over Prussia into the early 1880s. A navalist tendency already coloured historical writing during the nineteenth century, which bemoaned the supposed failure to create a powerful fleet earlier, blaming this on the lack of national unity and arguing that it had cost Germany opportunities to secure colonies and a greater share of the world's wealth. This view still influences some more recent writing and presupposes that powerful navies were necessary for national development, and that their absence was a sign of inferiority relative to other European states.

While navies indeed remained secondary to armies, even during the height of German naval power between 1898 and 1945, waterborne forces were nonetheless integral elements to German war-making throughout. Control of the seaways was important to Europe's Atlantic states with the development of new global trade routes from the later fifteenth century, but these were never instant sources of riches. The Mediterranean and Baltic trades grew considerably alongside the expansion of Asiatic and American commerce, while continental Europe itself remained the primary source of wealth, and consequently taxes and military power. Ships were also very expensive to build, crew and maintain, especially as they soon deteriorated if not kept repaired. Naval warfare had been changing significantly since the fifteenth century but had not reached the point where merchant ships could be just quickly fitted out with extra guns when required for war. While the Atlantic monarchies built specialized 'great ships' for war from the 1520s, these were costly prestige items, and most vessels, even if initially built as warships, were often used as merchantmen in peacetime to reduce their maintenance costs and keep them operational.[81] Concentration on land forces was thus a sensible use of scarce resources, particularly given that German rulers and elites continued to see Europe as their main area of interest.

Mediterranean Campaigns

The German lands and much of the Austrian Habsburg monarchy had long been connected to the sea, and the inhabitants had equally long seafaring traditions. Medieval emperors had also used naval power, but always to achieve specific objectives, such as Henry VI's conquest of Sicily in 1194. Mediterranean and Baltic pirates were often a problem for coastal communities, but these were always on the fringes of imperial power and of peripheral interest. Maximilian I certainly had ambitions to command the seas: his propagandistic works show imperial mastery of both galleys and carracks, the two principal types of seagoing vessels. However, he did not in fact possess such warships and it is noteworthy that the depiction of his war with Venice (1508–16) shows Landsknechts chasing the Venetian lion back across its lagoon (see Fig. 4).[82] The Ottoman advance through the Balkans posed a much more direct threat on land than at sea. The Empire's involvement in confronting the Turks in the Mediterranean only began after the Habsburgs inherited Spain in 1516, as it was on the cusp of acquiring a global empire and displacing Portugal as Europe's leading maritime power.

This coincided with the Ottomans' expansion westwards following their conquest of Syria and Egypt in 1517. Two years later, the sultan appointed Khayr ad-Din 'Barbarossa' as governor of Algiers, extending Ottoman suzerainty along the entire southern Mediterranean coast and prompting an upsurge in the activities of the Barbary corsairs, the north African sea raiders whose attacks on Christian shipping would continue for over three centuries. Charles V used his imperial authority to grant Malta to the Knights of St John in 1530, eight years after they had been ejected from Rhodes by the Ottomans. The Knights had a powerful fleet and initially cooperated with Charles against the Ottomans. In 1535 he launched an ambitious amphibious attack from Malta on Tunis, previously a Spanish tributary state, captured by Barbarossa the year before. Concerned that France might exploit the opportunity to renew its ambitions in Italy, Charles persuaded the pope to declare a crusade. The expedition was the largest maritime operation yet undertaken by an emperor and involved a fleet of seventy-five war galleys and 250 transports provided by Genoa, Spain, Portugal and the papacy, carrying an army of 27,000 men, including 8,000 south German Landsknechts.[83]

The fifteen Genoese galleys forming the core of the fleet were provided following Charles's agreement in 1528 with Andrea Doria, the Mediterranean's primary naval contractor and admiral, who exercised actual command under the emperor. The two-month campaign ended in August with the capture of Tunis, the liberation of 20,000 Christian captives, and the massacre of much of the local population. Although celebrated as a great triumph, it cost over 1 million ducats and had only been possible thanks to the huge haul of treasure seized from the Incas by the Spanish in 1533. Against Doria's advice, Charles tried to repeat his success by attacking Algiers in 1541 with around fifty galleys, 140 transports and 25,000 men, including 7,000 Landsknechts and 500 German cavalry, at the cost of about 800,000 ducats. A series of storms wrecked most of the fleet and forced a bedraggled Charles to retreat having lost 8,000 men. While his brother Ferdinand's failure to retake Buda that year lay partly in the incompetence of the siege operations, the diversion of funds to the Mediterranean certainly hindered Habsburg efforts to recover Hungary. The Ottomans captured Tripoli (1551) and, eventually, Tunis in 1569. Although Spain retook Tunis in 1573 following its great naval victory at Lepanto two years earlier, the Ottomans captured the city again in 1574 and held it until 1881.

The partition of Habsburg possessions in 1556 involved a division of military and naval labour against the Ottomans, whereby Austria shouldered the burden of landward defence, while Spain protected the Mediterranean with the assistance of Genoa, Venice, Tuscany, the papacy and the Knights of St John. The question of an imperial navy only emerged once it became clear to Spain that there was no swift solution to the Dutch Revolt after 1568. Although Spain's powerful Army of Flanders recaptured significant territory, the rebels shifted to the Channel and North Sea as 'sea beggars', or privateers attacking Spanish shipping. Spain petitioned the 1570 Reichstag meeting in Speyer for assistance on the grounds that, as Burgundian lands, the rebel areas were part of the Empire, which was bound to assist under the public peace legislation.

The request was sympathetically received by Maximilian II, who saw an opportunity to project imperial power into the *Oceano Germanico* (North Sea), and a joint squadron of seven ships was planned to be funded by the Burgundian, Lower Saxon and Westphalian Kreise. Discussions continued, but after 1576 with waning enthusiasm from Austria, which increasingly preferred a negotiated settlement to the Dutch Revolt. The crushing defeat of Spain's Armada in 1588 removed the scheme from the agenda for the next four decades.[84]

The Hansa

Protection of the Baltic coast, meanwhile, devolved on its inhabitants. The Hanseatic League emerged from an alliance between Lübeck and Hamburg in 1241, soon after the region had been conquered from the Slavs. The League expanded rapidly to encompass 170 towns from Ghent to Tallin, but the core always remained those in northern Germany. Its relationship to the Empire was ambiguous since, other than Lübeck, few members enjoyed the status of imperial city and consequently most were not represented directly in imperial institutions. While they cooperated to protect merchants and bargain trading concessions, they were also commercial rivals and the League came under increasing strain during the fifteenth century.

A major factor in this was the establishment in 1429 of the Sound Toll levied on ships passing through the Øresund, which separated the Baltic from the North Sea. The collapse of the Scandinavian Union of Kalmar in 1523, with the election of Gustav Vasa as the Swedish king, led to a struggle between Denmark-Norway and Sweden for control of this extremely lucrative source of revenue and pre-eminence in the Baltic more generally that lasted for over two centuries. The Hanseatic cities were drawn into this struggle unwillingly as they sought to maintain access through the Sound. Lübeck backed Denmark during the first of these so-called Northern Wars (1563–70), creating a squadron of six ships, including the prestige warship *Der Adler*, completed in 1566 and carrying 148 guns with 900 soldiers and sailors. Although retained after 1570, this ship was soon accidentally destroyed in a fire, while the other vessels were sold to spare the cost of their maintenance. The 1570 Reichstag also debated the defence of the Baltic coast, but Maximilian II preferred to mediate between the warring parties to preserve peace.[85]

After the mid-century imperial reforms, it was increasingly difficult for the Hanseatic cities to maintain their deliberately ambiguous status, and their continued refusal to pay Turkish Aid was a major reason why the emperor took little interest in protecting them. The increasingly obvious division of Europe into sovereign states also disinclined other monarchs to recognize the Hansa as a legitimate partner, with England no longer willing to treat with it after 1602. Whereas the League still mustered sixty-three members in 1557, only fourteen were still paying their dues by 1604.

With attention firmly focused on the Ottoman threat, the Empire refused responsibility for the former Teutonic Order lands in Prussia and Courland, which were forced to make their own accommodation with Poland, accepting its suzerainty in return for recognition of the Hohenzollern and Kettler families as hereditary dukes in 1525 and 1561 respectively. The requirement to assist the Polish king on land and sea drew them into his struggles with Danzig in 1577, when Prussia provided three warships, and later in a succession of conflicts with Sweden, which had conquered much of the southeastern Baltic shore after 1561. Prussia bought two Dutch-built warships in 1601 to fulfil its obligations to Poland, but again the cost of maintaining them in peacetime led to their disposal by 1608.[86]

The Danube Flotilla

Riverine warfare was an important element of land operations since waterways could serve both as defensible barriers and as major transport routes. The most important river was the Danube, which was essential to move troops and resources from southern Germany east to assist the Habsburgs to defend Hungary, as well as to support operations there against the Turks. A bureau was established in the 1520s to organize riverine transport, and the constant Ottoman threat resulted in this becoming permanent as the Ship Master's Office (*Schiffmeistereiamt*), formally subordinate to the Court War Council after 1557.

Emperor Charles's brother Ferdinand brought Italian experts to construct sixty gunboats to defend the Sava river, giving access to Croatia and Inner Austria, as well as the Danube. These were lost during the 1529 campaign when the Turks mustered 400 boats. A new flotilla of up to twenty-eight boats was constructed in Vienna after 1530 using timber from Upper Austria. These were called *Tschaiken*, after the Turkish word for water, and drew more on Hungarian expertise in their design, as well as their crews. Although some were lost in the defeats of the early 1540s, the flotilla remained permanent and expanded again during the Long Turkish War. Additional pontoon detachments were established in the major fortresses after 1572 to provide bridging equipment, to be supplemented with requisitioned barges in wartime.[87]

The Military Frontier also had a western, maritime section on the Adriatic coast, established at Senj after the loss of Klis and most of Dalmatia in 1537. The landward side was well protected by forests and mountains, but Senj itself was a poor harbour, shallow and exposed to sudden gales, which prevented its use as a base for galleys, the primary fighting ship in Adriatic and Mediterranean warfare. Instead, the Senj forces used small oared barks, each crewed by thirty to fifty men, which were ideal for darting out from between the numerous Dalmatian islands to attack shipping in the Adriatic, as well as raiding coastal communities. The crews were drawn from the Uskoks, or refugees settled in Senj as border guards. The Habsburgs' inability to pay the Uskoks led to their reliance on piracy, causing constant friction with Venice, which claimed supremacy in the Adriatic and whose shipping constantly suffered. Horrific stories of unorthodox Uskok practices led to a papal envoy investigating and his disturbing reports give a unique insight into this violent frontier community. Tensions escalated into full Venetian–Habsburg war from 1615 to 1618, fought mainly on land along the Isonzo river – where the front would be exactly three centuries later. Venice and the Habsburgs patched up a peace that entailed the Uskoks' resettlement inland.[88]

The development of specialist warships like galleys and gunboats added to the growing costs of warfare, which in turn was a key driver of political development, notably through the need to negotiate and collect taxes. Meanwhile, the emergence of professional forces encouraged new legislation to assert authority over them and resolve their innumerable disputes with the rest of society. These topics are addressed in the following chapter.

3

Going for a Soldier

GOOD AND BAD WAR

Military Knowledge

The emergence of a distinct 'Estate of Soldiers' (*Soldatenstand*) was one of the most profound changes affecting central European society, irrevocably ending the division into the three medieval corporate Estates of clergy, nobles and commons that was, in any case, loosening through economic changes. The claim of noblemen to be society's warriors was now challenged by men of humble birth, who simultaneously escaped many of the confines of settled society and claimed legal autonomy and a distinct identity. This process had long roots, but accelerated from the late fifteenth century, prompting the authorities to impose new laws to assert control and forge the new, professional soldiers into a more effective instrument of state policy. The flamboyant appearance of soldiers and the ambiguities surrounding their 'trade' attracted sharp commentary, not least because of the coincidence of these developments with the moral and political controversies of the Reformation, and the transformation of European affairs with the struggles between the Habsburgs, France, and the Ottoman Empire. The parallel emergence of the new technologies of printing and gunpowder weaponry were additional factors behind these changes, which were also manifested through new thinking about warfare.

Experience counted far more than bookish learning for most soldiers at this point, while there was no formal training in the art of war. Experience might be honed under guidance or acquired incrementally through successive campaigns. Prospective soldiers were not necessarily bereft of useful skills and knowledge, since familiarity with blade weapons was common and the largely agrarian life taught men how to care for animals, forage for food, and look after themselves outdoors. Foreign service both transmitted German ideas and practices to other parts of Europe and brought novelties back to the Empire and Switzerland. The Empire, and particularly the Habsburg lands, also served as a conduit for knowledge about warfare in eastern Europe and the Balkans to inform practice elsewhere; something that would persist until the Ottomans ceased to be feared in the eighteenth century.

Knowledge played a subordinate role in proving experience, which was measured more through the display of martial values, such as courage, bravery, fortitude, and discipline, as well as the demonstration of skills in personal combat and horsemanship. Much technical knowledge remained morally and socially suspect, particularly that relating to gunpowder weaponry, which was widely regarded as akin to alchemy and the 'black arts'. Master gunners were valued for their expertise, but also held in some disdain as technicians, as reflected in their pay being only four-fifths that of an ensign, the most junior infantry officer. They responded by presenting the invention of gunpowder as divinely inspired, hence the story that it had been discovered by a monk, and through the cultivation of St Barbara as the patroness of artillery. However, gunners also formed a closed guild, protecting their knowledge as trade secrets.[1]

The invention of printing around 1450, itself celebrated by Humanists as a German achievement, was already rapidly transforming the transmission of military knowledge by 1500, and with that also changing military practice and attitudes to war within the literate elite. Emperor Maximilian I was the first prominent European monarch to exploit the new medium to project a carefully crafted image of himself as a successful ruler and warlord.[2] His efforts to control print through censorship failed due to the new technology's diffusion to numerous imperial cities, and its coincidence with the onset of the religious schism after 1517. The Empire's media landscape remained more diverse and livelier than anywhere else in Europe before the 1630s, characterized by a broader range of opinion and continued technical innovation. Luther, himself the world's first bestselling author, published a strident condemnation of the *Murdering, Thieving Hordes of Peasants* (1525) at the height of the Peasants' War in response to the revolutionaries' own manifestos, while the Swabian League published pamphlets justifying its military action and harsh reprisals. Subsequent conflicts within the

Empire, such as the Schmalkaldic War (1546–7), the siege of Magdeburg (1551), and the struggle for Cologne (1583–8), generated hundreds of pamphlets, indicating both the range of opinions and level of interest.[3]

'War books' (*Kriegsbücher*) developed as a separate genre focusing on technical details and theory. Reception of ancient military writers, like Vegetius, remained limited throughout the Middle Ages, when written knowledge largely passed through the hands of clerics and the generally unlettered nobility were considered society's military specialists. Ancient works were put into print and discussed by Humanists, but their influence on a few prominent writers like Machiavelli has led some historians to exaggerate their contemporary impact. By contrast, war books began as practical manuals and compendia of information that gradually connected the world of skilled crafts with that of the literate elite. They emerged in the early fifteenth century as the accelerating spread of written culture encouraged the recording of oral traditions of knowledge. Two of the earliest war books were Konrad Kyeser's quirky *Bellifortis* (1405) and the anonymous *Feuerwerkbuch* (1420), both of which initially circulated in manuscript copies. The *Feuerwerkbuch*, which dealt with pyrotechnics, was later printed as *Büchsenmeisterei* in 1529, indicating the largely static state of written knowledge to that date. By then, however, the rapidity of actual military practice had rendered much of the older knowledge obsolete. This was now reflected in the proliferation of new works from around 1530, which expanded to include publications on military architecture and ways to fight the Ottomans. Around 170 new war books appeared in the Empire across the sixteenth century, compared to just twenty-nine over the previous hundred years.[4]

Printing produced both expensive, large-format, lavishly illustrated works and cheap pocketbooks that could be carried on campaign. That the new form of knowledge was valued is demonstrated by its close connection with the most prominent captains, who all had at least basic schooling. Sebastian Schertlin had studied at Freiburg and Tübingen universities, earning a master's degree, while Lazarus von Schwendi had been educated in Basel, Strasbourg, and possibly Paris. Georg von Frundsberg owned 634 books, mainly history and contemporary chronicles, while Reinhold von Solms acquired most of his military knowledge from reading, beyond his brief practical experience with Franz von Sickingen in 1515. Several captains wrote books, notably Conrad von Bemelburg and his collaborator, Solms, who published a seven-part comprehensive discussion of military theory and practice.[5] This work included detailed suggestions for a wargame using cards to assist military planning.[6] The most influential work was Leonhart Fronsperger's *Kriegsbuch*, illustrated with engravings by Jost Amman, which represented the high point of the late medieval tradition of trying to fix knowledge by compiling it as a compendium.[7] It remains a valuable source of information and recent histories of the Landsknechts often simply precis Fronsperger.

However, others were already writing more programmatic works, criticizing current practices, and advocating change. This was part of a broader trend of civic humanism, accelerating from about 1580, which applied learning and classical knowledge to solving current problems. It was also stimulated by the massive expansion of higher education, which saw the foundation of eighteen universities between 1502 and 1648, more than doubling the total and giving the Empire the most extensive provision in Europe. Reformers used well-established stereotypes of soldiers to argue for supposedly cheaper, more effective forms of organization. The impact of these works has been over-emphasized, notably in some versions of the Military Revolution argument, since few of their programmes were realized in practice. Nonetheless, they indicate the range of concerns and a belief in progress.

The most famous reformers were the counts of Nassau, who shaped actual practice through their roles in the army of the fledgling Dutch Republic. Johann VII von Nassau-Siegen's *Kriegsbuch* (1597) disseminated their call for better discipline inspired by a reading of Roman military history. These ideas spread through the Calvinist political network among northwest German princes and aristocrats, notably Landgrave Moritz of Hessen-Kassel, who wrote his own *Kriegsbuch* (1607), which was illustrated by his court historian, Wilhelm Schäfer.[8]

Johann's cousin, the leading Dutch general Maurice of Nassau, scored a narrow victory over the mutinous Spanish army at Nieuwpoort (1600), lending credibility to the reforms, but their apparent progressiveness is largely a creation of subsequent historical interpretation. For example, Johann served as adviser to the Swedish army during its campaigns in Livonia in 1601–2, which ended in defeat, while another Swedish army trained in the Dutch manner was routed within 20 minutes by Polish-Lithuanian cavalry at Kircholm in 1605. The Bohemian Confederates and their Protestant German allies were regularly defeated by imperial and Catholic League troops employing the supposedly now backward 'Spanish' methods in the 1620s.

Johann's other famous innovation, the military academy he established in Siegen in 1616, also had little practical impact. The count hired Johann Jacob Wallhausen to run it. Wallhausen had served in Hungary, Russia, and the Netherlands where he had worked closely with Maurice. Very few future officers had graduated before the academy closed by 1623, while its director failed to complete his planned six-volume work on the art of war. Nonetheless, he did publish an impressive eleven military books across 1614–21, which made his reputation and were widely translated, including into English, French, Russian, and German. He also collaborated with the engraver, Jacob de Gheyn, on an illustrated version of Johann's infantry drill manual in 1607, which appeared in German translation the following year.[9] The wide dissemination of these works ensured their lasting impact, not least because their illustrations were pirated for other works. However, they really represented the summation of sixteenth-century thinking rather than a wholly progressive new theory of war.

The disproportionate historical attention they have received distracts from other writers who were influential at the time. One of the most important was Schwendi, who played a major role in drafting the military regulations promulgated by the Reichstag in the 1570s. He drew inspiration from the Christian Middle Ages, advocating a revived crusading order to hold back the Turks and calling for moral reform so that soldiers could live from their wages without wasting their money drinking and gambling.[10] Another writer was Giorgio Basta, the most prominent of several Italians who disseminated experience of warfare against the Turks. Often highly critical of his Habsburg masters' treatment of their soldiers, Basta published books on generalship and the importance of light cavalry. Whereas Wallhausen ignored light cavalry and advocated the retention of lancers, who were now tactically obsolete, Basta favoured cuirassiers and mounted arquebusiers, which proved to be the mainstay of heavy cavalry for the next fifty years.[11]

Attitudes to War

The emergence of such technical books indicates a level of self-conscious professionalism encapsulated by Schertlin's motto *Dulce bellum inexpertis*: war is only beautiful for those who don't know it. Truchsess von

Waldburg, the Swabian League's commander, did not regard the peasants as worthy opponents, believing honour could only be gained by fighting a 'real' army.[12] Their works conveyed a sense of competence and presented war as the orderly application of controlled violence according to rational principles. This was most evident from the accompanying images, notably the drill manual illustrated by de Gheyn that explained how to handle firearms and pikes through separate pictures for each motion. Wallhausen broke the process of loading and firing a musket into 143 stages compared to de Gheyn's forty-three, reflecting not the actual procedure, which remained quite simple and easy to learn, but the desire to fix this scientifically.[13]

Other writers and artists addressed war as a moral issue. Printing also helped disseminate woodcut images more widely and cheaply. After around 1480, many of these responded to increased warfare and the emergence of soldiers as a new, distinct corporate group within society.[14] Easily identifiable by their flamboyant dress, soldiers swiftly became a malleable archetype who could be used for a variety of purposes, including general commentary on morality (see Figs. 1 and 2). Prints showing Landsknechts and Death pointed not simply to the risks of their profession, but also the futility of resisting fate. Death was often depicted as a Landsknecht wielding a two-handed sword, and religious art often showed the centurions at Christ's crucifixion as Landsknechts. Many prints revealed soldiers accompanied by women, often misidentified subsequently as sutlers, but in fact depicting prostitutes. Again, this was both a reflection of reality and a critique of material interest, lust, and desire in place of love and trust as the true basis of marriage. Another common figure was that of Fortuna, shown naked holding a sail and balancing on a ball, suggesting the fickleness of fate and that soldiers blasphemously believed that luck, not God, governed their lives. Some positively embraced the image, which appeared on several regimental flags after 1600. Another association with gambling was the appearance of a game known as 'Landsknecht', which appeared by 1534 using an Italian pack of only forty cards.

Other works addressed military matters more directly. Soldiers could appear positively as the Empire's defenders against the French and the Turks, but many works were openly critical like Sebastian Franck's pamphlet *Concerning the Arrival of Two Plagues in Germany* (1531), which, by juxtaposing the Landsknechts with the 'French disease', equated soldiers with syphilis to highlight their supposed degeneracy. Franck blamed 'that useless breed of men called Landsknechts' for 'seeking and causing war and visiting misfortune upon us all', arguing that 'if there were no Landsknechts, we would surely have fewer wars', which would also be smaller, shorter, and less costly.[15] This critique embodied the same cliché of the mercenary that had already drawn Machiavelli's ire in his commentary on the condottieri. Franck likewise advocated citizen soldiers as superior, thus using the same mercenary construct as, and drawing similar conclusions to, the Nassau counts.

The spread of foreign service stimulated criticism of mercenaries and by the 1490s many argued that soldiering was not an ordinary trade. Bernese burghers protested that they did not want to be associated with human trafficking (*hominum commercium*), suggesting that foreign service was an affront to God, as well as harming and corrupting those who engaged in it. Criticism grew louder with the string of costly battles: Novara (1513), Marignano (1515), Bicocca (1522), and Pavia (1525). Several humanists voiced concerns, including Erasmus and Willibald Pirckheimer, but the most famous critic was the Swiss reformer Huldrych Zwingli, who had served in the 1513 and 1515 campaigns as a chaplain. The experience of the disaster at Marignano had turned him against foreign service and set him on the path to breaking with Rome both theologically and politically. Zwingli's argument that soldiering was corrupting the country became a standard refrain that persisted even beyond the formal end to the service in 1859, and became woven with more secular arguments in the twentieth century presenting soldiers as unwilling wage slaves.[16]

However, most saw corruption differently. The bloody cost of Novara prompted popular protests in Bern, Luzern, and Solothurn, while Marignano was followed by the Gingerbread War (*Lebkuchenkrieg*), when 3,000 armed peasants broke into Zürich and intimidated the council, helping themselves to bakery goods at the same time as they negotiated across Christmas 1515. While those involved in these protests used the same language as the reformers, they attacked the unfair distribution of the benefits from foreign service rather than soldiering itself. Their principal grievance was against private pensions to selected individuals, not the public ones benefiting the wider community. Since Zürich had already banned private pensions in 1513, it was relatively easy for Zwingli to persuade the other, now Protestant, cantons to follow suit by 1521, but they nonetheless continued to support foreign service and only Zürich rejected the alliance with France. Soldiers also used the same language of having been sold on the butcher's block in order to demand fair pay and respect.[17]

Violence

The prominent place of theology and morality in the discussions of soldiers reflects Christianity's fundamental role in shaping attitudes to war and violence at this point. War was not inherently wrong, but to be considered 'just' it had to meet three criteria.[18] First, it could only be waged by a properly constituted authority. This question of legitimate power (*Potestas*) remained controversial within the Empire, given its multi-layered political structure that distributed sovereign powers unevenly. Nonetheless, the 1495 public peace signalled a major step towards clarifying this, which was consolidated through further legislation curbing the emperor's unilateral right to make war in the Empire's name. The Peace of Westphalia (1648) eventually reserved 'military sovereignty' (*Militärhoheit*) as an element of broader 'territorial sovereignty' (*Landeshoheit*), exercised only by the imperial Estates, and not by nobles, towns, or provinces within them. Powers remained shared, in the sense that their individual exercise was limited by the principle that they should not be directed against 'the emperor or Empire', and that actions taken in the Empire's name were subject to agreement through the Reichstag. The Swiss Confederation evolved along broadly similar lines, with the cantons also obliged to settle their differences peacefully through arbitration.

Second, there had to be a just cause for war, which should only be the last resort after all other efforts to right the wrong had been exhausted. This placed limits on war, because coercion should only continue until the wrongdoer desisted from their evil deeds and made amends. By suggesting war was a valid way to advance princely goals, Machiavelli's 'ends-justify-the-means' argument appeared shocking, delaying his reception in the Empire until the 1580s, when commentators still remained overwhelmingly hostile.[19] These restrictions applied primarily to conflicts among Christians where peaceful relations were supposed to be the norm. By contrast, peace was considered impossible with the Islamic world and conflicts were only punctuated by time-limited truces until 1699 when the emperor and the sultan agreed a peace intended to be permanent. Islamic views mirrored these beliefs, regarding the Empire and other Christian states as belonging to the House of War (*darüharb*) permanently at odds with the House of Islam (*darülislam*).[20]

Fear of the Turks had grown since the fall of Constantinople in 1453 and increasingly hardened through conflict and misunderstandings into the language of a 'clash of civilizations'. It reflected anxieties among Christians that they might be inferior and suffer defeat. Discussions of the Turks during the sixteenth century usually stressed their superior numbers and fearsome fighting qualities, but also their alleged brutality, cunning, and arrogance, which were given as further reasons why peace was supposedly impossible. Humanists and religious reformers used this image of 'the Turk' as a useful foil to criticize Christians, presenting the sultan's armies as a scourge sent by God to punish the impious for their sins.

While the threat was perceived as genuinely existential, it also legitimated Habsburg claims to leadership. They presented themselves as Christendom's bulwark, pointedly criticizing their French rivals for their temporary alliances with the sultan. Campaigns retained an element of the crusades, with volunteers from across Europe joining the imperial army as late as 1717.[21] The impossibility of permanent peace was used to underpin demands to the imperial Estates for equally permanent war taxes. Defence against the Turks was broadly accepted as an unavoidable duty, but few were prepared to surrender any say in the matter to the Habsburgs. The bulwark ideology also proved too abstract to suit the complex relations along the Habsburg–Ottoman border where, for example, the Uskoks preyed on the *Morlachi*, or Christian subjects of the sultan, as well as attacking Venetian shipping.

While the fascination with the Turks persisted, its character changed with the Ottomans' military decline from the end of the seventeenth century. The huge haul of exotic booty taken from the Ottoman camp outside Vienna in 1683 was instrumental in this, since its distribution around the German princely capitals suggested the Turks could be beaten. It also had a lasting cultural impact, manifest through coffee, food, music *alla turca*, and *turquerie* or porcelain figurines of exotic servants, all of which helped foster growing acceptance of Turks as fellow humans, even if the view remained founded on prejudice. No longer immediately feared, the Turks remained bogeymen whose alleged characteristics were now transposed on to other enemies, notably Louis XIV's France.

The third element of the theory behind just war was that operations should be conducted appropriately as the controlled application of force (*Gewalt*) rather than illegitimate, gratuitous *Violentia*.[22] Discussions already distinguished between two levels of warfare which differed in socio-cultural as well as military terms, and which remained fundamental in German ideas about war into the twentieth century. Major war (*Hauptkrieg*) involved large operations conducted by regular troops commanded by prominent figures and intended to achieve victory through battle or capturing important towns. This was always considered more honourable than the 'little war' (*Kleinkrieg*) of skirmishes, outposts, and raids. Whereas the former was associated with *decision* through swift victory, the latter was generally considered *attrition* often employed by the weaker party to prolong a conflict. Little war was already firmly associated with soldiers from the 'Wild East', such as Albanian Stradiots, Croats, Hungarians, Tartars, Cossacks, and Turks, long before it was critiqued in this manner by Scharnhorst, Gneisenau, and Clausewitz.[23]

In addition to overall methods, certain weapons were considered more honourable than others. As late as 1566, Fronsberger regarded handguns as 'unmanly', though he reluctantly considered them indispensable. Crossbows had encountered similar hostility in the fifteenth century, because they likewise enabled a humble foot soldier to shoot down an armoured nobleman at a distance. Light troops' tactics, such as feigned retreats, were also seen by many as lacking in honour. 'Good War' rested on the expectation that enemies would consider themselves as bound by the same norms, such as accepting defeated men's surrender. The refusal of the Swiss to do so during several 'Bad Wars' of the late fifteenth century led to reprisals, but violence generally remained within commonly accepted bounds and various practices, such as the rituals surrounding the surrender of besieged towns, carefully developed to de-escalate violence.[24]

THE TRADE OF WAR

Motives

Armies were rarely short of recruits during the sixteenth century, in contrast to those that followed, and usually at least twice as many men came forward as were required. Nonetheless, it is important to remember that compulsion played a role, such as mobilizing militia, while the economic and social factors behind the development of foreign service (see pp. 17–23) also propelled men to enlist in their own ruler's forces.

There were also positive pull factors. Soldiers' monthly pay rose during the later fifteenth century until it was stabilized by imperial legislation in 1507 at 4 fl for an infantryman and 12 fl for a cavalryman. This compared very favourably with 1.6 fl for a day labourer, 2.5 fl for a carpenter, and even the 5 fl paid to the middling sort of public officials and estate stewards. Specialists and well-equipped veterans could be classed as 'double pays' (*Doppelsöldner*), earning enough to attract patricians' sons and young noblemen. Moreover, unlike civilian wages, which were provided as a mix of money and materials like food or firewood, soldiers were paid in cash. Even after covering his living costs, an ordinary soldier could expect to keep up to 2.5 fl monthly, meaning a substantial sum could be accumulated during a campaign, which might also be supplemented through booty taken from civilians or defeated enemies.[25]

While soldiers were only paid during a campaign, this was not immediately a disincentive because many other jobs were also seasonal. More serious was the employers' frequent inability to pay men punctually, in full or even at all, leaving them little choice but to live off the land. Plundering was contrary to martial law and subject to tighter restrictions. The rise in the proportion of arquebusiers meant these were no longer counted as double pays whose overall proportion was fixed at 10 per cent by the 1530s. By then, inflation was beginning to bite, but soldiers' wages initially held up as they were still paid in gold, not silver, which devalued faster. This was no longer the case during the second half of the century when soldiering increasingly became just one of several options to earn a minimum wage.

Contracting involved high risks but potentially offered huge profits for captains and senior commanders, as well as a route to higher status and a noble lifestyle. Schertlin made at least 50,300 fl profit on his campaigns between 1518 and 1546, plus rewards and booty, chiefly from the Sack of Rome, worth over 19,300 fl. He was already knighted for his distinguished service at Pavia, but such titles required ownership of an appropriate estate to have full social value, so he invested 17,000 fl in buying the lordship of Burtenbach in 1532. Although he invested in agricultural improvements and fish farming, annual income from his estate rose only from 200 fl in 1534 to 1,320 fl in 1559, indicating the attraction of the huge windfalls that could be made from contracting.

Schertlin's fame ensured he was kept on retainer by several cities and princes, earning 1,140 fl a year by 1543. The final stage of his career illustrates the risks, since he was forced to flee the Empire after the defeat of the Schmalkaldic League, entailing a loss of 12,000 fl in unpaid expenses while his property was confiscated. His subsequent service for the princes in revolt in 1552 saw Schertlin lose another 1,000 fl, but he secured a pardon the following year and recovered his lordship, allowing him to retire. He continued to improve his property before selling it to his old comrade Conrad von Bemelburg for 102,000 fl in 1568. By the time of his death nine years later, Schertlin was reputed to be worth 1 million fl.[26]

Geographical Origins

Early modern Europeans had a concept of nationality, but the criteria were not firmly fixed, and the term was applied flexibly. We should be mindful of this when discussing soldiers' origins, and applying certain labels should not be construed as the presence of modern nationalist identities.[27] Contemporaries divided Germany culturally and linguistically into High (south) and Low (north), with the former identified most with providing Landsknechts, while the latter became increasingly known for providing cavalry from the 1540s. Within High Germany, Upper Swabia was famed as the main Landsknecht recruiting ground, distinguished politically more than linguistically from Germanophone Switzerland. In practice, Low German infantry were organized no differently, and it was only following the onset of the Eighty Years War (1568–1648) that men from the Netherlands were identified more clearly and separately as Walloons or Dutch.

'Nation', in keeping with its broader understanding, only assumed real significance for men serving outside the Empire. Louis XI already insisted that German-speakers be separated into Landsknecht units, but in practice 'Swiss' regiments often had a significant minority of 'Germans'. The segregation of soldiers by nationality was practised throughout Europe and reflected beliefs in national character and martial spirit. Within the Empire, the authorities preferred local men, meaning their own subjects, since these were bound by existing legal ties and loyalties. The contingent system used by the Empire and the various leagues within it ensured that armies were assembled from companies and regiments primarily composed of men from the territories that sent them. Likewise, Swiss tended to join units associated with their home canton. 'Foreigners', primarily meaning men from neighbouring territories, were recruited when larger numbers were needed. Contractors recruiting for imperial expeditions or for regiments intended for other powers were less selective about a soldier's place of origin.[28]

Religion increasingly became a factor after the 1520s, with Spain preferring men from Catholic areas like Austria, Bavaria, Cologne, and parts of southern Germany, but nonetheless it still recruited in Protestant Franconia and northern Germany. The Schmalkaldic League found it difficult to recruit in some areas in 1546 because the inhabitants were Catholics, or at least reluctant to fight the emperor, who was careful to avoid calling the conflict a religious war and provided Protestant chaplains for his army. While the imperial Estates acquired powers to supervise the Church in their territories in 1555, armies remained largely non-confessional zones, accepting recruits regardless of faith. Marx Sittich von Hohenems was a prominent exception in being such an ardent Catholic that he was awarded the title Defender of the Faith by the pope and launched his own armed intervention in the Swiss civil war of 1529. His entire family remained true to the old Church, as did other important contractors like Conrad von Bemelburg. Michael Ott and Lazarus von Schwendi converted to Protestantism, while Schertlin used his lordly powers to impose Lutheranism on his manor in 1546. Nonetheless, Schwendi worked closely with the Habsburgs, and while Frundsberg and Solms remained Catholic, they urged reconciliation.

Social Origins

Maximilian I strove to foster an elite group identity and already at Guingate in 1479 he and 200 nobles fought on foot; though medieval knights often dismounted in battle, it was unusual to stand among commoners. He continued to set a personal example, attracting wide attention when he dismounted to place himself at the head of his infantry as they entered Ghent on 7 July 1485.[29] Although he repeated this on several occasions, his action was not copied by his successors or other German princes. Nonetheless, young nobles did fight as double pays in the front rank, while many burghers served in their civic contingents sent against the Turks or as part of obligations to leagues. Allegedly a tenth of Bemelburg's 10,000-strong regiment were Ulm burghers in 1552, while even foreign service pulled respectable men, with the troops recruited by Wilhelm von Fürstenberg for France in 1536 comprising 'fine upstanding Knechte and many of them are noblemen'.[30]

Soldiering offered a route to upward social mobility. A humble infantryman who captured armour on one campaign could re-enlist as a double pay in the next. By skill, experience, or good fortune, it was possible to rise to captain's rank with command over 300 other men, many of whom might ordinarily be one's social superiors. Over half of Frundsberg's captains in his 1526 Italian campaign were commoners. Martin Schwarz, a cobbler from Augsburg, rose within about ten years to become captain of 200 Swiss in imperial service by 1485. His reputation was such that he was contracted to raise and command 2,000 Swiss and Germans in support of the Yorkist pretender Lambert Simnel, in whose service he was killed at Stoke in 1487. Sebastian Vogelsberger, the son of a smallholder, had worked as a journeyman baker and later as a language teacher before becoming a senior captain in French service.

Solms and Fürstenberg were unusual in that, as counts, they hailed from the Empire's aristocracy. Fürstenberg knew little of estate management and had squandered his inheritance. His notoriety for picking fights and being difficult to work with were factors forcing him into French service. That reputation, combined with growing ill-health, prompted the Schmalkaldic League not to hire him in 1546, despite his ardent Protestantism.[31] High birth did not guarantee success. Christoph of Württemberg, son of the reigning duke, signed a large contract with France in 1537, but his youth and inexperience meant he swiftly lost authority over his officers.

Frundsberg was more typical in coming from a family of minor nobles, only earning his personal knighthood through capturing the Bohemians' standard at Wenzensbach in 1504. His career shows the significance of personal reputation and charisma. A cultured and learned man, he deliberately cultivated the persona of a bluff, simple warrior. On his final campaign in 1526–7, when his army had not been paid for months, he rode a donkey as a symbol of poverty. Legends spread that he could ride any horse, break three coins on top of each other, and push a man over with his finger, but not even he could magic up money, and he died in 1528 having pawned his estates to pay his men.[32]

Schertlin's father was mayor of Schorndorf in Württemberg, though his mother was probably from a local noble family, and thus exemplified those from patrician backgrounds. The same was true of the Hohenems family from Voralberg that combined positions in the local Habsburg administration with contracting, though it was the latter that made their name and aided Marx Sittich II's acquisition of a cardinal's hat.[33]

'DISHONOURABLE TROUSER DEVILS'

Corporate Autonomy

Thus, sixteenth-century soldiers did not entirely match their subsequent depiction as rootless 'foreign' mercenaries. The majority were subjects of the territorial lord they served, or at least of the emperor. Nonetheless, their emergence as a profligate, outlandishly dressed group engaged in violence attracted condemnation from reform-minded clerics who preached against the 'lewd, undisciplined and dishonourable trouser devils'.[34] Beyond the moral and social challenges they posed, the new professionals threatened the political order. Their self-conscious solidarity and autonomy, which made them so effective on the battlefield, was at odds with the hierarchical ordering of power and status. This tension between horizontal association and vertical authority was common throughout Europe around 1500 and particularly acute in the Empire, where it was central to the broader controversies of the Reformation. At one extreme, there was the solidarity between neighbours and 'the community of all believers' at the heart of communal life and religious reform. At the other, there was the deep-seated belief in a divinely ordained worldly social and political hierarchy whereby true equality and harmony were only attainable in heaven.

Association and authority were always combined, but their exact balance varied and was often contested. The hierarchy of command was still in flux around 1500, but it already no longer corresponded with broader social stratification, because status was determined by the military function of each role rather than the holder's birth. Moreover, the strongly associative character of the Swiss and early Landsknechts bound officers within, rather than above, the ranks as first among equals. Ordinary soldiers were *Gemeine Knechte*, often shortened at this point to *Knechte*, though the term *Gemeine* persisted and re-emerged fully during the middle of the seventeenth century as the equivalent of 'private'. *Knecht* meant 'servant', but *Gemeine* had more positive associations with community.

Ordinary soldiers were grouped into a *Rotte* (squad) of usually ten men who elected their own *Rottmeister* to give them direction in battle and to act as their spokesman. This duality of command and representation continued up the hierarchy of ranks. Each month the company elected two intermediate superiors known as *Waibel*, a rank that eventually became *Feldwebel* or senior NCO, roughly equivalent to sergeant. The Waibel kept order, transmitted the captain's instructions, and organized watch duty, but also distributed rations and acted as the company's representatives when presenting grievances. If redress could not be obtained this way, the company could also elect special emissaries (*Ambassaden*) to negotiate. Each company also had a *Fourier* who acted as a clerk assisting the quartermaster keeping records, and a *Führer* (guide) whose role probably emerged from the task of carrying the flag to the battlefield before handing it to the ensign, but who could also act as legal adviser to the soldiers. The peasants also elected their captains in 1525, but already these positions among the Swiss and Landsknechts were being appointed by the cantonal authorities or regimental commanders.[35]

Soldiers constituted a corporate group, because they possessed their own law and the right to administer justice to their members, like the clergy or urban guilds. Unlike the latter, which were defined by their location in a specific town and operated as a closed shop, soldiers remained more temporary and itinerant and never possessed exclusive rights to determine who could belong to their company. Soldiers' legal identity rested on documents known as the 'articles of war', which developed from the disciplinary codes issued by the Reichstag for the forces raised against the Hussites in 1427 and 1431. The later imperial code of 1508, along with that of the Swabian League from 1519, developed into important models as these became more standardized and comprehensive around 1520. The articles specified harsh punishments for those unilaterally abandoning their comrades or breaching norms, such as plundering or harming clergy, women, children, or the elderly.[36]

While such clauses represented the articles' authoritative aspect, there were strong associative elements. All soldiers were admonished to respect the *Heerfrieden*, or the new military equivalent of the medieval *Burgfrieden* denoting the internal peace within the community, by avoiding violence and respecting their comrades. Moreover, becoming a soldier involved swearing an oath to obey the articles. This symbolized not merely subordination to authority, but membership of a community, exactly like the oaths sworn annually by urban burghers to be good neighbours and preserve their town. All oaths were contractual to some extent, understood as binding only while the other parties met their obligations. Soldiers' oaths lasted only so long as their unit and the collective swearing-in ceremony provided an opportunity to bargain for rights.[37]

The articles gave each unit a distinct legal identity, entitling it to convene its own court to judge cases among members. There were various forms of court, depending on what had been permitted in the articles by the warlord, but all were characterized by open hearings in front of the entire unit in which the soldiers were given considerable latitude in choosing jurors. Punishments were harsh, but the articles at this point allowed for death sentences to be carried out by beheading, which was considered more honourable than hanging and put common soldiers on a par with noblemen.

The artillery were the most like a guild, having their own articles in the Empire since 1444 and with their key command positions entitled 'master': master gunner (*Büchsenmeister*, equivalent to captain), and 'master of the ordnance' (*Feldzeugmeister*, equivalent to general). Infantry formations were larger and more 'proletarian' in the sense that they contained more ordinary soldiers who, by the 1520s, increasingly no longer owned the 'tools of their trade' as they were issued with weapons from public arsenals or by their officers. By contrast, cavalry units remained closer to the older feudal levy, with men, largely from rural backgrounds, enlisting individually without the ritual of a muster and shaking hands with their captain to signal acceptance of the articles, like the handshake in medieval vassalage.[38]

Mutiny and its Response

The central complaint of moralists and military reformers was that soldiers' corporate character made them unreliable and insubordinate. In contrast to the next two centuries, the main concern was mutiny rather than desertion, which was only a serious issue in the wake of defeats. Mutinies were primarily caused by the authorities' failure to pay soldiers or their requests to do something not previously agreed. Contemporary accounts stress the 'mercenary' character of soldiers' demands and present these as unreasonable. The Swiss were already notorious for pay mutinies before 1500 and they used the large size of their formations to enhance their bargaining power, since the armies in which they served would be drastically reduced in size if they left. Fear that his Swiss units would leave prompted the French commander, the vicomte de Lautrec, to launch his disastrous attack on the well-entrenched imperial army at Bicocca in 1522. His counterpart at Ceresole (1544) had to pretend that pay was on its way to persuade his Swiss to fight. The Landsknechts mutinied in 1516 when they discovered Maximilian had hired Swiss at a higher rate of pay, while the imperial army was wracked by a succession of mutinies during 1526–7, leading ultimately to the disastrous Sack of Rome.[39]

Rather than a sign of growing degeneracy, these problems were present from the start: Maximilian's Landsknechts refused to advance towards Buda after their victory at Stuhlweissenburg (1490), citing pay arrears, and instead took their booty and marched home. Some complaints were justified: no pay meant no food. Moreover, not all grievances were about money. Sickingen's Landsknechts refused to assault Mézières in September 1521, arguing the breach blown in the walls was not yet 'practicable' and the task was too dangerous.[40] However, it would be equally wrong to see the early Swiss and Landsknechts as forming some harmonious proto-socialist collective. Participation in mutinies entailed a breach of oath, risking personal honour and salvation. Mutineers' names were often recorded and sent to their home communities to be displayed on the gallows as a mark of disgrace, with possible further consequences when the men returned. Ringleaders usually seized on a scandal or emotive issue to mobilize support. Soldiers were reluctant to betray their comrades upon whom their lives depended in battle, imposing at least a moral compulsion to participate. Action was effective: battle and assault bonuses were not common before 1500 but became so within twenty years due to pressure from soldiers.

Warlords recognized that effective leadership required trust and respect, while fear and the threat of punishment alone were insufficient to instil discipline. However, the 1520s were a time of general turbulence associated with the challenges posed by the Reformation, which encouraged a hardening of attitudes by the 1540s. The frequent raising and disbandment of units prevented any continuity in collective bargaining and allowed the authorities to rewrite the articles of war. Those issued by Charles V in 1546 required men to serve as long as necessary, denying units the right to disband themselves. By the 1550s it was common to require soldiers to perform manual labour such as digging trenches, which they had previously refused as dishonourable. Courts martial no longer met in the open and were able to impose less honourable punishments like hanging. Imperial legislation proved decisive in this assertion of authority, since it carried the weight of the Empire and its legal mechanisms. The Reichstag issued sets of infantry and cavalry articles in 1570, which became widely copied models, including influencing the famous Swedish articles of 1632.[41] The infantry articles ran to seventy-four clauses to build on experience and close loopholes. In treating the cavalry as more 'noble', the Empire eventually lagged behind other powers, which dropped this distinction by issuing a single set of articles for all soldiers: Dutch Republic (1590), Sweden (1621), Denmark (1625), and eventually the Empire in 1642. The 1570 articles should be seen within the context of wider legislation regulating public behaviour, and which tightened surveillance through rules requiring travellers, including soldiers, to carry passports.[42]

The lengthening of the hierarchy of ranks formed a second element in this assertion of authority. Already in 1500 the Reichstag was requiring officers and men to swear different oaths.[43] Warlords pushed to control all appointments, but the extent to which they achieved this depended greatly on their relations with their colonels, who were concerned for their own authority and autonomy. By the later sixteenth century it was common for colonels to retain the right to nominate candidates to captaincies and often also lieutenancies, all subject to the warlord's formal approval. New arrangements with France in the 1560s deprived Swiss captains of the right to elect their colonels, who were now chosen by the king. However, matters often remained ambiguous: Hessian captains frequently received retainers from the landgrave, but maintained close connections with important contractors.[44]

Pay differentials reinforced the growing hierarchy. NCOs were paid the same as privates around 1500 but earned four times as much by 1550. The monthly pay of captains had doubled to 40 fl by 1543, or ten times that of a private. Double pays disappeared around 1570, while NCOs were no longer elected but appointed by the company commander. The Führer lost his function as the soldiers' legal adviser, while the position of Ambassaden disappeared and by the 1590s soldiers' committees were no longer tolerated. Meanwhile, unit sizes contracted, reducing the number of privates, but retaining that of NCOs and officers who were now collectively known as *prima plana*, because their names were recorded separately on the first page of the company roll. The French and Spanish were already doing this in the 1560s, followed by the Dutch rebels in 1573, while the imperial army followed suit in the 1590s, though Wallhausen and other theorists continued to recommend much larger company sizes.[45]

Landsknecht Culture

The associative character of martial law was complemented by a military culture that was collective rather than individualistic: Swiss troops and Landsknechts were *soldiers* rather than *warriors*. Individual skill, prowess, and daring were all important, but the nobility tried to claim these exclusively. The demands of soldiers for respect were largely a reaction to this. However, their skill lay in acting in close coordination with their comrades, since battlefield success depended on cohesion, not individual acts of bravery. Soldiers' honour was displayed through self-sacrifice, including acceptance of wounds and even death. Wounds became badges of courage and indicated participation in a common enterprise. The growing importance of gunpowder weaponry encouraged these beliefs, fostering a 'culture of endurance' as soldiers stood in massed formations under long-distance enemy fire, without immediately being able to retaliate until directed by their officers.[46]

This form of soldiers' culture developed first among the Swiss, for whom even looking backwards became a sign of cowardice. Relying on shock, the Swiss pike block had to keep advancing despite whatever the enemy threw at it, hence the practice of Bad War, since stopping to take prisoners would disrupt the formation. Like the Croatian cavalry of the seventeenth century, the Swiss deliberately fostered their fearsome reputation in the hope their enemies would break and run before contact. Solidarity was encouraged through rituals around the flag, which symbolized the company's unity and identity and could not be allowed to fall into enemy hands. They and the Landsknechts also cultivated their own customs and lore, some of which echoed pagan practices, such as throwing earth over their shoulder to appease the gods before battle.

Stripping the dead and defiling corpses was not only about plunder but could include a cultic element of gaining the powers of the deceased.[47]

Cohesion was also reinforced through peer pressure. Those showing fear would be mocked, while soldiers who fled could be cut down by their comrades. Men of higher birth serving in the ranks had to prove themselves worthy of their higher pay and better lifestyle, while their women were also closely observed and quickly criticized. Veterans who had seen three or more campaigns commanded respect and were expected to teach greenhorns the ropes. However, the omnipresence of violent death encouraged a culture of treating each day as the last, leading to the hard drinking and gambling that drew the ire of moralists. Competition for respect often led to fights within and between units, such as those involving Spanish and German troops in Charles V's army that left eighty-eight dead in 1546, while cavalry often camped separately from infantry for this reason, rather than out of tactical necessity.[48] The soldier's lifestyle was relentless and exhausting.

Landsknecht Dress

Swords were central to soldiers' identity through their association with martial values, manliness, and status, and officers remained reluctant to relinquish their right to carry them into the twentieth century, long after they had lost their military value. However, the ownership of weapons was widespread in the sixteenth century. Imperial law allowed people to be armed for self-defence and even women generally carried a knife. Handgun ownership spread quite rapidly among burghers after 1500, while territorial governments encouraged their subjects to arm themselves for militia service. Regulation centred on controlling only certain weapons, beginning with the imperial police ordinance of 1530 which banned stilettos and other arms that could be concealed. Further laws introduced increasingly sophisticated scales of fines and imposed requirements to compensate victims and their families.[49]

Thus, dress became soldiers' distinguishing feature and the flamboyance of Landsknecht costume that had emerged by 1510 was a direct expression of their fiery spirit. Suits were made from cloth of varying colours, so arms and legs could look different, while slashes to both and often to the chest revealed a contrasting lining. The hose was usually tight fitting around the knees and lower leg or cut short above contrasting stockings or a bare calf. This was replaced around mid-century by longer, baggy trousers called *Plunderhosen* because they were allegedly stuffed with booty. The large, broad-toed shoes called Bear's Claws (*Bärenklauen*) or Cow's Gobs (*Kuhmäuler*) were similarly multicoloured. Armour, if worn, could be fluted, mimicking the slashed cloth. Most wore large berets, sometimes over metal skullcaps, topped with feathers.

The classic explanation of the origins of this style was that the Swiss patched their ripped clothing with rich silks plundered from the defeated Burgundians, and some modern scholars believe it was an imitation of Burgundian court dress. Others see it as the expression of the Landsknechts' supposed individuality and desire to appropriate the rich clothing of the nobility.[50] It is more likely that the style emerged as an exaggerated form of more general fashions, stimulated by the soldiers' own competitive, showy culture. Soldiers were exempt from the sumptuary laws issued as part of the imperial police ordinance of 1530 that tried to restrict styles of dress to social groups, so that the maid could not be mistaken for her mistress.

Swiss soldiers were virtually indistinguishable from Landsknechts by 1520 beyond their cantonal banners and the white crosses sown on to the sleeves or chest of their clothing, while men in imperial service wore the red Burgundian cross. This gave troops from central Europe a distinctive appearance, differing from their Italian, Spanish or French counterparts, for instance. The engraved picture series showing soldiers already included separate plates for different ranks, with officers distinguished by their better armour and larger plumes.

By contrast, militiamen were more likely to wear uniforms, since these were purchased at public expense and because rulers appreciated the impact such a spectacle could make. Württemberg militia wore uniform hats and twill coats with black-and-white stripes and red sleeves in the 1480s, while at Duke Ulrich's wedding in 1511, 800 were dressed in red-slashed yellow, topped with red berets sporting white plumes, suggesting imitation of the Landsknecht style.[51] Some contractors were already making bulk purchases of cloth for their men in the 1530s, while it certainly became common for bodyguards to wear the livery of their master, such as Schertlin's sixty-strong cavalry troop dressed in yellow in 1545. German soldiers' appearance became increasingly drab by the 1580s, and what had been known as Landsknecht dress subsequently was termed the Swiss style when used for bodyguard units, notably and enduringly that of the pope.

The Campaign Community

The corporate legal status and distinctive dress of soldiers did not separate them entirely from society. The phenomenon of the 'soldier's child' (*Soldatenkind*) born in the barracks who followed his father into the ranks lay in the future with the permanent armies of the later seventeenth and eighteenth centuries. Even then, they were a tiny minority, and, like Catholic clergy, soldiers were not a self-reproducing group, but instead recruited from other parts of society. Foreign service was clearly a rite of passage for young, unmarried Swiss who used it to earn enough money to marry and settle down. The same was probably true for many Germans, as the absence of permanent armies removed any guarantee of continuous employment.

The bulk of soldiers came from the rural world and most returned to it, but relations with peasants were ambivalent. The Swabian League's infantry mutinied in March 1525, refusing to fight their 'brothers' during the Peasants' War. Having employed legal arguments about the need to crush rebellion, its commander Truchsess von Waldburg eventually regained his men's loyalty by offering an extra month's pay. Soldiers from the civic contingents continued to go home, but the League also recruited 1,000 men left unemployed after the Lake Constance peasants agreed to disband their forces in April 1525, while more peasant deserters enlisted the following month.[52]

Although emerging as a new Estate, soldiers nonetheless differed from the rest of society in being both itinerant and transient. Princes and cities held experienced captains and specialists on retainer, but these men did not live together, and beyond a handful of castle guards, soldiers were not kept permanently in service, but hired and discharged as needed. The Habsburgs preferred to retain Spanish troops for their permanent garrisons in the Netherlands and Italy from mid-century, though German professionals did serve along the Military Frontier in Hungary and Croatia after the mid-1520s. France retained Swiss rather than Germans or other foreigners between campaigns from the 1560s, but their numbers were still comparatively small compared to wartime strength.

Thus, most military units existed as 'campaign communities', generally only from spring to early autumn while weather permitted operations. Women and other non-combatants were a recognized element of this community, which depended on them for logistical and medical support, help with constructing camps, latrines, and entrenchments, looking after animals, foraging, and companionship. The Swabian League specified eight wagons for every 100 cavalry and three for a similar number of infantry in 1522.[53] The Hessian army invading Württemberg in 1534 comprised 4,215 cavalry, 16,343 professional infantry, 61 guns, and 15 war wagons, and was accompanied by 200 pioneers and 2,000 wagons, each pulled by four or six horses, including 614 transporting equipment and others with specially constructed pontoons, all escorted by 6,000 armed Hessian militia. The number of unarmed 'camp followers' is not recorded but is likely to have been around one for every three combatants.[54]

Women's presence went largely unremarked until the 1520s and their tasks did not differ substantially from those performed in the civilian sphere. Some were no doubt attracted by what critics termed a life of 'scoffing and boozing'. Others were pushed or pulled by the transformation of marriage driven by religious reform that saw four-fifths of the adult population legally married by the Church during the sixteenth century, compared to around one-fifth for much of the Middle Ages. Both Church and State cooperated in enhancing the legal position and moral authority of the household as the basic social unit to provide a stable tax base and a bastion against disorder. The ideal household was headed by a husband and wife who had different but complementary roles. The household was embedded within the political order at communal level, notably through the enfranchisement of most male householders for village and town council elections. Husband and wife were charged with keeping order over the other household members including live-in servants and apprentices. Thus, both husband and wife belonged to the 'public sphere', and the ideal of the home as a purely feminine domestic sphere only emerged during the later eighteenth century. The presence of women and 'boys' (servants) was important to soldiers' self-esteem and desire for the status of married men. The army tolerated 'May marriages', temporary liaisons lasting the campaign, while martial law granted army women the right to inherit their partner's property and gave them precedence over wives at home.[55]

Such pragmatism was condemned by the general moralizing drive from the 1520s, which also led to the closure of urban brothels. Women suffered by association and those with the troops were now routinely labelled 'whores', while the officer overseeing them in the camp was termed the *Hurenwebel*. Those joining the campaign community now risked being ostracized from their home communities and faced a permanent life on the road. However, the Reformation's tightening of parental control and the Church's refusal to marry many of the poor meant the campaign community remained attractive to some. Official toleration ended with the 1570 articles that banned 'lewd women' from camps, but the attempt to restrict their presence to lawful wives failed.

Welfare, Medical Care, and Mortality

Soldiers also differed from other social Estates in that they found it difficult to look after their own. The late medieval and early modern model of welfare was that each community provided for its own members with, for example, vagrants being forcibly returned to where they came from. In this sense, sixteenth-century soldiers were modern 'proletarians' whose employers felt they had discharged their responsibilities once they had paid them. Troops were usually paid off at the end of the campaign wherever they happened to be and were expected to make their own way home. They might be happy to do so if laden with booty, but this was frequently not the case. The 12,000 Swiss and Germans who had fought on opposing sides at Dreux, the opening battle of the French Wars of Religion in 1562, banded together after the campaign to plunder their way back to the Empire. Other units remained at least partly in service for self-protection, while individuals combined as unauthorized *Rotten* (bands) to survive the *Garte*, the time without pay between campaigns.

Marauders were regarded as a significant public order problem. Town walls were built as much to keep out or manage roving bands of strangers as to provide defence against set-piece sieges. The authorities became more prepared to accept responsibility for the sick and injured, even if their response remained woefully inadequate. Conscious of ancient Roman examples, as well as initiatives in contemporary Italy and the Netherlands, the Austrian Habsburg government discussed various ways of caring for former soldiers after 1529. Pensions for invalided veterans remained a matter of princely grace (*Gnadensache*), while widows and orphans generally remained at the colonel's mercy since the deceased was often owed considerable arrears that the warlord could not pay. The 1570 articles guaranteed soldiers that they would still be paid while recovering from injuries, and the 1594 Reichstag authorized church collections for those wounded fighting the Turks. The imperial army provided a field hospital in the 1597–8 campaign and considered introducing pay stoppages to create a hospital fund, something that became standard practice in the later seventeenth century.[56]

The development of gunpowder weaponry created new kinds of injuries, notably as black powder smoke and dirt from the discharge coated the projectile, thereby increasing the chances of infection. Surgeons were already recommending using silk to clean injuries in the 1490s, but the belief that lead bullets poisoned wounds encouraged doctors to remove them immediately using unsterilized instruments that added to the risks. Medical knowledge remained within the paradigm set by Hippocrates and Galen, guided by the theory of the need to balance the 'four humours', or bodily fluids believed to regulate human health and behaviour. While not matching modern knowledge, such beliefs should not be dismissed entirely as 'primitive'. Military medicine in fact advanced considerably around 1500, thanks largely to printing that allowed new ideas and experience about human anatomy to be disseminated more widely and rapidly.

German authors made significant, lasting contributions. Hans von Gersdorff, a trained surgeon from Alsace, carried out over 200 amputations during the Burgundian Wars and published an illustrated manual of military medicine, *Feldbuch der Wunderartzney* (Field Manual of Wound Treatment, 1517), which remained the standard work for over a century. Gersdorff recommended using a specially designed saw for amputations rather than the traditional blow with an axe, and demonstrated how wounds could be covered using flaps of skin. The apothecary Walter Ryff, who had been trained by Gersdorff, published over forty-eight books including *Die grosse Chirurgie* (1545), synthesizing surgical knowledge.[57] Despite these publications, wider society still regarded physicians (*Medici*) more highly, as these were university-trained, treated internal ailments, dispensed medicines, and claimed superiority over surgeons and orderlies (*Feldscherer*), who generally lacked formal qualifications and dealt with external problems, like wounds and pulling teeth.

The nature of wounds and the difficulties in treating them ensured high mortality among those injured in battle. The Swiss lost 30,000 killed during the campaigns between 1494 and 1500, with further heavy losses in the other battles of the Italian Wars.[58] However, military life was inherently unhealthy. A battle-sized army with its camp followers could easily number upwards of 40,000, equivalent to the population of Frankfurt or Cologne, the Empire's largest cities. This ratio persisted into the early nineteenth century as armies continued to grow, yet because they remained ambulant they lacked the facilities and infrastructure of cities, such as drainage and solid housing. Around four-fifths of the inhabitants of pre-industrial central Europe showed signs of disease and malnutrition in their bones, and cities were already breeding grounds for disease, so it is scarcely surprising that armies suffered even worse sickness and mortality rates.[59]

Like one in ten of the population, soldiers suffered from rickets, the causes of which (vitamin D deficiency and the lack of sunlight) were not diagnosed until the 1930s. Vitamin C deficiency as a cause of scurvy was not identified until 1912, and in the sixteenth century it was believed to be contagious. Bad diet also contributed to dental problems, which likewise affected many soldiers. Their dental health became important with the introduction of paper cartridges, which were supposed to be opened during the loading process by biting the end off. Armies carried tents and built huts when encamped for longer periods, but protection was often inadequate. Six Landsknechts froze to death on a particularly cold and wet July night at the siege of Pressburg (Bratislava) in 1542.[60]

The identification of campaign diseases is complicated by the confusions in contemporary diagnoses and labelling. Bubonic plague, spread by lice and rats, was the worst such disease, with mortality rates rising to 60 per cent during the regular epidemics that swept through Europe roughly each generation into the seventeenth century.[61] Typhoid, caused by bacteria in dirty conditions like camps, was often called *Morbus Hungaricus* because of its prevalence in campaigns against the Turks, but it may also have been confused with malaria, which was present along the Danube and its tributaries. Typhoid was the most common fatal disease affecting soldiers, with a monthly mortality rate of 10–20 per cent of strength and was especially rife when armies encamped for long periods, such as during sieges. Dysentery, commonly called *Ruhr* (flux), was another systemic problem of encampments and killed around 6 to 10 per cent monthly, generally striking in the late summer or early autumn. 'Plague' allegedly killed 5,000 Landsknechts and camp followers during the Sack of Rome in 1527. The 50,000-strong imperial army invading Provence in 1536 lost between 12,000 and 20,000 through disease, while Charles V's forces were allegedly halved from the same cause when campaigning along the Danube in Bavaria during September–October 1546.[62]

NO MONEY, NO WAR

War Costs

The common complaint 'No money, no Swiss' can be applied to sixteenth-century warfare generally: men and materials could nearly always be found provided they could be paid for, but all observers were concerned at the spiralling costs of conflict. 'Nowadays,' wrote Sebastian Franck, 'with Landsknechts employed everywhere, wars involve thousands of men as each prince tries to build a bigger and stronger army than his neighbour. It costs more nowadays to prepare for war than it used to require in the old days to fight and conclude one.'[63] The Swabian League's five-and-a-half-month campaign involving 9,000 troops against the peasants in 1525 cost 234,000 fl. Around a decade later the monthly costs of 4,000 infantry were put at 34,624 fl, but a similar number was estimated to cost 59,000 fl in 1607. Cavalry were around twice as expensive, while an artillery train of 130 guns was estimated at around 50,000 fl a month in the 1560s.[64]

Austria, including the silver-rich Tirol, had a normal annual revenue of 364,000 fl around 1500, making it the wealthiest member of the Empire, but this was less than half the income of Henry VII of England. Bavaria and the Palatinate were the next richest with revenues of around 100,000 fl each, while the medium principalities and large cities all received between 30,000 and 50,000 fl compared to 1.3 million fl enjoyed by Venice. If the numerous counts, prelates, lords, and smaller imperial cities are included, the Empire's public authorities probably had a total ordinary revenue exclusive of borrowing of about 2 million fl. While this was three times that enjoyed by the king of France, then Europe's wealthiest monarch, these resources were not centralized.[65] Maximilian I spent 25 million fl over the course of his reign, mainly on securing Milan during the Italian Wars, while Habsburg estimates from the later sixteenth century put the annual cost of an army of 55,000–60,000 at 7–8 million fl, or around four times the monarchy's normal revenue at that point.

It was clearly impossible to achieve the late medieval ideal that rulers 'live off their own' and fund their household, public administration, and war from domains and ordinary revenue. The combined debt of the imperial Estates was around four to five times their revenue by 1500, and the inability to balance budgets had encouraged the growth of the territorial and provincial Estates with whom rulers had to negotiate for new taxes. Obligations to the Empire were presented as unavoidable duties by princes to their Estates, who were often kept in the dark about their true value since, unlike their ruler, they were not party to discussions at the Reichstag or Kreis assemblies. The regularity of imperial tax demands led to new territorial taxes, which had become permanent by the 1550s. Revenue from the Empire played only a subordinate role in Habsburg war finance under Maximilian I and Charles V, mainly because much of the assistance was provided in kind as troops instead, who were maintained at the expense of the territories that had sent them.

Aid from the Empire became much more important after the partition of the Habsburg possessions by 1558 cut Austria off from Spain's wealth while leaving it with the burden of maintaining the Military Frontier. The costs of the latter nearly doubled to 1.67 million fl across 1556–76 as fortresses were strengthened and new permanent garrisons were established. Hungarian revenues covered no more than a third of this, leading to a system of regular subsidies from Austrian provinces, notably Styria, that provided 18.1 million fl between 1576 and 1606. The Reichstag agreed a succession of long-term grants from 1556, which effectively represented permanent war taxation since the money continued during the periodic truces with the sultan. Despite growing confessional tension, the proportion of the sums voted that was actually paid rose from about 70 per cent to 88 per cent. Combined with additional money provided by the Kreise, this aid totalled over 31 million fl and represented a substantial contribution to the Habsburgs' border defence.[66] By contrast, the members of the Schmalkaldic League paid under 52 per cent of their contributions to their common war chest in 1546, reflecting in part dissatisfaction among the weaker members with the princely leadership's belligerent policy.[67]

Tax grants were insufficient and often arrived late. The Habsburgs commuted traditional personal service obligations into cash taxes to boost revenue. Many nobles preferred this as cheaper and less dangerous than appearing in person, particularly as the actual cost could often be pushed on to their tenants. However, Estates distrusted rulers, recognizing that militia service might be reimposed on top of the new taxes should another conflict break out. Foreign aid was unreliable. French subsidies were significant in Philipp of Hessen's campaign to restore Duke Ulrich to Württemberg in 1534, and France also funded the Princes' Revolt in 1552.[68] While the money in both cases helped get operations started, it only met part of the total costs. Maximilian I was generally disappointed at his allies' failure to send the promised sums during the early stages of the Italian Wars. Papal and Spanish subsidies represented less than a tenth of the money raised by Austria during the Long Turkish War, compared to funding from the Empire, which provided 30 per cent.

Charles V borrowed heavily from German, Flemish and Italian bankers to fund his wars, but the scale of these loans was only possible thanks to his position as emperor and the extent of his lands. Partition of the Habsburg Empire cut Austria off from Spanish wealth just as imports of silver from the New World in the 1550s were beginning to make a substantial impact. The Austrian branch continued to borrow, but like other German princes, it lacked such access to international credit. Thus, German war finance increasingly differed from that in Spain or France, which relied heavily on bankers to bridge cashflow problems through large, expensive loans. Instead, the emperor and princes borrowed from the Estates, smaller bankers, and merchants to cover immediate shortfalls, while pushing other costs on to contractors by converting unpaid bills into additional debts. Philipp of Hessen's military adventures had pushed his debt to 956,988 fl by 1567, or six times that in 1529 and around three times his normal revenue.[69] Such debts accumulated across the Empire until the Estates could be persuaded to amortize them retrospectively.

This practice allowed the Estates to carve out their own fiscal autonomy within each territory, since they controlled the taxes linked to paying off the debts they assumed on their prince's behalf. They also used the opportunity to bargain additional rights and guarantees for their role in territorial affairs. In the Habsburgs' case this had fatal consequences, because they were forced to concede toleration to Protestant towns and nobles in most provinces in return for debt amortization from the 1560s. Attempts to restrict these new rights proved a cause of the Thirty Years War. Nonetheless, the provincial and territorial Estates remained junior partners to rulers who retained exclusive powers to start and end wars. By contrast, the electors, princes, and cities, collectively as imperial Estates, secured a say through the Reichstag and Kreis assemblies in directing imperial wars, but did not assume any debts on the Empire's behalf. While the Habsburgs and other princes remained indebted, the Empire was largely debt free, because each territory paid its own contingent and any war taxes voted went ultimately to the Habsburg treasury to subsidize the emperor's direct costs.[70]

The Swiss escaped these problems, because they did not make war on their own account after 1515 and instead obtained pensions on top of the pay the soldiers received directly. Although both pay and pensions were often in arrears or not met in full, the latter represented a substantial income stream for the cantonal authorities, who kept taxes very low and avoided debts. Overall, foreign service accounted for 6 per cent of Swiss GNP around 1500, while the proportion of cantonal revenue contributed by just the pensions ranged from 15 per cent in Bern and Zürich to over 40 per cent in the Catholic cantons, rising to 80 per cent in rural ones like Appenzell. Their impact was magnified by the general absence of war costs after the internal struggles ended in 1531. Although the Swiss continued to feel vulnerable, they dispensed with costly permanent forces, trusting instead in their militia, many of whom had experience in foreign service.[71]

Fiery Taxes

Warlords often had unrealistic hopes of making war at their enemies' expense. The legal structures established in the Empire in 1495 allowed those executing verdicts of the imperial courts and other official mandates to recoup their expenses from wrongdoers. The Swabian League's campaign against Duke Ulrich of Württemberg cost 300,000 fl of which only 82,000 fl was covered by the members' matricular contributions. Having successfully executed the imperial ban against the wayward duke, the League sold the conquered duchy to the Habsburgs for 210,000 fl, far below its true value.

Money could also be demanded from enemy populations by threatening to burn their homes. This 'fiery tax' (*Brandschatzung*) later became known as 'contributions' and was considered legal when used outside the Empire, but many Swabian League members doubted it was lawful against their own rebellious peasants in 1525. Unable to pay the troops that April, the League reluctantly authorized a levy of 6 fl per farm, presenting it as a fine rather than as contributions. Overall, 238,000 fl were raised, but this was pocketed by the members as reparations rather than given to the army, and the demand of the commander Truchsess von Waldburg for a 10 per cent cut was rejected.[72]

Fearing a Catholic plot, Philipp of Hessen persuaded the more cautious Saxon elector to agree a pre-emptive strike against the Franconian bishoprics of Bamberg and Würzburg in 1528, arguing the costs would be recouped at the bishops' expense. Although Saxony got cold feet and backed out, Philipp went ahead, only to discover that the whole affair was based on faulty intelligence provided by a Saxon official, Otto von Pack, and he faced a storm of protest and demands that he refund the money he had extorted. This 'Pack Affair' damaged him and Saxony politically, delaying the formation of the Schmalkaldic League.[73] The two princes nonetheless continued to act unilaterally without informing other League members, invading Brunswick-Wolfenbüttel in August 1542 in an operation that cost 800,000 fl. They then discovered that occupying the duchy cost them 70,000 fl monthly, or nearly 20,000 fl a month more than they could extract from it.[74] Moritz of Saxony managed to cover only 18 per cent of the 639,189 fl it cost him to lead the Princes' Revolt in 1552 from contributions levied on pro-Habsburg lands. Meanwhile attempts by his erstwhile ally Albrecht Alcibiades to fund his own operations almost entirely this way stirred his fellow princes against him and led to collective action that defeated him in 1553.[75]

Economic Impact

Monetizing war through taxes and debt redistributed some wealth, though German rulers relied heavily on contractors to purchase weaponry and war materials on credit and made few substantial purchases themselves. Armies consumed considerable resources. A force of 30,000 men required daily 330 to 600 cwt of bread and 225 oxen or their equivalent to provide each man with a ration of a 2 lb loaf and 2 lb of meat. A large cavalry horse consumed 4–5 kg of oats, 5–7 kg of hay, and 15–40 litres of water, meaning that the horses with such an army required the fodder from 160 hectares of meadow daily.[76] However, these men and animals would have eaten these resources anyway, so the overall impact was negligible; rather, it was how their presence in one place concentrated the demand that could benefit some producers while harming others.

Cashflow problems and logistical failure tended to accentuate war's negative impact, since armies without cash had no other means to sustain themselves beyond plunder. Deliberate destruction was also a strategy long employed in medieval wars when belligerents frequently avoided contact. The continued seasonal character of sixteenth-century conflicts often left parties with insufficient time to force their opponent to fight on favourable terms, making systematic destruction an attractive alternative. It was safer, as the targets were usually the enemy's subjects who were rarely able to resist, and it was frequently effective since most people lived at subsistence level so simple destruction of crops and farms inflicted lasting damage. While elites could escape, they nonetheless suffered indirectly as their tenants were no longer able to pay rent or taxes.

However, there were also limits, because a belligerent often had no desire to destroy what they might also find of value; a factor shaping the Swabian League's policy in 1525, when the victims of its extortion were the members' own subjects. The same principle applied to plundering at individual level, particularly when soldiers knew they would be in the target area for some time. They usually took household items, clothing, food, and cattle; all things that could either be directly consumed, used, or quickly sold on. Additional violence and destruction could occur, particularly if resistance was encountered, but it was also often perceived as counter-productive, while commanders sought to restrain plundering because it could quickly lead to indiscipline. Individual victims could suffer considerably, but plundering really made its impact through mass action and most sixteenth-century campaigns in the Empire were mercifully short and localized. This would change across the next century as Germans struggled to restrain the voracious demands of the growing scale and duration of warfare.

PART II

Accepting War as Permanent

4

Restraining the War Monster

THE THIRTY YEARS WAR, 1618–48

The War in German History

The conventional narrative of German military history is punctuated by
1648 as a supposed turning point between violent religious war and the
more 'limited' conflicts associated with an 'age of absolutism'. Exemplified by Louis XIV's France, absolutism in the German lands is most
associated with Prussia and Austria, with the other German rulers often
derided as 'petty princes' who just 'played at soldiers' (*Soldatenspielerei*)
by hiring their armies to foreign powers.[1]

The distinction between the Thirty Years War and subsequent conflicts in terms of scale, violence, and impact is more relative than absolute.
War was certainly not 'limited' in impact after 1648, nor was religion
totally removed as a political factor. The war did not create standing
armies. The Habsburgs already had one on their Military Frontier after
the 1570s, though the omnipresence of the Ottoman threat meant it
could not be easily deployed elsewhere. They were obliged to create a
new field army in 1618, which expanded greatly after 1625 and was the
only large force to remain permanent following 1648, albeit at reduced
strength, whereas other princes simply retained garrison companies
and militias. The Thirty Years War became entrenched in collective
memory as the archetypal 'absolute war' to be avoided at virtually all
costs, and the overriding desire was to return to peace and for that to
last (see Fig. 5).

Acceptance of war as a permanent, unavoidable part of life came only
grudgingly with the onset of renewed warfare from 1672, which finally
prompted the irreversible militarization of the component elements of

the Empire, though not of the Empire itself, which instead reformed its mechanisms for mobilizing forces when needed. That reform entrenched the Empire as a political hierarchy, fixing its political structure until its demise in 1806. Meanwhile, Switzerland's different experience resulted in a continued reliance on militias for its own defence, with regulars only raised for foreign powers, chiefly France, Spain, and later the Dutch Republic.

The Thirty Years War was nonetheless a defining episode in German history, profoundly affecting how subsequent generations thought about themselves and warfare more generally. While the war was initially remembered with horror and revulsion, its outcome in the Peace of Westphalia was broadly regarded positively as a successful compromise that restored the imperial constitution, enshrined religious co-existence, and protected German liberties. Only in the wake of renewed foreign invasion and defeat during the Revolutionary and Napoleonic era did the Westphalian peace become conflated with the Thirty Years War as a great national disaster that had supposedly left the country permanently weak and divided.[2] The question of who might be to blame for this became inextricably entwined with the mounting Austro-Prussian rivalry for mastery in Germany after 1815, which entrenched a set of partially contradictory and almost unshakable myths about the lessons of the Thirty Years War that endure in the popular perceptions of the conflict despite decades of new scholarship.

Foremost among these myths is that the war was inevitable, allegedly stemming from the compromise over religious rights in the Peace of Augsburg of 1555; a view that denies the historical actors any agency and ignores that the Empire enjoyed sixty-three years of relative tranquillity thanks to that settlement. Second is the view that the conflict rapidly spiralled out of control until 'it ceased to be war' because 'the soldiers alone ruled'.[3] Politically, this supposedly meant that the conflict expanded outwards to become a general European conflict, thereby minimizing issues in the Empire and reducing the importance of German actors.[4] Militarily, the Thirty Years War is widely perceived as having been outsourced to 'private' contractors, epitomized by the imperial general Albrecht von Wallenstein, who are thought to have acted on their own account with operations dictated by logistics, not politics.[5] Although the war has been considered the last and greatest of Europe's 'religious wars', those who fought it are paradoxically regarded as merely disinterested mercenaries. Finally, the result is considered an 'all destructive fury' of wanton violence and mayhem until the war supposedly burned itself out, at last making peace possible.[6] This final element of the traditional narrative profoundly influenced twentieth-century German views of national victimhood during both world wars.

The conflict was an imperial civil war that spread through the failure to restrict the initial crisis to Bohemia. It was prolonged by the unwillingness of its principal protagonists to compromise and through the successive intervention of external powers. Throughout, those involved regarded the war in the Empire as distinct from the struggles elsewhere in Europe, notably the resumption of the second phase of the Spanish–Dutch war in 1621, Sweden's war with Poland (1621–9), the Franco-Spanish War (1635–59), and Britain's civil wars (1638–51), as well as revolts in France and various parts of the Spanish monarchy. Several belligerents fought directly or indirectly in more than one conflict, but all were careful to demarcate their participation through agreements with their allies as well as declarations against their enemies.

Powers opposed to the Habsburgs provided financial and military aid to prolong the conflict in the Empire and prevent the emperor securing a victory that would have enabled him to aid Spain against the Dutch. Spain assisted the emperor to secure the opposite. Denmark and then Sweden intervened when they perceived their interests in northern Germany were threatened by imperial victories, and they received intermittent assistance from France, Britain, and others opposed to the Habsburgs. There were moments when it appeared that the war in the Empire might merge with that between Spain and the Dutch, notably in 1629 and 1632. France ramped up support for Sweden after 1635 as it also openly sided with the Dutch in its own war against Spain. Nonetheless, the three conflicts remained distinct: Sweden refused to declare war on Spain, a major trading partner; the emperor fought France only on imperial soil, but carefully demarcated cooperation with Spain elsewhere; and the Dutch abstained from all involvement in the Empire.[7]

All three conflicts were addressed separately in the peace negotiations at the Westphalian congress after 1643, with the Spanish–Dutch dispute settled by the Treaty of Münster on 15 May 1648. The Thirty Years War itself ended in a second Treaty of Münster between the emperor and France on 24 October 1648, and an imperial–Swedish agreement signed the same day in Osnabrück. That two agreements were necessary underscores how belligerents demarcated their involvement, as well as reflecting the Empire's own complexities. Although allies, France and Sweden had pursued separate objectives, while imperial territory was fought over in the Franco-Spanish War, because Spain's possessions in the southern Netherlands, Luxembourg, and the Franche-Comté collectively constituted the Empire's Burgundian Kreis. Consequently, this region was excluded by the second Treaty of Münster from the general peace in the Empire. France's failure to resolve its differences with Spain led to the break-up of the congress by April 1649 and ensured that Burgundy remained a war zone until the Peace of the Pyrenees in 1659.[8]

Causes

Just how the intricate character of the wars has been forgotten is demonstrated by the way Gerard ter Borch's famous painting of the Spanish–Dutch Peace of Münster has come to symbolize all three Westphalian treaties. The Franco-imperial treaty was celebrated by a similar ceremony in the same hall, as was that between the emperor and Sweden at Osnabrück. Anyone visiting the two rooms today will see the contemporary portraits of the envoys and their main political masters. The multitude of German representatives brings home how the conflict was always an imperial civil war over conflicting interpretations of the Peace of Augsburg and the constitution more generally. These issues remained central to the German belligerents throughout, since their resolution determined how the Empire would be governed, the status of the imperial Estates as its chief constituents, and the character of their constitutional liberties.

External intervention was always legitimated by reference to these liberties, rather than religion. Some participants felt personally summoned by God to fight, and religious conviction undoubtedly influenced decision-making, though this was hardly unique and featured in other early modern European conflicts, because religion remained central to personal values, legitimacy, and good government. However, most of those in authority remained pragmatic and saw religious goals as realizable only in the longer term and best achieved through peaceful persuasion rather than violence. Appeals were made to religious solidarity, but decisions to enter or leave the conflict were prompted by a much broader assessment of interests. Only some clergy and external observers – notably those in

Britain – simplified matters as a purely religious war. Rather than seeking to extirpate those of a different faith, the secular and ecclesiastical authorities broadly blamed the war on their own subjects' sinfulness, urging them to be more dutiful, pious, and obedient to retain divine favour and thereby secure victory.

The difficulty of disentangling religion and politics was demonstrated by the dispute over the imperial Church, which had been reserved for Catholics in 1555 by a separate imperial declaration that the Protestants did not regard as part of the Augsburg peace. Given the Empire's typically confused legal arrangements, the status of many of these lands was often unclear. Most of the Empire's princely families had converted to Protestantism by the 1560s and they refused to surrender their long-standing influence in these ecclesiastical principalities.

The situation was complicated by the spread of Calvinism which, unlike elsewhere in Europe, was primarily an elite phenomenon in the Empire, making most of its converts at the expense of the Lutherans among the imperial princes and counts, notably the Palatine and Brandenburg electors and the landgrave of Hessen-Kassel. These invoked their 'right of reformation', guaranteed under the Peace of Augsburg, to use their powers to supervise church affairs to promote their new faith among their subjects. In most cases this stirred strong opposition from their subjects, many of whom had only recently embraced Lutheranism and were bewildered and angered by another change. The Lutheran princes and counts, who remained the majority among the Protestant elite, objected that the Calvinists were endangering the compromise peace, while the Catholics saw the infighting as proof that heretics could not be trusted. These tensions and fears spilled out in numerous vicious public polemics in 1617, the Reformation's anniversary year, but the most vitriolic were those between Lutherans and Calvinists.

As the foregoing suggests, there was no neat division along religious lines in the Empire by 1618. Indeed, the rival branches of the Hessian princely family in Lutheran Darmstadt and Calvinist Kassel would fight their own intermittent inheritance dispute during the war with the emperor's backing for the former, largely dictating why the latter sided with the anti-Habsburg forces. Confessional tensions had appeared to peak with the formation of the Protestant Union (1608) and the Catholic League (1609), led by the Palatine and Bavaria respectively. This development mirrored the Hessian dispute, but on a much larger scale, since these were rival branches of the Wittelsbach family that had been at odds since the Landshut War of 1503–5.[9]

The Palatines' conversion to Calvinism damaged their standing in much of the Empire, adding to their sense of declining influence. Although an electorate, they took up the cause of those weaker princes and minor counts who felt disenfranchised within the Empire's hierarchical structure. The Palatines' demands for German liberties naturally included the most extreme Protestant interpretation of the Augsburg peace, but also greater influence for those princes, counts, and cities who were prepared to support them. The Protestant Union never attracted a majority among the Protestant imperial Estates and was always opposed by Saxony, which regarded itself as leader of the Lutherans and wanted simply to preserve the gains already secured in the Augsburg peace.

Duke Maximilian of Bavaria formed his League in direct response, rallying those church lands currently held by Catholics, who were the natural targets of the Protestant Union. Mainz cooperated to bring these into the League, but also pushed for Saxon membership to avoid polarizing confessional politics and to ensure Habsburg support. Duke Maximilian deliberately played up the purely Catholic character of his League to retain leadership, which would be threatened if he was joined by Saxony or the emperor, the latter being, regardless of personal faith, the ruler of many Protestant subjects.

The formation of these alliances did not make war inevitable or divide the Empire into armed camps. Other than Bavaria, all the princes were heavily in debt and maintained no forces beyond their militias, which they were struggling to organize and motivate. Both modelled themselves on the Empire's collective security arrangements, with members agreeing to pay into a common fund and to provide additional money to hire professional troops to augment their militias should mobilization be necessary. The Protestant cities joining the Union saw it as an insurance policy and opposed any action that endangered the peace, whereas most of the princely members hoped to enlist support for their own private interests, such as the duke of Brunswick's dispute with his main town, or Brandenburg's hopes to secure the entire Jülich-Cleves inheritance once this fell vacant in 1609.[10]

The Union and the League mobilized during the first Jülich-Cleves dispute in 1609–10, which briefly threatened to escalate into a major war. The huge expense involved deterred them from doing the same in a second emergency in 1614, when the Dutch occupied many of the strategic towns on the Lower Rhine. The Habsburgs managed to defuse tensions after 1615, compelling Maximilian to disband the League in 1617, while several of the Union's members dropped out or stopped paying their fees.

The Empire clearly had problems in 1618, but there was nothing to suggest war was imminent, at least not on the scale that followed.[11] That this occurred had much to do with the problems of the Habsburg monarchy itself, which lost direction under Rudolf II after 1576. His weak, inconsistent and devolved management of the hereditary lands allowed the family's three main branches to pursue their own policies. The Styrian branch took a hard line after 1579 against its Lutheran nobility, interpreting existing agreements in ways favouring Catholics, who were perceived as more likely to be loyal and were given preferment in civil and military appointments. This policy was interrupted as the Habsburgs turned in on themselves following the disappointing outcome of the Long Turkish War and Rudolf's refusal to marry and produce a legitimate heir. Under attack from his childless brother Matthias, Rudolf granted further concessions to the Bohemian Protestant nobility, who were permitted to establish a parallel government after 1608.

The Bohemian Revolt and its Aftermath

The attempt to roll back these concessions after Rudolf's death in 1612 stirred discontent among the Protestant elite, who lost court appointments and influence. A minority of malcontents staged the infamous Defenestration of Prague on 23 May 1618, throwing three Habsburg officials from their office window, deliberately to force the other Protestants to join more active opposition. No one was ready to fight. Only the Styrian branch, headed by Archduke Ferdinand, had professional troops, which were in the process of being disbanded following his brief war with Venice, while the omnipresent Ottoman threat prevented the Habsburgs from drawing many troops from the Military Frontier. The situation there soon deteriorated when the prince of Transylvania used the crisis to make his own bid to become Hungarian king, precipitating several rounds of fighting until 1626.[12]

Four aspects were clear from the outset. First, religious and political differences had not caused a 'communication breakdown' between the parties, who continued to seek a peaceful resolution throughout the war, especially when they felt in a position of strength.[13] Second, what they sought was 'peace with honour' rather than total victory. All recognized that they lacked the means to achieve everything they might desire, but more fundamentally they believed objectives should remain within accepted norms to be both politically legitimate and theologically and morally sound. Each party was a coalition of unequal elements with diverging interests. Those negotiating recognized they would not be able to achieve everyone's goals, and a major factor prolonging the war was balancing the need for peace with the desire not to alienate one's own supporters upon whom the continued military effort depended.

Third, military operations were always intended to secure the conditions necessary for a favourable peace by pressuring the enemy to negotiate.[14] The relative balance between the belligerents hindered the generals' ability to achieve this, particularly as foreign powers usually stepped up support when they felt their favoured party was on the brink of collapse. With none of the belligerents prepared for a large war, let alone a long one, foreign involvement began almost immediately when Spain sent money to help build a new imperial army in June 1618. However, the commitment of outsiders was always contingent on their own circumstances and many historians have exaggerated the scale and importance of external aid; it made a difference at several key points, but the war was fought primarily with German manpower and resources, while Danish, Swedish, and French intervention all depended on German collaborators who provided most of the troops.

Fourth, once operations began, the war was immediately brutal and destructive, rather than escalating in a roaring crescendo of violence as imagined in the 'all-destructive fury.' The violence had little to do with religious animosities. The belligerents used militia when they lacked funds for professionals, but they made no effort to call their subjects to a holy war that would have compromised their claims to be responsible, Christian rulers seeking peace. The violence was the inevitable consequence of the repeated failure of all parties to pay and supply their armies properly, as well as of the endemic difficulties of waging large-scale warfare in pre-industrial Europe. Occasionally, deliberate destruction and even massacre were used as terror tactics, but always with the intention of hastening the successful end of an operation by encouraging an enemy to cease resistance.[15]

There were many occasions when the war could have ended sooner, had one party not overplayed its hand, or if external support had not revived a flagging cause. The prospects for peace in Bohemia were not unfavourable. Saxony backed Emperor Matthias's efforts at mediation, which were supported by many in the Bohemian lands, notably Moravia, which had to be coerced into eventually joining the other provinces in their rebellion. However, the emperor's heir apparent, Archduke Ferdinand, was determined not to let the opportunity slip to assert the Habsburgs' authority in their own lands. His narrowly legalistic interpretation dominated Habsburg strategy until his death in 1637. His conscience dictated that he could not break existing agreements with Protestants who accepted his authority, but those who took up arms were, in his eyes, automatically outlaws who forfeited their rights and possessions. For him, the war offered a succession of opportunities to recover the previous generation's lost authority and increase his family's ability to manage the Empire.[16] Matthias's death in March 1619 allowed Ferdinand on his accession as Ferdinand II to assert his more hard-line policy, which was underpinned by the arrival of Spanish reinforcements.

The Bohemian rebels irrevocably placed themselves in the wrong in Ferdinand's opinion when they deposed him as their king and elected Frederick V of the Palatinate instead in July 1619. Frederick escalated the conflict by accepting the Bohemians' offer that autumn, since this linked the tensions in the Empire with those in the Habsburgs' hereditary lands. The Protestant Union refused to back him, though several members supplied troops, as did his British father-in-law, James I, without any of these formally becoming a belligerent.[17] The Bohemians carefully rewrote their constitution ahead of offering their crown, severely curtailing royal powers within what was now termed a Confederation. Most Austrian Protestant nobles and towns allied with the Confederation, threatening Ferdinand, who was in Vienna.

Maximilian of Bavaria seized his chance, persuading Ferdinand to allow him to revive the League in October 1619, in return using that organization to send an army to rescue him. Behind Maximilian's offer was the memory of the dispute within the Saxon Wettin family that had seen the transfer of their electoral title from the Ernestines to their Albertine rivals who had backed Charles V in 1546–7. For Maximilian, the Thirty Years War was about Bavaria definitively supplanting the Palatinate as the leading Wittelsbach branch.

Maximilian's intervention proved decisive, with his troops overrunning Upper Austria before joining the imperial army to invade Bohemia. However, Saxon support was also significant in surrounding Bohemia to the north and defeating resistance in Lusatia and Silesia. The campaign culminated in the battle of White Mountain, fought on a hill just west of Prague on 8 November 1620 (see Fig. 6). Although the slightly larger Confederate army was demoralized, it held a strong position and the result was far from a foregone conclusion.[18]

The Confederates' total rout made the battle arguably the most decisive in the whole war. Frederick fled, eternally mocked as the 'winter king', thanks to the brevity of his reign. Ferdinand moved swiftly to impose a settlement based on his interpretation of the law. The defeated rebels were treated as outlaws, and though most were pardoned, they were deprived of their lands, which were given to nobles who had remained loyal throughout the crisis, as well as being sold to help reduce the ballooning war costs. The transfers were so extensive that around half the population changed landlord and opened the way to Bohemia's re-Catholicization. The provincial Estates were eventually given revised constitutions in 1626–7, but there was little need for wider institutional changes now that the country was dominated by families who owed their wealth and influence to supporting the ruling dynasty. This informal alliance consolidated Habsburg power, underpinning it until the end of the monarchy in 1918.[19] It was to defend this victory that Ferdinand II and his son and successor, Ferdinand III, would keep fighting until 1648.

The war could have ended there had Frederick V renounced his lost crown, but he refused all offers of compromise, partly from sympathy with his supporters who had been driven into exile, but also from an unshakeable belief that God would eventually bring him victory. With the small imperial army busy pacifying Bohemia and fighting the Transylvanians, the task of dealing with the Palatinate was delegated to Bavaria backed by Spanish auxiliaries.[20] Saxony retained Lusatia in lieu of its war expenses and withdrew into neutrality. Maximilian's commander, the count of Tilly, made short work of Frederick and those minor princes who raised forces in his cause and who had all been defeated by the end of 1623. Maximilian extracted his reward when Ferdinand provisionally transferred the Palatine lands and electoral title to him after Frederick had been formally declared an outlaw.

Again, the war could have ended there, but Christian IV of Denmark then intervened early in 1625 when he occupied much of Lower Saxony to protect his interests in several church lands that now appeared threatened by the surge in Catholic influence.[21] Maximilian opposed the resumption of the war but accepted the continued deployment of the League army in the name of restoring the Empire's public peace. As Spain had already withdrawn its troops, Ferdinand authorized the relatively junior but wealthy Bohemian general Wallenstein to expand the imperial army, which reduced his dependency on Maximilian. Denmark's comprehensive defeat by 1629 enabled Ferdinand to extend his policies into northern Germany. Princes and nobles who had backed Christian IV were declared outlaws and their lands redistributed to Ferdinand's supporters and to compensate his unpaid senior officers, with Wallenstein being made duke of Mecklenburg in 1628.

On Wallenstein's advice, Denmark was offered generous terms in the Peace of Lübeck in June 1629, recovering all its own lands in return for renouncing pretensions in the Lower Saxon bishoprics. This secured lasting Danish goodwill, not least because Denmark feared Sweden far more than the Habsburgs. Unfortunately, Wallenstein's advice was ignored on other issues. Ferdinand sent detachments of the imperial army to assist Poland, with which he had a defensive alliance, against Sweden, thereby adding to that country's alarm at growing imperial power on the southern Baltic shore. Further troops were briefly sent to assist Spain against the Dutch, while others moved into northern Italy to uphold imperial rights in the disputed Mantuan succession where they clashed with French forces. This expansive policy frustrated Ferdinand's efforts to secure peace with France and to persuade the electors to accept his son as successor designate. Worse, Ferdinand unilaterally imposed his own interpretation of the dispute over the church lands in the Edict of Restitution in March 1629, abandoning the established practice of judicial review of individual cases and ordering the return of all property taken from Catholics since 1552. This was a major blunder, undermining pretensions to an honourable peace and alienating Saxony, which had largely ensured the Lutheran princes had remained neutral.

A resumption of war was far from inevitable, and Saxony and Mainz worked hard to soften Ferdinand's edict. Their efforts were cut short by

Gustavus Adolphus, Sweden's ambitious king, who invaded Pomerania in June 1630. Gustavus presented different reasons for his actions depending on whom he was addressing, and his goals expanded with his military successes. Primarily, he wanted Germans to pay for Swedish security. Some lands would be annexed, notably Pomerania, which, while Lutheran, was ruled by a childless duke. Gustavus ignored the objections of his own father-in-law, Georg Wilhelm, elector of Brandenburg, whom the Pomeranian duke had recognized as his heir. When Georg Wilhelm tried to remain neutral, Gustavus turned his artillery to face the electoral palace. Swedish propaganda may have presented the king as the saviour of German Protestant rights, but he expected absolute obedience from those he liberated. Saxony reluctantly re-entered the war, this time ostensibly in support of Sweden, but really to pressure Ferdinand into moderating the Edict of Restitution.

Gustavus's great victory over Tilly at Breitenfeld in September 1631 enabled him to expand into the rest of Germany. He now pursued the reverse of Ferdinand's policy, redistributing conquered land to German princes and aristocrats who supplied the bulk of his forces. These 'donations' were to be held as fiefs of the Swedish Crown, thereby undercutting imperial authority, and directly threatening the Empire's integrity. Sweden lacked the time or capacity to build a stable empire in Germany, and its structure was already creaking when Gustavus's death at Lützen in November 1632 robbed it of its chief architect. The system collapsed almost completely with the great imperial victory at Nördlingen in September 1634, facilitated by the brief return of Spanish forces to assist the emperor.[22]

This victory gave Ferdinand a second chance at a definitive settlement, resulting in the Peace of Prague in May 1635, which met most, though not all, of Saxony's demands, as well as confirming Bavarian possession of the Palatinate and the emperor's settlement in his hereditary lands from the 1620s. Bavaria accepted the dissolution of the League, in return for retaining its own army as an auxiliary supporting the emperor. Saxony received broadly similar rights. All other armies were to be dissolved and instead imperial Estates were to pay war taxes to support the emperor's army.[23] These arrangements greatly strengthened the emperor's formal military power, while the Peace accepted his interpretation that the original war had ended in 1629, and that events after 1630 had been an entirely new struggle begun by Sweden's invasion.

The legitimacy of the peace was undercut by its presentation to the imperial Estates as a fait accompli, rather than as a commonly negotiated compromise such as that reached in Augsburg in 1555. Worse, Ferdinand excluded the Palatinate, Hessen-Kassel and several other princes from his general amnesty, thereby allowing Sweden to claim it was still fighting for German liberty. He also seriously underestimated the task of persuading the Swedes to leave Germany, delegating this to Saxony, which was expected to prompt the Protestant imperial Estates to raise the money Sweden needed to pay off its army, now its officers had largely lost the lands they had been given by Gustavus.

France had subsidized Swedish intervention since 1630 and now incrementally moved towards direct involvement to shore up its ally during 1635. By 1636 it was obvious that Sweden could not easily be induced to leave, but neither side could secure a preponderance as a victory in one region was often offset by a defeat elsewhere. Ferdinand III made a final effort to bolster the legitimacy of the Prague settlement by summoning a Reichstag in 1640–1, the first since 1613, but the circumstances were by now far less favourable.[24] France and Sweden slowly evolved a more effective strategy of using their main army to block that of the emperor, while other forces coerced the imperial Estates into one-sided neutrality. Those who accepted these deals had to provide supplies to the allied armies and permit their transit across their lands, but were otherwise largely left alone. Brandenburg agreed this by 1642, followed by Saxony by 1646 in the wake of several imperial defeats. Bavaria wavered, but knew that only the emperor could guarantee its continuing possession of the Palatine electoral title.[25]

The Peace of Westphalia

The final years of the war were closely linked to the peace congress convened in the Westphalian towns of Münster and Osnabrück, which were declared neutral for that purpose. Envoys began gathering in 1643, but negotiations only began in earnest two years later once Sweden had launched a pre-emptive strike to remove Denmark as a hostile mediator. Having learned his lesson, Ferdinand III invited all the imperial Estates to participate, thereby undercutting accusations he was trampling on constitutional liberties. The bulk of the Estates, including most Protestants, had no desire to weaken the Empire, since it protected their own autonomy, and they voted against Franco-Swedish proposals to convert it into a looser aristocratic federation.

Like the war it settled, the Peace of Westphalia is the subject of enduring myths. It did not make the German principalities independent, nor inaugurate the modern international order based on state sovereignty.[26] The Empire remained a hierarchical order in which sovereign powers were shared unequally. The main change was that participation in external affairs was more securely sealed off at the level of imperial Estates, whose subjects were excluded from the exercise of the subsidiary powers known collectively as 'territorial sovereignty' (*Landeshoheit*). The presence of alliance rights among these powers was not new, because imperial Estates had previously exercised these. On the contrary, the previous limitation was restated more strongly that the exercise of these rights should not be directed against the interests of the emperor or the Empire.

Neither did the Peace secularize politics. Calvinism received formal inclusion in the rights established in the Peace of Augsburg, which was otherwise expressly confirmed. However, the imperial Estates lost the power to change their subjects' religion, which was henceforth to remain as it had been in 1624; a date deliberately chosen as a compromise to safeguard the Catholics' recovery of several church lands in the opening stage of the war. Extensive safeguards were extended to protect the dissenting minorities that existed in most territories. The Habsburg lands were expressly excluded from this, thereby allowing the emperor to continue his re-Catholicization measures introduced in the wake of White Mountain. All of this stopped short of modern toleration. The many 'religious cases' after 1648 involved the exercise of legal rights, such as the use of particular churches or sources of ecclesiastical revenue. In this respect, the Peace of Westphalia did take religion out of politics, as well as localizing disputes and making it much harder to polarize them along confessional lines. With a few notable exceptions, the imperial supreme courts successfully defused these disputes over the next century and a half.

The Peace did not entail the loss of the whole of Alsace, but merely Austria's part of it that passed wholly to France, while Strasbourg and the other cities and lordships remained part of the Empire. Sweden acquired the former bishoprics of Bremen and Verden, as well as the port of Wismar and the western part of Pomerania, all of which remained nonetheless imperial fiefs. Like Denmark, which still held Holstein, Sweden thus acquired representation in imperial institutions;

something that gave it influence, but also bound it within the imperial constitution. France and Sweden formally guaranteed the Peace, but in practice this added little to their ability to influence imperial politics, which still depended on their prestige and military power. In France's case, these were in the ascendency, whereas for Sweden they declined sharply from the 1670s.

Brandenburg-Prussia gained the most territory, receiving the eastern half of Pomerania, plus four former church lands as compensation for Sweden's acquisition of the western half. Although these gains boosted its revenue by a third, the elector remained aggrieved and the desire to acquire the missing half of Pomerania was a major factor dictating subsequent Prussian involvement in European wars. The elector had not in fact secured these gains through military victories, as his army had performed uniformly badly during its brief involvement in the war. Instead, he owed his new lands to the Habsburgs' desire to expand Brandenburg as a buffer to contain Swedish influence.

Bavaria retained the Upper Palatinate and the Palatine electoral title but was obliged to return the Lower Palatinate to Frederick V's son and successor, who was given a newly created eighth electoral title. This settlement cemented Bavaria's rise to the second tier of German principalities alongside Brandenburg and Saxony. Despite having been on opposing sides, the electors continued to function as a group.[27]

As the foregoing suggests, the war had not rendered the Empire ineffective. Although its interpretation had been hotly contested, the constitution retained its moral authority, while elements had continued to function, notably the Kreis structure that had facilitated a minimum of cooperation in several regions.[28] Ferdinand III's involvement of the imperial Estates, albeit conceded reluctantly, paved the way for a remarkable recovery of imperial authority after the war, which peaked at the mid-point of the War of the Spanish Succession around 1708.

Finally, the Peace of Westphalia did not make Switzerland an independent state, but merely removed Basel's obligation to pay fees to maintain one of the two imperial supreme courts. Around 80,000 Swiss had served France, Spain, Sweden, and Venice across the years of the Thirty Years War, but the Confederation preserved a precarious neutrality despite deepening tensions between the Protestant and Catholic cantons.[29] The emperor formally regarded the Swiss as still his subjects, and it took until the late seventeenth century for the view that Switzerland was a fully separate country to become widely accepted, even among its own inhabitants.

COLLECTIVE SECURITY, 1648–80

Peace Implementation

Over 42,000 printed copies of the Peace of Westphalia were distributed as part of a broader effort to ensure all parties adhered to it and there was no return to violence. The most pressing priority was to demobilize the 180,000 soldiers in the Empire whose presence was not only an intolerable burden on an exhausted population, but also hindered the territorial exchanges that had been agreed. This process was organized by the special congress convened in Nuremberg in 1649–50, which arranged a schedule and coordinated the collection and disbursement of funds raised through the imperial tax structure. Around 5.2 million tlr were paid to the Swedes, with a roughly comparable sum going to Austria, Bavaria, and Hessen-Kassel. At least twice as much was also paid directly by local communities to sustain the soldiers in the meantime; money was clearly still available to have continued the war, had the belligerents desired it.

Demobilization was achieved astonishingly quickly. Around two-thirds of the troops had already gone by autumn 1649, and overall numbers soon fell to 20,000, chiefly within the Habsburg army, most of which had moved into Hungary, and garrisons that Sweden retained in its new German possessions. The peace settlement prohibited transfer of soldiers to the ongoing Franco-Spanish War and covert Austrian efforts to support Spain were largely thwarted. A substantial proportion of the Bavarian army was recruited by Venice, which had been at war with the Ottomans since 1645. Germans and Swiss formed over two-thirds of the foreign units serving Venice until 1671. Meanwhile, the population decline had caused land prices to crash and placed a premium on labour, allowing most of the rest to reintegrate relatively swiftly into society. Widespread fears of marauding proved largely unfounded.[30]

Peace Preservation

The Empire had survived the war but was no longer the same. Imperial politics had become internationalized to an unprecedented degree through the successive external interventions to oppose or support the emperor's management of the Empire. Although distracted by its own internal problems and the ongoing war with Spain, France continued to cultivate a clientele among the German princes after 1648, spending the next three decades experimenting how best to manage them effectively. France was soon joined by its European rivals, including the emperor, who used bilateral arrangements with key princes to supplement his more formal political management through imperial institutions.

The electors and middling princes responded, because the external intrusion made them increasingly aware of their own inferior status among European royalty. They refused to be treated as simply Germany's aristocracy and wanted recognition across Europe as well as within the Empire. None wanted to leave the Empire, as they all recognized it protected their autonomy. Nor did they want fundamental constitutional amendments, because any collective change of status would not alter their own position relative to other princes. Instead, external sponsorship was welcomed as additional leverage when attempting to bargain with the emperor for exclusive benefits for themselves in terms of new titles and influence. Competition intensified during the 1690s as it became increasingly obvious that nothing short of a royal title would ensure the international respect which they now desired.[31]

These developments were related to France's resurgence and Spain's relative decline. European politics were increasingly dominated by the question of the succession in Spain, as it was not expected that the sickly Carlos II, who became king in 1665, would either produce an heir or live long himself (in fact, he lived to 1700). Rival Austrian and French claims raised the spectre of another single hegemonic power not seen since the days of Charles V, but Spain's elite opposed partition and the primary claimants were reluctant to discuss proposals openly for fear of compromising their own claims and international prestige.

France's insistence that Austria break with Spain by making a separate treaty had been a major factor delaying the completion of peace in 1648. A key provision of the Franco-imperial agreement at Münster in October 1648 was the exclusion from the peace of the Burgundian

Kreis, consisting almost entirely of Spanish territory. The Swiss and western German principalities remained fearful for the next decade that the Franco-Spanish War might spill across the Rhine. Meanwhile, the north remained troubled by tensions between Brandenburg and Sweden over the partition of Pomerania, as well as Sweden's attempts to annex the city of Bremen in addition to its recent acquisition of the surrounding archbishopric. To the east, growing Ottoman interference in Transylvania threatened to escalate into full war with the Habsburgs in addition to the ongoing war with Venice.

The Empire and Swiss Confederation responded to these threats by revising their existing collective security arrangements. The Swiss acted first but were extremely fortunate that their new defence structure never faced a serious challenge across the next century and a half. The Empire acted more slowly, employing a variety of improvised measures before implementing a comprehensive reform in 1681–2 that lasted until its demise in 1806. Although also imperfect, the imperial structure was repeatedly tested in war and served the Empire's needs reasonably well.

After nearly three decades of wrangling during which the Protestant and Catholic cantons made their own ineffective arrangements, the Swiss had been finally compelled to cooperate by the sudden appearance of a plundering Swedish army at Bregenz on their northeastern frontier in early January 1647. A meeting at the small town of Wil later that month established the basic structure of the Confederation's defence for the next two centuries. Known as the 'Defensional of Wil', this apportioned responsibility among the cantons to provide 36,000 men, organized into three levies with the first to be ready for immediate despatch. The decision to rely on their militia reflected the Swiss confidence in their innate martial qualities, despite Swedes having just routed the Tirolean militia, which rested on similarly cherished tradition.[32]

Subsequent revisions were limited to tinkering because the Confederation's multiple problems stymied any radical change. The cantons were not only divided by religion and politics, but all suffered from deep-rooted socio-economic tensions too. The latter erupted in rural Luzern in February 1653 and soon spread to much of northern Switzerland regardless of religion. The Luzern and Bernese governments capitulated to peasant demands, but the other cantons objected through the diet and initiated repression which had stamped out the protests by June.[33]

Popular resentment at the urban elites was strongest in the subject dependencies, which represented one of the more glaring inequalities within the Confederation. Lands such as Toggenburg and Thurgau had been conquered by cantons during the later Middle Ages, but were not fully incorporated due to the opposition of rivals, as well as the ruling elites' reluctance to share power. Unrest often expressed itself as protests by dissenting minorities, but it encompassed social and political as well as religious grievances. Rival cantons supported the minorities' cause to assert their own claims to the dependencies.

Unresolved tensions following the 1653 Peasants' War erupted three years later in the Villmergen War, fought over the key strip of Catholic lands dividing the Confederation north to south and preventing further expansion of Bern and Zürich, the two most aggressive Protestant cantons. Although outnumbered, the Catholic inner Swiss cantons were able to defeat a poorly coordinated invasion in a short war involving 2,000 deaths. In both emergencies, the Swiss only faced themselves, and though the militia performed poorly, there was no immediate pressure to reform it.[34]

The question of the Empire's defence arrangements was deliberately postponed by the Westphalian congress to stop discussions on their reform delaying peace. It was nonetheless clear that there were three options, each with radically different political implications. The Habsburgs' preferred solution was a version of what had been attempted in the Peace of Prague in 1635. The imperial Estates should pay war taxes to support a single army under the emperor's direct control. Had this been adopted, it would have pushed the Empire towards becoming a more conventional monarchy, which was why it was opposed by most imperial Estates. Whereas they had been prepared to fund Turkish defence through regular taxation before 1618, the experience of three decades of civil war, during which many imperial Estates had suffered from occupation by rapacious imperial troops, left them understandably reluctant to do this again.

The more powerful secular princes argued they should be funded by their weaker neighbours to provide a more decentralized defence. The development of small, permanent forces in several principalities by the early 1670s defined this option as that of the 'armed princes', who saw contributions from their unarmed neighbours as valuable additional means to maintain their troops alongside foreign subsidies and their own subjects' taxes.[35] Realization of this option would have federalized the Empire ahead of the changes that did not happen until 1806, as those communities which had failed to accept the burden of imperial taxes after 1521 had already long lost any real autonomy.

The third option was to involve all imperial Estates, thereby keeping the Empire's character as a multi-layered structure composed of unequal, diverse elements. The relative vitality of the Kreise offered a viable framework to achieve this, since these were already empowered to coordinate regional defence and peace enforcement. Their firm anchor in the imperial constitution made them more attractive than separate leagues or unions partially discredited by the recent war, which had revealed them as vehicles for sectional interests. The Kreis assemblies gave all members individual votes, unlike the Reichstag where arrangements favoured the electors and more powerful princes. However, the Kreise reflected the Empire's broader geographic variations. Those with the greatest territorial fragmentation, like Swabia and Franconia, proved more vibrant and effective than those dominated by one or two larger principalities, such as Lower and Upper Saxony.

The potential of the Kreise was already demonstrated in the early 1650s when several of them formed defence pacts, known as 'associations', agreeing to cooperate over wider regional security. The more powerful princes often found it expedient to participate, but their efforts to assert leadership hamstrung several of the associations. Nonetheless, Johann Philipp von Schönborn was successful in securing the backing of many of the smaller Rhenish and northwest German territories, thanks to his prestige as elector of Mainz and the fact that, as an ecclesiastical prince and therefore without children, he was not viewed as harbouring the same designs for regional hegemony as some of his secular, hereditary peers. The emperor viewed these autonomous regional initiatives with suspicion, particularly as Schönborn simultaneously opposed the Habsburgs' attempts at a more monarchical, less consultative management of the Empire.[36]

Initial Armaments

Most principalities relied on companies of professional garrison troops to be supplemented by militia in an emergency, but a few rulers added additional regular units, which fluctuated in size depending on need and available finance but were now maintained even in peacetime as a cadre.

Foremost among these armed princes was Frederick William, known subsequently as the Great Elector of Brandenburg. Sweden's invasion of Poland in 1655 placed the elector in an awkward position, as his possession of East Prussia made him a Polish vassal and obliged to assist. However, Swedish threats forced him to support the invasion, and Brandenburg troops represented around half of the army that defeated the Poles at Warsaw in July 1656. The battle was important as Brandenburg's first major success after its poor military performance during the Thirty Years War.[37]

However, the political benefits Frederick William derived from the war stemmed from his cooperation with Austria, which intervened in support of Poland after 1657. This occurred at a critical juncture. Ferdinand III's death in April of that year created an interregnum during which Louis XIV's candidacy complicated Habsburg efforts to secure the election of the late emperor's son Leopold. Frederick William changed sides and traded his vote in return for Austrian backing to free East Prussia from Polish and Swedish influence.[38] The Peace of Oliva, settling this Northern War in the spring of 1660, included international recognition of East Prussia as a sovereign duchy. The significance of this should not be exaggerated. European royalty regarded Prussia as a semi-barbaric place on the margins of civilization, while even Frederick William was more preoccupied with Cleves and Mark in Westphalia, which were still partly occupied by the Dutch and produced more revenue. Nonetheless, he was now the only German ruler alongside the Habsburgs to possess independent land beyond the Empire.

Brandenburg strength topped 25,000 in late 1655, but its army was generally between a sixth and half that across the 1650s and 1660s, while the Guelph dukes and Christoph Bernhard von Galen, the militant bishop of Münster, maintained similarly sized forces. Known as 'Bomber Bernard' for his knowledge of artillery, Galen besieged his own capital several times to break resistance to higher taxation and firmer rule. He also joined England in the Second Anglo-Dutch War, invading the republic from the east in 1666 before shortage of money and the defeat of his maritime ally forced him to withdraw. The episode demonstrated the dangers that the emerging armed princes posed to their subjects, neighbours, and foreign powers.[39]

France's desire to harness such assertive princes for its own interests prompted the formation of the Rhenish Alliance on 14 August 1658, just two weeks after Leopold I's coronation underscored Louis XIV's failure to become emperor. The Alliance included Schönborn and his two fellow ecclesiastical electors in Cologne and Trier, along with Sweden on behalf of its German territories, Galen and eventually another twelve princes. France was not yet universally regarded as a 'national' enemy, and Schönborn and many others hoped Louis would act as defender of their liberties against a potentially overmighty Habsburg emperor.[40]

By grouping the princes into an alliance, Louis hoped it would be easier to manage them as an anti-Habsburg block that would prevent the emperor from mobilizing the Empire against him. The arrangements reflected that France was dealing with princes, rather than the broader patrician elites in Switzerland. French subsidies went exclusively to the princes, and were not disbursed to their subjects, though additional pensions were sometimes paid to cultivate key advisers. The money went to improve fortifications and to boost the capacity to provide troops if France needed them, rather than to recruit soldiers as integral parts of the French army. Although France managed to get the Rhenish Alliance renewed twice, it was unable to control its members, several of whom like Schönborn and Galen saw it as a framework for military cooperation against their own recalcitrant subjects, notably the burghers of Erfurt and Münster.

The Turkish War, 1662–4

Although serious to those in their proximity, none of the threats in the 1650s was sufficiently acute to galvanize action across the Empire. The next two decades saw new dangers, first in the east and then in the west and north, which were on a scale that compelled a larger, more radical response leading to the defence reforms of 1681–2. The coincidence of renewed threats simultaneously to the east and west would consolidate the changes across the later 1680s and 1690s.

Eastern security had continued to rest on the structures developed since the 1570s, though the outbreak of the Thirty Years War had ended tax grants from the Reichstag, forcing the entire burden of the Military Frontier on to the Habsburgs. Fortunately, the Ottomans were distracted by problems of their own and renewed the truce of 1606 six times from 1615. For the emperor, the Ottomans posed an existential threat with the frontier only 100 kilometres from Vienna, whereas the sultan regarded the Habsburgs as only one of several relatively distant enemies. This asymmetry was reflected in the gifts exchanged at each renewal of the truce: the emperor handed over a large sum of hard cash, suggesting he was the Ottoman's tributary, whereas the sultan's envoys brought carpets and other items demonstrating their master's munificence.[41]

However, neither ruler fully controlled their 'men on the spot', while the truce permitted cross-border raiding on which the frontier communities depended for much of their livelihoods. Conflicts could easily escalate, particularly if one side saw an opportunity for quick gains. A surge in Ottoman raiding after 1655 increased the pressure on Leopold to act. Schönborn seized the opportunity to press for defence reform at a Reichstag that the emperor reluctantly convened in January 1663. The crisis mounted as the Ottomans launched a major offensive against Habsburg Hungary in July. Rejecting the emperor's call for taxes, Schönborn obliged Leopold to allow the Rhenish Alliance members to send contingents under their own generals to assist the hard-pressed Habsburg forces. The 13,600-strong Alliance corps included 6,000 French, more than twice the number Louis was obliged to provide under the 1658 agreement and who, uniquely in this engagement, fought alongside Leopold's troops. The French presence challenged the emperor's traditional claim to be Christendom's defender, though Louis continued France's covert cooperation with the Ottomans.

Most imperial Estates agreed with Schönborn in demanding a share in directing the war but remained suspicious of the Alliance and its armed members. Emperor Leopold rose to the challenge, appearing at the Reichstag himself to thank Schönborn for his efforts, but dodging the question of reform by promising to discuss this later. The Estates responded by sending 15,000 troops mobilized through the Kreise. Together with 4,500 men sent separately by Bavaria, Brandenburg, and Saxony, these measures provided a third of the total forces ranged against the Ottomans in the 1664 campaign. Commanded by the imperial general Raimondo Montecuccoli, these soundly defeated a much larger Ottoman army at St Gotthard on the Raab river on 1 August.[42]

Leopold ignored his advisers, who urged him to continue the war, and instead quickly bought an extension of the truce on 20 August, allowing the sultan to keep three fortresses and paying another 'free gift' of 200,000 fl. Hungarian discontent at this outcome led to a series of conspiracies and revolts, which grew more serious as the Habsburgs tried to reorganize the Military Frontier after 1671, triggering a decade of violence that tied down a significant proportion of the monarchy's army in gruelling counter-insurgency operations. Along with several princes and Louis XIV, Leopold sent some troops to Venice, now engaged in the final stage of its long war against the Ottomans, but these failed to prevent the fall of Candia in Crete after an epic siege in 1669.[43]

The results appeared disappointing, but the brief Turkish War already pointed to the compromise that would be reached after 1681. Moreover, though he had initially opposed its convention, Leopold ultimately chose not to dissolve the Reichstag, which was to remain now permanently in session until 1806. While no one yet predicted this would be an 'eternal diet', the emperor slowly realized he had more to gain than lose by cooperating with the mass of weaker imperial Estates who, by acting collectively through imperial institutions, counterbalanced the growing power of the armed princes.[44]

The Dutch War, 1672–9

The main reason why Leopold was so keen to cut his commitments in the east was his fear of France, which had emerged from a long period of internal and international war and was now ready to contest inheritance claims to Spain's possessions. Louis's first attempt came in 1667 when his armies swiftly overran the Spanish Netherlands and Franche-Comté, ostensibly as payment for the dowry promised when he married Philip IV's daughter Maria Theresa in 1660, as part of his 1659 peace settlement with Spain.[45] Leopold was ill-prepared and tried diplomacy to limit French gains. Eventually, Britain, Sweden, and the Dutch Republic combined to persuade Louis to evacuate most of the conquered territory in May 1668.

The episode damaged Louis's standing within the Empire, contributing to the failure to renew the Rhenish Alliance when it expired in 1667. This suited the king's more aggressive policy, freeing him from a framework formally dedicated to upholding the Peace of Westphalia, and allowing him to forge bilateral agreements with individual armed princes. These included Cologne and Münster, whose cooperation in 1672 allowed French armies simply to bypass the heavily fortified Spanish Netherlands when Louis launched a premeditated attack to punish the Dutch Republic for having opposed his plans.[46]

The main French attack swept through Cologne and its dependency of Liège, while Galen and an enlarged Münster army invaded the republic from the east, reaching Groningen. Further French subsidies to Bavaria, Hanover, and Pfalz-Neuburg secured their neutrality, hindering the Empire's response. Nonetheless imperial and Brandenburg troops occupied Koblenz, threatening the French right flank. When the French approached Amsterdam, the Dutch opened their sluices, flooding much of the republic and halting the invasion. Galen's offensive collapsed when he ran out of supplies in August. The struggle continued along the southern Dutch frontier into 1673. Brandenburg temporarily left the war as the French occupied Cleves, and by November both Cologne and Münster had abandoned France.[47]

The crisis exposed the tensions between activism and passivism in the Empire, which would continue until 1806. Activists saw involvement in the war as an opportunity to advance their dynastic goals. Austria was foremost among these, since the Spanish inheritance was at stake, while other princes sought to arm and secure sponsorship for their own goals. The further Louis moved from association with 'German liberties', the less attractive he appeared as a sponsor, yet his aggression inadvertently created alternative patrons eager for German military assistance. Leopold's alliance with the Dutch on 4 August 1672 laid the first foundation in what would become the 'Old System' of Austria's membership of a broad anti-French coalition lasting, with interruptions, until 1756. The Dutch had already hired German troops in 1666, followed by Spain once it declared against France in 1673. The number of hired auxiliaries rose from under 3,000 (1673) to over 61,000 (1678).

The Empire lacked a framework for an autonomous, activist policy, though Leopold ensured he was party to many of the troop treaties with the armed princes. While backed by the emperor, these agreements were outside the formal framework of collective security, which remained purely defensive with most imperial Estates regarding mobilization as a last resort if diplomacy had failed. Nonetheless, the public peace legislation already provided the basis for the western Kreise to coordinate defensive measures along the Rhine in 1672. Mobilization was not dependent on a declaration of war, since the French were already considered to have breached the peace through their incursions on to imperial territory. The Kreis contingents provided a valuable supplement to the imperial army, given that a significant proportion of Austrian troops were still tied down combating the Hungarian revolt.

The two forms of German involvement emerged unplanned in response to the widening of the war and were not entirely in harmony. Foreign subsidies and other payments rarely covered the true cost of supplying auxiliaries, while continued French military superiority prevented the Allies from taking the war into enemy territory. Operational necessity dictated troop movements and the occupation of strategic positions, yet the campaigns along the Rhine were waged in an area of complex overlapping jurisdictions, and the continued reverses meant that German forces usually wintered on imperial soil. French forces under the vicomte de Turenne overran the rest of Alsace in 1673 and began plundering across the Upper Rhine. Other forces conquered Franche-Comté in just six weeks in 1674.

Fear that conditions were returning to those of the Thirty Years War prompted Leopold to assert central coordination of the Kreis and auxiliaries, as well as his own troops, by assigning them territories from which they could draw money and supplies. These 'assignations' were rationalized on the grounds that the unarmed imperial Estates should support those fielding troops for the common cause. Brandenburg and other princes bullied smaller counties and priories into agreeing supplementary 'treaties of protection', whereby the armed princes provided substitute troops in return for regular cash contributions considerably above the actual costs. Attempts to assert greater influence prompted those who could to work through the Kreise to increase their forces, with the total rising from around 7,000 men in 1673 to over 16,000 after 1675. Montecuccoli's arrival as commander on the Rhine repelled further French attacks, but he was unable to recover much of the lost territory.

One factor hindering success on the Rhine was the opening of a new front in northern Germany when Sweden, after much prompting by France, attacked in December 1674, hoping to conquer eastern Pomerania. Elector Frederick William led a small force from Berlin to surprise and rout a similarly sized Swedish army at Fehrbellin on 18 June 1675.[48] The battle was celebrated as a great victory and proved better suited as a foundational myth for the Hohenzollern dynasty than that at Warsaw, where Brandenburg troops had fought as Sweden's auxiliaries. Later nationalist historians also used the incident to claim that Prussia achieved its greatness through building up its own army, contrasting this with the alleged ineffectiveness of the Empire.

Frederick William's appeals failed to solicit direct military assistance. The rest of the Empire remained unenthusiastic, partly because it was already burdened with defending the Rhine, but also because the Estates recognized that he was using the emergency to pursue his own expansionist aims to in turn conquer the rest of Pomerania from Sweden. Nonetheless, imperial mandates against Sweden had some impact, persuading some of its German troops to refuse to fight. Meanwhile, Brandenburg's success in conquering western Pomerania by September 1678 was greatly assisted by Denmark's decision to attack Sweden in 1675, and to use Münster and Hanoverian auxiliaries to capture Sweden's possessions of Bremen and Verden the following year.

Sweden's poor showing did not detract much from French successes elsewhere, enabling Louis to secure very favourable terms in the seven treaties making up the Peace of Nijmegen in 1678–9. Alongside minor changes in positions along the Rhine, Leopold was obliged to accept France's retention of Franche-Comté and key fortresses along the southern frontier of the Spanish Netherlands, such as Lille, Douai, and Oudenarde. While these losses came directly at Spain's expense, they were also formally imperial territory. Meanwhile, French pressure forced Brandenburg to return most of its gains to Sweden by the Treaty of Saint-Germain-en-Laye in June 1679, while Denmark had to return all its conquests. It seemed small compensation that the Dutch had finally abandoned their garrisons on Brandenburg's Lower Rhinish territories.

DEFENCE REFORM, 1681–2

The Réunions, 1679–81, and Switzerland's Response

France's annexation of Franche-Comté threatened Switzerland more directly than the Empire because it removed a long-standing, if weak, territorial buffer. Franco-Swiss relations had deteriorated with France's bankruptcy in 1648 when the country's crown jewels were temporarily transferred to Zürich as a pledge for the huge pay arrears owed the Swiss troops. The last extension of the 1521 treaty expired in 1651, and the arrangement was not renewed until 1663.

Despite the elaborate ceremony at that event, Louis XIV showed a similar disinclination to be bound by formal arrangements with the Swiss as he did to being tied to the German princes. He employed Giovanni Stoppa, a Rhetian colonel in his service, to recruit additional regiments outside the established agreements and on terms much less favourable to the Swiss. The Confederation protested and Stoppa was hanged in effigy in Luzern, but the recruitment was ramped up after 1671 with the outbreak of the Dutch War. Although some Protestant officers expressed opposition to fighting the Dutch, the Swiss continued to cooperate with France.[49]

Concerns grew as French expansion continued despite the Peace of Nijmegen. Using fabricated legal claims backed by force, France began occupying those parts of Alsace that still belonged to the Empire. The policy, known as the Réunions, escalated with the capture of Strasbourg in September 1681, ignoring that this was an imperial city and had a defence pact with the Swiss. The Réunions culminated in another war with Spain that saw France capture Spanish-owned Luxembourg in 1684, further encroaching on the Burgundian Kreis. Finally, in 1685 Louis revoked the Edict of Nantes that had guaranteed toleration to the Huguenots, France's Protestant minority since 1598. Although Swiss troops were formally exempt from this measure, the Protestant cantons regarded this as a sign of Louis's faithlessness, as did their coreligionists among the German princes, some of whom openly welcomed the many thousands of Huguenot refugees fleeing the king's repression.[50]

The Confederation's inability to agree defence reform hindered a more vigorous response. France's temporary occupation of Franche-Comté in 1668 finally prompted some minor revisions to the Defensional of Wil and contingents were temporarily mobilized when the French reappeared in 1674. However, within two years Schwyz opted out of the common defence, followed by five other cantons by 1679, all objecting to subordinating their militia to a central war council. The last Catholic canton left the system in 1702. This was the context of the Swiss declaration of neutrality in 1674, the first such statement issued by the diet.[51]

Many Swiss slowly came to realize that continued neutrality depended less on their ability to defend themselves than the rivalry of major powers seeking to employ them as soldiers. Spain's relative decline affected this. It recruited 47,000 Swiss across the seventeenth century, with numbers peaking at 10,800 in 1690, but by then Spain had ceased paying pensions and had lost much of its former influence. Savoy's constant vacillation and mounting persecution of the Waldensian sect alienated many Protestant Swiss, and even once it largely joined the anti-French camp after 1690, it was scarcely a counterweight to Louis XIV.

The vacuum was filled by the Dutch and the English, who signed alliances with the Protestant cantons after 1690. Mirroring those with France, these included a package of financial and economic measures in return for Swiss troops, who served the Dutch in large numbers between 1693 and 1795. Several cantons also allowed Prussia and other powers to recruit individual soldiers, pushing the total in foreign service at any one time to 50,000–60,000 across much of the eighteenth century.[52] The Confederation's treaty with France remained in force, though not all Protestant cantons still supplied troops, meaning the Swiss now had a variety of potentially conflicting agreements.

Thanks to their multiple commitments, Swiss troops fought on both sides after 1693, adding to the internal tensions over the subject territories. This time the Catholic Inner Swiss cantons were backed by Valais and Ticino and thus felt sufficiently strong to support the bishop of St Gallen in a dispute with Protestant peasants in the Toggenburg region east of Zürich. Bern and Zürich cooperated more effectively than in the Villmergen War. After initial successes in May 1712, they widened operations to an all-out effort to conquer the entire corridor of dependencies, which they had largely achieved by August at the cost of 3,000 killed. The outcome left lasting resentment among Catholics, while reinforcing the Protestants' conviction that their innate martial valour would always triumph and there was no need to reorganize the Confederation's defence structure. Only the Catholic cantons renewed with France ahead of the 1663 treaty's formal expiry in 1723, joined belatedly by their Protestant neighbours in 1777.

Imperial Defence Reform

The Réunions caused such alarm in the Empire because they coincided with similar Danish aggression in northern Germany, including attempts to seize Hamburg in 1679 and 1686, as well as repeated occupations of Holstein-Gottorp. Nonetheless, the loss of Strasbourg was a seismic moment, symbolically far more important than the early loss of Austria's part of Alsace. It stirred unprecedented hostility towards France and prompted the Reichstag to place a duty on the emperor to recover Alsace. Austria used this on occasion to reinforce requests for aid in wars against France, but there was little enthusiasm for an offensive war and there was no direct link between the seventeenth-century problems and the Franco-German War of 1870.

Instead, the Empire reacted defensively by reforming its collective security through a series of measures between May 1681 and March 1682.[53] By working through the Reichstag, Leopold signalled the abandonment of attempts to impose a purely monarchical solution to defence, as well as a positive response to the appeals of the weaker imperial Estates who sought to escape subjugation by the armed princes using the emergency to demand taxes and billets for their troops.

The reform followed the precedents set in 1664 and 1672 by using the public peace legislation as a legal basis for mobilization at national, regional, or territorial levels. There was no mechanism for a formal declaration of war, as this was a defensively orientated system to respond to dangers, not cause them for others. Provision of troops remained the responsibility of the imperial Estates whose actions were always limited by the proviso that they must not be directed against the interests of the emperor or Empire. The right as well as duty of all imperial Estates to contribute was reaffirmed, thereby stemming the slide towards a federal solution entailing the annexation of those who were being coerced into protection agreements by their armed neighbours. Equally, however, the reform did not prohibit additional forces, leaving the armed princes free to maintain separate 'household troops' (Haustruppen), either for their own defence or to be hired as auxiliaries to the emperor or his foreign allies. The Kreise and their members were also free to hire additional troops to make up their quotas, as often occurred from the 1690s.[54] The term Reichstruppen applied when Kreis contingents combined under the command of imperial generals who were to be named jointly by the emperor and the Reichstag.

The matricular system was adjusted by assigning each imperial Estate revised contingents that could be called out in multiples of the basic quota, known as the Simplum, which totalled 12,000 cavalry and 28,000 infantry. Unlike the Swiss, it was expected that the Estates would send professionals, not militia, but they were not obliged to maintain their contingents in peacetime. Additionally, money could be raised using the established tax assessment valued in 'Roman Months' using the system established in 1521. Theoretically, this left a door open to the monarchical solution, and the Empire did vote purely cash grants periodically across the next 120 years. However, Roman Month taxes were normally only levied to supplement the mobilization of troops, with the money going to a new Imperial Operations Fund to pay for specialist equipment and other campaign costs. Meanwhile, it remained the Estates' responsibility to pay and supply their own contingents, and most Kreise swiftly passed additional legislation to regulate this.

The reformed structure has often been criticized as decentralized, fragmented, and ineffective with the oft-cited examples of minor counties, abbeys, and cities, each responsible for providing only a handful of men each. Naturally, there were genuine problems of ensuring standardization of equipment, uniforms and training among units composed of multiple small contingents, and it is often argued, not always fairly, that the forces of the larger principalities were militarily more effective. However, it would be wrong to conclude that this meant there was 'no longer a viable German political unity'.[55]

Siding with the more powerful princes would have federalized the Empire by removing the weaker elements of its long political hierarchy. This would have undermined what their collective security was supposed to protect, and it made effective management of the Empire much more difficult. The system was tailored to the Empire's needs and it did not seek to wage aggressive wars of conquest. It was never intended to replace the armed princes' forces, but instead to protect the Empire's weakest elements while leaving the stronger ones free to pursue their own objectives, always provided these did not conflict with the collective good.

THE TURKISH AND FRENCH WARS, 1683–1714

The Siege of Vienna and the Great Turkish War

The system's limited objectives were met when it survived the severe test of a two-front war that developed after 1683. The immediate trigger was a renewed Hungarian revolt led by Count Thököly after 1681. Despite doubling the Habsburg army, Leopold was unable to suppress the revolt and, seeing this as an opportunity to capture the 'golden apple' of Vienna, the Ottomans rebuffed the emperor's offers to extend the truce and instead invaded with a massive army in 1683.[56]

Leopold lost credit by fleeing to Passau, abandoning his capital to a prolonged siege, but at least he was free to organize the relief effort. The Reichstag authorized a triple quota, but the parallel French aggression in the Burgundian Kreis, along with French subsidies to Brandenburg and Denmark, ensured a patchy response. Nonetheless, 33,000 troops arrived to join the Habsburg army and a large allied Polish contingent on the Kahlenberg hill west of Vienna on 12 September. It was not a moment too soon, as the Turks had exploded a large mine, wrecking part of the city's defences, and were preparing for an assault.

Unlike at St Gotthard, where the Ottomans had retreated in good order, they now collapsed in rout; a sign not only of the ferocity of the relief army's attack, but also of the growing problems in the sultan's empire. As in 1664, Leopold was keen to negotiate a renewal of the truce to be free to stop France gobbling up the Spanish inheritance. This time, however, his advisers persuaded him to capitalize on the opportunity to conquer Hungary, and he signed the Holy League with Poland, Venice, and the papacy in March 1684. Russia's adherence to this alliance after 1686 proved a mixed blessing, as its troops were too far away to be of direct assistance, while its participation allowed the tsar to contest Leopold's claim to be protector of the Balkan Christians.

The decision to continue the war in the east necessitated a compromise with Louis XIV, which Leopold reached with the Truce of Regensburg in August 1684, recognizing French gains to that point for the next twenty years. The arrangement caused considerable disquiet in the Empire, but the Kreise continued to maintain their contingents in Hungary, and even Sweden sent assistance on behalf of its German possessions. Meanwhile, Leopold agreed the League of Augsburg with Brandenburg and other leading princes to assist defence in the west should Louis renew his attacks. Additional contingents from the armed princes represented around two-thirds of the 20,000–40,000 Germans assisting Habsburg forces in Hungary between 1684 and 1688. A further 18,500 troops were supplied under separate arrangements with Venice for a costly campaign in Ottoman-ruled Greece (see Fig. 7).[57]

The capture of Buda in September 1686 followed by the victory at Mohacs the next year precipitated a partial Ottoman collapse. The

Habsburgs had advanced their frontier 350 kilometres in under four years. In October 1687 they convened the Hungarian diet at Pressburg, packed with loyalists who accepted the dynasty's interpretation of the kingdom's constitution, including that the Crown was hereditary in the Habsburg family and no longer elective. A special commission was established the following year to expropriate land from those who had previously rebelled, as well as distributing newly conquered areas to loyalists, mirroring the practices employed in Bohemia and Austria during the 1620s. With the capture of Belgrade on 6 September 1688, vast Balkan conquests appeared to beckon and there was even talk of reaching Constantinople.

The Nine Years War, 1688–97

Habsburg progress was violently interrupted by the outbreak of a new war in the west. Growing alarmed at Habsburg gains in Hungary, Louis XIV used a series of pretexts to invade the Palatinate on 24 September 1688, hoping to stiffen the sultan's resolve to continue fighting. However, the French king's underlying goal was to advance his wider claims to more Spanish territory, with the new act of aggression intended to intimidate Leopold into recognizing his most recent gains as permanent. The conflict was almost immediately complicated by the Glorious Revolution, which saw the Dutch stadtholder, William III, replace the Catholic James II as king of England, Scotland and Ireland in November 1688. Leopold had secretly encouraged Dutch intervention, supporting William's recruitment of 14,000 German auxiliaries to enhance the republic's security while he invaded England. William's diplomacy secured the cooperation of the Scandinavian kingdoms and prevented Louis from opening a far northern front, as he had achieved in the 1670s.[58]

William's success added Britain to the existing Austro-Dutch alliance, which had already been informally renewed in July 1688. The new combination was cemented as the Grand Alliance in May 1689, dedicated to opposing French hegemony in Europe. Britain and the Dutch Republic, collectively known as the Maritime Powers, were financially the most powerful European states, thanks to their growing, commercialized economies, and sophisticated tax and credit systems. Both relied heavily on foreign troops to expand their armies rapidly. France's aggression, following its recent revocation of the Edict of Nantes, made it relatively easy to find German princes willing to provide troops: the number of auxiliaries in Anglo-Dutch pay topped 38,000 by 1696, whereas France was unable to find anyone in the Empire with whom to cooperate.[59]

The Maritime Powers rapidly became skilled at balancing the German princes, dispersing their contingents to spread the risk in case one threatened a withdrawal to bargain for better terms; something that the duke of Savoy used to exert leverage while he cooperated with the Grand Alliance in the 1690s.[60] Meanwhile, Leopold asserted firmer control over defence by seeking the Reichstag's backing to declare an 'imperial war' (*Reichskrieg*) on France. This unprecedented act, on 3 April 1689, strengthened the legitimacy of the collective effort against a Christian opponent, setting it on a par with the duty to fight the Turks.[61] The impact of the recent defence reform was felt immediately. The Kreise had already deployed 30,000 troops on the Rhine in 1689, with over 3,000 more still serving in Hungary. The combined total was around double the maximum achieved in the Dutch War and increased to over 40,000 from 1694 following a renewed French incursion over the Rhine. While their record lacked glorious battles, the Kreis troops nonetheless retook positions previously lost to the French and held them at bay for the rest of the war, thereby also fulfilling their role in Leopold's plans by relieving his own army of defending the Rhine and allowing him to deploy it in Hungary and in support of Spain in the Netherlands and northern Italy.[62]

Compared to Nijmegen, the Peace of Rijswijk in autumn 1697 was quite favourable to the Empire. France was obliged to evacuate Lorraine and the Breisgau, both of which it had occupied for decades, as well as return key fortresses it had held in the Rhineland since the 1640s. Nonetheless, France retained Strasbourg and many of the other areas annexed through the Réunions, while its insistence on special religious arrangements (with the now Catholic elector's connivance) in the Palatinate breached the Peace of Westphalia and caused two decades of confessional squabbling among the German princes.

The End of the Great Turkish War

As Louis intended, his attack on the Palatinate sucked the energy from the Habsburg offensive in Hungary, enabling the Ottomans to retake Belgrade in October 1690. Leopold refused to abandon his expansive plans, however. Despite the withdrawal of all Kreis troops by 1690, the imperial commander, Ludwig Wilhelm von Baden, won a resounding victory at Slankamen in August 1691, consolidating his reputation as *Türkenlouis*.[63]

To make up for the shortfall in troops and to exploit this victory, Leopold signed new agreements with several armed princes for fresh contingents of auxiliaries to serve in Hungary. Central to these was an arrangement with Hanover in 1692. The emperor promised a new, ninth electoral title, in return for military support and assurances that Hanover would not support French efforts to foster a neutral 'third party' among the German princes that would split the Empire and damage the Grand Alliance. The agreement proved problematic for both parties. Hanover found its commitment expensive as it cost two to three times more to send a soldier to Hungary than to serve in the west, and the casualty rates were much higher. Meanwhile, the outcry from other old princely dynasties at the unprecedented favour shown toward the Hanoverian duke delayed the award of his new electoral title until 1708.[64]

The Hanoverians failed to tip the balance in the emperor's favour in Hungary, while Türkenlouis was switched to command on the Rhine after a French temporary breakthrough in 1693. Elector Augustus 'the Strong' (so named for his physical strength, not military ability) was appointed as his successor as part of a wider deal to secure substantial Saxon military support. Leopold also backed Augustus's successful election as the new king of Poland in 1697, which entailed his controversial conversion to Catholicism. Augustus was a poor general and made little headway against the Ottomans.[65] The situation only changed with the end of the war in the west, which enabled Leopold to switch troops and appoint a new commander, Prince Eugene of Savoy.[66] It proved a wise choice. Eugene crushed the Ottomans at Zenta on 11 September 1697, cementing his reputation as one of Austria's greatest generals.

The impending Spanish succession crisis prompted Leopold to quit while he was ahead, concluding peace with the sultan at Karlowitz on 26 January 1699. The Ottomans accepted the loss of all Hungary and Transylvania, the annexation of which increased the Habsburg monarchy by 60 per cent, pushing its centre of gravity outside the Empire. Now a great power regardless of possession of the imperial title, the monarchy's relationship with the Empire would increasingly change over the next century. In contrast to the earlier truces with the Ottomans, this agreement was intended as a genuine peace, prohibiting raiding, and establishing what was supposed now to be a permanent frontier between the two empires.

The Great Northern War, 1700–21

The settlements of 1697–9 reflected a wide desire for general peace after three decades of hot and cold wars. Unfortunately, a new conflict erupted on the Empire's northeastern frontier in 1700, followed shortly by the long-awaited war over the Spanish succession as the reign of the heirless and physically and mentally damaged Carlos II had finally ended. Poland had emerged empty handed from the Great Turkish War despite its role in relieving Vienna. Its new king, the Saxon elector Augustus, believed Sweden's Baltic possessions offered an easy target and attacked in 1700 in alliance with Denmark and Russia. He had not reckoned with the dynamism of Sweden's new warrior king, Charles XII, who soon knocked out Denmark, defeated Russia, and invaded Poland, turning what was supposed to be a short war of conquest into a protracted attritional struggle.

This indicated the limits to the military power of individual German princes. With 2 million inhabitants, Saxony roughly matched Sweden, and it also had the additional resources of Poland-Lithuania. However, despite prodigious efforts, its army remained permanently under-strength and unequal to the task of waging war on such a scale.[67] Charles XII split Poland by installing his own king, Stanislas Leszczyński, in 1704. A further major Saxon defeat at Fraustadt by a force half their size led to a Swedish invasion of their homeland in 1706, forcing Augustus to recognize Stanislas and abandon his Russian allies. Briefly, it appeared that Charles XII might plunge his victorious army deeper into the Empire, but instead he swung eastwards in 1708, embarking on an invasion of Russia that ended in his crushing defeat at Poltava in 1709 and subsequent flight into exile in the Ottoman Empire.

Augustus reopened the war, soon ousting Stanislas from Poland, but he lacked the power alone to attack Sweden's German territories. The situation only changed once the Russians conquered Sweden's eastern Baltic territories, including what became Estonia and St Petersburg, and advanced into Mecklenburg-Schwerin where they established an alliance with its duke who was embroiled in a dispute with his Estates. Two Russian regiments were briefly seconded to the Mecklenburg army.[68]

With the parallel War of the Spanish Succession finally winding down, Hanover and Prussia sent troops to claim a share of Sweden's German lands, bringing the northern conflict into the Empire in 1712. The emperor attempted to establish northern Germany as a neutral zone, partly to preserve the public peace, but also to contain the growth of Hanover and Prussia which he realized would become harder to manage. The Hanoverian succession in Britain in 1714 secured its elector the support of the Royal Navy in the Baltic, making him a major player in the conflict. His troops captured Bremen and Verden that year, while a combined army took Swedish Pomerania in 1715. Saxony was meanwhile distracted by the unsettled situation in Poland fuelled by Russia as the tsar extended his new influence. Meanwhile, Britain, France, and the Dutch were keen to preserve a balance in the Baltic and brokered a settlement in 1721 that confirmed Hanover's gains, but restored most of Pomerania to Sweden, leaving Prussia with little to show for its involvement.[69]

The War of the Spanish Succession, 1701–14

The Spanish succession crisis finally broke after a series of failed compromises led Carlos II to bequeath his dominions to Louis XIV's grandson Philip, in a bid to keep his empire intact. With French troops moving into the Spanish Netherlands and Italy in support of Philip, Leopold sent Prince Eugene to contest possession of Milan in June 1701.[70] Determined to oppose a Bourbon king in Spain, the Maritime Powers backed Leopold on the condition that, after victory, the two Habsburg empires could not be combined, but instead were to be split between the emperor's two sons, Joseph and Charles.

The Empire's involvement followed the template set by the Nine Years War, combining activist and defensive participation within the interlinked frameworks of a renewed Grand Alliance and another imperial declaration of war, sanctioning formal mobilization in 1702. Despite tensions, cooperation prevailed over individualist action. Leopold secured Brandenburg support in November 1700 by permitting Elector Frederick to style himself 'king in Prussia'. Although the 'in' rather than 'of' deliberately denoted a lesser quality of majesty, Frederick's elevation, so closely following the Saxon–Polish royal union, poured oil on to the fire of wider German princely ambition. Georg Ludwig of Hanover, not yet fully recognized as an elector, manoeuvred to safeguard his chances of acceding to the British crowns after he was recognized as potential heir in 1701.[71] His repeated demands to be allowed to command the imperial army on the Rhine were intended to raise his profile within the Grand Alliance.

Nonetheless, the Maritime Powers repeated their policy of the previous war, dispersing the German auxiliary contingents to different fronts. The primary theatre was the Spanish Netherlands, which the two allies were determined should not fall to the Bourbons. A second front opened in 1703 as the British and the Dutch sought to install Archduke Charles as king in Spain itself.[72] Further auxiliaries in Anglo-Dutch pay were sent to assist imperial troops in northern Italy, which remained Leopold's primary area of interest. Overall, the number of German auxiliaries rose from around 18,000 in 1701 to 80,000–90,000 after 1705, with a further 25,000 serving the emperor each year. This represented a considerable increase in military effort compared to the previous conflicts.

The imperial declaration of war was important in counteracting French efforts to persuade the imperial Estates to remain neutral. The western Kreise renewed their association from the previous war, obliging Leopold to join on behalf of the Austrian Kreis to ensure he contributed to the 40,000 troops mobilized to defend the Rhine as well. France only recruited Bavaria and Cologne as active supporters, in a reversal of the Wittelsbach family dispute that now saw the Palatinate siding with the emperor. The old princely houses of Gotha and Wolfenbüttel, disgruntled at Hanover's elevation to electoral status, both raised troops to back France, but swift imperial countermeasures obliged them to supply these to the Maritime Powers instead in 1702.

France's alliance with Bavaria saw it fighting alongside what appeared to be the Empire's second most powerful prince, since the Hohenzollerns' potential was not yet fully appreciated. Situated in the heart of the Empire, Bavaria posed a serious threat, especially once a French army broke over the Rhine to reinforce Elector Max Emanuel in 1703. Although an attack on the Tirol was repulsed, the Franco-Bavarian advance coincided with Austria's financial collapse, triggered by Leopold's inability to pay his principal military contractor. Simultaneously, Habsburg efforts to disarm the aristocrats' private armies and to promote Catholicism stirred another Hungarian revolt. Led by Prince Rákóczi, who received French money and military advice, this swelled into a mass movement pushing in directions increasingly at odds with the aristocrats' intentions. The parallel war in the west reduced the Habsburgs' ability to respond, while errors by several field commanders left the initiative with Rákóczi, until the tide turned as imperial generals developed a more effective counter-insurgency strategy. As in the 1670s, the revolt obliged the emperor to redeploy a large part of his army from the west, souring relations with his British and Dutch allies who were also angered by his suppression of Hungarian Protestantism. Nearly half a million Hungarians died, mainly through the spread of disease. Facing defeat, the rebel leadership accepted a compromise peace in 1711.[73]

Meanwhile, the Allied army under the duke of Marlborough made its famous march from the Netherlands to the Danube, joining the imperial forces under Prince Eugene and decisively defeating the Franco-Bavarians at Blenheim in August 1704. The campaign demonstrated Anglo-Dutch cooperation as well as that between the different elements of the Empire's collective defence: in addition to British, Dutch, and Austrian troops, the victorious army included German auxiliaries paid by the Maritime Powers, others sent by German princes, and Kreis contingents.[74] Bavaria's defeat greatly strengthened the emperor's power within the Empire. Max Emanuel was driven into exile and his lands were ruthlessly exploited to sustain Austria's own army.

Eugene's great victory over Bourbon forces at Turin in 1706 secured Habsburg control of Spain's possessions in northern Italy, achieving a key goal.[75] Habsburg power peaked in 1708–9 as a brief and successful war with the papacy cleared the way for the conquest of Naples and Sicily, securing the rest of Spain's Italian possessions and extending Austria's presence to southern Italy. Joseph I's unexpected early death in 1711 interrupted this run of success, leaving his younger brother Charles VI as sole heir of both Spain and Austria. Enthusiasm for the war was already waning among the political elites in Britain and the Dutch Republic, who recognized they had missed the opportunity of harvest failures and a financial crisis in 1709 to persuade Louis XIV to accept a favourable peace. Since 1708 the war had been going badly for the Allies in Spain, where Habsburg influence was increasingly confined to Catalonia. Keen to disengage, the Maritime Powers made their own peace with France at Utrecht in 1713, recognizing Philip V as king of Spain, with the Netherlands and Italian possessions being transferred to Austria.

Reluctant to abandon the Catalonians, Charles VI persuaded the Reichstag to continue the war alone, but Prince Eugene was now outnumbered nearly three to one as France turned its full might against him on the Rhine. Charles and the Empire were obliged to settle in the twin treaties of Rastatt and Baden in 1714, accepting the terms reached at Utrecht, as well as Max Emanuel's restoration in Bavaria.[76]

Charles VI remained bitterly disappointed, but his gains from Spain were equivalent to about half the Habsburg monarchy's extent in 1683 and were more populous and richer than the recent conquests in Hungary and Transylvania. The new territories were exposed, however, and the Barrier Treaty, imposed by the Maritime Powers on Austria in 1715, saddled the Habsburgs with maintaining Dutch garrisons in the now-Austrian Netherlands. The defeat of Charles's dream of uniting Spain and Austria, alongside the check on French hegemonic ambitions, signalled the underlying shift in European relations to a multipolar state system. Alongside Austria and France, Britain and Russia had emerged as great powers, while Spain had slipped to second rank, where the Dutch rapidly joined them, with countries like the Scandinavian kingdoms and Portugal in a third tier.[77]

Membership of this order was now firmly associated with sovereignty, as demonstrated by Prussia's international recognition as a kingdom as part of the Utrecht settlement. Although derided as a wasteful extravagance by his grandson Frederick II, Elector Frederick's costly acquisition of a royal title had bought him acceptance as an independent ruler and given him a place at the peace negotiations, unlike the duke of Lorraine, who was treated as merely a vassal of the Empire and politely shown the door. The failure of both Wittelsbach branches to secure royal titles from parts of Spain's inheritance during the war underscored Prussia's singular status, especially as its Crown was associated with its own territory and not held through a personal union, like those of the rival Saxon and Hanoverian electors.

The Empire had defended itself successfully, and most imperial Estates were content with Bavaria's restoration, which rebalanced imperial politics by stemming the growth of Habsburg influence. Nonetheless, the character of German involvement in European wars since 1672, together with Austria's dramatic growth, had sharpened the distinctions between the Empire's components. The imperial title remained vital to the Habsburgs' international prestige and self-worth, but it was now sustained primarily from their own dynastic resources including its new, extensive possessions outside the Empire. The military potential of the Empire itself had slipped to an auxiliary role, magnified by the creation of territorial standing armies that functioned as auxiliaries for other powers.

Switzerland's position had also changed. It did not become independent because of the Westphalian settlement, but instead evolved slowly as an entity separate from the Empire, with its inhabitants both seeing themselves as such and being considered so by others by about 1700. Like the Empire, the Confederation remained a complex structure composed of unequal parts. Whereas the Empire could defend its autonomy, that of the Confederation had become closely dependent on a set of contradictory military relationships with rival European powers that often impacted adversely on its domestic harmony.

5

Permanent Armies

GENERALISSIMOS

Field Command

Most discussions of seventeenth-century warfare overdraw the distinction between the supposedly disorderly 'mercenaries' waging the Thirty Years War and the more disciplined 'standing armies' of the subsequent 'age of absolutism'. In German history, the former era is associated with Wallenstein, while the latter is identified with the 'rise of Prussia'. This narrative aligns with the traditional view that the Empire was largely irrelevant after 1648 but obscures important lines of continuity. The Habsburgs already possessed permanent forces before 1618, albeit organized to defend their Military Frontier rather than as conventional western European troops. They remained the dominant military power, while other principalities, such as Bavaria and Saxony, played significant secondary roles earlier than Brandenburg-Prussia. Gunpowder weaponry improved in several stages around 1630, 1670, and 1700, both propelling and facilitating important changes in tactics. The Habsburgs were also at the forefront of German efforts to establish sea power in the 1620s, joined belatedly and equally unsuccessfully by Brandenburg three decades later.

A key change was the shift away from personalized command and towards its institutionalization in what would eventually become a general staff. As with all important long-term developments, this was largely unplanned and far from linear, as demonstrated by the reappearance of highly personal command in the form of Frederick II of Prussia after 1740. Throughout, rulers asserted their rights as warlords while in practice delegating much of their authority to generals, who were in turn integrated into a more coherent and stable hierarchy defined by an ascending order of ranks. Generals thereby now emerged as a distinct group of senior officers whose appointment and promotion were subject far more to the warlord's direct control than in the case of the much larger number of regimental officers where the colonels retained considerable, though gradually declining, influence.

Military victory remained important to rulers' prestige, but the risks of personal command were as high as during the sixteenth century. The decisive factors prompting more warlords to delegate command were new attitudes to monarchy and the onset of protracted warfare after 1618. The change was most pronounced among the Habsburgs, whereas German princes remained more likely to lead their troops in person. Monarchical courts became more settled in a single, primary residence. This process began in Spain with Philip II's promotion of Madrid as an administrative centre, formally inaugurating it as his capital in 1606. His two successors expanded the imposing royal residences and other official buildings in and around the city in a deliberate attempt to project an image of grandeur and power. Symbolizing monarchical stability in stone helped mask its financial instability and dependency on high-interest loans. The wars engulfing Europe during the first half of the seventeenth century slowed but did not interrupt this trend, which resumed with redoubled vigour and greater flamboyance under Louis XIV as France emerged from a deadly combination of civil and international wars after 1659. Louis's massive palace at Versailles asserted not only his claims to absolute authority, but also his command of nature itself, with the extensive gardens regimenting flora and fauna in a deliberately militaristic manner.[1]

The Habsburgs followed the Spanish model, which tended to emphasize political distance, whereas most German princes copied Louis XIV in asserting more direct control. Although more a matter of degrees than absolute, these differences were nonetheless important. They were expressed architecturally, with the princes building new baroque palaces in the style of Versailles from the 1680s, whereas the Habsburgs largely modified their existing residences. Politically, the Austrian Habsburgs followed the Spanish practice of governing through a chief minister, whereas the princes chaired their councils in person. The Spanish method was criticized at the time and subsequently for handing power to unaccountable 'favourites', but in fact it allowed monarchs to offload blame for mistakes or defeats, whereas direct control exposed rulers' reputations. German princes also relied on favourites, while the Austrian Habsburgs could also act directly, especially through their practice of entrusting individual provinces or tasks to different family members under the emperor's overall authority.[2] There were no firm constitutional rules dictating how far authority was devolved, and much depended on circumstance and personal preference.

During the Thirty Years War, the Habsburgs were most likely to delegate field command to a generalissimo or lieutenant general, whereas minor princes usually led their forces in person. The latter often had relatively few troops and, for those opposing the Habsburgs, their commitment to the war directly endangered their status as imperial princes and they saw their presence in the field as necessary to ensure Sweden continued to take their interests seriously. The Swedes rightly distrusted their German allies and usually assigned one of their own generals to accompany the more powerful princes, as well as trying to disperse their troops to different commands to weaken the German influence. Several princes were driven into exile, while the death of Landgrave Wilhelm V of Hessen-Kassel obliged his widow Amalia Elisabeth to hand command to a male general, though she continued to direct overall strategy.[3]

Frederick V of the Palatinate, Johann Georg of Saxony, and Maximilian I of Bavaria all accompanied their armies on occasion, however they delegated to a senior general who formally posed as their adviser but in practice exercised real command. While this allowed Frederick to escape direct blame for the disaster at White Mountain, his flight from Prague immediately after the battle irrevocably damaged his reputation. Like Amalia Elisabeth, Maximilian sought to direct operations through regular correspondence with his commanders and was closely involved in often quite detailed administrative matters. His long-standing relationship with Jean Tserclaes de Tilly demonstrates the importance of personal aspects. Both were aloof, cold men, yet they developed genuine sympathy and mutual understanding: Maximilian rarely expressed himself tenderly, yet showed concern for Tilly's well-being. Both were devout Catholics, but Tilly was more sympathetic towards Habsburg interests. The relationship worked, because Tilly shared his master's views on loyalty, dutifully subordinated himself, and was careful when voicing criticism.[4]

Tilly had overcome difficult family circumstances to work his way up from ordinary soldier in Spanish service to imperial field marshal by 1605, but he nearly wrecked his career because his loyalty to Rudolf II saw him end up on the losing Habsburg side during the Brothers' Quarrel of 1608. His transfer to Bavarian service as lieutenant general in May 1610 indicates the informal hierarchy that already existed between the more highly prized imperial posts and those in princely service, where the rewards were usually smaller and there were fewer opportunities for glory. From commanding an army against the Turks, Tilly now had to busy himself organizing the Bavarian militia and responding to Maximilian's penny-pinching and bureaucracy. Already aged fifty and suffering from previous wounds, Tilly could easily have slipped into obscurity had it not been for the onset of protracted warfare after 1618. His role in the victory at White Mountain consolidated Maximilian's faith in his abilities and ensured his continuation as Bavarian and Catholic League commander.

At around 30,000 men, the League army remained substantially larger than the emperor's own forces. Conscious of his dependency on his Bavarian ally, Ferdinand II tried to subordinate the League army to his own commander, Hieronymus de Caraffa, in spring 1622. Maximilian successfully rejected this move, citing the autonomy already granted him in the treaty of Munich (1619), which provided the legal basis of his assistance to the Habsburgs throughout the war.[5] Thereafter, Ferdinand accepted the League's autonomy and Tilly continued to act separately from the imperials, even after the expansion of the emperor's field army under Wallenstein in 1625. Coordination was provided by regular strategic planning conferences, often held in Regensburg or some other town on the Danube, as well as through correspondence between Vienna, Munich, and the generals.

Although cumbersome, this system worked much better than its equivalent among the shifting anti-Habsburg coalitions that had failed to establish a stable command structure prior to 1631. The League and imperial armies only briefly came under centralized command after Wallenstein's dismissal in August 1630 when Tilly was named general of both forces. It is testament to his skills and patience that he made this work at all, since the two forces remained administratively and politically separate, while he now had to answer to Vienna as well as Munich. With his personal reputation already ruined by the sack of Magdeburg in May 1631, Tilly's defeat at Breitenfeld four months later shattered the emperor's confidence in him and paved the way for Wallenstein's return as imperial commander.

Tilly's death following a further defeat at the Lech in April 1632 made it easier for Maximilian to swallow Wallenstein's reinstatement, but the elector remained determined to remain a separate warlord of the League, even if this entailed briefly assuming field command himself. Although eventually compelled to dissolve the League following the Peace of Prague in 1635, Maximilian had already negotiated continued military autonomy for what, effectively, became a Bavarian corps within the reorganized imperial forces. Saxony secured equivalent autonomy as part of its deal to switch sides, while a separate Westphalian corps emerged from the League's former northern branch exercised by Maximilian's brother Ferdinand of Cologne. Throughout, strategic direction remained collective, agreed through conferences of generals, imperial envoys, and princely representatives. Bavarian, Saxon, and Westphalian generals commanded in the theatres assigned to them and their forces, but combined forces brought together for battle were usually led by imperial officers.

Meanwhile, Sweden imposed its own structure after its victory at Breitenfeld, which allowed Gustavus Adolphus to insist on the 'absolute direction' of the war against the emperor. The king's death at Lützen in November 1632 weakened Sweden's control, since government devolved to Chancellor Oxenstierna on behalf of six-year-old Queen Christina. Oxenstierna's position underscores the continued significance of personal authority. While no one doubted his abilities as a statesman to decide strategic objectives, he lacked Gustavus's charisma and ability to command in the field. This contributed to Sweden's loss of control over its south German allies, whose remaining forces eventually detached under Bernhard of Weimar, who sought a closer relationship with France to advance his ambitions. France's growing military involvement in the Empire by 1643 further reduced Sweden's relative weight in directing the war and obliged it, like the emperor, to coordinate with its ally through conferences and correspondence.

Wallenstein's role in this story at first seems anomalous because it is usually considered that of a free agent acting largely on his own account with unprecedented powers. He was named *capo*, or head of the main imperial army in the Empire, on 7 April 1625 in a move intended to increase the emperor's weight relative to the League by consolidating imperial units into a force equivalent to that under Tilly. However, the Habsburgs continued their long-established practice of naming other generals to command elsewhere, notably Bohemia, Hungary, and Italy, as well as for specific operations such as crushing the Upper Austrian Revolt in 1626. Their army always remained polycentric like their monarchy, and neither Wallenstein nor the other generals following him ever held a supreme command with direct authority over all units. The separate commanders reported to the Court War Council to which Wallenstein was also subordinate.

Nonetheless, Wallenstein was given wide autonomy for his own command and was jealous of other generals, notably Count Collalto who retained considerable influence at court. The ever-grander titles granted to Wallenstein were to mollify his feelings after Ferdinand refused to subordinate all other generals to him. However, his power attracted criticism, especially as he proved a convenient target for the electors, princes, and others who were alarmed by the growth of Habsburg influence, as well as the growing cost of the war. These factors prompted Wallenstein's first dismissal in August 1630, which occurred at the point when Sweden did not yet pose an existential danger and confidence in Tilly's abilities was high. Wallenstein did not immediately recover his powers at his initial reinstatement at the beginning of 1632, and it was not until April that he forced the emperor not just to restore them, but to add the right to recommend colonels for promotion to the rank of general and to issue recruiting patents.[6]

The circumstances of Wallenstein's assassination on 25 February 1634 underscore the continued importance of personal relationships. Always haughty, he failed to maintain his relations with the imperial court, where his dwindling group of advocates found it increasingly hard to refute the malicious rumours that he was playing a double game in his negotiations to detach Saxony and Brandenburg from their alliance with Sweden. Chief among his critics was a group of Italian officers, including Matteo Gallas and Ottavio Piccolomini, who had risen thanks to Wallenstein's patronage but now opposed him for a mix of personal ambition and professional disagreements. Wallenstein was unable to shift the war from the Bohemian lands, while his complex game of diplomatic double bluff increasingly ran at odds with more promising initiatives by other imperial envoys to win over Saxony.

Once he realized the seriousness of these machinations in Vienna, the generalissimo pressured the officers under his direct command to swear personal loyalty to him on 12 January 1634. Many looked to their chief as the guarantor for their pay arrears and all were aware of the deleterious impact his first dismissal had made on the army and its finances. Although forty-nine officers signed a document pledging personal loyalty, many swiftly realized the situation was very different from that in 1630, as Wallenstein's demands on them contradicted their higher loyalty to the emperor. More directly, it was in their material interest to stick with Ferdinand as the source of legitimate authority, as any rewards Wallenstein could offer would lack legality. As more officers made their excuses and left his headquarters, Wallenstein finally decided to do what his enemies accused him of, and headed west to Eger, intending to defect to the Swedes. Unknown to him, the commander of the Eger garrison was already in touch with the party of officers charged with carrying out the emperor's secret orders to 'remove' Wallenstein. Alone in his bedroom in the Pachabel House in Eger, the generalissimo was murdered by Walter Devereux, an Irish dragoon captain in imperial service, while his four remaining loyal officers were killed as they dined in the castle as the commandant's guests.[7]

The circumstances of Wallenstein's death were hugely embarrassing for the emperor, particularly as the subsequent formal inquiry failed to unearth clear evidence of his treason, beyond the Pilsen Reverse. Nonetheless, the episode demonstrated the solidity of the established social and political hierarchy, despite the turmoil of the war. The confiscation of Wallenstein's extensive property gave the Habsburgs a welcome windfall with which to reward the senior officers for their continued loyalty.

A key factor prompting Wallenstein's murder was his constant opposition to the presence of Archduke Ferdinand, the emperor's son, with the army. The archduke was made nominal commander in April 1634, with Gallas as adviser until 1637, when he formally took over as Ferdinand succeeded his father as emperor. Gallas's abilities were eroded by his growing alcoholism and he was replaced in 1639 by the new emperor's younger brother, Archduke Leopold Wilhelm, who was given Piccolomini as his adviser. Leopold Wilhelm received broadly similar powers to Wallenstein to disband regiments, punish their colonels, and propose officers for promotion to the rank of colonel. Ferdinand III was already losing confidence in his brother's abilities when Leopold Wilhelm fought the second battle of Breitenfeld in November 1642 against

Piccolomini's advice. After the archduke's resignation, Gallas was reappointed on his past reputation, though without the powers granted to Wallenstein or Leopold Wilhelm.[8]

Further defeats and Gallas's incapacity obliged Ferdinand III to reinstate his brother Leopold Wilhelm as generalissimo on 1 May 1645, this time with even wider powers to bolster his authority within the army. Leopold Wilhelm's second command saw an even further decline of Habsburg fortunes, until the emperor found the face-saving device of securing his appointment as governor of the Spanish Netherlands early in 1647. Gallas briefly resumed command, because Ferdinand could not stomach the appointment of Peter Melander Count Holzapfel, a Calvinist and former Hessian general who had defected to imperial service in 1640 and currently commanded in Westphalia. Holzapfel was nonetheless named Gallas's deputy and formally assumed command on 17 April 1647, eight days before the alcoholic Italian's death. Holzapfel proved a capable commander but was killed at Zusmarshausen in May 1648. Ferdinand overruled advice from Count Schlick, president of the Court War Council, and chose Piccolomini as the new generalissimo. Although prickly and ambitious, Piccolomini nonetheless stabilized the front during the few months before peace was finally concluded.

Although these appointments did not achieve the desired victory, the emperor retained control throughout. He may not always have chosen wisely, but he at least had a freer choice than in France, where the Bourbons always had to balance the interests of the self-assertive princes of the blood who felt entitled to command.[9] Moreover, powerful field commanders were balanced by the growing efficiency of the Court War Council, itself boosted by the appointment of experienced and respected generals as its presidents, notably Collalto from 1624 to 1630 and Schlick between 1632 and 1649. The president sat ex officio on the emperor's privy council and provided a second opinion on strategy and military organization, often outweighing that of the generalissimo.

Later Habsburg commanders received more limited powers, partly from fear they might abuse them, but mostly from the ongoing bureaucratization of military administration that saw greater amounts of business handled by the Court War Council. The great influence wielded by Raimondo Montecuccoli in the 1660s and 1670s, and by fellow Italian Prince Eugene of Savoy after 1703, existed because both were simultaneously field commander and war council president. This was generally avoided subsequently because the growing workload rendered such a combination undesirable.

Brandenburg-Prussia was typical of the experience of the medium and smaller principalities in establishing a stable chain of command much later than Austria. Brandenburg's direct involvement in the Thirty Years War was brief and militarily unsuccessful, and it was not until the Northern War of 1655–60 that the elector named Baron Sparr, a former imperial general, as field commander. He was promoted to field marshal in June 1657, the title henceforth designating the most senior general, and remained in post until his death in 1668, but was not then re-placed.[10] The elector's decision to name both Prince Johann Georg of Anhalt-Dessau and Georg Derfflinger as field marshals in 1670 prompted a row over precedent, leading to the latter's resignation. Derfflinger was re-appointed to replace Anhalt-Dessau in 1673 and thereafter Prussia had a continuous line of commanding generals until 1919.

The First General Staffs

Baron Sparr is rightly credited with fostering a group of officers who functioned as Prussia's first general staff. However, in doing this, he was simply continuing a practice already embedded in the imperial army dur-ing the Thirty Years War. The general staff fused the commander's own entourage with other key officials and responded to the growing admin-istrative burden and need to coordinate multiple operations in different regions and to align these with the emperor's political objectives. Wal-lenstein's more personal style of management slowed development of the general staff, but it was fully in place by 1640 and included all the senior administrative personnel and specialists: war commissars who saw to logistics and communications with Vienna, engineers, the chief medical officer, masters of provisions and field postal services, and the 'general auditor', who was the army's senior legal officer. Combined, this num-bered thirty-nine individuals during Holzapfel's period as commander, while similar though smaller staffs developed in the Bavarian and West-phalian armies fighting for the emperor.[11]

Born in wartime, the general staff's task was to fight the war more effectively. Operational decisions remained with the commander, who consulted the senior officers currently with him in the field. Even Wallen-stein regularly held councils of war with his officers, relying particularly on Heinrich Holk.[12] Strategic planning was reserved for the emperor, advised by his privy council and Court War Council and, in practice, conducted through ad hoc conferences of selected officials, generals, and representatives from important allies. The general staff lacked the managerial structure distinguishing its nineteenth-century successors, and the term *Generalstab* after 1650 was primarily used to denote all officers with the rank of general.

Nonetheless, the staff as it had emerged by the 1640s was an important innovation, particularly as most of the specialist and administrative roles associated with it remained filled in the imperial army after 1648. The most important of these was that of Senior Quartermaster (*Oberster Quartiermeister*), first appointed in 1596, forty-one years earlier than in Brandenburg, where it did not immediately become permanent. Charged with organizing billets and route planning, the quartermaster developed as the precursor to what would later be called a chief of staff. The post was not consistently filled after 1648 but it reappeared in 1697 due to the ongoing Great Turkish War in the form of general quartermaster, the title that subsequently became standard for the role.

There was no framework for the systematic collection and analysis of intelligence. Strategic intelligence relied primarily on information provided by diplomats, an area in which the Habsburgs held a major advantage as they were represented by envoys in most of Europe's major courts, whereas the other German princes only began establishing more formal diplomatic relations with other powers during the 1660s. Tactical information derived from scouts, spies, and local inhabitants and was gathered by commanders in the field, who were required to send regular reports to their warlord. Although the Empire had had one of the world's first modern postal communications systems since the 1490s, the emperor made little attempt to use this to gather information. By contrast, the Swedes were swift to capitalize on the capture of Frankfurt, the Empire's postal and information hub, in 1631. One of their spies had already managed to penetrate the high security surrounding the conference between Tilly and Wallenstein at Güstrow in 1628, and they had an agent in Tilly's headquarters in 1631. Although postal communications were declared inviolable during the Westphalian peace congress, covert interception became common during the later seventeenth century when information gathering became more systematic and sophisticated.[13]

War Commissariats and Councils

Another important innovation was the centralization of logistics and war finance in the imperial army with the establishment of the General War Commissariat (*Generalkriegskommissariat*) in 1647 under Ernst von Traun. This created a specialized agency subordinate to the Court War Council and improved planning and accountability. Traun's department oversaw the complex transition from large wartime army to smaller but permanent peacetime force in 1648–9. Bavaria was another important innovator in this respect, having already developed a comparatively well-organized administrative structure before 1618. Tilly's death in 1632 exposed underlying personal and structural tensions between regimental commanders and the war commissars, who were supposed to monitor military administration and expenditure. These problems were widespread throughout early modern Europe, but unlike in the imperial or Swedish armies, Bavaria had already stopped allowing commissars to simultaneously hold regimental command to ensure their independence from the system they were supposedly monitoring.[14]

The development of war commissars in Brandenburg after 1640 merely followed these precedents with the difference that the elector gave them an important role in tax collection. A General War Commissariat was established in 1655, initially under Sparr as field marshal, but as an independent body after 1688; a process that followed the one in Austria but was in line with that in the other larger German principalities. The smaller ones followed later, with the commissariat functions only separated from Württemberg's war council in 1673.[15] Brandenburg also had a war council after 1631 to provide the elector with specialist advice on personnel, recruitment, war finance, and martial law. This mirrored similar councils already established elsewhere, notably in Bavaria. Such bodies became more common because of the Thirty Years War; one, for instance, was established in the bishopric of Würzburg in 1635, probably on the advice of the imperial general Melchior von Hatzfeldt, who was brother to the bishop.[16]

In this sense, war certainly 'made the state' by driving institutional development. However, this was neither as linear nor as dysfunctional as both the older and the newer historiographies of German bureaucracy suggest.[17] There was, of course, no blueprint as to what a 'modern' state should look like, though Habsburg practice remained strongly influential well into the eighteenth century, and Sweden and especially France provided important additional models during the later seventeenth century. Efforts to promote economic recovery after the Thirty Years War found theoretical expression as 'Cameralism' from the mid-1650s. This self-consciously 'scientific' approach to governance rapidly established itself as an academic subject in German universities; the seventeenth-century equivalent of today's business and management studies. Its advocates argued strongly for state intervention in society and the economy to promote the 'common good', defined in practice as greater revenue generated by thrifty, obedient subjects. Of course, this created new problems, notably through the criminalization of some practices that now appeared at odds with the state's objectives, for example labelling itinerants as 'work shy' and sending them to correctional institutes. Administration also developed an 'inner dynamism' as officials identified new fields of activity, expanding their remit, and adding to the mountains of paperwork.

What has often been described as 'reform' is thus best understood as learning from mistakes, omissions, and good practice, and the revision of existing structures, rather than radical change. Posts and institutions were reconfigured in different arrangements in response to recurring problems without fundamentally altering the basic administrative framework already in place by the 1650s in Austria and the larger principalities, and copied elsewhere during the 1670s. Fresh ordinances updated and expanded earlier ones, while establishing additional precedents that were built upon in turn, particularly as the prolonged renewed warfare after 1672 created an 'institutional memory' by the 1710s and established enduring routines.

FROM CONTRACT TO COMMISSION

Contracting

The Empire was largely at peace after 1554, and while its frontiers were exposed to various dangers across the next sixty years, these were never sufficiently threatening to dissuade its elite from the view that war should be an exception, not a norm. The Court War Council argued for a permanent army to confront the Turks, but the Reichstag only voted money to subsidize maintaining the Military Frontier and its regular garrisons. Most territories reorganized their militias after the 1570s to cope with short-term emergencies and provide a measure of security. Neither the Protestant Union nor the Catholic League created armies, relying instead on mobilized militia and hastily recruited professionals during the Jülich-Cleves crises of 1609–10 and 1614. Thus, it was natural to rely on these long-established methods when war broke out in 1618.

The unforeseen scale and duration of the Thirty Years War changed the nature of contracting in four important ways. First, the number of contractors rose substantially, with perhaps 1,500 involved in the Empire during the war.[18] This in turn prompted an influx of new, often relatively inexperienced men, especially as the end of the Long Turkish War (1606) and the start of the Twelve Years Truce (1609) between Spain and the Dutch rebels had reduced opportunities to enter the profession of arms. Wallenstein provides a typical example. He came from an established family of minor Moravian nobles. The Long Turkish War ended after he had barely two years' experience as a company officer. He next served in a short-lived regiment raised to support Matthias during the Brothers' Quarrel in 1608. Based on this relatively modest experience and his connections to important families, he was named colonel of a new regiment by the Moravian Estates in 1615, but this unit existed only on paper. His first foray into contracting was in 1617 when he raised two companies of cuirassiers to support Archduke Ferdinand during the Gradisca War.

However, Wallenstein's subsequent career departs from the norm and instead points to the third novel aspect: the appearance of the general contractor who raised entire armies, rather than just regiments or companies. Ernst von Mansfeld was the first to do this once he joined the Palatine army with around 2,000 Swiss financed largely by the duke of Savoy in 1618. While more units passed under his command across the next two years, these were mostly raised separately by other colonels, often with English money. The contacts he forged allowed him to recruit new regiments after 1620, again largely financed by England, though his forces were rarely much over 12,000.[19]

Wallenstein was in an entirely different league, contracting 24,000 men in May 1625 and commanding over 110,000 just three years later. This was not the emperor's original intention and was only possible thanks to Wallenstein's independent means, having married a very rich heiress in 1609, which also gave him an entrée into Moravian high society. He had already funded his first unit in 1617 by selling one of his estates worth 80,000 fl. His wife's money enabled him to raise two entire cuirassier regiments – the most expensive and prestigious of cavalry units – in 1619–20, followed by an infantry regiment in 1621. This made him colonel of three regiments simultaneously, the usual upper limit for most contractors; like them, he delegated command to trusted lieutenant colonels, which meant he missed the great triumph at White Mountain, though one of his cuirassier units was present.

Although eventually promoted to *Generalfeldwachtmeister*, the lowest general's rank, in June 1623, his repeated offers to raise more troops were rebuffed because the emperor could not afford them. Again, his wealth enabled him to take the next step. Having been left in command of the troops re-establishing Habsburg authority in Bohemia after 1621, he was ideally placed to profit from the confiscation of rebel property; something he accelerated through his role in the Mint Consortium that made fortunes for its directors by issuing debased coinage. He had already loaned over 1.6 million fl to the emperor by 1623, rising to over 8 million fl six years later. With much reluctance, Ferdinand entrusted the expansion of the imperial army to him in May 1625, but lingering doubts delayed the formal announcement until July.[20]

Wallenstein's role subsequently expanded as he used his own lands to supply beer, grain, and equipment to the field army, as well as assuming responsibility after 1627 for establishing the new imperial navy, leading to his formal appointment as admiral in April 1628. No one else ever acted on this scale. Christian of Halberstadt and Bernhard of Weimar both organized armies of up to 20,000 men, acting like Mansfeld and Wallenstein in that they subcontracted to colonels who recruited individual regiments.[21] Both were younger sons of German princes with little prospect of inheriting their family's main possession, while Mansfeld sought to remove the stigma of his illegitimate birth and recover access to his family patrimony. All had a direct stake in the war, as did the other princes like Wilhelm V of Hessen-Kassel, Charles IV of Lorraine, and the various Guelph dukes, who cannot be classed as 'military enterprisers' solely interested in money.

Wallenstein was different, though that did not make him simply a 'mercenary'. While controversy still surrounds his ultimate goals, it is clear he sought to ingratiate himself with the Habsburgs as a means for social advancement and always sought to convert his financial and military influence into land and titles. Already in 1623 he had persuaded Ferdinand to consolidate his accumulated properties as a new duchy of Friedland, making him a major Moravian aristocrat. Four years later Wallenstein was granted the duchy of Sagan in Silesia in lieu of 150,000 fl arrears of his general's salary. Neither of these duchies possessed the coveted status of imperial immediacy; something he secured in 1628 when Ferdinand transferred the sequestrated duchy of Mecklenburg to him in lieu of 4 million fl he had advanced to sustain the army's operations. Wallenstein built a series of lavish palaces to underpin each stage in his rise, and by 1630 was spending 750,000 fl annually maintaining his princely household. With failing health and no direct heirs after the death of his only son by his second wife in 1628, it is likely he wished to enjoy his new status, not prolong the war. He initially refused repeated requests to resume command after the first battle of Breitenfeld, only accepting once the Saxons' seizure of his Moravian palaces made the war directly personal.[22]

Since Wallenstein was given command over the existing regiments in the Empire, he initially only needed to recruit around 11,500 new troops to meet the agreed target. The scale of the Danish threat and the need to compete with the League's forces to minimize Bavaria's influence combined to rationalize further expansion through new formations. Of the 172 regiments raised between 1618 and 1630, 102 were formed during the five years of Wallenstein's first command. Of these, thirty lasted less than two years, and only sixty-six remained in being in December 1630.[23] This instability indicates the limits to general contracting that rested entirely on credit. His colonels advanced their own money to raise their regiments, with some of the costs recouped through permission to levy 'contributions' in the areas where the units were mustered. Expansion was too rapid, obliging Wallenstein to rely on inexperienced men whom the old campaigners criticized as greenhorns who did not know how to organize and run their regiments. The disbandment and amalgamation of these units reduced some of the liabilities, but the remaining colonels were owed 1 million fl by 1628. Jan de Witte, Wallenstein's banker, reported in March 1630 that he could no longer secure fresh loans, but his master had an aristocrat's business sense, and simply insisted money could be found. The generalissimo's dismissal that August caused the system to collapse, and de Witte drowned himself in the well of his Prague mansion.[24]

The tragic end to Wallenstein's first command obscures an underlying trend towards more permanent formations that proved another lasting change in contracting wrought by the war. While officers looked to the generalissimo to represent their interests, they also – like Wallenstein himself – regarded the emperor as their warlord and the only source of lasting, legitimate rewards. The Habsburgs were adept at retaining loyalty by issuing promissory notes, partial payments, lands, titles, and other favours. During the final decade of his reign alone, Ferdinand II created 70 counts and 100 barons, and named 400 individuals as court chamberlains.[25] These alternative forms of recompense were driven most immediately by the Habsburgs' perennial shortage of money, but also reflected their status as the imperial dynasty with powers of ennoblement denied to other princes.

It also reflected the transition from seasonal to protracted warfare. Contractors had profited previously from the difference in the cash advance and payments from their warlord, and the actual cost of recruiting and maintaining their regiment, particularly as they could often pocket the pay arrears of soldiers who had died or deserted during the campaign. Now, units had to be kept permanently up to strength, while the emperor and other warlords were no longer able to honour their promises to refund all expenses. Most colonels made good the shortfall through corruption and extortion, as well as looking to their warlord to transfer confiscated or captured property in lieu of payment.

These practices eroded the warlords' political legitimacy and military authority. The emperor used the opportunity of Wallenstein's murder to ban simultaneous colonelcies of multiple regiments in April 1634. This was reiterated to greater effect in 1642 and though exceptions continued to be made, retired officers and courtier generals not with their regiments were compelled to relinquish them. Promotion to general was another means to reward good service, with denial of this rank conversely a punishment for mismanagement of a regiment. Tilly was unusual among senior commanders in not having his own regiment until 1624, but generals without regiments became more common after 1648. Even powerful figures like Piccolomini were obliged to accept the emperor's authority to reassign, amalgamate, or disband regiments. While colonels continued to be referred to as 'proprietors' (*Inhaber*), this reflected their financial investment in raising and running regiments, rather than absolute ownership; their units were not 'private' armies.

Officer Appointment and Promotion

Control of officers' appointments was a key aspect to the growing power of warlords. By 1618, rulers already had the right to confirm or reject colonels' suggestions for new appointments and promotions. Appointments were always to fill a specific vacancy, rather than to the army in general, with any surplus officers either being attached (*aggregiert*) to an existing unit or put on half pay on a waiting list. This remained essentially unchanged into the nineteenth century when appointments were finally centralized. Throughout, commissions were prepared by the ruler's war council and issued in his name. Much depended on the personal relations between colonels and warlord, while change was gradual, not dramatic.

Wallenstein enjoyed considerable latitude in naming colonels who were retrospectively endorsed by the emperor, and his colonels in turn had significant influence over the selection of junior officers. The Court War Council exerted greater control after 1634, but Habsburg colonels continued to enjoy relative autonomy with their suggestions usually accepted. Other German princes took the opportunity of the demobilization in 1648–9 to establish more direct control, since their 'armies' were now only a few companies, rather than entire regiments. Bavaria was significantly ahead of other principalities in only appointing officers following recommendations from its Court War Council after 1651. The duke of Calenberg (Hanover) could even appoint NCOs in the late seventeenth century.[26] Imperial legislation issued during the Turkish War mobilization of July 1664 proved influential in strengthening rulers' authority over appointments.

The renewed expansion of forces during the second half of the century could interrupt this trend. The duke of Holstein-Gottorp appointed captains directly when his army comprised only six companies totalling 1,037 men in 1661. By 1702 it had grown to 5,383 soldiers in sixty-six companies grouped into several regiments; an expansion only possible because the newly appointed colonels had advanced the necessary money, obliging the duke to concede their right to appoint their subordinates.[27] Likewise, the growth of the Brandenburg-Prussian army during the Northern War (1655–60) forced the elector to rely on experienced colonels, who resisted his efforts to dictate to them.

By defending their influence, colonels were not always simply protecting their own clients, but wanted to prevent rulers imposing new officers on their unit who might not be popular with those already in post, especially as this disrupted the growing trend towards promotion by seniority (*Anciennität*) rather than by merit. Promotion was less of an issue when units only existed for a campaign. Officers had been appointed on their experience, birth, connections, or a combination of these factors. Senior commanders had the power to issue field commissions, appointing or promoting men to fill vacancies caused by casualties. Such powers persisted into the eighteenth century, though they were now only fully valid if subsequently approved by the warlord. The continuous existence of regiments across many years during the Thirty Years War created a more stable officer corps, with the French word *Officier* entering German usage around 1650 to distinguish the commissioned ranks from the rest of the *prima plana* including the NCOs. The 1664 mobilization proved significant, because many territories kept the officers from their contingents on retainers after the soldiers were demobilized at the end of the campaign.

The institutionalization of both permanent units and a stable hierarchy of ranks resulted in promotions generally following seniority defined by the date of commission, with an ensign vacancy filled by the longest-serving sergeant, the longest-serving ensign moving to fill the next lieutenant post, and so on up to colonel. This dead-man's-shoes approach has often been condemned by later historians, but the protracted and costly warfare after 1672 constantly created vacancies, and forty-three of the 378 men reaching the rank of colonel or general in Brandenburg-Prussian service between 1650 and 1725 were killed in action, while the army lost seventy-nine officers at the siege of Buda (1686), forty-five at Fleurus (1690) and eighty-one at Neerwinden (1693), to name just a few engagements. Promotion was relatively rapid, at least to the rank of major, when rulers tended to intervene more directly, rather than simply approving colonels' recommendations. Such interventions were always justified on grounds of merit, but this lacked a clear definition. From the 1660s, Brandenburg-Prussia specified that officers should be 'respectable' (*anständig*) and 'capable' (*tüchtig*), but this was open to wide interpretation. By the 1700s many princes were openly favouring noblemen whose presence it was thought would add lustre to their armies.[28] Understandably, 'merit' was often perceived as favouritism and unwarranted interference, whereas seniority reinforced solidarity among regimental officers. Merit often worked in reverse, as inefficient officers were selected for dismissal when armies were reduced at the conclusion of hostilities. Criticism of seniority only really set in with the return to longer periods of peace after 1714.

Recruitment

Recruitment remained primarily 'voluntary' enlistment, but the shift after 1593 to units retained for successive campaigns meant that this was no longer a phenomenon of the start of a campaign, but a regular activity. Initially this applied only to wartime when units had to be kept up to strength by fresh drafts who were normally collected during the winter lull in operations. This practice continued in subsequent wars, but was supplemented after 1648 by less intense, but continuous, recruitment in peacetime to maintain authorized strength. The opening of new hostilities prompted a major effort as existing units were expanded to war strength and additional ones were raised in a process like that during the sixteenth century, with men collected en masse and mustered, before heading to the front. Otherwise, men were recruited individually or in small groups, and were sworn in once ten to fifteen had been assembled, and then marched to join their regiment.[29]

Recruitment required the warlord's permission and most authorities rejected requests from other powers, particularly after the 1650s. The exception was the emperor, who claimed the right to recruit in imperial cities and lands of the imperial knights, and whose requests to do so in princely territories were rarely refused. The electors usually secured permission from their smaller neighbours but were less successful when looking further afield. The Swiss cantons also tightened controls over their subjects to conserve manpower for officially contracted regiments serving France, Spain, or the Dutch Republic.

Responsibility for recruitment lay with the captains, who were charged with raising new companies and keeping existing ones up to strength. Captains frequently delegated the task of finding replacements to their lieutenant, who went with a couple of trusted NCOs and the company musicians to a large town or imperial city where they lodged in an inn for the duration. Recruitment involved considerable effort: around ten men from the four regiments of Mainz's army were detached for this purpose in peacetime, with the total in wartime rising to twenty-one officers and 560 men in 1707.

Market days and church fairs provided good opportunities, since these drew men in from the surrounding country. Once a man accepted the bounty and donned an item of uniform, he was considered a recruit, even before he was formally sworn in, and could only back out of his promise if he could produce witnesses to testify that he had been duped. This liminal legal state between civilian and soldier led to numerous disputes, but while recruiters undoubtedly used free drink and tricks, the element of coercion and duplicity have been greatly exaggerated in subsequent fiction and histories.[30]

The shift to permanent units encouraged the spread of 'capitulations', or asymmetrical contracts specifying a minimum period of service without protecting the recruit from an early discharge if he was no longer required. Capitulations nonetheless offered some security, while their renewal often required the army to pay a renewed bounty. Trier used six-year capitulations during the 1670s, while a decade later Saxony required cavalrymen to sign for up to ten to fifteen years, as they were easier to recruit than infantry, who were offered eight to ten years. Recruiting difficulties forced the Franconian territories to cut service time to one to three years during the War of the Spanish Succession.

Militia and Conscripts

Several principalities already required their civil officials to assist recruitment during the 1670s, assigning quotas to each district, but often leaving it to the local authorities to decide whether to pay bounties to attract volunteers or use the militia registers to select conscripts. This practice had already begun in the Habsburg monarchy intermittently during the Thirty Years War, and continued more consistently from the 1650s when it was handled by the provincial Estates. The annual quota across the monarchy rose from 12,000 (1690) to 20,000 (1701), reflecting the army's growing manpower demands.[31]

This slide towards conscription drew on the territorial militia systems developed during the sixteenth century, because these provided a convenient way to identify men for the draft. All the belligerents relied on militia during the Thirty Years War. While numerous examples of poor performance can be found, it is easy to overlook the militia's continued utility. First, it enabled poor warlords to raise large numbers relatively cheaply. Of Würzburg's 170,000 inhabitants, around 30,000 were theoretically liable for service. The number under arms peaked at 10,000 in 1638, with the level more usually around 3,000–5,000. Although poorly trained and equipped, they nonetheless contributed to the successful defence of the bishop's small fortified towns of Forchheim and Kronach, which were never taken despite repeated Swedish attacks.[32]

It was thus natural that the disbandment of most professional troops after 1648 was accompanied by reorganization of territorial militias to provide peacetime security in their place, for example in Württemberg (1650), Bavaria (1651), Tirol (1652), Saxony (1663), and Hanover (1666). While the reformed militias were sometimes given new designations, such as *Landregiment*, in practice they remained like those of the 1570–1630 era with local officials maintaining registers of eligible men, divided into a select first levy who were to be trained on Sundays, and a second levy and reserve that remained largely on paper. Meanwhile, civic guards were suppressed in towns where rulers asserted tighter control, such as Münster (1661) and Brunswick (1671), though they survived in the imperial cities, and elsewhere as parts of the reorganized territorial militias.

The numbers remained impressive. The muster of Hessen-Kassel's militia in 1673 saw 12,000 men assembled, representing 9 per cent of the total population and 43 per cent of men aged twenty to fifty.[33] As these figures indicate, it was impossible to sustain such levels for long given the agrarian, labour-intensive economy. Militia could perform good service, notably the Tiroleans, who repelled a Franco-Bavarian invasion in 1703 by felling trees to block mountain passes. However, that celebrated success must be set against their abject failure to withstand a Swedish attack in the same area in 1647. Rulers and their military advisers knew militia were inferior to regulars, and often the repeated efforts to revive them were only as a fallback because their Estates refused to vote funds for professionals.

Mobilization against France in 1672–3 carried official sanction from the emperor, as did that in subsequent major wars, which also had the added weight of full backing from the Reichstag. This allowed princes to present military service as fulfilling imperial obligations, thereby overriding any objections from their own Estates. Bamberg and several other smaller territories already drafted militiamen to fill out their contingents to the imperial army in the 1670s, and larger territories followed suit during the Nine Years War, introducing more formal mechanisms for this purpose after 1702.[34] Conscripts were usually given a small bounty, thereby blurring the boundaries between the draft and voluntary enlistment.

Militiamen did not see themselves as citizens-in-arms and resistance was widespread, with some peasants regarding it as a point of honour to miss drill sessions or appear with defective equipment. Drafting prompted men to flee, sometimes permanently through emigration, and in extreme cases violent protest: militia summoned by the Swedish authorities in Bremen and Verden to resist invasion in 1711 mutinied and killed several officers and soldiers.[35] Local authorities sometimes connived to protect the population, with those in Württemberg sending so many lame individuals and cripples to be considered for the draft in 1733 that only a tenth of the 4,000 called up were considered fit for it.[36] Nonetheless, the constant repetition of these measures after the 1670s, combined with the backing of imperial law and an increasingly efficient territorial bureaucracy, established territorial militias across the Empire by 1700 as a means to both supply limited numbers of conscripts to regular regiments in wartime, and embody additional temporary units for home defence.

CLOSE ORDER AND FIREPOWER

Size

Armies fluctuated considerably into the 1670s when the differences between peace and war strength grew less pronounced. A force of 20,000–25,000 men was considered a formidable battle-sized army in the 1620s, as it had been a century before. While the numbers deployed on one side in major battles rarely exceeded this strength during the Thirty Years War, the participation of numerous princes and foreign powers enabled multiple such armies to be fielded simultaneously. Most engagements still involved fewer than 50,000 men in the wars between 1672 and 1714, though their conduct by large coalitions could result in much larger battles, notably during the War of the Spanish Succession.

The Habsburg army remained the largest of all German forces. The dynasty had only 1,050 regular troops in June 1618, in addition to the 20,000 or so garrisons and militia along the Military Frontier. The field force already totalled 14,200 by late July; testimony to the efficiency of contracting in raising armies. Spain provided around 7,000 auxiliaries between 1619 and 1623, while 8,000 Hungarians and Croatians were drawn from the frontier. Further new regiments nudged the overall total to about 28,000, but the range of dangers meant no more than half could be assembled in one place, forcing the emperor to rely on the League, which fielded 30,000, backed by additional militia. Wallenstein's recruiting pushed total effectives to at least 40,000 by the end of 1625, peaking at an official establishment of 130,200 in 1628. Actual strength was always lower, and both the emperor and League disbanded some units across 1629–30 when peace was made with Denmark. The League continued to muster about 25,000 into the mid-1630s, while the imperial army fluctuated between 74,000 and 125,000.[37] Numbers declined but in October 1648 the imperial army still numbered 51,000 with a further 12,500 in the associated Westphalian army, while Bavaria mustered 20,500.

Frederick V and his supporters mustered up to 45,000 during the early phase of the Thirty Years War but were unable to concentrate their armies. While rarely successful in battle, the Saxon army was the third largest force, with Hessen-Kassel also being significant at around 10,000 effectives after 1631. Brandenburg-Prussia forces fluctuated wildly in authorized strength, but rarely mustered more than 5,000. Denmark relied primarily on recruiting Germans, many of whom had fought already against the emperor in the earlier campaigns. These provided the bulk of the 'Danish' army, which consistently numbered around 25,000 from 1625 to 1629. Between 10,000 and 18,000 Britons also served in Danish forces across this period, but no more than 8,000 at any one time.[38]

Imperial forces were still stronger than those Sweden was able to deploy when it intervened in the war in June 1630. However, Sweden had already mustered 89,700 effectives by December 1631, and may have reached a staggering 200,000 by the middle of 1632. Adding the likely imperial and League forces, that meant there were around 350,000 men under arms; an unprecedented number that goes far in explaining why this phase of the war was the most destructive.

Sweden only reached this total by drawing heavily on its German collaborators who raised most of its soldiers, despite the better-known presence of Scots and other Britons, who totalled 30,000 across 1631–9. The regionalization of the war prevented Sweden from concentrating more than about 30,000 in any one place for long. Overall numbers declined substantially after Gustavus Adolphus's death in 1632 and again after Sweden's great defeat at Nördlingen in 1634, so that the army averaged around 90,000 effectives for most of the rest of the war, dropping to 64,000 by its end in 1648. Two-thirds or more of these were Germans, who also accounted for the separate army that broke away under Bernhard of Weimar in 1635 and was subsequently absorbed by France as its army in Germany. Together with some additional French regiments, this army added another 18,000 or so to anti-imperial forces, though it had fallen to only half that strength by the war's end.

The trajectory was one of rise and fall, rather than the steady increase in army size suggested by the Military Revolution thesis for this period. Nonetheless, at over 180,000 men still under arms across the Empire in October 1648, military growth was quite dramatic, considering there had been no more than a few thousand professional soldiers over the entire Empire in 1618, aside from the garrisons on the Habsburg Military Frontier. The war also did not create standing armies, since all principalities had drastically reduced or disbanded their troops by 1650, leaving only the Habsburgs with a field force. This was also reduced to a low point of 13,732 men in 1655, but while its strength continued to fluctuate thereafter, the underlying trend was always upwards with more men retained at the end of each conflict than had been under arms just prior to it.[39] By 1705 paper strength had grown to 160,000, of whom 113,000 were effective, thereby returning the army to roughly the size it had attained under Wallenstein.

Mobilization of contingents for the imperial army in the 1664 campaign against the Ottomans prompted the smaller principalities to raise new professional units, but the real 'birth' of the other German armies was the Dutch War, because this saw the first substantial employment of German auxiliaries hired by Spain, the Dutch, and other members of the anti-French coalition, as well as the coordination of contingents for the imperial army raised by the Kreise. Their combined total was around

163,000 in the later 1670s, of which 43,500 were Brandenburg-Prussians. As in Austria's case, these forces now waxed and waned with each successive conflict, but always with an underlying upward growth, while the internal composition changed with the reliance on permanent regiments retained as cadres in peacetime and the relegation of militia to secondary roles. Total strength of these armies was relatively stable at 100,000 for most of the 1680s and rising to 150,000 around 1697. These other armies peaked at a collective total of about 213,000 in 1710, but since Brandenburg-Prussia's army was no more than it had been across 1675–9, it was the medium-sized and smaller forces that saw the greatest growth. Moreover, the emergence of these forces since the 1670s changed the military balance in the Empire where the Habsburgs, while still the most potent power, were no longer the only one with significant forces.

However, the army's internal composition was now very different, since over half of the forty-two new Austrian regiments added across 1681–5 were retained despite the reduction in overall size in 1700. The army was thus not only permanent and incrementally growing larger, but it was institutionally more stable. Many of the units fighting the War of the Spanish Succession had existed for decades, most were to survive across much of the eighteenth century, and in some cases until 1918. These permanent formations served as a trained, experienced cadre, retained on a reduced establishment in peacetime, ready to be filled out with new recruits when new conflicts broke out.

The Habsburgs had an army of true European significance, but it was unusual in not including any elite 'guard' units. These had always been a feature of French forces, and became even more so under Louis XIV whose *maison du roi* emerged after 1671 as a privileged army within an army and became the model of similar household troops elsewhere, including Brandenburg-Prussia. By contrast, the Habsburgs had only a few ceremonial units at their court, which were dressed in deliberately archaic uniforms and were never intended for combat.

Infantry

The belligerents entered the conflict after 1618 with their forces organized as they had been during the Long Turkish War. The regiment had become the primary administrative and tactical unit, particularly for infantry, but combat deployment necessitated the amalgamation of understrength units to achieve formations of the required size. That size changed significantly across the war, partly in response to the difficulty of maintaining large regiments, but also as commanders sought greater tactical flexibility. Initially, large regiments of 3,000 were favoured, but most imperial and League units were half that during the 1620s, dropping to between 1,200 and 1,500 in the early 1630s, and varying even more sharply to between 520 and 920 by the later 1640s for the League, with their imperial counterparts now slightly smaller.[40]

Much ink has been spilt in the Military Revolution debate over the alleged contrast between the supposedly large, ponderous 'Spanish' formations, favoured by the imperial and League armies, and the smaller, more flexible ones of their opponents (see Fig. 6). There were indeed differences, though these narrowed considerably during the early 1630s, while neither system was inherently superior. Rather than an 'older Catholic' model being replaced by a 'modern Protestant' one, all commanders were trying to find the optimal balance between shock and firepower while accounting for the varying quality and size of their units.

Imperial and League regiments were certainly larger during the 1620s, but that reflected the superior capacity of their governments to recruit and sustain them. Formations were rectangular, rather than the squares shown on many contemporary engravings, which often reproduced information from old drill manuals rather than being based on eyewitness accounts. The first three to five ranks were musketeers, with anything up to twenty ranks of pikemen behind, and thin 'sleeves' of further musketeers on each end of the formation.

Driven by the necessity of matching superior Spanish numbers, the Dutch rebels had thinned the deployment of their smaller regiments to only ten ranks, grouping all the musketeers at either end, flanking the pikemen in the centre. The musketeers employed the 'counter march', whereby successive ranks moved through the gaps in the files to fire, and then returned to the rear to reload in a version of the caracole already used by mounted pistoleers in the sixteenth century. These practices were brought to the Bohemian Confederates and other anti-Habsburg forces in the 1620s by officers who had served in the Dutch army before the truce of 1609. Advocates of this method claimed it meant that 'a regiment not stronger than 1,000 men could match one of the enemy with 3,000'.[41]

The counter-march simply formalized the looser practice already used in the earlier sixteenth century whereby musketeers moved forward to fire once they were ready, and which was still employed in the imperial and Bavarian army.[42] The more controlled Dutch method was not so different from that advocated by Giorgio Basta based on the experience of the Long Turkish War, in which most of the senior commanders of the early stages of the conflict after 1618 had served, including those on the Bohemian side. Imposing tighter fire control placed a premium on discipline and training, because the experience of participating in a practised, choreographed movement that became disordered under battlefield conditions was far more demoralizing for those involved than if they just concentrated on firing and reloading at their own pace. Rather than representing a direct precursor to modernity, the Dutch methods proved decidedly inferior and armies employing them lost every major battle throughout the 1620s.

To understand why this was so, it is necessary to recognize the deficiencies of early seventeenth-century muskets. At 16 to 18mm, most were still large-calibre weapons. Muzzle velocity was quite impressive at 300m/second, enabling penetration of 2mm armour at 40m, but kinetic energy declined rapidly with distance and the same projectile would only dent armour at 200m, which represented the maximum effective range. However, windage ensured shots rarely travelled precisely where they had been aimed, and every second shot missed at distances over 75m. That mattered less against large, dense masses of troops than the misfire rate of a fifth, which reduced the realistic rate of fire to one round every two minutes. A few rounds of fire created dense clouds of powder smoke that soon hindered visibility. Soldiers only carried eight to fourteen measured rounds of powder and shot in pouches suspended from a bandolier, with around twelve further rounds in a satchel. From the 1640s, ammunition was combined in prepared paper cartridges now carried in a *cartouche*, or leather cartridge case stiffened with wood. Even at this point, the ammunition allowance remained no more than twenty-five to thirty rounds, indicating that soldiers were not expected to engage in sustained musketry.[43]

The proportion of pike to shot could vary considerably. Although most armies gravitated towards a ratio of 1:3 by the 1630s, it would be wrong to see a higher proportion of muskets as inherently more progressive. It is clear the League and imperial victories of the 1620s were due to a great extent to the larger size of their formations, which could absorb more casualties while remaining effective, and whose large bodies of pikemen both protected them against cavalry and proved intimidating to enemy infantry.

Sweden brought new methods to Germany after 1630, which had been developed during the fighting against the Poles over the previous two decades. Swedish tactics have often been presented simply as offensive, whereas they were a clever combination of defensive firepower and aggressive attacks with cold steel. Generally outnumbered by the Poles and Lithuanians, who also had far superior cavalry, the Swedes trained their infantry to fire 'salvoes' whereby entire ranks of musketeers discharged their pieces simultaneously at attackers once they entered within close range. Similarly, small squads of musketeers were 'interlaced' among the Swedish cavalry squadrons to fire at attackers simultaneously as the troopers discharged their pistols. The shock element of these tactics was the following counter-attack that was intended to hit an enemy reeling from the heavy close-range fire.

The Swedes also grouped their infantry in the centre of any battle deployment with the regiments arranged in two lines, while the cavalry were posted, also in two lines, on either flank. This represented a significant departure from the Spanish practice of posting small cavalry squadrons to support clusters of infantry regiments. However, the trend towards placing all the infantry in the centre flanked by cavalry was already well-advanced in Germany prior to the Swedes' arrival. Swedish infantry regiments, nominally about 1,200 men each, deployed as 'brigades' of four equal units of pikemen flanked by musketeers in checkerboard pattern. Lauded by some later historians as supposedly a trend towards more linear tactics in which more muskets could be brought to bear, this formation had in fact been developed to counter the more highly mobile Polish forces and provide mutually supporting, all-round defence.

Sweden's German allies copied its tactics, which were also widely disseminated through printed tactical manuals and commentaries on the war in the Empire, as well as by British officers who had served under Gustavus Adolphus and returned home after 1638 to fight their own civil wars. To be effective, however, these methods required a high level of training and discipline, as well as an enemy who obligingly attacked, rather than waiting on the defensive in a strong position. They also had serious inherent flaws. The supporting musketeer units slowed the advance of the Swedish cavalry and were extremely vulnerable if abandoned by their own horsemen. It is noteworthy that Sweden's enemies never copied the practice and its supposed use by Frederick II at Mollwitz (1741) resulted from accident rather than design and in any case did not stop the Prussian cavalry from being routed by the Austrians. The supporting fourth unit in the infantry brigade formation was soon abandoned, partly because regiments were often under-strength, but mainly because it served no real purpose when confronting the larger imperial and Bavarian formations.

Tilly's defeat at Breitenfeld (1631) was due primarily to his loss of control over his army as it became too widely dispersed during the opening stages of the battle, allowing Gustavus to hit his centre with a well-timed counter-attack. Gustavus was defeated at Alte Veste (1632) by Wallenstein, who remained on the defensive, and again at Lützen (1632), which only became a Swedish victory because the imperial generalissimo decided to abandon the field during the night.[44] In both cases, the Swedish infantry failed to break their imperial and League counterparts.

One factor in this was that imperial tactics had already adapted and were consolidated in a major reform undertaken by Wallenstein in the winter of 1631–2. The standard tactical unit was now a 'battalion' of 1,000 men, two-thirds of whom were musketeers who flanked pikemen in a line seven to ten ranks deep. Partly in response to Tilly's recent defeat, these changes also reflected an appreciation of the minor but steady improvements in weaponry over the last decade. Archaeological evidence has recently disproved the myth that the Swedes used lighter, smaller-calibre muskets by 1632; in fact, their weapons were generally the older type, whereas the majority of imperial infantry were armed with muskets produced in Suhl, which were about 15 cm shorter, weighed around 4.6 kg, and were used without needing a rest.[45] The brigade formation and the interlaced musketeers were both abandoned by 1634, as the Swedes and their allies adopted imperial methods, albeit usually deploying slightly smaller and thinner units. The fact that the armies of the British civil wars went through the same process, also switching from 'Swedish' to 'German' practice, indicates the ineffectiveness of both Gustavus's tactics and the old Dutch methods that provided part of their inspiration.

Infantry continued to provide the backbone of all German armies after 1648. The battalion remained the tactical unit and by the 1690s was usually around 500 to 600 men, subdivided for administrative purposes into four or five companies. Habsburg regiments had three or four battalions each, whereas those in other armies were generally only one or two battalions strong. The proportion of pikemen in the imperial army had fallen to only a fifth by June 1641, but this reflected the greater readiness of recruits to volunteer as musketeers, and pikemen were still regarded as a regiment's steady core. Some of the contingents sent against the Turks in 1664 were up to half pike-armed, while Brandenburg-Prussia still issued armour to pikemen in 1674.

Armies experimented with what were misleadingly called 'Swedish feathers' in contemporary English writing, but 'pig's feathers' (*Schweinsfedern*) in German, more accurately reflecting their origins in boar spears. These were double-ended short spears that could be embedded in the ground facing the enemy as a defensive barrier. Some had an additional fork mid-way to allow the musketeer to steady his weapon. Used during the 1660s and 1670s, they were soon supplanted by the plug bayonet, or long knife that could be stuck into a musket muzzle thereby lengthening it and giving the soldier a convenient defence against cavalry. Brandenburg-Prussia already stopped issuing pikes in 1691, and their proportion universally and rapidly decreased, disappearing altogether after the introduction of the socket bayonet around 1700, which could be fixed to the end of the musket without blocking the barrel.

The bayonet's introduction reduced the utility of infantry swords, which were shortened from up to 130 cm to below 100 cm and abolished entirely in the imperial army after 1704. Their reintroduction in 1769 reflected less their use as a defensive weapon than their cultural associations as the honourable badge of a soldier. Outside Switzerland, halberds had already disappeared by 1610, except as a weapon for NCOs, while officers carried a 'spontoon', or half-pike. Both were more badges of rank than practical weapons, though they could be held lengthwise and used to push men back into linear formation. The imperial army was the first to equip soldiers as grenadiers in 1663, four years ahead of this change in France, which provided the inspiration for these troops' introduction in the Swiss militia around 1686. Grenades had long been used in siege warfare and were small, hollow shells made of glass or thin metal containing a powder charge that was ignited by firing a short match fuse just prior to throwing them. Given their short range, and the fact that those throwing grenades were exposed to retaliatory fire, grenades remained a weapon restricted to attacks on fortifications.

Grenadiers were soon employed more generally as assault troops and were grouped together in separate companies attached to each regiment by 1700. Selected from the tallest and strongest recruits, they were regarded as a reliable elite and were distinguished by their distinctive tall headgear, which was less likely to be dislodged when throwing grenades than the broad-brimmed hats worn by other soldiers.

Meanwhile, firearms continued to improve significantly. New ignition mechanisms had already appeared around 1600, using a lever gripping a flint that was released by pulling the trigger to snap down on the priming pan and spark the charge. This dispensed with the need for a slow-burning match, thus reducing the chances of accidents, such as setting fire to the soldier's clothing, which was often covered in loose powder spilled during the process of hasty reloading. The mechanism also worked better in damp weather and the absence of a burning match helped conceal soldiers during nocturnal operations. Known as the snaphance, these early flintlocks were delicate and expensive, and their military use was restricted to equipping the guards of powder stores and the artillery. The proper flintlock emerged by 1650 with an adapted mechanism that now automatically released a metal cover protecting the priming powder, thereby improving reliability and reducing the misfire rate to 10 per cent, half that of a matchlock.[46] Improved manufacture further reduced costs and enabled all infantry to be equipped with flintlocks during the later seventeenth century; a factor further hastening the pike's disappearance.

The growing emphasis on firepower led to the successive thinning of formations from six ranks in the 1670s to four by the 1710s. The latter depth was the maximum in which all ranks could fire without having to change their positions, but even with only four ranks, those in the front had to kneel to allow those behind to shoot without injuring their comrades. Given that ranges and accuracy remained unchanged, the shots discharged by kneeling soldiers generally fell short, and they were often deployed with fixed bayonets as a defensive barrier, rather than adding weight to the fire of the other three ranks.

Once commanders realized that the range, accuracy, and volume of fire could not be improved, they increasingly emphasized its speed and control instead. No single European army can claim credit for introducing 'platoon fire', which became universal after 1710, since the prolonged wars from the 1670s waged by coalitions allowed the rapid dissemination of good practice between allies and enemies alike. None-theless, Leopold von Anhalt-Dessau is notable for already developing rapid-fire tactics and his introduction of iron ramrods in his regiment in 1699 was copied by all Prussian infantry in 1718. These speeded reloading because they were less likely to break than the wooden ones used till then. Platoon fire involved subdividing the battalion line into squads of about fifty to a hundred men, who loaded and fired in a con-trolled sequence to ensure that at least part of the line was firing at any one time. Each platoon was commanded by an officer who stood apart so he could supervise his men, while the NCOs remained in the rear to keep the ranks aligned and discourage men from fleeing. The battalion commander, holding at least the rank of major, was now mounted so he could see over the line. The separate placement of the officers increased their visibility and thus vulnerability to enemy fire and explains their disproportionately high casualties.

Although much modified over time, platoon fire remained the stand-ard method of delivering both offensive and defensive musketry into the twentieth century. However, it represented only an evolutionary advance on the previous, less tightly controlled methods. Prussian soldiers' ammunition allowance in 1660 was still only twenty-four rounds, and this was not increased to thirty until 1730, eventually doubling in 1750. Even with more ammunition, it was difficult to sustain prolonged fire without changing position, because the unit was still hopelessly shrouded in smoke after a few rounds.

Cavalry

There was no clear correlation between the development of linear firepower tactics and changes in the role of cavalry. Between a quarter and a third of the imperial army were cavalry across 1618–24, but this proportion was inflated by large numbers of Croatian and Polish light horsemen employed initially due to the difficulties of recruiting enough regular troops. Cavalry formed only a fifth to a quarter of the troops arrayed against the emperor, though that proportion swelled to half in the armies of Mansfeld and Christian of Halberstadt between 1622 and 1624, largely because both commanders lost much of their infantry through repeated defeats and abandoned garrisons. Wallenstein's expansion of the imperial army relied heavily on infantry, reducing the mounted proportion from 27 per cent (1625) to 14 per cent (1630). This trend reversed sharply during the later 1630s, with a third to half of all soldiers being cavalrymen by the later 1640s.[47] Other armies followed a similar trajectory: Bernhard of Weimar's force was supposed to be two-thirds infantry after 1635, but in practice half his men were cavalry who were famed as the best in Germany. Given that a substantial proportion of infantry were usually tied up in garrisons, field armies had more horse than foot by the end of the Thirty Years War.

This development was entirely at odds with the supposed trend since Gustavus Adolphus's time towards reliance on infantry firepower and has gone largely unnoticed. Commanders in the 1640s certainly did not favour greater numbers of cavalry. Instead, they bemoaned their lack of infantry. Foot soldiers were generally steadier in battle than cavalry, who were difficult to rally once routed or having rushed off in excited pursuit of defeated foes. One explanation for this trend is strategic: commanders needed to act swiftly in conjunction with diplomacy, especially once peace negotiations began in earnest after 1643. With dwindling overall numbers, cavalry-heavy armies offered a better rapid response, moving fast to block enemy moves or to exploit sudden opportunities. Infantry could be drawn from local garrisons to reinforce them when a battle seemed imminent. Logistics provides a second explanation, since cavalrymen could forage over wider areas and carry food and fodder on their mounts' backs.

Heavy cavalry remained between 27 and 30 per cent of regular imperial troops after 1648, but if the Croatians and other light cavalry are added, around half of total strength was mounted into the 1680s. The subsequent growth of the army was weighted towards infantry, but cavalry still formed 30 per cent of total strength during the War of the Spanish Succession. A major reason behind these numbers is the Habsburgs' dual commitments against the cavalry-heavy armies of the Ottomans, and western European opponents employing more infantry. Cavalry also formed over half of the Brandenburg-Prussian army when it faced the Poles in 1656, but that proportion dropped to a third when it engaged the French in 1672. By the outbreak of the next war in the west in 1688, fewer than one in five Brandenburg-Prussian soldiers was mounted.[48] Infantry dominated all Swiss forces, partly because their reputation rested on their prowess as foot soldiers, but largely because these were more useful in mountainous terrain. The 1647 defence pact required cantonal militias to include only three cavalrymen for every 100 soldiers, and though the proportion was doubled in 1668, it remained exceptionally low by European standards and the role of cavalry was limited to acting as scouts and messengers.

In contrast to their infantry, imperial cavalry regiments were initially quite small at between two and five companies, each of 100 men, with Wallenstein's thirteen companies of cuirassiers in 1619 being exceptional. League units remained around 400 cavalrymen each, but larger regiments became common in the imperial army once Wallenstein took command and the norm was fixed at ten companies in 1633, the same as in the infantry. Actual strengths fell increasingly below that, averaging 200 to 700 cavalry each in the 1640s, by which time Bavarian units were now much stronger at 700 to 1,000. Cavalry organization among the anti-Habsburg forces was broadly similar though, as with their infantry, regiments were generally somewhat smaller. Imperial regiments shrank to 400 cavalry each by 1655 but were double that size by the 1670s and thereafter remained consistently stronger than those in other German armies, which could not afford to maintain such large units. The squadron was already the primary tactical unit in 1618, formed by combining two or three companies. Wallenstein favoured squadrons of 500 cavalrymen, or roughly twice as many as those of his opponents, but already by 1634 this had reduced to 300–400 men, and thereafter strength fell by a further 100 men.

Cavalry were classed according to the troop types established by 1600 with the majority being arquebusiers, who were both cheaper and considered more versatile than the more heavily armoured cuirassiers. The ratio was reversed after Wallenstein's criticism of his arquebusiers at Lützen.[49] The change was partly nominal, because only the front rank of the imperial cuirassiers still wore three-quarters armour by that point, while many of the cuirassier regiments raised in support of Sweden after 1630 were equipped as arquebusiers. The last imperial arquebusier regiment was disbanded in 1644, and henceforth all heavy cavalry were designated cuirassiers and armed and equipped the same. Imperial and Bavarian cuirassiers continued to wear helmets, breast- and backplates into the 1730s, whereas other German armies opted for a cheaper set of equipment with just a breastplate and an iron skullcap worn under the now ubiquitous tricorne hat. These more lightly armoured units were often simply known as 'horse' (*Reiter*), but their tactical role remained the same as the better-protected cuirassiers.

The tactical employment of arquebusiers and cuirassiers was in any case already similar by 1618: they were to defeat their opposing numbers and then exploit opportunities to attack enemy infantry who were already wavering or were in exposed positions. Squadrons were drawn up in ten-rank lines, later thinned to eight ranks for cuirassiers and six for arquebusiers, but these differences were largely nominal and all imperial and League heavy cavalry were in six ranks by 1633. Swedish cavalry were generally a rank thinner, but the difference mattered less because their formations were weaker than their opponents who matched the length of their line. All parties deployed in three to five ranks after 1636, something that remained standard into the eighteenth century, but which initially stemmed from the difficulty of keeping units up to strength.[50]

Like their infantry, Swedish cavalry combined defensive fire with aggressive attacks with cold steel. The latter were not carried at full gallop, because the troopers had to wait in line with their attached musketeers, who in turn were obliged to withhold their fire to match the limited range of their mounted comrades' pistols. These restrictions meant that the famed Swedish 'charge' was really a sudden surge forward against an enemy who became disordered by close-range musket and pistol fire. This could prove effective, notably at Lützen where the Swedes repelled Field Marshal Pappenheim's imperial and League cavalry, whose attack was probably hindered by the fact their horses were already blown. Certainly, the abandonment of the practice of interlacing musketeers by 1634 freed the Swedish cavalry to copy the more general practice of a rapid advance launched from a greater distance at a trot, accelerating to a moderate gallop as it neared the enemy.

Imperial cavalry still relied on their pistols, slowing their advance to fire before the final gallop. The caracole was widely employed by both sides during the 1620s and was not ineffective, at least to soften up infantry prior to an attack. Its discontinuation around 1633 appears to have less to do with any greater success of Swedish cavalry tactics than because improved musketry and light artillery proved far more effective in confusing enemy infantry than pistol fire. Pistol fire against opposing cavalry was much more likely to prove counterproductive, since the need to reduce speed in order to fire inhibited momentum and could disorder or demoralize the attackers, particularly if their opponents surged forward at that point. Here, Gustavus's emphasis on attacking with drawn swords made sense, as it heightened the intimidating effect of the charge. Many cavalry combats were decided more by morale than actual blows, with one side either recoiling rather than pressing home against implacable foes or turning to flee as their opponents continued to advance. The latter occurred at the second battle of Breitenfeld (1642), where the flight of several imperial regiments (again arquebusiers!) caused their entire left wing to collapse in the face of the Swedish attack, deciding the battle. Nonetheless, cavalry remained equipped with pistols into the mid-nineteenth century as useful weapons for personal defence.

Cavalry's effectiveness always depended not only on tactics, training, equipment, and morale, but also on the quality of its horses, of which there were invariably fewer than the number of men. Wartime wastage rates were high, and it was common for a third or more of troopers to be dismounted at the end of the campaign season. As with manpower, the winter was used to bring the number of horses back to required strength by the time that fresh grass and better weather made large-scale operations easier again in the spring. It is a particular sign of the woeful state of the imperial cavalry in April 1647 that a quarter were still dismounted and many of the rest rode mules.[51]

Dragoons

The merger of arquebusiers and cuirassiers into a single form of heavy cavalry was also encouraged by the growth of a distinct troop type, known as 'dragoons' for reasons that have not been satisfactorily explained.[52] Mounted missile troops had already fought at times on foot during the sixteenth century, but around 1610 theorists began to advocate a specialist form of mounted infantry to seize or defend key points until supported by the rest of the army and who could be used in raids and other forms of small war. Although Wallhausen envisaged at least some of them carrying pikes, this appears rarely, if ever, to have been the case. Instead, they carried a short musket or carbine, and were dressed as infantry without high boots to enable them to move swiftly on foot. They were equipped relatively early with flintlocks because of the dangers of carrying a lighted match while mounted, and all Brandenburg-Prussian dragoons were so armed in 1672.[53]

The first imperial dragoon regiment was raised in 1622 and numbers peaked at only three regiments in 1627, with the last one disbanded two years later. One reason for their low numbers was their inferior status relative to heavy cavalry, since 'small war' operations lacked the prestige associated with battles. The imperial army was also amply supplied with highly effective Croatian and other light cavalry who, to a considerable extent, performed similar roles. Nonetheless, several cavalry colonels appreciated the potential of troops of dragoons and attached them to their regiments. Wallenstein raised a new, designated dragoon regiment in 1631, and there were nineteen by 1636, though they varied wildly in size from two to ten companies. The disappearance of arquebusier regiments cemented the place of dragoons alongside cuirassiers and one dragoon regiment was retained in the army reduction of 1649, with numbers fluctuating thereafter in line with overall army size, but climbing to ten regiments by the 1690s.[54] Given their absence of armour and their smaller, cheaper horses, dragoons were increasingly regarded as a useful supplement to cuirassiers as battle cavalry. Over a quarter of Brandenburg-Prussia's mounted troops in 1688 were dragoons. The requirements of this additional task led to dragoons being issued with thick leather boots, thereby hindering their employment in their original dismounted role.

Light Troops

A succession of rebellions and political opposition in Hungary and Transylvania prevented the Habsburgs from employing large numbers of light cavalry from these areas at the start of the Thirty Years War. Instead, they recruited Poles and Ukrainians between 1619 and 1623, with around 10,000 serving at any one time. A further 4,500 were recruited for the 1633 campaign, along with 1,500 Balkan light horse known as *Kapelleten*. These were all largely gone by 1634, whereas Croatians formed a consistently important part of the army, initially mobilizing around 10,000 men, with the total number peaking at twice that in the 1630s. Many of these served on the Military Frontier deterring Ottoman raids and combating Hungarian and Transylvanian opponents, notably from 1618 to 1622 and 1644–5. Wallenstein greatly expanded the number of Croat regiments after 1631, with the total peaking at twenty-five in 1636, falling to four by 1648. Regiments were usually small, numbering five to ten companies of only forty to fifty men each.[55]

Croatians and Hungarians excelled at scouting, raiding, and screening the movements of the main army. In battle, they attacked diagonally, swerving alternately right then left to fire their two wheellock pistols, and then right again to fire their carbine. Around a fifth to a quarter carried light lances, while all had curved sabres for close combat. Their swift horses enabled them to evade a larger enemy unit, allowing it to rush forward and become disordered, before pouncing back to attack it, as at Lützen. They appeared in their distinctive local costume of red cloaks and caps, the latter trimmed with fur, brightly coloured braided jackets, tight trousers, and tailored calf boots, all of which provided the model for the later hussar uniforms copied widely throughout Europe.[56]

Recruitment drained the Military Frontier, where effective strength had fallen dangerously low to 15,000 men by 1641, or nearly a third below the authorized level. Hungarians formed a significant proportion of these, and the monarchy relied increasingly on powerful magnate families like the Batthyány, Esterhazy, and Zrínyi, who held the border captaincies and were now allowed to expand their private armies to around 12,000 men. Reflecting their militia status, the Croatian regiments with the field army were disbanded in 1649, but one raised subsequently was retained on the regular establishment after 1660.

At that point, border forces totalled around 15,000 Hungarians and Croatians, generally serving as militia infantry, along with 6,000 German regulars, but there were still the private armies of magnates and senior churchmen numbering 10,000–20,000 and another 10,000 in the county militias. Given that Hungary was also paying for a sizable proportion of the Habsburg field army that was billeted on the kingdom, the local magnates demanded a greater political role. The monarchy responded by reorganizing the Military Frontier in 1671–2, regularizing the different formations and trying to integrate them more firmly into the army. These measures provoked the opposition that flickered with varying intensity until 1711, but nonetheless did not stop the Habsburgs raising up to 18,000 Hungarian troops during the initial campaigns against the Ottomans in 1683–5, rising to 25,000–30,000 over the next five years.

The bulk of these remained light cavalry and infantry in militia and irregular formations, but the first mounted 'hussar' and irregular infantry (*Haiduk*) regiments were added to the establishment in 1688. The foot units were smaller than their 'German' counterparts, but otherwise were organized and equipped the same and generally expected to take their place in the line of battle. By contrast, hussars, who now replaced 'Croatians' in official nomenclature, remained true light cavalry. Together these two types added 6,000–7,000 men to the regular troops serving on the Rhine and in Italy during the 1690s. Meanwhile, the victories over the Turks facilitated greater integration of Hungarian units and the army's new regulations from 1697 appeared in Hungarian translation two years later.

The reconquest of Hungary rendered the old Military Frontier largely redundant, prompting a major reorganization between 1699 and 1702. The old sectors around Raab, Kanisza, and other forts now well behind the new frontier were disbanded, while new captaincies were established at Karlstadt, Warasdin, Slavonia (Peterwardein), Banat (Temesvar), and Transylvania. Settlers and refugees from the Ottoman Empire were granted privileges in return for serving in the border militias, which were established largely on the previous model and guarded the new string of outposts and fortresses.

Buoyed by these successes, the Habsburgs ramped up centralization, targeting the numerous militias and private armies that had swollen to 100,000 men and whose legal privileges and association with the Hungarian magnates posed a serious potential danger.[57] The resulting Rákóczi Revolt delayed full implementation until 1711, and prevented the Habsburgs from deploying large numbers of Haiduks and hussars in the west. France was able to form its first hussar units from Hungarian deserters and exiles, having already had a unit originally formed from Croatian deserters since 1642. Bavaria also had a hussar regiment following its earlier possession of a 500-strong Croatian light cavalry regiment from 1635 to 1639.[58] The performance of the imperial hussar regiments, few though they were, nonetheless inspired other armies to raise similar units, including Prussia in 1721 (see Fig. 9). These were formed by princes generally using their own subjects, selecting shorter men on smaller horses, though some officers in the late eighteenth century still felt it necessary to say that soldiers did not have to be Hungarians to be good hussars.[59]

Artillery and Technical Troops

If infantry provided the mass, and cavalry enjoyed the prestige, artillery remained the junior branch, but the seventeenth century nonetheless saw it put on a regular footing and incorporated within the regular army. Cannon-founding techniques lagged behind the theoretical development of ballistics, because it proved difficult to cast barrels that were sufficiently strong without being excessively heavy. Not till the later seventeenth century did producers switch from casting around a solid core and instead made the barrel as a solid metal cylinder and drilled out the bore, which improved stability and accuracy. Cannon remained prestige weapons with the barrels still highly decorated with coats of arms, Latin dedications, and their own unique name, usually deriving from classical mythology. Such baroque flourishes gave way to more utilitarian designs in the eighteenth century, but barrels generally retained royal or princely monograms well into the next century when steel replaced bronze as gunmetal. The old designations by type gave place to a more standardized classification by weight of iron shot calculated in pounds around the 1650s, which remained the principal way to identify artillery for the next two centuries until this was replaced in turn by categorization by calibre.

German territories continued to store large arsenals of often obsolete pieces: Württemberg had 242 cannon in 1621, while Strasbourg had 336 in 1665, but 292 of these were in storage and the rest mainly placed on the city's ramparts for its immediate defence.[60] The belligerents entered the Thirty Years War with an average ratio of one cannon for every 1,000 men, meaning that each side deployed only around twenty pieces even in major battles during the 1620s. Large cannon trains were only assembled for sieges, such as the ninety-six guns placed before Magdeburg in 1631.[61] These included heavier pieces and mortars for indirect fire.

Sweden is usually credited with introducing the light 3 pdr 'regimental gun' that could be manhandled forward as the infantry advanced and used in close support. As we have seen (pp. 71–3), already in the sixteenth century German armies had a wide variety of infantry support weapons ranging from 'double muskets' mounted on stands and firing 30–40 mm balls, to wheeled falconets or falcons firing 1½ or 3 pdr roundshot. Wallenstein attached light cannon to all regiments by 1631, while the Bavarian army experimented with 8 pdrs as a compromise between hitting power and mobility but seem to have switched to 3 and 4 pdr cannon by the 1640s, by which time the imperial army had largely discontinued light artillery. The number of heavy guns remained the same, with any increased ratio of cannon to manpower during the latter part of the war deriving from the greater use of light artillery.

As with many of the other supposed innovations associated with the Swedes, the effectiveness of such weapons has been greatly exaggerated in subsequent accounts. Contemporary reports of Lützen all note the destruction wrought by the two imperial batteries of heavy guns on the advancing Swedish infantry, whereas neither the Swedes' preliminary bombardment from their heavy guns at long range, nor the regimental guns accompanying their infantry and interlaced musketeers, are noted for doing much damage, beyond a falconet ball being most likely responsible for mortally wounding Pappenheim.

Initial muzzle velocity was 300–500m/second, equivalent to modern semi-automatic weapons and meaning seventeenth-century artillery could break the sound barrier. However, cannon suffered similar problems of excessive windage to muskets, and even heavy field guns were rarely accurate beyond 1,000 metres, though their larger balls retained greater kinetic energy and could still be lethal compared to smaller-calibre pieces. Light artillery lacked range, while the rate of fire was not much better than for heavier pieces, and there are rarely reports of gunners running out of ammunition in battle.[62] Nonetheless, a lucky shot could still prove devastating to clusters of soldiers struck by it.

Shortage of trained gunners was another problem. The Saxon field army had 150 gunners and 426 support personnel, together with 66 drivers for 132 horses all serving 24 cannon and four mortars in 1620. Saxony was unusual in having already established its artillery as a permanent formation in 1602 which could be expanded in wartime. The imperial army centralized its artillery command at the end of 1635, and retained around 100 skilled gunners and technicians, along with 12 field guns, 68 wagons, and 576 horses when the army was reduced in 1649. Not until October 1697 did Brandenburg-Prussia finally detach its field artillery as a separate corps distinct from fortress artillery. Comprising nine companies of gunners and one of bombardiers for siege work, this still only totalled 409 men in 1700. It is indicative of artillery's subordinate role that the various Brandenburg contingents serving in the Nine

Years War and War of the Spanish Succession often took no cannon with them at all, yet there were over 2,000 pieces distributed in the country's fortresses for their own defence and in arsenals as reserves of valuable metal.[63]

As with artillery, Saxony was also ahead of most other German forces in creating technical troops, establishing a corps of engineers in 1681 and permanent units of miners and pontooneers with a bridging train by 1700. Having already recruited Dutch and French experts, it made a determined effort to expand these forces and assemble more specialized equipment ahead of embarking on the Great Northern War. Saxony's Russian ally relied heavily on Saxon experts and equipment throughout that conflict, particularly during sieges. The imperial army retained just one engineer and nine miners at the end of the Thirty Years War, but likewise had permanent corps of specialists by the later seventeenth century.

Fortifications

The primary task of technical troops was siege warfare. Political tensions in the Empire encouraged several princes to construct new fortifications for their residence towns or at strategic points, notably Mannheim (1606), Frankenthal (1608), Philippsburg (1615), Bonn (1622), and Tönning (1626). Hamburg, Frankfurt, Nuremberg, and several other major imperial cities also built new works. Some of these fortifications were on a huge scale. In Hamburg's case, these roughly doubled the city's size between 1616 and 1627 and proved significant in underpinning its successful neutrality throughout the Thirty Years War. Those at Frankfurt were poorly executed and the city was obliged in 1631 to surrender to the Swedes, who promptly built larger, better-designed defences that were eventually completed in 1650. Meanwhile, Mainz, Würzburg, and other princely residence towns were also extensively strengthened during the war.[64]

As these details already suggest, new fortifications took years to build and were correspondingly expensive. In addition to Hamburg, which was merely threatened, there are several important examples of cities successfully resisting determined sieges, notably Stralsund (1628), Ingolstadt (1632), and Brno (1645), though in the case of Stralsund it came at the price of accepting Swedish annexation. Conversely, Münden (1626), Magdeburg (1631), Würzburg (1631), and Donauwörth (1632) demonstrated the dangers of prolonged resistance, as all were sacked when their refusal of offers of surrender was followed by successful assaults leading to massacres of the garrisons and inhabitants.

These examples both for and against fortification could easily be extended, but the failures did not deter governments continuing to strengthen defences after 1648. While regular armies were largely disbanded during the 1650s, princes and some imperial cities spent heavily improving and expanding fortifications or, in Mannheim's case (1652), entirely re-founding the city after its destruction. Most principalities now had at least one major fortress, usually the residence town, plus a few minor towns with modern defences, as well as several older castles. Brandenburg-Prussia began extensive improvements after 1658 to ensure there was at least one strong position in each province.

These programmes were funded through taxes the Estates could no longer refuse after the 1654 Reichstag ruling that subjects were obliged to pay for 'necessary fortresses and garrisons'. Most of the few professional troops maintained after 1648 were garrison companies, which were to be supplemented by militia in wartime. This practice still determined the defence policies of most small and medium-sized territories at the end of the eighteenth century. Territories maintaining larger forces usually also established 'invalid companies' from soldiers too old or infirm for field service, who were expected to continue to perform guard duty in return for what was effectively their pension. Austria created independent garrison companies in 1675 to free its line troops for field service, until these were disbanded in 1747 and the regular regiments served in rotation in the major fortresses. Vienna had had its own professional garrison since 1582. Varying between 400 and 2,200 men depending on need, this was paid for by the Lower Austrian Estates and only passed under army command in wartime. This symbol of civic and provincial autonomy was abolished in 1741, with responsibility for defending the city passing fully to the army.[65] Other princes also compelled their towns to disband their civic guards and surrender control of fortifications as part of wider policies of asserting political authority. Although regular sieges were required in the cases of Brunswick (1605, 1671), Münster (1655, 1657, 1660–1), and Erfurt (1663), princes exerted firmer control over armed force from the 1670s.

By the later seventeenth century only a fifth of the Empire's 1,500 larger towns and cities remained unfortified, but the majority were

protected only by medieval walls and just ninety possessed modern fortifications while a similar number had reasonably modernized defences.
Only sixty towns had been defortified before 1688, mainly during the
Thirty Years War.[66] The French devastation of the Palatinate at the start
of the Nine Years War saw Mannheim's renewed destruction, with the
defences of Heidelberg and other towns blown up or demolished. Meanwhile, France had pursued a deliberate policy of defortifying towns in
its own interior to prevent their use in rebellions, while systematically
strengthening frontier defences, both to block potential invasion routes
and to serve as launchpads for attacks into the Empire, Spanish Netherlands, and Dutch Republic.

The Empire's decentralized structure devolved responsibility to the
imperial Estates to protect their own territories, but this did not prevent
a coordinated response that emerged swiftly after 1689 through the
Kreise along the western frontier. These cooperated to build massive
lines of earthworks and abatis that incorporated villages and churches
as strongpoints blocking the routes over the Rhine and across the Black
Forest. Peasants were conscripted as construction workers and militiamen to guard the finished defences. Having held during the 1690s, the
lines were breached by the French in 1703–4 and 1707 during the War
of the Spanish Succession, prompting the construction of additional
works. These colossal obstacles marked the landscapes for generations,
with traces persisting today, such as the Ettlingen Lines south of
Karlsruhe that are now a popular hiking route.[67]

Meanwhile, France had been compelled by the Peace of Rijswijk
(1697) to return Mont Royal (Trabach), Nancy, Bitche, Philippsburg,
Kehl, Breisach, and Freiburg, along with several key points in the Spanish Netherlands including Luxembourg. Long discussions eventually led
the Empire to assume collective responsibility for Philippsburg, blocking
the Rhine at the northern end of the Black Forest, as well as Kehl which
countered the French possession of the Rhine bridge at Strasbourg. These
became imperial fortresses (*Reichsfestungen*), maintained through collective imperial taxes and garrisoned by troops supplied by the Swabian
and Franconian Kreise. Other funds were eventually allocated to assist
Austria in strengthening Freiburg and Breisach, guarding the southern
stretch of the Rhine and the Black Forest. Meanwhile, the Upper Rhenish Kreis coordinated assistance for Mainz, which had been strengthened
by its elector and which blocked French access to central Germany along

the Main. Finally, the Westphalian Kreis organized reinforcements to assist Trier in holding both Koblenz and the Ehrenbreitstein fortress, blocking the Moselle route, as well as garrisoning Cologne to defend the Lower Rhine.

MAIDEN VOYAGES

Naval Developments

The seventeenth century saw two major developments of lasting import-ance to European navies. The first was the emergence of two types of purpose-built warship that reflected potentially complementary yet fun-damentally different naval strategies. Large, heavily armed warships were constructed from the 1590s that combined seaworthiness with firepower in batteries of cannon arranged in broadsides on several decks. These underwent numerous important changes in design and offered naval powers the tantalizing potential to clear the seas of enemy warships. Battle tactics changed mid-century to reflect this, with a grow-ing emphasis on broadside gunnery to disable or even sink opposing ships, rather than immediately closing to board them. Meanwhile, a second type of cruising warship known as the frigate emerged from the fast 'race-built' galleons developed by northern European maritime powers. Equipped with only a single gun deck with fewer, lighter guns, these ships relied on speed, and could be used either to support battle-ships or independently as commerce raiders and convoy escorts.[68]

The two options eventually became known as a battlefleet for a 'high seas' strategy and commerce raiders. The former appeared to promise victory through decisive action, while the latter suggested a longer, attri-tional struggle. Battleships were large and expensive but demonstrated monarchical power more clearly than frigates, which were cheaper and thus more attractive for weaker powers. Frigates were also preferred by privateers, contractors who were licensed by belligerents to raid enemy shipping in return for a share in the profits.

Frigates could be built easily in private yards, but battleships were more complex, and their development fuelled the emergence of per-manent naval infrastructures, which constituted the second major development of the seventeenth century. This included not only admin-istrative institutions to supervise the construction and maintenance of warships, and see to their manning and supply, but also extensive dockyards and warehouses for building, repairing, and equipping the vessels. The lure of riches from global trade and colonies had already fuelled rivalry between Europe's Atlantic states, encouraging these to establish overseas bases to sustain long-distance operations.

These two developments accelerated from the early 1650s and were consolidated in the decade of peace after 1679.[69] The total size of European navies more than doubled to 441,000 tons across 1650–80 and peaked at 770,000 tons during the War of the Spanish Succession, fuelled primarily by the emergence of Britain's Royal Navy as the world's largest, accounting for about 30 per cent of European tonnage. All German warships never totalled more than 5,000 tons, suggesting that naval matters were largely irrelevant.

The Imperial Navy

That conclusion would be wrong, as both the Empire and several of its associated territories became more active compared to the previous century, with the period after 1628 seeing the maiden voyages of genuine German navies. The origins of the first imperial navy date to 1624 when Spain mooted its 'admiralty project' intended to assist its war against the Dutch Republic. The original concept envisaged enlisting imperial military assistance to establish a naval base in the duchy of East Frisia on the North Sea coast. From there a Spanish squadron could intercept Dutch trade with the Baltic, which supplied the Republic with much of its wealth. Discussions stalled because Ferdinand II was reluctant to become embroiled in Spain's Dutch war while he was still engaged in the Thirty Years War.[70]

The emperor became more interested once Denmark's Christian IV had been defeated on land, yet his army had escaped to the Danish islands protected by his powerful navy. By 1627 the plan had widened to include Poland-Lithuania, whose king promised twelve warships, as well as a similar number of ships to be hired from the Hansa cities with Spanish money, while Ferdinand II provided a base in a Pomeranian port on the Baltic coast. This Baltic fleet would cooperate with a similarly sized Spanish fleet operating from Flanders in the Channel and North Sea, thereby cutting off both ends of the Dutch Baltic trade. The imperial court was sceptical by the time it named Wallenstein as

General of the Oceanic and Baltic Seas on 21 April 1628.[71] Concerned for their neutrality on which their trade depended, the Hansa had already rejected Spain's request for ships two months before, and definitively withdrew from discussions in September. Stralsund refused to be used as a naval base and Wallenstein eventually gave up in August 1628 after the Pomeranian town had withstood a prolonged siege.

Operations switched to Wismar in Mecklenburg, where Wallenstein had just been enfeoffed as duke. Spain sent Gabriel de Roy, a naval expert, and substantial funds, enabling Wallenstein to hire Baltic shipwrights, construct five warships, amass stores, and establish a cannon foundry. Additional funds were raised by levying 'ship money' taxes on Mecklenburg; a measure like that pursued simultaneously by Charles I in England, which later contributed to the outbreak of the English civil wars. Another six ships were hired, making eleven in total, amounting to about 5,000 tons, armed with 108 guns. Nine Polish warships arrived in January 1629 under Adrian van Dusen, a Dutchman who had previously served Hamburg. De Roy wanted the fleet to engage in commerce raiding to help subsidize the growing costs, but Wallenstein objected, fearing it would antagonize other powers and jeopardize the peace negotiations he had initiated with Denmark. He preferred his own project to redirect Baltic trade by building a canal using the Schwerin lakes to connect to the Elbe, thereby avoiding the high tolls levied by Denmark in the Sound. Although construction had already began in 1627, the scheme proved overly ambitious given the available technology and means.

The imperial fleet cruised the Baltic in spring and summer 1629, taking some Dutch, Danish, and Swedish ships, but Wallenstein's success in securing a compromise peace with Denmark that June removed its main purpose from Ferdinand's perspective. The fleet briefly sortied in August, successfully repelling a Swedish attempt to blockade Wismar. Poland's interest in the project had always been to solicit Habsburg aid for its own war with Sweden, which ended in the Truce of Altmark in October, whereupon it withdrew its ships from Wismar. Having made a final cruise, the crews were paid off and the remaining ships laid up to save money. Wallenstein's dismissal in November ended all activity, and the Swedes captured the ships and stores when they took Wismar in January 1632.

Facing mostly land-based opponents, Austria lacked any incentive to create another sea-going navy until after 1701 when it made a major effort to conquer Spain and its Mediterranean possessions. Since this was also in the interest of its British and Dutch allies, it enjoyed the support of their powerful fleets until the final years of the war, by which point there was neither time nor money to do anything. Meanwhile, the Danube flotilla was revived to oppose the Ottomans after 1662 but was used primarily to transport troops and supplies and to assist in bridging operations, including enabling the relief army to cross the Danube to free Vienna in 1683. New galleys and gunboats were built after 1684 to support the army's reconquest of Hungary. These included a sixty-gun two-decker crewed by Netherlands sailors, which was used to bombard Turkish fortifications. The flotilla had expanded to sixteen large and eleven smaller warships, and thirty oared gunboats by 1701, but these were largely idle as the Ottomans kept the peace after 1699.[72]

The Brandenburg Navy and Colonies

Brandenburg-Prussia emerged briefly as a second German naval power during the later seventeenth century. Although interpreted retrospectively as signalling Prussia's alleged mission to unite Germany and give it a 'place in the sun', this activity in fact stemmed from Brandenburg's exposed position in relatively cold northeastern Germany. Thanks to his dual position as duke of Prussia, the Brandenburg elector was a Polish vassal until 1660, obliging him to assist Poland in its protracted struggles against Sweden. Given that the Swedes saw Prussia as a potential addition to their own growing empire, it was in the elector's interest to cooperate with his overlord, but likewise he wished to avoid an open breach with Sweden that would give it a pretext to seize his lands. This explains what otherwise appears a weak and hesitant policy, while caution was also rational both because of the elector's lack of funds and because he was simultaneously trying to secure the entire Jülich-Cleves inheritance on the Lower Rhine, a territory worth far more in tax revenues than Prussia.

Having briefly maintained a warship from 1601 to 1608, Brandenburg's first real naval activity began in 1621 when it provided four small ships to assist the Poles. Reflecting its own lack of facilities and desire to avoid long-term costs, these ships were hired each summer when better weather made Baltic operations possible. The squadron in 1625 included the *Welcome*, registered in Newcastle, and crewed by thirteen Englishmen.[73] The Swedish capture of Pillau ended these operations in July 1626, and other than a coastguard ship maintained after 1637, activity ceased until the Northern War of 1655–60. The refusal of the Dutch to transport Brandenburg troops for an attack on Sweden's Baltic islands exposed the elector's lack of naval power and prompted him to buy two English frigates, which were immediately impounded by the local authorities.

These were replaced in 1660, and two small warships were used to support the army on the Lower Rhine in 1674 during the Dutch War. However, it was renewed war with Sweden the following year that encouraged the Elector Frederick William to create a navy. As in the 1620s, it seemed expedient to simply hire one and the Dutch shipper, Benjamin Raule, was licensed as a privateer to raid Swedish shipping. Raule's squadron soon grew to ten ships with 287 crew, and the lines between privateers and state navy became blurred when the elector provided a new regiment of marines and used the ships to support army operations against Swedish positions in Pomerania.[74]

Although Brandenburg came out of the war almost empty-handed in 1679, Raule's contract was renewed and he was sent to attack Spanish shipping in the Channel on the grounds that Spain owed 2 million tlr of subsidy arrears from its treaty of 1674. Already hostile to the emergence of another Baltic naval power, England and the Dutch Republic threatened retaliation, while Raule failed to cover his costs from his prizes and tried to escape his contract by offering to sell his ships to the elector. It cost 6,000 tlr a month to keep a ship in commission, while even one laid up required 800 tlr a month to maintain.

Reluctant to abandon his maritime ambitions, Frederick William decided to copy the Atlantic seaboard states by seeking a slice of the lucrative African slave trade. He was not the first 'German' prince to attempt this. The duchy of Courland, alongside Prussia, the other former German crusader order state under Polish suzerainty, had already established an outpost on Tobago in 1642, expanding operations by seizing part of the Gambia in 1650 and creating a fleet that by 1654 totalled forty-four warships armed with 1,416 guns and carrying around 3,000 sailors. Far more potent than Brandenburg, its duke saw no reason to cooperate with the elector, but a Swedish invasion in 1658 crippled the duchy, which subsequently lost its outposts by 1691.[75]

The removal of Courland as a competitor may have encouraged Frederick William's decision to begin his own operations in 1682, using a pretext to seize the port of Emden in East Frisia that was garrisoned by Brandenburg marines. A post, named Gross Friedrichsburg, was established in what is now Ghana in 1683, and Raule's surviving ships were transferred to the new Brandenburg African Company at considerable expense. By 1717 this had shipped 30,000 Africans to the Caribbean. Diversion of resources to sustain the Company's operations left Brandenburg without naval assets during its involvement in the European wars after 1688. The Company attracted hostility from its much more powerful Dutch and English rivals, and though it expanded its possessions in Africa and the Caribbean, it remained unprofitable. Its main assets were sold off to the Dutch between 1717 and 1720, while St Thomas, the last Prussian Caribbean outpost, was seized by the Danes in 1731.

The Hansa

The end to imperial and Brandenburg operations left the Hansa as the sole German seagoing naval power. The League was in terminal decline, holding its last congress in 1669, after which it was effectively reduced to Lübeck, Hamburg, and Bremen; they had already been relying more heavily on the Empire to protect their interests after 1648. All three cities nonetheless remained important commercial ports. The loss of ships to Barbary corsairs in the mouth of the Elbe in 1662 and 1667 caused considerable alarm and prompted the construction of new frigate-type escort ships using Dutch designs. The convoy system broke down during the War of the Spanish Succession and by 1742 Hamburg's shipping had declined by 60 per cent.[76]

The Swiss Flotilla

Switzerland's lakes and rivers had long been vital to its transportation and commerce. The imperial army created a gunboat flotilla after 1631 that contested Swedish control of Lake Constance and thwarted their siege of Lindau in 1647. However, the Swedes then captured most of the gunboats, securing command of the lake and threatening the small towns along its shores. Following this experience, Zürich considered building its own warships, but only Bern went ahead, constructing five galleys in 1667 to protect its control of the Vaud and support its ally, Geneva, by controlling the lake associated with that city. Like so many would-be naval powers, it decided by 1690 that the purpose-built warships did not justify their cost, and it reverted to the previous practice of hiring barges when it needed to transport troops.[77]

Bern employed Dutch and French experts to design, build, and maintain its flotilla. Spaniards, Italians, and Dutchmen played a major role in developing the imperial navy, as well as designing new vessels for the Danube flotilla. The same was true for Brandenburg, where Raule was both naval commander and director of the African company, while the crews were predominantly Dutch, Danes and Norwegians, as well as from Hamburg. Despite the strong German seafaring tradition, early naval development thus relied heavily on foreign expertise to launch it.

6

From Extraordinary to Ordinary Burden

FROM DIVINE PUNISHMENT
TO STATE NECESSITY

Military Knowledge

The development of standing armies across the seventeenth century transformed war from an intermittent to a permanent burden, forcing governments to find new ways to finance and accommodate their forces, and obliging soldiers and civilians to live together in more stable communities. This shift changed attitudes. The belief that war was sent by God to punish human sin remained strong throughout much of the century but was increasingly displaced by rulers' claims that war was a state necessity and that armies were rational instruments to advance legitimate goals.

The first half of the seventeenth century saw an acceleration in the growth of printed information about war, which was itself driven by the thirst for news during the protracted conflicts engulfing much of Europe. The primary innovation was the advent of a regular commercial news press, beginning in Strasbourg and Antwerp around 1605, which was facilitated by the Empire's extensive postal system that distributed papers quickly and cheaply. The Thirty Years War directly stimulated these developments and by 1648 there were around thirty regular German-language papers in circulation, providing far more comprehensive and varied news coverage than was available elsewhere.

Another development were the illustrated newsbooks combining retrospective summaries and extracts from official documents and treaties. The most influential was the *Theatrum Europeaum*, begun by Johann Philipp Abelin in 1633 with a volume on the opening years of the Thirty

Years War, and continued until 1738 covering events with a lag of around a decade. The early volumes were illustrated with spectacular engravings by Matthäus Merian, which have become some of the most iconic images of seventeenth-century warfare.[1]

News reporting was generally more accurate and neutral than the partisan pamphlets issued by governments and their supporters that were intended to influence opinion rather than generate sales.[2] Editorials only developed much later in the seventeenth century, by which time Amsterdam, London, and Paris had overtaken German cities as sources of information on European conflicts. Nonetheless, the permanence of the Reichstag after 1663 made its host city of Regensburg into an international 'information hub' where diplomats obtained and exchanged news. Solothurn assumed a broadly equivalent position in the Swiss Confederation thanks to its location as France's permanent embassy, which drew other powers to negotiate there and to seek news of their rivals' activities. The expansion of diplomatic networks across Europe, in which the Habsburgs took the lead, provided additional sources of information.[3]

The Reichstag also published its proceedings, as well as manifestos, position statements, and detailed regulations. The latter were replicated at Kreis level with no effort to keep these procedural and administrative ordinances secret. By the late seventeenth century these were being collected into compendia and were themselves the subject of commentary on best practice.[4] Treatises on war remained primarily in the late Humanist mould as descriptive practical handbooks, rather than reflective analyses. The most sophisticated and influential were the four major works produced by Raimondo Montecuccoli in the 1660s and 1670s whose ideas represented a bridge to equivalent works in the eighteenth century. Montecuccoli drew on his own extensive experience as a senior Habsburg commander from the latter stages of the Thirty Years War and subsequent conflicts against the Ottomans and French. He helped disseminate ideas about both eastern and western European warfare and was the foremost contributor from the German-speaking lands in a field otherwise dominated by French writers and, for siege warfare, also Dutch and Italians. Alongside Montecuccoli, other Italians in Habsburg service were also important in transmitting knowledge about the Ottomans, who remained a formidable military power; notably Luigi Marsigli, who wrote an influential study in the 1680s based on his experience of campaigning in Hungary.[5]

The impact of such writings on military practice remained limited since most officers still learned largely through direct experience. Habsburg plans after 1568 to establish a military academy came to nothing, and though Wallenstein hosted a small one at Jičin, capital of his duchy of Friedland, between 1628 and 1634, this had limited impact. Several smaller principalities established knights' academies (*Ritterakademien*) from the 1650s, which taught French, riding, dancing, fencing, and often mathematics, engineering, and technical drawing. While primarily finishing schools for young noblemen, these skills had a practical application for those pursuing military careers. Saxony established a cadet company in 1692, followed by Prussia in 1701, which provided essentially the same curriculum, but in a more obviously militarized setting with the strong expectation that graduates should become officers.[6]

Attitudes

Christian just-war theory still guided thinking more broadly, but it was increasingly interpreted through a secular lens as princes asserted a monopoly of violence and justified its use in terms of state necessity to achieve a 'public good', which was often a euphemism for their own dynastic interests. While this trend was general throughout Europe, discussions of it in the German lands remained framed by the Empire's public peace legislation that had already established norms guiding the use of force. This encouraged a highly legalistic approach, since even the exercise of religion rested on rights anchored on the imperial constitution.

Religion continued to guide rulers' behaviour well into the eighteenth century, with German princely dynasties preferring their co-religionists as marriage and alliance partners. However, already in the Thirty Years War, cross-confessional alliances were relatively common, especially among those favouring the Habsburg cause. Material interests weighed heavily, adding to a prevailing sense of uncertainty after 1648. Montecuccoli asserted 'there can be no real peace between powerful competing states, one must suppress or be suppressed, one must either kill or perish'.[7] Rather than prefiguring Social Darwinism, this reflected a sense that the international order had become more unpredictable as it shifted towards a multipolarity of major and minor states.

The later seventeenth century saw Louis XIV emerge as both a model of a powerful monarch and as *Mars Christianissimus*, or the Most

Christian War God, in Leibniz's biting satire, first published in 1683 following the French annexation of Strasbourg and the other Alsatian imperial cities.[8] The French threat joined that of the Turks in official justifications for the maintenance of armed force across the Empire. Rulers and their supporters also referred to the Thirty Years War as a warning of the dangers of not being armed, and of the need for soldiers to be disciplined and under proper authority. The decades following 1648 saw the peak of mechanistic views of the state as a rational, ordered construct intended to advance human good, and this translated into the military sphere as claims that only powerful princes, backed by solid finances, could guarantee security.[9]

Baroque courtly culture emphasized order and control, as well as the state's claims to monopolize violence, symbolized by the cannon, stands of arms, and other military motifs that decorated palaces. Significantly, the latter were no longer fortified castles because the prince was now protected, not by walls but by his disciplined soldiers who stood guard outside and whose uniforms signified their subordination to his authority.

Violence

Soldiers recounted violence and death with little emotion, ostensibly regarding it as an occupational hazard, but it clearly filled civilians with dread.[10] Attempts to discern a divine plan encouraged some to interpret portends, such as the famous comet of 1618 that in fact appeared six months after the Thirty Years War began. Most found this confusing, fearing they might misread the signs and take inappropriate action. Astrology was widely regarded as blasphemous and Wallenstein's fascination with it was used by his critics to condemn him for supposedly basing strategy on the stars.[11]

Looking heavenwards was an understandable response to the uncertainty caused by rumour and exaggeration that could not be allayed by reading the newspapers. Horror stories abounded throughout early modern Europe, relying on common tropes such as rape, infanticide, cannibalism, and captives roasted alive.[12] These stories provided templates for writers to express their own fears, and the incidence of real violence during the Thirty Years War made them readily believable. However, the violence in contemporary accounts becomes more graphic the further it supposedly occurred from the author's own direct observation.

Most of these accounts were written for private reasons, such as the edification of family or a community such as a convent, or as a means for an individual to cope with trauma. Oral traditions nonetheless transmitted stories of violence until about 1700 when these began to be recorded by local historians. Most of these sources remained largely neglected until the mid-nineteenth century when they became woven into a general horror narrative of a war out of control. This view was powerfully influenced by Hans von Grimmelshausen's novels, which were bestsellers during the 1660s and 1670s but were gradually forgotten until rediscovered by the German Romantics amid renewed foreign invasion during the 1790s.

Grimmelshausen exemplifies the prodigious German literary and poetic inventiveness in response to the Thirty Years War, which otherwise severely dislocated artistic and intellectual life.[13] His best-known novel, *Simplicissimus*, was not published until 1667, but drew on his own experiences as a soldier to present the conflict as a series of seemingly random events. One of the most evocative and influential scenes involves the plundering of a farm retold from the perspective of an innocent child. *Courasche*, his other major work, combines a stock misogynistic critique of the whore as the main protagonist, yet also depicts her as a strong, independent character who was among the war's victims. These ambiguities later attracted Berthold Brecht, who reworked the story as his anti-war drama *Mother Courage*.

While contemporaries perceived violence as all-pervasive, they could nonetheless distinguish different levels, and regarded some acts as more atrocious than others. Military and civilian laws were frequently breached, but they did not lose all moral authority, and the famous cycle of etchings by Jacques Callot entitled *The Miseries of War* ends with an image of military discipline being imposed through the mass hanging of soldiers. One sign of this is that accusations of opponents behaving 'worse than the Turks' still carried weight in propaganda.[14]

Another is the element of reciprocity in the treatment of prisoners. Under the conventions of 'good war', prisoners were the 'property' of their captors, who could sell them either to a comrade or directly back to their own side or families for a ransom. Retaining prisoners in captivity was expensive and only used for high-profile figures, who were either regarded as valuable hostages or malefactors such as rebels deserving punishment. The most prominent example was the French king, François I, who was captured by imperial troops at Pavia in 1525 and held by Charles V until he agreed peace. Usually, low-ranking prisoners were simply turned loose, as they were not considered sufficiently valuable to warrant the cost of holding them to ransom. Killing prisoners was generally considered justifiable only in the case of towns taken by storm which had previously refused offers for surrender, or in the case of enemies beyond the boundaries of Christian warfare, such as the Turks. The Swiss practice of 'bad war' around 1500 thus posed serious problems since enemies were now killed immediately while the battle was in progress. Refusal to give 'quarter' could easily prove counterproductive by encouraging opponents to fight harder and posed risks to soldiers on one's own side who might fall into enemy hands.

Senior commanders had an interest in encouraging reciprocity as this aligned with chivalric ideals and enabled them to appear magnanimous to defeated foes. They also wanted to control their own troops, both during battle and afterwards when valuable prisoners or war materials could be taken. Thus, changing attitudes to prisoners reflected desires for self-preservation and official attempts to assert control. Articles of war specified restrictions on prisoner-taking and treatment. The ransoming of women and children was increasingly forbidden during the later seventeenth century, while soldiers and war materials had to be handed over to the senior commanders, who now held them on behalf of their warlord rather than as personal property. The practice of 'self-ransoming' continued unofficially well into the eighteenth century: individual soldiers would buy their freedom from their captors immediately or soon after being taken, and then make their own way back to their home side. Captured officers were now generally given parole, released on their word of honour not to fight again for an agreed period. This practice was extended to surrendering garrisons of besieged towns in the later seventeenth century. However, the preferred option was redistribution through a formal agreement known as a cartel, which regulated the mutual exchange of prisoners, either on a like-for-like basis or in return for cash payment.[15] The Spanish–Dutch agreement from 1599 is often considered the first cartel, but it is clear such arrangements were made at least a century early, for example between France and Spain during the war over Naples in 1502. They were used intermittently during the Thirty Years War but became standard practice in subsequent conflicts.[16]

A PRECARIOUS EXISTENCE

Motives

The impressment of prisoners into their captor's army appears to have been less common than sometimes thought. Sweden did this following most of its victories during the Thirty Years War, though it only applied to ordinary soldiers and not officers. Bavaria generally avoided it, while the imperial army seems to have applied it selectively to German soldiers, rather than taking native Swedes or Frenchmen. Prisoners often saw joining their captors as the only way of securing food and their immediate survival. Garrisons that surrendered with the honours of war also frequently lost men as they marched out, since joining the victors could seem preferable to a long, hungry trek to find their own side. It is usually unclear from contemporary accounts how far pressure was applied in these situations, since victorious forces had often also suffered heavily and their commanders saw impressment as a quick way to rebuild strength. However, it was also widely recognized that pressed men were generally unreliable and often took the first opportunity to abscond and rejoin their own side.

The practice continued, though on a still more reduced scale, in the wars of the later seventeenth and early eighteenth centuries when greater efforts were made to ensure that prisoners were not obliged to fight their former comrades. The victorious Allies took a considerable haul of French and Bavarian prisoners at Blenheim in 1704. Saxony was permitted to recruit 1,600 of these, of whom around half actually joined its army campaigning against the Swedes. Similarly, Saxony recruited 500 of the 1,200 Swedish troops taken at Stralsund in 1715, though many of these were in fact Germans.[17]

Likewise, most armies avoided pressing criminals, even when facing recruiting difficulties. No more than 200 of the 10,000 or so recruits received by the Bavarian army between 1635 and 1648 were criminals sentenced to military service, and the authorities continued to prefer sending felons to Venice to suffer the terrible fate of serving as oarsmen in its galley fleet.[18] Bavaria was relatively unusual in already relying quite heavily on drafting militiamen to fill out its professional forces, notably during the early 1620s and periodically in the wars after 1688.

Some other territories also did this, notably Württemberg, which forcibly converted men mobilized as militia into regular regiments in 1691 with very mixed results.[19]

Thus, most soldiers were at least nominally 'volunteers' whom the secondary literature has generally classed as 'mercenaries' serving purely for pay, rather than any 'higher ideals'.[20] Given the paucity and ambiguities of the surviving evidence, it is difficult to discern why men enlisted, though we should not automatically assume that soldiers took their oaths of loyalty any more lightly than civilians who swore allegiance to their communities and lords. While very few soldiers were holy warriors, they were not indifferent to religion and its moral precepts.[21] Loyalty to comrades was also another significant factor, at least once men were already serving.

Soldiering remained a relatively attractive form of employment in the early seventeenth century, and one officer reckoned there were five recruits for every four vacancies in 1619. The protracted warfare engulfing the Empire after 1618 ensured armies were constantly looking for recruits, but the financial pressures meant few soldiers received regular pay. Rates varied considerably between armies, and between summer and winter months, reflecting the competition from civil employment. Soldiers now received rations, either directly, or through arrangements imposed on the areas where they were billeted. The daily rate was usually 2 lb bread, 1 to 1½ lb meat, 1 measure (1.4 l) of wine or 2 of beer. German army bread was usually 2/3 wheat and 1/3 rye, but flour was often mixed with grit and bleached with chlorine, while the meat ration contained skin and bone, meaning only about half was directly edible. Soldiers generally ate peas, beans, and semolina with the meat, plus cabbage or sauerkraut and dried fruit, depending on the season. Butter, cheese, and eggs had to be bought from wages, if not supplied by the local population. These rations remained broadly the same well into the nineteenth century and provided enough calories but were deficient in vitamins. During the seventeenth century they normally had to be shared with the soldier's non-combatant companions, who otherwise had to fend for themselves. The availability of food varied greatly according to the season, campaign theatre, and the outcome of military events. Hunger was a frequent companion, but one deadened with alcohol as the use of schnapps and other hard spirits, while already known in the Middle Ages, now became more common.[22]

Demobilization after 1648 drastically reduced opportunities, but also allowed governments to stabilize pay relative to civilian wages. German infantry now earned around 3 fl per month, with cavalry receiving about twice that. These rates remained unchanged into the early eighteenth century, but were subject to stoppages introduced as part of the 'company economy' by which captains managed the material welfare of their men by deducting money in lieu of uniforms, medicines, rations and, by about 1700, limited pension schemes. Much depended on how much was deducted and what was provided free, but the promise of more regular pay, plus basic subsistence, still attracted under-employed or seasonal workers.[23] For example, a uniform was worth the equivalent of six months wages for a day labourer.

The lure of plunder persisted into the later seventeenth century. Münster drew many recruits during the 1670s because of its bishop's previous raids into Dutch territory, which had netted rich booty.[24] While individuals certainly made their fortunes, many soldiers soon lost their plunder, either when their army's baggage was captured in the wake of a defeat, or because they found it hard to convert it into cash and were forced to sell it cheap. Tighter supervision also reduced opportunities for plunder during the later seventeenth century. Swiss recruiters were already offering small bounties (*Handgeld*) as an initial inducement to enlist in foreign service by the early seventeenth century. These became more common during the second half of the century when creeping inflation eroded the real value of soldiers' pay and it became harder to recruit as armies expanded faster than the growth in population.

The institutionalization of the company economy imposed some curbs on officers' profiteering, but there was still money to be made from the differential between the value of the stoppages and the true cost of clothing and provisions. Officers generally had better opportunities to acquire substantial plunder, though this was woven into hierarchical patronage relationships whereby subordinates passed on choice items to their superiors. Tighter regulations also narrowed these opportunities after the 1650s. Reduced profitability fuelled the emergence of split companies in the Swiss regiments in French service from the early seventeenth century as several contractors combined to finance and command a single unit.[25]

Geographic Origins

Nonetheless, military service remained attractive to nobles and many patricians' sons, while the proliferation of armies and protracted character of wars created numerous opportunities during the first half of the seventeenth century. Service in several different forces in succession was a recognized way of obtaining experience and securing promotion. Consequently, the officer corps was generally more cosmopolitan than the rank and file, who were increasingly their warlord's own subjects.

Around 1620 it was still common to commission trusted colonels to raise regiments in locations where the population had the reputation of making good soldiers, or where recruits were thought to be plentiful. The Catholic League army contained three infantry regiments of Walloons and another from the Rhetian republic in 1620, while Wallenstein's first major foray into large-scale contracting involved raising a cuirassier regiment, also from Walloons, in 1619. Such non-German regiments became less common within a decade, except in the imperial army, which drew on the Habsburgs' extensive possessions, especially in Croatia and Hungary. While the bulk of the Bavarian army in the 1630s were not the elector's own subjects, no more than a fifth were non-Germans. The situation was very different by the 1680s when most were Bavarians, with the remainder largely from neighbouring imperial cities and small territories. Large minorities of non-natives were now only found in the armies of smaller principalities, which either supplied auxiliaries for other powers, like Mecklenburg, or over-reached themselves by engaging in multiple conflicts, like Saxony.[26]

The Habsburgs' prestige and the size of their army enabled them to attract officers from across the Empire and beyond, including Scottish and Irish Catholics.[27] The powers intervening in the Thirty Years War relied heavily on German princes and aristocrats to raise the bulk of their forces, and these in turn drew on their own contacts and clientele when appointing officers. Doubts about the loyalty of some German officers after 1635 encouraged Sweden to prefer its own subjects, but the country's nobility was too small to fill all the posts. Germans remained a significant proportion of Swedish and Danish officers into the nineteenth century, though many of these came from those kingdoms' German possessions or families who were naturalized within their own nobilities.

Louis XIV's expulsion of the Huguenots in 1685 led many to take service in German armies, especially as these were usually fighting in the anti-French coalitions of the later seventeenth century. Huguenots comprised a fifth of all Prussian infantry officers and over a quarter of those in the cavalry between 1688 and 1713, but their overall share was already declining during the 1690s and their presence in other German armies was significantly lower. Bavaria had a small minority of Irish Catholic officers during the War of the Spanish Succession, but this was a consequence of the special circumstances of its army fighting in exile alongside that of the French who supported the Jacobite cause. Otherwise, usually no more than one in twenty officers in the smaller German armies came from outside the Empire once permanent armies were established during the 1670s. Princes increasingly asserted the right to determine whether their nobles, like their more humble subjects, could serve in foreign armies. Switzerland was the exception where the continued close ties between contracting and cantonal government meant local elite families monopolized officer appointments in the units in foreign service.[28]

Social Origins

The appointment and promotion of commoners to junior officer ranks remained widespread into the 1670s, but noble status placed a barrier on what could be achieved by talent alone and, compared to the next two centuries, proportionately far fewer men were ennobled through military service. The proportion of commoners (including those ennobled during service) among Bavarian colonels fell from a third between 1650 and 1670 to a seventh in the following four decades. While over a quarter of Saxon officers were commoners during the 1680s and 1690s, only one secured promotion to colonel, and noble predominance grew greater still after the elector became king of Poland in 1697.[29] Commoners continued to form a more significant proportion of the officers in the ecclesiastical and other smaller principalities whose forces offered fewer prospects for advancement and lacked the status of the larger armies.

Prussia was relatively unusual in seeing the proportion of commoners rise across 1688–1713, though nobles still accounted for nearly nine-tenths of the senior ranks. Commoners predominated among Swiss officers in foreign service, though the barriers to entry rose significantly from the early seventeenth century, effectively restricting appointments (and thus profits) to a few patrician families in each canton. They treated their companies as hereditary possessions but, in reality, only had 'right of usage' while ultimate ownership remained with the state they served, which could revoke their command and assign units to others of its own choosing.[30]

Religion was widely considered a test of political loyalty, and while it was possible for dissenters to become officers, confession likewise imposed limits on promotion prospects and it was relatively common for Protestants to convert to Catholicism while in Habsburg service. It was easier to insist on conformity in smaller than in large armies. Religion remained important in imperial politics well into the eighteenth century, but it also served other interests. This explains the prolonged controversy over commanders for the imperial army, which ended in the Reichstag ruling in 1704 that there had to be an equal number of Protestants and Catholics in each rank, thereby allowing Prussia to appoint some of its generals against Habsburg opposition. However, the Franconian Kreis members refused to segregate their collective forces and continued to mix contingents from Catholic and Protestant territories in the same unit after 1681. Less attention was given to the beliefs of ordinary soldiers, and the growing recruiting difficulties by the late seventeenth century encouraged further toleration.[31]

Information on the origins of ordinary soldiers remains patchy prior to the more detailed muster lists kept from the later seventeenth century. Recruits came predominantly from rural backgrounds, reflecting settlement and economic patterns, but could include a significant minority of former craftsmen, especially during wartime when trade was adversely affected. Nonetheless, recruiters preferred to operate in towns, since these drew migrants from the surrounding area who often failed to find the work they hoped for and could be persuaded to enlist instead. Imperial cities became especially favoured locations, given their political autonomy and the fact that many were located close to several different territories.

Swiss joining French service generally did so aged around twenty-four, but most armies took men up until their mid-thirties or even older, though they preferred those under thirty. Less than one-fifth of Bavarian recruits were nineteen or younger, while two-thirds were aged twenty to thirty-five. Archaeological data from mass graves of the Thirty Years War indicates most soldiers were in that age group, with around a tenth in their sixties.[32] Around half of Bavarian soldiers in the 1630s and 1640s had prior military service, partly because some had deserted other forces, but also because armies preferred veterans used to the rigours of campaigning. Mass demobilization around 1648, combined with the initial demographic recovery from the war years, meant that soldiers were predominantly younger when armies began seeking large numbers of new recruits in the 1670s. The permanence of armies thereafter, combined with growing recruiting difficulties, pushed the average age upwards by 1700, particularly as regiments retained a cadre of veterans at the conclusion of each conflict, and one Hanoverian unit included an old trooper who had fought at St Gotthard in 1664 before eventually being killed at Ramillies aged eighty in 1706.[33]

CAMPAIGN COMMUNITIES

Regulation

The greater permanence of armies was manifest in a more comprehensive regulatory framework intended to control soldiers and demarcate their status within a society composed of several distinct corporate groups. This process began first in the Habsburg forces, whose legal arrangements were generally copied by the other German armies, as well as influencing practice elsewhere, notably Sweden.

The Long Turkish War of 1592–1606 created a new dynamic, because units were no longer disbanded at the end of each campaign but kept in being close to the front to be ready for when operations resumed the following spring. The Habsburgs began imposing open-ended contracts, requiring soldiers to serve for as long as they were being paid, and denying them the right to disband themselves or stop fighting. This added to the financial pressures, since arrears had to be settled before troops could be discharged, prompting serious disorders in Vienna in 1606 when the emperor could not do this.

The Habsburgs already insisted on holding inspection and auditing parades known as 'musters' during the Long Turkish War, rather than simply at its start and termination. Musters became a crucial control mechanism as armies became more permanent from the 1670s, since they were now held at least annually in peacetime as well as wartime. At a muster the entire unit would parade before a commissioner sent for this purpose by the army's central administration. Each man had to step forward in turn to speak to the commissioner at his desk in confidence and was encouraged to be frank if he had complaints. Whistle-blowers whose accusations were substantiated by investigations received a year's pay or an honourable discharge. Increasingly, detailed personal information was recorded about each man in the muster rolls to assist in the detection of fraud, such as officers passing off their servants as missing soldiers whose pay they had been drawing. From the 1680s, regiments increasingly also had to submit single-sheet monthly returns summarizing the strength of each company and recording how many men were missing from strength and for what reason. Meanwhile, imperial legislation from 1664 required commanders to send regular 'conduct lists' (*Conduite Listen*) on their immediate subordinates. Copied by other German armies from the 1670s, this became a system of annual appraisal, complete with standardized forms and points systems that look strikingly familiar to anyone who has encountered similar processes in the modern workplace.[34]

The Habsburg army already used musters in the 1590s as opportunities to consolidate under-strength units, paying off difficult or incompetent officers and transferring their men to bring other companies up to strength. Several units mutinied when their men refused to be parted from popular officers whom they saw as better guarantors for their own pay arrears. Nonetheless, this practice of 'reforming' or 'reducing' regiments became common during the Thirty Years War and imperial law was changed in 1641 explicitly to confirm the warlord's powers in this respect. Thus, the state inserted itself in the contractual relations between officers and men. However, it proved impossible to dispense with colonels, since efforts to form regiments by issuing contracts separately to captains proved unsuccessful. Nonetheless, the Habsburgs had asserted greater influence over the appointment of junior officers by 1615. The greater latitude granted to Wallenstein between 1625 and 1634 did not reverse this long-term trend, and the retention of the army permanently at reduced strength after 1649 provided a renewed opportunity to strengthen central authority through the amalgamation of the remaining regiments.[35]

The new imperial articles of war, issued in 1642, ended the last vestiges of a freely negotiated contract and obliged soldiers to serve for as long as necessary and to accept any amalgamation of their regiment. The new code distilled those from the 1570s into a shorter format and removed the distinction between infantry and cavalry in that it applied to all soldiers equally. Following further revisions in 1673, a new, comprehensive set was promulgated by the Reichstag on 31 January 1682, which provided the basis for German military law since most territories followed its provisions closely in their own legislation. The articles continued to define soldiers as a distinct legal group, specifying norms and punishments for civil offences, like adultery, as well as more obviously military ones. The forces of the imperial cities were exceptions in this respect in that they remained civic employees, without their own courts martial, and fell largely under civil jurisdiction.[36] Their articles were supplemented from the 1620s by an increasing number of administrative ordinances regulating pay, provisions, procurement, transportation, accommodation, promotion, and a host of other issues that became more pressing as armies grew more permanent. Württemberg issued seventeen different sets from 1673 to 1692 alone.[37] The Kreise issued their own ordinances and often became models for disseminating good practice, resulting in considerable standardization in procedure, despite the existence of separate armies in each region. The rules became less innovative during the 1700s, and the basic legal and administrative framework that would last a century or more was in place by 1714, with new ordinances simply modifying those already in force.

Soldiers' Identities

One factor behind the tighter regulations was to crush the remnants of the autonomous Landsknecht culture that was perceived as threatening good discipline and proper subordination. After 1650 the authorities propagated the ideal of the 'good soldier', in contrast to the licentious soldiery of the Thirty Years War. While this partly reflected reality, it was also a device to garner acceptance of the now permanent war taxes, which continued into peacetime and which, it was claimed, were necessary to ensure soldiers were better behaved and more effective in defending their territory.[38]

The greater subordination of soldiers was reflected in their relative loss of individuality. In place of the nicknames used by Landsknechte, like 'Daredevil', 'Seven Fingers', or 'Weed', soldiers were now recorded by their baptismal names in the muster lists – contrasting with French practice where the assumption of a *nom de guerre* still remained central to becoming a soldier.[39] A more visual indication of this trend was the replacement of the individualistic Landsknecht dress with military uniforms. Slashing with contrasting lining and other finery had largely disappeared already around 1580, except for officers and a few bodyguard units. The men generally dressed in drab colours, indistinguishable from peasants other than by their weaponry and equipment.

The issuing of cloth in lieu of pay during the Long Turkish War already indicates the development of uniforms.[40] Colonels were concerned for their men's health and wanted them (and, by association, themselves) to avoid becoming objects of ridicule if dressed in rags. Rulers were also concerned for their reputations and many of the reformed militias already had uniform-coloured coats and breaches around 1600. The Saxon army issued standardized clothing with the coats matching the flag colours in 1620. Several other armies followed a similar practice at the opening of the Thirty Years War, and though financial constraints often meant soldiers wore civilian dress, the same pressures also encouraged the issuing of cheap clothing in lieu of pay. The Habsburgs already primarily issued 'pearl grey' coats in the 1630s, and this became their army's standard colour into the eighteenth century when the material was increasingly bleached white. Other armies largely followed imperial practice into the 1680s when they adopted distinctive colours: sky blue for Bavaria, red for Hanover and Saxony, dark blue for Prussia (since 1641), Hessen-Kassel, the Palatinate, and several other forces.

It was already common to organize bulk contracts, with coats made to three standard sizes to fit men of different stature. Regiments were distinguished by their 'facings'; at this point usually no more than the differently coloured linings of their coats revealed by turning back their sleeves. Regimental uniforms became more elaborate and distinctive around 1700 as the cut of the coat changed to reveal more of the lining, which was now decorated with lace, especially for guard units. The broad-brimmed hat, ubiquitous since the later sixteenth century, was now folded up to form the tricorne that would remain the standard headgear into the 1790s when it was briefly replaced by the bicorne, followed by the conical shako around 1806. Officers continued to dress differently until around 1710 when they were required to appear in uniform like their men.

The delay in officers adopting uniforms indicates the longer hierarchy of ranks established by the late sixteenth century. Officers considered themselves separate from their men, who had to remove their hats in their presence as a sign of respect. Relations were paternalistic, reflecting the reciprocal character of corporate society more generally. Echoing attitudes towards Georg von Frundsberg a century before, several senior generals during the Thirty Years War were called *Vater* by their men, including even the haughty Piccolomini, who was hailed as a saviour when he joined the demoralized imperial army in the summer of 1642.[41] Having lost much of their associative autonomy, soldiers now looked to their officers to represent them in dealings with the authorities and communities, including expecting their protection when accused by civilians of crimes. In turn, neither officers nor their princely masters expected soldiers to think for themselves, frequently referring to them as children.[42] Greater continuity of service encouraged men to regard each other as comrades, a word entering common usage during the seventeenth century and deriving from the Italian *camerata* for a group sharing a room or tent.

Armies remained itinerant campaign communities but, unlike those of the sixteenth century, these were now permanent as they stayed together throughout the protracted warfare, first during the Long Turkish War, and then on a far larger scale across the Thirty Years War. Elements already stood still as garrison communities, fixed in one place for years at a stretch. These emerged with occupation policies during the Thirty Years War when the belligerents garrisoned towns and castles to protect their own possessions, or to deny these to enemies. The imperial army used the excuse of local rioting in 1628 to occupy the imperial city of Lindau, strategically located at the east end of Lake Constance, and stayed for twenty years at the inhabitants' expense.[43]

After 1648, most territories retained a few companies lodged in castles or billeted on townsfolk. Military activity remained limited to short expeditions, such as the assistance provided against the Turks in 1664, and forces were reduced upon their return. The resumption of semi-permanent warfare after 1672 meant regiments were now retained as cadres during what proved to be brief intervals of peace. The seasonal rhythm of war remained active campaigning in the spring, summer, and early autumn, with a withdrawal to winter quarters, but these were now usually close to the front and thus the Rhineland saw a continued heavy military presence during the long wars with France, as did Hungary during the conflicts with the Ottomans.

Regiments nonetheless retained some connections to their home territories while away on campaign and parties would be sent back during the winter to recruit them back up to strength. They would also generally return at the conclusion of hostilities and be lodged in reduced numbers until being either fully disbanded or sent out on a new campaign. Most were billeted individually or in small groups with civilians who were given tax rebates intended to cover the costs. Soldiers were often unwelcome, and some communities resisted their presence, even with violence.[44] Few barracks existed beyond shoddy sheds, cramped rooms in old castles, or damp casemates in fortresses. Purpose-built barracks appeared around 1700 in princely residence towns or major administrative centres, like Düsseldorf, Stuttgart, and Ludwigsburg, but these only housed a small proportion of the troops.[45]

'Camp Followers'

The growing permanence of armies affected relations between soldiers and women. Contemporary comments about 'hordes' of camp followers reflect the often-hostile attitudes of the writers who increasingly saw these as 'the cause of disorder and confusion in the army.'[46] Wallhausen claimed in 1615 that a regiment of 3,000 men would have 4,000 followers, while Gronsfeld estimated the 40,000 Bavarian and imperial army had 140,000 non-combatants in 1648. Administrative records and demands for accommodation indicate that the numbers of followers were no more than equal that of soldiers in mobile units, and equivalent to between one-quarter and one-third of those in garrison, suggesting the presence of a permanent core with a fluctuating, more temporary population when in the field. German regiments were noted as having more women than Italian ones, while it seems that the Swiss had fewer followers when they left home, though they subsequently acquired them once in foreign service.[47]

Camp followers included women, children, a fair proportion of adolescents, and some adult males, most of whom performed essential tasks in transportation, animal welfare, laundry, foraging, cooking, and medical care, as well as offering companionship. Soldiers still had an aversion to digging, and male and female camp followers were often called upon as additional entrenchment workers. Soldiers and followers were mutually dependent. When Peter Hagendorf, an imperial soldier, was wounded during the storming of Magdeburg in 1631, his wife, Anna Stadler, entered the city instead to seize bedding, two silver belts, clothes, and a jug of wine from the burning houses. Absentee wives could also provide support, looking after business affairs as well as families, notably in Switzerland where they assisted their officer husbands by despatching replacement recruits and transferring the profits of the company economy through bills of exchange.[48] Women could also be taken, and Hagendorf, whose wife had meanwhile died, recorded in his diary that 'I got a pretty girl as my booty' after the capture of Landshut in 1634.[49]

These experiences contrasted sharply with the critique of moralists and a growing number of senior officers. One satire in 1621 claimed army women could live free and easy; they did not have to waste time and effort over their appearance, because there were more than enough men in the camp to compete for their favours, and they did not need an expensive wedding, since they could take all they needed from peasants.[50] Retreating armies were frequently forced to stop and fight in order to save their baggage and camp followers during the Thirty Years War, adding arguments of military efficiency to calls to reduce numbers.

Changes to the articles of war from the 1620s initially targeted only unmarried women, who were to be expelled from the camp. The tighter rules made little impact on numbers but did affect legal status. Whereas only a fifth of Bavarian recruits were married, four-fifths of veterans were in the 1640s. The Brandenburg articles from 1656 permitted all soldiers to be accompanied on campaign by their wives, and a significant number still did so in the 1680s (see Fig. 7). The re-establishment of larger forces during the 1660s and 1670s led to further restrictions, because the authorities recognized that soldiers' wages were insufficient to support families and feared these would become a public burden. This also aligned with the general post-Reformation desire to restrict marriages among the poor. Meanwhile, the more permanent presence of garrisons within communities attracted civilian critique. Soldiers were widely regarded as disreputable, dangerous, and associated with sexual offences, illegitimacy, and infanticide: 70 per cent of illegitimate births in Göttingen involved soldiers from the garrison during the early eighteenth century.[51] Officers were placed *in loco parentis* through new regulations issued during the late seventeenth century, requiring soldiers to seek their parents' permission before being allowed to marry. Clergy were forbidden to marry soldiers without such authorization, while officers were also discouraged from accepting recruits who were already married. The proportion of married soldiers in the Prussian army declined from around 70 per cent in 1660 to between a quarter and a third around 1700, with that in other armies being roughly similar.[52]

Medical Care and Welfare

The broader medical context changed significantly during the seventeenth century. The regular cycles of bubonic plague continued into the 1630s, exacerbated by troop movements, with the outbreak in northern Italy in 1630 carried north by the imperial army as it marched to confront the Swedes the following year. However, the northern Mediterranean was largely free after 1651, while the last major occurrence in the Baltic ended in 1713. The decline of the plague made the deadly presence of other diseases more obvious: typhus, typhoid, dysentery, and respiratory illnesses like *sinusitis maxillaris* caused by days of living around damp campfires.[53] Syphilis, known since the mid-1490s, also became firmly associated with soldiers around 1500 when its congenital element was first diagnosed. One in eight of the soldiers' skeletons found on the battlefield of Wittstock show third-stage syphilis. Finally, the development of permanent forces meant that men now endured years of the physical impact of drill, carrying heavy equipment, or countless hours in the saddle. Soldiers were more affected by arthritis to shoulders, elbows, and especially hips and knees, than peasants of equivalent age, and around one in four had serious joint problems.[54]

Military medical knowledge stagnated, but officers were well aware of the need to care for soldiers to reduce campaign losses. The Catholic League issued detailed instructions in February 1620, ahead of its campaign in Bohemia, explicitly citing the example of the costly Long Turkish War as demonstrating the need for improvements.[55] The army also probably drew on the experience of the new St Elizabeth Hospital, established in Munich in 1618. Experienced doctors were appointed, augmented by monks serving as volunteers, and different levels of care were arranged with mobile units accompanying the army for immediate assistance, and a base hospital for longer-term treatment. Each unit also had a few barber surgeons (*Feldscherer*) to offer initial treatment of wounds. The sick and injured were lodged in commandeered buildings, with soldiers detailed from their regiment to look after them and to provide special rations. These measures became standard practice.

Recovery depended greatly on the type of injury or disease, but limited evidence suggests it could be as high as 80 per cent. However, the Catholic League's army was overwhelmed by a virulent outbreak of 'Hungarian fever' that killed around half of its 22,000 men by the end of 1620. The imperial army besieging Belgrade in 1717 had 15 per cent of its strength incapacitated through dysentery in ten weeks, compared to modern refugee camps that rarely have rates above 10 per cent. Faulty understanding of the causes of disease, together with basic failings in camp hygiene, were all significant factors, but logistical failure and the unpredictability of military operations were important too. Units returning from Hungary were usually quarantined to stop the spread of disease, while the growing belief in the 1690s that infection spread through 'bad air' at least prompted some improvements in camp sanitation.

The development of permanent armies from the 1670s ensured there was no return to the pre-1618 phenomenon of the *Garte* ('time without pay'), in which large bodies of unemployed soldiers roamed the countryside between campaigns. Units were now reduced with men paid off over several months, rather than fully disbanded suddenly. Discharged soldiers swelled the numbers of itinerant poor, but armies also recruited from this group, and the frequent recurrence of fresh conflicts enabled the authorities to treat this as a systemic public order problem rather than one requiring special measures.

The lethality of combat and hospital care limited the numbers who survived with disabilities. Disabled and elderly ex-soldiers were treated like other poor and were expected to return to their home communities. The image of the disabled veteran begging was a common genre figure in contemporary art, and the authorities recognized it was not a good advertisement for military service. It reflected badly on the princes who employed them, and it became increasingly common to acknowledge a duty to care for those who had suffered 'for the fatherland', including foreign soldiers 'who have performed loyal and good service and exposed their lives and persons as much as natives'.[56]

From the mid-1670s old or injured soldiers were divided into three categories. Those deemed 'semi-invalids' were sent to garrison companies retained for home defence. The majority of 'full-invalids' were granted small pensions as a form of 'outdoor relief', while a minority were housed in special military hospitals. Funds were raised by introducing pay stoppages, supplemented by occasional windfall endowments. Sweden already had one in the 1640s, but the grand *Invalides* in Paris, opened in 1671, was the primary example, prompting similar, though smaller military hospitals to be opened in Germany, first in Celle (1684), followed by others at Eckernförde (1696), Karlshafen (1711), and Tönning (1712). Attempts to build one in Berlin after 1705 were abandoned in 1713 and it did not open until 1748. Prussia maintained around 2,000 invalids in 1709, or double the number supported in 1688, while Württemberg sustained between 200 and 300.[57] The growth in numbers simply reflected the increased scale of the problem, and there were always far more deserving cases than recipients. Although all were affected by stoppages, there was no universal entitlement and any assistance remained an act of the ruler's grace, while women and orphans generally had to make do with one-off gifts.

AN IRON CENTURY

Human Impact

Contemporaries regarded the seventeenth century as one of hardship and adversity. Few would have agreed with the historiographical convention of 1648 representing a sharp divide between a century and a half of destructive religious wars, followed by a similarly long period of supposedly limited 'cabinet wars'. Rather, the decade or so prior to 1618 was experienced as one of anxiety, and once genuinely destructive conflict followed, people increasingly looked back on the sixteenth century as a golden age of peace and prosperity, compared to the despair and decay they now saw around them.[58] The two decades following 1648 were also ones of unease given the ongoing Franco-Spanish War until 1659 and the permanent Ottoman threat. The resumption of protracted wars after 1672 was widely regarded as another Thirty Years War, and though the human and material damage was less than what was suffered across 1618–48, it was nonetheless severe. The ferocity and high stakes of these later wars have simply not found as clear a place in historical memory as the Thirty Years War.

Most assessments of the impact of war follow a simple 'before-and-after' approach already adopted in the early 1650s when the territorial authorities ordered local communities to take stock of the surviving population, livestock, and buildings. Related to efforts to revise tax registers and boost revenue, the censuses resulted in a certain amount of distortion as communities sought to dodge new obligations by contrasting their current dire straits with pre-war conditions. This led Sigfrid Henry Steinberg, a German émigré in Britain, to argue in an influential essay published shortly after the Second World War that the German population and economy had actually increased during the Thirty Years War.[59] We do need to treat contemporary evidence with caution, since the war provided a convenient excuse for any misfortune or mistake. For example, debts often stemmed from mismanagement, corruption, or profligacy: the Great Elector, Frederick William, often lauded for clear-sightedly developing the Prussian army, nonetheless managed to spend 29,209 tlr on jewellery, tapestries, and silks between 1641 and 1645, equivalent to a year's wages of an infantry regiment.[60] Few now accept Steinberg's view, but modern estimates nonetheless place the total lower than the popular belief, widely held since the 1850s, that the country lost between two-thirds and three-quarters of its inhabitants. The most likely overall decline, crudely measured against the pre-war level, was still staggering at around a fifth of inhabitants.

That figure is horrendous enough. However, it obscures a much more complex picture of spatial, temporal, socio-economic and gendered variations in impact. There was a diagonal swath of destruction running from Württemberg in the southwest through the Palatinate, Thuringia, and Saxony to Pomerania in the northeast, where overall losses were around half, compared to a 27 per cent decline in the Bohemian lands and a 14 per cent increase in Austria.[61] There were further variations within territories, with those parts of Brandenburg along transit routes losing up to 60 per cent of their inhabitants, compared to a fall of only 15–20 per cent in areas further from military operations. Displacement rather than death accounted for a significant proportion of these losses, as people moved to safer areas: refugees accounted for 10 per cent of Zürich's population in 1634.

Some areas were repeatedly affected, whereas others largely escaped destruction, or suffered intensely over relatively short periods. Württemberg was relatively unaffected until 1631 but lost the equivalent of

71 per cent of its pre-war population across the next decade. Wittstock lost a similar proportion through plague in the immediate aftermath of the battle there in 1636. Only five of the 699 deaths recorded in the parish of Elpse in Westphalia between 1622 and 1649 were directly war-related, but many of the others were lives cut short by malnutrition and disease at least exacerbated by war. Overall, there were perhaps 1.7 million military deaths during the Thirty Years War, of whom one in seven were killed in action, and the rest through disease. Most armies lost up to a quarter of their strength annually, though this also included deserters and prisoners.[62]

Soldiers were the most obvious casualties, but social and economic position also affected the likelihood of coming to harm. The rich were often targeted by soldiers, not merely because of their wealth, but as authority figures who could be taken hostage, or mocked, such as town councillors forced to dress in ridiculous costumes and dance to amuse their tormentors. Conversely, the rich could also escape harm by paying bribes. The clergy occupied a similarly ambivalent position, sometimes deliberately targeted, while spared or protected on other occasions. The poor had fewer resources, but also less to lose and so could find it easier to move to a safer area.

Children were sometimes taken hostage to extort ransoms from their families. The climate of fear fuelled witchcraft accusations, which peaked with the war's mid-point and primarily claimed female victims. Contemporary accounts highlight women's suffering, partly to convey a sense of horror and of violence escaping legitimate bounds, but also reflecting real injuries. There is ample evidence of rape, especially following the capture of cities that refused offers to surrender but, like other violence, this was primarily situational rather than being used as a deliberate tactic as in some twentieth-century wars. Women also resisted, such as the nuns of one Bamberg convent who drove marauders from their church.[63]

The resumption of prolonged warfare after 1672 slowed the demographic and economic recovery, and the Empire did not return to its 1618 population levels until around a century later. The Rhineland was especially hard hit during the Nine Years War, suffering a fall in population of up to 40 per cent. That conflict accelerated Protestant emigration from the Palatinate, which had already begun with official efforts to re-Catholicize the territory in 1685, and around 7,000 fled to Brandenburg and another 9,000 to Pennsylvania. However, about 5,000 Protestant Waldensians, displaced from conflict in Savoy, settled in Baden and Württemberg. The impact along the Upper Rhine after 1688 was worse than that during the Thirty Years War, because French forces systematically destroyed Heidelberg, Mannheim, and other towns, some of which only recovered their pre-war population levels in the nineteenth century. Further damage followed across 1701–14, but on a reduced scale. Military losses continued to be heavy. Units serving in Hungary and Greece during the 1680s and 1690s commonly lost 30–60 per cent of strength in a single campaign, while even in western Europe losses could be high. The Habsburg army inducted 280,000 recruits during the War of the Spanish Succession, meaning it replaced its initial strength twice over in fourteen years.[64]

War Finance

Most governments entered the Thirty Years War heavily indebted, with Bavaria exceptional in holding 891,000 fl in cash reserves. No one foresaw a conflict on that scale or duration, and governments employed the methods already developed across the previous century by attempting to meet initial expenses from taxation while accumulating more debt to be cleared at their enemies' expense or subsequently amortized through new agreements with their territorial or provincial Estates. This approach immediately ran into difficulties, because the conflict's character as an imperial civil war made it much more contentious than the previous struggles against the Ottomans or French. The emperor refrained from requesting aid through the Reichstag before 1641, while the opposition of many of his own subjects made it difficult to raise funds there either.

War cost far more than any other activity. Maintaining 100 cavalrymen for a month required 2,800 fl, compared to the annual cost of the newly founded university of Salzburg at 3,600 fl.[65] The imperial army cost around 4 million fl in 1619, tripling by 1625 and rising to 18 million fl for 1630. Incomplete official figures put the total cost at between 100 to 120 million fl, or about double what Bavaria and the League admitted. Both these figures are underestimates. Faced with spiralling costs, all belligerents swiftly resorted to expedients, of which coinage debasement in 1621–2 was the most disastrously counterproductive, causing brief hyperinflation before action through the Kreise brought this under control. The emperor, Bavaria, and their Bohemian and Palatine opponents all received foreign subsidies that proved important in enabling them to raise armies across 1618–20, but not to sustain them thereafter. France subsequently provided over 9 million tlr in aid to Sweden and its German allies, while Spanish and papal subsidies to the emperor and the Catholic League totalled 15.8 million tlr. The money eased cashflow but covered no more than 3 per cent of total costs across the war. Imperial victories by 1629 finally emboldened the emperor to decree war taxes across the Empire in consultation with the electors in 1630. These were renewed and supplemented by further measures agreed through some of the Kreis assemblies.[66]

However, none of these measures covered costs, and armies had already resorted to levying contributions from enemy and neutral territories within the first year of the conflict. 'Contributions' are most closely associated with Wallenstein. Although he did not invent the method, he employed it more systematically and ambitiously. Arrangements varied considerably depending on circumstances, but essentially forced communities to assume responsibility for sustaining parts of the army directly. In most cases, existing taxes were simply diverted at much higher rates from the territory's own treasury and paid to officers. A substantial proportion was paid in kind, both to sustain troops and to stockpile supplies for forthcoming operations. The imperial army had 2.6 million loaves of bread stacked in Passau in June 1634, enough to feed 34,000 men for twenty-two weeks.

Despite contemporary hopes, war did not 'feed itself'.[67] The policy of confiscations was both fundamental to sustaining the war and politically far more significant than contributions. The value of the property seized from the defeated Bohemian rebels in 1621 was 21 million fl, or equivalent to half the total raised in taxation across the entire Habsburg monarchy between 1618 and 1640. Another 13.73 million fl were seized from Wallenstein and his three closest associates after their murders in 1634. The Palatinate was transferred to Bavaria in 1628 in lieu of 13 million fl in war expenses claimed from the emperor. A similar deal, worth 5.9 million fl, occurred with the cession of Lusatia to Saxony in 1635. The bulk of Sweden's German troops were financed by transferring captured property to their officers during the 1630s.

The war left all belligerents even more indebted. Saxony already relied on borrowing for 40 per cent of its revenue in 1618 and was effectively bankrupt by 1624. Defeat and prolonged occupation pushed debts to over 25 million fl by 1657, despite another 10 million fl of interest arrears having been written off. Action through the Reichstag in 1654 eased the burden of debt without collapsing the credit market.[68] However, there was no peace dividend, because rulers refused to abandon many of the emergency wartime taxes and employed the language of necessity to justify this. The same Reichstag meeting also saw new legislation requiring territorial Estates to fund 'necessary fortresses and garrisons' required for defence. A small group of princes lobbied to extend this into the right to determine the level of military taxes, leaving the Estates only with the right to discuss how the required sums might be raised. Their efforts were eventually blocked by an imperial veto in 1670, stabilizing ruler–Estate relations and permitting the imperial supreme courts to continue intervening in territorial affairs to adjudicate disputes. Nonetheless, there was now no return to the previous situation where military expenses were 'extraordinary' and these were now permanent budget items.

Brandenburg-Prussia, Münster, and several other principalities used force to compel their Estates to accept higher taxes. Coercion became much more difficult after 1670 and several princes, including the duke of Mecklenburg, were deposed by the imperial courts during the eighteenth century for using force. The Great Elector persuaded his Estates to agree new excise taxes, enabling them to tap into economic growth. Far from representing a 'Historic Compromise' whereby the nobles allegedly surrendered influence over policy in return for greater control over their serfs, the agreements from the 1650s locked the Hohenzollerns into arrangements that proved hard to adapt to later circumstances. Brandenburg-Prussia continued to rely disproportionately on domains' revenue relative both to the rest of the Empire and to other European powers.[69]

The Habsburgs worked well with their Estates after restructuring their membership during the 1620s, replacing their opponents with loyalists who owed their wealth and status to the dynasty. While relations deteriorated in Hungary from the 1670s, the other provincial assemblies played an important part in sustaining Habsburg finances through the prolonged warfare across 1663–1718. The dynasty continued to rely heavily on credit, notably from Samuel Oppenheimer, who advanced cash and supplies worth 30 million fl from 1695 until his death in 1703, which brought the monarchy almost to the brink of bankruptcy. Administrative and financial reforms followed, including efforts to foster a more diverse banking sector.[70] Contributions remained important in wartime, but these were regulated more closely by imperial legislation that allowed the affected territories to offset aid given directly to troops fighting enemies of the Empire against imperial war tax demands. Actual costs usually exceeded what was refunded, meaning a considerable proportion of the cost of maintaining troops still fell on local communities.

The cost of the Bavarian army rose sevenfold between 1664 and 1683, faster than increased taxes voted by the Estates and other revenues. Most middling and larger German principalities were maintaining larger armies than they could afford by the 1680s and renting regiments out as auxiliaries had already become crucial to sustaining these forces a decade earlier. Foreign payments at best covered costs, and several princes knowingly entered financially disadvantageous agreements, regarding the potential political benefits as making them worthwhile. The total cost of the Empire's military effort during the War of the Spanish Succession was around 650 million fl, of which about 90 million fl was covered by Anglo-Dutch subsidies and direct payments to auxiliaries, and around 36 million fl in loans, while the rest was met domestically.[71]

Switzerland's experience was a sharp contrast, because the only permanent troops were the regiments in foreign service, while the cantons relied on their militias for home defence. Bern was obliged to borrow from England to cover its expenses during the brief conflict with its Catholic neighbours in 1656, but had accumulated such a large surplus that it could meet the entire cost of 437,500 tlr of the Toggenburg War in 1712 from cash reserves while also investing in British war debt floated on the London Stock Exchange.[72]

Economic Impact

War sucked money from the economy through taxation and extortion, and while much of it trickled back, its beneficial effects were uneven and blunted by the high levels of physical destruction. This was worst during the Thirty Years War, because the partial collapse of public administration combined with the climate of fear to produce despair at the seemingly unending violence. Most communities coped well enough with their initial encounters with troops, but the urgency of military demands encouraged rapacious and wasteful practices that destroyed valuable resources. The counts of Hohenlohe normally shot five animals a year in their game reserve, but imperial officers killed 232 in 1635 alone.[73] Repeated encounters demoralized inhabitants, who no longer repaired fences, ditches, dykes, or barns and were forced to consume precious seed corn or their remaining livestock. Many princes and lords fled early on to safe havens, such as the city of Cologne, leaving their affairs in the hands of administrators and stewards who often felt overwhelmed. The redistributive policies employed by the main belligerents meant some areas changed master several times in rapid succession. Personnel also changed and records were lost. As the population of the worst-affected areas dwindled, the rodent population exploded, further reducing food supplies, and accelerating the vicious cycle of decline and decay.[74]

The Empire was already affected by the general reorientation of trade towards northwest Europe and some economic sectors and regions were already in decline. However, some trades coped better than others, with, for example, beer brewing displacing viticulture across much of the southwest. A few made fortunes: the Swedish general Banér and his Bavarian counterpart Aldringen were both said to have around 1 million tlr deposited in foreign banks at their deaths. There was still horded wealth at the end of the war when the Swedes captured plunder worth a total of around 8 million fl from Bregenz (1647) and Prague (1648) alone.

Since the less fertile land was abandoned first, overall agricultural productivity declined less than total land use as the population contracted and people moved away. Land prices plummeted by up to three-quarters and benefited those survivors still with modest means. Governments offered tax breaks and began various programmes intended to stimulate the economy and boost tax revenues. Known broadly as 'cameralism', many of these measures proved counterproductive, but they nonetheless rationalized the princely state that emerged strengthened, with a greater capacity to influence the previously largely self-governing small towns and villages in which the bulk of the population still lived.

Amsterdam became the centre of Europe's arms trade between 1580 and 1620 at a time when that city effectively left the Empire through the independence of the new Dutch Republic. The prince-bishopric of Liège had already developed after 1492 as Europe's principal producer of small arms, retaining that status into the nineteenth century. German armies bought weaponry from both these suppliers, but the Empire was also a major arms exporter. Nuremberg and Ulm were major metalworking centres in the late fifteenth century and continued to produce armour into the seventeenth century. Both also made cannon, as did several other imperial cities, and south German arms production was sustained during the later sixteenth century by the high demand for weapons along the Habsburg Military Frontier.[75] Nuremberg produced between 15,000 and 30,000 small arms annually during the Thirty Years War, selling to both sides despite its nominal adherence to the pro-Swedish party. Its guns were stamped with an 'N' to indicate their good provenance.

However, the city was already being overtaken by Suhl in the county of Henneberg in Thuringia, which supplied 19,500 handgun barrels annually from the 1570s. Production remained decentralized in small workshops organized through craft guilds, but the concentration of expertise and specialized plant gave some economies of scale, while specialization enhanced the town's reputation and its guns were stamped 'SVL', an abbreviation of its name, as a sign of quality. Solingen near Düsseldorf acquired equivalent fame as a producer of blade weapons. Other, secondary gunmaking centres included Zelle (Thuringia), Essen, and Aachen. All these locations were imperial cities or in areas beyond the immediate control of powerful princes, enabling them to operate more freely. Suhl's freedom ended abruptly when it was ransacked by imperial troops in 1634, but production resumed within five years and by 1645 imperial orders totalled at least 36,000 muskets, plus other firearms. The Habsburgs established their own arms production centre at Steyr (a town with a long future in this field) in 1639 to free dependency on imports, but in practice they and the other princes continued to buy from multiple suppliers across the next two centuries, because most lacked the capacity to meet such large orders at short notice.

The Thirty Years War caused a surge in demand for munitions, with the imperial army alone requiring 5,000 cwt annually by the 1620s, or around forty times pre-war consumption. Gunpowder production relied on saltpetre imports from Poland, but these were disrupted by the Swedish blockades of Danzig from 1618 to 1629 and 1632 to 1634. An alternative was found by importing Indian saltpetre through Amsterdam after 1621, and India remained the mainstay of European explosives production until the introduction of Chilean nitrates in the 1830s.[76]

War in no way paid for itself, but instead weighed heavily on the population throughout the seventeenth century, reflecting the increased scale and duration of conflict and the emergence of permanent armies. Although the Empire had been a battleground during the Thirty Years War, this reflected that struggle's character as an imperial civil war. Subsequently, it managed to reform its system of collective security and defend itself during the long wars with France and the Ottoman Empire. That system would be severely tested again across the eighteenth century, which saw the emergence of Prussia as a second German great power alongside Austria. As the following three chapters will show, Prussia's challenge ultimately destabilized the Empire at the point when it faced an existential threat from France in the 1790s. Changes in organization, equipment, and tactical doctrine were modest after 1714, though all German armies were forced to adapt after 1792, chiefly through reforming their recruitment methods. Eighteenth-century conflicts would also prove burdensome, in no way corresponding to the cliché of 'limited wars'.

PART III

Professionalizing War

7

Habsburgs and Hohenzollerns

AUSTRIA OVERSTRETCHED, 1714–39

Inner German Rivalry in a European Context

The decision of the German princes to remain armed in 1714 after four decades of nearly continuous warfare contrasted with the rapid demobilization after the Thirty Years War. The possibility of war was now accepted as permanent, and it had become a sign of state power to be fully prepared to fight when necessary. Even the Empire's minor counties and cities maintained permanent cadres of regular troops in peacetime, both to be ready to provide their imperial contingents when required and as a symbol of their political autonomy. Only the Swiss continued to regard their traditional militia as their primary means of defence.

The two decades of relative peace after 1714 saw the consolidation of methods of military organization, recruitment, training, and funding that had been established since the 1670s. Soldiering had become a career, albeit a generally poorly paid one, and armies were now an accepted part of society. Training, career structures, pensions, and other arrangements became increasingly professional in the modern sense of adhering to a common set of standards, conduct, and practices. In turn, these were subject to tighter state regulation and supervision, and operated through formalized written culture rather than autonomous custom and ad hoc practices. Although adjusted in the wake of defeat and the Holy Roman Empire's collapse in 1806, the basic structures coalescing around 1714 endured well into the nineteenth century.

While military institutions changed comparatively little across the eighteenth century, the political balance within the Empire was irrevocably altered by the emergence of open Austro-Prussian rivalry in 1740, establishing the Hohenzollern monarchy as a second great power along-side the Habsburgs. As Prussia pulled ahead, the other electorates and middling principalities sank into the mass of minor territories as a 'Third Germany', outclassed militarily and politically by the two great powers whose policies increasingly determined the Empire's fate. The inter-nationalization of both imperial and Swiss politics proceeded apace, with the fate of both states becoming more dependent on the broader balance across Europe and the attitude of the continent's leading powers. While Switzerland had no realistic chance of being able to defend itself, the Empire might have averted its demise had Austria and Prussia cooperated to save it rather than save their own interests. Cast adrift, most of the middling princes threw in their lot with Napoleon, finally giving the Third Germany its own shape as an independent Confederation after 1806. Although this proved short-lived, the political changes it entailed made it impossible to restore the Empire once Napoleon had been de-feated, and Germany continued to be dominated by the unstable balance between its two leading powers into the 1860s.

The custom of reading German history through Prussia's story often reduces the eighteenth century to a teleology with the Hohenzollerns inevitably supplanting the Habsburgs as the leading power. In fact, des-pite its repeated setbacks after 1733, Austria remained the dominant power, consistently displaying far greater resilience than Prussia, which repeatedly only narrowly escaped catastrophic defeat and temporarily slipped into the ranks of Europe's second-rank states across 1806–13.

Prussia did not feature prominently among Austria's security con-cerns in the twenty-five years after 1714 and Frederick William I's efforts to expand his influence in the Empire were easily blocked.[1] Instead, Austria's priorities shifted from protecting the Rhine and Hun-gary to combating threats to its newly acquired possessions in the Netherlands and Italy, as well as dealing with Russia's growing influ-ence in the Baltic, Poland, and the Balkans. Emperor Charles VI continued the practice, established before 1714, of relying on the imper-ial Estates and Austria's allies to assume much of the burden, thereby keeping a large part of his own forces free to pursue his own objectives. However, the changed circumstance made this more difficult. Anglo-Dutch cooperation was weaker as the now-bankrupt Republic strove to remain neutral, while Britain periodically sought better relations with France into the 1730s. The Austro-Dutch Barrier Treaty from 1715 to defend the newly acquired Southern Netherlands served the Republic's interests more than the emperor's, while existing agreements prevented the Habsburgs from reviving Antwerp as a major commercial centre of a kind that would have made owning the new provinces worthwhile.[2]

Charles was further compromised by his desire to secure international guarantees for a change in Habsburg inheritance law in 1713. Known as the Pragmatic Sanction, this permitted succession in the female as well as the male line to the Habsburg hereditary lands and became more pressing after 1717 when Charles's sole heir was his daughter, Maria Theresa.[3] Prince Eugene famously declared that a full treasury and a strong army would be better guarantees than international treaties. However, the past four decades had taught that Austria required allies if faced by a major war, and the deficiencies in Habsburg finances and military forces derived from its numerous commitments rather than any naïve faith in the efficacy of written agreements. Charles's efforts appeared successful and by 1732 the Pragmatic Sanction had been accepted by the Reichstag and all major powers.

Meanwhile, Charles was assisted by the general adherence to constitutional norms within the Empire that deterred the resort to violence to settle disputes. Unilateral attempts to use force against neighbours drew immediate censure from imperial institutions and caused significant reputational damage, as Hessen-Kassel discovered when it invaded Schaumburg-Lippe in 1787.[4] Imperial Estates complied with court orders to send troops to enforce verdicts and to maintain order, and a similar system of collective internal security operated in Switzerland where cantonal authorities could call on their neighbours' militia for assistance. Of course, such public service was often abused by the powerful to extend their influence, notably Prussia, which occupied much of Mecklenburg-Schwerin between 1733 and 1755. Nonetheless, imperial politics were so complex that the patterns of local and regional rivalries tended to check any substantial shifts in power and, overall, these activities stabilized the Empire and its conservative socio-economic order, though not always with positive results for its inhabitants.[5]

The six western and southern Kreise renewed their Association in 1714, ensuring a minimum level of defence along the Rhine. The instability of international relations into the 1730s complicated the emperor's management of the armed princes, because the lack of Anglo-Dutch support weakened his hand in competition with French and Spanish efforts to recruit German allies. The Wittelsbach principalities of Bavaria and the Palatinate proved the most difficult as, having settled their own rivalries, they generally sided with France, hoping it would support their own claims in due time to the Austrian succession.[6]

Turkish and Mediterranean Wars, 1716–20

Initially, Charles's efforts were crowned with success as he mastered threats to the east and south. Venice had been at war with the Ottomans since 1714, but it was losing ground, despite recruiting 8,000 Germans, who represented a quarter of its army.[7] Austria intervened to support Venice in 1716, but deliberately made no arrangements with Russia or Poland to deny them influence. The subsequent conflict demonstrated Austria's changed relationship to the Empire, since its earlier victories over the Turks had made them a much more distant threat for the German princes. The lingering sense of unavoidable duty prompted the Reichstag to vote financial assistance, but no Kreis contingents were sent. Nonetheless, several armed princes saw an opportunity to court Habsburg favour and reduce their own military costs by hiring out parts of their armies.

In all, Austria obtained 25,500 auxiliaries, including a substantial Bavarian contingent sent in 1717 to demonstrate the elector's temporarily renewed loyalty after his opposition over the Spanish Succession. Prince Eugene of Savoy mustered around 80,000 men in the main army, with a further 40,000 protecting Transylvania. Having defeated an Ottoman offensive at Peterwardein in August 1716, he swiftly overran the Banat region and a third of Wallachia, thereby eliminating the Ottoman salient between Hungary and Transylvania. Eugene pushed on during 1717 to besiege Belgrade, which had been lost in 1690, only to be trapped by a large Ottoman relief army. Running low on supplies, he counter-attacked on 16 August, turning imminent disaster into a stunning victory, and forcing the fortress to surrender.

Spain had meanwhile taken advantage of Habsburg distractions to invade first Austrian-ruled Sardinia in August 1717 and then Sicily in June 1718, seeking to recover its former Mediterranean lands. Faced with this new threat, Charles quickly settled with the sultan at Passarowitz in July 1718. The Ottomans accepted the loss of the Banat, Belgrade, and two-thirds of Serbia, but retained the Morea (southern Greece) they had reconquered from Venice. Meanwhile, Charles confirmed Hanover's gains in northern Germany at Sweden's expense in return for British-Hanoverian naval support against Spain. Sardinia and Sicily were recovered after bitter fighting, which concluded in 1720 with a settlement favourable to Austria.

The War of the Polish Succession, 1733–5

Austria became increasingly isolated during the 1720s, prompting Charles to forge a defensive alliance with Russia in August 1726. The new balance between the two powers was expressed by Charles's reluctant recognition of Russia's status as an 'empire', though he claimed his own Holy Roman imperial title remained superior. Austria was satisfied with its recent gains from the Ottomans and had no desire to see the sultan weakened further, particularly as the newly conquered lands cost more to defend than they produced in revenue. However, the lack of Anglo-Dutch support after 1720 reduced Austria's leverage with its new ally.[8]

The difficulties became obvious following the death of Augustus 'the Strong', the Saxon king of Poland, in February 1733. Austria and Russia swiftly agreed to back the elector's son as his successor against the former king, Stanislas Leszczyński, who was endorsed by France and received limited support from the Polish nobility. However, Austria wished to avoid war, whereas Russia moved to block French military assistance reaching Stanislas through Danzig in September, because it wanted to settle matters in Poland quickly to be free to pursue its own further expansion in the Balkans.

France escalated the conflict, attacking the Upper Rhine in October in alliance with Spain, which renewed its efforts to conquer Austria's possessions in Italy. By deliberately avoiding aggression against the Austrian Netherlands, France ensured there was no reactivation of the Grand Alliance, and Britain and the Dutch Republic remained neutral. The Kreis Association summoned its members to provide a triple contingent on 9 November, ahead of this being decreed for the entire Empire when the Reichstag formally declared war on France on 9 April 1734. The Kreis troops totalled 34,000, while Austria obtained another 54,000 auxiliaries by calling in favours from the armed princes, including Prussia, which sent 10,200. Although these failed to prevent the loss of both Kehl and Philippsburg to the French, the front had stabilized by the beginning of 1735 when the imperial army was able to assume a modest offensive.

German support enabled Charles to deploy the bulk of his own army to Italy, where it was comprehensively defeated by Franco-Spanish forces. Russia belatedly honoured its commitments and sent 13,000 men, who arrived in southern Germany in August 1735 in time to influence the peace negotiations.[9] A preliminary settlement was reached in October whereby the Saxon candidate was recognized as the Polish king with Stanislas compensated with the duchy of Lorraine. The latter was reluctantly relinquished by its duke, Francis Stephen, who was mollified by his marriage to Charles's daughter Maria Theresa and eventual succession to the duchy of Tuscany, which was an imperial fief and became vacant with the extinction of the Medici family in 1737. Meanwhile, Austria ceded Naples and Sicily to a separate junior branch of the Spanish Bourbons. The agreement was one of the most complex of the eighteenth century, a period not short of intricate treaties, and it took until May 1739 before it had been ratified and fully implemented.

The Turkish War, 1735–9

The outbreak of a new Turkish War added urgency to Austria's peacemaking, since Russia insisted Charles support its ambitions to conquer the Crimea. Pressure mounted after Russia's initial campaign failed disastrously in 1735. The emperor resolved on a single campaign in 1736 as being all he could afford, but continuing financial and military problems delayed this until July the following year.[10] Once committed, he found it difficult to escape from what became another war of attrition.

The conflict reinforced the trend apparent since 1716 that the Empire now saw its duties as limited to defending the Rhine and regarded the east as Austria's responsibility. The Reichstag renewed its limited financial aid, but again no Kreis contingents were sent. The Habsburg army was 22 per cent below strength, and troops had to be left in the west as peace there was not yet formalized. Only 62,550 could be deployed in Hungary where they were joined by 28,000 hired auxiliaries. The Ottoman army had improved since 1718, whereas Austria's had not, and its generals mishandled the campaigns. Coordination with Russia was poor, while the Austrian generals quarrelled as their rivalries were fuelled by the growing uncertainty over the Habsburg succession.[11] A series of defeats culminated in the loss of Belgrade, forcing Charles to accept a French-brokered peace on 1 September 1739, ceding Serbia, but at least retaining the Banat from the earlier gains.

The accumulative impact of the wars since 1733 was to exhaust Austria's financial and political credit, leaving it acutely vulnerable when Charles VI died on 20 October 1740, aged fifty-five. The crisis far exceeded that of the last imperial interregnum in 1657–8, since the succession to the Habsburgs' hereditary lands was now at stake along with the imperial title. Austria's prospect of the latter was now much reduced since, as a woman, Maria Theresa could not compete herself, and her new husband lacked the centuries of ingrained loyalty that had secured the electors' support in the past.

IMPERIAL CIVIL WARS, 1740–63

Prussia's Seizure of Silesia

This volatile situation was ruthlessly exploited by Frederick II ('the Great'), Prussia's new king, who succeeded his father on 31 May 1740. To that point, Prussia had remained largely an unknown quantity. The military build-up under Frederick William I since 1713 was acknowledged, but the enlarged army had not seen combat since the siege of Stralsund in 1715 and though the contingent on the Rhine in 1734 looked impressive, many doubted whether they were much more than parade ground troops.

Frederick's unprovoked invasion of the Habsburg province of Silesia has remained controversial. Older accounts cited Prussia's 'historic mission' as necessitating this flagrant violation of the Empire's public peace; the Empire was dismissed as an irrelevant medieval relic, and with Austria allegedly incapable of uniting Germany, Prussia bravely assumed that responsibility. While shorn of this nationalist gloss, more recent accounts nonetheless retain the emphasis on the ruthless use of military might with Prussia's victory largely assumed as inevitable.[12]

The presentation of Frederick as the archetypal German militarist is doubly ironic, given that he took his cultural and military cues from France. Frederick had read the draft of Voltaire's *Age of Louis XIV* in the 1730s (published 1751) as well as his *History of Charles XII* (published 1731), the Swedish monarch who served as an additional warrior-king role model. Voltaire also cooperated in Frederick's *History of the House of Brandenburg*, which likewise voiced the view that 'great men' made their own success.[13] Frederick had learned the French way of war from books and was now determined to outshine the Sun King. The strike on Silesia emulated Louis XIV, who began all his wars across 1667–88 with premeditated aggression, but whereas the French king's generals had become bogged down besieging fortresses, Frederick believed he could avoid this by invading rapidly with overwhelming force.

Frederick was interested in long-established Hohenzollern goals, such as obtaining the other half of Pomerania and the full Jülich-Cleves inheritance, but these were not as central to his thinking as they had been to the previous three Prussian rulers, all of whom had remained conventional in only pursuing objectives to which they had a legitimate claim. Frederick thought both more strategically and opportunistically. He had no claim to anything beyond a tiny part of Silesia, but Austria's crisis offered a chance to seize one of its richest provinces, the possession of which would increase Prussia's territory by a third and its population by a half. These material calculations feature more prominently in the writings of nationalist historians than they did in Frederick's own mind, which was filled with visions of everlasting glory. Silesia was the only part of Austria's territory he could attack directly, and he had already resumed his father's programme of expanding the army by securing the services of the troops raised by German princes for Charles, troops who had now been returned, largely unpaid.

The wider circumstances seemed favourable. The death of Russian Empress Anna a week after that of Charles led to a period of instability prolonged by war with Sweden between 1741 and 1743, partly engineered by French diplomacy to keep Russia occupied. Meanwhile, Britain was already embroiled in a colonial struggle with Spain, while the Dutch had no desire for a fresh war. With Charles's death, Frederick knew he must act quickly, especially to forestall Saxony which had a better dynastic claim to Habsburg territory and coveted Silesia as a land bridge between the electorate and Poland. If Saxony took Silesia, it would increase its authority in Poland and create a powerful combined state capable of restricting Prussia to the Baltic coast.

Already on 29 October, Frederick resolved to attack, but he never articulated a long-term plan. Instead, he gambled on a bold stroke to achieve an initial advantage that would enable him to bargain for part of

Silesia in return for his support against Maria Theresa's other enemies, or at least neutrality. A large corps was posted on the Hanoverian frontier to deter intervention while 27,000 men were swiftly assembled to invade Silesia, which was defended by only 7,000 Austrians. The Prussians crossed the frontier on 16 December announcing they were coming to protect Maria Theresa's inheritance. The attack opened what became the War of the Austrian Succession, with Prussia's two interventions also known as the First (1740–2) and Second (1744–5) Silesian Wars.[14] The province was soon overrun but the Prussians found themselves stuck like Louis XIV's armies in front of the fortresses, which continued to resist.

A relief force was hastily assembled under Marshal Neipperg, who crossed the mountains to trap Frederick in the south of Silesia, obliging the king to attempt a breakout. The two armies clashed at Mollwitz on 10 April 1741. Steeped in history, Frederick had gone to war intending to emulate the 'hero-kings' he had read about. Like Alexander the Great, he posted himself at the head of his bodyguard on the right wing, instead of remaining behind the centre where he might have had some chance of directing events. The opening stages went well for Neipperg, who routed the Prussian cavalry. Entrusting his remaining troops to the experienced Marshal Schwerin, Frederick abandoned the field, narrowly escaping capture as he did so. The disciplined Prussian infantry proved they were more than show troops, eventually breaking their Austrian opponents, many of whom were poorly trained new recruits.

Neipperg's failure to achieve another Mühlberg or White Mountain emboldened France, Spain, Bavaria, and Saxony to join Prussia in a coalition by June. Maria Theresa offered parts of the Netherlands to Prussia if Frederick would return Silesia and vote for her husband as emperor. Other concessions were offered to France and Bavaria, but all were rebuffed in the expectation of making better gains by using force. Bavaria overran most of Bohemia where its elector was proclaimed king. Austria's prospects appeared much worse than they had in 1619, and the Bavarian elector was chosen as Emperor Charles VII in January 1742. Hanover reluctantly fell in line with the other electors, though Britain financed an army to protect the Austrian Netherlands against France.[15]

Charles's election was a major blow to the Habsburgs, who had held the imperial title continuously since 1438. Maria Theresa and her ministers regarded the imperial Estates' failure to support them as a betrayal, and the episode fundamentally changed Austrian attitudes to the Empire.

Habsburg forces were officially styled as 'Royal Hungarian', reflecting not only Maria Theresa's most prestigious remaining title but also the one part of her possessions no one else claimed.

Bavarian imperial rule was a boon to Frederick II, who used Charles's weakness to force him to enhance Prussia's autonomy within the Empire by removing many of its legal and ceremonial restrictions. Frederick did not, however, seek Prussia's independence and continued to rely on his constitutional rights and privileges to influence imperial politics.[16] Charles offered further concessions to win military support against Austria from the armed princes. Although only Hessen-Kassel and the Palatinate provided troops, even rumours of the proposed changes were enough to alarm the smaller imperial Estates at whose expense they would be made, and contributed to the lasting erosion of imperial power and prestige wrought by the war.

Maria Theresa was fortunate that the Ottomans were distracted by their other problems, thereby permitting her to concentrate on fighting her western foes. Her famous emotional appeal to the Hungarian nobility in September 1741 solicited 30,000 additional troops, mainly hussars who improved Austria's ability to interdict enemy supplies and hinder their operations. Counter-offensives temporarily overran Bavaria but proved unable to dislodge the Prussians, and Maria Theresa reluctantly accepted a British-brokered peace on 28 July 1742, ceding most of Silesia, plus the county of Glatz in the mountains, which strengthened Prussia's hold on the province.

The settlement established a strategic situation lasting until 1866. Prussia's territory now extended southeastwards, flanking Moravia, and pushing to the mountain nexus linking the three core Habsburg possessions of Austria, Bohemia, and Hungary. Silesia was long and narrow, with only a limited number of passes over the mountains into Habsburg territory. Prussia had the benefit of interior lines, but Silesia's shape prevented defence in depth should the Austrians break in. Saxony remained as a buffer between the core Hohenzollern province of Brandenburg and the Ore Mountains along Bohemia's northern frontier. If Saxony cooperated or was occupied, Prussia could access additional routes into Bohemia, but only at the cost of handing the benefit of interior lines to its opponent, since its own forces would now be stretched in a much longer arc on the northern and eastern side of the mountain ranges.[17]

The War of the Austrian Succession

Having obtained his prize, Frederick abandoned his allies and retreated into neutrality. Britain used its influence to restructure its alliance with Austria. In return for increasing its financial and military support, it forced Maria Theresa to cede a slice of Lombardy to Savoy-Piedmont, to add it as an ally against the French and Spanish in Italy. While the Savoyards helped Austria defend its remaining Italian possessions, all efforts to reconquer those lost in 1735 proved futile. The concession to Savoy meanwhile gave that state a firmer footing east of the Alps and was another step in the process by which its ruling house emerged as a serious challenger to Austria's influence in Italy a century later.

The overall improvement in Austria's position across 1743–4 prompted Frederick to re-enter the war in the summer of 1744, ostensibly in support of Charles VII and France, but really to forestall any Austrian attempt to reconquer Silesia. Invading Bohemia with 80,000 men, Frederick took Prague but was forced into a costly retreat when Austrian light troops cut his supply lines. He then fought a brilliant campaign to defeat a combined Austro-Saxon invasion of Silesia in 1745, with his victories at Soor and Hohenfriedberg demonstrating his maturity as a battlefield commander. Austria conceded again and renewed its recognition of Prussia's possession of Silesia.

Charles VII's early death amid a renewed Austrian invasion of his homeland in January 1745 abruptly ended Bavaria's dreams of greatness. The electors chose Maria Theresa's husband as Emperor Francis I, restoring Austria's possession of the imperial title. While this remained crucial to Habsburg prestige and the family's self-consciousness as *imperial*, their relationship to the Empire had grown more distant. This was symbolized by the designation of Habsburg forces as 'imperial royal' (*kaiserliche-königlich* abbreviated with the German initials k.k.). More fundamentally, the new relationship was expressed through the dualism in Habsburg government as Maria Theresa retained the final word in domestic matters and foreign policy, leaving her husband with only a limited role.[18] The dualism continued after Francis's death in August 1765 as his son and successor as emperor, Joseph II, continued to have to defer to his mother on key policy issues until her death in November 1780. By that point, relations with the Empire were already being treated more as if it were a separate state.

The smaller territories had collaborated through the Kreis structure since 1744 to maintain armed neutrality and likewise refused Austria's calls for aid against Prussia or France. Anglo-Dutch money secured the assistance of the previously hostile Bavarian and Hessen-Kassel troops, though some of the latter were sent to Britain to confront the Jacobites in 1745–6.[19] The main focus of the wider conflict shifted after 1744 to the Austrian Netherlands, which the French had conquered by 1747. Mounting reverses prompted Austria to renew its alliance with Russia, which despatched 37,000 troops, paid for by Britain and the Dutch. As with the force sent in 1735, their arrival in Franconia in 1748 was too late for the war but added to the pressure of other events on France to make peace.

A series of treaties was concluded in Aachen between April and November 1748. Although Austria recovered the Netherlands, the war had exposed that province's vulnerability and the inability of the Dutch to defend it. The outcome influenced Joseph II's plans to exchange it for Bavaria to reduce Austria's liabilities and rebalance the Habsburg monarchy as a more 'German' and compact state. The wider settlement confirmed Austria's loss of Silesia and part of the duchy of Milan, as well as adjusting the balance in colonial possessions among the western European belligerents.

Frederick was the clear victor, but his success had depended greatly on the wider circumstances of the War of the Austrian Succession diverting Habsburg resources elsewhere. He used the following decade to integrate Silesia within his monarchy, though his ability to exploit this new province was hindered by his belief that the largely Catholic population was inherently unreliable. With Bavaria clearly broken, France upgraded to a Prussian alliance, cooperating diplomatically to block Habsburg efforts to rebuild their influence in the Empire.[20] Meanwhile, the relative balance between the two German powers was partially restored by Austria's reform programme, which redressed many of the administrative and financial deficiencies that had undermined its military performance since 1733.

The Seven Years War

Austria's priority remained the recovery of Silesia, not merely as a valuable province, but because its loss had severely damaged the Habsburgs' standing in the Empire and Europe more widely. The new Austrian chief minister, Count Kaunitz, recognized that Britain and the Dutch would not support this goal, and took the bold step of inviting France, Sweden, and Russia to join Austria. The Hohenzollern monarchy was to be reduced to the electorate of Brandenburg, with Austria recovering Silesia and Russia and Sweden taking East Prussia and Pomerania respectively. France proved receptive as it was embroiled in a renewed colonial and trade war with Britain after 1754 and wanted to strike at its associated possession of Hanover in retaliation. Anticipating this, Britain had already signed a defence pact with Prussia to secure its support in the event of a French move against Hanover. Already distrustful of the wily Frederick, France interpreted this as a betrayal of the Franco-Prussian alliance and accordingly accepted Kaunitz's offer, allying with Austria and thus completing the famous 'reversal of alliances' in 1756, which finally broke the Old System dominating European relations since 1688.[21]

Diplomacy outpaced Austria's military preparations. Aware of the forces gathering against him, Frederick launched a pre-emptive strike in August 1756, opening what became known in Europe as the Seven Years War.[22] Austria's ally, Saxony, was swiftly overrun, and its army forcibly pressed into Prussian service, while smaller Prussian forces occupied much of Mecklenburg to create a wider buffer north of Brandenburg and to access additional sources of money and recruits. Frederick's response followed the logic of his actions in 1740: he moved first, hoping to secure a decisive advantage from which he could bargain himself out of a long war. As in 1740, however, this openly broke the public peace and created a new set of problems that negated much of the initial success. And this time, Austria again held the imperial title and made full use of its constitutional position to cloak its plans to dismember Prussia in the language of restoring tranquillity in the Empire.

Swedish and French support gave Austria the backing of both the Protestant and Catholic guarantors of the imperial constitution, thereby undercutting Frederick's efforts to present the struggle as a religious war. Despite Prussian and British-Hanoverian efforts, the Reichstag approved Austria's call for a mobilization to enforce the public peace. Hanover and five north German territories subsidized by Britain formed their own anti-French army, weakening the imperial mobilization. The other imperial Estates were well aware of Austria's plans and only supported the official purpose of liberating Saxony and Mecklenburg.

Nonetheless, the imperial army mustered between 25,000 and 33,000 soldiers each year between 1757 and 1762 and its presence allowed Austria to concentrate its forces on recovering Silesia. Meanwhile, France hired around 20,000 troops from the Wittelsbach principalities of Bavaria, the Palatinate, and Zweibrücken, as well as paying the 10,000-strong Saxon army once it reconstituted itself in 1758 having escaped Prussian service. Although the Wittelsbachs withdrew their auxiliaries in 1759, Württemberg supplied additional substantial forces to the coalition between 1757 and 1760.[23]

This was not a limited war: Prussia was fighting for its existence. Frederick tried to take the war to his enemies, invading Bohemia and defeating the Austrians in a costly battle outside Prague in May 1757. His weakened army was then severely beaten by an Austrian relief force at Kolin on 18 June, forcing him to abandon the siege of Prague and evacuate Bohemia.[24] The failure indicated the limits to Prussian power and the shortcomings of its 'front-loaded' strategy, which depended on securing a quick and decisive initial victory to avoid a protracted war.

Having swiftly occupied Prussia's Westphalian provinces, France persuaded Austria to let it attack Hanover in order to strike at Britain, its real enemy.[25] Following its defeat at Hastenbeck, the Hanoverian army and Britain's other German auxiliaries were stood down and the French occupied part of the electorate. Meanwhile, a Russian army conquered most of East Prussia, while the Swedes threatened Pomerania and blockaded the Baltic coast. Frederick's forces were reduced to Brandenburg, Silesia, and Saxony, which he still occupied.

Forced on to the defensive, Frederick fought his most brilliant campaign in the winter of 1757, first routing the combined French and imperial army at Rossbach in Saxony on 5 November before defeating a much larger Austrian force at Leuthen in Silesia a month later. The king's 'oblique attack' worked perfectly on both occasions, enabling him to maximize his inferior numbers by concentrating these to strike his opponents in the flank. The success was most complete at Rossbach where he caught the Franco-imperial army before it had deployed, whereas at Leuthen victory was only achieved after a costly struggle.[26]

These victories stabilized the situation and emboldened Britain to repudiate Hanover's neutrality, reactivate its German auxiliaries, and land a small expeditionary force to resume the war in northwest Germany in February 1758.[27] This tied down the French, whose assistance to Austria was now limited to financial aid. Nonetheless, the odds against Prussia remained high: by 1758, Frederick had 135,000 field troops against 150,000 Austrian and Kreis troops, as well as 98,000 Russians and Swedes (see Fig. 8).[28] Frederick shuttled his dwindling forces to meet each threat in turn, assisted by his enemies' inability to coordinate. Austro-Russian cooperation was undermined by the former's growing concerns at the prospect of Russian gains along the southern Baltic and the threat these would pose to Poland and the wider balance of power.[29]

Although on the defensive, Frederick still sought to shorten the war by seeking battle. This strategy led to near disaster after he was comprehensively defeated by a combined Austro-Russian army at Kunersdorf in 1759, again only narrowly escaping death or capture. He achieved further victories over the Austrians in 1760, but each time at considerable cost and was unable to prevent the Russians ransacking Berlin. He complained bitterly at what he perceived as insufficient help from Britain, which had largely achieved its goals in its parallel war with France in America by 1760 and whose exit from the Seven Years War was only delayed because France persuaded Spain to join the conflict. Increasingly desperate, Frederick urged the Ottomans to attack Austria, but the sultan was concerned at growing Russian influence in Poland and refused.

Ultimately, Prussia was saved by what Frederick termed the 'Miracle of the House of Brandenburg'. First, Austria and Russia failed to follow up their success at Kunersdorf and then, more decisively, Russia switched sides in March 1762 following the accession and brief reign of its erratic tsar, Peter III, who voluntarily evacuated East Prussia, and contributed 20,000 auxiliaries for the war against Austria in return for Prussia's acquiescence to a Russian attack on Denmark. Although a Russian palace coup soon ended this abrupt volte-face, its new ruler, Catherine II, reaffirmed peace with Prussia and left the war for good in June.[30] A Prussian army, commanded by Frederick's brother Prince Heinrich, defeated the imperial army at Freiberg in Saxony in October, prompting the imperial Estates to declare neutrality.

Britain's comprehensive victory in the colonial conflict had already prompted France and Spain to open negotiations, leaving Austria no choice but to follow suit. The war in the Empire was settled by the Peace of Hubertusburg in February 1763, restoring the pre-war status quo. Although Frederick had only narrowly escaped total defeat, his survival against such odds confirmed Prussia's status as a great power and fostered a dangerous belief in the efficacy of launching a bold first strike.

THE THREAT OF PARTITION, 1764–91

The Military Imbalance

The Empire had achieved its war aim of reimposing the pre-war status quo but was severely strained by the conflict. Habsburg prestige was damaged by the failure to defeat Prussia and the blatant manipulation of collective security for narrowly dynastic ends. Although there was a smooth transition following Francis I's death, the new emperor, Joseph II, regarded his role unsentimentally in utilitarian terms and his policies alienated many of the Habsburgs' traditional clientele among the weaker imperial Estates.[31]

Interest in collective security waned, given that the Ottomans were no longer considered a threat, while Austria's alliance with France removed the danger to the western frontier. The Kreis Association had been renewed in 1748, but the western territories were frustrated by the unwillingness of their more distant neighbours to share the costs of maintaining defences. Kehl was abandoned in 1754, followed by Philippsburg in 1782, leaving Mainz as the only imperial fortress on the Rhine. By 1763 virtually all imperial Estates were saddled with considerable debts after three decades of warfare and they welcomed the peace as an opportunity to reduce military expenditure. Having represented 40 per cent of total German strength in 1714, the combined forces of the smaller territories were outnumbered 3:1 by Austria and Prussia in 1770, reducing their influence in the Empire.

Although it retained all its territory in 1763, Prussia remained the weakest and least influential of the European great powers. Frederick now embarked on a range of domestic reforms intended to boost fiscal-military capacity, but he was acutely conscious of his state's vulnerability. His alliance with Britain terminated with the peace and coincided with the end of Saxon rule in Poland, opening that country still further to Russian influence. The spectre of Kunersdorf continued to haunt Frederick, who now feared Russia almost more than Austria's continued desire for revenge. He escaped isolation by securing an alliance with Russia in 1764 by dropping negotiations with the Ottomans and giving Catherine II a free hand in Poland, in return for her promise not to assist Austria.[32]

Prussia's influence in the Empire formed an additional line of defence as Frederick cynically presented himself as a constitutional champion to block Joseph's efforts to reform imperial institutions in Austria's interests. It was also important to maintain good relations with the smaller territories, which remained useful sources of recruits for the Prussian army. Force was a matter of last resort, since Frederick knew he could not afford a long war, especially if he lacked allies.

The First Partition of Poland, 1772

Poland's growing problems created a power vacuum that extended the 'eastern question' northwards and fuelled the rivalry between Austria, Prussia, and Russia. A vast, unstable space created potentially extraordinary opportunities for territorial growth for the voracious surrounding powers. Poland's descent into civil war after 1768 drew in Russia, thereby alarming the sultan and triggering a renewed Russo-Turkish conflict lasting until 1774, in which Catherine II's forces scored notable victories. Austria was increasingly alarmed by the prospect of a total Ottoman collapse, while both it and Prussia were concerned at Russian influence in Poland. Austria increased its forces in Transylvania as a warning to Russia and initiated unofficial cooperation with the Ottomans.[33]

Frederick and Joseph met at Neisse in Silesia in 1769, and the temporary rapprochement led to the three great powers settling their differences at Poland's expense three years later. While Russia took the largest share to the east, Austria annexed Galicia and Prussia acquired West Prussia, thereby linking Brandenburg and East Prussia, but still leaving Danzig as a Polish enclave. The Poles were in no position to resist as forces from the three powers swiftly occupied the designated areas. The settlement was extended by the Russo-Ottoman peace in 1774, whereby the sultan conceded access to the Black Sea. A year later he bowed to Austrian pressure and surrendered Bukovina, part of Ottoman Moldavia, to the Habsburgs. These events exposed how dangerous it was for small or weak states to rely on enmity between the great powers to preserve their own independence.

The Swiss failed to take notice thanks to their inability to discuss serious reforms.[34] At least 200,000 Swiss served in foreign armies across the eighteenth century, with a peak of 75,000 in 1748, falling to about 40,000 by the late 1780s. The spread was now broader across Europe than it had been for much of the seventeenth century. Significant numbers entered Spanish service after 1724 and the practice was further exported in 1735 with the establishment of Bourbon rule in Naples, where the Swiss formed a quarter of that state's infantry. Swiss and Rhetians (Grisons) accounted for about half the new infantry regiments added to the Savoyard army after 1733.

Traditionally, defenders of foreign service argued that placing troops with rival powers protected their own country's neutrality, but the diversification of clients failed to improve Swiss influence, especially as it was no longer possible to play off France against Austria after their alliance in 1756. The new French war minister, the duc de Choiseul, finally tackled the long-standing issues of pensions in sweeping reforms between 1762 and 1764, asserting greater control over the units in the French army and unilaterally rewriting their terms of service. After long, hard negotiations, the 1521 treaty between France and the Swiss Confederation was renewed in May 1777 for what proved to be the last time. France compelled the cantons to agree by cutting off salt supplies and dismissing their officers until they accepted the new conditions of service. As pension rates now remained fixed, their value was steadily eroded by inflation, while the progressive curbs on the autonomy of company commanders hit profits. These were lowest in units recruited under separate arrangements outside the framework of a formal alliance, such as those supplied to Naples. The cantons' limited influence was revealed in December 1789 when Naples unilaterally disbanded its four Swiss regiments, which were considered expensive and unreliable.[35]

The threat of partition was taken much more seriously in the Empire, where there was widespread fear among the weaker imperial Estates that Austro-Prussian cooperation might impose a 'Polish solution', either dividing the 'Third Germany' between them or splitting it into more clearly demarcated spheres of influence. France and Russia opposed this but, unlike Denmark or Sweden, neither possessed German territory and their support for the established order could not be relied upon. Instead, both powers saw the constitution merely as a device to prevent opponents accessing what French diplomats regarded as the 'inert forces' of the Third Germany.[36]

The War of the Bavarian Succession, 1778–9

These concerns stimulated interest among the weaker Estates to reform imperial institutions, reassert influence, and curb the damaging effects of Austro-Prussian rivalry. Princely interests continued to diverge, however, and six Estates seized the opportunity of the American Revolution to subsidize their military expenses by hiring out 30,000 troops to Britain in a series of controversial treaties after 1775.[37] Nonetheless, efforts to form a princely league were boosted by Joseph's attempts to persuade the Wittelsbachs to accept an exchange of Bavaria for the Austrian Netherlands.[38] The extraordinary opportunity offered by the extinction of the Bavarian line in 1777 allowed Joseph to press the surviving Palatine branch to accept his proposal. If realized, Austria's absorption of Bavaria would have offset the earlier loss of Silesia by greatly expanding Habsburg power in Germany.

With Britain and France distracted in America, Frederick decided to risk war to stop Habsburg expansion, having enlisted Saxon support to ease the problems of invading Bohemia. Prussia mobilized 253,000 troops, deploying 154,000 to which Saxony added 22,000. Their attack was blocked by 261,000 Austrians, leading to a stalemate. Both sides suffered supply problems, giving rise to the conflict's other name of the 'Potato War' as the hungry soldiers plundered a vegetable that had been recently introduced to boost Bohemian agriculture.

Maria Theresa opposed the war, ignored the humiliated Joseph, and opened her own negotiations leading to the Peace of Teschen in May 1779, which was brokered by France and Russia.[39] Austria retained a small slice of Bavarian territory but was obliged to permit a union of Bavaria and the Palatinate. Frederick had secured his immediate goal of blocking the exchange plan, but Prussia's underlying vulnerability remained. He resumed the policy of constitutional obstruction, playing on fears stoked by Joseph's attempt to curtail the spiritual jurisdiction of the ecclesiastical princes to seize leadership of the reform group. This was packaged as the League of Princes in 1785, which was far from being the attempt at German unity claimed later, but was instead a temporary measure to block Austria after Frederick had failed to persuade Russia to renew its alliance.[40]

Frederick left Prussia in a comparatively weak position when he was succeeded by his nephew Frederick William II in 1786. Factionalism and favouritism grew within Prussia's government under its new king, adding to the loss of direction. Dynastic solidarity prompted the despatch of 20,000 troops to rescue the Dutch stadholder, William V, from the bourgeois Patriot movement in 1787. The troops were withdrawn in April 1788 having achieved their objective, but at considerable cost to Prussia's fragile finances. William V still felt uneasy and increased the proportion of German troops in the Dutch army.[41] Only in August 1788 did an alliance with Britain temporarily allow Prussia to escape isolation.

Austria's Last Turkish War, 1788–90

Prussia's relative weakness was not obvious to the Habsburg government, which remained concerned that it would demand more Polish territory if either Austria or Russia made further gains at the Ottomans' expense. Polish territory was economically more valuable than lands in the Balkans. Austria wanted to preserve the Ottoman Empire; a goal that harmonized with that of its French ally. Yet further cooperation with Prussia seemed impossible, making it imperative to seek an understanding with Russia.

This was achieved in 1781, securing the immediate goal after the War of the Bavarian Succession, namely, isolating Prussia.[42] Austria was obliged to acquiesce at Russia's annexation of the Ottoman tributary state of the Crimea in April 1783 in return for diplomatic backing over a renewed attempt to persuade the Wittelsbachs to exchange Bavaria for the Netherlands. Again, Joseph was compelled to abandon his project, this time after Franco-Dutch pressure in 1784–5. The fiasco angered France and increased Austria's dependency on its Russian ally, which became embroiled in a new Turkish war in 1787.

As in 1737, Austria felt it had little choice but to intervene in the hope of limiting Russia's gains rather than making more of its own. Prussia's momentary distraction supporting the Dutch stadholder against internal opponents provided an opportunity, particularly as it had appeared at one point that Frederick William II might ally with the sultan. The situation became still more complicated when Sweden attacked Russia in 1788, leading to two years of inconclusive fighting in the Baltic.

Austria mobilized 282,000 troops, deploying an unprecedented 140,000 as its main strike force in Hungary in 1788. The Empire regarded the conflict as a purely Austrian affair and provided no assistance.

Nonetheless, the Austrians had observed the performance of the Russians across 1768–74 and were much better prepared than they had been in their last war. Belgrade was captured on 8 October after a massive bombardment from Austria's Danube flotilla and siege batteries. The success emboldened Joseph II to push on to Bucharest, sucking him deeper into a costly war as his army was decimated by disease. The burden of conscription added to the resentment at Joseph's reforming attack on the Catholic Church and other established institutions, prompting revolts in Hungary, Transylvania, and the Netherlands. These coincided with the French Revolution in the summer of 1789, which paralysed the French monarchy and removed Austria's primary ally since 1756.

Joseph's death allowed his successor, Leopold II, to make peace in 1790, surrendering all gains except for a small part of Bosnia, establishing a frontier with the Ottoman Empire that would remain unchanged until 1908. Russia was obliged to make a separate peace in 1792 but secured its goal of improved security for the Crimea and access to the Black Sea. Austria's restraint was largely driven by the necessity of denying Prussia grounds to claim more of Poland. Finding himself blocked, Frederick William II agreed the Convention of Reichenbach in July 1790, making a vague promise to cooperate with Austria. None of this proved of much benefit to Leopold, who would be unable to prevent Prussia joining Russia in the Second Partition of Poland in 1793, depriving that kingdom of over half its remaining territory. Frederick William's share included Danzig and Thorn and consolidated the link between Brandenburg and Prussia.

FIGHTING FOR SURVIVAL, 1792–1815

The French Revolutionary Wars, 1792–1802

Revolution in France coincided with unrest in the Habsburg lands, Saxony, Liège, and several smaller German principalities. The protesters' appropriation of French revolutionary slogans and symbols created the appearance of a general challenge to monarchical rule. However, the movements within the Empire remained primarily conservative and traditional. While Austro-Prussian rivalry hindered the restoration of order in Liège, imperial institutions otherwise proved effective in coordinating pacification and imposing measures like censorship to limit the spread of revolutionary ideas, so the situation did not pose a major threat to the Empire.[43] The French abolition of feudalism in August 1789 affected those minor German princes who still had lands in Alsace, but they preferred negotiation rather than war to recover their rights. Despite voicing concern for the French royal family, neither Austria nor Prussia wanted conflict with France, and both hoped the Revolution would mellow with time. The real crisis came when France's new government chose to escape its mounting domestic problems by declaring war on Austria, invading the Austrian Netherlands in April 1792.

The outcome of the opening campaign was instantly exploited by the revolutionaries as proof of their inherent superiority over their opponents, and their claims have ever since established a pervading sense of a seemingly inevitable victory of the new over the old order.[44] The real difference was cultural, rather than military, social, or political: the revolutionaries refused to conform to expectations, meaning their opponents consistently underestimated them.

Prussia agreed to support Austria in return for the latter's acceptance of its inheritance of the lands of the junior Hohenzollern branch in Franconia. Only 85,000 men were assembled for the invasion of France in July 1792; half were Prussians, a third Austrians, and the rest Hessians, together with a few émigrés. Two additional Austrian corps covered the advance to the north and south. The main force was commanded by Duke Karl of Brunswick and was accompanied by the Prussian king and the poet Goethe. Progress was delayed by heavy rain and dysentery, allowing two French armies to combine with a total of 54,000 men at Valmy south of the river Brionne to block further progress. Brunswick and the main corps of 34,000 advanced to dislodge them on 20 September, hoping to secure the area for winter quarters. The action that followed was more of a cannonade than a battle and the gunfire had little effect due to the wet ground.

Brunswick decided not to press home his advantage when the French did not break as expected, and instead he withdrew having lost only 164 men to 300 of the French. Such inconclusive confrontations had been common in early modern warfare. Brunswick failed to understand how his decision to retreat would be interpreted by the French as a huge victory, emboldening the new revolutionary National Convention to abolish the monarchy and embark on an expansive war, ostensibly to liberate the oppressed peoples of Europe. Louis XVI was executed in January 1793 and on 1 February France declared war on Britain and the Dutch Republic, followed soon afterwards by a similar declaration against Spain.

This led to the first of eventually seven successive coalitions intended to contain France. The first was closest to the old Grand Alliance with Britain and the Dutch again subsidizing part of the Allied war effort. However, it proved far less durable than its forerunner, largely because its members continued to act as they had before, whereas the French behaved differently. Another major factor was that Prussia's emergence alongside Austria as a German great power had destabilized the Empire's internal balance, and the two powers temporarily cooperated to exploit the emergency to force the Empire into war with France.

The southwestern Kreise had already mobilized in 1792 for their own defence. Correctly fearing that Austria and Prussia wanted to repeat the practice of the 1670s and oblige the smaller territories to fund their armies, the middling princes insisted on being allowed to send their own troops. The Reichstag authorized a triple quota in November 1792 followed by an official declaration of war on 23 March. Official strength increased to an unprecedented four-fold quota on 9 October 1794, and though this was not reached overall, many territories did meet their individual obligations until 1796.[45]

The war further radicalized the French revolutionary regime, which ruthlessly exploited the country's manpower to increase its army's effective strength to around half a million men. Conscription provided a seemingly endless flow of replacements, encouraging France's generals to continue their aggressive but costly tactics that ultimately defeated their more cautious opponents. The situation hung in the balance across 1793–4. Both Mainz and the Austrian Netherlands were lost, then recovered by Allied counter-attacks, only to be lost again in a renewed French offensive in autumn 1793 that saw French victories in the same locations in Alsace that would see German triumphs in 1870. A new Allied effort in 1794 fell apart due to inferior numbers and poor coordination. Suspicious of the Austrians, the main Prussian force pulled out in July 1794, opening a gap in the Rhineland that was swiftly exploited by another French offensive.

Relentless French attacks precipitated a total Dutch collapse in 1795, leading to the establishment of the Batavian Republic as a French satellite regime. Batavia followed France's 'nationalist' example and disbanded the Swiss and German regiments in its service, much to the disgust of many of the soldiers who protested they had 'shed their blood for the [Dutch] Republic, have never taken part in political affairs, and have always served with loyalty and honesty'.[46]

France's successes were aided by a major Polish rising that distracted Prussia and Russia after May 1794. Unable to fight on two fronts, Prussia prioritized its interests in the east and left the war against France through the Peace of Basel on 5 April 1795, ceding its Westphalian territory left of the Rhine and agreeing to neutralize all northern Germany, including Hanover, which had no choice but to cooperate. The crisis in the east was settled through a third and final partition of Poland in October 1795. Fearing it would be disadvantaged by further Prussian and Russian gains, Austria participated too, annexing Cracow and Lublin. Meanwhile, Hessen-Kassel and Saxony soon joined the Prussian neutrality zone, taking out the most potent of the armed princes.

As Spain also exited the conflict, Austria was left to fight on with only the rump of the Empire as support. Its growing desperation led to increasingly high-handed policies towards the lesser Estates, including forcibly disbanding the Swabian Kreis troops as Baden and Württemberg opened negotiations with France. Meanwhile, its victory over most of the First Coalition allowed France to concentrate its forces against Austria in the Rhineland and northern Italy. Archduke Charles repulsed two massive thrusts over the Rhine in September 1795 and the summer of 1796, but his victories were offset by parallel defeats in Italy. There, a French army under Napoleon Bonaparte conquered Savoy in April 1796, and then decisively defeated the Austrians, taking Lombardy and Mantua. Austria was forced to agree an armistice in April, which was converted into the Peace of Campo Formio on 17 October 1797. Austria accepted the loss of the Netherlands and Lombardy in return for French acquiescence in its annexation of Venice. As the hallowed polities collapsed, the survivors, in a pattern that would repeat over the next two decades, could not prevent themselves from undermining their own legitimacy by participating in the dismemberings. The settlement covered only the Habsburg lands, necessitating a congress which opened in Rastatt to discuss a definitive settlement for the Empire, but the pace of events slowed as Napoleon left to pursue his grandiose ambitions in Egypt.

Nonetheless, France maintained the pressure, invading Switzerland in January 1798 following disputes over foreign service. At the outbreak of the Revolution there had been 24,000 foreign soldiers who formed 15 per cent of France's army. Of these 13,770 were Swiss and most of the rest Germans. Their presence contradicted the new ideal of national sovereignty in which power was vested in the nation. Resentment mounted against the Swiss and German troops after the royal family selected some to accompany them on their abortive 'flight to Varennes' escape attempt in June 1791.[47]

Matters culminated in the infamous massacre at the Tuileries Palace. Abandoned by the French National Guards deployed to support them, around 1,000 Swiss Guards were attacked by revolutionaries on 10 August 1792. Most fought their way out, but 368 were killed, including sixty-eight after they had laid down their arms.[48] Ten days later the revolutionaries disbanded all foreign units, but 4,000 men continued to serve, partly to avoid unemployment, but also because many regarded France as their home. The Swiss elite were angry at France's unilateral repudiation of the hallowed alliance. Although the Confederation declared its neutrality in 1792, it continued to supply soldiers to the anti-French coalition, especially Spain. The diet responded to French protests that France had already disbanded these troops leaving the soldiers unemployed.

With Austria defeated, France could settle with the Swiss. The Confederation's collective security failed completely, with only Bern and Solothurn offering any resistance. The much-vaunted militia were soon routed by the hardened revolutionary troops. The cantons were replaced by French-style departments within a new 'indivisible' Helvetic Republic, which abolished many of the socio-economic inequalities bedevilling old-regime Switzerland. The Republic was forced to sign a new treaty with France in April 1798, replacing that of 1521, and to provide 18,000 men as an autonomous part of the French army. It is testimony to the efficiency of the former system that it had managed to recruit larger numbers for foreign service, while the Republic struggled to do so, obliging the French to agree it could halve its commitment in 1800. Elements of the force served in France, Germany, Italy, Corsica, and Santo Domingo, while one unit was destroyed serving as marines at the battle of Trafalgar in 1805.

For all their nationalist rhetoric, the French revolutionaries wound up employing foreign soldiers like the old regime they replaced, only they imposed far worse terms, since the previous treaty with the Swiss had exempted them from serving in the colonies or onboard ships.[49] Only 1,071 Germans joined the revolutionary *Légion germanique* formed in December 1792, ostensibly to spearhead the liberation of Germany from the feudal yoke. The unit was instead sent to suppress the clerical reactionary rising in the Vendée, where it was decimated in the bitter fighting. The French briefly employed other 'legions' of German troops until 1806, largely recruited from prisoners of war, while many other Germans served in the émigré forces raised by aristocratic French officers fleeing the Revolution. Virtually the entire Hanoverian army escaped the French occupation of the electorate in 1803 and served in exile as the King's German Legion in British service, mainly in Spain after 1808. It was joined by a Brunswick Legion after the failed rising against the French in 1809. Both these formations would fight with distinction at Waterloo. Swiss units continued to serve the Spanish until 1808, while two regiments entered British service, as did several German units, all mainly recruited from exiles and men wishing to continue a career without serving France.[50]

Exploiting Napoleon's growing difficulties in Egypt, Austria attacked in March 1799 and was joined by Russia and Britain in the Second Coalition. Britain subsidized the remaining armed princes in southern Germany, who represented what was left of the Empire's military effort. The initial successes were cut short by Napoleon's return in August as he reorganized the government along more authoritarian lies. The fighting spread to Switzerland, where the lack of support for the new regime led it to being mocked as the 'invisible republic'. An Austro-Russian attempt to liberate the Swiss was defeated by the French and prompted Russia to exit the war by the end of the year. Austria fought on into 1800, but suffered major defeats at Marengo and Hohenlinden, obliging it to agree the Peace of Lunéville on 9 February 1801.[51]

The End of the Empire

The new settlement confirmed that of Campo Formio, sanctioning the French annexation of all land west of the Rhine and permitting those secular rulers who suffered territorial losses there to be compensated at the expense of the ecclesiastical princes and imperial cities. Formally, the task of redistributing territory was entrusted to a special deputation of the Reichstag; however this had little choice but to follow a plan prepared by France and Russia which ensured their clients and allies benefited most. The process was completed in February 1803 and saw the annexation of 112 imperial Estates, reducing the overall number by a third.

The institutional structure remained, complete with Reichstag, Kreise, imperial supreme courts, and the system of collective security, but the political balance shifted because the surviving principalities acquired the votes and other rights associated with the territories they absorbed. Other than Mainz, all the ecclesiastical territories disappeared, while the imperial cities were reduced to just six. Several new principalities were created by amalgamating various small imperial cities and lordships, but the primary beneficiaries were the secular electors whose ranks were joined by several elevations from the armed princes and who, collectively, now held the majority of votes in the Reichstag and other institutions.[52] The destruction of the imperial Church ended the Catholic political majority, though the Protestant princes who acquired these lands were obliged to respect their new subjects' religion. The beneficiaries also had to assume all debts associated with their new possessions and to pay pensions to any civil or military personnel they dismissed. Mastering these problems accelerated the process of reform already underway in most principalities. Imperial institutions assisted this process by providing ways to resolve the innumerable disputes and, in many areas, legal practice remained guided by imperial law well into the nineteenth century.[53]

Despite claims from several intellectuals, notably Hegel, that the Empire had collapsed, most inhabitants still saw it as their home and considerable efforts were made to ensure it continued to function.[54] Nonetheless, the changes represented a decisive shift towards a more federal structure, while any chance of making the new arrangements work was frustrated by relentless pressure from Napoleon, who was determined to deny Austria a chance to recover from its recent defeats. Austria was obliged to recognize Napoleon as emperor of the French in May 1804, with the Habsburgs creating their own hereditary title (as 'Emperor of Austria') in December to ensure their own imperial credentials against any further erosion of the Empire.[55] In May 1805, Napoleon reorganized the various Italian satellites into a new kingdom of Italy with himself as monarch, but delegated authority to his stepson as viceroy.

Fearing he would attempt the same in Germany, Austria joined the new Third Coalition with Britain, Russia, Sweden, Portugal, and Naples. Prussia was conspicuous by its absence, which also prevented any mobilization as northern Germany remained in the neutral zone agreed in 1795. With the Empire sinking fast, Bavaria, Württemberg, and Baden sought metaphorical lifeboats by making pacts with France to supply over 32,000 auxiliaries for Napoleon.[56] The French emperor struck in August with the Russians still working their way across Poland. Austria's counter-thrust into Bavaria was bungled and the bulk of its army was surrounded and forced to surrender at Ulm in October in what was one of the Habsburgs' greatest military disasters. Napoleon pushed on, taking Vienna on 14 November, while the remaining Austrians joined their Russian allies in Moravia. Napoleon attacked them at Austerlitz on 2 December, scoring his most brilliant victory.[57]

The Rheinbund

With its forces also driven out of Italy and its other allies defeated, Austria made peace at Pressburg on 26 December 1805. It ceded the recently acquired Veneto to the Napoleonic kingdom of Italy. The Tirol was given to Bavaria, while Württemberg received Austria's remaining Swabian possessions. Both electorates were now recognized as kingdoms, while Baden – also enlarged – became a grand duchy. Napoleon pushed ahead with his plans to further reorganize the Empire, grouping Bavaria, Württemberg, Baden, and thirteen other allied principalities into a new Confederation of the Rhine (*Rheinbund*) on 12 July 1806 with himself as 'protector'. The signatories declared themselves as sovereign states outside the Empire. Fearing Napoleon would usurp the Holy Roman title to legitimate his plans, Emperor Francis II reluctantly abdicated and dissolved the Empire on 6 August 1806. Britain and Sweden refused to recognize this act, arguing that, as the ruler of a mixed monarchy, Francis lacked the authority to do this unilaterally.[58]

Later nationalists dismissed the Rheinbund as little more than Napoleon's German recruiting depot. Carl Theodor von Dalberg, the former elector of Mainz and nominal 'prince primate' of the new confederation, struggled to give it a constitution that would rescue what he saw as the best elements of the old Empire.[59] Although fewer than those in the Empire, the members of the new organization were as varied and status-conscious, and resisted curbs on their new sovereignty. Napoleon encouraged them, as he opposed anything that might give the Rheinbund a collective voice against his demands. All members were obliged to provide contingents at Napoleon's request, with the larger states fielding anything from a brigade (e.g. Baden) to an army corps (Bavaria), while the smaller principalities combined to provide regiments.[60]

Switzerland

Meanwhile, Napoleon imposed the Act of Mediation on the fractious Swiss on 19 February 1803, replacing the dysfunctional Helvetic Republic with a new Swiss Confederation. The thirteen original cantons were restored with an additional six created from their former subject territories: Aargau, Grisons, St Gallen, Tessin, Thurgau, and Vaud. The independent city of Geneva was incorporated into France, albeit with some privileges. The Valais was left as an independent republic to safeguard French access to the Simplon pass, until 1810 when Napoleon simply annexed this to France. The principality of Neuchatel, an associate of the old Confederation that had passed to Prussia in 1707, was entrusted to Napoleon's field marshal Louis-Alexandre Berthier in March 1806.

The new Confederation considered itself sovereign but was compelled to sign a new agreement with France on 27 September 1803 which, though officially fixed at fifty years, was deliberately called the 'perpetual alliance', echoing the arrangements from 1521. The Swiss were not permitted to have more than 20,000 militia for their own defence and had to supply over 16,000 troops permanently for Napoleon's forces, though this time it was agreed they would no longer be sent outside Europe. In addition, the Valais and Neuchatel each had to provide a battalion. Overall, around 33,000 served across 1805–13, representing a significant burden for a country with only 225,000 men of military age.[61]

The Confederation declared neutrality in the wars of 1805 and 1809. Austria accepted this on both occasions, but Napoleon stated he would respect it only while it suited him. Austria ignored a renewed declaration in 1813 and forced transit that amounted to an occupation until 1815. The Confederation unilaterally renounced the Act of Mediation in December 1813 once the war had turned against Napoleon, but it was unable to withdraw the surviving soldiers still with the emperor's army until his defeat in April 1814; an episode suggestive of the fallacy of Swiss claims that foreign service safeguarded their neutrality.

Settling with Prussia, 1806

Prussia's king clung to his neutrality, refusing a French offer to make him emperor of northern Germany, but equally he stood by without helping Austria after 1795.[62] Napoleon's reorganization of much of Germany into the Rheinbund finally pushed him into joining a Fourth Coalition with Russia, Britain, Sweden, and a rather reluctant Saxony. Prussia's peacetime army was nominally 247,000 but financial problems and concerns over the reliability of its new Polish subjects meant that only 142,800 could be deployed against France. Not all of these were available, because it was feared that the units stationed in Westphalia under Marshal Blücher would desert if they were moved eastwards to join the main army. Additional troops were left in East Prussia because Prussia distrusted Russia.

Napoleon advanced rapidly from central Germany with 180,000 troops, intending to smash the Prussians before the Russians could arrive. The French and their Rheinbund allies were organized into corps, each around 25,000 men with an appropriate balance between infantry, cavalry, and artillery to allow them to fight independently if necessary. The new structure improved Napoleon's ability to coordinate his large army and fight multiple engagements across a wider front than those of conventional early modern battles. The efficacy of this, together with his superior generalship, were amply demonstrated when he caught the Prussians and Saxons still scattered at Jena and Auerstädt on 14 October 1806. The battles were hard fought, but the Prussians and Saxons lost 25,000 casualties, twice those of their opponents. Worse, the Prussian army disintegrated during the retreat, with many units surrendering without further resistance. Considering the scale of the victory, Napoleon rightly concluded that he had avenged France's humiliating defeat by Prussia at Rossbach in 1757.[63]

Berlin was occupied on 25 October as the Hohenzollern court and government fled to East Prussia. Saxony changed sides, joined the Rheinbund, was elevated to a kingdom, and sent a contingent to reinforce the

66,000 Rheinbund troops now with the French army. Napoleon pressed on into Prussian Poland, winning further, more costly victories over the rump of the Prussian army, which had meanwhile been reinforced by the Russians. His enemies made peace at Tilsit on 7 July 1807. Russia accepted Napoleon's Rheinbund, which expanded to incorporate northern and central Germany including Nassau, Hessen-Darmstadt, and the Thuringian duchies. A new kingdom of Westphalia was created for Napoleon's brother Jérôme, from parts of Hanover, Hessen-Kassel, and several other territories. Along with the grand duchy of Berg, ruled by the French marshal Joachim Murat, Westphalia was intended to be a model loyal state to anchor the Rheinbund to France.[64] In return, Napoleon gave his blessing to a Russian invasion of Finland, which was successfully conquered from Sweden by 1809.

Prussia was treated punitively, losing nearly half its territory, including lands to Berg and Westphalia. Much of Prussian Poland, along with the Polish lands that Austria obtained under the Third Partition, were combined as the pro-French Duchy of Warsaw. Prussia was reduced to 119,000 square kilometres with 4.5 million inhabitants, effectively wiping out all the gains made since 1740. The subsequent Convention of Paris on 8 August 1808 added more conditions, limiting the army to 42,000 men with no reserves for ten years and imposing 140 million francs worth of reparations. Napoleon had achieved what Maria Theresa had failed to do in the Seven Years War: Prussia had been reduced to the status of a secondary power.

The catastrophe left Prussia in crisis. The government struggled to reform all branches of the state while silencing criticism of the monarchy, which was widely blamed for the debacle. Conservatives were no longer able to block reform, but still tried to shape it, while many of the reformers were naïve and there was insufficient time or funds for their proposals to be realized. Despite their disagreements, all at least were united by the belief that only a victory over France could restore Prussia and prevent its total loss of independence.[65]

The War of the Fifth Coalition

Napoleon now turned southwest, invading Spain in December 1807 to enforce his new Continental System intended to defeat Britain economically by closing Europe to its commerce. Spain's resistance from 1808 opened what became known as the Peninsular War and sucked in ever more French troops, including eventually 35,000 men from the smaller and medium-sized Rheinbund states, as well as several Swiss units, all of which suffered heavy casualties.[66]

Inspired by Spanish resistance, Austria joined Britain to form the Fifth Coalition, opening a new war on three fronts in April 1809. While one small Austrian army attacked the Duchy of Warsaw, another made good progress against the kingdom of Italy. The main effort was made along the Danube where Archduke Charles attacked with 175,000 troops against Bavaria, supported by an anti-Bavarian rising by Austria's former subjects in the Tirol. Few Germans answered Austria's call for a war of liberation against France, whereas the Rheinbund honoured its treaty and sent its full commitment of 122,000 men. Charles was forced back by the French counter-attack in a series of hard-fought battles but scored a tactical victory at Aspern-Essling on 21–22 May; the first success against an army personally commanded by Napoleon. However, Emperor Francis II rejected Charles's advice to negotiate peace. Austrian reverses in Italy assisted Napoleon in resuming his attack across the Danube, where he defeated Charles in a costly battle at Wagram on 5–6 July.[67]

Austria accepted the Peace of Schönbrunn on 14 October 1809, becoming a landlocked power by ceding Trieste and Dalmatia to France, as well as losing more territory to Bavaria. It was obliged to pay reparations and reduce its army to 150,000. While Napoleon soon lifted the latter requirement, the defeat was still a major blow and cleared the way for France to reorganize its European empire. Holland and northern Germany were annexed directly, with a reorganized Rheinbund, plus Switzerland, Warsaw, Italy, Naples, and (more nominally) Spain as satellites. Austria and Prussia were bound by asymmetrical alliances as junior partners. Conflict was reduced to Iberia where a massive build-up of French forces in 1810 repelled an Anglo-Portuguese advance, resulting in a stalemate along the Spanish–Portuguese border.

The significance of Napoleon's victories across 1805–9 was demonstrated by his ability to draw on German manpower for his disastrous invasion of Russia on 24 June 1812, intended to enforce compliance with his Continental System. Of the 449,000 soldiers in the initial invasion force, 177,300 were Germans, including 123,600 from the Rheinbund; its principal members were Bavaria, Saxony, Westphalia, and Württemberg. Austria and Prussia provided 31,000 and 19,000 soldiers respectively as forces flanking the main thrust, which thus missed most of the fighting. The remaining 3,800 came from German lands recently annexed by France. The main column defeated the Russians in the bloody battle of Borodino on 7 September that failed to produce the decisive victory Napoleon sought.[68] Having begun their retreat on 19 October, only 60,000 emaciated survivors of the main column straggled into Poland in December. Overall, the invasion force lost 380,000 killed, including many of the reinforcements that subsequently joined it.

THE WAR OF LIBERATION, 1813–15

The disaster encouraged some Prussian officers to change sides once their corps under Field Marshal Ludwig Yorck reached East Prussia. Aided by Carl von Clausewitz, who was already serving with the Russians, Yorck negotiated the Convention of Tauroggen on 30 December 1812, allowing Prussia to retreat into two months of neutrality. Signed without royal permission, the agreement bought time for the reform-minded officers to push the reluctant king, Frederick William III, into allying with Russia on 28 February and then finally declaring war on France on 16 March. The king's famous proclamation 'To my people' (*An mein Volk*), issued the next day, set the tone of a patriotic war of liberation.

Prussia struggled to mobilize, initially fielding only 80,000 soldiers under the seventy-year-old Marshal Blücher, while the Russians were slow to arrive in large numbers. Angered by French annexation of its Pomeranian lands in January 1812, Sweden also broke with Napoleon in March 1813 and formed the Sixth Coalition with Britain, Russia, Prussia, Portugal, and Spain. Austria initially abstained because it had struggled to provide even the small field force in 1812 and, despite his recent defeat, it was far from clear that Napoleon's days were numbered.

France still had a field army of 120,000 in eastern Germany, with another 50,000 men garrisoning towns along the rivers Elbe and Saale holding the Rheinbund states on Napoleon's side. Their rulers were reluctant to abandon the emperor without guarantees that the anti-French coalition would let them keep their new lands and titles, and while they also struggled to rebuild their armies after the Russian campaign, they nonetheless provided around 61,000 troops to the French army in August 1813.

Napoleon repulsed the initial Allied advance into Saxony in a series of costly battles, before requesting a ten-week truce on 4 June which allowed him to rebuild his forces with new drafts of conscripts from France. However, the truce benefited the Allies more, enabling Austria to complete its mobilization, mustering 300,000 troops by the time it joined the Fifth Coalition on 17 August. Austria continued to increase its forces, which totalled over 500,000 men by 1814 and made it the lead partner. Although Britain provided arms and cash, its own military effort remained restricted to Iberia and it had little influence over the strategy adopted to defeat Napoleon in Germany. Overall command was entrusted to Field Marshal Schwarzenberg, whose chief of staff, Joseph Radetzky, devised the Trachenberg Plan to avoid direct contact with Napoleon while defeating the secondary forces commanded by his marshals. Meanwhile, the Allies deliberately mixed their forces to create multi-national armies to spread the risk of casualties among the partners.[69]

This attritional strategy proved successful once war resumed in the late summer of 1813, particularly as Napoleon was less able to replace battle losses than his enemies. Westphalia collapsed in September when its army refused to fight as Russian troops surrounded its capital, forcing King Jérôme to flee. Having secured guarantees for most of its gains since 1805, Bavaria defected on 14 October. Two days later the Allies felt sufficiently strong to risk confronting the emperor, who had concentrated 190,000 men and 752 guns at Leipzig. Three Allied armies, totalling 350,000 and 1,314 guns, converged on the French, gradually forcing them back on the city over the next three days. The remaining Saxons defected to the Allies at the height of the battle, though this made little difference to the outcome as it was clear Napoleon had lost. Abandoning 24,000 wounded soldiers and 15,000 men trapped in Leipzig, he escaped westwards deeper into Germany, having lost a further 22,000 killed and wounded and half his artillery. Allied losses were also heavy at 44,200 killed, wounded, and captured, along with a further 9,000 casualties suffered at Hanau, where Napoleon brushed aside an Austro-Bavarian attempt to block his retreat on 30 October. Celebrated as the Battle of the Nations, the victory at Leipzig broke Napoleon's grip on Germany. Although isolated French garrisons clung on, the remaining Rheinbund princes now hastened to join the Allies.

The Allies crossed the upper Rhine on 21 December. Together, they mustered 350,000 field troops against Napoleon's 120,000, but the outcome remained uncertain, primarily because the Allies disagreed over their ultimate objective. Austria, Britain, and Sweden were prepared to see Napoleon remain ruler of a France reduced to its 'natural frontiers', whereas Russia and Prussia insisted on removing him and restoring the Bourbons. Schwarzenberg and Radetzky's continued caution reflected Vienna's desire for a compromise peace.[70] Napoleon's last allies, Denmark and Naples, defected and the emperor was forced back to Paris where he abdicated unconditionally on 6 April, four days ahead of the duke of Wellington's capture of Toulouse in the south of France.

A congress convened in Vienna to discuss the post-war settlement.[71] Napoleon's escape from exile in Elba restarted the conflict as the War of the Seventh Coalition in March 1815. The Prussian chief of staff, Count Neidhardt von Gneisenau, devised the Allied plan to invade France based on that used the previous year. Three Allied armies totalling 632,000 men stood in a wide arc from the Netherlands up the Rhine, with a further 50,000 deployed in Italy against Naples, which foolishly declared for France. Napoleon mustered 300,000 troops but these were still reorganizing and not all the French were pleased to see him back. He advanced rapidly northwards with 128,000 men intending to smash the Allied army in the Netherlands, gambling that a decisive victory would trigger dissension in the coalition ranged against him.

The famous Waterloo campaign that followed was a series of interrelated battles south of Brussels. Of the 222,000 Allied troops involved, only 34,000 were British and 29,000 Dutch-Belgian, with the rest being Prussians, Hanoverians, Brunswickers, and Nassau troops, leading one author to claim Waterloo as a 'German victory'.[72] That verdict is true in terms of the contribution in manpower, particularly as the bulk of the other Allied forces were Austrians, but Britain continued to provide valuable financial and material aid, and the coalition's resilience made an ultimate French victory unlikely.

Change and Continuity

In absolute terms, the Revolutionary and Napoleonic Wars were fought on an unprecedented scale, but this needs to be set into the context of Europe's exponential demographic growth since the 1730s, increased agricultural and industrial productivity, and the significantly improved (though still inadequate) road and canal network. The novelty of the conflicts lies less in the size of the forces engaged than in their political impact. Whereas Louis XIV had struggled over four decades without cracking the coalitions ranged against him, Revolutionary and Napoleonic France shattered five of the seven coalitions it faced. French victories wrought the kind of transformation in western, central, and southern Europe that Austria, Prussia, and Russia had imposed on Poland and the Balkans after 1772, only this time the changes had far greater social and economic repercussions, and occurred with a rapidity that proved deeply unsettling.

Germany and Switzerland were profoundly affected. The Empire, which had been in existence for over a millennium, was gone, and while the changes in Switzerland superficially looked less radical, their domestic impact was no less significant. Yet, there were also important continuities that were eventually consolidated in the Vienna settlement of 1815, which confirmed Swiss neutrality and established the German Confederation. Prussia survived as the second German great power alongside Austria, and both were still bound to the reorganized and now sovereign smaller German states through a looser framework of collective security.

8

Professionalizing War

BY ROYAL COMMAND

Army Command

The eighteenth century is usually regarded as either the apogee of old-regime 'limited war' or an era of accelerating innovation pointing towards the fundamental changes of the French Revolutionary and Napoleonic era. In either interpretation the commanding figure is Frederick II, leading inevitably to the reduction of German military history to that of Prussia. Much of the eighteenth century saw only modest changes to organization, armament, training, and tactics, all remaining strongly influenced by late seventeenth-century experience, which was consolidated during the two, largely peaceful decades following 1714. Austria remained the preferred model until the renewed warfare between 1733 and 1763, but its failure to defeat Prussia ensured the latter attracted growing attention within and well beyond the Empire.

The next three decades were largely peaceful, leaving the mid-century wars as the reference point in the increasingly intense discussions of best practice. German forces were not unprepared for war in 1792, nor was their defeat inevitable or solely due to inferior organization or tactics, but instead it lay in a more complex combination of factors in which political rivalry within the Empire proved the most fatal.[1] Defeats forced deep reforms, first in Austria, the medium-sized German principalities, and Switzerland, and then in Prussia; in each case combining a different mix of existing impulses, responses to French practice, and conservative resistance to change. The result was a new set of structures which, while still drawing on eighteenth-century experience, shaped German armies into the mid-nineteenth century and in some respects considerably beyond.

Meanwhile, Austria and, to a lesser extent, Prussia engaged in European naval developments as followers rather than leaders.

Military command remained determined by the mixture of collective and autonomous forces established during the seventeenth century and reflecting the fragmented sovereignty of both the Empire and the Swiss Confederation. Swiss cantons named their own militia commanders, with generals of collective forces appointed only in wartime. The prolonged warfare of the later seventeenth century led to the appointment of permanent collective commanders at both regional and overall imperial levels in the Empire, agreed through the Kreis assemblies and the Reichstag. Initially in the 1680s, the assemblies named generals for their contingents who remained in post until they died or resigned, while the emperor appointed the overall commander. Growing political rivalry, expressed partly in confessional terms, ultimately led to the formalization of this process at imperial level in 1704.[2] Senior officers were nominated by the leading armed princes and appointed to the available posts after discussion in the Reichstag, with each rank duplicated to ensure parity between Protestants and Catholics. The Habsburgs were forced to concede this, because of their reliance on auxiliaries supplied by Prussia, Saxony, Hanover, and Hessen-Kassel, all of which were Protestant principalities determined to have a voice in directing the Empire's wars against France.

Parity was nonetheless mitigated by the principle of seniority, ensuring a single hierarchy based on date of appointment to each rank. Moreover, the established reputations of, first, Ludwig of Baden-Baden, famed as *Türkenlouis* after his recent victories over the Ottomans, and then Prince Eugene of Savoy secured the respect of the other imperial generals. Eugene's commanding presence in the Habsburg monarchy ensured he led both the Austrian forces and the collective imperial army from 1733 to 1735, even though he was by now elderly and clearly past his best. Austria's subsequent temporary loss of the imperial title amid the 1740s created a bifurcation of command. The Habsburgs treated imperial forces in later wars as separate, subordinate adjuncts and ensured their own army was led by a general entirely of their own choosing. Nonetheless, they remained determined that command of collective forces went to one of their own generals, partly to sustain their prestige as the imperial dynasty, but primarily to retain access to wider German resources. This led to renewed friction with Prussia during the imperial mobilization after 1792, as the Hohenzollerns refused to subordinate their troops to Habsburg generals, while simultaneously demanding that a share of imperial appointments went to their own officers.[3]

Each imperial Estate remained responsible for appointing commanders for its own forces serving separately from Kreis or imperial contingents. Troops provided as auxiliaries to Britain, France, or other European powers usually marched under their own generals, though these in turn were subordinate to the command structures of the states they served. The same continued to apply even after the Empire's demise in 1806, because the Rheinbund armies were integrated into Napoleon's own imperial command structure. Other than Austria and Prussia, only Bavaria and Saxony made war on their own account in the eighteenth century, while Hanover occupied a hybrid position after 1714 as its elector was simultaneously Britain's monarch. In all five cases the ruler retained the final say in appointing commanders in both war and peace, as did the princes of the other German principalities, who usually named a senior officer as head of their armed forces in peacetime.

George II is famous for having been Britain's last monarch to lead an army personally in battle, commanding at Dettingen (1743) during the War of the Austrian Succession, where his force included many Hanoverians as well as British and Austrians. Frederick William I of Prussia, Max II Emanuel of Bavaria, and Augustus 'the Strong' of Saxony also led their armies in person, though without much success. Other reigning German princes served as generals, including George II's father while he was still only elector during the War of the Spanish Succession. However, most preferred the methods already developed during the seventeenth century to avoid personal and political risks by delegating command to a professional general who was bound by written instructions and obliged to consult his immediate subordinates before taking important decisions, such as giving battle.

Frederick II was exceptional in assuming direct and exclusive command in both peace and war. Clearly inspired by the example of Louis XIV, whom he deeply admired, the Prussian king nonetheless practised this in his own idiosyncratic and highly personalized way. Louis, and those who followed his example more faithfully, such as Max Emanuel or Augustus, made sure they were accompanied by an experienced professional to provide advice. By contrast, Frederick dispensed with almost all advice after 1741, insisting he alone knew best and instead expected his generals simply to execute his plans, though those he trusted more were given some latitude as to how they accomplished this. He was merciless in castigating those who failed him, notably hounding his younger brother, August Wilhelm, for mishandling operations after the defeat at Kolin (1757).[4]

Frederick's methods have been widely praised as enabling him to defeat his more ponderous opponents. Certainly, not having anyone to answer to allowed him to take risks.[5] However, he only narrowly escaped death or capture on many occasions and his monarchy, and perhaps Prussia's subsequent greatness, could so easily have come to a premature end, as occurred with Sweden's Charles XII, the only other European monarch pursuing a similarly reckless command style and who ended up shot dead in a trench.

War Ministries

Frederick applied the same methods to foreign policy and civil administration through his highly personalized style known as 'cabinet government'. In contrast to the modern meaning of that term, this had nothing to do with ministerial responsibility or initiative. Instead, the king took practices already developed under his father, but pushed them to extremes by governing from his 'cabinet', or writing bureau, through written orders in response to memoranda and reports from ministers and officials. Prussia's military successes across 1740–63 encouraged several other princes to copy his methods, though rarely with the same work ethic. However, Frederick remained heavily dependent on what information his officials chose to send him. Meanwhile, his denial of initiative and acerbic censure of perceived failures discouraged critical reflection or innovation.[6]

Micro-management remained just about possible, because Frederick William I's creation of the General Directory in 1722 had at last given the monarchy a centralized clearing house for communications with the individual Prussian provinces, which all retained their own administrations. Frederick's reorganization of the General Directory in 1746 created clearer subdivisions along functional lines, with military matters entrusted to the Sixth Department. Department chief General Wedel was named *ministre de guerre* in November 1760, the first use of this title, but his job remained overseeing logistics, billeting, and the Potsdam military orphanage. War funding remained part of the Second Department's business since this functioned in lieu of a finance ministry.

The growing volume of business, notably in personnel matters, forced Frederick to establish General Inspectors of infantry and cavalry in each province in 1763, but he soon made exceptions by allowing units he felt had distinguished themselves in the recent war to communicate again directly with him. Meanwhile, he increasingly relied on adjutants to transmit his orders and provide confidential reports on what his generals and officials were doing. Selected from junior officers who had caught his eye, the adjutants inevitably attracted adverse criticism from their older, more experienced colleagues who resented being bossed about.

Frederick's reputation, inflated by his own relentless self-promotion, held his next two successors in thrall, hindering any serious reform. A Supreme War Collegium (*Oberkriegskollegium*) was established in June 1787 to handle procurement and military pensions, along with separate departments for each service branch. An overlap with the General Directory's Sixth Department persisted until 1790 when this was absorbed along with military finance into the new body, but a further reorganization six years later failed to remove the duplication of functions and confused jurisdiction that continued to characterize Prussian military administration until 1918. Meanwhile, Frederick William II expanded his predecessor's use of adjutants, who were beginning to act in a manner like the infamous Military Cabinet that would exercise such malign influence during Wilhelmine Germany. Although initial efforts were made to establish brigade and divisional commands, this remained incomplete by 1806, at which point the army was still 'run like a platoon' by the king.[7]

Defeat at Jena-Auerstädt on 14 October 1806 finally forced genuine reform. The General Directory and Supreme War Collegium were replaced by ministries organized on functional lines during the second half of 1808. Fearing for his royal prerogatives, Frederick William III split military matters between two departments until finally compelled to establish a single War Ministry (*Kriegsministerium*) under Hermann von Boyen in 1814, which lasted until 1919.

Austria continued the established pattern of consultative decision-making through institutions dominated by civil officials who called on professional officers for advice, rather than ceding control to them. This contrast has generally been explained through the argument that, as a woman, Maria Theresa was unable to emulate Prussia's military monarchs.[8] The Habsburg empress in fact was heavily involved in military strategy and administration, playing a far more active role than her husband, and only gradually and reluctantly ceding ground to her son, Joseph II, once he became emperor and co-ruler in 1765.

Strategic coordination improved with the creation of the Council of State (*Staatsrat*) in 1761, which sat over the monarchy's administrative institutions. These were already organized along functional lines, but still conducted business according to early modern collegial principles, whereby each member voiced an opinion that was combined in a memorandum of advice presented to the ruler for a decision. Initiative remained restricted and the emphasis remained on administration and implementing decisions taken at a higher level. Military matters were still handled by the Court War Council, though the Commissariat was temporarily detached as a separate institution between 1746 and 1766. Officials were quite well paid by the 1750s to safeguard against corruption, while record-keeping improved with the establishment of a war archive in 1711; a move not followed by Prussia until 1816.

Relations between the War Council's president and the field commander could be difficult, but the situation was eased when these two posts were held by the same individual: Prince Eugene (1703–36), Count Daun (1762–6), Archduke Charles (1801–9), and Prince Schwarzenberg (1814–20). Personality greatly influenced how these arrangements worked in practice, notably suffering during the final decade of Prince Eugene's tenure. Relations between commander, council president, and monarch were another important factor. Emperor Francis II disliked his younger brother Archduke Charles, who was undoubtedly the most able Habsburg general of the French Revolutionary and Napoleonic era. Francis reluctantly appointed Charles as War Council President in 1801, and later to the new post of War and Navy Minister, but blocked his calls for reform until 1804 when the War Council was reorganized with civilian department heads. This made no real improvement, but at least the defeat in 1805 allowed Charles to introduce other measures, notably reorganizing the army into corps along the French model. Renewed defeat in 1809 led to Charles relinquishing his posts. Francis refused to reinstate him in 1813 when Austria turned against Napoleon, appointing instead Schwarzenberg, who had already commanded the corps previously assisting the French in Russia.

Charles's post of War and Navy Minister did not last, and the Court War Council continued to administer the army until 1848. The main objection to the ministerial system was its association with accountability to representative institutions. Thus, while Prussia, Bavaria, and most other medium-sized German states created war ministries in the 1800s, these institutions functioned broadly like the earlier war councils they nominally replaced. Ministerial accountability was introduced in the constitutions adopted by the south German states in the late 1810s, and by the two German great powers after 1848, though it remained circumscribed in all cases by the continuation of strong royal prerogatives in military matters.

General Staffs

The highly personalized command style of Prussia's monarchs inhibited the development of a modern General Staff, but even Frederick II was obliged to expand the traditional quartermaster's staff in 1758 to assist in the practical aspects of planning, such as cartography and paperwork. Austria had already done this a few months earlier when Field Marshal Franz von Lacy was named head of an expanded General Quartermaster's Staff, which now numbered thirty officers and nineteen engineers. Field commanders were expressly instructed to consult the staff when planning operations, and Lacy was empowered to second officers to work with individual generals. Lacy was also given command of new regiments of staff troops, which were soon expanded to 4,160 infantry and 1,000 cavalry who relieved other units of guarding headquarters, escorting convoys, and similar tasks.

The new staff worked well, but the associated troops were disbanded to save money in 1762 and the army returned to only a skeleton staff in peacetime.[9] This body concentrated on map-making, a task in which the Austrians had been deficient during the Seven Years War. The use of telescopes, spirit levels, barometers, and improved mathematics, as well as new ideas of knowledge emerging from the Enlightenment, all revolutionized cartography in the late eighteenth century. The combination of better maps and written rather than verbal orders were believed to improve command and control, and help make war more rational.

Archduke Charles again expanded the staff, renewing its place in operational planning after 1795, but it still concentrated on mapping.

Planning became its primary task in September 1805, though under the Court War Council's supervision in a structure that proved unnecessarily complicated. Karl Mack's appointment as Quartermaster General ended in his own imprisonment for surrendering to Napoleon at Ulm in 1805, but Count Radetzky ably fulfilled this role after 1809, contributing significantly to Schwarzenberg's successes in 1813–14. The contrast is instructive in warning against overemphasizing institutional structures when personalities and circumstances often made more difference.

Bavaria (1792), Saxony (1810), and several other armies also established permanent quartermaster staffs, often strongly influenced by the French *corps d'état*, created in 1783. These developments transformed the term General Staff to mean the body entrusted with planning and assisting command, rather than simply a collective term for the army's senior commanders. However, the integration of the Rheinbund armies within France's imperial structure ensured their staffs were limited to operational management, rather than strategic planning. The new Swiss federal army created in 1804 under French direction likewise included a permanent staff of thirty officers to handle logistics and map-making.

However, it was Prussia that ultimately developed the first fully modern General Staff, having benefited from insights brought by officers from the smaller German armies. Baron Massenbach, a former Württemberg officer who joined Prussia's quartermaster staff in 1782, pushed to expand its role, ultimately leading to a thorough reorganization of that body in November 1803. Gerhard von Scharnhorst, one of Massenbach's subordinates, had already made a name for himself as an innovative officer while serving his native Hanoverian army before being invited to join the Prussians in 1801. In keeping with prevailing practice, Scharnhorst was seconded to assist the Duke of Brunswick during the disastrous 1806 campaign, when he found his advice ignored.

The duke, like many senior generals, regarded staff officers as little more than junior assistants, but Scharnhorst already envisaged an entirely different role. Rather than simply relieving the commander of mundane tasks, Scharnhorst argued staff work should expand his ability to control and direct the army. He saw clearly that this would require a new kind of training, extending beyond technical proficiency in practical matters like mapping to encompass genuine strategic planning. As with so many other matters, the defeat in 1806 opened the door to change, allowing Scharnhorst to reorganize the staff in 1807–8, creating a functional subdivision into departments responsible for operational planning, administration, and logistics that were replicated in the separate staffs created in each of the new army corps and divisions. Already in 1809, staff officers prepared studies of the 1806–7 campaign to learn from its mistakes. The War School opened the following year to train future staff officers along the lines devised by Scharnhorst.[10]

Nonetheless, the full impact of these measures lay decades in the future. The king and conservative officers opposed them. The War School closed in 1812, not reopening until 1816, while Scharnhorst's early death in battle in 1813, aged fifty-seven, robbed the reforms of one of their key proponents. Above all, the impact of Prussia's new General Staff remained limited by the fact that the country only fought as a member of an international coalition in which Austria was the dominant German partner.

Intelligence

Intelligence-gathering remained unsystematic and largely detached from General Staff work. Prussian espionage was coordinated by General Winterfeldt, who recruited a retired Austrian lieutenant colonel to provide information, as well as personally travelling to Bohemia in 1750. Other Austrian officers were blackmailed into cooperating, while some criminals were released from prison in return for serving as spies. Austria also recruited former Prussian officers and Jacobite exiles serving in various armies. Plans of enemy fortresses were especially prized, since this allowed engineers to assess weak spots prior to siege operations.[11]

Information was often poor and even accurate reports were not always believed. Frederick II simply refused to accept that the Austrians had improved their artillery and entered the Seven Years War severely underestimating his opponents. Most information remained tactical and derived from scouts, deserters, and personal knowledge and observation. Frederick had ridden over much of the ground his armies fought on, and he excelled in spotting opportunities provided by the terrain. Until the development of effective observation balloons in the later nineteenth century, battles could often be won through concealing troops in dips in the land, or through knowledge of fast routes behind obstacles. Military cartography and effective scouting could bring decisive advantages and, like Frederick, Napoleon again proved the importance of exploiting the opportunities of the landscape, notably in his victories at Austerlitz and Jena.

THE CADRE SYSTEM

Officer Appointment

Recruitment underwent three important changes across this period. Limited forms of conscription became increasingly important from the 1720s, without fully displacing the reliance on volunteers for much of the manpower. This was combined with furloughing a growing proportion of soldiers for most of each year, thereby consolidating the cadre system that had begun to emerge during the brief periods of peace before 1714 whereby formations were maintained at reduced strength outside wartime. Pressures of renewed warfare after 1792 produced significant reforms, expanding conscription by removing many of the previous social and economic exemptions, and by introducing a regular annual draft that transformed military service into a cohort experience for each successive group of young men. While in response to the French Revolution, the reforms did not transform German soldiers into citizens-in-arms, though this concept was introduced into the ongoing discussions over how best to organize an army.

None of these changes substantially affected how officers were appointed or promoted, with the largely decentralized yet hierarchical structures of the previous century remaining in place. Older studies argued that Prussia's kings after 1713 forged a loyal 'service nobility' by compelling noble families to send their sons to serve as officers. In fact, like other German armies, Prussia had no formal system to recruit, train, and appoint officers, very few of whom had been to the cadet schools. Matters remained devolved to regimental colonels, who continued to enjoy wide autonomy in selecting candidates for the entry-level positions.

Although already practised earlier, it became common after 1714 for officers to enrol their sons as NCOs or cadets, allowing them to accumulate years of service that could give preferment when the next ensign position fell vacant. One Württemberg regiment contained a four-year-old boy who already had two and a half years' 'service', while another six children had nominally enlisted at age three or four.[12] Thereafter, promotion remained largely by seniority (*Anciennität*), which continued to run within each regiment, making it difficult for individual officers to advance their careers by transferring to vacancies in other units to jump the queue in their own. Both Frederick William I and Frederick II certainly took a keen interest in who their officers were, intervening on occasion to overrule colonels, or change appointments, though usually punitively, by sending officers who had displeased them to serve in less prestigious units.[13]

Officer posts had become semi-venal across the later seventeenth century, thanks to the consolidation of the company economy which relied on officers investing their own funds in keeping their units functioning. Outright purchase was expressly forbidden in Saxony (1687), Prussia (1700), and several other armies, while the sale of public office was far less common than in Spain or France, or indeed in Britain where commissions remained much more open to purchase until 1870. In an age where most public officials derived a substantial proportion of their income from charging fees for their services, purchase was not invariably regarded as corrupt, provided a higher authority retained final say in the process. The colonel's control of junior appointments combined with the seniority principle to ensure that positions were not openly for sale. Instead, movement up the hierarchy of ranks depended on financial transfer (*Verrechnung*), whereby a junior officer compensated his immediate superior for the investment he had made in the unit.

Thus, money changed hands at promotion from lieutenant to captain and from lieutenant colonel to full colonel, since these involved assuming responsibility for the company and regimental economies respectively. The associated costs could be substantial, amounting in Prussia to 500 to 800 tlr in the case of a company, 6,000 tlr for an infantry regiment, and 8,000 tlr for one of horse.[14] Promotion still depended on official approval, whereupon the successful applicant had to pay substantial fees to the government. The expense naturally prevented poorer officers from advancing, leaving them stuck on their present rank while a less senior but richer comrade overtook them.

The high officer casualties of the mid-century wars ensured relatively rapid turnover and opened chances for merit to be recognized, though there was still no clear definition of what made a 'good officer'. Promotion slowed considerably during the long peace after 1763 when it also became obvious that, despite annual performance reviews, most armies lacked effective mechanisms to remove incompetent or unfit officers. Renewed warfare after 1792 saw significant changes in most officer corps. That of Prussia was artificially preserved thanks to its decade of neutrality after 1795, making the shock of defeat in 1806 more profound. The Prussian Military Reorganization Commission, established in 1807, purged 1,971 of the 7,000 officers within two years. The senior ranks were the most affected, with only twenty-two of the 142 generals still in post. Meanwhile, both the company economy and promotion by seniority were abolished in 1808 to open up the army to talented commoners. As with so many of the liberal reforms, these measures were soon nullified and the army's reduced size after 1815 allowed nobles to resume their dominance of the officer corps.[15]

Volunteers

The two decades of relative peace after 1714 allowed the authorities to assert greater control over recruitment, because the reduced size of most armies lessened the urgency of finding manpower. Nonetheless, the military life offered few material attractions, and most armies were compelled to reintroduce 'capitulations', or fixed-term contracts allowing soldiers to leave rather than being obliged to serve as long as their commanders wanted. Bavaria did this in 1726 for its infantry, initially only offering eight-year terms, but reducing this to four or even three years when renewed warfare after 1733 increased manpower demands. Austria typically offered three- or four-year contracts when recruiting in the wider Empire but expected its own subjects to serve at the emperor's pleasure until 1757 when volunteers were offered six-year capitulations.

At the return to peace in 1763, most armies switched again to six- or eight-year terms, while Austria abolished capitulations altogether. Recruiting difficulties soon forced a return to more attractive terms, and within five years a third of Austria's soldiers were again serving on fixed-term contracts, which allowed men to bargain another bounty if they chose to re-enlist. However, after 1714 company commanders increasingly lost the freedom to negotiate separately with prospective recruits and had to offer standard contracts devised by the military administration. Civil officials were now called upon to witness these to ensure that men were not being duped and had received the promised bounty, while medical examinations were tightened up to assess fitness to serve.[16]

Militia

The traditional militia system remained central only to Swiss defence, where it was expected to provide the contingents each canton owed under the Confederation's system of collective security. Numbers were impressive on paper: the total for all thirteen cantons in 1798 was 196,125 men, or over 13 per cent of the population, compared to the 25,000 professionals away in foreign service. Geneva also had a large militia, totalling 2,750 in the city and 590 from its rural dependencies, in addition to a civic guard of 720 professionals in 1730.[17] While the Swiss were loud in their patriotic rhetoric, many were reluctant to turn out to train or accept military discipline. Efforts to reform Zug's militia in the 1750s provoked popular unrest.[18] The Catholic cantons largely disengaged from the collective structure and attempts among the Protestants to introduce reforms foundered on accusations of meddling in cantonal affairs. Bern counted as one of the best-organized cantons, but only trained its militia for fifteen days a year. It at least managed to mobilize its full 20,000 men when the French invaded in 1798, but these were soon defeated, partly because, other than Solothurn, the other cantons failed to assist.

The new constitution imposed by the French later that year left the militia largely unchanged alongside a small professional federal army. The militia performed poorly in the 1799 campaign, but the Swiss clung to the ideal that militia service expressed their liberties and martial traditions. The revised 1804 constitution retained it, fixing the first levy at 1 per cent of population, with the customary second and third levies available for emergencies. The militia were mobilized to uphold the Confederation's (pro-French) neutrality in 1808, 1809, and 1813, but were unable to prevent Austria from occupying the country in 1814–15. Still neutral, but now inclining towards the Allies, the Confederation eventually mobilized 40,000 men to protect its frontier during the Hundred Days of 1815, but the force took months to assemble, by which time Napoleon's defeat had ended the emergency.[19]

Militias also remained in the Habsburgs' Alpine territories and possessions in southwest Germany into the 1790s, as well as along the

Military Frontier, but were otherwise discontinued. The medium-sized and smaller German principalities retained them after 1714 as a potential supplement to their professional soldiers, whose overall numbers were reduced from a peak of 170,000 in 1710 to around 85,000 during the two decades of peace. Like several other principalities, Württemberg undertook repeated reforms across 1716–38, and most territories had skeleton professional staffs ready to command embodied militia in wartime. Hanover and Hessen-Kassel relied heavily on embodied militia regiments to supplement their regular forces during the mid-century wars, but their performance was mixed and Hanover abolished these regiments altogether in 1763, only to re-establish them five years later.[20]

Conscription

By that point, most principalities had adapted their militia organizations to serve as a form of limited conscription. Militia service already rested on obligations to defend the territory and assist in keeping order, while local communities were required to 'enrol', or register all male inhabitants according to the traditional three levies determined by a combination of age, occupation, marital and family status. Men registered in the 'select' first levy had already been drawn to augment and sustain regular units sent to fulfil imperial and Kreis obligations in the wars before 1714. It was natural to do this again during the mid-century wars and those after 1792. However, many territories were already doing this more systematically by the 1730s to keep their regular regiments up to strength.

The majority used the rolls to draft men while still formally retaining the militia as a distinct military formation alongside their regular units.[21] Prussia was unusual in formally abolishing its militia on 7 March 1713, having only recently reorganized it as a home defence force during the War of the Spanish Succession. However, its famous 'canton system' (*Kantonverfassung*) of limited conscription introduced by 1733 was simply a more systematic version of the ad hoc adaptations of militia structures used elsewhere. It emerged during the 1720s as the king tried to minimize the friction and social unrest caused by his officers who competed for the same pool of native recruits. Regiments were assigned 'cantons' as exclusive recruiting districts, and local officials were soon asked to assist by enrolling the eligible men and summoning them to an annual muster where the officers could select the number required to maintain strength. The exact origins of the canton system are not known, but it may well have been inspired by similar methods used already in Denmark and Sweden, and a major motive was to save the cost of paying bounties to volunteers.

Frederick William I had proclaimed a universal obligation to serve on 9 May 1714 and his successors continued to assert this periodically across the century.[22] However, such statements can be found in the preambles of most German militia and conscription ordinances since the sixteenth century. They reflect their common origins in the late medieval three-tier militias, in which all those not obliged to serve in the first two levies could still be called out in the third as a last resort. Thus, the numerous exemptions to the Prussian draft are not surprising, since these were common throughout the Empire and Switzerland, where the initial select levy was restricted to young, unmarried men in occupations that it was felt could be spared from the economy. Nobles, clergy, public officials, and key workers like miners were exempt, as were major towns such as Berlin, Potsdam, Brandenburg, and Magdeburg, and entire districts in Silesia, Westphalia, and Polish areas annexed after 1793, mainly because their inhabitants were distrusted. Collectively, 1.7 million adult males were covered by these protected categories when the canton law was revised in 1792.[23]

Most territories imposed draft quotas according to each district's population or tax levels, while Prussian cantons were based loosely on the number of 'hearths' as a crude assessment of the number of inhabitants. Where more men were eligible than required, those present had to draw straws or role dice, with low scores being 'bad numbers'.[24] Officers refused to accept those who were physically unfit, but they often connived with local officials to spare the sons of favoured or richer families. The practice of dodging the draft by paying a substitute to serve instead was technically illegal, though it clearly occurred quite often. Governments also interfered with inheritance law and employment contracts to ensure there were always enough recruits.[25] Prussia was unusually harsh in obliging those selected to serve simply 'at his majesty's pleasure' until 1792, when this was finally limited to twenty-five years. Other armies limited service to between three and six years, or the duration of current hostilities, thus making the draft like the contracts offered to volunteers.

In Prussia and the other territories, the burden of service was mitigated by granting conscripts an extended furlough of up to ten months each year after their initial training, which both saved paying their wages and lessened the economic impact by releasing their labour power back to the civilian economy. Prussia also mobilized additional units in four of its provinces during the Seven Years War. Called Provincial Militia, these were akin to the old second levy, being recruited from cantonists who had not been drafted into the regular units. Provincial Militia were disbanded in 1763, unlike the other conscripts who were retained.

Prussia's more systematic draft had four clear advantages over the more ad hoc versions used elsewhere. The army obtained a regular flow of men, friction between regiments was reduced, the furlough system was easier to operate with men being released in their regiment's local district, and the regularity of recruitment enabled families to accommodate it in their lives. Several territories reorganized their drafts along Prussian lines after the Seven Years War, notably Hessen-Kassel, Baden, and Münster. Hessen-Kassel was the first, already dividing its territory into twenty cantons in December 1762. However, it also retained a second-tier levy, requiring those not selected for its regular army to serve in so-called Garrison Regiments intended for home defence; but in practice several of them were deployed to make up the numbers required by commitments to Britain during the American Revolutionary War, a broad cross section of Hessen-Kassel's inhabitants being killed or having settled there. Hessen-Kassel also restricted service to ten years in 1793.[26]

Austria, meanwhile, relied heavily on a different kind of draft that was organized by its provincial Estates who had already been assigned manpower quotas in the seventeenth century and were left largely to their own devices regarding how to fill them. Volunteers were preferred, but the heavy losses across 1733–42 forced the Estates to draft ever larger numbers to meet the army's demands and, during the Seven Years War, they provided 215,546 recruits or their cash equivalent as bounties, with most conscripts given six-year terms. The government already discussed replacing this with a canton system in 1761, but the suggestion was strongly opposed by the Austrian chief minister, Count Kaunitz, who rejected it as epitomizing what he regarded as the evils of Prussian militarism.[27] Backed by Joseph II, the measure was eventually agreed in

February 1770, but it took two years to complete the necessary population census and the system was not fully operational until 1781.
Hungary, the Italian littoral, Further Austria (*Vorderösterreich*), and the
Tirol were all exempt, but the rest of the monarchy was divided into
thirty-seven districts that were expected to provide two-thirds of the
manpower, with the remainder coming from volunteers, including substantial numbers recruited across the Empire. The new system cut out
the Estates and meant that the army now had direct access to manpower; something which made many officers into advocates for social
and economic reforms to improve peasants' welfare and ensure they
were physically up to military service.

Austria suffered heavy casualties in its operations across 1788–90,
during which most of the long-service professionals were killed, meaning
that the army that met the revolutionary French forces after 1792 was
composed of fresh volunteers and new draftees. Renewed manpower
demands forced the army to draw beyond the set categories and take
married men, raising up to 750,000 soldiers annually during the 1790s.
A ten-year service term was introduced in 1802 for infantry, with cavalry
and artillery expected to serve another two and four years respectively.
The Empire's demise cut Austria off from important sources of additional manpower, including its Italian lands, which were annexed by
France. Nonetheless, it was still able to conscript an impressive 630,000
men in 1809.

Revolutionary Challenges

These huge numbers were required to meet those mobilized by revolutionary France. The ensuing clash has been widely seen as a fundamental
turning point in the history of warfare, not least because this is how it
was regarded by many at the time. Clausewitz wrote that 'suddenly war
again became the business of the people ... The full weight of the nation
was thrown into the balance', creating what some have interpreted as the
birth of 'total war'.[28] French numbers were certainly impressive: 1.25 million men were conscripted across 1792–8, followed by a further 2.5
million by 1814. When making comparisons with 'old regime' recruitment, these numbers need to be set into the context of the 25 per cent
growth in France's population across the eighteenth century, as well as its
rapid territorial expansion after 1795. Around 80,000 Rhinelanders were

conscripted into 'French' regiments in Napoleon's army between 1802 and 1814, serving more dutifully than native Frenchmen and especially Belgians, who had the highest proportion of draft dodgers. Additional manpower was obtained when France annexed Holland and much of northwest Germany in 1810.[29]

Beyond the increased numbers, French mobilization made a lasting ideological impact, creating the myth of the patriotically motivated 'citizen-in-arms', for whom military service was a duty owed to the nation in return for enfranchisement and other political rights. This had long antecedents and already formed a central part of Enlightened discussions of military reform in France, Germany, and elsewhere during the late eighteenth century.[30] Actual implementation in France fell far short of the ideal. The revolutionaries initially relied on volunteers to supplement the regular army when they declared war on Austria early in 1792. When this proved insufficient, they summoned a *levée en masse* in 1793, nominally putting the entire nation on a war footing, but in practice selecting an initial draft of 300,000 men drawn from quotas imposed on each administrative district. Draft dodging was widespread, and the system was replaced in September 1798 by regular conscription in annual cohorts of twenty-year-olds who were to serve five years or the duration of the war. Although the universal obligation was reiterated several times, exemptions were always made, and these were codified in April 1799 when the rich were also allowed to pay for substitutes.

The bloody victories of the 1790s lent these measures the mystique of military success, imparting a powerful legacy that endures today. By granting male suffrage, the Jacobin regime linked service with political rights, fostering the belief that the soldiers served the nation, not a monarch; something that Napoleon was careful to continue after assuming personal power. The measures appeared to extend freedom and equality yet expanded state power, while the supercharged patriotism delegitimized personal objections. This sleight of hand sustained the impression that French soldiers were motivated patriots whereas, after an initial flurry of enthusiasm, an average of only some 3,500 men actually volunteered each year for military service.

The German Response

These developments had three important consequences for German military practice. First, French superior numbers and successes convinced many that larger armies were necessary and that these could no longer be provided by established methods of recruitment. Second, the association of mass armies with revolution made them politically suspect, raising the spectre of a 'peoples' war' that would sweep away the established order, as appeared to be the case in France. This encouraged many officers and conservatives to argue that an alternative form of nation-in-arms had to be found. Third, the association of political liberty with the apparently voluntary nature of military service proved powerfully attractive to those favouring more liberal reforms. Notably, they took inspiration from the French National Guards, who formed, largely spontaneously, in 1790, both to protect the moderate, early revolution and to defend property against 'the mob'. These volunteers had served in separate units from line troops until 1793 and continued to exist as a middle-class home defence force after the expansion of conscription.

The German response was framed by the traditional militia structure of three levies, though there were considerable variations in how this was implemented and the extent to which the changes were influenced by French ideas. Broadly, traditional militias disappeared completely as conscription was expanded to sustain the regular army, which now relied almost completely on draftees rather than volunteers. For example, Württemberg abolished the distinction between regulars (*Haustruppen*) and militia (*Landmiliz*) on 17 August 1799, with the latter formally disbanded that December when the remaining militiamen had to relinquish their arms. Men were now drafted directly into the army from the pool of those who were eligible. Using an incident involving armed poachers as a pretext, the government then disarmed the entire population in June 1809; a measure that resulted in the surrender of large quantities of firearms including, startlingly, over 120 pieces of artillery, indicating just how imperfect the formal monopoly of violence had been. Meanwhile, the system of militia recruitment was repurposed as one for conscription, which was duly extended to the additional lands acquired in the territorial redistributions after 1803. Substitutions were initially permitted until the law was fully revised in August 1806 when cohort conscription was introduced, but in practice many still escaped the draft while those called up had to serve long terms: eight years in the infantry, or eleven in the cavalry.[31]

While Austria kept its existing conscription system unchanged, Saxony and Bavaria followed a similar path to Württemberg, initially consolidating militia service into a draft in the 1790s, and then revising this into cohort conscription in 1811 and 1812 respectively. Universal service was reaffirmed, and exemptions and substitutions were abolished. A significant proportion of soldiers were furloughed to save money and soften the impact of the expansion of armies to meet obligations to France. Demands increased as warfare became almost continual after 1808, forcing both Saxony and Bavaria to follow France and permit substitution. Westphalia adopted the French method immediately with its conscription law of 1808, drawing men at twenty to serve five years, with the option of substitution. Bavaria conscripted 25,000 men in 1808–9, followed by over 44,000 in 1812–14 when it was forced to call them up a year early, and Westphalia had drafted over 28,000 men by the beginning of 1813.[32]

While the new conscript regular army took the place of the traditional first levy, additional forces were raised as a secondary force, officially for home defence, but with the possibility of being called into the field to provide additional numbers. On completion of their term of service, Württemberg soldiers transferred to reserve units formed in 1808. Other states created similar units, but Austria proved more influential by creating a new, second-line force known as the *Landwehr* the same year. This was drawn from men who had not yet been drafted but was also open to those in exempted categories who could volunteer. The government did not trust Hungary and Galicia, both of which remained outside the system. Only seventy of the nominal 170 battalions were formed, and of these just 15,000 men served in 1809, representing 6 per cent of effective strength. Three-quarters of those drafted in Upper Austria deserted, and the army soon pressed the remaining Landwehr men into regular units. After his victory over Austria in 1809, Napoleon insisted that the Landwehr be completely disbanded, but the registers of available men were maintained. Fifty battalions were mobilized in 1813, but did not see action, because the army already had enough conscripts. Despite this limited role, the voluntary aspect of the Landwehr featured prominently in the patriotic propaganda issued in 1809 when Austria stood virtually alone against France and proved a powerful influence on Prussia.[33]

Prussian Conscription

Prussia had left its recruitment unchanged, though the territorial redistribution in the Empire since 1802 had cut off the supply of additional men from beyond its frontiers, on which it had relied heavily. The disaster of 1806 finally cleared the way to revise the canton system. Reformers like Scharnhorst advocated a liberal, middle way between what they perceived as the excesses of a Jacobin 'peoples' war' and their own king's conservative insistence on royal control of the army. Inspired by both Austria's example and that of the Spanish guerrillas opposing Napoleon since 1808, they argued that Prussia needed more motivated soldiers who could be trusted to fight in open order like the feared French skirmishers.

Like the king and conservative officers, the reformers were acutely conscious that Prussia was not yet ready to fight France and that any changes to its army had to be made within the tight constraints imposed by Napoleon in 1808, which had limited the regular army and banned reserves and militias. The first response was the introduction of what became known (for unclear reasons) as the *Krümpersystem* in 1809, whereby the army deliberately called up too many cantonists, discharging the surplus after a few weeks. This covert training programme system simply copied what had already been practised openly under Frederick II, and even including these reserves, total strength grew only modestly from 53,523 in 1807 to 65,675 in early 1813.[34] More radical measures were clearly needed.

The final breakthrough came in February 1813 once it became clear that Prussia was heading for war with Napoleon and the king now had no choice but to raise a large army. The package of measures is usually interpreted as introducing universal service but is better understood as Prussia's own variant of the broader German adaptation of the three-levy model to meet current conditions. Like Austria and the Rheinbund states, conscription supported the regular army as the equivalent of the old 'select' first levy. The 1792 canton regulations were suspended on 8 February for the duration of the war, removing all exemptions except for sole breadwinners, clergy, and on health grounds. Recognizing that this would be unpopular with the wealthy, Scharnhorst simultaneously sanctioned the formation of volunteer units open to men who could pay for their own arms and uniforms. This represented the Romantic, liberal element of the reform, and it was expected to provide units of motivated patriots who would form the equivalent of the second levy to assist the regular army. Scharnhorst entrusted the poet Ernst Arndt with framing a patriotic appeal calling for a 'national war' against the French by invoking a Romantic 'martial spirit' and myths like the Nibelung saga.[35]

Scharnhorst was obliged to accept additional, conscripted second-line units, because the East Prussia authorities had already begun to draft men from the old exempt categories into new formations modelled on the Austrian Landwehr. These were belatedly sanctioned by Frederick William III in his famous decree 'To my people' on 17 March. As in Austria, the Landwehr was open to volunteers, with resort to conscription ostensibly applying only if insufficient men came forward. Finally, the *Landsturm* was decreed as a temporary third-tier force on 21 April, to comprise all those, mainly older men not already serving in the other formations. Inspired partly by the example of the Spanish guerrillas, it was supposed to wage an insurgency against the French, who were still occupying much of Prussia.

Interpretation of these measures has been clouded by what they came to mean during arguments between liberals and conservatives after 1815. The Landsturm was not a novel idea; it had the same name as the third levy of traditional militias. The Reichstag had already decreed 'arming the people' (*Volksbewaffnung*) in 1794 in direct response to the French *levée en masse*, and over 33,000 militia had been raised by the southwest German authorities against Prussian objections that this was politically dangerous. The governments involved swiftly agreed after several mutinies, and the militias were stood down.[36] Prussia now went through the same process, disbanding the Landsturm on 17 July 1813 as too revolutionary.

The new volunteer units were also regarded with some suspicion, because of Prussia's experience with Major von Schill in 1809. Defying royal orders to observe Prussia's neutrality in Napoleon's war with Austria, Schill had taken his regular hussar regiment across northern Germany in the hope of raising the population against the French yoke. 'Cheered by many and supported by few', he was declared a deserter and was executed after being captured by Dutch and Danish troops serving France. He only became a popular hero after his deserter status was formally annulled in 1872.[37] By contrast, Major Lützow, who had served with Schill, was lauded as a patriot for leading a 3,000-strong all-arms volunteer *Freikorps* (free corps), raised in 1813 and operating independently of the regular forces. The personnel were solidly middle-class and included Friedrich Jahn, a Romantic nationalist who founded the German gymnastics movement, and Theodor Körner, who was killed in action and whose posthumously published poems immortalized the volunteers as youthful heroes fighting for the fatherland. The unit's black, red, and gold tricolour, replicated in its coat, facings, and buttons, was subsequently adopted as the national colours by German liberals.

In all, 49,372 men volunteered during 1813, an impressive number given Prussia's reduced population and a clear indication that Scharnhorst's appeal had found a positive response. Of these, 24,841 served in volunteer units, including Freikorps like Lützow's and the Hanseatic Legion, as well as the equally famous volunteer *Jäger*, or rifle battalions attached to regular infantry brigades. The remaining volunteers joined the line and Landwehr units.[38] However, overall, they represented less than a tenth of Prussia's manpower and their importance was due more to their inspiration to later liberal nationalists.

By contrast, conscription expanded the line army and reserves to over 140,000 and the Landwehr to 113,000. Overall, one in ten Prussian males was now in uniform. Prussia lacked enough muskets to arm so many, with available stocks going first to the regulars. Conservatives distrusted the Landwehr because local authorities were empowered to nominate the officers. However, such fears were unjustified, since appointments were still subject to royal approval and most of those selected were district officials and reactivated former officers, including many who had been dismissed in 1808. Rather than representing a 'peoples' army', the Landwehr was simply a mechanism by which Prussia could raise more conscripts than could be trained, equipped, and incorporated within regular units. Bavaria, Hanover, and other German states also organized Landwehr between 1813 and 1815, likewise relying on conscription to provide the manpower and arming them with muskets supplied by Britain, Austria, or Russia, or those captured from the French. Many served only reluctantly, notably the Saxons and Rhinelanders conscripted in 1815 after it had become known that the Congress of Vienna had assigned their homelands to Prussia. Nonetheless, the effectiveness of the Landwehr improved over time with more training and better equipment, and these troops formed a substantial proportion of the Prussian and Hanoverian forces at Waterloo.

HORSE AND MUSKET

Size

The eighteenth century saw a dramatic rise in the overall strength of German armies, from 343,000 at the peak of the War of the Spanish Succession in 1710 to about 700,000 in the last years of peace before the French Revolutionary Wars. This increase was around four times faster than demographic growth and contrasted with the armies of several other European powers, which either remained largely unchanged or, as in France's case, even declined slightly across this period. The total number of Swiss serving in foreign armies rose modestly from around 65,000 in 1690 to peak at 77,000 in 1748, before declining to 39,900 on the eve of the French Revolution. France's discharge of most of its Swiss troops in 1792 cut that total to about 25,000.[39]

As with all statistics, the overall numbers conceal a more complex picture. Whereas the smaller German armies collectively equalled the combined Austrian and Prussian strength in 1710, the two German great powers accounted for nearly seven of every eight soldiers by 1790. This disparity only emerged in the 1740s with the onset of open Austro-Prussian rivalry. Prior to that point, Austria's forces had fluctuated between a peacetime low of 108,000 (1740) and a wartime high of 205,000 (1735), with the smaller forces broadly following a similar trajectory, whereas Prussia's force had increased steadily from 46,100 (1714) to over 77,000 (1740). Thereafter, the smaller forces remained broadly within established parameters, peaking at a combined total of 165,000 towards the end of the Seven Years War, but both Austria and Prussia now significantly augmented their strength. The smaller territories disengaged from this process, maintaining only reduced establishments after 1763, while Prussia and Austria, after a drastic but brief cut in strength until 1775 to save money, both then substantially increased their forces. Throughout, Austria's army remained consistently larger than Prussia's, except during the self-imposed period of economies between 1762 and 1775, and by 1790 the Habsburgs had mustered 400,100 compared to their Prussian rivals' total of 195,000.[40]

Based on this data, the broader German lands were unquestionably the most heavily militarized part of Europe, but the overall population supporting these forces nearly doubled to 48.2 million in the century to 1800, chiefly thanks to Austria's and Prussia's annexation of much of Poland after 1772. The territorial acquisitions added twice as many people as would be expected from natural demographic growth, though it should be remembered that neither Austria nor Prussia drew as many recruits from their non-German possessions, in proportion to population, as they did from their German and Czech heartlands. It also needs noting that, outside Austria, between a third and a half of soldiers were on unpaid furlough for most of each peacetime year, substantially reducing the effective 'present' strength.

The Revolutionary and Napoleonic Wars saw the armies of both German great powers fall substantially in size, while those of the reorganized medium-sized states grew significantly after 1806. Austria's last Turkish War of 1788–90 decimated its army, which could muster only 230,000 effectives when it first faced France in 1792. Defeats and territorial losses by 1802 restricted it to 263,000 when it faced Napoleon again in 1805 during the War of the Third Coalition. Field forces totalled around 283,400 in 1809, backed by 310,000 reserves, but nearly half the latter were Landwehr who only existed on paper. Renewed defeat enabled Napoleon to impose a formal restriction of only 150,000 men and while the actual number remained higher, the army was in poor shape and lacked equipment, and now had a much smaller population to draw upon thanks to significant losses of territory. It is testimony to the monarchy's resilience that it eventually fielded 568,000 men in 1813.[41] Meanwhile, Prussia's army remained static at a nominal 235,000 until its defeat in 1806 at Jena-Auerstädt, after which, as we have seen, it was rebuilt to 281,000 by August 1813, also now supported by a much-reduced population, revenue, and territory.

By contrast, many of the smaller armies increased substantially after 1792, initially in response to the Empire's mobilization and then as their princes sought to survive the rapidly changing political order after 1802. Württemberg's army had doubled to around 7,000 by 1800, before growing more than fourfold to 28,600 by 1809, or substantially above the doubling of its population through the territorial redistribution. It sent contingents of 12,000–16,000 men in each of Napoleon's campaigns of 1806, 1809, and 1812, losing virtually its entire strength in the latter, yet still fielding 24,500 against France in 1814. This effort was considerably above that made in 1866, when it fielded 16,956 men, despite having over a third more inhabitants.[42]

While its growth was initially less spectacular, Bavaria now emerged as unquestionably the third German military power. At 15,000 men in 1799, its forces were scarcely larger than they had been for much of the past four decades, but reforms after 1804 substantially increased this and by 1815 it had 75,800 men under arms. Bavaria combined with Baden and Württemberg to provide 32,120 troops for Napoleon's war with Austria in 1805, with this support rising to 65,800 during the conflict against Prussia the following year. The Rheinbund fulfilled its full obligation to France by fielding over 122,000 in 1809. Like the Empire, the new federal structure still contained twenty-seven small states whose collective contingents amounted to only 15,600 men compared to the seven large ones which each fielded between a brigade and a corps. Nonetheless, the smaller contingents all suffered considerable casualties, especially in Spain and Russia between 1808 and 1812. Whereas the Austrians and Prussians were able to disengage without significant loss in 1812, the Rheinbund contingents suffered the full horrors of the infamous retreat from Moscow yet managed to rebuild its armies within six months by calling up more conscripts.[43]

Understandably, those involved felt the burden of war was unprecedented. However, even if various guard and other units retained at home are added to the field forces, collectively the Rheinbund states' armies probably did not exceed 150,000 men, or around 20,000 fewer than their predecessors in the Empire had maintained during the War of the Spanish Succession, when their populations were at least a quarter smaller, and they had lacked the administrative economies of scale secured through the territorial redistributions from 1802 to 1810. The Swiss Confederation presents a similar picture. Its treaty commitments with France after 1803 obliged it to provide 16,000 infantry, to which units from Valais and Neuchatel added about another 1,700. While up to 12,000 Swiss still served Bourbon Spain in 1808, many of these troops were in fact Spanish and their numbers soon declined. Overall, the total in foreign service was only marginally above the number after 1792, which was around a third of what it had been in the 1740s. The units in French service had consumed 32,849 recruits by 1813, thus replacing themselves twice over across a decade; horrendous enough, but less than the attrition suffered by many Austrian and Prussian regiments in the

Seven Years War, to give just one of several possible examples from these earlier, supposedly limited conflicts.[44]

Infantry

Infantry still formed the backbone of all armies after 1714, with its organization broadly unchanged from the late seventeenth century until the 1790s. Austrian regiments remained much larger than those in other armies, including Prussia's. The number of Hungarian regiments had tripled to nine by 1741, when they represented nearly a fifth of Habsburg regular infantry. The only significant change was the grouping of grenadier companies in separate battalions, though in most armies this was only an ad hoc tactical measure.

Improved manufacture enabled armies to standardize muskets to a greater degree, but these stayed much the same until Prussia's introduction of the double-ended ramrod in 1777, which marginally improved speed in reloading since soldiers no longer needed to remember which end to use. The M1780 Prussian musket had a conical touchhole, which made an equally marginal reduction in misfires. Muskets otherwise remained as heavy as those of the seventeenth century and had equally large calibres, limiting their effective range. Together with its bayonet, the average musket weighed about 5 kg, while the sixty rounds of ball and powder that had become the common ammunition allowance by mid-century added 4.5 kg. Belts and the fairly useless short sword increased this by a further 1.35 kg, with another 5 kg for a knapsack with its vital contents of spare clothing, cleaning materials, and food, plus a further 1 kg for a haversack with the bread ration. A tin water canteen, as well as each soldier's share of the common mess equipment like a kettle or tent pole, brought the average load to around 27 kg.[45]

Carrying full kit naturally slowed movement, which in any case was restricted due to the premium placed on keeping the ranks and files aligned to ensure effective platoon fire and for the officers to retain control of their men under battlefield conditions. Soldiers were often ordered to leave their knapsacks and other heavier equipment on the ground before taking position in the line of battle. While this reduced fatigue and facilitated swifter movement and firing, it could be disastrous for morale and health if the unit had to retreat quickly; the crippling losses to sickness suffered by the Württembergers assisting Austria was blamed on their having lost their knapsacks at the battle of Leuthen in December 1757 and then surviving by digging vegetables from the frozen ground without shelter for five days.[46]

The standard pace of advance was around 55 metres a minute, with 'at the double' for manoeuvring the unit being about 74 metres. Not until 1797 did Prussia's regulations increase speed to 100 metres a minute. Prussia introduced the cadenced step to make it easier to keep the ranks aligned, and this was copied by Austria in 1754. Marching for consecutive days over poor roads could cause sick rates to rise, and most armies tried to rest one day in every three or four. Even in an age that generally emphasized outmanoeuvring above outfighting an enemy, armies often spent long periods in billets: the Prussian musketeer Dominicus marched for only 1,598 hours between July 1756 when his unit was mobilized and the end of November 1759 when he was captured by the Austrians.[47]

The absence of significant changes in weaponry magnified the importance of minor adjustments in tactics and training. The main advance during the eighteenth century was to standardize drill so that musketry and manoeuvres were common to all regiments. Changes were always incremental and often minor because officers were reluctant to teach soldiers new tricks. Standardization began earlier in the smaller armies, where it was easier to impose uniformity. Bavaria had had a single manual since 1674, and the other south German forces had these by the 1720s, with the Kreise playing a major role in promoting uniformity among their members. All these manuals borrowed heavily from practice in the imperial army which, as the largest and most prestigious force, remained the model to follow. However, opposition from many colonels frustrated Prince Eugene's efforts to standardize Austrian drill and it was not until 1749 that the infantry had a single manual of arms.

This was unnecessarily complex in comparison to Prussia's 1726 regulations, which were already adopted, at least in part, by Württemberg and several other smaller territories ahead of Frederick II's victories in the 1740s that cemented Prussia's reputation. Revised in 1757, Prussia's regulations influenced France's manual from 1764 and were copied to a considerable extent in Austria's new manual in 1769. They were carried across the Atlantic by Friedrich von Steuben, an unemployed Prussian captain who convinced Benjamin Franklin to hire him as instructor to the new American army in 1777.[48]

Manuals might have become standardized, but their interpretation remained largely left to individual officers. New recruits were taught the basics individually by a veteran or an NCO, before being drilled together. Training could be intense, beginning at 2 a.m. for Prussians and not ending until midday, but after the initial few weeks of practice was restricted to around an hour daily. Most armies held at least battalion-sized exercises annually in peacetime from the 1680s, with summer encampments becoming relatively common after 1714. Although these were not as 'realistic' as modern exercises, they at least taught soldiers some basic field craft. Lack of suitable land and the cost of compensating farmers for damaged crops generally restricted their scope. Frederick William I had part of his capital's famous Tiergarten park cut down to make a 1 km² drill ground in 1730, which became known as the 'Berlin Sahara' on account of the sandy soil. Prussia became famous for its regular annual manoeuvres involving mock battles, held regularly from 1743 and copied by Austria after 1752, and by some other armies on a smaller, less regular scale.[49]

A major purpose of drill was the socialization of recruits into military life and to accustom them to subordination and to acting in choreographed unison.[50] It was widely believed that it took at least two years to turn a peasant into a soldier, but the extension of the furlough system made this difficult to achieve. Furloughed men were expected to become proficient in individual drill within eight days of rejoining their unit for the spring exercise months, but officers complained 'they are almost as ignorant as recruits'.[51] Concern that men returning from leave would disrupt their unit's performance in the king's presence at Prussia's autumn manoeuvres led to some lucky individuals not being recalled at all.

Johann Neubauer spent seven months in training in the Prussian army before he fired his first live round in 1726.[52] Lack of funds restricted live firing, though Prussia later used wooden bullets as practice ammunition, while the Austrians used targets shaped like Prussian grenadiers. Prussia emphasized speed over accuracy, but though it was possible to fire up to six rounds a minute using blanks, four was a more realistic bet with live ammunition, and rates dropped under battlefield conditions. Some Prussian regiments fired up to three times their standard allowance of sixty rounds during battles in the Seven Years War, indicating how sustained musketry had become a central part of linear tactics. However, firing often commenced at extreme range.[53] Prussian infantry already formed in three ranks in 1735, thereby ensuring all muskets could be brought to bear, but the use of two-rank lines on occasions in the Seven Years War was an expedient forced by insufficient numbers to match enemy deployment.

Austria had already noted the Prussians' proficiency in 1706, but Prince Eugene remained sceptical, doubting whether they were anything more than parade-ground troops. The battle of Mollwitz proved otherwise in 1741. The Austrian infantry lost formation as the numerous new recruits, trying to escape the withering Prussian fire, bunched behind their more stoical comrades, until some units were thirty ranks deep. However, following this the Austrians soon caught up, adopting iron ramrods and platoon fire in 1742, and three-rank deployment in 1757.

By that point, linear tactics had reached the limit of what was possible given the human and technological constraints, fuelling a long debate over the relative merits of shock tactics versus firepower. Beneath the arcane discussions of technical details was the simple question of whether a continuous, steady advance with levelled bayonets was more intimidating to an enemy than the attackers halting at close range to deliver disciplined musketry. Officers were concerned that it could be difficult to persuade their men to resume an advance if their fire failed to break opposing troops. Frederick II increasingly emphasized pressing ahead without pausing to fire. Fourteen battalions advanced with shouldered muskets at Prague in May 1757, only to falter in the face of intense Austrian musketry before being completely broken by a well-timed counter-attack. A similar massed attack by nine battalions failed at Kolin a few weeks later.

Cavalry

These difficulties increased the importance of effective cooperation between the different service arms. However, the emphasis on massed musketry made that difficult to achieve, since the infantry deployed in long lines in the centre, displacing the cavalry to the wings, while artillery remained in a largely supporting role. Cavalry's battlefield duties remained those of the proceeding century: defeat their mounted opponents and then exploit opportunities to attack enemy infantry at a disadvantage in the hope of converting a marginal success into a major victory.

Cavalry remained the most prestigious arm and still formed around a quarter of total strength into the early 1770s. Thereafter, the proportion in the Habsburg army dropped to 17 per cent, before slipping to 15 per cent during the Revolutionary and Napoleonic Wars, though medium-sized armies, like the Hanoverians and Saxons, still maintained the old proportion. The exception was, as ever, Switzerland where only around 2 per cent of cantonal militia were mounted, equipped as dragoons.[54] Austria always maintained large regiments of around 1,000 or more troopers, with Prussia gradually expanding to match it, while those in the smaller armies were only half that size. Austria finally abandoned the subdivision into companies in 1769, with the larger squadron hence-forth the primary administrative and tactical unit, though, given the Habsburg army's preference for mass, these were often paired as 'divisions' in battle.

Cavalry remained organized into the types established by the later seventeenth century, with roughly a third of Prussian cavalry being cuirassiers, dragoons, or hussars in the 1750s.[55] Cuirassiers were expensive, due to their armour and large mounts, and their numbers were halved in the Austrian army by 1780. The Habsburgs added a *chevau-léger* regiment in 1758; literally meaning 'light horse', this was intended as a hybrid medium type for both scouting and line of battle duties. Favoured by Joseph II, who was painted in his chevau-léger colonel's uniform, there were seven regiments by 1792 and the type was copied by several other German armies, notably the Bavarians.

Following the earlier example of the Saxon army, the Habsburgs also raised *Uhlan* (lancer) regiments after their annexation of Polish terri-tory, while Prussia also added a regiment of *Bosniaken*, or Balkan lancers.[56] Classed as light cavalry, Uhlans wore distinctive Polish square-topped caps, whereas chevau-légers and increasingly other cavalry types wore tall leather helmets. Lancers became much more common during the Napoleonic era, partly because they also found favour with the French and were adopted by several Rheinbund armies. Lancers had an initial advantage in an attack and could strike infantrymen, who often went prone to avoid cavalry sabres, but handling lances required skill and they were much less effective in melees with other cavalry.

Cavalry deployed in two ranks by the 1750s, riding boot-to-boot during attacks. Charles XII of Sweden had introduced the full gallop charge around 1700, relying on speed and shock, but this was not universally favoured. Riders could easily lose formation and their horses could blow or snort due to stress or fatigue, leaving them vulnerable to a counter-attack from an enemy who did not panic. Nonetheless, Frederick II adopted the full gallop charge in 1744, blaming the poor performance of his cavalry in earlier battles on their slowness. By 1754 Prussian cavalry were trained to commence their attack 860 metres from the enemy, accelerating to a full gallop across the final half. Troopers were ordered to hold their swords raised, ready to strike down at the enemy, adding to the intimidating impact. This proved highly effective against enemies who were already in disarray, or had not finished deploying, as at Hohenfriedberg (1745) and Rossbach (1757) respectively, but it was not noticeably superior in other situations to more conventional tactics.[57] The distance for the final gallop was shortened to only 180 metres in 1774 to conserve the horses' energy and the unit's alignment.

The wars between 1740 and 1815 were undoubtedly the heyday of European cavalry. Over 20,000 Prussian troopers beat 18,000 Austrians at Leuthen in December 1757 in the century's largest cavalry clash. Massed cavalry attacks became an essential feature of Napoleonic warfare, in which they involved columns of multiple squadrons lined behind each other, supported by horse artillery.

Austria copied this after 1805, but such attacks were often wasteful, even if they succeeded. The Saxon heavy cavalry brigade lost 652 of its 1,030 men charging the Rajevski Redoubt at Borodino (1812) in a desperate measure launched to break stubborn Russian resistance. While still allowing for massed attacks, Prussia's new cavalry regulations from that year already drew appropriate conclusions and assigned cavalry more of a supporting role, prefiguring later nineteenth-century tactics.

Light Troops

The development of chevau-légers and lancers alongside hussars reflected a desire to improve the capacity for scouting and skirmishing. However, both new types were established from the outset as regular units with a designated battlefield role. Already regularized around 1700, hussars followed the same trajectory as dragoons during the seventeenth century, increasingly called upon to supplement battle cavalry rather than being employed as skirmishers.

Thus, the development of light infantry as skirmishers supporting their 'heavy' counterparts in the 'line of battle' represents a more significant change in this period, though it stemmed initially more from a desire to increase manpower rather than a deliberate attempt to introduce new tactics. Austria, Prussia, and the smaller armies each took a different route, with the first of these leading the way. The Habsburgs applied their own version of a 'martial race' theory, regarding Hungarians, Croatians, and the peoples from the Balkans as somehow naturally suited to irregular warfare, but the monarchy's growing centralizing tendencies produced a series of ill-judged and counter-productive attempts to regularize the Military Frontier forces. Annexation of Serbia and the Banat in 1718 prompted a reorganization intended to assert tighter supervision and reduce costs. Another attempt followed in 1736, only to be disrupted by the disastrous Turkish War that saw the loss of Serbia. Finally, reforms were forced through after 1746, imposing a regimental structure on the border infantry, followed by a new legal code in 1754, curbing soldiers' privileges, but enhancing their officers' status. The Banat and Transylvania were formally incorporated within the Military Frontier in 1752, extending it to a strip 1,600 kilometres long by up to 120 kilometres wide. Each stage in the reorganization provoked mutinies that secured some concessions but failed to reverse the steady transformation of the borderers from privileged militiamen into regular soldiers.

The results were impressive in securing additional manpower. From a population of only 350,000 settlers, the Habsburgs were able to draw around 14,000 men permanently for their wars in the Empire across 1740–63. Since units served on rotation, no fewer than 88,000 borderers fought in the Seven Years War, while the total strength of the force rose from 42,000 in 1740 to about 75,000 in 1788. Borderers were often excellent boatmen, and they did useful service in raiding across rivers and covering retreats. They played a major role in hounding the Prussians out of Bohemia in 1744, but they were not considered steady enough to face disciplined troops in battle. General Laudon created a two-battalion Freikorps in 1759 of line troops to follow up once sniping from the borderers had thrown the enemy into disarray, but this unit was disbanded at the end of the Seven Years War and Austria failed to develop an integrated system of light and heavy infantry tactics.[58]

Prussia took a different course, believing that any recruits could be trained to fight irregular warfare. However, Frederick II was convinced that disciplined infantry would always prevail, and his use of light troops in the Seven Years War was mainly motivated by the shortage of manpower. Recruiting from occupied territories, deserters, and prisoners of war, Prussia eventually formed fourteen infantry regiments, five mixed infantry and cavalry corps, and two cavalry regiments, all distinguished by the prefix 'free', meaning independent of the regular army establishment. Somewhat smaller numbers were formed again during the War of the Bavarian Succession.[59] Although these were occasionally used in raids, their primary duty was to combat the Austrian borderers through conventional musketry and simply to make up the numbers on secondary fronts otherwise drained of the best units by the king for a major battle. In short, considering both the borderers and small wars generally as inferior, Frederick created his own inferior-class troops to handle them.

Whereas the two great powers sought mass, the smaller armies opted for quality, developing the detachments of 'huntsmen' (*Jäger*) appearing briefly in seventeenth-century wars into small, elite units of riflemen fighting as snipers in support of heavy infantry. Hessen-Kassel was particularly noted for this, not least for its riflemen's success in targeting officers, which especially earned the ire of the Americans in the Revolutionary War. Recruited from foresters, and often employed as such in peacetime, riflemen were already skilled in fieldcraft and marksmanship, but their numbers were always limited. Prussia and Austria had both established similar corps by the 1750s, but these likewise remained a small elite.

Several Hessians and other Germans returning from America in 1783 became advocates for regular light infantry who could fight conventionally in line or skirmish in loose order. Many officers remained sceptical, with some justification given skirmishers' vulnerability to cavalry, which had been virtually absent from American battlefields. Nonetheless, Prussia established twelve battalions of fusiliers as permanent light infantry in 1787 and trained ten men in each company as sharpshooters. Several other armies did likewise, but this simply continued the relegation of light tactics to units that were generally considered inferior to their line counterparts.

By contrast, Revolutionary France detached sections from each infantry unit forward in loose order as *tirailleurs* to screen the advance and to harass and disrupt the enemy through skirmish fire. Contrary to the myth, these were not invariably successful: massed French skirmishers were repulsed by disciplined Prussian musketry at Kaiserslautern in November 1793 and it was not until 1795, when French tactics had become a more sophisticated combination of light and heavy infantry, that they became more effective. Both Austria and Prussia adapted after 1806, likewise attacking in battalion columns screened by skirmishers. Such tactics required good training to be fully effective, and units often went forward as a mass without screens.[60]

Artillery

The artillery remained the smallest and least prestigious of the three main military arms, and limited to a supporting role, except in siege warfare. Austria maintained the largest establishment, but still only had 800 gunners in its field artillery in 1746. Numbers expanded dramatically as artillery's importance grew during the mid-century wars; by 1763, Austria had over 4,800 artillerymen, with this almost doubling by the 1780s. Prussia's field artillery likewise increased from 785 men in 1731 to 6,309 in 1768. However, the Saxon artillery, always the best among the smaller armies, grew from 2.4 per cent of total strength (1730), to 6.6 per cent (1791), a proportion not otherwise reached in German armies until the late nineteenth century.[61]

Later seventeenth-century science transformed ballistics through the development of modern calculus and an understanding of air resistance. The improved knowledge fed through into gun-founding, notably in the M1731 Prussian artillery system. However, neither the M1741 nor M1758 models were as good; a salutary reminder that technological development is not always linear. Already inferior in the 1740s, Prussian artillery was completely outclassed by the new M1753 Austrian system developed by Prince Wenzel Liechtenstein, who invested the fortune he inherited into designing new cannon. The M1753 was the world's first fully unified system, standardizing on 3, 6, and 12 pdr field guns using lighter, unadorned barrels, and more precisely cast roundshot that reduced windage. The new pieces were so effective that the type remained in service until 1859 and was copied by Saxony (1766) Prussia (1768), and Bavaria (1785), as well as influencing Jean-Baptiste de Gribeauval, who served as French liaison officer with Austria during the Seven Years War and subsequently reformed the French artillery.

Liechtenstein also introduced the first modern artillery manual in 1757, assigning specific duties to each man in the gun crew, and introducing annual target practice.

Prussia began the Seven Years War with only 360 field guns, 236 of which were small regimental pieces, indicating artillery's primary role as close support for the infantry. By 1768 the field artillery had 320 heavy guns and 88 heavy mortars to 358 regimental pieces, reflecting the greater role assigned to counter-battery fire to silence enemy artillery, as well as longer-range targeting of enemy formations in support of attacks. By 1760 each Prussian brigade had a supporting heavy artillery battery, and within two decades the ratio of guns to men had risen to five to six per 1,000, or roughly double that in 1700. The artillery train depended on conscripted peasants who were not accorded combatant status. Both Austria and Prussia found their artillery a hindrance during the War of the Bavarian Succession, slowing their own movement and discouraging offensive action.

Prussia established a battery of horse artillery in 1759 to provide more rapid support by mounting the gunners to accompany the horse-drawn gun team. There were twenty batteries by 1806, while the Austrians followed suit in 1760, with horse artillery forming a twelfth of their artillery by 1771. They also introduced the *Wurst* (sausage) elongated gun carriage in 1762, allowing the crew an uncomfortable ride. Innovative for its time, this had been replaced by the seated limber, with the gunners mounted on the ammunition box, by the Napoleonic era. True horse artillery only emerged in France after 1792, thanks largely to Gribeauval's improved, lighter gun carriages.

Prussian artillery's shortcomings were exposed in 1806–7 when most of its guns were captured. Although these were replaced with newer, better pieces, the army had only 1,659 guns of all types in 1812, less than a quarter of the total six years before, and only 236 were available for its field army in 1813. Austria also lost 800 cannon to France in 1809. Many of the captured pieces were distributed to the Rheinbund armies. Meanwhile, the ratio of guns to men in the French army rose from two to five per 1,000 across 1800–12. One factor was Napoleon's use of massed batteries to bombard the enemy before launching an attack. Another was the reintroduction of regimental guns in 1809. Abolished only four years previously as a drag on movement, these were now regarded as essential to support an infantry whose deteriorating training adversely affected their musketry. France continued to assign light guns to its infantry for several decades after 1815, whereas Prussia had already permanently discontinued this practice in 1812, adopting what would become the standard practice of assigning field batteries to each infantry brigade. Infantry would remain without close-support weapons until the introduction of machine guns in the 1890s, followed by trench mortars twenty years later.

Technical Troops and Fortifications

Technical troops acquired a distinct identity as they were separated from the artillery. In Austria, this process took place between 1718 and 1772 for the different specialist branches of engineers, pontooneers, sappers, and miners. Along with Saxony, the Habsburg army led the way, with Prussia considerably behind in terms of organization and capacity. Austria swiftly copied France by adopting the optical telegraph in 1799, using flags in the Habsburg colours of red and white to send messages across mountainous terrain in a matter of minutes and which could be seen by officers newly equipped with telescopes.[62]

Alongside bridging rivers and building earthworks, the primary tasks of specialists remained the design, construction, maintenance, defence, and capture of fortresses. A major reason for the constitution of a separate engineer corps in 1718 was Austria's acquisition of the Netherlands and Italian fortresses from Spain, in addition to the ongoing task of maintaining those of the Military Frontier. Long negotiations with the Dutch failed to secure an agreement to extend the Netherlands 'Barrier' up the Rhine to protect against France by incorporating places like Mainz and Kehl, which had been built after 1683 to block France's seizure of Strasbourg two years earlier. Instead, the Empire was left to continue its own arrangements based on the imperial fortresses established by 1714. Other than Mainz, these were poorly maintained after the 1750s and failed to stem French attacks following 1792.

Although Mannheim was again rebuilt in 1715, Baden-Durlach's new capital of Karlsruhe was left unfortified when it was founded the same year. Bremen, Hanover, Kassel, Leipzig, Münster, and several other major towns were deliberately defortified following the Seven Years War. Combined with those destroyed by the French in 1688–9, around 150 German towns lost their defences in the century to 1789. A further

350 followed by 1815, largely at the insistence of the French, including the former imperial fortresses of Kehl, Philippsburg, and Breisach, meaning that 60 per cent of German towns were now deliberately 'open', indicating that they would not be defended to avoid making them military targets.

Austria had already demolished many of the Barrier fortresses in the Netherlands after these failed to stop France in 1747. Although new works were built at Königgrätz, Josephstadt, and Theresienstadt after 1766 to protect Bohemia, Austria relied primarily on its army for defence. Prussia was thus exceptional in embarking on a major building programme in the 1720s, extending this after the conquest of Silesia and annexation of West Prussia. Berlin was defortified in 1734; something that Frederick II later regarded as a mistake after the Austrians and Russians twice raided his capital during the Seven Years War. Various minor or exposed forts were abandoned after 1752, but work continued to strengthen Magdeburg, Stettin, Wesel, Kolberg, Königsberg, Graudenz, and major fortresses in Silesia, notably Schweidnitz and Neisse.[63]

Fortresses played a major part in Prussia's defensive strategy under Frederick William I and Frederick II. Acutely conscious that their lands lay open to invaders, both kings saw fortresses as immovable rocks to prevent an enemy securing a firm foothold in any of their provinces. Separate garrison regiments were created in the 1720s from men considered too short, too old, or otherwise unsuited for field service, while the field army received the best recruits and was intended as the offensive element. This dichotomy worked during the mid-century wars but failed completely when the field army disintegrated in 1806, prompting most fortresses, after so many years of building and preparation, to surrender to the French after only minimal resistance.

VENTURES AT SEA

A Minor Role

Europe's navies grew from 614,000 tons in 1720 to 1,668,000 tons in 1815, thanks to an increase in the overall number of ships, and because the size of an individual battleship grew sixfold between 1650 and 1815 to reach 3,000 tons. Warships were sophisticated, purpose-built vessels, requiring specialized dockyard facilities. Merchantmen could no longer be substituted for warships, nor could the running costs of the latter be subsidized by using them for commerce in peacetime. Although Bremen, Hamburg, and Lübeck had 480 merchantmen in 1786, the total German mercantile fleet represented only 3.7 per cent of European tonnage, while German warships never exceeded 1.5 per cent of European naval power at this point.[64]

With maritime trade restricted and Prussia's colonial ventures abandoned by 1717, there was little economic incentive to invest in expensive naval forces. Hamburg's escort force declined by two-thirds to only 1,000 tons by 1775. Saxony briefly had some gunboats on the Elbe in the 1730s, while the Palatinate had maintained a couple of armed yachts on the Rhine since the 1680s, but these were largely for show. Austria revived its Danube flotilla during the 1716–18 Turkish War with new oared gunboats, but these were badly designed, and the force was outnumbered and defeated by the Ottomans across 1737–9. Although the flotilla was revived, it also failed to stop the French in 1805 and 1809.[65]

Austria's Mediterranean Fleets

Austria's acquisition of the Spanish Netherlands and Italian territories prompted it to establish a small seagoing fleet after 1714. Spain left no ships behind, and the few that Austria bought merely matched those of the Knights of Malta and were equivalent to only a sixth of the Venetian navy on which Austria depended in the 1716–18 Turkish War. Austria's impotence was demonstrated in the conflicts from 1718 to 1720 when it was obliged to rely on Anglo-Dutch support to oppose Spanish efforts to recover Sicily. A ship from the new Ostend Company was captured by Barbary corsairs in 1724 and its crew were sold into slavery. Austria paid bribes through its envoys in Constantinople to secure treaties with Tunis (1725), Tripoli (1726), and Algiers (1737) to stem their commerce raiding.

Meanwhile, efforts were made to build a fleet based at Trieste using British experts and Spanish and Italian officers to protect interests in the Adriatic and Mediterranean. This grew to a respectable 9,000 tons, with a total of 500 guns and 8,000 crew by 1735, or more than three times the personnel then manning the Danube flotilla, while an infantry regiment was deployed as marines. However, the Ostend Company, having invested heavily in new bases in the Bay of Bengal, failed by 1731 due to Anglo-Dutch opposition to its activities, and the loss of Naples and Sicily in 1738 removed the new navy's rationale. Most of the ships were sold to Venice, while the remaining personnel were transferred to the Danube flotilla.[66]

Austria renewed its tribute to the Barbary corsairs after 1748, but the same simple measures could not be employed against Prussia, which licensed several English ships as privateers in the Mediterranean and Baltic during the Seven Years War. Russia's Baltic fleet sailed to the Mediterranean in 1769, defeated the Turks at Chesme the following year, and landed troops in Greece. Conscious again of its impotence, Austria constructed another small squadron based at Trieste in cooperation with Tuscany, which had become a Habsburg secundogeniture in 1738. As previously, the new force was linked to broader efforts to emulate Anglo-Dutch success in global trade, this time by establishing the Trieste Company in 1774, run by an Englishman, which secured bases in Mozambique, the Malabar Coast, Pegu, and Canton. Regular patrolling proved too costly and several of the warships were sold, only for Austrian shipping to again fall prey to English privateers licensed by Prussia during the War of the Bavarian Succession. Joseph II now ruled against reviving the squadron, calling it a 'most useless and vain exercise'.[67] A new treaty with Morocco in 1783 finally succeeded in reducing the corsair attacks, and when the Trieste Company became overextended two years later, Joseph refused a bailout and it went bankrupt.

Austria's annexation of Venice in 1797 secured control of the republic's respectable navy, which totalled thirty-seven warships armed with 111 guns, but shortage of funds ensured these had only 787 crew, compared to the 365 men of the new Lake Constance flotilla of fifteen gunboats and patrol craft. Both these forces were lost along with their associated territories by 1805, while defeat in 1809 forced the cession of Istria as well, temporarily ending all maritime activity.

Prussia's Baltic Flotilla

In addition to licensing privateers, Prussia briefly organized a flotilla of oared gunboats at Stettin to protect the Pomeranian coast during the Seven Years War. An attempt to break the Swedish blockade of the Oder failed in September 1759. The flotilla was rebuilt, totalling fourteen galleys with 130 small guns and 650 crew by 1761, but it failed to prevent the Swedish capture of Usedom island or the loss of Kolberg and was already disbanded by May 1762. A few small warships were maintained in the early 1790s, and again ten years later; however, all but one were sold in 1808. Alliance with France required Prussia to enforce the Continental System, necessitating the acquisition of a few more gunboats. Sweden handed over six more when it transferred Stralsund to Prussia in 1815, but all bar one gunboat had been sold within five years.

Prussia resumed state-sponsored maritime trade in 1750 with the establishment of the Asiatic Company, while the more successful Maritime Company (*Seehandlungs Gesellschaft*) was formed after the annexation of West Prussia from Poland in 1772. The Swedish and Russian blockade halved Prussia's maritime trade during the Seven Years War, while the brief war over the annexation of Hanover in 1806 saw Britain seize 300 Prussian merchantmen.[68]

These incidents would later feature in justifications for developing a German battlefleet, but it is hard to see how Prussia, or indeed Austria, could compete with Europe's established naval powers at this point, given the huge disparity in expertise, experience, and resources. German military thought, together with the social, cultural and economic repercussions of conflict, would remain primarily determined by land warfare, though the overall impact of these discussions was far from limited, as the next chapter will show.

9

Socialization of the Military

ENLIGHTENED WAR AND ITS CRITICS

Military Knowledge

The eighteenth century saw armies become permanently embedded in society. Soldiers remained a distinct corporate group, but they lived among civilians, particularly in towns, and were the most visible sign of the state's presence and its claims to monopolize warfare. As with most aspects of German military history, this process has been subject to a variety of diverging interpretations. One influential view focuses on Prussia and other principalities, like Hessen-Kassel, which likewise maintained disproportionately large armies and argues that the presence of so many soldiers militarized society. Others instead argue soldiers remained detached as a despised, marginalized group whose profession was of little interest to wider society.[1] Neither perspective captures the more complex realities of military–civilian relations in this period, as will become clear throughout this chapter. However, both clichés do reflect important strands in contemporary debates on warfare and armed forces in German-speaking Europe.

Military thinking drew heavily on ideas already articulated in the seventeenth century, but increasingly gave greater consideration to the purposes of war and the relationship of soldiers to civilians. Frederick II's many contradictions included his concern for secrecy combined with a desire to demonstrate his mastery of military affairs. His *Instructions*, summarizing his thoughts on how best to conduct war, are now among his best-known works, but initially only fifty copies were issued to his generals in 1753 and it only reached a wider audience after the Austrians captured a copy in 1760. Yet he also wrote prolifically on military history and theory, including carefully crafted accounts of his own campaigns intended to protect his reputation for posterity. In doing so, he was engaging in the burgeoning military public sphere, which was in turn part of lively debates about politics and society conducted through new periodicals, reading clubs, and salons across the German lands.[2]

Discussions were characterized by a growing faith in the human capacity for progress that was at the heart of what has been termed the Enlightenment. While several Enlightened thinkers criticized war as irrational, most sought to reduce its impact by finding ways of achieving victory more efficiently.[3] Rather than taking inspiration from the past or seeking to return things to an imagined idealized state, problems were now addressed through reforms presented as improvements on current conditions. The strongly utilitarian approach shifted the emphasis to practical applications, rather than sticking with custom and established knowledge. The experimental aspect was most evident in ballistics where target practice was measured scientifically to improve performance. Although governments still regarded decisions for war and peace as exclusive prerogatives, they nonetheless released unprecedented volumes of information through new official publications, such as gazettes and court calendars that listed all senior officials and military personnel by name and gave details about the organization and strength of their armies. The Empire's common institutions, notably the Reichstag, published its proceedings, including debates on war and peace, as well as issuing innumerable printed ordinances and regulations.[4]

The existence of different armies ensured that this Enlightened military public sphere was decentralized and multivocal. Although the Prussian army was widely admired by the later eighteenth century, its officers were far from the leading figures. The most important of the new specialist periodicals was *Das neue militärische Journal* published in Hanover between 1788 and 1805, which had around 450 subscribers. Compared to the nineteenth century, the interest in military affairs remained fairly niche, with no more than twenty new books appearing annually by 1800, though Johann Wilhelm von Archenholz's history of the Seven Years War, published in 1791, was a bestseller and still remains in print. Discussions among officers were also part of the general fashion for sociability characteristic of the age. Like those in many other garrison towns, Würzburg officers selected a café and paid a monthly subscription to sustain regular meetings after 1774; a practice that developed as the officers' 'casino', or club, that remained an integral element in all German armies into the twentieth century. The Potsdam garrison had an active literary circle that included Major Ewald von Kleist, who was a friend of leading writers, including Lessing who himself had served as private secretary to General Tauenzien during the Seven Years War.[5]

While indicating that soldiers were not detached from broader cultural and intellectual life, such activities were nonetheless the pursuit of a minority of officers. Military education continued to be dominated into the later eighteenth century by the established emphasis on practical experience and on-the-job training. The curriculum at the Prussian cadet school, opened in 1717, remained narrower than those at the traditional knights' academies, thanks to Frederick William I's notorious hostility to bookishness. Academic subjects received greater attention under his son Frederick II, who established a separate *Académie Militaire* as an elite school for the most promising cadets in 1765, as well as separate branches of the ordinary school to serve the provinces. Overall, only 6,000 of the 45,000 Prussian officers serving between 1713 and 1807 had attended cadet school, and while the proportion was higher among those who became generals, this also reflected that such individuals usually came from a more privileged background and could afford the tuition fees.

Cadet schools were opened in many of the medium-sized principalities such as Bavaria (1756) and Münster (1763), but Prussia was far from being the only inspiration. The privately run Chaotic Institute, founded in 1666 through a bequest from the eccentric Baron Chaos, provided the Habsburg army with an engineering school that was reorganized as a state institution in 1717, with another college established in Brussels a year later. Whereas these charged high fees, the Austrian cadet schools opened in the 1750s offered free education to the sons of officers and noblemen. The same applied to the higher military academy established in 1752 at Wiener Neustadt, 45 kilometres south of Vienna, which had 200 students who also received free uniforms if they passed the three-year course and joined the army. While much of the teaching was delivered by monks, Wiener Neustadt graduates were considered a military elite by 1815. This relative openness to commoners was shared by some principalities, such as Hanover, and contrasted with Prussia's restriction of education to the nobility. France briefly became the model during the Napoleonic era, notably for the Westphalian War Academy

(1808) and artillery school (1810), and the polytechnical institutes opened in Prague (1806) and Vienna (1815).

Overall, cadet schools and military academies primarily served to educate officers' and noblemen's sons, many of whom subsequently went on to entirely different careers. Of the 1,496 graduates of Württemberg's *Karlsschule* from 1773 to 1794, only 140 became officers, though thirty-three of these rose to the rank of general. The proportion of Prussian generals with university education doubled to 12 per cent across 1730–1813, but for most officers military knowledge remained the practical skills to understand drill and minor tactics, manage subordinates, and run the company economy.[6]

Attitudes to War

War was broadly accepted as a necessary evil, and even the devout Pietists were prepared to accept standing armies provided they were led by humble, God-fearing men.[7] Nonetheless, those in authority remained concerned for their personal reputations, if no longer for their souls, and felt obliged to justify the use of force to their peers and their subjects. Frederick II resorted to various tortuous legal arguments to legitimate his entirely unprovoked attack on Austria in 1740 and tried to present both the first two Silesian wars and the Seven Years War as religious conflicts in defence of Protestantism in the Empire. The imperial army intervened to quell university students in Lutheran Jena who objected to the emperor's war with Prussia in 1759. However, most remained unconvinced by Frederick's efforts and the Protestant burghers of Heilbronn continued to taunt Prussian recruiting officers in their city long after 1763 by accusing the king of having stolen Silesia.[8]

Such instances show that the general population was far from indifferent to warfare. Military parades drew large crowds, such as the famous review of the Hanoverian army at Bemerode in 1735. The widespread popular admiration of Frederick II was due more to his prominence as a successful general than as an enlightened monarch, and the largest-selling image of him was the engraving by Daniel Chodowiecki from 1777 showing him in military uniform reviewing his troops. Pictures of the king and other military themes featured widely on snuffboxes and porcelain, creating a pool of images drawn upon by nineteenth-century artists to fashion enduring impressions of eighteenth-century warfare. Many of these items were relatively cheap, as were the 'victory ribbons' which first appeared in the early eighteenth century within days of a battle and showed the triumphant general and other patriotic motifs. Production peaked in the Seven Years War, though victory ribbons experienced a brief revival at the opening of the First World War.[9] However, it would be wrong to interpret this as evidence of any militarization of society; rather, they are manifestations of a broader culture of consumption, with similar items for sale at pilgrimage sites and after imperial coronations and princely weddings.

If war was broadly accepted as a fact of life, its excesses were not, and Prussia's growing prominence led it to attract most of the criticism. Archenholz, himself a former Prussian captain, condemned Frederick William I for having turned Berlin into a 'copy of Sparta . . . dedicated to Mars where despotism in its most grotesque form bared its teeth', though he praised Frederick II for turning the city into a new Athens by combining military prowess with arts and culture.[10] Perhaps under-standably, Austrians were more straightforwardly hostile. Maria Theresa presented the Seven Years War as essential to smash Prussian militarism before it forced other European powers into an intolerable arms race.[11] The Habsburg government was convinced the Prussian army was something exceptional, breaching civilized norms, and their internal discussions echoed the aphorism, variously attributed to Vol-taire, Mirabeau, and the Prussian minister Friedrich von Schrötter, that Prussia was an army with a state, rather than a state with an army. Para-doxically, that led the Habsburgs to pursue a more extreme form of warfare than Frederick himself, by arranging with their allies in 1756–7 to dismember Prussia.

Foreign service was a second aspect of war that attracted growing criticism in the later eighteenth century. Hessen-Kassel, the leading Ger-man supplier, signed thirty-eight conventions to supply soldiers to other powers between 1677 and 1815, mostly without attracting adverse com-ment prior to the 1770s. The despatch of auxiliaries to serve Britain during the American Revolutionary War (1775–83) prompted unpreced-ented criticism among German intellectuals, largely because the men were sent overseas against an enemy posing no obvious danger to their homelands. However, criticism remained broadly within established bounds, whereby the practices of individual princes were condemned, without the entire system being called into question. The involvement of cultural luminaries, such as the playwright Friedrich Schiller, provided an articulate critique that was instrumentalized after the 1830s as part of a far wider effort to condemn the surviving minor principalities as barriers to German unity, but had no impact at the time, with German princes continuing to hire out troops to other powers up to 1815.[12] Such criticism was also not representative of all opinion. The general perception among the troops was that Britain's cause was just and the Americans were ungrateful rebels. Service in America, as well as that of Hanoverians in India between 1782 and 1792, coincided with widening curiosity about faraway places. Letters home and subsequent books by veterans were received as travelogues that attracted considerable interest.[13]

Discussions in Switzerland differed because foreign service was associated with the Confederation's neutrality rather than with princely courts. Swiss regiments had encountered each other on opposing sides in several major actions during the War of the Spanish Succession, but the clash between Bernese units in French and Dutch service at Malplaquet in 1709 became notorious because of that engagement's status as the bloodiest battle of the eighteenth century. Of 20,000 overall casualties, 8,000 were Swiss including 2,000 dead.[14] The incident featured in arguments that foreign service endangered neutrality because it risked dragging the Swiss into other people's wars. Criticism grew after France unilaterally imposed a new set of terms in 1763–4, ending the hereditary ownership of companies and reducing soldiers' privileges. The Helvetic Society, formed in 1761, responded by sponsoring an essay competition in which the winning entry condemned foreign service as depopulating the country, while the Zürich economist Johann Waser was executed in 1780 for calling the practice a 'cancer in the womb of Helvetia'.[15]

Despite the emotive language, criticism largely remained selective and reflected wider struggles within the Swiss Confederation's elite over access to power and resources. Protestants condemned arrangements with France but supported those with the Dutch Republic. Most patricians continued to believe foreign service was necessary to avert over-population, while many of the objections came from officers who felt widening access to company commands threatened their shares of already dwindling profits. France's refusal to increase pensions since the seventeenth century forced the leadership of several Swiss cantons to restrict distributions to existing recipients, leading to prolonged disturbances in Zug between 1728 and 1736 that eventually broke the dominance of the powerful Zurlauben family.[16] The growing contro-versy over foreign service added to the factionalism of Swiss politics but, as in the Empire, it fell short of full condemnation of the practice.

Violence

We have far more sources about eighteenth-century soldiers' experience of violence than for the preceding two centuries, but what these tell us remains broadly the same. Johann Jacob Dominicus, a Prussian private during the Seven Years War, had his musket smashed in two by a can-non shot at the battle of Prague (1757). Two years later at Kay, bullets perforated his uniform in four places and he regarded the intensity of the Russian artillery fire as 'something that is not permitted in war'.[17] As with most soldiers, his diary is a record of his constant search to find food and dry shelter, while his experience of battle was that of constant thirst amid the acrid smoke as he sweltered in his woollen coat and bundles of equipment.

Most soldiers accepted that, as the Prussian Lieutenant Barsewisch put it, 'those who expect pleasant days in wartime should stay at home'.[18] Enlightened rationality made little impact on most soldiers' attitudes, which remained rooted in the same fatalism characterizing their forebears across the preceding two centuries who likewise put their faith in God. Some clearly became disillusioned. The veteran Col-onel von der Streithorst wrote to his master, the duke of Württemberg, in 1720 after four gruelling years campaigning against the Turks and Spanish that 'it is said that there is already a fresh war in Poland. The devil knows where all these wars come from. I've had enough now for a few years and will leave it to another who has itchy feet.'[19]

Official efforts to foster hatred of enemies had limited effect. The Turkish Bells were rung for the last time in Austria's unsuccessful war of 1737–9, which simply opened rifts in the Empire, with the Jesuits blam-ing the defeat on the decision to entrust command to the Protestant General Seckendorff. Many were uncomfortable with the mid-century wars pitting parts of the Empire against each other and Prussian sol-diers expressed admiration for the bravery of their Austrian opponents in the Seven Years War. Much depended on context and how soldiers behaved, rather than necessarily the power they served.

The authorities remained reluctant to endorse popular opposition to invaders, even when this occurred, as in Bohemia where peasants attacked Prussian and Saxon detachments in 1741. They were also ambivalent about employing irregulars, such as Trenck's Pandours in Austrian service in the 1740s, since their association with atrocities undermined official claims to be waging a legitimate war. Officers serving with such units increasingly petitioned for them to be taken into the regular establishment to protect their reputations and improve their status.[20]

The long peace after 1763 led to growing criticism of armies that focused on concerns that soldiers lacked enthusiasm. It was this Enlightened critique that fashioned the stereotype of soldiers as 'hired, thoughtless, will-less machines' which has so profoundly shaped subsequent interpretations of eighteenth-century armies.[21] Some writers simply developed the earlier Christian moral criticism of soldiers, but others used the same language to voice fears that brutal discipline had created an army of 'marionettes' that might break under the pressure of battle. Much of the discussion focused on making minor improvements to soldiers' conditions, but some writers drew inspiration from new ideas about the natural world to argue for the adoption of more fluid tactics requiring greater personal initiative.

A minority embraced the modish Romanticism of the end of the eighteenth century to argue that war could promote 'rebirth' through moral improvement and social renewal. Their arguments went far beyond the Enlightened call to integrate soldiers better into society, and instead demanded the fusion of army and nation in highly emotive language generally devoid of concrete suggestions as to how this could be achieved. They rejected efforts by Enlightened officers, such as Archduke Charles, Georg von Berenhorst, and Dietrich von Bülow, to avoid unnecessary casualties, arguing victory should simply be pursued at all costs.[22] However, most stopped short of 'people's war' in the manner of the Spanish guerrillas of the 1808–14 Peninsular War, and instead continued to see war as remaining under state direction.

These impulses fed into arguments by the Prussian military theorist Clausewitz and others after 1815, who retrospectively dismissed eighteenth-century conflicts as 'cabinet wars' that had been 'limited' in terms of objectives, scale, and impact. This interpretation rested on the belief that the French Revolution had unleashed popular forces which Napoleon then harnessed to fight a wholly new 'war of the nations' in place of what was derisorily dismissed as the 'sport of kings'. The influence of this view can be seen in much of the general writing on warfare between 1648 and 1789, but it caricatures and obscures the often-ferocious reality of pre-revolutionary warfare.

LIFE ON A MINIMUM WAGE

Motivation

Patriotic sentiments drew on established ideas about the 'German Fatherland' and long-standing dynastic and territorial loyalties, but were articulated with new vigour during the Revolutionary and Napoleonic Wars. Austria's war of 1809 against France set the template through proclamations and widely disseminated pamphlets that gave those who volunteered subsequently the rhetoric through which to express their motives, especially when they wrote their memoirs after 1815.[23] The expression of loyalty in more overtly nationalist terms around 1800 does not mean that soldiers prior to that date lacked ideological reasons for enlisting. However, mundane and material factors continued to predominate, as across the previous two centuries.

While limited forms of conscription grew in importance across the century, a significant proportion of soldiers remained volunteers, most of whom were seeking a better life. A key attraction of the Prussian army was its more relaxed attitude to soldiers' marriages, and the 1787 recruiting regulations expressly instructed officers to promise this as a means to lure men from other territories whose desire to marry had been frustrated by material circumstances or parental or clerical objections.[24] Others were drawn by a sense of adventure, such as Johann Caspar Schiller, father of the dramatist, who was dazzled by the glamorous uniforms of a Bavarian hussar regiment as it passed through his home town and joined up to see more of the world.[25]

The retention of units in peacetime after 1714 assisted the development of regimental identities that not only attracted recruits, but held them in the ranks, often despite adversity. Distinctive uniforms and collective rituals, such as ceremonies surrounding regimental flags, all fostered a sense of belonging and could find expression in violent brawls with men from other units in the same army.[26] Concerned to ensure loyalty remained focused on himself, Frederick II sought to suppress regimental histories when these first appeared in the Prussian army in the 1760s.

The king took a more relaxed attitude to regimental bands that were established during the later seventeenth century, considerably earlier than in France. The Swiss and Landsknechts had used fifes and drums to transmit signals in battle over the din of gunpowder weaponry and by the mid-sixteenth century it had become standard practice to include several musicians in each company. These were known collectively as *Spielleute*, who counted as regular soldiers and were paid as such, in contrast to *Hobisten* who were paid either by the regimental colonel or collectively by the officers and who appeared around 1680 with the spread of the *hautbois*, an early form of oboe imported from France, as well as the clarinet, invented in Nuremberg in 1694. Simultaneously, brass and percussion instruments were adopted in emulation of the famous Janissary bands of the Ottoman army.[27]

The combination of more varied instruments played by larger bands allowed for the development of modern military music, which also became a competitive form of display between regiments. Already in the 1660s, heavy cavalry regiments had kettle-drummers whose instruments were decorated with richly embroidered hangings displaying the commander's monogram. The Saxon and Prussian artillery switched their bagpipes around 1740 to drums that were so large they had to be mounted on special wagons. The *Dessauer March*, introduced by Leopold I of Anhalt-Dessau for his Prussian regiment in 1705, is one of the oldest specially composed military tunes, while the *Mollwitzer March* is attributed to Frederick II, Michael Hayden wrote *Der Pappenheimer* march for the Austrian army, and Beethoven produced a quick march for the Bohemian Landwehr in 1809. Other marches originated in their regiment's favourite songs, but the influences also flowed in the opposite direction as composers like Johann Joseph Fux and Mozart incorporated martial, 'Turkish' instruments into their performance works. Meanwhile, musical signals became more complex, especially with the introduction of the flugelhorn from Britain via Hanover in 1758, which became the chief way to transmit orders such as 'advance', 'halt', or 'retreat'. Prussia standardized signals in 1788, which had previously been individual to each regiment, and henceforth each soldier had to recognize eight different tunes, increasing to twenty with the 1812 regulations.

True to his aristocratic nature, Frederick II believed that only officers were motivated by honour, whereas the rank and file were primarily concerned about material rewards. In fact, his soldiers identified as a distinct group, bound by its own codes of conduct and expectations. Religion reinforced a sense of duty, especially for soldiers struggling to overcome fear during combat. Self-belief was fostered through training and experience, while trust in officers and commanders was bought by past victories, encouraging the Prussians to consider themselves as clearly superior to their opponents by the 1750s.[28]

The early eighteenth century saw German princes establish new chivalric orders with hierarchies of ranks and medals to reward good service, such as the Prussian Order of the Black Eagle, created to mark the acquisition of the royal title in 1701, or the *Militär St Heinrichsorden,* founded by the elector of Saxony in 1736 and named after his distant ancestor Emperor Henry II. Like their sixteenth-century forebears, these orders remained status honours granted only to a few, privileged senior officers.

Frederick II established the *Pour le Mérite* shortly after his succession in 1740. Intended to mark genuine achievement, the king regularly held it out as an incentive to bravery prior to battles.[29] It formally became the highest honour for bravery in 1810, and 5,415 had been awarded by 1918. By then, it was known as the Blue Max, combining a reference to its design as a blue enamel Maltese Cross, with its most famous later recipient the fighter ace Max Immelmann. In practice, it remained largely a status order restricted to officers, and a third of recipients during the First World War were generals or admirals.

The spread of Enlightened ideas around mid-century encouraged the belief that ordinary soldiers could also be courageous. Austria's Maria Theresa Order, introduced four days after the victory at Kolin (1757), marked a transition to more modern practice. While still restricted to officers, around a third of recipients were commoners. Bavaria introduced a bravery medal for ordinary soldiers in 1794, followed by Württemberg in 1806 when the practice was becoming more widespread among the medium-sized German states. Prussia belatedly introduced its famous Iron Cross in 1813, designed by Karl Schinkel, the country's leading architect, and modelled on the French *Légion d'honneur,* to recognize civilian as well as military merit. This broader remit was soon forgotten, as virtually all the 17,600 awards between 1813 and 1815 went to soldiers. It was intended as a one-off measure, and there were not even enough medals to go round, with those on a waiting list to 'inherit' their medal as older beneficiaries died out. Eventually, all 60,000 surviving veterans of 1813–15 were given a special campaign medal in 1863. Wilhelm I did not believe that the wars of 1864 or 1866 were sufficiently heroic to warrant resurrecting the honour, which only became fully Germanized with the award of another 45,000 Iron Crosses in 1870–1. As in 1813–15, recipients were still predominantly officers.[30]

Military service retained its attractions for the nobility as a way of demonstrating loyalty to their prince, securing status and reward, and obtaining honourable employment. Saxony's Lutheran territorial Church provided few job opportunities for the electorate's nobility, who petitioned for their sons to be given preference in officer appointments in 1763. While Catholic imperial knights still preferred church careers, those who were Protestant sought military employment: of the seventeen adult males of the Riedesel family in the second half of the eighteenth century, eleven became officers in various German and European armies, compared to five who became officials in imperial institutions or German territorial governments. By the late eighteenth century, many families had generations of service in the same army. The Beck, Bredow, Dohna, Goltz, Kleist, Marwitz, and Schwerin families collectively provided sixty-seven of the 895 generals who had served in the Prussian army by 1791, and even smaller forces had families with long traditions of service, including those from patrician and commoner backgrounds in the ecclesiastical principalities.[31]

While officers continued to enjoy much higher rates of pay than ordinary soldiers, they were also expected to purchase their own uniforms and horses and, when money was short, to accept long delays before receiving their salaries. The principal monetary attraction remained the profits from the company economy, or 'devolved management', which became entrenched during the long conflicts of the later seventeenth century and was consolidated in regulations issued around 1700–20.

Soldiers' pay was subject to multiple deductions for their bread ration, 'invalid money' (pensions fund), medicine, and clothing. The latter was divided into *Große Montour* comprising a coat, waistcoat, hat, and leather belts, which were supposed to be replaced every two to six years, depending on the practice in each army. The *Kleine Montour* consisted of shoes, stockings, gaiters, shirt, trousers, hair ribbons, and the stock, an uncomfortable collar stiffener that soldiers had to endure until they were discontinued in the 1800s. These items were replaced more regularly, generally annually or every two years.[32]

Regimental commanders usually handled purchasing the major items, with the acquisition of the 'small clothes' devolved to each captain for his company. Officers could profit from any surplus funds, but the opportunities for this declined as quality-control measures were tightened, while the allowances were often cut in peacetime when the soldiers were expected to wait longer for their uniforms to be renewed. Periodic experiments in centralized purchasing or state manufacture further disrupted profiteering. Officers could still withhold the pay of men on furlough; officially as a surety to encourage them not to desert, but most armies allowed company commanders to take a cut that was supposed to subsidize the recruiting costs associated with keeping their unit up to strength. These funds accumulated in the company chest, which officers often used as an unofficial bank, profiting by lending money to their men or civilians. Additional sums could be derived from abuse of power, such as demanding fees in return for granting a discharge or permission to marry.

Colonel proprietors in the Habsburg army were making up to 12,000 fl annually in the 1690s, but opportunities declined significantly with retrenchment and tighter supervision after 1714. Prussian infantry captains averaged 1,500 to 2,000 tlr annually, while those in the cavalry made a little more and regimental colonels received about 3,000 tlr. These sums nominally compare favourably with the profits from managing a landed estate; the Kleist family, for example, made about 5,700 tlr annually from their manor at Stavenow in Brandenburg in midcentury. However, much of the company economy was centralized in 1763, halving profits, whereas the value of a landed estate increased fivefold across 1717–1808. Moreover, most Prussian officers only became company captains in their forties and were in their sixties if they reached the rank of general, therefore they did not enjoy these incomes for their entire career. The majority were junior officers whose pay was around 11 tlr a month, or about five times that of a private, while their uniforms were expensive, with the gold and silver lace required for a guards' unit alone costing 105 tlr.[33]

Soldiers' pay remained static and was increasingly eroded by inflation across the century. Demobilization around 1714 left surplus manpower, prompting armies to reduce wages and bounties. The real value of Bavarian soldiers' wages fell by nearly a quarter relative to their position in 1702. Increased manpower demands during the mid-century wars resulted in higher bounties and coincided with a fall in food prices which eased the pressure. The situation declined again in the long peace after 1763, which also saw a sharp rise in the cost of living. A Prussian private received only eight pence (*Groschen*) a week, whereas the cheapest tavern meal with a glass of beer cost tuppence, and sentries in occupied Saxony during the Seven Years War were seen begging.[34] The Prussian army increased pay by a quarter in 1799, the first rise since 1713, but this failed to offset the overall decline, especially as civilian wages rose faster.

Despite the meagre pay, armies remained attractive to the poor. Men signed up for fixed terms, guaranteeing employment for four to eight years. While their pay was subject to the numerous stoppages, they at least received a bread ration, clothing, and accommodation. Prussia provided the bread free in wartime and added a supplementary meat ration. Prussian subjects liable for conscription often volunteered as 'foreigners', because this secured permanent service all year round, whereas conscripts were on unpaid furlough for much of the year.[35] As professionals, they were also entitled to find additional paid employment in their off-duty hours, something that was practised in all German armies. The Prussian army's prestige after the Seven Years War ameliorated its reputation for poor pay and harsh discipline, but its attractiveness to outsiders declined once Frederick II forbade foreigners from owning property and stopped honouring the service agreements by refusing to release men at the end of their contract.

Push factors continued to operate, with recruiting becoming easier during economic downturns or periods of famine, notably that in 1770–1 which led to prolonged problems. While Hessen-Kassel relied on conscripts to supply its auxiliaries during the American Revolutionary War, the other principalities primarily used volunteers, some of whom saw the chance of free passage to a life in the New World. Hanover had little difficulty finding 2,000 volunteers to form two regiments for the English East India Company in 1781, despite competition from those principalities recruiting for American service. Structural economic changes also drove men to enlist, notably the shift to cattle breeding and milk production in Switzerland that required less labour. Moreover, military service remained for many only one stage in their working life. Most

Swiss volunteering for foreign service did so around the age of twenty, serving abroad for an average of six years, before returning home with some money and life experience at what was considered the right age to marry, and settling down to some other form of employment.[36]

Geographic Origins

Swiss regiments in foreign service were still expected to recruit two-thirds of their manpower from the thirteen cantons and their allies, though a blind eye was turned to Germans who, in practice, often included Alsatians, Dutch, and Scandinavians. The remaining third were not supposed to come from the hiring country, so as not to compete with its own recruitment. The French war minister claimed in 1763 that only a sixth of the 18,000 'Swiss' then in service actually came from the Confederation. This is likely to have been an exaggeration, but it certainly became increasingly hard to adhere to the rules, especially for service in armies, such as the Neapolitan, where the conditions were less attractive than in France. Spain deliberately improved pay and conditions in 1804, hoping to recruit the Swiss recently discharged from French service, but simultaneously it relaxed the nationality requirement so that only a third now had to come from the Confederation.[37]

Likewise, German regiments sent abroad contained far more foreigners than those serving their own prince: around 30 per cent of the Hessen-Kassel soldiers in the American Revolutionary War came from outside the principality, compared to only 2.4 per cent in units stationed at home. The foreign proportion in the contingents from the other principalities ranged up to half and outsiders were generally discharged first when hired units returned home. The devolution of recruitment to regiments contributed to variations: only half of the men in German regiments in French service came from the Empire, with Swiss and Alsatians forming most of the rest, but Germans and Swiss could also be found in the Irish units.[38]

Prussia was exceptional in recruiting substantial numbers from beyond its frontiers. Around a fifth of personnel were foreigners during the War of the Spanish Succession; a high figure but not that exceptional compared to other German armies at that point. Frederick William I's expansion of the army after 1713 was initially met from within Prussia, but the introduction of conscription by 1733 made foreign recruitment essential, since draftees were furloughed for most of the year leaving only the cadre of 'foreigners' on duty. The foreign proportion had doubled to 40 per cent by 1740 and peaked at 50 per cent by 1756, before declining to 36 per cent by 1804.[39] In line with the situation in other German armies, the foreign proportion was much higher among the infantry than the cavalry or artillery, which also attracted more volunteers thanks to better pay.

Both Prussia and Austria recruited across the Empire but the bulk of foreigners came from neighbouring territories, except for regiments commanded by German princes, who were expected to recruit their own subjects. Since native volunteers were classed as 'foreign' in Prussian regimental records, a significant proportion (perhaps up to a fifth) were actually the king's subjects. Overall, only 4 to 6 per cent of total Prussian strength were non-Germans, chiefly Poles. While higher than in other German armies, this proportion is considerably lower than the usual clichés suggest.

A tiny proportion came from outside Europe. The Prussian and Saxon armies recruited small 'Janissary corps' from Turkish prisoners during the 1680s and 1690s. These units soon disappeared, and while the Saxon army briefly re-established its unit in 1730–2, only its uniforms, rather than personnel, were Turkish. Turks and north Africans, both universally termed 'Moors', also served as musicians in many German armies. The fifers of the Prussian guard infantry were traditionally Blacks across 1713–1806, supposedly descendants of the elector's African colony. The Hessen-Kassel and Ansbach contingents returned from America with Black musicians recruited from liberated slaves. However, only Prussia maintained a combat unit, initially established in 1744 from deserters of Balkan origin from the Habsburg army. Termed *Bosniaken* (Bosnians), they were dressed in Tatar costume and segregated from the rest of the army with their officers unable to transfer to other units for promotion. Frederick II entertained various schemes to recruit large numbers of Tatar cavalry and eventually a unit of 500 was added to the original Bosniaken in the period 1795–1806.[40]

In contrast to the rank and file, the officer corps remained more cosmopolitan, especially in the Habsburg army, where 39 per cent of infantry and cavalry officers came from outside the monarchy, principally from the Empire and concentrated in regiments commanded by German princes. Habsburg policy remained 'imperial' in the sense that officer recruitment was part of wider efforts to foster loyalty across the Empire, and in this respect the dynasty remained far more successful that their Hohenzollern rivals, whose army generally attracted only imperial knights and lesser nobles from neighbouring territories.[41]

Social Backgrounds

The demobilization in 1714 reduced the number of officer positions, which remained limited until renewed warfare after 1733 saw regiments being augmented and new units raised. Virtually all territories used this as an opportunity to restrict officer appointments to nobles, partly through long-standing prejudice that these had a natural aptitude for command, but also through the desire to bind the indigenous nobility to the dynasty. This was most pronounced in Prussia, where the monarch was able to compel a growing proportion of the nobility to serve after 1713, and despite the fivefold increase in the size of the army, commoners still accounted for fewer than one in ten of the 7,000 officers in 1806. However, the decreasing attractiveness of military service discouraged the wealthy from applying and the proportion of estate owners declined, leaving the officer corps dominated by lesser nobles, including many from outside Prussia.[42]

By contrast, the Habsburg army remained open to commoners, who constituted a third of officers in the second half of the eighteenth century, with the actual proportion of those of humble birth being higher still as commoner officers with thirty years of unblemished service were automatically ennobled after 1757. Attempts to restrict appointment to nobles caused problems in Württemberg, where the nobility had escaped ducal jurisdiction in the sixteenth century. Despite their continued hostility to the duchy's standing army, the patrician families dominating the Württemberg Estates continued to seek officer appointments and lodged formal complaints at the preferment given to foreign nobles. Commoners were always more prominent in the smaller armies, which lacked the prestige and promotion prospects of Austrian or Prussian service, with the proportion averaging around half, though it could be considerably higher in the ecclesiastical principalities where the Church offered better career alternatives for noblemen. Nonetheless, nobles dominated the senior positions everywhere: whereas 432 of the 712 Hessen-Kassel officers were commoners in 1764, only three of the twenty-seven regimental command-ers were non-nobles.[43]

One of the attractions of foreign service was that this usually resulted in the creation of new officer posts, except for regiments raised under contracts with the Swiss cantons, where company commands were monopolized by cartels of patricians and military families. Active service also offered good prospects, given the high proportion of officer casual-ties which could clear the logjam of promotion by seniority. Bravery in battle remained the primary determinant of 'merit', which otherwise lacked a formal definition and was open to abuse. Favouritism frequently determined the selection of generals, including Austria's disastrous reli-ance on Prince Charles of Lorraine, Maria Theresa's brother-in-law, in the opening stages of the Seven Years War. However, the application of merit was perhaps most arbitrary in Prussia, where Frederick II added his own idiosyncratic restrictions based on a scheme prepared in the 1720s that ranked regiments by seniority according to the date of their foundation. The king tweaked the rankings according to his whim, add-ing further difficulties as men from the senior units got preferment. Eventually, the army grew too large for the king to micro-manage, lead-ing to appointments and promotions at junior level becoming increasingly bureaucratized after 1763.[44]

The long peace after 1763 led to superannuation as promotion oppor-tunities declined and elderly officers were retained, often as additional supernumeraries. It now took around twenty-eight years for a soldier to rise from ensign to captain in Prussian service, or twice that before 1756, while all company commanders were over fifty, and half of Prussian gen-erals and a quarter of battalion commanders were over sixty by 1806. The smaller German armies adapted faster after 1792 as they were affected more profoundly by the pressures of mobilization and the consequences of political reorganization after 1802, during which most of the smaller forces were disbanded and their serviceable personnel absorbed by those of the surviving states. Commitments to the Rheinbund also involved significant expansion, notably in Bavaria, Württemberg, Baden, Hessen-Darmstadt, and Nassau, necessitating the appointment of more officers. Württemberg was exceptional in that its newly minted king, Friedrich I, now actively encouraged commoners to boost the proportion of his own subjects among the officer corps. Change was delayed in Prussia by the opposition of Fred-erick William III until the crushing defeat in 1806. Although the proportion of commoners among Prussian officers rose to 45 per cent by 1817, the underlying trend was less dramatic as around half of those in post in 1806 were still serving, including in the senior ranks which remained held by nobles. The real change was that the elderly had been mustered out.

Hans Joachim von Zieten resigned from the Prussian army in 1724 when he was passed over for promotion on account of his small stature. Although he later re-enlisted and rose to become one of Frederick II's most distinguished generals, he did so by joining the hussars, which accepted shorter men. Height became a significant factor determining recruitment after 1714 as armies began specifying minimum thresholds and recording each soldier's stature in the regimental rolls. The general minimum was around 165 to 167 cm for infantrymen and 168 to 173 cm for cavalrymen, or considerably above what was specified later; Austria took men as short as 153 cm in the early twentieth century.[45] Height served as an obvious, if crude, measure of physical fitness, while it had a practical purpose when muskets were about 155 cm long and heavy cavalry rode large horses. Big men also looked imposing and were preferred for grenadiers and other elite troops.

The obsession with height assumed an extreme form in Prussia where it was associated with Frederick William I, but in fact it had already begun during his father's reign and continued during that of his son. Governments seeking Prussia's favour sent exceptionally tall men as diplomatic gifts, while Prussian recruiters targeted large men, sometimes even kidnapping them, knowing they would be rewarded.[46] The concern for height unintentionally exempted many men from conscription. For example, Infantry Regiment No. 3 had 20,737 potential recruits enrolled in its canton in 1773, most of whom were children. Only 4,247 were over five foot, of whom only 124 reached the required minimum of five foot five inches (about 165 cm). Given that the unit needed 60 to 120 recruits annually to maintain strength, virtually all the tall men would automatically be drafted. No wonder mothers told their children: don't grow or the recruiter will catch you![47]

Conscription generally took younger, unmarried men, with most new recruits in Prussia aged just under twenty-one. Foreign recruits were around four years older, with the average age of men in the ranks being in the low thirties. The same was true in Münster where the bishopric's soldiers were around ten years older on average than their predecessors in the later seventeenth century. Grenadiers were considerably older than musketeers because they were selected from veterans. In short, eighteenth-century armies placed a premium on age, considering mature men as more reliable and better able to cope with the rigours of service. Austria's reduction of the minimum age for service from twenty (or twenty-one) to eighteen in 1746 was considered an emergency measure, rather than desired.[48] Nonetheless, as with officers, peacetime led to superannuation as men were retained because it was too expensive to pension them off and pay bounties to find replacements. The situation was usually worse in the smaller forces: less than half of Augsburg's civic guard were fit to take the field when the city had to provide its contingent to the imperial army in 1795.[49]

Older men tended to have previous military experience, particularly the foreign recruits who had often served in several armies.[50] Otherwise, recruits frequently gave no prior profession when their details were entered in the regimental rolls. Former textile workers usually formed the largest occupational group, reflecting that trade's often precarious character, but most regiments had a small minority of educated professionals who had perhaps fallen on hard times. There is little evidence, however, to substantiate the cliché that the ranks were filled with convicts or prisoners of war. Soldiers were far more likely to be sent to the workhouse for punishment than inmates be pressed into service. The exception was when units were being raised for foreign service, since this was often done at short notice and provided a convenient way of getting rid of undesirables.[51] Armies were reluctant to accept deserters from other forces, rightly suspecting they would abscond once they had received their enlistment bounty.

Prisoners of war were only recruited in large numbers during the Seven Years War. The entire Saxon army of 18,177 men was pressed into Prussian service after it surrendered in October 1756. More than half of the unwilling soldiers deserted within a month, and soon 10,000 had reassembled on Habsburg territory to reform their old units and continue the fight against Prussia. Prussia conscripted 18,800 Saxons to replace those who had left, but these soon fled as well, and the whole episode damaged its army's morale, since soldiers in the old units distrusted their unwilling comrades. Both Austria and Prussia also recruited each other's soldiers once prisoner exchange arrangements collapsed in 1759, with the latter using rather more coercive measures than the former. The Americans made considerable efforts to persuade captured Germans to enlist during the Revolutionary War, as did the Russians with captured Rheinbund troops in 1812–13, both with mixed results.[52]

GARRISON COMMUNITIES

Legal Status

Central to the cliché of eighteenth-century soldiers standing separately in society is the belief that they lived under a state of brutal discipline. Frederick II's remark that his men should fear their officers more than the enemy is widely cited.[53] There is certainly ample evidence for fear and brutality, particularly in the Prussian army. Not only did it feature in the public discussion of armies, as we have seen, but it was directly observed. After watching a parade during a visit to Berlin in 1764, James Boswell wrote that 'the soldiers seemed in terror. For the least fault they were beat like dogs.' Soldiers of one Prussian regiment were ordered not to cough on parade, while officers dreaded the annual reviews, visibly trembling when Frederick II approached, knowing he would test their knowledge by asking about minute details.[54]

Military life could drive men to despair: the suicide rate among late eighteenth-century Prussian soldiers was four times that of civilians, and the fact that most deaths occurred during the exercise months suggests higher levels of stress and a reluctance to serve. Troops were under tight surveillance and were forbidden to be on the streets after 7 p.m., while even officers had to ask permission to leave their garrison town. Soldiers in many armies were frequently banned from smoking, even off duty, though tobacco usage became widespread during the eighteenth century and Prussians could buy discounted 'soldiers' tobacco' from government stores. The civil authorities were required to report furloughed men who got drunk.[55]

However, the most notorious example was the punishment of 'running the gauntlet', in which the delinquent was forced to walk between two lines of 100 of his comrades who beat him with hazel switches while the drummers drowned out his cries. Sentences typically required this process to be repeated between six and thirty-six times, though anything over ten would be spread out over several days; over thirty times was considered a death sentence and a coffin would be carried out to the punishment ground.[56]

In keeping with criminal law in general, the process was deliberately intended to be shocking as a deterrent. It was reserved for serious cases, especially for repeat offenders who had previously been pardoned. Men were forced to walk because running was considered more dangerous for them. The process was certainly used, but there was a growing consensus around 1730 that the military codes were unduly harsh, particularly as those of the late seventeenth century, which generally remained in force, were in turn based on the 1532 imperial criminal code that looked increasingly antiquated. Courts martial continued to impose harsh sentences, but these always required higher confirmation, often from the ruler, who usually commuted them into other forms of punishment, such as hard labour. Unease about corporal punishment seems to have been greater among some officers than their subordinates, since privates and NCOs serving on courts martial often voted for harsher sentences than their superiors.[57] Prussian regulations in the 1720s already admonished officers and NCOs to treat soldiers with care, while all corporal punishment, including running the gauntlet, was abolished in 1808. Other armies followed suit, for example that of Bavaria in 1821. Nonetheless, soldiers remained under martial law and had very few opportunities to appeal beyond the formal military hierarchy to any independent body.

Serial deserters were the delinquents most likely to face the gauntlet. All armies had suffered from desertion, but the largely seasonal character of warfare held it in check, since most men stayed in the ranks until they were paid off at the end of the campaign. The consolidation of permanent armies during the later seventeenth century embedded desertion as a structural feature, in contrast to mutinies, which became increasingly rare. This shift reflected the authorities' success in breaking the horizontal, associative element in military culture: desertion involved individuals or small groups, whereas mutiny was a collective act. Mutinies still occurred, but only in exceptional circumstances, such as that by the two Ansbach-Bayreuth regiments at Ochsenfurt in March 1777, when the men mistakenly believed that they would be made to sail across the Atlantic to America in the leaky barges ferrying them down the Main River.[58]

Desertion rates have been greatly exaggerated in secondary accounts, and the problem features prominently in the cliché of the downtrodden, allegedly disinterested, mercenaries. Most German armies, including the

Prussian, lost only about 2 per cent of total strength annually through desertion, though some experienced rates of up to 6 per cent in peace-time.[59] Mobilization or relocation to a new garrison town could see a surge in desertion to 10 per cent, but while wartime rates were often around 6 per cent they could also be under 1 per cent.[60] Moreover, these rates compare favourably with those suffered by other armies: the French army lost 10.3 per cent annually during the Seven Years War, while the rate was often much higher among the supposedly more motivated soldiers of the Revolutionary era, when an additional 29 per cent of conscripts dodged the draft.[61]

Desertion was situational, rather than the result of recruiting the 'wrong' kind of soldier. Sudden changes in material conditions, such as lack of food, pay, or shelter, often drove men to leave, as had occurred in the wake of defeats in the sixteenth and seventeenth centuries. Conscripts, recent recruits, and thus younger men were the most likely to desert, often finding military service 'a wretched life', as the twenty-four-year-old Joseph Hiltersperger put it.[62] Foreigners also featured disproportionately. However, native veterans with unblemished service also deserted. Much depended on relations with comrades and especially NCOs and officers. The presence of an exceptionally violent sergeant in the city of Augsburg's professional guard was responsible for eighteen men deserting and another twenty-eight seeking a discharge in just six years. Collectively this represented nearly one in five of the unit's strength. Ironically, many of the reasons why men enlisted also drove them to desert: the illusion that prospects might be better elsewhere, rash decisions induced by heavy drinking, the desire to escape punishment and, especially, disappointed expectations such as the failure to obtain permission to marry. The annual desertion rate in Prussia soared to 9 per cent in 1714 when the king decided to expand rather than reduce the army at the onset of peace, dashing hopes of many men who wanted to quit.[63]

Desertion concerned all armies, because replacing men was time-consuming, expensive, and often difficult. Württemberg issued at least fifty-five mandates between 1660 and 1779, indicating the persistent difficulties, especially as these orders frequently simply repeated existing measures.[64] The legislation was essentially the same throughout the Empire, where all armies had adopted a similar package of measures by the late seventeenth century. The threat of harsh punishments, like running the gauntlet, was intended to deter desertion, but pardons were issued frequently to encourage men to return. The passport system, introduced already in the sixteenth century, was progressively tightened, and was coupled with regular patrolling of the highways by mounted gendarmes as part of more general policing. Bavarian police and military patrols arrested 62,132 deserters and draft dodgers, along with 64,379 civil criminals and 210,325 vagrants, in the period 1806–16.[65] Based on earlier arrangements to exchange prisoners, a sophisticated system of 'cartels', or extradition treaties, developed after 1714 between the German principalities, often coordinated at Kreis level, as well as between German governments and France. The bilingual agreements between France and Swabia in 1732 and 1741 became models for Franco-German cartels during the Rheinbund era and beyond as this practice continued into the mid-nineteenth century.[66]

However, probably the most effective measure was the introduction of property confiscation that began around 1700 in most territories and indicates the already impressive capacity of the state, even at local level. Deserters' names were passed to local officials, who seized any property they might own to recover the cost of their recruitment bounty and any uniform items or equipment they had taken. These rules could extend to forcing the man's parents to pay, as well as impounding any inheritance he was due, and the same measures were applied to subjects who enlisted in other armies without permission.[67]

Soldiers as a Corporate Group

A key factor aiding the hunt for deserters was that soldiers were an easily identifiable group. From 1725, furloughed Prussian soldiers were obliged to wear their uniform coat, or at least their waistcoat, to be distinguishable from civilians. Officers were instructed to ensure their men developed an appropriately martial bearing, and veterans were observed to walk and carry themselves differently from men who had never served. Supervision now extended to hairstyles. Prussian soldiers were required to wear pigtails wrapped in black ribbon from 1718. Supposedly introduced to protect their necks against enemy blows, this fashion was copied throughout the Empire until all armies abandoned it around 1806. Grenadiers and NCOs were further required to sport moustaches, but beards were usually banned, in contrast to Jewish subjects who were obliged to wear them. Hair had to be worn white on parade, with each Prussian company receiving 50 lb of powder for the annual review period under Frederick II.[68]

In contrast to the later seventeenth century, officers now also had to wear uniforms, with Hessen-Darmstadt adopting these relatively early in 1704, followed by all other armies from the early 1720s.[69] Austrian officers were already required to wear gorgets (largely symbolic neck armour) and sashes as markers of their rank around 1710. Civilians were forbidden from copying officers' uniforms or court dress, while other state officials, such as huntsmen, were given their own distinctive clothing. Prussia's famous 'break-in style', or transition from courtly to martial appearance associated with Frederick William I in 1713, was thus part of a general trend. Uniforms were now tailored more tightly and decorated with smaller cuffs and the coat-tails pinned as 'turnback'; both appear to be practices imported by Prussia from Charles XII's Swedish army (see Fig. 10). Rulers increasingly appeared in military dress in public and on portraits, and Joseph II was even buried in his field marshal's uniform.[70]

The requirement that officers wear uniform bound them visibly within a military hierarchy extending from the ruler to the lowest private and identifying all as state servants. It encouraged a measure of equality that crossed rank and social distinctions with, for example, noble-born officers serving as godparents to the children of their commoner comrades. However, the stultifying impact of the promotions system based on seniority, combined with the preferment given to nobles, all caused friction that worsened with the boredom of garrison life and clashes of personality. Heavy drinking and gambling continued to characterize the social life of all military personnel. Cultured rulers like Frederick II or Carl Eugen of Württemberg gave officers free entry to their new opera houses, though the Prussian monarch had to issue printed instructions on how they should behave and remind them not to bring their mistresses.[71]

Social distinctions continued to find expression in a myriad of subtle yet important ways. Ordinary soldiers played different card games to those of their superiors, for instance. Many officers unthinkingly regarded their men as their social inferiors, sometimes unfairly: Prussian Private Dominicus could correspond in French, something many of his superiors were unable to do, while captains relied heavily on NCOs to run their company administration. Soldiers' lives revolved around their 'comradeship', or group of usually eight men sharing a tent and cooking on campaign, while in peacetime they pooled their pay to buy food and spent time together drinking and smoking. Foreigners tended to seek each other out, as did those from similar backgrounds such as the former theology student Johann Neubauer, who found a fellow *studioso* in the same regiment to pray with.[72]

The distinctive legal status, appearance, and culture of soldiers did not separate them entirely from society. In contrast to those of the nineteenth century, most lived billeted in civilian homes. Civilians were obliged to house soldiers individually or in small groups, providing board and lodging, heating, and lighting in return for tax rebates. Efforts were made to rotate units between communities after 1714 to ensure no area was unduly burdened, but the system remained unfair because nobles, clergy, and the wealthy were exempt. Yet it was this elite that held power locally, generally had the requisite space, and negotiated with officers over assigning quarters. Cavalry represented an additional burden, since they required constant fodder for their horses, while civilians were obliged to transport soldiers' baggage when they changed quarters.[73]

The associated problems led communities to press the authorities to construct barracks, sometimes even offering to pay more tax to fund these. Prussia had already moved its cavalry into urban billets in 1719, and by 1747 all thirty-six towns in Magdeburg province accommodated at least a company of soldiers each. Altogether, thirty-two new barracks were built during Frederick II's reign, and the large military presence in Potsdam was responsible for that town's expansion from 1,500 inhabitants living in 220 houses, mostly built of clay, in 1713, to 5,640 people in 553 mainly stone buildings, together with over 2,000 troops, by 1730. However, even in Potsdam, accommodation remained inadequate, with soldiers still billeted on a quarter of civilian homes at the end of the century.[74] Other German territories had fewer barracks, but also smaller armies, so the situation was broadly the same. Accommodation was everywhere cramped and often unhygienic. All the barracks in Stuttgart shared the same stream for drainage. By 1760 this had become a morass, having not been dredged for two decades, and the stream flooded the cellars at the slightest rain, finally prompting action to clean it.[75]

While soldiers may not have always been welcome, they became a permanent presence across the Empire and Habsburg monarchy after 1714, with their 'garrison community' existing alongside similarly legally distinct groups, notably courtiers, clergy, and university students, who also had their own zones within towns. The significance of these garrison communities varied according to their numbers. Most German armies were concentrated at their prince's residence, usually with smaller detachments in one or two other towns, plus individual companies in obsolete castles and other military posts. Palatine soldiers accounted for nearly half of Mannheim's population in 1770.[76] Around 50,000 men, or a third of Prussia's army, were quartered in just seven primary garrisons: Berlin, Potsdam, Königsberg, Stettin, Magdeburg, Halle, and Breslau, which all had over 10,000 inhabitants, whereas most provincial towns had fewer than 4,000 people and the presence of a single regiment could often represent up to a third of the population.

In the absence of regular police, soldiers were the most visible representatives of authority. Sentries were posted outside public buildings and at town gates, where they collected tolls and checked passports. A reserve remained on duty at the guard house that was a regular feature in most town squares, and the garrison was expected to turn out in the event of rioting or fire. Insulting sentries was a common way to express discontent with authority, while drink often fuelled brawls between off-duty soldiers and other groups, notably journeymen and students. However, soldiers' involvement in violence was not unusual considering they were recruited from the same young, masculine, and largely poor section of the population most noted for this form of crime.

Their relative poverty was the primary cause of animosity, rather than their profession, and while there are examples of families harbouring deserters, there are numerous cases of civilians handing them over to the authorities in return for cash rewards. Soldiers were often seen begging, while they and their wives were rightly suspected of stealing vegetables, fruit, and firewood. Town councils and wealthy burghers objected to the military's use of valuable real estate for barracks, fortifications, and exercise grounds. As always, though, good relations left fewer traces in the records, but a genuine sense of community can be gauged from soldiers' letters, diaries, and memoirs. Ulrich Bräker, who had been duped into joining the Prussian army, recorded its departure for the front in 1756: 'Then the drums struck up; tears from civilians, tarts, pros etc, were flowing in torrents. Those warriors too, who were natives of the place and leaving behind wives and children, were really cut up, broken-hearted they were.'[77]

As this indicates, a significant proportion of soldiers were married, despite the official reluctance to accept this for fear that wages were insufficient to support families and that wives and children might become dependent on public welfare. Austria permitted only five married men per company in 1700, relaxing this to fifteen in 1785, though the number was cut to just four in the early nineteenth century and nine out of ten soldiers remained single. Restrictions on marriage extended to potential recruits in those territories adopting limited conscription where men enrolled on the draft registers had to seek the army's permission to marry, since this gave them more chances of exemption. Prussia was exceptional in relaxing these rules in the 1740s when it realized that married foreigners were less likely to desert. It also tolerated 'soldiers' sweethearts', or concubines, despite this being illegal under imperial law since 1577. Concubinage was phased out across 1786–97, but the rules on marriage were relaxed further, and the army always contained far more married men than the official quota of a third. The other German armies also removed or ignored restrictions, especially in the later eighteenth century when around a third of personnel were married. While that proportion generally applied to all ranks, Prussia went to the opposite extreme of usually refusing permission to officers, thanks to Frederick II's view that they should 'make their fortune with their sabres, not by marriage'.[78]

Professional soldiers, who usually included all the foreigners, were only expected to do duty two to four days a week, and, together with their wives, formed a significant proportion of many towns' pool of menial labour. Some had valuable skills from previous employment and could operate as master craftsmen outside the guild structure, thereby undercutting civilian rivals and leading to protests. Soldiers were also given various exemptions from tolls, often abusing this to profit from trading in cheap goods, including with the connivance of civilians. Very few soldiers' wives were employed as laundresses in barracks, forcing the majority to seek work as servants, hawkers, and in the textile industry. Württemberg wives had to be reminded not to steal the barracks' bed linen to make skirts, while a Berlin police raid in 1711 netted many soldiers' wives and daughters working as prostitutes.[79] Prostitution continued to be tolerated in Prussia, but the authorities shifted from a policy of restriction to one of trying to prevent infection among soldiers in the 1790s. As in other armies, Prussia had developed a limited safety net since the 1680s to support wives and families when their menfolk marched to war; another significant feature of the transition from 'campaign community' to 'garrison community'.[80]

Meanwhile, a significant proportion of native soldiers were able to return to their birthplace on furlough, only being recalled for two to three months each spring for the annual exercises and reviews. This practice began in the smaller German armies in the 1670s as an economy measure, since furloughed men were unpaid and expected to work as farm hands and day labourers. Around a fifth or a quarter of most armies were on such extended leave during the eighteenth century, with the proportion reaching a half in those armies adopting limited conscription, as in Prussia, Hessen-Kassel and, later, Austria. The Bavarian war minister, the American-born Count Rumford, was convinced that furlough 'served not a little to the establishment of harmony and a friendly intercourse between soldiers and the peasantry'.[81] Although men on furlough could cause trouble, the system certainly softened the impact of the draft and, together with billeting, marriage, and the widespread employment of off-duty soldiers, was a major element embedding the army within society.

Medical Provision and Welfare

The experience of prolonged warfare from the 1670s led to a modest improvement in medical provision that was consolidated as armies demobilized around 1714. Each company now had a barber surgeon (*Feldscher*), giving a ratio of one medic to about 100 soldiers. In addition, an army of 30,000 was supposed to have 160 trained doctors, though in practice the overall ratio of medical personnel was often only 1 to every 300 or 400 men. Austria benefited from reforms instituted at Maria Theresa's request by Baron Swieten in the 1750s. Even barber surgeons were now expected to pass a basic proficiency test, while the establishment of the Josephinium in Vienna in 1785 provided a specialized school of military medicine. Prussia belatedly founded its own, the Pépinière in Berlin (1795), but nonetheless failed to achieve the target of one trained doctor per battalion. Veterinary schools emerged somewhat later, for example in Bavaria in 1799. Recruitment of qualified personnel remained a real problem. The four preferred candidates as surgeon general in Württemberg in September 1757 all sought to avoid active service by claiming ill health or lack of experience. Shortage of doctors to tend the sick forced the army to rely on chaplains, ten of whom died following infection during 1757–8.[82]

Nonetheless, a basic hierarchy of treatment was already established by 1714 and lasted into the twentieth century. Each regiment was responsible for minor ailments and battlefield first aid. Mobile field hospitals, equipped with specialized wagons, treated serious casualties on or near the battlefield. Base hospitals formed a third line, providing longer-term care and convalescence. Whereas these had been established only in wartime, most territories now created permanent military hospitals, as in Berlin (1710), Dresden (1732), Asperg in Württemberg (1759), Potsdam (1772), Würzburg (1790), and Bamberg (1792).

The dissemination of specialized knowledge remained restricted and Prussia did not issue its first medical regulations until 1788. Soldiers were admonished to wash themselves regularly and keep uniforms, equipment, and barracks clean. Austria prohibited lodging the sick and injured in barns or civilian houses in Hungary and Serbia, because of the perceived higher risks of infection, and all armies practised basic quarantine during epidemics. Wounds to the head or torso generally remained fatal, but veterans' records indicate that injuries to bodily extremities were certainly survivable if properly treated. Prussian field hospitals enabled 220,000 injured and sick to return to duty during the Seven Years War, though a fifth of those hospitalized died, primarily due to poor sanitation. Standards remained dire into the Napoleonic Wars and many of Prussia's losses were due to want of care. Disease accounted for three-quarters of Austria's dead in the Seven Years War and a staggering 95 per cent of Bavarian fatalities in the same conflict. Mortality even in base hospitals ranged between 9 and 15 per cent across Germany between 1810 and 1815. Most soldiers would no doubt have agreed with the Prussian trooper Nicolaus Binn, who wrote home prior to the battle of Kunersdorf: 'Better dead than taken prisoner or badly wounded.'[83]

Most soldiers only served for four to eight years and were still reasonably fit when discharged and could generally find work. Problems only arose at the end of major wars when large numbers of men were discharged at once and competed for jobs, notably in 1714, 1736, 1748, and 1763. Historians have been highly critical of the poor provision for former soldiers, many of whom were forced into vagrancy.[84] The Swiss in French service were exceptional in being granted long-service pensions. Most German soldiers were lucky if they received an invalidity pension, which remained a matter of grace and favour, rather than entitlement, despite pay stoppages already being applied to fund this in the late seventeenth century. Old soldiers were often simply kept in the ranks or eventually sent to 'invalid companies' guarding fortresses.

Austria copied France and Britain by establishing an 'invalid house' in Pest in 1729 as a home for men incapable of any further service, though plans to create others were constantly postponed through lack of funds, and the monarchy continued to rely on decentralized, local relief from ecclesiastical charities. A system of general care was finally established in March 1750 using a mixture of endowments and pay deductions. Intended initially for 6,000 men, it maintained 19,559 by 1763, including 4,729 semi-invalids in thirty-two garrison companies, and 4,494 in Pest and other, smaller homes. However, 17,388 men were officially invalided out of the Habsburg army during the Seven Years War, and the actual number in need of care was probably considerably higher given that Prussia recorded 200,000 wounded and disabled in that conflict, of whom only 10,000 received state relief.[85] The Berlin invalid house only opened in 1747 and accommodated just 600, meaning that, as in Austria, the vast majority of former soldiers merely received 'outdoor relief' in the form of small regular gratuities (see Fig. 11).

Austria led the way in establishing full pension entitlement for officers, civil servants, and their widows in 1749, finally guaranteeing universal provision in 1781 by freeing individual grants from the availability of designated funds. France adopted a similar approach in 1790, followed by Bavaria in 1805 and other south German states. However, these benefits came with the requirement in Austria and Bavaria that officers deposit a substantial marriage bond before marrying, with the state retaining the money if it subsequently had to pay a widow's pension. Outside Austria, officers' wives usually only received three 'widow's months' pay as a one-off gratuity, though several armies established widows' funds in the 1770s. Arrangements for soldiers' widows remained haphazard.

Prussia acknowledged universal entitlement to former personnel in 1787 and accepted responsibility for another 16,000 previously unassisted veterans by 1791 but failed to assign additional funds to sustain this. Neither Austria nor Prussia allocated more than 2 per cent of their military budgets to veterans' care, and while the proportion was sometimes double for other armies like that of Bavaria, these lacked economies of scale. Governments fully recognized the deficiencies in provision and tried to find alternatives to funded care by encouraging the employment of former soldiers as teachers, policemen, and civil servants. Of the 4,258 disabled Prussian soldiers mustered out after the War of the Bavarian Succession in 1779, only ten sat the schoolteachers' exam and none passed.

Soldiers' children represented around 25–30 per cent of orphans. Military orphanages were established in Bavaria (1682), Prussia (1724), Saxony (1738), Austria (1772), and elsewhere. That in Potsdam was the most famous and housed 1,250 boys and 750 girls in 1758, but essentially remained a workhouse until 1780 when some effort was made to provide education. Boys were expected to become army drummers or apprentices, while girls became servants or textile workers. Basic schooling was provided in most garrisons, already early in the eighteenth century, often by chaplains.

Religion

The Empire, the Habsburg monarchy, and the Swiss Confederation continued to enforce the religious settlements of the previous century mandating an official faith alongside limited toleration for dissenters. While recruits of the official faith were preferred, this was rarely a barrier to enlistment and armies were relatively non-denominational compared to civilian communities. Governments ensured that their units entering foreign service were guaranteed freedom of worship and could bring their own chaplains, for example in the case of troops from Catholic Würzburg entering Protestant Dutch service in 1747.[86]

The Prussian army was formally detached from the Lutheran state Church in January 1717 by the establishment of a separate 'war consistory' to appoint army chaplains and oversee religious observance. The government built a church each for Catholics and Greek Orthodox, as well as three for Lutherans in Potsdam in 1722–3, allowing soldiers to attend according to preference. The famous *Garnisonskirche* was consecrated in 1732 to replace an earlier structure destroyed when a gunpowder store exploded. Chaplains were told to keep sermons clear and simple, and not to exceed fifteen minutes, though additional time was allowed for rousing hymns, which were especially encouraged. Nonetheless, the army's religious character remained strongly Lutheran, not least thanks to Frederick William I's encouragement to the Pietist movement, which combined devotion with a strong work ethic. The annexation of Silesia and later West Prussia significantly increased the proportion of Catholics, compelling Frederick II to open the military chaplaincy to priests in peacetime.

Austria followed Prussia in establishing a specialist chaplaincy department in its General Staff in 1721. By contrast, other Catholic territories left provision to the Church, with soldiers simply attending local services and chaplains only appointed in wartime. Jews were discriminated against under Habsburg conscription law, being sent to serve in the transport corps, though after 1789 those in Galicia were free to volunteer and the first known Jewish officer was appointed during the Napoleonic Wars. Since the Austrian Habsburg army did not yet cook for its soldiers, religious observance remained possible.[87]

Perhaps predictably, chaplains routinely despaired of their flocks as irreligious reprobates. A former theology student, Johann Neubauer, foolishly complained to the sentry on his second night in service that the other soldiers were playing cards; the sentry repeated this to the entire group, which collapsed in laughter. While they may not have reached the desired level of piety, most soldiers displayed conventional devotion and expressed a simple faith that God would aid victory. The famous Lutheran chorales were sung with genuine fervour after Frederick II's victories.[88]

NOT SO LIMITED WAR

The Human Impact

Eighteenth-century warfare was neither as limited nor as bloodless as often portrayed, though the onset of sustained demographic growth from the 1730s mitigated some of the impact relative to that experienced in the previous century. Armies needed to replace around a tenth of their strength annually to cover death, invalidity, discharge, and desertion, with the proportion rising significantly higher in wartime. The Habsburg army recruited 20,000 of the monarchy's subjects annually in the early eighteenth century but had 61,234 vacancies in 1744. The army drew another 3,000 men annually from the rest of the Empire, rising to 5,000 after 1763. Altogether, 220,000 recruits were inducted during the wars of 1733–9, equivalent to replacing the army's entire strength. By the end of the century, the army had doubled in size and 104,000 recruits were required from the monarchy alone in 1795.[89]

The Prussian army absorbed 140,601 recruits across 1713–40; an average of 5,200 annually, and this number likewise grew as the army continued to expand. By contrast, the other German forces remained static, or even contracted, meaning that the proportional burden decreased as the population grew, and it was this that shaped perceptions of the renewed high demand for manpower after 1792 as an especially heavy burden. Overall, German armies represented around 2 per cent of the population, roughly equivalent to the number of Swiss in foreign armies, which is estimated at between 135,000 and 500,000 across the century with the total probably closer to about 250,000.[90] These proportions are about double those experienced in the century after 1815.

Around a third of Bernese recruits in French and Savoyard service were killed or wounded during the eighteenth century, but most of the remainder, including those who deserted, returned home.[91] The mid-century wars were fought extensively in the Empire, causing considerable damage and population loss. The Seven Years War was worse than that of the Austrian Succession. Prussia suffered 180,000 soldiers killed, the heaviest loss of any belligerent, compared to Austria's 126,000 dead and another 28,000 from the smaller German forces. Several Prussian regiments consumed the equivalent of two or three times their initial strength; an attrition rate comparable to the First World War. Altogether, around 850,000 Habsburg soldiers died on active service during the eighteenth century, compared to around half a million Prussian and other German soldiers over the same period.

These losses put those of the Revolutionary and Napoleonic era into perspective: Swiss and Valaisan casualties were broadly comparable to those suffered under the old regime, and while higher at around 600,000 dead across 1805–15, German and Austrian losses were also not unprecedented as a proportion of population. Yet, after three decades of relative peace, they seemed shocking, and their impact was heightened by their concentration in a few major campaigns, particularly for the Rheinbund states that suffered horrendous casualties in Spain and

Russia. Almost three-quarters of Württemberg's 26,292 casualties of the Napoleonic Wars were lost in Russia during 1812. The shift to conscription after 1806 further concentrated the impact on men in their twenties: nearly a third of all men born in the Rhineland between 1776 and 1794 were drafted into the French army across 1802–14, and of these nearly half died.[92]

The Financial Burden

Switzerland contrasted sharply with the Empire and the Habsburg monarchy in escaping war debts, and instead accumulating large cash reserves in the cantonal treasuries. The pensions associated with foreign service remained an important source of income, but the Confederation's avoidance of war after 1712, together with its reliance on low-cost (albeit ineffective) militias rather than professionals, meant that even reduced tax levels produced surpluses. The near embarrassment of riches prompted Bern and some other cantons to invest on the London Stock Exchange, as well as lending to France and other governments.[93]

The per capita tax burden in Austria and Prussia doubled across the eighteenth century, and then leapt another two-thirds across 1790–1820. While this rate of increase was broadly in line with that elsewhere in Europe, returns were much lower than in France and especially Britain, both of which had much wealthier populations and more dynamic economies. War dominated government expenditure. Tight control over soldiers' pay, cheese-paring economies, and the extension of the furlough system all served to limit the rise in per capita annual costs from about 75 fl in the 1720s to around 100 fl by 1800.[94] However, overall costs rose because many armies grew in size and because all governments failed to surmount the problem of accumulated war debt.

It is easy to write this story as one of failure, contrasting with that of Britain and the Dutch Republic, which established funded national debts and a sophisticated system of commercialized credit. Recent discussions of 'fiscal-military states' have tended to emphasize the importance of representative institutions, notably the British Parliament, as explanations for why such regimes coped better than absolute monarchies.[95] In fact, the territorial and provincial Estates continued to function in most German principalities and the Habsburg monarchy, not merely to assist in raising revenue, but also in providing important sources of relatively cheap loans. Indeed, their comparative success was one of the reasons why German governments were less concerned about developing banks and commercialized credit. For example, the Bavarian elector repeatedly persuaded his Estates to assume tranches of accumulated war debt, enabling him to function with an almost permanent budget deficit across the century.

Prussia was unusual in continuing the medieval practice of trying to fund war from accumulated tax surpluses, which consisted literally of barrels of cash in the royal vault rather than invested profitably in foreign banks or bonds. This method suited Prussia's first-strike strategy, but soon foundered once the reserves were spent and a war dragged on. Moreover, Prussia's monarchs were reluctant to disturb the agreements their predecessors had reached with their provincial Estates in the later seventeenth century. Frederick II's involvement in the War of the Austrian Succession was relatively brief and resulted in the capture of the rich province of Silesia. He managed to fight using accumulated reserves, regular taxation, and a modest loan from the Brandenburg Estates, removing the incentive to make major changes. Consequently, Prussia entered the Seven Years War poorly prepared and rapidly resorted to a range of traditional expedients, including coinage debasement, paying public officials in promissory notes, and levying over 20 million tlr in contributions from occupied Saxony and Mecklenburg. These measures pushed much of the burden on to neutral and enemy territory, causing widespread damage to the Saxon and Polish economies. Prussia was also fortunate in receiving 28 million tlr in British subsidies, which covered an unusually high proportion of its total war costs of 125 million tlr and allowed Prussia to exit the war still with a cash reserve.

By contrast, Austria's debt increased only modestly by 7 million fl to 106 million fl during the War of the Austrian Succession, but the monarchy initiated a major reform programme, associated with finance minister Count Haugwitz, combining moderate centralization, renegotiation of Estates' tax grants, and a package of measures intended to stimulate the economy. Habsburg finances continued to look creaky, because the monarchy failed to commercialize its debt and relied on the old practice of asking their provincial Estates periodically to assume responsibility for paying at least some of their creditors. It further suffered in contrast to Prussia in that its ally, France, provided a smaller subsidy during the Seven Years War, which cost the monarchy 390 million fl. Military failures also prevented Austria from shifting the cost on to Prussia. Nonetheless, the system muddled through with nearly two-thirds of the cost met from taxation and Estates' loans, with part of the remainder covered by the introduction of paper currency.

Prussia entered the Revolutionary Wars wedded to its traditional methods of austerity, expedients, and exploitation of neutrals and enemies. The massive extension of furlough in peacetime suppressed the true costs, which ballooned as soon as the men were recalled to the colours. Defeats and the retreat into neutrality after 1795 denied Prussia opportunities to push costs on to others or to obtain foreign subsidies. Further defeat in 1806–7 cut Prussian territory by half and left it saddled with 32.4 million tlr in reparations owed to France. The crisis was such that the government contemplated surrendering Silesia to Napoleon to clear the debt. Supporting the emperor in 1812 cost 85 million tlr, not counting the expense of sending an auxiliary corps to Russia, while fighting France between 1813 and 1815 consumed another 61 million tlr. The monarchy finally accepted the need for reform, but the ongoing crisis limited what could be achieved and the country again faced bankruptcy by 1815.

Joseph II's reforms disturbed the working relationship with the Estates just as he embarked on the costly Turkish War of 1788–90 and faced revolt in the Netherlands. His government rapidly resorted to expedients, including coinage debasement and substantial issues of paper money. Like those in France, Austrian banknotes soon lost value because the public faith in their convertibility quickly evaporated, unlike in Britain, where confidence was sustained by a stronger financial sector and the government was already able to abandon the obligation to convert notes into cash in 1797. The nominal value of Austrian paper currency ballooned from 12.9 million fl (1785) to 1.1 billion fl (1811), while total debt climbed from 339 million fl (1790) to 689 million fl (1815), continuing to rise into 1820. The monarchy teetered on the brink of bankruptcy several times, but avoided disaster, partly thanks to foreign loans (worth 118.5 million fl) and 31.3 million fl in British subsidies, but also to its Estates, which secured 160 million fl of debt through low-interest bonds, as well as providing the emergency loans used to pay reparations to France after the defeats of 1805 and 1809.

The smaller German lands all entered the Revolutionary era with large, accumulated debts. War soon upset their precariously balanced budgets, but the real problem was the requirement imposed by the territorial redistributions of 1803–10 to assume the debts of mediatized territories, thereby shifting the burdens of the vanished governments on to those that survived to become sovereign states. Nearly half of Baden's 31 million fl debt by 1820 derived from this process, while Bavaria's existing 20 million fl liabilities grew by 93 million fl, equivalent to its entire military spending across 1804–15, all indicating that territorial expansion could be a mixed blessing. However, Westphalia's declaration of bankruptcy in 1812 was unusual and most governments followed Austria's policy of suspending interest payments and issuing paper currency. As in Prussia, the war forced modernization through the consolidation of public debt, ending the previous duality of separate liabilities of prince and Estates, unifying the debts of different state institutions, funding it from general rather than specifically assigned revenue, and commercializing it through conversion to government bonds tradable on financial markets.

Economic Impact

Alongside taxation and indebtedness, the impact of war was felt primarily through the burden of military occupation and the levying of contributions by raiding parties. Depredations by both side during the Seven Years War cost the electorate of Cologne and its dependencies of Münster and Paderborn a total of 21.2 million tlr.[96] Efforts were already being made to mitigate these costs through improved logistical support and switching from cash contributions to forced requisitioning in which armies issued receipts for supplies that communities could then present to their authorities to claim tax rebates. Already employed by French forces operating in Germany during the Seven Years War, this became the primary method used by the Revolutionary and Napoleonic regimes to sustain their armies in Germany and Switzerland after 1792.[97]

The situation remained chaotic during much of the 1790s, due to the rapidly changing military situation, comparable to that experienced during the Thirty Years War when communities faced successive and mounting demands from different armies. One contemporary estimate valued the damage inflicted on Swabia, Baden, and Württemberg by 1802 at 70 million fl.[98] However, the territorial redistribution after 1803 created some economies of scale, while Napoleon's arrangements with the

Rheinbund, and Austria and Prussia, made his demands more predictable and hence manageable. The level remained challenging: much of the logistical burden of Napoleon's invasion of Russia fell on Prussia, which was expected in 1812 to provide 50 million daily rations for the 480,000 soldiers, 15 million rations for the 140,000 horses, plus to supply 2 million bottles of beer, a similar quantity of schnapps, 44,000 cows, 15,000 horses, and 3,600 wagons, all on top of the 77,920 horses, 22,772 oxen, and 13,394 wagons directly requisitioned by the French.

These figures give some indication of the resources required to sustain armies, and also that the primary source of supply remained the rural, agrarian world, rather than towns or industry. Armies needed to replace around 10 per cent of their horses annually to cover losses to sickness, injury, and old age; roughly the same proportion as for manpower. Wartime greatly increased demand: the Austrian army lost 35,314 horses during the Seven Years War, half of which were captured, and the rest killed or injured.[99] Horses were taken at three to four years old and served for up to ten years. Light cavalry horses were generally 1.55m high and weighed 450 kg, while heavy cavalry required mounts of 1.65 to 1.75m, weighing between 600 and 700 kg. Northern Germany developed as a primary supplier of heavy cavalry horses to European armies by 1700, thanks to selected breeding programmes at commercial stud farms, notably in Holstein, Halberstadt, Celle, and Magdeburg. Light cavalry horses were sourced from Hungary, Ukraine, and Wallachia. Governments increasingly established their own studs, such as Bavaria in 1807, but never escaped dependency on imports, even in peacetime.[100]

The stabilization of permanent garrison communities had a significant impact, not least because the payment of soldiers' wages was the most important way that taxes circulated back into the economy. The brewing and tobacco industries were notable beneficiaries, especially from the 1720s.[101] Merchants and representative institutions like the Estates generally opposed state monopolies and lobbied to ensure that food, clothing, and arms contracts were open to competition. Governments remained concerned to secure supply and often harboured unrealistic hopes that state industries would be profitable. Consequently, the production of military goods shifted between private and public operators, generally each time in the belief that new arrangements would somehow prove more satisfactory than those currently employed.

Austria established arms production in Steyr in 1655 to free its army from dependency on foreign imports. Operated by the Mittenmayr family (later ennobled as 'von Waffenberg'), this used proto-industrial techniques to boost production, but declined after 1700, seemingly due to the difficulties of retooling to make Austria's new pattern musket. Arms production was revived in 1726 by a new entrepreneur, who accepted it on the guarantee that the government would purchase 6,000 muskets annually, but production remained insufficient, and Austria had to import 25,000 muskets from Liège, which remained Europe's primary gunmaker during the eighteenth century, employing 6,000 workers in 1788. A separate Viennese arms factory managed to produce 17,000 muskets annually across 1806–15, but this also failed to meet the demand.[102]

Production in Prussia was concentrated in the Potsdam-Berlin area, not simply because of its importance as a political and military centre, but also thanks to the good connections by rivers and canals to Hamburg, the Netherlands, and Sweden, which supplied key raw materials. The imposing new arsenal (*Zeughaus*) was opened on the river Spree in 1690, while a powder mill was established in Jungfernheide in 1717, as well as iron, copper, and brass works in Neustadt and Eberswalde in the Mittelmark region. The Zehdenick foundry (in the Uckermark), operating since the 1660s, produced artillery shot. The most famous sites were the Lagerhaus clothing factory, established in Berlin in 1714, and the Potsdam musket factory, opened in 1722.

The Lagerhaus employed 500 workers on site and another 8,000 through the putting-out system, making it one of Europe's largest textile producers. However, the army's ninety or so regiments had over 500 different patterns of lace and braid, requiring specialist silk workers and hindering moves towards more modern production techniques. The Potsdam factory was a public-private partnership headed by David Splitgerber and Gottfried Daum, who operated it in return for the exclusive contract to supply muskets and swords to the Prussian army. As was quite typical elsewhere, production was split, with the barrels, ramrods, and bayonets made in a separate plant in Spandau, and then assembled with the wooden stock at Potsdam. Splitgerber and Daum had a 33 per cent profit on each musket, allowing them to expand to become the exclusive operators of the Eberswalde and Zehdenick works. Their annual turnover more than quadrupled to 4 million tlr between 1740 and 1762, and they cleared 1 million tlr in profit during the Seven Years War.

However, the factory was tooled to produce beyond what the army required in peacetime yet could not supply its wartime needs. Quality control was often poor, and it only retained profitability during the long peace after 1763 because the Prussian government allowed it to export to Spain and Poland. Even in 1803, it employed only 400 workers and its overall impact on economic growth, along with the other arms production sites, remained relatively low. Total production across the Empire in 1800 was around 20,000 muskets annually, compared to 55,000 in France and up to 200,000 in Britain, while there was nothing in the German lands to match the scale of the British, French, Dutch, or Spanish warship-building industries.

The eighteenth century saw Prussia's emergence as a second great power alongside Austria, thereby relegating the other principalities collectively to the status of a 'Third Germany' increasingly marginalized politically and militarily. The Holy Roman Empire was unable to master the twin challenges of internal Austro-Prussia rivalry and external pressure from France. The Empire's demise by 1806 destroyed central Europe's political balance, reorientating this from a hierarchical order, headed by the Habsburgs, to a flatter structure composed of sovereign states grouped within a looser confederation. Prussia nearly disappeared along with the rest of the old order, and though it re-emerged as one of Europe's great powers by 1815, it was smaller than it had been just seven years earlier. After 1815, the smart money was still on Austria remaining the pre-eminent central European power, signalling an element of continuity amid the changes.

While the wars after 1792 had transformed central Europe's political balance, the struggles of the mid-eighteenth century were far from limited in their social and economic impact. Armies had professionalized, with a regular career ladder, routine administrative practices, a corporate ethos, and a distinct identity. Soldiers were not isolated from society, but linked to it in multiple ways, not least by living among civilians and through the extended furloughs that saw many working part-time in the wider economy. This would change significantly after 1815, and more so from the 1860s with the switch from long to short service conscription and the ideals of military service as the 'school of the nation'.

PART IV

Nationalizing War

War and Nation-Building

GUARDIANS OF ORDER, 1815–51

Central Europe after Napoleon

The years after 1815 in Central Europe are known variously as the Restoration, *Vormärz* (Pre-March), or Biedermeier eras, respectively highlighting the apparent return of an old political order, the supposed inevitability of the revolutions that came in March 1848, and the culture of cosy bourgeois domesticity during relatively peaceful decades. All three labels indicate important aspects of a period that is often ignored by military historians who leap forward to the mid-century 'wars of unification' between 1864 and 1871, which saw Austria's definitive exclusion from Germany and Prussia's victory over France. The subsequent four decades are then in turn usually covered from the perspective of 1914, with authors disagreeing primarily over the inevitability of the First World War and the roles of Germany and Austria-Hungary in causing it.

Without minimizing the significance of the mid-century conflicts, it is important to note how the legacy of the Napoleonic Wars continued to exercise an influence throughout the nineteenth century. Following 1815, war and revolution were regarded as dangerously entwined, with many fearing that one would automatically lead to the other. Although monarchs were restored throughout Europe, few sat as easily on their thrones as those before 1789. Popular discontent over mundane matters like food prices could escalate into armed attempts to overthrow those monarchs, while revolution in one state might be exported by war to others.

Soldiers were now expected to be guardians of order prepared to crush internal opposition and, if necessary, to intervene elsewhere to support imperilled regimes. Simultaneously, there was an appreciation that the potential scale of warfare had grown and that countries needed to harness their human and material resources more effectively. Heightened patriotism offered governments opportunities to justify greater burdens on their inhabitants, but these ideals could not be disentangled from liberal demands for more representative government. The default response was a reliance on proportionally small armies recruited from long-service conscripts who rarely represented more than a fifth of those theoretically eligible.

Reliability against domestic opponents was to be achieved politically, by ensuring that command remained in the hands of the 'right sort' of men, and socially, by isolating soldiers from civilians. Neither of these objectives was fully realized, while soldiers were untrained and ill-equipped for an effective gendarmerie role. Military proficiency remained rated in the traditional terms of being able to defeat similarly armed, trained, and organized armies in battle.

Meanwhile, the legacy of war debts necessitated austerity and the avoidance of risk. German rulers shared the hope that a Concert of Europe would secure lasting peace through cooperation to preserve the political balance established by the Congress of Vienna in 1815. While national interests still took precedence and could justify going to war, it was widely believed they would be better served through peace, or at least by curbing the escalation of conflict. Even authoritarian regimes felt obliged to pay some attention to popular opinion and to make at least some show of consulting other powers rather than acting unilaterally.[1]

Before proceeding, it is worth placing the German experience in its global context. Although conventional Western military history focuses on the German 'wars of unification', which are often regarded as a step towards 'total war' after 1914, the largest conflicts of the nineteenth century were fought outside Europe. The most extensive, protracted, and bloody was the Chinese civil war known as the Taiping Rebellion (1850–64), in which 20 to 30 million people died. The most devastating proportionally was the conflict between Argentina, Brazil, and Uruguay against Paraguay (1864–70), in which the latter lost three-quarters of its entire population. Those with the most far-reaching territorial impacts were the wars of imperial conquest pursued by Britain (especially in South Asia), France (north Africa and later Indochina), and Russia (central Asia). Although involving far smaller forces, the United States meanwhile expanded westwards to become the continental hegemon in

North America, annexing half of Mexico in the process (1846–8). Finally, though America's own civil war (1861–5) involved an approximately similar number of combatants as the Franco-German War of 1870–1, it lasted four years, compared to just ten months.

The German Confederation

The political reconfiguration of central Europe underpinned the entire Vienna settlement, because this area had to be sufficiently strong to hold the continental balance between France and Russia, while remaining incapable of actually threatening either through aggressive war. Both Austria and Prussia agreed with this. Prussia had been enlarged to 278,000 square kilometres and 10.3 million inhabitants, or more than twice the size to which Napoleon had reduced it in 1807. Although still a tenth smaller than it had been before the defeat at Jena in 1806, Prussia was clearly one of the major beneficiaries of the peace and had no immediate territorial ambitions. Austria remained the dominant German power with 26 million subjects in 1815, but the conflict with Revolutionary and Napoleonic France had been a gruelling experience that convinced the ruling elite of the necessity to avoid under almost any circumstances anything endangering the monarchy's continued stability. The architect of this conservative course was Prince Metternich, foreign minister since 1809, who headed the government after 1821 and pursued a policy of containment until his dismissal in 1848.[2] Domestic concerns drove policy, with the army tasked with policing the Habsburgs' Italian possessions to deny France an excuse to make trouble, as well as cooperating with Russia against a potential Polish rising.

The German Confederation was created on 10 June 1815 to provide a framework for Austro-Prussian cooperation while simultaneously denying either power the chance to dominate the Third Germany of the small states that had survived the wreckage of Napoleon's Rheinbund. The Confederation's boundaries largely followed those of the old Empire, with parts of both the Habsburg and Hohenzollern monarchies remaining outside it. Although Sweden had surrendered its last German possessions to Prussia, Denmark retained the duchies of Holstein and Lauenburg as dependencies within the Confederation. Hanover was initially still linked to Britain by personal union, and Luxembourg was part of the Confederation while simultaneously belonging to the new, much larger kingdom of the Netherlands created by combining the former Habsburg Low Countries and the territory of Liège with what had been the Dutch Republic.

Considerably fewer than half of Habsburg subjects were within the Confederation, compared to most Prussians. With its priorities elsewhere, Austria had little interest in developing the Confederation beyond the minimum necessary to maintain a credible deterrent against France. Deeply in debt, Prussia had no desire to supplant Austria as German leader. The Third Germany remained heterogeneous, comprising seven medium-sized states with a combined population of 9.5 million and thirty-two smaller ones with only 2 million inhabitants. Hessen-Kassel was reconstituted as *Kurhessen* ('Electoral Hessen' as an echo of the old Empire) from the Napoleonic kingdom of Westphalia, which was abolished, but most of the other states were Rheinbund survivors. Bavaria and Württemberg were the natural leaders, with Hanover in Britain's shadow until the personal union ended in 1837, and Saxony was still smarting after losing a third of its territory to Prussia in the Vienna settlement. While they appreciated the Confederation as necessary for their continued existence, they were reluctant to surrender too much of their precious sovereignty to it.[3]

Austria's imperial status rested on its own new hereditary title created in 1804, but the permanent presidency it held in the Confederation offered little influence. German government remained monarchical at state level, with Bremen, Frankfurt, Hamburg, and Lübeck being the only surviving civic republics. There was no national parliament, but the states were urged to establish their own constitutions with representative assemblies. By 1824, only fifteen of the thirty-seven monarchies had done so, mainly those in the south. States were represented by their governments in the Federal Assembly (*Bundestag*), with sovereignty preserved by ensuring all had at least one vote while even the two great powers had no more than four each.

As under the Empire, states were free to pursue their own foreign policy provided it did not harm the other members. The Vienna settlement ensured that the Confederation's constitution permitted states to defend themselves but not to initiate wars. A two-thirds majority in the Federal Assembly was required to trigger mobilization, further encouraging passivity in the interests of the general European balance. Nonetheless, following the recent prolonged wars against France, policymakers believed collective defence remained necessary.

These general principles were implemented through the Confederation's 'military constitution' completed in 1822 after four years of discussions.[4] Austria and Prussia agreed most matters beforehand but respected the smaller states' desire to preserve their sovereignty. The established practice of organizing territorial contingents was again adopted, but in modified form to reflect the changed character of warfare. Unlike before 1806, the states had to maintain their full force in peacetime. Quotas were fixed at 1 per cent of population based on an estimate in 1818, giving an active Federal Army of 300,000. A further 0.83 per cent of population was supposed to be ready as reserves. While most states met their quotas, these were considerably under the fixed percentages, because the population had been underestimated in most cases. Like the Empire, the Confederation never satisfactorily resolved the problem of revising official quotas to take account of demographic growth, though matricular assessments were eventually increased in 1855 to 1.17 per cent of the 1818 population to reflect this. Austrian and Prussian territory outside the Confederation (for example in northern Italy or Prussia itself) was excluded from these obligations. While states were free to maintain additional troops, few other than Austria, Prussia, and Bavaria did so.

Each contingent was to be composed of 77 per cent infantry (including 5 per cent rifle-armed light infantry), 14.3 per cent cavalry, 1 per cent pioneers, and the rest artillery with a ratio of two guns per 1,000 men. In another response to the Napoleonic era, the combined force was divided into ten corps, each subdivided into two or three divisions of two infantry brigades with attached cavalry and artillery. However, there were no mixed contingents as no state was to provide fewer than 400 infantry, 300 cavalry, or a battery of six to eight guns. This was relatively straightforward for the three largest states: Austria and Prussia designated parts of their armies to form three corps each, while Bavaria provided a seventh. The remaining states combined to form the other three corps, with the smaller states redistributing elements of their quotas in the different troop categories to ensure their units reached the minimum thresholds.

Although the contingents were now permanent, the other arrangements only existed in wartime, not least because Austria and Prussia wanted to keep their forces free from interference from the smaller states. However, a small Federal Military Commission did emerge from the debates on the new structure and remained a permanent advisory body that acquired some oversight of the fortresses and training.

The Swiss Confederation

Broadly similar arrangements were made in Switzerland, which was reorganized by the Vienna Congress on 7 August 1815 by adding Geneva, Neuchâtel, and Valais to give it twenty-two cantons. Simultaneously, the last elements of the 1798 constitution were removed to return Switzerland to decentralized government in which each canton was represented equally in the diet regardless of its size.[5] As with its German counterpart, the new structure was not without its echoes of old-regime complexity as Neuchâtel would remain bound by personal union to Prussia until 1848.

Like their German counterparts, the cantons retained the right to make treaties provided these did not breach their collective obligations. However, the great powers declared Switzerland to be 'perpetually neutral' on 20 November 1815 to ensure no one dominated the Alpine passes.[6] Swiss neutrality was part of a wider strategy to help preserve peace by creating buffer states between the great powers. A nominally autonomous region known as Congress Poland was also established to defuse rivalry between Austria, Prussia, and Russia, but at the Poles' expense.

Obliged to uphold their neutrality, the Swiss also reorganized their collective security. On 20 August 1817 the diet agreed this as the Defensional of Wil in direct reference to its famous forebear of 1647. Defence rested on the traditional militia, with each canton required to mobilize 2 per cent of its population when required. Cantons were permitted to maintain their own professional forces for local defence and public order, but some, like Aargau, dispensed with such troops.[7] Although all cantons had been compelled to participate in common training by 1825, the stubborn determination to cling to autonomy frustrated various efforts to standardize uniforms, arms, and equipment.[8] The Confederation carried out partial mobilizations during all nineteenth-century wars and crises near its frontiers.

Foreign Service and its Complications

One sign of adaptation to the new European order was the decline of foreign military service, which was increasingly regarded as incompatible with the ideals of national sovereignty and citizenship. Other than Nassau, which briefly provided two regiments for the Netherlands, the German states no longer hired out auxiliaries to foreign powers and restricted their inhabitants' freedom to join other armies. The Swiss were slower to change. The Helvetic Republic did not cancel existing contracts with other powers after 1798, while the new Confederation saw foreign service after 1815 as removing the need for it to care for veterans demobilized after the Napoleonic Wars by encouraging them to re-enlist in other armies. New agreements were made with France, the Netherlands, the Papacy, and Naples. The last contract was signed in 1825 with Naples under Austrian, French, and Russian pressure to provide reliable troops for the restored Bourbon regime, thereby relieving Austria of that duty after it had intervened there during 1821 against a coup by liberal army officers (see Fig. 12).

The Neapolitan contract continued, but those with the Netherlands and France were cancelled in 1829–30 following growing criticism depicting foreign troops as tools of despotism.[9] France also disbanded its sole surviving German regiment, which had been formed from the remnants of other foreign units in 1816. However, the liberal critique did not remove the need for foreign manpower, not least because compulsory military service remained deeply unpopular throughout Europe. Men from the disbanded German regiment became the nucleus of France's new Foreign Legion organized in 1831 during the conquest of Algeria. Germans and Swiss provided most of the initial manpower, and there was even briefly a separate Swiss Legion (1855–9). Of the 600,000 Legionnaires who served across 1831–1963, 35 per cent were Germans and 5 per cent Swiss, including French and Italian speakers, compared to only 1 per cent from Britain.[10]

The German Confederation permitted enlistment for those who had completed their own state's military service, but this too was banned in 1853. Despite this, Britain recruited 13,000 Germans and Swiss along with 3,500 Italians for its own foreign legion in 1854 as it struggled to sustain its expeditionary force during the Crimean War. That conflict ended before the legion saw action and many of its members were instead disposed of by sending them as settlers to South Africa.[11] By that point, individual emigration had replaced organized units as the primary route into foreign service. The failure of the 1848–9 revolutions saw a surge in emigration to America. Unable to adjust to their new life, many joined the

American filibustering expeditions in the 1850s, such as those of William Walker in Nicaragua. Rather more joined the US army, which did not make an ability to speak English a requirement until 1894. Overall, 256,000 first- and second-generation German and Swiss immigrants served in the Union army during the Civil War, forming 13 per cent of its strength, compared to 10 per cent represented by African Americans. Another 15,000 German and Swiss immigrants served the Confederacy.[12]

Meanwhile, opinion in Switzerland swung significantly against foreign service after the Neapolitan and papal use of Swiss troops to crush domestic opponents. The new Swiss constitution of 1848 banned any new treaties, and the Neapolitan contract was terminated in 1859 when two of the four regiments mutinied because the Swiss diet ruled that they could no longer carry Swiss flags. Naples and the Papal States followed the French example and reorganized their units as 'foreign', rather than expressly German or Swiss, but the demise of both those states through the process of Italian unification removed them entirely. Only the pope's small Swiss guard in the Vatican remained after 1870 under a special exemption granted by the diet.[13]

The decline of the professional foreign soldier coincided with the rise of the freedom fighter who volunteered to assist others in their liberation struggles. In practice, the lines between these two types were frequently blurred, since professionals did not necessarily lack ideals, while volunteers often had more mundane motives for their actions. Much depended on how the authorities regarded the cause being fought for. Germans showed little enthusiasm for Italian unity but were much taken with Greek efforts to escape Ottoman rule after 1821. Panhellenism proved particularly attractive given Romanticism's celebration of Greek rather than Roman antiquity while, outside the Habsburg government, the Ottomans were widely regarded as despotic.

In practice, few Germans followed the example of England's Lord Byron and joined the Greek cause before 1832, by which point independence had been won and it had become a matter of stabilizing the new country's monarchy. The Greeks chose the second son of Bavaria's Ludwig I, Otto, himself an ardent philhellene, as their new king. A Bavarian expeditionary force of 3,500 regular troops was despatched to act as his bodyguard early in 1833 and remained until July 1835, by which time another 5,410 mainly Bavarian volunteers had arrived to form the core of a new royal army. The Bavarians failed to apply the lessons of the 1809 Tirolean uprising during their gruelling counter-insurgency against Greek opponents of the new order.[14]

The Greek expedition was a precursor to the better-known Austrian involvement in Mexico between 1864 and 1867, which resembled it in many respects. Keen to win favour with the Habsburgs and extract himself from an increasingly costly entanglement in Mexico's affairs, France's Emperor Napoleon III persuaded Archduke Ferdinand Maximilian, Franz Josef's younger brother, to accept a new Mexican imperial title from that country's embattled conservatives. An expeditionary force of 6,000 volunteers from the Habsburg army was despatched along with 1,500 Belgians recruited on behalf of Maximilian's Belgian-born wife, and backed by 25,000 French troops. The initial sense of adventure rapidly evaporated once it became obvious that the French army itself was pulling out, leaving Maximilian to fight the liberal insurgents with his own inadequate forces. The bulk of the Austrians accepted the offer to depart in December 1866, but around 1,000 remained with Maximilian, who refused to abandon those Mexicans who had supported him, fighting on until he was captured and executed in June 1867.[15]

The Challenge of Revolution

Both expeditions involved volunteers fighting for established governments and causes that were, at least in part, conservative. However, many volunteers were associated with liberal and nationalist ideals that German governments regarded with suspicion. The German Confederation initially sought to silence criticism by tightening censorship through the Karlsbad decrees in 1819. These were fiercely condemned by liberals but were intended to avoid renewed war and violence as the liberal-nationalist rhetoric was often virulently both anti-French and anti-Semitic.[16]

The German Confederation had adopted much of the old Empire's legal culture with its emphasis on administrative review and judicial arbitration to settle disputes pragmatically and peacefully, rather than through the over-hasty use of force or definitive court verdicts. As with the Empire, this largely removed violence from the level of disputes among member states, and between them and the Confederation. Trouble between states and their own subjects proved a different matter, as the Confederation did not develop an appeals mechanism equivalent to the Empire's supreme courts. Governments were encouraged to settle problems peacefully, but in practice often lacked adequate police forces and were obliged to rely on their armies when confronted by serious disturbances. The Confederation copied the Empire's system for intervention, with all members obliged to assist neighbours to maintain order and to comply with any collective action agreed at the Federal Assembly. The procedures were deliberately slow to allow those threatened by them to respond to negotiations instead. Collective action only proved necessary on five occasions, with another three resolved diplomatically.[17]

These mechanisms were first tested in 1830 when renewed revolution in France saw the conservative Bourbons replaced by the Orleanist liberal constitutional monarchy. Momentarily, the clock appeared to reset to 1789 as civil wars erupted in the Netherlands, Portugal, and Spain, and revolution challenged Russia's control of Congress Poland. While Russia had crushed the Poles by February 1831, the Netherlands civil war ended in the partition of that kingdom through the establishment of an independent Belgium, which was eventually recognized internationally in 1839 as another neutral buffer state alongside Switzerland. In the process, Luxembourg was partitioned, with most of it going to Belgium and only the rump left as a grand duchy within the German Confederation but linked by personal union to the Netherlands.

Meanwhile, unrest swept across much of Germany, including serious disturbances in Brunswick, Kurhessen, Saxony, and Baden, and a failed coup by liberal army officers in Württemberg.[18] Over 20,000 liberals gathered in a self-styled 'national festival' at Hambach Castle in May 1832, but in reality the protests were uncoordinated and much of the discontent stemmed from opposition to the kinds of economic changes many liberals advocated. The sense of danger had been magnified because the new Orleanist regime appeared to harbour expansionist ambitions and briefly mobilized 80,000 troops after Austria had again intervened in Italy to crush protests in Modena and the Papal States. Austria responded by increasing its forces its northern Italian territories (Lombardy) to 100,000. Concerned at its ability to sustain such a force as well as defend Germany, it renewed efforts to reform federal collective security. The contingents from eighteen small states were regrouped into an additional reserve infantry division intended to garrison the cities that had been designated federal fortresses. However, more far-reaching proposals foundered on the desire of the medium-sized states to preserve their autonomy.

Austria fell back on a bilateral defence pact with Prussia in December 1832. It was renewed in 1840 amid a new war scare prompted by further sabre-rattling from France, which had backed an Egyptian revolt against Ottoman rule and found itself isolated when Austria and Britain supported the sultan.[19] The momentary fear of invasion encouraged the smaller states to improve military coordination and prompted an out-pouring of Romantic patriotism manifest in the composition of *Die Wacht am Rhein*. These lyrics were set in 1841 to a tune composed by Haydn to celebrate Emperor Francis II's birthday in February 1797 and subsequently became the German national anthem.

The Sonderbund War, 1847

Switzerland was also affected, as liberals demanded a more unitary state which they hoped would open their country to economic progress. A wave of unrest resulted in the rewriting of many cantonal constitutions, reducing the grip of the patrician oligarchy. Simultaneously, long-standing confessional tensions resurfaced because the liberals saw the Catholic cantons as socially conservative and tied to Rome, while Catholics resented the secularization of church property and the requirement that priests swear loyalty to the new constitutions.

The scale of the unrest is indicated by the despatch of thirteen federally coordinated expeditions between 1818 and 1844 to restore order, mainly in the Catholic Forest Cantons, as well as in Basel where town-country tensions proved so deep that the canton was partitioned into urban and rural halves in 1832 as Basel and Basel-Landschaft respectively.[20] These conflicts attracted the attention of Switzerland's neighbours, raising fears that they might intervene. Austria objected to the anti-Catholic measures, while France posted a large force on Geneva's doorstep in 1838 after the Confederation refused to extradite Napoleon's nephew, the future Napoleon III, who at that point was regarded as a radical liberal and was attending the federal officer training school in Thun. The crisis was resolved by Napoleon departing for temporary exile in America.

The situation grew much worse as impatient radical liberals took matters into their own hands. Led by Johann Ochsenbein, a captain in the Federal General Staff, around 3,500 self-styled *Freischärler* (insurgents)

invaded Luzern in March 1845 intending to expel the Jesuits and secularize church property. Luzern called in aid from its Catholic neighbours and
the insurgents were swiftly defeated, losing 300 killed and wounded.[21]

The incident nonetheless understandably alarmed the Catholics, and
Fribourg, Luzern, Schwyz, Valais, Unterwalden, Uri, and Zug formed a
Sonderbund (separate alliance) in December. Intended as secret, the
news leaked out in June 1846, causing uproar among liberals. Ochsenbein was elected to head Protestant Bern's government just as it became
that canton's turn to hold the federal presidency, something that undermined efforts to resolve matters by negotiation. Following moves by the
liberal majority in the diet to dissolve their alliance and to expel the
Jesuits, the Sonderbund followed the example of earlier Catholic alliances in Swiss history and launched a pre-emptive strike on 3 November
1847 intended to improve their bargaining position.

Both sides mobilized using the contingent system from 1817. It was
an unequal contest. The Sonderbund members had only a fifth of the
Confederation's inhabitants and mustered four divisions totalling 34,000
men with forty guns under Colonel de Salis, backed by 50,000 Landwehr
(home guard). Although three small cantons declared neutrality, the rest
supplied their contingents to the federal army, which totalled 98,000 and
172 guns in seven divisions. Command was entrusted to Henri Dufour,
an engineer officer from Geneva who had served France loyally until
Waterloo and who, after much lobbying, had persuaded the diet to adopt
the white cross on a red background as the federal emblem.

Both commanders were keen to avoid unnecessary bloodshed.
Dufour fought a model campaign, first surrounding Fribourg, which
was isolated from the rest of the Sonderbund, and forcing it to surrender. Already unenthusiastic, Zug now capitulated, allowing Dufour to
mass 34,000 troops against Salis's 15,000 at Gisikon, west of Luzern,
on 23 November (see Fig. 15). The last battle fought by Swiss troops, it
ended after just forty-five minutes with the complete rout of the Sonderbund army. The remaining Catholics capitulated six days later. Dufour
and Ochsenbein stressed the need for reconciliation and the diet soon
remitted over a third of the 4 million francs in reparations imposed on
the defeated cantons.

The swift, convincing victory deterred potential Austrian intervention and cleared the way for the liberals to remake the Confederation
with a new constitution in April 1848. Modelled on that of the United

States of America, this created an elected lower house with the number of representatives proportional to population, balanced by an upper house where each canton had two senators. Both houses elected a seven-man federal council on a four-year term, with each councillor heading one of the new government departments, including defence. This constitution has remained largely unaltered, except for the right to call a referendum if sufficient support could be demonstrated, which was adopted in 1874, and the extension of the franchise to Jews (1866) and, very belatedly, women (1971).

Government became more centralized, with Bern as the national capital and the introduction of standardized currency, customs, and weights and measures. Defence was declared a federal matter, with no canton itself permitted to maintain more than 300 men. However, the army remained a militia composed of cantonal contingents and much of the earlier devolved system remained largely unchanged before some modest centralization in 1874. The reformers stopped short of writing neutrality into the constitution, but it nonetheless provided an ideal around which all Swiss could unite regardless of language or religion.

Revolutionary War, 1848–51

The revolutions of 1848–9 represented a far greater challenge to the established order than those of 1830–2. Protests began in parts of Italy in January 1848 and spread rapidly thanks to the faster and broader dissemination of news through the electric telegraph and mass-circulation press.[22] In most cases, violence rapidly escalated because the authorities lacked alternatives to deploying troops once they were confronted by armed protesters. Berlin, a city with 400,000 inhabitants, had just 242 policemen in 1848.[23] Although soldiers were under strict rules about using live ammunition, they were not trained in public-order roles, despite the authorities repeated reliance on them to break strikes and quell bread riots.

The protests were as much against change as for it, since many ordinary people blamed those in power for economic shifts that were eroding the old corporate social order. Radical liberals struggled to assert leadership and direction, though nationalism provided a focus in Italy, Hungary, and Poland, where rulers were perceived as foreign as well as monarchical. It is easy to dismiss the revolutionaries as doomed to fail, but the sense of crisis was heightened by the fusion of domestic strife and international conflict, with 60,000 deaths across Germany and Italy and many more in Hungary.

The Habsburg monarchy was at the epicentre, facing violent domestic upheaval while struggling against independence movements in Hungary and its Italian possessions. Metternich misread the situation as a repeat of 1789, remaining focused on a threat from France, where the liberal monarchy was replaced by a republic in February. He was forced to resign after the government lost control of Vienna following rioting on 13 March 1848. A series of successors proved unable to master the situation, while their confusing and often contradictory policies further undermined confidence in the regime and emboldened the revolutionaries to demand more. Already on 15 March, Hungarian liberals led by Lajos Kossuth declared themselves to be their country's government. While still recognizing Hungary as bound by personal union to Austria through the Habsburgs, they proceeded to establish their own volunteer army, called the *Honvéd*, backed by a national militia. Around 30,000 Hungarian soldiers, including about 1,000 officers, defected to the new regime. Meanwhile, Habsburg forces under Joseph Radetzky were driven from Milan, their main Italian garrison, after five days of street fighting. During the retreat, around 10,000 Italians deserted, further impairing the army's ability to respond.[24] The news prompted Venice to declare itself an independent republic on 26 March, seizing much of Austria's small navy and hindering the flow of reinforcements to Radetzky. Piedmont's king, Charles Albert, bowed to domestic and broader Italian pressure and declared war on Austria in the name of liberating Italy.

Across Germany, angry crowds stormed civic arsenals, formed revolutionary national guards, and constructed barricades. Baden's government swiftly conceded demands on 27 February. Bavaria's King Ludwig I abdicated, other rulers fled, and several states received revised constitutions. Prussia's army proved no more capable of confronting civilian protesters, losing control of Berlin during mid-March in a sequence of misunderstandings and irresolution that led to 230 deaths. King Frederick Wilhelm IV was deeply shaken and obliged to convene a popular assembly to draft a constitution, and to accept the formation of a citizens' militia.[25]

The government's situation was not as bad as it first appeared since most troops remained loyal, while the crowds soon dispersed once their immediate objectives appeared to have been achieved. The Confederation mobilized its VII and VIII Corps, officially to secure the frontier against a possible French invasion, but the presence of these troops helped the Baden and Palatine governments crush a series of small, ill-coordinated risings in April and September 1848.

However, the authorities hesitated to rescind their initial concessions and felt obliged to permit a national parliament to convene in Frankfurt in May 1848. Dominated by liberals, this body sought to reform the Confederation in line with their ideals. A skeleton central government was established, including a war ministry entrusted to the Prussian General Peucker, while a small federal navy was formed in June. Both were hamstrung by the states' refusal to place their troops under Peucker or vote new money. Support for the parliament rapidly dwindled among the smaller states' rulers once it became clear that many liberals wished to remove their military autonomy.

Questions of language and culture initially only assumed secondary place in their project but became prominent as the Frankfurt liberals grappled with the practicalities of converting the Confederation into their ideal of a nation state.[26] Despite noble expressions of fraternity, they felt no real affinity with non-German speakers. Proposals for a 'Little Germany' solution, defining the country linguistically, threatened the integrity of the Habsburg monarchy, not least because around half of its 11 million subjects within the Confederation were Czechs, Slovaks, Slovenes, and Italians. The Hohenzollerns were not happy either, given the sizable Polish population in their eastern lands. The parliament had no choice but to endorse the alternative 'Greater Germany' option based on the existing Confederation.

While the parliamentarians debated, the princes acted. Confronted by multiple threats, the Habsburgs were forced to prioritize. The new regime in Hungary was tacitly accepted while small forces were directed against Galicia and Bohemia, silencing local protests by June 1848.[27] The main effort was directed at recovering the position in Italy where Radetzky had retreated into the area in central Lombardy known as the Quadrilateral, protected by the four fortresses of Verona, Legnano, Mantua, and Peschiera. Reinforcements allowed him to mask Venice while counter-attacking the Piedmontese to the west in June. Overstretched after their initial successes, the Piedmontese were decisively defeated at Custoza between 22 and 25 July and agreed an armistice. Radetzky swiftly restored the ducal regimes in Modena and Parma, and reoccupied Venice's Terra Firma, subjecting the city itself to a close blockade in August 1848.[28]

Radetzky's victory in Italy enabled Austria to switch attention to Hungary, where the revolutionaries had been struggling to establish a viable state. The refusal of the Magyars to grant equal rights to minorities prompted a rising in Transylvania and armed opposition from Croatia. The latter was organized by the governor, Josip Jelačić, who saw an opportunity to loosen Croatia's ties to Hungary and attacked with 45,000 men in September 1848. The Habsburg government had little choice but to co-opt Jelačić's action as its own offensive. Hungary decreed conscription, expanded the Honvéd to 170,000 men by July 1849 and, supported by 6,000 German, Italian, and Polish volunteers, pushed the Habsburg forces up the Danube towards Vienna.[29]

Senior officers were growing concerned at the vacillating government in Vienna. A battalion mutinied rather than march against the Hungarians while Austria's war minister was killed during a renewed revolutionary outburst in Vienna. Believing a collapse was imminent, Field Marshal Windisch-Grätz withdrew the other units from the capital, leaving it to the revolutionaries, and joined Jelačić between the city and the approaching Hungarians. After Vienna refused to surrender, Windisch-Grätz attacked the city on 28 October 1848. Resistance collapsed after the Hungarians were defeated at Schwechat two days later, removing the possibility of relief. The capital was placed under martial law, but few reprisals were taken. A new government was installed under Windisch-Grätz's brother-in-law, Prince Schwarzenberg. Emperor Ferdinand I, who was widely regarded as feeble-minded, was compelled to abdicate on 2 December in favour of his youthful nephew Franz Josef.

The new emperor recognized it was impossible to set the clock back, but nonetheless sought to emulate Joseph II's technocratic government by adopting a style of centralized, undemocratic government, which survived until 1862 and has become known as 'neo-absolutism'.[30] The new direction was signalled on 4 March 1849 when he proclaimed a new, unitary constitution for the entire monarchy, indicating that he would not split it along linguistic or cultural lines to please the nationalists. Hungary responded by declaring itself an independent republic under Kossuth. Windisch-Grätz advanced with 176,000 soldiers down the Danube, taking Buda and Pest, but was removed from command after the offensive stalled in the face of fierce Hungarian resistance. The situation shifted with the arrival of 190,000 Russians in June 1849. Perennially short of arms and ammunition, the Hungarians struggled on until forced to surrender in August. Kossuth and many of the leaders escaped into Turkey.

One factor stalling the Austrian advance in spring 1849 was the resumption of war in Italy, where Piedmont re-entered the struggle, pitting 80,000 men against Radetzky's 75,000. The old marshal swiftly launched his own counter-attack, crushing the Piedmontese after tough fighting at Novara on 23 March 1849. The Piedmontese king was obliged to abdicate in favour of his son, who agreed another armistice. Radetzky was now free to detach 5,000 men to join a combined French, Spanish, and Neapolitan army, which restored the pope who had been obliged to flee Rome. Meanwhile, the main effort switched to Venice where operations were stepped up from blockade to full siege in May, though it took until 28 August before the defenders submitted after being hit by 120,000 shells from Radetzky's siege guns.

The collapse of the revolutionary movements in Hungary and Italy coincided with a similar fate in Germany. A brief lull in threats elsewhere allowed the Prussians to double the forces concentrated outside Berlin, thereby strengthening the hand of the hawkish 'camarilla' which included Crown Prince Wilhelm. All resistance swiftly collapsed as troops entered the city on 9–10 November, emboldening the government to close the popular assembly and declare martial law. Despite this, the Frankfurt parliamentarians continued to hope that Prussia would lead a reformed Confederation and elected Frederick William as the new head of state on 27 March 1849. He rejected their 'crown from the gutter' a month later after Austria had already repudiated the parliament and refused further cooperation.

Largely disconnected from these events, Baden's army mutinied in May, forcing the grand duke to flee, and reviving liberal hopes of a genuine popular rising. The mutiny was prompted by the decision to induct three times the usual number of conscripts to meet a new federal quota agreed by the Frankfurt parliament. Violence was directed against unpopular officers but soon escalated, especially after the failure of the initial government countermeasures. More vigorous action in similar circumstances averted mutiny in Württemberg.[31] Most Badenese officers refused to serve under the revolutionaries, obliging them to promote

NCOs to take their place. Unrest spread to the Palatinate, where local Bavarian units joined the rising, and to Saxony where the insurgents included a young Richard Wagner.

Prussian troops stormed the barricades in Dresden, but southern Germany was considered Austria's sphere. With the Habsburgs preoccupied, Prussia decided to act, not least from fear that unrest would spread north along the Rhine to its possessions in Westphalia. Two Prussian corps joined a composite force of south German troops whose presence was mainly to ensure the operation retained the character of a federal intervention. Opposition soon collapsed in the Palatinate, but the Baden revolutionaries offered stiff resistance, thanks in part to the presence of that state's mutinous army, until the fall of Rastatt on 23 July.

The restored grand duke disbanded virtually his entire army, reraising new units in its place. Most revolutionaries were permitted to escape, and only twenty-seven death sentences were carried out in Baden. Nonetheless, the upheaval was profound and 5 per cent of the population emigrated, mostly to America.[32] Improved economic conditions gradually mollified popular grievances, while governments developed more sophisticated responses to public disorder, establishing state gendarmeries armed with sabres and rifles but trained in crowd control: the Habsburgs already mustered 19,000 in 1850. Although the army remained hated by the left, German authorities were much less likely to call in troops during the second half of the nineteenth century than their French or Italian counterparts.[33]

The Schleswig-Holstein War, 1848–51

While the expected war with France failed to materialize, the Confederation became embroiled in a conflict with Denmark which ran alongside the revolutionary upheavals, as well as Prussia's plans to replace the Confederation with its own Lesser German union of states in only loose association with Austria. Danish liberals decreed a new unitary constitution that threatened the autonomy of its duchies of Schleswig and Holstein. This coincided with a change of monarch, emboldening one of the ruling family's relations to proclaim the duchies as independent with himself as ruler on 24 March 1848.[34] As most of the Schleswig-Holstein population were German-speaking, their cause was swiftly embraced by German liberals whose calls for action became too loud for their governments to ignore. Several hundred Prussian and other German officers were given leave of absence to assist in the formation of a Schleswig-Holstein army, which was then defeated by Danish troops on 9 April.

The Federal Assembly interpreted this as a hostile act, and authorized Prussia and other German states to respond. Intervention offered a convenient way to redirect liberal aspirations away from domestic matters towards nationalist expansionism, and 22,000 Prussian and other troops swiftly arrived in Schleswig under the Prussian General Wrangel. The Danes were driven from their peninsula but clung on to fortified points on the east coast at Dybbøl and Fredericia while their superior navy blockaded German ports, cutting German overseas trade by three-quarters. Britain and Russia had no desire to see Denmark defeated and forced the Confederation to suspend operations in August. The war resumed once the truce expired in February 1849, but despite increasing Federal forces to 46,000 in addition to the now 20,000-strong Schleswig-Holstein army, no better progress could be made.

The conflict was becoming embarrassing for Prussia, which agreed another truce in July, leading to the withdrawal of all Federal forces while Denmark suspended its own operations. With the revolutions crushed, liberal hopes focused on Schleswig-Holstein itself, which increased its new army through conscription and 5,000 German volunteers to 44,000. Prussia nonetheless agreed peace with Denmark. Ratification by the Federal Assembly was delayed by rising tensions with Austria, which, having defeated Piedmont and the Hungarians, was now free to block Prussia's plan to split the Confederation.

Denmark seized the opportunity to settle with its recalcitrant duchies, defeating the Schleswig-Holstein army at Idstedt on 25 July 1850. Further minor victories finally broke all resistance by November. An agreement in London in May 1852 confirmed Denmark's victory but left the two duchies their traditional autonomy. Austria meanwhile deployed 250,000 troops in southern Germany and Bohemia, supported by 90,000 men from those states that opposed Prussia's plan. Frederick William IV ordered a mobilization on 5 November 1850 and three days later Prussian and Bavarian troops briefly exchanged fire. Matters remained tense for three weeks until Prussia backed down and agreed at a conference in Olmütz to simply restore the Confederation to its pre-1848 state.[35]

EXCLUDING AUSTRIA, 1852–69

Austro-Prussian Rivalry

The debacle cost Prussia much of the credit it had won among liberals and nationalists during the Schleswig-Holstein War, and it was far from obvious that it would re-emerge to challenge Austria's leadership of the Confederation. Economic trends were benefiting Prussia more than Austria, where trade within the monarchy was always more important than between it and the rest of the Confederation. Frederick William IV replaced the more liberal arrangements of 1848 with a modified constitution in January 1850, restricting the franchise for the diet through a three-tier system with votes weighted towards rich property owners. This conservative structure remained in place until 1918 but, in the 1850s, seemed more progressive than Austria's neo-absolutist government and enabled Prussia to recover the support of most German liberals who looked to it to reorganize the Confederation. However, the liberals remained a minority throughout Germany, with their cause damaged by association with revolutionary violence, and while the economic changes hindered Habsburg efforts to maintain the political balance in Germany, it did not make the partition of 1866 inevitable.

Prussia's growing military leadership was a far more significant factor. Austria had been much more heavily engaged in the wars of 1848–9 than Prussia, but this was not how things were perceived within Germany. Habsburg forces had fought in Italy and Hungary whereas Prussia had led the federal operations against Denmark and the revolutionaries. Prussia's army was now clearly the model to follow, and the smaller states increasingly adopted its uniforms, drill, and weaponry. However, in aligning themselves with Prussia, they hoped their battalion and regiment-sized contingents would remain viable contributions to the federal army, and they remained broadly suspicious of Hohenzollern ambitions.[36]

Austria's Setbacks in the 1850s

Austria failed to offer an alternative because it was preoccupied with its own problems. The main force remained deployed in Italy, while the ongoing financial problems discouraged an active policy elsewhere. When the Habsburgs did feel obliged to act, it was not in Germany but the Balkans after the outbreak of the Crimean War in 1853. As in the eighteenth century, Austria feared that Russia's expansion endangered its own southern frontier. A partial mobilization was ordered to lend weight to mediation intended to preserve the integrity of the Ottoman Empire. Forced to evacuate its occupying forces from Wallachia and Moldavia, Russia felt betrayed after its own support for the Habsburgs during the Hungarian revolution. Meanwhile, Austria's refusal to join the war against Russia displeased Britain and France, who had backed the Turks.[37]

Austria was therefore left isolated for unrelated reasons just as it faced a new challenge to its dominance in northern Italy. Neither it nor France were keen to fight, but by 1859 the Habsburg government felt it had no choice after Piedmont undermined its authority in Lombardy by openly harbouring draft dodgers.[38] Franz Josef planned a swift punitive expedition to humble Piedmont and damage its standing among Italian nationalists, as in 1848–9. This strategy was wrecked by Austria's slow mobilization. Despite beginning preparations in November 1858, shortage of funds and a desire to avoid prematurely breaking the peace delayed the offensive until 29 April when the army in Lombardy was still 30,000 below its intended strength of 200,000. Many were conscripts, and enough Hungarians deserted to enable the Piedmontese to form them into a separate unit.

Unlike in 1848–9, the Germans were not distracted by their own problems and showed some interest in Austria's cause. Many believed a Habsburg defeat in Italy would encourage France to invade the Rhineland, but Prussia was unwilling to cooperate unless it was given exclusive command in Germany. Around 250,000 Prussian and federal troops assembled in June, but the mobilization merely lent weight to Prussia's mediation efforts, rather than directly supporting Austria. Piedmont eventually mustered 89,300 including a small corps of nationalist volunteers operating against the Tirol. The decisive factor was France's decision to back Piedmont, followed by an efficient and speedy French mobilization that rushed 128,000 reinforcements by land and sea in time to meet the Austrians.[39]

The hesitant Austrian commander, Ferenc Gyulai, lost more time. Defeats in initial encounters demoralized the Austrians, but Franz Josef rejected the idea of retreating to the Quadrilateral. The main armies clashed at Magenta on 4 June. Although neither side committed their full force, Gyulai became concerned he was being outflanked and retreated. Franz Josef took personal command and combat was renewed at Solferino on 24 June where the forces were evenly matched at around 150,000 each. Austrian logistical problems had left their men hungry and thirsty, and some temporary advantages were thrown away in a series of poorly coordinated attacks. Although the 28,000 men killed and wounded represented proportionately lower losses than in many early modern engagements, the battle attracted wide attention as the largest since the Napoleonic Wars and was considered exceptionally bloody. As will be discussed later, the battle prompted the founding of the Red Cross movement.

The Austrians retreated in good order to the Quadrilateral, but Franz Josef decided to sacrifice Lombardy to end the war quickly, especially as he feared another uprising in Hungary. Napoleon III was also keen to settle. Both emperors agreed preliminary peace with France on 11 July, which left the situation in Italy in flux. Piedmont exploited this vacuum to use Garibaldi's nationalists to topple the Bourbons in Naples and Sicily. By 1861, other than the Austrian Veneto and a truncated Papal States, all Italy had been combined into a new kingdom under Piedmont's House of Savoy.

Austria introduced limited political reforms, ending neo-absolutism by 1862 through the introduction of new elected provincial assemblies and a national parliament (*Reichsrat*) with control over the military budget. The concessions failed to appease nationalist demands, especially among the Magyars and Slavs who boycotted the parliament, which was suspended temporarily in 1865. Amid spiralling debt, the new parliament distrusted the military, which did not help itself by making little effort to present its case for more funds or to engage constructively with a political system it despised. The army's budget was cut drastically to save money, and funds were redirected towards building a respectable navy to meet the new Italian challenge in the Adriatic.

The momentary fear of a French invasion prompted the formation of the *Nationalverein* in September 1859, which was dedicated to achieving the Little Germany model of federal reform. The association was a vocal but small liberal elite that accepted Prussia's leadership only as a default option and espoused utopian views, such as regarding permanent armies as superfluous.[40] The Prussian government thought quite differently after that year's mobilization had exposed serious weaknesses.

Acting as regent for his incapacitated father, Crown Prince Wilhelm was determined to increase the army's peacetime strength, which had remained unchanged since 1815 at 150,000. Most deputies were prepared to compromise, but extremists to the left and right escalated the issue into a test of power between the diet and the monarchy.[41]

Despite the skewed electoral system, the conservatives steadily lost ground. On the advice of General Roon, the embattled war minister, Wilhelm called on Otto von Bismarck, who had established a reputation as an able diplomat, to form a new government. Bismarck initially tried to compromise, appearing before the diet's budget committee on 30 September 1862 when he made his famous 'Iron and Blood' speech. Having failed to persuade it, Bismarck simply ignored the diet and continued without an authorized budget. Largely excluded from the franchise, most Prussians remained indifferent to the crisis, which appeared to be a squabble among the country's ruling elite. Reluctant to stir revolution, the Prussian liberals bided their time, expecting Bismarck to fail.

The government's disregard for the constitution damaged Prussia's standing within the Confederation, while its support for Russian repression in Poland in 1863 again disappointed German liberal opinion. Austria's standing improved, meanwhile, thanks to the end of neo-absolutism, and its proposals for federal reform appeared more constructive than those offered by Prussia.

The Second Schleswig-Holstein War, 1864

A new crisis in Schleswig-Holstein gave Bismarck a welcome opportunity to recover the initiative and create a distraction from Prussia's constitutional impasse. The cause was a rerun of that in 1848 as liberals renewed their efforts to integrate Schleswig fully into the Danish state, prompting more angry protests at the disregard for the rights of the German-speaking minority.[42] This time, the Danes completely misjudged the situation because Britain and France blamed them for not leaving the problems alone, while German governments were no longer distracted by revolution.

The smaller German states felt obliged to act, partly to appease liberal opinion, but also to uphold the Confederation's integrity. On 7 December 1863 the Federal Assembly authorized Hanover and Saxony to occupy Holstein and Lauenburg, Denmark's two duchies within the

Confederation. Hanover's reluctance to act without more substantial support allowed Prussia to become involved. Austria was determined not to cede leadership and obliged Prussia to accept it as partner. However, Prussia's proximity to the war zone and superior financial position allowed it to field 63,500 men to Austria's 31,000, and to assert operational control. The two duchies were swiftly occupied without violence as the Danes withdrew northwards across the Eider River into Schleswig. The smaller states believed the mission accomplished, but Austria and Prussia demanded Denmark rescind its new constitution. The ultimatum was sharply criticized in the Federal Assembly, and Prussian troops nearly came to blows with the Hanoverians as they unilaterally entered Holstein.

As in 1848, the prospect of war against foreigners triggered an outburst of popular nationalism and the two German powers pushed ahead. However, Austria merely wanted Denmark to restore the arrangements agreed in 1852, whereas Bismarck secretly planned to annex at least part of Schleswig. Boxed into a corner, the Danish government felt obliged to fight, though the war was not popular among the 40,000 conscripts hastily called to duty. The political leadership placed unrealistic hopes in the line of entrenchments along the frontier known as the Dannewirke, expecting the army to hold this until Britain and other powers came to the diplomatic rescue.

Bismarck needed Prussia's army to deliver a quick and easy victory. The task fell to Helmuth von Moltke, chief of staff since October 1857. Often later referred to as 'the Elder' to distinguish him from his similarly named nephew holding the same post after 1906, Moltke was in many ways an atypical Prussian officer.[43] Hailing from Denmark's German-speaking nobility, he had a decade's service in the Danish army before transferring to Prussia in 1822. A bookish man, he spent most of his time in the army's topographical department and then the historical section writing an account of the Seven Years War. Having served four years as adviser to the Ottoman army, Moltke returned in 1839 to resume a sequence of mundane staff roles. Although these secured him the favour of the equally conservative Wilhelm I, he remained overshadowed by General Roon.

War with Denmark gave Moltke the chance to prove himself. Unfortunately, he had been obsessed with France, a country he despised after French troops had burned his childhood home, and he had not considered the possibility of fighting Denmark before 1863. His historical studies convinced him of the need to pin down and then envelop an enemy to achieve a decisive victory. The Danish strategy played into his hands by concentrating their forces along the Dannevirke close to the Prussians and Austrians. Moltke planned to strike quickly and destroy them before they could retreat to their fortresses at Dybbøl and Fredericia.

Although he devised the plan, as chief of staff Moltke had to defer to the commander, the elderly General Wrangel, who was appointed largely because the king believed he had won the previous war. Things went awry from day two of the offensive on 2 February 1864 when the Prussians were repulsed at Mysunde, while the Austrians won glory with costly attacks elsewhere. Rightly guessing Moltke's plan, the Danish commander ignored his government's orders, abandoned the Dannevirke, and retreated to the fortresses. Wrangel then defied Bismarck by occupying Jutland to the north, prompting serious Anglo-French protests. Concerned that 1848 was repeating itself, Bismarck insisted the army capture Dybbøl before international pressure forced him to end the war. The Austrians obligingly agreed to mask Fredericia to allow the Prussians to concentrate on Dybbøl, which was subjected to a formal siege. Wrangel was replaced by his deputy, General Falckenstein, who was conscious time was running out. On 18 April the fortress finally fell to an assault preceded by a six-hour bombardment that thoroughly demoralized the defenders.

Diplomatic pressure obliged the belligerents to agree a truce four weeks later. Safe on their islands and protected by their superior navy, the Danish government saw no reason to compromise. On 29 June, four days after the truce expired, the Prussians captured Als island by amphibious assault against ineffective resistance from the garrison, which received no aid from their navy. Even the most obstinate members of Denmark's government now knew they had lost. Long negotiations concluded with the Peace of Vienna in October when Denmark surrendered Schleswig, Holstein, and Lauenburg, which had collectively comprised a third of its territory with two-fifths of its inhabitants.

Moltke had delivered the decisive victory Bismarck had required, but much had depended on Danish mistakes and Austria's acquiescence. Despite his protestations to the contrary, Moltke had paid little regard to the 'fog of war' and had planned as if the Danes would behave only as he expected. He neglected wider strategy and focused on details, claiming that, once operations began, the army should be left alone to achieve victory, before handing over to the politicians to negotiate the peace. The course of the war already demonstrated the difficulties of separating war and politics, as well as the dangers of allowing the army simply 'to do its job' free of political supervision. The victory obscured these dangers and encouraged Prussia's government to trust Moltke and the army. The war of 1864 proved to be the template for Prussia-Germany's future conflicts, with the successes in 1866 and 1870–1 embedding the flaws ever deeper into the country's institutions, only to be repeated with ever more disastrous results in the subsequent two world wars.

The Confederation's Destruction, 1866

Denmark entrusted its former duchies to joint Austro-Prussian admin-istration. The Confederation, on whose behalf the war had nominally been waged, was excluded from these arrangements. The smaller states protested loudly, but Hanover and Saxony had little choice but to with-draw their forces from Holstein and Lauenburg. Austria and Prussia divided the spoils in the Gastein Convention of August 1865, with the former responsible for Holstein while the latter took charge of Schleswig. This compromise failed to dampen criticism in the Confederation and Bismarck decided to settle matters with Austria before the international situation turned against Prussia.

Tensions persisted as France negotiated with both German powers, seeking the best deal in return for its support. Napoleon III inclined towards the Habsburgs, which he still rated the stronger of the two powers, but he expected the impending struggle to be protracted like the Seven Years War and wanted to choose his own moment to inter-vene after Austria and Prussia had both weakened themselves in a preliminary round of fighting. Italy's government felt their country's unification remained incomplete and believed another success against Austria would quell popular discontent, including a long-running insur-gency in the south. It concluded a secret pact with Prussia in April 1866 after Austria rejected their offer simply to buy the Veneto and remain neutral. The Italians rightly distrusted Bismarck, fearing he might leave them in the lurch to fight Austria alone, and stipulated that the war had to begin within three months or the deal was off.

Meanwhile, Moltke was already displaying the anxiety that would characterize German strategic thinking until 1945. Convinced that Prussia could not afford a long war, he pressed the government to launch a pre-emptive strike against Austria. Wilhelm I was very reluctant to fight people he regarded as fellow Germans and Bismarck knew that war was a huge gamble in which Prussia risked its existence whereas Austria only had its leadership in Germany at stake. He nonetheless deliberately manipulated problems with the Gastein Convention to push Austria towards war. The army began mobilization on 18 May, completing this within three weeks. Prussia declared its hand by occupying Holstein on 6 June, with the Austrian garrison withdrawing to avoid conflict, but Moltke lost his chance to strike because Bismarck felt this was premature.

Over the next two weeks opinion swung decisively against Prussia in the diet, which authorized military assistance to Austria on 18 June after Prussia declared the Confederation dissolved. Prussia had already commenced offensive operations against Saxony and Hanover after 15 June, but neither it nor Austria wanted to reduce their diplomatic options by declaring war, which only Italy did on 20 June. Fourteen small German states declared neutrality while another six backed Prussia militarily, heightening the conflict's character as a German civil war.[44] The middling states had refrained from mobilizing so as not to provoke Prussia, but Hanover assembled 18,400 for annual manoeuvres to be ready. Although understrength, they collectively mustered 137,000 men in support of Austria. Austria knew they were deficient and poorly led, and expected them to be defeated, yet appreciated their support in isolating Prussia politically as well as militarily.

Only 374,000 of Austria's theoretical war strength of 850,000 men were available, and 25,000 of these were retained to deter unrest in Hungary and 100,000 were deployed in the Veneto against the 166,000 Italians. Accounting for others in garrisons, only 175,000 could be concentrated in Bohemia against the expected Prussian attack. However, the Austrians were widely considered Europe's best soldiers after the French and the Paris betting shops put the odds of a Habsburg victory at 4:1.[45]

Moltke had planned for war since 1865, recognizing the need to defeat Austria before the rest of the Confederation came to its aid. Prussia eventually mobilized over 437,000 troops. Of these, 254,000 were initially available to attack Austria, while 46,000 were concentrated under General Falkenstein to deal with the Hanoverians. Policy and operational control remained poorly aligned. Formal command lay with the king, still nominally a warlord, while each army was under its own general, two of whom were royal princes who could not be simply ordered about. Co-ordination remained with Moltke, who secured the right to bypass the war minister and talk directly to Wilhelm I. Wilhelm also formally retained the final say in politics, yet policy was really made by Bismarck, who still ran the government without a budget approved by the diet.

Falkenstein ignored orders and mishandled operations against the Hanoverians. Although the latter were eventually surrounded and forced to surrender on 29 June, it was only after they had saved their honour by defeating the Prussians at Langensalza two days before. Matters might have been worse for the Prussians had the southern states deployed quicker and pushed northwards, but their governments preferred to assemble their troops on the river Main and left the Hanoverians to their fate.[46] Compared to the reluctant south Germans, the Saxons were eager to fight, intending to recover the territory annexed by Prussia in 1815. Delays in the Prussian advance allowed the 32,000 Saxon troops to escape and join the Austrians in Bohemia.

The bulk of Prussia's forces were now stretched across a 500-kilometre arc along the Saxon and Silesian frontiers with Bohemia, much as Frederick II's armies had been in 1757. Moltke had studied that king's campaigns in detail and was concerned that the Austrians would catch his forces before they could concentrate into a more unified whole. The Prussians finally crossed into Bohemia on 23 June, but Moltke still lacked a clear idea of his enemy's positions or intentions. The next day, Archduke Albert scored a convincing though not decisive victory at Custoza over the Italians, who had divided their forces and were caught off-guard. It looked as if Moltke's carefully laid plans were unravelling, and he remained apprehensive over the next five days as the advance guards of his main columns scored a string of costly victories over the Austrian and Saxon detachments along the frontier.

The Austrian commander, Ludwig von Benedek, had only accepted his assignment reluctantly and was struggling with logistical problems and contradictory advice from men in Vienna whom he despised. He fell back to a strong position west of the Elbe near Königgrätz. Prussian reconnaissance remained poor, and Moltke still believed Benedek was east of the river until 1 a.m. on 3 July, just hours before commencing his attack. The battle pitted 220,000 Prussians against 215,000 Austrians and Saxons and was the largest engagement since the Allied victory over Napoleon at Leipzig in 1813, until that at Mukden between Russia and Japan in 1905. Both Moltke and Benedek struggled to direct the action, which stretched along a 16-kilometre front. Matters hung in the balance until the fortuitous arrival of Prussian reinforcements tipped the scales in the late afternoon.[47]

Moltke failed to achieve the desired victory by envelopment because Benedek succeeded in extracting three-quarters of his army in good order. Meanwhile, the concentration of all three main Prussian armies overstretched their logistical support, exacerbating an outbreak of cholera and slowing their pursuit of the Austrians. Archduke Albert arrived with reinforcements from the Italian front, stabilizing the situation. Nonetheless, Franz Josef took the same decision as in 1859 to settle quickly rather than risk more by prolonging the war and opened negotiations on 5 July. It is testimony to the strength of anti-Prussian sentiment that Austria's German allies continued fighting until 2 August following a series of defeats in minor, but sometimes hard-fought engagements.

Bismarck and Moltke recognized the need for peace, particularly to forestall potentially hostile French and Russian intervention. Prussia's victories dispelled Wilhelm I's earlier reluctance and he demanded territorial concessions. However, recognizing these would cause the same problems as Frederick II had experienced after annexing Silesia, Bismarck settled for an indemnity of 40 million fl. The other Germans were dealt with more harshly. In addition to taking Schleswig, Holstein, and Lauenburg, Prussia annexed Hanover, Hessen-Kassel, Hessen-Homburg, Nassau, Frankfurt, and part of Hessen-Darmstadt. Bavaria ceded two small districts and, along with Saxony, Württemberg, and Baden, paid 59 million fl in reparations. Liechtenstein was declared independent of Austria, which also ceded the Veneto to Italy. But Austria retained Trieste and the Adriatic coast, which the Italians had hoped to receive.

The German Confederation was formally dissolved on 24 August, destroying a key pillar of the Vienna settlement. Prussia's annexations increased its population from 17.2 million to 24.6 million and left its immediate neighbours little choice but to join it in a new North German Confederation, which was formally constituted on 1 July 1867. Only

Luxembourg escaped, detaching itself completely from military cooperation with the German states. Saxony and the other twenty smaller members had a combined population of just over 8 million. Although they had twenty-six of the forty-three votes in the new federal council, Prussia's king held a permanent presidency. Bismarck compromised with the liberals by establishing a Reichstag elected by universal male suffrage, giving the new organization a semblance of democratic control. Most accepted this and those in Prussia retrospectively approved Bismarck's unconstitutional measures since 1862. Prussia's weight was greater still because, other than Saxony, Brunswick, and Mecklenburg-Schwerin, its new partners relinquished their military rights and allowed their contingents to be incorporated within an expanded Prussian army.

Hessen-Darmstadt occupied a hybrid position, accepting the incorporation of its northern territory within the new Confederation, while otherwise remaining separate. This arrangement reduced the chances of the remaining southern states forming a separate confederation, which might ally with Austria or France. Baden, Bavaria, and Württemberg failed to agree military cooperation and were persuaded by Bismarck to sign defensive treaties with Prussia.

Unlike its defeat in the 1740s, Austria did not rebound with renewed vigour and determination to confront Prussia. All pretensions to German leadership were abandoned, and instead Austria finally conceded Hungarian demands to be treated as an equal partner. The *Ausgleich* (Compromise) of 1867 restructured the Habsburg state as a Dual Monarchy dominated by Germans and Magyars under a common dynasty.[48] Both halves had their own parliaments and administrations, as well as home guards: the Landwehr in Austria and Honvéd in Hungary. The army, navy, and foreign policy remained common concerns exercised through separate central ministries still based in Vienna. The dualism was expressed in the official redesignation of the armed forces as 'imperial and royal' (abbreviated in German as *k.u.k.*). Delegates from both parliaments met annually to agree a budget, but there was no real debate, and the respective shares of Austria and Hungary were fixed on a 70:30 split, with the Hungarians only reluctantly accepting just a little more in 1907.

It is easy to write off Austria-Hungary as doomed from the outset, and it certainly had numerous problems. Greatest among these was the widespread dissatisfaction among the Czechs, who resented being denied a similar autonomy, and among the other peoples who felt disenfranchised by the Magyars in Hungary. The emergence of new Slav states in the Balkans from the Ottoman Empire after 1876 increased nationalist agitation among their compatriots in Hungary. The Magyars manipulated arrangements to widen their autonomy without ever actively seeking full independence. It took about a decade for the arrangements to bed, down and while economic growth was quite impressive after the 1880s, it stimulated the rise of socialist movements which added to the monarchy's already complicated political landscape. Austria's introduction of universal male suffrage in 1907 isolated German-speakers in its parliament, where the Czechs and other nationalities were becoming increasingly uncooperative.

On the surface, the army remained a solid pillar holding the monarchy together and the officers stayed loyal even as support from other groups fell away. However, Germans held nearly three-quarters of the posts, yet represented less than half the total population. A significant proportion among them increasingly believed that Austria should shed its troublesome minorities and merge with Germany. Officers from other regions continued to identify with the dynasty, but their relationship was personal and persisted only while Franz Joseph lived.

Serious though these problems were, it is important to remember that political instability and popular discontent were scarcely uncommon in late nineteenth-century Europe. While the great powers accepted the emergence of the new Balkan states, there was little to indicate they would countenance similar moves from Austria-Hungary's minorities. The various separatist movements failed to unite, and their presence encouraged the Austrian Germans and Magyars to cooperate sufficiently to at least preserve their respective dominance.

FORGING IMPERIAL GERMANY, 1870–1

War with France

There was no direct path from Prussia's victory in 1866 and the war with France only four years later. Bismarck was sceptical about Prussia's ability to absorb the south German states and while he felt 'unification' was inevitable, he believed it would be better if this was gradual rather than through a war that might stir opposition from other powers. As late as February 1870 he rejected an application from Baden to join the North German Confederation. Four months later a crisis over Spain's choice of its future king rapidly escalated into a conflict over French objections to a possible Prussian monarch in Madrid. Widely known as the Franco-Prussian War, this involved all Germany because France's declaration of war on 19 July triggered Prussia's defensive treaties with the southern states. Bismarck contributed directly to the crisis by releasing the infamous Ems telegram, a press release he deliberately edited to antagonize France, to suggest a French diplomatic insult, but much of the blame falls to Napoleon III and his ministers, who believed a successful war would bolster the regime after a series of domestic and international setbacks.[49]

France's decision was ill-advised. Napoleon III had been unable to persuade Austria to support him as Franz Josef rejected advice from some hawkish officers for a war of revenge and instead declared his neutrality on 18 July. France's army still enjoyed high prestige despite its recent failure in Mexico, which was suitably far away to be ignored by European observers. It eventually mobilized just over 2 million men, but less than half of these were regulars and there were never more than 710,000 under arms at any point. Mobilization proved chaotic, despite the French long-service system being intended to enable the army to fight from a standing start. Only 300,000 had been mobilized by the end of July, and most of the new formations were national guards and other reservists. France's navy was vastly superior but was accorded a minor role in French planning and did little beyond blockading the German coast.[50]

The German mobilization was not quite as smooth as sometimes supposed, but nonetheless far surpassed that of the French, with an initial deployment of 434,000 men from the North German Confederation and 85,000 from their southern allies, in addition to 199,000 garrison troops. Overall, 1,494,412 men were mobilized during the war, of whom three-quarters served at some point in France. Considering there were 41 million Germans, including those in the south, compared to 36 million French, Germany mobilized a much smaller proportion of its population, but employed this far more effectively, reaching a maximum strength that exceeded that of France by nearly 240,000 men.[51]

Troops on both sides were initially highly motivated, but French enthusiasm soon waned as many were sceptical of the Napoleonic regime, whereas the Prussians at least were buoyed by self-belief following the wars of 1864 and 1866. Men from the recently annexed northern states and southern Germany were more ambivalent, leading some Prussian officers to doubt their effectiveness. Not all were convinced victory would be easy and the Berlin stock exchange crashed at the news of war.[52] There were no clear war aims beyond somehow punishing perceived French affrontery. The patriotic rhetoric masked a variety of motives, with the rulers of Baden, Bavaria, and Württemberg all expecting significant territorial gains as their reward for supporting Prussia.

Preoccupied with repeatedly re-evaluating 1866, Moltke had given little attention to planning war against France. Like Wilhelm I, he feared the French would be ready quickly and he would be forced to fight defensively. Accordingly, German mobilization prioritized the movement of infantry and artillery, leaving them initially short of cavalry. The image of Prussian lancers terrorizing the countryside is one of the lasting French memories of the war, but German reconnaissance remained deficient throughout, and Moltke often only had a sketchy idea of where his enemies were. It was not until 28 July that he realized German numerical superiority on the frontier would enable him to attack first.

His brief remained the same: to achieve a sufficiently swift and decisive victory that Bismarck could dictate peace before other powers intervened. As before, he planned to achieve this by a battle of envelopment from which the French could not escape. Three German armies, initially totalling 309,000, were deployed along a 100-kilometre front to converge on Metz and Strasbourg, the two main railheads in eastern France, in the hope of catching the French as they concentrated on attacking the Rhineland.

A weak French attack at Saarbrücken caused momentary panic on 2 August, but the Germans assumed the offensive two days later, defeating the French at Wissembourg, Froschwiller-Wörth, Spichern, and Bomy across the next ten days. German generals ignored Moltke's orders, acting as they saw fit, while the Third Army managed to miss the French altogether for three weeks. Fortunately for Moltke, French coordination was even worse, and Marshal Bazaine, the senior commander, repeatedly threw away opportunities to catch the Germans at a disadvantage, particularly in the hard-fought battles of Mars-la-Tour (Vionville) and Gravelotte (St Privat) on 16–18 August. Moltke's plans for envelopment disintegrated into brutal frontal assaults against superior French rifle fire, with the Germans winning because their officers at all levels continued to press their men forward.

French morale plummeted as it became clear they were fighting such determined enemies, and as logistical breakdowns and command indecision shattered confidence in their leaders. Bazaine's retreat into Metz finally allowed Moltke to trap around half of France's regular army in the city. Having failed to relieve Metz, Napoleon III was driven northwards to Sedan, where he too was surrounded and forced to surrender after an unequal battle on 2 September in a disaster even greater than that at Pavia in 1525. In addition to its emperor, France had lost half a million men, including 260,000 prisoners, in just six weeks.[53]

War with the French

According to the accepted European rules of warfare, France should have capitulated. To his horror, Moltke now found himself facing a nation in arms. Long-term resentment at the Napoleonic regime merged with renewed patriotic fervour as a new government declared France a republic and refused to submit. The country had plenty of weapons, the harvest was in, and many Frenchmen were not averse to getting paid and fed at government expense.[54] Meanwhile, the Germans were suffering from exposed and over-extended supply lines, and the presence of Metz and other fortresses still holding out behind the front.

Moltke's solution was conventional: take the French capital to reinforce the point that the Germans had won (see Fig. 16). Around 250,000 men had surrounded Paris by 23 September but were outnumbered by the defending troops and national guards, who had the benefit of modern fortifications. Moltke was compelled to begin a siege while Bismarck fretted that each delay increased the likelihood of unwelcome foreign intervention. Fortunately for him, the new French government believed the city could not hold out for long and launched a series of disorganized relief efforts with troops who had not completed their training. Bazaine's surrender of Metz on 27 October freed German forces just as other French armies were approaching to the northwest, south, and east of Paris. The increasingly bitter and desperate fighting continued throughout the winter. Isolated garrisons became symbols of French defiance, but efforts to relieve the important border fortress of Belfort failed and the army under General Bourbaki, which had been sent to its aid, disintegrated, with the remnants retreating into Switzerland. With its population on the verge of starvation, Paris surrendered on 27 January, obliging the French government to sign an armistice.

Peace preliminaries were agreed on 26 February but events were interrupted by the Paris Commune, which rejected the peace and sought to prevent a German occupation of the city. The Germans allowed French government troops into Paris to crush the insurrection. The war formally concluded with the Treaty of Frankfurt on 10 May. Wilhelm I and Moltke insisted on substantial territorial gains, both as a marker of victory and to increase Germany's security. Unlike 1866, Bismarck agreed, recognizing that the war's protracted, bloody final stage had made lasting enmity inevitable and increased the need to satisfy German opinion that the sacrifice had been worthwhile. The French offered their colonies in Indochina but were forced to cede Alsace and Lorraine instead. In addition, France was to pay 5 billion francs in reparations within five years, during which time the German occupation would continue. To the Germans' astonishment, France paid almost three years early. At the army's insistence, it had held a victory parade in Paris, which proved a distinctly unsatisfying affair compared to the Allied celebrations after Napoleon's fall in 1814.[55]

The German Empire

Before the war ended, Bismarck had recognized the necessity of creating a more stable framework to secure Prussia's predominance. Careful negotiations led to the proclamation of a new German Empire on 18 January 1871 in the Hall of Mirrors at the Palace of Versailles. The location was chosen because it was the army's headquarters during the siege of Paris, which was still underway. The event was immortalized in Anton von Werner's famous painting of the assembled German princes, all in military unform, hailing Prussia's King Wilhelm I as their emperor (see Fig. 17). The staging echoed the highly romanticized historical understanding of the acknowledgement of early medieval emperors by their warrior lords, but otherwise no effort was made to claim the Holy Roman Imperial legacy, which was too closely associated with the

Habsburgs, and the designation 'Second Empire' only emerged subsequently through the conventions of German historical chronology.

Werner's painting captures the contrast with the earlier attempt at Little German unity in 1848, as Wilhelm now received his status from the princes, not a parliament. Ordinary Germans were only represented through the carefully choreographed presence of small detachments of officers and men from each regiment in the army. Bavaria had been particularly reluctant to join, but its support was bought by secret cash payments to its king and special privileges within the new Empire, which was formally constituted on 16 April.[56]

Although called an empire, the new polity was essentially a Prussian-dominated federation created by adding the four southern states to the eighteen monarchies and three cities of the North German Confederation, whose constitution it adopted largely unchanged. The emperor and princes retained sweeping powers within their own states, including the right to appoint or dismiss ministers and to dissolve parliaments and call fresh elections. Foreign policy was reserved to the Federal Council (*Bundesrat*), composed of representatives of the states, who deliberated in secret. In contrast to 1867, and at the insistence of Bavaria and Württemberg, the council's agreement was necessary to declare war.

Nonetheless, Prussia's king was automatically also now emperor and held the powers of supreme warlord. The army was renamed the *Kaiserheer*, but Baden, Hessen-Darmstadt, and Mecklenburg-Schwerin allowed their forces to be submerged within an expanded Prussian army. Brunswick followed suit in 1886, leaving just Bavaria, Saxony, and Württemberg with separate forces, all of which were now reorganized and equipped along Prussian lines and integrated within a common command structure dependent on the emperor. The three states retained their own war ministries and general staffs, but all necessarily deferred to their Prussian counterparts. The other princes had to be content with minor distinctions like local badges on the helmets of regiments raised from their subjects.

The army's peacetime strength was fixed by the new constitution at 1 per cent of population, the same proportion as in 1818 and 1867. This theoretically allowed the army to expand in line with demographic growth, but in practice it continually lagged behind, because the desire to avoid wrangling with political parties encouraged the government to accept budgets fixed on seven-year cycles.[57] The army also had to compete for funds with the imperial navy, created on 1 February 1872 as a genuinely national institution under a new navy ministry.

A new office of imperial chancellor was created to represent the emperor in dealing with the Reichstag, which could only debate budgets and legislation proposed by the chancellor and ministers, all of whom were appointed by the emperor. The structure reflected Bismarck's conservative vision of benign government standing above factions and petty self-interest. However, Germany rapidly developed elements of modern participatory politics that he had sought to avoid. The National Liberals, who had backed his version of unification, soon fragmented, as did the conservatives, while powerful new organizations emerged in the form of the Centre Party, representing Catholics, and the Marxist Social Democratic Party (SPD), which had become the largest faction in the Reichstag by 1914.[58] Prussia's Polish minority remained troublesome, while many Württembergers and Bavarians were lukewarm at best towards the new empire. Since they lacked their own prince, Alsace and Lorraine were treated as a separate area held in common by the other states and were consequently denied representation in imperial institutions. They were eventually given their own assembly in 1911 but this failed to dispel their perception of being occupied, while the Germans regarded the locals as ungrateful after their 'liberation' from French rule.[59]

Historians remain as deeply divided about imperial Germany as they are over Austria-Hungary, but the disagreements are less about its long-term viability than whether it deviated from 'normal' European social and political developments. It experienced dramatic economic and demographic growth, which was not only a sign of success, but also presented considerable challenges, notably the social consequences of rapid industrialization and urbanization. Like imperial Japan, with which it is often compared, Germany coped relatively well with this process of modernization and its problems were a more extreme example of those experienced elsewhere, rather than genuinely exceptional.[60]

As in Austria-Hungary, the principal issue was managing the competing sectional interests that grew more pronounced as modernization advanced. Much of the constitution had been left deliberately vague. The emperor's authority rested primarily on Prussia's preponderance. Although lacking substantial powers, regular elections and growing media attention made the Reichstag the forum for national politics. With the military budget dependent on the Reichstag's approval, it fell to the chancellor to find a majority among the parties, none of which bridged Germany's existing social, religious, and regional divisions. Matters were complicated from the 1880s by a growing number of extra-parliamentary single-issue pressure groups.

STRATEGIC DILEMMAS, 1872–1914

New Alliances

The absorption of the southern states removed them as intermediaries between Prussia, Austria, and other European powers.[61] Whereas before 1870, Prussia had only shared a short stretch of border with France, the rest being Bavarian or Badenese, after 1871 Imperial Germany was a massive presence, as well as now occupying a chunk of formerly French territory. Prussia meanwhile lost its former role as defender of German liberties against the Habsburgs or external threats and struggled to find another purpose. Forging the Second Empire unbalanced the post-1815 order, which had depended on the German Confederation as a passive central European core. Within years of the creation of Imperial Germany, events largely outside its control dictated its future. Bismarck responded by seeking alliances but his initially loose cooperation with Austria-Hungary and Russia foundered on tension between these two powers over the fate of the Ottoman Empire in the Balkans after 1875.

Russia's victory over the Ottomans by 1878 led to the creation of Montenegro, Romania, and Serbia as independent states, as well as Bulgarian autonomy by 1878. Friedrich Beck, the rising star among Habsburg military advisers, was convinced it was necessary to acquire the Ottoman provinces of Bosnia and Herzegovina to safeguard possession of Dalmatia, which was otherwise almost cut off from the rest of the monarchy and might fall victim to Serbian or Montenegrian expansion. Austria-Hungary occupied the Ottoman provinces in 1878, ostensibly to safeguard these for the sultan, but despite eventually deploying 278,000 troops, it took until 1882 to crush local opposition and associated risings in Dalmatia.[62] The situation stabilized because

Serbian hostility towards Russia's ally Bulgaria kept it from allying with the tsar until 1903.

Austria-Hungary joined Germany in the Dual Alliance in October 1879. Although it had abandoned thoughts of revenge against Prussia, few Austrians were enthusiastic about cooperation, which they saw as an admission of their own weakness. General Beck, who became chief of staff in 1881, rejected all suggestions for preventative wars and saw cooperation as vital in deterring potential Russian aggression. Concerns about a two-front war eased in 1882 when the alliance expanded to include Italy, which at that point feared France. Bismarck attempted to balance the now Triple Alliance with an understanding with Russia to reduce the risk of war and kept all arrangements deliberately vague to leave his diplomatic options open.

The 'Short War Illusion'

Such uncertainties were anathema to military planners. The Austrians continually fretted at their allies' reluctance to specify what aid they would provide in the event of war, while the Germans were caught in a contradictory mix of entitlement and anxiety. The victories of 1864–71 had enabled Prussia to step out of Austria's shadow as a more fully German great power. Politicians and staff officers shared ordinary Germans' belief that their country was entitled to respect and influence, and they felt little compulsion to forgo short-term national advantages in the interests of longer-term international peace. However, they also felt acutely vulnerable, initially to possible French revenge and later to encirclement by superior enemies.

Politicians accepted that the armed forces needed to prepare in peace for war. They often had direct personal experience of war and appreciated its increased scale. Leo von Caprivi, who was navy minister (1883–8) and then chancellor (1890–4), fought in all three wars and had risen to the rank of general of infantry. Bernhard von Bülow, chancellor from 1900 to 1909, had killed a French soldier in personal combat in 1870. It seemed obvious to leave planning to the professionals, whose recent (although ever more distant) victories appeared to confirm they could be trusted with the fate of the nation. The General Staff readily accepted this task, which accorded with their own self-perception. Their own willingness to die for their country led them to conflate their interests with those of the nation. Their professionalism gave them an innate sense of superiority. In a world increasingly dominated by scientific expertise, they were the military specialists and claimed unique and exclusive knowledge. They did not seek to escape political control but were impatient with what they saw as unwelcome constraints on their ability to complete their mission. They increasingly embraced the belief that 'military necessity' justified the disregard of domestic control and international laws and conventions.

Their confidence was brittle, however. Although the General Staff had won, they were haunted by the spectre of a 'peoples' war' (*Volkskrieg*) in which a popular insurgency might rob them of their 'rightful' victory over an enemy's regular army. Their planning was not based on an illusion that a future war would be 'short' but rather the fear it would prove 'long'.[63] Victory had to be so swift and overwhelming that it would leave a defeated foe incapable of anything other than immediate and total surrender. The General Staff believed they could achieve this through superior planning, organization, and morale. Their growing obsession with meticulous preparations was to assuage the underlying anxiety that things might go wrong. This inadvertently placed operational above strategic concerns and encouraged a fatalistic acceptance of risk. It also ignored experience elsewhere in the world. A few observers reported on the length of the American Civil War, but this conflict's duration was blamed on its protagonists being amateurs.[64] No account was taken of the Mexican War (1864–7), or the long, devastating wars in China and Latin America.

After 1871, Moltke regarded war as inevitable, but his innate conservatism led him to oppose a wider militarization of the country in case this opened the armed forces to socialism and other suspect influences. He became increasingly pessimistic and by 1880 no longer believed that a pre-emptive strike against France would succeed. However, he doubted France would attack without allies and broadly agreed with Bismarck that security would be better served through diplomacy than war. Opinion shifted under his successor Alfred von Waldersee, whose term as chief of staff from 1888 to 1891 coincided with Wilhelm II's accession (1888) and Bismarck's dismissal (1890). The new emperor was 'gaffe prone and frequently charmless', and his impulsive behaviour added a new element of uncertainty.[65]

Critically, he did not renew Bismarck's understanding with Russia, which then forged an alternative alliance with France in 1894. From being an unstable, multipolar system, Europe was now divided into the Triple Alliance of Germany, Austria-Hungary, and Italy flanked by France and Russia, with Britain at that point still detached in 'splendid isolation' as a global maritime imperial power. This seismic shift did not make war inevitable, but it nonetheless narrowed German war planning to the problem of a two-front war against France and Russia, whose combined military and naval strength was far greater.

Waldersee and Wilhelm II were convinced that the superiority of German *Kultur* would outweigh numerical inferiority and ensure victory. They continued to believe in a short war as this removed the need to address how a long conflict might be won. In his recommendations, Waldersee masked this subjective argument by stressing 'rational' planning and technical expertise. Convinced he should become chancellor, Waldersee squandered the emperor's goodwill by criticizing his performance at the 1890 manoeuvres.

However, his successor as chief of staff, Alfred von Schlieffen, shared his conviction in the inevitability of war and determination to win it through superior planning. Like Waldersee, Schlieffen had risen rapidly thanks to favourable staff appointments that brought him powerful patrons. An austere man who read military history as bedtime stories to his children, he is forever associated with the infamous 'Plan' which has been widely blamed for both the outbreak of the First World War and why Germany lost it. The destruction of most of his papers in the bombing of the war archive in Berlin in 1944 makes it difficult to reconstruct what he really intended and has led to claims that there never was in fact a coherent plan.[66]

Schlieffen believed that Germany could win a two-front war, but only if it fought defensively, at least in the initial stage. His famous 'plan' to attack France was devised in December 1905 after Russia had just been defeated by Japan and was not an immediate threat. Seven armies were to deploy in the west, two of which were to hold the expected French attack on Alsace-Lorraine. The other five would strike in a wide arc through Luxembourg, Belgium, and the Netherlands to hit France from the north as a hammer that would slam their forces against the anvil of the armies defending Alsace-Lorraine.[67] Avoiding the deep thrust into northeastern France envisaged by Moltke, Schlieffen believed his plan would win the war in six weeks. Troops could then be switched by rail to reinforce the single army deployed to protect East Prussia against Russia should it attack.[68]

The plan took some account of changes in weaponry which made frontal assaults more costly by seeking to wrong-foot the French through the sheer scale of the envelopment to the north. However, the idea also reflected Schlieffen's own obsession with a battle of annihilation, which he derived from his historical studies of the Carthaginian victory at Cannae in 216 BC, as well as Moltke's triumph at Sedan.

Schlieffen left some scope for diplomacy, hoping that a swift victory over France would prompt Russia to sue for peace and deter Britain from intervening. However, the disregard for three neutral states' rights was justified as military necessity which precluded any preliminary negotiations lest these warn the French of German intentions. Worse, his plan brooked no half-measures: victory over France had to be total, meaning operations would be detached from diplomacy until the generals had succeeded. Like Moltke, he lacked an alternative in case his enemies did not behave as expected. Rather than considering variables, Schlieffen focused on detail, notably the capacity of Germany's railways to move troops rapidly. Everything depended on immediate success, and virtually no attention was given to how a long war might be sustained; that was simply too awful to contemplate. Prussia's war ministry made separate plans to feed the population for three years, but these were not integrated with the staff strategy. Meanwhile, Schlieffen's focus on swift victory on land led him to assign the navy the task of relieving the army of the duty of defending Germany's coast, rather than assisting the offensive. He simply assumed Britain would not intervene, and therefore did not consider how the navy might be required to prevent British assistance to France.

Chancellor Caprivi and many generals doubted whether Schlieffen could really win in just forty days, but they were unable to think of an alternative plan for victory.[69] However, Caprivi at least hoped this would not be necessary. Far more than the General Staff, he recognized that industrialization was making Germany more dependent on access to overseas markets, as well as the ability to import food. Yet, he also appreciated that the vast bulk of German trade was still with its European neighbours and he remained deaf to the small, but vocal lobby demanding colonies.[70] He attempted to adjust to Germany's deteriorating international position by compromising with Britain in

1890. German influence in Zanzibar was abandoned in return for Britain surrendering Helgoland Island in the North Sea, which improved German maritime security.

WELTPOLITIK

Caprivi lost Wilhelm's confidence and resigned in 1894. His successor, Prince Hohenlohe, struggled to continue a more pacific foreign policy, but he too eventually resigned in 1900 to be replaced by Bülow, who shared Wilhelm II's vision of *Weltpolitik*, that a country could only truly be a great power if it acted globally. Bülow had already famously expressed this in a speech to the Reichstag 1897: 'We don't want to put anyone in the shade, but we too demand our place in the sun.'[71] The new course was not immediately directed against Britain, but increasingly became perceived as such because the opportunities were shrinking as other powers completed the process of carving up the world. Weltpolitik's popularity grew among voters until around 1907, by which time it had lost any strategic rationale and it was clearly far more in Germany's interests to compromise with Britain to keep global trade open.[72]

Weltpolitik was welcomed by Alfred von Tirpitz, whom Wilhelm had placed in charge of the navy's construction and finance department in 1897. Unlike his army counterparts, Tirpitz was from middle-class origins. While he shared their conservatism, he embraced elements of modernity, notably technological change, and industrial management techniques. He cultivated a loyal following among his close collaborators, but was stubborn and refused to admit mistakes.

Tirpitz strongly condemned the previous naval planning, which had concentrated on breaking the expected enemy blockade of the coastal ports. Arguing that war at sea differed from war on land in that there were no physical features to capture or control, he felt policy should be redirected to commanding the oceans through destroying the enemy fleet in battle. Subsequently known as navalism, this concept was already fashionable in Britain and the United States. Although conceived for the sea, it was essentially the same as the army's belief that the purpose of war was to annihilate enemy forces. Likewise, it was emotional more than rational, believing that naval power was not only essential to great-power status, but that it could only be achieved through the possession of a modern battlefleet that was itself a totem of national pride and technological prowess. In a secret speech to naval officers in October 1913, Tirpitz argued that it was 'more honourable to fight for the most honourable aim and to go under honourably instead of accepting a future without glory'.[73] Like the army, he saw war as inevitable, but regarded Britain, not France or Russia, as the primary enemy.

Receiving enthusiastic backing from Wilhelm II, who fancied himself as a naval architect and admiral, Tirpitz immediately set about emancipating the navy from its junior place in German military strategy. Recognizing it would be expensive, he carefully framed his ideas as supposedly defensive by presenting his Risk Theory (*Riskogedanke*) that a large German fleet would deter Britain, which would not want to chance a battle in case its Royal Navy was left too badly damaged to fight another power. The simplicity of this appealed to the Reichstag deputies, who had grown tired of being asked to fund various types of ships without any clear overarching purpose, while Tirpitz's carefully managed media campaign won over industrialists and the wider public eager to see more German battleships. The Reichstag's passage of the Navy Law in March 1898 provided funding for an ocean-going battlefleet.

This indirect challenge to Britain was swiftly followed by further antagonism during the South African War (1899–1902). Believing conflict made Britain vulnerable, Wilhelm II was disappointed when his offers of an alliance were rebuffed and responded by adopting an aggressively pro-Boer stance. Tirpitz exploited the situation to persuade the Reichstag to pass a second Navy Law in June 1900 mandating funding to maintain a ratio of 2:3 in battleships to those of the Royal Navy. This directly challenged Britain, which had adopted the 'two-power standard' in 1889 that its navy should be equal to the next two largest fleets and initiated the 'naval race'.[74] Britain looked elsewhere for allies, making agreements with Japan (1902), France (1904), and Russia (1907) that completed the division of Europe's major powers into two rival blocks.

Calls for War

The next decade saw the German and Austrian chiefs of staff growing increasingly vocal in their demands for pre-emptive war, but their respective targets continued to diverge. The first calls came during 1905–6 in the wake of Japan's victory, which left Russia seriously weakened while Germany became embroiled in a new dispute over Anglo-French influence in Morocco. Schlieffen insisted on seizing the moment to attack France but he was overruled by Wilhelm II and replaced in 1906 by his deputy, the elder Moltke's nephew, who had enjoyed a similarly accelerated career thanks to having been the emperor's adjutant. While maintaining a facade of cool professionalism, the younger Moltke was wracked by self-doubt and was even more pessimistic than his uncle had been, writing privately in January 1905 that a future conflict 'will be a peoples' war, which won't end in a decisive battle, but will become a protracted, exhausting struggle'.[75]

Unlike Schlieffen, the younger Moltke paid more attention to the maritime dimension and was not convinced by Tirpitz's assurances that the navy could break a British blockade. Accordingly, he modified his predecessor's plan to avoid infringing Dutch neutrality in the hope Germany could circumvent a blockade by importing through the Netherlands. The change narrowed the route to be traversed by the main strike force, increasing the risk of logistical difficulties and the likelihood of even much smaller opposing forces fighting successful delaying actions. He also shifted some of the weight from the main force to strengthen the two armies assigned to defend Alsace-Lorraine. These modifications subsequently attracted fierce criticism with their architect being blamed for losing Germany the war.

The debate over the Schlieffen Plan misses the point that the details mattered less than the General Staff's inability to think objectively about the broader strategic context. They remained trapped within their own logic. They all knew that war was extremely risky but could not admit the possibility of failure without undermining their own claims to professional expertise and demands for resources. They ignored reality by focusing on purely operational matters for a best-case strategic scenario while attempting to reduce complexities by excluding those factors that would have made their plans appear unrealistic and by stressing intangible, and therefore unquantifiable, factors like their soldiers' aggression and offensive spirit. The outward appearance of calm confidence and professional competence was sustained by the annual *Kaisermanöver*, which conveyed a false impression of what war would be like, including choreographed massed cavalry charges.

Meanwhile, Austro-Hungarian planners also became convinced of the need for 'preventative war'. After a period of relative stability, the monarchy's internal problems grew, and it was a sign of the regime's distrust of its own forces that the new Muslim Bosnian units were deployed to Prague, Vienna, Graz, and Budapest after rioting in 1897, because they were considered more loyal. Fearing an imminent repeat of 1848, the General Staff prepared plans to invade Hungary in 1905.[76] Franz Ferdinand, the heir apparent since 1896, was concerned that the monarchy might fragment. Energetic, but inconsistent, he played an increasingly important role in deciding Habsburg policy, favouring the alliance with Germany but wishing to avoid war with Russia.

His main concern was Italy, which had turned to the Adriatic after a disastrous colonial failure in Abyssinia in 1896 and was now threatening Habsburg interests in Montenegro and Albania. Franco-Italian relations improved after 1902, while Italian irredentist agitation increased as nationalists demanded Trieste and parts of the Tirol to complete their country's unification. A part of the Habsburg government still believed Italy was committed to the Triple Alliance, but Franz Ferdinand was not convinced and in 1906 he compelled the elderly Beck to resign as chief of staff and replaced him with his own favourite, the mercurial Conrad von Hötzendorf.

A self-conscious modernizer, Conrad, like Schlieffen, advocated preventative war, but he had Serbia and Italy in his sights, not France or Russia.[77] Whereas Beck and others had become alarmed at the prospect that Germany would leave them to face Russia and any other enemies to the south or east, Conrad quietly welcomed this since it gave him a free hand to plan war against Italy or Serbia. He was convinced a quick victory over either country would strengthen Austria-Hungary in any future conflict with Russia. His chance appeared to come in 1908 when a change of government in the Ottoman Empire prompted the Habsburgs to complete the annexation of Bosnia-Herzegovina to forestall Serbian designs. Conrad sought to widen the crisis and launch a preventative war against Serbia but was overruled. As with Germany's sabre-rattling two years before over Morocco, the episode antagonized Austria-Hungary's potential enemies without improving its security.

In Germany, Bülow, whose reputation had already been damaged by a succession of public scandals, was forced to resign after the Reichstag refused to increase the navy budget due to the growing expense of battleships. The new chancellor, Bethmann-Hollweg, opposed navalism and sought better relations with Britain but, like his predecessor, proved unable to form a stable majority in the Reichstag or to resolve Germany's strategic dilemmas. Tirpitz refused to admit his Risk Theory was wrong for fear the government would cut his budget, and the theatrical staging of naval reviews by Britain and Germany sustained popular enthusiasm for big battleships and contributed to the continued sense of antagonism and suspicion.[78] Contrary to the popular view, the naval race did not lead to war in 1914. During the Agadir Crisis in Morocco in 1911, Tirpitz's request for more money was denied and he was forced to compromise by accepting an amended Navy Law the following May. By December 1912 he had lost his government's support, and the army again took priority in defence spending. Later, in July 1914, no one wanted his advice.

Conrad demanded to be allowed to attack Italy once it became embroiled in a war with Turkey over Libya in 1911 and resigned when he was overruled. Austria-Hungary's situation deteriorated rapidly with the Turks' renewed defeat in the two Balkan Wars of 1912–13. Serbia emerged as the biggest winner among the anti-Ottoman coalition while the war deepened ethnic tensions within the Habsburg monarchy.[79] Independent Slavic, Italian, and Romanian states now created serious alternative loyalties. The Austrian and Hungarian parliaments were sufficiently alarmed to vote a major credit for new armaments and to pass the War Service Act to enable the government to rule by decree in wartime. Conrad was reappointed chief of staff in December 1912 but, in contrast to his German counterparts, lost out to the Habsburg navy, which received a considerable proportion of the new money.

Believing Austria-Hungary to be unreformable, the German General Staff had largely ignored it in their calculations since the 1890s. Growing concern at Russia's revival after 1905 prompted some effort to improve coordination and the Triple Alliance was renewed for the fourth and last time on 5 December 1912. The younger Moltke doubted Italy's commitment because it now claimed the defence of Libya meant it could no longer send troops to the Rhine in the event of war with France. A naval pact was agreed in June 1913 to cooperate in the Mediterranean to prevent France moving its colonial army from north Africa to reinforce its home forces, but both the German and the Habsburg staffs were thinking primarily in terms of a land war.[80] Already in February 1913, Austria-Hungary had accepted Germany's war plan and agreed to deal with Russia and any enemies in the Alps or Balkans while Germany crushed France. This decision curtailed its options, hastening its slide into a subordinate role already before war broke out on 28 July 1914.

The July Crisis

Throughout the war scares and crises since 1871, the German and Austro-Hungarian governments had repeatedly stepped back from hostilities, often against the advice of their general staffs. Why they took a different course in 1914 continues to cause controversy.[81] Opinion divides broadly between those stressing long-term factors, like systemic rivalry trending towards war, who usually see the conflict as inevitable, and those arguing that the European powers had overcome crises before but failed to do so in July because of miscalculations and mistakes. The crisis broke during July 1914 when Wilhelm was on his yacht and Austria's war minster was among the many key figures away on holiday. The severity of the situation was not immediately obvious to the wider public.

Conrad and Moltke the Younger had doubts and felt unprepared for war: Moltke expected Germany to run out of shells within forty days. However, both were convinced that war now offered better chances of victory than waiting for a future moment. They used their technical expertise to provide detailed memoranda that appeared convincing, notably that current armament programmes would give France and Russia a decisive advantage within two years. However, such advice was subjective and driven by their belief in the inevitability of war, along with the Germans' view that national honour dictated standing by Austria-Hungary after the shock of Franz Ferdinand's assassination by Serbian nationalists in Sarajevo on 28 June. This led to Bethmann-Hollweg sending the infamous 'Blank Cheque' note to Vienna on 6 July to that effect.[82] At that point, matters remained a political rather than a military gamble, since the chancellor hoped that either Russia would be deterred from backing Serbia, or an Austro-Hungarian invasion of that country would succeed fast enough to forestall intervention.

Austria-Hungary's next missteps proved critical. Franz Ferdinand's murder had removed a key advocate of caution, increasing the influence of hawkish officers who were determined to crush Serbia to demonstrate power and preserve its waning great-power status.[83] Germany distrusted British mediation as compromising its Habsburg ally, but pushed Vienna to make concessions to secure Italy's adherence to the Triple Alliance, rather than to make peace with Serbia. Austria-Hungary's over-hasty declaration of war on Serbia in turn triggered Russian mobilization, thereby ending efforts by the tsar's government to settle the crisis peacefully.

I I

Nations in Arms

A GENIUS FOR WAR? THE RISE OF THE GENERAL STAFF

Napoleon's Legacy for Germany

The French Revolution and Napoleon cast a long shadow over military affairs, as in so many other aspects of nineteenth-century Europe. Austria and the Empire had only been defeated after a decade of gruelling warfare. In turn, it had taken a further three-year war of attrition to liberate Germany by 1814. That experience informed the widespread desire to avoid further costly wars and to impose tight limits on military expenditure in the three decades following 1815. However, Napoleon's rapid victories over Austria and Prussia between 1805 and 1807, as well as his own definitive defeat at Waterloo, also left a powerful memory of martial glory and a conviction that warfare had changed irrevocably. This contradictory legacy of suffering and celebration interacted with disagreements between conservatives and liberals over the post-Napoleonic political and social order to shape defence policy and military organization until the fresh revolutionary upheavals of 1848–9.

From that point, matters were increasingly influenced by rapid technological changes, propelled in turn by industrialization which made the mass production of precision-engineered weaponry possible for the first time, as well as introducing such innovations as steam power, railways, and the electric telegraph, which revolutionized transport and communications. Prussia's short-service conscription proved the best response to the competing demands of economy, efficiency, quality, and quantity. Its triumphs over Austria and France established it as the model to follow, even though its own commanders continued to argue over how best to adapt to further, still more rapid technological change. Meanwhile, both Austria and Prussia joined the ranks of the world's leading naval powers, with the former initially leading the way, only to be belatedly overtaken by imperial Germany after 1898.

Prussia's victories across 1864–71 were widely attributed at the time and subsequently to superior planning that allowed it to maximize its army's potential and achieve the desired quick, decisive victories. This aspect, more than any other, has shaped the lasting popular belief that Germans possessed a peculiar 'genius for war', as noted in the Introductory chapter. Combined with widespread admiration for Clausewitz, whose writings were believed to have shaped war planning, this consolidated the belief that the Germans generally, and Prussians in particular, were Napoleon's true interpreters and heirs, and that they had unlocked the secret of victory which could be distilled into a set of timeless formulae. Nowhere is this truer than in the United States, where Clausewitz remains the only non-American to be honoured with a portrait in the National War College in Washington.

Closer examination reveals more complex explanations for German successes – and failures – during the nineteenth century, with the myth widest of the mark regarding command and control. Critics of German militarism have long argued that the absence of fully democratic structures allowed the army to escape political control and irresponsibly prepare for what became a self-destructive war. This, too, is a distortion, but it does pinpoint the key problem that none of the German states solved satisfactorily after 1815: how to establish clear, accountable structures to handle the related tasks of command, administration, and planning. Imperial Germany's problems lay less in the army's desire to escape constitutional control than in its inheritance of Prussia's unhappy division of these three aspects between competing institutions, which it proceeded to exacerbate still further.

States' Rights

The conservative atmosphere of the Restoration era after 1815 thwarted liberal hopes of subordinating military power to constitutional control. German monarchs remained warlords who insisted on command as their personal prerogative. This, as much as rivalry between Austria and Prussia, ensured that the new German Confederation did not create an overall commander in peacetime, but instead arranged for this only to be done in wartime when the Federal Council would name a general and staff, as well as approving the overall plan of operations.[1]

A Military Commission was appointed in 1819, with Austria, Prussia, and Bavaria each having a representative, along with three more chosen by the states composing the three mixed army corps. Intended as a temporary advisory body, the Commission effectively became permanent and assumed more responsibilities, including oversight of the federal fortresses, organizing inspections of contingents, and appraising technological developments like railways.[2] Beyond this, the Confederation briefly had a war ministry and admiralty between 1848 and 1850, both of which fell victim to the reassertion of states' rights once the revolutionary emergency had abated.

The Swiss Confederation followed an identical pattern, indicating that this was not purely a production of monarchical reaction, but was also strongly driven by particularism and the desire to preserve cherished political autonomy. Federal commanders were only appointed by the diet in emergencies and there was initially no war ministry or General Staff. Each canton maintained its own war council to supervise its federal contingent and small professional guard. A permanent Military Supervision Board was appointed in 1817 with six officers charged with inspecting cantonal contingents and advising the diet on technical matters. Following the Sonderbund War of 1847, the Board was replaced in 1850 by the Military Department, which initially only had four staff, but gradually expanded to handle military administration at the federal level by 1866. Meanwhile, the new Federal Council, established by the 1848 constitution, subsumed the function of the previous ad hoc confederal war councils to decide on strategy in emergencies. Repeated recommendations from Baron Jomini, Friedrich Rüstow, and other respected experts eventually led to the establishment of the Staff Bureau in 1865, which incorporated the topographical office from the General Staff, as well as providing an archive and a military history section, and gathering intelligence on foreign armies.[3]

Command during the Restoration Era, 1815–48

Most German states maintained only the forces required by their obligations to the Confederation. As these usually remained small, there was no incentive to change existing command and administrative arrangements.[4] It took the revolutionary upheavals of 1831 before Hanover and Saxony finally replaced their old, collegial war councils with ministries responsible to parliament. Monarchs remained nominally commanders but routinely delegated the actual exercise of authority to a senior general. These arrangements were attacked not only by liberals seeking to subordinate command to constitutional control, but also often from within the army and civil administration.

The defects of the Bavarian army were widely attributed to the supposedly malign influence of Field Marshal Wrede, who was slowly stripped of his authority until 1829, when he was sidelined as inspector general, and command was entrusted to the war minister. This matched the liberal ideal, since ministers were accountable to parliament, but they were also often officers appointed by the king. The move also effectively merged command with administration and left the divisional staffs (and briefly the corps staffs, 1848–55) as the only permanent, higher-level commands. This pattern was broadly followed in Baden, Saxony, Württemberg, and the other medium-sized states whose forces were at least of brigade strength.[5]

In Prussia, the king reluctantly accepted the establishment of a single war ministry in 1814, replacing the previous division of tasks between separate institutions. Nonetheless, these roles were still assigned to separate departments within the ministry. Command and personnel were the most sensitive since these were traditionally royal prerogatives and the king took a keen interest in the selection of senior officers. Attitudes were more relaxed towards finance and administration, since these aspects were regarded as simply finding the means to implement rather than decide policy, and because it was accepted that the Prussian diet had to be consulted in setting budgets and agreeing taxes. War planning was considered the least glamorous task, given the return to peace, prevailing austerity, and the association of this function with mundane, technical matters like logistics and cartography.

The subsequently famous Greater General Staff (*Großer Generalstab*) was formally constituted under Rühle von Lilienstern in 1821, thereby institutionalizing Gerhard von Scharnhorst's distinction between staff as a central planning body, and the Troop General Staff (*Truppengeneralstab*), or staffs of the army's higher formations: corps, divisions, and brigades. Comprising only forty-five officers, half of whom were in the troop staffs, the General Staff was separated from the war ministry in 1825, but its head still reported through the minister to the king. Prussia's war minister was obliged after 1850 to swear an oath to the constitution as well as his customary personal loyalty as an officer to the king, leading him to be mistrusted by politicians because he was a general, distrusted by the army because he was involved in politics, and held in suspicion by the monarch because his views often differed from those of field commanders.[6]

Mid-Century Disorganization

Prussia's arrangement was one of several unsatisfactory outcomes from the 1848–9 revolutions. These upheavals finally forced the Habsburgs to replace their venerable Court War Council with a war ministry in April 1848. Franz Josef's imposition of neo-absolutist government the following year led to no fewer than sixteen reorganizations of the ministry by 1866 as the emperor struggled to reconcile his desire for personal rule with the realities of complex, modern administration. His assertion of personal command in 1849 led to the creation of a General Adjutant's Office headed by Count Grüne to relay orders, as well as a Military Chancellery to handle paperwork. Full of men from well-connected families, Grüne's office considered itself superior to the Quartermaster General's Staff, nominally responsible for planning, which remained subordinate to the war ministry. Increasingly marginalized, the latter disappeared completely in 1853, before being reconstituted in 1862 following Austria's defeat in Italy. Meanwhile, the navy had remained under army command until 1856, when the emperor's younger brother, Ferdinand Max, secured the establishment of a separate ministry, but his departure for Mexico saw that body reabsorbed into the war ministry as the Marine Section.[7]

Matters became still more complex following the disaster of 1866 and the establishment of the Dual Monarchy. There were now separate Austrian and Hungarian war ministries, responsible for the Landwehr and Honvéd respectively, with a superior imperial war ministry for the regular army and navy. The liberals heading the war ministry across 1866–74 followed Bavaria's earlier example and sidelined the conservative Archduke Albrecht, whom Franz Joseph had appointed commander in 1866, by creating the post of inspector general three years later. The position of Quartermaster General now substituted for that of commander, but the emperor refused to relinquish his prerogatives so easily and still exerted influence through a revived Military Chancellery. Arguments among the liberals meanwhile led to the temporary disappearance of the Quartermaster General's staff altogether in 1871, before its re-emergence as the General Staff four years later. Thanks to his reputation as the victor at Custoza and to personal fortune, Archduke Albrecht continued to exert disproportionate influence on affairs until his death in 1895.

Some clarity was only established through the emergence of Count Beck, whose appointment successively to head the Military Chancellery (1867), General Adjutant's Office (1874), and chief of the General Staff (1881) gave him such a commanding position that he was nicknamed *Vize-Kaiser*. Steering a middle course between liberals and conservatives, Beck ensured the war ministry concentrated on finance and administration while the staff handled planning. However, the increasingly elderly emperor permitted his nephew and heir apparent, Archduke Franz Ferdinand, to form his own military chancellery in 1899, which became a vehicle for his wider efforts to reform the monarchy and reshape defence policy. After a long struggle, the archduke secured Beck's replacement by Conrad von Hötzendorf in 1906. Critically, the General Staff had been removed from the war ministry's supervision in 1895 and given direct access to the emperor, thereby weakening constitutional control while increasing the number of highly personalized institutions competing for influence over strategy.

If historians have often, somewhat unfairly, dismissed such confusion as typically Austrian, they have equally inaccurately presented Prussia as the ideal, streamlined 'power state'. Prussia differed only because it institutionalized the division between the three elements of command, planning, and finance to a much greater degree. The war ministry's relative impotence was already demonstrated during the constitutional crisis of 1859–61, when Wilhelm I used a special commission to circumvent the war minister Eduard von Bonin, a liberal who opposed the plans to reform the Landwehr, prompting Bonin's resignation and replacement by Albrecht von Roon. The next, more critical step came on 2 June 1866, when Moltke the Elder secured the right to communicate directly with the king as nominal commander, rather than through the war minister. Intended to speed decisions in wartime, this effectively removed planning from any constitutional oversight.

These structures were carried over into Imperial Germany because the surviving states all signed military conventions accepting Prussia's supremacy. The new empire simply used Prussia's war ministry to manage its army, with the still autonomous Bavarian, Saxon, and Württemberg ministries implementing Prussian directives applying to their own forces. Prussia's minister was now paid by the empire and had to negotiate with the Reichstag for funds but was appointed by the emperor to whom he owed personal loyalty. Whereas the army remained composed of contingents still associated with the surviving states, the navy became an entirely imperial institution. The Prussian Navy Ministry, created in 1861, was now dissolved and replaced by a new Imperial German Admiralty on 1 January 1872. Under the chancellor's oversight, this was one of the few common institutions, though formal command was reserved to the emperor, and was in practice exercised by the navy minister, who was a Prussian officer.[8]

At this point, Germany's structures looked more rational than Austria's, but matters took a decided turn for the worse on 28 April 1885 when Wilhelm I decreed that the chancellor and war minister were no longer to countersign any order that did not explicitly involve the military budget. Officer appointments and promotions were henceforth handled by a new Military Cabinet, like Austria's Military Chancellery and which had its origins in the Prussian kings' reliance on adjutants to control their army regardless of formal institutions. Wilhelm II complicated the situation further in April 1889 when he dissolved the Admiralty and replaced it with three bodies of nominally equal status under his overall authority. A new position of commander was now responsible for tactics and operations, with personnel matters handled by a Navy Cabinet, and design, construction, maintenance, and finance all entrusted to the *Reichsmarineamt* (RMA – Imperial Marine Office).

So far, the changes had been driven more by the monarch's concern to preserve his royal prerogative than by the military's desire to emancipate itself from political control, though Alfred von Waldersee, the new chief of staff from 1888, had pushed for this.[9] As in Austria, personalities mattered at least as much as institutions, with section heads competing for influence and resources, exercising patronage, and fighting turf wars with other departments. These personal rivalries are glossed over in the standard critiques of German militarism, which interpret the armed forces as homogeneous and with a single will and agenda. Perhaps the most fatal example was Tirpitz, whose lobbying persuaded Wilhelm II to abolish the naval command in 1899, replacing it with the Admiralty Staff, nominally responsible for tactics and operational planning. While Tirpitz eliminated a position he had regarded as hindering his plans to expand the navy, he deepened the division between those responsible for deciding how warships should actually be used and his own department that designed and built them.

General Staffs

The personal character of monarchical government also affected the development of Germany's famous staff system. Monarchs remained supreme commanders, while officer promotion was still broadly guided by seniority. Army and corps commands went to generals who either had long service records or were the ruler's relations. Scharnhorst had accepted that this was unlikely to change when he envisaged staff officers as a commander's experienced guides. Staff officers had an entirely different and, to their critics, privileged, career path. Both the Prussian and Austrian war colleges insisted on exacting standards, with only a minority of applicants graduating with a staff posting. However, those that did so were still young, junior officers now serving as Troop Staff officers with senior generals who were often princes or even kings.

Unlike most of their peers, they had the chance to be noticed and to win favour. August Mackensen, from modest middle-class origins, impressed Wilhelm II while a staff officer and became the first commoner to become a royal adjutant, later being ennobled on the emperor's fortieth birthday, given command of the 1st (Death's Head) Hussars and ultimately becoming a field marshal.[10] Others rising through staff service included Paul von Hindenburg, Erich Ludendorff, the future chancellor Franz von Papen, and all chiefs of staff. The risk of 'groupthink' increased as Prussia's staff acquired control of the War Academy in 1872, leading to an increasingly narrow curriculum focusing on purely technical matters.

Staffs expanded as armies grew, but primarily because the German model made their chief into a shadow commander, substituting for the monarch who refused to relinquish overall authority, yet was incapable of exercising it in the field. Prussia's staff totalled only sixty-four officers in 1853, but had expanded to 794 by 1914, of whom 169 were Troop

Staff liaising with corps and fortress commands or serving as military attachés. Austria's staff meanwhile grew from around sixty in the early nineteenth century to 434 on the eve of the First World War.[11] Prussia's success ensured its methods were copied elsewhere. Bavaria had already introduced a troop staff in 1826, while the small Swiss staff, established on the French model in 1804, totalled 400 officers by 1874 when it was reorganized along Prussian lines to provide liaison with the army's new brigade and divisional structures.[12] Prussian training methods were also adopted, including the staff rides developed by Moltke the Elder, following Frederick II's example of traversing likely campaign theatres and testing officers' ability to cope with potential operational problems.

However, the Bavarian, Saxon, and Württemberg staffs remained departments within their war ministries, as did staffs in other countries, like France, which adopted some of Prussia's methods. Bavaria had already agreed in 1870 to surrender operational command to Prussia in the event of a future war, and duly disbanded its staff in 1914, only briefly reconstituting it to help with demobilization in 1919. The Swiss staff grew so large because it was the only permanent formation of the federal militia and included the army's engineers and other specialists, as well as officers seconded for training.

Operational Command

By contrast, Prussia, followed by Austria, used the staff to direct as well as plan operations. Troop staff officers morphed from assistants to shadow generals thanks to their plenipotentiary powers, entitling them to issue orders if they felt the field commander was deviating too far from their chief's plan. The increase in capacity emerged unplanned in response to the difficulties encountered in the wars of 1866 and 1870–1 and was at odds with Moltke's original intentions.

Recognizing he was dealing with an army led by princes and experienced generals while he had never commanded even a platoon in battle, Moltke developed the model of 'command by directive' (*Weisungsführung*) in which the chief of staff devised the overall plan but allowed army and corps commanders some latitude in how to implement this. This took account of Clausewitz's 'fog of war', recognizing that, as men on the spot, field commanders were often better placed to know what was happening and should be allowed to respond to changing circumstances without always referring upwards for instructions. Wilhelm I, while still crown prince, and his brother, Fredrich Carl, both contributed substantially to this method, with the latter urging it be replicated at the tactical level. However, lower-level command remained that of 'tactics by order' (*Befehlstaktik*) in keeping with the army's ingrained sense of hierarchy.[13]

However, Moltke quickly became frustrated at what he saw as the generals' failure to follow his instructions. He managed to remove General Falckenstein from corps command after numerous mistakes in 1866 but found his carefully laid plans repeatedly disrupted during 1870. General Steinmetz openly defied Moltke's orders, leading to the unintended battle of Spicheren on 6 August, while a meticulously planned encirclement of General Patrice MacMahon's French army at Wörth nearby on the same day began prematurely and was eventually only won through superior artillery fire.

Technological developments merely fuelled Moltke's urge to micromanage operations further, because the electric telegraph promised almost instantaneous communications. He was not alone in this, of course, with Napoleon III famously trying to direct the Crimean War by cable from Paris. However, German war-planning acquired a noticeable rigidity when combined with the insistence on swift, decisive victory. After 1871, German war planning was guided by the fear that, for want of the proverbial nail, the entire country's future would be lost. Moltke and his successors focused on details, believing these to be their professional remit. They did not see themselves as beyond political control, because they saw that as exercised by the monarch, not parliament, which was there merely to provide whatever money and legislation they judged necessary.

Intelligence

For all the concern over the fog of war, intelligence was given scant attention. Prussia established a Secret Information Service as a subsection of the General Staff in 1835 to process reports from officers on leave and those prepared by the military attachés attached to embassy staff since 1830. Waldersee held that post in Paris in 1870, while by 1914 there were attachés in nine European countries, including Switzerland but not Austria-Hungary, as well as in Turkey, China, Japan, and the United States. Naval attachés were also appointed after 1871, though none was posted to London until 1886. Attachés reported directly to the monarch, sometimes without informing the foreign minister.[14]

The disconnect widened because the foreign ministry ran its own intelligence network, though the closure of the other German states' embassies at least centralized this somewhat after 1871. The Prussian Post Office monitored telegraph communications from the 1880s and later also the phone network, providing information to the foreign ministry, but the navy developed its own intelligence service. The situation was similar in Austria, which established the Evidence Office as a subsection of the General Staff, but also gathered information through diplomatic channels. Its service was so poor in 1848 that the navy had to consult an encyclopaedia for information about the Sardinian navy.[15]

Verification checks were weak, and there was a tendency to pass on information that confirmed accepted views, including about one's own forces. Bavaria's war ministry routinely told the king that all was fine, conveying the impression it had secured good value for public expenditure, with the result that the monarch saw no reason to back its calls for more money.[16] Intelligence on foreign enemies was limited to collecting information on their numbers, structure, tactics, and weaponry, and neither the German nor the Austrian staffs made much effort to correlate their technical knowledge with diplomatic assessments of other countries' likely intentions. Counter-intelligence was rather better, with German agents enjoying selling false war plans to France and Russia in 1906. However, no attempt was made to develop an effective decryption service.

LINE AND LANDWEHR

The Politics of Recruitment

Recruitment was the most contested aspect of Napoleon's legacy, since resolving this strongly shaped the relationship of armies to society and how future wars would be fought. It was not a simple question of either a small professional army or a mass force of citizens-in-arms, as opinions differed so widely on both quality and quantity. Universal service had already been declared, but few supported its full implementation. In an era of austerity, war ministers remained mindful to retain enough money for training and equipment. Professional officers recognized that it had only been the declining quality of the French army that had masked the manifold deficiencies among the volunteers and Landwehr across 1813–15. Regarding them as a temporary expedient to defeat Napoleon, German governments welcomed the returning volunteers and Landwehr as patriotic heroes but told them their task was over and they should return to civilian life.[17]

Most were only too happy to do so, and there was little enthusiasm for continuing military service in peacetime. Liberals, meanwhile, argued about defence. Many agreed with conservatives that mass armies could only be sustained through popular enthusiasm, which in turn threatened radical, aggressive policies such as those associated with the Jacobins in France. The liberals wanted to avoid war and regarded defence as resolved by 1820 as the German Confederation concluded its collective security arrangements, fixing strength at a modest 1 per cent of population, composed of regulars with a small reserve. Most liberals opposed universal service and demanded a continuation of French-style conscription as had been practised in the Rheinbund states, which allowed the middle class to buy exemption through paying for substitutes.

Militias and Civic Guards

Only a small, Romantic minority advocated citizens' militias (*Volksbewaffnung*) with elected officers. Such calls were strong on polemical rhetoric and weak on practical ideas, but they appealed to local patriotism and the desire among many burghers to demonstrate their own civic martial masculinity distinct from the largely proletarian conscripts. Several German states relaxed the restrictions imposed on gun ownership during the Napoleonic era and allowed the re-establishment of civic guards (*Bürgerwehren*) and shooting clubs in the 1820s. These organizations also provided a way in which veterans from 1813–15 could continue a militarized social life and assert claims to status and recognition. Guards existed in sixty-three Württemberg towns by 1829, but total membership was only 2,103 and enthusiasm was already waning.[18]

The revolutionary upheavals of 1830–1 provided a renewed boost, particularly as guard membership appeared patriotic in the face of a feared French invasion and fitted the liberal ideal of military service as a temporary civic duty. Each state's guards were under the jurisdiction of its interior ministry, thereby heightening their appeal to liberals as independent of the army, while reconciling the authorities to their existence, since they usefully supplemented the limited civilian police. Enthusiasm soon waned but redoubled with the renewed twin dangers of revolution and a possible French invasion in 1848. Crowds gathered demanding to be armed. In the fevered atmosphere, it was difficult to distinguish radicals from moderates, but arming the middle class seemed the least-worst option and most governments swiftly conceded laws mandating the formation of civic guards in March 1848.

The civic guards remained primarily an urban phenomenon, dominated by affluent, mostly young political activists who held elaborate, emotional ceremonies where women presented black, red, and gold banners they had made, and all sang rousing, patriotic hymns. Tensions soon surfaced between the guards as symbols of liberty and their practical duties as paramilitary police. Complaints about the cost of buying arms and uniforms obliged governments to raise taxation, prompting fresh resentment. Professional officers objected to having to salute their amateur colleagues and saw the guards as a dangerous, expensive rival, especially as some guardsmen deserted to the Baden revolutionaries in 1849. Enthusiasm again soon faded, this time definitively as the experience of even the limited warfare of 1848–9 raised awareness that Sunday soldiering no longer matched the realities of modern war.[19]

The guards were disbanded across 1851–3 as most liberals accepted the regular army as both cheaper and more effective. However, further to the left, Friedrich Engels was exceptional in advocating Prussia's short-service system, and most socialists looked to Switzerland as the model for their 'people's army' (*Volkswehr*).[20] Like the liberals, the socialists saw what they wanted to see; in reality, Switzerland's militia rested on tradition rather than new political ideas. The Confederation's 1815 constitution reiterated the long-standing obligation of all males to defend the country, but the 1817 regulations left it to the cantons to implement this, like all common measures since 1647. The traditional three levies persisted, with the first, composed of younger men, designated the elite for immediate service (*Auszug*), the second as a Reserve of the middle-aged, and the last as a home guard of older men. Although called Landwehr, this third levy equated with what in Germany was designated Landsturm. The upper age limit for service varied from fifty to sixty-five, depending on the canton, since each followed its own conscription law.

The 1817 law only specified arrangements for the first two levies, fixed at 33,758 men each, and divided into units of standard size. The latter required some deviation from the rule that the first two levies each represented 2 per cent of available manpower, as cantonal contingents were varied to ensure they filled complete units, so that men from different cantons would not have to serve together. This further reflected Switzerland's strongly decentralized constitution. Following the Sonderbund War, conscription law was finally standardized across all cantons in May 1850, with those aged twenty-two to thirty liable for the first levy, thirty-one to thirty-eight for the reserve, and between thirty-nine and forty-four for the Landwehr. Actual implementation remained a local matter and the question of exemptions often proved highly controversial, while militiamen had to provide their own arms and uniforms and only got paid if they were mobilized.[21]

Arrangements were finally centralized in November 1874, when the combined strength of the first two levies was increased considerably, while the Landsturm was re-established in 1886 to mobilize those aged seventeen to fifty who had been excused service on health or professional grounds. Contemporary observers regularly counted Switzerland as the most highly militarized country in Europe but, while the strength of the two first levies rose to 281,000 by 1907, this was only 0.8 per cent of the total population, equivalent to the proportion in Germany. Whereas German soldiers were regulars, backed by additional reservists with at least some training, the Swiss remained militia with only a few weeks annual drill.[22]

Long-Service Armies in Austria and the German States

The German states adopted one of three variants of a cadre system, of which Prussia's ultimately proved the more successful. That this would be so was far from obvious immediately after 1815 when Austria's long-service conscription found widespread professional approval. This rested on the system introduced in the 1770s and revised in August 1827 when a form of cohort draft replaced the previous method of conscripting men as needed to maintain strength. Henceforth, those aged nineteen to twenty-nine were liable for selection by a lottery held every three years. Service remained fourteen years until 1845 when it was shortened to eight, in both cases followed by up to twenty more years in the Landwehr.

Although nobles were liable after 1848, clergy, officials, teachers, students, and independent farmers all remained free, while anyone could buy exemption by paying 500 to 800 fl for a substitute. Exemptions were significantly curtailed in 1858, while the largely nominal Landwehr was abolished in 1852 and replaced with two years' service in a new system of reserves.[23]

On paper, this system gave Austria a large, well-trained army which could bring most of its strength to bear quickly without having to call up large numbers of reservists or Landwehr who had forgotten how to be soldiers or had never learnt properly. Although one-fifth of the 64,000 horses were missing from official strength in January 1859, manpower was just 8 per cent below the authorized 334,000, or a much better ratio than often achieved in the eighteenth century. The relatively high present strength also allowed the army to deploy units outside their recruiting districts without fear that large numbers of reservists would need to travel to join them at mobilization. Each draft was quite large at 76,000, but this could be absorbed by Austria's substantial population.

The system worked, because Austria faced relatively small armies in 1848–9 and was able to overawe Prussia in 1850. Unfortunately, budgetary pressures had already led to recruits being furloughed after initial training, thereby reverting to the eighteenth-century practice of the standing army as a peacetime cadre. The army's dispersal to protect Austria's extensive possessions inhibited its concentration against specific enemies, prompting the hasty call-up of 250,000 largely untrained men in 1859 in a bid to match superior Franco-Piedmontese forces. Further economies following that defeat prevented an increase in the draft intake, leading to a repeat of this problem in 1866.

In contrast to Austria's limited cadre system, the medium-sized German states used the French methods adopted in the 1810s with annual drafts, selected by lot from each cohort, with only limited exemptions, but permitting substitution. In most cases, men served nominally for six years, but were usually discharged after eighteen months to save money, before transferring to a nominal reserve which received little or no refresher training. Furloughed men took menial jobs, like their eighteenth-century predecessors. Hanover abolished its Landwehr in 1820, but Bavaria, Württemberg, and several others retained theirs on paper incorporating exempt, rejected, and older men. Everywhere, exempted or rejected men remained theoretically liable for service in wartime but underwent no training to prepare them. These methods aligned with the German Confederation's defensive orientation and its common structures to mobilize, rather than maintain large armies. The 1820 law only required two-thirds of cavalry and one-sixth of infantry to be present at any time.

Like its Swiss counterpart, the German Confederation failed to revise its members' contingents in line with demographic growth, with the result that these soon fell short of the 1 per cent of population envisaged in 1820. The annual intake remained static, or even fell as in Württemberg. Most armies inducted only a fifth of each cohort, and while this rose to a third in the medium-sized states after 1849, it remained unchanged in smaller ones like Saxe-Coburg. Baden rejected two-thirds as unfit in the 1820s, while that figure in Saxony was three-quarters two decades later. A significant proportion of these men were excused as too short; 10,000 of Bavaria's eligible cohort of 40,000 escaped the draft this way each year, compared to 800 declared physically unfit.

Middle-class men were far more likely to be excused this way than the poor, indicating the prejudices and connivance of those involved in the draft. They were also better placed to afford to buy exemption, which generally cost the equivalent of a day labourer's annual wage. Insurance schemes appeared in several states, with those drawing 'bad numbers' in the draft lottery receiving payouts to hire a substitute. Around 15,000 Württembergers secured exemption across 1817–49, while nearly a fifth of Hanoverian infantry were paid substitutes. Since men volunteering as substitutes were supposed to have completed their own service, the majority simply re-enlisted at the end of their term, effectively becoming professional soldiers like their eighteenth-century predecessors.[24]

These arrangements suited most liberals, who regarded constitutions as the way to control military power and did not feel the need to serve themselves, particularly as there were far more attractive civilian occupations to pursue. The relatively low annual intake eventually won grudging public acceptance, and the number of Württemberg draft dodgers fell from 643 a year to only sixty a year across the 1820s, before rising to around 3 per cent as the burden increased modestly in the 1850s. Emigration, illegal for those who had not yet served, nonetheless offered a way out, with many of those going to America illicitly dodging the draft.

Prussia's Short-Service Model

Prussia's different course was the product of compromise and austerity, rather than far-sighted planning. Given its subsequent adoption across Germany, Austria, and many other countries globally, it is worth examining it more closely. Its architect was Hermann von Boyen, one of the exiled Prussian liberals serving Russia in 1812–13 who was made war minister shortly after his return. His conscription law of 3 September 1814 remained in force, with few modifications, until 1919 and used the established three-tier system to integrate the different military organizations created by the hasty mobilization at the start of 1813.

Prussia's famous canton system (providing long-service conscripts who spent much of their time furloughed) was definitively replaced by new military districts handling conscription and the mobilization of reserves. Cohort conscription was introduced, with men inducted at twenty years of age for three years' service followed by two years in the reserve, which could be summoned upon mobilization to fill out the line units.[25] All men remained theoretically liable, but the system allowed those with means to serve as one-year volunteers who paid for their own arms and equipment and were subsequently liable for a call-up as Landwehr officers or NCOs. The Landwehr remained organizationally separate but service in it directly followed that in the line and reserve. The Landwehr's first levy, consisting of those aged twenty-six to thirty-two and all twenty- to twenty-five-year-olds who had not been drafted, was intended to almost double the field army by adding a similar number of additional regiments to those of the regulars. The second levy, comprising men aged thirty-two to thirty-nine, was essentially akin to the old third tier of militia and was to replace line troops as static fortress garrisons in wartime.

These measures represented a compromise between the conservatives' desire for a politically reliable and militarily efficient army with the need for large numbers and the liberals' advocacy of patriotic volunteers. The subsequent controversies surrounding the Landwehr proved so heated in Prussia because that organization symbolized the liberal hopes for wider change that faded rapidly after 1819 as the king refused to grant a constitution and embraced the reactionary Karlsbad decrees. Boyen and Karl von Grolman, chief of staff, resigned after the Landwehr's autonomy was eroded through the brigading of its regiments with those of the line army.

Intended to tighten the army's control over its own reserve, this inadvertently increased the concern of many officers that the Landwehr's deficiencies would damage the entire army and make mobilization dependent merely on the prevailing popular mood. These fears appeared confirmed during the call-up to confront the revolutionary disturbances of September 1830, when the Landwehr were sent home after a month because of their perceived unreliability.

Meanwhile, tight financial constraints kept the Prussian army proportionately smaller than that of the eighteenth century. Already by 1825 there were far more men in each annual cohort than the army could take, and recruits were now selected by lottery. Officially, there were still no exemptions, but men could obtain deferment on various grounds, such as being a family's sole breadwinner. Overall strength remained unchanged, and the army continued to draw around 40,000 men annually, but population growth meant that the proportion of eligible men drafted declined from half to a fifth across 1820–50.

By 1832, the Landwehr comprised 3,000 professional officers and instructors, 80,000 former soldiers, 75,000 men who had been drafted directly into it and received some basic training, and 19,000 completely untrained men.[26] It was retained, because Prussia could not afford a better system of reserves, and it was still supported by the liberals like Boyen who returned as war minister in 1840, and saw it as a counterweight to monarchical reaction. The general population remained indifferent. Crowds no longer turned out to watch training or stand drinks for Landwehr soldiers. Applications for Landwehr officer appointments declined and by 1841 around half of the company commanders were seconded regulars. The Landwehr collectively aged after 1814 as men remained liable into middle age, by which time they had usually married. The cost of supporting the families of mobilized men fell on their home communities, which also had to provide horses for the cavalry, the least effective element of the Landwehr.

Conscious of these growing problems, and concerned to save money, the army followed the practice elsewhere and began discharging conscripts six months early after 1820, with the balance of their obligation transferred as reserve service. Line service dropped to only two years in September 1833 to train more, still young, reservists, rather than rely on the Landwehr. Many officers objected, still considering three years the minimum needed to make proper soldiers; this argument was not merely confined to conservatives but was shared by progressives who realized that new weaponry required longer training. Thirty battalions of Landwehr were mobilized in 1848–9, partly to ensure the army had enough manpower, but also to prevent trained men from joining the revolutionaries. Those deployed against Denmark proved willing, but other units were often unreliable, and all were less effective than regulars. The army and government saw this in political terms, but many of the problems stemmed from men's unwillingness to leave their families, poor-quality uniforms, bad food, and wholly inadequate training. The problems exposed the reality gap compared to the ideal of a 'people's army', while the fact that nearly four-fifths of young men largely escaped service altogether added to the prevailing resentment and calls for reform.

The Roon Reforms

The war minister Eduard von Bonin advocated merging the Landwehr with the reserve as a common pool of trained men to fill out line units in wartime, while also cutting the upper age limit to reduce the likelihood of having to call up married men. Many officers backed this simple solution, but Crown Prince Wilhelm, who increasingly acted in place of his incapacitated father, flatly refused, regarding the Landwehr as little more than dangerous amateurs. The still highly personal character of Prussia's government was demonstrated through Wilhelm's ability to circumvent Bonin, who was forced to resign in 1859, by calling on Albrecht von Roon, only recently promoted general, yet known and trusted by the regent since his own days as a junior officer. Roon shared Wilhelm's belief that recruitment was an internal army matter beyond the remit of the Prussian diet, which could only discuss funding.

Roon has often been depicted as a far-sighted professional, yet what he really wanted was more long-service soldiers, which Prussia could not afford. His famous reform in fact represented a compromise between this and Bonin's proposals. Three-year service was restored, reserve duty extended to five years, followed by eleven years in the Landwehr, with only the youngest being expected to form separate brigades and garrison units in wartime. The expensive Landwehr cavalry were disbanded. These measures might have been accepted by the diet had Roon and Wilhelm not covertly tried to expand the line army without first securing approval for the necessary additional funds. Seizing the opportunity presented by

1. Swiss defiance after their defeat at Marignano in 1515, as depicted by Ferdinand Hodler, 1900.

2. Imperial heavy cavalry and Landsknechts shown attacking from the right during their victory over the French at Pavia in 1525.

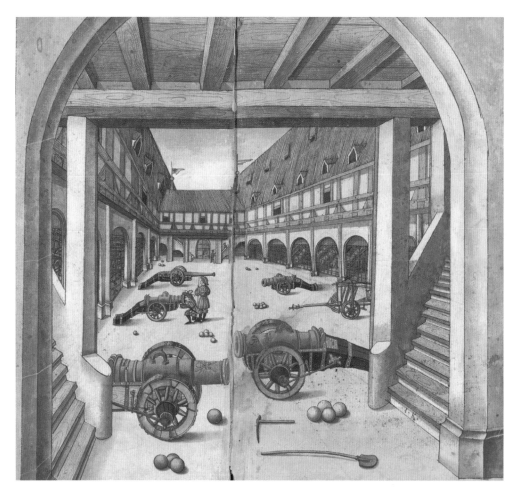

3. The entrance and courtyard of Maximilian's arsenal at Innsbruck.

4. Landsknechts chasing the Venetian lion back across its lagoon, an allegory of the Habsburg triumph of land power over sea power in 1510.

5. Imperial infantry and cavalry, accompanied by artillery, advance at the Battle of White Mountain, 1620.

Abbildung deß vnbarmhertzigen/abschewlichen/grausam vnd grewlichen Thiers/

Welches in wenig Jahren / den grösten Theil Teutsch-

landes erbärm vnd jämmerlichen verheeret/außgezehret vnd verderbet. Beneben einem Bericht/
Woher daßelbige seinen Vrsprung/wer solches erzogen/ernehret/ꝛc. Endlich durch was Mittel
seiner wider loß zu werden. Männiglich an Tag gegeben.

6. The Thirty Years War, depicted in a contemporary broadside as a 'ruthless, loathsome, cruel and abominable beast', 1635.

7. A drummer summons Saxon infantry and their wives to prayers held by their regimental chaplain, during their service with the Venetians at the siege of Modone, 1686.

8. Austrian troops surprise the Prussians at Hochkirch, 1758. Note the wives and children, bottom left.

9. Officers of the Prussian Royal Hussar Lifeguard showing off their riding skills, *c.* 1736. The main figure is the unit's commander, Colonel Alexander Ludwig von Wurmb.

10. Landgrave Friedrich II of Hessen-Kassel reviews his guards, *c.* 1770.

12. Self portrait of a Valaisan soldier in Neapolitan service in a letter home, also showing Vesuvius and a steam train, 1830s.

11. Adolph Menzel's depiction from the 1850s of eighteenth-century Prussian cadets with an invalid soldier.

13. The ignominy of defeat. Uniforms and equipment of the Westphalian Garde du Corps are reused as carnival costumes in Cologne after 1815. The tall 'classical style' helmets were fashionable *c.* 1790–1840, but always impractical.

14. The Baden Artillery Brigade exercising at the Gottesau barracks, Karlsruhe, 1846.

15. Switzerland's last battle, Gisikon, 1847. Federal infantry advance heroically in the foreground, green-coated staff officers stand in the middle distance, while a battery fires from the hill behind.

16. The ideal of the omniscient general staff: Moltke directs the German siege of Paris, 1870.

17. The proclamation of the German Empire on 18 January 1871.

18. Britain's Royal Navy makes way for the 'Germans to the front' at Tianjin, China, 1900, as celebrated in Carl Röchling's contemporary painting.

19. The Schutztruppen on patrol in German South West Africa, 1908. Their camels' descendants still roam the Kalahari Desert.

20. Austro-Hungarian Railway and Telegraph Troops, 1895. The men already wear the blue-grey uniforms which became standard for the whole army during the First World War.

21. The four Austro-Hungarian dreadnoughts of the Tegetthoff class, photographed during the First World War.

22. The Škoda arms factory in Pilsen, showing 30.5 cm mortars awaiting delivery to the front late in the First World War.

23. German stormtroopers preparing to attack, Western Front, 1917.

24. Freikorps troops in action in Berlin, March 1919. The tank is one of those captured from the British before 1918.

Leutnant   Feldjäger (Melder zu Rad)
Tiroler Landesschützenregiment
Feldadjustierung

25. A lieutenant and cycle messenger of the Tirolean Feldjäger, 1934. The cyclist's forage cap and other minor uniform details were intended to distinguish these Austrians from their German counterparts.

26. Ju-87 'Stuka' dive bombers over Poland, 1939.

27. A team in action with an MG34 machine gun, Russia, 1942.

28. Blitzkrieg at a slow pace. Infantry on foot alongside an armoured column headed by a tank destroyer, Russia, 1941.

29. Members of the Wehrmacht's 'Free Indian Legion' training for duties along the Atlantic Wall, 1943.

30. Russian auxiliary 'HiWis' dig out a motorized column stuck in Ukrainian mud, summer 1941.

31. Female Wehrmacht signals personnel in occupied Paris, August 1940.

32. Execution tourism. A soldier adjusts his camera during the hanging of alleged male and female partisans at Orel, Russia, 1941/2.

33. A Red Army soldier steals a woman's bicycle in occupied Eastern Germany, c. 1945/6.

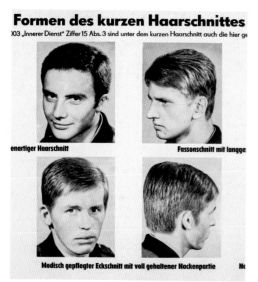

34. A selection of the officially approved haircuts for East German conscripts, 1960.

35. 'Our navy' recruiting poster for the Bundeswehr, 1972. The plane at the top right is one of the infamous Starfighter 'Widow Makers'.

36. A Bundeswehr transport helicopter during a rescue exercise as part of Mission Resolute Support, near Mazar-e Sharif, Afghanistan, August 2019.

the mobilization of June 1859, Landwehr units were retained, but their older personnel were discharged and replaced by increasing the annual intake of conscripts to 63,000. New cavalry guards and logistics units were created, adding 58,560 men to the line army, while substantially reducing the Landwehr.[27] The reorganization was completed in May 1860, by which time Wilhelm I had become king. His decision to present flags to the new regiments made their existence obvious, provoking loud protests from the diet, which refused to grant the additional 9.5 million tlr needed to pay for the reform.

Most accounts focus on the subsequent constitutional crisis, while assuming the reforms achieved what the army wanted. This was not the case. In 1864 units were deliberately sent to the front 20 per cent below strength, because the Second Schleswig-Holstein War broke out just after one cohort had been discharged and the army did not want to send the new conscripts into the field.[28] Two Landwehr divisions were deployed in 1866 but performed very poorly at Langensalza, where they were defeated by the Hanoverians. Six divisions were fielded in 1870–1, again because of insufficient line troops, but most Landwehr were used to guard lines of communications rather than at the front.

Later Nineteenth-Century Pressures

The experience of 1848–9 had already prompted reforms in Saxony that made it the most effective of the medium-sized armies by 1866. Attempts in Bavaria to move to Prussian-style short service were blocked by parliamentary opposition, and though the army was reorganized following the deficiencies revealed in the 1859 mobilization, it only managed to mobilize 22,000 of the 114,000 reservists in 1866 when field strength remained considerably below the nominal establishment of 72,000.[29] Württemberg performed marginally better, but Prussia's victory in 1866 silenced those who still opposed adopting its system. Saxony and the other states joining the North German Confederation aligned with Prussia, which modified its conscription law in 1867 with three years' line service, followed by four in the reserve and only five in the Landwehr. The Landwehr's second levy was abolished and all men over thirty-two now belonged to a nominal Landsturm; a far cry from Gneisenau's original vision of youthful partisans. The four southern states all conformed following the creation of Imperial Germany in 1871.

Austria-Hungary incorporated many features of Prussia's system in its new conscription law of 5 December 1868: annual cohort conscription, no substitutes or (theoretically) exemptions, three-year service with the option of paying to volunteer only for a single year, followed by ten years in the reserves, five in the Landwehr and finally Landsturm duty until the age of forty-two. As part of the Dual Monarchy system, Austria's Landwehr was entirely separate from Hungary's equivalent, the *Honvédség*, usually shortened to *Honvéd*.[30] Regarding it as a potential national army, the Hungarian parliament provided relatively generous funds, but the Honvéd remained small, rising from 10,500 to 30,000 by 1914, and it lacked officers and was not permitted artillery until 1913. Austria's parliament lacked a similar political incentive to develop the Landwehr, though its equipment and organization was considerably improved after 1889.

Although their short-service system had triumphed over the Austrian and French long-service armies, Prussian officers were aware of the lethality of modern weaponry and knew that future wars would require armies that were both large enough to absorb potentially huge casualties and still sufficiently well-trained to win. However, the unsteady political compromise at the heart of Imperial Germany's foundation in 1871 made achieving both quantity and quality very difficult. The Reichstag was generally prepared to pay for new weaponry but would not budge from the provisions of the 1867 law, which fixed army strength at 1 per cent of the population; the same as agreed by the German Confederation in 1820. All subsequent 'increases' in strength agreed by the Reichstag were simply adjustments of the army's present strength intended to align with the country's rising population. As the increments failed to keep pace, the army's peacetime strength had fallen to 0.8 per cent of the population by 1910.[31] Essentially, Roon's reform changed nothing, and Imperial Germany faced the same problem as Prussia had done in the 1850s.

Austria-Hungary had a similar problem, because the 1868 law allowed parliament to fix the annual intake, which remained 100,000 until 1889 while, even following a further modest increase in 1903, it still totalled only 127,600, of whom 103,100 went to the regular army and the remainder were drafted directly into the Landwehr or Honvéd. As in Germany, around 2 per cent of conscripts were drafted into the navy. The total represented 0.29 per cent of the population, compared to

Germany's draft at 0.47 per cent, and 0.75 per cent in France, where the burden of conscription was consistently higher. Around two-thirds of each cohort still escaped actual service in 1890; a proportion that declined only marginally across the next two decades.

Many conservative officers in Austria-Hungary opposed taking more men from each cohort, believing that growing urbanization and industrialization were increasing the proportion likely to be 'infected' with socialism. A major concern was the shortage of men considered suitable as officers. The ratio of officers to men was fixed at 1:23 in 1867 in peacetime, increasing the reliance on reserve officers to help the army expand. Germany had 30,029 professional officers by 1914, including 6,583 in the Bavarian, Saxon, and Württemberg armies, but Austria-Hungary mustered only 18,500 with a further 1,000 in the navy, and it struggled to recruit enough reserve officers.[32] Although the Austro-Hungarian and German parliaments authorized substantial increases in 1912–13, these would take around three years to implement, and the peacetime strengths of both their armies remained significantly below those of France and Russia in 1914.

Given these constraints, all subsequent changes in both Germany and Austria-Hungary focused on increasing the capacity of the reserves to provide the necessary trained manpower, with the regular army essentially acting as a cadre to be expanded in wartime. Germany's February 1888 law finally abandoned Roon's model and returned to Bonin's proposals, in that the Landwehr was fully integrated within the reserve system as the element encompassing older men. The regimental structure was replaced by Landwehr districts, which were to mobilize whatever formations might be needed from whatever men were available at the time. Now planning for a two-front war, the German General Staff envisaged adding a division each of older reservists and Landwehr to every corps, roughly doubling the army's size upon mobilization.[33] The re-equipping of the regulars with new rifles in 1888 and 1897 created sufficient surplus older arms enabling the men intended for these formations to be trained. Meanwhile, three-year service was cut to two years in 1893; a move followed by Austria-Hungary in 1912, which also attached a Landwehr division to each corps, increasing the wartime field army by a third.

Although the German intake increased, many men were discharged prematurely, as had occurred earlier in the century. German reservists returned for two periods of eight weeks' refresher training during their five years, while the Landwehr's first levy mustered only twice for up to two weeks in their four-year term with no training offered to the older men. Those who escaped the draft were assigned to the Landsturm, the younger portion of which was dubbed the *Ersatz* (replacement), which assumed growing importance in German war planning after 1890. They were to drill four times for a total of twenty weeks across their twelve-year liability to prepare them to be drafted to replace the high casualties that were now expected. Austria-Hungary's arrangements were broadly similar, but in neither country were they fully implemented, and few of Germany's 5 million Ersatz had received even basic training by 1914.

When assessing these measures, it must be remembered that, like their anticipated European opponents, both Germany and Austria-Hungary did not intend to fight a long war of attrition. The prolonged Revolutionary and Napoleonic Wars were regarded with horror: for their radicalism, destructiveness, and repeated failure (despite Napoleon's acknowledged brilliance) to achieve a decisive, final outcome. Any future war had to avoid a repeat, but this was always an assertion rather than something inherent in modernity. The wars between 1848 and 1871 offered examples which appeared to support arguments that quick victory was possible. The subsequent expansion of reserves was to enable the rapid mobilization of what was hoped would be overwhelming force for a swift and decisive blow. Older reservists and Landwehr were intended for home defence, thereby maximizing the number of younger, fitter, and better-trained men who could be deployed for offensive action. Only from the 1890s did plans envisage using more reservists and even Landwehr to augment the strike force. The German and Austro-Hungarian populations tripled in the century to 1914, and both states became much richer and more effective in resource extraction. Both could have maintained larger regular armies but chose not to. A major reason for that was the desire to spend their money on other things, but one important factor was that the generals constantly reassured the politicians that they could win a future war, even if the odds might appear daunting.

RIFLES AND RAILWAYS

Size and Higher Organization

As the foregoing suggests, overall peacetime strength across German-speaking Europe remained no more than 1 per cent of population across the century. Austria-Hungary's army totalled 478,000 in 1914 compared to 800,000 civil servants, indicating the changing character of the state as it assumed more non-military functions.[34] A significant proportion of soldiers had been furloughed during the first half of the nineteenth century, and while the expansion of reserve systems increased the number affected by military service at some point in their lives, for most it remained a relatively brief episode. While eighteenth-century armies had also been cadres, they generally represented nearer 1.5 per cent of population and contained a substantial minority of men serving on relatively short contracts. Meanwhile, large numbers of men had belonged to militias and civic guards, at least until the 1760s. The proportion affected by military service was undoubtedly higher overall by 1900, but the difference from a century before was not as marked as the standard narrative of militarization might suggest.

In a similar continuity with the previous century, Austria's army remained the largest until 1866, though its margin over Prussia's had shrunk to less than a fifth more men, down from twice as many in 1815. Together with Bavaria, these three states counted for over two-thirds of German Confederation forces and were the only ones to maintain substantially more than their official contingents. If the smaller numbers of additional Saxons, Hanoverians, Württembergers, and others are included, the thirty-four weaker members together maintained 150,000 troops, equivalent to their eighteenth-century forebears, though the paper total including reservists was much larger. These forces were absorbed after 1867 into what became the Prussian-dominated Imperial German army that swelled to around 770,000 on the eve of the First World War.

The higher formations previously used only in wartime were adopted permanently by the larger armies after 1815, using the hierarchy standardized by Napoleon. Implementation was most complete in Prussia, where the corps structure was integrated with the regionally organized conscription system introduced in 1814 for eight of the army's nine corps. The guards' corps drew men from across the country, meaning it too was composed of conscripts, unlike its equivalent in France and several other European states, which siphoned off the best men from the line units. The corps structure doubled as a framework for military government during civil emergencies and wartime. Each corps was subdivided into two divisions, each of two brigades of two infantry regiments, signalling the infantry's central importance in structuring the army. Cavalry, artillery, and specialists were attached to these formations in different ways across the century, with the balance shifting from brigade to corps level and then back to division level, which would become the primary higher formation after 1914. There were also separate cavalry divisions intended as a battlefield strike force.

Austria created regional army commands but, outside Italy, did not establish a corps structure until 1849. The intermediary divisional level was temporarily abandoned after 1859 in favour of much larger brigades, but defeat in 1866 revealed this had been a mistake by making it harder to control units in battle. Prussia's regional structure was adopted in 1882 when the monarchy was divided into fifteen corps commands, with another added in 1909.

Of the other German states, only Bavaria's army was large enough to have a permanent higher structure after 1815. The Confederation's military structure overlay those of its members, with Austria and Prussia each responsible for three corps, while around half of Bavaria's army made up the VII Corps. The remaining states combined to field the other three corps, plus a reserve infantry division. The paired subdivision into two divisions each of two brigades was broadly followed with some variations in the composite corps. Prussia simply designated three of its corps as its contingent, but in practice mobilizations after 1848 resulted in all armies deviating from the formal allocation of units to specific higher formations.

Annexation of most of the north German states in 1867 allowed Prussia to establish three more corps, while the Saxon army now formed its own. The remaining south German armies were integrated into this system in 1871, with a new corps for Alsace-Lorraine. Augmentation to the army thereafter resulted in the creation of new higher formations, usually through adding a third division to existing corps and then later expanding this into a new corps. There were twenty-five corps by 1914, plus fourteen and a half more corps of reservists, one of Landwehr, six and a half divisions of Ersatz, and eleven cavalry divisions. The strength of each corps was around 25,000 men, only slightly higher than those of the mid-century wars.[35] Switzerland followed this trend, using ad hoc brigades and divisions until 1874 and finally adopting a permanent corps structure in 1891, reflecting the growth of its army across the century.

Infantry

As in the eighteenth century, most soldiers were infantrymen, with the proportion highest in Switzerland at nine out of ten, compared to three out of four elsewhere. The proportion among reservists was greater still, because regular cavalry were generally retained closer to full strength in peacetime, while Prussia's expensive Landwehr cavalry disappeared in the Roon reforms and only 4 per cent of its Austro-Hungarian equivalent after 1868 was mounted.

One major change was the convergence towards a homogeneous 'general infantry', replacing the specialist types that had emerged since 1670. Austrian grenadiers lost their expensive bearskin hats in 1852, while the reorganization of 1859 standardized all companies in each battalion as infantry, reserving the title 'grenadier' to denote long-service veterans. Likewise, Prussia applied the term for its twelve most senior regiments and no longer to denote a separate tactical role. Austria disbanded its garrison infantry in 1855 and had converted its border regiments to conventional line troops by 1881.[36] Some symbolic markers persisted through distinct uniforms, but only the Jäger remained genuinely different as elite, rifle-armed light infantry, until the universal adoption of breach-loading rifles of a standardized design and calibre in the 1860s meant all foot soldiers were similarly armed and trained. A new type of infantry belatedly emerged when Austria reorganized its Tirolean Landwehr as specialized mountain infantry in 1906, though their initial impact was blunted by their deployment in 1914 eastwards against the Russians, leaving only poorly trained reservists to defend their homeland when Italy entered the war a year later.

It is easy to criticize officers for failing to adopt what, with hindsight, appear obvious technological advances and superior practices, but the merits of new weaponry and ideas were rarely clear at the time. New technology repeatedly proved highly disruptive across the nineteenth century, since adopting one superior weapon might provide a temporary advantage over likely opponents but came at the cost of making one's own existing arsenal also obsolete, as well as usually requiring different ammunition and new tactics and training. There was always the additional risk that the costly and lengthy transition to a new weapon might be interrupted by a new international crisis, or indeed by a further breakthrough. Those advocating new technologies were also not necessarily 'progressive' in other aspects. Indeed, one of the peculiar distinguishing features of many of Germany's most conservative officers in the late nineteenth century was their fervent embrace of technologies that they thought would give their army the necessary qualitative edge, so that this would lessen the need to open the ranks to social and political undesirables.[37]

Another major brake on adopting new weapons was that, in their initial iterations, they were frequently inferior to existing ones. All armies entered the peace after 1815 with large stockpiles of smoothbore muskets and artillery which they saw no immediate need to replace, especially in an era of austerity. The adoption of the percussion cap proved relatively easy because existing muskets could be converted to this new ignition system that reduced the likelihood of misfire and improved operation in bad weather. Several German states were already fitting this system within two years of it becoming commercially available in 1822. The subsequent delays stemmed from the need to amass enough weapons to avoid units being armed and trained differently. Austria began issuing percussion muskets in 1835, followed by Prussia (1839) and Switzerland (1842).[38]

Johann von Dreyse first demonstrated his revolutionary breachloading rifle in 1827, but it was not formally approved until 1838. Dubbed the 'needle gun' after its lever-and-pin system used to ignite the charge in a prepacked paper cartridge, this was effective up to 600m, or three times that of percussion muskets, and could allow soldiers to fire and reload while prone, thereby presenting less of a target themselves. However, the firing mechanism took several attempts before it became reliable, while officers were concerned that the improved rate of fire – twice that of the muzzle-loading muskets – would encourage soldiers to waste ammunition, and that it would be difficult to get them to stand and resume an advance once they had gone prone. Even once approval had been granted, the limitations of Dreyse's factory meant that only 45,000 rifles had been stockpiled by 1848.

The crisis that year prompted Prussia to issue the new weapon to its best units, and it soon proved its superiority against the revolutionaries and the Danes who remained armed with percussion muskets. Now convinced, Prussia boosted production at Dreyse's factory, but reservists remained equipped with the M39 percussion musket in the war of 1864. Prussia's new rifle was meanwhile challenged by the alternative muzzle-loading Minié system, adopted by France in 1849, using a specially designed soft-lead conical bullet that slid easily down the barrel and was forced into the rifle grooves by the percussion ignition process. Although this was harder to fire from prone, it was otherwise easier to use as the loading process was similar to how soldiers were already trained, while the needle gun still suffered from the difficulty of securing a gas-tight seal on its firing mechanism.

Austria swiftly introduced the Lorenz rifle, an improved version of the Minié, in 1854, which outranged the needle gun by 300m, and within four years most German states as well as Switzerland had re-equipped their troops with similar weapons. Many Prussian officers believed they had chosen the wrong rifle and the government began converting stocks of muskets to the Minié system until they were blocked after 1858 by Crown Prince Wilhelm, a convinced supporter of the needle gun. The political and financial investment meant that Prussia clung to the needle gun even when the Union army was already using some magazine repeating rifles with metallic cartridges during the American Civil War, while France adopted the Chassepot in 1866: the pinnacle of breach-loading, paper-cartridge technology with a range up to 1,500m.

Reading only this chronology would suggest that Prussia should have met with defeat in its wars across 1864–71. An initial examination of Prussian infantry tactics would also point to this as a likely outcome. The 1812 regulations remained in force, with some modification in 1847, until 1888, and still informed practice after that. Battalions could deploy either in a three-rank line or as an assault column with their four companies of 250 men each arranged in two pairs behind one another, with each company composed of three platoons, each in three ranks, one behind the other. During the initial advance, the third platoon from each company would break into open order and move ahead of the battalion as skirmishers, falling back as the column closed with the enemy. Prussian officers doubted the efficacy of the light-infantry tactics, developed in France after 1838, because they seemed to promote a dangerous individualism. The number of skirmishers was halved in 1854, because the needle gun's increased rate of fire enabled the smaller number to deliver the same firepower. Since the needle gun's high parabolic arc meant the bullet travelled above a man's height for much of the distance, officers emphasized precision rather than speed, encouraging soldiers to aim and not waste ammunition.[39]

Austria's regulations were not so different on paper, allowing, for example, entire companies to be deployed as skirmishers and combined company columns to advance with a mix of mutually supporting fire and movement. However, training was much worse in Austria than Prussia, despite efforts since 1819 to hold at least brigade-level exercises annually. Fire control remained poor, with soldiers inclined to open at long range, while the long furlough hindered the learning of more complex skirmisher tactics. Like the Revolutionary French around sixty years before, Austrian officers concluded – probably unfairly – that large, massed columns moving at speed were better suited to their men's limited skills. Austria's defeat in 1859 ironically appeared to prove this, since the French also relied on rapid, determined attacks, though these were also combined with superior use of skirmishers. Bavaria also held six large training camps between 1823 and 1852, which became more regular from 1856, but were hindered by budget cuts limiting the available practice ammunition. These problems affected the other German armies, with those contributing to the VIII and X Federal Corps holding joint exercises only once each in 1840 and 1845 respectively, while the IX Corps did not assemble until 1866.[40]

Matters were worse still in Switzerland, where most militiamen trained in small groups, like eighteenth-century recruits. Although 2,800 officers and NCOs completed the two-month basic course at Thun between 1819 and 1828, most of the learning was by rote. The Swiss Confederation held fourteen exercise camps between 1820 and 1852, with up to six cantons participating at any one time, though only a fraction of the elite contingents of each were involved and many officers instructed them by reading directly from the drill manual. Recruits received only two weeks' training before 1875, and though this was then extended and short refresher courses were introduced for reservists, Switzerland relied on the wider new Europe-wide trend of introducing compulsory physical education at school to socialize its future soldiers.[41]

The consequences were obvious during the Sonderbund War of 1847 where units got lost, even though they were fighting in their own country, opened fire at imaginary targets, and when they finally met, blazed away at long range until they had exhausted their ammunition, with the outcome often decided by the bold action of a few determined troops who intimidated the others. No one took notice of the Swiss, who were universally derided as amateurs, but while foreign officers closely observed the belligerents in 1864, the verdict was mixed. Prussian officers and NCOs struggled to control their conscripts and reservists in battle, and the needle gun only proved itself in defensive fire at Lundby on 3 July when a minor Danish attacking force was repulsed with heavy losses.[42] Prussia's great success was the conventional infantry assault at Dybbøl, and while the Austrians had suffered considerable losses in the opening battles of the campaign, they too had triumphed by attacking with cold steel.

Moltke had already taken note, having carefully studied the Crimean War and that of 1859, where in both cases the large Russian and Austrian assault columns had been defeated by superior defensive fire. He concluded that Prussian infantry should fight defensively, only counter-attacking once their superior fire had damaged their opponents. This worked very well in the opening battles in Bohemia in 1866, because the Austrians obligingly behaved as expected, losing 30,000 casualties in four days. Their Saxon allies performed rather better, thanks to their synthesis of Austrian and Prussian approaches. The boot was on the other foot at Königgrätz because the Austrians were on the defensive and Moltke could only win by attacking. However, the Prussians were now convinced of their inherent superiority, while their opponents were demoralized by their recent defeats, and the Austrian commander Ludwig von Benedek threw away much of his advantage by launching costly counter-attacks.

France's defeat in 1870–1 had multiple causes and cannot be explained alone through superior Prussian tactics. Prussian troops were buoyed by a belief in victory that in fact rested on relatively infirm foundations. Their higher command was far from perfect, but it was at least superior to that of the French, particularly in ensuring cooperation between infantry, cavalry, and artillery. The French generally fought on the defensive, providing opportunities to maximize the effectiveness of their superior rifles. Many Prussian infantry assaults stalled, and this arm suffered by far the heaviest casualties in the war.[43] The worst case was the Prussian guards' attack on St Privat on 17 August 1870, where 8,000 men were killed or wounded; more than either the Austrians in their assault on Chlum Heights at Königgrätz (1866) or the better-known Pickett's Charge by the Confederates at Gettysburg (1863). Crucially, however, unlike those two occasions, the Prussian guards eventually prevailed, providing the prime example for those who, across the next forty-five years, would argue that a determined bayonet attack could still succeed despite mounting evidence to the contrary.

The onset of Prussia's victories in 1864 distracted attention from the American Civil War, not least because Europeans still viewed conflict on their own continent as always more advanced. North Americans mean-while interpreted 1866–71 through their own recent experience, applauding Prussians as citizen soldiers triumphing over the lackeys of autocratic regimes. Whereas Prussia's extra-European influence had been limited to a small military mission to Turkey in 1836, it now became the primary model to follow, displacing France in Peru (1872), Japan (1878), Chile (1886), Bolivia and Mexico (both around 1910), as well as making a significant impact in Argentina, Brazil, and China. Influence was strong-est in Chile, where it was associated with Emil Körner, a former Saxon captain who reorganized the army on the German model, complete with a General Staff and war academy, and promoted massive purchases of Krupp weaponry. Chile became known as the Prussia of Latin America, buoyed by its own victory over Peru and Bolivia across 1879–84, and extended German influence indirectly by in turn sending its own military missions to reform the smaller South American armies.[44]

Much of the impact was superficial, such as Peru's adoption of Pickel-haube helmets, which still bore the German imperial eagle when Peruvian soldiers were captured by the Chileans. Moreover, German influence was also promoted more broadly through emigration and trade, notably in the case of Chilean nitrates. Nonetheless, the widespread emulation of their methods reinforced the Germans' own conviction of their sup-eriority. By contrast, Austria's influence was limited to sales of Mannlicher rifles and the adoption of the *Radetzky March* by the Chilean military school for its passing-out parade.

The relative lull in technological developments meanwhile helped sus-tain faith in the offensive. It was no longer possible to modify the thirty-year-old needle gun, so the army finally switched to a new rifle, known as the G71. Made by Mauser, this was precision-made with inter-changeable parts and had a faster bolt-action loading and ejection system using 11 mm metallic cartridges, improving range and accuracy, but it was still only single shot. Although modified in 1884 as a magazine rifle, it was not until the end of the decade that significant improvements came with the invention of smokeless powder by French, German, and Swedish scientists, including Alfred Nobel. In addition to making it harder to spot enemy firing positions, this created greater chamber precision, permitting the switch to 8 mm ammunition, but requiring an entirely new rifle, with Germany adopting the G88 made by Loewe as a 'common rifle' for all troops. Inferior to its equivalents in several other armies, this was then replaced by the Mauser G98, which was widely adopted around the world and remained in use into the 1950s.[45]

Switzerland had already adopted its own Vetterli magazine rifle in 1869, while Austria-Hungary had the Mannlicher repeating rifle from 1888. Officers had purchased their own revolvers since the 1850s, and these became standard issue after 1879 following improvements in design. The semi-automatic Mauser C96 'broomhandle' could fire thirty rounds per minute and was widely used during the first half of the twentieth century, as was the famous Walther P08, better known as the Luger after its designer, which replaced the sword as the iconic weapon of the German officer until 1945. Finally, after Bavaria had briefly used an early prototype from 1867 to 1871, like France's *Mitrailleuse*, both Germany and Austria-Hungary adopted machine guns in 1899 and 1903 respectively, drawing on models developed in Britain and the United States which had finally solved significant technical problems. Machine guns were heavy, requiring a four-man crew, and were regarded as the modern equivalent of the earlier regimental guns as close-support weapons for infantry, rather than an invention requiring tactics to be rethought.

The Russo-Turkish War (1877–8) offered a portent of what was to come, especially as it had been the Ottoman army, widely derided as inferior, which had caused such serious losses among the Russian attackers at Plevna. The advantages of defence were again noted during the South African War (1899–1902), where the Boers, armed with Mausers, had inflicted heavy casualties on Britain's professional army employing conventional assault tactics. The Russo-Japanese War (1904–5) indicated these risks on an even greater scale with its massacres of attacking troops. The German army issued a new infantry manual in May 1906, which claimed to incorporate these lessons by modifying those from 1889 to employ a three-phased attack. The initial advance would still be made in large, dense formations to allow officers to maintain control while moving at speed. The lead units were to disperse by companies into open order with multiple supporting lines as they came under enemy small-arms fire. The advance would continue, but now in 80m dashes, using the terrain for cover, with alternating fire and movement between companies commencing at between 1,200 and 800m from their opponents. Return fire emphasized speed and volume, with aimed fire only starting at around 400m. After one or two more dashes, the volume and accuracy of fire was expected to have either broken the enemy troops or suppressed them so that they went prone or cowered in their trenches, permitting the final attack to be launched with a hurrah and the bayonet.[46]

It is easy to criticize these tactics with the benefit of hindsight of what came after 1914. The problem was already clear during the Balkan Wars (1912–13). However, the German and Austro-Hungarian armies were not alone in their 'cult of the offensive', which gripped their contemporaries in Britain, France, Russia, and elsewhere.[47] Improvements in breach-loading weaponry simply magnified the concerns since the 1840s that once soldiers had gone prone under fire, it would be hard for their officers to persuade them to resume the advance and they would simply blaze away ineffectively against protected targets until they had run out of bullets. Ammunition resupply in combat was already a concern during 1870–1, when the Germans had fired over 30 million rounds, or about 400 shots for every French casualty.[48] Although weight increased with the switch from paper to metallic cartridges in the 1870s, the reduction in calibre offset this during the following decade, meaning the average infantryman's load – which now included a spade as an entrenching tool – was about the same in the 1890s as it had been during the eighteenth century, except that improvements in the design of belts and pouches (in which Germany was world-leading) meant the weight was now better distributed.[49]

Officers, therefore, retained some confidence that their men could keep moving forward, provided they did not stop too long to open fire. Further weight was added to this view by the fact that Russia, Britain, and Japan all eventually triumphed successively in their wars after 1877, despite their losses; and the Japanese had done so with tactics based on the 1889 German field manual. In all three cases, observers were convinced that the victors had succeeded thanks to their superior 'martial spirit', enabling them to overcome horrendous losses and triumph against a supposedly culturally inferior foe.

Finally, when judging tactics on the eve of the First World War, we need to recognize that those advocating the defensive were not necessarily more realistic. Europe's great powers were convinced long wars were politically and economically unsustainable, and required their generals to secure swift, decisive victory. At first sight, the logical conclusion might seem to be to follow Moltke's thinking from the 1850s and assume a tactical defensive until the enemy was sufficiently bloodied to ensure a counter-attack had a reasonable chance of success, but the Turks, Boers, and Russians had all ultimately failed with this strategy.

Only Switzerland based national defence entirely on renouncing the offensive, because it relied on the fear of attritional warfare deterring any attackers. Many Swiss officers, together with most of the population and politicians, were in thrall to the country's sharpshooter myth; as the hardy descendants of the equally mythical William Tell, the Swiss were supposedly born marksmen who could defeat any invader. This attitude was encapsulated by the apocryphal story widely circulated after Wilhelm II had questioned a Swiss soldier during his state visit in 1914:

> You have 10,000 men here. What would you do if I came against you with 10,000 men?
> Your Imperial Majesty, every one of us would fire once.
> And if I came at you with 20,000 men?
> We would fire twice.[50]

Cavalry

Switzerland was the only country where calls to abolish cavalry as an unnecessary expense were seriously entertained, but nonetheless advocates of this arm were increasingly forced to justify its place in modern warfare. Hanover was unusual in that around a quarter of its soldiers were cavalry who were considered the finest in Europe, thanks to the quality of their horses. Austria's peacetime proportion was only 12.3 per cent in 1847, while that in Germany had fallen to 11.1 per cent by 1914, despite the establishment of new regiments pushing the total to 110.[51] The wartime proportion was always lower, since most reservists were infantry, but Switzerland was exceptional in maintaining only 1 per cent as cavalry.

As with infantry, cavalry became increasingly homogenized as all were armed and trained the same, regardless of their nominal type and distinctive uniforms. All Prussian cavalry carried short carbines after 1819, and a standardized sword was adopted in 1852, removing the previous differentiation between long, straight-bladed heavy cavalry weapons and shorter, curved sabres carried by the light horse. Pistols were no longer issued after the Napoleonic era, except to trumpeters, who were given revolvers after 1879 for personal protection. Opinions continued to differ on the utility of the lance. Bavaria disbanded its Ulan regiments in 1822, while Austria-Hungary discontinued use of the weapon in 1884, even for those regiments still nominally designated 'lancers'. By contrast, all Prussian cavalry were equipped with a lance from 1890 in addition to their sabres. One of the hardest-fought metaphorical cavalry battles was the Prussian cuirassiers' defence of their right to continue wearing their traditional breastplates, despite these offering little protection against modern rifles, until they finally accepted in 1888 that these would now be restricted to parades; something their Austrian counterparts had already done in 1860.

The Napoleonic era distinction between heavy battle cavalry and their lighter scouting counterpart remained into mid-century, though Austria was already beginning to instruct its heavy cavalry to skirmish after 1854. The traditionally large Austrian regiments proved unwieldy in the 1859 war and were cut to four field squadrons, plus a depot to train recruits and remounts. Austria's cavalry outperformed its Prussian opponents in 1866, but suffered heavy losses mounting traditional-style attacks. The remaining cuirassier regiments were disbanded and by 1869 all cavalry regardless of their nominal designation were armed the same and mounted on similar horses, while training emphasized the 'light' roles of skirmishing, raiding, and screening movements, all of which made sense given the likelihood that the next war would be fought in Poland against Russia.[52]

German officers had already noted the significance of these roles during the American Civil War but felt they did not translate to Europe. The war against France saw several heroic cavalry charges in the Napoleonic manner, the most famous of which was 'Bredow's Death Ride' at Mars-la-Tour on 16 August 1870. Recognizing that it was a suicide mission, Friedrich von Bredow led his 800 troopers against French artillery that was enfilading the main Prussian position, using the terrain and smoke to conceal his advance. He managed to burst through the gun line and penetrate the enemy front by up to 3,000m before withdrawing, having lost half his men. Generally considered the last great cavalry charge in western European warfare, Bredow's costly attack nonetheless did relieve the pressure at a critical stage in the battle and, like the assault of the Prussian guards two days later at St Privat, provided an example celebrated by those still advocating conventional cavalry tactics.

Again, it is easy to condemn such opinions with the benefit of hindsight. Prussia's 1876 regulations still mandated massed attacks with drawn swords and, as in Switzerland, the cavalry faced increasing criticism from those on the left in the Reichstag that they were nothing more than expensive, obsolete parade-ground troops.[53] Given the cavalry's prestige, this branch was disproportionately represented in the high command with two-thirds of corps commanders in 1880 having reached senior general's rank from this service. Most remained convinced that cavalry still had a role, if only the right tactics could be found. Unlike Britain, France, the United States, Mexico, or several Latin American states, Germany lacked the experience of 'colonial' campaigns in open terrain against mobile opponents, which encouraged these states' armies successfully to refashion cavalry into the original dragoon role of mounted infantry. The average German cavalry horse was already laden with over 51 kg of equipment and ammunition, even before its trooper mounted it, leading many officers to doubt that relying on firepower would answer the tactical dilemma. In any case, it was not until 1909 with the adoption of the K98 carbine, a slightly shorter and lighter version of the Mauser G98, that the German cavalry had a rifle which almost matched those of most infantry. Nonetheless, cavalry remained the most conservative branch, with most of its officers dreaming that the infantry and artillery would somehow damage the enemy sufficiently to create the opportunity for a glorious charge that would convert battlefield advantage into decisive victory.

Artillery

The artillery grew in both size and status across the nineteenth century, but it would be wrong to see its personnel as wholly progressive and it was not entirely free of the foibles displayed by the other two military arms. It was smallest in Switzerland when the 1817 law mandated a ratio of one gun per 1,000 men, but nonetheless stipulated that the team horses had to be maintained in peacetime so that the artillery was fully mobile when required.[54] Austria and the German states retained the Napoleonic ratio of around three guns per 1,000 men into mid-century, but substantially increased this proportion across the 1860s, and again after the 1890s. Germany was already mustering 72,000 artillerymen in 1888, and by 1914 these considerably outnumbered its cavalry, whereas the two branches were roughly on a par in Austria-Hungary at around 11 per cent each of total strength.

Conscious of its deficiencies in the recent wars, Prussia re-equipped its entire artillery after 1816, and again in 1842, but the other armies largely continued with existing stocks to save money. The experience of 1848–9 revealed that the crews manning conventional bronze smooth-bore artillery were vulnerable to infantry armed with the new longer-range, rapid-firing, breach-loading rifles. Like their infantry counterparts faced with competing types of rifle, gunners had to decide between long-ranged rifles or short-ranged smooth-bore cannon. The former had a theoretical maximum of around 3,500m, far exceeding any other rifle, but practical ranges remained constrained by artillery's reliance on direct fire at targets within sight. Rifled artillery suffered from the same problems as its infantry counterpart in achieving a gas-tight seal for the breach, meaning that most designs remained muzzle-loaders.

These difficulties encouraged the widespread adoption of large-calibre smooth-bore cannon designed to fire either shells or shrapnel. The first modern shell was invented in 1823 by Henri-Joseph Paixhans, a French artillery officer seeking a way for his country's navy to neutralize Britain's superior wooden fleet. He solved the problem of flattening the projectile's trajectory and took an important step towards creating the conical shell, which improved range and accuracy. Paixhans' 'shell guns' were fitted on French warships in the 1840s, but it was the Russians who first used them with devastating effect at Sinope, where they burned the Ottoman fleet at the start of the Crimean War.[55] Shrapnel was a hollow spherical shell with a fuse timed to burst over enemy troops. First adopted by the British army in 1803, it had an initial misfire rate of one-in-three, but subsequent improvements made it considerably more reliable after 1845. France adopted both types of ammunition for large-calibre smooth-bore cannon, which became known as Napoleons and were widely used throughout Europe and North America in the 1860s.

France rapidly supplanted these weapons with the La Hitte system adopted by 1859, which used rifled, bronze, muzzle-loading guns to fire improved shells. Following its defeat to Prussia, Austria in 1863–4 entirely re-equipped its artillery with its own rival Lenk system, which was also adopted by Saxony and Württemberg. Austria also uniquely developed military rocketry after 1808, expanding this to eighteen batteries by 1854, but was unable to solve continuing technical problems. The notorious inaccuracy of rockets meant that General Dufour refused to deploy them in the Sonderbund War on the grounds they were a terror weapon. Austria disbanded its rocket corps once its artillery had received the new Lenk guns.

Unlike its adoption of the breach-loading rifle, Prussia jumped what proved to be a technological transitory stage by immediately adopting the steel-rifled cannon. Whereas the needle gun had soon been outclassed, the new Krupp steel 6 pdr proved more successful. The use of steel had been delayed by technical problems which Alfred Krupp had solved, allowing more precise rifling and a better breach mechanism. However, it had taken its inventor over a decade to convince the army, and the first use of the steel-rifled cannon in the Second Schleswig-Holstein War was hardly decisive. What did impress everyone were the old, large, iron siege guns, which had been recently rifled and were used with devastating effect against Dybbøl, where their fire demoralized the defenders prior to the infantry assault. Austria's artillery outclassed that of the Prussians in the initial battles of 1866, when it became obvious that too much attention had been spent on deciding which gun to adopt, rather than how to use it. The Prussians learned quickly, and already at Königgrätz they were making better use of their longer-range artillery.

Artillery doctrine was swiftly altered. Gunners and their weapons were now to march at the head of the column so they could be brought into action immediately. Reserve artillery was reduced, with the surplus batteries redistributed to double the allocation for each brigade so as to overwhelm the enemy with fire ahead of the infantry assault. What clinched the matter was the experience of 1870–1, when Germany encountered a French army still using La Hitte guns, which were inferior to the Lenk system and still used timed fused shells, whereas Krupp cannon now fired percussion shells that burst on impact at any range.

German and Austro-Hungarian artillery followed a similar development after 1871, but the latter increasingly fell behind in terms of quantity and quality. German artillery was reorganized into field and fortress branches, with field artillery fully mounted on horses so they could accompany an advance, while fortress artillery was equipped with heavier guns and provided the extra power needed for sieges. In comparison to their infantry, the German artillery responded more fully to the problems revealed in 1878 when the Russians and Romanians attacked Plevna after three-and-a-half days' bombardment, only to find the Turkish earthworks and trenches still intact. Analysis of the South African and Russo-Japanese wars revealed that shrapnel had little effect on entrenched troops. The Germans responded by adding heavier guns and high-trajectory howitzers to their field artillery, enabling long-range plunging fire.

They also noted the development of quick-firing (QF) guns in the 1890s. A four-gun battery of this type could fire up to eighty shots per minute, compared to fifteen rounds from a battery of six conventional guns. Further technological improvements followed swiftly, notably pneumatic recoil, which removed the need to reposition after each shot, as well as a gun shield to protect the crew. The French adoption of all these innovations in its famous 75 mm cannon in 1897 immediately outclassed the new Krupp models introduced only the year before, creating a temporary panic until improved versions could be produced. Nonetheless, each German division had seventy-two guns in 1914, compared to forty-eight and forty-two in its respective Russian and Austro-Hungarian equivalents, as well as having a superiority in heavy and medium artillery of 7:1 over the French. No army had stockpiled enough ammunition, but at least Germany had allocated 1,000 rounds per gun, six times that in 1870, and four times the amount supplied in Austria-Hungary.[56]

Despite the massive increase in the number and potential of artillery, tactics closely followed earlier practice. The emphasis remained on mobility, to keep up with the advancing infantry and achieve the fire superiority necessary for an assault. Guns were deployed in more dispersed lines, but little attention was paid to protecting them against enemy fire. The need for speed discouraged the development of indirect fire since this required setting up forward observation posts and telephone lines to communicate with gunners who could no longer see their target. Like cavalrymen, many gunners still dreamed of a heroic race forward to engage the enemy at close range.

Specialist Troops

The proportion of specialist troops grew from around 1 per cent of all troops in 1815 to over 5.5 per cent by 1914; a rate even faster than that of the artillery, reflecting the greater complexities of logistics and the importance of field engineering. The most substantial increase was in the pioneers who, by mid-century, were attached in battalion strength to each corps to support its advance by building bridges and clearing roads, and to entrench when on the defensive. Transport was increasingly militarized as part of the army rather than hired when needed and expanded to handle the larger quantities of ammunition required after the 1850s. Austria had maintained a permanent transport cadre since 1776, but its support troops remained weaker than those in Germany, because of the limitations on conscription imposed by parliament after 1868. A German corps required 2,400 vehicles and 14,000 horses by 1914 for its food, munitions, and hospital.

The traditional method of mounted couriers for communications was supplemented by the electric telegraph after 1853 in Austria, followed by Prussia the next year. Both relied heavily on civilian officials to operate the system. This functioned well enough during 1864 where the fighting was brief and geographically contained, but it broke down in 1870–1 when the disruption of telegraph lines by the francs-tireurs added greatly to the Germans' sense of losing control. The army had nine battalions of telegraph troops by 1913, having also adopted radios in 1905, and though there were still too few personnel and the devices often failed, Germany was better equipped than France.

Railways

The most significant expansion of specialists was the creation of railway troops, who grew rapidly in line with the expanding potential of this form of transport. The first German railway opened in 1835 between Nuremberg and Fürth, twenty years after the first experimental locomotive. Several economists and railway promoters solicited state aid by arguing that developing a national network would enable Germany to mobilize faster than its opponents. Seemingly far-sighted, such arguments assumed other countries would not be able to do the same.

The Austrian army began evaluating the military potential of railways in 1837 shortly after the country's first line opened, while Captain Pönitz of the Saxon army swiftly became a leading expert, publishing three books advocating a national German system.[57] The Federal Military Commission made several recommendations after 1836, but railway development remained a state matter, driven by commercial rather than military concerns. By mid-century there were over fifty different companies throughout the Confederation, while the total amount of track grew from 469 km (1840) to 17,215 km (1870). Most lines ran north-south aligned with trade; this proved useful to Prussia in 1866, but less so when it had to move westwards against France in 1870.

Military use was hindered by the technical limitations of early railways. Locomotives were underpowered and fragile, while track-laying was hugely expensive. Prussia made the first large-scale movement, transporting 8,000 guardsmen by locomotive back to Berlin after the September exercises in 1839. Saxony (1840) and Austria (1841) followed, but these movements were all in peacetime. The first combat deployment came in March 1846 when Austria rushed reinforcements by train to suppress a rising in Galicia. Austria also made more substantial use of rail transport than Prussia during 1848–9, but the networks remained insufficiently developed for this to make much difference strategically. A decade later, matters were different, and Austria moved 45,000 men, 10,000 horses, 1,008 wagons, and eighty-eight guns from Prague to Verona by locomotive in thirteen days in May 1859; a journey that would otherwise have taken sixty-four days on foot.

France had more track and rolling stock than Germany in 1870, but the latter made much better use of its network, thanks to the establishment of specialist railway troops in 1867; a measure soon adopted by Austria-Hungary, but not in time by France (see Fig. 20).[58] Moltke also learned from the experience of 1866, when railways had hindered rather than assisted the concentration of troops by encouraging the dispersal of Prussian forces along separate lines heading south. However, Prussia's growing use of railways stemmed from its reliance on short-service conscription, which increased the number of reservists who had to assemble to mobilize the army. Thanks to better planning, mobilization was completed two days ahead of schedule in August 1870.

Railways now assumed a central place in the German General Staff's war plans, prompting the government to embark on a costly nationalization programme after 1880, buying up smaller or uncooperative companies, and double-tracking many of the lines. European track tripled between 1871 and 1914, with Germany having 12 km per 100 km² of territory, compared to 10 km in France, 7 km in Austria-Hungary, and only 1 km in Russia. The growing cost added to the friction between Prussia and the other states after 1890, notably Bavaria, which jealously guarded the autonomy of its own railway. The army experimented with electric trains to increase speed but then abandoned this, having decided they were more vulnerable to sabotage; a curious example of how military priorities hindered national development.

Railways undoubtedly speeded mobilization: even in Austria-Hungary, this had been halved to three weeks by 1914. Nonetheless, armies were by then much larger with more artillery, ammunition, and equipment. An infantry division required thirty-two trains each 500m long, while the weight of equipment prevented speeds over 30 kmh, scarcely faster than those in 1866. Loading and unloading was only possible with special ramps, and one of the chief tasks of the railway troops was to adapt civilian infrastructure to military needs. The apparent potential of railways blinded planners to other problems, notably what happened to troops moving beyond the railheads and how to maintain supplies to them as they marched ever further away.

Fortifications

If railways promised movement, fortresses represented defensible barriers, and their importance to the German Confederation's military strategy is another indication of the significance of Napoleon's legacy, since most of the effort was concentrated on protecting the western frontier against France after 1815. A series of treaties between 1816 and 1819 named Mainz, Luxembourg, and Landau as Federal Fortresses (*Bundesfestungen*) and set aside 60 million francs of the French reparations to strengthen these and to construct others. There was not enough money to fortify all the options and support among the smaller states soon waned. After prolonged wrangling, Rastatt and Ulm were chosen as new Federal Fortresses and extensive works were completed after 1842. All five fortresses remained property of the state where they were situated, but command and garrisons were a collective duty. Around 15 per cent of federal forces were allocated as garrisons, with the burden falling particularly heavily on Bavaria, Baden and Kurhessen, though Prussia insisted on sharing responsibility for Luxembourg, Mainz, and Rastatt to increase its strategic influence.[59]

Prussia had invested heavily in strengthening Koblenz, Cologne, and Deutz after 1815, while Bavaria built up Gemmersheim and Ingolstadt from the 1830s and Austria repaired the area in central Lombardy known as the Quadrilateral. Prussia's short-service system necessitated the repurposing of ecclesiastical buildings and factories as arms depots for the reservists, while other states expanded their arsenals. The most spectacular was that in Vienna built between 1850 and 1856 in direct response to the recent revolution. Covering 33 hectares and requiring 177 million bricks, this was an entire military town intended to over-awe the capital and deter future unrest.[60]

The Gastein Treaty of 1865 envisaged adding Rendsburg in Holstein as a sixth federal fortress, but this was negated by the demise of the German Confederation the following year. Luxembourg had expanded to a network of twenty-four forts linked by 22 km of tunnels, earning it the sobriquet of the 'Gibraltar of the North'. The changed strategic priorities, including that principality's exit from the Confederation, led to the works being demolished after 1867; an enormous task that took until 1883. Annexation of Alsace-Lorraine rendered Landau redundant, and it too was slighted in 1871 and Koblenz demilitarized in 1890.

Railways and industrialization had relatively little to do with the demolition of the defences of around 180 other German cities between 1816 and 1866 which no longer met strategic requirements. These included Vienna, which had already been declared an open city in 1817, and where the fortifications were finally replaced in 1857 by the Ringstraße, designed to allow troops to move rapidly around the city to confront rebellious citizens. Like their early modern counterparts, many citizens resented the military's presence, which became more rigid, especially in Prussia where a zoning law was imposed in 1814 restricting civilian construction and land use. These were relaxed in towns within the interior, many of which also lost their arms depots after the 1870s, but again only because these no longer served military purposes.[61]

Whereas improved rifled artillery had demonstrated its potential at Dybbøl in 1864, the ineffectiveness of an even larger bombardment at Paris only six years later indicated that fortifications had not lost their military value, provided their design and construction matched contemporary standards. Fortress design had already shifted to outlying fortlets, expanding the defensive perimeter and obliging the enemy to commit even greater resources to besiege them – although, of course, they also necessitated ever larger garrisons to defend them. The development of heavier explosive shells in the 1880s was countered by using reinforced concrete, which was tougher and cheaper than traditional construction methods. Steel gun turrets on fortresses, like those on warships, provided better protection at half the previous cost.

A prime example was Mainz, which had been allowed to expand beyond its existing defences in 1872. The old walls were demolished in 1904–5 and replaced by a 26 km circle of 318 concrete bunkers and detached forts connected by their own railway. Germany and Austria-Hungary built new coastal fortifications to protect their naval bases after the 1880s, while Przemysl in Galicia was expanded once its strategic importance as a key rail junction was realized.[62] Whereas Germany and Austria-Hungary saw fortresses as freeing forces for offensive action elsewhere, they assumed central importance in Swiss national defence. Having already strengthened its frontier defences from the 1850s, the Swiss Confederation massively expanded these later, notably with the Gotthard Fortress, begun in 1885 three years after the opening of the strategic rail tunnel.

Colonial Forces

In comparison to western European armies, overseas colonial troops represented only a very minor element of Germany's forces and were completely absent from Austria-Hungary. Germany entered the competition for colonies relatively late and without government backing. What became German South West Africa (now Namibia) was originally a private venture of Franz Lüderitz, a tobacco merchant from Bremen, who handed over his struggling project to government control in 1884 as Imperial Germany's first colony. Togo, the Marshall Islands (bought from Spain), and parts of Cameroon and New Guinea were soon added, as was German East Africa in 1891.

Colonies were acquired because it suited the few investors and traders who might get rich, and because it was easy to sell them to an increasingly jingoistic public as symbols of great-power status and new sources of national wealth. South West Africa was touted as Germany's answer to Australia as a white settler colony, but only 24,000 Germans moved to all the colonies between 1883 and 1914, compared to the 1.8 million who emigrated to the United States alone across 1880–93. The colonies failed to provide a market for German goods and by 1914 had required 646 million Marks in subsidies to maintain themselves.[63]

The navy had already acquired coaling stations in Tonga (1876) and Samoa (1879), and eventually also Kiaochow Bay (modern-day Jiaozhou) in 1897 under very different circumstances, but most senior naval officers were sceptical of larger colonial ventures, especially as they were divided over the role their service should play in German defence.[64] The collapse of the German East African Company in 1888 forced the government's hand, because this commercial debacle had been triggered by what was termed the 'Arab Revolt'; in reality a complex series of violent adjustments by local powerholders to growing European intrusion in the region. Efforts to quell the disturbances and reassert authority through a naval blockade had failed by February 1889, and Bismarck reluctantly authorized Hermann Wissmann to organize a private army to operate deeper inland.

A former army lieutenant, Wissmann had secured leave in 1879 to work for the Belgian king Leopold's private slave empire in the Congo and counted as one of Germany's few 'Africa experts'. Like today's use of private military and security companies, the outsourcing of colonial warfare allowed the government to deny actions it found distasteful or politically inexpedient. Wissmann recruited Sudanese and Shangaan professionals, whom the Germans inaccurately called Zulus, and who were officially known as *Askaris* (soldiers). Although he claimed success, the ongoing violence and the German East African Company's inability to pay his troops obliged the government to assume direct control in March 1891.

Neither the army nor the navy wanted responsibility for colonial defence, so Leo von Caprivi, who had just replaced Bismarck as chancellor, converted Wissmann's force into the Imperial Protection Force (*Kaiserliche Schutztruppe*). This was unique in being the only element of the German armed forces directly under parliamentary control, with the navy minister responsible for organization and discipline, while local command devolved to the colonial civil governor, with tactical leadership entrusted to officers and NCOs seconded from the German army who were under navy regulations during their colonial service (see Fig. 19). Typical of Imperial Germany, this complex arrangement worsened after 1896 as the navy ministry managed to shed all responsibility to a new Colonial Department, a branch of the foreign ministry.

The Schutztruppe expanded to absorb the previously private forces in South West Africa (1894) and Cameroon (1895). Training followed that for the German infantry, though in common with practice in other European colonial armies, they always received older weapons than those carried by the small white cadres. Askaris were barracked separately from their families to control them, and great efforts were made to foster the sense of being a military elite distinct from the rest of the population. The forces in East Africa, Cameroon, and Togo totalled around 400 Germans and 4,000 Askaris in 1914, together with an approximately similar number of police, while in keeping with its official character as a white settler colony all 2,500 personnel in South West Africa were German.

The forces of other imperial powers were equally thinly stretched, but most developed the capacity to despatch expeditionary forces to confront major threats. Germany's ability to do this remained limited. The Imperial German constitution mandated the army for national defence, preventing the despatch of conscripts overseas, unlike Italy or Spain, and obliging the authorities to rely solely on volunteers, as in the case of the Schutztruppe cadres. A small marine corps was established in 1852 from army volunteers, expanding to two battalions in 1889 with a third added after the acquisition of Kiaochow Bay. After 1895, marines no longer served on German warships, but instead were kept in Kiel as a rapid-reaction force. The Boxer Rebellion in China (1899–1901) and subsequent wars in West and East Africa required the organization of separate expeditionary corps, which proved difficult given the time it took to process volunteers' paperwork. Proposals after 1905 to create a permanent rapid-reaction force all foundered on the reluctance of the army, navy, and colonial ministry to carry the cost.[65] Unlike the empires of Britain, France, and Russia which, regardless of their manifold problems, continued to provide substantial manpower and resources towards metropolitan defence after 1914, Germany's colonies were always a strategic liability and distraction.

LUXURY FLEETS

Developments to 1851

In 1914, Germany ranked as the second-largest navy after Britain, while Austria-Hungary was in seventh place after Italy, but ahead of Russia.[66] These positions had been achieved by Germany and Austria-Hungary in under two decades at considerable effort and expense and represented the pinnacle of each state's maritime power, which they would lose completely within the next four years. For both, the rapid developments from the late 1890s rested on solid foundations laid much earlier, while the high drama of Germany's naval race with Britain obscures Austria's much longer heritage as the more powerful navy of the two continental powers.

Having briefly lost its navy with the surrender of Venice in 1809, Austria captured the entire royal Italian fleet when it retook the city in April 1814.[67] Although in a poor state, this gave the Habsburgs a force roughly equivalent to the one they had five years before, consisting of eighteen large warships many of which were still under construction. The force was almost wholly Italian, including the naval college. The college had been founded in Venice by the Napoleonic regime in 1810 and was taken over almost unchanged. Italian was the language of command, with officers from other parts of the monarchy being required to learn it on joining the navy. The senior appointments were mostly given to officers from the old Trieste squadron, lost in 1809, who had meanwhile served in the army. Although also mainly Italians, their appointment over the heads of the Venetians caused tensions.

However, the main problem was shortage of funds, with the Austrian navy never receiving more than 4 per cent of military spending before 1848, meaning that only two of the larger ships were completed, in reduced format as frigates. The overall size of the fleet had declined by more than half to a low point by 1845. Austria's Levant trade nonetheless expanded, and the navy was deployed against Greek pirates during Greece's war of independence against the Ottomans (1821–32). These problems continued until the establishment of a new Greek monarchy in 1863. The Austrian navy earned rather more prestige by joining Britain in operations to support the Ottomans against Egypt along the

Syrian and Lebanese coasts in 1839–40. A vessel from the Danube Steamship Company, founded in 1829, was the first steamer to sail in the Mediterranean only five years later, and by 1848 the navy had two steamers.

The small size of the Austrian officer corps, numbering no more than 150 together with around fifty cadets, fostered a close-knit community, especially as the Trieste officers retired. It proved harder to insulate naval personnel from Italian nationalist agitation than in the army, where units served with soldiers from other parts of the monarchy. Four-fifths of the 5,000 sailors defected to the revolutionaries in March 1848, capturing the admiral and ten of the twenty-two warships. Nonetheless, a third of the officers remained loyal, including many Italians, and the remaining ships operated from Trieste to support the subsequent successful siege of Venice.

While modest, Austria's navy had nonetheless offered some protection to German vessels against Mediterranean pirates, leaving the Confederation with little incentive to develop its own forces. Prussia's navy consisted of four officers, one training ship, and a few gunboats, while Hanover had one old warship and the Hanseatic cities none in 1847. Germany's mercantile fleet of 6,808 ships and 45,000 sailors was suddenly exposed and helpless when Denmark blockaded the North Sea and Baltic ports at the start of the Schleswig-Holstein War in April 1848.

German nationalists immediately embraced the idea of a navy as a symbol of unity and a federal endeavour, unlike the army which remained composed of separate contingents. With Austria unable to lead, Prussia filled the void, particularly as its own trade was hit by the blockade. A navy league raised money to buy four ships, including one named *Frauenlob* (ladies' praise) to honour its female subscribers.[68] The Frankfurt Parliament formally authorized the establishment of a *Reichsflotte* on 14 June, diverting money allocated to construct the federal fortresses, and imposing extra levies on the states. Prussia and northern Germany paid, but not the southern states, nor Austria which claimed its own fleet was already serving the common interest. Most states refused to accept naval service as a substitute for military conscription, while the lack of experienced officers led to a Dutchman being given the initial command.

The real driving force was Prussia's Prince Adalbert, who had advocated the creation of a Prussian navy since 1835 and was appointed by the Frankfurt Parliament to head its new naval commission. He oversaw the integration of the few existing ships into a common force that had expanded to 1,800 men with nine steam warships and two sailing warships, plus twenty-seven gunboats, by autumn 1849. Schleswig-Holstein meanwhile collected sixteen small ships. Adalbert was forced to resign by his cousin Frederick William IV of Prussia, who opposed the parliament's revolutionary programme, and command passed to Karl Brommy, a Saxon who had previously served in the Chilean and Greek navies.

Britain backed Denmark over Holstein and threatened to treat the new German fleet as pirates, claiming it did not recognize the black, red, and gold tricolour chosen by the Frankfurt Parliament as a national flag. After a few ineffectual sorties, Brommy's squadron was defeated by the Danes off Helgoland on 4 June 1849. The inability to break the Danish blockade was an important factor in the Confederation's abandonment of Holstein and the latter's subsequent defeat in 1850.

Mid-Century Reorganization

The collapse of the liberal efforts to reform the German Confederation spelled the end to its navy, which was formally disbanded on 31 March 1853. Adalbert ensured that Prussia bought the best ships as a nucleus to create its own navy. Oldenburg was persuaded to surrender a patch of territory on Jade Bay later that year, giving Prussia its first deep-water port on the North Sea coast, subsequently renamed Wilhelmshaven in the king's honour. The acquisition of Kiel in 1865 provided a second base in the Baltic.

Meanwhile, Austria reorganized its navy both to modernize it and to ensure political reliability by recruiting Germans and Scandinavians in place of the suspect Venetians.[69] Brommy was hired as a technical adviser, while command went to Vice Admiral Dahlerup, a Dane. German became the official language of command in 1858, though in practice Italian influence remained strong. Seeking a more secure base than Venice, the navy relocated to Pola on the Croatian coast, which as a result had expanded from a small village to a town of 50,000 by 1914. A secondary base was established at Cattaro (modern-day Kotor in Montenegro) in the 1880s. After this initial period of consolidation, the navy expanded greatly after 1854 under Archduke Ferdinand Max, Franz Josef's younger brother, who was as enamoured by the sea as his Prussian counterpart, Adalbert.

Both princes assumed command amid the first of what was to prove a succession of technological changes, with each of the next six decades bringing new or improved forms of propulsion, construction, and armament. The dilemmas were even greater than those on land, given the growing complexity and cost of warships and the understandable reluctance to invest in unproven designs that might soon become obsolete. Generally, Austria made better choices into the early 1880s, thanks to its longer maritime experience compared to Prussia's navy, which remained dominated by army officers.[70]

In the 1850s steam switched from being auxiliary to sails to become the main form of propulsion, freeing ships from dependency on the winds. Adalbert chose a paddle engine for the *Danzig* in 1851, the first Prussian-built steam warship. Although this had seemed the most promising technology in the 1840s, it required large wheels amidships which were vulnerable to gunfire, while reducing the space available for the ship's own armaments. It was already being superseded by screw propellers fixed to the stern, the superiority of which was definitively demonstrated in 1857. Austria bought a British-built screw corvette in 1854 as a model to copy. The Stabilimento Tecnico Triestino (STT) was founded as a private yard in 1857, but largely relied on government contracts, while the navy built its own yard at Pola. This infrastructure enabled Austria to design and build most of its own warships, whereas Prussia relied primarily on Britain and France until 1875. Austrian ships were also better maintained: Prussia's new prestige battleship, *König Wilhelm*, only made two-thirds of its design speed in 1870 shortly after its launch because its hull was fouled by 60 tons of barnacles.[71]

Austria also switched earlier to ironclad warships, already ordering three in September 1861, only shortly after France and Britain had proven the viability of their construction. By 1866, Austria had seven in service, compared to Prussia's two, neither of which was as well-designed. Meanwhile, the Danube flotilla was reorganized after a long period of reliance on the ships of the Danube Steamship Company. Drawing on the experience of the American Civil War, the first of ultimately six armoured steam monitors was launched in 1871.[72]

The new construction reflected Ferdinand Max's determination to create a battlefleet, whereas Adalbert settled initially for the more realistic goal of commerce protection and coastal defence. Unfortunately, it was difficult to decide between these two options as they were not as distinct as they first appeared. Austria already outnumbered the Piedmontese navy in 1859, but French intervention nullified any advantage. The race to build more of the ironclads than the recently united Italy after 1861 obliged Austria to divert money from the army budget, and apart from the occasional voyage by individual ships to show the flag, the fleet was concentrated in the Adriatic, where it could do little to enhance the Habsburgs' pretensions to lead Germany. Meanwhile, Prussia swiftly followed the British and American example by sending its small squadron to force China, Japan, and Siam to agree trade treaties. However, its navy was too small to prevent a renewed Danish blockade in 1864.

Mobilization difficulties affected navies too, and most of Austria's new fleet did not reach the North Sea until Denmark was already defeated on land. The small advance guard of three wooden ships under Captain Tegetthoff was defeated off Helgoland on 9 May when his flagship caught fire, underscoring the vulnerability of traditional warships to shell guns.[73] Tegetthoff's force nonetheless fought bravely and he was promoted to rear admiral the next day. By now, he was the main figure in Austria's navy, his patron and chief having departed for what proved his unhappy reign as Emperor Maximilian of Mexico.

Tegetthoff commanded when Austria's navy finally faced its Italian rival at Lissa on 20 July 1866. The largest sea battle since Trafalgar and the first involving large numbers of ironclads, Lissa was the only contest between roughly evenly matched fleets before the battle of the Yalu River in the Sino-Japanese War (1894), and it attracted considerable attention from naval experts and the wider public. Italy's defeat at Custoza prompted its government to push Admiral Persano into doing something with the new, expensive ironclad fleet, so he bombarded Lissa island. Tegetthoff attacked, catching the Italians at a disadvantage as some of their ships had been damaged the day before by fire from the Austrian forts. However, he was outnumbered both in ironclads (twelve to seven) and overall, while the Italians' French- and British-built ships had better guns. He decided to steam directly for the Italians, intending to ram them, based on information he had received about naval engagements during the American Civil War.

The results were spectacular. Tegetthoff's flagship, the *Ferdinand Max*, rammed and sank its counterpart, the *Re d'Italia*, while another Italian ironclad, the *Palestro*, exploded after being hit by shellfire. Although Persano had in fact switched to another ship, the high drama of the clash between the two flagships caught more attention than the loss of the *Palestro*, while most observers downplayed the fact that accurate Austrian gunfire had already disabled the *Re d'Italia*'s steering gear, making it an easier target. Faith in the efficacy of ramming shaped naval design and tactics for the next thirty years.[74]

Strategic and Technical Dilemmas after 1871

Further technological developments added to the difficulties of learning lessons from Lissa. Improved designs, construction, propulsion, and armaments together ensured that ships launched in the 1870s already outclassed the first generation of ironclads. The switch to steel construction in the 1880s in turn rendered most of the earlier ships obsolete, not least because the change was combined with improved armour protection and engines. The latter removed the need for auxiliary sails, allowing for further design innovations, but the larger coal consumption placed limits on the operational radius of warships and increased the importance of possessing overseas bases to ensure that ships on the high seas could refuel without having to return to their home port. The new ships found themselves leashed to vulnerable bases in ways that had global implications, but which also show the unpredictable impact of technological innovation. Meanwhile, the uneven pace of change between naval artillery and armour protection caused a shifting balance between offence and defence.[75]

Naval experts struggled to devise the best combination of the different warship types and to reconcile these choices with strategic needs and financial means. Discussions increasingly focused on three options during the 1870s. The preferred choice of most officers was to acquire a battlefleet to command the oceans by defeating any rivals in a great battle like Lissa. The model remained Britain's Royal Navy, whose uniforms, regulations, and ships were widely admired and copied. The Prussian war minister, Albrecht von Roon, pressed for a battlefleet after 1862, managing to persuade the Reichstag of the new North German Confederation in 1867 to approve an ambitious ten-year plan for sixteen ironclads and fifty-four smaller vessels. Few of these were ready in

1870, and the navy's confinement to port by the French blockade damaged its standing, especially as the army earned the glory. Meanwhile, Tegetthoff's early death at forty-three from pneumonia robbed Austria-Hungary's fleet of its chief advocate in 1871, and his successor Friedrich von Pöck was unable to persuade the cash-strapped monarchy to continue the building programme. Neither Germany nor Austria-Hungary was unusual at this point. By 1876, every country that was to possess an armoured ship in 1914 already had one; proliferation had stopped due to expense and continued uncertainty over warship design.

The opposing strategic option was to engage in commerce raiding, which appeared to offer the chance to attack, but on a tighter budget. While harking back to early modernity, commerce raiding was rethought following the international convention of 1856 banning privateering, and the growing belief that all modern states needed navies as well as armies. Already articulated in the 1870s, this strategy achieved its greatest influence in the decade after 1885, when it was associated with a group of French officers known as the *Jeune École*.[76] They seized on the appearance of a new type of warship, designed as a speculative commercial venture by Armstrong of Newcastle in 1882. Termed a 'protected cruiser', this was an updated version of the old sailing frigate: lightly armoured, carrying a few big guns to deal with most enemy ships, while also being fast enough to outrun those it could not match. Fully powered by steam, these ships were expected to roam the oceans, disrupting enemy trade, and forcing the dispersal of battlefleets to convoy duty. After Chile bought Armstrong's first cruiser, Austria-Hungary bought the next two, which were completed in 1885–6.[77]

However, neither Austria-Hungary nor Germany felt comfortable with the Jeune École, whose ideas appeared ill-suited to great-power pretensions, and they were unable to assuage an acute German sense of strategic vulnerability. Consequently, both pursued variants of the third, middling option of a coastal-defence navy, combining smaller (and thus cheaper) battleships, shore batteries, and forts, all intended to relieve the army of the burden of protecting vulnerable shorelines.[78] Generally associated with weaker powers, the adoption of this strategy by Germany and Austria-Hungary has often been dismissed as simply a prelude to their later construction of battlefleets; indeed, this is how several of their leading officers interpreted it. However, it was in fact a period of innovation that contributed more broadly to naval warfare.[79]

Again, Austria-Hungary led the way, though for the last time. Maximilian von Sterneck, who assumed the position of commanding admiral in 1883, saw the Jeune École as a vindication of his own ideas which in fact relied on new technology to create a small, aggressive fleet capable of denying the Adriatic to the Italians. Influenced by his experience as captain of the *Ferdinand Max* at Lissa, Sterneck naturally favoured the ram, adding five Austrian-built light cruisers designed to sink Italian battleships. These proved a technological and tactical dead end, but his promotion of torpedo warfare was very different.

Torpedoes developed from early ramming technology as explosives attached to poles projecting from small, fast vessels that had to strike their opponent to sink it, thereby exposing themselves to considerable risk. Captain Luppis had been seeking a way to make a self-propelled torpedo since 1859, but the breakthrough came in 1866 when he collaborated with Robert Whitehead, a British engineer operating a machine-tool factory at Fiume in the northern Adriatic. Initially relying on clockwork, early torpedoes had a limited range, but nonetheless caused considerable alarm among all navies that their expensive battleships were now vulnerable to relatively cheap weapons travelling beneath the surface. In typical Habsburg fashion, the government could not afford an exclusive licence and, accepting that the invention would not stay secret, permitted Luppis and Whitehead to sell to other navies after 1871. All types of warships were soon equipped with torpedoes, with specialized torpedo boats developed by 1879 and any gain to the Habsburgs thereby completely lost.[80]

Sterneck's vision of flotillas of torpedo boats led by his ram cruisers foundered on the limitations of the available technology. Whitehead's addition of a gyroscope transformed the torpedo in 1896, giving it an effective guidance system, while improved propulsion had increased its range from 400m (1872) to 10 km (1914). Germany rapidly developed its own flotillas, becoming a world leader in torpedo-boat design. However, like Austria, it failed until just prior to 1914 to follow Britain's lead and build larger, better-armed versions known as 'destroyers' intended both to combat torpedo boats and launch such attacks themselves.[81]

Meanwhile, Germany developed a more aggressive version of coastal defence under Albrecht von Stosch, who replaced Adalbert when Prussia's navy was re-designated the *Kaiserliche Marine* in 1872. Although an army general, Stosch was an energetic organizer who played a key role in establishing the modern German navy. Convinced that a navy was essential for Germany's commercial development and flush with French reparations payments, the liberals in the Reichstag voted substantial funds to complete the navy plan from 1867.

However, Stosch recognized that a battlefleet was beyond the country's means and doubted its strategic utility. He restructured the building programme to meet the dual requirements of coastal defence and commerce protection. The core of the navy would be a 'sortie fleet' (*Ausfallsflotte*) of small battleships that could attack from heavily fortified bases to break a future blockade. The second element consisted of light cruisers designed for long-distance voyages to show the flag and represent German interests abroad. He recognized that the shift from sail to steam required overseas coaling stations and lobbied the government to acquire them, but he saw such bases as necessary to sustain naval operations and not as the start of a new colonial empire. Nonetheless, there was a perversity in building warships to guard coaling stations which only existed to power warships. The third element was a 'flying squadron' of fast but better-armed ships that would lend weight to Germany's global reach: anyone foolish enough to oppose one of Germany's cruisers would know it would soon be reinforced by the additional ships.

The problems with this plan were not strategic, since it reflected the country's current needs, but technological. Stosch's projections were based on outdated experience and envisaged each ship having a service life of thirty years, whereas the rapidity of change had reduced this to ten or even five years. Ships could be refitted with new engines, boilers, and armaments, but this was often poor value for money. The four *Sachsen* class 'sortie corvettes' added to the fleet by 1880 revealed that German designers and shipbuilders still had much to learn. Stosch's own difficult personality harmed his ideas and he suffered greatly when the brandnew ironclad *Großer Kurfürst* was accidentally rammed and sunk off Folkstone by another German battleship during a summer training voyage in 1878 with the loss of over half her crew. Stosch's repeated interference in the investigation, which involved no fewer than four courts martial, added to the tensions in the navy just as it entered a period of reduced funding.[82]

Blocked by Bismarck, Stosch resigned in 1883 and was replaced by Leo von Caprivi, another former general. Caprivi was widely criticized by those who wanted a larger navy. His order of November 1888 that naval landing parties were, by definition, not authorized to advance inland beyond the range of their ships' guns attracted notable derision. However, he essentially tailored Stosch's strategy to suit more reduced funds and the belief that German interests were primarily in Europe. He secured the money to build the Kiel Canal, which opened in 1895 and allowed Germany to shift warships freely between the Baltic and the North Sea without having to use the exposed and readily blocked route around northern Denmark. He also expanded the torpedo-boat flotilla and promoted the construction of protected cruisers from 1886, which became the backbone of Germany's global naval presence until 1914.[83]

Heading into Open Waters, 1891–1905

One of Caprivi's final acts as navy minister in 1889 was to approve the construction of the *Brandenburg* class of battleships, which entered service by 1894.[84] Their appearance signalled the end of the ironclads and the onset of what became known as the pre-dreadnought era, which opened with Britain's *Royal Sovereign* class of battleships in 1889 and lasted until the launch of the revolutionary *HMS Dreadnought* in 1906. Tactics shifted from ramming to gunnery as battleship design stabilized with primary and secondary armaments for long- and medium-range fire against enemy ships, plus tertiary light artillery and machine guns to combat torpedo boats. Naval guns became more powerful, but so did the capacity of armour protection, while improved engines and boilers increased speed (greatly complicating targeting) and operational radius, at last providing a true ocean-going large warship capable of meeting the expectations of those who advocated a battlefleet strategy.

Germany had not invented the new type of warship but was quick in following Britain's lead, and training and maintenance improved by the late 1890s when British observers considered that 'the German navy is the best-kept in Europe'.[85] While the *Brandenburgs* incorporated some innovative features, they and the next four classes of pre-dreadnoughts were under-gunned and generally inferior to their British equivalents. Austria-Hungary followed in Germany's wake once Sterneck changed tack in 1891, and built the *Monarch* class of small pre-dreadnoughts and two armoured cruisers.[86]

In both states, the construction of larger battleships was in response to their appearance in other navies, rather than from a fundamental reappraisal of strategic needs. The Habsburg monarchy's merchant marine expanded dramatically across the later nineteenth century, and the completion of new railways from Austria and Switzerland to Trieste between 1906 and 1909 further boosted exports, one-sixth of which went by sea in 1914, mostly in the country's own ships. Nonetheless, total tonnage was only 2 per cent of world shipping, and the Hungarians (who controlled the monarchy's Adriatic possessions) repeatedly opposed increased naval expenditure as unnecessary, prompting Admiral Spaun, Sterneck's successor, to resign in 1904. No new ships were ordered until 1909, and work slowed on those already under construction. Austria-Hungary was left with a slightly enlarged coastal-defence navy that still lacked a clear role.[87]

Germany took a different course following Wilhelm II's accession in 1888. An honorary admiral in Britain's Royal Navy since 1889, the new Kaiser wanted a suitably large fleet of his own and pushed for more seagoing battleships. The publication of Alfred Thayer Mahan's influential history of British sea power in 1890 added weight to Wilhelm's arguments through its linking of command of the oceans and great-power status. Mahan's ideas found such ready acceptance because they simply reinforced what many German naval officers were already thinking.[88]

Foremost among these was Captain Tirpitz, one of many officers who felt disappointed at the navy's ignominious role in 1870–1 and longed for glory. His role as head of the torpedo inspectorate from 1877 to 1888 failed to convert him into an advocate of the Jeune École but did enable him to collect a loyal 'torpedo gang' of followers. His subsequent posting to Germany's small East Asia cruiser squadron in 1896 was Tirpitz's only active command and he initially hesitated when offered the job of heading the *Reichsmarineamt* (RMA) responsible for naval design the following year.

He took office at a moment when conditions were unusually favourable for building a battlefleet. Not only did this project have Wilhelm's backing, but Germany had seized Kiaochow Bay from China in November 1897, claiming it as compensation for the murder of two missionaries, which at last gave a secure base for the East Asia squadron.[89] Crucially, the pace of innovation seemed to have slowed, making it possible to plan a fleet based on pre-dreadnoughts and assorted cruiser types.

Tirpitz's strategy owed much to Stosch whom he respected.[90] Ironically, what became known as the High Seas Fleet was not intended to contest control of the oceans directly, but to destroy the Royal Navy in Germany's home waters. Tirpitz mistakenly believed a future war would see Britain's fleet establish a close blockade of the German coast, and he planned to sortie and smash it with his new battleships. He engineered the navy reorganization of 1899 to silence those who opposed his views. Officially, operational planning remained the responsibility of the Admiralty Staff, but Tirpitz's RMA designed and built the ships according to their master's strategic and tactical thinking. Command remained reserved to Wilhelm, who delegated it to admirals of his choosing. They included his younger brother Prince Heinrich, who led the High Seas Fleet from 1906 to 1909 and opposed rivalry with Britain until Tirpitz removed him through 'promotion' to fleet inspector.

More seriously, Wilhelm urged Tirpitz after 1903 to change battleship design to that of the 'all big-gun ship', eliminating the secondary armaments and increasing the heavier guns for longer-range engagements. Austria-Hungary's chief naval architect, Siegfried Popper, reached the same conclusions, which were confirmed by the lopsided naval battles of the Russo-Japanese War. Whereas Austria-Hungary pushed ahead with conventional pre-dreadnoughts, because it lacked the money to build anything larger, Tirpitz objected that bigger ships would not fit through the Kiel Canal and risked opening his policy to objections from the Reichstag that he was seeking to construct a 'limitless fleet'.

Dreadnoughts, 1906–14

Britain pulled ahead of Imperial Germany with the launch of *HMS Dreadnought* in 1906, the world's first all big-gun ship that outclassed all existing battleships, if not quite yet rendering them obsolete. Tirpitz refused to concede and rejected Chancellor Bülow's call to switch to a Jeune École strategy, arguing that Britain had inadvertently levelled the field and both powers were now starting from scratch. Wilhelm backed his admiral, refusing to let Britain dictate how many battleships he could have. Tirpitz got the new dreadnought construction through the Reichstag by presenting it as replacements for older vessels. Germany belatedly launched its own, inferior version in 1908, but its designers and constructors displayed an impressive ability to adapt and innovate, and the two *Bayern* class 'super dreadnoughts' begun in December 1913 surpassed even the Royal Navy's best ship, setting the standard in battleship design lasting into the 1930s.[91]

It was too late, however, as Germany had already lost the naval race. It had thirteen dreadnoughts at the outbreak of war in 1914, with four more entering service later that year, whereas Britain had twenty-two, rising to thirty in 1915, as well as more battlecruisers, the faster, more lightly armoured version of the new ships. The cost of battleships tripled between 1900 and 1910, while that of cruisers doubled. Total German naval expenditure doubled across 1905–13, while that of Austria-Hungary rose by 55 per cent, but Britain added only 40 per cent more expenditure and yet still spent twice as much as Germany in 1913, while both Russia and the United States were also now outspending Germany.[92]

Austria-Hungary added dreadnoughts once Admiral Montecuccoli, Spaun's replacement and another Lissa veteran like all the fleet's commanders, persuaded STT to start building one before he had secured parliamentary approval. Eventually four dreadnoughts entered service, the largest of all Austria-Hungary's warships (see Fig. 21).[93] They were well-designed, but Italy's navy was still twice as large. The new ships required much larger crews, necessitating a doubling of personnel between 1904 and 1914, when there were around 20,000 sailors, or roughly the same as in the country's merchant marine that the navy was supposed to protect.

Tirpitz refused to change course, even though some officers realized that inventions such as radios, aircraft, and submarines were making it more likely that the Royal Navy would keep its fleet safely out of reach by maintaining a distant blockade, closing off the North Sea between its base at Scapa Flow and Norway, while using minefields and torpedo boats to shut the English Channel. Tirpitz's critics already advocated what would, by necessity, become German strategy in the First World War: keeping the 'fleet in being' safe in port as a potential threat, while pursuing commerce raiding to interdict Britain's maritime supply. Although money was belatedly invested in developing submarines and a naval air service, Tirpitz refused to abandon the High Seas Fleet, arguing that the fast battlecruiser squadron could be used to lure the Royal Navy into the long-desired battle of annihilation.

The View from 1914

The German army was relatively well-prepared and equipped by 1914 for the war it planned to fight, but Austria-Hungary's was considerably less so. Germany's navy was highly proficient but was configured for a strategy that stood little chance of success. Austria-Hungary's navy was more efficient and better equipped than its army, but too small to challenge its most likely opponent in the manner its commanders envisaged: a re-run of their glory days at Lissa. This fixation on decisive victory through conventional battles dominated German and Habsburg planning, reflecting the influence of Napoleon's legacy and the experience of the fast-moving and decisive mid-nineteenth-century wars. This was common among Europe's armed forces but exercised a more destructive influence because both countries' senior staff disdained diplomacy yet had no real alternatives to offer once their own plans comprehensively failed on contact with their enemies on the outbreak of war in July 1914.

12

Serving the Nation

DREAMS OF SHORT WARS

Military Knowledge

The experience of the Revolutionary and Napoleonic eras stirred more critical attitudes to war and the place of the military in society. Victory over France enhanced the Prussian army's reputation, but many were now less happy with its continued close association with monarchy and unrepresentative politics. Liberals and conservatives clashed over alternative ways of organizing defence, while being equally unwilling to release significant funds, especially given the long decades of relative peace into the 1860s. Both sides of the political debate were loud in voicing their patriotism but wanted relatively little to do with professional soldiers, who remained widely despised. This changed dramatically with the violent process of German unification in 1871, which tied patriotism and military service more closely together and enhanced soldiers' social standing, despite the resumption of another long period of peace. The army remained closely associated with monarchy, especially in Austria-Hungary, while Switzerland fashioned its own republican military tradition. Yet, military values were far from universally predominant, and the armed forces continued to feel underfunded and looked to the future with a volatile mixture of doubt and over-confidence.

Disagreements over the changing character of war were fundamental to these debates and anxieties. The overriding concern after 1815 was how best to interpret Napoleon's legacy, since virtually all commentators were convinced that the scale, conduct, and impact of war had changed irrevocably. For much of the century the most influential writer was Baron Jomini, who hailed from the political elite of Vaud in the

Swiss Confederation, yet became an enthusiastic supporter of the Helvetic Republic (established in alliance with France in 1798), and later joined the French army, rising to become chief of staff to Marshal Ney. Jomini incurred the hostility of Marshal Berthier, Napoleon's own chief of staff and, briefly, prince of Neuchâtel. Finding his career blocked, Jomini transferred to the Russian army in 1813, before retiring to Brussels in 1829. Already a prolific writer on military theory while a serving officer, Jomini now emerged as the leading 'interpreter' of Napoleon. Although he used the geometric abstractions favoured by late eighteenth-century writers, Jomini argued that war was an art, not a science, while the descriptive, conventional character to much of his work at least ensured it was accessible and acceptable to a wide readership. His texts became required reading at military academies, including West Point where they were read by the generation of officers who went on to command during the Civil War.[1]

Jomini's reputation contributed to the relative obscurity of Carl von Clausewitz, whose now famous work, *On War*, remained largely unread long after his own premature death from cholera in November 1831. Clausewitz joined the Prussian army as a cadet aged twelve and went on to study at the new War Academy under Scharnhorst, who became his mentor. Along with Gneisenau and Hermann von Boyen, he resigned in protest at Prussia's forced alliance with France in 1812 and joined the Russian army, heading the team that negotiated the Convention of Taurogen which pushed Frederick William III into the war against Napoleon. Having served as a liaison officer, he rejoined Prussia's War Academy in 1818, this time as its director. At that point the post was considered a relatively dull, junior appointment and he spent much of his time compiling what was to be his great work. This remained unfinished at his death and was published posthumously by his widow, who attempted to give the relatively jumbled mass of notes greater coherence.

Like that other great nineteenth-century German theorist Karl Marx, Clausewitz changed his mind on several points, while leaving others cryptic or unfinished, thus opening the door to diverging interpretations. His 'centre of gravity' (*Schwerpunkt*) principle, urging the concentration of military resources to achieve a breakthrough, was subsequently celebrated as a major contribution to strategic thought, but was scarcely original. Nor was his attempt to distil general principles, since that characterized much of the work of other authors associated with the military enlightenment. Rather, it was how Clausewitz did this and the conclusions he reached. Rejecting rational, abstract systems, he embraced the Romantic spirit of his age to argue that war could not be detached from its wider context. Ultimately, it was a struggle to force an opponent to submit to one's will, in which morale played a significant role alongside material factors. Although he did not directly coin the phrase the 'fog of war', he nonetheless stressed how uncertainty and inadequate information made war complex and unpredictable.[2]

Senior Prussian officers certainly read Clausewitz, but there is little evidence that his thinking influenced Moltke's planning during the Wars of Unification.[3] Moltke's stress on defeating the enemy's army decisively reflected the broader reception of Napoleonic strategy, as well as his own study of military history. In practice, Moltke and his successors in the Prussian General Staff paid scant attention to the fog of war, and their schematic and detailed planning, involving calculating troop and train movements precisely, resembled seventeenth-century thinkers, such as Vauban, who claimed to be able to predict exactly how much time would be needed to besiege and take a town. Based on his experiences in 1864 and 1866, Moltke compiled detailed guidelines on practical tasks ranging from forming a skirmish line to loading and unloading railway wagons. Issued to all officers from regimental commander and above in 1869, these instructions were intended to enable Prussian commanders to cope with unexpected situations, but they also inadvertently fostered a stifling love of proper procedure.

Professional literature became more developed but likewise remained preoccupied with narrow technical matters. Since 1808, Austria had been publishing its own professional paper, the *Österreichische Militärische Zeitung*, which carried commentary on current and recent wars, as well as disseminating good practice, but this critical discussion was curtailed for fear of offending state censors until the 1860s. Prussia followed with the *Militär-Wochenblatt* (*MWB*) in 1816, but that remained staid compared to the *Allgemeine Militär Zeitung*, published in Darmstadt between 1826 and 1902, which rapidly became the main professional paper because of its readiness to air controversial views. Moltke's encouragement of debate, combined with Prussia's greatly enhanced reputation, eventually led the *MWB* to take the lead, especially once it began publishing book reviews and commentary on foreign armies from the 1880s. The navy had to wait until 1890 before the *Marine Rundschau* provided a regular professional journal.[4]

The Prussian General Staff was already studying past practice by 1816 and soon had the largest military history section in the world. Its account of the 1866 war had already appeared the following year and is often considered the first modern official history. Austria followed in 1818, embarking on a multi-volume history of the wars of Prince Eugene in 1876, followed by histories of other eighteenth-century and more recent conflicts. Prussia replied after 1890 with a series on the wars of Frederick II to replace that issued in the 1830s, as well as studies of the South African and Russo-Japanese wars. Staff histories concentrated on operations and battles, seeking historical examples to justify strategies that had already been resolved upon. The latter trait particularly characterized the Prussian account of the Seven Years War, in which Frederick was interpreted as a successful risk-taker, winning by a decisive war of movement. Ironically, the outbreak of the First World War interrupted the official history in 1761 at the point where the Prussian king was bogged down in a war of attrition.

The present-minded approach was strongly criticized by Hans Delbrück, who had served in 1870–1, then became tutor to one of the Hohenzollern princes and finally university professor in Berlin. Delbrück wrote on a wide range of topics but made his name through his six-volume history of warfare, published between 1900 and 1920 and widely translated. Like Clausewitz, he believed war could only be understood when set in a wider context, but it was his distinction between the strategies of decision and attrition that had the greatest impact, because he used his association with the Free Conservative Party to intervene in pre-1914 debates, arguing that the General Staff had misinterpreted Frederick II and risked dooming Germany to an unwinnable war.[5]

While European monarchs had long been taught as children the rudiments of military manoeuvres using toy soldiers, German officers developed the modern wargame (*Kriegsspiel*) to test tactical and strategic thinking. Georg Heinrich von Reiswitz is usually credited with devising the first set of rules, published in 1824, and based on weapons data from the Napoleonic Wars collected by Scharnhorst. In fact, Reiswitz borrowed from his father's rules, as well as several much earlier examples. Hanoverian and Brunswick officers were already practising tactics using figures on a tabletop by 1781 when inclement weather prevented exercises outside. Wargames became widespread by the 1830s, offering a more sober and cheaper alternative to the usual pursuit of gambling for junior officers stuck in boring garrison towns. German success in 1871 led to other armies adopting wargaming for training, notably in the United States. The practice changed significantly in 1876 with the introduction of less rigid rules by Prussian war minister Verdy du Vernois, allowing umpires to confront students with more realistic problems of command and control. A set of rules for naval wargames appeared that year and the practice likewise soon spread to other navies.[6]

Higher-level officer training was formalized through the development of war academies in addition to the cadet corps, which continued to offer more basic education. Prussia led the way with the establishment of its General War School (*Allgemeine Kriegsschule*) in 1810, eventually renamed the *Kriegsakademie* in October 1859. The curriculum was broadened after 1816 under the influence of Rühle von Lilienstein and especially Eduard von Peucker, who abandoned the narrow, technical focus initially advocated by Scharnhorst and Clausewitz, and ensured officers received a more rounded education. Peucker also insisted on high standards and normally only two-thirds of entrants completed the three-year course, while successful graduates had to pass another test before being accepted as staff officers. However, Peucker's retirement in 1872 cleared the way for a return to a narrow focus on practical military matters, deliberately selected to improve the chances of noblemen relative to their commoner classmates, who generally had superior schooling prior to admission. The anti-intellectual ethos, stressing the development of character, hindered the German army's ability to absorb modern technology or appreciate its potential.[7]

These flaws largely went unnoticed as other armies created their own higher academies, notably Austria (1852) and Bavaria (1867). Switzerland had already opened an academy in Thun in 1819 led by Henri Dufour. Students included the future Napoleon III but, despite Dufour's efforts, standards remained poor. Conscious that the decline of foreign service reduced opportunities to gain experience, the Swiss army began sending officers to observe foreign manoeuvres after 1857 and eventually opened its own higher-level staff college in 1876. By 1830 most cantons at least required aspirant officers to pass a test before being commissioned, but this generally consisted of demonstrating proficiency in the drill regulations.

Officers often remained poorly educated into the later nineteenth century. Efforts to require professional training prior to appointment in Bavaria failed, though after 1872 all prospective officers were obliged to have a higher school leaving certificate.[8] Only around 15 per cent of graduates from Prussia's cadet schools became officers, compared to three-fifths of Habsburg officers who had attended one of the monarchy's nineteen schools. From 1844, Prussian officers were at least expected to have completed junior school and to sit an exam, but Boyen's efforts to insist on higher standards were thwarted, and the minimum thresholds were relaxed after 1870 to admit more noblemen. By contrast, training in Austria's Wiener Neustadt academy improved once it was finally freed from the dominance of Catholic monks in 1868, and only a fifth of applicants passed the examinations for the higher General Staff courses.[9]

Austria already had a naval academy in Venice after 1814, which was eventually relocated to Fiume in 1857, though officer education still relied heavily on practical experience gained on long training voyages. The Prussian navy opened a navigational school in Danzig in 1817, but only created a naval war academy in 1872, soon followed by specialist engineering, medical, and torpedo schools. Training was thorough, but as in the army, it focused increasingly on practical matters.[10]

Attitudes to War

The term 'militarism' first appeared in France in 1816 during debates on Napoleon's controversial legacy and had entered German usage by 1870.[11] All commentators were convinced that wars were now waged between nations and no longer just kings, but the diversity of experience prevented an easy consensus. Radicals had often sided with France across 1792–1815 in the hope of wider social and political change and much of their agenda was now discredited by its association with revolutionary terror. However, conservatives were compromised too, since virtually all the surviving regimes had collaborated with France at some point, notably Rheinbund members like Bavaria, Westphalia, Nassau, and Hessen-Darmstadt whose soldiers had fought and died on the French side.[12] Many of the inhabitants of areas annexed by Prussia resented their loss of identity, as did those in the former Austrian lands now held by Baden and Württemberg.

Discussion remained relatively muted during the tight censorship immediately following 1815, when writers remained generally deferential to the surviving dynasties. The period before 1813 was neglected in favour of celebrating the final three years as a combined patriotic effort to free Germany from the evil French. Liberals regarded these as 'wars of freedom' (*Freiheitskriege*) in which the people called and the monarchs followed, whereas conservatives reversed this, presenting instead a story of 'wars of liberation' (*Befreiungskriege*) directed by kings and generals. The liberal symbol was the black, red, and gold flag of Lützow's volunteers, in contrast to the conservatives' appropriation of the iron cross and Prussia's black, white, and red cockade introduced in 1813 as a deliberate riposte to the French revolutionary red, white, and blue tricolour.[13]

The memory of these conflicts underwent several changes during the nineteenth century. Veterans' associations formed during the 1820s to sustain camaraderie and to demand respect from those who had not fought. Numerous memoirs and campaign histories appeared across the next three decades, many of which were illustrated thanks to the invention of lithography in Germany in 1796, which enabled the mass reproduction of engravings, which in turn were often hand-coloured through the putting-out process. The memory of the disastrous 1812 campaign was profoundly shaped by the publication between 1831 and 1843 of ninety-nine pictures drawn by Christian Faber du Faur, a former Württemberg artillery officer, graphically showing the decline of the Grande Armée from an imposing force to a few huddled, emaciated survivors.[14]

However, numerous other artists depicted more heroic, martial images. Schematic depictions of each regiment's uniform had already appeared in the 1720s, with no fewer than eight printed sets on the Saxon army produced across 1779–1811. These found a growing market from the 1830s. Louis Sachse, later one of Germany's first commercial photographers, published seventy-two plates showing the Prussian army in 1830, followed by Heinrich Eckert and Dietrich Monten's monumental 421 colour plates illustrating the uniforms of the armies of the German and Swiss Confederations, published between 1835 and 1843.[15]

Adolph Menzel, one of Sachse's assistants, produced his own series depicting the uniforms of the army of Frederick II, as well as illustrating a bestselling biography of the great king (see Fig. 11). Menzel's pseudo-baroque engravings are still widely reproduced and have been fundamental in shaping popular perceptions of the Frederician era. Their power lies in their ambiguity, with Frederick frequently appearing gaunt, alone, and even despondent. However, there are enough pictures of determined soldiers and bold attacks to convey a lasting image of Prussian prowess in the face of adversity.[16] Menzel took great pains to ensure accuracy, borrowing original uniform items from the Prussian arsenal, thereby initiating 'uniformology' (*Uniformkunde*), the detailed study of historical uniforms later exemplified by Richard Knötel's mammoth eighteen-volume study. Knötel's pictures and those of other artists were mass-produced as cigarette cards and in other cheap formats, adding to the pervasiveness of military images in late nineteenth-century Germany.

Uniforms now assumed greater prominence alongside arms and armour, which had been traditionally collected by monarchs and aristocrats. The Viennese arsenal, built between 1850 and 1856, alongside its main role intimidating potential future urban revolutionaries, also included Austria's earliest and largest purpose-built museum. Initially intended to display the Habsburgs' collection of militaria, the museum was opened to the public in 1869 and broadened into a modern military museum after 1885 to celebrate the armed forces. Saxony, Bavaria, and other states all opened similar museums, as did the Swiss cantons from the 1880s, often on the initiative of local families donating heirlooms from foreign service as a way of recording their place in history.

The numerous memoirs from the Napoleonic Wars were far from universally positive, often recounting harsh struggles for individual survival, but collectively they contributed to an emerging consensus of 1813–15 as a specifically German version of peoples' war, drained of its revolutionary fervour in favour of a story of personal heroism against a foreign invader. Both liberals and conservatives accepted war as a morally valid policy instrument to forge and defend national interests. Horror and suffering became sublimated as patriotic duty.

The limited experience of combat in 1848–9 did little to disturb this trend. News reporting of wars in the Crimea, America and elsewhere presented a sanitized image relying on engravings, rather than photographs, and texts which, while acknowledging the destructive effects of improved weaponry, nonetheless focused on patriotism and heroism. Despite their relative brevity and victorious outcomes, the reality of the wars across 1866–71 left many shocked and disillusioned by the appallingly high numbers of casualties. The impact was felt vicariously by civilians, who were informed through the efficient German field postal service that delivered 90 million letters during 1870–1. In contrast to the Napoleonic era, writers were less reticent about the horrors of war. However, they used the earlier memoirs and images as templates to frame their experiences, and to legitimate their suffering and own acts of violence as necessary to secure national unity. New associations of veterans were formed, and the book market was flooded with patriotic histories expressing confidence in German prowess and success.

Numerous monuments were constructed, notably the huge figure of Germania above Rüdesheim on the Rhine, the victory columns in Berlin and Munich, and the massive equestrian statue of Wilhelm I at the Deutsches Eck in Koblenz. All were dwarfed by the towering monstrosity of the 'Battle of the Nations' memorial opened by Wilhelm II shortly before the First World War at the centenary of the victory over Napoleon at Leipzig. These remain, as do the streets in many cities still named after Sedan and other victories. Although defeated, Austria nonetheless erected imposing monuments in Vienna to Archduke Charles and Prince Eugene in the 1860s, followed by a massive statue of Radetzky in 1892.[17]

Given this trend, it is perhaps surprising that the German Army League only emerged in 1912 during the Reichstag debates on increasing the military budget. It mustered 90,000 members within two years, more than double the size of the Colonial Society and considerably more than the 18,000 in the anti-Semitic Pan-German League. The Navy League, established a few weeks after Tirpitz secured the First Navy Law in 1898, had 331,000 members, making it the largest of all pressure groups, but even its impact on policy was relatively modest, as popular support for (or at least acceptance of) the armed forces was both broader and more diffuse, largely displayed as pride in local units and family members who were serving, rather than strident militarism or navalism. The Social Democrats were the world's first million-strong mass party, dwarfing all others, while millions of Germans belonged to trades unions, church groups, or both. Support for pressure groups was weaker still in Austria-Hungary, where a Navy League was established in 1904 with thirty-nine members, growing to over 43,000 by 1914, but this was in a state with 52 million inhabitants, and the League struggled to recruit members beyond German-speakers.[18]

Militarism was thus far from simply an elite phenomenon or a device to foster acceptance of war. The armed forces themselves lacked a clear consensus on their purpose, organization, and relationship to society. While 90 per cent of German reserve officers joined clubs to listen to lectures on military topics, only a small proportion of middle-class men held such positions and military service did not constitute an 'enfeudalization of the bourgeoisie' as critics of Wilhelmine Germany once claimed.[19]

The two most notorious incidents of alleged civilian subservience to the military reveal, on closer inspection, that Germany had its own specific mix of contradictions stemming from the incomplete processes of modernization. The case of the 'Captain of Köpenick' involved Wilhelm Voigt, a petty criminal recently released from prison who had just lost his job to over-zealous police interference. Having purloined a second-hand captain's uniform, Voigt took command of a small group of off-duty soldiers on 16 October 1906, marched to Köpenick town hall, placed two municipal officials under arrest for fraud, and made off with the contents of the local treasury, for which, in proper Prussian manner, he issued a receipt. Voigt was eventually arrested only after a tip-off from a former cellmate. Wilhelm II pardoned him in 1908, allegedly pleased that the case confirmed public subservience to military authority, and the incident has been widely interpreted in those terms. However, Voigt also became a folk hero who duped the authorities, while most German newspapers at the time focused on his hard-luck story and the judge gave him a reduced sentence on the grounds that he had been a victim of unjust police surveillance.[20]

The other case occurred in Saverne (Zabern) in Alsace in 1913 and involved Lieutenant von Forstner, whose ill-treatment of local recruits swiftly attracted hostile press attention. Forstner inflamed the situation by ostentatiously strolling around town. The local commander in fact reacted quickly, placing Forstner under arrest and transferring the recruits but, concerned for the army's reputation, did not make these measures public. Goaded by continual press criticism, the commander declared martial law in the town on the grounds that the civil authorities had lost control. This was soon rescinded, but again the army refused to publish details of its subsequent investigation, fuelling suspicions that it considered itself beyond democratic control.[21]

'Militarism' also had its critics. Indeed, that term only emerged during the 1860s as Catholic Germans attacked what they perceived as the army's undue influence. The liberal historian Ludwig Quidde was briefly imprisoned for publishing a short work comparing Wilhelm II to Caligula and, though he went on to form the German Peace Society, this attracted little support. As liberals and Catholics largely accepted the Second Empire by 1890, anti-militarism became primarily associated with socialism. Karl Liebknecht attacked the perceived 'normality' of military preparations and argued that if there had to be a war, it should be waged between classes, not nations. The army's fears of socialist infiltration were partly genuine, as the Social Democratic Party encouraged activists to seek promotion as NCOs to influence the troops and to expose the very real abuses, such as conscripts forced to chew their socks on inspection parades or eat their own excrement.[22] However, the party remained reformist rather than revolutionary, intending to improve soldiers' conditions rather than subvert the high command.

The Fear of Peoples' War

The long memory of the Revolutionary and Napoleonic era encouraged fears that war could escape political control, a fear that paradoxically encouraged recourse to extreme violence. Ironically, it was the moment of triumph over France in 1870–1 that cemented these anxieties and left a fatal legacy of brittle confidence, contributing to German actions in 1914.

The German bombardments of Strasbourg and Paris were widely criticized as inhumane innovations breaching the laws of war. Concerned that the siege of Strasbourg was tying up too many troops, General August von Werder fired 195,000 shells over five days in August 1870, reducing much of the city to rubble in the futile hope of terrorizing it into surrender. The great cathedral was damaged and huge quantities of precious medieval and Renaissance art and other material incinerated. Having run out of ammunition, Werder switched to a regular siege that eventually forced the defenders to capitulate on 28 September. Keen to avoid repeating the mistake, and confident that Paris would soon surrender, Moltke adopted a more hesitant approach when he surrounded the French capital that month. However, the German press called for tough measures as retaliation for perceived French aggression, while Bismarck grew concerned that delay might allow the other European powers to intervene and dictate peace. Reluctantly, the army began a general bombardment on 5 January 1871 using 230 heavy guns and mortars, some of which were worn out by the work. Around 1,400 buildings were destroyed or damaged, but casualties were relatively light at around 400 killed and wounded and, as at Strasbourg, the shelling simply stiffened the defenders' resolve, which only collapsed after 133 days once it became obvious the city would never be relieved and was running out of food.

The outcry reflected more changed sensibilities – given that this was the first conflict fought between signatories of the Geneva Convention, as well as the difficulty of besieging cities which had grown much larger – than changed practices in warfare, since such bombardments had been common in previous centuries.[23] The German shelling did far less damage than the French government's brutal crushing of the Paris Commune a few months later, and it was soon overshadowed by the outcry over the bombardment of Alexandria in 1882 by the British navy, which also indicated that the problem was a general, widespread one.

A major factor behind the use of terror bombardments was the concern that continued French resistance might rob Germany of its hard-earned victory. Having defeated France's regular armies and captured its monarch, the Germans found themselves confronted from October 1870 by a revolutionary republican regime that refused to give up. The German command interpreted the new French mobilization as a repeat of the Jacobin *levée en masse*. They particularly objected to the use of *francs-tireurs*, a term originating in 1792 to denote snipers and other irregulars who waged guerrilla warfare, cutting telegraph lines, damaging railways, and ambushing patrols. At the most, there were around 60,000 francs-tireurs who inflicted no more than 1,000 casualties. The French did not regard them as successful and abandoned insurrectionary warfare after 1871 in favour of enhancing their regular army.[24]

The psychological impact of the francs-tireurs on the Germans was considerable. Over 105,000 troops were detached to guard lines of communication. Although the actions of francs-tireurs differed little from those of classic European 'small war', German soldiers regarded them as treacherous, accusing them of failing to wear identifiable uniforms and, as one officer admitted, 'naturally, we killed a lot of innocents in reprisal'.[25] Contributions were also levied as fines, though partisan activity was often used as an excuse to avoid paying for requisitioning on which the Germans depended as their own transport could not supply the armies in France. However, relations between the Germans and French civilians were not invariably bad and improved considerably once the immediate fear of violence was removed.

Historical opinion remains divided over the longer-term impact, with some seeing 1870–1 as a step towards 'total war' in which the invaders were confronted by a nation in arms.[26] One factor suggesting the opposite is that the German army failed to develop a counter-insurgency doctrine or even train for occupation duties in the years following 1871. It was not alone in this, since all major powers regarded small wars as secondary to major operations and something they only really expected to encounter in colonial conflicts. The German delegations at the Brussels Conference of 1874, and those in The Hague in 1899 and 1907, pushed for tighter rules governing volunteers and irregulars, which resulted in the requirement that they wear uniforms. Britain, Switzerland and those states without large, regular armies prevented the legal prohibition of mass mobilization, since they feared they would not otherwise be able to defend themselves.[27] Moltke and his successors in the General Staff remained sceptical of these efforts to codify international laws of war, arguing that civilian attempts to limit violence constituted a 'false humanitarianism', since it merely made war more protracted and costly. This was the kernel of the 'military necessity' argument, indeed partly rooted in the latent fears of a peoples' war, but also influenced by strategic concerns that Germany could not afford to fight a war of attrition. To the German high command, laws remained guidelines only, to be ignored where these conflicted with the necessity of securing a quick victory.

Colonial Violence and Genocide

Even less attention was paid to rules during colonial operations. Germany expanded its possessions rapidly, primarily through the establishment of protectorates in East Africa (encompassing what is now Rwanda, Burundi, and most of Tanzania), and South West Africa (modern Namibia) in 1884–5. Initial development was driven by Carl Peters, founder of the German Colonial Society, who acted like a conquistador negotiating unequal treaties with local people on behalf of his own private company.

Even after his acquisitions were retrospectively approved by Bismarck, private enterprise continued to play a significant role in expanding the territories and imposing authority, notably through the Wissmann-Truppe between 1889 and 1891.

From May 1889 to June 1910, German colonial forces conducted 231 military operations, notably against the Hehe in East Africa, who offered stiff resistance, routing the newly formed Schutztruppe at Rugaro on 17 August 1891 in just ten minutes. Hermann Wissmann already employed Askaris as the core of any combat group to be used for difficult tasks such as storming fortified villages, while supplementing these with *ruga-ruga* irregulars, often recruited from tribes with a grudge against Germany's current local enemies, who were sent on search-and-destroy missions, rounding up cattle and taking hostages. This division of military labour continued throughout the era of German rule and established a plausible deniability whereby German officers blamed the irregulars for atrocities committed under their command.[28]

Like those serving other Western colonial powers, German officers were acutely conscious that they were heavily outnumbered with no prospect of immediate help from home. They shared common racist prejudices, regarding most Africans as savages who would only respond to violence and justifying their own extreme brutality by reference to real or alleged actions by their opponents, such as the mutilation of corpses. The same argument was employed to legitimate the use of so-called 'African' practices, such as seizing women and children as booty and as a way of calculating victory in operations where the enemy often evaded contact. News of this method eventually caused protests in Germany and led to it being officially suspended in June 1897 but, while some officers voiced concerns at the continued use of violence, most felt justified. Colonial service was only open to volunteers and was heavily over-subscribed: 1,500 men volunteered for the handful of officer and NCO positions when the Wissmann-Truppe was formed in 1889, while after 1891 the Schutztruppe required three years unblemished service before accepting soldiers seconded from the German army.

It was not necessary for German officers to evade civilian authority, because such control was so deficient, with no fewer than five government agencies involved in military operations in South West Africa. Conscious that Germany's political elite had little interest in their colonies, administrators were reluctant to ask for more money in case it prompted the home government to abandon the entire project as too expensive. This encouraged a certain restraint, but equally the belief that, if an operation had to be launched, it had better be quick and successful.

Germany's first major overseas expedition was not to Africa but China, where it sent troops in August 1900 to suppress the anti-foreigner revolt known as the Boxer Rebellion. The murder of the German ambassador in June 1900 was one factor, but Wilhelm II was also determined not to be outdone by Austria, Britain, France, Italy, Japan, Russia and the United States, which also sent forces and collectively constituted the world's naval and colonial powers. At 19,093 men, the German contingent was the size of an army corps and constituted nearly a third of the combined force. Despatching his soldiers, the Kaiser made his notorious 'Hun Speech', in which he praised them for their brutality when he stated that the German mission in China was to punish rather than colonize. The Germans largely lived off the land during their occupation of Zhili province, outdoing even the other contingents in their looting. For those who took part, the expedition was an exciting adventure, while the German public saw it as demonstrating that their country had assumed its rightful place on the world stage; a sentiment encapsulated in Carl Röchling's painting 'Germans to the front!', showing Britain's Royal Marines standing aside to let their German comrades lead the advance (see Fig. 18).[29]

While the behaviour in China was bad, it was not far out of line with that of other imperial powers, in contrast to the second expedition, despatched in May 1904 to confront the revolt of the Herero in German South West Africa. Governor Theodor Leutwein wished to avoid violence, but he underestimated the difficulties facing local inhabitants and was unrealistic in his expectations of their willingness to accommodate demands for grazing land from the colony's 4,600 white settlers.[30] The settlers were soon besieged, forcing Leutwein to request aid. As with China, the army drew on volunteers, despatching 14,000 to the colony under Lothar von Trotha, who had experience of campaigning in East Africa. Leutwein had already contained the situation by the time Trotha arrived. Having surrounded the Herero at Waterberg, Trotha attacked on 11–12 August, but the majority escaped into the Omaheke Desert.

While Trotha's intentions remain a matter of controversy, he refused Herero requests to surrender and had prisoners shot. On 2 October 1904 he issued his infamous Annihilation Order (*Vernichtungsbefehl*), instructing his troops to drive the Herero into the desert, and to shoot any who resisted, including women and children. The measures were extended against the Nama once they also revolted that month. Although Schlieffen, chief of the General Staff, approved the order, the government eventually forced Trotha to rescind it in December and it produced a storm of protest from the SPD once it was leaked to the press in August 1905. Having halted deliberate genocide, Chancellor Bülow instructed Trotha to imprison the 30,000 remaining captives in three concentration camps, but they were soon used as forced labour, including being rented out to the railway and other businesses. The army was short of food and keen to punish the Herero, but starvation soon became policy.[31] Around 45 per cent had died by 1908 and some settlers grew concerned they would soon have no workers left. Overall, around 65,000 of the 80,000 Herero died, along with half of the 20,000 Nama.

Meanwhile, the separate Maji-Maji revolt began in east Africa in July 1905, triggered by a new tax system, the imposition of a plantation economy on a previously nomadic population, and the claims of a medium that his war medicine would turn German bullets into water (*Maji*). The government sent two cruisers, which landed marines equipped with machine guns, enabling Governor Count Götzen to crush the revolt by August 1907. Unlike Trotha, Götzen did not explicitly intend to destroy his opponents, but his response was likewise shaped by earlier experience of east African warfare in which starvation seemed the only way to defeat an enemy who avoided battle. His forces suffered 470 casualties, of whom only fifteen were white, but between 200,000 and 300,000 of the colony's population died.

Although higher than the death toll in South West Africa, the campaign attracted less attention, largely because it involved fewer German troops. Of the 19,000 Germans deployed to South West Africa across 1904–5, 1,500 became casualties, along with 250 settlers. The war cost 600 million Marks compared to the 14.5 million normally spent annually subsidizing the colony. Trotha was promoted, but Götzen was recalled, and limited efforts were made to respond to the grievances of surviving east Africans. The Colonial Department was removed from the Foreign Ministry in 1907 and elevated to ministry status as the *Reichskolonialamt* to promote economic development and avoid further costly rebellions.

Interpreting these events is difficult. The deliberate measures against the Herero undoubtedly constituted genocide, but attempts by several authors to draw a direct line 'from Windhoek to Auschwitz' imply a false continuity and inevitability that risks denying agency to those involved and thereby exculpating them.[32] Claims that the extreme violence was inherent in German military culture are also overdrawn. The German high command did not believe it could learn anything from African warfare and the events had little impact on its planning, which remained dominated by European conceptions of future conflict. The fears and aspirations of the civilian settlers exercised a malevolent influence, not least pressure from those who were keen to expropriate Herero farmland. German soldiers generally shared their commander's racism, seeing the Herero as simply part of a hostile environment rather than as people. These attitudes were imperial rather than specifically German, and were present during other 'asymmetrical' colonial conflicts, such as those in Cuba, British South Africa, and the Belgian Congo, where extraordinary levels of violence prevailed. The 'situational dynamism' encouraged a rapid escalation to extreme violence: imperial forces feared the personal consequences of defeat in a conflict where they did not believe 'normal' rules applied, and were concerned not to show weakness, not only towards their opponents but also to their colonial rivals.[33]

While the Germans' behaviour attracted some adverse press commentary, none of the other colonial powers protested until Britain published the so-called *Blue Book* in August 1918, based on documents captured by South African forces during the conquest of German South West Africa. This publication was part of a wider attempt to justify the seizure of Germany's colonies by cloaking imperial aggrandizement in the language of humanitarian intervention, which became the basis of the mandate system eventually endorsed in the peace treaties ending the First World War. The Germans responded with their *White Book* in 1919. Recognizing their own record was appalling, they made no attempt to refute the British claims directly, but instead argued violence was systemic to colonialism and that the other imperial powers had behaved equally badly. The Germans had a point, as even some Britons were forced to acknowledge. Ultimately, the controversy was self-defeating and contributed to a general undermining of colonial rule, but the parallel discussion surrounding German atrocities in Belgium in 1914 helped sustain the widespread belief that Germany's record was exceptionally violent. The Federal Republic apologized to Namibia in 2004, but has so far refused to pay reparations, though recently it has offered some compensation.[34]

DUTY AND REWARD

Motivation

Both liberals and conservatives expected soldiers to be motivated by patriotism, with the former believing that their personal commitment to victory would encourage them to use their initiative and mean they could be trusted to fight even when not directly supervised by officers. In practice, abstract concepts of the nation found little traction among soldiers who largely thought in traditional terms of duty to God and their ruler, loyalty to comrades, and the fear of being perceived as a coward.[35] Rather than motivating volunteers, appeals to patriotism largely served to make conscription more palatable after 1815, and there was often a wide discrepancy between high-flown rhetoric and actual commitment, especially as the draft still largely fell on the poor.

Bi-annual training camps in Switzerland attracted considerable public interest, with 15,000 spectators attending the 1822 exercises, and provided a rare chance for men from different cantons to meet. Patriotic speeches and songs gave these events the character of national festivals, but local and confessional animosities persisted beneath the surface. Zürich, for example, objected to the requirement that participants wear the federal armband, and the regularity of the exercises declined as tensions mounted prior to the Sonderbund War of November 1847.

Matters changed with the expansion of conscription during the 1860s and the concomitant adoption of short service in Austria and the south German states, all of which resulted in a broader cross section of society being required to serve. Although defeated in 1866, Austria could still draw on relatively recent glories, such as the victory over Italy at Custoza, while Radetzky's memory provided a positive father figure to help integrate soldiers from different ethnic backgrounds, though its attraction even among Czechs waned in the later nineteenth century.

Victories in 1864 and 1866 enhanced the military's standing in German society. Whereas soldiers' songs had previously been primarily bawdy, reservists summoned to fight France in 1870 sung *Die Wacht am Rhein* and other patriotic hymns. The story of national victory was far easier to tell in Prussia than in Hanover, Bavaria, and the other states which had been defeated in 1866. In October 1869, Prussian soldiers demolished the monument erected to the Hanoverians killed in 1866. Hanoverians felt disadvantaged in Prussian service and animosities persisted into the First World War. The Prussian general, Ferdinand von Stülpnagel, appointed to lead the Württemberg army in 1871, was recalled just two years later after his arrogance alienated his subordinates. The Prussian commander at the 1898 joint manoeuvres with the Saxons had to halt his men within twenty paces in a mock battle to stop a real fight breaking out. Conscripts from most of the surviving smaller states were now inducted directly into Prussian regiments, while the few remaining armies were increasingly uniformed and organized along Prussian lines. The national cockade, introduced by Wilhelm II in March 1897, used the Hohenzollern colours of black, white, and red. The old multi-layered sequence of identification continued to work for many who felt their local and regional identities were secured by their wider belonging in the new German Reich. However, Sedan Day, chosen as united Germany's national day after 1871, met with a mixed response, especially in areas like Württemberg that retained a strong sense of their own identity.[36]

Regimental traditions provided another focus for loyalty, which often sat uneasily between region and nation. Eighteenth-century rulers had been ambivalent towards such sentiments, fearing they might focus on ties to the regimental commander rather than themselves. Nonetheless, traditions developed around the ceremonies held to mark the award of new flags, which provided opportunities to commemorate past glories and signal dynastic and national loyalty. From the 1820s, German armies deliberately conserved flags that had become damaged or worn out, adding to the militaria collections that became the basis for museums later in the century. Neither Austria nor the German states followed Britain's practice of stitching the name of victories on to flags as 'battle honours', but instead each unit received streamers which recorded its designation and date of foundation. Austrian regiments also held official special days marking key events in their history. From 1873, German units received metal rings attached to the stave to record the names of ensigns killed carrying the flag in battle. Flags remained emotive symbols: all captured banners of German origin were removed from Les Invalides church by the Nazis after the fall of France in 1940, but the Allied Control Commission required their return in 1947.[37]

Regiments developed their own musical traditions. The introduction of valves for brass instruments allowed for more balanced bands and a more varied and appealing repertoire. Austrian playing differed from the German style, and the army's Hoch und Deutschmeister infantry regiment was famous for its band, for which over 100 pieces were written. Wilhelm Wieprecht, a member of Berlin's orchestra, reorganized Prussian military music after 1827 and introduced the concerts that soon became an inseparable element of all public martial display. This reached its zenith in the four decades prior to the First World War, when the musical establishment of the Prussian army expanded to 600 bands with 15,000 members, with additional bands in the navy and colonial troops. Wieprecht also reorganized military music in Turkey (1847) and Guatemala (1852). Prussian bands still played during the assault on Dybbøl in 1864, while the Austrians fought at Königgrätz two years later to the sound of the *Radetzky March*, composed by Johann Strauss the Elder in the summer of 1848 in the wake of victories over the Italian and Hungarian revolutionaries. Thereafter, the purely utilitarian element of military music declined to bugle signals, until these were finally displaced by the introduction of the telegraph, field telephones, wireless radio, and flares during the First World War.[38]

Prior to 1871, civilians had often maintained that civic honour at least matched that of soldiers, but thereafter it was widely acknowledged in Germany that the army occupied a privileged place in society. Service became more attractive, particularly to the middle classes, who had previously often sought to avoid the draft. A growing number came forward as one-year volunteers, despite the considerable financial outlay this entailed: 174 Marks for the uniform and at least 300 Marks a month to cover food and lodgings. Max Weber disliked his year's service but believed it was his duty and succeeded in getting his reserve officer certificate when it finished in 1884. Whereas reserve officers were merely 'demigods', in the words of Friedrich Meinecke, officers were 'young gods' who were now the most desirable dancing partners at balls. For the lower ranks, at least the army taught men personal hygiene and how to sew and do laundry, perhaps also improving their chances as better prospective husbands.[39]

Social status offset officers' relatively poor pay, which stagnated into the 1870s. Austrian officers fared worst, waiting nearly a century before a pay rise in 1851, at which point they earned only two-thirds of what their counterparts in the German medium-sized states received. A Bavarian second lieutenant was on a par with a postman or deputy locomotive driver, and though the ranks from captain upwards were better paid, military salaries were eroded by inflation. Three subsequent pay increases progressively closed the pay gap between junior and senior Habsburg officers by 1900, but a lieutenant still earned barely 20 per cent more than a skilled industrial worker. German officers were somewhat better off, but their increases after 1871 accumulatively totalled 66 per cent, compared to the 250 per cent wage rise enjoyed by industrial workers across the same period. A third of a junior officer's pay was deducted as the cost of his uniform. The Swiss army suffered the same problem, even after epaulettes were abolished in 1868 to make uniforms cheaper. By the 1880s a German junior officer needed 30 Marks a month from his family to supplement his monthly pay of only 75 Marks, and this subsidy could rise to 150 Marks if he was in a guards regiment. Regimental commanders began demanding proof of independent means before appointing new officers.[40]

The absence of any serious educational requirements at least removed that as a barrier to entry, in contrast to other careers which now required long and expensive professional training, but an officer's life was scarcely a route to riches. Indeed, low pay increasingly became almost a badge of honour by the later nineteenth century, since conservative and aristocratic officers felt it deterred social undesirables. The trend towards ostentation and expensive display around 1900 similarly reflected a move towards social exclusion that, perversely, made the service more desirable to some, because even junior officers commanded respect from civilians as well as their subordinates.

Armies still attracted volunteers even in the decades before conscription became more comprehensive. The four decades following 1815 saw several cyclical economic downturns disrupting traditional craft production before the growth of new industries provided increasingly attractive alternatives. Foreign service continued to draw recruits from Switzerland and parts of Germany, especially where communities already had established patterns of sending men to individual armies. Service in France became less popular with the growing local hostility towards foreigners, but that in Naples and the Papal army remained attractive (see Fig. 12).[41] Pay was low, but Prussia offered good incentives for NCOs, who were recruited from men who had volunteered for an extra four-year term following their three years' compulsory draft. Even after the expansion of conscription, around 3,000 men who were unable to pay their way as one-year volunteers nonetheless presented themselves for the full three years ahead of being called up, since this allowed them to choose which regiment they joined.

Daily routines were long and often arduous, boring or both. Those in the German navy began at 5 a.m., when sailors had to stow away their hammocks, and continued with a repetitive cycle of cleaning themselves, the ship and its equipment, drill and parades until lights out at 9 p.m. Austrian and German armed forces provided lunch as the only hot meal of the day, expecting men to survive on their bread ration plus coffee for breakfast and dinner. Additional iron rations, including bacon, biscuit, and rice, were issued on active service. Greater attention was paid to food preservation from mid-century, especially to stop bread spoiling before it reached the front, and to provide canned meat and vegetables. The captain, paymaster, and ship's doctor had to taste the food before it was served to sailors on German warships, though they ate their own meals separately from the crew. The German army introduced mobile field kitchens in 1908. Capable of preparing a warm meal for 250 men in just two hours, these were known as *Gulaschkanonen* because their chimney resembled a cannon barrel. Austria finally introduced hot evening meals five days a week in 1905.[42]

Around 200 Prussian soldiers took their own lives each year between 1876 and 1914, a figure which the army's critics used to support accusations of brutality towards conscripts. While suicide rates were higher among soldiers than civilians of similar age, this was common to nineteenth-century armies. Given that the army numbered around half a million men, the rate was still relatively low, and the proportion was higher among NCOs, perhaps due to 'career stress', rather than conscripts. Austria-Hungary suffered twice as many suicides as Germany, but these still only represented 0.1 per cent of strength annually. What is often overlooked is that virtually all suicides involved firearms, and ready access to guns is widely cited in explanations for the higher rates suffered by modern police forces with armed officers, such as in the United States.[43] Desertion and unauthorized absence remained a problem, accounting for 22 per cent of the 6,974 individual breaches of the

German military code in 1913, but the rate was lower than in Britain and much smaller than the US, amounting to only 0.2 per cent of total strength.[44] In short, military service remained tough, but for most men it now only occupied a few years of their lives thanks to the introduction of short-service conscription.

Social Origins

Conscription significantly reduced the already small number of foreigners serving. Geneva's professional *Garde Soldée*, established in November 1814, remained open to foreigners, but in practice the only outsiders were men from other cantons.[45] Foreigners could still be found in the senior ranks of the smaller German armies before 1870, mainly as a legacy of professionals entering service during the Napoleonic era. Only one-fifth of Bavarian generals came from the kingdom's old aristocracy, while a similar proportion of Hessen-Darmstadt generals were born outside Germany. Transfer between armies was less common than in the previous century, with most of those who did so joining Austrian rather than Prussian service.[46] The exception was the Schleswig-Holstein army which, during its brief existence from 1848 to 1851, relied heavily on Prussians on secondment, who accounted for half its officers, while Prussian and other German volunteers formed 12 per cent of enlisted men.[47]

Conscription also ensured that armies broadly reflected the national or regional composition of their populations, though with some variations. Hungarians remained proportionately under-represented in the Habsburg army, whereas Croatians and Italians featured disproportionately in the navy. Germans accounted for over half of Habsburg naval officers, but only 16.3 per cent of sailors, followed by a long margin by Magyar officers at 12.9 per cent including Rear Admiral Miklós Horthy who subsequently became regent of Hungary from 1920 to 1944. Ethnic stereotypes influenced the roles assigned to recruits, with Germans and Czechs predominating among engineers, electricians, and heavy-gun crews, while Croats were tasked as stokers and with other forms of hard manual labour. The situation was even more extreme in the army where Germans formed 79 per cent of Habsburg career officers and 60 per cent of those in the reserve by 1910. Nonetheless, regional recruitment mitigated the problems posed by a state with eleven languages and five major religions, though around a fifth of regiments were composed of at least two linguistic groups. So-called 'army German' provided a limited lingua franca on both land and (after 1848) at sea with about eighty commonly understood words of command. Most Habsburg officers were multilingual, and many knew English and French as well.[48] These issues affected Prussia as well, where some regiments contained Polish and Lithuanian speakers, recruited from the eastern provinces.

In contrast to the continuing poor standards among officers, the educational backgrounds of ordinary soldiers improved broadly in line with those in society generally. Already by 1866, 97 per cent of Prussian soldiers were literate, and just over 13 per cent had at least a high school education, compared to only one in ten Habsburg soldiers who could read and write. However, even at the end of the century, only one in four German soldiers regularly read a newspaper, and most could not name the chancellor (i.e. Hohenlohe), though they had at least heard of Bismarck. Literacy among Austrian soldiers now almost matched that in Germany but was much poorer across the other Habsburg provinces, notably in Dalmatia, which posed considerable problems for the navy, because this region provided most of the sailors.[49]

As the discussion of conscription revealed, the burden fell disproportionately on the poor before the 1860s, and while the balance shifted somewhat thereafter, nearly two-thirds of men still escaped the draft on grounds of health, short stature, or for family reasons. By contrast, the officer corps remained dominated by the nobility and affluent upper-middle class, largely because it remained self-recruiting. Four-fifths of Prussian officers applied directly to a regiment for their initial appointment. In Austria there was the additional barrier that ensign positions remained dependent on buying out the existing incumbents, though six posts per regiment were reserved for Wiener Neustadt graduates, and colonels lost their powers over officers' promotion and marriages in 1868. However, the qualities required of aspirant officers remained ill-defined, allowing social prejudice to continue to influence appointments.

The Prussian officer corps remained the most socially exclusive, particularly once bourgeois officers were weeded out during the 1820s. By contrast in Austria, officers with thirty years unblemished service, or who had been awarded a medal, were automatically ennobled, meaning a significant proportion of those who remained were of common birth, as in the eighteenth century. While nobles continued to be a slight majority among cavalry officers, they constituted only 14 per cent of those in the infantry by 1897. Commoners increasingly dominated the senior ranks as noble families, especially those from the non-German provinces, turned away from military and naval service after 1849 while, in another contrast with the German states, only two of the twelve war ministers between 1864 and 1918 were noblemen.

The medium-sized German states posed fewer social barriers to entry, and most officers came from upper-middle-class rather than aristocratic backgrounds, with that proportion greatest in Bavaria, where it rose from around half in 1800 to 70 per cent after 1812, followed by a modest decline until 1849, when it rose again to five-sixths by 1883. Despite this, the senior ranks remained dominated by nobles: of the 1,241 generals who served in the armies of thirteen medium-sized German states across 1815–70, 70 per cent were noblemen. Sons of officers and government officials generally constituted two-thirds of officers, signalling the continued close ties between army and state, except in Bavaria, where only a small proportion came from military families. The smaller German states required fewer officers and could afford to be more exclusive in recruiting them, with noblemen forming two-thirds of officers in the Saxon duchies.

The process of unification changed matters significantly. Many Hanoverian officers remained loyal to the defeated dynasty and refused to serve Prussia, and while the numbers transferring were higher in other annexed states, like Nassau, there were still too few officers for the new regiments formed from these areas, necessitating the appointment of more commoners. Elsewhere, Prussianization after 1871 reversed previous trends and made the officer corps more aristocratic, notably in Baden and Saxony, with only Bavaria remaining the outlier. Nonetheless, the expansion of the Prussian army from the 1880s forced it to admit more commoners as officers, because there simply were not enough noblemen available, while the non-noble proportion was already higher in the navy. Even the senior ranks were affected, with the proportion of nobles among colonels and generals declining from 86 per cent in 1860 to 53 per cent by 1913, and this figure included those who had been ennobled during service.

Partly from necessity, Wilhelm II called for those who were 'nobles by conviction' (*Adels der Gesinnung*) to be treated the same as 'nobles by birth'. To some extent, each force's officer corps cohered as a distinct social group, though it would be wrong to label them as a caste, given the heterogeneity of background, means, marital status, wealth, and age. Commoners already embraced the same codes of honour as their noble-born colleagues, and even in Switzerland great emphasis was placed on a smart appearance and correct behaviour. Although the Austro-Hungarian army was less status-conscious than Prussia's and it was common for officers to use the informal *Du* form when addressing one another, they maintained their distance from the rank and file, who they were only obliged to address formally as *Sie* in 1868, twenty years after this became required in Prussia and Mecklenburg-Schwerin. By contrast, Swiss officers remained citizen-soldiers who combined civilian careers with short periods of duty. Republican values encouraged them to view their subordinates as fellow citizens who should be persuaded rather than coerced to do their duty.[50]

However, prejudice persisted, especially in the Prussian guards and cavalry regiments. The one-year volunteers also remained a privileged group among ordinary soldiers, living separately in private accommodation, whereas their comrades were quartered in barracks. Corporal Friedrich Engels had his own valet and enjoyed his year attending the theatre, concerts, and university lectures, and indulging in fine dining. Likewise, Theodor Fontane preferred the company of officers during his year in 1844–5. Class distinctions were probably worse in the German navy, which shared the tensions common to many nineteenth-century navies between engineering and executive officers, with the former being primarily commoners and the latter more affluent and aristocratic. The situation was exacerbated by Tirpitz's open preference for nobles and his expectation that engineer officers pay for their own training. Engineers ate separately and were excluded from social functions reserved for executive officers. Deck officers formed a middle layer, socially on a par with their executive colleagues, but excluded from command, except on submarines, which were unpleasant vessels considered tactically and socially inferior. Deck and engineering officers protested by refusing to attend the Kaiser's birthday celebrations in 1912 and petitioning the Reichstag, but Tirpitz ignored them, believing this to be the work of a few malcontents.[51]

Peacetime contraction after 1815 reduced promotion prospects in all armies which remained governed by seniority, including in Prussia, where Boyen's reforms were reversed in the 1820s. By 1835 the average

Prussian lieutenant had to wait over twenty-one years to become a captain and a further fourteen to be promoted to major; three times as long as in 1815. Promotion above captain after the 1820s was judged more by merit, but this was assessed narrowly as the ability to think clearly on specific practical matters. Commoners were not unduly disadvantaged until they reached the 'major's corner' (*Majorsecke*), where they tended to get stuck while noblemen were promoted faster over their heads. The rank of major remained a sticking point, even once promotion accelerated with the mid-century wars and again during the subsequent expansion from the 1880s.

Officer appointment and promotion remained cantonal responsibilities in Switzerland until 1874 when it was federalized, though in practice initial recruitment still depended on nomination by the cantons. The situation was complicated by the importance attached in patrician circles to the acquisition of experience through foreign service. The proportion who had served abroad declined from about 45 per cent prior to 1831, to only 19 per cent across the next two decades, before falling off sharply once this practice was banned by the Federal government. The vacancies were increasingly filled by men from respectable burgher backgrounds, such as small traders, craftsmen, and farmers. These in turn were displaced from the 1880s by men from the urban, educated, technical, and mercantile backgrounds who were often younger than their predecessors, leading to their portrayal in the press as social climbers.[52]

The political changes in Germany across 1803–15 broke the linkage between dynasty and religion since the territorial redistribution left the surviving states with significant dissenting minorities. Although the differing Christian confessions were granted legal equality, pre-Enlightenment suspicions surrounding political loyalty persisted, leading rulers to continue to favour co-religionists as officers. Catholics now formed over a third of Prussian subjects, but only 16 per cent of army and 14 per cent of naval officers. The imbalance was mirrored in Austrian-Hungary where Catholics formed 86 per cent of career officers, but only two-thirds of the population in 1911. Austria continued to attract Catholics from across southern and western Germany until these connections were broken by the defeat in 1866. Again, Bavaria remained the exception where up to half of officers were Protestant, compared to only a fifth of the population. In 1844, Bavaria abolished the requirement for Protestant soldiers to kneel as Catholic religious processions passed, but Catholics were still required in Prussia to attend some Protestant services on special occasions, such as the Kaiser's birthday.

The Habsburgs were more tolerant of religious diversity among enlisted men, with many regiments having more than one chaplain from the 1830s to serve the different faiths within the ranks, while the army was even able to accommodate the formation of four Muslim regiments after the annexation of Bosnia-Herzegovina in 1885. Jews remained slightly under-represented among soldiers, and distinctly so for regular officers, but accounted for a disproportionate number of reserve officers and military administrators. Jewish officers faced prejudice, but conversion was not essential for promotion and twenty-three achieved the rank of colonel or general prior to 1911. By contrast, anti-Semitism remained strong in the Prussian army, where Jews were liable for conscription following the Emancipation Edict of 1812, but they remained barred from officer appointments. The hostility of local officials ensured that Jews were also often excluded from those drafted between 1813 and 1815, and in 1827 there were just 189 Jewish soldiers in the Prussian army, representing only 0.1 per cent of total strength, whereas Jews numbered 1 per cent of the population.

From the 1830s, Jews lobbied to be conscripted to prove their value as Prussian citizens, but even in 1907 they only formed 0.3 per cent of the army. Although even the guards regiments officially accepted Jewish recruits after 1874, conscription law allowed officials to reject 'undesirables' without explanation. Viktor Klemperer was very disgruntled at being declared unfit to serve, though he later became a decorated volunteer during the First World War. Around 30,000 Jews, including Walther Rathenau, the future foreign minister, served as one-year volunteers between 1880 and 1910, comprising 5 per cent of those who did so, but not one was commissioned as a reserve officer. The sons of Gerson Bleichröder, Bismarck's banker, were only reluctantly accepted as reserve officers after they had been baptized. Bavaria, otherwise more accommodating, no longer commissioned Jews after 1885, and the last Jewish officer had left by 1906. The army's anti-Semitism was shared by the Pan-German League, which had a strong presence within the civil service but was otherwise out of line with Wilhelmine society more generally and contrasted with the presence of Jews among the country's senior diplomats, which was proportional to their share of the population.

Many officers readily accepted the simplistic scaremongering that conflated Jews and socialists as deadly threats to the nation.[53]

PART OF LIFE

Martial Law

The process of codifying military law, itself part of a wider programme of legal codification, continued long into the nineteenth century with new codes appearing in Baden (1803) and Prussia (1845), for example. One impulse came from the desire for greater precision; within four years of issuing a new code in 1819, the Swiss Confederation initiated further revisions, resulting in a fresh ordinance of 506 articles in 1834.[54] Another factor was the desire among south German states to ensure that military service did not deprive citizens of the rights they were now acquiring through the new state constitutions adopted in the 1820s. Bavaria transferred civil cases involving soldiers to the civil courts after 1828 and made military tribunals more transparent in 1862 by permitting the accused's relations to attend.[55] Prussia adopted the principal of innocent until proven guilty in 1845 but otherwise upheld the army's exclusive jurisdiction over soldiers, who were denied key rights while serving, including being disenfranchised to insulate the army from politics. Disenfranchisement was adopted across the North German Confederation in 1869 and extended to the rest of Germany five years later.

Prussia's code formed the basis of the new imperial code of June 1872, completing the process of codification of military law well ahead of its civil counterpart that eventually produced the famous *Bürgerliches Gesetzbuch* of January 1900, which continues to inform German legal practice today. Württemberg and Saxony retained their own codes, but these were closely modelled on Prussia's. Only Bavaria's 1869 code remained aligned to civil practice and separated the roles of judge and prosecutor. Liberal efforts to reform the imperial code along Bavarian lines failed in 1897–8, though the other states forced Prussia to modify its procedural rules to permit open hearings and equality among jurors.

The Prussian code at least ended the corporal punishments that remained legal in other states. Württemberg abolished the practice of running the gauntlet in 1819, around the time when other German states moderated some penalties, but it was retained by Austria until 1855. Lesser forms of corporal punishment remained legal in the smaller German states until 1848 and for another twenty years in Austria where military courts continued to meet in secret. A key reason for the retention of harsh measures was that officers believed soldiers needed them. Discipline remained relatively poor in the decades after 1815. Most conscripts served long terms but spent the bulk of their time on furlough and regarded their time with the colours as disrupting their lives. They remained socialized in the general male alcoholic culture and proved difficult to control when they returned to their unit. Reservists and Landwehr men were under civil jurisdiction and they resented passing back under martial law when recalled to duty, notably in 1848–9. Prussia's shorter service proved more acceptable, especially as many served considerably less than the official three years, which contributed to better discipline.

Officers continued to consider themselves above the law to a considerable extent. Duelling emerged as a problem in the later seventeenth century largely through the reception of French and Italian ideas. Official efforts to limit interpersonal violence among soldiers and university students created a legal distinction in 1668 between drawing weapons in the heat of a fight (termed a *Rencontre*), and a duel as a premediated and arranged combat. The distinction inadvertently strengthened the association between duelling and personal honour. Princes issued repeated prohibitions, but already in 1713 the Württemberg government tacitly accepted that a new law was unlikely to have much effect, though they renewed it anyway and it remained in force until 1839. By then, most governments had abandoned outright bans in favour of requiring officers to put their case to an 'honour court' (*Ehrengericht*) to decide whether a duel was justified. Prussia finally gave way in 1874 and ruled that officers who refused a challenge were to be dismissed on the grounds that their failure to defend themselves dishonoured the entire army. Attempts to reverse this, including an anti-duel league among Bavarian officers, all foundered on official resistance.[56]

Soldiers' Identities

The Kaiser's defence of duelling is indicative of the highly personalized relationship between the monarchy and its army. The monarchy defeated efforts by the reformers to extend the oath of allegiance to include the fatherland in the 1810s, and instead military personnel continued to swear purely personal loyalty to the monarch until 1918. Oaths were controversial since they highlighted the wider issue of who held power. Liberals wanted soldiers to swear obedience to the constitution, thus putting them on a par with civil officials. Not all officers accepted this. Colonel Wurstemberger's refusal to swear an oath on Bern's new liberal constitution in 1832 was followed by the mass resignation of seventy-two other officers who agreed with him.[57] In Germany, liberals in Kurhessen (1831), Bavaria (1848), Württemberg (1848), and some other states succeeded in requiring this, though these measures were sometimes reversed, as in Bavaria (1852). Frederick William IV promised this in Prussia in 1848, but never enacted it, while Austria changed its oath in November 1850, removing the reference to the constitution introduced two years earlier.[58]

Personal ties to monarchs were further symbolized through military flags, shako and helmet badges, which all bore royal cyphers and coats of arms, while officers wore sashes in the dynasty's personal colours. Uniforms remained broadly 'Napoleonic' in style until 1848, with soldiers stuffed into tight-fitting tailcoats and breeches, with large bell shakos on their heads. Heavy cavalry wore the 'classical' style metal helmets introduced in the 1790s (see Fig. 13). Those of the Prussian cuirassiers were so impractical that men had to be sent to collect lost helmets after their unit had practised a gallop.[59]

In 1842, Prussian soldiers received uniforms of a revolutionary new design based on a single-breasted tunic that was more comfortable and offered better covering in inclement weather. The old arrangement of carrying ammunition pouches, bayonets, and other equipment using leather crossbelts was replaced in 1848 by a new system of hooking shoulder belts to a waistbelt, thereby achieving a better weight distribution. Both these innovations were rapidly copied by other armies throughout Europe and later globally. However, it was the new spiked leather helmet, introduced in 1842, that became the iconic symbol of the Prussian army and, to its critics, of German militarism (see Fig. 16). The exact origins of this *Pickelhaube* remain a matter of dispute, deriving either from a similar helmet already adopted by the Russian army or as a design by the Berlin historical painter Heinrich Stilke. Initially 37 cm tall without the spike, later models became progressively lower, but it remained in service until replaced by the equally iconic steel helmet (*Stahlhelm*) in 1916.[60]

Adoption of the Pickelhaube became a symbol of the shifting balance of power in Germany, with those states aligning with Prussia already using it by 1848. Austria, Saxony, Württemberg, and the Swiss Confederation instead followed France in replacing the tall bell shako with smaller, tapered versions around 1850, soon followed by cloth kepis which were lighter still. Bavaria typically pursued its own course, retaining the leather crested 'caterpillar' helmet (*Raupenhelm*) already adopted in the 1790s. Landwehr and reserve units wore regular-style uniforms, with those in Prussia distinguished by an iron-cross device on their headgear. However, the civic guards and other revolutionary formations in 1848–9 deliberately adopted clothing closer to civilian dress and wore their hair loose, in contrast to soldiers, whose hairstyles remained closely monitored, with only pioneers and drummers permitted beards prior to the 1860s. The contrast between soldiers' and civilians' appearance grew more pronounced from mid-century as male attire became increasingly sombre compared to military uniforms, which remained brightly coloured.[61]

Soldiers were now also increasingly housed separately in a process which, while taking a century to complete, demarcated civilian and military spheres more clearly. Billeting predominated into the 1820s and lasted in some garrisons into the next century: Bavarian soldiers in Regensburg only moved into barracks in 1912 (see Fig. 14). However, barrack construction accelerated from the 1820s as governments both addressed local complaints about soldiers' behaviour and sought to isolate military personnel from the feared 'contagion' of revolution. Town councils came to regard a garrison as a boost to the local economy and the Bavarian army received ninety-one petitions in 1913 alone requesting that one be created. The army was also keen, because the shift from individual drill to field training required concentrating troops in places with better access to exercise grounds, while moving into major towns connected them to the rail network and speeded up mobilization.

Armies initially used monasteries acquired during the secularization of the imperial church lands in 1803, but even the purpose-built barracks were often unsuitable and unhealthy, particularly during the cholera epidemics of the 1830s. The Bavarian army replaced wood with coal heating in 1846 and introduced oil lamps for lighting in 1865, but conditions still contrasted sharply with the comfortable bourgeois domesticity of the Biedermeier era. The expansion of conscription in the 1860s increased the pressure for improvements, leading to a second wave of new construction from the 1880s, and by 1903 all Prussian soldiers were lodged in barracks. Austria lagged considerably behind, and outside Italy and Vienna, over half the troops remained in billets or rented accommodation into the 1880s, with the cavalry even having to sleep in tents over the summer months.[62] Switzerland, with its militia army, managed to dispense with large-scale barracks construction.

Marital Relations and Social Life

Barracks accentuated the distinctiveness of the garrison within its urban setting, but as cities grew soldiers formed a declining proportion of most of their populations, falling from just over 14 per cent of Berlin's inhabitants in 1790 to only 2.8 per cent by 1871. Meanwhile, the composition of the garrison community was transformed with the switch from long-service professionals to short-service conscripts. Soldiers' families still accounted for nearly half of Berlin's garrison in 1803, but by 1871 four out of five members were serving soldiers, as all women were now excluded from the barracks except the wives and daughters of NCOs, and these were no longer under military jurisdiction, from which all soldiers' dependents had been freed in 1809.[63]

Thus, conscription largely ended the phenomenon of the soldier's wife, because only young, unmarried men were drafted. Reservists and Landwehr men could marry, tying them more clearly to the civilian sphere and distinguishing them from the regulars. Officers were still expected to be 'married' to their career, especially as the state wanted to avoid responsibility for their widows. In 1843, Baden repeated an earlier prohibition on junior officers marrying, while their senior comrades had to prove independent means to maintain their families. Austria required lieutenants to deposit the equivalent of thirty-three years' pay into the widow's fund before permission would be granted, whereas colonels were asked for somewhat over six times their salary. Not surprisingly, officers often married beneath their social status, seeking rich but humble brides to boost their finances. Over two-thirds remained single and those who married did so much later than civilians and correspondingly had smaller families. Concubinage and illicit liaisons were common into the 1890s, as was the use by all ranks of brothels, which remained legal across Germany and Austria-Hungary. Bavaria imposed similar requirements on its officers until 1872 when these were replaced by the Prussian policy of simply asking junior officers to provide affidavits proving they had the means to support a family.[64]

Conscription made military service a cohort experience, since men were called to the colours annually in year groups. Most had already left school at fourteen and had up to six years in an apprenticeship or employment prior to call-up, unlike their counterparts for much of the twentieth century who were drafted around the time they completed education. Men travelled to the barracks together, following a noisy, alcoholic send-off, in which those declared unfit had to buy drinks for the others. Arrival in the garrison involved often degrading initiation rituals and new recruits were assigned the worst places in the dormitory. Army life remained bawdy, part of a communal bonding process that many found distasteful.[65] However, once in the army, conscripts generally accepted its socialization and regarded themselves as distinct from, indeed superior to, male civilians, whom they sometimes despised as 'shirkers'. They took advantage of their status to make trouble, but it should be remembered that this was not inherently 'military', as they were predominantly young, unmarried men, with few responsibilities, for whom soldiering was a relatively brief step outside the conventions of civilian life.

The extension of reserve systems and veterans' associations provided a succession of militarized organizations for the male lifespan, though experience still varied greatly, especially depending on whether the cohort had seen active service at some point. The experience was also far from universal, given the large proportion of men who were either exempted altogether or who passed directly into the reserves with only nominal and occasional training. Civilian life continued to offer competing masculine role models, such as those of missionaries, public officials, and businessmen, while the military life was subject to a variety of critiques from religious organizations and the trades union movement.

Classical allusions to female fighters had been common until the late eighteenth century, as was the trope of a city as a virgin under siege from an unwelcome suitor. The best-known example was Magdeburg, besieged twice in 1551 and 1631, where the meaning of the city's name,

'Maiden's Castle', lent itself to literary and artistic devices. Writers tended to praise the city's alleged self-sacrifice as akin to Lucretia, immolating itself rather than face further dishonour during the sack of 1631. Some writers celebrated women who offered active resistance, such as the 'Viragoes of Biberach', who repulsed General Ossa's imperial army during the Thirty Years War 'with scalding water, stones, and such feminine weapons, beating his men from the walls of their city, and encouraging their husbands'.[66] Most dwelt on the final element of this story, describing women's resolve as shaming cowardly men into action. Attitudes to the very few real-life Amazons were ambivalent, especially as these cross-dressing female soldiers had sometimes passed for years without detection, making their male comrades feel duped when their identity was revealed. They too tended to be held as examples to encourage men to fight, rather than as roles for women to follow.

These stories still circulated around 1800 when central Europe was again engulfed by foreign invasion. The Bernese war council told women to remain at home, but several did fight and were killed, while others suffered from the deliberate revolutionary violence of the French in 1798.[67] The prolonged warfare saw a surge in female activism across Germany, with 573 women's patriotic associations appearing between 1813 and 1815, particularly in Prussia, where they were encouraged by the monarchy to foster acceptance of the new forms of conscription. Elite women, including Hohenzollern princesses, were prominent in leading these organizations, which raised substantial funds for war. Their efforts were recognized in 1814 by Frederick William III's foundation of the *Luisenorden*, a special medal for women named after his late wife, but only 166 awards were made.

In this way, the 'wars accelerated and intensified the nationalisation of the gender order and the "gendering" of the nation'.[68] Women were offered a role in nation-building that fitted with the emerging bourgeois model of the family, in which they were largely excluded from public life and confined to a private, domestic sphere. Three patriotic ideal types replaced the earlier heroic Amazon: the self-sacrificing 'heroic mother' who allowed her son or husband to go to war; the 'warrior's sweetheart' who was being defended; and the 'caring nurse' who, at this point, was expected to work in a base hospital and not at the front. The Wars of Unification saw a new surge of female activism along these lines, and by 1914 female patriotic associations had 600,000 members and there was even a women's version of the Navy League; but, in contrast to Britain, women were offered only a subordinate role in the festivities surrounding the launch of new warships.[69]

Not all women meekly accepted this. Some Bavarian women took up arms to prevent their menfolk being conscripted during the Napoleonic Wars, while others continued to prevent their husbands or sons from volunteering, arguing for an alternative patriotism in which the man did his duty as husband and taxpayer. Some sought a more active role in the citizens' militias during 1848–9, but even liberals mocked the idea that women could bear arms, despite their being legally entitled to carry guns for self-defence and hunting. The introduction of universal suffrage for all men over twenty-five in 1871 consolidated the gendered division of the nation into militarily active, enfranchised men and passive, disenfranchised women. No middle-class party supported the cause of female suffrage. The female figure of Germania symbolizing the nation might have been an armed and furious Valkyrie in Friedrich von Kaulbach's famous painting from 1914, but German women were not expected to fight.[70]

Medical Care

The transformation of medical care during the nineteenth century eventually gave women a place again in military organizations. Care remained largely devolved to individual units and languished in the long peacetime years following 1815, primarily due to shortage of funds. The Swiss federal army entered the Sonderbund War in 1847 with only 494 medical personnel for 98,861 men, but the obvious inadequacy prompted Zürich to send a voluntary aid detachment of doctors and nurses equipped with coaches to evacuate the wounded. The revolutionary wars of 1848–9 forced other armies to reorganize provision, with Austria, Bavaria, Prussia, and others copying French practice and establishing separate medical corps tasked with removing the wounded, to stop soldiers leaving the firing line to help injured comrades to safety.[71]

Changes in weaponry resulted in horrific wounds from large-calibre, soft lead bullets, and from shell fragments. Amputation remained the preferred treatment, placing a premium on safe and swift casualty evacuation. The widespread calls for reform across Europe produced two, partially conflicting solutions. One, exemplified by Florence Nightingale in Britain, advocated the expansion and improvement of army medical services, whereas the other stressed charity and voluntarism.

The latter was best exemplified by the Swiss initiative that led to the foundation of the Red Cross in 1863.[72] The leading figure was Henri Dunant, a businessman from Geneva who witnessed the aftermath of the battle of Solferino in 1859. Dunant recognized that war could not be eliminated but argued the suffering it caused could be alleviated. Nonetheless, he was an idealist whose vision was given practical shape by others, notably Henri Dufour, who wrote the preface to Dunant's famous book *Memory of Solferino* and did much of the organizing, including presiding at the meeting in Geneva that founded the movement, as well as chairing the following one that agreed the first Geneva Convention. The others were Gustave Moynier, president of a local philanthropic society, and Dr Louis Appia, who had worked as a surgeon in Italy in 1859. Moynier explicitly cited the inspiration of the Zürich voluntary aid detachment, which had helped the wounded of both sides in 1847. Their vision, endorsed at the 1863 meeting, was of nationally organized charitable societies, coordinated by the Swiss international committee (ICRC), which would train volunteers in peacetime who would accompany their army on campaign and assist the wounded of both sides. The 1864 Convention secured the neutrality of these personnel, who were to be identified by the famous armband with a red cross on a white background. This symbol, reversing the Swiss national colours, was seemingly adopted on a whim, but became problematic when Turkey joined the movement in 1876 and objected that it was a Christian device, choosing instead the Red Crescent.

Christian philanthropic impulses were indeed a strong influence on the movement, especially those of Dunant, who envisaged that well-minded, compassionate aristocrats and clerics would lead the army of volunteers. Gustave Moynier was also unrealistic in basing the plans on the experience of 1847, ignoring that conflict's peculiar character as a civil war in which neither party particularly wanted to fight. The Swiss also took no notice of the American Civil War in which the US government had already guaranteed the neutrality of medical personnel of both sides in April 1863. Nonetheless, the emphasis on Christian, elite leadership was immediately appealing to the royal and princely courts of Germany, where the first three Red Cross societies were formed by February 1864: Württemberg, Oldenburg, and Prussia. Austria initially boycotted the movement, claiming it was unnecessary because it had its own Patriotic Society for Aid to Wounded Soldiers, War Widows, and Orphans, established in April 1859.

The Swiss also responded quickly to the Schleswig-Holstein War, despatching observers to both sides.[73] The Prussians went out of their way to be helpful, while large numbers of civilian volunteers from various philanthropic organizations assisted the army's small medical corps. Their presence was credited with the improved survival rate of sick and wounded, of whom only just over 1 per cent died. Several German states now ratified the Geneva Convention, but Austria refused to cooperate, rightly regarding Prussia's activities in this field as a challenge to its claims to leadership. Defeat in 1866 finally forced Austria to abandon unilateralism, particularly as its own voluntary society failed miserably and Prussia captured so many of its wounded soldiers, obliging the Habsburgs to ratify the Geneva Convention.

Nonetheless, Prussian medical services were overwhelmed by the high casualties at Königgrätz when nearly half of the wounded died of postoperative infections, while their army lost more to typhus and cholera than the Austrians. Part of the Red Cross movement's success was that, by bringing care of the wounded to international attention, it shamed governments into making improvements. A comprehensive review led to major reforms. Many of the voluntary groups were brought more firmly under the umbrella of a Pan-German Red Cross in 1869 as a single 'national' society under government supervision, militarizing charity and removing the self-appointed 'delegates of humanity' from the battlefield. Although they remained volunteers, all members had to follow Prussian military medical regulations. Austria-Hungary caught up after 1868, initially subjecting volunteers to official coordination, then cooperating with the German Red Cross after 1874, before finally combining voluntary organizations in its western provinces into a separate Austrian Red Cross five years later.[74]

In 1868, Prussia revised its medical regulations, which now applied to the new North German Confederation. Prussia saw cleanliness as a sign of good discipline and an expression of its soldiers' superiority over those of other nations. Water canteens finally became standard issue in 1867 while, after resistance from Wilhelm I, who told the war minister Albrecht von Roon, 'for my whole life I have considered underpants superfluous', these were now provided too.[75] Alongside the Netherlands,

Prussia was the first state to require compulsory vaccination of its soldiers, reducing the fatal incidence of smallpox.

The new practice of antiseptic surgery, pioneered by Louis Pasteur in France and Joseph Lister in Britain, was adopted by Prussia in 1867, significantly reducing the post-operative death rates. Prussia made its own contribution through Friedrich von Esmarch, who had served as a junior doctor in 1848 and by the end of his career was recognized as the father of modern military surgery. His triangular bandage, invented in 1869, is still included in field medical kits. He also pioneered new techniques in resuscitation and swiftly adapted first-aid practices developed by Britain's St John Ambulance to write a first-aid manual in 1882 that was translated into thirty languages.[76]

Prussian soldiers were issued with first-aid kits, including the triangular bandage and sterile lint, in time for the 1870 campaign, greatly improving the primary level of care on the battlefield. They were also given tin dog tags to assist identification if they became casualties. The second level was also reorganized as Prussia expanded its separate medical corps, assigning detachments as corps troops to evacuate serious casualties. Doctors were granted officer status and could command other medical personnel, something the Swiss army had done in 1862. The medical corps now had stretchers and ambulances, while specialized hospital trains connected the war zone with the tertiary level of care in the base hospitals in the rear or at home. These were staffed by the numerous female volunteers, indicating the gendered character of medical care, as male doctors still doubted women's capacity to work at the front. This division contrasted with the prominent status of elite women, notably Queen Augusta of Prussia, as patrons of the voluntary organizations.[77] To further demonstrate its good intentions, the army distributed 80,000 copies of the Geneva Convention to the troops as they marched into France in 1870.

The efficacy of these reforms was already demonstrated during the 1870–1 war when medical care only seriously broke down after the battle of Gravelotte, though the death rate among wounded admitted to hospital was still over 11 per cent. The Prussian Red Cross's 250,000 members raised nearly 19 million tlr in aid, including a large donation sent to Switzerland to care for the sick and wounded among General Bourbaki's army when it was interned, though the French government paid most of the costs. The Swiss were also active, interceding to secure safe passage for 4,000 women and children trapped in the siege of Stras-bourg, and organizing a missing and tracing service to inform families of the fate of killed and captured soldiers; this was something already pioneered by Clara Barton in the American Civil War, and which would be copied in Austria in 1886.

The German army found the presence of fourteen different national aid societies, including from Britain and the United States, in the war zone unwelcome, especially as it suspected spies of abusing the Red Cross armband. The experience reinforced its efforts to militarize volun-teers who now trained with soldiers on peacetime manoeuvres; a practice also followed in Austria and Switzerland. The colonial Schutztruppe was given a relatively large medical establishment due to the high incidence of infections, especially typhoid, and knowledge gained on its campaigns, including in China, was applied in disease prevention during the First World War. Meanwhile, the collection of detailed statistics on soldiers' physical fitness profoundly influenced broader thinking about national health.[78] Austria-Hungary deployed 145,000 troops during the occupa-tion of Bosnia-Herzegovina in 1878–9, losing 1,191 killed and 4,013 wounded in ten weeks of heavy fighting, but while 110,000 men fell sick, only 2,006 died, and health improved further with the establishment of a bacteriological research department in 1890.[79]

German military medical regulations were revised in 1878 and 1887, but the high command became increasingly concerned at the growing destructiveness of modern rifles. The switch to smaller-calibre weapons in the 1880s increased their range, making it harder to evacuate casualties to safety. The character of gunshot wounds changed, increasing the num-bers of men with treatable, yet potentially fatal, injuries. The war ministry estimated that a fifth of total strength would be wounded in future bat-tles, and that the ever-larger armies and growing scale of the battlefield all greatly complicated the problems of casualty evacuation. The medical corps expanded to over 6.5 per cent of strength, primarily to remove battlefield casualties and staff the field hospitals, with volunteers serving those in the rear. Alternative methods were sought and, drawing on the Swiss traditions of mountain rescue, the German army began training dogs in 1885 to find injured soldiers and alert stretcher parties.[80]

Care of Veterans

The territorial reorganization of 1802–6 left many states overburdened, since they became responsible for the welfare of former military and civil personnel in the mediatized areas. The duration and scale of the conflicts across 1792–1815 added considerably to this by creating another generation of disabled ex-soldiers, including traumatized and frost-bitten survivors of the Russian disaster of 1812. Governments responded by expanding existing efforts to reintegrate former soldiers into society by providing civil service employment. The measure was also intended to encourage men to volunteer for an extra term in peacetime and thus assist the recruitment and retention of NCOs. From August 1820, Prussia guaranteed government employment to all those with nine years' service, provided they were literate and numerate. Most former soldiers were completely unsuited, and the adverse impact on administrative efficiency forced the programme to be drastically curtailed in 1827, limiting it to those with a high school education. Baden also imposed greater restrictions and in 1829 introduced pensions for its gendarmerie to prevent this consisting only of superannuated ex-soldiers.[81]

The real problem was the absence of genuinely universal pension rights, since these remained largely a matter of princely grace. During the 1831 revolution the Kurhessen Estates granted pensions to the veterans who had served Britain in America in the 1770s and their widows because of the political controversy surrounding their ruler having profited from foreign subsidies. The storm of protest from veterans of more recent wars forced the government to concede universal entitlement.[82] The shift to short-service conscription eased the problem, since few men other than officers now made the army a lifetime's career. With proportionately fewer older men to care for, both Prussia and Austria relaxed the restrictions on employing former NCOs in government posts during the 1860s, helped also by the fact that these were now usually better educated. After 1855, Austria allowed officers with fifty years' service to retire on full pay, with pro rata rates for those forced out earlier due to ill health, thereby establishing a retirement age for the first time. Pension rates were improved subsequently but remained worse than those granted to civil servants until 1907. The situation in Germany was meanwhile revolutionized by the increasingly comprehensive package of social insurance introduced for all employees after 1883, including basic universal pension entitlements guaranteed by the state in 1889.

The status of veterans became more politicized with the Wars of Unification linking the ideal of national sacrifice more closely to conservative politics. By 1908 fewer than one in seven veterans had seen actual combat, and their associations were more about sustaining warm memories of past comradeship than welfare provision to their members. Soldiers were given their uniforms upon discharge and wore them at weddings and funerals, where their womenfolk also sported regimental colours.

Veterans' organizations merged into the *Kyffhäuserbund*, named after the mountain that had become a focus for the conservative sentiment of national renewal. The Kyffhäuser mountain was both the notional tomb of the twelfth-century Emperor Frederick Barbarossa and the location of a monumental complex devoted to Kaiser Wilhelm I to link the new Imperial Germany to the romanticized glories of its medieval forebear. The Kyffhäuserbund had over 2.8 million members on the eve of the First World War and its political leanings were clearly indicated by the formal exclusion of socialist veterans. The expansion of conscription in Austria-Hungary saw the number of veterans' associations grow more than tenfold across 1868–1914, but the monarchy's ethnic diversity made it more difficult for the authorities to manipulate these to promote acceptance of military service.[83]

The Treatment of Prisoners

The German states followed the established European practice of redistributing prisoners, either through formal exchange cartels, or releasing them on parole. All the wars before 1870 were relatively brief, and only in 1866 were the numbers of prisoners substantial, as Prussia captured over 50,000 Austrians and other Germans, including almost the entire Hanoverian army, while losing only 910 of its own men this way. The 1870–1 war was on an entirely different order of magnitude. The Germans had captured over 260,000 French troops by the end of October 1870, with the total rising to 383,860 by the end of the war, in addition to the 90,192 interned in Switzerland and 6,300 in Belgium, whereas the French had taken just 8,000 men. Exchange was clearly impossible, but after some initial problems, French prisoners were housed in 242 camps across Germany. Around 2.7 per cent of French prisoners died in German captivity, mainly from tuberculosis and lung infections; a rate only marginally above that among those interned in Switzerland, and the French inspectors were pleased, though concern was voiced at German treatment of captured francs-tireurs.[84]

The impetus for change came from America where exchanges during the Civil War collapsed after the Confederacy refused to treat Black troops as belligerents. The United States issued the famous Lieber Code in 1863, notable less for any specific innovation, and more as the first attempt to codify common standards of treatment of prisoners in captivity. While care of prisoners was a concern of the founders of the Red Cross, attempts to create a parallel Green Cross voluntary organization, based in Basel, foundered and eventually the ICRC assumed the coordinating role during the First World War. Although the convention drafted by lawyers at the 1874 Brussels congress remained unratified, the German government treated it as international law, and it eventually became the basis for the 1899 and 1907 conventions. Henceforth, belligerents were forbidden to deny quarter or kill soldiers who had surrendered and were required to treat prisoners humanely and not as criminals. They could compel them to work, provided this was not directly for their own war effort. However, German public acceptance of these rules was undercut by the army's belief that they should only be observed so long as they did not undermine the chances of victory. The General Staff's 1902 legal handbook permitted the killing of prisoners who posed an existential threat, reflecting the underlying fear of francs-tireurs. Moreover, like other European forces, the army did not consider the rules applied to the colonies, where it persistently denied that conflicts constituted formal war.[85]

LIMITED WAR

Human Losses

The army's fear of existential total war was at odds with the actual character of most of the wars it fought during the nineteenth century. The 'wars of nations' in fact remained relatively limited in scope and immediate impact, especially compared to previous and future conflicts.

Switzerland's three-week civil war in 1847 saw 126 fatalities and 634 wounded. The conflicts between 1848 and 1850 were protracted, but they were also punctuated by truces and far less destructive than those of the Napoleonic era. The belligerents in the First Schleswig-Holstein War suffered around 14,500 killed and wounded, with casualties marginally heavier on the Danish side, though the Germans lost more prisoners. Austria lost 12,309 killed, wounded, and missing in its two brief wars with Piedmont, which suffered 7,400 casualties. Crushing the Rhineland revolutionaries cost the German Confederation's forces 154 killed and 1,184 wounded. Austria's suppression of Hungarian independence was bloodier with a collective death toll of 98,000, but this was an outlier in the general trend that continued in 1859. Although noted for the suffering at Solferino, Austria's overall total loss in this conflict of 30,000 killed and wounded was proportionately lower than in many early modern wars, while Austria and Prussia together suffered 3,500 killed and wounded in 1864 compared to Denmark's 6,200.[86]

The full impact of improved weaponry began to be felt in 1866, which saw over 85,000 killed and wounded in six weeks, as well as over 25,000 fatalities from disease. The escalation continued in 1870–1, which cost the German forces over 135,000 dead and wounded, compared to 282,000 on the French side. Casualties in some units were acute, especially in the costly assaults at Gravelotte and St Privat. The memory of these losses underlay much of the high command's subsequent anxiety about future wars, and with good reason given the continued improvements in the lethality of weaponry. However, both wars were brief compared to those of the preceding three centuries, and they resembled the ideal of 'limited war' as the application of armed might to achieve a defined goal far more closely than the 'cabinet wars' of the eighteenth century, which had often been prolonged and bloody. The relative 'success' of both wars in this respect acted as a counterweight to the memory of the casualty returns by sustaining faith in the chimera that future wars might be equally swift and decisive.

War Finance

All German states entered the peace after 1815 heavily indebted, but Prussia's position was considerably worse than Austria's. Tax reforms produced modest results and the Hohenzollern monarchy was only saved by a loan of nearly 33 million tlr brokered in London in 1818 by Mayer Amschel Rothschild. With debts still double those of 1810, the monarchy was finally forced to admit the extent of the crisis to the public in 1820, enabling liabilities to be consolidated at lower rates of interest, thus halving the cost of debt servicing to the equivalent of one-tenth of revenue.[87]

Austria's debt continued to rise, from 706.5 million fl to over 1 billion fl, between 1818 and 1848, or more than three times that of Prussia's, while the cost of servicing this consumed a quarter of revenue. Nonetheless, it benefited from the windfall of French reparations and revenue from territory occupied until 1818, deriving 122.8 million fl from this, compared to Prussia's share of about 75 million fl. It also avoided a public admission of its difficulties. Like other powers, Austria slashed defence spending during the long years of relative peace after 1815, reducing it to 50 million fl a year by 1848, or around a fifth of government expenditure, compared to half three decades earlier.

The reluctance of both great powers to abandon traditional financial secrecy contrasted with the south German states, which adopted constitutional government with parliamentary scrutiny of budgets. Nonetheless, parliaments showed little interest in military spending, beyond brief moments of patriotism during the war scares of 1840 and 1859, and the general emergency in 1848–9. Bavaria's annual army budget declined from 8.2 million fl in the 1820s to around 7 million fl, before rising modestly to 8.5 million fl in the 1840s, 11 million fl during the next decade, and finally 16 million fl after 1859. Foreign envoys were convinced Bavarian kings were squandering the money on their lavish palaces, and funds assigned to fortress construction had to be diverted to meet essentials like soldiers' pay, while the army budget remained burdened with a large pensions bill, despite veterans' allowances remaining unchanged between 1822 and 1871.[88]

The relative weakness of the German powers in European terms is demonstrated by the fact that Britain coped well after Waterloo despite having a debt nearly nine times larger than Austria's, while even France, the defeated power, managed well enough despite owing more than three times as much. Steady population growth after 1815 helped generate more revenue, but the German economies remained weaker in per capita terms. Defence continued to consume the lion's share of the budget alongside debts. Prussia was at the upper limit, devoting a third of expenditure to the army, compared to a fifth in Württemberg, but even the cost of maintaining its federal contingent of just 180 men took nearly one-seventh of the Free City of Lübeck's expenditure. The same was true in Switzerland where, for example, well over 40 per cent of the Genevan budget went on defence and security costs in the 1820s.[89]

With little room for error, even modest military action threatened to destabilize budgets. The costs of partial mobilizations during the 1830–1 revolutions prompted Prussia to cut military service from three to two years as an economy measure in 1833. Each state continued to meet its own expenses under the German Confederation's system of collective security, making it difficult to calculate the cost of the wars across 1848–50, but Denmark's experience gives some indication: it spent 140.4 million tlr on defending its claims to Schleswig-Holstein, or not far short of the equivalent of Prussia's entire national debt.[90]

Although the Prussian monarchy swiftly jettisoned many of the promised reforms, its acceptance of parliamentary budgetary control in 1848 significantly improved its finances, enabling nearly half of its accumulated debts to be paid off. Government borrowing added significantly to debts that had reached 290 million tlr by 1866, but over half of these new loans were invested in railway construction, which contributed significantly to economic growth and finally enabled the government to produce a surplus by 1863. The mobilizations of 1854–5 and 1859 each cost over 30 million tlr, or considerably more than the 22.5 million tlr spent fighting Denmark in 1864, which was covered from existing revenue without recourse to fresh borrowing. Prussia was thus in a strong position to fight Austria in 1866. That war cost 146 million tlr, but 55.6 million tlr was recouped from reparations, and most of the rest covered by reserves and the sale of railway shares.[91] Overall debt rose only modestly to 321 million tlr. France was obliged to pay 2 billion francs after 1871, or two and a half times the cost of the war. The surplus fuelled the *Gründerzeit* economic boom that soon stuttered in 1873 as Germany followed most of the world into prolonged economic difficulties wrought by profound changes in the global economy. However, the country's dynamic growth during the last two peacetime decades absorbed the spiralling armaments and defence costs, despite the fierce debates in the Reichstag over spending.

Austria's experience both reflected and contributed to its decline relative to Prussia. Austria spent over 2 billion fl on defence between 1848 and 1858, or twice as much as its northern rival and almost equal to France, which had a much stronger economy. Yet, though annual revenue more than tripled to 502 fl million across 1848–66, it failed to keep up with rising expenditure. The war of 1859 cost 295 million fl, causing a deficit of 51 per cent, or five times the usual level. Unsurprisingly, by 1865, Austria's debt was 2.9 billion fl, and it was forced to borrow 90 million fl at extortionate rates from French bankers to fight Prussia in 1866, which cost another 230.5 million fl. The continued burden of debt after 1848 prevented Austria from investing in growth, thereby widening its gap with other European powers, and it was not until the 1880s that the budget returned to surplus. Complex regulations intended to prevent fraud proved counterproductive. Officials avoided the burdensome paperwork by relying on informal contacts, leading to over-pricing and corruption. The problems had already been obvious since the early 1860s, but the government and army feared a full investigation would harm their reputations. Meanwhile, civilian politicians seized the opportunity of recovering budgetary control in 1861 to take their revenge on the military men who despised them by halving expenditure on the army by 1865.[92]

Austria-Hungary's population grew three times faster than the rise in defence expenditure. Germany spent twice as much, but despite increasing this faster than either France or Russia, its defence spending also fell behind its rising wealth. By 1890, Italy was spending over a fifth more on defence than Austria-Hungary. As in Germany, the Habsburgs' development of a powerful navy created a rival for scarce funds. Naval expenditure climbed slowly from 15.85 million fl (1868) to 35.68 fl (1899), before averaging 58 million fl across the next decade with the switch from an Adriatic to a Mediterranean fleet. The decision to add dreadnoughts pushed the annual bill to over 170 million fl by 1912, when it represented around 22 per cent of total defence spending, or three times the proportion in 1868. Despite these increases, defence remained only just over a quarter of total state expenditure. The growing complexity of weaponry and the armed forces generally meant that war was rapidly becoming more expensive. Austria-Hungary's occupation of Bosnia-Herzegovina cost a relatively modest 75 million fl, but the two partial mobilizations of 1908 and 1911–12 consumed the equivalent of a staggering 2 billion fl.[93]

When assessing the impact of military expenditure, it is necessary to remember that all nineteenth-century states remained 'small' compared to their twentieth- and twenty-first-century counterparts. Prussia was highly unusual in spending about 14 per cent of GDP during the 1820s, as the average across nineteenth-century Europe was rarely above 10 per cent. Much of public expenditure remained devolved to the communal, level where it was spent on welfare, education, infrastructure, and policing. Communal expenditure rose more proportionately across the nineteenth century, even after central governments became more active in these fields as well, notably in Germany after 1883 with the introduction of universal welfare entitlements. Including the communal level, overall public spending climbed to 17 per cent of GDP, but that was still only between half and two-thirds of what has been common after 1919. Moreover, the growth of non-military expenditure reduced the proportion consumed by defence from 27 per cent (1874) to 22 per cent (1913). These figures underscore the more 'limited' character of nineteenth-century warfare relative to earlier and future conflicts.[94]

Economic Impact

Beyond taxation and the commercialization of debt through the sale of bonds, defence primarily affected the economy through procurement policies. Austria, Prussia, and medium-sized states like Bavaria continued to rely on state factories to produce much of their arms, uniforms, and equipment after 1815, while smaller states and the Swiss cantons generally bought from commercial firms, notably those in Liège, which remained Europe's primary centre for small arms production. The arms business remained risky, given the unpredictability of demand and the high costs of developing new products, while the long period of relative peace deterred new entrants. Prussia spread its orders after 1815 to encourage private firms to boost capacity, but most had folded, merged, or been taken into state ownership by the early 1850s.[95]

By then, industrialization was gathering pace and forced governments to find new ways of working with manufacturers, usually against the initial wishes of officers. Innovations in design and production techniques increased the tempo of change, adding to the uncertainties in choosing between rival types of the same weapon. Prussia created a testing commission to assess new weaponry in 1809, but the growing volume of business meant this was reorganized in the 1850s. Similar bodies were introduced in other states, while the Swiss Confederation centralized inspection at its main depot in Thun. Politics continued to hinder standardization in Germany and Switzerland into the 1870s, since each state or canton wanted to control its own purchasing. However, firms also competed to demonstrate the superiority of their designs, most of which remained unproven before the wars between 1859 and 1871.

Württemberg retooled its government arms factory, established in a former Augustinian convent at Oberndorf in 1812, to convert its existing rifles to the Dreyse system in 1867. However, even this urgent task merely increased the work force from fifty to 200, and the factory remained in deficit until it was sold to the Mauser family, who had been its chief gunsmiths since its foundation. Franz Mauser had worked for Remington in the United States and had secured a patent to develop a superior bolt-action version of the Dreyse rifle using metallic cartridges. After failing to interest France or Austria, his brother Peter Paul secured the contract to replace the increasingly obsolete needle gun in the Prussian army with what became the G71 Mauser. The success of this weapon ensured that Mauser remained the German rifle of choice well into the twentieth century, but domestic orders were never sufficient to sustain the business and it was the 1887 deal to supply 550,000 rifles and carbines and 100 million cartridges to Turkey that secured the company's fortunes.[96]

The same was true for Krupp, the most famous of all German arms manufacturers, which had started in 1811 as a steel producer. Alfred Krupp, son of the firm's founder, secured international attention by casting a flawless two-ton steel ingot in 1851, but it was not until May 1859 that Prussia placed its first order for his revolutionary cast-steel rifled artillery. The superior performance of Krupp's guns in 1866 and 1870–1 resulted in a flood of orders, earning him the sobriquet of the 'cannon king', while his factory in Essen became the 'arsenal of the Reich'. The company had expanded from 122 employees in 1847 to over 43,000 by 1902, or more than all the state factories and shipyards combined. Krupp built the grandiose Villa Hügel, connected to his factory by its own railway station. He ostentatiously supported the monarchy and right-wing politics, but in reality only made parsimonious donations to lobby groups like the Navy League, while extorting government loans to overcome temporary financial difficulties in 1865, 1870, and 1874 by threatening to let French banks assume a controlling stake in his firm. However, the government refused to grant him a monopoly, while its own purchases were insufficient to keep him in business, forcing him to rely heavily on exports. Krupp was also unusual in being one of the few large firms for which arms production remained the core business, leaving it quite vulnerable to market fluctuations.[97]

There were relatively few other large arms producers. The Deutsche Waffen- und Munitionsfabriken (DWM) began as a merger of two other firms in 1896, one of which had begun as a sewing-machine company founded by Ludwig Loewe. The Loewe firm maintained a separate existence to spread its risk, and invested heavily in developing the Belgian state arms producer, Fabrique Nationale Herstal, making Mausers under licence, while DWM was linked directly to other foreign arms firms in Budapest, Liège, and Newcastle. Rheinische Metallwaren- und Maschinenfabrik was co-founded in 1889 by Heinrich Ehrhardt who, like Dreyse, Mauser, and Krupp, was an inventor turned entrepreneur. Ehrhardt beat Krupp to the 1897 and 1905 contracts to re-equip the German army with field artillery, but his firm continued to engage in other markets, including being one of the pioneers of the automobile industry.

The same was broadly true for Austria, though on a much-reduced scale, reflecting its lesser importance as an industrial economy. The Werndl rifle factory began as a family business in 1821 and only switched to rifles in 1864, becoming the Österreichische Waffengesellschaft five years later. Although it produced over 6 million rifles between 1871 and 1914, and remained the Habsburg army's primary small-arms supplier, its most successful element was the Steyr Mannlicher subdivision, named after Ferdinand Mannlicher, inventor of a new repeating rifle in 1890, which relied heavily on export sales, notably to Chile. Meanwhile, heavy weapons were supplied by Škoda, which began in 1859 by making sugar-mill machinery in Pilsen and, like the Mauser factory, achieved its success once it was bought out by its chief engineer, Emil Škoda, who connected it to the railway in 1886. Within four years the firm had become the principal supplier of artillery and machine guns to the Habsburg forces, as well as producing forgings for warships and liners.[98]

Switzerland's small domestic market led to the continuation of the state as the primary arms producer far longer than in Germany or Austria. The imposition of greater uniformity over clothing and weaponry in 1848 encouraged the centralization of production and led to the development of gunpowder and weapons production at Thun, the Confederation's principal arsenal, after 1856. Full centralization was completed in 1874 and saw the reorganization of production along business lines as K&W Thun. Meanwhile, uniforms were produced after 1871 by another state firm that became W&F Bern, and which also made small arms, including the Vetterli rifle, an adaptation of the American Winchester repeating rifle that was also adopted by the Italian army. Reluctance to invest heavily in research and development, given the state's own limited needs, hindered the growth of both firms and left the army dependent on German imports for artillery and machine guns until these were cut off in 1915 by the First World War.[99]

With motor transport still in its infancy, armies relied heavily on horses, both for cavalry and for transport, with a ratio of roughly one animal for every four soldiers. Unlike the eighteenth century, cavalry and artillery units maintained a full complement of horses in peacetime, but mobilization still required additional animals for the units composed of reservists. The expansion of cavalry and especially the artillery with additional ammunition wagons all increased the number of animals required. By 1914 the German cavalry alone needed nearly 9,000 remounts annually. There were around 4 million horses each in Germany and Austria-Hungary at that point, but selective breeding programmes had encouraged the military to accept only large animals and only two in five horses met the required size. While state stud farms supplied most peacetime needs, those in wartime were now to be met by conscription, which would severely damage all agriculture during the First World War.[100] The 7th Field Company of the South West African Schutztruppe represented an exotic exception in being mounted on camels imported from the Sudan, whose descendants still roam the Kalahari Desert as the only ones in Sub-Saharan Africa.

Naval Construction

Warship-building only emerged as a significant industrial sector with the establishment of the German navy in 1872. The new Admiralty ruled that all warships had to be built in Germany using local materials, but the navy's small size discouraged firms from specializing in this sector, and the navy continued to rely on ships constructed in state yards. The total value of warship construction increased significantly after

1895, but around 40 per cent of warships built in private yards were for export. Admiral Tirpitz turned to private firms for his massive building programme after 1898, since only their yards could handle the new, larger warships, and because he wanted to win their support as a pro-navy lobby. However, he created a highly competitive tendering process, forcing firms to undercut each other to secure contracts. This directly affected Krupp, which saw naval construction as an opportunity to off-set the fall in army contracts, as well as to sell its revolutionary nickel-steel armour plate. Tirpitz forced Krupp to slash its prices for armour plate by 31 per cent across 1900–7, making a considerable saving given that armour represented a third of the cost of a large warship. The unit price for guns, which accounted for another third, was also reduced by encouraging Krupp and Rheinmetall to bid against each other. Krupp's bankers forced the firm into a cartel with other warship builders that seriously threatened Tirpitz by 1914, but the outbreak of war prevented this from having any real impact.[101]

Profits could be high on individual components, but overall German firms did not make much from warship-building and only six of the sixty-three biggest yards engaged in this by 1914, while just 4 per cent of Germany's steel production was used for warships, compared to 30 per cent in Britain. Britain increased its share of global shipbuilding to nearly 70 per cent, whereas Germany's share grew only modestly to about 11 per cent during the great naval race when the country also ceased to be a significant warship exporter. Around 1,000 firms supplied the German army, but purely military products rarely counted as core business, and their share even in Krupp's overall turnover declined to 34 per cent. The handful of major arms manufacturers survived primarily through exports, though these were buoyed by the German army's high reputation. While important for a few prominent firms, arms production employed no more than 2 per cent of the total industrial workforce and arms sales were only significant in trade relations with Turkey and Romania.

The sector was even smaller in Austria where, in 1911, there were only twenty-one firms specializing in arms production with a combined work-force of 30,000, of which Škoda and the warship builder STT were the largest. There were another four firms in Hungary employing 10,000 workers, while a further 150 businesses benefited indirectly from naval construction. The government deliberately awarded contracts to Austrian and Hungarian firms to appease the monarchy's two parliaments and ensure they passed the navy budget, even though buying foreign-built warships would have been some 8.5 per cent cheaper per ton.[102]

Thus, both Germany and Austria-Hungary were comparatively late in developing military-industrial complexes, which also remained relatively weak both economically and politically. In Austria's case, influence was limited to where contracts were awarded, not the decision to construct ships in the first place. Firms also operated internationally, with German companies being particularly dependent on exports, which in turn relied on their government remaining on good terms with potential purchasers. German firms joined British, French, and American companies in the Harvey syndicate of 1894, which attempted unsuccessfully to fix prices for armour plate, while the Austro-Hungarian torpedo manufacturer Whitehead established a factory in Weymouth to sell its products to the Royal Navy.[103] Military expenditure thus only made a modest impact on economic development and for many firms the outbreak of war in 1914 proved bad for business.

PART V

Democratizing War

13

Demagogues and Democrats

THE FIRST WORLD WAR 1914–18

The 'Spirit of 1914'

In 1914, Imperial Germany and Austria-Hungary embarked on a conflict requiring an unprecedented level of popular mobilization. Beneath the rhetoric of nations in arms, nineteenth-century armies had declined proportionately to population. Military service had been a short episode in most men's lives, if they had donned a uniform at all, and few had seen action. Women had overwhelmingly been civilians, most of whom expected to remain unaffected by warfare. After 1914, Germans engaged in what soon became termed 'total war', leaving no part of life unaffected. Although directed from above, this effort was sustained to a considerable extent by self-mobilization and a willingness to accept hardship and loss.[1]

This argument is increasingly accepted in the scholarship on the First World War, but it remains controversial when applied to the 1939–45 war. Yet, as this and the following chapters will show, the scale of the German effort in both conflicts depended on the readiness, albeit often reluctant, of ordinary men and women to participate. That preparedness did not evaporate with the total defeat in 1945, but was revived and sustained throughout the Cold War, though it was now open to greater criticism and was often performed much less willingly, notably in the German Democratic Republic (DDR). Only since 1990 has national defence ceased to play such a determining role in most German people's lives to the point that some now fear that the positive attributes of a citizen army are being lost.

That Germans are not alone in Europe in sharing this trajectory is an important reminder not to detach their military history from its broader context.[2] This chapter examines the German experience across the five major periods from 1914 to the present: the unprecedented mobilization of the First World War; the contested demobilization and gradual re-armament of the interwar era; the violence of genocidal war between 1939 and 1945; the renewed rearmament under the very different circumstances of the Cold War; and the downsizing and near-constant restructuring since 1990 as all countries have sought to adapt to what is increasingly termed a new 'security environment'.

Imperial Germany and Austria-Hungary, known collectively as the Central Powers, had a combined population of 118 million in 1914, against 266 million in Britain, France, Russia, and Serbia, who together controlled a further 448.4 million colonial subjects, compared to the Germans' 10 million. Although the Central Powers initially mobilized 3.485 million troops, they were already far outnumbered by their enemies' 5.726 million, backed by a further 500,000 colonial soldiers. Bulgaria and the Ottoman Empire joined the Central Powers later in 1914, but their assistance was more than offset by the intervention of Japan (1914), Italy (1915), Portugal and Romania (1916), and most notably by the United States in 1917, which added a further 103 million people on the Allied side. Brazil, various Central American states, China, and Siam also joined the Allies after 1917.[3]

These odds were not unexpected by German and Habsburg planners, who counted on superior organization and morale to secure a decisive victory before the Allies could bring their full human and material resources to bear. The mounting international crisis across late July 1914 sparked a run on the banks and panic buying. Beyond a few patriotic demonstrations in Vienna and Berlin, the 'spirit of 1914' was characterized more by grim resolve than popular enthusiasm. Most inhabitants knew war was dangerous, but while socialists and trades unions attracted strong support for their anti-war rallies, Germans and Austrians generally did not blame their own governments for the breakdown of peace and saw military service as a patriotic duty.[4]

Germany was better prepared militarily and politically than Austria-Hungary. Standing on the balcony of his Berlin palace at 7.30 p.m. on 31 July, Kaiser Wilhelm II famously announced that 'I no longer recognize any parties or confessions; today we are all German brothers and only German brothers.'[5] This declaration was especially aimed at the Social

Democratic Party (SPD) and the Catholic Centre Party (*Zentrum*), both of which had made electoral gains across the past decade at the expense of conservatives and Protestants. The call to a *Burgfrieden* (Civic Truce) was underpinned by keeping the Reichstag in session, despite simultaneously enacting the 1851 state of siege law, which empowered the army regional commanders to assume wide civilian powers. The SPD responded positively, with only fourteen of its ninety-two Reichstag deputies opposing the vote on war credits on 3 August.

By contrast, Emperor Franz Josef and the Habsburg elite showed little inclination to invite their subjects to participate in the war effort. Austria-Hungary's Reichsrat, or common parliament, had already been suspended in March 1914 following raucous disputes between the different nationalist parties, and the building was converted into a military hospital. The Habsburgs soon realized their mistake but were never as successful as their German counterparts in rallying popular support. The Austrian government ruled by decree, and while the Hungarian parliament remained in session, this simply served as a platform to criticize Habsburg management of the war. The Austrians distrusted the Hungarians, many of whom saw an opportunity to bargain for greater autonomy in the Dual Monarchy, while the army regarded civil servants as hinderers, not helpers, in national mobilization. While comparing favourably with its ally, Germany nonetheless failed to engage its citizens as effectively as the British, French, Belgian, Serbian, and later American governments. The Reichstag delegated legislative power to the empire's upper house, the Bundesrat controlled by the monarchs and princes, while the failure to involve the SPD in government or grant trades unions a meaningful say in war management fuelled a growing sense of disenfranchisement.[6]

Unlike that of 1870, mobilization in 1914 was the first of a genuinely mass army, involving the call-up of reservists into new formations, as well as strengthening existing ones. It was here that German preparations excelled. Boots fitted, food was available, and troop trains ran on time, all boosting confidence. Whereas German trains heading west sported optimistic slogans about dining out in Paris, those leaving Habsburg Bohemia for the Eastern Front were daubed 'meat export abroad' by their unwilling occupants. Austria-Hungary was so unready that it gratefully accepted the donation of 2.5 million old rifle cartridges which the Germans had condemned as 'suitable only for the Chinese army'.[7]

Meanwhile, Switzerland also mobilized on 5 August having been informed by Germany that it would invade Belgium. The parliament elected Ulrich Wille the Elder as federal general, despite misgivings that he favoured the Central Powers. Since the Sonderbund War of 1847, religious differences had been largely replaced by the country's linguistic division along the north-south *Röstigraben* (Potato Pancake Ditch) between French and German speakers. France, however, remained confident that the Swiss would defend themselves, and ruled out any idea of crossing their territory to outflank the Germans. Most militiamen were soon sent home, with a reduced number serving on rotation to guard the frontiers. Two intelligence officers were dismissed for passing information to Austria, but otherwise both army and society remained united behind their neutrality and obeyed their government's appeal to set an example.[8]

The Global War

The odds against the Central Powers increased still further with the swift loss of Germany's colonies. Australian and New Zealand forces captured the Pacific islands by mid-September 1914. The Japanese, with some British assistance, captured Jiaozhou Bay in November, the heavily outnumbered German defenders having been assisted by the crew of an elderly Austrian cruiser.[9] Of the African colonies, Togo surrendered after three weeks' resistance to British and French troops, while German South West Africa was taken by the South Africans in July 1915. German Cameroon held out six months longer, but only German East Africa proved a major challenge. Colonel Lettow-Vorbeck, the local commander, disobeyed the civilian government and pursued his own ruthless war of attrition against a range of enemies which eventually totalled 160,000 British, Belgian, Portuguese, South African, and colonial troops, backed by 1 million African porters, a tenth of whom died. Lettow-Vorbeck's forces never numbered more than 15,000, mostly locally recruited Askaris whose loyalty he retained by allowing their families to accompany them and to live off the land. He only surrendered on 14 November 1918, three days after the war had ended in Europe.[10]

Lettow-Vorbeck was later celebrated as an exemplar of German determination, but his resistance made little difference to the wider course of the war. The Allies were able to deploy large numbers of Indian and African colonial troops on the Western Front, as well as against the

Ottoman Empire once it joined the Central Powers on 29 October 1914. Germany's two modern warships in the Mediterranean had already escaped to Constantinople, where their commander, Admiral Souchon, assumed the direction of the Ottoman navy.[11] Other German advisers soon arrived, notably Admiral von Usedom and General Liman von Sanders, both of whom subsequently played important roles in directing operations. The Ottomans' entry into the war diverted Allied resources, notably during the costly attempt to force the Dardanelles in the Gallipoli campaign of 1915. However, the Ottomans faced numerous difficulties and were eventually forced to abandon their Middle Eastern empire by October 1918.

The importance of these setbacks was not so much the loss of Germany's colonies themselves, but that within weeks of the war breaking out the Allies controlled most of the world's shipping lanes and resources. The escape of the two warships to the Bosphorus looked like a major coup, but the fact remained that the Mediterranean (like the Pacific, Indian, and South Atlantic oceans) had become Allied lakes, while Germany lacked a rational plan to challenge that.

Stuck in the Mud

Important though these theatres were to the wider story of the war, the fate of the Central Powers was always going to be determined in Europe. Germany mobilized according to its modified 'Schlieffen Plan' with seven armies totalling over 1.5 million men in the west. The first two, containing over a third of that total, formed the main strike force intended to outflank the French by invading Belgium to the north, with another three armies (totalling 560,000) advancing through Luxembourg and the Ardennes in support. The remaining two armies (347,000) deployed further south to defend Lorraine and Alsace. The 8th Army (150,000) was positioned to defend East Prussia, while another 350,000 reservists were still being formed into units in home depots.

The German plan depended on breaking through the fortified Liège sector and on to the Belgian plain fast enough to swing southwards towards Paris before the British Expeditionary Force (BEF) could reinforce the French, and before the Russians overwhelmed the defenders of East Prussia. The schedule slipped immediately and though the first two armies punched past Liège, most of the Belgian army escaped to Antwerp and after a further retreat to the coast continued to resist for the rest of the war. The Germans pressed on, assisted by poor Anglo-French coordination and the fact that the BEF largely lacked a plan of what to do once it arrived on the northern French coast. By late August the BEF had been outflanked at Mons and compelled to retreat, but only after adding to the Germans' delay. Rather than swinging south-west round Paris, General Kluck, commanding the 1st Army, was compelled to advance more directly southwards to maintain contact with the slower-moving 2nd Army to his left. Shortage of cavalry prevented adequate reconnaissance and added to the mounting anxiety of Moltke the Younger and the rest of the General Staff, which had been mobilized as the High Command (*Oberste Heeresleitung*, OHL). A combination of stiff French resistance and a renewed advance on the river Marne by the BEF outflanked Kluck, who fell back on 9 September. Germany had already lost 50 per cent more combat deaths than during the entire Franco-German War.[12]

Moltke suffered a nervous breakdown and was replaced on 14 September by Erich von Falkenhayn, a trained staff officer who had previously advised the Chinese army, before being promoted over the heads of thirty more senior generals as Prussia's war minister in 1913.[13] Concerned that the morale of the 1st Army might collapse if it retreated further, Falkenhayn pushed westwards along the Franco-Belgian frontier, fighting a sequence of battles in what became known as the 'race to the sea' hoping to turn the Allied flank before the front line closed the last gap by reaching the coast. By 25 November he was forced to accept that the Allies had blocked his every move and he instructed the army to take up positional warfare (*Stellungskrieg*) by digging in. Intended as a temporary measure, it characterized the Western Front until the end of the war.

Moltke's tinkering with Schlieffen's plan had little to do with its failure, though he was swiftly blamed for it. The root cause was the army's conviction that its overall strategy stood any reasonable chance of success at all. Their opponents certainly provided them with some opportunities, but the whole enterprise was a huge gamble 'requiring too many things to go impossibly right, and too many opponents to make obliging mistakes'.[14] None of the Germans' errors was individually fatal, but their accumulative impact removed any slim chance of success. Worse, the Germans stuck to their strategy, whereas the Allies, notably the French commander Joseph Joffre, accepted their original plans had failed and adapted.[15] Although their failure was systemic, the Germans blamed individuals rather than how they took strategic decisions: Moltke, Kluck, and thirty-two other generals were removed, but no fundamental reforms were undertaken.

The Duo

Success proved even more dangerous since it appeared to confirm all would ultimately be well. In addition to the Marne, the battle of Tannenberg provides a key part of the explanation why the Germans ultimately lost the war by sustaining a false belief that decisive victory was possible. Russia began its offensive on 4 August, opening what became known to the Germans and Austrians as the Eastern Front. The attack came much sooner than the Germans had expected, because the Russians advanced before their army was fully mobilized. At around 600,000 men they nonetheless outnumbered the German defenders of East Prussia four to one. Initial incursions into German territory caused widespread panic, prompting Moltke to goad the local commander, General Prittwitz, into an ill-considered counter-attack. Once this failed, Prittwitz was removed and replaced by Paul von Hindenburg.

Hindenburg met Erich Ludendorff, just appointed as his new chief of staff, as they headed east by train to the front. The two men soon became known as the Duo, thanks to their close working relationship and complementary but contrasting characters. Hindenburg, the senior of the two, had been brought out of retirement at the start of the war, having fought in the Wars of Unification as a junior officer. He looked so much the part of an archetypal Prussian general that he was open to caricature. His outward calm masked a cunning and manipulative character who was deeply concerned for his own image and determined to ensure someone else took the blame for any mistakes.[16] The mercurial Ludendorff had played an important role in preparing the Schlieffen Plan and later in pressuring Moltke the Younger to modify it. He counted as the Duo's brains, even though he 'never rose above the intellectual level of a regimental colonel'.[17] Like Hindenburg, he hailed from eastern Prussia and had graduated from the War Academy, but by contrast came from a family of small businessmen, rather than the landholding Junker class. Strong-willed and highly strung, he had an almost limitless capacity for desk work, while the subsequent deaths of two of his stepsons redoubled his determination to win the war.

Unlike the secretive and prickly Falkenhayn, Ludendorff was open to ideas and encouraged debate among his staff, though he tended to fall out with clever subordinates like Fritz von Lossberg, who would emerge as one of Germany's foremost tacticians, and who bluntly pointed to the flaws in his grand schemes. Ludendorff preferred to work with men like his friend and factotum Max Bauer, who literally had a rubber stamp of his boss's signature to issue orders. Like Bauer and Admiral Tirpitz, Ludendorff was convinced Germany was battling shadowy, conspiratorial forces that he increasingly associated with Jews and socialists. He was obsessed with the Siegfried myth, recently popularized by Wagner's operas, and named many of the army's major operations after characters in the story.

Arriving at the Eastern Front, the Duo had to act quickly, prompting Hindenburg to adopt a plan already drafted by Prittwitz's staff, notably Colonel Max Hoffmann, though this did not prevent him from subsequently taking the credit. The following operations saw the two Russian armies smashed in quick succession at Tannenberg (Stęberk) (26–31 August) and Masurian Lakes (9–11 September), losing 270,000 casualties, or five times more than the Germans.[18] Ludendorff was going to name the first battle after the village of Frögenau in his report, until one of his staff pointed to the proximity of Tannenberg, where the Poles had defeated the Teutonic Knights in 1410. The choice of name added to the victory's symbolism, especially as it coincided with the costly defeats in the west. Tannenberg forged the public perception of Hindenburg as embodying not just military skill, but the masculine virtues of determination, strong nerves, readiness for sacrifice, and a sense of duty. Across the next four years, the Duo would argue that the war could be won despite the odds if other Germans applied the same characteristics.

Habsburg Failure

Austria-Hungary's failure negated whatever might have been gained strategically from Tannenberg. Conrad von Hötzendorf, the Habsburg chief of staff, amended the monarchy's war plan at the last minute, making a bad compromise between the two options of concentrating his forces either against Serbia or Russia. His decision was driven by the recognition that the Habsburgs had to please the Germans, who had left their own Eastern Front inadequately defended. The Habsburgs would remain the tail to the German dog throughout the war.

Russia had invested huge resources in improving its railways in Poland and was able to concentrate 1 million troops to invade Galicia. While the Habsburgs were better led at unit level than their opponents, soldiers in both armies were unenthusiastic.[19] Conrad's belated alterations created absurdities, such as Tirolean mountain infantry, equipped with ice picks and other items for winter warfare, joining their equally reluctant comrades trudging through Galicia in the sweltering heat. Outnumbered and outgunned, the Habsburg offensive soon stalled and then collapsed suddenly on 5 September when the army evacuated Galicia and retreated behind the Carpathian Mountains. Over 120,000 men were trapped in the new fortress of Przemyśl. Another offensive across February–March 1915 failed to relieve them and they eventually surrendered after six months' defence. The psychological blow has been dubbed Austria-Hungary's Stalingrad.[20]

Meanwhile, Serbia – Austria-Hungary's real target – stoutly repelled two invasions by over-confident Habsburg generals. The successive failures alarmed Germany, which feared the Russians might strike directly into Silesia. A new 9th Army was created by pulling men from the west along with new reserve formations, while three divisions were sent directly to join Habsburg units in a combined *Südarmee* under German command to strengthen the southern front along the Carpathians. Habsburg units were gradually beefed up with German heavy artillery and planes as these became available.

Falkenhayn reluctantly agreed to prioritize the Eastern Front in 1915. While Hindenburg pinned down part of Russia's forces in the north, a combined German-Habsburg offensive finally recovered Galicia by June, before pushing into Russian Poland, taking Warsaw on 4 August, and finally seizing Lithuania the following month, having inflicted over 1 million casualties on the enemy. These successes prompted Bulgaria to declare for the Central Powers on 6 September, assisting Habsburg troops in conquering most of Serbia and Montenegro.

However, the Allies opened new fronts in Macedonia and at Salonika, negating much of the advantage derived from Bulgaria's intervention. Worse, the Central Powers' success failed to persuade Italy to honour the pre-war Triple Alliance, and it instead joined the Allies by invading Austria on 23 May. The Italians attacked before they were fully prepared and, despite their vast numerical superiority, were repulsed from the Tirol and blocked at the Isonzo gorge on the high plateau between the Adriatic and the Alpine foothills. The front would remain in roughly the same place until June 1917, by which time Habsburg forces had repelled eleven offensives at a total combined cost to both sides of 1 million men. Locally, this can be considered a success, and the troops were notably more committed to defending their homeland than when invading Serbia or Russia. However, the new Italian front was a distraction the monarchy could not afford and undermined its already flagging efforts elsewhere.[21]

Already by the end of 1914, Germany had suffered 800,000 casualties, including 116,000 killed, or two and a half times the entire cost of the 1870–1 war. At nearly 1 million, Austria-Hungary's losses were even higher, while it suffered another 870,000 casualties and prisoners during the 'Carpathian Winter' and fall of Przemyśl. Over four-fifths of the pre-war infantry had become casualties or prisoners, as had half of the regular officers. Another million men were lost during the recovery of Galicia and conquest of Poland. There were no trained reserves, and by mid-1915 Habsburg forces consisted of untrained conscripts led by equally inexperienced junior officers. For the Habsburgs, the switch to positional warfare was a necessity as the army was in no condition to resume the attack.[22]

The Victory Peace

These horrendous losses occurred while the German and Habsburg elites were expanding their war aims. Pre-war planning lacked any strategic vision and merely concentrated on how to achieve victory, not what to do with it if it could be obtained. The German chancellor, Bethmann-Hollweg, wanted to keep his options open to allow scope for diplomacy, but was persuaded to accept a draft list of objectives on 9 September 1914. France was to be partially demilitarized, compelled to pay a huge indemnity, and cede its best mining regions to Germany. Liège would be annexed and Belgium reduced to a satellite. A German-led customs union would be created to include France, Belgium, the Netherlands, Denmark, Poland, Austria-Hungary, and perhaps Italy and Scandinavia. The intention was to make Germany 'blockade proof', meaning it could withstand Britain's naval power. Additional African colonies would also be demanded from France, Belgium, and Portugal. These goals vastly exceeded Habsburg ambitions, which were limited to some strategic border areas and the desire to reduce, but not annex, Serbia.

The Allies had their own expansive plans, notably Russia, but Germany's were excessive and contradicted the government's claim to be fighting a defensive war. Intellectuals broadly endorsed this 'September Programme', but industrialists and German royalty had their own ideas. Bavaria's king felt he should rule Belgium, while those of Saxony and Württemberg saw themselves as future Polish monarchs. The German navy wanted Belgian and Baltic ports, as well as more overseas bases. Already in autumn 1914, Falkenhayn recommended renouncing annexations to split the Allies, but he was overruled, especially as Tannenberg and the subsequent conquest of Poland and Lithuania later in 1915 encouraged the elite to expand their ambitions still further. Desperate to sustain the fraying Burgfrieden, the government tended to add each major lobby's pet project to its list, while conservatives pushed the idea of a Victory Peace to silence leftist critiques and persuade Germans that their continued sacrifices would be rewarded.[23]

The desire for more deterred the Central Powers from using their not inconsiderable gains to bargain for favourable terms, despite opportunities across 1915–16. By the end of 1915, Austria-Hungary held three-quarters of Serbia and, together with Germany, had conquered Russia's Polish and Lithuanian lands. Germany held most of Belgium, and large parts of northeastern France with its 2 million inhabitants. The conquest of two-thirds of Romania during the second half of 1916 pushed the area under German control to 525,000 square kilometres with 27 million people, or equivalent to almost its entire national territory and 40 per cent of its own population.

Conquered territory was placed under military administration. Poland was belatedly declared a kingdom in November 1916, as yet without a king or confirmed independent future. Limited concessions were offered in the hope that Poles would volunteer to fight Russia. Ludendorff hoped for 1 million soldiers, but only 4,700 under Józef Piłsudski had been mustered by the spring of 1917; however, they were rightly suspected of being unreliable nationalists.[24]

Stalemate

Falkenhayn remained convinced the war could only be won in the west, especially as the country's primary objectives lay there. With Austria-Hungary having lost offensive capacity, the task fell largely to Germany. Throughout 1915 both sides had experimented with ways to break the deadlock in the west, without success. Falkenhayn concluded it was better to let the enemy waste their strength in futile attacks and decided to prompt them into this by threatening Verdun at the northeast angle of the Allied defensive line. It remains unclear how far this was a coherent plan, or simply a subsequent justification for his own failure to take the town.[25]

Both sides poured in reinforcements from February 1916, thereby contradicting Falkenhayn's ostensible goal. Nearly four-fifths of French infantrymen served on rotation at Verdun, elevating the battle to a truly national struggle. Around 1.35 million tons of shells had been fired by the time Falkenhayn finally abandoned the operation in December, having lost 337,000 men killed, wounded, captured, or missing, or marginally fewer than the French at 378,000.

Meanwhile, British forces attacked along the Somme river in the summer, in part to relieve pressure on the French. The ensuing sequence of battles has become a byword in Britain for the futility of war, yet British and Allied troops performed creditably under terrible conditions, putting the Germans under great strain, and contributing to the decision to abandon the attack on Verdun. The five-month campaign cost the Allies 615,000 men while the German defenders, who included both Adolf Hitler and Otto Frank, father of the diarist Anne, probably lost nearly as many soldiers.[26] Both sides reacted to casualties similarly, believing it was necessary to press on so that the initial cost would not have been in vain. Neither had an accurate method for assessing how much their opponent was suffering and tended to believe the more optimistic reports.[27]

Franco-British appeals prompted Russia to attack again, despite having failed in a renewed offensive in March–April 1916. The new Russian commander, Aleksei Brusilov, reluctantly agreed, striking south on 4 June against the Habsburg armies, which rapidly collapsed, losing another 1.5 million casualties and prisoners. Although the offensive eventually stalled, the Russians had again captured Galicia and Bukovina.[28] The disaster caused near panic at Habsburg headquarters, obliging Falkenhayn to switch nine more divisions to bolster the Austrians.

The pressure mounted as Romania attacked weakly defended Habsburg Transylvania on 27 August in support of the Allies. A scion of Germany's Hohenzollern dynasty, Romania's king had wanted to honour treaties with the Central Powers, but his government believed it could get a better deal backing the Allies. The delay prevented Romania from coordinating its entry with Brusilov's offensive. The Romanian army was poorly prepared, badly equipped, and so incompetently led that even the Allies expected it to be defeated. Nonetheless, its entry increased Austria's dependency on Germany, which despatched reinforcements and took command of the counter-attack in September. This was planned by Falkenhayn, who was disgruntled that Hindenburg took the credit. By the end of the year Romania had lost 250,000 men and two-thirds of its territory. Distractions elsewhere prevented the Central Powers from advancing further, giving the Romanians six months to reorganize and to finally receive Russian assistance. German overconfidence further contributed to the failure of their attack in 1917, and Romania continued to defend its remaining territory into 1918.[29]

Bad Choices

Romania's entry into the war was the final straw for the many senior German officers who had lost confidence in Falkenhayn. Bethmann-Hollweg reluctantly agreed, hoping that a change of command would convince the Allies that Germany was determined to win. An equally reluctant Wilhelm II finally appointed Hindenburg as head of the OHL on 29 August. Jealous of Hindenburg's popularity, Wilhelm was named supreme commander of all Central Power forces; a largely nominal role reluctantly accepted by Austria-Hungary. Ludendorff was named First General Quartermaster with the brief to boost production of war goods. The weakness in Germany's political structure now fully emerged, since the Duo became 'silent dictators' with civilian control reduced to Wilhelm's fragile grasp on their loyalties. National well-being was subordinated to the army's operational requirements, all in the name of the long-promised victory.[30]

Austria-Hungary moved in the opposite direction during 1916. After Conrad's repeated failures, the Austrian and Hungarian prime ministers forced Franz Josef to allow them greater insight into the direction of the war. The elderly emperor's death on 21 November further destabilized the monarchy. His great-nephew and successor, Charles (Karl Franz Josef), failed to attract the same degree of personal loyalty and affection, and nationalist separatist movements gained ground.

Charles lacked the confidence to remove Conrad immediately, but gradually restructured the high command, finally replacing the hopeless general with Arz von Straußenburg, who had skilfully defended Transylvania against the Romanians in 1916 but was out of his depth in his new position. New articles of war were issued, abolishing harsh punishments to boost morale, while the Reichsrat was finally recalled in May 1917 to rally political support and restore greater civilian control.[31]

Despite their differing trajectories, neither Germany nor Austria-Hungary made a serious attempt at peace. Both had failed to manage the deteriorating public mood amid growing food shortages, overwork, and social dislocation. In a bid to rally industrialists to his call for greater war production, Ludendorff removed the ban on any public discussion of war aims in November 1916. The measure rebounded badly by exposing the true extent of the elite's annexationist goals at a time when most Germans were cold and hungry, and simply wanted peace.

Following President Woodrow Wilson's re-election on a ticket to keep the United States out of the war, Bethmann-Hollweg made a lukewarm offer to the Allies in December 1916, which was rejected. With no end in sight, on 9 January 1917 the chancellor reluctantly accepted the Duo's endorsement of the navy's demand to wage unrestricted submarine warfare in defiance of internationally accepted norms. The OHL grossly underestimated American capacity, not expecting the US to expand its 128,000 professional soldiers into a 2 million-strong expeditionary force. It was undoubtedly 'the worst decision of the war', particularly as it was rendered potentially unnecessary by the Russian Revolution of March 1917, which could have ended the two-front war and forced the remaining Allies to negotiate.[32] Pouring fuel on the fire, the German foreign ministry clumsily tried to foment war between Mexico and the US. Wilson switched from calling for 'peace without victory' to fighting a 'war to make the world safe for democracy' by bringing the United States into the war in April 1917, and later articulating his grand vision in his famous 'Fourteen Points' on 8 January 1918.

Rather than responding to the Allies' new threat of forcing regime change by democratizing their systems, the German and Habsburg elites refused meaningful concessions to their inhabitants. Growing discontent fuelled a wave of strikes that swept Germany in 1917, with twice as many workers downing tools as in the previous year.[33] Led by Matthias Erzberger, the Centre Party now abandoned its support for annexations and swung behind the SPD's call for peace. Dissatisfied with Bethmann-Hollweg's inability to manage the Reichstag, the Duo threatened to resign unless Wilhelm removed him. The chancellor resigned on 13 July to save the emperor embarrassment and was replaced by a succession of nonentities widely regarded as the OHL's stooges. The combination of the SPD and Centre Party was sufficient to secure a Peace Resolution in the Reichstag on 19 July. Although they had no way of forcing the government to follow it, their action directly challenged the established order.[34]

The OHL countered by supporting the Vaterland Party, formed in September 1917 to rally conservatives against the Peace Resolution by relentlessly blaming Jews, socialists, and 'shirkers' for undermining the war effort. Although chaired by Tirpitz, the prime movers were Wolfgang Kapp, an East Prussian official and future Putschist, and Anton Drexler, who went on to found the anti-Semitic German Workers Party, the forerunner of the Nazis. They had claimed 1.2 million members by the end of the year but most of these were already supporters of the old order. While banning other groups from proselytizing among their personnel, the OHL distributed the Vaterland Party's material as patriotic 'political instruction'.[35]

Russia's Defeat

The Duo inspected the Western Front in September 1916; Ludendorff had not been there for two years, while it was entirely new for Hindenburg. Both were shocked by the army's condition after the Verdun and Somme battles. Their concern at the Allies' obvious material superiority added impetus to what became known as the Hindenburg Programme, a set of wholly unrealistic production targets imposed on German industry. The Duo decided to wait on the defensive throughout 1917 until the new weaponry and munitions arrived and to allow the unrestricted submarine warfare to achieve its promised results. This strategy made sense in narrow military terms, but reduced the country's options, especially by negating any role for diplomacy.

Ludendorff commenced Operation Alberich in March 1917, withdrawing 30 kilometres to five interlinked prepared positions named after

Wagnerian gods, which the Allies soon dubbed the Hindenburg Line. This shortened the Western Front by 60 kilometres and freed thirteen divisions to augment the reserves. Improved defensive tactics enabled the Germans to repel repeated Allied assaults across 1917. They remained unaware of the extent of the mutinies these failures caused in the French army and were unable to exploit this potential opportunity.[36]

Following the overthrow of Tsar Nicholas II in March 1917, the new Russian provisional government under Alexander Kerensky launched a fresh offensive to demonstrate its continued commitment to the western Allies. Advancing in July, the main thrust to the south soon pushed Habsburg forces further back. The Germans had been expecting the offensive and allowed the secondary thrust to the north to run out of steam before counter-attacking, triggering a complete collapse, as the Russians abandoned not only their recent gains but those made by Brusilov the year before. The exhausted Austrians were unable to follow up, but Ludendorff wanted complete victory over Russia to renew operations in the west. Supported by their navy, German troops advanced along the southern Baltic, taking Riga in August and then Ösel (Saaremaa) and the other islands off the coast, exposing Russia's vulnerability to further amphibious attack.

The Russian defeats emboldened the Bolsheviks to seize control in November and open peace negotiations early the following month. Leon Trotsky, heading the Russian delegation, spun out the talks, expecting revolution to sweep westwards and render any territorial concessions unnecessary. Impatient, Germany recognized the Ukrainian nationalists, who were already engaged in an independence struggle against the Bolsheviks. Citing the Ukrainians' plight as an excuse, the Germans resumed their advance in February 1918. Fearing Germany would seize the entire region for itself, Austria-Hungary reluctantly joined the offensive.

The Bolsheviks were obliged to accept the Peace of Brest-Litovsk on 3 March 1918, ceding 2.5 million square kilometres inhabited by 50 million people and containing 90 per cent of Russia's coal and 54 per cent of its industry, as well as promising an indemnity of 5 billion gold roubles. Additional land was ceded to Bulgaria and Turkey. These punitive terms blatantly contradicted the Reichstag's Peace Resolution and demonstrated the OHL's disregard for civilian control. Russia's collapse exposed Romania, which also made a separate peace in May, requiring it to provide oil and food, but allowing it greater autonomy than that accorded the now nominally independent Ukraine.[37]

That country was subjected to a harsh occupation policy intended to extract food to feed hungry Germany and Austria. The commander of the occupation, Hermann von Eichhorn, was assassinated on 30 July, the only German field marshal to die violently in the war. Ukraine only supplied a tenth of the grain demanded, and most of this was consumed by the 750,000 German and Austrian occupation troops, who were losing control of the countryside as a vicious local civil war spread there and in Russia's former Baltic provinces.[38]

Austria-Hungary did not ratify Brest-Litovsk for fear it would inflame nationalist sentiment among its own inhabitants, but nonetheless cooperated with Germany's policy due to its growing dependence on its ally. The Italians had forced Habsburg forces back on the Isonzo front. Following renewed appeals for help, Germany took charge of directing a counterattack at Caporetto, or the Twelfth Battle of the Isonzo. The outcome was a disaster for the Italians, who lost 700,000 casualties and prisoners; only the victors' physical exhaustion and the swift arrival of more British and French reinforcements prevented a complete collapse.[39]

The OHL interpreted the outcome as proof of its strategic genius and the improved training of the troops, whereas Austria-Hungary simply wanted to leave the war. German war aims had progressively expanded, whereas those of the Habsburgs contracted, though they remained naïve by thinking that the future conversion of the monarchy into a looser federation would satisfy Allied demands for national self-determination for the Slavs. A blunder by the Austrian foreign minister prompted France to reveal in April 1918 that Charles had secretly made peace overtures early the previous year. The emperor had no choice but to apologize to Wilhelm and renew his promise of close cooperation with the OHL's directives.[40]

The Final Throw

Following the capture of Riga in August, Ludendorff had switched fortytwo divisions and over 1,000 guns from east to west where there were now 207 of Germany's 251 divisions, giving a nominal superiority over the Allies' 173 divisions. In fact, the Germans were already outnumbered, as their units were understrength, while American reinforcements were rapidly arriving. Hoffmann, Lossberg, and other key advisers all agreed with Wilhelm that Germany must exploit what they saw as a narrow time window to attack before the odds were ever greater. The final decision was taken on 21 January 1918, when Ludendorff made his famous remark that 'we talk too much about operations and too little about tactics', unwittingly exposing his limited conception of warfare.[41]

The Germans launched Operation Michael on 21 March, the first of five successive attacks that became known as the Ludendorff Offensive.[42] Ludendorff had prepared carefully, with roads improved behind the front to bring up supplies. Around 1.4 million men in seventy-four divisions attacked along an 80-kilometre front supported by 6,473 guns and 730 warplanes, hitting the British sector at St Quentin and Cambrai. The British were driven back, losing 3,100 square kilometres, or nearly ten times the ground they had taken five months to capture on the Somme two years earlier. However, much of the effort simply recovered areas that Ludendorff himself had abandoned in Operation Alberich the year before. Heady with success, Ludendorff pushed on in a sequence of further, ever more improvised and reckless attacks. Each time the exhausted Germans outran their supplies and were hit hard by Allied counter-attacks. German morale plummeted when the code name for the final attack given to the troops was *Friedenssturm* (Peace Storm), suggesting that this would be the last effort required of them.

By the time he cancelled further attacks on 21 July, Ludendorff had lost nearly 1 million men, including 125,000 killed and 100,000 missing. American forces in Europe had meanwhile grown from 320,000 to 1.293 million, and would reach 2.1 million by November, of whom 1.3 million were at the front. Meanwhile, Habsburg forces were already disintegrating, in part due to the Russians' release of prisoners who had no desire to renew the fight and added to the widespread defeatism. Austrian replacement units mutinied, soldiers shot their officers or dispersed to loot civilians. The few remaining effective divisions suffered heavily when the Italians routed an ill-advised offensive along the Piave river in June 1918. By that autumn, though the army still nominally numbered 4.6 million, fewer than 900,000 remained at the front.[43]

Collapse

The Central Powers crumbled as the Allies started their 'Hundred Day's Campaign' along the Western Front on 8 August; a date that became known as the 'Black Day of the German Army', because 30,000 troops surrendered after minimal resistance. Others continued to fight stoutly, and the Allies suffered a million casualties, but nonetheless broke through the Siegfried Line, the key sector of Ludendorff's Alberich positions, in October. The Germans had lost another 1,171,700 men, a third of whom surrendered. At least a further 500,000 were temporarily incapacitated by the flu pandemic, and of the 3.4 million in the west only 1.4 million were at the front, while the Allies had a 32 per cent superiority in guns and 20 per cent advantage in warplanes.[44]

Meanwhile, Bulgarian and Ottoman morale plummeted as German troops were switched to plug gaps in the west. Both powers agreed armistices with the Allies by October. Emperor Charles belatedly announced his plan to federalize the monarchy, authorizing his subjects to form national committees. This inadvertently accelerated separatism as Czechs, southern Slavs, Poles, Hungarians, and even German Austrians had declared independent states by 31 October. Defeated by a new Italian offensive at Vittorio Veneto on 24 October, the army disintegrated as entire units now simply went home. Desperate to reassert control, the Habsburg high command agreed an armistice on 3 November. Sensing imminent total collapse, the Italians pressed on regardless, capturing another huge haul of prisoners and equipment as they occupied areas that they intended to keep in the coming peace.[45]

Since August, the Duo had been preparing their own exit, which would preserve their reputations and that of the army they loved, while shifting the blame for the inevitable defeat on to the politicians they hated. They used the opportunity of Bulgaria's armistice on 29 September to inform an astonished Wilhelm II that the war was lost and they threatened to resign unless he authorized a suicidal Final Battle (*Endkampf*) to salvage the army's honour. To his credit, the Kaiser called Ludendorff's bluff on 26 October, replacing him with Wilhelm Groener, who had previously coordinated the war economy, before being made a scapegoat for the failure of the Hindenburg Programme and being sent as chief of staff in the east during 1918.[46] Ludendorff's removal was broadly welcomed within the officer corps. He fled initially to Sweden, before turning to writing profusely to fashion his image as a god of war, assisted by his second wife until their divorce in 1925. The wily Hindenburg kept his post by deliberately staying aloof.[47]

Having reluctantly appointed Max von Baden as the new chancellor, Wilhelm arrived at the OHL's headquarters in the Belgian town of Spa. Sensing imminent revolution, the OHL ordered troops to secure the Rhine bridges and key buildings in Berlin. The sailors of the High Seas Fleet mutinied to stymie the admirals' unauthorized plans for a suicidal final battle. The unrest had spread rapidly by 4 November, when the supposedly loyal troops in Berlin and on the Rhine declared for the growing revolution.

The son of a Württemberg NCO, Groener's pragmatism outweighed his innate conservatism, and he recognized that counter-revolution was impossible. On 9 November he summoned an 'Army Parliament' at Spa, consisting of thirty-nine officers from front-line units, knowing that more senior commanders would not give an honest assessment of the soldiers' mood. They confirmed that the men would no longer fight. Ever conscious of his reputation, Hindenburg ensured it fell to Groener to tell Wilhelm the unpleasant news. Hindenburg then told the Kaiser not to allow himself to be taken to Berlin, where he might share the fate of Tsar Nicholas II, who along with his whole family had recently been murdered by the Bolsheviks. Without having yet relinquished the throne, Wilhelm left by train for the Netherlands early the next morning, while Hindenburg informed the politicians in Berlin that the army would obey their instructions. The officers remained monarchists, but many, especially the younger and junior ones, had lost patience with Wilhelm and the other German rulers and, collectively, they preferred to sacrifice the monarchy to save the army.[48]

Without authorization, Max von Baden announced on 9 November that Wilhelm had abdicated and named the SPD leader, Friedrich Ebert, as chancellor. Equally without authority, or even agreeing it with Ebert, Philipp Scheidemann of the SPD proclaimed a republic later that day. He later claimed he had done so to forestall a similar move by the Spartakists, led by Karl Liebknecht and Rosa Luxemburg, who had split from the SPD over its earlier support for the war and were widely considered to be Germany's Bolsheviks.

The improvised founding of the German Republic robbed it of legitimacy in the eyes of many of the population, but most did not care at that point given their overriding concern for peace. The new government lacked a firm mandate, but was at least acknowledged by the workers', soldiers', and sailors' councils that mushroomed across Germany and throughout the armed forces. These likewise lacked clear authorization but had roots in the corporate structures developed during 1916 to encourage the trades unions to cooperate with the Hindenburg Programme. Although they were immediately compared to the soviets, the similar councils that had played a central role in Russia's revolution, most were concerned only with local issues, such as enabling their unit to return home safely, or seeing that their community had sufficient food. Most saw their function as ensuring that the existing authorities discharged their responsibilities, not seizing power themselves.[49]

Fearing disruption to the army's food and transport and concerned 'that the wagon does not skid further to the left', Groener used the OHL's phone line to call Ebert during the night of 10/11 November. He regarded Ebert, who had lost two sons in the war, as 'an honest and decent character'.[50] Exactly what was promised remains unclear, as the only source is Groener's memoirs, but it is probable they agreed to cooperate to bring the army home and maintain domestic order.

The Allies did not know how close Germany was to collapse and insisted on harsh terms at the armistice talks, which had opened at Compiègne in northern France on 8 November. To prevent Germany from exploiting a respite to recover, its army was to evacuate the areas of France, Belgium, and Luxembourg that it still occupied within fifteen days, and pull back across the Rhine within thirty-one days. The left bank would then be occupied by Allied troops, who would establish three bridgeheads at Cologne, Koblenz, and Mainz. The Saarland, with its vital coal mines, was also to be surrendered. The bulk of the navy would be interned, offshore fishing would cease, and the Allied blockade would continue until peace had been agreed. Hindenburg consented to these terms, even though to save face he ensured that it was Matthias Erzberger who signed the armistice as head of the German delegation on 11 November.[51]

REVOLUTION AND DICTATORSHIP, 1919–38

Stabbed in the Back?

The armistice terms deprived Germany of the means of further resistance, lending weight to the later accusation that the peace was a *Diktat*, imposed on a helpless country. Many officers already considered themselves 'undefeated in the field', yet 'stabbed in the back' by a home front that had allegedly failed to emulate their steely resolve. Initially, this myth was fanned by Ludendorff and other senior commanders to ensure they escaped personal blame for the defeat, but many ordinary personnel condemned their 'criminal, conscienceless officers'.[52] Later, as the myth became more entrenched during the 1920s, it interpreted the war as a political rather than a military defeat, blaming the old monarchist order, as well as the 'shirkers', and others already accused by the Vaterland Party propaganda. This allowed the junior officers, who had largely retained the loyalty of their men, to emerge with their reputations intact, alongside Hindenburg and a very small number of senior officers. While the armed forces felt the bitterness of defeat, they absolved themselves of any responsibility for it.[53]

Austria-Hungary had its own variant of this myth, blaming the nationalists who had 'been working against us for months'.[54] However, its forces were more visibly in a state of complete collapse. The General Staff hid in the war archives, while Emperor Charles, who refused to abdicate, was eventually persuaded to sign the demobilization order. That proved unnecessary since most of the soldiers simply went home. Charles soon went into exile, but the fate of his monarchy remained unclear, because the Allies could not agree on how to implement self-determination for its diverse inhabitants. In the vacuum, fragments of the former Habsburg army, backed by citizens' 'home guards' (*Heimwehr*), fought each other, as well as Bulgarians, Romanians, and Russians, to determine the size of the future independent states and their form of government.

These violent civil wars would rage across this 'shatterzone of empires' until the early 1920s, characterized by pogroms, massacres, and political murders.[55] Austria's Social Democrats, who had similarly stumbled into power, organized a new *Volkswehr* (People's Army) as a national force distinct from the Heimwehr, which were generally more conservative. Intended as a socialist militia, the Volkswehr in practice relied heavily on the surviving cadres of the old imperial army, composed of junior officers facing an uncertain future and other men who found it hard to reintegrate into civilian life.[56] These disparate forces repelled Czech and Yugoslav incursions, as well as establishing the new border with Hungary by 1920.

The task of demobilization seemed far more daunting in Germany, which still had 3.5 million men in the west, 750,000 in the east and southern Baltic, 200,000 in former Habsburg and Ottoman territory, and 1.5 million in the home army. The OHL's refusal to face reality across 1918 meant little had been done to plan for a defeat. Following the armistice talks, it was obvious the Allies would require Germany to reduce its forces in any peace treaty. Like his counterparts in Austria, Ebert was determined that his government secure the Allies' respect and trust as a reliable negotiating partner in the hope this would achieve better terms. He also wanted to maintain public order to enable his government to implement democratic reforms; a process he began immediately after 12 November by lifting martial law, restoring civil liberties, establishing universal male and female suffrage, and agreeing a new compact between employers and trades unions.[57]

Hindenburg and other senior officers did little to disabuse Ebert of his belief that he did not need their expertise. While the front-line units in the west generally remained orderly and refrained from violence, many arranged their own withdrawal. They were supposed to collect in depots east of the Rhine and wait for their discharge papers, but with Christmas approaching at least a million simply went home. By January 1919 there were only a million soldiers left, over two-thirds of whom were in the east, where things were much more chaotic. Several units in Poland surrendered their weapons to Piłsudski's forces in return for transport home. Concerned that the Poles might seize Germany's eastern provinces, the government despatched reinforcements, but the units simply disintegrated as 'everyone wants to hang up their uniform and go back to their civilian job'.[58]

Demobilization appeared orderly to German civilians, since the disorders largely occurred during the evacuation of enemy territory, and Ebert and the SPD considered they had delivered their promise to bring the boys back home. However, the improvised character hindered formal public receptions for the returning troops, adding to many soldiers' sense of grievance and betrayal by a seemingly indifferent population. Ebert was keen to secure the army's goodwill and managed to stage a parade on 10 December 1918 for the Guards divisions as they returned to Berlin, where he told them 'no enemy has defeated you', thereby inadvertently promoting the stab-in-the-back myth.[59]

Fear of the Left

The apparently abrupt collapse of the old order fuelled the expectations of violence. Events were read through the historical understanding of the French (1789 and 1871) and especially more recent Russian revolutions. Even the Swiss were perturbed, mobilizing 95,000 militia to quell a general strike in November 1918. Suspicion of Bolshevik agitators deepened the hostility that most Swiss felt towards the left and prompted the government to break diplomatic relations with Russia's new regime.[60]

In Germany, the actions of the far left heightened fears by conforming to their opponents' expectations, for instance through inflammatory speeches and demonstrators' use of red flags and Bolshevik slogans. The Spartakist leadership were also victims of their own ideology, believing that they must act like Lenin in Russia and use violence to remove Ebert and others whom they deemed the last vestiges of the bourgeois order. A surge of thefts and deepening poverty added to the general sense of anxiety and insecurity.

Senior army officers encouraged Ebert's fears to convince him they remained indispensable after demobilization.[61] Later left-wing historiography accepted such statements at face value, since they fitted the interpretation of a Communist revolution having been 'betrayed' by the SPD moderates.[62] In fact, Ebert had successfully outmanoeuvred the Spartakists, who never controlled the revolution. Nonetheless, the army's disintegration left a vacuum filled by paramilitaries. As in Austria, most of these were Heimwehr concerned primarily with maintaining local order and protecting property.[63] Ebert provided legality for these spontaneously formed units by authorizing 'self-defence' forces, especially to protect the eastern frontier. Both the mainstream SPD and its more radical splinter, the Independents (USPD), formed 'republican guards' from demobilized soldiers and armed civilians. Both were small, ineffective, and politically unreliable. A separate unit of armed sailors, calling themselves the Volksmarine Division (People's Marines), arrived in Berlin, ostensibly to defend the revolution.

The bulk of the recently returned Guards units simply went home for Christmas, leaving only a few thousand regular troops in Berlin. The government suspected the unpaid sailors of stealing art treasures from the palace where they were barracked. The Guards were sent to disarm them on 23 December. Accounts are conflicting, but the operation ended in ignominious failure, with the officers excusing themselves by saying they stopped firing to avoid hitting civilian bystanders. Casualties were far fewer than claimed in the local papers, but Ebert was alarmed that what appeared to be growing disorder would undermine his credibility with the Allies.[64] Meanwhile, the Spartakists merged with other leftist factions as the German Communist Party (KPD), heightening fears of a second 'Bolshevik revolution'.

The Freikorps

Following the resignations of the USPD members of his cabinet, Ebert invited the former basket-maker and long-standing SPD member Gustav Noske to assume the new post of national war minister on 27 December. Recognizing he would become unpopular, Noske remarked 'someone has to be the bloodhound'.[65] As the Prussian army still formally existed as a separate entity within German forces, Colonel Walther Reinhardt was promoted to what proved to be Prussia's last war minister. Another pragmatic Württemberger like Groener, Reinhardt was considered an essential expert in a time of crisis. Meanwhile, Hindenburg, still nominally commander, continued to threaten to resign unless Ebert definitively rejected the peoples' militia model embraced by Austria and advocated by the far left.[66]

Concerned to avoid a repeat of the events on 23 December, Noske and Reinhardt began attaching ad hoc units known as *Freikorps* on to the government payroll (see Fig. 24). These formations had heterogeneous origins. Some were simply Heimwehr who put 'Freikorps' in front of their local title. 'True' Freikorps were units accepting central government command and prepared to serve wherever required. Some were formed around the remnants of old imperial formations, such as the Garde Kavallerie Schützen Division, whereas others were recruited from scratch, usually by relatively junior officers, with the bulk of the manpower coming from cadets and teenagers who had just missed out on the war. Germany was still awash with weaponry, and most Freikorps were well-equipped with the latest machine guns, flamethrowers, and even a few tanks.[67]

An attempted rising by the KPD in Berlin swiftly collapsed on 7 January, but the OHL warned the government that the situation resembled that of 1848 and both sides lost the opportunity to de-escalate tensions. Four days later, government troops shelled and stormed the Vorwärts building, the publishing house of the SPD newspaper which had been seized by the KPD. The soldiers believed that Rosa Luxemburg had fired the machine gun that killed five of their comrades. She and Liebknecht were arrested and then murdered by a squad of ex-naval officers. Overall, 200 people were killed, including many after they had surrendered. The atrocity defined the revolution for the far left, which remained bitterly opposed to the SPD throughout the life of the German Republic. The government excused its soldiers' actions on the grounds that the KPD were using 'Russian terror tactics'.[68]

The violence forced the government to relocate temporarily to Weimar, where the new parliament convened following national elections on 19 January. The SPD emerged the clear winner, but without an overall majority, and formed a coalition with the Centre Party and DDP, a new moderate liberal group. Together, they represented 76.2 per cent of the vote, indicating both the strength of popular support for Ebert's moderate revolution, and the extent to which his fears of the far left were exaggerated. Although the government soon returned to Berlin, the designation 'Weimar Republic' was increasingly used by those on the right to undermine the new state's legitimacy.

The KPD responded by escalating strike action which began after the January atrocities. Determined to demonstrate to the Allies that it controlled the country, the government despatched Freikorps and other government troops in a series of rapid but violent campaigns. The new commander of the Berlin garrison, General Lüttwitz, crushed a general strike there in early March, killing 1,200, of whom 200 were civilians executed following Noske's order to kill anyone holding a weapon. After the Bavarian workers' councils declared their region a 'free state', government forces stormed Munich in May, citing the execution of ten hostages by the Bavarian Red Army as grounds for their own brutality.

Concern for the security of the eastern frontier added urgency to the government's desire to assert control. Estonia, Latvia, and Lithuania declared themselves independent as soon as the Germans departed, and were swiftly recognized by the western Allies, who saw them as a buffer against Bolshevik Russia. As in Poland and Ukraine, local factions fought for control of the new states, which also suffered incursions from the forces engaged in Russia's escalating civil war. The new Polish government encouraged its compatriots in Prussia's eastern lands to form militias and fight for their freedom.

These efforts were countered by German Heimwehr, backed by Freikorps. Many senior German generals, including Walther Reinhardt, saw a chance to contest pressure from the western Allies by preserving some of Germany's wartime influence in eastern central Europe. The OHL decamped to Kolberg on the Baltic coast in February 1919 to direct operations, the largest of which was the campaign waged by Rüdiger von der Goltz, whose force grew to 50,000 Freikorps, complete with warplanes. The Allies tolerated Goltz's intervention in Latvia's civil war because they knew their own populations were war weary and saw the German presence as a means of checking Bolshevik influence. As Goltz increasingly acted independently, collaborating with Latvia's German minority, the Allies lost patience and pressured the German government to recall his troops. Most returned in September. Intermittent fighting dragged on in Silesia into 1922 when the Allies obliged Poland to accept the outcome of a plebiscite determining that the area remained German. Although these campaigns failed to sustain Germany's eastern empire, they contained enough small, local victories to validate the myth that the German army had remained undefeated.[69]

While Goltz had acted independently, the central government did assert control over many of the paramilitaries and Freikorps. Since the future size of the German army remained to be decided at the peace conference, existing units were combined into the 'Provisional Reichswehr' on 6 March 1919, the country's first truly national army as the separate Prussian, Bavarian, Saxon, and Württemberg forces were abolished. Many of the Freikorps were absorbed into it, either forming one of the twenty-four new brigades like Ehrhardt's Marines, created from conservative sailors and ex-officers, or amalgamated into new formations. Overall, there were 340,000 men in May 1919, of whom 220,000 were in the east, around 60,000 under Lüttwitz in Berlin, and 50,000 in the west. Groener, Reinhardt, and other senior officers hoped the Allies would permit at least 350,000 soldiers but were prepared to accept a peace strength of 100,000, with double that in wartime using reservists.[70]

Versailles

These hopes were not wholly unrealistic as Germany entered the peace talks in Paris, which represented a serious attempt to establish a new liberal democratic world order. Unfortunately, this objective was hindered by participants' insistence on national honour, the legacy of wartime propaganda that had stirred expectations, the complexity of the issues, and the sheer bitterness of societies trying to deal with such an unparalleled catastrophe. The tone was set by the opening address from France's President Poincaré, pointedly held on 18 January 1919, the forty-eighth anniversary of Germany's declaration of its Second Reich: 'You are assembled in order to repair the evil that it has done and prevent a recurrence of it.'[71]

The starting point was that the war was Germany's fault, encapsulated in Article 231 of the final treaty, known as the War Guilt Clause, which underpinned Allied demands for reparations, further justified by reference to those imposed by the Germans on France (1871) and Russia (1918). The ideal of war guilt was central to the Allies' perception of their own suffering and of having waged a just war. Concerned that undertaking this themselves might destabilize the new German Republic, the Allies required Germans to prosecute themselves. Popular demands to 'hang the Kaiser' were dropped after the Netherlands refused to extradite him, while Hindenburg, Ludendorff, and other high-ranking figures were removed from the initial list of 3,000, leaving just 854, mainly chosen by France and Belgium. Eventually, 113 were tried by the German supreme court in 1921, but only six were convicted. The process backfired badly, allowing German personnel to articulate arguments of 'military necessity' to defend themselves against charges of atrocities against civilians and prisoners. Exclusion of the senior figures meant there was no proper debate over why Germany had gone to war.[72]

The other terms added to the sense of unfairness, though much of this was the Germans' own fault. Ludendorff had not bothered to read Wilson's Fourteen Points when he had urged the imperial government to open negotiations, but for anyone who had done so it was already obvious during the war that the Allies' goal of 'self-determination' would entail the truncation of Germany and dissolution of Austria-Hungary.[73]

Germany was required to return Alsace-Lorraine to France, to cede Eupen and Malmédy to Belgium, Memel to Lithuania, and Hultschin to the new state of Czechoslovakia, and to return West Prussia to Poland. Loss of the latter created the 'Polish Corridor', giving Poland access to the Baltic but again detaching East Prussia from the rest of Germany. Plebiscites were held in Upper Silesia and northern Schleswig, and whereas the former voted to remain German, the latter chose to rejoin Denmark, thereby removing the gain from the war of 1864. Combined, these changes reduced Germany's territory by 13 per cent and its population by about 10 per cent, and though many of these belonged to national minorities, around 2 million Germans became Polish citizens in what was considered by many as a contradiction of the right to self-determination. All colonies were also surrendered. France was permitted to control the Saar coalfields for fifteen years, while the Rhineland would remain occupied until 1935 as surety for the reparations payments and German disarmament.[74]

The Allies dealt with the former Habsburg lands in separate treaties, rejecting the Austrians' and the Hungarians' claims that they should be treated like the other successor states of Czechoslovakia, Poland, and Yugoslavia, rather than defeated enemies. The stipulation eventually agreed with Austria at St Germain on 10 September 1919 transferred the southern Tirol to Italy, while Hungary was obliged by the Treaty of Trianon in June 1920 to cede two-thirds of its territory to Czechoslovakia, Romania, and Yugoslavia. The outcome was deeply resented by most Hungarians, who wanted to recover the lost territory, whereas most Austrians were ready to accept their new frontiers, but not their independence. Austrian Germans had already become dissatisfied with Habsburg multiculturalism before 1914, and the new Social Democrat government petitioned the Allies to permit the 'union' (Anschluß) with Germany. This was immediately vetoed, turning the idea from a left-wing project based on the right of self-determination into a conservative nationalist dream.[75]

Allied generals were prepared to be less severe on the military terms, with the British feeling that none of the defeated powers could afford a professional army, while the French wanted a system based on short-service conscripts to convert their forces into citizens' militias, like that of the Swiss. This was also the preference of the German and Austrian socialist governments. However, Allied politicians, notably Britain's David Lloyd George, had read about how Prussia had supposedly circumvented the restrictions imposed by Napoleon in 1808 by using short-service conscription to build up trained reserves. They overruled the generals and fixed the German army at 100,000 long-service professionals, with Austria restricted to 30,000 and Hungary to 35,000, all without heavy artillery. Germany's navy was to be cut to a coastal defence force with 15,000 men, and warplanes were banned.[76]

These restrictions were part of a political project to eliminate 'militarism', but there was no accepted definition as to what that meant. They were supposed to be steps towards general disarmament and the renunciation of war in favour of international arbitration through the new League of Nations. At President Wilson's insistence, that body's headquarters were established in Geneva. Switzerland agreed to join, thereby abandoning its 'fundamental neutrality' in favour of international engagement to uphold peace.[77] However, the US Congress defied the president by rejecting League membership, eventually signing a separate peace treaty with Germany in 1921. This action encouraged the belief that the peace was not solid and might be revised. German dissatisfaction was heightened by their country's exclusion from the League, making this appear even more of a victors' club. Although the Allies accepted some limits on the size of their navies in separate agreements in 1922 and 1930, these were soon ignored once Japan resumed construction.[78]

To the defeated powers, disarmament thus appeared a hypocritical effort to leave them defenceless. The longer-term effect proved destabilizing, because the German and Austrian governments tolerated the presence of paramilitaries as providing potential wartime reserves, while the Allies, other than France, increasingly saw the terms as unfair and unenforceable. Waning enthusiasm and disagreements among the Allies over monitoring further fuelled the belief that the restrictions could be circumvented or ignored.[79]

Peace Implementation

All that was not immediately obvious to the German delegation at Versailles when these terms were presented on 7 May 1919. Many officers, including Reinhardt, urged a resumption of war to enable them and their men to die honourably. Groener had anticipated such a reaction and had prepared a sober assessment of the futility of further resistance, particularly as the Allies still blockaded hungry Germany.[80] Ebert felt the country had no choice and accepted the treaty on 28 June. The decision shattered confidence in the government among many officers who had been prepared to cooperate with the Republic until then.

The naval terms were easily implemented because on 21 June 1919 the Germans had scuttled their warships which had been held at the Royal Navy's base at Scapa Flow. This action, taken unilaterally by the commanding admiral, was broadly celebrated as redeeming national honour.[81] The air force had relatively few personnel and its warplanes were scrapped during 1920. Dealing with the land forces proved far more difficult. The OHL was disbanded in July 1919 when Hindenburg finally stood down, his reputation still untarnished, enabling him to secure election as president after Ebert's death in 1925. Groener deliberately kept the command regionalized to control the remaining generals until September, when the government implemented the republic's new constitution by establishing a single war ministry with authority over both the army and navy. Groener then stepped down, with Reinhardt becoming army commander, the navy entrusted to Vice Admiral Trotha, and Noske remaining national war minister.[82]

At 200,000 in early 1920, the army still exceeded the limit allowed by the Versailles Treaty, and the Allies were growing impatient, suspecting that the Germans were deliberately trying to dodge their obligations. In fact, Groener had made serious efforts to reduce army strength since June, but several units refused to disband, notably the Freikorps, which had served in the Baltic. The reductions also had the unfortunate consequence of increasing the army's conservative character, since those handling officer selection used the opportunity to purge the few genuine republicans in favour of retaining those from the Freikorps. Reinhardt lost the army's respect and was unable to reassert his authority.

Ehrhardt's Marine Brigade and another ex-Freikorps unit refused Noske's orders to disband and declared for a new government proclaimed in Berlin on 13 March 1920 by Lüttwitz and Kapp, the former Vaterland Party leader. Ludendorff, Lettow-Vorbeck, Max Bauer, and other conservatives rallied to the putschists, while senior army officers refused to assist the government, saying that their units would not fire on their comrades. Ebert responded by endorsing a general strike, which found overwhelming public support, forcing the putschists to flee abroad on 18 March. The KPD tried to steer the strike as a new revolution, finding some support in the Ruhr, Saxony, and Thuringia, but this movement soon collapsed following negotiations and the deployment of troops.[83]

The Reichswehr

The army's refusal to assist the government discredited Reinhardt and Noske, who were replaced by Hans von Seeckt and Otto Gessler respectively. Whereas Gessler was a liberal who served the Republic loyally until forced to resign in 1928, Seeckt had been prominent in opposing the use of the army against the Kapp Putsch. However, he had also distinguished himself in directing operations in Poland, Serbia, and the Ottoman Empire, and enjoyed the officers' confidence.[84] Beyond dismissing Trotha and a few other officers who had backed the Putsch, the government missed an opportunity to purge anti-republicans.

Ebert and Gessler recognized that soldiers no longer served a hereditary monarch, but a republic with a government that might change with each election. They wanted an army above party politics that would loyally serve any constitutionally elected government, whereas Seeckt wanted an apolitical army to insulate it against democracy. As Gessler later noted, 'the army's relationship to the state is and remains problematic as long as the state itself is problematic'.[85] Seeckt's view represented a continuation of the nineteenth-century ideal of a professional army that should be left alone to do its job as it saw best.

Seeckt completed the army's reduction, using the divisional structure imposed on Germany by Versailles as an excuse to break up the provisional brigade structure and disband those units he distrusted. The new Reichswehr was formally inaugurated on 1 January 1921, followed by the Reichsmarine on 11 April. Seeckt rejected Reinhardt's conclusion that Germany needed a mass army backed by heavy artillery. Not only was this impossible given the Versailles restrictions, but he believed that the recent war indicated that smaller units of tough professionals could defeat larger numbers of poorly trained citizens-in-arms. He argued that Germany's army in 1914 had been too large to implement the Schlieffen plan, whereas the small professional forces had thrashed the revolutionaries in 1919.

Stressing quality over quantity, Seeckt envisaged the Reichswehr as a highly mobile force, relying on superior training, leadership, and weaponry to counter-attack rapidly. He has been hailed as a visionary and originator of the Blitzkrieg, or lightning war, supposedly characterizing German tactics in the Second World War.[86] However, his ideas were only superficially realistic. Even he thought the 100,000-man limit too small, and all his plans envisaged a force two or three times that, without ever fully addressing where the missing manpower would come from, nor how any casualties could be replaced, while the planes, tanks, vehicles, and heavy artillery he wanted were all banned by Versailles. Like Ludendorff, he focused on tactics, not operations, let alone strategy, underestimating airpower's potential and paying no attention to the role of the navy.[87]

Shortage of manpower obliged Seeckt and the government to tolerate the persistence of paramilitaries. The Heimwehr units allowed themselves to be disbanded during 1920, but other armed organizations, notably the eastern border guards, were initially retained. Allied pressure and Seeckt's hostility to unprofessional forces led to this 'Black' or hidden Reichswehr being disbanded in 1923. Seeckt nonetheless remained concerned to promote 'defence capacity' and permitted landowners and former officers to train local militias. Often disguised as sporting gun clubs, these groups foundered in the later 1920s as boredom set in when members discovered there was little to do beyond meet in the backrooms of beer halls.[88]

The Ruhr and Rearmament

Seeckt's focus on tactics exemplified the armed forces' inability to contribute positively to German foreign policy. Regardless of ideology, most politicians wanted to recover independence by reducing or eliminating reparations, ending the foreign occupation of the Rhineland and the Saar, and, if possible, recover the lands lost to Poland. The disagreements were over how to achieve this. The army's leadership remained locked in a late nineteenth-century mindset: pre-war policy had been correct and the failure to achieve victory was due to mistakes by individuals like Schlieffen or Falkenhayn. Germany was surrounded by enemies and diplomacy should only be used to disrupt potentially hostile coalitions, not improve relations with neighbours. At no point did the generals seriously consider anything other than recovering great-power status, arguing instead only over what risks were acceptable while pursuing this goal.

There were some grounds for this hostile world view. The Allies had temporarily occupied additional towns following the Kapp Putsch and when Germany defaulted on reparations in 1921. Further defaults prompted France and Belgium to occupy the Ruhr region in January 1923, deepening Germany's economic crisis and hyperinflation. Seeckt had to admit that the Reichswehr only had sufficient ammunition for an hour's fighting, while the total French army was ten times larger. Rather than fight, the government encouraged civil disobedience to disrupt the Franco-Belgian occupation. The French responded by deporting over 100,000 inhabitants, eventually obliging the German government to end passive resistance in October.[89]

The chaotic atmosphere encouraged Adolf Hitler to hijack a conservative monarchist effort and proclaim Bavaria as independent. Hitler's National Socialists (Nazis) party was one of the more successful of several extreme right-wing parties emerging after 1919, but while it had 50,000 members these were concentrated in Bavaria and it had not yet become a national movement. Inspired by Mussolini's 'March on Rome', which had seen the Italian fascists seize power in October 1922, Hitler hoped to achieve the same on 9 November 1923. He got no further than the environs of a beer hall in Munich; a failure that is an important reminder that the German Republic remained resilient despite what many interpreted as a year of national crisis.[90]

Although there were eight changes of coalition government over the next six years, there was greater stability within several of the important ministerial portfolios. The commanding figure was Gustav Stresemann, who remained foreign minister across 1923–9. Anti-Western, yet pragmatic, Stresemann recognized that military force was not a viable way to achieve national goals, and instead he used partial fulfilment of the Versailles terms to widen the differences among the Allies. France's behaviour in the Ruhr stirred international sympathy for Germany's plight, notably within the United States, allowing Stresemann to secure a succession of international agreements between 1924 and 1929. These saw reparations payments reduced, the Ruhr evacuated, and Germany's admission to the League of Nations in 1926 following its formal acceptance of its new western frontiers. The last Allied troops departed the Rhineland in June 1930, five years early, though the region was to remain demilitarized.

The Allies' new conciliatory attitude reflected a growing sense that they had treated Germany unfairly and they made the concessions despite their knowledge that the Reichswehr was secretly rearming. The story of rearmament is generally told teleologically from the perspective of 1939, rather than that of 1923 when it began amid the Ruhr crisis. The Reichswehr's obvious inability to defend the country convinced even the SPD to create a secret budget to pay for modern weaponry. Germany's access to such equipment in turn derived from its continued military reputation. General Franco, then newly appointed director of Spain's military academy, requested permission in 1928 to visit Germany to see how the Reichswehr had overcome defeat to punch above its weight on a small budget.[91] Meanwhile, former German officers were hired as advisers, notably by the Chinese Nationalists under Chiang Kai-shek, who recruited around 120 Germans between 1927 and 1938, including Max Bauer and, eventually, Seeckt. Whereas the Germans in China trained over 80,000 Nationalist troops, who were used against the Japanese invasion after 1931, their counterparts in Bolivia proved far less successful, with the faulty direction of Hans Kundt contributing to that country's disastrous defeat by Paraguay in the Chaco War (1932–5).[92]

Among the other countries keen to obtain German expertise was Soviet Russia (USSR), which likewise felt itself to be an international pariah after 1918. The two states agreed a trade deal at Rapallo in April 1922, which provided cover for the secret testing of tanks at Kazan, planes at Lipezk, and gas at Tamka, together with associated training for German personnel and opportunities for firms like Krupp to develop prototypes. It was a truly 'Faustian bargain' in which the Reichswehr and German industry ensured they remained leaders in designing certain types of weaponry, but at the cost of providing similarly vital technology and expertise to the power that would play a key role in destroying Germany in the Second World War. While some German officers returned favourably impressed, the majority simply had their prejudices confirmed, contributing to the fatal underestimation of the Soviet Union in 1941.[93]

While the full scope of these activities was not known, their existence was public knowledge, with the SPD agreeing not to make too much of a fuss, because it also saw them as essential for national security. Hans Zenker, the navy's new commander, was forced to resign in 1928 when it was discovered he had tried to buy a film company to influence public opinion in favour of more battleships. His fall took Gessler with him, leading to Groener's return to public life as the new war minister. He allowed the secret programmes to continue so that he could monitor and influence the Reichswehr's activities.[94]

However, there was no progressive fusion of army and state, or 'smooth transition' from a small, defensively orientated Reichswehr and an aggressive, supposedly well-prepared Wehrmacht.[95] Many officers had become dissatisfied with Seeckt by the time he was forced to resign in 1926 for having allowed the Kaiser's grandson to attend manoeuvres in full imperial uniform. Although now able to develop more realistic plans for a bigger army, the largest most envisaged was 300,000 men including reservists, backed by some tanks and a small air force. The Reichswehr did not prepare an offensive war plan until 1929, and this focused solely on how to capture the new Polish port of Gdynia. The armed forces' leadership remained preoccupied with how to defend the country against possible combinations of hostile neighbours. Some would have liked to aim higher but were usually worried about the risks of failure. Groener, and the Reichswehr's new commander, Wilhelm Heye, continued to see war only as a matter of last resort, and co-operated to assert political authority over the generals.[96]

In July 1932, General Schleicher, Groener's successor as war minister, announced that Germany would no longer be bound by the Versailles restrictions, unless other powers also accepted limits at the international disarmament conference that had just opened in Geneva. Four months later, following the general refusal to accept such restrictions, Schleicher authorized a modest increase to 149,000 men, plus reserves and a small number of planes and tanks. While the Reichswehr's leadership wanted more, this was because, like their Wilhelmine predecessors, they feared they could not defeat Germany's potential invaders and did not value diplomacy as an alternative to the country's security concerns.[97]

Nazi Germany

The reasons for the Nazis' seizure of power during 1933 are complex and the outcome was far from inevitable. A major factor was that those leading the Republic did so little to defend it. Following the definitive exit of the SPD from the governing coalition in 1930, leadership passed to men who despised democracy. Politics shifted from the Reichstag, which met increasingly infrequently, and on to the streets, which saw a surge in violent clashes between party armies.

These had emerged from the same roots as the veterans' organizations and combat leagues formed after 1918, of which the largest and most influential was *Stahlhelm* (Steel Helmet), the league of former front-line soldiers. Although most veterans shunned political organizations, the numbers joining were still substantial because so many Germans had served. The disbandment of the border guards and other paramilitaries around 1923 removed competitors, while Stahlhelm's membership surged from 150,000 to 260,000 when it opened membership to younger men without military service. The Reichswehr remained ambivalent towards Stahlhelm, less on account of its blatant anti-democratic views and more because it clearly saw itself as an alternative army. Nonetheless, in the absence of a formal reserve, it was tolerated to instil martial values into potential future recruits.

The Nazi Stormtroopers (SA) claimed the same front-line military pedigree, but they were developed after 1921 explicitly as a party army to protect leaders and intimidate opponents. Many of the early members had belonged to the Freikorps, notably the organization's leader, Ernst Röhm, who also briefly served as a military adviser in Bolivia. However, the Nazis saw Stahlhelm and the other veterans' organizations as rivals and sought to surpass them in both membership and violence.

The SPD was hindered by its own antimilitarism from mounting an effective response. It collaborated with the Centre Party, the DDP, and trades unions to establish the *Reichsbanner* (Republican Flag) organization in 1924, which soon numbered nearly a million members, or three times the total achieved by Stahlhelm at its peak. Nonetheless, its trust in the official order and reluctance to embrace violence ceded the streets to the Republic's opponents. The latter also included the rival *Rotfront-kämpfer* (Red Front Fighters) league, established by the KPD, whose brawling with the SA fostered a sense that the left had to be neutered to restore German unity.[98] The Republic's conservative leadership squandered several opportunities to disband the SA, while its infighting across 1932–3 opened the door, first to Hitler becoming chancellor in January 1933, and then to dictatorial powers by agreeing the Enabling Act on 24 March 1933.[99]

Despite promising order, the new regime was violent from the outset as political opponents were taken into 'protective custody' for 're-education' in concentration camps; just two of the Nazis' chilling use of euphemisms. Other parties and organizations were banned or Nazified, often with carefully choreographed ceremonies to demonstrate the new *Volksgemeinschaft* (People's Community), such as that when most of the surviving Freikorps leaders surrendered their flags to the SA in November 1933.[100]

Germany's regions lost their autonomy as the country was reorganized into the party's administrative subdivisions. Nazi ideology extolled the values of hierarchy and firm leadership, but in fact the state rapidly became polycentric through the proliferation of competing party organizations and the surviving institutions of the previous order, including the armed forces, government ministries, civil service, judiciary, and police. The party's emphasis on endless struggle and the survival of the fittest encouraged ruthless competition between all elements of the party and government. Cabinet meetings ceased after February 1934 as Hitler disliked paperwork and preferred personal audiences and verbal reports. Hindenburg's death six months later enabled him to combine the positions of president and chancellor. His cultivation of personal loyalty opened numerous informal channels alongside official structures, as well as fostering a culture of graft, including among the armed forces' leadership, who were rewarded with lavish gifts of cash and property. This was merely the pinnacle of a pyramid of corruption and opportunism, fuelled increasingly through plundering the regime's victims.

While murderously efficient in some respects, the Nazi state was also dysfunctional. Keen to keep his options open, Hitler's response to a problem was either delay a decision in the expectation that it would resolve itself or appoint a new commission of experts to prepare technical advice. Each organization produced its own statistics and recommendations, often driven by its own immediate leader's ambitions.

Although the churches were permitted to continue, only the armed forces had the potential capacity to oppose the new order. Hitler inherited a senior staff recently appointed by Hindenburg prior to his death. General Fritsch, the new commander, was widely admired within the army as a model officer and, though an anti-Semite, he openly despised the Nazis. Werner von Blomberg, the new war minister, by contrast cooperated in purging Jewish officials and officers and his apparent compliance earned him the nickname 'Rubber Lion' among those still sceptical of the Nazis. Nonetheless, Blomberg shared his colleagues' concern that Röhm intended to replace the Reichswehr with the SA which, following its absorption of the Stahlhelm and new members, now totalled

4.5 million men, vastly outnumbering the regular forces. Keen to secure the generals' cooperation and recognizing that Röhm had made too many enemies within the party, Hitler sanctioned his murder in the Night of the Long Knives on 30 June 1934, which also saw the deaths of around 200 others whose lives the regime now found inconvenient.[101]

The Black Order

The action was carried out by the black-clad *Schutzstaffel* (Protection Squad, SS), established in 1929 as Hitler's personal bodyguard and headed by Heinrich Himmler, an utterly ruthless early convert to Nazism who doggedly pursued his own vision despite repeated setbacks. Himmler exceeded Röhm in wishing not only to replace the Reichswehr but to refashion the entire Nazi state along his own, supposedly more pure, ideological lines. The SS expanded rapidly, creating several distinct branches. The *Sicherheitsdienst* (Security Service, SD) grew from a party organization in 1931 to become by 1938 the state's primary counter-espionage agency, eventually also absorbing military intelligence. By 1936, Himmler also secured control of the regular police, reorganized as the *Ordnungspolizei* (Orpo), as well as the plainclothes investigation branch (Kripo) and the new secret police (Gestapo). Possession of armed force was central to Himmler's agenda, and the neutralization of the SA was an important step. After 1934 the SA were disarmed and reduced to 1.2 million thugs to enforce the regime's anti-Semitic and other repressive policies. The concentration camps were transferred to the SS, which established the paramilitary *Totenkopfverbände* (Death's Head Units) to run them.

The primary force, however, was the new *Verfügungstruppe* (Special Duty Force, VT), established in March 1933 and paid from the police budget but trained by the army. The regime's internal rivalries slowed the expansion of the VT, which still only comprised a tenth of the total 223,000 SS personnel in 1938. Hitler saw the force as an elite guard who would set an example to Germany's other soldiers, but his continual dissatisfaction with his generals pushed him into conceding Himmler's incessant demands to expand the force, which was officially renamed *Waffen-SS* (Armed SS) in December 1939. By then, it had already absorbed the Death's Head Units, whose concentration-camp duties were assumed by the nominally civilian *Allgemeine-SS* (General SS).

Predictably, the army despised Himmler's 'asphalt soldiers', who enjoyed higher pay and better rations once the war began, as well as priority for new weapons after 1940 with their own procurement programme. Although they were under the army's operational command, the creation of separate SS divisions strengthened the autonomy of the Waffen-SS and their own sense of elite status. The latter was manifest in their refusal to follow normal safety protocols against the use of live ammunition in training.[102]

The Wehrmacht

In October 1933, Germany withdrew from the Geneva disarmament talks and from the League of Nations, but it refrained from openly rearming. A year later Hitler authorized the secret expansion of the army to 300,000 men in twenty-one divisions, the total that most generals had always wanted. A succession of measures between February and October 1935 announced the creation of an air force (*Luftwaffe*), renamed the navy as the *Kriegsmarine*, reintroduced conscription, and revealed new weapons such as submarines and light tanks. The armed forces now assumed the name *Wehrmacht*, which had its own higher staff and command, with the army simply designated *Heer*, deliberately using the old Germanic term, rather than *Armee*, the French loan word used predominantly since the early eighteenth century. These measures were enthusiastically welcomed by the armed forces' leadership.[103]

The next four years saw a succession of escalating acts of aggression that intimidated Germany's neighbours, emboldened its military leadership, and consolidated Hitler's domestic power. The new forces had yet to be fully trained and armed, but Germany's neighbours were reluctant to risk war. The remilitarization of the Rhineland in March 1936 was conducted by just 22,000 lightly equipped troops backed by 14,000 police. France grossly overestimated German strength and decided not to act once Britain withheld its support. Belgium renounced its defence pact with France and retreated into neutrality. The establishment of the 'Rome-Berlin Axis' in July and the despatch of assistance to Franco's nationalists in the Spanish Civil War all suggested growing German strength.[104]

Hitler repeatedly told his senior commanders that he regarded war as inevitable, but he remained vague as to its scope or timetable. A conference of senior commanders and the foreign minister was convened in the Reich Chancellery in November 1937, which has become known by the name of the officer taking the minutes, Colonel Hoßbach.[105] Hitler outlined his plans to seize *Lebensraum* ('living space') in Eastern Europe that would not only accommodate the country's growing population but would make it 'blockade proof' by providing the food and raw materials that the Allied navies had cut off during the First World War. This was explicitly justified on ideological terms in line with Nazi claims that the Germans were a 'master race'.

The meeting exposed the armed forces' persistent and critical weakness: fixated with *how* to achieve victory, the senior command paid scant regard to *why* they should want one. Their deep-seated, narrow professionalism accustomed them to expect political leaders to provide the grand strategic vision, while their ingrained conservatism inclined them to see Hitler as a populist version of their own nationalism. Moreover, he remained relatively close to their own thinking by proposing to expand incrementally, hitting Poland and Czechoslovakia first as weaker targets, before confronting the western powers. There was still no coherent plan, and subsequently each operation was planned separately in response to Hitler's requests.

Although they were concerned at his tight schedule requiring them to be ready by 1944, none of the commanders voiced moral objections and their remaining hesitancy largely stemmed from a concern that moving too rapidly might result in defeat. Only the chief of staff, Ludwig Beck, fundamentally disagreed, believing that Britain and France did not have to be enemies and diplomacy might secure much of what Germany wanted.[106]

The doubters were swiftly removed. Blomberg was blackmailed into resigning his post as war minister, which was assumed by Hitler, while Fritsch was suspended on trumped-up charges and replaced by Walther von Brauchitsch who was considered more pliant. A supreme command (*Oberkommando der Wehrmacht* – OKW) was created to improve coordination between the three service branches. Another sixty senior officers were sacked or retired. Beck kept his objections largely to himself, and then resigned in September 1938, being replaced by Franz Halder, a Bavarian who, like the other senior officers of his generation, had served as a staff officer in the First World War and subsequently in the Reichswehr.

Anschluss

Germany's annexation of Austria in March 1938 further encouraged the army's willing cooperation with the regime, because the operation was not without risks yet proved successful. The Austrian Republic had shared many of the problems afflicting its larger neighbour since its formal foundation in November 1919. Although overall the peace terms were not as harsh as those imposed on Germany, Austria was nonetheless saddled with reparations and restrictions on the size and composition of its armed forces. The army was reorganized in 1920, and officially named the *Bundesheer* two years later, but remained below even its modest authorized strength of 30,000 because the country was virtually bankrupt.

Austrian politics polarized between the Social Democrats, who lost power in 1920, and the conservative Christian Social Party, which increasingly rejected union (*Anschluß*) with Germany in favour of a separate Austrian identity.[107] This alienated some of the Heimwehr paramilitaries who persisted beyond the Bundesheer's foundation and became increasingly anti-republican. However, unlike their German counterparts, Austria's Social Democrats organized their own, effective paramilitary 80,000-strong *Schutzbund*, which held the 60,000-man Heimwehr in check.[108] The growth of a rival National Socialist movement eventually pushed the Heimwehr into an alliance with the Christian Social Party under Chancellor Dollfuss. Leftist opposition was crushed in February 1934 when the Schutzbund was disbanded after the army shelled the Karl-Marx Hof, a vast workers' housing complex in Vienna. Citing the emergency, Dollfuss secured the Allies permission to add 8,000 men to the army, which was finally brought up to strength. Meanwhile, the Heimwehr was reorganized as the 100,000-strong Front Militia to enforce this new 'Austro-fascist' corporatist state, a more Catholic clerical version of Mussolini's Italy. A coup attempt by Austria's National Socialists was crushed in July, though Dollfuss was assassinated.

His successor, Dr Schuschnigg, dissolved the Front Militia in favour of expanding the country's regular forces, openly revealing the existence of a small air force in 1936. The army was well-trained, and though leaning to the right, remained loyal to the Republic. Nonetheless, many officers had been demoralized by the political violence of 1934, while the new Rome-Berlin Axis increased Austria's vulnerability, because Mussolini softened his opposition to a possible German annexation.

That came on 12 March 1938 when 100,000 troops crossed the frontier, backed by 400 planes. The operation had been improvised at forty-eight hours notice. Many German reservists lacked complete uniforms, while their vehicles ran out of fuel, because the army relied on refilling at Austrian service stations, which soon ran dry. Austria's army offered no resistance as they could see how enthusiastically much of the population welcomed the invaders.[109] Subsequently confirmed by a plebiscite, the annexation increased Germany's population by over 6.7 million, and substantially strengthened its armed forces and war industries.

THE SECOND WORLD WAR, 1939–45

From Munich to War

Czechoslovakia knew it was next on Hitler's list and began immediate defensive preparations. Its army was approximately equivalent to Germany's in size, training, and equipment, plus the country had a defence pact with France. Italian diplomatic support for Hitler weakened Anglo-French resolve and led to the Munich agreement in September 1938, allowing Germany to annex Czechoslovakia's mountain frontier region and leaving the country defenceless. By mid-March 1939 further German threats dismembered Czechoslovakia, reducing Bohemia and Moravia to a protectorate and detaching Slovakia as a one-party, pro-German satellite. A week later Lithuania was compelled to return to Germany the territory of Memel, which it had received in the Versailles peace agreement.[110]

Hitler pushed ahead on 3 April 1939, ordering the General Staff to prepare Case White, the code name for the invasion of Poland. While he dictated the relentless pace, his strategic thinking broadly aligned with the Wehrmacht's leadership and, indeed, that of the General Staff in the later Wilhelmine era. All saw Germany as surrounded by real, not merely potential enemies, whom they assumed likewise saw the world as inherently competitive and were arming against them. Hitler simply pushed this to logical extremes on a global scale. By the summer of 1939 it was obvious that Germany would never match the resources of the Western powers which, together with the United States and Soviet Union, were also accelerating rearmament. Meanwhile, Germany's alliances with Italy and Japan were loose and did little to tip the broader strategic balance.

Germany embarked on war with its economy already fully stretched whereas its main opponents were only just gearing up and possessed vast, under-utilized capacity. As in 1914, Germany remained a regional power taking on countries with global resources and, again, the key military decisions hinged on pretending this was not the case. The leadership believed there was a narrow 'window of opportunity' to strike before their enemies would be too strong. That window momentarily widened when Stalin agreed the Nazi-Soviet Pact on 23 August, dividing East Central Europe into spheres of influence and guaranteeing the flow of vital oil and raw materials to Germany in return for cash and armaments. The deal cushioned the likely impact of any British naval blockade. Meanwhile, the strongly isolationist sentiment of Americans removed any immediate threat of US intervention.[111]

Previous experience had already conditioned the German armed forces to accept that 'military necessity' legitimated extreme measures, while their jealously guarded sense of professionalism inculcated an ethos of 'technocratic ruthlessness'.[112] Nonetheless, their actions after 1939 were quantitatively and qualitatively different. The conviction that Germany was locked in a struggle for national survival before even a shot had been fired fostered the Wehrmacht's broad acceptance of the regime's racial and Manichaean ideology, which in turn pushed violence to ever greater extremes.

Poland

The recent extension of territory southeast through the annexation of Austria and much of Czechoslovakia, as well as Slovakia's collaboration, transformed the strategic situation against Poland, which had previously been rated a dangerous opponent, and enabled Germany to deploy its superior numbers along far wider borders: over 1.5 million troops and 1,900 warplanes against 1.3 million and 900 respectively. The feeble Anglo-French response removed any hopes Poland might have had of successful resistance, as well as dumbfounding many in the Wehrmacht command who feared Germany's western frontier was inadequately defended. An additional Soviet invasion from the east began on 17 September hastening the end for Poland, though it only surrendered on 16

October, forty-six days after the initial German attack. That was none-theless short enough to enable German troops to be switched westwards in time to block a potential Anglo-French counter-attack.[113]

Polish forces suffered 120,000 dead, or ten times those of the Germans, who captured 587,000 prisoners, while the Soviets took another 200,000. The German occupation was immediately brutal and over 100,000 civilians had been killed by the end of the year. In accordance with the pact with Stalin, the country was partitioned, with Germany annexing the lands lost in 1919 and expelling 1 million Poles. The rest of the country was entrusted to a General Government, headed by Hans Frank, the self-styled 'king of Poland', who behaved worse than any absolute monarch.[114]

In contrast to former Czechoslovakia, which was to be gradually assimilated, Poland was to be cleared to facilitate German colonization.[115] Any assimilation was purely an expedient, driven by the growing labour shortage after 1941. Polish children in the annexed areas were taught ungrammatical pidgin German so they could follow orders but would always appear inferior. Their fate was determined by a complex mix of intent and improvisation, while the regime's polycentric character acted as an accelerant on violence as different individuals and groups competed for influence. The construction of Auschwitz began in April 1940, and it soon became the largest of around forty concentration and death camps in Poland. Over the next five years, the occupiers killed 5 million inhabitants, including 3 million Jews, and deported a further million to Germany as slave labourers. Another 6 million people elsewhere in occupied Europe were also murdered, including 600,000 Germans, who were mainly Jews.[116]

War in the North and the West

Most Germans hoped the victory would be followed by a return to peace, but Hitler soon abandoned ideas of reaching an accommodation with Britain. Neutral Denmark and Norway were attacked on 9 April 1940. Neither was prepared. Denmark surrendered after only eighty minutes' resistance once the German ambassador threatened that Copenhagen would be bombed. Norway received British assistance and held out until 10 June. Fearing it would be next and heavily dependent on Germany for its trade, Sweden granted transit for German forces across its territory and promised to supply vital raw materials. These successes appeared spectacular, but the Scandinavian conquests were vast, largely empty spaces, which now had to be defended against the Allies, meaning in Norway's case that when the war ended there were around 400,000 German troops marooned there.[117]

The long-expected main attack in the west finally came on 10 May. Most senior German commanders were pessimistic. Around 45 per cent of the army were First World War veterans over forty years old, while about half lacked adequate training.[118] Whereas the Wehrmacht had a numerical superiority of 2.5 million to the 2 million British and French soldiers, the Allies had a 44 per cent superiority in tanks, many of which were also heavier and better armed than their German counterparts.

The General Staff initially produced a warmed-up version of the Schlieffen Plan to avoid France's new fortified Maginot Line protecting its eastern frontier, by striking through the Liège sector again to the Channel and then swinging south. After much argument, Erich von Manstein, a junior rival to Halder within the staff, persuaded his superiors to accept his *Sichelschnitt* (Scythe Cut) idea to detach the main thrust (forty-five divisions) through the difficult terrain of the Ardennes to turn the French flank much sooner. Meanwhile, nineteen divisions would pin the French down on the Maginot Line and another twenty-nine would invade Belgium and the Netherlands. This modification is often celebrated as 'proof of the brilliance of German military doctrine'.[119]

It was a huge gamble, with much of its success stemming from Allied errors and sheer luck. Most notably, the 41,000 vehicles of the main thrust soon backed up in huge columns, which were vulnerable to air attack. As with Ludendorff's offensives, the Germans outran their supplies on several occasions, leaving them vulnerable to counter-attacks. However, the Germans *believed* they would triumph having just crushed Poland. Although brief, that campaign provided invaluable experience, particularly in coordinating units at the tactical and operational levels, whereas few Allied officers had seen combat since 1918. Allied morale had waned during the long 'Phoney War', while the sudden invasions of neutral Belgium and the Netherlands swiftly saw both these countries conquered, adding to a sense of inevitable defeat. Britain's evacuation of its forces from Dunkirk between 27 May and 4 June, while successful in escaping imminent capture by the Germans, further undermined French morale and led to a ceasefire on 25 June, deliberately staged by Hitler at

Compiègne in revenge for the 1918 armistice. France was partitioned into a German-occupied north and west, with the rest of the country neutral under a new, conservative government based at Vichy.

Switzerland

France's rapid fall exposed Switzerland, which was now surrounded, as fascist Italy had joined the war on the German side on 11 June. The failure of the Geneva disarmament conference in 1934 had already convinced many Swiss that liberal universalism had failed and that the country should abandon its engagement with the League of Nations and retreat to its earlier 'fundamental neutrality'. While conscious that its neighbours were rearming, Switzerland still struggled with the aftermath of the Great Depression, which had cut its foreign trade by two-thirds. The army was already starved of funds during the 1920s, but the power of the militia ideal convinced the government to reject recommendations from the General Staff that the country should reorganize its defence with a smaller but more professional and better-equipped force.[120]

As in 1914, France wanted Swiss neutrality to work and had no intention of infringing it.[121] Italy appeared more of a threat after Mussolini's support for the Anschluss, as he was rightly suspected of now wanting to partition Switzerland. However, the southern frontier was secured by the precipitous Alps, leaving Germany as the only obvious but very real danger to the north and east. As in Austria, Germany had promoted a Swiss National Front to agitate for annexation. From having been primarily preoccupied with a fear of communism since 1918, the Swiss government belatedly banned party uniforms and insignia, and promoted a common national culture transcending linguistic divisions. History played a major part in this, including reviving memories of the 1499 war against the 'Swabian pigs' to the north.

The influential Swiss general Ulrich Wille the Younger was prevented from following in his father's footsteps as commander on account of his blatantly pro-German sympathies. The government selected instead Henri Guisan, who was strongly opposed to appeasement. Guisan's defiant speech on 25 July 1940 caught the public mood, which was equally determined to preserve independence, and he emerged as the key figure.

The militia had already been mobilized on 1 September 1939, and since then units had served on rotation along the northern frontier. Guisan knew the Germans were likely to attack without warning and authorized the Swiss air force and anti-aircraft batteries to use force against German aircraft. The Swiss first opened fire on 10 May, and across the next four weeks got the better of several dogfights, shooting down eleven German planes to their loss of only three. Meanwhile, ten German saboteurs were caught trying to destroy Swiss aircraft on the ground and imprisoned. Then reality hit as German ground forces arrived on the frontier, prompting Guisan to order his forces to avoid further clashes.

The Germans knew the Swiss were poorly prepared but believed they would nonetheless fight hard. France's rapid collapse on 22 June 1940 removed the immediate need to cross Swiss territory, and the Germans became increasingly concerned that an invasion would cause them unnecessary casualties and could prompt the Swiss to dynamite the Gotthard and Simplon tunnels, which provided a strategic route to Italy. The invasion plan, dubbed *Operation Tannenbaum* (Christmas Tree), was repeatedly shelved as the Germans settled for economic and transit rights and used the threat of severing vital coal supplies to force Swiss compliance. Germany's growing distractions elsewhere ensured Swiss defences were never fully tested.[122]

From West to East

Victory in the west left Germany facing Britain and its global empire. The OKW was at a loss how to respond when Britain refused to make peace, while the German army expected the navy and air force to deal with it. An air campaign was launched, developing across the summer into terror bombing ('the Blitz'), which degraded the Luftwaffe's capacity and damaged its standing within the German armed forces.[123] An amphibious assault (dubbed Operation Sealion) was just one of the options that Hitler considered, before deciding that a conquest of Britain would cause its empire to disintegrate to the benefit of the United States and Japan. He felt Germany was becoming too dependent on Soviet deliveries of oil, grain, cotton, and other raw materials which it was struggling to pay for. By late July 1940 he had decided it was time to end this 'unnatural' alliance and instead attack the USSR. According to Hitler's tortured logic, defeating Stalin would encourage Japan to attack the USA, thereby isolating Britain further. As in 1939, the conviction that time was short strongly influenced this decision, since he felt that America would be ready for war within two years.

Overruling the army's and navy's plans for a global war against Britain, Hitler ordered them on 18 December to prepare to invade the Soviet Union.[124] The OKW initially thought of a short strike to conquer the Ukrainian 'breadbasket' and neutralize Russia as a military threat, but Hitler planned genocidal war. He made this chillingly clear in a two-and-a-half-hour speech to 250 selected senior commanders on 31 March 1941, when he stated it would be an 'existential war' in which the normal rules and international laws would not apply.[125]

This was hardly news to his audience since he had already used similar language. The main tension among planners was between those who overestimated the resources that could be seized, and those who remembered the difficulties experienced in Ukraine during the First World War. A few advocated a more conciliatory attitude towards the local population, but the majority rejected this, citing the failure of securing effective collaboration during 1917–18. The infamous 'Hunger Plan', prepared by the Ministry of Food, was formally adopted on 2 May 1941. The forested and more urbanized northwest of the USSR was to be left to starve, while Germany used the southern 'black earth' region to feed itself. The population was to be deported or exploited as slave labour. An estimated 20–30 million people were expected to die. Leningrad, Moscow, and other major cities were to be denied the opportunity to surrender and instead be bombed to rubble.[126] Well before the 'Final Solution' was agreed at the Wannsee conference on 20 January 1942, which accelerated the murder of Europe's Jewish populations, the regime's broader genocidal objectives were clear, even if the exact means remained undecided. Rather than raising moral objections, planners simply debated how far genocide should dictate military operations with the OKW arguing victory needed to be secured first, whereas Himmler and others saw a chance to accelerate extermination while simultaneously carving out further influence for themselves.[127]

Despite having a year to plan, German preparations were disorganized and inadequate. The regime's highly competitive atmosphere led to duplication and wasteful inefficiency, as well as attempts to outflank rivals by claiming that unrealistic objectives could be achieved. The department tasked with occupation administration and headed by

Alfred Rosenberg, a leading Nazi ideologue, was known as the 'Ministry of Chaos'. Those voicing concerns about risks were immediately shut down with arguments that alleged racial superiority guaranteed German victory.

Whereas prior to 1914 planners had overestimated Russia's strength, they now did the opposite, believing that Stalin's purges had destroyed the Red Army's cohesion. It had indeed performed poorly against the Finns in the 'Winter War' of 1939–40, but that experience was prompting reforms. For now, it was still a colossus with feet of clay: badly managed, ill-prepared, and poorly led, but mustering 2.7 million men, 13,000 tanks, nearly 35,000 guns and 9,000 planes in the west. The Germans massed 145 divisions (3.05 million men), but their other sixty divisions were fully committed elsewhere holding down occupied western and northern Europe (fifty-one divisions) or supporting Italy (nine divisions), leaving no strategic reserve, in contrast to the Red Army, which had an additional 2.8 million men. The Soviets had a huge superiority in materiel, as the Germans could only field 3,638 tanks, 7,146 guns, and just 2,770 warplanes because the Luftwaffe was already also committed in the Mediterranean helping Italy.[128]

The disparity increased the significance of Germany's allies, who provided a further thirty-seven divisions (930,000 men) for the initial invasion force. The German leadership was even more dismissive of their allies than their forebears had been during the First World War. International relations were now seen even more narrowly as a zero-sum game in which only Germany should come out on top. Nazi ideology reinforced the earlier prejudice by ranking foreigners in a crude hierarchy based on supposed racial characteristics and taking no account of the interests or capabilities of their allies.[129]

Only Finland was treated as a credible ally, but mutual distrust still prevented either side formalizing the arrangement, with the Finns simply operating in support by striking towards Leningrad. The Balkan states were at loggerheads, with their own rivalries shaping their interaction with Germany. Romania was the most committed, eventually sending 585,000 troops against Russia. Hungary and especially Bulgaria were more cautious. None were properly consulted, yet Romanian and Hungarian participation was crucial, compensating for Turkey's refusal to cooperate by extending the front line southwards to the Black Sea. As in 1939, Slovakia participated willingly in the hope of preserving its fragile autonomy, as did Croatia, resurrected as a puppet state from the wreckage of Yugoslavia which Germany had swiftly invaded in April 1941. The Germans did distribute some of the vast haul of weapons they had captured across 1939–40 to help their allies improve their obsolete arsenals, but their own forces were under-equipped and much of the booty was squandered as the Wehrmacht's three service branches squabbled over the spoils.[130]

Italy was Germany's sole formal ally, but Hitler only bothered to inform Mussolini on the eve of attacking Russia. Italy had mobilized barely 1.6 million soldiers from its 44 million inhabitants, and these were in many ways even more poorly equipped than those in 1915. Mussolini had fought his own parallel war in the Mediterranean since June 1940, increasingly frustrated at Hitler's inability to forge an alliance with Fascist Spain and block British reinforcements to Malta and North Africa. The Italians' planning was at least as unrealistic as that of the Germans, but there was some justification for their complaints that the Wehrmacht refused to heed their advice and instead unfairly blamed them for setbacks. By 1941, Hitler recognized Italy had become a liability, but nonetheless despatched two divisions to assist in North Africa, and Mussolini felt obliged to respond by sending an elite force to Russia. The struggle in the Mediterranean, like the failure to cross the Channel, revealed the continuing provincialism of German power. Too many countries remained hostile, neutral, or simply beyond the reach of Berlin. Ultimately, it was a 'world war' through the involvement of the USSR, USA, and Britain, not because of Germany.[131]

The attack against Russia was given a thin veneer of an anti-communist crusade, but in fact there was little solidarity between Germany and its allies, which were also governed by authoritarian regimes embracing similarly selfish and aggressive policies. It was impossible to conceive of any serious, lasting gains that these countries would have made had Germany's attack on the USSR succeeded. All were aware of Germany's previous disregard for formal treaties and had no illusions about its ultimate intentions. Indeed, they soon saw Germany's difficulties in the east as providing welcome leverage in their asymmetrical relations with the Nazi regime.

Operation Barbarossa

Displaying a crass misunderstanding of history, Hitler named the invasion Operation Barbarossa after the twelfth-century German emperor who had campaigned against the Slavs, not appreciating that he had died in Turkey in a failed bid to liberate the Holy Land.[132] The need to bail out Italy in the Balkans, combined with bad weather, delayed the start until 22 June 1941. Nonetheless, the OKW assured Hitler it would secure complete victory within three months before the feared Russian winter set in. Moscow was 1,000 kilometres away, with Russia's industrial zone a further 1,500 kilometres safely behind that. The front was 3,000 kilometres wide and split by the Pripet Marshes in the centre. Russia's railways used a different gauge and would have to be re-laid before they could be used. The OKW had proposed various options for concentrating German resources, but Hitler compromised by accepting all of them and ordering three thrusts spread along the whole front.[133]

Initially, the Germans' confidence appeared justified. Abandoning Russia's traditional defence in depth, the Red Army had concentrated close to the frontier, enabling the Germans to exploit their early breakthroughs to surround and defeat much of it. By mid-July the Soviets had lost 2 million men, 3,500 tanks, and 6,000 planes, including 1,200 destroyed on the ground during the first day by surprise attacks. Having overrun eastern Poland, the former Baltic states, and Ukraine, including the industrial Donets Basin, the Germans temporarily regrouped in August. Heady with success and mesmerized by the prospect of even greater gains, they pushed on, only to grind to a halt as the weather worsened, Soviet resistance stiffened, and their own forces suffered huge losses.

The Soviets had lost a staggering 4.47 million killed, wounded, and captured by the end of 1941 – the equivalent of 229 divisions. However, they adapted rapidly, reorganizing their forces with a simpler command structure, and mobilizing another 5 million replacements, enabling them to counter-attack at the start of 1942. By March of that year Germany had suffered 1.1 million casualties. A further 900,000 were sick and only eight divisions remained fully combat ready. Of the 3,492 tanks and self-propelled guns lost, only 740 were replaced immediately, while the Luftwaffe had lost 4,948 planes since June 1941, equivalent to a third of the new aircraft production, which also had to replace losses on other fronts.[134] Germany was eventually able to make good its losses with fresh conscripts and new equipment during 1942, but the disparity in forces merely increased, especially as German casualties on the Eastern Front averaged 2,000 men a day, or the equivalent to a division each week between 1941 and 1944.[135] Across the war, the Soviet Union mobilized over 34 million men and women, or nearly double that achieved by Germany on all fronts. What had already appeared a huge gamble in June 1941 was now a losing bet.

The odds worsened when Japan's unprovoked attack on Pearl Harbor on 7 December 1941 brought the United States fully into the war. The US had already adopted a pro-Allied neutrality in November 1939 and within a year had accepted it would have to enter the war against Germany. During the spring of 1941 it provided weaponry and vehicles to Britain under the Lend Lease scheme and declared an exclusion zone in the western hemisphere to safeguard vital convoys to Britain. Cooperation was strengthened with the signing of the Atlantic Charter in August 1941, which became the basis for the modern United Nations (UN). In October 1941, Lend Lease was extended to the Soviets as well.[136]

Following these events, it becomes understandable why Hitler felt war with the United States was inevitable, but Germany's actions had triggered the sequence, while Japan's unilateral attack speeded them up. Strategic cooperation between Germany and Japan was virtually non-existent, while Hitler's argument that Japanese intervention would keep the US occupied was wholly unrealistic.[137] The Japanese had failed to destroy the US Pacific Fleet at Pearl Harbor, and though they conquered many of the Allies' South East Asian territories, they became bogged down in their own unwinnable war. America had nearly two and a half times more per capita GDP than the Japanese Empire in 1941. It produced 41.7 per cent of the world's capital goods, giving it a huge potential to make armaments, compared to Japan with only a 3.5 per cent share and a crippling dependency on imported food and raw materials.[138]

Case Blue

Germany's leadership at least made some adjustment to the new reality. The goals of smashing Bolshevism and securing Lebensraum were temporarily shelved in favour of the more immediate needs of seizing sufficient resources to sustain the war. A small German detachment had reached the Russian oilfields at Tiflis back in September 1918, and the OKW was convinced this could be achieved again. Seeing what they wanted to, they significantly overestimated the proportion of oil the Caucasus region contributed to total Soviet production, as well as underestimating the difficulties of conquering it and exploiting it to improve Germany's global position.

Code-named Case Blue, the massive offensive began on 5 April 1942 and by August the oilfields had been taken. Those on the ground were now confronted with factors the planners had ignored: the Russians had destroyed the facilities, and the Germans had only obtained 1,000 tons of oil by the time they evacuated the region in December.[139] Meanwhile, secondary operations initially intended to cover the northern flank of the main attack were expanded by Hitler into a costly attempt to capture Stalingrad, a major centre of Soviet arms production. General Paulus's 6th Army was soon enmeshed in bitter street fighting while its Romanian supports were too weak to contain a Soviet counter-attack in November. Paulus's 291,000 men were trapped by over three times that number of Soviet troops. All relief efforts failed, forcing him to surrender on 31 January 1943. The total losses, including Romanians, amounted to 800,000 men. Although the Red Army lost around 1.1 million, it could absorb such punishment better than its opponents.[140]

Stalingrad is often seen as a turning point, not least because Paulus's surrender damaged German morale. However, the meeting of Allied leaders in Casablanca the same month was arguably more significant. The Anglo-American commitment to fight until Germany's unconditional surrender reduced the likelihood that the Nazi regime could use any future victory to bargain terms.

Defeat in the Mediterranean

A meeting in Casablanca was possible because the Allies had opened a new front in North Africa by landing in Morocco in November 1942. Italy's main army now faced attacks from Morocco to the west and Egypt through the Libyan Desert from the east. Overall, 260,000 Germans served in the *Afrikakorps* under Erwin Rommel, which was sent in February 1941 to reinforce the Italians. Rommel twice temporarily turned the tide but was already facing total defeat by the time he handed over command to General Arnim on 9 March 1943. Two months later the surviving 275,000 Axis troops surrendered.[141]

The Allies followed up by landing on Sicily in July, eventually prompting the Italian high command to remove Mussolini and seek an armistice in September.[142] The German response was swift and brutal as they turned on their former comrades, whom they now despised. Much of the Italian army was disarmed and deported as slave labour to Germany, while SS commandos rescued Mussolini to head a rump fascist state in northern Italy. The Allies landed in the south in October, beginning what would prove a long, gruelling campaign to fight their way northwards up the Italian peninsula.[143]

Retreat in the East

The impact of these setbacks was magnified by further Soviet offensives early in 1943 that regained lost ground in Ukraine. Keen to recover the initiative, Hitler and the OKW decided to attack a bulge in the Soviet front around Kursk. The operation was delayed until the arrival of new, heavier, but largely untested German tanks. German numbers were still impressive at 900,000 men backed by 2,000 planes, but Soviet forces were a third larger and had far more and superior tanks. Famed as history's largest tank battle, opinion remains divided as to whether the Germans could have won, had not the operation been called off after eight days on 13 July because of the Allied landings in Sicily.[144]

However, the numbers were already overwhelmingly stacked against the Wehrmacht, which had now lost much of its remaining offensive capacity. The Soviets had lost 15,000 tanks by the end of the year to 3,841 German tanks, but they still outnumbered their opponents. German strength in the east declined from 3.14 to 2.53 million men, with many of the surviving troops now being poorly trained conscripts. The OKW remained reluctant to retreat in case this encouraged the country's eastern European allies to defect like Italy. The obvious conclusion – that this meant Germany sooner or later would lose – was resisted.

Renewed Soviet offensives from January 1944 finally liberated Leningrad after an epic 900-day siege, and shattered German forces in the south, retaking most of the Ukraine and breaking into Romania.[145] With Germany now firmly on the defensive, Hitler ordered his generals to establish a line of fortified positions from the Baltic to the Black Sea.

Intended to act as breakers against the sea of future Soviet offensives, these were ordered to hold out at all costs. The policy was not without potential, but was pursued to an ideological extreme, forcing isolated garrisons into futile resistance that wasted Germany's dwindling manpower.[146]

Meanwhile, Germany treated its remaining allies ever more ruthlessly. Little effort had been made to cooperate with local fascists, who were invariably disappointed at the Germans' behaviour in their countries. The central government was largely excluded from occupation policy, which was handled through dysfunctional competition between the Wehrmacht and a variety of separate administrations, especially in the east. Denmark was exceptional in being allowed to retain its own government.[147] Vichy France had already been occupied late in 1942 following the Allied landings in Morocco. Hungary was occupied in March 1944, followed by Slovakia in August. Finland had been seeking an exit since early 1943 and used the German retreat as an opportunity to agree its own armistice with the Allies in September 1944. A communist coup in Bulgaria that month saw that country change sides, soon followed by Romania.

Two powerful Allied offensives in June 1944 expedited this process. Landing in Normandy on 6 June, the western Allies mustered 1.5 million men in France within a month. Outnumbered three to one, the Germans suffered from a divided command, inadequate air cover, and a crippling fuel shortage. Having mounted a strong defence around Caen, German resistance collapsed as the survivors raced to escape east of the Seine. A second landing in southern France in mid-August hastened the German exit. German losses totalled 500,000, or twice that of their opponents. An effective response to the Normandy landings was further hindered by the Soviet offensive just over two weeks later. Marshalling 2.4 million men, the Red Army cracked the German centre held by 886,000 troops and reached the Vistula by the end of July.[148]

The End

The obvious futility of fighting on finally prompted a small group of officers to attempt to assassinate Hitler in July 1944.[149] The plot's failure seriously undermined the Wehrmacht's influence within the polycentric Nazi state. Political loyalty assumed an even larger role in senior appointments, such as the choice of the wholly unsuited Panzer commander

Heinz Guderian as chief of staff. Himmler was permitted to expand his SS empire, securing command of the 1.9 million-strong Replacement (*Ersatz*) Army, composed mainly of untrained recruits. In September he also secured control of the 'Wonder Weapon' programme developing the rockets and jet fighters that the regime still believed could win the war. A levy of teenagers and old men was summoned as the *Volkssturm* to fanaticize the home front and demonstrate Germany's continued resolve to the Western Allies in a futile attempt to persuade them to negotiate. Jealous of Himmler's influence, Hitler's private secretary, Martin Bormann, ensured that the Volkssturm was organized by the party, but trained by the army.[150]

Collectively, these measures betrayed an obstinate belief that a combination of superior skill, technology, and willpower could still bring victory. In fact, Germany was deficient in all these respects, as well as now overwhelmingly outnumbered. It also suffered from the central problem of the entire war – that Germany had created enemies (most clearly Britain and the United States) that it never had the means or even the plans (in America's case) to defeat. Nonetheless, morale held up. While few people now believed the regime's claims that it would still deliver total victory, the majority thought their country could achieve an acceptable peace, most likely through an accommodation with the Western powers in an alliance against communism.

This hope was entirely unrealistic but was sustained by the Allies' inability to breach Germany's western defences despite heavy fighting between September and December 1944. The German counter-attack in the Ardennes (Battle of the Bulge) at the end of the year demonstrated that the Wehrmacht remained a dangerous opponent but the assault cost it more casualties than it inflicted. The defeat led to the evacuation of the remaining territory west of the Rhine and finally convinced most people that the war could not be won. Further Soviet offensives meanwhile completed the liberation of the Balkans and Baltic region.[151]

In January 1945, Germany still mustered 7.5 million personnel, though significant portions were now isolated in 'pockets' such as Courland, Memel, and Budapest. By May, 1.54 million of these would be dead, equivalent to the entire losses across 1942–3 and close to the total killed in the First World War. Many fought on because they had nowhere else to retreat to, while the regime ramped up repression and terror. Himmler made secret peace overtures through the Swedish Red Cross, while the SS commander and governor of Italy since September 1943, Karl Wolff, also opened secret talks, all of which were rebuffed.

German resistance faltered once the Western Allies finally broke across the Rhine on 7 March, trapping the main army in the Ruhr region. General Model gave his 320,000 men their discharge papers and committed suicide.[152] Concerned at the speed of the Anglo-American advance, Stalin ordered his forces to take Berlin first in what proved a costly but ultimately successful battle. General Jodl surrendered much of the remaining field army to the Americans on 7 May. Although the following day was celebrated as Victory in Europe, or VE Day, it took some time before the Wehrmacht's other remnants capitulated. Admiral Dönitz, to whom Hitler had entrusted Germany before committing suicide, was not arrested until 23 May.[153]

The Second World War has been endlessly refought in numerous books, often by individuals who admire the Wehrmacht. Such discussions generally focus on supposed 'turning points', speculating that if the outcome of individual battles had been different, the entire course of the war could have been changed. Like the scapegoating of Schlieffen, Kluck, and others during the First World War, such an approach replicates the German General Staff's own narrow view of warfare as primarily tactical. The early victories certainly demonstrated the power of shock and awe, intimidating Germany's opponents, just as the country's sabre-rattling prior to 1939 had encouraged the dangerous policy of appeasement. By 1941, Germany controlled 180 million people in occupied Europe, and together with its own population and those of its allies, it had an economic potential twice that of the Soviet Union. At that point, however, the USSR was still gearing up, whereas the Nazi economy was fully stretched and increasingly reliant on forced and slave labour. Even if the regime had been capable of more rational and effective decision-making and use of resources, it is likely that the war would have merely lasted longer, but with the same outcome. The US economy was three times larger than that of Germany, and combined with Britain and the USSR the Allies had a fivefold economic advantage. By 1944 they fielded a combined 28 million soldiers to Germany's 9.4 million and Japan's 5.4 million. Germany was consistently outproduced in weaponry, while Allied superiority at sea and in the air ensured their greater resources could be brought to bear far more effectively.

THE COLD WAR, 1945–90

Civilian Powers?

In contrast to 1918, the totality of Germany's defeat was obvious to its population, hardly any of whom actively supported the Werewolf underground movement organized by Himmler to resist the inevitable Allied occupation.[154] Other than some officers, few Germans wanted to remain in uniform. As the Cold War among the victors led to the east-west partition of their country, Germans' attention focused on reunification, not revenge. Germany's apparent rejection of militarism was echoed in postwar Japan and has led to both countries being characterized as 'civilian powers'.[155]

Defeat supposedly compelled both Germany and Japan to recognize the systemic interdependence of states and the futility of pursuing unilateral power politics for selfish advantage. Consequently, both sought to civilianize their external relations by making these more like their domestic politics: remove violence and accept a rules-based order, even if this necessitated transferring some sovereignty to supranational bodies. While renouncing war as a foreign political tool, both countries nonetheless used their post-war economic recovery to lend weight to attempts to influence international behaviour.

The primary support for this interpretation comes from the formal renunciation of aggressive war in the Japanese (1947) and West German (1949) constitutions. German politicians have embraced the term 'civilian power', particularly during the twenty-first century, but it only partially matched their country's post-war trajectory. Both West Germany and Japan aligned with the West as the Cold War deepened after 1945. Japan created a Self-Defence Force in 1954, which has yet to fire a shot in anger, though it has participated in peacekeeping missions since 2004. Germany also rearmed within the Cold War blocs, with the eastern German Democratic Republic (DDR) becoming particularly highly militarized. German forces have been progressively and substantially reduced since Reunification in 1990, but have simultaneously engaged more actively in foreign missions, including since 1994 in combat roles. Individual Neo-Nazis and other right-wing Germans also volunteered for the Croatian and Serbian armies during the Yugoslav civil wars.[156] Moreover, the military downsizing is deceptive, since it applies to virtually all states globally, while the changing character of war has created less visible ways of coercing enemies than the tank-heavy mass armies of the Cold War and, indeed, pre-1945 eras.

Occupation and Denazification

The idea that Germany might willingly become a civilian power seemed absurd to the victorious Allies, whose policies were guided by their experience of the aftermath of the First World War. This time, Germany had surrendered unconditionally and was fully occupied, giving the Allies far greater freedom to dictate policy. They had begun planning for this outcome in 1941 and intensified preparations as victory grew more likely across 1943, when regime change and complete demilitarization became key objectives. Henry Morgenthau, the US Treasury Secretary, proposed achieving this through deindustrializing Germany and occupying it for twenty years. Although initially a favoured option, this was soon dropped for fear that Germany would be unable to support itself and remain dependent on foreign aid.[157] This tension between the desire to punish Germany and the need to reconstruct it remained fundamental to how the country was treated by the victors after 1945.

Japan, Italy, and the other defeated powers were compelled to pay reparations but were given peace treaties and retained their sovereignty. By contrast, German sovereignty was abolished on 5 June 1945 by a decree of the Allies, who no longer recognized any German government. The victors deliberately avoided describing their presence as an occupation, which would have bound them to adhere to the restrictions enshrined in the 1907 Hague Convention. Instead of a peace treaty, they passed a series of measures at their conference in Potsdam across the summer of 1945 to administer Germany.[158]

Germany lost its territory east of the Oder and Neisse rivers, which Stalin promptly transferred to Poland as compensation for Russia's westward expansion at the Poles' expense. Russia also annexed part of East Prussia, including Königsberg, now renamed Kaliningrad. The Saarland was transferred to French control, while other smaller border areas went to Belgium and the Netherlands. The rest of Germany was divided into four unequal zones, as were Berlin and Austria, ensuring that Britain, France, the United States and the Soviet Union had a share in each case. These arrangements were intended as provisional until Germany could be trusted to behave. Their impermanence fuelled the worsening relations between the USSR and three major Western Allies, because Stalin wished to keep the new arrangements in the east, whereas the others had more sympathy for the Germans' own wish to restore a unified state within its pre-1937 frontiers.

Nonetheless, all four Allies agreed that Germany's fundamental transformation was a precondition of a permanent peace and they shaped their initial occupation policies to this end, articulated as a series of 'D-words': disarmament, demilitarization, decentralization, democratization, decartelization, and deindustrialization. The last was envisaged to make Germany pay, while simultaneously reducing its war-making potential. Denazification was fundamental to all measures, and swiftly became dominant as the Allies realized the drawbacks to the Morgenthau Plan. There were no common guidelines: each of the four powers acted in its own zones according to its own world view and attitudes towards Germans. All Allied administrations were improvised and understaffed, and soon had to scale back their ambitions.

The Nazi penetration of society had extended well beyond the party's 12 million members, since virtually all organizations had been Nazified, forcing the Allies to try and distinguish those individuals to be deemed dangerous or even criminal from those who had simply conformed to the regime's demands. It was immediately agreed that party membership was insufficient grounds alone to condemn someone, necessitating a laborious screening process of those occupying influential positions. Those considered fanatics or willing adherents lost their jobs and were barred from holding public office for ten years.[159]

To facilitate this, at least 470,000 civilians were interned without trial across Germany's four zones, of whom 190,000 were held in ten 'special camps' in the Soviet zone, including several repurposed former concentration camps. Over 43,000 inmates had died by the time these were finally shut in 1950, mainly of tuberculosis and other camp diseases. The Soviets deported a further 270,000 Germans to the USSR.[160] Punishment was a core objective, as the victors agreed that their handling of war crimes after 1918 had failed. Existing international law had no measures to deal with genocide, the definition of which only emerged during the process of prosecuting crimes from the Second World War. To cope, the Allies agreed new rules which broke national sovereignty by permitting external agents to prosecute a state and its officials for crimes against their own population as well as others.[161]

The process has been heavily criticized. It was certainly rushed. Britain deployed two different teams with little coordination or attempt to use police investigative expertise. In addition to the main trials held at Nuremberg, each power operated separate military tribunals in their own zones. The cases were not always well-prepared and even the Allies often underestimated the scale of German war crimes. There were separate trials for the regime, government, armed forces, industrialists, doctors, and others who were implicated.

The murder of the Jews was also handled as a special case, unwittingly helping those who wished to portray the Holocaust as an entirely separate event. Like the other branches of the SS, the Waffen-SS was designated a criminal organization, but this did not cover those who joined it after 1943 on the grounds that these had been conscripted, thereby creating an ambiguity its members exploited subsequently to portray themselves as simple soldiers. The SA and General Staff were acquitted on this charge, though individuals were condemned.[162] This selectivity unintentionally created a small group of 'Nazi war criminals' who became the scapegoats for the wider population, enabling others to disassociate themselves from violence and claim (at least to themselves) that they had either been 'following orders' or were misled by evil leaders, as will be discussed further in Chapter 15.

In addition to Hitler, propaganda minister Joseph Goebbels and Luftwaffe chief Hermann Göring, at least sixty-seven generals and admirals committed suicide to escape capture or incriminating verdicts. The three western Allies executed around 500 war criminals by hanging, with the total in the Soviet zone being around twice that. The Soviets imprisoned or deported around 40,000, mainly low-ranking officials and military personnel; again, far more than in the three western zones. Enthusiasm for the process rapidly waned as the Allies sought to re-establish German self-government, which the initial wave of dismissals had rendered ineffective. Soon, even senior figures were released from prison early, and by January 1952 only 1,258 were still held by the Western Allies. West German courts resumed prosecutions of individuals in several waves after 1958. By 2005, 106,000 people had been investigated, of whom 6,000 were convicted and just 166 given life sentences.

It is understandable why some feel that the entire process has been an ignominious failure.[163] It should be remembered, however, that this result was not intended, and there were some important achievements, not least in rescuing many of the victims from potential oblivion and in establishing a new benchmark in international jurisprudence. The tribunals rejected the 'following orders' excuse and sought to explain as well as punish. Finally, attitudes shifted significantly in the decades following 1945, most notably after the Yugoslav Wars (1991–2001), when engagement with the legacy also became part of the memorialization of the Second World War to ensure the crimes were not forgotten.[164]

Two Germanies

The growing rivalry between the USSR and its former Allies hastened the end of denazification, especially in the West, where it lost impetus after being entrusted to the local German authorities. Both sides in the deepening Cold War loosened the restrictions they had placed on German political life as they sought the population's support and cooperation. The SPD was soon allowed to re-emerge. The conservatives and Catholic Centre Party regrouped as the Christian Democratic Union (CDU – with its Bavarian sister party, the CSU), while the free-market liberals established the Free Democrats (FDP). The ability of these parties to operate nationally was curbed by the forced merger of the SPD and communists in the Soviet zone as the Socialist Unity Party (SED) in April 1946. Likewise, the communists' presence in the west of the country soon collapsed.

The Western Allies shifted from punishment to capacity building, including Germany in the financial aid package known as the Marshall Plan in 1947, intended to promote Europe's economic recovery. The USSR became increasingly obstructive as the Western powers pressed ahead with the merger of their zones into a friendly German state. Tensions escalated with the Soviet blockade of West Berlin in June 1948, leaving only the three air corridors the USSR had previously agreed with the Western Allies. US Douglas DC3 transport planes became known to Berliners as 'candy bombers' as they flew in vital supplies, though well over half of the 2.3 million tons of aid was actually coal to heat the city over the winter. Recognizing its blockade was counterproductive, the Soviets lifted restrictions on 12 May 1949.[165]

Two weeks later the western zones were combined as the Federal Republic of Germany (BRD), followed in October by the conversion of the Soviet zone into the German Democratic Republic (DDR). The former restored considerable local autonomy to Germany's regions, now constituted as Federal States (*Bundesländer*), of which there were ten once the Saarland was returned by France in 1957. The provincial town of Bonn was selected as the capital because West Berlin remained a self-governing entity. The government was accountable to an elected *Bundestag* (Federal Parliament) and headed by a chancellor, with a president as representative head of state. The DDR was organized as a centrally controlled unitary state with the Soviet sector of East Berlin as its de facto capital. Despite its name and the legal existence of other political groups, the DDR was a one-party state from its inception, with government organized on the Soviet model and headed by a Politburo. All four powers retained powerful forces in their respective zones, though their presence was soon regulated by agreements with the relevant German government.

Germany's partition was part of the wider Cold War divide. The West forged two overlapping alliances. Military cooperation was established with the North Atlantic Treaty Organization (NATO), combining much of Western Europe with the United States and Canada in 1949. Meanwhile, a longer process of economic and political cooperation was initiated in 1950, which resulted in the formation of the European Union (1993). The USSR responded with the Warsaw Pact (1955) and Comecon (1949) respectively for the Eastern European states within its sphere of influence. International relations were now primarily bi-polar, dominated by the USA and USSR as rival superpowers, though other states, notably China and India, exercised significant independent influence in their regions. Germany was at the epicentre of Cold War tensions since the front line ran along the inner German border, which saw the largest concentration of rival forces.

Rearmament

Despite their ideological differences, East and West Germany shared similar goals: to recover full sovereignty, win international acceptance, and provide security for their citizens. By 1954 the West had definitively rejected the USSR's proposal to restore Germany only as a largely demilitarized, non-aligned country. Both East and West Germany now accepted that reunification had slipped to a longer-term objective and henceforth could only be achieved through cooperation with their respective Cold War sponsors. The tension between these objectives was never fully resolved. The obligation to accept integration within the rival blocs threatened to curtail sovereignty and make partition permanent. For this reason, the SPD initially opposed Konrad Adenauer's CDU government's policy of *Westbindung*, or greater integration within Western Europe. Meanwhile, East Germany's governing SED soon came to depend on Soviet support against its own population. Regime survival displaced reunification as the existential goal and the term 'German nation' was dropped from the revised 1974 constitution as the DDR presented itself as an entirely different state from its Western counterpart.[166]

Rearmament was a priority for both governments, but the absence of a peace treaty meant neither was free to decide this alone. Each saw a chance to increase its weight with allies, while the superpowers expected Germans to contribute manpower to their own defence. While these factors largely determined the process of rearmament, its character was also influenced by the individuals involved, especially in the West. The use of two atomic bombs against Japan in August 1945 radically changed the global security context, which was further altered by the USSR's first successful nuclear test in 1949, as well as Mao Zedong's communist victory in China.

The task was far greater than the organization of the Reichswehr in 1919, because the process of disarmament in 1945 was far more comprehensive than that after the First World War. The Wehrmacht had been formally abolished on 30 August 1945, and though several thousand former personnel were used for mine-sweeping and rubble clearance, there was no institutional continuity between Germany's former armed forces and those established after 1945.[167] Police forces were soon re-established, though these initially operated under tight Allied supervision.

The Western Allies considered allowing Austria to reform its own army in 1946, but they dropped this in the absence of a peace treaty. The communist coups in neighbouring Czechoslovakia and Hungary led to the formation of the *B-Gendarmerie* in October 1949 in Austria's three Western zones. The 'B' was deliberately never explained, but its use implied the new force was part of Austria's federal police (*Bundesgendarmerie*). Organized as motorized light infantry, it was intended as a rapid reaction force against possible communist insurgency.

Although they rejected Soviet proposals on Germany's future, the Western powers accepted them for Austria in the State Treaty of 15 May 1955, which re-established sovereignty on the condition the country remained outside the rival alliances. Austria was only permitted self-defence 'based on the Swiss model'. The B-Gendarmerie, which had only numbered 7,000, was swiftly absorbed into the new *Bundesheer* (Federal Army), which initially totalled 25,000 in 1956. The army was already deployed on Austria's eastern frontier later that year when Soviet troops invaded Hungary to crush an anti-communist rising. While Austria remained officially non-aligned, it was essentially pro-Western and its limited defence forces were primarily orientated as a tripwire against a potential Soviet invasion.[168]

Switzerland continued the policy of 'fundamental neutrality' that it had already adopted immediately prior to the Second World War, but in practice, like Austria, it remained pro-Western after 1945, cooperating with Western European economic – but not political – integration and supporting UN sanctions against Rhodesia (1966) and South Africa (1977), ahead of becoming a full member in 2002.[169] The Soviet Union established its military alliance, the Warsaw Pact, on 14 May 1955, a day ahead of the State Treaty to make it clear to the other states it occupied that they could not expect such generous treatment.

While the superpowers had been prepared to compromise over Austria, they promoted separate armies in their respective parts of Germany. The Soviet occupiers formed paramilitary units thinly disguised as police from May 1948. Unlike their counterparts in the western zones or Austria's B-Gendarmerie, these were equipped with heavy weapons, including 1,000 tanks by 1953, as well as a small navy and air force. Almost from the outset, East German forces were configured as a trained cadre to lead a much larger force. Expansion was accelerated after 1952 as the West rejected Stalin's first set of proposals for reunification, and the force was reorganized as the *Kasernierte Volkspolizei* (Barracked People's Police – KVP), a designation intended to mask rearmament from East Germans as well as the West.[170]

Rearmament was spurred by the mass protests of 17 June 1953, caused to a considerable extent by the diversion of scarce resources from consumer goods into militarization, but triggered by the impos-ition of unrealistic targets on construction workers. Around half a million East Germans took to the streets demanding free elections and reunification. The Soviets activated three of their sixteen divisions in the country, but the East German civilian police (the *Volkspolizei*) remained loyal and suppressed the rising at the cost of twenty-eight dead and over 400 injured.[171]

The event haunted the SED for the rest of its existence. It immedi-ately accelerated rearmament, formally converting the KVP into the National People's Army (NVA). Its security policies blended external defence against the capitalist West with internal repression of potential counter-revolution. All armed organizations shared this dual role to at least some extent. The first line of defence was the provision of con-sumer goods to mollify the population. Much of the extensive internal surveillance by the Ministry of State Security (Stasi) was intended to enable the government to head off discontent by arranging the import of scarce but desirable items. The Volkspolizei, Stasi, and other para-military organizations like the 'Armed Groups of the Working Class' – a party militia – collectively formed a second line of defence intended to deploy 'ordinary police measures', as in 1953. If these failed, the govern-ment would bring in the army, with the Soviet occupying forces as a final reserve.[172]

These measures were employed effectively to prevent opposition to the construction of the Berlin Wall in August 1961. Unlike the citizens of other Soviet-occupied countries, East Germans had an obvious alter-native home in West Germany, where many already had relatives. The inner German border was closed in May 1952, but it was still possible to cross in Berlin. By 1961, 3.5 million had left, prompting the SED to seal the frontier completely, initially around West Berlin, but later else-where along the inner German border, two-thirds of which was blocked with wire fencing, minefields, and tripwire-triggered machine guns by the 1970s. Improved internal surveillance stopped most potential escap-ees reaching the frontier, though 915 were killed trying to cross by 1989.[173] Construction of the Berlin Wall enabled the SED to complete the DDR's militarization, switching from volunteers to conscription for the NVA in 1962.

Whereas the Soviets had been free to promote rearmament in their zone, friction between Britain, France, and the United States slowed that process in the West. France was particularly opposed to a new German army. However, Western intelligence considerably overestimated the size of the Soviet threat, prompting Britain and the US to favour enabling their zones to defend themselves. Pressure increased with the redeployment of American troops at the outbreak of the Korean War in September 1950. As an interim, West Germany was permitted to establish a lightly armed border defence force (*Bundesgrenzschutz*) controlled by the interior ministry in 1951. Comparable to Austria's B-Gendarmerie, this only totalled 20,000 men by 1953.

France now accepted German rearmament provided it was accompanied by greater integration within multilateral European structures. Known as the Pleven Plan after the French premier who proposed it, this mirrored France's agreement to Germany's reindustrialization, which was to take place within the European Coal and Steel Community, the economic organization that developed with the Treaty of Rome (1957) into the European Economic Community (EEC). Paradoxically, France eventually vetoed its own plan after four years of negotiations when it believed greater European defence integration would curb its own military autonomy.[174]

France's reluctance prompted Adenauer to proceed cautiously. He wanted to avoid suspicions that rearmament entailed recreating the Wehrmacht, but that made it hard to choose professional advisers from among the 3,200 former generals and admirals. In December 1948 he turned to Hans Speidel, who had been Rommel's chief of staff. Although he was not closely involved in the July 1944 bomb plot, Speidel had been arrested because he had frustrated orders to destroy Paris as the German army retreated. His good French connections were immediately useful, while his intervening experience as a history professor at Tübingen University added to his seemingly 'civilian' character. Speidel also already enjoyed good contacts with West Germany's leadership, including Theodor Heuss, the country's first president. Speidel's close collaborator was Adolf Heusinger, who had been the army's chief of operations staff but – despite being injured in the blast – had been suspected as disloyal after the bomb plot and removed. Both men had worked for American military intelligence immediately after the war, adding to their useful connections. While they had seen action as junior officers in the First World War, neither had held senior field command, and they were criticized by some other Wehrmacht veterans as 'office generals'. They exploited Adenauer's trust to act as gatekeepers, deciding who would be involved in the new armed forces, and they eventually outmanoeuvred several more senior former officers.[175]

Speidel and Heusinger steered a semi-conspiratorial meeting of fifteen former Wehrmacht officers at Himmerod Abbey in the Eifel Mountains in October 1950 to endorse their plan for the future armed forces. Those present agreed to oppose France's proposals to integrate Germans only at battalion strength, fearing this would make them simply NATO's cannon fodder. They were quite willing to accept rearmament within a European army, believing that no single country could defend itself against the USSR, but wanted twelve divisions, plus relatively powerful air and sea forces to assert German influence. However, what exercised them most was the need for the rehabilitation of 'German soldiers', including former Waffen-SS.[176]

Speidel and Heusinger met Eisenhower, NATO's supreme commander and later president of the United States, on his visit to Germany in January 1951, and persuaded him to sign a document they had prepared articulating their distinction between 'Good German Soldiers' and 'Bad Nazis'. Adenauer subsequently endorsed this and persuaded the Bundestag to alter the constitution to allow former career soldiers and officials to receive pensions. These measures secured the elite's acceptance of rearmament under the conditions imposed by the West.[177]

Following the failure of the Pleven Plan, the impasse was broken by Britain's proposal to admit West Germany into NATO. The suggestion pleased the United States, as it effectively ended the likelihood of a separate European military alliance and was welcomed by Adenauer as a step towards recovering sovereignty. West Germany joined NATO on 9 May 1955, formally establishing its new *Bundeswehr* (Federal Armed Forces) six months later. As with its East German counterpart, and indeed also Austria's army, it took around a decade for this to reach its authorized strength.

Cold War Strategy

The leadership of both East and West Germany believed that rearmament would secure their territorial security and increase their international influence, but swiftly found that strategy was dictated from outside by their superpower sponsors. NATO believed at least fifty divisions would be necessary to deter invasion by the Red Army's 175 divisions stationed across Eastern Europe, but even by 1962 it still only mustered twenty-four divisions, mainly Americans and Canadians. The USSR also enjoyed much firmer control over its allies (other than Romania), especially after it reorganized the Warsaw Pact in 1961, and it could more easily reinforce its armies in East Germany and Czechoslovakia than the United States could aid its Western European allies. By contrast, America's allies were more genuine, and its forces were not required to suppress local populations. The US enjoyed superior airpower and, despite the USSR's growing nuclear arsenal, America possessed 'overkill' superiority through its ability to destroy its opponent several times over.

Contrary to Western fears, the USSR mainly planned defensively, with the priority being to retain its grip over Eastern Europe. It focused more on conventional warfare before 1961, upgrading its forces with new weaponry and vehicles to boost capacity and compensate for a significant reduction in personnel.[178] Conscious of its inferiority in conventional forces, NATO already resolved to prioritize nuclear defence before West Germany rearmed, intending to station most of its troops west of the Rhine and bomb Soviet forces as they advanced from East Germany.

West German planners accepted they would not be permitted their own nuclear arsenal, but the full reality of the new conditions only hit home when details of the NATO exercise Carte Blanche were revealed in the press in June 1955. In this simulation NATO dropped 268 nuclear bombs on Germany to stop a Soviet advance, causing an estimated 5.2 million civilian casualties. It was now obvious to Bundeswehr planners that their role was simply to delay the Red Army so that it could be bombed more effectively.[179] The deployment of new, tactical nuclear weapons to US forces in Europe in 1958 increased fears that NATO would resort immediately to their use. Weighing just 55 kg (compared to 4 tons for the Hiroshima bomb), these could be fired by modified artillery and offered a way to destroy advancing troops rather than having to rely on long-range missiles to retaliate against the USSR.

Both strategic options were, for obvious reasons, now unpalatable to West Germany's leadership: reliance on nuclear weaponry would turn the country into a wasteland, whereas conventional defence would make it a battlefield. NATO relented, modifying its strategy with the adoption of 'Forward Defence' by the early 1960s, shifting its intended battleline eastwards to run roughly halfway across West Germany, and now targeting the nuclear blast at Soviet troop assembly areas east of the inner German border. NATO moved further in line with German desires with its new 'Flexible Response' strategy, adopted in December 1967, which allowed greater scope for conventional warfare, shifting the battleline to just behind the inner German border, and emphasizing nuclear weaponry more for deterrence. The new strategy coincided with the change in West German government from the CDU to an SPD-led coalition under Willy Brandt and later Helmut Schmidt as chancellors. It assisted their task of making the Bundeswehr both more effective and socially acceptable, as well as increasing Germany's weight within NATO, particularly now that France had distanced itself from that organization in 1966.[180]

East German forces were integrated within Soviet plans, which changed under Nikita Khrushchev to a more offensive strategy by 1961. Greater mechanization meant the Red Army expected to advance 90 kilometres a day, or around three times faster than envisaged during the 1950s. The USSR now planned to pre-empt NATO with a first strike to be followed by a rapid advance of conventional forces, which would occupy much of Western Europe and present the United States with a fait accompli. East Germany and Czechoslovakia formed the forward combat zone in these plans. The NVA was always kept at a high state of readiness as the planned first wave of the northern and central thrusts, while Soviet and Czech forces would strike southwards through Bavaria. Additional Soviet and NVA units would seize West Berlin. The growing unreliability of Poland within the Warsaw Pact by the 1980s increased the burden on the NVA and the East German navy (the *Volksmarine*) to cover the northern flank.

East German forces held regular joint exercises with their Soviet, Czech, and Polish comrades from 1961. However, the plans were seriously flawed, especially from the East Germans' perspective. The bulk of the NVA was expected to advance in the first wave, including bringing its mobile air-defence capacity, thereby exposing both national territory and the Soviet lines of communications. Logistical capacity would be further undermined, because the SED envisaged using its paramilitaries to crush the anticipated counter-revolution. Soviet planners expected the West to use nuclear weapons only once it had lost 100 kilometres of territory, whereas under Flexible Response the tactical button would have been pressed much earlier. They also underestimated the potential impact on morale by believing poorly protected troops would advance through radioactive areas, only abandoning this when the Chernobyl nuclear disaster in April 1986 raised public awareness of the dangers. While fashioned for the atomic age, Soviet and East German planning continued the traditional German fixation with swift, decisive victory against impossible odds. Preparations in the 1980s included field marshal epaulettes and bravery medals to be distributed to East Germany's leader, Erich Honecker, and Stasi chief Erich Mielke, in the event of the expected triumph.[181]

Warsaw Pact forces mobilized to crush an effort by Czech communists to liberalize their regime in August 1968. Ever loyal, the SED prepared two NVA divisions, but these remained at home after hardline Czech communists objected that a German presence would harm their cause by reawakening memories of Hitler's invasion just thirty years before.[182] Three months later the USSR indicated that all Warsaw Pact members were obligated to crush counter-revolution. These actions reminded Western Europeans of NATO's value and led to regular annual military exercises in Germany from 1969 (until 1993). Training focused on the 'Fulda Gap', a salient of East German territory that was expected to be the main Soviet invasion route. The US army constructed a replica of Hattenbach village at Fort Leavenworth in Kansas, its main training facility, to practise defence.[183]

These preparations continued amid the thaw in East-West relations that set in during the late 1960s. West Germany's new government contributed to this. The SPD dropped its opposition to the country's rearmament at its party conference in 1959. Although initially unpopular among members, the decision gained adherents because Brandt combined it with a new approach to the problem of reunification. Whereas Adenauer had refused to recognize East Germany, Brandt sought a better understanding, appreciating that reunification was impossible without agreement from the USSR. Known as *Ostpolitik* (Eastern Policy), this rapprochement included treaties in which Poland and the USSR recognized Germany's post-1945 eastern frontiers, as well as the mutual recognition of the existence of two German states in 1972. Also, in contrast to Adenauer, Brandt was prepared to embrace the concept of Germany's collective guilt for the Second World War, symbolized by falling to his knees on a visit to the site of the Warsaw Ghetto in 1970.

Russia's rapidly deteriorating relations with China after 1969 prompted it to open a dialogue with NATO, leading to the Strategic Arms Limitations Treaties (SALT) process and the Conference for Security and Cooperation in Europe (CSCE) agreements. The latter, also known as the Helsinki Accords, stabilized the Cold War divide through a mutual agreement not to interfere with each system's way of life. However, progress on nuclear disarmament remained slow and stalled with the Soviet invasion of Afghanistan in 1979.

Already in 1976 the Soviet Union had announced plans to deploy a more modern type of nuclear intermediate ballistic missile (IBM) known as the SS20. Helmut Schmidt, now the German chancellor, advocated forcing the USSR to reduce its nuclear arsenal by threatening to deploy the US equivalent, called the Pershing II, to replace its predecessor introduced in 1962. This strategy had an economic dimension that was less obvious to the public on either side of the Cold War divide. The US had substantially reduced its defence budget following the Oil Crisis of 1973 but was still spending proportionally far less of its GNP than the Warsaw Pact countries, which were becoming dependent on Western loans to sustain the limited supply of consumer goods to quell domestic discontent. The East could not afford a new arms race and would be forced to negotiate.

Schmidt's proposal was adopted as NATO's Double-Track Decision on 12 December 1979. It proved highly unpopular among voters, leading to the re-emergence of the peace movement and of the Greens as a fourth major element in West German politics alongside the SPD, FDP, and CDU/CSU. Consequently, Schmidt's governing coalition with the FDP collapsed in 1982 and was replaced by what proved to be sixteen years of CDU-led governments.[184] Concerned not to lose their financial lifeline to the west, the SED and their counterparts in Hungary and Poland acted to moderate Russia's response, which remained primarily confined to anti-Western propaganda.

Increasingly, the SED saw the main threat as coming from their own people rather than the West. They were alarmed by the growth of the Solidarity movement, which challenged the Communist Party's leadership in Poland. Erich Honecker advocated Operation Winter March, which envisaged one NVA division joining seventeen Soviet and Czech divisions in what would have amounted to a re-run of the simultaneous German and Soviet invasions in 1939. Like his Czech counterparts in

1968, Poland's premier, General Jaruzelski, objected to German involvement and forestalled intervention by declaring martial law in 1981.[185]

Reunification

The SED's position worsened with the renewed thaw in the Cold War by the mid-1980s. NATO's new AirLand Battle Doctrine of 1982 improved the coordination of conventional forces, which had meanwhile been strengthened. Planners were increasingly confident they could block the Warsaw Pact's expected first wave and then use airpower to destroy the second before it got moving.[186] Unable to compete with higher NATO defence spending, the new Soviet leadership under Mikhail Gorbachev signalled a change of direction, renouncing its right of intervention in favour of 'freedom of choice' for socialist countries in 1988.

Incapable of reform, the SED faced an existential crisis. Despite its extensive internal surveillance, it was surprised by the rapidity of events following Hungary's opening of its frontier with Austria on 10 September 1989. Gorbachev's state visit on East Germany's 40th anniversary, 7 October, emboldened the opposition rather than strengthening the regime. A change in leadership to Egon Krenz failed to stop the surge in public demonstrations. Doubting the regime's ability to act, some senior NVA officers considered a coup to allow them to follow China's example earlier that year in Tiananmen Square and use force. Some troops were deployed, but the SED leadership forbade the use of live ammunition. A bungled attempt to introduce new travel laws inadvertently opened the Berlin Wall on 9 November. Over 5.2 million East Germans visited the West across the next four days. Nothing could save the SED state now and the party polled only 16 per cent in the country's first free elections in March 1990.[187]

Germany's lack of sovereignty meant that reunification could only be achieved through agreement with the victors of the Second World War. The next West German chancellor, Helmut Kohl, agreed in July 1990 to pay the costs of the Soviet garrison in East Germany until it could be evacuated. No nuclear weapons or foreign troops would be stationed in East Germany and Bundeswehr units there would only count as part of NATO's forces once the Red Army had left. Finally, Kohl agreed to reduce the Bundeswehr from its current 480,000 men to 370,000 by 1995. This was a relatively easy concession to make, since he had already planned cuts due to the easing of international tensions and

Germany's falling birth rate which was affecting conscription. Nonetheless, it entailed acceptance of a formal limit to German forces.[188] The agreement paved the way for the Two Plus Four Treaty between East and West Germany and the wartime Allies on 12 September, which led to reunification on 3 October.

Any hope among East Germans that the more positive aspects of their state might carry over were already dashed before reunification: this was a Western takeover. The entire SED state and its socio-economic system was to be dismantled, while the country was reorganized as six new federal states within an expanded Federal Republic that moved its capital to Berlin. Morale plummeted within the NVA, especially among its 25,000 regular officers who had enjoyed a privileged position within the SED system. Having already been cut by 50,000 men as an emergency economy measure in 1989, the NVA required a tenth of its strength just to guard the huge haul of weapons handed over as the regime's paramilitaries were disbanded. There was also its entire infrastructure to dispose of, including sports clubs, a football team, its own phone network, hunting grounds, choir, orchestra, and ballet troupe, in addition to a vast arsenal of relatively modern weaponry.

Kohl's government allowed the Bundeswehr to resolve this task within general guidelines set by the Defence Ministry. Matters were overseen by a new Eastern Command under Jörg Schönbohm, who took over at reunification. The NVA had already detached itself from Warsaw Pact command and removed ammunition from its weapons. It had been disbanded by the end of 1991 when most of its personnel had been discharged, and integration was completed in 1993 when the new Bundeswehr units were activated. The departure of the final Russian troops in August 1994 completed this process, though disposal of East German weaponry took another year.[189]

NEW CHALLENGES SINCE 1991

The Elusive Peace Dividend

The merger of the two German armies suggested that the end of the Cold War would bring a new era of stability and prosperity. The removal of the Soviet threat disinclined voters to accept continued high defence spending, while the vogue for neo-liberal economic thinking encouraged an unrealistic faith that privatization would enable the state to discharge its public responsibilities more cheaply by greater involvement of private enterprise. Whereas NATO's thirteen European members had 3.5 million soldiers in 1990, there were fewer than 2.1 million under arms twenty years later, despite the addition of twelve new countries.[190]

Although undoubtedly driven by economic and political pressures, force reduction reflected the changing security environment rather than improved peace and stability. The end of the Cold War was followed by a new international impasse as cooperation between the United States and the new Russian republic swiftly broke down. The prospect of a Third World War faded, only to be replaced by numerous 'New Wars' within 'Failed States' whose internal problems, combined with malevolent external pressures, led to their collapse into civil conflicts.[191] Initially, it looked as if international organizations would respond effectively. The Cold War's division had often paralysed the UN's Security Council, inhibiting the despatch of armed peacekeepers. Whereas there had never been more than 10,000 troops acting as UN 'Blue Helmets' during the Cold War, over 95,000 were deployed by 1995. After a brief decline, numbers surged again to a total of 100,000 by 2015, mainly on missions in Africa.[192]

These developments compelled not only Germany to modify its multilateralism, but Austria and Switzerland to reconsider the neutrality they had adopted throughout the Cold War. Prior to 1991, Germany had refused to support 'out of area' operations, meaning beyond NATO's traditional focus on defending Central Europe. It rejected American calls for support during its intervention in the Vietnam War (1961–75), though it did increase its subsidies supporting the American presence in Germany and bought more American military equipment. Likewise, it refused support during the Soviet-Afghan War (1979–89) for fear that antagonizing Russia would endanger reunification.[193]

It became harder to argue that Germany was contributing its share to NATO with the end of the Soviet threat. Germany's self-fashioning as an *Ordnungsmacht* – a power supporting the international order – made it difficult to resist American calls to contribute more. The desire to assert sovereignty encouraged this, since Germany wanted to prove itself as a 'capable alliance partner' (*Bundnisfähig*).

Military downsizing increased interdependency, since even Europe's nuclear powers (Britain and France) were losing the capacity to act uni-laterally. Germany's rejection of unilateralism after 1945 was reinforced by the process of reunification. Conscious of the need to allay fears that Germany might again become Europe's unstable core, as it had been from 1866 to 1945, Kohl accepted greater integration by supporting the formation of the European Union (EU) in 1993 and the adoption of the euro as a single currency six years later.[194] Endorsing these measures, Defence Minister Volker Rühe announced his country was now 'encir-cled by friends'.[195]

German policy was increasingly torn after 1991 between a pro-American 'Atlanticist' option and a 'Europeanist' agenda, with the prospect of a possible third alternative of a more unilateral policy emerg-ing only more recently. The tension between the two main options was not immediately obvious. Kohl saw NATO's eastwards enlargement after 1991 as an extension of his own government's rules-based multi-lateralism, particularly as the former Warsaw Pact states presented themselves as now aligned with Western democratic values. Manfred Wörner, previously defence minister and the first German to be NATO's secretary general, initiated the Partnership for Peace (PfP) programme in 1994, which extended military cooperation to other democratic states that otherwise did not want to become NATO members, such as Austria, which joined the scheme in 1995.[196]

From Kosovo to Afghanistan

Preoccupied with reunification, Kohl sent 18 billion DM to mollify the United States during the Gulf War (1991), representing a tenth of the total international aid towards the cost of the conflict.[197] However, there were already calls from within the CDU that the constitution should be modified to permit the 'out of area' deployment of German forces. This became more pressing with the collapse of Yugoslavia into civil war a few months later, a calamity hastened by Germany's quick recognition of Slovenian and Croatian independence. Pressure to inter-vene grew as Serbian forces overran the UN safe havens in 1992. Initially, Kohl was only prepared to agree deployment provided this was backed by a UN resolution and was restricted to areas where the Wehr-macht had not operated, effectively ruling out a mission to Yugoslavia.

The use of airpower appeared to offer a solution, allowing Germany to support the NATO-led operations with surveillance planes operating from Italy, a NATO member. The despatch of armed troops to support the UN mission in Somalia (1993–5), albeit in a non-combat role, added to the growing controversy surrounding these actions. Following a case brought by the FDP, the German constitutional court ruled on 12 July 1994 that out-of-area missions were permissible if they met three conditions: agreement by the Bundestag, multilateral rather than unilateral action, and that they supported peace and stability.[198]

Ideally, it was felt that such action should be underpinned by a UN mandate; however, the public mood swung briefly in favour of intervention following the Srebrenica massacre of Bosnian Muslims by Serbian forces in 1995. From being an argument in favour of Germany remaining a 'civilian power', the Nazi past suddenly became central to legitimating intervention when the new foreign minister after 1998, Joschka Fischer, argued that responsibility for Auschwitz obliged the country to act to prevent any repetition.[199] Four of the Luftwaffe's Tornado jets attacked Serbian air defences on 24 March 1999, Germany's first combat mission since 1945. Significantly, this took place as part of the NATO intervention in the former Yugoslav republic of Kosovo and without a UN mandate.[200] Germany's willingness to support similar actions grew exponentially across the next two decades. By January 2011, 250,000 Bundeswehr personnel had served on numerous missions worldwide, with a peak commitment of 10,434 in May 2002.[201] Austria also increased its participation, deploying 1,250 personnel on eighteen missions in 2005–6 alone.[202]

Such missions assumed a different character in the wake of the 9/11 attacks. Gerhard Schröder, who succeeded Kohl as chancellor in the new SPD/Green coalition government in 1998, responded to the US invocation of NATO's Article 5 by promising 'unlimited solidarity'. The article had never been triggered before and obliges NATO members to assist a member state under attack. Framed at the start of the Cold War against the USSR, it was unclear how it would operate in the era of New Wars, particularly as the United States had been attacked by terrorists harboured by the Afghan government. American and NATO-led missions had struggled since 1991 to secure support through the UN. Germany, Austria, and America's other allies were confronted with the prospect of acting outside the formal international peacekeeping framework.

Germany and Austria eventually decided to participate in the International Security Assistance Force (ISAF), which was underpinned by a UN mandate to stabilize a new Afghan government, rather than the US and NATO Operation Enduring Freedom (OEF) tasked with the 'war on terror'. In practice, it proved difficult to keep the two missions distinct, especially as the bulk of ISAF forces were provided by the powers also supporting OEF and both operated under NATO command. Meanwhile, Germany also participated in missions in other global regions to which OEF expanded, such as anti-piracy patrols off Somalia. Germany's contribution was nonetheless substantial, with the 4,812 men and women deployed in June 2011 giving it the third largest of forty-eight contingents (see Fig. 36).[203]

German forces were assigned to Afghanistan's Kunduz province from 2003 and were ill-prepared for a growing insurgency four years later. Georg Klein, at that point the colonel commanding the German contingent, called in US air strikes when two tankers were believed to have been hijacked. These exploded, inflicting 102 civilian casualties. The ensuing public outcry indicated just how far German public opinion had shifted, especially since the end of the Cold War. Operations in a conflict zone were expected somehow to remain bloodless stabilization and peace-building missions. The defence minister and chief of staff resigned, but the Bundestag nonetheless authorized additional troops and extended its own mandate for the mission, and the Defence Ministry began to refer to operations as 'war', thereby gradually normalizing this as a policy instrument.[204] Germany continued to participate even after ISAF was replaced by a smaller Resolute Force to train the new Afghan army in 2014, when Foreign Minister Frank-Walter Steinmeier affirmed that there was no intention 'to leave the country like the Americans left Vietnam in 1975'.[205] The imminent withdrawal of US forces from Afghanistan left Germany no choice but to evacuate its remaining forces in June 2021. Over 150,000 Bundeswehr personnel had served there since 2002 at the cost of €12.5 billion and fifty-nine lives, the country's longest and costliest mission to date since 1945.[206]

European Security

Although Germany supported its NATO allies in Afghanistan, Schröder's government was already alarmed at the fundamental shift in US policy in 2002, when the Bush administration asserted a unilateral right to determine what posed a threat and to take whatever action it considered appropriate. Simultaneously, it articulated the Responsibility to Protect (R2P), legitimating unilateral intervention in other countries on humanitarian grounds. Sensing that there was little public support to follow this course, Schröder reorientated from Atlanticist to Europeanist multilateralism. The rundown of US forces in Germany, from over 248,000 (1989) to 69,000 (2000), added impetus to this, by making it clear that Europeans would have to shoulder more of their own defence.

The first manifestation of this explicitly *Deutsche Weg* was Schröder's refusal to support the United States in the Iraq War (2003–11), which initially put Germany at odds with several other NATO allies, notably the UK. Meanwhile, Germany sought to make the EU's security structure more effective. Through the 1990s, Germany had held a middle position between those EU members favouring Atlanticism (chiefly the UK, Denmark, and the Netherlands), and those (notably France) favouring greater integration of European forces. The Franco-German Brigade was already established in 1987 as a force outside NATO command and this was gradually expanded with the accession of other countries to create a European Corps in 1992. A command structure was slowly developed by 2003 to support missions outside NATO. These measures have been criticized as hollowing out NATO, but they were continued by the new CDU-led coalition government under Angela Merkel after 2005. Cooperation was given greater coherence with the adoption of the Common Security and Defence Policy (CSDP) in 2009, and several existing missions, such as the anti-piracy patrols, were switched to be under this umbrella.[207]

The new European security framework has encouraged Austria and Switzerland to participate in missions aligned with NATO but outside its immediate framework. The Yugoslav War proved a shock to Austria, which mobilized to protect its frontier, reminding the population why an army might still be useful. Although chronically underfunded, the Austrian army saw opportunities to gain valuable experience and demonstrate its purpose. It created a special company-sized unit to undertake more challenging missions as part of an international force, participating in Kosovo and ISAF. Switzerland also provided logistical support for the intervention in Bosnia after 1996. Following a 2002 referendum, it changed its military law to permit personnel to carry offensive weapons on foreign missions, with thirty-one soldiers serving in Afghanistan from 2003 to 2008. Like Austria, it established a special unit to improve its ability to contribute forces.[208]

Germany cooperated with France when it invoked the CSDP's common defence clause after the 2015 Paris terror attacks, but while it has supported EU sanctions against Russia since the occupation of the Crimea in 2014, it has refrained from joining NATO in bolstering the defences of Poland and the Baltic states. There have been other signs suggesting that Germany might pursue a more independent course. It refused to mutualize debt following the 2008 financial crisis, which would have entailed a further loss of sovereignty through greater political integration within the EU. Angela Merkel announced in 2011 that neither NATO nor the EU could solve global problems alone, and that Germany needed to seek new allies. Reiterated in 2012, this has been interpreted as a desire to act more independently, something that was also suggested by Germany's refusal to support the international intervention in Libya in 2011.

Germany has remained active, but in looser 'coalitions of the willing' which preserve its autonomy and agency. The level of participation has been scaled back, with Germany contributing around 2,700 personnel on eleven missions in 2019, or around a quarter of the total in 2002.[209] The new freedom has been facilitated by exempting training missions from requiring Bundestag approval since 2015, after five years of lobbying by the CDU, which argued this restriction was limiting the country's ability to act flexibly.[210] Currently, the largest overseas mission is the deployment of 900 personnel assisting France to train the Malian army.

A major factor behind this policy shift has been the migrant crisis. Whereas Germany received 438,000 asylum applications from refugees fleeing Yugoslavia in 1992, the country accepted 1.8 million between 2015 and 2018. Alongside terrorism, migration has become the German public's primary security concern, creating a new 'home front' for international relations. Overseas missions are increasingly presented as building the capacity of 'failing states' to cope with their own problems, thereby stemming the flow of potential refugees towards Germany. The country is not alone in this. The EU revised its security strategy in 2017 to expand the non-military dimension, with most of its missions now involving police and civilians.[211]

Austria, Switzerland, and Germany have all acted to a certain extent as 'civilian powers' since 1945. Arguably, Switzerland has long pursued a 'civilian' foreign policy, despite being relatively highly militarized in terms of the proportion of its population who trained as militiamen. While relatively well armed, West Germany conformed to the 'civilian power' model in terms of remaining defensively orientated and pursuing its foreign political goals through multilateralism and economic power. Reunified Germany has continued this course, having acted alone in only two of its seventy-six overseas missions across 1990–2015, whereas France has engaged either alone or in ad hoc partnerships ninety-eight times over the same period.[212] Although that contrast has become less pronounced more recently, Germany still does not match the capacity of either France or the UK for larger-scale unilateral action and, unlike both those states, remains a non-nuclear power. Progressive force reductions since 1990 mean that Germany, like Austria and Switzerland, can no longer defend unaided its territory against a significant conventional attack. The same applies to most European countries, making Germany's 'civilian' character seem less exceptional. Meanwhile, the changing security environment has seen most European governments develop a variety of responses in which the conventionally configured armed forces play a less prominent role, alongside cyber defence, intelligence cooperation, and the strategic use of humanitarian aid.

14
From Total War to the End of War?

COMMAND IN THE INFORMATION AGE

The Last Warlords

The influence of technology on warfare has grown markedly since 1914. Germans perceived the First World War as a 'Materiel Battle' (*Materialschlacht*), the outcome of which would be determined by vast quantities of armaments and munitions. Throughout, however, it was clear that sheer quantity would never suffice and that quality, in terms of both the weaponry itself and how it was used, was also crucial. The tight restrictions imposed on German armaments at Versailles in 1919 compelled an even greater emphasis on quality, which continued despite its rapidly increased strength as Germany rearmed after 1933. The dive-bombers, tanks, and other new weapons introduced during that decade have become integral to the iconography of the Third Reich and symbolic of German militarism more broadly to the extent that they distract from important continuities in armaments, organization, tactics, and logistics across the first half of the twentieth century. They also failed to win the Second World War.

Total defeat in that conflict was followed immediately by the onset of the nuclear age, which profoundly influenced Cold War strategy. Although West Germany developed nuclear energy, both it and its Eastern neighbour were limited to conventional forces whose structure, armaments, and doctrine were profoundly shaped by their membership of the rival Cold War blocs. While reunification and the end of the Cold War freed Germany from some of the external constraints on its defence policy, the escalating complexity and cost of conventional weaponry simultaneously imposed new limits. These had already long been felt in

Austria and Switzerland, where the high cost of modern weaponry weighed heavily on already tight defence budgets and increasingly alienated voters.

Throughout, German armed forces have been composed of citizens whose motivation and opinions always mattered to some extent, even in the dark days of dictatorship. The ability of established methods of recruitment to mobilize and train personnel was progressively eroded by the increasing sophistication of weaponry, particularly from the 1980s. As threats to national territory became more distant and diffuse after the Cold War, it proved harder to convince citizens to pay for armaments and to accept casualties. Germany has followed other Western powers in relying on new weapons systems as a substitute for exposing its personnel to risks. The recent defeat in Afghanistan has revealed the limits to this policy, while the emergence of new 'hybrid' forms of warfare, such as terrorism and cyberattacks, have increased the challenges of delivering national security in a form and at a cost acceptable to electorates.

The tasks of command had never been easy, but undoubtedly grew more complex, particularly as the need to mobilize productive capacity and to sustain public support became crucial after 1914. The outbreak of war immediately exposed the deficiencies in Germany's and Austria-Hungary's structures, which reflected their partially modernized, authoritarian characters. In both, command was still personal, with the emperor as supreme warlord. Neither Wilhelm II nor Franz Josef was suited to lead in person, while the political risks of doing so were demonstrated by Tsar Nicholas II, whose assumption of direct command associated him more closely with defeats and hastened revolution in Russia.

The elderly Franz Josef had delegated to Archduke Friedrich as head of the army's supreme command (*Armeeoberkommando* – AOK). In practice, actual direction of operations devolved to the chief of staff, the incompetent Conrad von Hötzendorf who lived in isolated luxury at Friedrich's country seat in Teschen, only visiting the front three times before his removal in 1918, by which time it was far too late to avert total defeat.[1] Whereas Franz Joseph was widely revered, Wilhelm II was already considered a liability before the war, to be sidelined once the real business began. The other German monarchs lost their peacetime commands, as the Bavarian, Saxon, and Württemberg general staffs handed over to that of the Prussians, which was mobilized as the

Supreme Army Command (OHL). Although formally only an adviser, the chief of staff in practice directed operations.

Command was not fully centralized, however. A separate, Supreme Command East (Ober-Ost) was established in November 1914 and entrusted to Hindenburg, who had already acted in this role since August. Hindenburg's assumption of the OHL role in August 1916 gave him overall direction, but there was still the separate command for the navy and the complex range of competing agencies that had mushroomed since the 1880s. Wilhelm exercised a moderating influence even into 1917, for instance delaying the full adoption of unrestricted submarine warfare, but was unable to give any real direction and was not motivated to defend civilian oversight. He increasingly became a 'shadow emperor', preoccupied with designing medals and other minor matters.[2]

Not only did Germany's various executive agencies fail to coordinate effectively, but its leaders invested little in their relationship with Austria-Hungary, despite their promise of support being a key factor prompting Austria to open the war. There was no common war plan. Moltke the Younger refused to provide information about events on the Western Front, allowing Conrad later to use the Germans' difficulties to excuse his own failures. Falkenhayn established a branch of Ober-Ost close to the AOK in Teschen but refused to subordinate German divisions to Habsburg command. These tensions worsened as the war lengthened.[3]

The fall of both monarchies ended personal command in the successor states, which adopted republican governments. Germany's first national war ministry was created at General Reinhardt's insistence on 1 October 1919 with the dissolution of the separate institutions in Prussia, Bavaria, Saxony, and Württemberg.[4] Civilian control was asserted by the rule that the war minister could not be a serving officer and was answerable to parliament. The complex structures of the Wilhelmine era were replaced by unified army and navy commands. The General Staff was formally abolished, but in practice persisted as the Troop Office (*Truppenamt*) created in October 1919. Ostensibly concerned with routine administration, this continued its predecessor's planning role.

Like the rest of the republican constitution, these structures were not necessarily deficient, had the will existed to make them work. Senior officers accepted civilianization to circumvent the Versailles restrictions. Whereas Wilhelmine bureaucrats had often been serving officers, posts were reclassified as civilian so as not to count towards the limit of

115,000 army and naval personnel. Likewise, other functions previously handled by the military were transferred to civilian departments, such as the railway ministry.

Hitler abolished the war ministry, merging its functions with those of command as a new supreme command (*Oberkommando der Wehrmacht* – OKW) in 1935 over the now three service commands: army (*Heer*), navy (*Kriegsmarine*), and air force (*Luftwaffe*). While looking centralized as an organization diagram, this proved dysfunctional thanks to the competitive culture fostered by the new regime. Each service branch had its own staff which regarded the others as rivals for influence and resources. Overall planning was supposed to be done by the OKW, but this was headed by increasingly subservient chiefs and remained chronically understaffed, having only fifty clerks even in 1944. The army staff did most of the planning during 1939–40, relegating the nominally superior OKW staff to secondary fronts like Norway. The OKW reasserted a role in the West from 1941, but the army staff ran the Eastern Front which consumed the bulk of Germany's resources. The OKW only recovered influence after the 1944 bomb plot increased Hitler's distrust of the army. A separate personnel department was established under General Jodl in 1939, which soon detached itself from the OKW's supervision as it developed as Hitler's personal headquarters.[5]

As this outline makes clear, personal command had returned with Hitler, whose self-appointed role as Leader (*Führer*) resembled that of a monarch. Hitler ignored the formal bureaucratic structure and communicated with the different service branches directly. Dissatisfied with his generals, he assumed personal command of the army in December 1941 and lived at his headquarters in the east, always a considerable distance from the front, which he rarely visited. He issued Directives (*Weisungen*) rather than precise orders. Superficially, this resembled the German Mission Tactics (*Auftragstaktik*), which supposedly had their origins in Moltke the Elder and devolved initiative to the 'men on the spot' to decide how best to achieve the commander's objectives. In practice, Hitler's Directives were intended to be part of his personal legacy to demonstrate his allegedly unique insight into world historical forces.[6]

Germany's elite would subsequently excuse themselves by blaming Hitler's 'corporal's mentality' for their defeat.[7] Hitler was hardly the first German commander to interfere in minor operational matters, and he had certain strengths. Unlike most of the senior officers, he had a grand strategic vision, but one shaped by Nazism's perverted world view. In contrast to Wilhelm II, Hitler had too much power, because the rest of the elite lacked an alternative vision and ceded the ground to him.[8]

Civilian Control

The fatal dangers of personal warlords finally ended with Germany's total defeat in 1945. Germany and Austria readopted republican structures of control as they rearmed, albeit with some important differences. East Germany was the least innovative in that the new position of defence minister created in 1956 was combined with that of general inspector, thereby continuing the duality of civil and military roles which characterized Imperial and Nazi Germany. Nonetheless, civilian control was exercised collectively through what became the National Defence Council in 1960, chaired by the minister for state security (i.e. the Stasi chief) and staffed by politburo members.[9]

West Germany self-consciously fashioned a 'parliamentary army' when it changed its constitution in 1955 to permit rearmament. Control rests in peacetime with the defence minister, who hands over to the chancellor in wartime; something that has yet to occur subsequent to 1945 since all military action has remained at the status of 'operations short of war'. A two-thirds majority in the Bundestag is necessary to declare a 'state of defence', a term deliberately selected to demonstrate the country's character as a 'civilian power'. In Austria, command rests with the federal president, with control exercised through the defence minister. In both countries, serving officers only have an advisory role through a defence council. Austria created an army command only in 1973, but this is still subordinate to the ministry. Switzerland retained its existing structure whereby a commander would only be elected in wartime, with the armed forces otherwise subordinate to the defence ministry.

West Germany deliberately abolished the traditional senior titles, such as field marshal and general of infantry, partly because they had become too closely associated with Prussian militarism, but also to align its rank hierarchy with that of NATO. Each of the three service branches was headed by a general inspector with a fourth added in 2001 for the new logistics branch. A senior general inspector is the professional head of the Bundeswehr. An attempt by Ulrich de Maizière to assert greater autonomy while he was senior general inspector (1966–72) was firmly rebutted by Helmut Schmidt, then defence minister, who did not want another General Seeckt. More recently in 1997, the government has demonstrated civilian control by dismissing a lieutenant general after a Neo-Nazi speaker was invited to address the military academy, while in 2003 the head of the special forces was removed after he praised a speech by an extreme right-wing MP.[10]

Neither West nor East Germany re-established a General Staff, partly because such an organization was now too tainted with aggressive war-making, but more practically because rearmament took place within the Cold War alliances, which left no scope for independent action or the development of a national doctrine. Although much is sometimes made of the German concept of Mission Tactics, German forces remain within NATO and EU multilateral structures and are guided by their doctrines. However, the growing burden of overseas missions necessitated the establishment of a Joint Forces Operational Command in 2001 to coordinate out-of-area deployments.

Unofficial defence ministries emerged around five years ahead of re-armament. Konrad Adenauer was forced to remove his first military adviser, former tank general Gerhard von Schwerin, for being too open about his new role to the press.[11] His replacement was Theodor Blank, a former carpenter who had served as a Wehrmacht lieutenant and was a member of a Christian trades union, which gave him political credentials appealing also to the German left to some extent. Nonetheless, around 250 former Wehrmacht officers comprised most of the initial staff of what became known as Amt Blank (Blank's Office) until it was formally constituted as the defence ministry on 7 June 1955.[12] Subsequently, the post has not always been a happy one. Of the eighteen individuals serving by 2021, seven have been dismissed or forced to resign following scandals, including one who was (wrongly) accused of being an East German spy. The first woman, Ursula von der Leyen, was appointed in 2013, serving until 2019, when she became EU Commission president, and was succeeded by Annegret Kramp-Karrenbauer.

In a further deliberate break with the past, West Germany created an entirely civilian Federal Defence Administration in October 1955 to handle procurement, infrastructure maintenance, legal services, recruitment, welfare, and pensions, all of which are governed by civil and business rather than martial law. The growing volume of activity was reflected in its expansion from 15,000 civil servants (1956) to 230,000 in the wake of reunification, though a greater reliance on the private sector has seen this fall to 75,000 (2011).[13]

Intelligence

Information gathering and management became more challenging across the twentieth century as those directing war had less time to react to more rapidly changing events, while public opinion exerted more influence on the capacity of states to sustain conflict. The German and Habsburg intelligence services during the First World War reflected their countries' structural flaws: a concentration on the tactical and operational levels to the neglect of strategic information, as well as poor coordination with civilian agencies and government.

German intelligence was led by the controversial Walter Nicolai after 1912. Although his staff rose from eleven to 188 across the First World War, they were overwhelmed by the task, and relied on open-source material, gossip, and personal observation. Espionage only really functioned on the more fluid Eastern Front, whereas in the West the intelligence chief relied on Germans who had served in the French Foreign Legion. German behaviour in the East discouraged locals from cooperating, while little effort was made to coordinate with the equally deficient Habsburg intelligence service. Poor intelligence contributed to Germany's bad decisions, notably the hopelessly over-optimistic assessments of the potential of unrestricted submarine warfare.

The interception of enemy radio traffic prior to the battle of Tannenberg (August 1914) was the most notable success and only possible because Russian security was even worse. Germany's most famous spy, Mata Hari, the stage name of a Dutch exotic dancer, was betrayed by the insecurity of German codes, though it is possible this was deliberate as it was known she also worked for the French. The Royal Navy broke German codes early in the war and generally had forewarning of naval operations.

Counter-intelligence (*Abwehr*) developed rapidly, especially to foster dissent and subversion among enemy populations, including efforts to raise a holy war among Muslims in the British and French empires, and sponsoring the Irish nationalists led by Roger Casement, who was given some obsolete rifles. Rather more effective was the coordination with Swiss communists to move Lenin and thirty fellow Bolsheviks from

Switzerland to Russia once it became obvious that the new provisional government would not make peace in 1917.[14]

The dark side to Germany's Burgfrieden was the suppression of contrary opinion. This had already begun in August 1914 with the establishment of the War Supervisory Office. Nicolai expanded his role to include censorship, public relations, and propaganda, which rapidly assumed critical importance once the army failed to achieve the promised quick victory. Whereas before 1914, pro-war messages had been largely conveyed by sectional lobby groups, like the army and navy leagues, they were now nationalized and centrally coordinated. Both Germany and Austria-Hungary made full use of the new medium of film, as well as posters, exhibitions, rallies, and other methods to persuade their populations to support the war.[15] Perhaps the most striking object was also the most deliberately archaic: the huge wooden knight erected early in 1915 in Vienna for members of the public to hammer in nails while donating money to the war effort. Similar figures soon appeared in German cities, notably the 'wooden titan' built in Hindenburg's honour in Berlin.[16] While successful up to 1916, such propaganda failed to adjust to the dramatic decline in public morale and became increasingly counterproductive. Nonetheless, the armed forces' leadership largely believed their own message, which they continued to push, first through the Vaterland Party after 1917, and then with 'political instruction' to the troops waiting in depots to be demobilized in 1918–19. Hitler was one of the lecturers at the Lechfeld camp in Bavaria.[17]

Nicolai's prominence made him widely detested by the public and led to his exclusion from the post-war intelligence service, which initially remained even poorer. The navy did establish its own decryption department in 1919, while in 1928 the Reichswehr adopted the Enigma machine, a commercially available encryption device. Although the Germans made some modifications to their military machines, their codes were broken during the Second World War, even if the decryption process was sometimes too slow to be of immediate use. Admiral Dönitz failed to realize this possibility and instead blamed treason for the Allies' apparent ability to second-guess his operations.[18]

The polycentric character of the Nazi state adversely affected its intelligence-gathering and information-management services consisting of several competing agencies with overlapping functions. In addition to the foreign ministry and diplomatic service, there were separate units in the three service branches, the various SS security agencies, and the Abwehr, the military counter-intelligence unit established by the Reichswehr in 1921 and reorganized in 1935 when it was placed under Wilhelm Canaris, a conservative nationalist naval officer who enjoyed Hitler's confidence, but was himself increasingly disillusioned with Nazism. Canaris tried to undermine Nazi foreign policy and passed some information to the Allies before he and his senior staff were murdered in the wake of the July 1944 bomb plot, thereby clearing the way for the SS to assume control of military intelligence.[19]

The politicization of intelligence was far worse than in the First World War. Information was interpreted according to the regime's warped and conspiratorial world view, with the army intelligence unit on the Eastern Front long being over-optimistic in assessing the chances of defeating the Red Army. Very few intelligence officers spoke Russian and they even lacked detailed maps of the USSR. Soviet air superiority by 1944 prevented aerial reconnaissance, which had already largely replaced the traditional reliance on scouting cavalry during the First World War.

The Nazi regime established a propaganda ministry under Joseph Goebbels, who regarded the truth as secondary to ideological guidance of the nation. In practice, all belligerents used similar methods of disinformation, often deliberately omitting details to soften the blow of bad news and to give a more positive impression of the chances of victory. The primary difference was that Allied populations had access to more varied media, while German propaganda contained more blatant lies.[20] The Swiss authorities also presented a carefully fashioned image through newsreels to bolster public confidence and to counter German propaganda. The Swiss intelligence service had already expanded before 1939 to monitor its neighbours' intentions, and to foster the belief that the country would defend itself if attacked.[21]

Elements of the Nazi intelligence services persisted into the post-war era in the West, based on an informal network of former General Staff officers, Abwehr, police, and SS intelligence personnel, coordinated by Reinhard Gehlen, the former head of the army intelligence unit on the Eastern Front. Gehlen had been dismissed by Hitler in April 1945 after sending too many pessimistic reports; something that improved his credibility to the Western Allies, to whom he surrendered having carefully microfilmed fifty boxes of secret files gathered on the Red Army. A tireless self-promoter, he convinced not only Western secret services but also Adenauer that he was indispensable in the developing Cold War. He saw the provision of information to the West as a way of ensuring the former General Staff could survive denazification and re-emerge within a rearmed Germany. Hans Speidel and Adolf Heusinger, the main architects of the new Bundeswehr, initially regarded Gehlen as an ally, but distanced themselves once it became clear a rearmed Germany would not be allowed a General Staff, and he increasingly became a liability through his shady associates.[22]

Gehlen's organization, known simply in its abbreviated form as the Org, was based at Pullach on the outskirts of Munich and expanded with generous CIA funding to a network of 4,000 agents. Despite repeated misgivings about the dubious backgrounds of many of its employees, the Org was formally established as the Federal Intelligence Service (*Bundesnachrichten Dienst* – BND) in April 1946. Mounting scandals over its penetration by East German secret services ultimately led to Gehlen's retirement in 1968, along with the dismissal of 200 staff. The BND continues to provide foreign and counter-intelligence services, while another civilian agency, established in 1950, combats domestic threats, notably that presented by terrorism since the 1970s. A separate military counter-intelligence unit was also established in Cologne for the Bundeswehr in 1956, with parliamentary oversight strengthened in 1978.[23]

East German security services were organized on more military lines with the creation of the Ministry for State Security (Stasi) in 1950, whose minister always held senior military rank. Numbering initially 1,100, this had grown to 91,000 full-time staff with 173,000 'unofficial co-workers' (i.e. informants) by 1989. It was embedded in all public organizations, including the NVA, and had its own university and (until 1982) economic concerns. The Stasi primarily spied on its own population, but as the SED increasingly distrusted its socialist neighbours, it began covert operations there too. The NVA had its own agency with 2,100 officers studying NATO. The NVA gathered relatively accurate information but misinterpreted this through the party's ideology, which believed the imperialist West was inherently belligerent.[24]

The Bundeswehr responded, perhaps belatedly, to the rapid growth of new information technology by establishing a Strategic Reconnaissance Command, which became operational in 2008. Delays in commissioning new equipment forced it to lease its first drones, but the force was expanded into the Cyber and Information Space Command in April 2017 with the full status of a fifth service branch. Meanwhile, the German government tightly regulates the information market by creating high barriers to entry to foreign firms in a bid to establish 'cyber sovereignty'.[25]

CITIZEN SOLDIERS

Conscription

Twentieth-century recruitment relied on conscription framed as a patriotic duty rather than a burden. Volunteers were always sought as well and were used by necessity during the era of the Versailles restrictions (1919–35), while conscription methods varied considerably. Fundamental changes have only been made since the 2010s.

Both Germany and Austria-Hungary entered the First World War with systems intended to mobilize large numbers of at least partially trained men to achieve a swift victory. The losses of the opening campaigns already forced them to draw on men who had previously been assigned to the *Ersatz* (Replacement Pool) with little or no training. By 1915 the German army needed 300,000 replacements each month just to maintain strength, or nearly double the General Staff's worst prediction. The attritional battles of 1916 increased demands still further since units became exhausted more quickly and needed to be rotated through the front line faster. In short, even more men were required just to maintain strength.

Both powers began calling up the regular age cohorts ahead of schedule from 1915, accelerating the pace by 1917 and creating a looming manpower crisis by 1918. Those previously exempted on employment, social, or physical grounds were repeatedly reassessed, with many being drafted, as were many convalescents despite their often-fragile mental state. Throughout, the situation was more extreme in Austria-Hungary, where the opening losses were six times the size of its peacetime army and consumed its entire pool of trained manpower. Germany mobilized 13.2 million men, the equivalent of 81 per cent of its pre-war adult male population, while Austria-Hungary had called up 8.42 million of the eligible 9.2 million males by early 1918. These proportions exceeded those of their opponents, who nonetheless collectively drafted nearly double the combined total mustered by the Central Powers.[26]

Germany suspended conscription in November 1918, a factor fuelling volunteering among teenagers for the new Freikorps. At least 400,000 served in the Freikorps during 1919, but the peak strength was no more than half that, comparable to the size of the Provisional Reichswehr and much smaller than the million or so Home Guards.[27] The Versailles restrictions required all new personnel to enlist for twelve years, to prevent early discharge as a way of building up trained reserves. Officers had to sign on for twenty-five years. The army used illness and other excuses to replace men early, but the numbers involved remained small. Economic conditions ensured there were always at least fifteen volunteers for every vacancy, enabling the armed forces to select those they considered politically reliable. Conditions in Austria were similar.[28]

Many German parliamentarians initially welcomed the formal abolition of conscription in 1920 as ending 'militarism', but they wanted an alternative 'school of the nation' to instil republican values and patriotism. The idea eventually found expression in the compulsory labour service introduced late in 1931 as part of measures to mitigate the impact of the Depression.[29] The armed forces were enlarged after 1933 simply by recruiting more volunteers, of whom there were still enough. Göring, who headed the (at that point unofficial) air force, and Himmler, in charge of the SS, wanted their formations to be elites and developed modern marketing techniques to attract volunteers, including posters, magazine articles, and engagement through schools and youth organizations.[30]

Military Service under National Socialism

The reintroduction of conscription was announced in March 1935 and implemented in May with men initially serving only one year. Intended to expand the reserves rapidly, this proved too short a time to train recruits adequately, and was lengthened to a two-year term after August 1936. After over a decade of politicized street violence, many older Germans welcomed the reintroduction of conscription as a way of disciplining the country's youth. Meanwhile, the existing labour programme was reorganized in June 1935 along more militarized lines as the *Reichsarbeitsdienst* with a six-month compulsory service for all men. The Hitler Youth, established in 1926, became a state organization in July 1936, when already nearly two-thirds of children over ten were enrolled for compulsory preparatory military training and indoctrination.

Austria had reintroduced conscription in April 1936, simultaneously reorganizing the induction of recruits to prevent infiltration from banned National Socialist organizations. The country was integrated within the German system after 1938, considerably boosting the manpower pool. Other organizations were also absorbed. Germany's provincial police were largely recruited into the army in October 1935 to increase numbers. The civilian police (OrPo), by now controlled by Himmler, was used to field Police Battalions from men aged twenty-four or older in September 1939. There were 244,500 men serving in such units by the middle of 1940. Deployed mainly to Poland and then further east, they played a significant part in the Holocaust.[31]

The expansion of the Waffen-SS after 1934 created a competitor to the three established service branches, all of which now relied on conscription. Himmler saw volunteering as a sign of ideological commitment, and the SS targeted teenagers before they reached the age when they would be drafted into the Wehrmacht. Hitler eventually authorized the formation of five divisions of seventeen-year-olds in 1943. Many lacked the physical development and resilience required. The pretence of volunteering was abandoned altogether after July 1944 when Himmler secured control of the Ersatz and could draft men, especially those who would otherwise have gone to the Luftwaffe. Meanwhile, large numbers of foreigners were recruited into separate SS units after 1940.[32]

Over 4.67 million Germans had served in the Wehrmacht by 1939, with a further 12.626 million inducted by the end of the war out of a population of 75.97 million (including 6.65 million Austrians). Of these, 13.5 million served in the army, 2.5 million in the Luftwaffe, and 1.2 million in the navy. Another 900,000 served in the Waffen-SS with well over another million in various militarized auxiliaries like the labour organizations, air defence, Red Cross, and the Volksturm improvised after July 1944. Of the 20 million total, no more than a tenth volunteered. The numbers inducted annually steeply declined after 1942, despite calling up cohorts early. As in the First World War, many who had been rejected or exempted were reclassified to fill the ranks.[33]

New Citizen Soldiers

After 1945 only East Germany came close to such a high level of militarization. Conscious that its citizens could still emigrate westwards, the

SED initially relied on volunteers, requiring recruits after 1948 to sign up for three years in its paramilitary police, and continuing this when the National Peoples' Army (NVA) was formed in 1956. It also employed many of the techniques already used by the Nazis and, also, other 'totalitarian' regimes, to encourage recruitment. In addition to the party's youth organization, a Society for Sport and Technology was established in 1952. Offering exciting opportunities like parachuting and diving, this essentially provided preparatory military training to boys aged six to eighteen. Like the regime's other mass organizations, the results were disappointing. Although nearly 1.3 million boys were trained between 1964 and 1967, only half achieved the required proficiency and just 56,000 volunteered for military service.[34]

The construction of the Berlin Wall enabled a switch to conscription in January 1962. The system betrayed its origins in that of Imperial Germany, having been devised by Vincenz Müller, one of the few senior former Wehrmacht officers accepted by the SED, who had served as a junior officer in the First World War.[35] The NVA was to be a cadre of career officers, NCOs, and specialists, filled out with cohorts of conscripts every six months who passed into the reserves after their eighteen-month service. The ratio of officers to men was one to three, compared to one to twelve in the Bundeswehr, because the NVA was expected to be supplemented in wartime by additional manpower from the regime's numerous paramilitaries. Stasi and customs officials underwent military training, while all police were armed with at least pistols and carbines. After October 1978 all fourteen- to sixteen-year-olds underwent compulsory military training, and 85 per cent of six- to fourteen-years-olds joined the party's Young Pioneers, who were required to practise 'children's manoeuvres'. Conscription meanwhile also provided manpower to the paramilitary border guards and riot police. By 1989, East Germany had 2.5 million trained reservists, a million of whom were younger than thirty-five, of whom 400,000 would be called up immediately in wartime, out of a population of just 16.4 million.[36]

Military service was initially also unpopular in the West, where news of possible rearmament prompted the *Ohne Mich* (Without Me) movement in 1951, when 9.1 million people signed a petition objecting to an army. Volunteers were preferred, and it was hoped they would provide over half the target strength of 500,000 men. Nonetheless, conscription was also introduced in July 1956, though with only a twelve-month term, as Adenauer was facing an election and rejected his generals' request for more. The service period varied thereafter, rising to eighteen months in response to the Berlin Wall in 1962, but it was cut again to a year in 1972 as the rising birth rate provided enough recruits. Proposals to increase it once again in response to a demographic dip were overtaken by reunification. The smaller, reunified army prompted a steady reduction in the term to nine months by 2002, with the option of serving for only six months, followed by two blocks of six weeks refresher training as a reservist.[37]

Austria meanwhile followed the requirement imposed by the wartime Allies in 1955 and organized its army on the Swiss model, with a very small professional cadre to train a modest annual cohort of conscripts, backed by a largely nominal reserve. However, it did not adopt the traditional three-tier system which Switzerland retained until 1995 and which distinguished between an active army of younger militiamen, backed by two categories of older reservists. In practice, neither country's reserves were fully trained or organized; a problem also experienced in Germany where men who had completed their military service were assigned to a Territorial Army, which partly only existed on paper. Service in Austria was only nine months, which was cut to six in 1971. As in Switzerland and Germany, subsequent refresher training was brief.[38]

Eighteenth- and nineteenth-century officers had considered three years the minimum necessary to train a soldier. Although conscripts were now much better educated before they began their service, weaponry and tactics had become more complex and sophisticated. Essentially, the methods used in Austria, Switzerland, and – by 2002 – Germany were only sufficient to socialize men into military life, not train them to fight. These deficiencies became more obvious with the growth of overseas missions after 1990, which demanded a higher level of skill and experience than acquired by most conscripts.

Overall numbers were substantial. By 2005 over 7.85 million men had served in the Bundeswehr, which had become a normal rite of passage, just like conscription in Imperial Germany. Meanwhile, 1.8 million Austrians served across 1956–2000, or proportionately far more relative to population size than in Germany. However, the proportion serving was eroded by the growth of civil service as an alternative to the draft. Conscientious objection had not been permitted before 1955, and around 300 Jehovah's Witnesses had been executed for refusing to join the Wehrmacht. East Germany permitted objectors to join unarmed, but nonetheless uniformed, labour battalions after 1964. Around 15,000 served this way in deliberately unpleasant tasks selected by the regime, including in lignite mines, chemical works, and railway construction.[39] From 1974, Austria offered alternatives as medical orderlies or in the country's civil service, whereas West Germany had already provided this in 1956. Initially, only 1 per cent of potential West German conscripts chose this, but the numbers soared with the social changes of the 1960s, and by 1984 the army no longer challenged applications but, instead, working for the civil service was made six months longer than the draft in a futile effort to dissuade recruits from choosing it. The growth of the peace movement, followed by the end of the Cold War, combined to push the numbers of German objectors to 190,000 in 2002, or 40 per cent of those eligible.[40]

Meanwhile, the progressive reduction in the size of the Bundeswehr after 1990 cut the proportion who were drafted each year. The possibility of overseas service also forced the army to raise fitness requirements and to exempt men older than twenty-three, enabling some to escape service by remaining in education. By 2010 only 16 per cent of the cohort served, fuelling the same kind of resentment that had occurred with selective service during much of the nineteenth century.[41] Austria and Switzerland experienced similar pressures, leading to a prolonged public debate in all three countries about whether to abandon conscription altogether and instead adopt a purely professional army.

The debates were characterized by emotive language. Proponents of abolition argued that conscription compromised individual freedoms and was no longer appropriate in a modern society. Defenders stressed its continued value as a civic duty, the educational benefits of service, and the democratic value of an army of citizens.[42] The party alignment differed, with the left favouring retention of conscription in Germany, but opposing it in Austria. Both Austria and Switzerland voted narrowly for retention in 2013, whereas Germany formally suspended it in 2011. That step has not been unusual in Europe where Belgium (1994), The Netherlands (1996), France (2001), and Serbia (2011) have either abolished or suspended conscription.

In contrast to earlier generations of German officers, those of the modern Bundeswehr also favoured ending conscription because 20,000 regular personnel were required to train each cohort, the last of which numbered only 55,000 conscripts. It was initially hoped that men would nonetheless still voluntarily perform a slightly longer version of the old draft, but the take-up has remained disappointing, despite efforts to offer more attractive benefits like free medical care. Only 8,547 'voluntary conscripts' were serving in August 2021, with merely 302 others choosing the alternative civil service option. The rest of the Bundeswehr at that point comprised 53,164 career soldiers and 122,114 professionals on shorter contracts.[43]

Female Volunteers

Just under 13 per cent of this total were women, who now serve in combat roles and no longer only as unarmed auxiliaries. Women had been mobilized in large numbers during both world wars, but primarily to provide medical care and as substitute workers to free men for the front. Although women had performed these roles in earlier wars, their mobilization after 1914 differed in both scale and through a higher level of militarization and integration with the (otherwise male) armed forces.

One key shift was the increasingly direct role of the state. Mobilization in 1914 followed the format set by the mid-nineteenth-century wars, with women joining voluntary organizations, such as the Red Cross, and the War Committee for Warm Underwear headed by Germany's empress. The call-up of reservists meanwhile accelerated the pre-war trend of a rising female presence within the German labour force, which reached 38 per cent by 1918, lower than that in Britain, France, or Russia. The main change was that women moved from low-paid jobs in textiles, agriculture, and domestic service and replaced men in better-remunerated work in factories and transport. Around half of the 2 million female industrial workers were employed in arms factories.[44]

The growing manpower shortage by 1916 forced both Germany and Austria-Hungary to form women's auxiliary corps to switch men from administration and logistics to the front line. By March 1917 there were 56,900 women military administrative staff, whereas there had been only one (a teacher) among the 1,733 officials in the German navy in 1899. A new Women's Department was established in the war ministry, headed by Marie-Elisabeth Lüders, one of Germany's first female graduates, who also commanded the new War Auxiliary Corps, established in 1917 to provide logistical support behind the front. This mustered around 20,000, with a further 10,000 'spade women' digging trenches and filling sand-bags behind the main lines. Austria-Hungary had 107,000 female administrative staff by the end of the war, with another 33,000 uniformed, but unarmed, personnel in the rear areas. Germany established a female signals corps in July 1918 as the first formal women's military unit, but this never reached the planned strength of 100,000.[45]

The Versailles restrictions encouraged the Reichswehr to employ women in its supply departments, administration, and communications so that these roles would not count against the overall force numbers. Women were also included in the covert civil defence organization developed in the 1920s but were excluded from combat formations. The numbers expanded dramatically under the Nazis, who construed women's work in civil defence and hospitals as part of their 'motherly duties'. Around 70 per cent of civil defence personnel were women who also assumed leadership positions. The Wehrmacht already had 140,000 female clerks and logistics workers by 1940, with the total hitting 470,000 by 1944 (see Fig. 31). At that point there were also 160,000 women in air-defence batteries and 275,000 firefighters. As casualties were initially lower than expected, 10,000 auxiliary nurses were retrained as signals personnel in 1940. Serving with the field army, they wore uniforms but were not classed as combatants. The SS employed another 29,000 women, including 4,000 as concentration camp guards (a tenth of the total). A further 10,000 women worked in the colonial administration of occupied Eastern Europe. All wore uniforms, but were not considered combatants, unlike the half million or more women soldiers in the Red Army, of whom at least a quarter served at the front.[46]

Switzerland also established a female auxiliary corps in 1939, in response to pressure from women's organizations keen to contribute more to national defence. Its strength peaked at 23,000, or around a tenth of its unarmed auxiliaries, but like their German equivalents, these remained uniformed but non-combatant. The corps was retained on a much smaller scale after 1945.

Women remained excluded from military service during rearmament, with the West German constitution expressly forbidding their call to arms.[47] The Bundeswehr's medical corps was opened to female volunteers in 1975, the UN Year of Women, but this was primarily because there were 1,300 vacancies. The growth of the peace movement deterred volunteers and the first female army doctor was not commissioned until

1989. East Germany's revised conscription law of 1982 opened military service to female volunteers, but interest was low, and the regime also struggled to attract women to the police and paramilitaries. As under the Nazis, women preferred to conform by joining the party's less obviously military organizations, forming 30 per cent of civil defence personnel and 70 per cent of the East German Red Cross.[48]

A reunited Germany opened all positions in its medical corps to women in January 1991, while Austria permitted female volunteers for most roles in 1998. Changing public attitudes accelerated this process. Tanja Kreil, a qualified electrician, appealed successfully to the European Court after she was rejected from a maintenance job by the Bundeswehr on gender grounds. As a result all posts were opened to women after January 2001. Senior commanders broadly welcomed the move, believing that the presence of women on overseas missions would assist in de-escalating potentially dangerous situations. Women are still found predominantly in the medical corps, especially among its officers thanks to their generally superior education. Overall, their proportion is higher than in the British and Scandinavian forces, but below that in those of France and the United States.[49] Switzerland followed by opening all roles to women in 2004, disbanding its small auxiliary corps as superfluous the following year. However, at 0.8 per cent of strength women remain a tiny proportion compared to Germany and below even Austria, where 2 per cent of professional personnel are female.[50] Germany is one of eighteen Western militaries to permit transgender soldiers.

MATERIAL BATTLES

Size

The progressive opening of military service to women as well as men reflected both changing attitudes to gender equality and the need to sustain recruitment. As the preceding section has shown, conscription enabled huge numbers to be mobilized during both world wars, but it still proved a struggle to maintain strength. The forces of the Central Powers peaked in 1916, with nearly 6.8 million Germans and 4.88 million Austro-Hungarians under arms. Combined strength had fallen to below 6.6 million by November 1918, of whom only 1.9 million remained at the front. Nazi Germany managed to expand from an initial mobilized total of 4.722 million in 1939 to a peak of over 12 million by 1944. Thereafter, strength declined sharply, but the Wehrmacht still mustered 9.4 million at the start of 1945. The army's proportion of this total shifted from four in every five to just over half, largely due to the diversion of manpower to the Luftwaffe and other militarized organizations.[51]

These numbers were never matched subsequently, a fact contributing to the perception of Germany as a 'civilian power'. The Bundeswehr totalled only 68,000 men by October 1956 and it took around two decades before it reached the planned 500,000-man target. That represented about 0.8 per cent of the population, or roughly the same level of militarization as peacetime Wilhelmine Germany. Of these, 25,300 were professional officers and 155,000 NCOs, with the remaining 317,000 composed of conscripts. Mobilized strength, including reservists, was intended in 1980 to be 1,055,000 soldiers and 281,000 sailors and air force personnel, or considerably below the numbers achieved by Imperial Germany, which had had a slightly larger population.

Post-war Austria initially mustered only about 25,000 men, or approximately the strength of the interwar republic's army. A reserve structure was established in 1968, and plans a decade later envisaged a mobilized strength of 84,000 active personnel and 300,000 reservists. This target was never achieved and was officially abandoned in 1990. Subsequent restructuring progressively reduced strength to 15,000 professionals with an annual cohort of 10,000 conscripts, backed by 945,000 largely nominal reservists.[52] Switzerland has followed a similar trajectory. At its peak, 924,000 men and women were mobilized in 1945, or one-fifth of the entire population, though a fifth of these were unarmed auxiliaries and the total was sustained only briefly. Strength remained high after 1945, at around 650,000, but these were militia, very few of whom were present with their units. The radical reorganization of 1995 cut numbers to 400,000, and this was soon reduced further. The reorganization of 2018 left 140,000, of whom only 15,000 would be undergoing training at any point, supervised by a cadre of 8,800 professionals.[53]

East Germany was exceptional in continuing a high level of militarization, though it also struggled to achieve the intended strength until after the introduction of conscription in 1962. By late 1989 the NVA had 99,300 soldiers, 4,700 air force personnel, 29,500 air defence troops,

14,100 sailors, and 20,400 administrative staff, with a planned mobilized strength of 350,000 including reservists. These were backed by the party militia of about 189,000, of whom 80,000 were equipped as motorized light infantry and the rest as police.[54] There were an additional 14,000 riot police, 110,000 Volkspolizei, 158,000 police reservists, and 491,500 civil defence volunteers. Even omitting the less heavily equipped of these groups, the country's armed forces totalled around 2 per cent of the population.[55]

Reunification saw not only the disbandment of these forces, but the progressive reduction in the strength of the Bundeswehr, especially after 2003, to a total of 184,127 active-duty personnel, 80,374 civilian workers, and approximately 144,000 reservists in August 2021.[56] The cuts saw the army's proportion of the total drop from 70 per cent to 62 per cent as greater emphasis was given to the navy and air force, while new logistical, medical, and cyber branches were created. Downsizing has been a global phenomenon, with the total number of military personnel falling from 29 million (1989) to 9 million (2005), and though overall numbers rose again around 28 million by 2021, the proportion among high-income states is still considerably below that prior to 1989. The US military as a proportion of population dropped to 0.5 per cent by 2011, compared to 2 per cent in the Vietnam era and 9 per cent in the Second World War. At currently 0.22 per cent under arms, Germany is obviously considerably below this, but its 'civilian' character is not so marked as it still has the European Union's second largest force after France and ranks thirtieth globally by size.[57]

Tactics

The reduction in size has been matched by one in Germany's influence on military practice. German rearmament after 1945 took place within the Cold War blocs with the forces of East and West Germany required to conform to the requirements of their respective superpower sponsors. In West Germany's case there was also a significant break in continuity. In 1945 the Wehrmacht was still a dangerous opponent from which the United States believed it could learn how to fight the Red Army. A decade later, it was obvious that nuclear weapons had changed warfare fundamentally and the new Bundeswehr had to work hard to catch up.

By contrast, Germany had retained more of its military reputation after its defeat in the First World War, thanks largely to its innovations in land warfare. Although it had lacked a viable strategy in 1914, its tactical doctrine was not as deficient as the popular clichés of the Western Front suggest, and like the other belligerents both Germany and Austria-Hungary had learned something from observing more recent conflicts in South Africa, Manchuria, and the Balkans. The critical problem was the strategic emphasis on a swift, decisive victory, which necessitated rapid mobilization of often poorly trained men. Many German reservists still carried the obsolete M88 rifle and wore the old blue uniforms, rather than the 'field grey' (*Feldgrau*) service dress introduced in 1910. They were often unfamiliar with the latest tactical manual and there were not enough officers or NCOs to lead them effectively. As in almost every case, matters were even worse in the Habsburg army.[58]

Under these circumstances, officers often ignored the official, more complex fire and movement tactics, and led their men forward, trusting that a rapid, determined advance would nonetheless succeed. Whereas, for the British public, the full consequences of this approach only became obvious with the first day of the Somme (1 July 1916), for Germans it was already clear with the 'Massacre of the Innocents' (*Kindermord*) of Langemarck on 10 November 1914. While many of those killed were indeed young, largely untrained volunteers, others were older reservists. By the end of 1914, Germany had lost over 800,000 killed, wounded, or captured. Attrition in these opening campaigns exceeded even the material battles of 1916 and was over four times higher than the average monthly rate of 3.5 per cent suffered between 1915 and July 1918.[59]

Austria-Hungary's army was also gutted and never fully recovered, but Germany managed to adapt. Falkenhayn's switch to positional warfare (*Stellungskrieg*) on 25 November 1914 was intended as temporary until another suitable opportunity to attack should arise. The growing length of the stalemate on the Western Front prompted the OHL to issue formal regulations for defensive warfare in October 1915. As with all German doctrine, this focused narrowly on the operational and especially tactical level. It only made sense as a way of clinging on to those parts of France and Belgium that happened to have been seized in the war's opening weeks but offered no access to any conceivable war-winning strategy. Falkenhayn and the leading tactician, General Fritz von Lossberg, advocated forward defence with a strong front line backed by reserves – the same approach as the Western Allies.

By September 1916, Lossberg was proposing a more flexible defence in depth, which was adopted by Ludendorff with the backing of Max Bauer and Captain Hermann Geyer, who produced a new manual in December 1916. This incorporated the new appreciation of the heavy machine gun as a defensive weapon. In 1915, Germany had 8,000 machine guns, including 1,400 captured from the enemy. By 1918 the army had 100,000, including the slightly lighter version designated 08/15, which became so ubiquitous that its name remains a colloquialism for 'ordinary' (*null-acht-fünfzehn*).[60]

The manual divided the battlefield into three zones, with the first being a thin line of fortified outposts to disrupt the enemy's initial attack. The second, main battleline was up to 1,100m deep with two sets of multiple trench lines and pillboxes, with supporting artillery positioned behind it. The final rear area was several kilometres further back with the reserves sheltered in deep bunkers. The infantry received new, light artillery for direct support during 1917, as well as trench mortars, copied from the Turks, which gave them portable, short-range weapons. Meanwhile, the heavier artillery was reallocated from corps to divisional level to improve coordination. Austria-Hungary's deficiency in such infantry support weapons was another factor in its many defeats.[61]

The new tactics were not invariably successful, but were improved with experience and reduced German losses, especially as the greater depth allowed most of the infantry to wait in bombproof shelters during the enemy's preliminary bombardment, re-emerging in time to hold their lines or counter-attack if an opportunity presented itself. The Allies only adopted German methods when their own defences were breached during the first Ludendorff offensives in 1918.

Discovering how to achieve that breakthrough cost much time and many lives. By 1915 the best chance appeared to be in the East where the front was four times longer and the force-to-space ratio only a third of that in the West. The German and Habsburg victory over Russia at Gorlice in Poland (May 1915) involved a prolonged barrage followed by a concentrated attack that broke the enemy's centre.[62] Such a conventional approach stood little chance in the West against a well-entrenched opponent. The preliminary bombardment alerted the enemy and usually failed to destroy his defences. It proved difficult to coordinate the infantry's advance with the artillery's supporting 'creeping barrage', which was supposed to stay just ahead. Attacks usually lost impetus and became vulnerable to counter-attack.

Gas Warfare

The use of gas appeared a way to break the deadlock. Although chemical weapons were banned by the 1899 and 1907 international conventions, the OHL investigated their potential after the defeat on the Marne in 1914. The French army's use of gas grenades and modified bullets gave the German command sufficient excuse to employ methods developed by Fritz Haber, the director of the country's leading institute for chemistry. Haber had already perfected a way to synthesize ammonia that enabled Germany to manufacture both munitions and crop fertilizer despite the Allied blockade (he would be awarded the Nobel Prize for this in 1918). Bavaria's Crown Prince Ruprecht objected on moral grounds, but Falkenhayn and other senior commanders backed Haber, who hoped that chlorine gas would incapacitate rather than kill, and its use would save lives by shortening the war.

It took a month for the new *Stinkpioniere* to prepare Haber's canisters before they were first used at the Second Battle of Ypres on 22 April 1915, when they killed 1,200 Frenchmen and incapacitated a further 3,000. While this attack had the advantage of surprise, it achieved relatively little. Having protested, the Allies soon used gas as well. A further 400 cloud attacks had been used on the Western Front by 1918, but they depended on the wind direction and were generally ineffective, especially as both sides developed masks and other countermeasures. A fiercely patriotic German Jew, Haber had been denied the coveted reserve officer status, but was now given the Iron Cross and made a captain. His wife opposed his involvement and committed suicide, though the marriage was already unhappy.[63]

It took a new method of delivery before gas became more effective. This was provided by Colonel Bruchmüller, who, like Hindenburg and many others, had been brought out of retirement in 1914 and subsequently transformed artillery tactics. By 1916 he had evolved a method of firing three different types of gas shell. The initial barrage combining tear gas and a vomiting agent would force enemy troops to remove their gas masks, exposing them to the next round of lethal choking gas. Improved gas masks mitigated some of the impact of this tactic, and like the initial employment of gas it failed to be decisive. Overall, the Allies had over 700,000 gas casualties, nearly ten times those suffered by Germany, of whom only 3,000 died.[64]

Nonetheless, the use of gas was widely reviled, and the possession of such weapons was prohibited in the Versailles Treaty, which also required Germany to dispose of its heavy artillery. Chemical warfare was subsequently banned in more precise terms in the 1925 Geneva Convention, but the Reichswehr secretly tested weapons in collaboration with the Red Army. German scientists continued to invent new agents, including Zyklon B, initially intended as a pesticide, but later used to deadly effect in the Holocaust. The leading chemical conglomerate IG Farben created the far more potent sarin gas in 1938. Likewise intended for agriculture, this was produced in limited quantities after 1939, but fear that the Allies would retaliate prevented its use in the Second World War.[65] Sarin was subsequently adopted by NATO and the Soviet Union as the standard chemical weapon and was stored in huge quantities in both East and West Germany until finally banned as a weapon of mass destruction in 1993 – a measure that sadly has not prevented its use in some more recent conflicts.

Breakthrough Tactics

Bruchmüller made a greater impact through devising more effective tactics for conventional artillery. He incorporated a method invented by Captain Pulkowski to improve predicting where shells would land without having to fire ranging shots, which would alert an enemy to an attack. He also dispensed with the long preliminary bombardment in favour of a short, massive barrage to disorientate an opponent and destroy his communications, followed by carefully coordinated use of targeted suppression fire to prevent an effective response to the attacking infantry. These methods were first used against the Russians at Riga in September 1917, and subsequently at Caporetto and in the Ludendorff offensives. They remain the basis for current American and Russian practice, while NATO employs a computerized version of Pulkowski's method.[66]

More effective artillery still required infantry to win battles. What became known variously as 'stormtrooper', 'shock', or 'infiltration' tactics emerged from several independent efforts to find less costly ways of attacking an entrenched enemy. The best known was the first 'storm detachment' (*Sturmabteilung*) created on the Western Front in March 1915 to devise new tactics and then train other infantrymen, but broadly similar methods were developed on the Southern (Italian) front by the Württemberg Mountain Infantry, which included Erwin Rommel, then a lieutenant (see Fig. 23).[67]

Initially unsuccessful, the small storm detachment was reorganized in August 1915 by Captain Willy Rohr, who equipped the soldiers with the new steel helmet, trench mortars, flamethrowers, and hand grenades. Whereas previously men had been assigned to platoons according to their stature so that the unit looked good on parade, the men were now divided into squads in which each soldier had a specific task. Squad leaders were expected to use their initiative, especially in selecting how they crossed the ground to minimize casualties, and in responding to immediate threats. This command philosophy was known as 'mission tactics' (*Auftragstaktik*), characterized by the senior officer defining the objective, but allowing subordinates considerable latitude in deciding how best to carry this out.

While undoubtedly significant, it is important not to overestimate the broader impact of these methods. Some extravagant claims have been made for mission tactics as the secret of all Germany's military successes since Moltke the Elder, with the senior commander as the strategic genius whose subordinates were 'dogs of war' who instinctively knew what to do and only needed unleashing to achieve victory.[68] The main impact of mission tactics was, as the name suggests, at the local, tactical level, though higher unit commanders were also allowed greater latitude to decide when to summon reserves or artillery support. To be successful, mission tactics required motivated, skilled junior officers and well-trained soldiers, all of whom were in short supply. Even by February 1917, there were only fifteen battalions of stormtroopers, or roughly one per German army.

Nonetheless, the new methods were undoubtedly deliberately aggressive. The assault would be led by a line of squads of ten to twelve soldiers advancing independently, often under the cover of smoke, and using grenades to silence pockets of enemy resistance. Those that could not be subdued easily would be skirted and left to the following supporting troops to deal with. Following the successes at Riga and Caporetto, fifty divisions were trained in the new tactics, or around a fifth of the total. They got the best equipment and higher rations, but there were not enough young men, necessitating the drafting of those in their thirties to assault divisions whose quality did not match that of Rohr's model unit. Moreover, the diversion of recruits and resources adversely affected the performance and morale of the remaining infantry, most of whom now only received two months training, rather than the two years considered necessary prior to 1914. Stormtrooper tactics also proved extremely costly, especially when the advance troops outran their supports and became vulnerable to local counter-attack. Attrition during the Ludendorff offensives was nearly double that over the previous three years.[69]

Nonetheless, the spectacular success in the opening offensives of 1918 left a profound impression on post-war officers, as well as prompting the Nazis later to appropriate the name Sturmabteilung for their party army. Seeckt's response to the Versailles restrictions was to make every member of the Reichswehr into an elite stormtrooper. The groundwork was laid in his tactical manual, issued in two parts between 1921 and 1923, and known as *Führung und Gefecht* (FüG – Leadership and Combat), which in turn strongly influenced its replacement, *Truppenführung* (TF – Troop Leadership), written by Ludwig Beck a decade later. Often lauded as a manual for Blitzkrieg, these documents codified and refined First World War experience.[70] Mission tactics were indeed emphasized by stressing that senior commanders had to explain the *why* as well as the *what* when issuing orders. However, the emphasis remained on small-unit tactics, not the operational or strategic command levels.

The principal focus was still the ten-man squad, which was now reorganized around the machine gun to provide the main firepower, rather than simply acting as a supporting weapon. This development was facilitated by a new, lighter, and hence more portable type known as the MG34, which was issued in 1936 and was the world's first, general-purpose machine gun (see Fig. 27). Weighing only a sixth of the old 08/15, this could be operated by a single man, though it had a team of three, backed by six riflemen and a NCO squad leader. A new, significantly improved version was issued as the MG42, which had about twice the rate of fire as its Allied equivalents and was widely copied after 1945 in versions that remained in use in NATO armies until 2005.

Three (from 1942, four) squads made up a platoon under a junior officer. An advance would be made in short rushes using the terrain and relying on the vastly increased rate of fire to suppress the enemy and prevent effective countermeasures. These tactics benefited from being delivered by an army that in 1939–40 contained a relatively high proportion of reasonably well-trained soldiers and fighting men who were often demoralized or trained in more conventional tactics, or both. The British had already translated the TF just before the war, and sections were included verbatim in the US field manuals of 1940 and 1943, continuing to influence American practice until the end of the century.

However, like their opponents, Germans experienced combat as a long sequence of rapid actions, leaving little time to think. Most focused on personal survival and were largely oblivious to anything beyond their weapons and immediate comrades. Wehrmacht soldiers generally agreed that no more than six of every ten men were fully committed during battle. Well-trained troops coped well, though even supposedly elite and Waffen-SS units were gripped by panic and fled, notably during the winter of 1941–2.[71] Meanwhile, the focus on the machine gun encouraged an over-reliance among the rest of the squad, who were unable to cope if it failed; for example, in Stalingrad where the close-quarters street fighting negated its advantages.[72]

Training paid only lip service to personal initiative, with the emphasis remaining on obedience; something heightened by Nazi ideology. Mission tactics thus primarily rested on the junior officers and squad leaders whose men were increasingly ill-prepared. The horrendous losses suffered after June 1941 led to units being continually reconstituted, reorganized, or amalgamated, thereby significantly eroding cohesion. By late 1944 even basic training had been cut to three months or less. The importance of this was graphically demonstrated by the decline in soldiers' survival chances from an average of four years' service before death for those conscripted in 1939 to barely a month for those joining in 1945.[73]

Belated efforts were made to improve weaponry to offset the infantry's qualitative and quantitative decline. The army began the war with an inadequate infantry support gun, which soon proved incapable of destroying enemy tanks. Better guns were rapidly employed, notably the famous 88 mm originally developed as an anti-aircraft (AA) weapon, but which proved versatile in other roles.[74] There were never enough, while the introduction of armoured self-propelled guns (SPGs) competed with tank production, since these used the same chassis. Shortage of general artillery, largely caused by the Versailles ban on heavy weaponry, prevented the use of Bruchmüller's barrage tactics on a grand scale, and forced the army to rely instead on the Luftwaffe to provide ground attack 'flying artillery' with the famous 'Stuka' dive-bomber. Progressive loss of air superiority during 1942 thus severely restricted offensive capacity.

In 1942 infantry received the *Panzerfaust*, the world's first portable rocket-propelled grenade (RPG) weapon, followed by the *Panzerschreck* reusable rocket launcher based on American bazookas captured in Tunisia. The StuG44 assault rifle was introduced in 1944, another world first that offered a more versatile version of the submachine guns developed since 1918. The Soviets soon copied this as their own, considerably superior AK47 assault rifle, which remains a standard infantry weapon around the world. Like the rest of the Nazi armaments programme, these weapons could not turn the tide and simply lengthened the time it took to defeat the Wehrmacht.

Cavalry

Although most soldiers were infantrymen, cavalry remained important into the 1940s. It proved impossible to employ cavalry effectively on the Western Front in 1914 where they failed in their primary task of scouting and screening the advance. Matters were different on the more open battlefields in the East, but Austria-Hungary was compelled to dismount most of its cavalry by early 1915, because it could not replace the 150,000 horses killed in the opening campaigns. German cavalry were also largely dismounted before the end of the war.[75]

The Versailles terms fixed German cavalry at an anachronistically high proportion of three of the army's ten divisions. Nonetheless, the arm retained some significance, not least because Poland and the USSR still employed cavalry effectively in their war of 1920. While German cavalry carried sabres until 1941, they abandoned the lance in 1918 and were no longer intended to exploit an infantry breakthrough. Instead, the horse was now seen primarily for mobility and cavalry were combined with bicycle-mounted infantry in a role reminiscent of the original dragoons of the seventeenth century: to move rapidly to seize key ground or block enemy advances.

Bicycles only emerged as a viable form of mass transport in the 1890s. Austria-Hungary already taught its officers to ride them after 1881 and they were regarded as a good alternative to horses, not least because they did not require feeding or watering (see Fig. 25). The Habsburgs adopted motorcycles and cars in 1912 but used these at this point primarily to speed up messengers. Following experiments during the 1920s the Wehrmacht created several light divisions combining motorized infantry, including some on motorbikes, and light tanks that were intended to replace cavalry entirely. The most famous of these divisions were the two despatched as the Afrikakorps in 1941, but they were also exceptional in being fully motorized.[76]

Shortage of motor vehicles gave cavalry a reprieve after 1941 and they were expanded again to total four divisions by 1944 supporting the army on the Eastern Front. However, the greater potential of modern weaponry now restricted their use to combating poorly armed partisans, especially in the Pripet Marshes.[77] The Swiss army not only lacked motor vehicles but suffered a serious shortage of fodder during the Second World War. From having defended the retention of cavalry against parliamentarians who had seen horsemen as an expensive anachronism, the Swiss senior command proposed disbanding them altogether in 1947 but dropped this in the face of a public protest from what was still a largely rural population who could not imagine an army without horses. Parliament finally approved the motion in 1972, despite a renewed outcry. As another anachronism, bicycle-mounted infantry remained part of the Swiss army until 2001.[78]

Motorization

The persistence of cavalry is a reminder not to overestimate the significance of motorization and mechanization before the later twentieth century. Despite the place of tanks (*Panzer*) in popular literature and imagination, the Wehrmacht scarcely differed from its imperial forebear in terms of transport and mobility. Prior to the 1930s, mechanization was driven primarily by logistics, not tactics, and Germany lagged considerably behind its major rivals. Germany had experimented with steam traction as early as 1870–1, followed by Switzerland and Austria, but it switched in 1911 to petrol engines. Despite the Kaiser's enthusiastic support and Germany's innovative motor industry, there were only

61,000 vehicles, including 9,000 trucks, in Germany in 1913, compared to 91,000 in France and 209,000 in Britain. By 1918 the German army on the Western Front had 23,000 trucks to the Allies' 100,000.[79]

The lack of adequate transport was felt immediately in 1914. Germany's efficient use of its railways speeded its mobilization but did not solve the problem of how to supply the army once it advanced from the railheads into enemy territory. General von Kluck's 1st Army alone had 84,000 horses requiring 2 million tons of fodder daily. Meanwhile, increased ammunition expenditure had already doubled the size of the ammunition train compared to 1870. Although 3,700 trucks were initially mobilized from the beer industry, two-thirds of those assigned to Kluck's army had already broken down by 12 September. These problems immediately returned with the resumption of more mobile warfare at the end of 1917, as successful offensives soon outran their supplies. Meanwhile, the army continually struggled to resupply ammunition even to static fronts.

These problems persisted during the Second World War, when there was only one motor vehicle in Germany for every two in Britain and France, and ten in the United States. Germany built 800,000 trucks and other military vehicles during the war, but there were never enough, forcing it to rely heavily on horses. Given the scarcity of oil, this was not necessarily a disadvantage, because fuel could be diverted to the Luftwaffe and navy. However, no more than a tenth of the army was motorized, including the artillery, which largely remained horse drawn. The regime's endemic infighting compounded the problem by making poor use of what was available. The Luftwaffe and navy each had one vehicle for every ten men in January 1944, or nearly twice the allocation to the army, while the latter had 1.2 million horses to the 80,000 of the air force.[80] Even a tank division had 1,000 horses for its supply transport.

Operation Barbarossa in the summer of 1941 was only possible thanks to the huge haul of vehicles captured from the Western Allies the year before, but the plethora of different types required a bewildering range of spare parts, and 85 per cent of the 500,000 vehicles accompanying the invasion had broken down by November 1941. For the rest of the war, the army relied mainly on carts stolen from the local population. Unsurprisingly, the Wehrmacht largely moved at the same pace as the *Kaiserheer* in 1914, with their speed dictated by the foot-slogging infantry and horse-drawn transport. Napoleon's army covered the ground faster during its invasion of Russia in 1812, reaching Moscow in under twelve weeks, half the time it took the Wehrmacht – which failed to capture that city (see Fig. 28). As late as 1952, the former chief of staff, Franz Halder, was still advocating the horse as the primary means of transportation.[81]

Tanks

These remarks apply even more strongly to the role of tanks and other mechanized armoured vehicles that have become fetishized as totemic symbols of Blitzkrieg. Günther Burstyn, a lieutenant in the Habsburg army, designed an armoured car in 1903, as well as the first modern tank, complete with tracks and a swivelling gun turret in 1911. Although the armoured car was tested in 1906, Emperor Franz Josef forbade its adoption on the grounds it frightened the horses, and it was sold to the more appreciative French. The tank never made it off the drawing board.[82]

The German army showed little interest in armoured vehicles, even after Britain's first use of tanks at the Somme in 1916. Instead, the initiative came from the war ministry and led to the adoption of Germany's first tank in October 1917. A tall, armoured box on an Austrian Caterpillar-Holt chassis, this was designated A7V and has been called the 'clear winner for the title of "ugliest tank ever built"'.[83] No more than twenty of the projected 100 entered service and they made no impact on the war. By contrast, France and Britain developed tanks as both offensive and defensive platforms, employing nearly 400 at Cambrai on 20 November 1917. Although they achieved surprise, the Germans adapted quickly and their anti-tank tactics, which relied on defensive pits, hand grenades, and light artillery, were sufficient to contain what was still an emerging technology.[84]

Tanks were among the weaponry banned at Versailles in 1919, though the Reichswehr continued to test prototypes in Russia and used dummies mocked up on trucks to practise during field manoeuvres. To divert attention, development was entrusted to the motor transport department, imparting a different culture than in other armies where tanks were largely regarded as caterpillar-tracked cavalry with tactical doctrine profoundly influenced by that heritage. Although less bound by convention, German tank development had much in common with that of other armies during the 1920s: the main role of tanks was for infantry support. In addition to borrowing from British and French experience, the primary influence was Seeckt's operational concept of mobile defence, namely, tanks assisting infantry counter-attacks.

That these origins are not those popularly remembered has much to do with Heinz Guderian, who owed his rapid promotion to become Germany's first tank general in 1938 to his ardent National Socialism. His subsequent fame rested on his book *Achtung Panzer!* (1937) and his post-war memoirs, which were endorsed by Liddell Hart, Britain's leading theoretician and tank advocate.[85] Guderian only first saw a tank while on secondment to Sweden in 1929, and his ideas typified the unrealistic faith shared by many officers in interwar Europe that this weapon had revolutionized warfare and would win all future battles.

German tank tactics essentially copied those of the stormtroopers. A spearhead would deploy in several waves to punch through an enemy position, relying on motorized infantry for a rapid follow-up. The full potential of these ideas was constrained by an inability to resolve technical problems fast enough, and the impossibility of ever producing sufficient numbers of vehicles. Early tanks frequently broke down, and even in 1939 Germany lost a quarter of those deployed. Later models were also often unreliable because they were rushed into service before being fully tested.

Like other states, Germany envisaged light, medium, and heavy tanks, mirroring the old classifications of cavalry, with each intended for different battlefield roles. The first model (PzKw I) was based on a secretly imported British 'tankette' in 1932. This was a light tank, adopted because it was easier to produce than a heavier version, rather than because it was particularly good. Five other main designs followed by 1943, each progressively larger, better armoured, and more powerfully armed. All suffered serious design flaws, which were exacerbated by the often chaotic and competitive way they had been planned by rival agencies and arms firms. The obsession with technical perfection slowed development and led to a plethora of different versions of the same model. Arguably the best was the Panther (PzKw V), designed by Ferdinand Porsche, who had also created the iconic VW 'Beetle'. The Panther only entered service in 1943 and was Germany's first all-purpose 'main battle tank'. It was a more sophisticated version of the Soviet T34, which had already entered service four years early and outclassed all the older German tanks. Armoured cars were also developed from 1932 for scouting, while a variety of armoured half-tracks were produced to mechanize the infantry and tow supporting artillery.[86]

Initial German successes in 1939–40 depended more on superior coordination than numbers or quality. Unlike those of their opponents, German tanks already had radios. Tanks were first grouped into mass formations for the invasion of France, and though Panzer Armies were later created, armoured formations never totalled more than a tenth of the ground troops. Their impact was hindered by the shortage of other vehicles, limiting the number of supporting *Panzergrenadier* divisions to a maximum of twenty-two, most of which were merely motorized infantry in unarmoured trucks, rather than mechanized troops protected in armoured half-tracks. Meanwhile, production failed to replace losses and the number of tanks in a division declined from 324 (1939) to 144 (summer 1944), and even these numbers were rarely reached.

Effective use was impaired by the competitive allocation of resources. Although comprising less than 5 per cent of ground forces, the Waffen-SS ultimately controlled nearly a quarter of tank divisions and a third of the mechanized and motorized infantry.[87] The hording of resources by the SS eroded the tank force's impact, from being a strategic asset to becoming Hitler's personal guard that he was reluctant to risk. Meanwhile, the Wehrmacht's armoured units were reduced from a strike force to firemen, rushing to plug gaps in the increasingly brittle front line.

Ultimately, the Wehrmacht was defeated by the tactics for which it is usually credited. German armoured forces were never sufficiently large to make a decisive difference on their own, and their successes in the opening campaigns were only possible as part of a wider set of factors, including air superiority and enough conventional infantry to match their opponents' numbers. Germany produced 46,800 tanks and SPGs during the war, as well as 315,000 half-tracks across 1940–3 alone. However, the production runs of just the T34 (57,300) and the US Sherman tank (60,000) on their own both dwarf the entire German output. While the Panther may have been marginally better than the T34 and definitely superior to the Sherman, with only 6,043 often unreliable tanks made, it was never going to win the war.

Fortifications

Fixation with tanks has obscured the continued significance of fortifications to German doctrine and practice into the later twentieth century. The most obvious manifestations of this were the trench systems of the First World War, which became ever more sophisticated and extensive. Construction of the Siegfried Line, just one of Operation Alberich's five defensive positions, involved moving over half a million tons of rock and gravel, 100,000 tons of cement, and 12,500 tons of barbed wire. It was built in just four months using 6,000 construction workers, backed by 34,000 forced labourers and prisoners. Entire towns and villages were razed, and 140,000 civilians deported to clear the ground.[88]

The Treaty of Versailles required the demolition of all the fixed fortifications built during the last years of Imperial Germany. This chiefly affected Mainz, especially as the Americans decided that the works at Koblenz and Ulm were no longer of military value. Although the Wehrmacht ultimately circumvented France's Maginot Line in 1940, the emphasis on mobile warfare did not lead to a neglect of fixed defences. A paramilitary construction company was established in 1933 under Fritz Todt.[89] Backed by workers supplied through the compulsory labour service, the Todt Organization built Germany's famous autobahns, but its main effort was constructing airbases and fortifications. The largest of these was the *Westwall* built between 1937 and 1940 opposite the Maginot Line across the Rhine. The perceived value of such structures is demonstrated by the fact that further resources were poured into extending this in 1944 to reach 630 kilometres with 18,000 bunkers and positions.

Todt's organization also constructed the *Atlantikwall* along the continent's western coast from France to Norway, consuming 1.2 million tons of scarce steel, as well as mountains of concrete.[90] The huge effort added to the difficulties anticipated by the Allies when planning to invade France, influencing the choice of 'softer' targets in North Africa (1942) and Italy (1943), but it failed to prevent the Normandy landings in June 1944. Likewise, the Westwall slowed but did not stop the Allied advance into Germany at the beginning of 1945.

Germany's use of fortifications was secondary compared to Switzerland, which made them its primary form of defence. The Limmat Line of blockhouses and small forts was built along the Rhine between 1935 and 1939, while the older works in the high Alps were strengthened, notably the fortresses of St Maurice, St Gotthard, and Sargans. Inspired by Athens during the Peloponnesian War (431–404 BCE) and Belgium's resistance around Antwerp during the First World War, General Guisan adopted a strategy of the *Réduit National* (National Redoubt), expecting the Limmat Line merely to delay a German invasion and give time for an orderly withdrawal into the mountain fastness of the Alps. As with Guisan's two inspirational examples, such a strategy would have abandoned most of the country to the ravages of the enemy, and was far from popular among the Swiss, but it nonetheless caught the public mood of defiance and signalled a willingness to resist to the bitter end.[91] Switzerland continued to place great reliance on fixed defences into the 1990s, but otherwise the purpose of fortifications shifted to protect civilians from aerial bombardment, as we shall see later in the discussion of air power.

Post-War Dilemmas

After 1945 the German, Austrian, and Swiss armed forces were not only proportionately smaller than before but had to respond to the new strategic environment created by nuclear weapons, which none of them possessed. Both East and West Germany drew on the doctrines of mobile warfare established since the 1920s and aimed for tank-heavy, mechanized forces capable of flexible defence and swift attack. Austria and Switzerland mainly opted for territorial defence, intending to use their comparatively poorly equipped forces to hold as much of their territory as possible. Austria attempted to adopt mobile defence after 1971 but could not afford to mechanize much of its small army.

In all four countries, defence strategy was hindered by the spiralling cost of 'big ticket' items like tanks and fighter jets and their associated equipment and facilities, which had assumed a key role in determining force structure. Furthermore, all continued to rely heavily on conscripts whose service was usually too short to train them in sophisticated tactics. In part, the greater emphasis on hi-tech equipment mirrored the Wehrmacht's efforts in the Second World War to compensate for its soldiers' declining proficiency.

These problems grew more pronounced during the 1960s. Initially, weaponry was plentiful and cheap as Europe was awash with surplus equipment. The paramilitaries in immediate post-war Austria, and both East and West Germany, relied on ex-Wehrmacht light weapons, like the G98 rifle and MG42 machine gun. Tactical doctrine and training also initially followed Wehrmacht practice. East Germany switched to more modern Soviet weapons, notably after 1956, but its paramilitaries still used worn-out Wehrmacht small arms and wartime Red Army surplus into the 1970s.[92] There was an acute shortage of communications equipment, and in the 1950s East German troops were forced to use whistles and signal flags like their predecessors in the Imperial Army. Matters improved considerably during the 1970s when the NVA reached the peak of its proficiency and was able to mobilize up to 85 per cent of its war strength at just an hour's notice.[93]

Austria received some surplus Soviet tanks to help re-establish its armed forces in 1955 and to demonstrate its non-aligned status between the Cold War blocs. However, the bulk of its arms came from the United States, which supplied enough equipment for 28,000 men. Switzerland also looked westwards, buying considerable quantities of surplus American, British, and French weaponry, notably tanks and warplanes. The US supplied the bulk of the Bundeswehr's requirements in 1955, while the first issue of uniforms was almost universally hated as too American in style, as well as thin and cold. Later issues remained styled on those of the US, but the newly created full-dress uniform deliberately sought to reference German traditions while distancing the new army from the Wehrmacht, for instance by adopting a lighter, more silvery version of the old *Feldgrau*. By contrast, East German forces initially copied the Red Army, but later adopted uniforms much more like those of the Wehrmacht, though greener than grey in colour. Austria reintroduced a modified version of the uniforms its army had worn across 1933–8, which in turn referenced colours and styles of the old Habsburg army, also in a deliberate effort to distance it from the Wehrmacht.[94]

The source of weaponry and inspiration for uniforms were important markers of each state's international orientation, as well as responses to a problematic military past. West Germany still had significant arms industries which soon met the needs of its army and navy, though not the air force. The country also produced innovative weapons, notably the Leopard main battle tank in 1965, and the Marder, the world's first successful infantry fighting vehicle, which allowed troops to fire their weapons while moving as well as offering light artillery support. Both sold well abroad, with Austria and Switzerland among the sixteen countries adopting the improved Leopard II tank following its introduction in 1979.

However, neither East nor West Germany was able to pursue a fully independent course, since force structure and doctrine, as well as weaponry, had to align with those of its major allies. These pressures grew during the 1970s, especially in the West where NATO members were allowed more latitude than their Warsaw Pact counterparts, which largely had to follow the Soviet model. NATO's contingent system necessitated agreement on matters such as common calibre small arms to reduce problems of ammunition resupply and improve 'interoperability' – the capacity of the different members' forces to fight alongside each other. The growing cost and sophistication of major weapons systems, notably warplanes, also forced countries to collaborate on major projects, which could take a decade or more to develop and represented significant slices of their defence budgets.

East German forces adopted Soviet military doctrine and training by 1950. Command was hierarchical, inflexible, and highly politicized, with the ruling SED assuming a position equivalent to 'papal infallibility', making it impossible to question its ideological directives.[95] West Germany drew directly on the Reichswehr and Wehrmacht by reworking the earlier tactical manuals in the light of wartime experience into the new version designated HDV 100/100, issued in 1956. In contrast to East German practice, this emphasized mission tactics and devolved leadership as hallmarks of the new ideal of citizen soldiers. However, both German armies struggled to train their short-service conscripts, with only one in ten Bundeswehr soldiers able to hit a man-sized target at normal battle ranges in 1969.[96]

The Bundeswehr followed the outline sketched at the Himmerod meeting in 1950 and accepted as the basis of West Germany's admission into NATO five years later. The army was organized as six armoured divisions, initially with American M48 tanks and later the Leopard, and six Panzer Grenadier divisions of infantry riding in armoured US halftracks, later replaced by the Marder. There were additional units of paratroopers and mountain infantry. The balance between the different components varied somewhat into the 1990s, but change was modest beyond the issue of improved weaponry. East Germany's smaller NVA essentially followed the same pattern, but with Soviet tanks and generally fewer vehicles. A key feature was the persistence of distinct units aligned directly with the party. In addition to the SED's militia recruited from workers in state-owned enterprises, there was the elite guard unit, named after Feliks E. Dzierzhynski, the founder of Russia's secret police, which was controlled by the Stasi and organized as a light-infantry division with 2,500 professionals and 8,500 conscripts.[97] The forces of Austria and Switzerland remained largely conventional infantry, but by the 1960s they recognized their initial mix of weaponry was obsolete or inappropriate and belatedly sought to catch up without ever achieving the same standards of equipment or mechanization.[98]

Reform and Transformation

Whereas the Bundeswehr changed its structure four times across 1955–92, all of which left the basic twelve-division organization intact, it went through six major reorganizations between 1992 and 2011, several of which were superseded by new structures before they had been fully implemented. Although less pronounced, the pace and scope of change also accelerated in Austria and Switzerland with a similar direction of travel from 'reform' of the existing structure to more fundamental 'transformation' intended to produce something wholly new.[99] These revisions were driven by the general sense of a rapidly changing security environment following the end of the Cold War, but they occurred with a significantly longer time lag than their equivalents in the United States, Britain, and France, and likewise have been more reactive than attempting to pre-empt expected developments.

The initial delay is understandable. The Gulf War and the Yugoslav Wars did not immediately challenge the way European forces had been configured for the Cold War. Western participation in the Gulf War employed tank-heavy forces geared for rapid, mobile warfare, while intervention in the Yugoslav Wars relied initially heavily on air power. Germany, Austria, and Switzerland had all invested relatively large sums in modern weaponry, including some long-running development programmes, and did not want to have to spend more money reconfiguring their forces, especially if that did not appear immediately necessary. The federal structure in all three states added a further complication, because changes that might involve base closures or other cutbacks were often opposed by regional politicians. Public opinion remained largely wedded to the belief that the duty of citizen soldiers was territorial defence and was hostile to the despatch of conscripts or militiamen abroad. It was much easier for Britain and the United States, which relied on professionals, to reconfigure their forces around expeditionary warfare, requiring integrated all-arms units with good sea and airlift capabilities to operate rapidly beyond national frontiers.

Of the three, Germany had the largest forces and engaged earlier and more heavily in 'out of area' operations than either Austria or Switzerland. The Bundeswehr already found it challenging to support the missions to the former Yugoslav states after 1992. Its initial response was to create a 'rapid reaction force' to handle such operations, while leaving the bulk of its forces still configured for territorial defence. When that proved insufficient, a more wide-ranging defence was initiated after 2001, only to be redirected in the wake of 9/11 and the US invasion of Afghanistan by the new German defence minister, Peter Struck, who declared in July 2002 that 'Germany will be defended on the Hindu Kush'.[100] Self-consciously styled a 'transformation', the subsequent changes expunged the remnants of the older structures, and radically reorganized the entire Bundeswehr into three task-orientated components. The first were the three primary branches of land, sea, and air forces, in turn divided into around 35,000 front-line personnel for high-intensity operations, and 70,000 for low-to-medium stabilization and peacekeeping missions. These were in turn supported by a new, common logistics branch, called the Joint Support Service, and a similarly combined Central Medical Service, together with another 147,500 personnel.[101]

Austria adopted a broadly similar structure around nine years later, while Switzerland initiated this process in 2018. Meanwhile, Germany scaled back its ambitions after 2010, reducing the maximum numbers of troops capable of being deployed overseas to no more than 10,000 in up to three missions simultaneously.[102] Partly driven by financial pressures and the public debate that led to the suspension of conscription in 2011, this was also a response to the experience in Afghanistan. German troops had arrived there in 2002 bound by very tight rules of engagement and expecting a stabilization mission in line with their country's 'civilian power' orientation. One British officer described the German presence as resembling an 'aggressive camping organization' rather than an army.[103] The army lacked a counter-insurgency doctrine or training. The rapidly worsening situation after 2007 compelled a significant rethink, including the creation of advanced training units with American and British instructors at at Pfullendorf, the Bundeswehr's special forces school.[104] The extent of the ongoing transformation is underscored by the declining numbers of the army's iconic Leopard II main battle tank from 2,400 in 2004, or still around half the strength in 1989, to just 400 by 2014.[105]

IN SEARCH OF A ROLE:
THE GERMANS AT SEA

The Surface Fleets

Respectively second and seventh in the world rankings in 1914, the German navy declined dramatically within four years, while that of Austria-Hungary disappeared altogether. Although Germany attempted to recover its position rapidly after 1927, its naval command repeated many of the mistakes of its imperial predecessors. Rebuilt in the 1950s, the then two German navies remained primarily for coastal defence, though the post-reunification force has recently assumed a more global role.

Despite their relative rankings, the disparity at sea was even greater than that on land in 1914. Germany and Austria-Hungary had a combined naval tonnage of 1.29 million, compared to the 3.826 million tons of their immediate enemies. The entry of Italy (1915) and then the United States (1917) into the war added well over another 1.3 million tons. Britain's Royal Navy was alone twice as large as Germany's navy, and though many of its ships were elderly, it had twenty-seven modern battleships to the Germans' seventeen; a ratio that shifted to thirty-nine to twenty-one within nine months of the outbreak of war.[106]

Both Central Powers suffered further from the fact that their pre-war construction had been geared increasingly towards creating high-seas battlefleets, rather than developing the capacity to hit Allied shipping. As some German naval officers had already expected, Britain dumbfounded Admiral Tirpitz's plan by establishing a distant blockade, closing off the Channel and the North Sea between Scotland and Norway. The 1856 Paris Declaration had stipulated that, to be legal, a blockade had to be 'close', near the target's coast. The world's leading naval powers, including Germany and Austria-Hungary, issued the London Declaration in

1909, expanding belligerents' rights to intercept neutral shipping on the high seas. Although this remained unratified, Britain acted accordingly, and compelled neutral states like Switzerland, the Netherlands, and Scandinavian countries to accept tight quotas restricting their imports to what was needed for national consumption, in order to choke off any re-export of international goods to Germany or Austria-Hungary.[107]

The German navy was not directly affected by the blockade, because – unlike Britain's – it had not yet converted from coal to oil to fuel its surface ships and drew sufficient oil for its submarines from Romania.[108] However, the blockade immediately damaged the Central Powers in ways that underscored how ordinary citizens coped in warfare, even for authoritarian governments. Not only did their growing hunger affect morale on the home front, but the inability to break the blockade threatened the imperial regimes' credibility as military powers. Both the German and Austro-Hungarian navies came under growing pressure 'to do something', and their high commands increasingly lost respect and influence through their inability to respond effectively to these demands.

In Germany's case the situation was exacerbated by the tripartite division of its navy's command structure. Tirpitz became a victim of his own machinations: having persuaded Wilhelm II to abolish the post of supreme commander in 1899, the emperor unsurprisingly refused to let his admiral assume this role once war broke out. Tirpitz continued to offer critical, inconsistent advice until a mistake by one of his subordinates in the navy design office (RMA) gave the chancellor Bethmann-Hollweg the opportunity to dismiss him in March 1916.[109]

Germany's Baltic fleet under Heinrich, Wilhelm's younger brother, successfully supported the army's operations on the Eastern Front and kept Russia's navy at bay until that country collapsed in revolution in 1917. Meanwhile, Austria-Hungary's Danube monitors supported its army's operations against Serbia and the later Allied intervention in the Balkans. Although useful, it was clear to both naval commands that such operations would not be decisive.[110]

The German navy squandered several opportunities to implement Tirpitz's 'Risk Theory' strategy of luring the Royal Navy into battle close to Germany's North Sea coast in the opening months of the war. After that, the Royal Navy refrained from risking its large ships too close to the main German base at Wilhelmshaven. Meanwhile, Germany's surface raiders caused alarm disproportionate to their numbers.

In addition to its East Asia Squadron under Vice Admiral von Spee (two large and two smaller cruisers), Germany had three other modern cruisers off East Africa and in the Caribbean. These regular forces were eventually supplemented by sixteen converted civilian vessels, including fast liners. The Royal Navy had decided that convoys would simply create bigger targets, and instead despatched substantial forces to hunt the Germans down.

Spee was primarily trying to get home. Having managed to defeat one British force at Coronel off the Chilean coast, he was eventually killed and his force destroyed in December 1914 at the Falkland Islands, which he had planned to attack in the hope of finding more coal for his ships.[111] The other three cruisers caused more damage to Allied shipping, notably SMS *Emden*, which added a fourth, false funnel to make itself resemble a Royal Navy ship. It sank twenty Allied vessels, before being destroyed at the Cocos Islands in November 1914. The armed merchantman *Wolf* was more successful, sinking 140,000 tons of Allied shipping before returning safely to Germany.[112] The elimination of Germany's surface raiders by the spring of 1915 gave the Allies command of all the world's oceans outside the North Atlantic. Meanwhile, Germany had lost a quarter of its merchant marine to Allied action. Another 30 per cent had been forced into neutral waters and interned, while the rest now sat idly in port. Austria-Hungary similarly lost a third of its shipping.

U-Boats

Only in retrospect do submarines (*Unterseeboote* – U-Boats) appear the obvious answer to this situation. Germany's activities under the sea date from the appearance of the *Brandtaucher* ('Fire Diver') in 1850 during the first Schleswig War with Denmark. News of this infernal device prompted the Danes briefly to suspend their blockade of German ports, but the submarine sank on its first test dive on 1 February 1851. Although its inventor, the Bavarian Wilhelm Bauer, built another two equally unsuccessful submarines for Russia in 1856, Germany did not experiment with them again until 1890. Development was driven by Krupp using Spanish expertise, and the German navy only took note when compelled to by Wilhelm II, who had been impressed on a visit to the dockyard at Kiel.[113]

There were only twenty-nine submarines in service in August 1914, compared to the Royal Navy's seventy-six, while Austria-Hungary had just six of which only four were operational. Tirpitz envisaged submarines assisting the battlefleet attacking the Royal Navy once it approached the German coast. Initial submarine operations did score some notable successes against unprotected Allied warships. As the blockade began to bite, Tirpitz believed that sinking a few merchant ships would be enough to scare neutral merchantmen into remaining in port. Combined with minelaying, Germany's use of submarines constituted a counter-blockade intended to cut supplies of food and other key resources to Britain, and to demonstrate to its own inhabitants that it could retaliate. However, he and other senior officers underestimated how much their actions would antagonize the United States, which suffered from trade disruption even when its own ships were not being targeted.

Initially, submarines operated according to the rules established by The Hague Convention of 1907, by remaining on the surface and giving warning to their target, sinking it only once the crew had been evacuated. The Allies responded by deploying so-called 'Q-ships', merchantmen with concealed guns that would swing into action as a submarine surfaced. Citing this as a breach of the rules and claiming British ships were falsely flying neutral colours, Germany began sinking any ships in British waters without warning on 4 February 1915. However, Wilhelm II and Chancellor Bethmann-Hollweg opposed fully unrestricted submarine warfare, particularly as it would harm relations with the United States if American ships were hit. Restrictions were periodically reimposed, notably after the liner *Lusitania* was sunk in May 1915, killing 1,198 civilians, including 128 Americans.

To his credit, Tirpitz realized that submarine warfare would only be successful if the vessels were considered expendable and introduced elements of mass production to enable losses to be replaced and the fleet expanded. Germany built 369 U-boats during the war with another 138 unfinished and 204 on order in 1918.[114] Improved numbers made restricted submarine warfare more sustainable, enabling Wilhelm and Bethmann-Hollweg to counter repeated calls from the army for more vigorous action.

These operations were ongoing when the High Seas Fleet finally engaged the Royal Navy in the long-awaited great battle off Denmark's Jutland peninsula on 31 May–1 June 1916, known as Skagerrak to the

Germans. By now, operational command was held by Admiral Scheer, who supported Tirpitz's ideas. Scheer deployed 101 warships, including twenty-one dreadnoughts and battlecruisers, to the Royal Navy's 151 (including thirty-seven dreadnoughts and battlecruisers) under Admiral Jellicoe. Jellicoe outwitted his opponent, avoiding falling into the planned entrapment and placing the Germans at a potentially decisive disadvantage. However, Scheer skilfully extricated his ships and escaped to port. Each side had made tactical errors, but the battle also exposed longer-term problems like poor intelligence and design flaws, notably in some of the larger British ships. German gunnery had been superior, and British losses in terms of tonnage and personnel were double those of their opponents, enabling Scheer to claim victory.[115]

Both commanders were disappointed by the outcome, but for the Germans the failure to achieve decisive victory proved critical. Many large German warships had suffered extensive damage, which took time to repair and increased the commanders' reluctance to risk another battle. The next major operation was not undertaken until a futile cruise off Norway in April 1918. Morale had remained high after Jutland, which German sailors regarded as a tactical victory, but it plummeted with the enforced subsequent inactivity. Able or ambitious officers petitioned for transfer to the previously despised submarines, which also now took the pick of the sailors, further undermining morale on the surface ships. Boredom merely heightened the crews' perceptions of the manifold petty injustices of the German navy, in which officers ate separately with better rations and more shore leave.[116] Matters were similar in the Habsburg fleet, which stopped attacking the Allied blockade across the southern Adriatic after an Italian torpedo boat sank one of Austria-Hungary's only four dreadnoughts in June 1917.

Conscious of these problems, and under growing pressure to act, Scheer backed other officers' calls to unleash unrestricted submarine warfare, including in the Atlantic. As discussed in the previous chapter, German planners vastly overestimated the damage they would inflict on Allied shipping. Although German submarines sank an impressive 834,549 tons of Allied shipping in the four months before the United States declared war in April 1917, their capacity to hit American troop ships proved wholly inadequate: just six were sunk, of which four were returning to the US empty, drowning only 300 of the 2 million Americans who had crossed the Atlantic by late 1918.

The unrestricted submarine warfare campaign was soon countered by the belated introduction of convoys, now using specially designed escort vessels, in May 1917. Allied forces also employed an increasingly sophisticated range of anti-submarine technology, including hydrophones to detect submerged vessels, better sea mines, aircraft, and improved radio interception. Submarine losses increased to the point where Germany had to crew them with conscripts rather than volunteers by January 1918.[117] German U-boats made 3,274 voyages, sinking 6,394 Allied ships (over 11.9 million tons), with a further 108 destroyed by Austria-Hungary's submarines. Britain's imports fell by a third, while shipping losses began to outstrip new production during 1916, only to be vastly offset by America's entry into the war. With no more than thirty still relatively small submarines at sea at any one time, Germany could not hope to block the entire Atlantic. Meanwhile, Germany's international reputation suffered far more than that of the Allies, because its sinking of liners like the *Lusitania* was far more visible to foreign opinion than the effectiveness of the Allied blockade on German civilians.[118]

The Grand Scuttle

Scheer and other senior commanders ignored rising discontent among the crews, especially those of the larger ships, instead blaming problems on the work of a few socialist agitators; a view they retained after 1918 as the maritime version of the army's 'stab in the back' myth.[119] The growing mutiny foiled the high command's 'Death March Plan' of late October 1918 to go down fighting, as Tirpitz had already urged officers to do prior to the war, and Admiral Spee's crews had done at the Falklands.[120]

Naval officers felt honour was only restored when Admiral Reuter scuttled the bulk of the surface fleet that had been interned at Scapa Flow after the Armistice. The incensed Allies compelled Germany to surrender another five modern cruisers and 400,000 tons of dock equipment as compensation. The surviving ships, including those that could be salvaged, were distributed among the victors, who used most of them for target practice or scrap.[121] The entire German submarine fleet was surrendered separately, and likewise distributed among the Allies. After protests, the Allies returned Germany's first commissioned U-boats, the U1 and U2 dating from 1905 and 1908 respectively. Both long obsolete, the U1 was preserved as a museum piece (which still survives), while the U2 was scrapped.[122]

Austria-Hungary's fleet was similarly divided up, dashing the hope of the newly constituted Yugoslavia of inheriting most of it. The Allies eventually returned four patrol boats in 1921, which were operated by the new republican army's pioneer corps as a reconstituted Danube flotilla. This was incorporated as part of Germany's navy after 1938, until the surviving vessels were seized by American troops in 1945. A 'navy' was re-established in 1958 with one patrol boat, followed by a second in 1970, until both, now ageing vessels, were transferred to the Vienna army museum in 2006 with the police assuming responsibility for the Danube.[123]

Reichsmarine

Germany's fleet was meanwhile reduced to a coastal defence navy with its strength fixed by the Treaty of Versailles at 108,000 tons, including six old battleships, six light cruisers, and twenty-four destroyers and torpedo boats. Most were already around twenty years old and thus the age at which it was permitted to replace them, but with new vessels obliged to remain within strict tonnage limits and to remain a similarly long time in service. The Allies had relented already in March 1920, and permitted Germany to retain a third more ships, provided these were laid up in peacetime as a reserve. The number of personnel was fixed at no more than 15,000, a tenth of whom could be officers; only a fraction of the 275,000 men mustered by the imperial navy at its peak.[124]

The navy followed the army's pattern, initially constituted as a provisional force in April 1919, before formally becoming the *Reichsmarine* on 31 March 1921. The old imperial naval flag was replaced by the Republic's black, red, and gold national colours nine months later, but the force remained as conservative as the army. Personnel numbers were kept to strength, but the government could not afford to replace warships, several of which were kept far longer in service than specified by the Versailles restrictions, notably the battleship *Schleswig-Holstein*, which had the dubious honour of firing the opening shots of the Second World War thirty-one years after it was built.[125]

The first few post-war years were spent clearing mines, with overseas voyages resuming in 1924 primarily for training purposes and as an effort by Admiral Behncke, who replaced the conservative Admiral Trotha in 1920, to divert sailors from right-wing politics by giving them something to do. Beyond the lack of resources, the key issue was how to learn from the war without criticizing Tirpitz, who remained an important figure in right-wing circles and was openly admired by most naval officers. Many believed Tirpitz's claim that the navy could have won the war if it had been used more aggressively from the start. The submarine campaign was generally regarded as a failure, further heightening the fixation on the traditional strategy of seeking victory through a decisive action rather than a campaign of attrition. Germany secretly sold submarine technology to several minor powers and attempted to keep abreast of developments elsewhere, but most officers prioritized rebuilding the battlefleet and dreamed of refighting the battle of Jutland.

The navy suffered from remaining secondary to the army in defence strategy, politics, and public awareness. Officers largely supported the conservative nationalist DNVP, while the Nazis showed little interest in sea power, only using naval issues when they wanted to score points against their opponents.[126] The navy signalled its ambitions under Behncke's successor, Admiral Zenker, with the start of the 'pocket battleship' programme in 1927, a year before the scandal over covert rearmament led to his dismissal and replacement by Erich Raeder.[127] Raeder had served as chief of staff to the battlecruiser squadron on which the new design was based. Only nominally within the treaty limit of 10,000 tons, the new battleship was planned as a fast, powerful cruising warship intended to cause the kind of havoc wrought by Spee and the other surface raiders in 1914.

Raeder's embrace of this project represented an attempt to adapt Tirpitz's vision, switching the focus from a single, victorious battle to a decisive operation. Rather than trying to command the seas, as Tirpitz had sought, he wanted to deny them to Britain. He realized that Germany could not hope to match the Royal Navy in the North Sea and argued fast battlecruisers would enable it to escape to the oceans and interdict British trade. By focusing on big ships, Raeder appeared close to Tirpitz, but in fact his plan represented advocacy of the entirely opposite strategy of *guerre du course*.

Kriegsmarine

Raeder's ideas were fundamentally at odds with those of the Nazis after 1933, even though he embraced much of their ideology. Hitler regarded Germany primarily as a land power, supposedly destined to rule Eurasia, and wanted an accommodation with Britain. Germany's navy received greater resources and was renamed the *Kriegsmarine* as rearmament accelerated in 1935, but it remained subordinate in Hitler's calculations. It did not help Raeder's cause that he had incurred Himmler's enmity, while Göring saw the navy merely as a competitor to the Luftwaffe for scarce steel and oil.

Raeder accepted the Anglo-German Naval Agreement in June 1935, which revised the Versailles Treaty by permitting the Kriegsmarine to build up to 35 per cent of the Royal Navy's strength in every warship type except submarines, which were now permitted and where Germany could have 45 per cent. Hitler saw this as a step towards possible accommodation, while British officers had mistaken Raeder for a second Tirpitz and believed the agreement would contain any German expansion. While Britain genuinely tried to make it work, it had no effective way of verifying German compliance. Raeder saw it only as a temporary expedient to secure more resources, still intending to challenge Britain in the future.[128] He was alarmed at the Hossbach meeting in 1937, when Hitler indicated he expected war by 1944. Germany unilaterally renounced the Naval Agreement in April 1939, potentially paving the way for a larger fleet.

Compelled to prepare for this shorter timetable, Raeder presented Plan Z to Hitler in January 1939, which aimed to add six super battleships (each 56,000 tons), eight battlecruisers (each 20,000 tons), four aircraft carriers, 202 destroyers and smaller vessels, and 240 submarines within five years. Wholly unrealistic, it also represented a compromise between Raeder's more conservative preoccupation with large surface warships and younger officers who advocated submarines and smaller cruisers as surface raiders. Chief among the second group was Captain Dönitz, who had served on cruisers before transferring at his request to submarines in 1916. At this point, Dönitz nonetheless agreed with Raeder that submarines were only a temporary substitute until the surface fleet could be completed.[129] However, only three pocket battleships and two battlecruisers were finished by 1939, and the rest of the navy included just five light cruisers, thirty-three destroyers and torpedo boats, and fifty-seven submarines. Various other vessels were under construction, but few would be completed.

Raeder hoped the compromise would convince Hitler that the navy would not repeat the mistakes of the previous war and was worthy of the huge quantities of resources it requested. Conditions were more favourable in some respects in 1939 than they had been in 1914. The Nazi-Soviet Pact ensured the flow of vital resources, undermining the impact of a renewed British blockade. Nonetheless, Germany's merchant fleet was soon lost or largely confined to port. At different times, six surface raiders were set loose, sinking 1.44 million tons of Allied shipping before the last one was eliminated in 1943.[130] This campaign cost Germany two of its pocket battleships, as well as one (*Bismarck*) of only two of the planned super-battleships that were completed. Worse, the first of these losses, the *Graf Spee*, was scuttled by its captain in December 1939 after it was cornered by superior British forces off the Uruguayan capital, Montevideo. The bitter irony of this involving a ship named after the First World War admiral who had gone down fighting infuriated Hitler, damaging the navy's already weak position within the polycentric Nazi state.

Matters deteriorated further with the significant losses of smaller surface warships during the invasion of Norway in 1940. Raeder went along with Hitler's intention to invade Britain, preparing Operation Sealion to maintain the navy's credibility while continuing to lobby for resources. Postponement of that plan in October 1940 coincided with Mussolini's unilateral expansion of the war in the Mediterranean, which further stretched the navy and the Luftwaffe. After *Bismarck*'s loss in May 1941, Hitler dismissed capital ships as 'useless', and Raeder increasingly slipped into a 'fleet in being' mentality, trying to avoid further debacles that would damage the navy's influence.[131] The major units, like the other super-battleship *Tirpitz*, increasingly became liabilities that needed protection against Allied aircraft and submarines while contributing little beyond acting as targets for ever more ingenious Allied bombs. The redirection of valuable resources into building the Atlantic Wall was an acknowledgement of the navy's inability to defend the coast. On 6 January 1943, Hitler subjected Raeder to a ninety-minute monologue, castigating the navy's role in German history since 1866. Raeder promptly resigned and was formally replaced by Dönitz at the end of the month.[132]

The U-Boat War

Germany entered the Second World War with submarines only slightly better than those it possessed in 1918. By May 1945 it had completed the construction of 1,107 seagoing U-boats and around 1,000 smaller coastal U-boats. Effectiveness was hindered by Dönitz's initial belief that existing designs were satisfactory, and it was not until July 1943 that new construction concentrated on two new types: larger diesel vessels for the Atlantic, and smaller electric boats for the Mediterranean and Baltic. Operations benefited from the conquest of most of western Europe's coastline, giving easier access to the Atlantic. Germany followed the 1907 rules until 17 August 1940, when Hitler ordered unrestricted warfare to interdict the flow of goods from the United States, thereby initiating what became known as the Battle of the Atlantic.

The Allies introduced convoys from the start of the war. Anti-submarine technology had greatly improved, while the Allied use after 1942 of smaller 'escort carriers' extended air cover into the open seas. Whereas most targets had been sunk in the First World War by submarines on the surface using their deck guns, those after 1939 were destroyed mostly by torpedoes fired by submerged vessels. Torpedoes had increased greatly in range and accuracy, while Dönitz adopted 'Wolf Pack' tactics. Already proposed in 1917 but not employed, these deployed submarines in groups rather than singly and scored some spectacular successes. Overall, the campaign sank 14.69 million tons of Allied shipping, or ten times that destroyed by the surface raiders.

However, there were never enough U-boats – in fact, the campaign involved more Italian than German submarines. The reduction of Germany's naval strategy to a single weapon by 1943 allowed the Allies to concentrate their superior resources against it. May 1943 was perceived by submariners as the turning point. The introduction of the snorkel, allowing U-boats to see the surface while submerged, briefly raised hopes, but losses were now so great that a mission was regarded as a 'suicide operation'. Overall, three-quarters of German submarine crews were lost.[133]

Nonetheless, the Kriegsmarine continued to fight doggedly like the other parts of the Wehrmacht. Its last major operation was the evacuation of troops, equipment, and civilians from the eastern Baltic in the face of the Red Army's advance. Most of the ships carried a mixed civilian-military cargo and many were sunk, most notoriously the three overcrowded liners *Wilhelm Gustloff*, *General Steuben*, and *Goya*. All were torpedoed by Soviet submarines at the cost of 15,000 lives, or six times the combined loss of the *Titanic* and the *Lusitania*, and constituted the world's greatest maritime disaster. It was also the largest evacuation by sea, with over 2.2 million people landed in northern Germany.[134]

Post-War Navies

Unlike the imperial navy, which was still largely intact in 1918, the bulk of the Kriegsmarine's ships and submarines had been sunk or disabled by 1945, notably by Allied bombing. Britain employed some former personnel and smaller ships to clear mines immediately after the war, with part of these forces being used to establish a fishery protection service on 1 July 1951. This represented the maritime counterpart of the paramilitary border police and was intended to provide both immediate protection against the Soviets and the potential nucleus of a new navy. The USSR had already taken this step, adding a naval section to the East German paramilitary police in 1950. Both forces subsequently became the new navies: the Western *Bundesmarine* (1955) and the Eastern *Seestreitkräfte* (Maritime Armed Forces, 1956), renamed *Volksmarine* when it became a fully separate service branch in 1960.[135]

The bulk of the initial equipment of both forces consisted of small patrol craft from the former Kriegsmarine, supplemented within a few years by surplus destroyers and frigates provided by the respective Cold War sponsors. East Germany's efforts to salvage sunken U-boats failed, and its navy remained without submarines throughout its existence. Similar efforts were more successful in the West, where the Bundesmarine incorporated two U-boats which were raised and repaired in 1957. West Germany also benefited from possessing the two primary naval bases (Wilhelmshaven and Kiel) and the bulk of Germany's shipbuilding capacity. Once initial restrictions were lifted in 1961, West Germany built its own warships and submarines, the latter based on late wartime designs that soon became a major export success. By contrast, East Germany remained dependent on Soviet weaponry, while plans to turn Rügen Island into a major base were abandoned in the economies following the 1953 rising and widespread strike action against the East German government. The navy remained restricted to Rostock, the country's primary port.[136]

The Bundesmarine's first commander was Vice Admiral Ruge, who had played a leading role in the Grand Scuttle of 1919 and was subsequently head of construction for the Kriegsmarine. As one of only four senior naval officers assisting US intelligence after 1945, he joined the inner circle of those planning the new Bundeswehr. He wanted a greater role than coastal defence and the acquisition of old American destroyers in 1958 provided the capacity to join other NATO navies in Atlantic convoy duties. The first exercise conducted that August was named 'Wallenstein', referencing the commander of the original imperial navy in 1628 and signalling renewed ambitions. New, German-built replacements soon followed, while personnel grew from 7,700 (1956) to 35,000 (1966). However, the strength of the USSR's Baltic fleet was such that NATO assessments reckoned the Bundesmarine would be destroyed within forty-eight hours. Expansion was halted, and the navy remained primarily intended to protect the left flank of NATO's land forces. A variety of small, fast attack boats were built to assist this task, but the navy suffered from a shrinking budget as NATO prioritized land and air forces after the 1970s.[137]

The smaller Volksmarine was assigned a similar role. Its numbers grew by 1989 to 14,200 personnel with ninety-five relatively modern vessels, primarily rocket boats, and a small naval air service (established in 1985). Like the NVA, it disappeared with reunification, when most of its equipment was sold. The merged navy, renamed *Deutsche Marine* in 1991, immediately found a new role with the onset of more active overseas missions. Minesweepers were deployed to the Gulf in 1991, and from the following year the navy joined other NATO warships enforcing the arms embargo against Serbia. Continued budgetary pressures led to plans to halve the navy by 2005. Actual strength fell even lower to 24,657 personnel with seventy-five vessels, while the remaining naval aircraft were transferred to the Luftwaffe. The decline was almost immediately reversed with the expansion of the Western 'war on terror' to include anti-piracy and anti-people-smuggling missions in the Mediterranean and off the Horn of Africa. The new, more global role led to the construction of eleven frigates and corvettes built to standard NATO designs, as well as the development of the Class 125 frigate during the 2010s, which is capable of remaining on mission for two years without needing to return to port. Meanwhile, greater automation has facilitated this expanded role despite personnel numbers slipping to 16,300.[138]

AIR POWER

First Flight

The development of aerial warfare added a third dimension to conflict and led to the creation of an entirely new service branch alongside armies and navies. German participation in this process broadly followed that of other countries until it was abruptly stalled by defeat in 1918. Germany subsequently played a significant role in developing air power during the 1930s and 1940s, but without achieving a fully effective balance of the necessary components. Thereafter, as with military and naval developments, it slipped from leader to follower and the air forces of both East and West Germany modelled themselves on those of the two superpowers, the USA and the USSR. Within the armed forces, the air force's significance grew relative to the other two services after the 1950s, while throughout, Austria and Switzerland have seen air power as integral to sustaining their neutrality.

Switzerland had first tested balloons in 1794, eleven years after the Montgolfier brothers' first flight. Technical difficulties delayed military use, though the Austrian navy deployed observation balloons from the steamer *Vulcano* in a world first on 12 June 1849 during the siege of Venice.[139] Prussia briefly had two balloon detachments during the 1870–1 war, but the first permanent unit dated from 1884, initially as part of the railway troops, before becoming an independent formation three years later. The institutional origins exerted an important influence on future development, with aerial warfare rooted in the army's technical services, rather than immediately as a separate branch.

Development accelerated after 1898, with the first powered flight of a dirigible tested over Lake Constance on 2 July 1900, which permanently associated its designer's name, Count Ferdinand von Zeppelin, with this type of 'airship', even though other companies soon produced them. The successful test greatly influenced early German air power, convincing the army that Zeppelins were more promising than heavier air machines, the first of which only flew successfully in December 1903. Attracted by the idea that Zeppelins were a German invention, the government concentrated on their development until pushed by mounting public enthusiasm and the Kaiser's endorsement into buying the army's first plane in May 1910.[140]

As in other countries, public support played a major role in development, with the purchase of planes subsidized by popular subscription. Likewise, the early aircraft industry grew from enthusiastic inventors who produced new designs for the growing sport-flying market. A notable pioneer was Anthony Fokker from the Dutch East Indies, who moved to Germany and established a flying school in 1912. The technology was still in its infancy and it was far from clear how to exploit its potential for military purposes. Planes still only had a top speed of 80 to 100 kmh and while they could reach 2,400m their usual operating ceiling was 1,000m, or like that of balloons. Technology was changing rapidly, and most governments were concerned about investing in designs that would soon become obsolete. Reflecting its origins within the army, the first German statement of air doctrine, issued in March 1913, envisaged reconnaissance as the primary role, though plans were already being considered for bombing, interception, transport, and anti-aircraft defence.[141]

Austria-Hungary embraced these innovations much later, not testing military balloons until 1893, but it soon caught up and had thirty-nine warplanes, forty trainer aircraft, and eighty-five pilots by 1914, compared to the 220 warplanes and twelve airships of Germany's *Fliegertruppe* (Flying Troops). The Habsburgs had already established a naval air service in 1910, one of the few areas in which they were more advanced than Germany, where the navy only possessed a single Zeppelin in 1914. The Swiss remained sceptical, believing their country's winds were too strong, only realizing the potential for aeroplanes after the outbreak of war in 1914 made it difficult to buy the machines.[142]

Air Power in the First World War

The First World War saw the rapid development of air forces in both size and potential, as well as their emancipation as independent service branches with Germany's Fliegertruppe reorganized as the *Luftstreitkräfte* (Aerial Armed Forces) under its own command (General Hoeppner) on 8 October 1916; this was about two years ahead of Britain's formation of the Royal Air Force from a merger of the army and naval air services.[143] In 1914 half of Germany's aircraft were Austrian-built planes, which were already obsolete and had the unwarlike name of *Taube* (Pigeon). By 1918 the speed and operational ceiling of most planes had doubled, while new specialist types were developed as the belligerents increasingly mastered the challenges of fighting in a three-dimensional battlespace where features like towns, roads, and bridges were navigational aids rather than tactical objectives. A key challenge for all belligerents was to assert control over pilots who were still enamoured with the joys of flying and initially took a highly individualistic approach to their duties. Their experience was generally at odds with the institutional origins of air forces within armies commanded by generals who thought in terms of two-dimensional fronts. France not only began the war with the world's largest air force, but also thought more conceptually about how to use it, in contrast to Germany and other belligerents who largely improvised air doctrine from experience.

Contrary to the myth of chivalrous 'knights of the air', all belligerents sought to exploit the lethal potential of air power immediately, not least because this had already been tested during the Mexican Revolution (1911–20) and the Balkan Wars (1912–13), which saw aircraft used for bombing and strafing of ground and maritime targets. German Zeppelins bombed Liège on 6 August 1914, with further attacks soon made on Antwerp, Paris, and London. Although Franz Joseph refused permission for Habsburg planes to bomb Venice, they nonetheless had the dubious distinction of making the first aerial attack on refugees when they bombed Serbian fugitives on the Kosovo plain in November 1915.[144] Overall, targets in Britain were hit fifty-one times, with a total of 300 tons of bombs that killed 1,400 civilians and wounded another 5,000, compared to the more limited Allied bombing of western German towns which killed 740 and injured 1,900. The attacks added to the Allies' sense of moral outrage and conviction that they were waging a just war. They tied up a sizable proportion of Britain's air force to provide defence, but otherwise made little impact beyond spurring further development of more lethal methods. With gas-filled Zeppelins vulnerable to phosphorous ammunition, Germany joined other belligerents in developing larger aircraft to deliver bombs. Meanwhile, the Royal Navy created the first effective aircraft carriers to raid German Zeppelin bases on the North Sea coast, while the Royal Air Force had produced a heavy bomber that would have been capable of hitting Berlin if the war had not ended.[145]

German aircraft were already equipped with machine guns from late 1914, like those of the other belligerents, leading to the development of the two-seater fighter in which the second crewman operated a rear-mounted weapon. Tactics were transformed by the introduction of interrupter gear, which permitted a forward-mounted gun to fire through the rotating propellor. Invented by the Swiss engineer Franz Schneider, the Prussian war ministry had ignored this in 1913, but relented during 1915. Mounted on the new *Eindecker* single-seater monoplane designed by Fokker, this temporarily transformed aerial warfare in the 'Fokker Scourge' as the Germans cleared the skies of enemy aircraft, until their opponents caught up by May 1916.

The new technology enabled the emergence of the fighter pilot as a modern warrior, fusing man and machine to engage opponents in single-combat 'dogfights' above the scarred battlefields. Pilots saw killing primarily in terms of downing enemy machines, regardless of what happened to their crew. Combat was highly dangerous. In addition to the almost constant risk of mechanical failure, German aircrew were not issued with parachutes until April 1918, though at least this was ahead of their French and American counterparts, for whom this only became standard issue after the war. Compared to the anonymous masses in the trenches, or sailors on warships, fighter pilots were identifiable individuals. Three accounts by pilots were among the six bestselling war books in Germany after 1918, notably that by Manfred von Richthofen, the fighter ace also known as the Red Baron. The early stories still referred to loneliness, alienation, depression, and other more negative aspects of combat experience, but these elements were largely expunged in the popular retelling of these tales in the 1930s, which saw the lionization of fighter pilots as modern heroes.[146]

While many pilots experienced isolation and disorientation, what made them effective was the greater coordination and control provided by new organizational structures introduced after 1916, which saw an increase in the number of 'hunting groups' (*Jagdstaffeln*, shortened to *Jasta* and approximating to 'squadrons' in other air forces) and then their combination in larger 'fighter wings' (*Jagdgeschwader*) after June 1917. The first and most famous was Richthofen's 'Flying Circus'. The larger force enabled more complex tactics, but while innovative, the change was driven by the necessity of matching the growing number of Allied aircraft, which threatened to achieve air superiority and prevent the Germans from carrying out what was, still, air power's primary role of supporting the army by assisting the artillery to locate targets.

Germany built 48,000 aircraft across the war, including 17,000 in 1918 alone as part of the Hindenburg Programme's attempt to double production, but the high attrition rate to accidents and enemy action meant peak strength was only 3,975 planes (March 1918). Austria-Hungary built only 5,300 aircraft, achieving a maximum strength of 850, including its naval air service (1917). By contrast, Britain, France, and Italy alone built 119,000 planes, many of which were superior technologically to all but the Fokker DVIII biplane, only introduced in January 1918.[147]

Flight of the Phoenix

The Armistice forced Germany to surrender 1,700 planes, but though its air force command was dissolved in January 1919, several new squadrons were formed using aircraft fresh from the factories which served in the Baltic campaigns that year. Others were attached to the police. All were disbanded by 8 May 1920, which marked the official end of the air force, with the remaining planes being scrapped. Military and naval aviation were banned for Germany and Austria under the peace terms, but public enthusiasm for the new technology continued unabated and provided welcome cover for both countries' armed forces to train officers as pilots through sport-flying clubs. Moreover, Germany's aircraft industry was permitted to resume and the remaining limits on the size and capacity of aircraft were lifted in 1926, enabling the establishment of a state airline (*Lufthansa*).

Austria's right-wing paramilitary Heimwehr established a flying corps in 1927, while the regular army began training pilots the following year. Italian-built warplanes were bought in 1933 and initially entrusted to 'sport clubs', which soon became military formations ahead of being formally revealed as an air force in 1936. The Western powers tolerated this because Austria's modest rearmament was regarded as enhancing its neutrality. Likewise, Switzerland saw air power as indispensable to maintain its independence in an increasingly hostile world. Unlike Austria, it did not face international restrictions, but was equally short of funds. Having finally established an air force in October 1916, Switzerland struggled to equip it with sufficient planes before 1936, when it became a fully separate branch of service. In addition to several obsolete types of French planes built under licence, Switzerland produced its first genuinely home-made warplane, the two-seater C36 fighter, of which 152 were built between 1942 and 1948. However, the core of the new air force were the ninety Messerschmitt Me109 single-seater fighters bought in 1938.[148]

These were the first German military aircraft to be exported since 1918 and symbolized the innovation and capacity of that country's aero industry. The export licence was issued by the new Air Ministry established by the Nazis early in 1933 and headed by Hermann Göring. First serving in the Bavarian infantry, Göring had transferred to the air force in 1915 and risen to command the Flying Circus after Richthofen was shot down over France in April 1918. A decorated fighter ace credited with twenty-two 'kills', Göring was an early convert to Nazism and owed his new position and influence to this, rather than his war service or leadership qualities. He preferred men who shared a similar background as fighter pilots and who did not question his authority, like Ernst Udet, a fellow Flying Circus alumnus whose hands-on approach as head of the Luftwaffe's technical department extended to personally testing new planes. Göring was almost permanently at odds with Erhard Milch, the Lufthansa boss who was his deputy in the air ministry. Naturally cautious and permanently anxious about his Jewish heritage, Milch nonetheless managed to exploit Göring's growing laziness to widen his own influence.[149]

Göring and his protégés would exert a considerable, often negative influence on the development of Germany's new *Luftwaffe*, which was officially unveiled in 1935 after two years disguised as an organization for sport flyers. However, while the personal failures of its pilots are important, structural factors were also instrumental, notably the inherently competitive character of the Nazi state which wasted effort and scarce resources. Even more than the navy, which at least had enjoyed continuous existence across the interwar era, the Luftwaffe struggled with Hitler's impossibly tight timetable; something that Göring exacerbated by continually over-promising what could be achieved.

Germany also faced the same problems as other powers in devising an appropriate force structure and air-power doctrine. Although an independent branch of the military service, the Luftwaffe betrayed its origins within the army. Seeckt had placed several noted wartime flyers in the Truppenamt, the covert General Staff. These included Walther Wever, Hellmuth Felmy, and Albert Kesselring, all of whom would play significant roles in the Luftwaffe. Wever, who was to die in an air crash in 1936, is generally seen as the Luftwaffe's great lost hope. He was certainly more prepared to cooperate with the army and navy, and – like Seeckt – rejected the idea of using gas bombs as contrary to international law. Instead, Wever favoured tactics that mirrored those devised by Bruchmüller for the artillery: Germany should launch a massive first strike to destroy an enemy's air force while it was still on the ground, and then support the army's follow-up attack.[150]

Although the Luftwaffe mustered an impressive 1,888 planes and 18,000 personnel in 1935, France's air force was ten times larger and most German commanders were pessimistic. Their mood was transformed by Germany's intervention in the Spanish Civil War, which proved foundational for the Luftwaffe. Responding to appeals from the Nationalist rebels under General Franco in 1936, Hitler and Mussolini competed to assist a fellow fascist overthrow the liberal Spanish Republic. Italy's contribution was numerically larger, but Germany's made more impact, not least on its own air force. Overall, 19,000 men served in the specially formed Condor Legion, which had an average strength of 5,000. As these figures indicate, men were rotated through the Legion to maximize the number gaining experience. In 1940 this extensive combat experience was probably more important than qualitative difference in aircraft in explaining the Luftwaffe's domination of the skies during the invasion of France.[151]

The Legion was accompanied by a small battalion with the already ineffective light PzKw I tanks, while the 200 aircraft were initially mostly obsolete biplanes that were outclassed by Soviet fighters serving the Republicans. The situation changed within months as Germany sent to Franco's Nationalists its latest aircraft fresh from the factories and by the end of the deployment in 1939 the Legion had shot down five times as many aircraft as it lost. German pilots swiftly mastered the new conditions created by the dramatic technological advances since 1918. Speeds had doubled again, and planes were now equipped with radios, allowing the development of looser, more flexible tactics.

Clearing the skies allowed the Legion to support Franco's ground operations. Like the German army, the Nationalists were short of heavy artillery and requested air support as a substitute. The most infamous incident was the bombing of Guernica on 26 April 1937 by German and Italian aircraft, which exemplified both the potential and limitations of bombing at that point. The operation was supposed to block a Republican retreat by hitting the Rentena bridge, but instead the planes strafed panicked civilians and destroyed half the town.

The international outcry simply reinforced the Luftwaffe's faith in the potency of terror bombing which the now-dead Wever had opposed. Meanwhile, the German army welcomed the result, because it wanted to tie the new air force into a ground support role. Germany's new, fast, medium bomber (the Heinkel He111) had encountered little opposition from Spanish Republican forces, prompting the Luftwaffe to deem it sufficient and to abandon the development of a heavy, four-engine bomber, which threatened to take scarce resources from other projects. Worse, the additional resources were invested in producing more of the infamous 'Stuka' dive-bombers (Junkers Ju 87), which appeared to offer a substitute for heavy artillery through their ability to descend rapidly towards a fixed target (see Fig. 26). Over-engineered and heavy, the Stuka only had a 500-kilometre operational radius. It caught the public imagination as a terror weapon, but it was already being outclassed by other aircraft.

It also symbolized aggression, suiting the Nazis' ideological goals and reflecting the Wehrmacht's fixation on swift, decisive victory. Consequently, defensive preparations were disdained, meaning that German air defences remained under-developed prior to 1939. Wever had been followed by three successive chiefs of staff, inhibiting coherent planning. The job proved too much: Udet (1941) and his successor Jeschonnek (1943) both committed suicide following failures. Consequently, the Luftwaffe remained guided by Göring's fixation with weight of numbers. Production rose dramatically from 160 planes monthly (1934) to 700 (1939), but this was primarily achieved by concentrating on existing types that were rapidly becoming obsolete. In addition to 6,000 Stukas, Germany ultimately made over 33,000 Me109 fighters; a superb plane in 1936, this would be outclassed by 1941 and its limited range gave it only thirty minutes of flying time over Britain even when using bases in Western Europe.[152]

Special Forces

Alignment with the army resulted in the neglect of naval aviation, which had already proved deficient in the First World War. Göring saw naval aviation as a threat to his own empire, while Raeder failed to develop a coherent strategy and constantly interfered with the design of the *Graf Zeppelin*, the only one of the planned four aircraft carriers that came close to completion. The inadequacy of naval aviation contributed to the loss of the Battle of the Atlantic.[153]

Air transport initially proved more successful. The airlift of Franco's rebels from Morocco to Spain in July 1936 was a world first for this kind of operation. Germany repeated this during the annexation of Austria by flying troops to Vienna. Both operations succeeded because they faced minimal opposition, encouraging the Wehrmacht to place a faith in airlift that exceeded the capacity of the available aircraft. The principal transport plane, the Ju52, only carried twenty passengers, and though later models were better, they remained inadequate for the tasks to which they were assigned. The operations in North Africa after 1941 already demonstrated that the Luftwaffe was overstretched, but Stalingrad provided even more compelling proof. Although it flew 21,500 sorties to Field Marshal Paulus's army in the fourteen months from August 1942, it carried only 43,000 tons of supplies, equivalent to just 19 per cent of the total delivered by the Western Allies in the much shorter Berlin Airlift, though admittedly this did not face active Soviet opposition. The Stalingrad operation cost the Luftwaffe 488 planes and 4,000 aircrew. The failure did not prevent the Wehrmacht continuing to believe that air supply would enable isolated pockets to resist the Red Army, contributing to Hitler's repeated refusal to sanction evacuation and condemning the trapped soldiers to death or captivity.[154]

A similarly unrealistic faith was placed in the creation of paratroopers (*Fallschirmjäger*), copied from the Red Army in January in 1936. Conceived as special forces, these were intended to land behind enemy lines to capture key infrastructure and foster panic. They scored some spectacular successes in 1939–40, notably the capture of Fort Eben Emael, the lynchpin of Belgium's defences, but these were generally achieved against relatively light and confused opposition. The mass airdrop over heavily defended Crete in May 1941 eventually secured the island, but at the cost of 40 per cent casualties. Large-scale operations were now abandoned, but little was done to address the faulty coordination with the navy that also contributed to the disaster.[155]

The development of specialist capacity was hindered by the Luftwaffe's structure. Unlike the British and American air forces, it was organized territorially into air fleets (*Luftflotten*) assigned to the different fronts in support of the army and lacked a separate strategic bomber force or (until March 1944) a fighter command. Each air fleet had around 1,000 planes, and though aircraft production struggled to keep up with attrition after 1939, operational strength remained around 6,000 planes until a sharp fall in the last months of the war to 1,500 by May 1945. Long before then, shortages of fuel and pilots grounded much of the capacity for long periods.

Flight training was good, though no better than that of the world's other major air forces. It took two years to train a fighter pilot and double that time for a bomber crew, and quality declined as these times were cut after 1942. By that point, there were 1.9 million personnel, and the Luftwaffe was increasingly regarded by the army and navy as bloated and inefficient. Pressed to release manpower, Göring compromised by agreeing to the formation of twenty divisions of ground troops. The army refused to second officers or provide heavy weapons, leaving these units inexperienced and ill-equipped. Along with the equally grounded paratroopers, this represented a poor use of Germany's scarce manpower. Overall personnel numbers peaked at 2.8 million (August 1944), but the diversion of men as light infantry meant prisoners of war, women, and teenagers had to be drafted into air-defence batteries.[156]

Bombing

The Luftwaffe's primary role in the opening campaigns was in support of ground attacks. Warsaw (September 1939), Rotterdam (May 1940), and Belgrade (April 1941) were attacked in line with the doctrine of terror bombing adopted after Guernica, but these cities were poorly defended, and the swift capitulation of their governments simply reinforced the Luftwaffe's belief in its own prowess. This was shattered after July 1940 during the Battle of Britain and the subsequent 'Blitz' campaign.

Tasked with bringing Britain to heel after the fall of France, the Luftwaffe initially sought to secure air superiority by targeting the Royal Air Force's bases. Three of Germany's then five 'air fleets' (*Luftflotten*) were deployed, but these never mustered more than 1,200 operational aircraft and raids typically involved no more than 200 planes. Initial successes were wasted by inconsistent tactics, and the switch to the Blitz against London and other cities from early September represented a tacit admission of the impossibility of securing control of the skies. No air force had the capacity for precision targeting at that point, and the Germans' use of incendiaries reflected their faith in terror tactics, hoping that the destruction of civilian homes would force Britain to negotiate. A total of 53,595 tons of bombs were dropped, killing 43,000 civilians. By the time the campaign was suspended in May 1941, the Luftwaffe had lost 5,599 aircraft and 8,200 personnel, or 60 per cent of its entire losses to that point in the war.[157]

The Allies in turn bombed Germany across 1940–1, chiefly to bring home the reality of the war to its population. The campaign was stepped up with the arrival of the US air force in July 1942. The Allies' greater capacity was already demonstrated with the first 1,000-plane raid launched by the Royal Air Force against Cologne in May 1942. These became regular across 1943, with the Americans attacking during the day and the British at night. Key infrastructure was targeted, notably in the 'Dambusters Raid' against the Möhne and Eder dams to flood the Ruhr industrial region in May 1943. However, major cities were also hit, including Berlin throughout the war, as well as Hamburg (July 1943), and south German centres like Stuttgart and Munich from February 1944. The most notorious was the attack on Dresden, which was firebombed in February 1945. By the end of the war, around 60 per cent of Germany's urban space had been destroyed, including at least 3.8 million of the 19 million homes.

Controversy surrounds the death toll, with several influential post-war works uncritically citing Goebbels' claim that 200,000 people died in Dresden alone, whereas contemporary assessments by the SS put the total at 25,000; a figure confirmed by an inquiry commissioned by the city's mayor in 2004. The most likely overall total was up to 380,000, including civilian air defence personnel, slave workers, and prisoners of war, plus around 60,000 Italians and 75,000 other civilians in German-occupied Europe. Around half the German deaths were caused in the final months of the war when defeat was clearly inevitable. The keenly felt impact fed into Germany's post-war sense of victimhood, which was articulated by the East German authorities as part of their anti-Western propaganda.[158]

This line was continued by Jörg Friedrich, whose bestselling account of the Dresden firebombing was translated into English as *The Fire* in 2006. Friedrich presents the attack as deliberate murder, using provocative language such as calling the Allied bomber squadrons *Einsatzgruppen*, the term denoting the Nazi death squads in the Holocaust, while describing the civilian shelters as 'crematoria'. Such language decontextualizes the episode from the genocidal violence of Nazi Germany, while exculpating the country's own leadership for their wholly inadequate efforts to protect their own citizens.[159]

Nonetheless, it is important to remember that carpet bombing was a crude and cruel method. One of its chief architects, Arthur 'Bomber' Harris, certainly had an almost pathological hatred of Germans, regarding the First World War as unfinished business. He also recognized that precision targeting was beyond the available technical capacity of bombers and believed that incendiaries would kill the workers of the factories his planes could not destroy, and that civilian losses would break German morale. Rather like Haber's use of gas in 1915, Harris believed mass German casualties would shorten the war.[160]

Like the Luftwaffe senior command, he miscalculated in that relentless bombing stiffened civilian resolve to carry on in the belief a victory would make the suffering worthwhile. The Allied campaign was not without a real strategic impact. It forced Germany to change production priorities from offensive to defensive weapons, and to switch assets to home defence. Between 1942 and 1944 the impact primarily was one of destabilizing indecision as the Luftwaffe struggled to balance resource allocation between fighters, bombers, and ground-attack aircraft. It switched to prioritize fighter production in March 1944, by which time it was already too late as the Allies had vastly superior escort planes for their bomber fleets.

Second, the bombing campaign slowed German arms production across 1943–4, largely by forcing its dispersal into more remote locations and into new, underground factories staffed by slave labour and Italian prisoners of war. Bombing was particularly effective against those sectors that could not be moved, notably oil and synthetic fuel production. In turn, this crippled the Luftwaffe's capacity to operate against the advancing Allied armies. Given the Nazi regime's refusal to admit defeat, the Allies had little choice but to continue bombing into 1945, when it wrecked Germany's transport infrastructure and contributed to the

Wehrmacht's conviction that unconditional surrender remained the only option.[161]

Although it did not break German civilian morale, the bombing significantly affected it. Nazi propaganda had over-exaggerated the impact of the relatively feeble Allied attacks in 1940 to foster outrage, and this impaired the regime's ability to manage responses to the vastly more serious later bombing. Unlike the 1914–18 naval blockade, bombing did not noticeably raise German hatred of Britain or America, but equally it did not divide people from party as occurred in fascist Italy. Instead, it fostered a sense of a 'community of fate' (*Schicksalgemeinschaft*), reinforcing solidarity, but largely in forms that the regime found hard to convert into fanatical activism. Instead, many Germans saw bombing as divine punishment, including for their own behaviour towards the Jews, which was then common knowledge, though largely denied after 1945.[162]

Air Defence

Bombing also exposed the regime's inability to protect its own population. Some preparations were impressive. A civilian Air Defence League (*Reichsluftschutzbund* – RLB) had been established in 1933 by nazifying an existing organization founded five years before. The RLB expanded rapidly, reaching 22 million members, or more than one in four Germans, by 1942. Intended to provide first aid and to clear rubble, the RLB cooperated with a specialist Air Raid Police, established in 1935, and a fully national fire service, created in 1938 with standardized equipment – a genuine innovation soon copied in Britain and elsewhere. While these measures provided a good first response to the aftermath of attacks, they were also part of the regime's efforts to police its own population and did little to protect people against bombing.[163]

The first Allied raid on 11 May 1940 belatedly prompted the construction of civilian shelters from September, but these never provided for more than a tenth of the inhabitants of major cities, most of whom had to rely on cellars, which often became traps during bombardment. Survival increasingly depended on learning for oneself how to stay safe.

Having briefly moved people from the western frontier in August 1939, the regime prohibited evacuation as 'defeatist'. When it subsequently relented, the efficacy of the measures was reduced by a struggle between the Hitler Youth and the Nazi People's Welfare Organization to control it. Some 2 million children were moved, followed in April 1943 also by adults, since it now proved impossible to rebuild their homes. The number of evacuees reached 8.9 million by the beginning of 1945, many of whom had moved without permission. Mass evacuation exposed the regime's manifold shortcomings as it proved incapable of providing medical supplies, heating, or alternative accommodation. Nazi organizations redistributed Jewish homes and goods to victims, but this stolen largesse often fuelled resentment among recipients who felt others had got more.[164]

Active air defence suffered from the endless conflicts over resource allocation. Once the war began, Hitler prioritized anti-aircraft (AA) artillery since this was more visible to the public than fighter aircraft and German experience in Spain across 1936–9 had instilled false confidence in its effectiveness. AA defence grew to 889,000 personnel with 56,400 guns by 1944. Women represented nearly one in five of the crew members, but their participation was subsequently overshadowed by the memory of the 80,000 Flakhelfer (AA-helpers). Mainly recruited from grammar schoolboys – their working-class peers were already doing industrial apprenticeships – the 'Flakhelfer generation' went on to play a disproportionately significant role in German political and cultural life, including the future chancellor Helmut Kohl, foreign minister Hans-Dietrich Genscher, critical theorist Jürgen Habermas, and Joseph Ratzinger, who became Pope Benedict XVI.

The AA batteries were part of a coordinated system created only after July 1940, five years later than Britain's. Overseen by Josef Kammhuber, this used the still relatively new radar technology, searchlights, and aircraft which, from 1941, included specially modified night fighters to combat British bombers. Defence remained relatively effective until the summer of 1943, when the Allies began dropping 'window', or rolls of tinfoil, which confused German radar. Kammhuber was removed and eventually air defence was added to Himmler's growing empire in August 1944. Shortage of aircraft resulted in just 180 fighters assigned to air defence in 1942. Although numbers were belatedly increased, the core of the 'Kammhuber Line' remained AA guns whose ammunition expenditure consumed a third of all production, with on average 16,000 shells fired to down just one plane.[165]

Wonder Weapons

As the tide of the war turned, the regime placed growing faith in its 'wonder weapons' programme to secure the elusive qualitative edge over its enemies. Never coherent or fully coordinated, the development of new military technology had multiple origins in the Reichswehr's earlier sponsorship of covert rearmament, as well as the initiatives of individual scientists and inventors. It was pursued inconsistently, not least because the army and air force ran their own projects. Göring halted the development of jet propulsion in February 1940, believing Germany's early victories made it unnecessary.[166] Although the jet-propulsion programme resumed in 1941, Germany lost the opportunity to gain a technological edge. It eventually produced 1,888 jet warplanes by 1945, just 2 per cent of total production. These included, in yet another pyrrhic world first, the first operational jet fighter (the Me 262), of which there were never more than 200 in service at any time. The world's first operational helicopter (Fi282 Kolibri) likewise represented the diversion of resources into advanced technology that stood little chance of immediate application.

The rocket programme was the most ambitious and far-reaching of all the projects. As an entirely new technology, it had not been antici-pated in the restrictions imposed by the Versailles Treaty, allowing the Reichswehr to sponsor several enthusiasts who hoped government money would further their dream of landing on the moon. Foremost among these was Wernher von Braun, a brilliant if controversial figure who joined the NSDAP in 1937 and was promoted to SS captain, but later claimed he had conformed out of necessity. Braun worked on the A4 programme, better known as the V2 ballistic missile once Hitler characterized the project as *Vergeltung* (Vengeance) for Allied bombing. Development was initially overseen by Colonel Becker, who had worked on the 'super guns' in the First World War, including the long-range 'Big Bertha' guns produced by Krupp to bombard Paris, the shells from the largest of which were the first human-made objects to enter the strato-sphere in 1918.[167] The army continued to see rockets as an extension of long-range conventional artillery, a view shared by Hitler and many of the senior figures who failed to appreciate their strategic potential and only belatedly prioritized the project.

The V2 programme ran alongside the Luftwaffe's parallel efforts.

This produced several rocket-propelled planes more dangerous to their pilots than the enemy, and the more successful V1 cruise missile ('Doodle-bug' flying bomb). Unlike the V2 which had an arced trajectory, the V1 remained in the atmosphere. Both used liquid fuel for propulsion and were pilotless, remaining essentially 'point and shoot' weapons due to the difficulties of developing accurate guidance systems. The scientists continually over-promised in the hope of securing more resources, while the regime underestimated the technical challenges. The V2 required no fewer than 20,000 different components.

Both programmes were moved to Peenemünde on the Baltic island of Usedom by 1939, but operated on adjacent sites, typical of the regime's wasteful competitiveness. Production increasingly relied on slave labour, particularly after Allied bombing forced the relocation of much of the work to underground factories, notably the notorious Mittelwerk north of Nordhausen in Saxony, which was built by SS General Kammler, the constructor of Auschwitz.

The V1 was deployed first in June 1944. Around 22,400 were fired from batteries crewed by retrained AA gunners. Most rockets were directed against Belgium, but many were also fired at southeast England, where they destroyed or damaged nearly 1.5 million homes before the Germans' retreat moved them out of range by September. The V2 commenced offensive operations from July with the SS having already seized control of the batteries from the army. The missile's high altitude prevented any effective countermeasures beyond bombing production sites. Only a third of the 10,000 that were produced had been fired before the war's end. As with the German bombing campaign in the First World War, the need to protect their civilians forced the Allies to redirect resources, but by that point in the conflict this made little difference. The rocket campaign killed 15,500 Allied civilians, or at least 5,000 fewer than the number of slave labourers who died at the Mittelwerk. US intelligence later estimated that the V-programmes cost the equivalent of 24,000 fighter aircraft, compared to the 53,728 fighters produced during the entire war.[168]

Nuclear Weapons

Although the wonder weapons failed to prevent German defeat, the Allies were impressed by the ingenuity of their enemy and the innovations also displayed in their conventional weapons. Already before the war's end, they had scrambled to secure German technology and expertise. Within a week of Germany's surrender, the British and Americans established a joint programme to test captured weaponry using Krupp's proving grounds at Cuxhaven.[169] The denazification process was used to identify those with potentially useful knowledge or skills. Scientists were deported from Eastern Germany to the USSR in 1946, but the Soviets were far less successful than their Western rivals, mainly because, like Reinhard Gehlen, so many key figures deliberately surrendered themselves to the British or Americans. US forces ran multiple operations, the best known being Project Paperclip, which transferred 1,600 technicians from the V-programmes to America. They and numerous others were shielded from war crimes charges and given doctored papers to enable them to settle in the USA. Foremost among them was von Braun himself, who developed an improved version of the V2 which entered service in 1958 as Redstone, the world's first nuclear-armed missile, in addition to his better-known achievements of launching the first satellite and involvement in NASA's space programme. The French and Soviet nuclear missile programmes also owed much to V2 expertise.[170]

Germany's own nuclear programme had made little progress, despite its physicists' expertise. Development was led by Werner Heisenberg, and though he later claimed he had tried to slow it, the project was abandoned once Hitler lost interest in 1942. Fear that Germany might harness nuclear fission for military purposes had prompted the United States to develop its own programme after 1939. In contrast to the Germans' incessant infighting, the Allies cooperated, with Britain abandoning its own efforts and instead collaborating with the Americans, whose Manhattan Project had a staff of 150,000 and a $2 billion budget – a further indicator of how far Germany was qualitatively and quantitatively outmatched.[171]

West Germany subsequently renounced the development of nuclear weapons on its soil in 1954, but the growing awareness of how they had transformed the strategic situation prompted cooperation with France and Italy just three years later to create a nuclear weapon outside the country. Franz-Josef Strauss, who succeeded Theodor Blank as defence minister in 1956, was convinced that the possession of nuclear weapons was essential to demonstrate German sovereignty and he vigorously promoted the formation of the new Luftwaffe to have the capacity to use them. German ambitions only abated in 1966 when the United States agreed to equip the Bundeswehr with artillery modified to fire tactical nuclear shells. West Germany abandoned the joint programme with France and Italy and belatedly signed the Non-Proliferation Treaty in 1969 but, like France, interpreted the terms loosely to avoid retarding its expertise which was now openly displayed through the operation of civilian power stations, making it a 'virtual nuclear power'.[172]

While East Germany did not seek such independence, its army was nonetheless equipped with rocket batteries capable of launching tactical nuclear weapons in 1962.[173] In both East and West Germany, the super-powers retained the warheads in peacetime, on the understanding they would be issued to the delivery systems in wartime. The strategic arms reduction process led to the removal of the vast Cold War arsenals after 1990, except for around twenty gravity bombs stored in the US airbase at Büchel in the Rhineland-Palatinate. Subject to a dual key under a NATO agreement, these can be released in the event of war for delivery by a Luftwaffe fighter-bomber wing. The arrangement has proved a constraint on Germany's choice of new warplanes by limiting it to air-craft able to carry out this role.

As a neutral state, Switzerland was free to pursue its own nuclear pro-gramme, which began before 1945. Advocates argued it was equivalent to investing in fortifications to defend the country. A joint project com-menced with Sweden in 1956, and though attempts to buy bombs from Britain and France failed, the latter considered providing some assistance if Switzerland bought Mirage jets for its air force. Two Swiss referenda rejected the purchase of the jets, and the deal collapsed once some of the politicking around it became public in 1964. The 'Mirage Affair' strength-ened public opinion against nuclear weapons and Switzerland signed the Non-Proliferation Treaty in 1969, though the government committee considering the nuclear programme continued to meet intermittently until 1988.[174] Austria, meanwhile, abandoned its nascent atomic energy programme in 1978 following public opposition and declared itself 'nuclear free', subsequently playing a leading role in promoting non-proliferation and disarmament.

New Air Forces

The spiralling cost of increasingly sophisticated warplanes challenged all powers after 1945, but it hit smaller countries especially hard, because the cost of upgrading their air forces threatened to unbalance their entire defence budgets. Switzerland initially benefited from cheap wartime surplus to re-equip its air force with 500 relatively modern American, British, and French planes in 1949. Further purchases of newer aircraft followed but, by the 1960s, the growing costs forced Switzerland to keep older material long past its use-by date. There were over 300 requests from museums across the world in 1994 when Switzerland finally mustered out the last of the British-built Hunter jets, first purchased in 1958.

Austria faced similar constraints, and like Switzerland, it cooperated with Sweden as another, suitably neutral, country, to procure equipment and provide flight training. Declining public support after the end of the Cold War put further pressure on defence budgets in both countries. Austria was compelled briefly to lease planes from Switzerland to maintain air cover after 2005. It subsequently upgraded its equipment, buying new fighters and transport planes to NATO specifications to ensure continued capacity in order to cooperate with European partners. Switzerland's capacity continued to decline to the point where some question whether it can still police its air space.[175]

East Germany developed a clandestine air force after 1950, cloaking it as a flying club like those of interwar Austria and Germany, before officially revealing it in 1956.[176] West Germany planned one after 1950, strongly influenced by the old Luftwaffe's tactical roles. From having been jet pioneers, Germany was overtaken by developments elsewhere, notably in the United States after 1945, and the new West German Luftwaffe relied heavily on American technology and doctrine from its inception. In contrast to the surplus weaponry given to the army and navy, the US supplied 450 modern jets worth $315 million free of charge to equip the new Luftwaffe on its formation in 1956. The Luftwaffe became a major agent of Americanization, especially as there were fewer ex-Wehrmacht personnel than in the other branches, though Kammhuber was the first commanding general.[177]

The new Luftwaffe only reached target strength in the 1960s when it was plunged into crisis by the adoption of the new Lockheed F104 Starfighter multirole combat plane (see Fig. 35). Essentially a rocket tube with short wings, this swiftly became known as the 'Widow Maker' as 292 of the 912 in service crashed, killing 116 pilots by 1972.

A long-running scandal developed from 1966, leading to the successive sacking of the Luftwaffe's commander and the defence minister after it became known that design modifications had been delayed, while it was rumoured the manufacturers had bribed officials with $10 million going to the CSU in return for choosing the aircraft. Subsequent investigations also blamed a shortage of engineers and incorrect pilot training, all of which were eventually rectified.

As Austria and Switzerland also discovered, air sovereignty was hard to maintain in a world with intercontinental weapons capability. Both East and West Germany were integrated within their respective Cold War alliances, necessitating cooperation with their allied forces. While the East German air force had modern Soviet jet fighters, most of its personnel were employed in air defence. Great efforts were made to engage the population in civil defence, which expanded to incorporate the fire service (1958) and the East German Red Cross (1970). Although considered the least worst of the regime's defence organizations, the public remained unenthusiastic, regarding it as a continuation of the Nazi RLB, which was widely viewed as a failure, and deterred by the regime's own propaganda about the horrors of nuclear war. A vast bunker building programme was initiated in the 1960s, but like so many of the SED's other projects, this was wholly unrealistic and remained incomplete by 1989.[178]

The Bundeswehr's Luftwaffe briefly swelled to 110,000 men as it absorbed the remnants of East Germany's air force in 1990, including a squadron of new MiG29 jets retained to play the role of the enemy in NATO exercises, before these were sold to Poland in 2004. NATO's growing reliance on air power ensured the Luftwaffe remained more relevant than much of the rest of the Bundeswehr during the 1990s, but it was also trimmed during the successive reorganizations after 2002. Airlift capacity was improved in line with the expeditionary character of overseas missions, while the number of pilotless drones rose from eleven (1994) to 292 (2014) as these became increasingly important elements of modern arsenals.[179]

The current discussion around the legality of drones and other Lethal Autonomous Weapons (LAWs) is just one way in which public attitudes have influenced the organization and employment of armed force since 1914 to an unprecedented extent. Although governed by authoritarian and dictatorial regimes for much of this period, Germans were nonetheless citizen soldiers with a greater stake in national politics than those of previous centuries. The significantly larger scale of warfare and the growing reach of weaponry placed civilians at greater risk while simultaneously increasing their significance in sustaining the war effort. Assessing how this changed attitudes to war, military-civilian relations, and war's wider impact is the task of the next chapter.

15

Citizens in Uniform

TOTAL WAR AND ITS LEGACY

Military Education

The two world wars combined lasted just over ten years and were exceptional in their intensity and impact. Two successive generations were scarred by mass death, horrendous violence, deprivation, and suffering. The scale and scope of these conflicts led to their being termed 'total wars', though the apparent uniformity suggested by that common label obscures considerable differences between them. The violence of the Second World War is inexplicable without reference to that of the First, but it also differed in many ways. The deliberately genocidal character of much of the violence in 1939–45 left a legacy that still shapes how Germans think and respond to war today. Although not a belligerent, Switzerland was also directly affected by both world wars. However, from the perspective of the twenty-first century, it is possible to discern other important trends. Outside the decade or so of world war, Germans and Swiss experienced military service broadly as their predecessors had done during the nineteenth century: indirectly as part of their tax burden, other than for a relatively modest proportion of young men who served briefly as conscripted citizens in uniform.

The basic structure of military education established in the later nineteenth century persisted with training schools for NCOs and junior officers, primarily offering instruction in leadership and tactics, separate centres for specialists like engineers, and higher-level war academies educating staff and senior officers. Reflecting broader strengths and weaknesses, provision at the lower and specialist levels has generally proved more effective than that of the war academies, which long remained preoccupied with tactics and operations at the expense of strategy and the broader political and social context of war.

Armed forces benefited from the rising levels of general education within the societies from which they recruited. The proportion of Swiss militia officers with university education rose from 60 to 90 per cent across 1875–1945.[1] The situation was much less favourable in Germany, but the enforced reductions after the First World War also enabled it to be more selective, and over 90 per cent of new Reichswehr officers arrived with at least a high-school certificate. Higher war academies had been prohibited, but Germany simply devolved the old staff officer training to divisional level. NCOs were also trained to the level of former junior officers to provide a cadre for a much larger force. Nonetheless, overall numbers remained relatively small, and the Wehrmacht struggled to find enough qualified officers once the initial pool of talent had been deployed during the first wave of expansion after 1933. Training drew on past practice, with the new Luftwaffe also adopting wargaming. Courses were more intellectually demanding, but all service branches continued to stress willpower and a sense of duty over intellect or expertise; something that grew more pronounced with the pernicious influence of Nazi ideology.[2]

The focus also remained primarily on tactics. A higher *Wehrmachtsakademie* was established in 1935 as a serious attempt to break the silo mentality of the service branches by providing combined arms training, and to address the lack of strategic thinking. Courses were only two years (instead of three years in the old imperial academy) and the institution was closed in March 1938 without completing its statement of grand strategy, partly as this threatened to criticize Hitler's policies as too risky.[3]

Professional military education resumed with rearmament during the 1950s. Standards in East Germany were low before the establishment of sixteen training schools in 1956 and the Friedrich Engels Military Academy in Dresden in 1959, the latter having university status. By the mid-1980s, 2,400 officers had attended the Soviet military academy, which functioned in the manner of the old German General Staff in giving its alumni accelerated promotion. Overall, results were mixed since half the curriculum at all levels consisted of political indoctrination.[4]

In West Germany the Wehrmacht's legacy lingered through the subsequent service and promotion of men who had been trained as junior officers under the previous system, as indeed had already been the case with the transition from the imperial to the republican armies after 1918. Austria reopened its old academy at Weiner Neustadt in 1955, while West Germany re-established training schools for the three service branches a year later. A fourth school was added for the new logistics branch in 2006. A higher Leadership Academy (*Führungsakademie*) opened in Hamburg in 1957, but innate conservatism initially restricted the curriculum to technical aspects. Helmut Schmidt, the defence minister of the new SPD government in 1969, overhauled the system as part of his wider efforts to align the Bundeswehr more closely with the official ideal of citizen soldiers.[5] The curriculum was broadened and two Bundeswehr universities were opened in 1973 in Munich and Hamburg, with the latter later renamed Helmut Schmidt University in honour of its founder. Only 1.5 per cent of each university cohort go on to a two-year staff course at the Leadership Academy, which is the prerequisite for promotion to the rank of general. By 2020 the Academy had trained 5,000 German and 3,000 foreign officers (from 100 countries).[6]

Military Thought

For much of the first half of the twentieth century, German military thinking was dominated by an obsession with escaping perceived hostile encirclement and conquering the resources believed necessary to ensure independent national survival (autarky). In some respects this represented a continuation of earlier ideas in more extreme form, but there were important new impulses stemming from the First World War. The experience of the 'Hunger Blockade' fundamentally altered the understanding of security, which was no longer primarily seen in terms of frontiers and alliances, but was now focused on access to resources.

The shift was already present in the idea of a German-dominated customs union included in the September 1914 list of war aims but was more forcefully articulated in Friedrich Naumann's bestselling book, *Mitteleuropa* (*Central Europe*), published in 1915. A Protestant liberal politician, Naumann wanted to avoid socialism by finding an alternative way to satisfy the material desires of Germany's growing working class. He reframed the debate in terms of Germany's global position. Pre-1914 Weltpolitik had been couched in terms of status, with Germany's acquisition of colonies primarily intended to demonstrate that the country had joined the great powers. Naumann was conscious that the United States had 'closed' its frontier in 1890, civilizing the 'Wild West' and becoming a truly continental hegemon. He argued that Germany should follow this example and issue its own version of America's Monroe Doctrine by staking an exclusive claim to Eastern Europe as its 'Wild East'.[7]

The wartime occupation of Poland and the asymmetrical trade agreements with Romania for oil and other key resources all added impetus to these arguments. They amounted to a supercharged version of seventeenth-century Mercantilism, which regarded the world as a constantly sized cake and advocated that Germany should seize a bigger slice. Another source of inspiration was the concept of 'geopolitics' developed by the geographer and ethnographer Friedrich Ratzel, who also coined the term *Lebensraum* ('living space') to denote the physical area inhabited by a distinct people. Ratzel in turn influenced the Swedish political scientist Rudolf Kjellén, who regarded autarky as essential to national survival. The former Bavarian general Karl Haushofer founded the Institute of Geopolitics in 1922 to propagate these ideas, giving them a greater racist spin. Rudolf Hess, Hitler's future deputy, was Haushofer's research assistant.[8]

Meanwhile, the First World War's scale and intensity provided an additional impetus to the desire for autarky. Clausewitz had framed his concept of 'absolute war' as the concentration of military effort to achieve victory but did not advocate subordinating society and economy to this end. 'Total war' had remained feared as the unravelling of the controlled application of regular forces into a chaotic, autonomous 'peoples' war' (*Volkskrieg*). This also represented a potential threat to Germany's class system. Colmar von der Goltz was one of the few officers to advocate popular mobilization in his book *Volk in Waffen* (*People in Arms*, 1883), and was promptly shunted off to be military adviser to the Ottomans. Arming the people to avoid signing the Armistice was rejected in 1918, and Joachim von Stülpnagel faced similar hostility when he proposed this to resist the French occupation of the Ruhr in 1923.[9]

These fears framed the German concept of 'total war'. As will be shown towards the end of this chapter, the country's leadership entered the struggle in 1914 without a clear idea how to manage such a large-scale conflict. Far from being sought, total war was improvised from the failure to achieve decisive victory through conventional means.[10] It was retrospectively given greater coherence in 1935 by Ludendorff in light of his experience with Hindenburg in attempting to militarize the economy after 1916. Ludendorff simply radicalized the existing idea of 'military necessity' and the belief that the high command should be allowed to do its job free from constraints. Monarchs, politicians, industrialists, trades unions, and other organizations were to obey orders and marshal national resources as required. These arguments were written through the bitterness of defeat and the conviction that the armed forces would have triumphed had they not been 'stabbed in the back' by a 'weak' and unwilling home front.

Significantly, Ludendorff's statement on 'total war' was self-published, indicating both how marginal he had become and how his arguments were an attempt at self-justification.[11] Nonetheless, he gave shape to how many others felt that the war's totalizing impact had collapsed civilian-military boundaries. Civilians had been targeted in earlier conflicts like the Thirty Years War, which had also had a devastating effect on society, economy, and culture. However, the exponential expansion in the scale of war after 1914, combined with far more potent weaponry, enabled the enemy's population to be targeted more systematically and with deadlier effect. The resource-intensive 'materiel battles' encouraged a spuriously rational detachment among war planners, dehumanizing military personnel and civilians in statistical tables as 'resources' to be mobilized and callously employed or targeted.

The German military were not alone in thinking like this. For all its rhetoric of popular mobilization, Soviet 'war communism' during Russia's civil war (1917–22) involved a similarly ruthless top-down coordination of society.[12] However, Germany's experience created a distinct potential for extreme radicalization through most commanders' distrust of political control. Not wanting to lose a second time, the military embraced the Nazis, because it looked initially as if the new regime would let them get on with winning the next war.

In fact, Nazism was ambivalent towards total war. The regime's rhetoric of endless struggle coexisted uneasily with its promises of peace and prosperity. Likewise, its mass organizations and self-consciously 'revolutionary' credentials clashed with its insistence on absolute obedience to hierarchical authority. The population was to be encouraged to embrace militarism to facilitate mass mobilization but, like Imperial Germany, the

Nazi state dreamed of swift victory. Goebbels' infamous 'total war' speech on 18 February 1943 attempted to reconcile these tensions. By arguing that the USSR had ruthlessly mobilized all its resources, the propaganda minister stressed that Germany could not wage a 'bourgeois' war which protected its own middle class. However, the huge banner behind him on the stage in Berlin's Sportpalast read 'Total War – Short War': essentially, he sought to sustain the illusion that victory could still be swift if Germans made an extra effort.[13] Conscious that its legitimacy rested on the promise to give the loyal members of the Volksgemeinschaft a good life, the regime refrained from total mobilization, and struggled to ensure cinemas remained open and there was sufficient ice cream and other luxuries. In turn, this encouraged ever greater exploitation of other peoples who were regarded as expendable.

Blitzkrieg

Although Nazi Germany is indelibly associated with the concept of Blitzkrieg, this was never a coherent doctrine. The term occasionally appeared in professional military journals after 1936, but only as a warning to avoid positional warfare. It first gained popular currency when used by *Time* magazine on 25 September 1939 in its reporting on the campaign in Poland and the term was fashioned subsequently in the propaganda of both the Axis and the Allied powers. Retrospectively, its intellectual origins were traced to Moltke the Elder via Schlieffen's obsession with decisive battles of encirclement. The Wehrmacht's use of tanks and planes made it appear modern, but Germany's use of new weaponry was inconsistent thanks to the inability of the three service branches to coordinate procurement, doctrine, or strategy, as well as the country's insufficient industrial capacity. The real innovations remained those at the squad level, which grew from the stormtrooper tactics of the final years of the First World War. Otherwise, operational thinking remained within the mould set in the 1860s of making a rapid attack and hoping that opportunities would present themselves. The unexpected scale of the initial victories in 1939–40 led the Wehrmacht to believe its own propaganda and think that it really possessed a strategy.[14]

Total defeat did not shake the generals' self-belief, because they convinced themselves that they had again been robbed of victory, this time by Hitler's alleged meddling in command decisions. Impressed by the

Wehrmacht's ability to fight well against tough odds, and convinced it possessed a unique insight into the Red Army, US military intelligence recruited over 2,000 former senior officers after January 1946 to assist the US Army Historical Branch. Initially intended to provide the view from the other side of the battlefield for its own army's official history, the US expanded the programme to provide advice on how to combat the Soviet threat.

The work was coordinated by Franz Halder, whose dismissal by Hitler from his post as chief of staff in September 1942 and subsequent imprisonment in July 1944 made him appear 'clean'. Halder exploited the Americans' trust to secure the early release from captivity of men he approved of and to maintain contacts with those like Speidel and Heusinger who were forging the Bundeswehr. He shared their objective of defeating what they all regarded as the unfair defamation of German soldiers. By the time Halder retired with a US Meritorious Civilian Service Award in 1961, his team had produced 2,500 publications that not only placed their own individual service careers in the best possible light, but collectively presented the Wehrmacht's commanders as apolitical professionals whose advice had consistently been ignored by Hitler and other Nazi 'amateurs'.[15]

Their work profoundly influenced US doctrine during the early Cold War, but the impact waned with the development of tactical nuclear weapons which transformed the battlefield. However, many of their pamphlets were reprinted in the 1970s and contributed to the growing admiration for the Wehrmacht among sections of the US military and wider public. Although written largely from memory, the German-authored pamphlets had the air of authenticity and their narrow focus on operations and tactics fuelled the uncritical view of the Eastern Front, where war was waged seemingly in total detachment from the Holocaust.[16]

Germany's official use of military history after 1945 was much more cautious and formed part of a wider process of 'coming to terms with the past' (*Vergangenheitsbewältigung*) – to be discussed in more depth shortly. The new West German interior ministry founded an Institute for Contemporary History in Munich in 1949 solely to study the period 1914–45. A Military History Research Institute (*Militärgeschichtliches Forschungsamt* – MGFA) was established in Freiburg in southwest Germany in 1959. Its first head, Hans Meier-Welcker, was a former

Wehrmacht junior staff officer who subsequently trained as a historian and was instrumental in ensuring that the new institute pursued broader academic rather than narrow operational history. The MGFA absorbed East Germany's equivalent Marxist-Leninist institution in 1990 and was merged in 2013 with the Bundeswehr's Social Sciences Studies Centre as a combined research institute. These changes have not always been happy, but the MGFA has nonetheless contributed to the gradual rehabilitation of military history as a valid field of study in Germany.[17]

Violence

The German fear of a people's war found an immediate, violent expression in the killing of 6,500 French and Belgian civilians during the initial advance in 1914. The most notorious incident was in the Belgian town of Louvain as reprisals for alleged *francs-tireurs* attacks. This was, most likely, a friendly-fire incident among nervous German soldiers but it resulted in the great university library being burned down, the destruction of 2,000 buildings, the murder of 248 civilians, and the deportation of the 10,000 survivors. Such incidents gave substance to Allied claims that they were fighting a just war against 'the Huns'. German intelligence arranged for ninety-three intellectuals (including Max Planck, Siegfried Wagner, Wilhelm Röntgen, and Fritz Haber) to write 'An Appeal to the Cultural World' in response. This helped cement the country's belief it was fighting to defend their unique *Kultur* and contributed to the defensive denial of any wrongdoing.[18]

Crucially, these atrocities occurred as it became increasingly obvious that a swift victory would prove elusive. Subsequent occupation policies were oppressive, but not deliberately genocidal. The American mining magnate and future president Herbert Hoover was permitted to send 5 million tons of food aid to occupied Belgium. While this relieved the Germans of ensuring civilians were fed, they also stopped requisitioning food. Habsburg forces executed at least 11,400 civilians without trial in occupied Serbia, where the population declined by over a fifth, mainly through disease. However, the army also imported food to prevent starvation.[19]

The German presence in Poland was initially welcomed by the Jewish population as a liberation from Tsarist tyranny and some efforts were made to govern benevolently. However, deeply held views about the

'Wild East' led the army to blame the local population for the spread of disease, and the occupation became harsher and more rapacious from 1916 as racist views intensified. Negotiations with the Rockefeller Foundation for aid collapsed as the Americans believed the Germans might appropriate the food. No preparations were made for the occupation of conquered Romanian territory where the army lived off the land. The growing need for assistance from local nationalists in Poland, Ukraine, and the Baltic states prompted the army to abandon its protection of the Jewish population, which was exposed to pogroms during 1918. Austria-Hungary was less harsh, but it remained Germany's junior partner and lacked influence, while the flood of Jewish refugees sparked violent anti-Semitism in Vienna. Overall, the impact was a 'minor apocalypse' compared to what was to occur in the region after 1939, and while horrendous, most civilian deaths were not deliberate.[20]

It is equally hard to draw a direct line from military violence in the First World War to that of the Second, though likewise the earlier experience provided an important frame of reference for later atrocities.[21] Most soldiers found that the reality of war after 1914 was unrelated to the pre-war ideal, but experiences were very varied, with negative aspects like horror, alienation, disorientation, and loathing coexisting uneasily with more positive feelings of comradeship. The latter became celebrated after 1918 as an allegedly unique 'front experience' that actually owed more to the solidarity of defeat than wartime service. Front-line duty was mythologized as an imaginary community of men who had been forged through battle into superior beings, morally superior to those on the home front.[22]

Some have linked this militarized hyper-masculinity directly to support for Nazism. Certainly, many of the young Freikorps volunteers who embraced these ideas later joined the Nazis and participated in the Holocaust.[23] However, claims that this was a uniquely collective solidarity appear exaggerated, and friendships between German soldiers appear to have differed little from those between 'pals' or 'mates' in the Allied armies.

Moreover, Ernst Jünger, the leading exemplar for the 'front experience', remains a complex and contradictory figure. Having rebelled against his affluent middle-class parents by joining the French Foreign Legion in 1913, Jünger got cold feet and returned home, subsequently serving throughout the war, and rising to the rank of junior commander of stormtroopers. He reworked the most famous of his post-war auto-biographical works, *Storm of Steel*, several times eliding his initial expressions of disorientation and stressing glory and nationalism more clearly. His emphasis on the 'steel bath' forging 'new men' fitted the broader, conservative 'stab-in-the-back' myth of an undefeated army betrayed by the socialist Republic, and his anti-democratic nationalism remained mainstream into the 1970s. Yet, he refused to conform, behaving like a bohemian radical, taking cocaine and LSD, and hanging out with Picasso and Cocteau while posted as a staff officer to occupied Paris in the Second World War, when he wrote an essay advocating peace and became associated with the conservative resistance to Hitler. Jünger's longevity contributed to his being celebrated as a major literary figure and he received the Goethe Prize in 1982.[24] He was clearly exceptional. For most soldiers, war exposed masculinity's fragility, and it left many with horrific wounds that civilians often found repulsive.[25]

War Crimes

Thus, there is no simple explanation for why so many Germans participated in genocidal violence after 1939. As in the First World War, experience varied considerably even between brothers if they were posted to different fronts, as well as between service branch and type of unit with, for instance, significant contrasts between submariners and fighter pilots. Some units were almost continually in combat, others only briefly, while a fifth of personnel never fired a single shot.[26] As citizen soldiers, Wehrmacht personnel embodied their society's wider contradictions. They could be thoughtful, educated, considerate of their families, patriotic, dutiful – but also Nazis. Alcohol abuse proved important in socializing troops to become accustomed to killing.[27]

No soldier could plead ignorance of the '10 commandments of chivalrous warfare' that were printed inside their paybook, including the imperative to respect international law, and to refrain from looting or harming civilians. Yet, they were specifically instructed to do so, most notoriously by the Commissar Order, issued on 6 June 1941, directing that captured Soviet political officers were to be executed. The response proved patchy, not least since news of the order stiffened Soviet resistance, ultimately leading to it being rescinded on 5 May 1942. Other instructions were issued in 1942 to execute captured Allied commandos and anyone endangering German security in occupied Europe.[28]

Compliance likewise varied, and generally there was greater observation of international norms in the west than in the east of Europe. German troops massacred captured Black French personnel in 1940, but the army conducted operations against resistance fighters roughly within the rules until it lost influence to the SS after June 1942. Some restraint continued to be shown in Italy after 1943 from the need to cooperate with Mussolini's rump regime. Much depended on circumstances and personalities. The high proportion of teenagers among Waffen-SS troops contributed to the greater proclivity of these units to commit atrocities in France, including the Oradour Massacre. Conversely in Italy, greater moderation was shown after the ruthless ideologue General Kesselring relinquished command subsequent to being wounded in 1944.[29]

Those heading East were in no doubt that such considerations had been suspended. Troops preparing for Operation Barbarossa were already informed on 13 May 1941 that the goal was the 'total elimination of all active and passive resistance', and that they would not be prosecuted for war crimes unless their behaviour threatened military discipline. Many took this as a licence to do 'whatever we want'.[30] Not only did the regime and high command disregard the needs of the local population, but they paid insufficient attention to their own troops who, for example, lacked adequate supplies or winter clothing. Even those otherwise critical of National Socialism embraced the 'kill or be killed' mentality in the East, where mass violence rapidly became so commonplace it scarcely attracted comment.

Crucially, such violence did not stem from lax control, or a sense of disorientation while lost in the vastness of Russia. Nor was it the product of a progressive brutalization, because it was present from the outset.[31] It was rooted in Nazi ideology and was explicitly encouraged by the senior command, who had embraced the regime's genocidal goals. Ideological indoctrination was integral to Wehrmacht training and broadly accepted by its personnel, especially junior officers and squad leaders, who saw the extermination of a dehumanized enemy as part of their 'mission'.[32] All branches of the Wehrmacht were involved, including the Luftwaffe.[33]

The advance in the East was followed by SS *Einsatzgruppen* (task groups) and the paramilitary police battalions who, collectively, were responsible for the murder of up to 2 million civilians, including 1.2 million Jews. Another 500,000 'partisans' were killed. German forces were thinly spread in the East, which they regarded as a hostile environment. Based on the earlier experience with francs-tireurs, German counter-insurgency doctrine stressed swift, harsh measures. The refusal to grant partisans the option of surrender proved as counterproductive as the Commissar Order, as did occupation policies more broadly.[34] Some Wehrmacht personnel expressed disquiet, especially as things began to go badly by 1942, but the army's refusal to regard partisans as combatants helped blur the boundaries between counter-insurgency, depopulation, and genocide.[35]

The Wehrmacht's advance in the East was welcomed by the German-speaking population (which the Nazis termed *Volksdeutsche*, or ethnic Germans), as well as many local nationalists, who instigated their own pogroms. Most soldiers believed that the killing of Jewish men of military age was acceptable. Those involved in the mass shootings were given double rations. 'Execution tourism' was so rife that the army repeatedly had to order off-duty personnel not to take photographs or report back what they saw for fear of upsetting Germans at home (see Fig. 32).[36]

German Resistance to the Nazis

The opportunities for ordinary personnel to resist these policies were extremely limited, though around 100 risked their own lives to help others and their courageous actions show what could be achieved through determination and disregard for self-interest. The most prominent example was Sergeant Anton Schmid, a former Austrian electrician who saved 350 Jews in 1941–2 and even supplied arms to the Warsaw underground, before being discovered and executed.[37]

Resistance among senior officers was hobbled for the same reasons so many of them willingly collaborated with the Nazis. They were overwhelmingly conservatives, with those expressing unease about Nazism primarily doing so because they saw it, like socialism, as the product of the erosion of traditional society through industrialization and urbanization. Given their anti-modernist outlook, anti-Nazi conspirators were unable to think of a viable alternative beyond replacing Hitler with a more acceptable, conservative leader. Most senior military resisters were anti-Semites, including several of the leading – and later celebrated – figures, all of whom contributed through their desk work to coordinating the Holocaust. They simply felt that Nazi genocide was exceeding propriety, and that the criminal regime had failed to deliver the promised peace and prosperity. Above all, they feared Hitler's reckless polices would cost Germany the war and bring catastrophe to the nation.[38]

Western appeasement over Czechoslovakia in 1938 ended the hopes of senior figures like Ludwig Beck and Admiral Canaris that an international reverse would shift German opinion and enable them to remove Hitler. The subsequent rapid victories deterred any further action, but disquiet grew with Hitler's refusal to make peace after the fall of France in the summer of 1940, because it was now clear Germany was locked into a long war.

Unease was greatest among intelligence and staff officers who had more insight into the reality of the mounting odds, but little was done beyond private discussions. General Tresckow, a staff officer who had married Falkenhayn's daughter, emerged as the coordinator of a plot to kill the Führer. After a failed attempt to blow up Hitler's plane in 1943, Tresckow cooperated with Canaris's deputy in the Abwehr, Colonel Oster, on Operation Valkyrie. Disguised as countermeasures in the event of an uprising by slave workers, this prepared the seizure of key infrastructure in the event of another attempt on Hitler's life succeeding. Count von Stauffenberg, who had been wounded in Tunisia, replaced Tresckow as coordinator when the latter was posted to the front. After others refused, Stauffenberg volunteered to carry out the assassination attempt. Unlike modern suicide bombers, he did not wait to see if the device would succeed, and the assassination attempt failed because another officer unwittingly moved Stauffenberg's briefcase after he had left the room on 20 July 1944. To their credit, both he and Tresckow acted even though they doubted they would succeed and knew that the Allies were unlikely to negotiate. For Tresckow, taking a moral stand had come to outweigh purely strategic considerations.

Many of the other conspirators continued even though the situation was hopeless, and they were soon crushed. Himmler exploited the failed plot to expand his empire at the expense of the Wehrmacht and other institutions. Over 7,000 people were arrested, of whom 5,000 were executed. Several of those implicated, like Beck and Rommel, were permitted to commit suicide. Suspicion also fell on others who had fallen foul of Hitler, like Halder and Manstein, even though they had refused to support the plotters. Most Germans, including civilians, regarded the plotters as treacherous oath breakers who had undermined the war effort.[39]

Coming to Terms with the Past

The violence of the Second World War continued to trouble Germany into the twenty-first century. Unlike 1918, the totality of defeat was clear to all, but the public willingness to accept any responsibility rapidly evaporated. Allied occupation and denazification policies inadvertently encouraged the growing sense of denial and victimhood. Germans rejected the Allies' concept of collective guilt as failing to accommodate the variety of their actual experience. Following the devastating bombing of cities like Hamburg, Dresden, and Berlin, the Allies' requisitioning of homes, continued food shortages, prolonged internment of German civilians, and slow release of prisoners all stoked the conviction of Germans that they were also victims.[40]

This sentiment was most pronounced in Austrians, who came to regard the Anschluss as instrumental in making them Nazism's 'first victims'. Germans in the Western zones rapidly sought to draw a line under the past, presenting 1945 as 'zero hour' (*Stunde Null*), a tabula rasa for an entirely new beginning. The Church reinforced this with its message about the return of God following both Nazism *and* the decadent Weimar Republic. The political right expressly reconstituted itself as Christian (the CDU and CSU). Germany's subsequent 'economic miracle' recovery enabled 'zero hour' to become a success story, which increasingly few Germans wanted to besmirch by talking about the war. Disappointed that German workers had not rebelled against Nazism, the new Communist regime in East Germany also distanced itself from the past, trying to rally public support by focusing criticism on leading Nazis who, conveniently, were now largely living in West Germany.[41]

In his final radio broadcast to the nation on 9 May 1945, Admiral Dönitz, appointed in Hitler's last will and testament to be the new head of state, asserted that Germans had fought an honourable war against impossible odds and that, in contrast to the First World War, the armed forces had been supported to the end by the home front.[42] Dönitz's linkage of the armed forces to the nation at large reflected the wider sense of the war as a common effort in which all Germans had suffered. Increasingly, the Wehrmacht's reputation became the touchstone for the broader question of Germans' responsibility for the war and mass deaths.

In November 1945, Halder, Manstein and three other senior officers were asked to prepare an account of the Wehrmacht's conduct for the War Crimes Tribunal convened in Nuremberg. The resulting document articulated what has become known as the 'clean Wehrmacht myth'. The authors accepted that individual soldiers might be guilty of misdeeds but rejected any notion of collective responsibility. Crucially, they did not deny the Holocaust, but argued this was entirely separate from the war and organized solely by Hitler and leading Nazis. Denial of war crimes was thereby linked to defence of their professional competence, and hence also of their hopes that they could play a role in rearming Germany. They claimed they had always been patriotic, apolitical professionals whose advice had been ignored by the regime. Above all, they were honourable men who had kept their oath, unlike the July 1944 plotters whose actions had endangered the nation and sullied the honour of the armed forces. Over the coming months, they forged extensive alliances among other former officers, including those working for US and British intelligence, while closing ranks to marginalize men they disliked, like Alfred Jodl or Wilhelm Keitel, whom they singled out as scapegoats to be sacrificed to Allied justice.[43]

Manstein was convicted on nine of seventeen charges by a British military tribunal and sentenced to eighteen years' imprisonment in 1949. By that point British opinion had mellowed, with the public largely accepting the Wehrmacht's distinction between 'good German soldiers' and 'bad Nazis'. Those protesting against Manstein's conviction included not only Basil Liddell Hart, who considered him a military genius, but such diverse public figures as T.S. Elliot, the Labour MP Michael Foot, and Winston Churchill, who helped pay for a defence lawyer.[44] Manstein's early release in 1953 was widely interpreted as vindication of the clean Wehrmacht myth. Manstein continued his double denial in 1955 by publishing *Lost Victories*, arguing that the Wehrmacht was not responsible for either losing the war or implementing the Holocaust. Endorsed by Liddell Hart, Manstein's book was swallowed largely uncritically in the anglophone world.[45] The memoirs of Hitler's armaments minister and favourite architect Albert Speer made a similar impact: if someone so close to the inner circle knew nothing of war crimes, then how could ordinary Germans be expected to have known, let alone have done anything to prevent them?[46]

War service was impossible to deny, given that one in four Germans had belonged to the Wehrmacht or other armed organizations, but most had experienced other important milestones during this time, like falling in love, or leaving school. Post-war films and literature 'normalized' the war as part of 'ordinary' experience. Germans had been simple *Landser* (squaddies), no different from their (Western) opponents.[47] Meanwhile, East Germans were exculpated by their government, which presented the working class as the victims of 'fascists' and 'imperialists' responsible for the war. The Holocaust was elided by the refashioning of the Eastern Front as the start of socialism in Germany through the contacts forged with the Soviet Union: 'Stalingraders', like former general Paulus, presented their service as a cathartic conversion to socialism while in Soviet captivity.[48]

East and West German leaders announced the end of the post-war era in major speeches respectively in 1963 and 1965, in a clear attempt to consign the conflict firmly to history. Professional historians contributed to this, notably Gerhard Ritter, a conservative monarchist veteran of the First World War, whose influential history of German militarism presented Nazism as an aberration, disconnected from the earlier, especially Prussian past.[49]

These efforts were challenged immediately, and since the 1960s Germany has undergone three major cycles of agonized discussion about the Second World War, roughly coinciding with generational shifts. The discovery of caches of letters or photos removed from family albums have forced successive generations to question what they were told by their parents or grandparents.[50] Major incidents have stimulated this by pushing the past into the media limelight. An early and important example was the trial of Adolf Eichmann in Israel in 1961–2, when the term Holocaust entered public discourse – though still largely considered separately from how Germany prosecuted the war. Another was the broadcast of the US miniseries with that name in 1979, as well as the visit of US President Reagan in the company of Chancellor Kohl to the Bitburg cemetery on the fortieth anniversary of the end of the war, which reignited the debate over whether the Waffen-SS could be included in the rehabilitation of German soldiers.[51]

In Austria, a wave of warm nostalgia for the lost Habsburg era masked any serious consideration of the war while assisting the revival of the country's tourist industry. The cosy *Kaffee und Kuchen* image was finally shattered in 1986 by accusations of complicity in war crimes levelled against Kurt Waldheim, previously UN Secretary General and then a candidate in Austria's presidential elections. Waldheim was subsequently elected, but doubts about the veracity of his denials led to him becoming the first head of state to be barred from entry to the United States.[52]

Attitudes shifted during the 1990s as the question of direct personal responsibility waned with the gradual extinction of the war generation. Reunification offered another opportunity to consign the war to history. Germany's leadership continued to reaffirm a duty to remember the past, but some found their public pronouncements hollow and ritualistic, while generalized warnings about the dangers of war risked creating a homogeneous sense of universal victimhood. The peace movement's wholesale rejection of war inadvertently fostered acceptance of the clean Wehrmacht myth among the younger generation, many of whom believed that 'bad things' inevitably happen in war and that consequently their grandparents were no worse than any other soldiers.

The growing consensus was challenged by the Wehrmacht Exhibition, organized by the Institute for Social Research, an independent think tank. Timed for the fiftieth anniversary of the end of the war, the exhibition opened in March 1995 and toured thirty-seven German and Austrian cities over the next four years, accompanied by wide media coverage and discussion. It displayed copies of original documents and around 800 photos taken by Wehrmacht personnel that had been discovered in family albums and collections, including numerous examples of 'execution tourism'. There were some minor inaccuracies in presentation which were soon corrected, but they were seized upon by growing opposition, orchestrated by the CDU, CSU, extreme right NDP, and veterans' organizations. Protests escalated into violence in Munich, Vienna, and Dresden, and the end of the tour was hastened by an attempted bombing by neo-Nazis in March 1999.

The level of emotion underscored how many Germans were reluctant to accept that their grandparents might have committed war crimes, as well as how discussions of the past had shifted from 'old Nazis' defending their personal reputations to neo-Nazis with their own radical agenda.[53] The suspension of conscription and the shift to a smaller, professional army after 2011 has been accompanied by a growing concern that the armed forces are being infiltrated by the extreme right. The anti-immigrant Alternative for Germany (AfD) party actively promotes itself as the Bundeswehr's natural 'home', and around 2,100 of the 35,000 long-service professionals were members in 2019. Despite the official rejection of the Wehrmacht as a model for the Bundeswehr, several notorious examples of open admiration have been exposed by the press, notably among the special forces and other elite units. One case involved the adoption of a palm tree symbol by a unit serving in Afghanistan, which was criticized as reminiscent of the device used by the Afrikakorps.[54] While troubling, it should be noted that the proportion of AfD membership in the Bundeswehr (6 per cent) is several points below that party's latest vote share (10.3 per cent in 2021).

The Peace Movement

The modern peace movement emerged in the late nineteenth century from the existing socialist and Catholic critique of militarism. Rather than merely trying to mitigate war's effects, like the Red Cross, peace activists sought to eliminate militarism altogether. An early example was the formidable Bertha von Suttner, the daughter of a Habsburg field marshal, whose pacifist novel *Die Waffen Nieder!* (*Lay Down Your Arms!* 1889) was translated into sixteen languages and led to her becoming the first female recipient of the Nobel Peace Prize (1905), an award she had persuaded Alfred Nobel to institute four years earlier. German (1892) and Austrian (1893) Peace Societies were founded, and though these remained much smaller than those countries' army and navy leagues, Suttner and others were active in the International Women's League for General Disarmament, established in 1896, which numbered 1 million members and lobbied the conferences promulgating new laws of war in 1899 and 1907.[55]

The wartime 'civil truce' (*Burgfrieden*) largely silenced pacifism in 1914, but it swiftly re-emerged as hardship and hunger alienated much of the population from the German and Habsburg imperial regimes. Protesters asserted their own patriotism by criticizing their government for leading them towards disaster. While the interwar era is remembered mainly for paramilitary violence and the rise of militaristic fascism and

Nazism, only one in six Bavarian former soldiers joined a veterans' organization, while the members of the anti-military Veterans, Disabled and Dependents' Association outnumbered the total serving in the Freikorps by two to one. Many had simply had enough of war. Organized pacifism was stronger than prior to 1914, but still dwarfed by militaristic groups like Stahlhelm.[56]

Erich Maria Remarque's anti-war novel *All Quiet on the Western Front (Im Westen Nichts Neues)* sold 3.5 million copies in twenty-five languages within eighteen months of publication in 1929 and was quickly made into a Hollywood film the next year. It expressed a widely felt belief that the conflict had been futile and had dehumanized those who had fought it. Remarque was forced into exile by the Nazis, but his novel later served the narrative of German victimhood and the general belief that all powers had stumbled into the First World War.[57]

Anti-militarism became official policy when the victorious Allies banned German uniforms and insignia in August 1945. Nazi statues and symbols were swiftly removed, though the regime's monumental buildings and flak towers were usually too substantial to be demolished.[58] The rival Cold War blocs fostered reconciliation between the nations within their alliances at commemorative ceremonies to which veterans' organizations were increasingly invited as their members grew older. In contrast to the interwar era, veterans largely rejected overt militarism since this conflicted with their primary goal of securing pensions, and the focus for those clinging to a more conservative interpretation of the war increasingly narrowed to old comrades' associations meeting in smoky beer halls.

The basis of anti-militarism also changed. Before the mid-1930s it had primarily been the trades unions and socialist parties who opposed armies because soldiers were used to crush strikes.[59] In the 1950s this changed initially to opposition to military service, but once conscription was introduced, protesters switched their attention to nuclear weapons. Recognition that Germany was the prospective battlefield for a Third World War prompted the formation of Fight Against Atomic Death in 1957. This was strongly influenced by the memory of the Allied bombing campaign, as well as Christian fatalism. It copied Britain's Campaign for Nuclear Disarmament (CND) in organizing the Easter Marches. The first of these in 1960 saw demonstrators marching from the British missile base at Bergen-Hohne to the site of the Bergen-Belsen concentration camp, indicating the sometimes problematic relationship between the

German peace movement and the post-war victim narrative. Mass protests soon subsided, especially as the development of atomic energy appeared a more positive development, while inter-generational tension found expression in campaigning against the Vietnam War and the American presence in West Germany.[60]

NATO's Double Track decision in 1979 to deploy medium-range missiles to Germany prompted the emergence of a new peace movement, as well as the foundation of the Green Party (*Die Grünen*) in 1980, which soon became a third force in West German politics. Activists were now predominantly younger and quite innovative. Alongside demonstrations and petitions, protesters formed human chains between major cities, and produced literature to warn people of the dangers of 'atomic death on your doorstep'.[61] The protests drew in some serving members of the Bundeswehr, notably Gert Bastian, who formed Generals for Peace and Disarmament in 1981 and was a Green MP between 1983 and 1987.[62]

The movement contributed to the collapse of the SPD/FDP coalition government in 1982 and within a decade over half the population favoured unilateral disarmament. Faced with a surge in applications for conscientious objection, the Bundeswehr adapted how it presented itself, avoiding images of weaponry in favour of posters showing a smiling hedgehog. Nonetheless, while often finding them inconvenient, the country's governing elite could accept the protests as proving that West Germany was a peace-loving country. The peace movement lost momentum once the medium-range missiles were deployed in 1983 and soon diverted its energies into a myriad of environmental causes.

The East German authorities were less tolerant. Most of the population were unenthusiastic about rearmament, but the church establishment avoided confrontation with the regime so as not to jeopardize its continued ability to operate among the population.[63] The only pacifism permitted was that of militant socialist 'fighters for peace' opposed to the machinations of the capitalist West.[64] The ruling SED's programme to militarize the country's youth proved counterproductive, contributing to the country's worsening malaise and the emergence of a home-grown peace movement by the 1980s, inspired in part by its Western counterpart, and which included a young Angela Merkel.[65]

Although a few intellectuals, like the playwright Friedrich Dürrenmatt, criticized Switzerland for having stood by during the Holocaust, most Swiss celebrated their country's successful preservation of its neutrality in both world wars and remained favourable towards militia service. A succession of scandals surrounding procurement, as well as awareness of peace movements elsewhere, significantly shifted opinion and led to the formation of the Society for a Switzerland Without an Army (*Gesellschaft Schweiz ohne Armee* – GSoA) in 1982. This secured a cross-generational alliance of those on the left by arguing that unilateral disarmament was simply a logical extension of the country's traditional neutrality. Although it failed to secure a mandate for abolition, it garnered sufficient support in several referenda to influence the progressive downsizing of the armed forces since 1995, as well as blocking possible Swiss membership of NATO.[66]

In common with similar movements elsewhere in Europe, the German peace movement lost direction as the end of the Cold War removed the immediate threat of atomic death, while armed forces became less visible through downsizing and the decreasing proportion of citizens performing military service. Approval ratings for the Bundeswehr remained quite high into the 2010s but dropped off significantly. However, while opposition to foreign missions grew, only the Left Party (*Die Linke*) currently oppose them and there are signs that the public is taking less notice of them.[67]

ORDINARY MEN AND WOMEN

Motivation

The tensions between obligation and motivation already characterizing military service during the nineteenth century became more pronounced after 1914. The truly mass armies depended overwhelmingly on conscription to provide the necessary numbers, but the demands of modern warfare could only be met if soldiers were highly motivated. Traditional appeals to patriotism were supplemented by more overtly ideological messages intended to fire hatred of opponents, intensify a sense of duty, or both. In contrast to Britain, where volunteering was more a question of age, in Germany it was determined largely by class, reflecting social differences in patriotism's appeal.[68]

The State replaced the Church in articulating images of the enemy. In Germany during the First World War this swiftly focused on 'perfidious Albion', already identified by the population as the cause of their hardship through the 'Hunger Blockade'. The feeling was mutual, with a wave of anti-German sentiment in Britain involving dachshunds being kicked or stoned in the street, 'German Shepherd Dogs' becoming 'Alsatians', and the country's thoroughly Germanic royal family anglicizing itself from the House of Saxe-Coburg-Gotha to the 'House of Windsor' while their equally German relations, the Battenbergs, became the Mountbattens. In both cases the bitterness was stoked by the belief that the other had betrayed a 'natural' cultural and political affinity. By contrast, attitudes to France largely replicated those felt in earlier conflicts.[69]

Both German and Austro-Hungarian propaganda presented Russians as dangerous, yet inferior foes. The racist and ideological aspects grew once Russia was also identified with Bolshevism after 1917. Nazi ideology left no room for leniency or compassion, since that would imply others were racial equals, but the regime was inconsistent in its messaging, which adapted to some extent to circumstances. Anti-communism remained strong in post-war West Germany and indeed had long been so in Switzerland; however, it is doubtful that this significantly influenced recruitment in either country.

East German soldiers were schooled to hate 'the mercenaries of imperialism who have been whipped up into anti-communism and drilled for aggressive war', thereby endangering peace and 'a life worth living'. Ideological commitment rose in line with rank. Whereas only a third of soldiers felt the NVA met their expectations of a socialist army, the proportion was two-fifths among NCOs and at least half of the officers.[70]

The role of ideology is most controversial for the Wehrmacht, particularly given the subsequent reluctance to accept responsibility for war crimes.[71] In addition to numerous letters, diaries, and official documents, insight is provided by over 250,000 pages of transcripts of secret wiretaps of conversations between German prisoners of war made by British and American intelligence officers.[72] Nationalism, anti-Semitism, and anti-bolshevism were already deeply rooted in German society but were usually expressed unreflectively by men who otherwise thought of themselves as unpolitical, 'decent Germans'. Most soldiers held inconsistent views and often had a poor grasp of National Socialism, something that was not surprising given its inherently shifting and contradictory nature. In a country where 95 per cent of the population still belonged to a Christian church, Nazism never entirely displaced other, deep-rooted ideas. A key difficulty in identifying motivation is how these ideas – traditional conservative, nationalist, Christian, Nazi, and even more liberal beliefs – were often compatible and mutually reinforcing.

Unsurprisingly, ideology was strongest among the Waffen-SS, but the Volksturm people's militia, the regime's other overtly ideological military project, suffered from high rates of absenteeism. The self-fashioning of the Waffen-SS as an elite has also misled some later interpretations because it suffered higher desertion and suicide rates than the Wehrmacht, especially after 1943.[73] Respect for Hitler among the Waffen-SS remained widespread to the end, but ideological commitment flagged, leading to the creation of 'leadership officers' in December 1943, modelled on Soviet commissars and intended to raise commitment. Crucially, ideology proved far less central to cohesion in battle, where soldiers were themselves in danger, than as a factor sustaining collective action in atrocities against civilians who could rarely defend themselves.

Based on their own interrogations of German prisoners, Edward Shils and Morris Janowitz, two sociologists working for US intelligence, argued that ideology was only a secondary factor, and that cohesion depended on loyalty within the small 'primary group' of the squad. Their core argument was later popularized as the 'band of brothers' idea and proved hugely influential, not only as an explanation for why the Wehrmacht continued fighting until 1945, but also as an exemplar of 'small group cohesion' which could be adopted by other militaries.[74] The interpretation is partly substantiated by other evidence indicating that most German soldiers wanted to live up to their comrades' expectations, which in turn were defined conventionally as a 'soldierly ethos'. The overriding desire was to 'fit in' as a 'good comrade' who was neither a 'shirker' nor a reckless 'hero' capable of endangering the unit by selfish foolhardiness. Medals were the markers of this ethos and part of the Wehrmacht's deliberately competitive spirit. The Iron Cross was revived in 1939 and was now awarded on a mechanistic points basis, with at least 5 million distributed by 1945, or roughly one to every four soldiers.

However, the primary group did not function quite as Shils and Janowitz imagined, not least because its membership often fluctuated violently as men died, were transferred, or joined. Rather, soldiers formed smaller friendships within both their unit and the wider platoon. Cohesion also depended greatly on the quality of the squad's NCO or junior officer, which declined with the rising casualties. The year 1944 saw the reappearance of behaviours characterizing the German and Habsburg armies towards the end of the First World War, as soldiers adopted unobtrusive shirking, feigned illness, applied for transfer to less dangerous posts, and other survival strategies.

Defeatism became widespread, especially among troops on the Western Front. By January 1945 only one-fifth of SS personnel still believed the regime's claims that defeat was not inevitable.[75] Chaos and disorder reigned in the final weeks as civilians and Volksturm militiamen destroyed their official papers and insignia, often in rage at their misplaced trust in the regime, and that their suffering and hardship was in vain. These feelings of self-pity contributed to the post-war sense of victimhood.[76]

Given these conditions, many have wondered why the Wehrmacht generally continued to resist to the end. The primary reason, at least in the East, was that they no longer had anywhere else to retreat to. Another was the sharp escalation in official repression during 1944, stimulated by the memory of the disintegration of German forces in 1918. Under the 1872 military code only those who deserted to the enemy were liable for the death penalty, with all others facing a five-year prison term. There were around 50,000 official cases of desertion and unauthorized leave during the First World War, of which 8,000 were tried in the military courts, with only eighteen men executed, compared to the 269 deserters who were shot in the British army. While the German army was less harsh, it also suffered far higher desertion rates than officially recorded, because many soldiers simply surrendered during the final months of the war, which also saw a surge in the numbers reporting sick.[77]

Whereas the First World War prompted Britain to adopt a more pragmatic response to deserters, Germany took the opposite course after the republican interlude when military jurisdiction had been curtailed. The

1872 regulations were reissued in tougher form in 1934, while the use of the death penalty expanded after 1939. Around 30,000 soldiers were condemned to death, including 22,000 for desertion, of whom at least 16,000 were executed; roughly the same number as in Japan, but compared to just 288 in Britain, France, and the United States combined, and still less than the staggering 150,000 killed in the Soviet Union. In addition, the Nazis extended punishment to deserters' families after November 1944, and now considered those who surrendered to be traitors as well.[78] Shockingly, the victorious Western Allies permitted the defeated Wehrmacht to continue to execute some deserters in the weeks immediately following the German surrender. Those convicted of 'war treason' were belatedly and retrospectively officially exonerated in September 2009.[79]

The two post-war German armies consciously sought to distance themselves from such brutal practices, as well as to market service as an attractive career choice rather than simply a patriotic duty. This was particularly important in East Germany, which had to rely on voluntary enlistment longer than its western counterpart, but the regime's deficiencies and general lack of sufficient resources made this an uphill struggle. The occupying Soviet forces had seized the Wehrmacht's infrastructure, obliging the East Germans to create virtually everything from scratch. There were few barracks, with the initial volunteers obliged to live in tents while they built their own accommodation. Shower blocks were only added in the 1970s and even then, there was usually no hot water, especially in winter, whereas the army's tanks were kept in heated garages. Men slept eight to ten in a room where the temperature in winter was not above 12° thanks to the inefficient and unhealthy lignite heaters.

The day began at 6 a.m. with physical exercise, before a roll call and short breakfast, followed by training from 8 a.m. until 5.45 p.m. with an equally short lunch break. Soldiers had to endure a further ninety minutes' political instruction before finally being allowed off duty until 10 p.m. with lights out. They had only eighteen days of annual leave and were otherwise under constant supervision from their officers who could impose punishments for infractions like a lack of class consciousness or not understanding Marxism. Accessing Western media was forbidden and the families of serving personnel had to cut ties with their Western relatives. A brief effort at Chinese-style equality was abandoned in 1961, after which the officers adopted some of the worst traits of their old Imperial German forebears, living and eating separately from their men and spending their free time hunting on special game reserves (see Fig. 34).

Desertion reached 14 per cent of total strength in 1953, and though it declined, it nonetheless remained high until the construction of the Berlin Wall in 1961. Significant efforts were made to improve pay, and to offer sports and cultural activities. However, the army struggled constantly with alcohol abuse, which worsened as each cohort of conscripts neared the end of their service. Discharge days were frequently chaotic. To maintain their authority officers were compelled to tolerate a series of brutal rituals that characterized conscripts' last six months of service. After some modest improvement during the 1970s, morale declined with the worsening economic problems of the 1980s.[80]

Conditions in the Bundeswehr and Austrian armies were considerably better, though both likewise relied on conscription for the bulk of their manpower. The Bundeswehr made a sustained effort to appear attractive, adjusting its message in line with changing public opinion. The initial stress on manliness was not so different from that presented in the 1930s, but later greater emphasis was placed on service as an opportunity to gain valuable life experience and skills. Pay and living conditions remained below those in the civilian economy, particularly in Austria, and both forces have struggled to recruit sufficient specialists, like doctors or engineers. These pressures have increased in Germany following the suspension of conscription in 2011.[81]

Geographical Origins

Conscription laws were designed around social categories, leading to some unevenness in their geographical application. East Prussia provided 40 per cent more recruits proportional to its population for the Imperial German army, while in Württemberg that figure was 10 per cent, compared to 8 per cent and 22 per cent below average from the Rhineland and Alsace-Lorraine respectively. Nazi Germany conscripted 1.651 million men from areas annexed after 1938, as well as 1.305 million Austrians; combined, these represented 17.3 per cent of its total manpower, though Austria's share was slightly above average. Due to its perverse definition of Germanness, the SS preferred men from western rather than eastern Germany. Rural recruits were more likely to be sent to the artillery or cavalry because of their familiarity with horses. Previously distrusted as unreliable socialists, industrial workers found themselves preferred for the infantry after 1914 because commanders believed they could cope better with the noise and confined spaces of trench warfare, leading to urban recruits suffering disproportionate casualties.[82]

The linkage between service and citizenship did not immediately exclude foreigners. Although Ernst Jünger returned to serve his country in 1914, many Germans and Austrians chose to remain in the French Foreign Legion and were permitted to stay in North Africa rather than fight their compatriots on the Western Front. The Legion saw a surge in Germans volunteering during the 1920s when they formed 55 per cent of its strength. Around 3,000 Germans, Austrians, and Swiss served in the famous International Brigades on the Republican side during the Spanish Civil War. Although far smaller than the French, Italian, or Polish presence, they became important subsequently to the East German regime's anti-fascist tradition. Many leftist exiles also joined the French Foreign Legion during the 1930s. The Nazis demanded their extradition after 1940, but the Legion protected most of them by issuing false papers.[83]

Far more foreigners served Nazi Germany, where the voracious demand for manpower forced the regime to loosen its definition of Germanness after 1940. Ironically, the Waffen-SS went the furthest because it was excluded from the conscription quotas and finding foreign volunteers was the only way it could expand. The proportion of foreigners among Waffen-SS recruits rose from 4 per cent (April 1941) to nearly 56 per cent (April 1944) and, overall, barely 40 per cent of its personnel came from the Third Reich. The largest group (300,000) were what the regime defined as ethnic Germans (*Volksdeutsche*) recruited from the minorities across Eastern Europe, with another 250,000 non-Germans split roughly equally between Western and Eastern Europe. 'Nordic' recruits were preferred, but Croatians, Ukrainians, Bosnian Muslims, and 2,500 Indian Army soldiers captured in North Africa were also accepted (see Fig. 29). Only around fifty Britons volunteered, compared to 1,900 Swiss. Growing concerned at the number of foreigners, Himmler ordered them to wear special 'national' badges to distinguish them from the 'pure' Waffen-SS in July 1942, but within two years it proved impossible to maintain such distinctions.[84]

The Wehrmacht also recruited large numbers of foreigners. At least 251,000 Red Army soldiers deserted to the Germans and, overall, 1.2 million Soviet citizens served Nazi Germany, providing about 6 per cent of its total manpower. These included the 150,000 (mainly Ukrainians) in the Waffen-SS, 300,000 in the SS police battalions, and a significant number of 'Cossacks', whose precise total is difficult to determine because several units subsequently transferred to the Waffen-SS. The Wehrmacht often enrolled Soviet prisoners and citizens as 'Cossacks' to circumvent Hitler's prohibition on Slavs in German uniforms: bizarrely, the Führer believed the Cossacks were descendants of the Ostrogoths and therefore acceptable. Recruitment of Caucasian and Crimean Muslims was officially sanctioned in November 1941. Altogether, half a million Balkan and Soviet Muslims served Germany during the war. Most Soviet citizens, however, remained unarmed *Hiwis* (helpers), acting as drivers, cooks, pioneers, messengers, interpreters, and ammunition carriers attached to front-line units, including those of the Luftwaffe (see Fig. 30).[85]

The difficulties encountered with Polish and Ukrainian units during the First World War encouraged the Wehrmacht to accept the regime's additional ideological arguments against separate client armies, despite there being some support for these among the conquered populations in 1941. The growing crisis prompted Hitler to reverse this and permit the captured Soviet General Vlasov to form an anti-communist army in November 1944, which grew to 50,000 men but was distrusted and deployed in the west.[86] The Wehrmacht also recruited 30,000 Greeks into anti-partisan units and conscripted 130,000 Alsace-Lorrainers directly. Vichy France sent an 'Anti-Bolshevik Legion' of 6,600 as part of a campaign to bargain for greater autonomy, while fascist Spain supplied over 40,000 men to the Wehrmacht's 250th 'Blue Division' serving on the Eastern Front across 1941–4.[87]

Ideology was important to the first wave of volunteers. For example, 80 per cent of Norwegians joining the Waffen-SS belonged to the local fascist party, while Nationalist Spaniards saw serving in the Blue Division as a continuation of their own anti-communist 'crusade'. The majority, however, sought to escape the privations of occupied Europe or, for many of the East Europeans, simply to survive. They were regarded as traitors in their own countries. Most Soviet citizens captured by the Red Army during the war were executed. Vlasov also suffered this fate in

1946, but Stalin spared many of the 35,000 'Cossack' troops and their families handed over by Britain and the United States, recognizing that they had largely been compelled to join the Wehrmacht. Croatian collaborators were massacred by Tito's Yugoslav partisans. Fear of reprisals was among the factors prompting the refusal of 1.2 million East European forced labourers to go home after 1945. Around 250,000 settled in West Germany, while the rest emigrated, mainly to Britain, Australia, and the US. Many foreign and German Waffen-SS personnel volunteered for the French Foreign Legion, forming 60 per cent of its strength in 1946 and fighting subsequently in the unsuccessful defence of French Indochina against the communist Vietnamese. In their efforts to secure inclusion in the rehabilitation of German soldiers during the 1950s, SS generals Paul Hausser and Felix Steiner used their memoirs to present the Waffen-SS as a pan-European army and forerunner to NATO. However, most foreign volunteers faced considerable hardship after 1945, except those from Spain, who were given preferential employment opportunities by Franco's government.[88]

Around half a million Germans and Austrians fled the Nazis across 1933–9. Most were interned as enemy aliens once war commenced, but around 10,000, mainly Jewish volunteers, served in Britain's forces, while many others joined American units. The Soviet Union was the most willing to accept Germans, but only provided they were communist. These were allowed to establish a National Committee of Free Germany in July 1943, which provided the nucleus of the later SED government in East Germany. A League of German Officers was formed, largely for propaganda purposes, from captured Wehrmacht personnel in August 1943. A few officers joined willingly, like Vincenz Müller, who was convinced the war was lost and Germany would need Soviet goodwill later. News of the July 1944 plot convinced General Paulus also to join the League and he later served as a prosecution witness against his former comrades at the Nuremberg Tribunal.[89]

Jewish Soldiers

A significant proportion of German and Austrian anti-fascist volunteers came from their countries' Jewish minorities. These had faced mounting prejudice since the middle of the First World War. Jews had broadly welcomed the outbreak of war in 1914 as an opportunity to demonstrate their patriotism and finally secure full inclusion within society. Around 100,000 German Jews served, or one in every six, of whom 35,000 were decorated and 2,000 became officers. Three times that number served in the more tolerant Habsburg forces, where 25,000 became officers, including twenty-four generals.[90] Despite their disproportionate contribution, Germany's elite was largely convinced Jews were shirking and undermining the war effort. The critics were dumbfounded when the actual numbers were revealed by the notorious 'Jewish census' of November 1916 when the army required all units to report how many Jews were in the ranks.

Nonetheless, Ludendorff, Max Bauer, and other influential officers increasingly conflated Judaism and Bolshevism as shadowy forces responsible for the impending defeat. Ordinary soldiers did not yet share these views, despite the strongly anti-Semitic tone of the army's 'patriotic instruction' programme begun in 1917. Anti-Semitism surged more violently in the wake of defeat, though the situation in Austria was slightly better than that in Germany or Hungary. Excluded from Stahlhelm and other veterans' organizations, Jewish ex-combatants formed their own league, which had 55,000 members, a far higher proportion than achieved by the other groups.

The Reichswehr's small size enabled Hans von Seeckt – who remained an anti-Semite despite having married a Jewess – to exclude Jews along with republicans. However, the population broadly respected Jewish veterans. The names of the 12,000 Jewish war dead were recorded alongside their Christian comrades on war memorials and later Nazi campaigns to remove them often met with local resistance. Jewish veterans enjoyed some initial exemptions from the Nazi race laws, though these were progressively removed by 1941.[91]

The leadership of the new Wehrmacht generally shared conventional anti-Semitism and were ambivalent towards Nazism's more virulent policies. While still wanting to exclude Jews from the officer corps, senior officers felt they could serve as pioneers in wartime. The armed forces shared the same problems as the rest of German society, where many families had at least some degree of Jewish heritage, and the Wehrmacht continued to tolerate serving soldiers of mixed parentage: in all, up to 3,000 Jews and 200,000 so-called 'half-Jews' (those with two Jewish grandparents) served during the war, including several hundred as officers, despite this officially being prohibited. Around twenty became generals.[92]

Social Origins

The dramatic expansion of armed forces after 1914 not only saw a temporary surge in the number of Jewish officers, but also accelerated the terminal decline in the proportion of noblemen which had set in during the later nineteenth century. Commoners, like Ludendorff and Groener, composed 55 per cent of senior commanders and 72 per cent of all German officers by 1918. In addition to heavy casualties (one in four adult male nobles were killed), the war severely damaged the aristocratic officer ideal. Old-style monocles and swords were replaced by the archetypes of the cool, proficient staff officer and the steel-forged, hardened squad leader as the technicians of modern war.[93]

The new Austrian Republic abolished aristocratic titles in April 1919, but the country remained acutely status conscious. Although former Habsburg officers dominated the new army, the initial appointments were made by soldiers' committees who preferred junior commanders with front-line experience. Conservatives gravitated to the paramilitary Heimwehr, while a serious effort was made to filter out fascists after 1935. The Anschluss saw a purge of most of the senior officers, though around 220 former Habsburg officers eventually became generals in the Wehrmacht.[94]

By contrast, the German Republic missed several opportunities to purge the new Reichswehr of hostile conservatives, particularly once Seeckt assumed control in 1920 and favoured former staff officers like himself. This policy resulted in a temporary revival in the proportion of noblemen to 24 per cent by 1932, something that could not be sustained once the army expanded rapidly thereafter. Nonetheless, promotions through the career ladder ensured that aristocrats formed a significant proportion of the Wehrmacht's senior officers, including seven of the eighteen field marshals. One in five of Hitler's ministers also hailed from old noble families. Only the SS was initially shunned by nobles and the upper middle class.[95]

The Wehrmacht's rapid expansion, followed by the mounting officer casualties after 1941, produced similar pressures to those in the First World War. The army was reluctant to open the officer corps to those it considered socially undesirable and only granted temporary 'war commissions' to most new appointees. Although Hitler urged the army to widen selection for ideological reasons, it is likely this happened more from necessity as the number of army officers expanded from 23,000 (1938) to over 243,000 (1943), of whom over a fifth now came from working-class backgrounds. Widening the net also lowered educational standards, especially among the Waffen-SS where ideology trumped other criteria, and already before 1938 fewer than one in five officers had even elementary schooling. The naval officer corps also lost much of its earlier class stratification.[96]

The sheer size of the Wehrmacht posed problems when Austria and West and East Germany rearmed. Former personnel felt they had fought valiantly against communism and found it hard to see why anyone would object to their presence in the new armed forces, especially when these so clearly needed expertise. Austria and West Germany addressed this by imposing an upper age limit of fifty-four when they formally established their new armed forces in 1955, thereby effectively disbarring most who had held senior positions in the Wehrmacht. The Bundeswehr received 235,000 applications in 1955, including 160,000 with prior service, of whom 4,386 had belonged to the Waffen-SS. Around half the applicants were accepted, including 63,000 former Wehrmacht soldiers and about 1,000 Waffen-SS. Only forty-four of the 3,000 or so former Wehrmacht generals and admirals eventually joined the Bundeswehr, and though four-fifths of all officers had war service, most had only been NCOs. The proportion was lowest in the Luftwaffe. While 6,000 pilots survived the war, their experience was no longer even relevant ten years later and only 181 were taken on. Overall, noblemen still represented 15 per cent of Bundeswehr officers in the late 1960s, while a further 42 per cent came from civil service backgrounds, and just 4 per cent from the working class. These proportions altered radically with the generational shift around 1968 and by the mid-1970s noblemen had largely disappeared, while those from civil service backgrounds had dropped to 26 per cent and working-class officers had risen to 17 per cent.[97]

East Germany was much less accommodating towards the Wehrmacht, but there were too few old comrades from the International Brigades to command its new forces. Vincenz Müller and around 600 officers and specialists were initially employed. They had all undergone political 're-education' through the wartime League of German Officers, but most were already discharged in 1952, though Müller became the first chief of staff and was used to rally the middle class to the new

SED regime until he was retired in 1958. Around 5,000 former ordinary soldiers from working-class backgrounds were enlisted into the paramilitaries during the later 1940s.[98]

The early East German officer corps regarded itself as a professional military body serving the new state, but the ruling SED feared it might rival their pre-eminence and immediately sought to politicize the armed forces. Progress was slow and only a third of career soldiers were party members by the end of the 1960s. A decade later this rose to 97 per cent, or well above the proportion in other Warsaw Pact countries. Educational standards grew considerably, ironically making the force much less of a working-class army.[99]

A similar screening process was initiated following unification in 1990, with 1,500 East German officers immediately discharged as being too compromised politically. Around 10,800 former regulars (only around a sixth of the total) were eventually accepted into the Bundeswehr, but their pay initially remained at only 92.5 per cent of their Western colleagues, and their previous service was classed as having been in a 'foreign' army, severely retarding their careers. Unsurprisingly, most former NVA personnel saw themselves as shoddily treated by the Western takeover.[100]

Women in Arms

Whereas most men became soldiers through conscription, women primarily joined voluntarily. This experience was not always emancipatory. While female nurses broadly conformed to the expected gender roles during the First World War, the uniformed auxiliaries appeared transgressive. Most of those volunteering were young, unmarried middle-class women who incurred the ire of ordinary soldiers by preferring the company of male officers. Their comparatively high pay raised doubts about their motives, leading to sexual innuendos and comparison with prostitutes.[101]

Attitudes to sex generally affected how women volunteers were perceived. The Imperial German army exhorted soldiers to remain celibate but was sufficiently realistic to have installed prophylactic vending machines in barracks after 1900, despite Wilhelm II's efforts to get these removed. Like soldiers of other belligerents, Germans expected their women to remain chaste, while for the men themselves their loyalty was to their nation and their comrades, not their wives. Prostitution grew in the major cities and in occupied France, with official brothels strictly segregated and sentries posted outside those reserved only for officers. Despite the precautions, doctors estimated that 50,000 soldiers were incapacitated by venereal disease in January 1915, equivalent to more than an entire corps. Moralists criticized soldiers' loose morals as undermining the war effort, while soldiers suspected their wives of infidelities with prisoners of war and foreign workers.[102] Such concerns added to the tensions between the home and war fronts.

As in Britain, women were 'rewarded' with enfranchisement by the new republican governments in Austria and Germany, but to many (especially men) this merely added to the sense that the war had dislocated society. Unease was fuelled by the New Woman (*Neue Frau*) image of the 1920s: self-confident, short hair, and more daring clothing.[103] Demobilization forced women from the better-paid jobs, but they remained a significant proportion of the workforce, which was roughly equivalent to that reached by Germany's enemies during the Second World War. That conflict saw only a modest increase of 300,000 to 14.9 million female workers by September 1944, reflecting the inelasticity of the Nazi economy. Although the Reich Statistics Office estimated there were still 15 million women available for war work, the regime refused to require them to serve. The Nazi belief in fixed gender roles was one factor, but the regime recognized that domestic service also provided childcare, enabling some women to work. Above all, it feared that conscripting women would appear a desperate measure and undermine the morale of men in uniform.[104]

The relative protection of German women was not extended to those in occupied Europe, where the Wehrmacht established 500 brothels in which at least 34,000 women were forced to work. Some concern was shown for the army's reputation in Western Europe, but that was given scant attention in the East, where sexual licence was considered a 'reward' for arduous service and there were numerous cases of mass rape, such as in the wake of crushing the Warsaw rising in 1944. Nazi race laws deterred some soldiers, but it was common for soldiers simply to shoot women they had slept with to avoid any repercussions for themselves. Relations were not invariably so violent, and the term 'ethnic German' was sometimes interpreted loosely to enable soldiers to marry Polish women. German women who had liaisons with foreigners faced stiff penalties and their partners were hanged.[105] Foreign women suffered twice over, as they were frequently punished for their 'collaboration' once the war was over.[106]

A third of Germany's female population joined one of the nominally voluntary Nazi welfare organizations, while around a million women served in uniformed but officially non-combatant units and administrative positions. These *Blitzmädel* (Lightning Girls) attracted similar male hostility to their forebears during the First World War. Most were still young, had grown up with National Socialism, and wanted a good life, material possessions, and adventure. Few had any idea of what awaited them, especially those heading east. Some were appalled, many disillusioned, but a significant number participated willingly, especially the wives of male personnel, for instance staffing the refreshment tables for the men working at the deportation sites and shooting pits of the Holocaust.[107]

Those who mentioned their wartime service after 1945 presented it as an unavoidable necessity. By contrast, post-war Germany embraced the heroic image of the *Trümmerfrauen* (Rubble Women) clearing the way for a new society. In fact, concentration-camp inmates were used to clear bomb damage during the war, while most of the work after 1945 was done by large firms with machinery, or the labour battalions recruited from former Wehrmacht personnel. The Trümmerfrau myth was nonetheless instrumental in securing retroactive pension rights for many women.[108] Meanwhile, the fraternization of German women with Allied soldiers reinforced the sense of defeat, especially for veterans. The subsequent embrace of the American consumerist ideal during West Germany's 'Economic Miracle' restored something of the old gender order with the man as provider and assisted the reintegration of men into the workforce to the detriment of women. As the previous chapter indicated, women were only gradually permitted to volunteer for the new armed forces created in the 1950s and are still exempt from conscription in Austria and Switzerland.

ARMED FORCES AND SOCIETY

Legal Status

Soldiers remained citizens throughout the twentieth century, though not always with full legal rights. Their relationship to state and society was mediated by an oath of allegiance that proved highly problematic.

717

Whereas Habsburg personnel retained a strong sense of personal loyalty to their emperor, at least until the accession of Charles in 1916, their German counterparts increasingly saw their duty as being to the nation, not the ineffective Wilhelm II. As Wilhelm Groener explained to the astonished Kaiser on 9 November 1918, 'Oath to the colours? Warlord? These are only words, an idea.'[109]

Seeckt encouraged this trend in the post-war Reichswehr by suggesting it owed a deeper loyalty to the nation, thereby allowing officers to reconcile breaches of their formal oath to the constitution with their sense of duty. To further insulate the army, he persuaded the government to issue a new military law in March 1921, disenfranchizing serving soldiers and forbidding them from joining parties. The Social Democrats mistook this as a means of genuinely neutralizing the army, whereas it simply distanced personnel further from republican ideals.[110]

Soldiers' civil rights remained nominally safeguarded by the continued civilian jurisdiction over the armed forces and their entitlement to elect committees to represent their interests in negotiations with their officers – a relic of the revolutionary council movement of 1918–19. This right was abolished in July 1933 by the Nazis, who also ended civilian jurisdiction and required all personnel to salute uniformed NSDAP members. A new personal oath to Hitler was introduced after Hindenburg's death removed the last vestige of the republican order in August 1934. In contrast to their attitude towards Wilhelm II, Wehrmacht personnel felt bound by this oath, reflecting their generally high esteem for Hitler, which far exceeded the regard they felt towards the regime.[111] The Waffen-SS emerged as a party organization funded by the interior ministry after 1933, and at Himmler's insistence its personnel were removed from martial law in October 1939 to prevent the army imposing discipline to curb their activities.[112]

The reference to God in the oath, reintroduced by the Nazis after the secular Republic, was again abandoned when Austria and West and East Germany rearmed – though those in West Germany retained the option to include it. All three states now required oaths of loyalty to their constitutions, with that in East Germany also including 'brotherhood' with Warsaw Pact forces. In West Germany the oath just applied to professionals, with conscripts only obliged to make a 'solemn promise'. Soldiers remained enfranchised citizens with the right to complain about their superiors. West Germany created the post of Military Ombudsman

(*Wehrbeauftragte*) in 1957, copying Sweden, where this had been established in 1915 as an independent monitor responsible to parliament.[113] Bundeswehr personnel were also permitted to join civil service trades unions after 1966. Switzerland continued its earlier arrangements of treating its militiamen as civilians, only requiring an oath if they were mobilized.[114]

Innere Führung

Central to West Germany's wish to create a genuinely new army was the concept of *Innere Führung*, which can be variously translated as 'inner' or 'internalized' leadership. It was devised by Count Baudissin, who was involved at the Himmerod meeting in 1950 but was significantly younger and more junior to the other former Wehrmacht officers present. Whereas they had served in the Imperial German army and had preserved its conservative traditions through their time in the Wehrmacht, Baudissin only joined the Reichswehr in 1926 and had subsequently been captured in North Africa in 1941. His Protestant background had emerged more strongly while in captivity in Australia and he saw himself as a civic humanist, even considering becoming a farmer.[115]

He rejected Western armies as potential models, regarding their conventional hierarchical structure as insufficiently democratic to prevent Germany's strongly conservative military tradition reasserting itself. He wanted to replace the blind 'corpse obedience' (*Kadavergehorsamkeit*), in which allegedly even those who had been killed remained in the ranks, with discipline rooted in the law. To avoid becoming a separate soldierly caste, Bundeswehr personnel were to remain civilians at heart. The traditional reliance on oaths, drill, and ceremonies was to be replaced by moral integrity and civic duty. Crucially, Baudissin argued that a truly democratic army could also be militarily effective, and he linked Innere Führung to the initiative and devolved responsibility inherent in the doctrine of mission tactics.[116]

Baudissin's ideas were not entirely new because the Wehrmacht (in May 1942) and even the Prussian drill manual (1726) had admonished officers and NCOs that they had a duty of care towards their subordinates, whose trust they had to earn. However, whereas those ideas expressed Prussia's traditional paternalism, Baudissin built his argument from the ground up and stressed the fundamentally civilian character of citizen soldiers.

British observers dismissed Baudissin's ideas as an example of the Germans 'as usual, taking themselves rather too seriously'.[117] Predictably, most of Baudissin's colleagues were even less impressed once Innere Führung was adopted as the official leadership ethos in 1957. Former Wehrmacht personnel found it hard to shake off ingrained attitudes, for example continuing the old method of saluting (though at least not the Nazi Party salute). Other concessions were made to conservative opinion. An honour guard battalion was established for state occasions in 1957, adopted the old Prussian arms drill, and appeared at the funeral of the arch-conservative colonial general Lettow-Vorbeck in 1964. Former Wehrmacht personnel were permitted to wear decorations like the Iron Cross, though with the swastika removed. Units were again presented with flags in 1965.

Considerable controversy surrounded the reintroduction of martial music, which reformers wanted banned along with the other traditional pomp. The Reichswehr had regarded military bands as so essential to sustaining tradition that it assigned 3,600 personnel to that duty, despite the tight limit on numbers. The new Luftwaffe immediately adopted bands after 1933 to create its own identity, and East Germany's NVA swiftly did the same during the 1950s, believing this would not only boost morale but render rearmament more publicly acceptable. Its importance to the Bundeswehr is demonstrated by the fact that it established a new music corps in January 1956, ahead of forming the first combat units.[118]

Tradition

Music, flags, and rituals were all clearly no longer simply means to motivate soldiers, but now contested markers of the new armed forces' relationship to wider society. Austria eventually distanced itself from the Wehrmacht by reconnecting with its Habsburg heritage after 1967, when units were permitted to style themselves as successors of famous imperial regiments, like the Kaiserjäger.[119]

Both West and East Germany found it hard to jettison the Prussian past entirely and sought to instrumentalize the era of liberal reform with the first edition of Baudissin's Innere Führung considering Stalingrad, the bombing of Dresden, and the final battle of Berlin as collectively constituting 'our Jena-Auerstädt', referring to the defeat in 1806 to assert that the new Bundeswehr would likewise be born from the ashes of defeat. The induction of the first 101 men was hastily improvised to coincide with the bicentenary of General Gerhard von Scharnhorst's birth on 12 November 1955. The NVA also instrumentalized the 'Wars of Liberation' (1813–15) as a 'good Prussian' tradition, but significantly did not name any of its units after 'bourgeois' reformers like Scharnhorst, choosing instead to commemorate the German Peasants' War (1525), the communist militias of the German Revolution (1918–20), the International Brigades, and the Soviet Red Army.[120]

The Bundeswehr's founding generation discovered that it was much harder to break with the past. Defence Minister Franz-Josef Strauss praised Schlieffen, Falkenhayn, Hindenburg, Ludendorff, Seeckt, and Beck in his speech at the opening of the Bundeswehr's new Leadership Academy in 1957. The new navy likewise held up Raeder and Dönitz as role models while both were still alive and unrepentant about their support for Hitler. The army, navy, and Luftwaffe all named units after Werner Mölders, the innovative fighter ace who had served in the Condor Legion and on the Eastern Front. Although senior officers saw utility in showing outward respect to the July 1944 plotters, it was obvious many of them still inwardly condemned them as treacherous oath-breakers. Meanwhile, despite Innere Führung, the Bundeswehr's training generally treated conscripts as 'soft civilians' who needed to be 'toughened up'.[121]

A sequence of scandals eventually forced a change. Strauss was sacked in 1962 after he ordered a raid on the offices of *Der Spiegel* Magazine, which had criticized his corruption and incompetence. The deaths of recruits in training in 1963 was followed by more critical press coverage, while two senior officers were eventually forced to resign after they called for Innere Führung to be replaced by the 'old soldierly ethos'. The Bundeswehr's officially civilian character was forcefully restated by the new SPD government after 1969, but the revised instructions on tradition, issued in 1982, were only partially enforced.[122] Change remained painfully slow. Uncritical references to the Wehrmacht were only systematically removed from units' 'tradition rooms' after 1995. However, it took until May 2000 before a barracks was named after Anton Schmid, the Austrian who had heroically defied the Wehrmacht to help Polish Jews (and was subsequently executed) – and only then after three other installations had refused to accept the honour. The 1982 instructions were reissued in revised form in 2018, re-emphasizing that the Wehrmacht and also now the NVA offered no basis for tradition, and that the Bundswehr should instead draw on its own history and democratic credentials.[123]

Occupation

While Germans struggled to define relations with their own soldiers, they also had to deal with the prolonged presence of foreign troops, something that distinguished the twentieth century from earlier experience. American, Belgian, British, and French forces occupied the Rhineland between 1919 and 1930, with French troops staying another five years in the Saarland as part of the Versailles peace terms. The initial strength of 750,000 soon declined, particularly as the Americans withdrew altogether in 1923, and by late 1927 there were only 59,000, of whom four-fifths were French. France was always the most hawkish, also unsuccessfully trying to foster separatist movements in the occupied areas. The presence of Black French colonial troops, whose numbers peaked at 40,000, was interpreted by Germans as a national dishonour and contributed to Germans' later acceptance of Nazi racism.[124]

This first occupation provided a template for that which followed the Second World War, though the context was fundamentally different because Germany was now completely overrun and lacked a formal peace treaty. The earlier accusations of rape levelled against French colonial soldiers were completely surpassed by the trauma of the initial Soviet occupation of eastern Germany where around 1.9 million women were violently assaulted. The proportion in Berlin may have been as high as one in five, and around 10,000 died. There were 80,000 female victims in Austria. The scale even exceeded the atrocities committed by Japan in Korea and China. Trouble continued until 1947 when Soviet commanders were increasingly concerned at the indiscipline and so segregated troops from the civilian population (see Fig. 33).[125]

While the victims almost invariably remained silent, knowledge of what had happened was widespread and reinforced Germans' sense of victimhood, as well as deepening the Cold War divide, because it contrasted sharply with the behaviour of the Western Allies. Although not without its problems, the Western occupation was swiftly perceived as relatively benign. Allied troops occupied a privileged place in bombed-out Germany, and by 1947 most of them believed the Germans had suffered enough.

There were initially 3.5 million Western and 1.1 million Soviet troops in Germany. These numbers were soon run down, not least when both sides switched manpower to East Asia during the Korean War (1950–3). Thereafter, US forces never fell below 200,000, while the Soviet garrison was generally twice that. Britain's Army on the Rhine was around 50,000, while French forces were smaller. Dutch and Canadian troops were also stationed as part of NATO forces from the late 1950s.[126] These numbers were inflated by the presence of soldiers' families and civilian workers. The US army was consistently in the top twenty employers in West Germany, with a local labour force that peaked at 220,000 in 1951, before stabilizing at around 60,000 or about double the number working for the other Western powers.[127] Austria's State Treaty of 1955 ended its foreign occupation.

Many Germans were initially hostile towards the Americans and the French due to the presence of Black troops: Black people had featured prominently and negatively in Nazi propaganda, while around 2,000 people of African descent had perished in the Holocaust.[128] However, the need to disassociate themselves from National Socialism muted German racism, while 'the absurdity of attacking Nazi race hatred with a Jim Crow army' forced Americans to confront their own prejudices.[129] Colin Powell, posted as a junior officer to Germany in the 1950s, experienced it as a 'breath of freedom' after a still-segregated America.[130] As the richest of the occupiers, the Americans soon became the most favoured, particularly in West Berlin where they were regarded as protectors of the city's freedoms. Armed Forces Radio proved important in Americanizing German culture in the 1950s.[131]

Thereafter, attitudes to the US presence acted as a good barometer of American-German relations, though with a few distinctive features. The initially positive mood soured with German hostility to the Vietnam War and American opposition to the unionization of local workers employed on its bases. The end of the draft in 1973 changed the character of American personnel and coincided with force reductions, pressures on US military spending, and a decline in the value of the dollar. From affluent victors, Americans had become impoverished occupiers who no longer engaged with local communities and instead remained on their bases, where they could buy duty free from the government 'PX' (Post Exchange) store. Low morale, drug use, and petty crime deepened hostility amid the popular opposition to the stationing of Pershing II missiles during the early 1980s. Nonetheless, only Germany's small *Rote Armee Faktion* (Red Army Faction) terrorists protested violently, initiating what proved a twenty-year campaign of bombings against US installations in 1972. Other Germans simply accepted the American presence as a fact of life.[132]

The Red Army commandeered the former Wehrmacht's installations in East Germany, including the former General Staff's bunker at Wünsdorf, near the old exercise ground at Zossen 50 kilometres from Berlin, which became the headquarters of what was known as the Group of Soviet Forces in Germany. Most of Wünsdorf's population was removed as it expanded into a huge base with its own schools, bakery, print works, theatres, museum, sports clubs, and accommodation for 35,000 troops and administrators. Combined with the other 1,025 military installations, the Red Army controlled 2.7 per cent of East German soil. From the 1950s, the force received the latest equipment and counted as a prestige posting for officers. Conditions for the rank and file were even worse than those of East German conscripts. Soviet soldiers served a two-year tour, fifteen hours a day, with no leave, and were only allowed off base in groups accompanied by an officer. Living up to 120 per dormitory, they subsisted on bread, potatoes, cabbage, and tea, supplemented by regimental pig farms. Discipline was brutal and morale low, with high suicide and desertion rates, though, as there was nowhere to escape to, those absconding invariably faced stiff penalties. Conditions were concealed from the local population but were well known to the Stasi, who were powerless to stop soldiers wantonly destroying property or carelessly strewing live munitions while on exercises. Morale plummeted still further during the 1980s as it became harder to shield conscripts from Western media and they became convinced that capitalism had won the day.[133]

Only at the very end did the Russians earn the Germans' respect by remaining in their barracks, rather than help the SED hardliners use force to cling to power during 1989. The USSR's dissolution in December 1991 made its garrison homeless because it was composed of men from regions that had become independent states, and which refused to supply further conscripts. The now united Germany agreed to pay the soldiers' wages and fund the construction of flats in their home-lands to be ready for when they could be evacuated. The task was immense and involved the removal of 387,000 troops, 208,400 family members and civilian workers, 4,116 tanks, 7,948 armoured and 94,129 other vehicles, 3,578 artillery pieces, 623 warplanes, 615 heli-copters, and 2.6 million tons of equipment and munitions. Evacuation took three years and required 14,984 train and 1,878 ship loads.[134] Other than 2,600 armoured vehicles scrapped in Germany, Russia took everything, including the fixtures and fittings of the bases, which were so dilapidated that the German government subsequently found it hard to find buyers for the land.

The British, French, and Canadians had also gone by 1994, while American forces were substantially reduced, with units deployed to Iraq and the Balkans not being replaced. By 2012 strength had dropped to 50,000, with the last tanks leaving the following year, and just two air-bases remained. Combined with the Bundeswehr's own force reductions, the military presence in Germany has shrunk to about a tenth of that at the end of the Cold War, with often serious economic consequences for communities that once had bases, especially as not all municipalities have used the windfall of surrendered real estate wisely.

Medical Care and Military Welfare

The occupying powers cared for their own soldiers, and the hospital next to the Ramstein airbase in the Rhineland-Palatinate is still the larg-est American military medical facility outside the United States. German provision varied considerably across the twentieth century. The country entered the First World War leading medical research, exemplified by Wilhelm Röntgen's development of radiography, and Ludwig Rehn's new treatment for wounds to the heart, while Austria's Sigmund Freud pioneered psychoanalysis. Meanwhile, the shift from round to point-tipped bullets after 1898 had improved range but also increased survival chances, because they left cleaner wounds.[135]

The public's growing expectation that soldiers would be well cared for proved hard to meet as all facilities were rapidly overwhelmed by the terrifying number of casualties: the German army of the First World War treated an average of 175,000 wounded at field hospitals, 66,000 more at evacuation facilities, and a further 86,300 at base hospitals, for each month of the four years of war.[136] Around 18 per cent of wounds were inflicted by small arms, 3 per cent from gas, and just 0.1 per cent from close-quarter combat, with the rest due to shelling, reflecting the changed character of warfare that had not been anticipated by medical staff who had expected that 90 per cent of wounds would be from rifle fire. Casualty evacuation was hampered with the positional warfare on the Western Front, which left a 'No Man's Land' danger zone between the opposing lines. The army also treated 7 million cases of serious illness over the same period, with the return of the diseases of early modern warfare, like dysentery and typhoid, followed soon by typhus fever, cholera, and finally 'Spanish flu' in 1918. Typhus was also rife on the Eastern Front and men transferring westwards had to pass through delousing and cleansing stations to reduce the risk of spreading infections.[137]

Nearly three-quarters of Germany's 33,000 male doctors served during the war, with serious consequences for civilian health. Germany had already trained half a million women in first aid by 1914 and the outbreak of war produced a flood of patriotic volunteers for the Red Cross. Almost immediately, this existing model of voluntarism under female royal and aristocratic patronage struggled to cope, especially as donations to the Red Cross declined with the growing civilian hardship by 1916. Overall, 120,000 women served as Red Cross nurses, but the numbers immediately behind the lines were proportionately fewer than in the British and French armies, and the forty-six female German doctors were sent home in 1915, despite there being a shortage of qualified staff.[138]

There were some remarkable achievements. Wound mortality declined from 8.8 per cent in the opening months of the war to 1.8 per cent by the end of 1915, but this simply allowed more injured men to be sent back to the front. Even those who were too badly injured were 'recycled' by being given desk jobs or industrial work to sustain the war effort.[139] Army doctors were initially more attuned to the psychological effects of modern war, recording 300,000 cases of severely traumatized soldiers, compared with only 80,000 recognized by Britain. However, the growing shortage of manpower prompted them to change their diagnosis in 1916 when they began accusing men of malingering or identifying their symptoms as the product of 'weak' constitutions, which required cathartic treatment to learn self-reliance. Recovery rates declined as food and medicines became scarcer after 1916, particularly in Austria-Hungary, which managed to return only 62 per cent of its sick and wounded to the front, compared to about 90 per cent in Germany.[140]

Medical advances also created their own problems by enabling men to survive despite horrific injuries. By 1918 over 4 million German men were crippled, half of whom were amputees, with a further 2.7 million physically disfigured. War wounded, widows, and orphans initially attracted sympathy and the government accepted that its military dependents' law from 1907 was unfair in tying benefits to the deceased serviceman's rank, rather than to survivors' needs. State benefits were improved, and even extended to unmarried mothers and illegitimate children, especially as charitable donations fell sharply.[141]

The new Republic redoubled efforts after 1918, prioritizing welfare to win popular support and legitimacy. Germany spent three times as much as Britain on its own war wounded, while even during the Depression disabled veterans were twice as likely to retain their jobs as other workers. Britain's meagre welfare state was compensated by greater charitable support, which embedded veterans deeper within society, in contrast to those in Germany, but also in France and Italy, where they felt their personal sacrifices were publicly ignored.[142]

Nearly 7 per cent of the Reichswehr's officers belonged to its medical corps, offering relatively good provision.[143] Efforts to expand capacity after 1933 were hindered by the Nazis' wider policies, which prompted many talented scientists and doctors to flee. The German Red Cross cooperated fully with the regime in return for the prohibition of a rival communist welfare organization, established in 1921. While retaining a titular head, the effective leader after 1934 was Ernst Grawitz, a senior SS doctor who ensured the Red Cross resumed its role as an auxiliary military medical service. The Red Cross trained 650,000 women across 1933–45, of whom two-thirds served during the war alongside around 13,000 mainly male professionals.[144]

Germany entered the Second World War no longer at the forefront of medical science. Whereas the Allies collaborated to develop antibiotics, Germany failed to incorporate advances in blood transfusion, lacked blood banks, and had an inadequate supply of medicines. Troops were issued with 35 million methamphetamine tablets during the invasion of France in 1940 – an impressively large-sounding number, but equating to just fourteen tablets per man. Only invented two years earlier, these were known as 'tank chocolate' and 'pilot's salt', but their consumption was not that widespread, and recent claims that the regime and the Wehrmacht were full of addicts risk implying that they were not responsible for their actions, including war crimes.[145] Selected use of methamphetamines by the Bundeswehr continued into the 1970s and by the NVA until 1988.

The unexpectedly low casualties during 1939–40 fostered complacency and left the Wehrmacht wholly unprepared for the horrendous losses after 1941. The imperative of swift victory, combined with Nazism's ideological emphasis on toughness, led commanders to neglect their own men: in the five months to November 1941, the Wehrmacht had lost more men to frostbite and illness than to Soviet weaponry. The official hospital death rate was 10 per cent, or double that in the First World War, while the Wehrmacht was even more ruthless in returning convalescents to the front.[146]

Veterans' organizations were banned in West Germany until 1951 and, in contrast to the interwar era, no dominant body emerged. Around 2.5 million joined groups lobbying for disability benefits, another 500,000 belonged to the association of relatives of those missing in action or captivity, and a similar number joined the more overtly nationalistic old comrades' associations. Traditional groups, like the Kyffhäuserbund and Stahlhelm, re-emerged, while 60,000 former Waffen-SS formed their own association once they had been cold-shouldered by their fellow veterans. In contrast to the 1920s, all organizations pledged loyalty to the new Federal Republic. The restoration of pension rights to former Wehrmacht personnel by 1954 mollified many members who drifted away, while politically active veterans preferred to join the mainstream parties.[147] Former members of the Bundeswehr refused to join the other veterans' organizations, establishing their own association, which had 200,000 members in 2021.[148]

Both West and East Germany struggled to recruit enough qualified medical personnel after they rearmed. East Germany planned to have a capacity of 100,000 beds, or equivalent to a third of its mobilized strength, but its nine base hospitals could only accommodate 2,000 casualties. Although West Germany disdained the NVA's expertise and traditions, it guaranteed its personnel's pension rights during Reunification in 1990, significantly easing the task of merging the two armed forces. The subsequent restructuring created a Central Medical Service in 2000, which became fully operational within five years and reflects the wider process of establishing combined support services for the Bundeswehr.[149]

Prisoners

In addition to horrendous casualties, belligerents in the First World War were overwhelmed by what eventually amounted to 8 million prisoners, or two out of every fifteen combatants. Germany lost 1.265 million to the Western Allies and a further 250,000 to Russia, while that power captured 1.8 million Habsburg troops. Germany captured at least 2.5 million prisoners, including 1.5 million Russians, while Austria-Hungary took between 1.8 and 2.3 million prisoners – its inefficient record-keeping prevents a precise total. Reflecting the character of a conflict between citizens, all belligerents interned civilians who were now deemed 'enemy aliens'. Although unprecedented, the numbers affected were relatively small: Germany held 4,000 Allied civilians, while Britain interned 50,000 Germans, Austrians, Turks, and Bulgarians across its global empire.[150]

Whereas the possibility of interning civilians had not been considered in pre-war agreements, there was now a substantial body of international law governing the treatment of military prisoners. All belligerents claimed to be civilized nations, and the fate of prisoners quickly became a key issue in the propaganda war. Real or alleged mistreatment rapidly led to a cycle of reprisals; indeed, Germany only interned civilians once Britain had done so. The International Committee of the Red Cross (ICRC) in Geneva swiftly established a missing and tracing service and mediated – along with the Spanish government – to arrange the exchange of wounded or sick prisoners, and to persuade countries to adhere to international rules.[151]

All belligerents shot surrendering men, though they disputed the number of victims and who was more to blame for this. However, the issue was rarely deliberate maltreatment but that the initial hauls, especially on the Eastern Front, far exceeded the capacity of the captors to care for their captives. Most prisoner deaths were from camp diseases like typhus and lung infections. Mortality was generally 2–3 per cent, except for Russians held by Germany (6 per cent), Germans held by France (16 per cent), and those held by Russia (20 per cent). Poor record-keeping hinders such calculations for Austria-Hungary, though mortality was undoubtedly high among those prisoners it held.

Germany and Austria-Hungary put prisoners to work early in 1915. Initially intended to move them from unhealthy camps, this rapidly became forced labour essential to their war efforts. German-held Russian prisoners were sent to clear battlefields, build roads, and move supplies on the Western Front. France also employed German prisoners, including in munitions factories, but generally it adhered to the official rule to keep them at least 30 kilometres from the front; a guideline that Germany frequently breached.[152] Germany initially offered good wages to Belgian, French, and Polish civilians in occupied areas to move to its factories and farms, resorting to conscription and deportation when this failed to secure sufficient manpower. By 1918 there were 2.5 million foreign workers in Germany, mainly in agriculture, while Austria-Hungary employed around 1.3 million Russian prisoners in similar roles.[153]

Both Germany and Austria-Hungary were disappointed in their attempts to recruit Polish and Ukrainian prisoners and civilians into their forces as soldiers, whereas around 100,000 Czechs and other Habsburg soldiers volunteered to form a legion on the Allied side. This stayed in Russia when the new Bolshevik government agreed to release German and Habsburg prisoners at the Peace of Brest-Litovsk in March 1918. The Central Powers broke their promise to reciprocate, claiming it would fuel Russia's growing civil war. Repatriation of prisoners was delayed until 1920 by the war's messy end and complex peace settlement, despite protests from the ICRC.[154]

Public pressure compelled the Swiss government to accept 67,700 sick and wounded prisoners, who were distributed around the country's sanatoria and hotels. Another 26,000, mainly Italian, deserters and draft dodgers were also sheltered. However, all foreigners were required to work to earn their keep, while the public mood turned more hostile with the worsening food shortage by 1917.[155] Nonetheless, generous Swiss donated $5.8 million in food, clothing, and free holidays for German children between 1917 and 1925.[156]

The difficulties of aiding civilians and prisoners accelerated the prewar trend towards international cooperation and shifted the focus of humanitarianism from Christian charity to the ideal of universal human rights enshrined in law. Great hopes were placed in the League of Nations, founded in 1919. Germany's new republican government backed the ICRC's effort to plug the loopholes in the prisoner-of-war conventions through more comprehensive rules. The result was watered down in the new Geneva Convention agreed in 1929, which drew on looser proposals from Britain and the United States.[157] Prisoners remained under their captors' martial law which, in Nazi Germany's case, was much harsher than among the Western Allies. This meant, for instance, that it was legal during the Second World War for the Wehrmacht to punish Allied prisoners for such things as insulting the Führer.[158]

After 1939, Germany saw little compulsion to cooperate with the Western Allies, who only took a substantial number of its men prisoner with the surrender in Tunisia of the Afrikakorps in 1943. Most of the French and Belgian prisoners were retained as forced labourers on the legal technicality that no peace treaty had been signed. The same fate befell the 710,000 Italians taken when their country switched sides in 1943 and who were singled out for particularly harsh treatment. Minimal attention was paid to the huge hauls of Polish and Soviet prisoners, whose fate was considered largely irrelevant. Initially, few records were kept of the 3.35 million captured Russians, around 2 million of whom had died of starvation and neglect by March 1942. The Soviet Union had initially offered to observe the 1929 Convention, despite having not signed it, but the Nazi regime mistrusted Russia, mistakenly believing that 40 per cent of German prisoners had died in Tsarist captivity during the First World War.[159]

As in that conflict, prisoners during the Second World War were also put to work, but their treatment was much harsher and guided by Nazi ideology, which regarded most of them as expendable. Russians captured later in the war at least had slightly improved survival chances thanks to the switch in policy during 1942 to exploit their labour. Altogether, Nazi Germany employed 13.6 million forced and slave labourers, with the total rising from 3.5 million at the end of 1941 to 7.7 million by 1945. The concentration-camp system supplied 1.65 million slave labourers after March 1942, when Himmler saw an opportunity to increase influence within the war economy by providing inmates as workers rather than killing them immediately. Only 550,000 survived. Around two-thirds of the forced labourers were Western Europeans who generally fared better. The other third were mainly women from Eastern Europe recruited or conscripted as maids and farmhands. Slave and forced labourers were often deployed in crucial war industries, such as tank, aircraft, and rocket production, but they were treated appallingly because the Nazi regime believed there was an infinite supply and saw no need to look after them. Productivity was correspondingly low.[160]

A small contingent of pro-Nazi Swiss medical personnel accompanied Operation Barbarossa in 1941, yet otherwise Switzerland opposed Nazi policies but felt powerless to act. The ICRC was constrained by international law, which left Swiss medical personnel dependent on the cooperation of the Nazi German Red Cross, but feared that vigorous protests would endanger Switzerland's precarious neutrality. Concern that the country would be overwhelmed by refugees encouraged a restrictive policy that led to around 5,000 being turned away. Border controls were eventually relaxed in July 1944, and altogether the country sheltered 295,381 documented refugees, equivalent to about 7 per cent of its population. Nearly 1.2 billion Swiss francs in aid had been distributed by 1950, but the ICRC later admitted it could have done more and it was not until the 1990s that two major Swiss banks released 1.25 billion Swiss francs from the frozen accounts of Holocaust victims.[161]

Overall, the Allies captured 11 million Germans, half of whom were taken in the final months. Mortality among those held by the Western Allies was the same as in 1914–18, at 2–3 per cent, but around a quarter of the 3 million taken by the Soviet Union died. The Soviets treated captured Austrians better and released them much earlier – in 1950. Britain and the United States released their prisoners by the end of 1946, but France held some until 1948, and the last prisoners were not returned by the Soviets until 1956. The slow release fuelled Germany's post-war victim narrative. The Wehrmacht's faulty statistics were a significant factor in this. By 1944 it had no clear idea of its own casualties and greatly underestimated fatalities by recording men as merely missing, thereby giving their families false hopes and fuelling suspicions that their loved ones were still in Soviet captivity after the war.[162]

SPIRALLING COSTS

Death and Displacement

The two world wars stand out in terms of their human impact, not only within the twentieth century but in comparison to previous conflicts, such as the Thirty Years War, the prolonged struggles against France and the Ottomans across 1672–1718, or the French Revolutionary and Napoleonic Wars. The difference lies less in the proportion of the population who suffered death or injury, but in the overall scale as well as the intensity and character of these losses, which occurred within much shorter timespans and more directly through targeted killing, rather than indirectly through disease and malnutrition. Moreover, sickness and hunger were generally unintended consequences during early modern and nineteenth-century warfare, but were 'weaponized' as deliberate strategies after 1914.

Of the 60 million soldiers who served in the First World War, over 9.5 million were killed and around 20 million wounded, of whom 8 million were permanently disabled. A further 8 million civilians died, while the flu pandemic in 1918–19, exacerbated by the movement of demobilized soldiers, killed at least a further 17 million people. Germany's death toll was revised several times by the country's statistical office, which incrementally included those originally listed as missing. The total was between 1.6 and 2.05 million, with a further 4.248 million wounded, while 1,000 civilians were killed by direct military action (mainly aerial bombardment). Up to 478,500 German civilians died from malnutrition and other consequences of the Allied blockade and general mismanagement of the country's food supply, while tuberculosis and the flu killed another 360,000. Children growing up during the war remained noticeably shorter than average as adults. Austria-Hungary lost at least 1.1 million military dead and 1.943 million wounded, as well as around 300,000 civilian deaths – the latter largely to disease and malnutrition.[163]

The war also displaced significant numbers, either as refugees, or forcibly deported from their homes. By September 1918 there were around 1.8 million displaced persons in France who were predominantly refugees from the German-occupied north and east. Over 800,000 East Prussians fled the initial Russian invasion in August 1914, or about a third of the province's population. A further million Galicians fled into Hungary, which refused to accept them and shunted them into Austria, where their relief consumed 2.36 per cent of war expenditure. Russia also deported 200,000 ethnic Germans, along with 1.5 million Poles and Jews when it evacuated Poland in 1915.[164] France expelled 200,000 Alsace-Lorrainers back into Germany in 1919 on the grounds that they were insufficiently French. Far fewer Germans were affected by the loss of their country's colonies. The largest group, the mere 12,000 settlers in South West Africa, were allowed to remain because the white South African government hoped to assimilate them. Those in the other colonies, totalling just 6,000, were expelled and returned home to become some of the most vocal opponents of the Versailles Treaty.[165]

Although marred by paramilitary violence, the interwar era was far less bloody, with Germany and Austria also suffering far less severely than the lands immediately to their east. The German Revolution claimed over 2,000 lives and left 12,000 wounded, while Germany's border conflict with Poland (1918–20) cost it 1,240 killed and 1,000 wounded, with a further 3,000 Germans and Poles killed in the fighting in Silesia (1918–22).[166] Several hundred were killed during Austria's brief civil war in 1934. The violence appeared so shocking because much of it occurred in major cities of both Germany and Austria and was accompanied by a high rate of politically motivated murders. By contrast, at 876 killed and wounded, the Condor Legion's casualties in Spain were far fewer than anticipated, amounting to less than 5 per cent of those who served. Most of these were caused by accidents rather than enemy action, and the relatively light losses contributed to the Wehrmacht's subsequent over-confidence.[167]

The Second World War saw up to 80 million deaths globally, of which civilians accounted for a third, compared to just over a tenth in the First World War.[168] German military deaths numbered 5.318 million, including 261,000 Austrians, falling 79 per cent on the army, 8.1 per cent on the Luftwaffe, 2.6 per cent on the navy, 5.9 per cent on the Waffen-SS, and the remainder on the Volkstrum, police battalions, logistical and other supporting services.[169] Nearly two-thirds of the army's fatalities occurred on the Eastern Front. Around 195,000 foreigners died serving Germany, most of whom had been Soviet citizens, but also including 300 Swiss. Germany's allies lost over 1.5 million killed, wounded, and missing, with Romania and Hungary hit hardest, but Italy also suffered, incurring a third of its total wartime casualties supporting Germany on the Eastern Front.[170]

Men of conscription age suffered disproportionately, especially as cohorts were called up early. A quarter of the German army was under twenty-one by 1918. The burden of the Second World War fell heaviest on those born between 1911 and 1925, a third of whom were killed, but at least 1.5 million men over forty also died.[171] Young widows already stood out during the 1920s, but the impact was far greater immediately after 1945 when there were 7 million 'surplus women', with more than twice as many women as men among those in their twenties. However, Germany's genocidal war in Eastern Europe created an even greater imbalance and women formed up to two-thirds of the population of some Soviet cities. The birth rate fell, while that for divorce rose, notably among returning prisoners of war – at least partly because (according to church organizations) four out of every five wives had committed adultery during the war. The presence of 2.5 million 'half orphans' growing up with one parent contributed to the inter-generational tensions that peaked in 1968.[172]

Germany's collapse in the east triggered the largest population movement in world history as 9 million fled the advancing Red Army, followed by a further 14 million who were expelled from Czechoslovakia, Poland, Hungary, Romania, and the Soviet Union. The latter figure also included many of the surviving Jews who fled renewed local pogroms in the wake of the German retreat. Around 4 million German refugees and expellees settled in what became East Germany, forming around a quarter of its population, 430,000 moved to Austria, and the rest went to West Germany, where 2.3 million joined the League of Expellees (*Bund der Heimatvertriebene*), founded in 1957 to demand a restoration of the 1937 frontiers. Their numbers made them a powerful force in West German politics, while the government's endorsement of their claims that 2.2 million had died during their flight westwards became a central element in the broader victim narrative. The more likely total of half a million is bad enough. However, Konrad Adenauer refused to endorse their cause, which declined with the 'Eastern Policy' of reconciliation initiated by Willy Brandt in 1969, while the process of reunification included a definitive renunciation of claims to the 1937 frontiers.[173]

After 1945 the fear of nuclear annihilation co-existed with almost bloodless military service, and most fatalities now occurred through accidents rather than combat. During the 1950s over 100 East German soldiers committed suicide annually, while another 300–400 died accidentally, together representing 0.4 per cent of total strength. These rates far exceeded those in Austria or West Germany, whose greater engagement in foreign missions since the early 1990s has exposed their personnel to potentially hostile forces. Of the 80,000 Austrians who have served abroad since 1960, just fifty have died, whereas the Bundeswehr suffered 3,200 fatalities between 1955 and 2019, including 114 on overseas missions, of whom thirty-seven were killed in action. A further 1,988 serving personnel have committed suicide.[174] The latter statistic is also indicative of the mental-health impact of military service more broadly – and particularly combat – which has only been recognized more recently.

War Finance

Germany planned a short, victorious war in 1914, thinking the costs would be recouped by imposing reparations on France, as in 1871. By 1915 the conflict was costing 2 billion Marks monthly, equivalent to the entire 1870–1 war. Ostensibly, the country continued with business as usual, maintaining convertibility of the Mark into gold and presenting regular budgets to the Reichstag. In reality, taxation covered only 8 per cent of expenditure and the government funded the war by printing money, and by pushing extraordinary costs like veterans' and social care on to the municipalities. It also borrowed 97 billion Marks from its citizens through nine war loans. Austria-Hungary used a similar mix of expedients, but increasingly relied on a 100 million Marks monthly subsidy from Germany.

Officially, the war cost Germany 194 billion Marks, or thirty-five times its 1914 revenue and nearly a hundred times more than that of the 1870–1 conflict. The real cost was far higher, as national wealth fell by a third and industrial output by 40 per cent. The territorial losses and cost of the subsequent occupation of the Rhineland and Saarland reduced wealth by a further tenth. Shorn of its empire, Austria was on the verge of financial collapse until it was bailed out by an Allied loan in 1922. Preservation of its neutrality increased Switzerland's debt sevenfold and, like Austria, it severely curtailed military expenditure into the mid-1930s as a necessary economy. Switzerland's debt increased more than sixfold during the Second World War, forcing the country to accept a new direct tax that remains in force.[175]

The most controversial financial consequence of the war was the imposition of reparations on Germany, finally fixed in 1921 at 132 billion Marks ($31.4 billion). Critics have argued that these were too onerous and crippled the new Republic, whereas others interpret them as bearable economically, but not politically. Certainly, acceptance of reparations was tied to the hated War Guilt clause and inflicted significant damage on the German left, who were simultaneously condemned for a raft of measures that finally modernized the country's finances – notably, centralizing taxation and imposing a fully national income tax to fund the new welfare measures. It is also often overlooked that nationalizing the railways in 1921 accounted for half the government deficit, not least because all the rolling stock had been forcibly surrendered to the Allies and had to be replaced. Reparations initially took 10 per cent of GDP, but that proportion fell to 2.5 per cent after the payments were rescheduled in 1924. Meanwhile, the restrictions imposed by the Versailles Treaty saved roughly the same amount of money: German defence spending in 1924 was 0.93 per cent of GDP, compared to 0.84 per cent in Austria, 0.88 per cent in Switzerland, but 2.56 per cent in France and 2.77 per cent in Britain.[176]

Inflation had already been stirred by the Imperial government's wartime monetary policies. The new government prioritized welfare and hoped that continued inflation would reduce debts and blunt the impact of reparations. France's invasion of the Ruhr triggered hyperinflation in 1923, which inflicted further political damage on the Republic, though it was mastered relatively swiftly with the introduction in 1924 of a new currency, the Reichsmark (RM). The underlying change was a substantial growth in the state within the national economy, thanks to the massive increase in social spending, which displaced defence as the primary budget item. By 1928 the state represented 22.7 per cent of GDP, compared to 14.2 per cent in 1914.[177]

The Nazi seizure of power saw the state expand to 43 per cent of GDP by 1938. Although the new regime continued high-profile projects like building the autobahns, it secretly abandoned most of the Republic's promising measures that had brought the country out of the global Depression. Instead, resources were poured recklessly into rearmament, which consumed at least a seventh of GDP across 1933–9. Defence spending rose from 5 per cent of the official budget to 63 per cent. Budgets, however, lost their meaning as the regime resorted to increasingly secretive and criminal ways to fund itself. A parallel paper currency, known as Mefo bills, was created to pay armaments firms and other businesses, while Germans' savings accounts were secretly raided as a covert forced loan.[178]

War in 1939 represented a huge gamble, because Germany had no plan to pay for it other than through a swift and total victory enabling it to plunder its defeated opponents. By 1945 it had spent 1.47 trillion RM, of which 414 billion went directly on the Wehrmacht, 200 billion as civil expenditure, and the rest on servicing debts that were also largely caused by the war. Even civil expenditure was militarized, since it included 28 billion RM in welfare payments to soldiers' families and 85 billion on air defence, evacuation, and compensation for bombing victims.[179]

Around 77 billion RM were raised in forced contributions from defeated countries, around half of which came from France and represented 30 per cent of that country's national income. Only a tenth came from the east, indicating the total lack of realism in the belief that conquering that region would make Germany self-sufficient. Manipulation of exchange rates and trade netted another 45 billion RM, while 13 billion was derived from direct plunder. Germans took far more than that, since individual soldiers seized goods or bought them cheaply using the deliberately distorted exchange rates. The rest came simply from printing money and the continued raiding of savings accounts, with the circulation of money between the state and the compliant banks preserving the illusion of a stable currency.[180]

The Soviet Union estimated it had suffered $128 billion worth of damage and secured the Western Allies' agreement to 'demontage' – the systematic dismantling of German infrastructure in 1945 to the value of $23 billion to be shared by all four victors. The Soviets removed 4,500 factories from their zone, or about a third of the industrial capacity, and also plundered systematically, carrying off 450,000 radios, 60,000 pianos, 940,000 items of furniture, and other goods worth $14 billion in total. The Western powers soon halted demontage in their zones.[181] Germany was not required to pay additional reparations, but still had the outstanding bill from the First World War, of which only 14 per cent had been cleared by the time instalments ceased in 1933. Payments resumed in 1953 and were completed in 2010. Adenauer saw value in making additional voluntary payments to rehabilitate Germany internationally, beginning with a transfer to Israel in 1957. Over 63 billion, now calculated in the new Deutsche Mark (DM) introduced in 1949, had been paid to Jewish victims of Nazi terror by 2005.[182]

As in 1919, Germans had to pay the costs of their own occupation until the late 1950s, when the victors agreed to cover this themselves, though the USSR still expected East Germany to build and maintain its bases. West Germany had benefited from the aid package known as the Marshall Plan, and its economy was soon reorientated westwards again with the growing integration within what would eventually become the European Union. Annual growth during the 'Economic Miracle' recovery years was an impressive 5 per cent, but, like its republican predecessor in 1919, the new Federal Republic saw generous social welfare as central to securing acceptance among the population, as well as to make it appear more attractive than its Eastern communist rival. Provision of pensions to the former Wehrmacht in 1954 added another 4 billion DM to the annual budget, while payments to expellees totalled 145 billion DM by 2001. Social welfare continued to outstrip defence, though the purchase of major items like the Leopard tanks or Tornado jets periodically increased military spending.[183]

East Germany officially spent only 5 per cent of its budget on defence, but the cost of the numerous paramilitaries was disguised as civil expenditure. Expenditure declined but remained 11 per cent of GDP in the 1980s – far more than the country could afford and compelling the SED regime to rely on West German loans.[184] Defence spending in reunited Germany declined by 35 per cent across 1990–2015. Although the state now constituted around half of GDP, defence amounted to just 1.3 per cent during most of the 2000s. This was by choice and reflected the country's partial character as a 'civilian power', preferring instead to push through a major welfare reform. Nonetheless, the size of the economy ensured that expenditure was still considerable and in 2021 Germany ranked as the world's seventh largest military spender, just behind the UK, but ahead of France and Italy. Austria's spending rose from a modest 0.55 per cent of GDP in 1955 to 1.12 per cent a decade later, but then flatlined before dropping to 0.6 per cent in 2016 when money was so short that the armed forces had to restrict fuel consumption. Like Germany, Austria embarked on a relatively costly modernization programme. Switzerland's official budget was misleading since the civilian economy still carried much of the cost of the militia, and the true burden was 1.1 per cent in 2018.[185]

The War Economy

The First World War's perceived character as 'total' had not been anticipated, and it profoundly affected Germany's subsequent policy until

1945. Thereafter, the advent of nuclear weaponry transformed what was understood as 'total' from the mobilization of all resources to sustain mass conventional warfare, to the potential for humanity's complete destruction. Nonetheless, post-war governments remained mindful of the economic dimension of war preparations, especially in East Germany, where the SED regime continued a state-directed 'command economy' intended to sustain a high level of military readiness. Reunification in 1990 coincided with the global shift towards neo-liberalism, which argued that private enterprise could deliver public functions more cheaply and efficiently than the state. While Germany has been relatively restrained in adopting this approach, it has also outsourced some aspects of defence provision.

None of the belligerents during the First World War fully established a command economy and all regarded their measures as exceptional, temporary expedients. On balance, the authoritarian approach adopted by Germany and Austria-Hungary, but also Italy and Russia, proved less successful than the more democratic methods employed in Britain and France, which emphasized financial inducements rather than compulsion to shape behaviour. Britain and France still faced difficulties, but their approach encouraged better compliance with government policy.[186]

The most immediately military pressure was the huge consumption of weapons and munitions during the 'materiel battles' on both the Western and Eastern fronts. By December 1914 the Habsburg army was firing shells four times faster than its industry could replace them. Although shell output nearly quadrupled by 1916, it was still less than 50 per cent of Germany's output, and production declined significantly from the second half of 1917. The output of weaponry followed a similar trajectory.[187]

Germany established a War Raw Materials Department on 13 August 1914 at the suggestion of Walther Rathenau, chief executive of the electrical engineering giant AEG and future foreign minister of the German Republic. Rathenau's involvement indicates both how little thought the German General Staff had given to the matter prior to 1914 and how civilian industrialists played an important role despite the army's growing influence, particularly once the Duo of Hindenburg and Ludendorff asserted direction of the war effort. The Hindenburg Programme, announced on 31 August 1916, essentially used the production targets already devised by Prussia's war ministry, but attempted to replace the free market with a command economy to deliver them. Prepared by his assistant, Max Bauer, Ludendorff was convinced the Hindenburg Programme would match Allied material superiority.

The war ministry reluctantly agreed to the establishment of the *Kriegsamt* (War Office) under Wilhelm Groener in November to run the programme. Groener recognized that Ludendorff's idea of treating workers like soldiers was unlikely to work, and he softened the approach by seeking to involve trades unions in the implementation of the new Auxiliary Service Law, which imposed a compulsory sixty-hour week for men and a voluntary one of fifty-seven hours for women. The scheme added another layer of bureaucracy, while the Kriegsamt was a Prussian institution with little influence in Bavaria, Saxony, or Württemberg, all of which had important industries. Hindenburg's targets were unrealistic, and little effort was made to rationalize production: the number of different types of artillery pieces grew from fourteen in 1914 to seventy-seven by April 1917. More fundamentally, the economy was wholly unprepared in 1914 for this kind of war. Industrialists and workers scored unprecedented achievements: steel output doubled, shell production rose more than fivefold, and Krupp made 10,843 new artillery pieces and 9,439 spare gun barrels – but all this was still not enough to match the Allies, especially once the United States entered the war in April 1917.[188]

The Hunger Blockade

The Allied naval blockade begun in August 1914 weaponized food and is considered one of the most effective of such measures in human history. It was intended to force Germany to negotiate by creating mass unemployment, but in fact it operated more slowly to strangle food and munitions production.[189] The new process to synthesize nitrogen from air, only invented by Fritz Haber in 1913, enabled Germany to replace the Chilean nitrates cut off by the blockade and continue its munitions production. Nonetheless, the switch to armaments seriously compounded the blockade's impact on civilians because munitions also needed glycerine, which derived from fat, while mobilization took men and horses away from agriculture.

Germany relied on imports for a third of its food (items from which, in turn, the soldiers derived half of their daily calories), most of which came by sea. Austria-Hungary should have fared better, since it was self-sufficient in food in 1914, but mobilization also severely reduced production. Neither country's armed forces had stockpiled raw materials prior to 1914, yet they hoarded food once the war began, further harming civilians. Both countries only introduced rationing in 1915, after attempts to regulate the market through price fixing failed. Germany established a War Food Office and a Central Purchasing Company, both in 1916. The latter was a publicly funded private firm to monopolize imports and was the world's largest trading company. Neither the War Food Office nor the Central Purchasing Company proved effective.[190]

Meanwhile, 9 million pigs (a third of the total) were needlessly slaughtered in 1915 because the government believed they competed with humans for food. Germany's world-leading chemical industry produced soul-destroying Ersatz products including 511 substitutes for coffee, 837 different types of meatless sausage, and no fewer than 6,000 alternatives to beer, wine, and lemonade. Cold weather, a bad harvest, and a potato blight combined in the harrowing 'turnip winter' of 1916/17, shattering public confidence in the government, which was now blamed more than the Allies for deprivation. By 1917 the army consumed nearly a third of the country's grain, or three times its share relative to the size of population, whose rations were barely half the soldiers' daily 2,500 calories – which was itself not much more than half what combat personnel required. Mismanagement continued to exacerbate a deteriorating situation, while hope that Ukraine would somehow act as a breadbasket proved wholly unrealistic in 1918.[191]

Popular resentment at the blockade surged after November 1918 because the Allies continued it to pressure Germany, Austria, and Hungary into accepting the terms offered at the Paris conference – a major reason why the Peace of Versailles was reviled subsequently as a Diktat. German and Austrian appeals for aid prompted the foundation of Save the Children, though its efforts were poorly coordinated compared to that of Herbert Hoover, who supplied 1.2 million tons of food, while German Americans sent $120 million in aid to relatives.[192]

The Nazi War Economy

Senior German officers remained haunted by the belief that the blockade had broken morale on the home front and cost them the First World War. The public's loathing for Ersatz products, decline of living standards, and genuine hardship were all compounded by post-war instability and hyperinflation. Conditions remained tough and 16 million Germans (a quarter of the population) remained on welfare in 1924. These conditions fostered a lasting anxiety about the morale of civilians, which had much less to do with concern for their well-being than ensuring that popular discontent did not undermine a future war effort.

One major consequence was the determination to make Germany blockade-proof through the radical expansion of the *Mitteleuropa* plan of the First World War into the permanent conquest of Eastern Europe and the subordination of Western states. The Nazi regime encouraged various belt-tightening measures like economical 'one-pot Sunday' meals, but anxiety about civilian morale reinforced the ideological drive to exploit Europe's resources for the benefit of Germans. The ruthless measures in Eastern Europe proved even less effective than those of the First World War, and levels of supplies from the occupied Soviet territories were below those that Germany had obtained by trade prior to 1941. Hunger was integral to German planning and became a central aspect of occupied Europe's experience: in January 1943, Italians received 55 per cent of Germans' calory intake, Greeks got 31 per cent, while Jews were permitted a mere 2 per cent. Germany's war effort depended on mass starvation elsewhere.[193]

The new understanding of total war at least prompted the Nazis and Wehrmacht to start stockpiling food and raw materials in 1939, but these reserves were wholly inadequate for anything longer than the elusive swift victory. A massive investment in the chemical industry created an impressive capacity to produce synthetic fuels and rubber from coal. This served the army and Luftwaffe fairly well, though the navy's reliance on heavier oil left it vulnerable. The destruction or immobilization of all major surface units subsequently alleviated the navy's oil shortage. However, Allied bombing severely affected coal output, which had dropped to a fifth of pre-war levels by 1945, as well as hitting ammonia production, which was essential for munitions and fertilizers.[194] As in the First World War, the expectations of securing additional oil supplies in Eastern Europe were totally unrealistic. The US entry into the war in December 1941 gave the Allies control of 79 per cent of world oil output compared to the 3.5 per cent held by the Axis powers. Even if the Wehrmacht had seized the Caucasian oilfields intact, this would have only reduced the odds to 5:1. The Luftwaffe was intermittently grounded after 1943, despite receiving priority allocation.[195]

The clash between the Nazi regime's mania for centralized coordination and its obsession with competition seriously undermined its management of the war and any slim chance of ultimate victory. Whereas fostering competition had helped Tirpitz drive down the cost of naval shipbuilding before 1914, it proved wasteful and counterproductive after 1933, creating duplication, high prices, and serious production delays. The polycentric character of the Nazi state added to this. No fewer than five competing agencies were responsible for arms procurement. Firms were invited to submit rival bids for the same project and were often awarded contracts to make variants of the same type of weapon. The endless search for technical perfection delayed some projects, whereas others were rushed into production too soon.[196] Above all, planning was reactive after 1941 as Germany lost the initiative, while infighting between the Wehrmacht's service branches often delayed crucial decisions over the allocation of scarce resources. By contrast, the Western Allies also made serious procurement errors but they ended the war nonetheless with an array of weapons and systems vastly improved since 1940 – not least atomic bombs.

Göring proved a hopeless figurehead for the war economy and was replaced by Fritz Todt in 1940, who in turn was succeeded after his death in an air crash by Albert Speer. Speer attempted some reorganization and compiled impressive figures to substantiate his claims for a miraculous rise in production, which in fact rested on improvements already underway. Although elements of mass production had already been adopted after 1914, other than the American-owned Opel motor manufacturer, German firms had largely relied on scaling up traditional techniques and were inefficient compared to their American and Soviet rivals. Output peaked late in 1944, before the loss of occupied Western Europe and the relentless bombing campaign caused a sharp, terminal decline.[197] Overall output grew fivefold between 1939 and 1944, a proportion matched by the much larger Soviet Union, and beaten by Britain's tenfold and America's fiftyfold increases. Moreover, German reliance on slave labour seriously undermined quality and many weapons were deliberately sabotaged by workers who, for instance, put sand into aeroengines as they assembled them.

Post-War Economies

Only East Germany continued a centrally planned war economy after 1949, though one modelled on Soviet state socialism. As the Warsaw Pact's forward assembly area, East Germany had to supply pre-positioned logistical support to the Red Army and its allies, as well as its own forces. Additionally, the command economy was supposed to maintain the flow of consumer goods that the SED regime deemed essential to pacify its population and avoid a repeat of the 1953 rising. State-directed production was inefficient and never provided nearly enough to enable the regime to achieve its goals. Around a third of the army's total strength was drafted into state enterprises, with entire units working in the lignite mines, chemical works, and other industries by 1989, which seriously impaired combat readiness and exemplified the mounting crisis.[198]

Nothing like this was attempted in West Germany, which self-consciously fashioned itself as a 'social market economy', where workers were given a say in how businesses were run, and the state provided generous welfare, training, and financial incentives. The long-term consequences of the Second World War nonetheless exerted a significant economic impact. Germany's partition disrupted its domestic economy and prompted the Federal government to pay substantial subsidies to the communities suffering from their proximity to the inner German border.[199] Whereas East Germany had to provide the Red Army with its infrastructure, the United States spent 101 billion DM on building bases or renovating old Wehrmacht ones in the 1950s, while its expenditure in Germany during the following decade contributed 0.8 per cent of German GNP, which combined proved a significant element in the post-war 'economic miracle'.[200]

The costs of reunification in 1990 exceeded even the most pessimistic estimate and included 14 billion DM spent on evacuating the former Soviet garrison as part of the 57 billion transferred to Russia in return for its acceptance of the changes. Very little of this was recouped from the disposal of East Germany's huge arsenal, a process that has been described as resembling 'a yard sale' in which it was possible for even private clients to buy a light machine gun for $60 or a missile attack warship for $200,000. Many vehicles and uniform items were simply given away or donated to aid agencies or to several African armed forces.[201]

While enabling Germany to sustain a high level of social spending, the cut in the defence budget hit some areas quite hard. Force reductions led to the closure of 930 bases in 1990–1 alone, with a significant impact where annual per capita spending per soldier had been worth 60,000 DM to the local economies. The suspension of conscription in 2011 adversely affected social care because the numerous conscientious objectors cost only about a quarter of what the state would have had to spend on employing people to do these tasks.[202]

By 1985, West German arms procurement involved 150,000 separate contracts worth 14 billion DM.[203] Efforts were made to streamline the process and ensure better value for money, but the country's political elite remained sceptical towards the neo-liberal economics that gripped Thatcher's Britain and Reagan's America. Ultimately, it was the new left-leaning SPD/Green coalition that cautiously adopted the ideas in 2000, allowing more private enterprise in procurement. Four major public-private partnerships were established between 2000 and 2006 to outsource the provision of uniforms, IT services, and the leasing of unarmoured vehicles. The Federal Audit Office already concluded in 2004 that the modest initial savings were largely derived from pushing the real costs into the future. Nonetheless, outsourcing has continued and become particularly necessary with the importance of cyber warfare where, like other Western powers, the German state lacks the expertise to develop the necessary capacity.[204]

The shrinking military presence has transformed the landscape. Whereas the Wehrmacht had controlled 3,860 square kilometres in 1939, the Bundeswehr had used 4,230 square kilometres, with a further 1,500 square kilometres held by its NATO allies, while the NVA and Soviet garrison held 5,000 square kilometres in East Germany, all of which together represented 3 per cent of the total national territory. By 2005 the combined land held had dropped to 3,500 square kilometres, still larger than four of the sixteen federal states.[205] Some former military land has been preserved for environmental reasons, notably along the old inner German border, where the prolonged exclusion of humans had encouraged rewilding.

War Industries

The ban on arms production in 1919 forced German weapons manufacturers to turn swords into ploughshares – literally in the case of the Rheinische Metallwaren- und Maschinenfabrik, which switched in 1920 to making these along with locomotives and typewriters. Austria's Steyr shifted from rifles to cars, as did several other firms keen to expand into the new automotive market. Although some specialist firms were initially hard hit, overall Germany's industry was at full capacity again by 1920, stimulated by the need to replace rail infrastructure and shipping, as well as a revival of exports. Other than Krupp, most firms already had diversified portfolios prior to 1914, so that the wartime switch to arms production represented an aberration, not their norm.

Krupp was also a notable exception in engaging in the Reichswehr's covert arms programme, establishing a secret research department in Berlin in 1922 and cooperating with the Swedish firm Bofors, in which it held a 33 per cent stake. Several aircraft manufacturers established subsidiaries outside Germany to develop new designs, but the aero industry was subject to fewer restrictions and expanded significantly during the 1920s. At that point the differences between civilian and many military aircraft types were not so marked as later, and experience gained in civil aviation could be put to military use after 1933.

Rearmament offered desirable new business, but German industry's relationship with the Nazis was complex like that of much of the country's establishment, and not all welcomed the relentless, reckless ride towards aggressive war. Steel firms like Krupp were pushed into collaboration because they suffered most during the Depression and wanted to avoid further losses. Alfred Krupp only donated to the Nazis after 1933, but his firm relied heavily on exports, which were threatened by the regime's drive for autarky. Several family firms suffered directly from Nazi racism, notably Simson, the only arms manufacturer that had been legally permitted after 1919 and had supplied the Reichswehr, but which was seized from its Jewish owners in 1938, when the Loewe family were also kicked off the board of the rifle manufacturer DWM.

Arms producers resented the Nazi regime's attempts at centralized planning and price fixing, while they hedged their bets after 1939 by being restrained towards companies in Western and Northern Europe, knowing that Germany might not win the war and any future recovery would require foreign goodwill. No such consideration was shown for Eastern Europe, from where all arms firms drew slave workers, or indeed towards the western forced labourers either. Krupp was one of the largest employers of slave labour, even establishing a subsidiary at Auschwitz, but slave workers were used in all sectors, including submarine construction. Like most industrialists, Alfred Krupp was imprisoned only briefly and soon became a key figure in the post-war 'economic miracle'.[206]

That recovery was assisted by the relatively light restrictions placed on West German industry by the Allies. The initial prohibition on naval construction was essentially unnecessary because, unlike in 1918, the shipbuilding infrastructure had been entirely wrecked by Allied bombing. The shipbuilding ban was lifted in 1949 and the Western Allies soon permitted the new Federal Republic to produce and export arms. The Soviets' implementation of 'demontage' in their zone also wiped out any arms manufacturing capacity. East Germany subsequently developed a modest shipbuilding industry, though it still relied on the USSR for its warships' armaments and electronics, as it did for all other major weapons systems. Austria's Mannlicher firm also resumed small-arms production during the 1950s.[207]

Some firms struggled initially, like Messerschmitt, which did not resume aircraft manufacturing until 1968. The Bundeswehr's need for weaponry offered much new business, and some items like submarines and Leopard tanks became major export successes. However, the increasingly sophisticated character of weaponry, notably aircraft, forced a series of mergers and consolidations during the 1960s and 1970s, which were also encouraged by NATO's standardization programme to ensure inter-operability of equipment between its members. One example was the Panavia consortium, founded in 1969 by British and Italian firms with MBB, itself a merger of Messerschmitt, another aircraft manufacturer (Bölkow), and a division of the shipbuilder Blohm und Voss. Panavia developed the Tornado to replace the ill-fated Starfighter as NATO's primary jet, in turn using this experience to develop the Airbus passenger and transport planes.[208]

Such projects have proved lengthy, expensive, and somewhat risky commercially. Their sheer scale has also squeezed out many of the smaller arms producers, as well as ending most of Switzerland's small weapons industry, whose ambitious projects in the 1950s to make tanks and warplanes all foundered on the inability to solve the technical difficulties inherent in modern equipment. Smaller firms have nonetheless benefited from the long supply chains created by big-ticket items like the Leopard tank, which involved 2,700 different companies, including Swiss firms building it under licence.[209]

News of German tank sales to Israel in 1964 prompted calls that Germany should unilaterally renounce arms exports to sustain its 'civilian power' character. At that point West Germany had only a 0.5 per cent global share, but nonetheless it ranked as the world's tenth largest arms exporter in a market dominated by the USA, the USSR, and the UK, which collectively had an 88.6 per cent global share.[210] Domestic purchases declined as the Bundeswehr had been fully equipped by the late 1960s, encouraging firms to compete more aggressively for exports. The Brandt government issued new guidelines in 1971, permitting sales to NATO members, but restricting them elsewhere, especially to conflict zones. Rising unemployment during the 1970s saw a growing violation of the spirit, if not the letter, of these rules. Continued public hostility prompted revised guidelines in 1982 which in fact created more export opportunities, leading to a succession of major scandals, such as the sale of weaponry to Apartheid South Africa as firms routed business through other NATO countries to circumvent the restrictions.

The return of a left-leaning German government led to further guidance in 2000 incorporating the EU's code and requiring greater transparency. Although the sale of iconic items like tanks or submarines still periodically prompts a public outcry, exports remain a useful governmental policy instrument largely beyond the Bundestag's control. The loose application of the rules led *Der Spiegel* magazine to dub this the 'Merkel Doctrine' of not intervening abroad, but nonetheless fuelling conflict through arms exports.[211] Sales surged in value and Germany by 2020 had secured a 5.5 per cent global share, second only to France within Europe, and ahead of Britain and Italy.[212] On this basis Japan has better 'civilian power' credentials, only ranking fifty-fourth in global arms sales. However, as in the case of Imperial Germany's war industries, this should be put in perspective because this sector contributed less than 1 per cent of GDP. Moreover, while Germany – like virtually all states – lacks robust laws governing the provision of private military or security services, commercial efforts to provide military training in

Libya and Somalia failed in the 2000s, and the country is not a major player in this market.[213]

Outlook

The twentieth century opened with a significant growth of the state prompted directly by the stresses of the First World War. The aftermath of that conflict saw the state remain a major factor in the national economy through the expansion of social welfare, which was driven, in Germany's case, by the urgency of securing legitimacy among its own population as well as providing more effectively for their needs. These pressures persisted through the 1930s and into the Second World War. Although defence spending declined relative to social welfare in the post-war budget, the state remained the major player in the national economy through the redistributive and stimulating effects of its fiscal and investment policies.

These trends have been common throughout much of the world. The perception of the Federal Republic of Germany (alongside Japan) as a uniquely 'civilian power' relies to a considerable extent on its self-fashioning as it sought to distance itself from its Nazi past. Many observers have accepted this contrast, because pre-1945 Germany appears to have been a leading example of extreme militarization and militarism. As this work has argued, there is some substance to the claim that the pre-1945 German past was unusually militaristic, while subsequently Germany has been significantly less so. However, such a conclusion is only valid for selective aspects of both experiences.

Germans have not been alone in emphasizing military over civilian values and objectives, nor have they consistently done so themselves. While individual German monarchs, princes, and lesser authorities pursued wars and feuds into the eighteenth century, the broader orientation of the Holy Roman Empire was defensive. Security was collective and multilateral, and German participation in wars beyond their own frontiers was invariably in partnership with other allies. Swiss security was also collective, and while the Confederation ceased attacking its neighbours after 1515, its subsequent neutrality was directly linked to it providing other European powers with soldiers; something it continued to do rather longer into the nineteenth century than the German states.

The primary aggressor operating from central Europe was not Prussia, but the Austrian Habsburg monarchy, which made war on its own account, though frequently dragging much of the Empire with it. Its forces were also consistently the largest and, often, the best organized and most successful. It became an independent European power through its conquests during the later seventeenth and early eighteenth century, and successfully defended this position, first against Prussia in the mid-eighteenth century, and then against the far more powerful opponent represented by Revolutionary and Napoleonic France. The Habsburg monarchy's survival in both cases depended heavily on securing allies, and the margin of that survival was far greater than Prussia's, which faced complete destruction around 1757–61 and again in 1806–7.

Prussia was generally less successful in finding allies and relied more heavily on its army for security after 1713 than Austria, though its survival in the Seven Years War and the Revolutionary and Napoleonic era also depended heavily on external support. Its high level of militarization was relative to its own meagre resources and was mitigated by the part-time character of its standing army, much of which was furloughed for most of the year. That practice was common throughout the German lands, while Switzerland relied on its traditional militia structure, only belatedly adding a very small professional cadre in the nineteenth century. These aspects are important reminders of the continued and lasting civilian element within German military power.

Prussia's ultimate displacement of Austria as the leading German power in the 1860s was far from inevitable and was partly contingent on wider circumstances within Europe. Prussia did not possess a unique 'genius for war', but importantly foreign observers came to believe that it did after its unexpected victory over France in 1870–1. That success reinforced the tendency among its military leaders to seek a swift, decisive victory to ensure success was not snatched from their grasp by the spectre of a 'people's war', or that a conflict did not slide into a prolonged attritional struggle they believed they could not win. Concern for their jealously guarded professional prestige led the generals of the now Imperial Germany to consistently disdain potentially promising diplomatic solutions and to underestimate the dangerous odds they would face in a war. Again, they were not alone in this, as much of Austria-Hungary's military leadership shared the same delusion by 1914.

Despite defeat in the First World War, German officers largely refused to abandon their obsession with achieving a swift victory. That was the only 'lightning' element to a Blitzkrieg that never existed as a coherent strategy because the General Staff largely lacked a strategy at all, thinking primarily in operational and especially tactical terms. Although both Imperial Germany and, to a lesser extent, Austria-Hungary had become important naval as well as land powers, the two dimensions of warfare remained poorly coordinated. An even greater defeat for Germany in the Second World War finally exposed the fallacy of this approach, though it took the full realization of the implications of the nuclear age to finally expunge its last vestiges during the mid-1950s.

Far from representing an ideal model of how to win a modern war, the German experience serves as an exemplar of how to lose catastrophically. The unprecedented scale of both world wars ensured that the consequences of these defeats were felt far beyond Germany. Among the many other reasons behind the failure, the disregard of diplomacy ranks highly. Diplomatic options that might have rendered conflict unnecessary altogether were frequently ignored, while Germany twice embarked on major wars without a clear link between the intended purpose of victory and the means to achieve it. The interests of real and potential allies were repeatedly ignored both prior to hostilities and once these had begun. The elusiveness of the swift, easy victory prompted the country's leadership to widen each conflict, thereby merely adding to the number of enemies and stacking the odds further against themselves.

The Second World War consolidated Germany's reputation for excessive militarism. Again, this was partially justified because its military leadership had collaborated with the Nazis to militarize society to an unprecedented extent, and then to embark on a genocidal war with fatal consequences for millions of people, as well as for their own nation. The sheer scale of Germany's conquests against significant odds fostered a lasting admiration for the Wehrmacht in parts of the anglophone world and beyond, which draws on the mythical 'genius for war' while eliding how its actual conduct across 1939–45 was inextricably entwined with genocide and exploitation. To an extent, a positive image of the Wehrmacht has persisted in Germany too as successive generations have struggled to accept how the population could have been so deeply involved (many albeit reluctantly) in the Holocaust. That dreadful event, while drawing on ideas and practices already present in

Germany, was also contingent on specific circumstances. German history should not be read backwards from it as a teleologically 'Special Path' deviating from a civilized norm, since that contrast between Germany and its Western European neighbours rests on an equally simplistic interpretation of those countries' history.

Conversely, the contingency and horrific scale of genocidal war between 1939 and 1945 should not blind us to important continuities across the twentieth century and, to some extent, with the earlier past. One is the place of military service in the lives of ordinary people which, outside the extreme levels of mobilization in the two world wars, has been one that has not been shared equally by all men. Another is the importance of the expansion of uniform legal rights throughout the population and, hence, also for those who were serving. These rights were abused by authoritarian regimes, something that continued to characterize life in East Germany until 1989, but they were never completely ignored by governments and military leaders conscious that modern warfare required popular support.

Germany's character as a 'civilian power' relies heavily on its formal renunciation of war as a policy instrument, yet its sheer economic weight enables it to spend comparatively heavily on defence. The contrast with other countries is not so striking in the case of Switzerland and Austria, which have also pursued 'civilian' foreign policies and spend far less on defence. The renewed involvement of German personnel in combat since 1994 – and particularly in Afghanistan after 2002 – has been at the centre of discussions of whether the country was, or remains, a 'civilian power'. However, there seems little prospect that it will return to being a 'military power' in the manner manifest before 1945. Indeed, attachment to the 'civilian power' ideal combined with an understandable desire to spend less on defence has removed Germany's capacity to act unilaterally and raises doubts about its ability to meet its international obligations in a conventional war. The country's vulnerability was exposed by Russia's invasion of Ukraine in February 2022, which also revealed its dangerous dependency on gas imports. Though the new SPD-led government more than doubled defence spending in response, the new money is unlikely to alter the strategic balance significantly in the short term. The question remains how far Germany will continue to emphasize multilateralism and a rules-based international order or seek more flexible (and hence potentially more volatile) arrangements tailored to its own direct interests.

The character of war has also changed profoundly since 1990, reducing the importance of conventional defence while adding new, less clearly defined elements of security in which states pursue objectives with less obviously military means. The declining involvement of the German, Austrian, and Swiss populations in conventional military institutions has added to their reduced attentiveness to their governments' development of non-conventional ways to project power, such as arms exports, foreign training missions, and strategic use of overseas aid – something that is far more pronounced for Germany given its greater resources. Again, this development is not unique to Germany, but it is one that all democratically minded citizens should consider.

Notes

Abbreviations

ADB	*Allgemeine Deutsche Biographie*
AEG	Archives d'Etat de Genève
BMWB	*Beiheft zum Militärwochenblatt*
CEH	*Central European History*
CRE	*Consortium on Revolutionary Europe*
DBKH	*Darstellungen aus Bayerischen Kriegs- und Heeresgeschichte*
Doc Bo	M. Kouřil et al. (eds.), *Documenta Bohemica bellum tricennale illustrantia*, 7 vols. (Prague, 1971–81)
EcHR	*Economic History Review*
EHQ	*European History Quarterly*
EHR	*English Historical Review*
ERH	*European Review of History*
FBPG	*Forschungen zur brandenburgischen und preußischen Geschichte*
Feldzüge	*Feldzüge des Prinzen Eugen von Savoyen*, 21 vols., issued by the Austrian Kriegsarchiv (Vienna, 1876–96)
GH	*German History*
GSWW	*Germany and the Second World War*, issued by the Militärgeschichtliches Forschungsamt, 9 vols. (Oxford, 1990–2017)
GWU	*Geschichte in Wissenschaft und Unterricht*
HDM	*Deutsche Militärgeschichte 1648–1939*, issued by the Militärgeschichtliches Forschungsamt, 9 vols. (Munich, 1983)
HJ	*Historical Journal*
HJb	*Historisches Jahrbuch*
HJLG	*Hessisches Jahrbuch für Landesgeschichte*
HSAS	Hauptstaatsarchiv Stuttgart
HZ	*Historische Zeitschrift*
IHR	*International History Review*
JCH	*Journal of Contemporary History*
JMH	*Journal of Modern History*
JMilH	*Journal of Military History*
JSS	*Journal of Strategic Studies*
LAM	Landesarchiv Münster
MGFA	Militärgeschichtliches Forschungsamt
MGM	*Militärgeschichtliche Mitteilungen*
MIÖG	*Mitteilungen des Instituts für Österreichische Geschichtsforschung*
MZ	*Militärgeschichtliche Zeitschrift*

NASG *Neues Archiv für sächsische Geschichte*
NS New series
NSJB *Niedersächsisches Jahrbuch für Landesgeschichte*
NTSR J.J. Moser, *Neues Teutsches Staatsrecht*, 20 vols. (Frankfurt, 1766–75)
PC H. Virck et al. (eds.), *Politische Correspondenz der Stadt Strassburg*, 4 vols. (Strasbourg, 1882–1933)
Reyscher A.L. Reyscher (ed.), *Vollständige, historisch und kritisch bearbeitete Sammlung der Württembergischen Gesetze*, 29 vols. (Stuttgart, 1828–51)
StAD Staatsarchiv Darmstadt
VSWG *Vierteljahrsschrfit für Sozial- und Wirtschaftsgeschichte*
WiH *War in History*
WVJHLG *Württembergische Vierteljahresheft für Landesgechichte*
WZ *Westfälische Zeitschrift*
ZBLG *Zeitschrift für Bayerische Landesgeschichte*
ZGO *Zeitschrift für die Geschichte des Oberrheins*
ZHF *Zeitschrift für Historische Forschung*
ZSRG *Zeitschrift der Savigny Stiftung für Rechtsgeschichte*
ZWLG *Zeitschrift für Württembergische Landesgeschichte*

Introduction

1. Otto von Bismarck, *Bismarck: Die gesammelten Werke*, 15 vols. (Berlin, 1924–35), X, pp. 139–40. 2. 'Denn nur Eisen kann uns retten, uns erlösen kann nur Blut von der Sünde schweren Ketten, von des Bösen Übermut'. See generally, E.A. Hagen, *Max v. Schenkendorfs Leben, Denken und Dichten* (Berlin, 1863). 3. A. Jähne, 'Blut und Eisen', in K. Pazold and M. Weißbecker (eds.), *Schlagwörter und Schlachtrufe aus zwei Jahrhunderten deutscher Geschichte* (Leipzig, 2002), pp. 76–82. 4. J. Wintjes, 'German army culture, 1871–1945', in P.R. Mansoor and W. Murray (eds.), *The culture of military organisations* (Cambridge, 2019), pp. 100–20; T.N. Dupuy, *A genius for war: The German Army and General Staff 1807–1945* (New York, 1984); W. Görlitz, *The German General Staff: Its history and structure 1657–1945* (London, 1953); R.M. Citino, *The German way of war from the Thirty Years War to the Third Reich* (Lawrence, KS, 2005), and *The path to Blitzkrieg: Doctrine and training in the German Army, 1920–1939* (Boulder, CO, 1999). 5. X. Qiyu, *Fragile rise: Grand strategy and the fate of imperial Germany, 1871–1914* (Cambridge, MA, 2017). The author is an officer in China's People's Liberation Army. 6. I.V. Hull, *Absolute destruction: Military culture and the practices of war* (Ithaca, NY, 2004); R.M. Citino, *The Wehrmacht's last stand: The German campaign of 1944–1945* (Lawrence, KS, 2017), esp. pp. 307–11; E. Willems, *A way of life and death! Three centuries of Prussian-German militarism* (Vanderbilt University Press, 1986); J. Laffin, *Jackboot: The story of the German soldier* (London, 2003), esp. pp. 254–6. The recent positive endorsement comes from S. Neitzel, *Deutsche Krieger vom Kaiserreich zur Berliner Republik: Eine Militärgeschichte* (Berlin, 2020). 7. As argued, for instance, by P. Haldén, 'From total to minimal transformation: German oaths of loyalty', in ibidem et al. (eds.), *Transforming Warriors* (London, 2016), pp. 163–82. 8. Classic versions of this thesis include H.U. Wehler, *Deutsche Gesellschaftsgeschichte 1700–1990*, 5 vols. (Munich, 2008), and F. Fischer, *From Kaiserreich to Third Reich* (London, 1990). For a recent, influential restatement of the Sonderweg, see H.A. Winkler, *Germany: The long road west*, 2 vols. (Oxford, 2006–7). Critical overviews of the debate in J. Kocka, 'Looking back on the *Sonderweg*', *CEH*, 51 (2018), 137–42; H. Walser Smith, 'Where the *Sonderweg* debate left us', *German Studies Review*, 31 (2008), 225–40; W.W. Hagen, 'Descent of the *Sonderweg*: Hans Rosenberg's history of

old-regime Prussia', *CEH*, 24 (1991), 24–50. **9.** M. Kitchen, *A military history of Germany* (London, 1975); R.M. Citino, *The German way of war from the Thirty Years War to the Third Reich* (Lawrence, KS, 2005), esp. p. xiii; J.M. Kolkey, *Germany on the march* (Lanham, MD, 1995); J.R. White, *The Prussian Army 1640–1871* (Lanham, MD, 1996); B. Perrett, *Why the Germans lose at war* (Barnsley, 2014); K. Simpson, *History of the German Army 1648–present* (London, 1985); C.H. Hermann, *Deutsche Militärgeschichte* (Frankfurt am Main, 1968). **10.** For example, D. Stone, *Fighting for the fatherland: The story of the German soldier from 1648 to the present day* (London, 2006), p. 19. **11.** Several major research projects are correcting this for early modern Swiss history. See also R. Jaun, *Geschichte der Schweizer Armee* (Zürich, 2019), which covers the more recent past. For Austrian historians' sometime wilful neglect of their country's martial past, see M. Hochedlinger, 'The early modern Cinderella', *Austrian History Yearbook*, 32 (2001), 207–13. While representing an attempt to correct this, R. Bassett, *For God and Kaiser: The imperial Austrian Army, 1619–1918* (New Haven, CT, 2015), is an error-laden conventional narrative. **12.** Further discussion of this in W.J. Astore, 'Loving the German war machine: America's infatuation with Blitzkrieg, warfighters, and militarism', in M.S. Neiberg and D.E. Showalter (eds.), *Arms and the man* (Leiden, 2011), pp. 5–30; R. Smelser and E.J. Davies, *The myth of the Eastern Front: The Nazi-Soviet War in American popular culture* (Cambridge, 2008). Neitzel, *Deutscher Krieger*, decontextualizes the Wehrmacht from the Holocaust to create space to admire its ruthless efficiency. **13.** The point that German doctrine was overly concerned with tactics, not strategy, has been made by others, for example, K. Macksey, *Why the Germans lose at war* (London, 1996). **14.** https://www. bundespraesident.de/SharedDocs/Reden/DE/Joachim-Gauck/Reden/2015/01/150127-Bundestag-Gedenken.html (accessed 19 November 2021).

1. Warlords

1. The latter has been termed 'extra-territorial violence'. See J.E. Thomson, *Mercenaries, pirates and sovereigns: State-building and extra-territorial violence in early modern Europe* (Princeton, NJ, 1994). **2.** The state-building literature is now vast. For an influential example, see C. Tilly, *Coercion, capital and European states, AD 990–1992* (Oxford, 1992). **3.** P.H. Wilson, *The Holy Roman Empire: A thousand years of Europe's history* (London, 2016). **4.** W. Dotzauer, *Die deutschen Reichskreise (1383–1806)* (Wiesbaden, 1998). **5.** G.F. v. Blum, *Tabellarische Anstellung der Reichs-Matrikulauschläge zum Behuf einer Reichs-Usual-Matrikel ...* (Frankfurt, 1795). **6.** H. Carl, *Der Schwäbische Bund 1488–1534* (Leinfelden-Echterdingen, 2000); E. Bock, *Der Schwäbischer Bund und seine Verfassung (1488–1534)* (Breslau, 1927); C.W. Close, *State formation and shared sovereignty: The Holy Roman Empire and the Dutch Republic, 1488–1696* (Cambridge, 2021), pp. 24–55. **7.** See Wilson, *Holy Roman Empire*, pp. 445–54, and the sources cited there. **8.** G. Benecke, *Maximilian I, 1459–1519* (London, 1982). **9.** P.S. Fichtner, *Ferdinand I of Austria* (Boulder, CO, 1982); A. Kohler, *Ferdinand I, 1503–1564* (Munich, 2003). The numerous biographies of his elder brother are now surpassed by G. Parker, *Emperor: A new life of Charles V* (New Haven, CT, 2019). **10.** For a full list of all imperial Estates with their territories and populations, see P.H. Wilson, *From Reich to revolution: German history, 1558–1806* (Basingstoke, 2004), pp. 364–81. **11.** W. Schaufelberger, *Der alte Schweizer und sein Krieg*, 3rd ed. (Frauenfeld, 1987), pp. 152–68. See generally T. Scott, *The Swiss and their neighbours, 1460–1560* (Oxford, 2017). **12.** Scott, *Swiss*, pp. 23–44; Carl, *Schwäbische Bund*, pp. 451–5; H. Wiesflecker, *Kaiser Maximilian I*, 5 vols. (Vienna, 1971–86), II, pp. 314–57. **13.** T.A. Brady, *Turning Swiss: Cities and Empire, 1450–1550* (Cambridge, 1985). **14.** H. Zmora, *The feud in early modern Germany* (Cambridge, 2011), and his

State and nobility in early modern Germany: The knightly feud in Franconia 1440–1567 (Cambridge, 1997); H. Ulmschneider, *Götz von Berlichingen* (Sigmaringen, 1974). **15.** R. Scholzen, *Franz von Sickingen* (Kaiserslautern, 1996); V. Press, 'Kaiser und Reichsritterschaft', in R. Endres (ed.), *Adel in der Frühneuzeit* (Cologne, 1991), pp. 163–94. **16.** P. Blickle, *The revolution of 1525* (Baltimore, MD, 1975); T. Scott and B. Scribner (eds.), *The German Peasants' War: A history in documents* (Atlantic Highlands, NJ, 1991). **17.** P. Blickle, *Der Bauernjörg: Feldherr im Bauernkrieg* (Munich, 2015); S. Hoyer, *Das Militärwesen im deutschen Bauernkrieg, 1524–1526* (Berlin-DDR, 1975). **18.** W. Schulze, 'Die veränderte Bedeutung sozialer Konflikte im 16. und 17. Jahrhundert', in H.U. Wehler (ed.), *Der deutsche Bauernkrieg, 1524–1526* (Göttingen, 1976), pp. 277–302. **19.** K.B. Mayer, *The population of Switzerland* (New York, 1952), pp. 191–7. For an analysis of the different categories, see P.H. Wilson, 'Mercenary contracts as fiscal-military instruments', in Svante Norrhem and Erik Thomson (eds.), *Subsidies, diplomacy and state formation in Europe, 1494–1789: Economies of allegiance* (Manchester, 2020), pp. 68–92. **20.** P. de Vallière, *Treue und Ehre: Geschichte der Schweizer in fremden Diensten* (Neuenburg, 1912), p. 3. Discussion in H.R. Fuhrer and R.P. Eyer (eds.), *Schweizer in 'fremden Diensten': Verherrlicht und verurteilt* (Zurich, 2006); N. Furrer et al. (eds.), *Gente ferocissima: Merenariat et société en Suisse (XVe–XIXe siècles)*, (Zurich, 1997). **21.** An old but still influential example of this interpretation is M. Braubach, *Die Bedeutung der Subsidien für die Politik im Spanischen Erbfolgekrieg* (Bonn, 1923). Further discussion in P.H. Wilson, 'The German "soldier trade" of the seventeenth and eighteenth centuries: A reassessment', *IHR*, 18 (1996), 757–92. **22.** Examples in M. Harsgor, 'Die Spieße unter der Lilienblume: Deutsche Söldner im Dienste Frankreichs (14.–16. Jh.)', *Tel Aviver Jahrbuch für deutsche Geschichte*, 16 (1987), 48–81; G. Callejo Leal (ed.), *La presencía suiza en la milicia Española* (Madrid, 2017). **23.** F. Lot, *Recherches sur les effectifs des armées françaises des Guerres d'Italie aux Guerres de Religion, 1494–1562* (Paris, 1962), pp. 15–21, 33; D. Potter, *Renaissance France at war* (Woodbridge, 2008), pp. 155–99. **24.** Useful summary in J. Casparis, 'The Swiss mercenary system: Labor emigration from the semi-periphery', *Review* (Fernand Braudel Centre), 5 (1982), 593–642. **25.** A. Axelrod, *Mercenaries: A guide to private armies and private military companies* (Los Angeles, CA, 2014), p. 89. Other examples include the influential E.R. Huber, *Heer und Staat in der deutschen Geschichte*, 2nd ed. (Hamburg, 1943), pp. 65–72; S. Fiedler, *Kriegswesen und Kriegführung im Zeitalter der Landsknechte* (Koblenz, 1985), pp. 95–6. **26.** K. Pfaff, *Geschichte des Militärwesens in Württemberg* (Stuttgart, 1842), pp. 10–11. See generally, R. Baumann, *Das Söldnerwesen im 16. Jahrhundert im bayerischen und süddeutschen Beispiel* (Munich, 1978), pp. 73–84. **27.** Useful overview in M. Mallett and C. Shaw, *The Italian Wars, 1494–1559* (London, 2012). **28.** Details in ibid, pp. 50–2. Fuller discussion in P. Rogger, *Geld, Krieg und Macht. Pensionsherren, Söldner und eidgenössische Politik in den Mailänderkriegen, 1495–1516* (Baden, 2015). **29.** Potter, *Renaissance France*, p. 64. For the following, see H. Harkensee, *Die Schlacht bei Marignano* (Göttingen, 1909); W. Schaufelberger, *Marignano* (Zürich, 1993), pp. 48–57. Some accounts put the total Swiss dead as high as 16,500, but that is unlikely. **30.** G. Miège, *Marignan: Histoire d'une défaite salutaire, 1515–2015* (Bière, 2015); P. Paret, *Imagined battles: Reflections of war in European art* (Chapel Hill, NC, 1997), pp. 93–8. **31.** The classic interpretation of Swiss neutrality is P. Schweizer, *Geschichte der schweizerischen Neutralität* (Frauenfeld, 1895), which was endorsed and extended in the monumental study by E. Bonjour, *Geschichte der schweizerischen Neutralität. Vier Jahrhunderte eidgenössischer Aussenpolitik*, 9 vols. (Basel, 1965–76). **32.** G. W. Locher, *Die Zwinglische Reformation im Rahmen der europäischen Kirchengeschichte* (Göttingen, 1979); G.R. Potter, *Zwingli* (Cambridge, 1976), esp. pp. 398–418; R. Hauswirth, *Landgraf Philipp von Hessen und Zwingli* (Tübingen, 1968), pp. 65–95, 236–52. **33.** A. Gotthard, *Der liebe und werthe Fried. Kriegskonzepte und Neutralitätsvorstellungen in der Frühen Neuzeit* (Cologne, 2014). **34.** Scott, *Swiss*, pp. 45–7. **35.** Detailed examples in

L. Gally de Riedmatten, 'A qui profitait le service étranger? Une étude de la repartition des pensions en Valais au xvième siècle', in R. Jaun et al. (eds.), *Schweizer Solddienst* (Birmensdorf, 2010), pp. 139–70, and the contributions in K. v. Greyerz et al. (eds.), *Soldgeschäfte, Klientelismus, Korruption in der Frühen Neuzeit* (Göttingen, 2018). See also S. Rageth, *Sold und Soldrückstände der Schweizer Truppen in französischen Diensten im 16. Jahrhundert* (Bern, 2008); H. Romer, *Herrschaft, Reislauf und Verbotspolitik. Beobachtungen zum rechtlichen Alltag der Zürcher Solddienstbekämpfung im 16. Jahrhundert* (Zurich, 1997). **36.** J. Giono. *The battle of Pavia* (London, 1965). **37.** J. Hook, *The sack of Rome, 1527* (London, 1972); I. Sherer, *Warriors for a living: The experience of Spanish infantry during the Italian Wars* (Leiden, 2017), pp. 150–74. **38.** Quoted in Hook, *Sack of Rome*, p. 254. **39.** See R. Murphey, *Ottoman warfare, 1500–1700* (London, 1998); and P. Fodor (ed.), *The battle for Central Europe* (Leiden, 2019), which focuses on 1566 but also ranges more widely. **40.** J.B. Szabó and F. Tóth, *Mohács (156): Soliman le Magnifique prend pied en Europe centrale* (Paris, 2009). For imperial assistance, see W. Steglich, 'Die Reichstürkenhilfe in der Zeit Karls V.', *MGM*, 11 (1972), 7–55; G. Pálffy, 'The origins and development of the border defence system against the Ottoman empire in Hungary', in G. Dávid and P. Fodor (eds.), *Ottomans, Hungarians and Habsburgs in Central Europe* (Leiden, 2000), pp. 3–68. **41.** Parker, *Emperor*, pp. 226–30; F. v. Rexroth, *Der Landsknechtsführer Sebastian Schertlin* (Bonn, 1940), pp. 39–41. **42.** K. Brandi, *The Emperor Charles V* (London, 1939), pp. 501–4. **43.** E. Fabian, *Die Entstehung des Schmalkaldischen Bundes und seiner Verfassung 1524/29–1531/35* (Tübingen, 1962), pp. 65ff; G. Haug-Moritz, *Der Schmalkaldische Bund 1530–1540/41* (Leinfelden-Echterdingen, 2002); Close, *State formation*, pp. 48–112. **44.** A. Keller, *Die Wiedereinsetzung des Herzogs Ulrichs von Württemberg durch den Landgrafen Philipp von Hessen 1533/34* (Marburg, 1912). **45.** H.A. Schmidt, 'Landsknechtswesen und Kriegführung in Niedersachsen 1533–1545', *NSJB*, 6 (1929), 167–223; H.-J. Behr, 'Wider "die schendlichen Vergardungen der Knecht". Der Vertrag norddeutscher Fürsten und Städte zu Hannover 1546', *Lippische Mitteilungen*, 53 (1984), 19–50; J.W. Hunterbrinker, *'Fromme Knechte' und 'Gartenteufel'. Söldner als Soziale Gruppe im 16. und 17. Jahrhundert* (Konstanz, 2010), pp. 173–99; P. Burschel, *Söldner im Nordwestdeutschland des 16. und 17. Jahrhundert* (Göttingen, 1994), pp. 304–17; H. Preuß, *Söldnerführer unter Landgraf Philipp dem Großmütigen von Hessen (1518–1567)* (Darmstadt, 1975), pp. 28–62; H. Carl, 'Landfriedensbrecher und "Sicherheitskräfte": Adelige Fehdeführer und Söldner im 16. Jahrhundert', in C. Kampmann and U. Niggermann (eds.), *Sicherheit in der Frühen Neuzeit* (Cologne, 2013), pp. 273–87. For examples of rumours, see *PC*, vols. II and III. **46.** *PC*, III, nos. 624, 641. **47.** Ibid, nos. 105, 160–1, 176, 229. Around 12 companies of Swiss nonetheless entered League service. R. McEntegart, *Henry VIII, the League of Schmalkalden, and the English Reformation* (Woodbridge, 2002). For the war, see A. Schüz, *Der Donaufeldzug Karl V. im Jahre 1546* (Tübingen, 1929); A. Querengässer and S. Lunyakov, *Die Heere des Schmalkaldischen Krieges* (Berlin, 2019); Parker, *Emperor*, pp. 319–26. **48.** *PC*, IV, no. 330. **49.** W. Held, *Die Schlacht bei Mühlberg/Elbe* (Beucha, 2014); K. Frhr. v. Bothmer, 'Die Schlacht vor der Drakenberg am 23. Mai 1547', *NSJB*, 15 (1938), 85–104. **50.** L. Schorn-Schütte (ed.), *Das Interim 1548/50* (Heidelberg, 2005); H. Rabe, *Reichsbund und Interim: Die Verfassungs- und Religionspolitik Karls V. und die Reichstag von Augsburg 1547/1548* (Cologne, 1971). **51.** M. Fuchs and R. Rebitsch (eds.), *Kaiser und Kurfürst: Aspekte der Fürstenaufstandes 1552* (Münster, 2010). **52.** G. Kleinheyer, 'Die Abdankung des Kaisers', in G. Kohler (ed.), *Wege europäischer Rechtsgeschichte* (Frankfur-am-Main, 1988), pp. 124–44. The Franco-Spanish War of 1551–9 is summarized in Mallett and Shaw, *Italian Wars*, pp. 250–85. **53.** G. Biegel and H.J. Dorda (eds.), *Blutige Weichstellung: Massenschlacht und Machtkalkül bei Sievershausen 1553* (Braunschweig, 2003). **54.** M. Heckel, 'Politischer Friede und geistliche Freiheit im Ringen um die Wahrheit, *HZ*, 282 (2006), 391–425, with a less upbeat assessment in A. Gotthard, *Der Augsburger Religionsfrieden*

(Münster, 2004). **55.** A.P. Lutterberger, *Kurfürsten, Kaiser und Reich. Politische Führung und Friedenssicherung unter Ferdinand I. und Maximilian II.* (Mainz, 1994); M. Lanzinner, *Friedenssicherung und politische Einheit des Reiches unter Maximilian II. (1564–1576)* (Göttingen, 1993); H.-J. Behr, 'Die Exekution des Niederrheinisch-Westfälischen Kreises gegen Graf Johann von Rietberg 1556–1566', *WZ*, 128 (1978), 33–104. **56.** J. Lavery, *Germany's northern challenge: The Holy Roman Empire and the Scandinavian struggle for the Baltic, 1563–1576* (Boston, MA, 2002). **57.** G. Parker, *The Army of Flanders and the Spanish Road, 1567–1659* (Cambridge, 1972), p. 271; F. Edelmeyer, *Söldner und Pensionäre: Das Netzwerk Philipps II. Im Heiligen Römischen Reich* (Cologne, 2002), pp. 235–58, and his 'Lansquenetes del Sacro Imperio al servicio de la monarquía católica en el sigloi xvi', in E. García Hernán (ed.), *Presencía germánica en la milicia Española* (Madrid, 2015), pp. 29–61. **58.** Chapters by M. Ressel and T.P. Becker in A. Rutz (ed.), *Krieg und Kriegserfahrung im Westen des Reiches 1568–1714* (Göttingen, 2016). **59.** J. B. Wood, *The king's army: Warfare, soldiers and society during the Wars of Religion in France, 1582–1576* (Cambridge, 1996), pp. 18–27, 64, 72–3; E. May de Romainmotier, *Histoire militaire de la Suisse et de Suisses dans les différens services de l'Europe* (Lausanne, 1788), p. 59. **60.** J.A.M. van Tol, *Germany and the French Wars of Religion, 1560–1572* (Leiden, 2018), pp. 197–222; O. Bezzel, *Geschichte des Kurpfälzischen Heeres*, 2 vols. (Munich, 1925), I, pp. 30–40; de Vallière, *Treue und Ehre*, pp. 186–8, 210–11; W.A. Heap, *Elizabeth's French Wars: English intervention in the French Wars of Religion, 1562–1598* (London, 2019), pp. 73–7, 80; D.S. Gehring, *Anglo-German relations and the Protestant cause* (London, 2013), pp. 89–145. **61.** W. Schulze, *Reich und Türkengefahr im späten 16. Jahrhundert* (Munich, 1978). **62.** J.D. Tracy, *Balkan wars: Habsburg Croatia, Ottoman Bosnia and Venetian Dalmatia, 1499–1617* (Lanham, MD, 2016), pp. 284–337; G. Pálffy, *Hungary between two empires, 1526–1711* (Bloomington, IN, 2021), pp. 113–21; P.H. Wilson, *Europe's tragedy: The Thirty Years War* (London, 2009), pp. 97–106, and the sources cited there. **63.** E. Heischmann, *Die Anfänge des stehenden Heeres in Österreich* (Vienna, 1925), esp. pp. 187–8. Brief details of the Kreis troops in J. Müller, 'Der Anteil der schwäbischen Kreistruppen an dem Türkenkrieg Kaiser Rudolfs II. von 1595 bis 1597', *Zeitschrift des Historischen Vereins für Schwaben und Neuburg*, 28 (1901), 155–262; G. Tessin, *Die Regimenter der europäischen Staaten im 'Ancien Régime' des XVI. bis XVIII. Jahrhunderts* (Osnabrück, 1986), pp. 89–90, 152–4, 241, 243, 250–1, 308, 310, and his 'Niedersachsen im Türkenkrieg 1594–1597', *NSJB*, 32 (1964), 66–106. **64.** J.F. Pichler, 'Captain John Smith in the light of Styrian sources', *The Virginia Magazine for History and Biography*, 65 (1957), 332–54; C.F. Finkel, 'French mercenaries in the Habsburg-Ottoman war of 1593–1606', *Bulletin of the School of African and Oriental Studies*, 55 (1992), 451–71. **65.** L. Toifl and H. Leitgab, *Oberösterreich im Bocskay-Aufstand, 1605* (Vienna, 1990). **66.** B. Rill, *Kaiser Matthias* (Graz, 1999). **67.** Wilson, *Europe's tragedy*, pp. 106–15, 239–61.

2. Forming Armies

1. C. Rogers (ed.), *The military revolution debate: Readings on the military transformation of early modern Europe* (Boulder, CO, 1995). **2.** K.H. Marcus, *The politics of power: Elites of an early modern German state* (Mainz, 2000); V. Press, *Calvinismus und Territorialstaat. Regierung und Zentralbehörden der Kurpfalz 1559–1619* (Stuttgart, 1970). **3.** W. Burr, 'Die Reichssturmfahne und der Streit um die hannoversche Kurwürde', *ZWLG*, 27 (1968), 245–316. **4.** A. Maçzak (ed.), *Klientelsysteme im Europa der frühen Neuzeit* (Munich, 1988). **5.** L. Eppenstein, 'Beiträge zur Geschichte des auswärtigen Kriegsdienstes der Deutschen in der zweiten Hälfte des 16. Jahrhunderts', *FBPG*, 32 (1920), 283–367. **6.** H. Neuhaus, 'Reichskreise und Reichskriege in der Frühen Neuzeit', in W. Wüst (ed.), *Reichskreis und Territorium* (Stuttgart, 2000), pp. 71–88. **7.** D. Miller, *The army of the*

Swabian League, 1525 (Warwick, 2019), p. 20.   **8.** E. Schubert, *Fürstliche Heerschaft und Territorium im späten Mittelalter*, 2nd ed. (Munich, 2006); B. Arnold, *Princes and territories in medieval Germany* (Cambridge, 1991).   **9.** F. Wintterlin, *Geschichte der Behördenorganisation in Württemberg*, 2 vols. (Stuttgart, 1904–6), I, 44.   **10.** J.D. Hittle, *The military staff*, 2nd ed. (Harrisburg, PA, 1949), pp. 29–31, 42–3.   **11.** Good overviews in G. Pálffy, 'The Habsburg defense system in Hungary against the Ottomans in the sixteenth century', in B.L. Davies (ed.), *Warfare in eastern Europe, 1500–1800* (Leiden, 2012), pp. 35–61 at 49–50, 53–7; O. Regele, *Der österreichische Hofkriegsrat, 1556–1848* (Vienna, 1949).   **12.** Examples in L. Auer, 'Der Kriegsdienst des Klerus unter den sächsischen Kaiser', *MIÖG*, 79 (1971), 316–407, and 80 (1972), 48–70; T. Reuter, '*Episcopa cum sua militia*: The prelate as warrior in the early Staufer era', in idem (ed.), *Warriors and Churchmen in the High Middle Ages* (London, 1992), pp. 79–94; B. Arnold, 'German bishops and their military retinues in the medieval Empire', *GH*, 7 (1989), 161–83; K.L. Krieger, 'Obligatory military service and the use of mercenaries in imperial military campaigns under the Hohenstaufen emperors', in A. Haverkamp and H. Vollrath (eds.), *England and Germany in the High Middle Ages* (Oxford, 1996), pp. 151–68.   **13.** G. Ortenburg, *Waffe und Waffengebrauch im Zeitalter der Landsknechte* (Koblenz, 1984), pp. 27–9.   **14.** Reyscher, XIX/I, p. x; E. Pflichthofer, *Das Württembergische Heerwesen am Ausgang des Mittelalters* (Tübingen, 1938), pp. 3–6.   **15.** J. Zimmermann, *Militärverwaltung und Heeresaufbringung in Österreich bis 1806* (Munich, 1983), pp. 18–20. For the following, see also P. Leukel, '*All welt wil auf sein wider Burgundi*': *Das Reichsheer im Neusser Krieg 1474/5* (Paderborn, 2019), pp. 79–92.   **16.** K. Pfaff, *Geschichte des Militärwesens in Württemberg* (Stuttgart, 1842), pp. 6–7.   **17.** H. Schnitter, 'Die überlieferte Defensionspflicht', in R.G. Foerster (ed.), *Die Wehrpflicht* (Munich, 1994), pp. 29–37; D. Götschmann, 'Das Jus Armorum. Ausformung und politische Bedeutung der reichsständischen Militärhoheit bis zu ihrer definitive Anerkennung im Westfälischen Frieden', *Blätter für deutsche Landesgeschichte*, 129 (1993), 257–76.   **18.** E. v. Frauenholz, *Das Heerwesen der Schweizer Eidgenossenschaft* (Munich, 1936), which includes useful documents.   **19.** B.A. Tlusty, *The martial ethic in early modern Germany* (Basingstoke, 2011), pp. 16–56; U. Crämer, 'Die Wehrmacht Strassburgs von der Reformationszeit bis zum Fall der Reichsstadt', *ZGO*, 84 (1931), 46–95 at 49–51.   **20.** Pflichthofer, *Württembergische Heerwesen*, p. 65; Pfaff, *Militärwesens*, p. 10; E. Naujoks, 'Stadtverteidigung und Wehrverfassung Esslingens im 16. Jahrhundert', *Esslinger Studien*, 5 (1959), 16–30 at 22–6.   **21.** Examples in K.F. Wernet, 'Der Hauensteiner Landfahnen', *ZGO*, NS 56 (1943), 301–95; R. Baumann, *Das Söldnerwesen im 16. Jahrhundert im bayerischen und süddeutschen Beispiel* (Munich, 1978), p. 54.   **22.** For an example of a militia escort, see G. Richter, 'Württemberg und der Kriegszug des Herzogs Johann Wilhelm von Sachsen nach Frankreich im Jahre 1568', *ZWLG*, 26 (1967), 252–63.   **23.** W. Schulze 'Die deutschen Landesdefensionen im 16. und 17. Jahrhundert', in J. Kunisch (ed.), *Staatsverfassung und Heeresverfassung* (Berlin, 1986); O. Bezzel, *Geschichte des kurpfälzischen Heeres von seinen Anfängen bis zur Vereinigung von Kurpfalz und Kurbayern 1777*, 2 vols. (Munich, 1925–8), I, pp. 50–1; G. Thies, *Territorialstaat und Landesverteidigung. Der Landesdefensionswerk in Hessen-Kassel unter Landgraf Moritz (1592–1627)* (Darmstadt, 1973); H. Schnitter, *Volk und Landesdefension* (Berlin-Ost, 1977). Documents printed in E. v. Frauenholz (ed.), *Das Heerwesen in der Zeit des Dreißigjährigen Krieges*, 2 vols. (Munich, 1938–9), II.   **24.** A. Axelrod, *Mercenaries: A guide to private armies and private military companies* (Los Angeles, CA, 2014), pp. 49–59; S. Percy, *Mercenaries: The history of a norm in international relations* (Oxford, 2007), pp. 73–4, 83–5, 87.   **25.** S. Franck, *Chronica* (1531), printed in G. Strauss (ed.), *Manifestations of discontent on the eve of the Reformation* (Bloomington, IN, 1971), p. 217.   **26.** Machiavelli, *The Prince*, ch. 12; C. v. Clausewitz, *On war*, eds. M. Howard and P. Paret (Princeton, NJ, 1984), p. 587; see J. France (ed.), *Mercenaries and paid men* (Leiden, 2008), p. 6.   **27.** M. Mallet, *Mercenaries and their masters: Warfare in Renaissance Italy* (London,

1974), pp. 31–6; S. Selzer, *Deutsche Söldner im Italien des Trecento* (Tübingen, 2001), pp. 18–20, 388. **28.** Pflichthofer, *Württembergische Heerwesen*, pp. 75–7. **29.** U. Tresp, *Söldner aus Böhmen im Dienst deutscher Fürsten* (Paderborn, 2004). **30.** E. Richert, *Die Schlacht bei Guinegate* (Berlin, 1907). **31.** M. Nell, *Die Landsknechte. Enstehung der ersten deutschen Infanterie* (Berlin, 1914), p. 166; see also G. Kurzmann, *Kaiser Maximilian I. und das Kriegswesen der österreichischen Länder und des Reiches* (Vienna, 1985), pp. 63–71, 89–96, and generally R. Baumann, *Die Landsknechte* (Munich, 1994). **32.** S. Xenakis, *Gewalt und Gemeinschaft: Kriegsknechte um 1500* (Paderborn, 2015), pp. 53–4; Baumann, *Söldnerwesen*, pp. 43–7. **33.** W. Rose, 'Die deutschen und italienischen Schwarzen (Großen) Garden im 15. und 16. Jahrhundert', *Zeitschrift für Historischen Waffenkunde*, 6 (1914), 73–97; M. Arfaioli, *The Black Bands of Giovanni: Infantry and diplomacy during the Italian Wars (1526–1528)* (Pisa, 2005); W. Lammers, *Die Schlacht bei Hemmingstedt* (Neumünster, 1953). **34.** Older view in F. Redlich, *The German military enterpriser and his workforce*, 2 vols. (Wiesbaden, 1964–6); new approach in D. Parrott, *The business of war* (Cambridge, 2012); R. Baumann, 'Die deutschen Condottieri', in S. Förster et al. (eds.), *Rückkehr der Condottieri?* (Paderborn, 2010), pp. 111–26. **35.** J. Day, *Money and finance in the age of merchant capitalism* (Oxford, 1999), pp. 59–109; M.A. Denzel, *Das System des bargeldlosen Zahlungsvehrkehrs europäischer Prägung vom Mittelalter bis 1914* (Stuttgart, 2008), pp. 47–71, 93–174; O. Gelderblom, *Cities of commerce* (Princeton, NJ, 2013), pp. 81–140. **36.** H. Preuß, *Söldnerführer unter Landgraf Philipp dem Großmütigen von Hessen (1518–1567)* (Darmstadt, 1975), pp. 9–233; H.M. Möller, *Das Regiment der Landsknechte* (Wiesbaden, 1976), pp. 14–31, summarizing the contemporary literature. **37.** D. Potter, 'The international mercenary market in the sixteenth century: Anglo-French competition in Germany, 1543–50', *EHR*, 111 (1996), 24–58 at 27–8. **38.** P. Burschel, *Söldner im Nordwestdeutschland des 16. und 17. Jahrhunderts* (Göttingen, 1994), pp. 115–29. **39.** H. Gäse, 'Sebastian Schertlin von Burtenbach', *Ludwigsburger Geschichtsblätter*, 27 (1975), 69–88 at 76. **40.** Leukel, '... wider Burgundi', p. 521; Bezzel, *Geschichte des Kurpfälizischen Heeres*, I, 14–22; H. Fahrmbacher, 'Das Kurpfälzische Heerwesen im 15., 16. und 17. Jahrhundert', *Mannheimer Geschichtsblätter*, 11 (1910), 20–47 at 33–4; Pflichthofer, *Württembergische Heerwesen*, pp. 71, 77. **41.** *PC*, III, no. 399; F. v. Rexroth, *Der Landsknechtsführer Sebastian Schertlin* (Bonn, 1940), p. 56; A. Schuz, *Der Donaufeldzug Karl V. im Jahre 1546* (Tübingen, 1930), pp. 89–94; Preuß, *Söldnerführer*, pp. 395–6. **42.** G. Parker, *Emperor: A new life of Charles V* (New Haven, CT, 2019), p. 440; M.F. Alvarez, *Charles V* (London, 1975), p. 159. **43.** P. Rauscher, *Zwischen Ständen und Gläubigern. Die kaiserlichen Finanzen unter Ferdinand I. und Maximilian II. (1556–1576)* (Munich, 2004), p. 58; G. Pálffy, 'Türkenabwehr, Grenzsoldatentum und die Militarisierung der Gesellschaft in Ungarn in der Frühen Neuzeit', *HJb*, 123 (2003), 111–48 at 131, 136. **44.** B.S. Hall, *Weapons and warfare in Renaissance Europe* (Baltimore, MD, 1997); Ortenburg, *Landsknechte*, pp. 48–52. **45.** H. Schwarz, *Gefechtsformen der Infanterie In Europa durch 800 Jahren* (Munich, 1977), pp. 74–6, 117, 120. For the following, see also W. Ried, *Buch der Waffen* (Düsseldorf, 1976), p. 101; W. Boeheim, *Handbuch der Waffenkunde* (Leipzig, 1890), pp. 450–5; W. Rüstow, *Geschichte der Infanterie*, 2 vols., 3rd ed. (Leipzig, 1884), I, pp. 222–5, 233–4. **46.** Pflichthofer, *Württembergische Heerwesen*, pp. 52–9; Fahrmbacher, 'Kurpfälzische Heerwesen', p. 34. **47.** Rüstow, *Infanterie*, I, pp. 164–5. **48.** W. Meyer, 'Also griffen die Eidgenossen das Volk an. Die Schlacht bei St. Jakob an der Birs – Hintergründe, Verlauf und Bedeutung', in W. Meyer and W. Geiser (eds.), *Ereignis, Mythos, Deutung. 1444–1994 St. Jakob an der Birs* (Basel, 1994), pp. 9–57; D. Hardy, 'The 1444–5 expedition of the Dauphin Louis to the Upper Rhine in geopolitical perspective', *Journal of Medieval History*, 38 (2012), 358–87. **49.** For this and the following, see Rüstow, *Infanterie*, I, 168, 230–1, 251–4, 323–60; Schwarz, *Gefechtsformen*, pp. 58–9, 69–79. **50.** O. Bangerter, '"Le bien passoit le mal?" La performance des mercenaires Suisses en Italie en 1494–1496', in

R. Jaun et al. (eds.), *Schweizer Solddienst* (Birmensdorf, 2010), pp. 41–60. **51.** Ortenburg, *Landsknechte*, pp. 40–3. **52.** J.B. Wood, *The king's army: Warfare, soldiers and society during the Wars of Religion in France, 1582–1576* (Cambridge, 1996), p. 111; P. de Vallière, *Treue und Ehre: Geschichte der Schweizer in fremden Diensten* (Neuenburg, 1912), p. 183. **53.** The average strength of the 34 infantry companies in the imperial army at the start of the 1542 campaign was 588 each: *PC*, III, no. 258. **54.** S. Gunn, *The English people at war in the age of Henry VIII* (Oxford, 2018), p. 43; M. Neuding Skoog, *I rikets tjänst: Krig, stat och samhälle i Sverige 1450–1550* (Lund, 2018), p. 510; J. Albi de la Cuesta, *De Pavía a Rocroi. Los Tercios de infantería Española en los siglos xvi y xvii* (Madrid, 1999). **55.** Quoted in Schwarz, *Gefechtsformen*, p. 126. **56.** Rüstow, *Infanterie*, I, 329–31. **57.** Möller, *Regiment*, p. 76; A. Williams, *The knight and the blast furnace: A history of the metallurgy of armour in the middle ages and the early modern period* (Leiden, 2003); Kurzmann, *Kriegswesen der österreichischen Länder*, pp. 98–119. **58.** F. Chauviré, 'Le problème de l'allure dans les charges de cavalerie du xvie siècle au xviiie siècle', *Revue historique des Armées*, 249 (2007), 16–27; J.J. v. Wallhausen, *Kriegskunst zu Pferdt* (Frankfurt-am-Main, 1616), pp. 13, 20. **59.** J. Heilmann, *Kriegsgeschichte von Bayern, Franken und Schwaben von 1506–1651*, 2 vols. (Munich, 1868), I, pp. 30–1. **60.** E. v. Frauenholz, *Das Heerwesen in der Zeit des freien Söldnertums*, 2 vols. (Munich, 1936–7), II, pp. 210, 213. **61.** Burschel, *Söldner im Nordwestdeutschland*, p. 267; see also Boeheim, *Waffenkunde*, p. 483. **62.** F. Lot, *Recherches sur les effectifs des armées françaises des Guerres d'Italie aux Guerres de Religion, 1494–1562* (Paris, 1962), pp. 140, 143, 181; D. Potter, *Renaissance France at war* (Woodbridge, 2008), pp. 143–6. **63.** Z.P. Bagi, 'Westeuropäische Reitertruppen auf ungarischen Kriegsschauplätzen', *Militär und Gesellschaft in der Frühen Neuzeit*, 19 (2015), 47–70; C. Beaufort-Spontin, *Harnisch und Waffe Europas. Die militärische Ausrüstung im 17. Jahrhundert* (Munich, 1982), pp. 69–80. **64.** Baumann, *Söldnerwesen*, pp. 93, 132; S. Birtachas, 'Stradioti, Cappelletti, Compagnie, or Milizie Greche', in G. Theatokis and A. Yildiz (eds.), *A military history of the Mediterranean Sea* (Leiden, 2018), pp. 325–46. **65.** R. Atzbach, 'Die Belagerung der Burg Tannenberg bei Darmstadt 1399', *Fundberichte aus Hessen*, 50 (2013), 707–28. Not to be confused with Tannenberg in East Prussia, the site of the battles of 1410 and 1914. **66.** J. Kraus, *Das Militärwesen der Reichsstadt Augsburg, 1548–1806* (Augsburg, 1980), pp. 326ff. See generally K. DeVries, *Guns and men in medieval Europe, 1200–1500* (Aldershot, 2002). **67.** S. Fiedler, *Kriegswesen und Kriegführung im Zeitalter der Landsknechte* (Koblenz, 1985), p. 129. **68.** *PC*, III, no. 258. **69.** R.D. Smith and K. DeVries, *The artillery of the dukes of Burgundy, 1363–1477* (Woodbridge, 2005); M. Depreter, *De Gavre à Nancy (1453–1477): L'artillerie bourguignonne sur la voie de la 'modernité'* (Brussels, 2011); G. Agostan, *Guns for the sultan* (Cambridge, 2005), pp. 44–7. **70.** H. Wiesflecker, *Kaiser Maximilian I*, 5 vols. (Vienna, 1971–86), I, p. 97; H. Neumann, *Das Zeughaus*, 2 vols. (Bonn, 1992), I, p. 93; II, pp. 97, 140, 176; Kurzmann, *Kriegswesen der österreichischen Länder*, p. 147. **71.** *Zeugbuch*, copy in the Bavarian State Library (BSB cod.icon 222 digitized at https://daten.digitale-sammlungen.de/~db/0002/bsb00020956/images/ (accessed 15 October 2020). **72.** P. Dollinger, *La ville libre à la fin du Moyen Âge (1350–1482)* (Strasbourg, 1981), p. 126; U. Crämer, 'Die Wehrwesen Strassburgs von der Reformationszeit bis zum Fall der Reichsstadt', *ZGO*, 84 (1931), 46–95; Fiedler, *Landsknechte*, p. 130. **73.** *PC*, III, no. 310. **74.** Ibid. no. 354; Schuz, *Donaufeldzug*, pp. 38–45. **75.** J. Wille, 'Neue Berichte über die Kämpfe bei Laufen 1534', *Württembergische Vierteljahreshefte für Landesgeschichte*, 3 (1880), 171–4. **76.** See the detailed account in *PC*, III, no. 624. **77.** Rüstow, *Infanterie*, I, pp. 288–307; B. de Montluc, *The Valois-Habsburg wars and the French Wars of Religion* (London, 1971), pp. 104–15. **78.** C. Duffy, *Siege warfare: The fortress in the early modern world 1494–1660* (London, 1979), pp. 23–42; S. Pepper and N. Adams, *Firearms and fortifications: Military architecture and siege warfare in sixteenth-century Siena* (Chicago, IL, 1986). **79.** For example, the Hohentwiel in Württemberg: K.

v. Martens, *Geschichte von Hohentwiel* (Stuttgart, 1857). See generally Neumann, *Das Zeughaus*, I, pp. 51–2, 69–70. **80.** For the following, see G. Agostan, 'Habsburgs and Ottomans: defense, military change and shifts in power', *Turkish Studies Association Bulletin*, 22 (1998), 126–41; T. Szalontay, 'The art of war during the Ottoman-Habsburg long war 1593–1606 according to narrative sources' (PhD, University of Toronto, 2004); G.E. Rothenberg, *The Austrian military border in Croatia, 1522–1747* (Urbana, IL, 1960); G. Pálffy, *Der Anfänge der Militärkartographie in der Habsburgermonarchie* (Budapest, 2011), and his 'The origins and development of the border defence system against the Ottoman empire in Hungary', in G. Dávid and P. Fodor (eds.), *Ottomans, Hungarians and Habsburgs in Central Europe* (Leiden, 2000), pp. 3–68. **81.** J. Glete, *Warfare at sea, 1500–1650: Maritime conflicts and the transformation of Europe* (London, 2000); P. Padfield, *Guns at sea* (London, 1973), pp. 19–69; for an example, see B. Mozejko, *Peter von Danzig: The story of a great caravel, 1462–1475* (Leiden, 2020). **82.** E. Michel and M.L. Sternath (eds), *Emperor Maximilian I and the age of Dürer* (Munich, 2012), pp. 29, 66, 228–9. **83.** S. Haag and K. Schmitz von Ledebur (eds.), *Kaiser Karl V. erobert Tunis* (Vienna, 2013); R. Gonzales Cuerva and M.A. de Barras Ibarra, *Túnez 1535: Voces de una campaña europea* (Madrid, 2017); for this and the following, see J.D. Tracy, *Emperor Charles V: Impresario of war* (Cambridge, 2010), pp. 153–4, 170–82. **84.** A.E. Sokol, *Das Habsburgische Admiralitätswerk des 16. und 17. Jahrhunderts* (Vienna, 1976), pp. 26–32; K. Höhlbaum, 'Die Admiralsakten von Pfalzgraf Georg Hans, Graf zu Veldenz', *Mitteilungen aus dem Stadtarchiv von Köln*, 18 (1889), 1–55. **85.** M. Widner, *Die Hanse und ihre Seekriege* (Munich, 2001); R. Hammel-Kiesow and M. Puhle, *Die Hanse* (Darmstadt, 2009); for *Der Adler*, see B. Greenhill (ed.), *The evolution of the sailing ship, 1250–1580* (London, 1995), pp. 240–9. **86.** K. Petsch, *Seefahrt für Brandenburg-Preussen, 1650–1815* (Osnabrück, 1986), pp. 3–4. **87.** W. Aichelberg, *Kriegschiffe auf der Donau* (Vienna, 1982), pp. 7–10. **88.** C.W. Bracewell, *The Uskoks of Senj: Piracy, banditry and holy war in the sixteenth-century Adriatic* (Ithaca, NY, 1992); J.D. Tracy, *Balkan wars: Habsburg Croatia, Ottoman Bosnia and Venetian Dalmatia, 1499–1617* (Lanham, MD, 2016), pp. 159–61, 169–72, 266–9, 337–46; H. Valentinitsch, 'Ferdinand II., die innerösterreichischen Länder und die Gradiskanerkrieg 1615–1618', in P. Urban and B. Sutter (eds.), *Johannes Kepler (1571–1971)* (Graz, 1975), pp. 497–539.

3. Going for a Soldier

1. R. Baumann, *Das Söldnerwesen im 16. Jahrhundert im bayerischen und süddeutschen Beispiel* (Munich, 1978), pp. 155–63. **2.** L. Silver, *Marketing Maximilian* (Princeton, NJ, 2008); P. Terjanian, *The last knight: The art, armor, and ambition of Maximilian I* (New Haven, CT, 2019). **3.** T. Kaufmann, *Das Ende der Reformation: Madgeburgs 'Herrgotts Kanzlei' (1548–1551/2)* (Tübingen, 2003); N. Rein, *The chancery of God: Protestant print, polemic and propaganda against the Empire, 1546–1551* (Aldershot, 2008). **4.** R. Leng, *Ars belli: Deutsche taktische und Kriegstechnische Bilderhandschriften und Traktate im 15. und 16. Jahrhundert*, 2 vols. (Wiesbaden, 2002); P. Brugh, *Gunpowder, masculinity and warfare in German texts, 1400–1700* (Rochester, NY, 2019), esp. pp. 43–69. **5.** H. Gäse, 'Sebastian Schertlin von Burtenbach', *Ludwigsburger Geschichtsblätter*, 27 (1975), 69–88 at 75–7; F. Uhlhorn, *Reinhard Graf zu Solms, Herr zu Münzenberg, 1491–1562* (Marburg, 1952); E. Richter, *Frundsberg* (Munich, 1968), pp. 74–8; W. Küther and G. Seib, 'Konrad von Boyneburg (Bemelburg)', *HJLG*, 19 (1969), 234–95 at 273–6; E. Solger, *Der Landsknechtsobrist Konrat von Bemelburg* (Nördlingen, 1870), pp. 75–7. **6.** J. Wintjes, 'Europe's earliest Kriegsspiel? Book Seven of Reinhard Graf zu Solms's *Kriegsregierung* and the "prehistory" of professional war gaming', *British Journal of Military History*, 2 (2015), 15–32. **7.** L. Fronsperger, *Kriegsbuch* (Frankfurt, 1566), available online through the

Bayerische Staatsbibliothek. Discussion in Brugh, *Gunpowder*, pp. 74–93. **8.** H. Ehlert, 'Ursprünge des modernen Militärwesens: Die Nassau-oranischen Heeresreformen', *MGM*, 38 (1985), 27–56; G. Thies, *Territorialstaat und Landesverteidigung. Das Landesdefensionswerk in Hessen-Kassel unter Landgraf Moritz (1592–1627)* (Darmstadt, 1973), pp. 34–66. Count Johann's book is reprinted in W. Hahlweg (ed.), *Die Heeresreform der Oranier* (Wiesbaden, 1973). **9.** J. de Gheyn, *The Renaissance drill book* (London, 2003, first published 1607); C. Beaufort-Spontin, *Harnisch und Waffe Europas. Die militärische Ausrüstung im 17. Jahrhundert* (Munich, 1982), pp. 24–7; D. Lawrence, *The complete soldier: Military books and military culture in early Stuart England, 1603–1645* (Leiden, 2008), pp. 8, 48, 140–4, 282; O. Rusakovskiy, 'Das erste russische Militärrecht für fremde Söldner?', *Militär und Gesellschaft in der Frühen Neuzeit*, 19 (2015), 11–45. **10.** F. Sauter, 'Lazarus von Schwendi', in *Schwendi: 850 Jahre* (Laupheim, 1978), pp. 54–64. See generally J.W. Huntebrinker, *'Fromme Knechte' und 'Gartenteufel'. Söldner als soziale Gruppe im 16. und 17. Jahrhundert* (Konstanz, 2010), pp. 321–47. **11.** G. Basta, *Il maestro di campo generale, das ist: außführliche Anzeig, Bericht und Erklärung von dem Ampt eines General-Feldt-Obersten* (Frankfurt, 1617), and his *Il governo della cavalleria, das ist: Bericht von Aufführung der leichten Pferde* (Frankfurt, 1614). **12.** G. Wunder, 'Sebastian Schertlin. Feldhauptmann und Kriegsunternehmer', *Lebensbilder aus Schwaben und Franken*, 13 (1977), 52–72 at 54; P. Blickle, *Der Bauernjörg: Feldherr im Bauernkrieg* (Munich, 2015), p. 166. **13.** J.J. v. Wallhausen, *Kriegskunst zu Fuß* (Frankfurt, 1615), pp. 43–7. **14.** M. Rogg, *Landsknechte und Reisläufer: Bilder von Soldaten* (Paderborn, 2002); L. Silver, 'The Landsknecht', in J. Clifton and L.M. Scattone (eds.), *The plains of Mars* (New Haven, CT, 2009), pp. 16–19; Huntebrinker, *'Fromme Knechte'*, pp. 55–172. **15.** S. Franck, *Chronica* (Strasbourg, 1531), printed in translation in G. Strauss (ed.), *Manifestations of discontent on the eve of the Reformation* (Bloomington, IN, 1971), pp. 215–18. **16.** D. Vogelsanger, 'Ulrich Zwingli als Feldprediger in der Lombardei', in R. Haudenreich (ed.), *Marignano 1515–2015* (Lenzburg, 2014), pp. 79–94. **17.** P. Rogger, *Geld, Krieg und Macht. Pensionsherren, Söldner und eidgenössische Politik in den Mailänderkriegen 1494–1516* (Baden, 2015), and his 'Aufstand gegen die "tütschen Franzoßen": Der Lebkuchenkrieg in Zürich 1515/1516)', in Haudenreich (ed.), *Marignano*, pp. 95–106. **18.** A. Tischer, *Offizielle Kriegsbegründungen in der Frühen Neuzeit* (Münster, 2012). **19.** H. Münkler, *Im Namen des Staates* (Frankfurt am Main, 1987). **20.** J. Guilmartin, 'Ideology and conflict: The wars of the Ottoman empire, 1453–1606', *Journal of Interdisciplinary History*, 18 (1988), 721–47. For the following, see N. Malcolm, *Useful enemies: Islam and the Ottoman empire in western political thought, 1450–1750* (Oxford, 2019), pp. 51–274; A. Höfert, *Der Feind beschreiben: 'Türkengefahr' und europäisches Wissen über das Osmanische Reich 1450–1600* (Frankfurt am Main, 2003); R. Born (ed.), *The sultan's world: The Ottoman orient in Renaissance art* (Brussels, 2015). **21.** *Feldzüge*, XVII, 47–8. **22.** R. Pröve, 'Gewalt und Herrschaft in der Frühen Neuzeit', *Zeitschrift für Geschichte*, 47 (1999), 792–828. **23.** M. Rink, *Vom 'Partheygänger' zum Partisanen: Die Konzeption des kleinen Krieges in Preussen, 1740–1813* (Frankfurt am Main, 1999), pp. 79–100. **24.** P. Burschel, *Söldner im Nordwestdeutschland des 16. und 17. Jahrhunderts* (Göttingen, 1994), pp. 27–53. **25.** Richter, *Frundsberg*, p. 144; Baumann, *Söldnerwesen*, pp. 112–24; Burschel, *Söldner*, pp. 165–83, 192–9. **26.** F. v. Rexroth, *Der Landsknechtsführer Sebastian Schertlin* (Bonn, 1940). **27.** Fuller discussion of identities in P.H. Wilson, *The Holy Roman Empire* (London, 2016), pp. 233–92. **28.** Baumann, *Söldnerwesen*, 32–5, 54–7, 62; chapters by Z.P. Bagi and B. Sarusi-Kiss in K. Csaplár-Degovics and I. Fazekas (eds.), *Geteilt – Vereinigt. Beiträge zur Geschichte des Königreichs Ungarn in der Frühneuzeit* (Berlin, 2011), giving rich detail on the origins of Germans in Habsburg service. **29.** M. Nell, *Die Landsknechte. Enstehung der ersten deutschen Infanterie* (Berlin, 1914), pp. 150–3. **30.** PC, II, no. 346; Solger, *Bemelburg*, pp. 94–9; see also Z.P. Bagi, 'The life of soldiers during the Long Turkish War (1593–1606)', *Hungarian Historical Review*, 4 (2015), 384–417. Good short biographies of 22 officers and soldiers in R. Baumann, *Mythos Frundsberg* (Mindelheim, 2014). **31.** J.V. Wagner, *Graf Wilhelm von Fürstenberg, 1491–1549 und die politisch-geistigen Mächte seiner Zeit* (Stuttgart, 1966); R. Peter, 'Les lansquenets dans les armées du roi: Le Capitaine Général Guillaume de Fürstenberg', in *Charles-Quint, Le Rhin et la France* (Strasbourg, 1973), pp. 95–109. **32.** R. Baumann, *Georg von Frundsberg: Vater der Landsknechte und Feldhauptmann von Tirol* (Munich, 1984). **33.** Baumann, *Söldnerwesen*, pp. 97–8, 252–3; *ADB*, 13 (1881), 512–16. **34.** F. Blau, *Die deutschen Landsknechte* (Görlitz, 1882), pp. 112–21. **35.** H.M. Möller, *Das Regiment der Landsknechte* (Wiesbaden, 1976), pp. 50–1, 95–100; R. Baumann, *Landsknechte* (Munich, 1994), pp. 98–102; Blau, *Landsknechte*, pp. 31–5. **36.** W. Erben, 'Ursrung und Entwicklung der deutschen Kriegsartikel', *MIÖG*, supplement 6 (1901), 473–529. **37.** S. Lange, *Der Fahneneid: Die Geschichte der Schwurverpflichtung im deutschen Militär* (Bremen, 2002), pp. 25–38. The legal arrangements are discussed in Möller, *Regiment*, pp. 132–52, 183–259. **38.** H. v. Zwiedineck-Südenhorst, *Kriegsbilder aus der Zeit der Landsknechte* (Stuttgart, 1883), p. 52; S. Fiedler, *Kriegswesen und Kriegsführung im Zeitalter der Landsknechte* (Koblenz, 1985), p. 96. **39.** These and other examples in S. Xenakis, *Gewalt und Gemeinschaft: Kriegsknechte um 1500* (Paderborn, 2015), pp. 140–230; Huntebrinker, '*Fromme Knechte*', pp. 210–35; Baumann, *Söldnerwesen*, pp. 201–5, 217–20; I. Sherer, *Warriors for a living: The experience of the Spanish infantry during the Italian Wars* (Leiden, 2017), pp. 102–41. **40.** W. Friedensberg, 'Franz von Sickingen', in J. v. Pflugk-Hartung (ed.), *Im Morgenrot der Reformation* (Stuttgart, 1927), pp. 557–666 at 600–1. **41.** J.C. Lünig (ed.), *Corpus juris militaris des Heilgen Römischen Reiches* (Leipzig, 1723), pp. 68–76; E. v. Frauenholz, *Das Heerwesen in der Zeit des freien Söldnertums*, 2 vols. (Munich, 1936–7), II, pp. 355–424. **42.** M. Weber, *Die Reichspolizeiordnungen von 1530, 1548 und 1577* (Frankfurt am Main, 2002). **43.** Lünig, *Corpus juris militaris*, p. 199. **44.** J. McCormack, *One million mercenaries: Swiss soldiers in the armies of the world* (London, 1993), p. 74; H. Preuß, *Söldnerführer unter Landgraf Philipp dem Großmütigen von Hessen (1518–1567)* (Darmstadt, 1975), pp. 15–17. **45.** E. Swart, 'From "Landsknecht" to "soldier": The Low German foot soldiers of the Low Countries in the second half of the 16th century', *International Review of Social History*, 51 (2006), 75–92 at 81–4; Baumann, *Landsknechte*, pp. 111–12, 209–10. **46.** Xenakis, *Gewalt*, pp. 70–80, 111–19. For this concept more generally, see J. Lynn, *Battle: A history of culture and combat* (New York, 2003). **47.** G. Franz, 'Von Ursprung und Brauchtum der Landsknechte', *MIÖG*, 61 (1953), 90–1, 97–8; Blau, *Landsknechte*, pp. 49–50, 98–111. **48.** Burschel, *Söldner*, pp. 161–3. **49.** B.A. Tlusty, *The martial ethic in early modern Germany* (Basingstoke, 2011), pp. 56–87, 134–45. **50.** Rogg, *Landsknechte und Reisläufer*, p. 19. **51.** E. Pflichtofer, *Das Württembergische Heerwesen am Ausgang des Mittelalters* (Tübingen, 1938), p. 62; K. Pfaff, *Geschichte des Militärwesens in Württemberg* (Stuttgart, 1842), p. 8. **52.** Blickle, *Der Bauernjörg*, pp. 133–8, 160–2, 190, 235–6. **53.** J. Heilmann, *Kriegsgeschichte von Bayern, Franken und Schwaben von 1506–1651*, 2 vols. (Munich, 1868), I, p. 234. See generally, Burschel, *Söldner*, pp. 226–58, and J. Lynn, *Women, armies and warfare in early modern Europe* (Cambridge, 2008). **54.** A. Keller, *Die Wiedereinsetzung des Herzogs Ulrich von Württemberg durch den Landgrafen Philipp von Hessen 1533/34* (Marburg, 1912), pp. 50–1; K. v. Martens, *Geschichte der innerhalb der gegenwärtigen Gränzen des Königreichs Württemberg vorgefallene kriegerischen Ereignisse* (Stuttgart, 1847), p. 233. **55.** H. Wunder, *He is the sun, she is the moon: Women in early modern Germany* (Cambridge, MA, 1998), esp. pp. 38–55; J.F. Harrington, *Reordering marriage and society in Reformation Germany* (Cambridge, 1995); Baumann, *Landsknechte*, pp. 154–65, 201–2. **56.** Baumann, *Söldnerwesen*, pp. 214–19; E. Heischmann, *Die Anfänge des stehenden Heeres in Österreich* (Vienna, 1925), pp. 213–22; Möller, *Regiment*, pp. 100–11; Z. Bagi, 'Pedro de Illanes and a field hospital to be established in Hungary during the Long Turkish War (1593–1606)', *Kaleidoscope History*, 6 (2015), 14–24. **57.** M. Panse, *Hans von Gersdorffs 'Feldbuch der*

Wundarznei' (Wiesbaden, 2012); B. Di Matteo, 'Art and science in the Renaissance: The case of Walter Hermann Ryff', *Clinical Orthopaedics and Related Research*, 472 (2014), 1, 689–96. **58.** W. Schaufelberger, *Der alte Schweizer und sein Krieg*, 3rd ed. (Frauenfeld, 1987), p. 26. See generally, S.D. Bowd, *Renaissance mass murder: Civilians and soldiers during the Italian Wars* (Oxford, 2018). **59.** S. Eickhoff and F. Schopper (eds.), *Ihre Letzte Schlacht. Leben im Dreißigjährigen Krieg* (Zossen, 2012), p. 33. **60.** *PC*, III, no. 270. **61.** P. Lenihan, *Fluxes, fevers and fighting men: War and disease in ancien regime Europe, 1648–1789* (Warwick, 2019), pp. 18–27, 169. **62.** Rexroth, *Schertlin*, pp. 29, 56; J.D. Tracy, *Emperor Charles V: Impresario of war* (Cambridge, 2010), p. 112; K. Brandi, *The Emperor Charles V* (London, 1939), p. 554. **63.** Franck, *Chronica*, p. 217. **64.** Blickle, *Der Bauernjörg*, pp. 314, 338; Zwiedineck-Südenhorst, *Kriegsbilder*, pp. 49–54, 107; Heischmann, *Anfänge*, pp. 119–21. **65.** H. Boockmann, *Stauferzeit und spätes Mittelalter: Deutschland 1125–1517* (Berlin, 1998), pp. 320–1. **66.** Wilson, *Empire*, pp. 445–51; P. Rauscher, 'Kaiser und Reich. Die Reichstürkenhilfen von Ferdinand I. bis zum Beginn des "Langen Türkenkrieges" 1548–93', in F. Edelmeyer (ed.), *Finanzen und Herrschaft* (Munich, 2003), pp. 45–83. **67.** T.A. Brady, *Protestant politics: Jacob Sturm (1489–1553) and the German Reformation* (Boston, MA, 1995), p. 299. **68.** Brady, 'Princes Reformation vs urban liberty: Strasbourg and the restoration in Württemberg 1534', in I. Bátori (ed.), *Städtische Gesellschaft und Reformation* (Stuttgart, 1980), pp. 265–91. **69.** K. Krüger, *Finanzstaat Hessen* (Marburg, 1980), pp. 241–2. **70.** A. Sigelen, *Reichspfennigmeister Zacharias Geizkofler* (Stuttgart, 2009). **71.** P. Rogger, 'Pensions in Switzerland: Practices, conflicts, and impact in the sixteenth century', in S. Norrhem and E. Thomson (eds.), *Subsidies, diplomacy and state formation in Europe, 1494–1789* (Lund, 2020), pp. 146–71. **72.** H. Carl, *Der Schwäbische Bund 1488–1534* (Leinfelden-Echterdingen, 2000), pp. 361–3; Blickle, *Der Bauernjörg*, pp. 289–90. **73.** R. Hauswirth, *Landgraf Philipp von Hessen und Zwingli* (Tübingen, 1968), pp. 27–50, 264–5; E. Fabian, *Die Entstehung des Schmalkaldischen Bundes und seiner Verfassung 1524/29–1531/35* (Tübingen, 1962), pp. 33–7, 338–42. **74.** *PC*, III, nos. 305, 394. **75.** A. Querengässer and S. Lunyakov, *Die Heere des Schmalkaldischen Krieges* (Berlin, 2019), p. 14. **76.** J. Pohl, 'Die Profiantirung der Keyserlichen Armaden ahnbelangendt': Studien zur Versorgung der kaiserlichen Armee 1634/35* (Kiel, 1991), p. 15; P. Broucek, 'Logistische Fragen der Türkenkriege des 16. und 17. Jahrhunderts', in H. Boeg (ed.), *Die Bedeutung der Logistik für die militärische Führung von der Antike bis in die neueste Zeit* (Herford, 1986), pp. 35–60.

4. Restraining the War Monster

1. For a typical, but influential example, see M. Braubach, *Die Bedeutung der Subsidien für die Politik im Spanischen Erbfolgekrieg* (Bonn, 1923). Further discussion in P.H. Wilson, *Absolutism in Central Europe* (London, 2000). **2.** For example, F. Dickmann, *Der Westfälische Frieden*, 7th ed. (Münster, 1998), p. 494. For the contemporary, more positive views see V. Meid, *Der Dreißigjährige Krieg in der deutschen Barockliteratur* (Stuttgart, 2017), pp. 356, 192, 200; C. Gantet, *La Paix de Westphalie (1648)* (Paris, 2001). **3.** Quotes from M. Howard, *War in European history* (Oxford, 1976), p. 37; C.V. Wedgwood, *The Thirty Years War* (London, 1957), pp. 362, 383. For the war's legacy see K. Cramer, *The Thirty Years War in German memory in the nineteenth century* (Lincoln, NE, 2007). The most recent interpretations are surveyed by C. Gantet, 'Guerre de Trente Ans et Paix de Westpahlie', *Dix–Septième Siècle*, 277 (2017), 645–66; P.H. Wilson, 'The Thirty Years War 1618–48: A Quatercentenary Perspective', *GH*, 37 (2018), 227–45. New general studies include G. Schmidt, *Die Reiter der Apokalypse: Geschichte des Dreißigjährigen Krieges* (Munich, 2018); P.H. Wilson, *Europe's tragedy: The Thirty Years War* (London, 2009). **4.** Critique in P.H. Wilson, 'The causes of the Thirty Years War 1618–48', *EHR*, 123 (2008),

554–86. 5. M. van Creveld, *Supplying war* (Cambridge, 1977), pp. 5–18. 6. R. Ergang, *The myth of the all-destructive fury in the Thirty Years War* (Pocono Pines, PA, 1956). Discussion of the war's religious dimension in M. Asche and A. Schindling (eds.), *Das Strafgericht Gottes* (Münster, 2002); P.H. Wilson, 'Dynasty, constitution and confession: The role of religion in the Thirty Years War', *IHR*, 30 (2008), 473–514. 7. P.H. Wilson, 'Habsburg imperial strategy during the Thirty Years War', in E. García Hernán and D. Maffi (eds.), *Estudios sobre guerra y sociedad en la Monarquía Hispánica. Guerra maritima, estrategia, organizacíon y cultura militar (1500–1700)* (Valencia, 2017), pp. 291–329. 8. D. Croxton, *Westphalia: The last Christian peace* (London, 2013); M. Rohrschneider, *Der geschieterte Frieden. Spaniens Ringen mit Frankreich auf dem Westfälischen Friedenskongress* (Münster, 2007). 9. A. Ernst and A. Schindling (eds.), *Union und Liga 1608/09* (Stuttgart, 2010); A.L. Thomas, *A house divided: Wittelsbach confessional court cultures in the Holy Roman Empire, c. 1550–1650* (Leiden, 2010). 10. A.D. Anderson, *On the verge of war: International relations and the Jülich-Kleve succession crises (1609–1614)* (Boston, 1999); M. Groten et al. (eds.), *Der Jülich-Klevische Erbstreit 1609* (Düsseldorf, 2011). 11. J. Burkhardt, *Der Krieg der Kriege* (Stuttgart, 2018), stresses the continued possibility of peace, contrary to H. Duchhardt, *Der Wege in die Katastrophe des Dreißigjährigen Krieges* (Munich, 2017), with its more pessimistic assessment. 12. R. Rebitsch (ed.), *1618: Der Beginn des Dreißigjährigen Krieges* (Vienna, 2017). 13. The claims for a communication breakdown advanced by A. Gotthard, *Der Dreißigjährige Krieg* (Cologne, 2016), are refuted by J. Burkhardt, *Der Krieg der Kriege* (Stuttgart, 2018). 14. D. Croxton, 'A territorial imperative? The Military Revolution, strategy, and peacemaking in the Thirty Years War', *WiH*, 5 (1998), 253–79; P.H. Wilson, 'Strategy and the conduct of war', in O. Asbach and P. Schröder (eds.), *Ashgate Research Companion to the Thirty Years War* (Farnham, 2014), pp. 269–81. 15. M. Kaiser, 'Pappenheim als empirischer Theoretiker des Krieges', in H. Neuhaus and B. Stollberg-Rilinger (eds.), *Menschen und Strukturen* (Berlin, 2002), pp. 201–27. 16. T. Brockmann, *Dynastie, Kaiseramt und Konfession* (Paderborn, 2011); R. Bireley, *Ferdinand II* (Cambridge, 2014). 17. M. Rüde, *England und Kurpfalz im werdenden Mächteeuropa (1608–1632)* (Stuttgart, 2007); J. Polišenský, *Tragic triangle: The Netherlands, Spain and Bohemia, 1617–1621* (Prague, 1991); B.C. Pursell, *The winter king: Frederick V of the Palatinate and the coming of the Thirty Years War* (Aldershot, 2003). 18. O. Chaline, *La bataille de la Montagne Blanc* (Paris, 2000). 19. R.J.W. Evans, *The making of the Habsburg monarchy, 1550–1700* (Oxford, 1977); K. Keller and M. Scheutz (eds.), *Die Habsburgermonarchie und das Dreißigjährige Krieg* (Cologne, 2020); T. Knoz, 'Die Konfiskationen nach 1620 in (erb)länder-übergreifender Perspektive', in P. Mat'a and T. Winkelbauer (eds.), *Die Habsburgermonarchie 1620 bis 1740* (Stuttgart, 2006), pp. 99–130; H. Louthan, *Converting Bohemia: Force and persuasion in the Catholic Reformation* (Cambridge, 2009). 20. H.A. Cañete, *Los Tercios de Flandes en Alemania: La Guerra del Palatinado, 1620–1623* (Malaga, 2014). 21. P.D. Lockhart, *Denmark in the Thirty Years War* (Selinsgrove, PA, 1996). 22. I. Schmidt-Voges and N. Jörn (eds.), *Mit Schweden verbündet – von Schweden besetzt* (Hamburg, 2016). 23. H. Haan, 'Kaiser Ferdinand II. und das Problem des Reichsabsolutismus', *HZ*, 207 (1968), 297–345. 24. M. Hengerer, *Kaiser Ferdinand III. (1608–1657)* (Vienna, 2014); L. Höbelt, *Von Nördlingen bis Jankau: Kaiserliche Strategie und Kriegführung, 1634–1645* (Vienna, 2016). 25. D. Croxton, *Peacemaking in early modern Europe: Cardinal Mazarin and the congress of Westphalia, 1643–1648* (Selinsgrove, PA, 1999); R. Rebitsch et al., *1648: Kriegführung und Friedensverhandlungen* (Innsbruck, 2018). 26. This myth emerged among political scientists and international lawyers in the 1860s: Croxton, *Westphalia*, pp. 351–5, 367. 27. A. Gotthard, *Säulen des Reiches. Die Kurfürsten im frühneuzeitlichen Reichsverband* (Husum, 1999). 28. F. Schulze, *Die Reichskreise im Dreißigjährigen Krieg* (Berlin, 2018). 29. Useful summary of Swiss policy at this point in H. de Weck, 'La neutralité du corps helvétique avant, pendant et après la Guerre de Trente Ans', in R. Haudenschild (ed.), *Marignano*

1515–2015 (Lenzburg, 2014), pp. 235–52. **30.** A. Oschmann, *Der Nürnberger Exekutionstag 1648–1650* (Münster, 1991); B.R. Kroener, '"Der Krieg hat ein Loch ..."' Überlegungen zum Schicksal demobilisierter Söldner nach dem Dreißigjährigen Krieg', in H. Duchhardt (ed.), *Der Westfälische Friede* (Munich, 1998), pp. 599–630. **31.** L. Pelizeaus; *Der Aufstieg Württembergs und Hessens zur Kurwürde 1692–1803* (Frankfurt am Main, 2000); B. Stollberg-Rilinger, *The emperor's new clothes: Constitutional history and the symbolic language of the Holy Roman Empire* (New York, 2015). **32.** P. Broucek, *Die Eroberung von Bregenz am 4. Jänner 1647* (Vienna, 1981). **33.** J. Stüssi-Lauterburg et al., *Verachtet Herrenpossen! Verschüchet fremde Gast! Der Bauernkrieg 1653* (Lenzburg, 2003). **34.** H.R. Fuhrer (ed.), *Villmerger Kriege 1656/1712* (Bern, 2005). **35.** R. Fester, *Die armirten Stände und die Reichskriegsverfassung, 1681–1697* (Frankfurt am Main, 1886). For an example of an armed prince, see A. Querengässer, *The Saxon Mars and his force: The Saxon army during the reign of John George III, 1680–1691* (Warwick, 2019). **36.** P.H. Wilson, *German armies: War and German politics, 1648–1806* (London, 1998), pp. 150–201. **37.** C. v. Jany, *Geschichte der Preußischen Armee vom 15. Jahrhundert bis 1914*, 4 vols. (Berlin, 1928–9), I, pp. 120–30. **38.** E. Opitz, *Österreich und Brandenburg im Schwedisch-Pölnischen Krieg* (Boppard, 1969). **39.** W. Kohl, *Christoph Bernhard von Galen* (Münster, 1964); C. Frhr. V. Bönninghausen, *Die Kriegerische Tätigkeit der münsterschen Truppen, 1651–1800* (Coesfeld, 1978). **40.** J. Bruser, *Reichsständische Libertät zwischen kaiserlichen Machtstreben und Französischen Hegemonie. Der Rheinbund von 1658* (Münster, 2019); R. Schnur, *Der Rheinbund von 1658* (Bonn, 1955). **41.** G. Wagner, 'Österreich und die Osmanen im Dreißigjährigen Krieg', *MIÖG*, 14 (1984), 325–92; M. Baramova, 'Non-splendid isolation: The Ottoman empire and the Thirty Years War', in O. Asbach and P. Schröder (eds.), *Ashgate research companion to the Thirty Years War* (Farnham, 2014), pp. 115–25; M.H. Cevrioglu, 'Ottoman foreign policy during the Thirty Years War', *Turcica*, 49 (2018), 195–235. **42.** F. Tóth, *Saint-Gotthard 1664* (Panazol, 2017); H. Forst, 'Die deutschen Reichstruppen im Türkenkrieg 1664', *MIÖG*, supplement 6 (1901), 634–48; A. v. Schempp, *Der Feldzug von 1664 in Ungarn* (Stuttgart, 1909); K. Peball, *Die Schlacht bei St-Gotthard-Mogersdorf, 1664* (Vienna, 1964); Wilson, *German armies*, pp. 38–43. **43.** E. Eickhoff, *Venedig, Wien und die Osmanen*, 2nd ed. (Munich, 1973), pp. 230–64; W. Kohlhaas, *Candia 1645–1669: Die tragödie einer abendländschen Verteidigung* (Osnabrück, 1978); B. Mugnai, *The Cretan War, 1645–1671* (Warwick, 2018). **44.** A. Schindling, *Die Anfänge des Immerwährenden Reichstag zu Regensburg* (Mainz, 1991). **45.** J. Lynn, *The Wars of Louis XIV, 1667–1714* (London, 1999). **46.** P. Sonnino, *Louis XIV and the origins of the Dutch War* (Cambridge, 1988); C.J. Ekberg, *The failure of Louis XIV's Dutch War* (Chapel Hill, NC, 1979). For German military involvement, see Wilson, *German armies*, pp. 44–57. **47.** O. v. Nijmegen, *The Dutch army and the Military Revolutions, 1588–1688* (Woodbridge, 2010), pp. 438–513; A. Koller, *Die Vermittlung des Friedens von Vossem (1673)* (Münster, 1995). **48.** Jany, *Preußischen Armee*, I, pp. 240–4. **49.** O. Chalines, *Les armées du roi* (Paris, 2016), pp. 153–63. **50.** F.L. Ford, *Strasbourg in transition, 1648–1789* (Cambridge, MA, 1958), pp. 28–54; K.O. Frhr v. Aretin, *Das alte Reich 1648–1806*, 4 vols. (Stuttgart, 1993–2000), I, pp. 273–80. **51.** For this and the following, see G. Rapp and V. Hofer, *Von den Anfängen bis zum Sonderbundskrieg* (Basel, 1983), pp. 34–40, and the contributions by A. Riklin and J. Stüssi–Lauterburg in Haudenreich (ed.), *Marignano*. **52.** M. Bundi, *Bünder Kriegsdienste in Holland um 1700* (Chur, 1972); R. Gugger, *Preußische Werbungen in der Eidgenossenschaft im 18. Jahrhundert* (Berlin, 1997); G. Calleja Leal (ed.), *Presencia suiza en la milicia española* (Madrid, 2017). **53.** H. Angermeier, 'Die Reichskriegsverfassung in der Politik der Jahre 179-1681', *ZSRG*, 82 (1965), 190–222; Aretin, *Das alte Reich*, I, 280–301. **54.** P.H. Wilson, 'The Holy Roman Empire and the problem of the armed Estates', in P. Rauscher (ed.), *Kriegführung und Staatsfinanzen. Die Habsburgermonarchie und das Heilige Römische Reich vom Dreißigjährigen Krieg bis zum Ende des habsburgischen*

Kaisertums 1740 (Münster, 2010), pp. 487–514. For the legal arrangements more generally, see *NTSR*, XVI. **55.** E.R. Huber, *Heer und Staat in der deutschen Geschichte*, 2nd ed. (Hamburg, 1943), pp. 72–84 (quote at p. 84). Similar negative assessments in H. Weigel, *Die Kriegsverfassung des alten deutschen Reiches von der Wormser Matrikel bis zur Auflösung* (Bamberg, 1912); A.G.W. Kohlhepp, *Die Militärverfassung des deutschen Reiches zur Zeit des Siebenjährigen Krieges* (Greifswald, 1914). For more nuanced discussions of how it worked in practice, see P.C. Storm, *Der schwäbische Kreis als Feldherr* (Berlin, 1974); J.A. Vann, *The Swabian Kreis: Institutional growth in the Holy Roman Empire, 1648–1715* (Brussels, 1975); B. Sicken, *Das Wehrwesen des fränkischen Reichskreises* (Nuremberg, 1967). **56.** J.W. Stoye, *The siege of Vienna* (London, 1964); T.M. Barker, *Double eagle and crescent: Vienna's second Turkish siege and its historical setting* (Albany, NY, 1967); I. Parvev, *Habsburgs and Ottomans between Vienna and Belgrade, 1683–1739* (New York, 1995); P. Broucek et al., *Der Sieg bei Wien* (Vienna, 1983). **57.** Details in Wilson, *German armies*, pp. 68–86. **58.** L. Schwoerer (ed.), *The revolution of 1688: Changing perspectives* (Cambridge, 1992); C. Kampmann, 'The English crisis, Emperor Leopold I, and the origins of Dutch intervention in 1688', *HJ*, 55 (2012), 521–32; S. Oakley, *William III and the Northern crowns during the Nine Years War* (London, 1987); D. Onnekink, *The Anglo-Dutch favourite: The career of Hans Willem Bentinck, First Earl of Portland (1649–1709)* (Aldershot, 2007), pp. 40–52; J. Stapleton, 'Forging a coalition army: William III, the Grand Alliance and the confederate army in the Spanish Netherlands, 1688–1697' (PhD thesis, Ohio State University, 2003). **59.** Details in Wilson, *German armies*, pp. 87–100. **60.** C. Paoletti, *William III's Italian ally: Piedmont and the War of the League of Augsburg, 1683–1697* (Solihull, 2019). **61.** C. Kampmann, 'Reichstag und Reichskriegserklärung im Zeitalter Ludwigs XIV', *HJb*, 113 (1993), 41–59. **62.** M. Plassmann, *Krieg und Defension am Oberrhein. Die vorderen Reichskreis und Markgraft Ludwig Wilhelm von Baden (1693–1707)* (Berlin, 2000). **63.** D. Hohrath and C. Rehm (eds.), *Zwischen Sonne und Halbmond. Der Türkenlouis als Barockfürst und Feldherr* (Rastatt, 2005). **64.** L. v. Sichart, *Geschichte der königlichen hannoverschen Armee*, 5 vols. (Hanover, 1866–71), I, pp. 592–610, II, p. 68; G. Schnath, *Geschichte Hannovers im Zeitalter der neunten Kur und der englischen Sukzession 1674–1714*, 5 vols. (Hildesheim, 1938–82), I, pp. 597–642. **65.** T. Sharp, *Pleasure and ambition: The life, loves and wars of Augustus the Strong* (London, 2001); P. Haake, 'Die Türkenfeldzug Augusts des Starken 1695 und 1696', *NASG*, 24 (1903), 134–54. **66.** M. Braubach, *Prince Eugen von Savoyen*, 5 vols. (Munich, 1963–5), I, pp. 258–60. **67.** A. Querengässer, *Das kursächsische Militär im Großen Nordischen Krieg 1700–1717* (Paderborn, 2019). **68.** P. Wick, *Versuche zur Errichtung des Absolutismus in Mecklenburg in der ersten Hälfte des 18. Jahrhunderts* (Berlin, 1964); G. Tessin, *Mecklenburgsiches Militär in Türken- und Franzosenkriegen, 1648–1718* (Cologne, 1966). **69.** W. Mediger, *Mecklenburg, Russland und England-Hannover, 1706–21*, 2 vols. (Hildesheim, 1967). **70.** M. Pohlig and M. Schaich (eds.), *The War of the Spanish Succession: New perspectives* (Oxford, 2018); Wilson, *German armies*, pp. 101–29. **71.** F. Göse, *Friedrich I. (1657–1713): Ein König in Preußen* (Regensburg, 2012), pp. 202–60; A. Schwencke, *Geschichte der Hannoverschen Truppen im Spanischen Erbfolgekrieg* (Hanover, 1862). **72.** J. Albareda Salvadó, *La Guerra de Sucessión en España (1700–1714)* (Barcelona, 2010); F. Garcia Gonzáles (ed.), *La Guerra de Sucessión en España y la Batalla de Almansa* (Madrid, 2009). **73.** F. Theuer, *Brennendes Land. Kuruzzenkriege* (Vienna, 1984); G. Pálffy, *Hungary between two empires, 1526–1711* (Bloomington, IN, 2021), pp. 231–40. For Habsburg policy, see M. Hochedlinger, *Austria's wars of emergence, 1683–1797* (Harlow, 2003), pp. 174–93. **74.** *Die Schlacht bei Höchstädt*, special issue of *Jahrbuch des Historischen Vereins Dillingen an der Donau*, 105 (2004). **75.** R.S Giachino et al. (eds.), *Torino 1706: 300 anni dall' assedio e dalla battaglia di Torino* (Turin, 2006). **76.** R. de Bruin and M. Brinkman (eds.), *Peace was made here: The* *treaties of Utrecht, Rastatt and Baden, 1713–1714* (Petersberg, 2013). **77.** H. Duchhardt, *'Balance of power' und Pentarchie, 1700–1785* (Leiden, 1997).

5. Permanent Armies

1. J. Brown and J.H. Elliott, *A palace for a king: The Buen Retiro and the court of Philip IV* (New Haven, CT, 1980); P. Burke, *Fabrication of Louis XIV* (New Haven, CT, 1994); C. Mukerji, *Territorial ambitions and the gardens of Versailles* (Cambridge, 1997). **2.** J.H. Elliott and L. Brockliss (eds.), *The world of the favourite* (New Haven, CT, 1999); M. Kaiser and A. Pecar (eds.), *Der zweite Mann im Staat* (Berlin, 2003). **3.** T. Helfferich, *The iron princess: Amalia Elisabeth and the Thirty Years War* (Cambridge, MA, 2013). **4.** M. Junkelmann, 'Tilly: Eine Karriere im Zeitalter der Religionskriege und die "Militärischen Revolution"', in P.C. Hartmann and F. Schuller (eds.), *Der Dreißigjährige Krieg*, 2nd ed. (Regensburg, 2018), pp. 59–79; M. Kaiser, *Politik und Kriegführung: Maximilian von Bayern, Tilly und die Katholische Liga im Dreißigjährigen Krieg* (Münster, 1999), pp. 16–56. **5.** T. Brockmann, *Dynastie, Kaiseramt und Konfession* (Paderborn, 2011), pp. 236–7; Kaiser, *Politik und Kriegführung*, pp. 252–3. **6.** P. Suvanto, *Wallenstein und seine Anhänger am Wiener Hof zur Zeit des zweiten Generalats, 1631–1634* (Helsinki, 1963), pp. 32–41; M. Ritter, 'Die Kontributionssystem Wallensteins', *HZ*, 90 (1903), 193–249 at 203–9; F. Konze, *Die Stärke, Zusammensetzung und Verteilung der Wallensteinischen Armee während des Jahres 1633* (Bonn, 1906), pp. 10–12. **7.** C. Kampmann, *Reichsrebellion und kaiserliche Acht* (Münster, 1992); H. Ritter v. Srbik, *Wallensteins Ende*, 2nd ed. (Slazburg, 1952). Contemporary accounts in A.E.J. Hollaender, 'Some English documents on the end of Wallenstein', *Bulletin of the John Rylands Library Manchester*, 40 (1957–8), 359–90; G. Irmer (ed.), *Die Verhandlungen Schwedens und seiner Verbündeten mit Wallenstein und dem Kaiser*, 3 vols. (Stuttgart, 1888–91), III, pp. 286–96. **8.** For this and the following, R. Rebitsch, *Matthias Gallas (1588–1647)* (Münster, 2008); P. Broucek, 'Erzherzog Leopold Wilhelm und der Oberbefehl über das kaiserliche Heer im Jahre 1645', *Schriften des Heeresgeschichtliches Museum in Wien*, 4 (1969), 7–38; M. Hengerer, *Kaiser Ferdinand III. (1608–1657)* (Vienna, 2014), pp. 126–8, 219–20, 250; R. Rebitsch et al., *1648: Kriegführung und Friedensverhandlungen. Prag und das Ende des Dreißigjährigen Krieges* (Innsbruck, 2018), pp. 49–50, 89–94. **9.** G. Rowlands, *The dynastic state and the army under Louis XIV: Royal service and private interest, 1661–1701* (Cambridge, 2002). **10.** F. Göse, *Otto Christoph Freiherr von Sparr 1605–1668* (Berlin, 2006). **11.** Rebitsch, *Gallas*, pp. 241–50; E. Höfer, *Das Ende des Dreißigjährigen Krieges* (Cologne, 1998), pp. 69–73; O. Hackl, *Die Vorgeschichte, Gründung und frühe Entwicklung der Generalstäbe Österreichs, Bayerns und Preußens* (Osnabrück, 1997), pp. 41–8; H. Salm, *Armeefinanzierung im Dreißigjährigen Krieg* (Münster, 1990), pp. 93–5, 182–5. **12.** H.J. Arendt, *Wallensteins Faktotum. Der kaiserliche Feldmarschall Heinrich Holk (1599–1633)* (Ludwigsfelde, 2006). **13.** M. Fredholm von Essen, *The lion from the north: The Swedish army during the Thirty Years War*, vol. I, *1618–1632* (Warwick, 2020), pp. 227–33; M. Pohlig, *Marlboroughs Geheimnis: Strukturen und Funktionen der Informationsgewinnung im Spanischen Erbfolgekrieg* (Cologne, 2016). **14.** K. Saito, *Das Kriegskommissariat der bayerisch-logistischen Armee während des Dreißigjährigen Krieges* (Göttingen, 2020). For Traun, see P. Hoyos, 'Die kaiserliche Armee 1648–1650', *Schriften des Heeresgeschichtlichen Museums in Wien*, 7 (1976), 169–232. **15.** HSAS, A202 Bü.2189. **16.** C. v. Jany, *Geschichte der Preußischen Armee*, 4 vols. (Berlin, 1928–9), I, p. 54; R. Weber, *Würzburg und Bamberg im Dreißigjährigen Krieg* (Würzburg, 1979), p. 220. **17.** M. Raeff, *The well-ordered police state* (New Haven, CT, 1983). Further discussion in P.H. Wilson, *From Reich to revolution: German history, 1558–1806* (Basingstoke, 2004), pp. 234–89. **18.** F. Redlich,

The German military enterpriser and his workforce, 2 vols. (Wiesbaden, 1964–6), I, pp. 205–10. **19.** W. Krüssmann, *Ernst von Mansfeld (1580–1626)* (Berlin, 2010). **20.** Patents and other relevant documents printed in G. Lorenz (ed.), *Quellen zur Geschichte Wallensteins* (Darmstadt, 1987), pp. 84–94, 97–8. See also J. Kollmann, *Valdštein a Evropská politika* (Prague, 1999), pp. 72–6. See generally also J. Polišenský and J. Kollmann, *Wallenstein* (Cologne, 1997). **21.** H. Wertheim, *Der tolle Halberstädter* (Berlin, 1929); A. Ackermann, 'Vom Feldherrn zum regierenden Fürsten? Optionen im Reich und in Europa für Herzog Bernhard von Weimar und die Ernestiner', in M. Rohrschneider and A. Tischer (eds.), *Dynamik durch Gewalt?* (Münster, 2018), pp. 207–27. **22.** J. Kollmann, *Valdštejnů konec: Historie 2. generalátu 1631–1634* (Prague, 2001), pp. 28–34. See generally E. Fučíkova et al., *Waldstein: Albrecht von Waldstein – Inter arma silent musae?* (Prague, 2007). **23.** P.H. Wilson, *Europe's tragedy: The Thirty Years War* (London, 2009), p. 395. **24.** A. Ernstberger, *Hans de Witte, Finanzmann Wallensteins* (Wiesbaden, 1954), esp. p. 216. **25.** M. Hengerer, *Kaiserhof und Adel in der Mitte des 17. Jahrhunderts* (Konstanz, 2004); J. Krebs, *Aus dem Leben des kaiserlichen Feldmarschalls Grafen Melchior von Holzapfel* (Breslau, 1926), pp. 95–6, 205. **26.** K. Staudinger, *Geschichte des kurbayerischen Heeres*, 5 vols. (Munich, 1901–9), I, p. 395; F. Schirmer, *Nec aspera terrent! Eine Heereskunde der hannoverschen Armee* (Hanover, 1929), pp. 50, 57. See generally H. Meier-Welcker (ed.), *Untersuchungen zur Geschichte des Offizierskorps* (Stuttgart, 1962), pp. 38–92. **27.** G. Knüppel, *Das Heerwesen des Fürstentums Schleswig-Holstein-Gottorf, 1600–1715* (Neumünster, 1972), pp. 184–93. **28.** P.M. Hahn, 'Aristokatisierung und Professionalisierung: Der Aufstieg der Obristen zu einer militärischen und höfischen Elite in Brandenburg-Preußen von 1650–1720', *FBPG*, NS 1 (1991), 161–208; Jany, *Preußische Armee*, I, pp. 193, 206; A. v. Pfister, 'Das Regiment zu Fuß Alt-Württemberg im kaiserlichen Dienst auf Sizilien in den Jahren 1719 bis 1720', *BMWB*, 5 und 6 (1885), 157–268, at 187, 205, 236. **29.** Overviews of recruitment methods in Redlich, *Enterpriser*, II, pp. 170–267; M. Füssel, 'Stehende Söldner-Heere? Europäische Rekrutierungspratiken im Vergleich (1648–1789)', in K. v. Greyerz et al. (eds.), *Soldgeschäfte, Klientelismus, Korruption in der Frühen Neuzeit* (Göttingen, 2018), pp. 259–78; P.H. Wilson, 'The politics of military recruitment in eighteenth-century Germany', *EHR*, 117 (2002), 536–68. Detailed studies include R. Harms, 'Landmiliz und stehendes Heer in Kurmainz namentlich im 18. Jahrhundert', *Archiv für hessische Geschichte und Alterumskunde*, NS 6 (1909), 359–430; R. v. Schroetter, 'Die Ergänzung des preußischen Heeres unter dem ersten Könige', *FBPG*, 23 (1910), 81–145; W. Thum, *Die Rekrutierung der sächsischen Armee unter August dem starken (1694–1733)* (Leipzig, 1912). **30.** See W. Schüssler, 'Das Werbewesen in der Reichsstadt Heilbronn, vornehmlich im 19. Jahrhundert' (PhD, University of Tübingen, 1951), pp. 247–50; W. Thensius, *Die Anfänge des stehenden Heerwesens in Kursachsen unter Johann Georg III. und Johann Georg IV* (Leipzig, 1912), pp. 65–6. **31.** M. Hochedlinger, *Austria's wars of emergence, 1683–1797* (Harlow, 2003), pp. 105–11; *HDM*, III, 96–8. Much useful material on the militia is printed in E. v. Frauenholz, *Das Heerwesen in der Zeit des Dreißigjährigen Krieges*, 2 vols. (Munich, 1938–9), II. For the following, see also H. Schnitter, *Volk und Landesdefension* (Berlin, 1977). **32.** Weber, *Würzburg und Bamberg*, esp. 227–8 **33.** H.T. Gräf, 'Landesdefension, Miliz, Solddienst und stehendes Heer – (personelle) Schnittstellen am Beispiel der Landgrafschaft Hessen-Kassel im 17. Jahrhundert', in P. Rogger and R. Schmid (eds.), *Miliz oder Söldner?* (Paderborn, 2019), pp. 233–50. **34.** Examples in H. Caspary, *Staat, Finanzen, Wirtschaft und Heerwesen im Hochstift Bamberg (1672–1693)* (Bamberg, 1976), pp. 321–2; Thensius, *Anfänge*, pp. 62–4; E. Hagen, 'Die fürstlich würzburgische Hausinfanterie von ihren Anfängen bis zum Beginne des Siebenjährigen Krieges 1636–1756', *DBKH*, 19 (1910), 69–203 at 94–6; H.G. Böhme, *Die Wehrverfassung in Hessen-Kassel im 18. Jahrhundert bis zum Siebenjährigen Kriege* (Kassel, 1954), pp. 11–17 **35.** J. Nowosadtko, *Stehendes Heer im Ständestaat. Das Zusammenleben von Militär- und Zivilbevölkerung im Fürstbistum Münster, 1650–1803*

(Paderborn, 2011), pp. 293–4; H. Eichberg, *Festung, Zentralmacht und Sozialgeometrie* (Cologne, 1989), pp. 493–6. **36.** HSAS, A202 Bü.2278. **37.** *Doc Bo*, IV, pp. 414–46; Konze, *Wallensteinischen Armee*, pp. 9, 46–7, 51. The following statistics also draw on D. Pleiss, *Bodenständige Bevölkerung und fremdes Kriegsvolk. Finnen in deutschen Quartieren, 1630–1650* (Turku, 2017), pp. 337–8; L. Stiano-Daniels, 'Determining early modern army strengths: The case of electoral Saxony', *JMilH*, 79 (2019), 523–56, and Wilson, *Europe's tragedy* and the sources cited there. **38.** R. Frost, *The Northern wars: War, state and society in northeastern Europe, 1558–1721* (Harlow, 2000), pp. 139–42; G. Tessin, *Die Regimenter der europäischen Staaten im 'Ancien Régime' des XVI. bis XVIII. Jahrhunderts* (Osnabrück, 1986), pp. 159–60, 337, 343–4; S. Murdoch, *Britain, Denmark-Norway and the House of Stuart, 1603–1660* (East Linton, 2003), pp. 203–15. **39.** More detailed numbers for all German forces, 1650–1790, can be found in Wilson, *Reich to revolution*, pp. 227–8. **40.** Konze, *Wallensteinischen Armee*, pp. 14, 40–2; J. Heilmann, *Das Kriegswesen der kaiserlichen und Schweden zur Zeit des Dreißigjährigen Krieges* (Leipzig, 1850), pp. 1–3; P. Engerisser, *Von Kronach nach Nördlingen* (Weißenstadt, 2004), p. 503. **41.** J.J. v. Wallhausen, *Kriegskunst zu Fuß* (Oppenheim, 1615), p. 97. **42.** H. Kleinschmidt, *Tyrocinium militare. Militärische Körperhaltungen und -bewegungen im Wandel zwischen dem 14. und dem 18. Jahrhundert* (Stuttgart, 1983), p. 111. **43.** C. Beaufort-Spontin, *Harnisch und Waffe Europas. Die militärische Ausrüstung im 17. Jahrhundert* (Munich, 1982), pp. 95–142. For the following discussion of weaponry and tactics see also O. Groehler, *Das Heerwesen* (Berlin, 1993); H. Müller, *Die Bewaffnung* (Berlin, 1991); E. Wagner, *European weapons and warfare 1618–1648* (London, 1979); J.A. Meier, 'Halbarte oder Bajonett? Zur Vorgeschichte des bernischen Sieges in der 2. Schlacht bei Villmergen 1712', *Waffen- und Kostümkunde*, 47 (2005), 43–82. **44.** P.H. Wilson, *Lützen* (Oxford, 2018). **45.** A. Schürger, 'The archaeology of the battle of Lützen' (PhD, University of Glasgow, 2015), p. 157; L. Spring, *In the emperor's service: Wallenstein's army, 1625–1634* (Warwick, 2019), p. 65. **46.** The various mechanisms and their development are nicely illustrated in J.P. Puype and M. van der Hoeven (eds.), *The arsenal of the world: The Dutch arms trade in the seventeenth century* (Amsterdam, 1996), pp. 71–5. **47.** Calculated from *Doc Bo*, IV, 414–46. **48.** Jany, *Preußischen Armee*, I, pp. 300–1. **49.** C. Tepperberg, 'Das kaiserliche Heer nach dem Prager Frieden 1635–1650', in *Der Schwed ist im Land!* (Horn, 1995), pp. 113–39 at 121–2. **50.** Heilmann, *Kriegswesen*, pp. 34–40. **51.** W.P. Guthrie, *The later Thirty Years War* (Westport, CT, 2003), pp. 252–3. **52.** For possible explanations, see Beaufort-Spontin, *Harnisch*, p. 85. **53.** J.J. v. Wallhausen, *Kriegskunst zu Pferd* (Frankfurt am Main, 1616), pp. 39–41; Müller, *Bewaffnung*, p. 72. **54.** J.C. Allmayer-Beck and E. Lessing, *Die kaiserlichen Kriegsvölker, 1479–1718* (Munich, 1978), pp. 237–8. **55.** M. Weise, 'Gewaltprofis und Kriegsprofiteure: Kroatische Söldner als Gewaltunternehmer im Dreißigjährigen Krieg', *GWU*, 68 (2017), 278–91; D. Stanic, 'Who were these "terrible Croats"? On the origins of Croatian soldiers in the Thirty Years War', unpublished paper, Zagreb, 10 April 2018. **56.** G. Somogyi, *Warriors of the Hungarian frontier, 1526–1683* (Zrínyi Kiadó, 2014). **57.** I. Czigány, *Reform vagy kudarc? Kíserletek a magyarországi katonság beillesztésére a Habsburg Birodalom haderejébe 1600–1700* (Budapest, 2004). **58.** R. Boissau, *Histoire des Hussards de l'ancien régime* (Paris, 2017); C. Kapser, *Die bayerische Kriegsorganisation in der zweiten Hälfte des Dreißigjährigen Krieges 1635–1648/49* (Münster, 1997), p. 223. **59.** E. v. Warnery, *Remarks on cavalry* (London, 1791), pp. xix–xx, 4–6. **60.** L.I. v. Stadlinger, *Geschichte des württembergischen Kriegswesens* (Stuttgart, 1856), pp. 277, 577; U. Crämer, 'Die Wehrmacht Strassburgs von der Reformationszeit bis zum Fall der Reichsstadt', *ZGO*, 84 (1931), 46–95 at 74. **61.** Heilmann, *Kriegswesen*, p. 61. **62.** S. Bull, *The Furie of the Ordnance: Artillery in the English Civil Wars* (Woodbridge, 2008), p. 25; P. Englund, *Die Verwüstung Deutschlands. Eine Geschichte des Dreißigjährigen Krieges* (Stuttgart, 1998), pp. 424–5. **63.** O. Schuster and F.A. Francke, *Geschichte der sächsischen Armee*, 3 vols.

(Leipzig, 1883), I, p. 17; Tepperberg, 'Das kaiserliche Heer', p. 136; Groehler, *Heerwesen*, p. 92. **64.** J. Ehlers, *Die Wehrverfassung der Stadt Hamburg im 17. und 18. Jahrhundert* (Boppard, 1966); E. Padjera, 'Die bastionäre Befestigung von Frankfurt am Main', *Archiv für Frankfurts Geschichte und Kunst*, 3rd series, 12 (1920), 230–303; F. Willax, 'Das Verteidigungswesen Nürnbergs im 17. und 18. Jahrhundert', *Mitteilungen des Vereins für Geschichte der Stadt Nürnberg*, 66 (1979), 192–247; E.P. Kahlenberg, *Kurmainzische Verteidigungseinrichtungen und Baugeschichte der Festung Mainz* (Mainz, 1963), pp. 104–16. **65.** A. Veltzé, 'Die Wiener Stadtguardia', *MIÖG*, supplement 6 (1901), 530–46. **66.** Y. Mintzker, *The defortification of the German city, 1689–1866* (Cambridge, 2012), pp. 86–7. **67.** H. Schmidt, 'Die Verteidigung des Oberrheins und die Sicherung Süddeutschlands im Zeitalter des Absolutismus und der französichen Revolution', *HJb*, 104 (1984), 46–62; K. Lang, *Die Ettlinger Linien* (Ettlingen, 1965). **68.** P. Padfield, *Guns at sea* (London, 1973), pp. 71–83; A. Thrush, 'In pursuit of the frigate, 1603–40', *Historical Research*, 64 (1991), 29–45. A Brandenburg frigate from c. 1650 is illustrated in J. Wheatly and S. Howarth, *Historic sail: The glory of the sailing ship* (London, 2000), plate 72. **69.** J. Glete, *Navies and nations: Warships, navies and state building in Europe and America, 1500–1860* (Stockholm, 1993), pp. 173–212. **70.** O. Schmitz, *Die maritime Politik der Habsburger in den Jahren 1626–1628* (Bonn, 1903); R. Rodenas Villar, *La politica Europea de España durante la Guerra de Treinta Años (1624–1630)* (Madrid, 1967), pp. 83–92, 119–47; J. Alcala Zamora, *España, Flandres y el mar del Norte (1618–1639* (Barcelona, 1975), pp. 236–42, 267–82; E. Straub, *Pax und Imperium. Spaniens Kampf um seine Friedensordnung in Europa zwischen 1617 und 1635* (Paderborn, 1980), pp. 218–51, 288–314. For the following, see also M. Wanner, 'Albrecht of Wallenstein as "General of the Oceans and the Baltic Seas" and the northern maritime plan', *Forum Navale*, 64 (2008), 8–33; A.E. Sokol, *Das Habsburgische Admiralitätswerk des 16. und 17. Jahrhunderts* (Vienna, 1976), pp. 40–61. **71.** Brockmann, *Dynastie*, pp. 257–66, 303–10. **72.** W. Aichelburg, *Kriegsschiffe auf der Donau* (Vienna, 1982), pp. 12–15. **73.** K. Petsch, *Seefahrt für Brandenburg-Preussen 1650–1815* (Osnabrück, 1986), pp. 5–6. For the following see ibid, pp. 7–150; L. Huttl, *Friedrich Wilhelm von Brandenburg, der Große Kurfürst, 1620–1688* (Munich, 1981), pp. 296, 445–6. **74.** Jany, *Preußischen Armee*, I, pp. 224, 232, 248–50, 256, 259. **75.** A.V. Berkis, *The reign of Duke James in Courland, 1638–1682* (Lincoln, NE, 1960), pp. 62–80. **76.** C.F. Gaedechens, 'Hamburgs Kriegsschiffe', *Mitteilungen des Vereins für Hamburgische Geschichte*, NF 1 (1885), 115–26; Glete, *Navies and nations*, pp. 542–3. **77.** P. Bloesch, 'The Bernese navy, 1660–1690', *Mariner's Mirror*, 63 (1977), 9–23.

6. From Extraordinary to Ordinary Burden

1. L.H. Wüthrich, *Das druckgraphische Werk von Matthaeus Merian d. Ae.*, 3 vols. (Hamburg, 1993); P.H. Wilson and C. Gantet, 'Battles, images and cultures of remembrance in the Thirty Years War', in C. Denys et al. (eds.), *Le Champ de bataille après la bataille: Mémoires et usages* (Paris, 2022), forthcoming. **2.** H. Böning, *Dreißigjähriger Krieg und Öffentlichkeit* (Bremen, 2018). **3.** S. Friedrich, *Drehscheibe Regensburg: Das Informations- und Kommunikationssystem des Immerwährende Reichstags um 1700* (Berlin, 2007); K. Müller, *Das kaiserliche Gesandschaftswesen im Jahrhundert nach dem Westfälischen Frieden, 1648–1740* (Bonn, 1976). **4.** Examples include J.G. Kulpis, *Eines hochlöbl. Schwäbischen Crayses alte und neue kriegsverordnungen und Reglementen* (Stuttgart, 1737); J.C. Lünig (ed.), *Corpus juris militaris des Heiligen Römischen Reiches* (Leipzig, 1723). **5.** T.M. Barker, *The military intellectual and battle: Raimondo Montecuccoli and the Thirty Years War* (Albany, NY, 1975); J. Stoye, *Marsigli's Europe 1680–1730* (New Haven, CT, 1994). **6.** E. Heischmann, *Die Anfänge des stehenden Heeres in Österreich* (Vienna,

1925), pp. 210–13; O. Schuster and F.A. Francke, *Geschichte der sächsischen Armee*, 3 vols. (Leipzig, 1883), I, pp. 120–1; F.K. Tharau, *Die geistige Kultur des preußischen Offiziers von 1640 bis 1806* (Mainz, 1968), pp. 11–56. 7. Quoted in G. Rothenberg, 'Maurice of Nassau, Gustavus Adolphus, Montecuccoli and the "Military Revolution" of the seventeenth century', in P. Paret (ed.), *The makers of modern strategy* (Princeton, NJ, 1986), pp. 30–63 at 60–1. 8. P. Riley (ed.), *Leibniz: Political writings* (Cambridge, 1988), pp. 121–45. 9. B. Stollberg-Rilinger, *Der Staat als Maschine* (Berlin, 1986), pp. 86–8. 10. G. Mortimer, *Eyewitness accounts of the Thirty Years War, 1618–48* (Basingstoke, 2002); H. Medick, *Der Dreißigjährige Krieg: Zeugnisse vom Leben mit Gewalt* (Göttingen, 2018); M. Meumann and D. Neufänger (eds.), *Ein Schauplatz herber Angst: Wahrnehmung und Darstellung von Gewalt im 17. Jahrhundert* (Göttingen, 1997). 11. A. Bähr, *Der grausame Komet: Himmelszeichen und Weltgeschehen im Dreißigjährigen Krieg* (Reinbeck bei Hamburg, 2017); A. Geiger, *Wallensteins Astrologie* (Graz, 1983). 12. J. Thiebault, 'The rhetoric of death and destruction in the Thirty Years War', *Journal of Social History*, 27 (1993), 271–90. 13. K. Otto (ed.), *A companion to the works of Grimmelshausen* (London, 2003). 14. P.H. Wilson, 'Atrocities in the Thirty Years War', in M. O'Siochrú and J. Ohlmeyer (eds.), *Ireland 1641: Context and reactions* (Manchester, 2013), pp. 153–75; D. Wolfthal, 'Jacques Callot's *Miseries of War*', *The Art Bulletin*, 59 (1977), 222–33. 15. F. Redlich, *De praeda militari: Looting and booty, 1500–1800* (Wiesbaden, 1956), pp. 29–37; P.H. Wilson, 'Prisoners in early modern European warfare', in S. Scheipers (ed.), *Prisoners in War* (Oxford, 2010), pp. 39–56. 16. See for example the imperial-Danish cartel of 1626, printed in J. Heilmann, *Das Kriegswesen der kaiserlichen und Schweden zur Zeit des Dreißigjährigen Krieges* (Leipzig, 1850), pp. 270–1. 17. W. Thum, *Die Rekrutierung der sächsischen Armee unter August dem Starken (1694–1733)* (Leipzig, 1912), pp. 14–17, 25; Schuster and Francke, *Sächsischen Armee*, I, p. 191. 18. C. Kapser, *Die bayerische Kriegsorganisation in der zweiten Hälfte des Dreißigjährigen Krieges, 1635–1648/49* (Münster, 1997), pp. 64–74. 19. P.H. Wilson, *War, state, and society in Württemberg, 1677–1793* (Cambridge, 1995), pp. 115–22. 20. For a classic statement of this view, see E. v. Frauenholz, *Das Heerwesen in der Zeit des Dreißigjährigen Krieges*, 2 vols. (Munich, 1938–9), I, pp. 14–15. Further discussion in M. Sikora, 'Söldner: Historische Annährung an einen Kriegertypus', *Geschichte und Gesellschaft*, 29 (2003), 210–38. 21. N.M. Funke, 'Religion and the military in the Holy Roman Empire, c.1500–c.1650' (PhD, University of Sussex, 2012). 22. J. Pohl, '*Die Profiantirung der Keyserlichen Armaden ahnbelangendt*': *Studien zur Versorgung der kaiserlichen Armee, 1634/35* (Kiel, 1991), pp. 63–9, 100; B.A. Tlusty, *The martial ethic in early modern Germany* (Basingstoke, 2011), pp. 38–43. 23. P. Burschel, *Söldner im Nordwestdeutschland des 16. und 17. Jahrhunderts* (Göttingen, 1994), pp. 97, 183–92; F. Redlich, *The German military enterpriser and his workforce*, 2 vols. (Wiesbaden, 1964–5), II, pp. 241–58; H. Steffen, *Die Kompanien Kaspar Jodok Stockalpers: Das Beispiel eines Soldunternehmers im 17. Jahrhundert* (Brig, 1975). 24. T. Verspohl, *Das Heerwesen des münsterschen Fürstbischofs Christoph Bernhard von Galen 1650–1678* (Münster, 1908), p. 10. 25. B. Hitz, *Kämpfen um Sold. Eine Alltags- und Sozialgeschichte schweizerischer Söldner in der Frühen Neuzeit* (Cologne, 2015), p. 182. 26. G. Tessin, *Mecklenburgisches Militär in Türken- und Franzosenkriegen, 1648–1718* (Cologne, 1966), pp. 175–7; E. v. Frauenholz, *Die Eingliederung von Heer und Volk in den Staat in Bayern, 1597–1815* (Munich, 1940), pp. 14–15, 19. 27. D. Worthington, *Scots in Habsburg service, 1618–1648* (Leiden, 2004); R.D. FitzSimon, 'Irish swordsmen in the imperial service in the Thirty Years War', *Irish Sword*, 9 (1969–70), 22–31. 28. R. v. Schroetter, 'Das preussische Offizierskorps unter dem ersten Könige von Preussen', *FBPG*, 26 (1913), 429–97, and 27 (1914), 97–167 at 102–3; J.L. Garland, 'Irish officers in the Bavarian service in the War of Spanish Succession', *Irish Sword*, 14 (1981), 240–55. 29. Karl Staudinger, *Geschichte des kurbayerischen Heeres*, 5 vols. (Munich, 1901–9), I, pp. 137–8, 171, 213–15, 299; II, pp. 28–30; W. Thenius, *Die Anfänge des stehenden Heerwesens in Kursachsen unter Johann*

Georg III. und Johann Georg IV. (Leipzig, 1912), pp. 53–5.   30. Examples in M. Höchner, *Selbstzeugnisse von Schweizer Söldneroffizieren im 18. Jahrhundert* (Göttingen, 2015), pp. 33–5, 159–67; P. Rogger, 'Kompaniewirtschaft, Verflechtungszusammenhänge, familiale Unternehmensorganisation', in K. v. Greyerz et al. (eds.), *Soldgeschäfte, Klientelismus, Korruption in der Frühen Neuzeit* (Göttingen, 2018), pp. 211–37; F. Cojonnex, 'Entre parentèle et clientèle, l'example de la création et de l'apogée d'un reseau de solidarités: La famille de Chandieu au service de France (1640–1728)', in R. Jaun et al. (eds.), *Schweizer Solddienst* (Birmensdorf, 2010), pp. 123–38.   31. Kapser, *Bayerische Kriegsorganisation*, pp. 82–101; B. Sicken, *Das Wehrwesen des fränkischen Reichskreises* (Nuremberg, 1967), pp. 293–7; M. Kaiser, 'Cuius exercitus, eius religio? Konfession und Heerwesen im Zeitalter des Dreißigjährigen Krieges', *Archiv für Reformationsgeschichte*, 91 (2000), 316–53.   32. R. Chaboche, 'Les soldats français de la Guerre de Trente Ans', *Revue d'histoire moderne et contemporaine*, 20 (1973), 10–24 at 20; N. Nicklisch et al., 'The face of battle: Trauma analysis of a mass grave from the battle of Lützen (1632)', *PLOS One*, 12 (2017), 1–30.   33. F. Schirmer, *Nec aspera terrent! Eine Heereskunde der hannoverschen Armee* (Hanover, 1929), p.1.   34. For example, Schuster and Francke, *Sächsischen Armee*, I, pp. 142, 203–4.   35. E. Heischmann, *Die Anfänge des stehenden Heeres in Österreich* (Vienna, 1925), pp. 195–209   36. For example, T. Schwark, *Lübecks Stadtmilitär im 17. und 18. Jahrhundert* (Lübeck, 1990), pp. 128–44.   37. Reyscher, XIX/I, nos. 143ff.   38. B.R. Kroener, 'Soldat oder Soldateska?', in M. Messerschmidt et al. (eds.), *Militärgeschichte* (Stuttgart, 1982), pp. 100–23.   39. Burschel, *Söldner*, p. 319.   40. For the following, see L. Spring, *The Bavarian army during the Thirty Years War, 1618–1648* (Solihull, 2017), pp. 55–65; W. Kohlhaas, *Württembergische Uniformen von 1638 bis 1854* (Wuppertal, 1978); W. Friedrich, *Die Uniformen der Kurfürstlich Sächsischen Armee, 1683–1763* (Dresden, 1998); R. Hall, *Uniforms and flags of the armies of Hanover, Celle and Brunswick, 1670–1715* (Farnham, 2016); R. Hall and G. Boeri, *Uniforms and flags of the imperial Austrian army, 1683–1720* (Farnham, 2009); K.P. Merta, *Das Heerwesen in Brandenburg-Preußen von 1640 bis 1806*, vol. II (Berlin, 1991); C.P. Golberg and R. Hall, *The army of the electorate Platinate under Elector Johann Wilhelm, 1690–1716* (Farnham, 2004).   41. O. Elster, *Piccolomini-Studien* (Leipzig, 1911), p. 77.   42. Examples in J. Nowosadtko, *Stehendes Heer im Ständestaat. Das Zusammenleben von Militär- und Zivilbevölkerung im Fürstbistum Münster, 1650–1803* (Paderborn, 2011), pp. 1, 435; J. Dietz, *Memoirs of a mercenary* (London, 1987), p. 31.   43. O. Mayr, *Die schwedische Belagerung der Reichsstadt Lindau 1647* (Lindau, 2016).   44. Examples in O. Elster, *Geschichte der stehenden Truppen im Herzogtum Braunschweig-Wolfenbüttel*, 2 vols. (Leipzig, 1899–1901), I, p. 162; H. Streng, *Tuttlinger Geschichtsbuch* (Tuttlingen, 1962), p. 98.   45. P. Wentzcke, 'Düsseldorf als Garnisonsstadt', *Schriften des Hist. Museums und des Archivs der Stadt Düsseldorf*, 6 (1933), 1–15.   46. Bernhard of Sachsen-Weimar quoted in G. Droysen, *Bernhard von Weimar*, 2 vols. (Leipzig, 1885), II, p. 45.   47. J.J. Wallhausen, *Kriegskunst zu Fuß* (Frankfurt am Main, 1615), pp. 7, 16; Heilmann, *Kriegswesen*, p. 199; P. Engerisser, *Von Kronach nach Nördlingen* (Weißenstadt, 2004), pp. 505–15; G. Hanlon, *The hero of Italy: Orlando Farnese, Duke of Parma, his soldiers, and his subjects in the Thirty Years War* (Oxford, 2014), pp. 76–7, 155, 178.   48. N. Büsser, 'A family affair: Das Soldgeschäft als erbliches Verwandtschaftsunternehmen', in Jaun et al. (eds.), *Schweizer Solddienst*, pp. 105–22.   49. J. Peters (ed.), *Ein Söldnerleben im Dreißigjährigen Krieg* (Berlin, 1993), pp. 138, 145. See generally M.E. Ailes, *Courage and grief: Women and Sweden's Thirty Years War* (Lincoln, NE, 2018), pp. 17–58.   50. J.W. Huntebrinker, *"Fromme Knechte" und "Gartenteufel". Söldner als soziale Gruppe im 16. und 17. Jahrhundert* (Konstanz, 2010), pp. 93–4.   51. R. Pröve, *Stehendes Heer und städtische Gesellschaft im 18. Jahrhundert* (Munich, 1995), p. 114.   52. C. v. Jany, *Geschichte der Preußischen Armee*, 4 vols. (Berlin, 1928–9), I, p. 169.   53. Q. Outram, 'The socio-econommic relations of warfare and the military mortality crises of the Thirty Years War', *Medical History*, 45 (2001), 151–84; E.A. Eckert, *The structure of plagues and pestilences in early modern Europe* (Basel, 1996); R.J.G. Concannon, 'The third enemy: The role of epidemics in the Thirty Years War', *Journal of World History*, 10 (1967), 500–11. **54.** S. Eickhoff and F. Schopper (eds.), *Ihre letzte Schlacht. Leben im Dreißigjährigen Krieg* (Zossen, 2012), pp. 34–5, 94–5, 129. **55.** For this and the following see S. Riezler (ed.), 'Kriegstagebücher aus dem ligistischen Hauptquartier 1620', *Abhandlungen der Phil.-Hist. Klasse der Bayerischen Akademie der Wissenschaften*, 23 (1906), 77–210 at 84, 86–9, 109; Peters (ed.), *Söldnerleben*, pp. 117, 122; Burschel, *Söldner*, pp. 268–72; P. Lenihan, *Fluxes, fevers and fighting men: War and disease in ancien regime Europe, 1648–1789* (Warwick, 2019), pp. 81–91. **56.** Duke Eberhard Ludwig of Württemberg, 3 March 1704, HSAS, A202 Bü.2284, and 18 April 1716 in Reyscher, XIX/I, no. 303. **57.** HSAS, A202 Bü.2284; L6.22.6.38. See generally O. Breitenbücher, *Die Entwicklung des württembergischen Militärversorgungswesens nach dem Dreißigjährigen Krieg bis zum 1871* (Tübingen, 1936); C.H. Colshorn, *Die Hospitalkassen der hannoverschen Armee. Ein Vorläufer der Sozialversicherung seit 1680* (Hildesheim, 1970). **58.** P.H. Wilson, 'Was the Thirty Years War a "Total War"?', in E. Rosenhaft, E. Charters, and H. Smith (eds.), *Civilians and war in Europe, 1640–1815* (Liverpool, 2012), pp. 21–35. **59.** S.H. Steinberg, 'The Thirty Years War: A new interpretation', *History*, 32 (1947), 89–102. He presented his arguments in book form in 1966. For the following see J. Thiebault, 'The demography of the Thirty Years War revisited', *GH*, 15 (1997), 1–21; Q. Outram, 'The demographic impact of early modern warfare', *Social Science History*, 26 (2002), 245–72; W. v. Hippel, *Das Herzogtum Württemberg zur Zeit des Dreißigjährigen Krieges im Spiegel von Steuer- und Kriegsschadensberichten, 1629–1655* (Stuttgart, 2009), pp. 11–29. **60.** D. McKay, *The Great Elector: Frederick William of Brandenburg-Prussia* (Harlow, 2001), p. 71. **61.** T. Winkelbauer, *Ständefreiheit und Fürstenmacht*, 2 vols. (Vienna, 2003), I, p. 14; M. Cerman, 'Bohemia after the Thirty Years War', *Journal of Family History*, 19 (1994), 149–75. Fuller discussion of this and the following in P.H. Wilson, *Europe's tragedy: The Thirty Years War* (London, 2009), pp. 779–821. **62.** Eickhoff and Schopper, *Letzte Schlacht*, pp. 28, 153; H. Conrad and G. Teske (eds.), *Sterbezeiten: Der Dreißigjährigen Krieg im Herzogtum Westfalen* (Münster, 2000), pp. 57–60. **63.** M. Sjöberg, 'Transformation into manhood: Sex, violence, and the making of warriors, women, and victims in early modern Europe', in P. Haldén and P. Jackson (eds.), *Transforming warriors* (London, 2016), pp. 88–108; J. Thiebault, 'Landfrauen, Soldaten und Vergewaltigungen während des Dreißigjährigen Krieges', *Werkstatt Geschichte*, 19 (1998), 25–39; J. Kilian, 'Military violence in towns during the Thirty Years War', *Studia Historica Nitriensia*, 22 (2018), 79–103 at 90–2; M.A. Junius, 'Bamberg im Schwedenkrieg', *Bericht des Historischen Vereins zu Bamberg*, 53 (1891), 169–230 at 213. For soldiers' involvement in sexual violence later in the seventeenth century, see M. Lorenz, *Das Rad der Gewalt* (Cologne, 2007), pp. 207–18. **64.** H. Musall and A. Scheuerbrandt, 'Die Kriege im Zeitalter XIV. und ihre Auswirkungen auf die Siedlungs-, Bevölkerungs- und Wirtschaftstruktur der Oberrheinlande', in H. Eichler (ed.), *Hans Graul Festschrift* (Heidelberg, 1974), pp. 357–78; E. Dosquet, 'Between positional warfare and small war: Soldiers and civilians in the "Devastation of the Palatinate" (1688–89)', in A. Dowdall and J. Horne (eds.), *Civilians under siege* (London, 2018), pp. 109–36; J. Luh, *Ancien regime warfare and the Military Revolution* (Groningen, 2000), pp. 48–65; P.H. Wilson, 'Financing the War of the Spanish Succession in the Holy Roman Empire', in M. Pohlig and M. Schaich (eds.), *The War of the Spanish Succession: New Perspectives* (Oxford, 2018), pp. 267–97 at 273–4. **65.** R.R. Heinisch, *Paris Graf Lodron: Reichsfürst und Erzbischof von Salzburg* (Vienna, 1991), pp. 101, 111. See generally P.H. Wilson, 'War finance, policy and strategy in the Thirty Years War', in M. Rohrschneider and A. Tischer (eds.), *Dynamik durch Gewalt? Der Dreißigjährige Krieg (1618–1648) als Faktor der Wandlungsprozesse des 17. Jahrhunderts* (Münster, 2018), pp. 229–50; Pohl, *Profiantirung*, pp. 90–144. **66.** F. Schulze, *Die Reichskreise im Dreißigjährigen Krieg* (Berlin, 2018), pp. 99–276. **67.** K.R. Böhme, 'Lennart Torstensson und Helmut Wrangel in Schleswig-Holstein und Jutland 1643–1645', *Zeitschrift der Gesellschaft für Schleswig-Holsteinische Geschichte*, 90 (1965), 41–82 at 82. **68.** U. Schirmer, *Kursächsische Staatsfinanzen (1456–1656)* (Stuttgart, 2006); C. Hattenhauer, *Schuldenregulierung nach dem Westfälischen Frieden* (Frankfurt am Main, 1998). **69.** P. Baumgart (ed.), *Ständetum und Staatsbildung in Brandenburg-Preußen* (Berlin, 1983). **70.** G. Ammerer et al. (eds.), *Bündnispartner und Konkurrenten der Landesfürsten? Die Stände in der Habsburgermonarchie* (Vienna, 2007); B. Höll, *Hofkammerpäsident Gundaker Thomas Graf Starhemberg und die österreichische Finanzpolitik der Barockzeit (1703–1715)* (Vienna, 1976). **71.** P.H. Wilson, 'The German "soldier trade" of the seventeenth and eighteenth centuries: A reassessment', *The International History Review*, 18 (1996), 757–92, and 'Financing', 292–3. **72.** S. Altorfer-Ong, 'State investment in eighteenth-century Berne', *History of European Ideas*, 33 (2007), 440–62 at 446, 448. **73.** T. Robisheaux, *Rural society and the search for order in early modern Germany* (Cambridge, 1989), p. 61. **74.** Examples in T. Klingebiel, *Ein Stand für sich? Lokale Amtsträger in der Frühen Neuzeit* (Hanover, 2002), pp. 189–211; U. Ludwig, 'Strafverfolgung und Gnadenpraxis in Kursachsen unter dem Eindruck des Dreißigjährigen Krieges', *Militär und Gesellschaft in der Frühen Neuzeit*, 10 (2006), 200–19; F. Kleinehagenbrock, *Die Grafschaft Hohenlohe im Dreißigjährigen Krieg* (Stuttgart, 2003). **75.** G. Pálffy, 'Kriegswirtschaftliche Beziehungen zwischen der Habsburgermonarchie und der ungarischen Grenze gegen die Osmanen in der ersten Hälfte des 16. Jahrhunderts', *Ungarn Jahrbuch*, 27 (2004), 17–40. See generally J. Zunckel, *Rüstungsgeschäfte im Dreißigjährigen Krieg* (Berlin, 1997). **76.** D. Cressy, *Saltpeter: The mother of gunpowder* (Oxford, 2013), pp. 12–35.

7. Habsburgs and Hohenzollerns

1. P.H. Wilson, 'Prussia and the Holy Roman Empire 1700–40', *Bulletin of the German Historical Institute London*, 36 (2014), 3–48. **2.** R. Hatton, *Diplomatic relations between Great Britain and the Dutch Republic, 1714–1721* (London, 1950); A.C. Carter, *Neutrality or commitment: The evolution of Dutch foreign policy, 1667–1795* (London, 1975). **3.** The numerous works on the future empress are surpassed by the magisterial biography by B. Stollberg-Rilinger, *Maria Theresa: The Habsburg empress in her time* (Princeton, NJ, 2022), which adds much new material on her relationship with her army and its generals. **4.** T. Hartwig, *Der Überfall der Grafschaft-Lippe durch Landgraf Wilhelm IX. von Hessen-Kassel* (Hanover, 1911). **5.** Fuller discussion of the latter point in P.H. Wilson, *The Holy Roman Empire: A thousand years of Europe's history* (London, 2016), pp. 603–54. For public order interventions, see M. Fimpel, *Reichsjustiz und Territorialstaat. Württemberg als Kommissar von Kaiser und Reich im Schwäbischen Kreis (1648–1806)* (Tübingen, 1999); M. Hughes, *Law and politics in eighteenth-century Germany* (Woodbridge, 1988); H.C. Peyer, *Verfassungsgeschichte der alten Schweiz* (Zürich, 1978), pp. 139–41. **6.** R. Graf v. Neipperg, *Kaiser und Schwäbischer Kreis (1714–1733)* (Stuttgart, 1991); P.C. Hartmann, *Geld als Instrument europäischer Machtpolitik im Zeitalter des Merkantilismus, 1715–1740* (Munich, 1978). **7.** I. Parvev, *Habsburgs and Ottomans between Vienna and Belgrade (1683–1739)* (Boulder, CO, 1995), pp. 168, 184. For the following, see J. Odenthal, *Österreichs Türkenkrieg, 1716–18* (Düsseldorf, 1938); *Feldzüge*, XVI and XVII; P.H. Wilson, *German armies: War and German politics, 1648–1806* (London, 1998), pp. 215–18. **8.** K. Roider, *Austria's eastern question, 1700–1790* (Princeton, NJ, 1982). For the following, see J.L. Sutton, *The king's honor and the king's cardinal: The War of the Polish Succession* (Lexington, KY, 1980); M. Hochedlinger, *Austria's wars of emergence, 1683–1797* (Harlow, 2003), pp. 208–12. **9.** M. Köster, *Russische Truppen für Prinz Eugen* (Vienna, 1986). **10.** K. Roider, *The reluctant ally: Austria's policy in the Austro-Turkish War, 1737–1739* (Baton Rouge, LA, 1972); L. Cassels, *The struggle for the*

Ottoman empire, 1717-1740 (London, 1966); C. Duffy, *Russia's military way to the west* (London, 1981), pp. 44-54; P.H. Wilson, *German armies: War and German politics, 1648-1806* (London, 1998), pp. 234-40. 11. E. Lund, *War for the everyday: Generals, knowledge and warfare in early modern Europe, 1680-1740* (Westport, CT, 1999), pp. 168-87. 12. For a good summary of the debates on Frederick 'the Great' in German history, see P.M. Hahn, *Friedrich der Große und die deutsche Nation* (Stuttgart, 2007). 13. J. Kunisch, *Friedrich der Große* (Munich, 2004); A. Storring, 'Frederick the Great and the meanings of war, 1730-1755 (PhD, University of Cambridge, 2018). 14. M.S. Anderson, *The War of the Austrian Succession, 1740-1748* (London, 1995); R. Browning, *The War of the Austrian Succession* (New York, 1993). Habsburg policy is covered also by Hochedlinger, *Austria's wars*, pp. 246-64, while Prussia's involvement can be followed in D.E. Showalter, *The wars of Frederick the Great* (London, 1996), pp. 38-89. For a sound guide to international relations in this period, see H.M. Scott, *The birth of a great power system, 1740-1815* (Harlow, 2006). 15. P.C. Hartmann, *Karl Albrecht, Karl VII: Glücklicher Kurfürst, unglücklicher Kaiser* (Regensburg, 1985); W. Handrick, *Die Pragmatische Armee, 1741-1743* (Munich, 1991). For Hanoverian policy see also U. Dann, *Hanover and Britain, 1740-1760* (Leicester, 1991). 16. P.H. Wilson, 'Prussia's relations with the Holy Roman Empire, 1740-86', *HJ*, 51 (2008), 337-71. 17. Fuller discussion of the strategic situation with good maps in C. Duffy, *Frederick the Great: A military life* (London, 1985), pp. 89-100. 18. R. Zedinger, *Franz Stephen von Lothringen (1708-1765)* (Cologne, 2008), pp. 179-214. 19. C. Duffy, *The best of enemies: Germans against Jacobites, 1746* (London, 2017). For the impact of the war on the Empire, see Wilson, *German armies*, pp. 247-60. 20. O.C. Ebbecke, *Frankreichs Politik gegenüber dem deutschen Reiche in den Jahren 1748-1756* (Freiburg, 1931). 21. L. Schilling, *Kaunitz und das Renversement des Alliances* (Berlin, 1994); S. Externbrink. *Friedrich der Große, Maria Theresa und das Alte Reich. Deutschlandbild und Diplomatie Frankreichs im Siebenjährigen Krieg* (Berlin, 2006). 22. D. Baugh, *The global Seven Years War, 1754-1763: Britain and France in a great power contest* (London, 2011); F.A. Szabo, *The Seven Years War in Europe, 1756-1763* (London, 2007); M. Füssel, *Der Preis des Ruhms: Eine Weltgeschichte des Siebenjährigen Krieges* (Munich, 2019). The campaigns are covered from Austria's perspective by C. Duffy, *By force of arms* (Chicago, Il, 2008), and Hochedlinger, *Austria's wars*, pp. 330-48, for Prussia by D.E. Showalter, *The wars of Frederick the Great* (Harlow, 1996), pp. 135-320, and for the Empire in Wilson, *German armies*, pp. 264-80 with a more detailed, if overly negative account in A. Brabant, *Das Heilige Römischee Reich teutscher Nation im Kampf mit Friedrich dem Großen*, 3 vols. (Berlin, 1904-31). 23. P.H. Wilson, 'The Württemberg army in the Seven Years War', in Alexander Burns (ed.), *The changing face of Old Regime warfare: Essays in honour of Christopher Duffy* (Warwick, 2022), forthcoming. 24. P. Broucek, *Der Geburtstag der Monarchie: Die Schlacht bei Kolin, 1757* (Vienna, 1982). 25. H. Carl, *Okkupation und Regionalismus: Die preußischen Westprovinzen im Siebenjährigen Krieg* (Mainz, 1993). 26. A. Querengässer (ed.), *Die Schlacht bei Roßbach* (Berlin, 2017). 27. R. Savory, *His Britannic Majesty's army in Germany during the Seven Years War* (London, 1966); P. Doran, *Andrew Mitchell and Anglo-Prussian diplomatic relations during the Seven Years War* (New York, 1986); R.N. Middleton, *The bells of victory: The Pitt-Newcastle ministry and the conduct of the Seven Years War, 1757-1762* (Cambridge, 1985); K.W. Schweizer, *England, Prussia and the Seven Years War* (Lewiston, ME, 1989), and his *Frederick the Great, William Pitt and Lord Bute: The Anglo-Prussian alliance, 1756-1763* (New York, 1991). 28. C. Duffy, *Instrument of War* (Warwick, 2020), p. 398. 29. L.J. Oliva, *Misalliance: A study of French policy in Russia during the Seven Years War* (New York, 1964). 30. J. Kunisch, *Das Mirakel des Hauses Brandenburg* (Munich, 1978). 31. D. Beales, *Joseph II*, 2 vols. (Cambridge, 1987-2009). 32. H.M. Scott, *The emergence of the Eastern powers, 1756-1775* (Cambridge, 2001). 33. B.L. Davies, *The Russo-Turkish War, 1768-1774* (London, 2016); C. Scharf, *Katharina II., Deutschland und die Deutschen* (Mainz, 1995), pp. 371–95; Hochedlinger, *Austria's wars*, pp. 350–8. See generally J. Lukowski, *The Partitions of Poland* (Harlow, 1999). **34.** A. Holenstein, 'Miliz im Reformstau. Das Scheitern einer nationalen Verteidigungsorganisation als Spiegel der schweizerischen Integrationsblockade im späten Ancien Régime', in P. Rogger and R. Schmid (eds.), *Miliz oder Söldner?* (Paderborn, 2019), pp. 173–93. **35.** M. Höchner, *Selbstzeugnisse von Schweizer Söldneroffizieren im 18. Jahrhundert* (Göttingen, 2015), pp. 30, 199–205; R.P. Eyer, *Die Schweizer Regimenter in Neapel im 18. Jahrhundert (1734–1789)* (Frankfurt am Main, 2008), pp. 419–82. **36.** E. Buddruss, *Die französische Deutschlandpolitik, 1756–1789* (Mainz, 1995); Wilson, *German armies*, pp. 280–97. **37.** H. Dippel, *Germany and the American Revolution, 1770–1800* (Chapel Hill, NC, 1977); R. Atwood, *The Hessians: Mercenaries from Hessen-Kassel in the American Revolution* (Cambridge, 1980); H.T. Gräf et al. (eds.), *Die 'Hessians' im Amerikanischen Unabhängig-keitskrieg (1776–1783)* (Marburg, 2014). **38.** P.P. Bernard, *Joseph II and Bavaria* (The Hague, 1965); H. Temperley, *Frederick the Great and Kaiser Joseph: An episode of war and diplomacy in the eighteenth century* (London, 1915); Hochedlinger, *Austria's wars*, pp. 364–70. **39.** Stollberg-Rilinger, *Maria Theresa*, pp. 720–9. **40.** M. Umbach, *Federalism and Enlightenment in Germany, 1740–1806* (London, 2000); K.O. Frhr v. Aretin, *Das alte Reich 1648–1806*, 4 vols. (Stuttgart, 1993–2000), III, pp. 301–51. **41.** O. Bezzel, *Haus-truppen des letzten Markgrafen von Ansbach-Bayreuth unter preußischen Herrschaft* (Munich, 1939), pp. 25–44; K.U. Keubke and H. Köbke, *Mecklenburg-Schweriner Truppen in den Niederlanden 1788–1795* (Schwerin, 2003). **42.** Roider, *Eastern question*, pp. 155–92. For the following see also O. Criste, *Kriege unter Kaiser Joseph II* (Vienna, 1904). **43.** K. Härter, *Reichstag und Revolution 1789–1806* (Göttingen, 1992); Wilson, *German armies*, pp. 298–340. For Austrian policy, see K. Roider, *Baron Thugut and Austria's response to the French Revolution* (Princeton, NJ, 1987); Hochedlinger, *Austria's wars*, pp. 401–43. Prussian policy is covered by L. Kittstein, *Politik im Zeitalter der Revolution: Untersuchungen zur preußischen Staatlichkeit, 1792–1806* (Stuttgart, 2003). **44.** T.C.W. Blanning, *The origins of the French Revolutionary Wars* (London, 1986), and his concise overview: *The French Revolutionary Wars, 1787–1802* (London, 1996). Also invaluable is S.S. Biro, *The German policy of revolutionary France: A study in French diplomacy during the War of the First Coalition, 1792–1797* (Cambridge, MA, 1957). **45.** H.-G. Borck, *Der schwäbische Reichskreis im Zeitalter des Französischen Revolutionskriege (1792–1806)* (Stuttgart, 1970); P.H. Wilson, 'Armies of the German princes', in F.C. Schneid (ed.), *Armies of the French Revolution* (Norman, OK, 2015), pp. 182–210. **46.** General Daendals quoted in M. Geerdink-Schaftenaar, *For Orange and the States: The army of the Dutch Republic, 1713–1772*, 2 vols. (Warwick, 2018), I, p. 111. **47.** M. Rapport, *Nationality and citizenship in Revolutionary France: The treatment of foreigners, 1789–99* (Oxford, 2000), pp. 48–50, 91–103; C.J. Tozzi, *Nationalizing France's army: Foreign, Black and Jewish troops in the French military, 1715–1831* (Charlottesville, VA, 2016), pp. 19–21, 53–72, 226–7. **48.** F.S. Scott, *The response of the royal army to the French Revolution* (Oxford, 1979), pp. 166–7; J. Bodin, *Les Suisses au service de la France* (Paris, 1988), pp. 243–91; Höchner, *Selbstzeugnisse*, pp. 209–17. **49.** J.R. Bory, *Regiments suisses au service de France (1800–1814)* (Sion, 1975); Tozzi, *Nationalizing France's army*, pp. 158–61. **50.** R.W. Gould, *Mercenaries of the Napoleonic Wars* (Brighton, 1995); G.C. Dempsey, *Napoleon's mercenaries* (London, 2002); M. Wishon, *German forces and the British army: Interactions and perceptions, 1742–1815* (Basingstoke, 2013), pp. 165–92; B. v. Schwert-feger, *Geschichte der Königlich Deutschen Legion* (Hanover, 1907). **51.** C. Duffy, *Eagles over the Alps: Suvorov in Italy and Switzerland 1799* (Chicago, IL, 1799); J.R. Arnold, *Marengo and Hohenlinden: Napoleon's rise to power* (Barnsley, 1999). **52.** G. Walter, *Zusammembruch des Heiligen Römischen Reiches deutscher Nation und die Problematik seiner Restauration in den Jahren 1814/15* (Heidelberg, 1980); Aretin, *Das alte Reich*, III, pp. 489–98. **53.** Wilson, *The Holy Roman Empire*, pp. 649–66. **54.** W. Burgdorf,

Reichskonstitution und Nation: Verfassungsreformprojekte für das Heilige Römische Reich deutscher Nation im politischen Schrifttum von 1648 bis 1806 (Mainz, 1998), and his *Ein Weltbild verliert seine Welt: Der Untergang des Alten Reiches und die Generation 1806*, 2nd ed. (Munich, 2009). **55.** P.H. Wilson, 'Bolstering the prestige of the Habsburgs: The end of the Holy Roman Empire in 1806', *IHR*, 28 (2006), 709–36. **56.** F.C. Schneid, *Napoleon's conquest of Europe: The War of the Third Coalition* (Westport, CT, 2005). The latest overview of what followed is A. Mikaberidze, *The Napoleonic Wars: A global history* (Oxford, 2020). I am much obliged to Jack Gill and Frederick Schneid for kindly supplying detailed information on the numbers of German troops serving France across 1805–14. **57.** C. Duffy, *Austerlitz 1805* (London, 1977). **58.** A. Forrest and P.H. Wilson (eds.), *The bee and the eagle: Napoleonic France and the end of the Holy Roman Empire, 1806* (Basingstoke, 2009). **59.** K.M. Färber, *Kaiser und Erzkanzler: Carl von Dalberg und Napoleon am Ende des Alten Reiches* (Regensburg, 1994); M. Rowe, 'Napoleon and the "modernisation" of Germany', in P.G. Dwyer and A. Forrest (eds.), *Napoleon and his empire: Europe, 1804–1814* (Basingstoke, 2007), pp. 202–20. **60.** J. Angelelli and A. Pigeard, *La Confédération du Rhin* (Entremont-le-Vieux, 2002); J.H. Gill, *With eagles to glory: Napoleon and his German allies in the 1809 campaign* (London, 1992). **61.** For service see Dempsey, *Napoleon's mercenaries*, pp. 276–309; A.J. Tornare, *Les Vaudois de Napoléon: des Pyramides à Waterloo, 1798–1815* (Morges, 2003). **62.** For Prussian policy, see C. Clark, *Iron kingdom* (London, 2006), pp. 284–311; B. Simms, *The impact of Napoleon: Prussia high politics, foreign policy and the crisis of the executive, 1797–1806* (Cambridge, 1997). **63.** F.C. Schneid, 'The campaign of 1806–07 in Prussia and Poland', in A. Mikaberidze and B. Colson (eds.), *The Cambridge history of the Napoleonic Wars*, 3 vols. (Cambridge, 2022), II, ch. 41, forthcoming. **64.** S.A. Mustafa, *Napoleon's paper kingdom: The life and death of Westphalia, 1807–13* (New York, 2013). **65.** The considerable literature on this is admirably summarized in K. Hagemann, *Revisiting Prussia's wars against Napoleon* (Cambridge, 2015), pp. 37–60, and D. Walter, 'Reluctant reformers, observant disciplines: The Prussian military reforms, 1807–1814', in R. Chickering and S. Förster (eds.), *War in an age of revolution, 1775–1815* (Cambridge, 2010), pp. 85–99. **66.** C. Esdaile, *The Peninsular War* (London, 2002). **67.** J.H. Gill, *1809: Thunder on the Danube*, 3 vols. (Barnsley, 2008–10). For Austrian policy, see H. Rössler, *Graf Johann Philipp Stadion. Napoleons deutscher Gegenspieler*, 2 vols. (Vienna, 1996); G.E. Rothenberg, *The emperor's last victory: Napoleon and the battle of Wagram* (London, 2004). **68.** C. Duffy, *Borodino and the war of 1812* (London, 1973); A. Zamoyski, *1812: Napoleon's fatal march on Moscow* (London, 2012). **69.** Detailed coverage of the campaign in M. Leggieri, *Napoleon and the struggle for Germany*, 2 vols. (Cambridge, 2015), with more on the plans in A. Sked, *Radetzky* (London, 2011), pp. 32–69. **70.** M. Leggiere, *The fall of Napoleon: The Allied invasion of France, 1813–1814* (Cambridge, 2007). **71.** A. Zamoyski, *The rites of peace: The fall of Napoleon and the Congress of Vienna* (London, 2012). **72.** P. Hofschroer, *1815. The Waterloo campaign: The German victory* (London, 2004). For a concise guide to the battle and its place in history, see A. Forrest, *Waterloo* (Oxford, 2015).

8. Professionalizing War

1. P.H. Wilson, 'German military preparedness on the eve of the Revolutionary Wars', *CRE*, (2004), 16–30. **2.** H. Neuhaus, 'Das Problem der militärischen Exekutive in der Spätphase des Alten Reiches', in J. Kunisch and B. Stolberg-Rillinger (eds.), *Staatsverfassung und Heeresverfassung* (Berlin, 1986), pp. 297–346, and his 'Prinz Eugen als Reichsgeneral', in J. Kunisch (ed.), *Prinz Eugen und seiner Zeit* (Würzburg, 1986), pp. 163–77. **3.** K. Härter, *Reichstag und Revolution, 1789–1806* (Göttingen, 1992), pp. 383–6. **4.** M. Lavater-Sloman, *Der* *vergessene Prinz: August Wilhelm Prinz von Preussen* (Zürich, 1983). **5.** J. Kunisch, *Friedrich der Große* (Munich, 2004), pp. 77–80. **6.** H.M. Scott, 'Prussia's royal foreign minister: Frederick the Great and the administration of Prussian diplomacy', in R. Oresko et al. (eds.), *Royal and republican sovereignty* (Cambridge, 1997), pp. 500–26; H.C. Johnson, *Frederick the Great and his officials* (New Haven, CT, 1975). **7.** P. Paret, *The cognitive challenge of war: Prussia 1806* (Princeton, NJ, 2009), p. 25. **8.** C. Duffy, *Instrument of war: The Austrian army in the Seven Years War* (Warwick, 2020), pp. 20–35. Revised interpretation in B. Stollberg-Rilinger, *Maria Theresa* (Princeton, NJ, 2022), pp. 127–37, 419–33. For Habsburg institutions see M. Hochedlinger, 'Das stehende Heer', in ibidem et al. (eds.), *Verwaltungsgeschichte der Habsburgermonarchie in der Frühen Neuzeit* (Vienna, 2019), I, pp. 655–763, which has extensive further references. **9.** Duffy, *Instrument of war*, pp. 418–21. See generally O. Hackl, *Die Vorgeschichte, Gründung und frühe Entwicklung der Generalstäbe Österreichs, Bayerns und Preußens* (Osnabrück, 1997), pp. 49–189; G. Rapp and V. Hofer, *Der schweizerische Generalstab*, vol. I (Basel, 1983), pp. 90–129. **10.** C.E. White, 'Setting the record straight: Scharnhorst and the origins of the nineteenth-century Prussia general staff', *WiH*, 28 (2021), 25–45. **11.** Duffy, *Instrument of war*, pp. 151–5, 321, 421–4. For the following, see also A. Storring, 'Subjective practices of war: The Prussian army and the Zorndorf campaign, 1758', *History of Science* (2020); https://doi.org/10.1177/0073275320958950 **12.** HSAS, C14 Bü.338, muster of the Kreis Regiment, September 1741. **13.** C. Winkel, *Im Netz des Königs. Netzwerke und Patronage in der preußischen Armee, 1713–1786* (Paderborn, 2013), pp. 34–76. Examples of the earlier view in R. Wohlfeil, 'Ritte – Söldnerführer – Offizier: Versuch eines Vergleichs', in J. Bärmann (ed.), *Geschichtliches Landeskunde* (Wiesbaden, 1966), pp. 45–70 esp. 59–70; K. Demeter, *Das deutsche Offizierskorps in Gesellschaft und Staat, 1650–1945*, 4th ed. (Frankfurt am Main, 1965), pp. 116–53. See also Duffy, *Instrument of war*, pp. 162–75. **14.** R. v. Schroetter, 'Das preussiche Offizierskorps unter dem ersten Könige von Preussen', *FBPG*, 26 (1913), 429–97, and 27 (1914), 97–167 at 125–34; J. Kloosterhuis (ed.), *Bauern, Bürger und Soldaten: Quellen zur Sozialisation des Militärsystems im preußischen Westfalen, 1713–1803*, 2 vols. (Münster, 1992), I, pp. 350–77. **15.** W.O. Shanahan, *Prussian military reforms, 1786–1813* (New York, 1945), pp. 104–9. Further discussion of the social composition of the officer corps can be found on pp. 336–8, 495–500. **16.** K. Staudinger, *Geschichte des kurbayerischen Heeres*, 5 vols. (Munich, 1901–9), III, pp. 240–2, 253, 488; O. Heinl, *Heerwesen und Volksbewaffnung in Vorderösterriech im Zeitalter Josefs II. und der Revolutionskriege* (Freiburg im Breisgau, 1941), pp. 15–16, 20; Möllmann [sic], 'Zur Geschichte des Kurtrierischen Militärs', *Trierisches Archiv*, supplement 1 (1901), 60–87 at 69–70, 74. **17.** H. Foerster, 'Die ewige Neutralität der Schweiz 1815', in R. Haudenreich (ed.), *Marignano 1515–2015* (Lenzburg, 2015), pp. 269–94 at 269, 280; AEG Militaire E3, *Tablature de la garde et des compagnies bourgeois.* **18.** D. Schläppi, 'Kompensation statt Korruption. Fremdes Geld, symbolische Legitimation und materielle Redistribution am Beispiel des Zuger Stadtrats im 17. und 18. Jahrhundert', in K. v. Greyerz et al. (eds.), *Soldgeschäfte, Klientelismus, Korruption in der Frühen Neuzeit* (Göttingen, 2018), pp. 123–52 at 148–50. **19.** J. Stüssi-Lauterburg and H. Luginburg, *Vivat das Bernerbiet bis an d'r Welt ihr End! Berns Krieg im Jahre 1798 gegen die Franzosen* (Baden, 2000), pp. 21–50; Rapp and Hofer, *Schweizerische Generalstab*, pp. 91–118. **20.** HSAS, A28 Bü.99; L6.22.6.34; F. Schirmer, *Nec aspera terrent! Eine Heereskunde der hannoverschen Armee* (Hanover, 1929), pp. 139–40, 203–5. **21.** Examples in HSAS, A6 Bü.34; A202 Bü.2005–2007 L6.22.7.5a. For the following, see P.H. Wilson, 'Social militarisation in eighteenth-century Germany', *German History*, 18 (2000), 1–39, and the sources cited there. **22.** E. v. Frauenholz, *Das Heerwesen in der Zeit des Absolutismus* (Munich, 1940), pp. 225–7. **23.** P. Paret, 'Conscription and the end of the old regime in France and Prussia', in W. Treue (ed.), *Geschichte als Aufgabe* (Berlin, 1988), pp. 159–82. **24.** Examples in HSAS, A8 Bü.59, and H. Weisert, *Geschichte der Stadt Sindelfingen, 1500–1807* (Sindelfingen, 1963), pp. 225,

260. 25. Examples in HSAS, A2020 Bü.2257, 9 January 1739; A202 Bü.2276 13 November 1741; P.K. Taylor, *Indentured to liberty: Peasant life and the Hessian military state, 1688–1815* (Ithaca, NY, 1994), pp. 57–74. 26. C. Ingrao, *The Hessian mercenary state: Ideas, institutions and reform under Frederick II, 1760–1785* (Cambridge, 1987), esp. pp. 132–5. 27. Duffy, *Instrument of war*, pp. 214–21; F. Szabo, *Kaunitz and Enlightened absolutism, 1753–1780* (Cambridge, 1994), pp. 278–93. See also M. Hochedlinger and A. Tantner (eds.), *'Der grosste Teil der Unterthanen ist elend und muhselig'. Die Berichte des Hofkriegsrats* (Innsbruck, 2005). 28. *On war* (transl. and ed. M. Howard and P. Paret, Princeton, NJ, 1976), p. 591. Examples of this classic interpretation include C. Tilly, *Capital, coercion and European states, AD 990–1992* (Oxford, 1992), pp. 80–4, 106–14; D. Bell, *The first total war: Napoleon's Europe and the birth of warfare as we know it* (New York, 2007). For a critique, see D.D. Avant, 'From mercenary to citizen armies: Explaining change in the practice of war', *International Organization*, 54:1 (2000), 41–72; M. Sikora, 'Die französische Revolution der Heeresverfassung', in P. Baumgart et al. (eds.), *Die preußische Armee zwischen Ancien Régime und Reichsgründung* (Paderborn, 2008), pp. 135–63. 29. J. Smets, 'Von der "Dorfidylle" zur preußischen Nation. Sozialdisziplinirung der linksrheinischen Bevölkerung durch die Franzosen am Beispiel der allgemeinen Wehrpflicht (1802–1814)', *HZ*, 262 (1996), 695–738. 30. T. Hipper, *Citizens, soldiers and national armies: Military service in France and Germany, 1789–1830* (Abingdon, 2008); D. Moran and A. Waldron (eds.), *The people in arms: Military myth and national mobilisation since the French Revolution* (Cambridge, 2003). 31. P. Sauer, 'Die Neuorganisation des württembergischen Heerwesens unter Herzog, Kurfürst und König Friedrich (1797–1816)', *ZWLG*, 26 (1967), 395–420, and his *Revolution und Volksbewaffnung. Die Württembergische Bürgerwehren im 19. Jahrhundert, vor allem während der Revolution von 1848/49* (Ulm, 1976), pp. 27–9. Recruitment ordinances in Reyscher, pp. 797, 859–99, 1004–13. 32. W.D. Gruner, *Das bayerische Heer 1824 bis 1864* (Boppard am Rhein, 1972), pp. 37–43; P. Bunde and M. Gaertner, *The Westphalian army in the Napoleonic Wars, 1807–1813* (Berlin, 2019), pp. 23–6 33. G. Rothenberg, *Napoleon's great adversaries: The Archduke Charles and the Austrian army, 1792–1814* (London, 1982), pp. 118–19, 137–9, 175. 34. Shanahan, *Prussian military reforms*, pp. 159–78. See ibid, pp. 159–60, for possible origins of the term. For the following, see also P. Paret, *Yorck and the era of Prussian reform, 1807–1815* (Princeton, NY, 1966). 35. U. Frevert, *A nation in barracks: Conscription, military service and civil society in modern Germany* (London, 2004), pp. 25–7; K. Hagemann, *Revisiting Prussia's wars against Napoleon* (Cambridge, 2015), pp. 52–7. 36. P.H. Wilson, *German armies: War and German politics, 1648–1806* (London, 1998), pp. 314–19. 37. M. Rink, 'The German Wars of Liberation, 1807–1815', *Small Wars and Insurgencies*, 25 (2014), 828–42, quote at 814; S.A. Mustafa, *The long ride of Major von Schill: A journey through German history and memory* (New York, 2008). Schill's force never exceeded 1,910 men. 38. Hagemann, *Prussia's wars*, pp. 62, 178–93. 39. Statistical data presented in more depth in P.H. Wilson, *From Reich to revolution: German history, 1558–1806* (Basingstoke, 2004), p. 227, and 'Warfare under the old regime, 1648–1792', in J. Black (ed.), *European Warfare, 1453–1815* (Basingstoke, 1999), pp. 69–95 at 80; P.G.M. Dickson, *Finance and government under Maria Theresia, 1740–1780*, 2 vols. (Oxford, 1987), II, pp. 345–55; J. McCormack, *One million mercenaries: Swiss soldiers in the armies of the world* (London, 1993), p. 147. 40. Full breakdown of Austrian strength in HSAS, A74 Bü.202, Bühler's report 16 August 1788. 41. Rothenberg, *Archduke Charles*, pp. 24, 81, 126, 174–9. 42. G. Cordes, 'Das württembergische Heerwesen zur Zeit Napoleons', in *Baden und Württemberg im Zeitalter Napoleons*, 3 vols. (Stuttgart, 1987), II, pp. 275–96; E. Jäger, *Das Militärwesen des Königreiches Württemberg* (Stuttgart, 1869). 43. J. Gill, *With Eagles to glory: Napoleon and his German allies in the 1809 campaign*, 2nd ed. (Barnsley, 2010); J. Angelelli and A. Pigeard, *La Confédération du Rhin* (Entremont-le-Vieux, 2002). I am extremely grateful to Jack Gill and Frederick

Schneid for sharing their detailed research into the strength of German forces in Napoleon's armies on which this and much of the following paragraph is based. **44.** Data on Swiss strengths from A.J. Tornare, *Les Vaudois de Napoléon: Des Pyramides à Waterloo, 1798–1815* (Morges, 2003). **45.** C. Duffy, *Military experience in the age of reason* (London, 1987), pp. 168–9. For firearms, see H. Müller, *Die Bewaffnung* (Berlin, 1991), pp. 86–95; R. Wirtgen, *Handfeuerwaffen*, Part II, *Preußen (bis 1870)* (Rastatt, 1979), pp. 50–63. **46.** HSAS, G230 Bü.58, reports of various officers and doctors, 25 February 1758. **47.** J.J. Dominicus, *Aus dem Siebenjährigen Krieg. Tagebuch des preußischen Musketiers Dominicus* (Munich, 1891), p. viii. **48.** HSAS, A6 Bü.21; A202 Bü.2278; C14 Bü.121, 123a; F. Münich, *Geschichte der Entwicklung der bayerischen Armee seit zwei Jahrhunderten* (Munich, 1864), pp. 25–34; P.D. Lockhart, *The drillmaster of Valley Forge: Baron de Steuben and the making of the American army* (New York, 2008). **49.** W. Ribbe (ed.), *Geschichte Berlins*, 2 vols. (Munich, 1988), I, p. 410. This remained in military use until 1850. See also O. Elster, *Geschichte der stehenden Truppen im Herzogtum Braunschweig-Wolfenbüttel*, 2 vols. (Leipzig, 1899–1901), II, pp. 171–5; J.C. Frhr. v. Allmayer-Beck, 'Die friderizianische Armee im Spiegel ihrer österreichischen Gegner', in O. Hauser (ed.), *Friedrich der Große und seine Zeit* (Cologne, 1987), pp. 237–54. **50.** H. Kleinschmidt, 'The military and dancing', *Ethnologia europaea*, 25 (1995), 157–76, and his 'Mechanismus und Biologismus im Militärwesen des 17. und 18. Jahrhunderts', in D. Hohrath and K. Gerteis (eds.), *Die Kriegskunst im Lichte der Vernunft*, 2 vols. (Hamburg, 1999–2000), I, pp. 51–73. **51.** E. v. Warnery, *Remarks on cavalry* (London, 1798), pp. xvii–xviii. See also Munich, *Bayerischen Armee*, pp. 135–9; J. Nowosadtko, *Stehendes Heer im Ständestaat. Das Zusammenleben von Militär- und Zivilbevölkerung im Fürstbistum Münster, 1650–1803* (Paderborn, 2011), pp. 30–1, 47–8. **52.** Neubauer's diary reprinted in H. Bleckwenn (ed.), *Kriegs- und Friedensbilder, 1725–1759* (Osnabrück, 1971), pp. 230, 248. **53.** E. Hagen, 'Die fürstlich würzburgische Hausinfanterie vom Jahre 1757 bis zur Einverleibung des Fürstbistums in Bayern 1803', *DBKH*, 20 (1911), 1–142 at 44–5; J.C. Frhr. v. Allmayer-Beck, *Das Heer unter dem Doppeladler: Habsburgs Armeen, 1718–1848* (Munich, 1981), p. 55. More detail in B. Nosworthy, *The anatomy of victory: Battle tactics, 1689–1763* (New York, 1989). **54.** Calculated from Dickson, *Finance and government*, II, pp. 345–51; Duffy, *Instrument of war*, pp. 278–98; R. Müller, *Die Armee Augusts des Starken: Das sächsische Heer von 1730 bis 1733* (Berlin, 1984), pp. 63–90; R. Müller and W. Rother, *Die kurfürstlich-sächsische Armee um 1791* (Berlin, 1990), pp. 15, 21–8; article on 'cavalry' at http://his-dhs-dss.ch/de. **55.** O. Groehler, *Das Heerwesen* (Berlin, 1993), pp. 83–90; M. Guddat, *Kürassiere, Dragoner, Husaren: Die Kavallerie Friedrichs des Großen* (Hamburg, 1989). **56.** For the Uhlans in Saxon service, 1730–63, see S. Summerfield, *Saxon army of the Austrian War of Succession and Seven Years War* (Huntingdon, 2011), pp. 149–57. **57.** C. v. Jany, *Geschichte der Preußischen Armee*, 4 vols. (Berlin, 1928–9), II, p. 317. **58.** Rothenberg, *Archduke Charles*, pp. 24–5, 72–3, 119–21, and his *The military border in Croatia, 1740–1881* (Chicago, IL, 1966); Austrian Kriegsarchiv, *Österreichischer Erbfolgekrieg, 1740–48*, 9 vols. (Vienna, 1876–1914), I, pp. 491–502; Duffy, *Instrument of war*, pp. 33–48, 433–6; J. Kunisch, *Feldmarschall Laudon* (Vienna, 1972), esp. pp. 28, 83. **59.** F. Wernitz, *Die preussischen Freitruppen im Siebenjährigen Krieg, 1756–1763* (Wölfersheim-Berstadt, 1994); M. Rink, *Vom 'Partheygänger' zum Partisanen: Die Konzeption des kleinen Krieges in Preussen, 1740–1813* (Frankfurt am Main, 1999), pp. 149–74. For the following, see also B. Heuser, 'Lessons learned? Cultural transfer and revolutionary wars, 1775–1831', *Small Wars and Insurgencies*, 25 (2014), 858–76. **60.** B. Nosworthy, *Battle tactics of Napoleon and his enemies* (London, 1997); Paret, *Yorck*, pp. 186–7. **61.** M. Guddat, *Kanoniere, Bombardiere, Pontoniere: Die Artillerie Friedrichs des Großen* (Herford, 1992); Müller, *Armee Augusts des Starken*, pp. 91–8; R. Müller and Rother, *Armee um 1791*, pp. 25–7; S. Summerfield, *Saxon artillery, 1733–1827* (Nottingham, 2009); A.L. Dawson et al., *Napoleonic artillery* (Marlborough, 2007), pp. 28–41. **62.** Kriegsarchiv,

Österreichischer Erbfolgekrieg, I, pp. 447–51; Austrian Kriegsarchiv, *Krieg gegen die Französischen Revolution, 1792–7*, 2 vols. (Vienna, 1905), I, pp. 562–3; Groehler, *Heerwesen*, pp.98–101. For the optical telegraph, see J.B. Müller, 'Kriegstagebuch 1799–1902', *Schriften des Vereins für Geschichte und Naturgeschichte der Baar und der angrenzenden Landesteile*, 8 (1893), 68–115 at 112–13. 63. Y. Mintzker, *The defortification of the German city, 1689–1866* (Cambridge, 2012), pp. 55–182; C. Duffy, *The fortress in the age of Vauban and Frederick the Great, 1660–1789* (London, 1985), pp. 112–47. 64. J. Glete, *Navies and nations: Warships, navies and state building in Europe and America, 1500–1860* (Stockholm, 1993), p. 241. 65. O. Schuster and F.A. Francke, *Geschichte der sächsischen Armee*, 3 vols. (Leipzig, 1883), I, p. 202; O. Bezzel, *Geschichte des kurpfälzischen Heeres von seinen Anfängen bis zur Vereinigung von Kurpfalz und Kurbayern 1777*, 2 vols. (Munich, 1925–8), I, pp. 291–2; *Feldzüge*, XVII, 26–9; T. Tupetz, 'Der Türkenfeldzug von 1739 und der Friede zu Belgrad', *HZ*, 40 (1878), 1–52 at 20–1; W. Aichelberg, *Kriegsschiffe auf der Donau* (Vienna, 1982), pp. 17–24. 66. F. Pesendorfer, *Österreich – Grossreich im Mittelmeer? Das Königreich Neapel-Sizilien unter Kaiser Karl VI.* (Cologne, 1998); K. Roider, *Austria's eastern question, 1700–1790* (Princeton, NJ, 1982), pp. 60–1. 67. Quoted in Szabo, *Kaunitz*, p. 302. See also his 'Unwanted navy: Habsburg naval armaments under Maria Theresa', *Austrian History Yearbook*, 17–18 (1981–2), 29–54. Two cutters were bought in 1784, reconstituting the Trieste squadron. 68. K. Petsch, *Seefahrt für Brandenburg-Preussen, 1650–1815* (Osnabrück, 1986), pp. 93–128; F. Gottmann, 'Prussia all at sea? The Emden-based East India companies and the challenge of transnational enterprise in the eighteenth century', *Journal of World History*, 31 (2020), 539–66.

9. Socialization of the Military

1. O. Büsch, *Military system and social life in old regime Prussia, 1713–1807* (Atlantic Highlands, NJ, 1997); E. Willems, *A way of life and death: Three centuries of Prussian-German militarism* (Nashville, TN, 1986), esp. pp. 38–40. 2. A. Pecar, *Die Masken des Königs. Friedrich II. von Preußen als Schriftsteller* (Frankfurt, 2016). 3. P.H. Wilson, 'War in German thought from the Peace of Westphalia to Napoleon', *European History Quarterly*, 28 (1998), 5–50; D. Hohrath and K. Gerteis (eds.), *Die Kriegskunst im Lichte der Vernunft. Militär und Aufklärung im 18. Jahrhundert*, 2 vols. (Hamburg, 1999–2000); C.E. White, *The Enlightened soldier: Scharnhorst and the Militärische Gesellschaft in Berlin, 1801–1805* (New York, 1989). 4. K. Härter, 'War as political and constitutional discourse: Imperial warfare and the military constitution of the Holy Roman Empire in the politics of the Permanent Diet (1663–1806)', in A. De Benedictis and C. Magoni (eds.), *Teatri di guerra* (Bologna, 2010), pp. 215–37. 5. E. Hagen, 'Die fürstlich würzburgische Hausinfanterie vom Jahre 1757 bis zur Einverleibung des Fürstbistums in Bayern 1803', *DBKH*, 20 (1911), 1–142 at 47; F.K. Tharau, *Die geistige Kultur des preußischen Offiziers von 1640 bis 1806* (Mainz, 1968), pp. 116–22; J. Kloosterhuis (ed.), *Bauern, Bürger und Soldaten: Quellen zur Sozialisation des Militärsystems im preußischen Westfalen, 1713–1803*, 2 vols. (Münster, 1992), I, pp. 561–2. For the following, see also K.H. Brand and H. Eckert, *Kadetten*, 2 vols. (Munich, 1981). 6. R. Uhland, *Geschichte der Hohen Karlsschule in Stuttgart* (Stuttgart, 1953); D. Hohrath and R. Henning, *Die Bildung des Offiziers im Aufklärung* (Stuttgart, 1990), pp. 28–63; E. Stockinger, 'Vorbildung, Herkunft und Werdegang militärischer Führer in Deutschland von 1730–1813', *Wehrkunde*, 24 (1975), 592–7. 7. C. Hinrichs, *Preußentum und Pietismus* (Göttingen, 1971), 126–73; R.L. Gawthrop, *Pietism and the making of eighteenth-century Prussia* (Cambridge, 1993), 1993, pp. 223–46. 8. H. Patze and W. Schlesinger (eds.), *Geschichte Thüringens*, vol. V (Cologne, 1982), p. 377; W. Schüssler, 'Das Werbewesen in der Reichsstadt Heilbronn, vornehmlich im 19. Jahrhundert' (PhD, University of Tübingen, 1951), p. 296; M. Schort, *Politik und*

Propaganda. Der Siebenjährige Krieg in der zeitgenössischen Flugschriften (Frankfurt am Main, 2006). **9.** J. Niemeyer, *Die Revue bei Bemerode 1735* (Beckum, 1985); K. Vanja, *Vivat-Vivat-Vivat! Widmungs- und Genkbänder aus drei Jahrhunderten* (Berlin, 1985). **10.** F.W. v. Archenholz, *Gemälde der Preußischen Armee* (Berlin, 1791), pp. 7, 15. **11.** Maria Theresia to Field Marshal Daun, 24 July 1759, printed in J. Kunisch, *Das Mirakel des Hauses Brandenburg* (Munich, 1978), pp. 95–100. For the following, ibid, pp. 17–43, 101–41. **12.** H.T. Gräf, 'Die "fremden Dienst" in der Landgrafschaft Hessen-Kassel (1677–1815)', in R. Jaun et al. (eds.), *Schweizer Solddienst* (Birmensdorf, 2009), pp. 89–102; P.H. Wilson, 'The German "soldier trade" of the seventeenth and eighteenth centuries: A reassessment', *The International History Review,* 18 (1996), 757–92. Many of the arguments against subsidies had been voiced already long before: T. Helfferich, '"Unter den Schutz Frankreichs": German reception of French subsidies in the Thirty Years War', in S. Norrhem and E. Thomson (eds.), *Subsidies, diplomacy and state formation in Europe, 1494–1789* (Lund, 2020), pp. 43–67. **13.** C. Tzoref-Ashkenazi, *German soldiers in colonial India* (London, 2014), pp. 49–167. **14.** A. Corvisier, *La bataille de Malplaquet 1709* (Paris, 1997), pp. 33, 36, 90. **15.** R. Bolzern, 'The Swiss foreign service and Bernese reform politics in the late eighteenth century', *History of European Ideas,* 33 (2007), 463–75; M. Höchner, *Selbstzeugnisse von Schweizer Söldneroffizieren im 18. Jahrhundert* (Göttingen, 2015), pp. 183–98, 218–19, 229–33. **16.** C. Huber and K. Keller, 'Französische Pensionen in der Eidgenossenschaft und ihre Verteilung in Stadt und Amt Zug durch die Familie Zurlauben', in K. Greyerz et al. (eds.), *Soldgeschäfte, Klientelismus, Korruption in der Frühen Neuzeit* (Göttingen, 2018), pp. 153–82. **17.** J.J. Dominicus, *Aus dem Siebenjährigen Krieg. Tagebuch des preußischen Musketiers Dominicus* (Munich, 1891), pp. 16, 56, 61–3; see also K. Latzel, '"Schlachtbank" oder "Feld der Ehre"? Der Beginn des Einstellungswandels gegenüber Krieg und Tod 1756–1816', in W. Wette (ed.), *Der Krieg des kleinen Mannes* (Munich, 1995), pp. 76–92. **18.** E.F.R. v. Barsewisch, *Von Rossbach bis Freiburg, 1757–1763. Tagebuchblätter eines friderizianischen Fahnenjunkers und Offiziers* (Krefeld, 1959), p. 65. **19.** Quoted in A. v. Pfister, 'Das Regiment zu Fuss Alt-Württemberg im kaiserlichen Dienst auf Sizilien in den Jahren 1719 bis 1720', *BMWB,* 5 and 6 (1885), 157–268 at 233. **20.** T. Horstmann, *Generalleutnant Johann Nikolaus von Luckner und seine Husaren im Siebenjärigen Kriege* (Osnabrück, 1997), pp. 2–11; P. Batelka et al., 'Berufsmäßiger Gewalttäter: Wie Söldnergewalt in der Frühen Neuzeit entfesselt und begrenzt wurde', in W. Speitkamp (ed.), *Gewaltgemeinschaften in der Geschichte* (Göttingen, 2017), pp. 83–100. For Austria's qualms about Trenck, see B. Stollberg-Rilinger, *Maria Theresa* (Princeton, NJ, 2022), pp. 141–50. **21.** Herder quoted in A.H.F. Vagts, *A history of militarism* (London, 1938), p. 78. **22.** L.W. Eysterlid, *The formative influences, theories, and campaigns of the Archduke Charles of Austria* (Westport, CT, 2000); A. Kuhle, *Die preußische Kriegstheorie um 1800 und ihre Suche nach dynamischen Gleichgewichten* (Berlin, 2018). **23.** L.S. James, 'For the fatherland? The motivations of Austrian and Prussian volunteers during the Revolutionary and Napoleonic Wars', in C.G. Krüger and S. Levison (eds.), *War volunteering in modern times* (Basingstoke, 2011), pp. 40–56. For further discussion see pp. 477–9. **24.** Printed in E. v. Frauenholz, *Das Heerwesen in der Zeit des Absolutismus* (Munich, 1940), pp. 298–308 at 304. **25.** O. Brosin, *Schillers Vater* (Leipzig, 1879), pp. 3–9. **26.** J. Nowosadtko, *Stehendes Heer im Ständestaat. Das Zusammenleben von Militär- und Zivilbevölkerung im Fürstbistum Münster 1650–1803* (Paderborn, 2011), pp. 97–8, 198–9. **27.** R. Müller and M. Lachmann, *Spielmann – Trompeter – Hoboist: Aus der Geschichte der deutschen Militärmusiker* (Berlin, 1988); G. Kandler, 'Zur Geschichte der deutschen Soldatenmusik', in B. Schwertfeger and E.O. Volkermann (eds.), *Die deutschen Soldatenkunde,* 2 vols. (Berlin, 1937), I, pp. 473–523. **28.** K. and S. Möbius, *Prussian army soldiers and the Seven Years War* (London, 2020), pp .33–7, 57–168. **29.** Examples in Barsewisch, *Von Rossbach,* pp. 29, 45–6, 83, 114–15. **30.** K.F. Hildebrand and C. Zweng, *Die Ritter des Ordens Pour le Mérite,* 4 vols. (Osnabrück, 1999–2003);

M. Hochedlinger, 'Mars ennobled: The ascent of the military and the creation of a military nobility in mid-eighteenth-century Austria', *GH*, 17 (1999), 141–76.   **31.** O. Rudert, *Die Reorganisation der kursächsischen Armee 1763–69* (Leipzig, 1911), pp. 35, 39–43; K.S. Baron v. Galéra, *Vom Reich zum Rheinbund. Weltgeschichte des 18. Jahrhunderts in einer kleinen Residenz* (Neustadt a.d. Aisch, 1961), pp. 211–13; Vagts, *Militarism*, p. 66; B. Haas Tenckhoff, *Das fürstbischöflich münsterische Militär im 18. Jahrhundert* (Münster, 1930), pp. 149–51; E. Herter, *Geschichte der kurkölnischen Truppen in der Zeit vom Badener Frieden bis zum Beginn des Siebenjährigen Krieges* (Bonn, 1914), p. 19.   **32.** Comparison of Württemberg and Hessen-Kassel practice in 1764 in HSAS, A8 Bü.51. See more generally F. Redlich, *The German military enterpriser and his workforce*, 2 vols. (Wiesbaden, 1964–5), II, pp. 47–56.   **33.** Figures from W. Hagen, 'The Junkers' faithless servants', in R.J. Evans and W.R. Lee, *The German peasantry* (London, 1986), pp. 77–86; D. Kotsch, *Potsdam: Die preußische Garnisonsstadt* (Braunschweig, 1992), pp. 64–5. For Austria, see C. Duffy, *Instrument of war: The Austrian army in the Seven Years War* (Warwick, 2020), pp. 180–5.   **34.** O. Groehler, *Das Heerwesen* (Berlin,1993), p. 31; H. Schlechte (ed.), *Das geheime politische Tagebuch des Kurprinzen Friedrich Christian von Sachsen, 1751 bis 1757* (Weimar, 1992), pp. 361, 387.   **35.** M. Winter, *Untertanengeist durch Militärpflicht? Das preußische Kantonsystem in brandenburgischen Städten im 18. Jahrhundert* (Bielefeld, 2005).   **36.** E. v. Knesebeck, *Geschichte der chur-hannoverschen Truppen in Gibraltar, Minorca und Ostindien* (Hanover, 1845); M. Höchner, 'Selbstzeugnisse von Schweizer Soldaten im Siebenjährigen Krieg', in Jaun et al. (eds.), *Schweizer Solddienst*, pp. 61–103 at 77.   **37.** H. Suter, *Innerschweizerisches Militär-Unternehmertum im 18. Jahrhundert* (Zurich, 1971), p. 44.   **38.** C. Ingrao, *The Hessian mercenary state: Ideas, institutions and reform under Frederick II, 1760–1785* (Cambridge, 1987), pp. 153–5, 159 n.136; C.J. Tozzi, *Nationalizing France's army: Foreign, black and Jewish troops in the French military, 1715–1831* (Charlottesville, VA, 2016), pp. 221–5; see also Duffy, *Instrument of war*, pp. 39–109, 223–6.   **39.** C. v. Jany, *Geschichte der Preußischen Armee*, 4 vols. (Berlin, 1928–9), I, p. 711; II, pp. 77–8, 240–8; III, pp. 5–6, 50, 55–7, 184, 436.   **40.** G.F. Jones, 'The Black Hessians: Negroes recruited by the Hessians in South Carolina and other colonies', *The South Carolina Historical Magazine*, 83 (1982), 287–302; S Theilig, 'Migration, identitäre Transformationen und Integration tartarischer Soldaten in das preußische Militär 1795–1800', in C. Rass (ed.), *Militärische Migration* (Paderborn, 2016), pp. 71–90.   **41.** T.U. Roeder, 'Professional identity of Army officers in Britain and the Habsburg monarchy, 1740–1790' (PhD, University of Cambridge, 2018), pp. 19–40; M. Hochedlinger, 'Adlige Abstinenz und bürgerlicher Aufstiegswille. Zum Social- und Herkunftsprofil von Generalität und Offizierskorps der kaiserlichen und k.k. Armee im 17. und 18. Jahrhundert', in G. Pfeiler and K. Andermann (eds.), *Soziale Mobilität in der Vormoderne* (Innsbruck, 2020), pp. 271–349; P.H. Wilson, 'Prussia's relations with the Holy Roman Empire, 1740–86', *The Historical Journal*, 51 (2008), 337–71.   **42.** K. Demeter, *Das deutsche Offizierskorps in Gesellschaft und Staat 1650–1945*, 4th ed. (Frankfurt am Main, 1965), p. 5; F. Göse, *Rittergut, Garnison, Residenz. Studien zur Sozialstruktur und politischen Wirksamkeit des brandenburgischen Adels, 1648–1763* (Berlin, 2005).   **43.** HSAS L5 Tom.145 fol. 568–9; H.G. Böhme, *Die Wehrverfassung in Hessen-Kassel im 18. Jahrhundert bis zum Siebenjährigen Kriege* (Kassel, 1954), p. 25.   **44.** C. Winkel, *Im Netz des Königs. Netzwerke und Patronage in der preußischen Armee, 1713–1786* (Paderborn, 2013), esp. pp. 36–8. For the following, see also J. Brüser, 'Zwischen Kronprinz Friedrich Wilhelm und Napoleon: Das württembergische Offizierskorps im Russlandfeldzug 1812', in W. Mähle and N. Bichhoff (eds.), *Armee im Untergang: Württemberg und der Feldzug Napoleons gegen Rußland 1812* (Stuttgart, 2017), pp. 31–45; P. Paret, *Yorck and the era of Prussian reform, 1807–1815* (Princeton, NY, 1966), pp. 263–6.   **45.** See generally J. Komlos, *Nutrition and economic development in the eighteenth-century Habsburg monarchy* (Princeton, NJ, 1989), pp. 228–39.   **46.** W.R. Fann, 'Foreigners in the Prussian army, 1713–1756',

CEH, 23 (1990), 76–85; J. Kloosterhuis (ed.), *Legendäre 'Langen Kerls'* (Berlin, 2003); K. Zeisler, *Die 'Langen Kerls'. Geschichte des Leib und Garderegiments Friedrich Wilhelm I* (Frankfurt am Main, 1993). **47.** A. Skalweit, 'Die Eingliederung des friderizianischen Heeres in den Volks- und Wirtschaftskörper', *Jahrbuch für Nationalökonomie und Statistik*, 160 (1944), 194–220 at 210–11; C. v. Jany, 'Die Kantonverfassung Friedrich Wilhelms I.', *FBPG*, 38 (1926), 225–72 at 248–9. **48.** W.R. Fann, 'On the infantryman's age in eighteenth-century Prussia', *Military Affairs*, 41 (1977), 165–70; W. Hanne (ed.), *Rangirolle, Listen und Extracte ... von Saldern Infanterie Regiment Anno 1771* (Osnabrück, 1986), p. 23; Nowosadtko, *Stehendes Heer*, p. 182. **49.** J. Kraus, *Das Militärwesen der Reichsstadt Augsburg, 1548–1806* (Augsburg, 1980), p. 208. **50.** Examples in HSAS, A6 Bü.27–30, containing Württemberg muster rolls from 1728. **51.** Examples in B. Sicken, 'Müßiggänger und liederliche Burschen. Beobachtungen zur militärischen Aushebungen ländlicher Außenseiter im Hochstift Würzburg Mitte des 18. Jahrhunderts', in P. Leidinger and D. Metzler (eds.), *Geschichte und Geschichtsbewußtsein* (Münster, 1990), pp. 269–307; K. Staudinger, *Geschichte des kurbayerischen Heeres*, 5 vols. (Munich, 1901–9), III, pp. 247–9. **52.** M. v. Salisch, *Treue Deserteurer: Das kursächsische Militär und der Siebenjährigen Krieg* (Munich, 2009); Duffy, *Instrument of war*, pp. 185–91, 239–42; D. Krebs, *A generous and merciful enemy: Life for German prisoners of war during the American Revolution* (Norman, OK, 2015); H.A. Vossler, *With Napoleon in Russia, 1812* (London, 1969), pp. 126–41. **53.** Frederick expressed this slightly differently on several occasions: J. Luvaas, *Frederick the Great on the art of war* (New York), pp. 16, 77–8. Examples of the stereotypical interpretation in M. Kitchen, *A military history of Germany* (London, 1975), p. 23; C.H. Hermann, *Deutsche Militärgeschichte* (Frankfurt and Main, 1968), pp. 112–13. **54.** F.A. Pottle (ed.), *Boswell on the grand tour: Germany and Switzerland, 1764* (Melbourne, 1953), p. 80; A. v. Witzleben, *Aus alten Parolebüchern der Berliner Garnison zur Zeit Friedrichs des Großen* (Berlin, 1851), pp. 10–11. **55.** HSAS, A30a Bü.12, instructions from 1779; F. Beck, *Geschichte der alten Hessen-Darmstädtischen Reiterregimenter* (Darmstadt, 1910), p. 389; J. Muth, *Flucht aus dem militaärischen Alltag: Ursachen und individuelle Ausprägung der Desertion in der Armee Friedrichs des Großen* (Freiburg, 2003), p. 14 n.5, 157. **56.** Archenholz, *Gemälde*, p. 28. **57.** Nowosadtko, *Stehendes Heer*, pp. 122, 126, 139, 220–3; Möbius, *Prussian army soldiers*, pp. 29–32; P.H. Wilson, 'Early modern German military justice', in Davide Maffi (ed.), *Tra Marte e Astrea. Giustizia e giuridizione militare nell' Europa della prima età moderna (secc. xvi–xviii)* (Milan, 2012), pp. 43–85. **58.** E. Städter, *Die Ansbach-Bayreuther Truppen im Amerikanischen Unabhängigkeitskrieg, 1777–1783* (Nuremberg, 1956), pp. 22–3; see also P.H. Wilson, 'Violence and the rejection of authority in eighteenth-century Germany: The case of the Swabian mutinies in 1757', *German History*, 12 (1994), 1–26. For desertion generally, see M. Sikora, *Disziplin und Desertion* (Berlin, 1996). **59.** The statistics cited here have been calculated from numerous army and regimental histories; see also W.R. Fann, 'Peacetime attrition in the army of Frederick William I, 1713–1740', *CEH*, 11 (1978), 323–41; M. Winter, 'Desertionsprozesse in der Preußischen Armee nach dem Siebenjährigen Krieg', in J. Nowosadtko et al. (eds.), *Militär und Recht* (Göttingen, 2016), pp. 187–207. **60.** For example, the Saxon corps in 1792–6: O. Schuster and F.A. Francke, *Geschichte der sächsischen Armee*, 3 vols. (Leipzig, 1883), II, pp. 190–221. **61.** A. Forrest, *Conscripts and deserters: The army and French society during the Revolution and Empire* (Oxford, 2001). **62.** HSAS, A6 Bü.63, June 1734. **63.** Kraus, *Augsburg*, pp. 290–1; Jany, *Preußischen Armee*, vol. I, p. 659. **64.** Reyscher, XIX. Further individual notices and measures in HSAS, A6 Bü.63; A30c Bü.1; E31 Bü.1324. **65.** Examples of pardons in HSAS, A6 Bü.63; A202 Bü.2278, 2281; StAD, E8 B107 and 18, 27 November 1718. C. Küther, *Menschen auf der Straße. Vagierende Unterschichten in Bayern, Franken und Schwaben in der zweiten Hälfte des 18. Jahrhunderts* (Göttingen, 1983, 1987), pp. 19–22. **66.** HSAS, C14 Bü.70; cartel between Hessen-Darmstadt and Prussia from 1818 in StAD, E8 B107/13; K. Härter, 'Die

Formierung transnationaler Strafrechtsregime', *Rechtsgeschichte*, 18 (2011), 36–65. **67.** Examples in HSAS, A30c Bü.1; StAD, E8 B108/2. **68.** E. Vogt, *Unter der Herrschaft des Zopfes im 17. und 18. Jahrhundert* (Neugreifenburg, 1974); Witzleben, *Aus alten Parolebüchern der Berliner Garnison zur Zeit Friedrichs des Großen* (Berlin, 1851), pp. 28–39. **69.** A. Keim, *Geschichte des Infanterie-Regiments Großherogin (3. Großherzogl. Hessisches) Nr.117* (Berlin, 1903), p. 42n. **70.** H. Bleckwenn, *Unter dem Preußen-Adler. Das brandenburgisch-preußische Heer 1640–1807* (Munich, 1978), pp. 81–6; K.P. Merta, *Die Uniformierung* (Berlin, 1991), pp. 55–65; A. Ritter v. Arneth, *Geschichte Maria Theresias*, 10 vols. (Vienna, 1863–79), VII, p. 185. **71.** Witzleben, *Parolebüchern*, pp. 42–4; R. Weltrich, *Friedrich Schiller* (Stuttgart, 1899), p. 76. **72.** Neubauer's diary reprinted in H. Bleckwenn (ed.), *Kriegs- und Friedensbilder, 1725–1759* (Osnabrück, 1971), pp. 220, 250. **73.** Examples in F. v. Schroetter, 'Die Entwicklung des Begriffs "Servis" im preußischen Heerwesen', *FBPG*, 13 (1900), 1–28; O. Bezzel, *Geschichte des kurpfälizischen Heeres von seinen Anfängen bis zur Vereinigung von Kurpfalz und Kurbayern 1777*, 2 vols. (Munich, 1925–8), I, pp. 71–5. **74.** Kotsch, *Potsdam*, pp. 19–22, 36, 58–60; Muth, *Flucht*, pp. 114–17; B. Engelen, *Soldatenfrauen in Preußen* (Münster, 2005), pp. 248–82. **75.** HSAS, A32 Bd.248 fol. 181–2. **76.** H.T. Gräf, 'Militärisierung der Stadt oder Urbanisierung des Militärs?', in R. Pröve (ed.), *Klio in Uniform?* (Cologne, 1997), pp. 89–108, 92. For the following, see also K. Schwieger, 'Militär und Bürgertum. Zur gesellschaftlichen Prägekraft des Preußen Militärsystems im 18. Jahrhundert', in D. Blaius (ed.), *Preußen in der deutschen Geschichte* (Königstein, 1980), pp. 179–200 at 185–7; W. Neugebauer, 'Staatsverwaltung, Manufaktur und Garnison. Die polyfunktionale Residenzlandschaft von Berlin-Potsdam-Wusterhausen zur Zeit Friedrich Wilhelms I', *FBPG*, NS 7 (1997), 233–57. **77.** U. Bräker, *The poor man of Toggenburg* (Edinburgh, 1970), p. 132. **78.** Engelen, *Soldatenfrauen*, pp. 109–27; Duffy, *Instrument of war*, pp. 50, 209, 230–1; P.H. Wilson, 'German women and war, 1500–1800', *War in History*, 3 (1996), 127–60. Quotation from Jany, *Preußischen Armee*, III, p. 38. **79.** Barracks regulations from 1777, printed in Reyscher, no. 436; L. and M. Frey, *Frederick I: The man and his times* (New York, 1984), p. 142. **80.** Engelen, *Soldatenfrauen*, pp. 438–50; O. Elster, *Geschichte der stehenden Truppen im Herzogtum Braunschweig-Wolfenbüttel*, 2 vols. (Leipzig, 1899–1901), I, p. 208. **81.** B. Thompson Count Rumford, *The collected works of Count Rumford*, 5 vols. (Cambridge, MA, 1968–70), V, p. 8. **82.** HSAS, A202 Bü.2006; Von Kolb [sic], 'Feldprediger in Altwürttemberg', *Blätter für württembergischer Kirchengeschichte*, 10 (1906), 22–51, 117–42 at 132. Prussian provision is summarized in M. Guddart, *Kürassiere, Dragoner, Husaren: Die Kavallerie Friedrichs des Großen* (Hamburg, 1989), pp. 68–9, 82–3, while that for Austria is covered by Duffy, *Instrument of war*, pp. 364–78. See generally P. Lenihan, *Fluxes, fevers and fighting men: War and disease in ancien regime Europe, 1648–1789* (Warwick, 2019), pp. 140–67. **83.** *Preußischer Soldatenbriefe* (Osnabrück, 1982), pt 2, p. 22. Statistics from Urlanis, *Bilanz der Kriege*, pp. 241, 249–50, 303–4; Staudinger, *Kurbayerischen Heeres*, III, p. 1,070. **84.** E.g. E. Schubert, *Arme Leute, Bettler und Gauner im Franken des 18. Jahrhunderts*, 2nd ed. (Neustadt a.d. Aisch, 1990), pp. 138–46. **85.** For this and the following, see B. Wunder, 'Die Institutionalisierung der Invaliden-, Alters- und Hinterbliebenenversorgung der Staatsbediensteren in Österreich, 1740–1790', *MIÖG*, 92 (1984), 341–406; W. Hubatsch, *Frederick the Great of Prussia* (London, 1975), pp. 134–5, 205–6; Engelen, *Soldatenfrauen*, pp. 503–30; M. Meumann, 'Soldatenfamilien und unehrliche Kinder: Ein soziales Problem im Gefolge der stehenden Heere', B.R. Kroener and R. Pröve (eds.), *Krieg und Frieden* (Paderborn, 1996), pp. 219–36. **86.** E. Hagen, 'Die fürstlich würzburgische Hausinfanterie von ihren Anfängen bis zum Beginne des Siebenjährigen Krieges, 1636–1756', *DBKH*, 19 (1910), 69–203 at 193. See more generally P.H. Wilson, 'Militär und Religiosität in Württemberg, 1677–1797', in M. Kaiser and S. Kroll (eds.), *Militär und Religiosität in der Frühen Neuzeit* (Hamburg, 2003), pp. 71–96. **87.** B. Marschke, *Absolutely Pietist: Patronage, factionalism and* *state-building in the early eighteenth-century Prussian army chaplaincy* (Berlin, 2005); I. Deák, *Beyond nationalism: A social and political history of the Habsburg officer corps, 1848–1918* (Oxford, 1990), pp. 172–3; Duffy, *Instrument of war*, pp. 224, 379–80. **88.** Neubauer in Bleckwenn (ed.), *Kriegs- und Friedensbilder*, pp. 218–19; *Preußischer Soldatenbriefe*, esp. pp. 11–16, 20, 23, 27–8, 34; Dominicus, *Tagebuch*, pp. 6–7. **89.** Öst. Erb., vol. I, 463, 468–9, 539; P.H Wilson, 'The politics of military recruitment in eighteenth-century Germany', *EHR*, 117 (2002), 536–68 at 539–40. **90.** Höchner, *Selbstzeugnisse*, p. 30. **91.** W. Pfister, *Aargauer in fremden Kriegsdiensten*, 2 vols. (Aargau, 1980–4), I, pp. 55–72; R. Feller, *Geschichte Berns*, 4 vols. (Bern, 1946–60), III, p. 516. The following statistics derive largely from B.Z. Urlanis, *Bilanz der Kriege* (Berlin-DDR, 1965). **92.** A. v. Pfister, *Denkwürdigkeiten aus der württembergischen Kriegeschichte des 18. und 19. Jahrhunderts* (Stuttgart, 1868), p. 560. Austria lost a further 165,000 killed in action during the French Revolutionary Wars, considerably above Prussia's losses which were mainly due to disease. **93.** S. Altorfer–Ong, 'State investment in eighteenth-century Berne', *History of European Ideas*, 33 (2007), 440–62. **94.** Some of the evidence for these figures is set out in more detail in P.H. Wilson, *War, State and Society in Württemberg, 1677–1793* (Cambridge, 1995), pp. 37–42. For tax burdens, see P.C. Hartmann, *Das Steuersystem der europäischen Staaten am Ende des Ancien Régime* (Munich, 1979). **95.** For critical engagements with this literature, see W. Godsey, *The sinews of Habsburg power* (Oxford, 2018); C. Storrs (ed.), *The fiscal-military state in eighteenth-century Europe* (Aldershot, 2009). For the following, see also E. Klein, *Geschichte der öffentlichen Finanzen in Deutschland* (Wiesbaden, 1974), pp. 67–103; P.G.M. Dickson, *Finance and government under Maria Theresia, 1740–1780*, 2 vols. (Oxford, 1987); H.P. Ullmann, *Der deutsche Steuerstaat: Geschichte der öffentlichen Finanzen vom 18. Jahrhundert bis heute* (Munich, 2005), pp. 124–31. **96.** C. Becker, 'Von Kurkölns Beziehungen zu Frankreich und seiner wirtschaftliche Lage im Siebenjährigen Kriege (1757–1761), *Annalen des Historischen Vereins für den Niederrhein*, 100 (1917), 43–119; A. Stoffer, 'Das Hochstift Paderborn zur Zeit es Siebenjährigen Krieges', *Zeitschrift für vaterländische Geschichte und Altertumskunde Westfalens*, 69 (1911), 58–182. **97.** F. Redlich, *De praeda militari: Looting and booty, 1500–1800* (Wiesbaden, 1956), pp. 58–77; T.C.W. Blanning, *The French Revolution in Germany: Occupation and resistance in the Rhineland, 1792–1802* (Oxford, 1983). **98.** J.G. Pahl, *Denkwürdigkeiten zur Geschichte von Schwaben während des beyden Feldzüge von 1799 und 1800* (Nördlingen, 1802), p. 19. See generally U. Planert, *Der Mythos vom Befreiungskrieg. Frankreichs Kriege und der deutsche Süden* (Paderborn, 2007); M. Rowe, *From Reich to state: The Rhineland in the revolutionary age* (Cambridge, 2003). **99.** Jany, *Preußischen Armee*, I, p. 800; Muth, *Flucht*, p. 40. **100.** F. Krippenstapel, *Die preußischen Husaren von den ältesten Zeiten bis zur Gegenwart* (Berlin, 1883), pp. 80–1; O. Chaline, *Les armées du Roi: Le grand chantier XVIIe–XVIIIe* (Paris, 2016), pp. 259–61. **101.** Examples in Kotsch, *Potsdam*, pp. 46–7, 82–96; Schwieger, 'Militär und Bürgertum', pp. 187–8, 197. **102.** L. Auer, 'Wirtschaftliche Aspekte des Spanischen Erbfolgekrieges', in J.I. Ruiz Rodriguez et al. (eds.), *La guerra de sucesión española* (Munich, 2008), pp. 73–90 at 84; A. Dolleczek, *Monographie über die k.u.k. österr.-ung. Blank- und Handfeuer-Waffen* (Vienna, 1896), p. 80. See also for the following G. Krause, *Altpreußische Militärbekleiderungswirtschaft* (Osnabrück, 1983); A. Wirtgen, 'Die Handfeuerwaffen der preußischen Armee 1740–1786', in *Die Bewaffnung und Ausrüstung der Armee Friedrichs des Großen* (Rastatt, 1986), pp. 35–50; W. Treue, 'David Splitgerber. Ein Unternehmer im preußischen Merkantilstaat 1683–1764', *VSWG*, 41 (1954), 253–67.

10. War and Nation-Building

1. P.W. Schroeder, *The transformation of European politics, 1763–1848* (Oxford, 1994), p. 52. 2. W. Siemann, *Metternich: Visionary and strategist* (Cambridge, MA, 2019). 3. The number of member states fluctuated with the accession of Hessen-Homberg in 1817 and the merger of several minor principalities. G.S. Werner, *Bavaria in the German Confederation, 1820–1848* (Cranbury, NJ, 1975); B. Ashton, *The kingdom of Württemberg and the making of Germany, 1815–1871* (London, 2018); P. Burg, *Die deutsche Trias in Idee und Wirklichkeit vom Alten Reich zum Zollverein* (Mainz, 1989); R.D. Billinger, *Metternich and the German question: States' rights and federal duties, 1820–1834* (London, 1991). 4. J. Angelow, *Von Wien nach Königgrätz: Die Sicherheitspolitik des Deuschen Bundes im europäischen Gleichgewicht, 1815–1866* (Munich, 1996), pp. 33–52; M. Kotulla, 'Die Entstehung der Kriegsverfassung des deutschen Bundes vor dem Hintergrund verfassungs-rechtlicher und verfassungspolitischer Kontroversen in der Bundesversammlung, 1816–1823', *ZSRG GA*, 117 (2000), 122–237. *HDM*, IV/II, 226–358, gives a good overview of the organization and structure of the contingents. 5. AEG Confédération F2. 6. Printed in H. Foerster, 'Die ewige Neutralität der Schweiz 1815', in R. Haudenreich (ed.), *Marignano 1515–2015* (Lenzburg, 2015), pp. 299–94 at 289–90. 7. *Eidgenößisches Militaire-Reglement von 1817* (Bern, 1817). 8. AEG F7 to F10 papers. See generally A. Lenherr, *Das schweizerische Militärwesen der Restaurationszeit* (Osnabrück, 1976); G. Rapp and V. Hofer, *Der schweizerische Generalstab*, vol. I (Basel, 1983), pp. 131–4. 9. AEG France, 28–30; H. Amersfoort, 'The end of an enterprise: Swiss regiments in the Royal Dutch Army, 1814–1829', in S. Rial (ed.), *De Nimègue à Jave* (Morges, 2014), pp. 189–202. For the wider context, see P.H. Wilson, 'Foreign military labour in Europe's transition to modernity', *ERH*, 27 (2020), 12–32. 10. D. Porch, *The French Foreign Legion* (London, 1991); M. Windrow, *Our friends beneath the sands: The French Foreign Legion in France's colonial conquests, 1875–1935* (London, 2010); C. Koller, *Die Fremdenlegion* (Paderborn, 2013), esp. pp. 47–8. 11. C.C. Bayley, *Mercenaries for the Crimea* (Montreal, 1977); J. Leband, 'From mercenaries to military settlers: The British German Legion, 1854–61', in S. Miller (ed.), *Soldiers and settlers in Africa, 1850–1918* (Leiden, 2009), pp. 85–122. 12. R.E. May, *Manifest destiny's underworld: Filibustering in antebellum America* (Chapel Hill, NC, 2002), pp. 98–100; A.J. Cade II, 'Why they fought: The initial motivation of German-American soldiers who fought for the Union during the American Civil War', *ERH*, 27 (2020), 65–87. 13. J. Steinauer and R. Syburra-Bertelletto, *Courir l'europe: Valaisans au service étranger, 1790–1870* (Sion, 2009); D.J. Alvarez, *The pope's soldiers: A military history of the modern Vatican* (Lawrence, KS, 2011). 14. W. St Clair, *That Greece might still be free: The Philhellenes in the War of Independence* (London, 1972); O. Bezzel, *Die königliche bayerische Armee vom 1825–1866* (Munich, 1931), pp. 13–43. 15. E. Pitner, *Maximilian's lieutenant. A personal history of the Mexican campaign, 1864–67* (London, 1993). 16. K. Hagemann, *Revisiting Prussia's wars against Napoleon* (Cambridge, 2015), pp. 79–129. 17. Angelow, *Von Wien*, pp. 52–6; E. Wienhofer, *Das Militärwesen des Deutschen Bundes und das Ringen zwischen Österreich und Preussen um die Vorherrschaft in Deutschland, 1815–1866* (Osnabrück, 1973), pp. 80–3. 18. G. Arnsberg, '… *über die Notwendigkeit einer deutsche Republik.' Die württembergische Militär- und Zivilver-schwörung 1831–1833* (Stuttgart, 2017). 19. O. Ozavci, *Dangerous gifts: Imperialism, security, and civil wars in the Levant, 1798–1864* (Oxford, 2021), pp. 211–26; J. Niemeyer, *Das österreichische Militärwesen im Umbruch. Untersuchungen zum Kriegsbild zwischen 1830 und 1866* (Osnabrück, 1979), pp. 59–60. The Federal Fortresses are discussed on pp. 453–4. 20. For a summary overview of the interventions, see AEG F10.1 Kreisschreiben, 5 June 1844. 21. J. Remak, *A very civil war: The Swiss Sonderbund War of 1847* (Boulder, CO, 1993), pp. 34–45. For the following, see also AEG F11; R. Weaver, *Three weeks in November: A military history of the Swiss civil war of 1847* (Solihull, 2012); Rapp and

Hofer, *Schweizerische Generalstab*, pp. 193–228. **22.** M. Rapport, *1848: Year of revolution* (New York, 2009); J. Sperber, *The European revolutions, 1848–51* (Cambridge, 1991); W. Siemann, *The German revolution of 1848–49* (Basingstoke, 1998); H.J. Hahn, *The 1848 revolution in German-speaking Central Europe* (Harlow, 2001). **23.** G. Wittling, 'Zivil-militärische Beziehungen im Spannungsfeld von Residenz und entstehndem großstädtischen Industriezentrum', in B. Sicken (ed.), *Stadt und Militär* (Paderborn, 1998), pp. 215–42 at 224. See generally, A. Lüdtke, *Polices and state in Prussia, 1815–1850* (Cambridge, 1989). **24.** I. Deak, *The lawful revolution: Louis Kossuth and the Hungarians, 1848–1849* (New York, 1979); G. Bona (ed.), *The Hungarian Revolution and War of Independence: A military history* (Boulder, CO, 1998); J.C. Allmayer-Beck, 'Die bewaffnete Macht in Staat und Gesellschaft', in A. Wandruszka (ed.), *Die bewaffnete Macht* (Vienna, 1987), pp. 1–141 at 6, 28–9; A. Sked, *The survival of the Habsburg empire: Radetzky, the imperial army and class war, 1848* (New York, 1979), pp. 55–82; L. Sondhaus, *In the service of the emperor: Italians in the Austrian armed forces 1814–1918* (Boulder, CO, 1990), pp. 37–47. **25.** For Prussian policy at this point, see D.E. Barclay, *Frederick William IV and the Prussian monarchy, 1840–1861* (Oxford, 1995). **26.** B.E. Vick, *Defining Germany: The 1848 Frankfurt parliamentarians and national identity* (Cambridge, MA, 2002). **27.** S. Pech, *The Czech revolution of 1848* (Chapel Hill, NC, 1969). **28.** A. Sked, *Radetzky* (London, 2011), pp. 133–58; M. Embree, *Radetzky's marches: The campaigns of 1848 and 1849 in Upper Italy* (Solihull, 2011); J. Keates, *The siege of Venice 1848* (London, 2005). **29.** G. Rothenberg, 'Jelacic, the Croatian military border and the intervention against Hungary in 1848', *Austrian History Yearbook*, 1 (1965), 45–68; W. v. Rüstow, *Geschichte des ungarischen Insurrektionskriegs in den Jahren 1848 und 1849* (Zürich, 1860); K. Sitzler, *Solidarität oder Söldnertum? Die auslädischen Freiwilligenverbände im ungarischen Unabhängigkeitskrieg 1848–49* (Osnabrück, 1980). For other Germans who supported revolution in Italy, see F.N. Göhde, 'German volunteers in the armed conflicts of the Italian Risorgimento, 1834–70', *Journal of Modern Italian Studies*, 14 (2009), 461–75. **30.** S. Beller, *Francis Joseph* (London, 1996). **31.** R.C. Canevali, 'Armies in revolution: The Badenese mutiny of 1849', *CRE*, 14 (1985), 632–43; L.E. Lee, 'The peoples' armies or princely armies: The German revolution of 1848–9', *CRE*, 18 (1989), 644–58; S. Müller, *Soldaten in der deutschen Revolution von 1848/49* (Paderborn, 1999); P. Sauer, *Das württembergische Heer in der Zeit des Deutschen und des Norddeutschen Bundes* (Stuttgart, 1954), pp. 130–41. **32.** K.H. Lutz, *Das badische Offizierskorps, 1840–1870/71* (Stuttgart, 1997), pp. 280–99. **33.** W. Wagner, 'Die k.(u.)k. Armee: Gliederung und Aufgabenstellung', in Wandruszka (ed.), *Die bewaffnete Macht*, pp. 142–633 at 237–9; A. Johansen, *Soldiers as police: The French and Prussian armies and the policing of popular protest, 1889–1914* (Aldershot, 2005); J. Gooch, *The Italian army and the First World War* (Cambridge, 2014), pp. 12–13. **34.** W. Carr, *Schleswig-Holstein, 1815–1848* (Manchester, 1963); N. Svendson, *The First Schleswig-Holstein War, 1848–50* (Solihull, 2007); G. Stolz, *Die Schleswig-holsteinische Erhebung* (Husum, 1996); 'FN' [sic], *Die Feldzüge des Deutsch-Dänische Krieges in den Jahren 1848 und 1849* (Leipzig, 1853). **35.** For Austrian policy, see the articles by L. Sondhaus and R.A. Austensen in *IHR*, 13 (1991), 1–37; W. Carr, *The origins of the wars of German unification* (London, 1991), pp. 96–101. **36.** Example in U. Heer, *Das Militär des Herzogtums Sachsen-Coburg und Gotha unter Herzog Ernst II. (1844–1867)* (Berlin, 2018), pp. 35–7, 47–9, 88–94. **37.** W. Baumgart, *The Crimean War, 1853–1856* (London, 1999). **38.** F.J. Coppa, *The origins of the wars of Italian unification* (London, 1992), pp. 59–111. **39.** Angelow, *Von Wien*, pp. 216–18; F.C. Schneid, 'A well-coordinated affair: Franco-Piedmontese war planning in 1859', *JMilH*, 76 (2012), 523–56, and his *The French-Piedmontese campaign of 1859* (Rome, 2014). **40.** F. Müller, 'The spectre of the people in arms: The Prussian government and the militarisation of German nationalism, 1859–1864', *EHR*, 122 (2007), 82–104. **41.** D.E. Barclay, 'The court camarilla and the politics of monarchical restoration in Prussia, 1848–58', in J. Retallack (ed.),

Between reform, reaction and resistance (Providence, RI, 1993), pp. 123–56. Useful summary of events in D.E. Showalter, *The wars of German unification* (Harlow, 2004), pp. 75–87, with more detail in E.N. Anderson, *The social and political conflict in Prussia, 1858–1864* (Lincoln, NE, 1954). **42.** Background in Carr, *Origins*, pp. 41–9, 64–84, 112–18. For the war, see T. Buk-Swienty, *1864: The forgotten war that shaped Europe* (London, 2015); M. Embree, *Bismarck's first war* (Solihull, 2006). **43.** T. Zuber, *The Moltke myth: Prussian war planning, 1857–1871* (Lanham, MD, 2008), offers a more critical view than the usual emphasis on professional expertise which is stressed by A. Bucholz, *Moltke and the German wars, 1864–1871* (Basingstoke, 2001). Balanced assessment in P.G. Gross, *Mythos und Wirklichkeit. Geschichte des operative Denkens im deutschen Heer von Moltke d.Ä. bis Heusinger* (Paderborn, 2012). Further discussion in ch. 12, **p. xxx. 44.** The states supporting Prussia were Brunswick, Mecklenburg-Schwerin, Oldenburg, Sachsen-Gotha, Schwarzburg-Rudolstadt and Schwarzburg-Sondershausen. **45.** S. Fiedler, *Kriegswesen und Kriegführung im Zeitalter der Einigungskriege* (Koblenz, 1991), p. 123. For the war, see G. Wawro, *The Austro-Prussian war: Austria's war with Prussia and Italy in 1866* (Cambridge, 1996); Showalter, *German Unification*, pp. 161–200. Austria eventually mobilized 528,000 men. **46.** M. Embree, *Too little, too late: The campaign in west and south Germany, June–July 1866* (Solihull, 2015). **47.** G. Craig, *The battle of Königgrätz* (Philadelphia, PA, 1964). **48.** Contrasting interpretations in P. Judson, *The Habsburg empire* (Cambridge, MA, 2016); S. Beller, *The Habsburg monarchy, 1815–1918* (Cambridge, 2018). **49.** D. Wetzel, *A duel of giants: Bismarck, Napoleon III and the origins of the Franco-Prussian War* (Madison, WI, 2001). For the debate on the war's causes, see the contributions from David Wetzel and Josef Becker in *CEH*, 41 (2008), 93–124. For the ostensible cause, see L.D. Steefel, *Bismarck, the Hohenzollern candidacy and the origins of the Franco-Prussian War* (Cambridge, MA, 1962). **50.** T.J. Adriance, *The last gaiter button: A study in the mobilisation and concentration of the French army in the war of 1870* (Westport, CT, 1987); G.P. Cox, *The halt in the mud: French strategic planning from Waterloo to Sedan* (Boulder, CO, 1994); R. Holmes, *The road to Sedan: The French army, 1866–70* (London, 1984). For the war, see G. Wawro, *The Franco-Prussian War: The German conquest of France, 1870–1871* (Cambridge, 2003), and the classic study by M. Howard, *The Franco-Prussian War* (London, 1962). **51.** Prussian General Staff, *Der deutsch-französische Krieg, 1870–1*, 5 vols. (Berlin, 1874–81). **52.** F. Stern, *Gold and iron: Bismarck, Bleichröder, and the building of the German Empire* (London, 1977), pp. 130–1. **53.** D. Fermer, *Sedan 1870: The eclipse of France* (Barnsley, 2008). **54.** B. Thaite, *Citizenship and wars: France in turmoil, 1870–1871* (London, 2001). **55.** D. Wetzel, *A duel of nations: Germany, France and the diplomacy of the war of 1870–1871* (Madison, WI, 2012), pp. 185–215. **56.** D. Albrecht, 'König Ludwig II. von Bayern und Bismarck', *HZ*, 270 (2000), 39–64. The spendthrift Ludwig II was given an annual life pension of 300,000 marks. For the Second Empire generally, see V.R. Berghahn, *Imperial Germany, 1871–1914* (Oxford, 1994); T. Nipperdey, *Deutsche Geschichte, 1866–1918*, 2 vols. (Munich, 1990–2). **57.** H. Müller, 'Das Reichmilitärgesetz von 1874 als erstes deutsches Septennat', in P. Baumgart et al. (eds.), *Die preußischen Armee* (Paderborn, 2008), pp. 229–46. **58.** J. Sperber, *The Kaiser's voters: Electors and elections in Imperial Germany* (Cambridge, 1997). **59.** C.J. Fischer, *Alsace to the Alsatians? Visions and division of Alsatian regionalism, 1870–1939* (New York, 2010), pp. 7–81. **60.** S. Berman, *Democracy and dictatorship in Europe from the ancien regime to the present* (Oxford, 2019), pp. 146–68; V.R. Berghahn, *Imperial Germany, 1871–1918* (New York, 2005). **61.** P. Schroeder, 'The lost intermediaries: The impact of 1870 on the European system', *IHR*, 6 (1984), 1–27. **62.** G.E. Rothenberg, *The army of Francis Joseph* (West Lafayette, IN, 1976), pp. 90–104; S.W. Lackey, *The rebirth of the Habsburg army: Friedrich Beck and the rise of the General Staff* (Westport, CT, 1995), pp. 59–82. For the following, see also F.R. Bridge, *From Sadowa to Sarajevo: The foreign policy of Austria-Hungary, 1866–1914* (London, 1972). **63.** See

S. Förster, 'Der deutsche Generalstab und die Illusion des kurzen Krieges, 1871–1914', *MGM*, 54 (1995), 61–95, and I.V. Hull, *Absolute destruction: Military culture and the practices of war in Imperial Germany* (Ithaca, NY, 2006), pp. 93–181, in contrast to L.L. Farrar, *The short war illusion: German policy, strategy and domestic affairs, August–December 1914* (Santa Barbara, CA, 1973). **64.** J. Luvaas, *The military legacy of the Civil War: The European inheritance* (Chicago, IL, 1959); J. Scheibert, *A Prussian observes the American Civil War* (London, 2001). **65.** F.J. Müller, 'The German monarchies', in M. Jefferies (ed.), *The Ashgate research companion to Imperial Germany* (Abingdon, 2015), pp. 55–76 at 69. See J.C.G. Röhl, *The Kaiser and his court* (Cambridge, 1994); L. Cecil, *Wilhelm II*, 2 vols. (Chapel Hill, NC, 1989–96). **66.** As argued by T. Zuber, *Inventing the Schlieffen Plan: German war planning, 1891–1914* (Oxford, 2002), and his *German war planning, 1891–1914: Sources and interpretations* (Woodbridge, 2004). This claim is challenged by R.T. Foley, 'The real Schlieffen Plan', *WiH*, 13 (2006), 91–115; A. Mombauer, *Helmuth von Moltke and the origins of the First World War* (Cambridge, 2001), and her 'Der Moltkeplan. Modifikation des Schlieffenplans bei gleichen Zielen', in H. Ehlert et al. (eds.), *Der Schlieffenplan* (Paderborn, 2007), pp. 79–99; Gross, *Mythos*, pp. 75–98. **67.** Dutch territory would be crossed if the Germans advanced via Maastricht, which projected south into Belgium. **68.** T.M. Holmes, 'Back to the sources: An attempt to resolve the Schlieffen Plan controversy', *WiH*, 28 (2021), 525–43. The idea that Schlieffen intended to fight *both* France and Russia derived from the assessment of German officers after 1918, who claimed it would have succeeded had it not been modified by his successor, Moltke the Younger. The various iterations of Germany's war plans across 1893–1914 are printed in H. Ehlert et al. (eds.), *The Schlieffen Plan* (Lexington, KY, 2014), pp. 346–525. **69.** H.H. Herwig, 'Germany and the "short war" illusion', *JMilH*, 66 (2002), 681–93 at 688. **70.** R. Hobson, *Imperialism at sea: Naval strategic thought, the ideology of sea power and the Tirpitz plan, 1875–1914* (Leiden, 2002), pp. 117–31. For the accuracy of Caprivi's assessment, see M. Hewitson, *Germany and the modern world, 1880–1914* (Cambridge, 2018). **71.** Quoted in J. Steinberg, *Tirpitz and the birth of the German battlefleet* (London, 1968), p. 60. **72.** E. Grimmer-Solem, *Learning empire: Globalisation and the German quest for world status, 1875–1919* (Cambridge, 2019). **73.** Quoted in M. Epkenhans, *Tirpitz: Architect of the German High Seas Fleet* (Washington, DC, 2008), p. 53. See also P.J. Kelly, *Tirpitz and the Imperial German Navy* (Bloomington, IN, 2011), which supersedes the still useful V. Berghahn, *Der Tirpitzplan: Genesis und Verfall eine innenpolitischen Krisenstrategie unter Wilhelm II* (Düsseldorf, 1971). **74.** P. Padfield, *The great naval race: Anglo-German naval rivalry, 1900–1914* (London, 1974), with the recent modification that Britain was also concerned at German commerce raiding potential: M.S. Seligmann, *The Royal Navy and the German threat, 1901–1914* (Oxford, 2012). **75.** H.J.L. v. Moltke, *Erinnerung, Briefe, Dokumente 1877–1916* (Stuttgart, 1922), p. 308. For the 1905–6 crisis, see A. Moritz, *Das Problem des Präventivkrieges in der deutschen Politik während der ersten Marokokrise* (Frankfurt am Main, 1974). **76.** Rothenberg, *Army of Francis Joseph*, pp. 128–37. **77.** L. Sondhaus, *Conrad von Hötzendorf: Architect of the Apocalypse* (Leiden, 2000); W. Dornik, *Des Kaisers Falke. Wirken und Nach-Wirken von Franz Conrad von Hötzendorf*, 2nd ed. (Innsbruck, 2013). See also G. Kronenbitter, '*Krieg im Frieden*'. *Die Führung der k.u.k. Armee und die Großmachtpolitik Österreich-Ungarns 1906–1914* (Munich, 2003). **78.** J. Rüger, *The great naval game: Britain and Germany in the age of empire* (Cambridge, 2007), pp. 244–50. **79.** R.C. Hall, *The Balkan Wars, 1912–1913* (London, 2000); T. Scheer, 'The Habsburg empire's German-speaking public sphere and the First Balkan War', in D. Geppert et al. (eds.), *The wars before the Great War* (Cambridge, 2015), pp. 301–19; A. Hannig, 'Austria-Hungary, Germany, and the Balkan Wars', in K. Boeckh and S. Ruter (eds.), *The wars of yesterday* (New York, 2018), pp. 113–36. **80.** T. Hadley, *Military diplomacy in the Dual Alliance: German military attaché reporting from Vienna, 1879–1914* (Lawrence, KS, 2016); M.N. Vego, *Austro-Hungarian naval* *policy, 1904–14* (London, 1996), pp. 114–33. **81.** C. Clark, *The sleepwalkers: How Europe went to war in 1914* (London, 2012); G. Martel, *The month that changed the world: July 1914* (Oxford, 2014). R.F. Hamilton and H.H. Herwig (eds.), *Decisions for war, 1914–1917* (Cambridge, 2004). Good summaries for the Central Powers in A. Watson, *Ring of steel: Germany and Austria-Hungary in World War I* (London, 2014), pp. 28–52; H. Strachan, 'Germany in the First World War: The problem of strategy', *GH*, 12 (1994), 236–49. **82.** Printed in M. Montgelas and W. Schücking (eds.), *Outbreak of the world war: German documents collected by Karl Kautsky* (New York, 1924), pp. 78–9. **83.** G. Wawro, *A mad catastrophe: The outbreak of World War I and the collapse of the Habsburg empire* (New York, 2014), especially stresses that Austria-Hungary's behaviour was reckless because it was wholly unprepared for a major war.

11. Nations in Arms

1. Bavaria played a key role in blocking the peacetime appointment of a commander: W.D. Gruner, *Das bayerische Heer, 1824 bis 1864* (Boppard, 1972), pp. 77–82, 212–20; E. Wienhofer, *Das Militärwesen des Deutschen Bundes und das Ringen zwischen Österreich und Preussen um die Vorherrschaft in Deutschland 1815–1866* (Osnabrück, 1973), pp. 55–6, 62; M. Kotulla, 'Die Entstehung der Kriegsverfassung des deutschen Bundes vor dem Hintergrund verfassungsrechtlicher und verfassungspolitischer Kontroversen in der Bundesversammlung, 1816–1823', *ZSRG GA*, 117 (2000), 122–237 at 200–7. **2.** W. Keul, *Die Bundesmilitärkommission (1819–1866)* (Frankfurt am Main, 1977). **3.** *Eidgenössisches Militaire-Reglement* (Bern, 1817), pp. 24–37; V. Hofer, *Der schweizerische Generalstab*, vol. II (Basel, 1983), pp. 16–17, 37–44. **4.** For an example: K.U. Keubke and R. Munn, *Mecklenburger Truppen in Schleswig-Holstein, in Baden und bei inneren Unruhen im eigenen Lande 1848/49* (Schwerin, 2012), p. 107. **5.** O. Bezzel, *Die königliche bayerische Armee vom 1825–1866* (Munich, 1931), pp. 9–15; R. Bauer, *Handbuch der bayerischen Ämter, Gemeinden und Gerichte, 1799–1980* (Munich, 1983), pp. 340ff; K.H. Lutz, *Das badische Offizierskorps, 1840–1870/71* (Stuttgart, 1997), pp. 165–9. **6.** J. Steinberg, *Tirpitz and the birth of the German battlefleet* (London, 1968), pp. 49–50. **7.** For this and the following, see W. Wagner, 'Die k.(u.)k. Armee: Gliederung und Aufgabenstellung', in A. Wandruszka (ed.), *Die bewaffnete Macht* (Vienna, 1987), pp. 142–633 at 144–58, 351–73; L. Höbelt, 'Die Marine,' in ibid, pp. 687–763 at 730–4; G. Rothenberg, *The army of Francis Joseph* (West Lafayette, IN, 1976), pp. 38–41, 59–61, 78–80, 105–25. **8.** W. Hubatsch, *Der Admiralstab und die obersten Marinebehörden in Deutschland, 1848–1945* (Frankfurt am Main, 1958). **9.** G. Craig, *The politics of the Prussian army, 1640–1945* (Oxford, 1955), pp. 227–31; M. Kitchen, *The German officer corps, 1890–1914* (Oxford, 1968), pp. 7–12. For the following, see also H.H. Herwig, *'Luxury' fleet: The Imperial German Navy, 1888–1918* (London, 1980), pp. 21–4; Steinberg, *Tirpitz*, pp. 53–4, 62–4. **10.** T. Schwarzmüller, *Zwischen Kaiser und 'Führer'. Generalfeldmarschall August von Mackensen* (Paderborn, 1997). **11.** U. Herr and J. Nguyen, *Die deutschen Generale sowie Kriegsministerien und Generalstäbe von 1871 bis 1914* (Vienna, 2012), pp. 363–6; J. Niemeyer, *Das österreichische Militärwesen im Umbruch. Untersuchungen zum Kriegsbild zwischen 1830 und 1866* (Osnabrück, 1979), pp. 147–53; Wagner, 'Armee', pp. 158–67, 373–89. **12.** Bauer, *Handbuch der bayerischen Ämter*, pp. 336–7; R. Jaun, *Das Eidgenössisch Generalstabskorps, 1804–1874* (Basel, 1983), pp. 203–48, and his *Das schweizerische Generalstabskorps, 1875–1945* (Basel, 1991), pp. 432–5; Hofer, *Der schweizerische Generalstab*, pp. 17–34. **13.** T. Zuber, *The Moltke myth: Prussian war planning, 1857–1871* (Lanham, MD, 2008), pp. 99–100; S. Leutenschneider, *Auftragstaktik im preußischen-deutschen Heer, 1871–1914* (Hamburg, 2002). **14.** L. Cecil, *The German diplomatic service, 1871–1914* (Princeton, NJ, 1976), pp. 124–38. **15.** Höbelt, 'Die

Marine', p. 689.   16. Gruner, *Das bayerische Heer*, p. 333.   17. D. Moran, 'Arms and the concert: The nation in arms and the dilemmas of German liberalism', in D. Moran and A. Waldron (eds.), *The people in arms* (Cambridge, 2003), pp. 49–74; K. Hagemann, *Revisiting Prussia's wars against Napoleon* (Cambridge, 2015), pp. 221–7.   18. K. v. Rotteck, *Über stehende Heere und Nationalmiliz* (Freiburg, 1816); U. Frevert, *A nation in barracks: Conscription, military service and civil society in modern Germany* (London, 2004), pp. 50–65, 113–17; J. Forderer, 'Das Bürgermilitär in Württemberg', *Tübinger Blätter*, 23 (1932), 1–27 at 7–10; K. Pfaff, *Geschichte der Stadt Stuttgarts*, 2 vols. (Stuttgart, 1845), vol. II, pp. 245–6.   19. P. Sauer, *Revolution und Volksbewaffnung. Die Württembergische Bürgerwehren im 19. Jahrhundert, vor allem während der Revolution von 1848/49* (Ulm, 1976); M. Wettenengel, *Die Wiesbadener Bürgerwehr 1848/49 und die Revolution im Herzogtum Nassau* (Taunusstein, 1998); J. Schlürmann, 'Das Militär der Freien und Hansastadt Lübeck 1623–1867', in E.S. Fiebig and J. Schlürmann (eds.), *Handbuch zur nordelbischen Militärgeschichte* (Husum, 2010), pp. 165–204 at 191–7.   20. Frevert, *Nation in barracks*, pp. 132–8, 205–6.   21. O. Meuwly, *Armée Vaudoise. Evolution et démocratisation au XIXe siècle* (Yens sur Morges, 1995), pp. 50–85; Jaun, *Eidgenössisch Generalstabskorps*, pp. 260–1.   22. D. Woodward, *Armies of the world, 1815–1914* (London, 1978), p. 176.   23. Niemeyer, *Das österreichische Militärwesen*, pp. 37–42; Wagner, 'Armee', pp. 200–4, 240–3; A. Sked, *The survival of the Habsburg empire: Radetzky, the imperial army and class war, 1848* (New York, 1979), pp. 34–5. Conscription was finally extended to the previously exempt parts of the monarchy (Hungary, Lombardy, Venetia, Dalmatia, and Tirol) in 1852–3.   24. Anon, *Die bayerische Armee 1866* (Berlin, 1866), pp. 5, 18–19; Gruner, *Das bayerische Heer*, pp. 147–52, 267, 346, 360–74; P. Sauer, *Das württembergische Heer in der Zeit des Deutschen und des Norddeutschen Bundes* (Stuttgart, 1958), pp. 27–39, 90–7; Lutz, *Badische Offizierskorps*, pp. 22–5; J. Niemeyer, *Königlich Hannöversches Militär, 1815–1866* (Beckum, 1866), pp. 12, 17; Keubke and Mumm, *Mecklenburger Truppen*, pp. 7–8; U. Herr, *Das Militär des Herzogtums Sachsen-Coburg und Gotha unter Herzog Ernst II. (1844–1867)* (Berlin, 2018), pp. 49–56   25. Those drafted into the cavalry served four years, with only one in reserve. See *HDM*, IV/I, 59–109; D. Walter, *Preußische Heeresreformen, 1807–1870* (Paderborn, 2003).   26. W. Petter, 'Die Roonsche Heeresorganisation und das Ende der Landwehr', in P. Baumgart et al. (eds.), *Die preußischen Armee* (Paderborn, 2008), pp. 215–28 at 221.   27. Details in C. v. Jany, *Geschichte der preußischen Armee*, 4 vols. (Berlin, 1928–9), IV, pp. 219ff.   28. W. Vogel, *Entscheidung 1864* (Koblenz, 1996), p. 26.   29. Gruner, *Das bayerische Heer*, pp. 201, 314–15.   30. W. Wagner, 'Armee', pp. 417–30, 493–4; T. Pape, 'Die Königlich ungarische Landwehr (Honvéd) 1868 bis 1914', in Wandruszka (ed.), *Habsburger Monarchie*, pp. 634–86. In common with this model elsewhere, those drafted into the cavalry and artillery served one or two years longer respectively, with their reserve service shortened correspondingly. The Tirol retained special privileges within Austria's Landwehr.   31. S. Fiedler, *Kriegswesen und Kriegführung im Zeitalter der Millionenheere* (Koblenz, 1993), pp. 39–43.   32. F. Buchholz et al., *The Great War dawning: Germany and its army at the start of World War I* (Vienna, 2013), p. 177; I. Deák, *Beyond nationalism: A social and political history of the Habsburg officer corps, 1848–1918* (Oxford, 1990), p. 174.   33. The arrangements are summarized in Buchholz et al., *Great War*, pp. 168–73. Landwehr service was increased to six years in 1888, while reserve service rose by a year in 1893 to compensate for the cut in line duty. Similarly, Austria-Hungary's 1912 law increased reserve duty from seven to ten years.   34. Figures from Fiedler, *Millionenheere*, p. 76.   35. List in Buchholz et al., *Great War*, pp. 125–38. See also Bauer, *Handbuch der bayerischen Ämter*, pp. 341–53; Wagner, 'Armee', pp. 389–99.   36. Wagner, 'Armee', pp. 183–99, 415–17.   37. See generally D.E. Showalter, *Railroads and rifles: Soldiers, technology, and the unification of Germany* (Hamden, CT, 1975); D.E. Brose, *The politics of technological change in Prussia: Out of the shadow of antiquity, 1809–1848* (Princeton, NJ, 1993), and his *The Kaiser's army: The politics of military technology in Germany during the machine age, 1870–1918* (Oxford, 2001). **38.** Niemeyer, *Das österreichische Militärwesen*, pp. 113–21; R. Wirtgen, *Handfeuerwaffen*, Part II, *Preußen (bis 1870)* (Rastatt, 1979), pp. 66–9; AEG F9, *Révision des règlements sur l'armament de l'armée fédérale*, 1841; J.A. Meier (ed.), *Des milices Genevoises* (Zürich, 2008), pp. 121–3. For more detail on weaponry see G. Ortenburg, *Waffe und Waffengebrauch im Zeitalter der Einigungskriege* (Koblenz, 1990), and his *Waffe und Waffengebrauch im Zeitalter der Millionenheere* (Bonn, 1992). **39.** Zuber, *The Moltke myth*, pp. 74–94. **40.** W. Wagner, *Von Austerlitz bis Königgrätz: Österreichische Kampftaktik im Spiegel der Reglements, 1805–1864* (Osnabrück, 1978), pp. 31–122; Niemeyer, *Das österreichische Militärwesen*, pp. 82–95, 110; Bezzel, *Bayerische Armee*, pp. 119–23; Gruner, *Das bayerische Heer*, pp. 76, 275–6, 324. **41.** A. Lenherr, *Das schweizerische Militärwesen der Restaurationszeit* (Osnabrück, 1976); R. Jaun, *Preussen vor Augen: Das schweizerische Offizierskorps im militärischen und gesellschaftlichen Wandel des Fin de Siècle* (Zurich, 1999), pp. 57, 69–70, 89–90, 419–38; Hofer, *Der schweizerische Generalstab*, pp. 56–73, 89–108; E. Meyer, *Solothurnische Geschichte in Einzelbildern* (Olten, 2002), pp. 226–32. **42.** M. Embree, *Bismarck's first war* (Solihull, 2006), pp. 325–30. **43.** G. Wawro, *The Franco-Prussian War* (Cambridge, 2003), pp. 306–9. **44.** C. Kamiessek, *Kriegslust und Fernweh: Deutsche Soldaten zwischen militärischen Nationalismus und imperialer Nation (1770–1870)* (Frankfurt am Main, 2018), pp. 121–300; W.F. Sater and H. Herwig, *The grand illusion: Prussianization of the Chilean army* (Lincoln, NE, 1999); F.M. Nunn, 'Emil Körner and the Prussianization of the Chilean army', *Hispanic American Historical Review*, 50 (1970), 300–22; E.B. White, *German influence in the Argentine army, 1900–1945* (New York, 1991); W. Schiff, 'German military penetration into Mexico during the late Diaz period', *Hispanic American Historical Review*, 39 (1959), 568–79; E. Kaske, *Bismarcks Missionäre: Deutsche Militäinstrukteure in China, 1884–1890* (Wiesbaden, 2002). **45.** D. Storz, *Deutsche Militärgewehre*, 2 vols. (Vienna, 2011–12), and his *Gewehr und Karabiner 98: Die Schußwaffen 98 des deutschen Reichsheeres von 1898 bis 1918* (Vienna, 2006). **46.** Analysis in A. King, *The combat soldier: Infantry tactics and cohesion in the twentieth and twenty-first centuries* (Oxford, 2013), pp. 105–6, 130. **47.** J.A. Dredger, *Tactics and procurement in the Habsburg military, 1866–1918* (Basingstoke, 2017); M. Samuels, *Command or control? Command, training, and tactics in the British and German armies, 1888–1918* (London, 1995). **48.** M. Clodfelter, *Warfare and armed conflicts: A statistical reference to casualty and other figures, 1500–2000* (Jefferson, NC, 2001), p. 210. **49.** The total load in 1895 was 27.6kg: Ortenburg, *Millionenheere*, pp. 143–4. **50.** Quoted in Woodward, *Armies of the world*, p. 175; see also Jaun, *Preussen vor Augen*, pp. 105–12. **51.** Niemeyer, *Hannöversches Militär*, pp. 19–21; Sked, *Survival*, pp. 44–5; Fiedler, *Millionenheere*, p. 58. **52.** Niemeyer, *Das österreichische Militärwesen*, pp. 52–4, 134–7; Wagner, *Von Austerlitz*, pp. 52–3, 159–69, and his 'Armee', pp. 206–9, 436–8. **53.** Brose, *Kaiser's army*, pp. 7–16. **54.** *Eidgenößisches Militaire-Reglement*, pp. 10–19, 43. **55.** P. Padfield, *Guns at sea* (London, 1973), pp. 149–63. **56.** D. Stevenson, 'The field artillery revolution and the European military balance, 1890–1914', *IHR*, 41 (2019), 1301–24; M.C. Ortner, *The Austro-Hungarian artillery from 1867 to 1918* (Vienna, 2007), pp. 24–353; Ortenburg, *Millionenheere*, pp. 158–62, 196–206. **57.** B. Köster, *Militär und Eisenbahn in der Habsburgermonarchie, 1825–1859* (Munich, 1999), pp. 75–100; A. Mitchell, *The great train race: Railways and the Franco-German rivalry, 1815–1914* (New York, 2000), pp. 43ff; Showalter, *Railroads and rifles*, pp. 28–37. For Pönitz, see *ADB*, XXVI (1888), 411. **58.** Jany, *Preußischen Armee*, IV, pp. 316–17. **59.** J. Angelow, *Von Wien nach Königgrätz: Die Sicherheitspolitik des Deuschen Bundes im europäischen Gleichgewicht, 1815–1866* (Munich, 1996), pp. 57–64; Wienhofer, *Militärwesen*, pp. 65–73; K.J. Rößler, 'Kampf um den Bau und die Besatzung der Festung Rastatt', *Die Ortenau*, 42 (1962), 264–73; O. Schäuffelen, *Die Bundesfestung Ulm und ihre Geschichte* (Ulm, 1980). **60.** H. Neumann, *Das Zeughaus*, 2 vols. (Bonn, 1992), I, pp. 171–6. **61.** Y. Mintzker, *The* *defortification of the German city, 1689–1866* (Cambridge, 2012), pp. 89, 185–200, 235–9; K.T. Weber, 'Rayon – eine Kunstlandschaft', in ibid (ed.), *Leben in und mit Festungen* (Regensburg, 2010), pp. 126–38; T. Tippach, 'Garnison und kommunale Politik in Koblenz in der zweiten Hälfte des 19. Jahrhunderts', in B. Sicken (ed.), *Stadt und Militär, 1815–1914* (Paderborn, 1998), pp. 243–62. **62.** A. Watson, *The fortress: The great siege of Przemysl* (London, 2019), pp. 54–62. **63.** S. Conrad, *German colonialism* (Cambridge, 2012); H. Gründer, *Geschichte der deutschen Kolonien*, 5th ed. (Paderborn, 2004). For colonial forces, see T. Bührer, 'Chartergesellschaft, privatrechtliche Wissmann-Truppe, Kaiserliche Schutztruppe. Deutsche-Ostafrika 1885–1918', in S. Förster (ed.), *Rückkehr der Condottieri?* (Paderborn, 2010), pp. 237–50; J. Kraus and T. Müller, *The German colonial troops from 1889 to 1914* (Vienna, 2009). The violent operations of these forces are covered on pp. 484–9. **64.** W. Nuhn, *Kolonialpolitik und Marine: Die Rolle der kaiserlichen Marine bei der Gründung und Sicherung des deutschen Kolonialreiches, 1884–1914* (Bonn, 2002). **65.** T. Bührer, 'Ein "parlamentsheer" ohne "preußische Erbstücke"? Der zivil-militärische Konflikt um die Führung der Kaiserlichen Schutztruppen', *Militärgeschichtliche Zeitschrift*, 71 (2012), 1–24. **66.** F.T. Jane (ed.), *Jane's fighting ships* (London, 1914). **67.** For the following, see L. Sondhaus, *In the service of the emperor: Italians in the Austrian armed forces, 1814–1918* (Boulder, CO, 1990), pp. 62–87; A. Sokol, *The imperial and royal Austro-Hungarian navy* (Annapolis, MD, 1968), pp. 10–15. **68.** W. Hubatsch (ed.), *Die erste deutsche Flotte, 1848–1853* (Herford, 1981); Wienhofer, *Militärwesen*, pp. 73–8; H.J. Hansen, *Ships of the German fleets, 1848–1945* (New York, 1975), pp. 12–35. **69.** Höbelt, 'Die Marine'; Sondhaus, *Italians*, pp. 88–95. **70.** D.H. Olivier, *German naval strategy, 1856–1888* (London, 2004), pp. 41–76; L. Sondhaus, '"The spirit of the army" at sea: The Prussian-German naval officer corps, 1847–1897', *IHR*, 17 (1995), 459–84. **71.** M. Epkenhans, *Tirpitz: Architect of the German High Seas Fleet* (Washington, DC, 2008), p. 11. The technical details in the following are drawn mainly from R. Gardiner (ed.), *Conway's All the world's fighting ships, 1860–1921*, 2 vols. (London, 1979–85); A. Dodson, *The Kaiser's battlefleet: German capital ships, 1871–1918* (Barnsley, 2016). The first German-built armoured ship, *Hansa*, used a British design and took four years to construct (1868–72). **72.** G. Pawlik, *Des Kaisers schwimmende Festungen: Die Kasemattschiffe Österreich-Ungarns* (Vienna, 2003); G. Pawlik et al., *Die k.u.k. Donauflotille, 1870–1918* (Graz, 1997). **73.** G. Pawlik, *Tegetthoff und das Seegefecht vor Helgoland* (Vienna, 2000). **74.** For example, G.H.U. Noel, *The gun, ram, and torpedo* (London, 1885), pp. 50–79, 97–100. For Lissa, see H.W. Wilson, *Ironclads in action*, 2 vols. (London, 1896), I, pp. 211–51; J.P. Greene and A. Massignani, *Ironclads at war: The origin and development of the armoured warship, 1854–1891* (Conshohocken, PA, 1998), pp. 213–39, 251–4. **75.** W. Hovgaard, *Modern history of warships* (London, 1920). **76.** The de facto manifesto was written by C. Charmes, *Naval reform* (London, 1887). See also T. Ropp, *The development of a modern navy: French naval policy, 1871–1904* (Annapolis, MD, 1987), pp. 155–80, 253–74; L. Sondhaus, *Naval warfare, 1815–1914* (London, 2001), pp. 139–57. **77.** M.J. Bastable, *Arms and the state: Sir William Armstrong and the remaking of British naval power, 1854–1914* (Aldershot, 2004), pp. 176–8; E. Sieche, *Kreuzer und Kreuzerprojekte der k.u.k. Kriegsmarine, 1889–1914* (Bonn, 2002) **78.** G. Paloczi-Horvath, *From monitor to missile boat: Coast defence ships and coastal defence since 1860* (London, 1996). **79.** Reappraisal in L. Sondhaus, *Preparing for Weltpolitik: German sea power before the Tirpitz era* (Annapolis, MD, 1997); R. Hobson, *Imperialism at sea: Naval strategic thought, the ideology of sea power and the Tirpitz plan, 1875–1914* (Leiden, 2002); Höbelt, 'Die Marine', pp. 705–13. **80.** F.F. Bilzer, *Die Torpedoschiffe und Zerstörer der k.u.k. Kriegsmarine, 1867–1918* (Graz, 1997), pp. 10–16; E. Thomer, *Torpedoboote und Zerstörer* (Oldenburg, 1954); G.E. Armstrong, *Torpedoes and torpedo-vessels* (London, 1896). **81.** L.D. Lyon, *The first destroyers* (London, 1996). **82.** L. Sondhaus, *Preparing for Weltpolitik: German sea power before the Tirpitz era* (Annapolis, MD, 1997), pp.

125–40; Wilson, *Ironclads in action*, II, pp. 192–6. **83.** T.D. Gottschall, *By order of the Kaiser: Otto von Diederichs and the rise of the imperial German navy, 1865–1902* (Annapolis, MD, 2003), pp. 99–103; G. Koop and K.P. Schmolke, *Die Großen Kreuzer Kaiserin Auguste bis Blücher* (Bonn, 2002), and their *Kleine Kreuzer, 1903–1918* (Bonn, 2002). **84.** D. Nottelmann, *Die Brandenburg-Klasse* (Berlin, 2002); Sondhaus, *Preparing for Weltpolitik*, pp. 179–84. **85.** G.W. Steevens, *Naval policy with some account of the warships of principal powers* (London, 1896), p. 136. **86.** P.J. Kemp, *Austro-Hungarian battleships* (London, 1991), pp. 9–20. **87.** Sokol, *Austro-Hungarian navy*, pp. 57–60, 65–8, 81; M.N. Vego, *Austro-Hungarian naval policy, 1904–14* (London, 1996), pp. 35–6. **88.** Hobson, *Imperialism at sea*, pp. 136–47. **89.** Gottschall, *By order of the Kaiser*, pp. 134–78. **90.** Steinberg, *Tirpitz*, p. 66; see also Herwig, *'Luxury' fleet*, pp. 33–53. **91.** G. Koop and K.P. Schmolke, *Von der Nassau- zur König-Klasse* (Bonn, 1999), and their *Die Linienschiffe der Bayern–Klasse* (Bonn, 1996). **92.** Jane (ed.), *Jane's fighting ships*, pp. 33–45, 117–24; N.J.M. Campbell, *Battlecruisers: The design and development of British and German battlecruisers of the First World War era* (London, 1978); O. Parkes, *British battleships 1860–1950* (London, 1957), pp. 466–624; Herwig, *'Luxury' fleet*, pp. 69–83. **93.** W. Aichelburg et al., *Die 'Tegetthoff' Klasse* (Vienna, 1979); Vego, *Austro-Hungarian naval policy*, pp. 68–86.

12. Serving the Nation

1. J. Shy, 'Jomini', in P. Paret (ed.), *The makers of modern strategy* (Princeton, NJ, 1986), pp. 143–85, and more generally A. Gat, *A history of military thought* (Oxford, 2001), pp. 97–381. **2.** D. Stoker, *Clausewitz: His life and work* (Oxford, 2014); V.E. Bellinger, *Marie von Clausewitz: The woman behind the making of On War* (Oxford, 2016), pp. 219–38; H. Strachan, *Carl von Clausewitz's On War* (London, 2012); J. Jędrysiak, *Prussian strategic thought, 1815–1830: Beyond Clausewitz* (Leiden, 2020). **3.** T. Zuber, *The Moltke myth: Prussian war planning, 1857–1871* (Lanham, MD, 2008), pp. 80–1. **4.** K. Floring, 'Zur Geschichte der Allgemeinen Militärzeitung, 1828–1902', *MGM*, 18 (1975), 11–32; H. Schnitter, *Militärwesen und Militärpublizistik. Die militärische Zeitschriftenpublizistik in der Geschichte des bürgerlichen Militärwesens in Deutschland* (Berlin, 1967). **5.** M. Raschke, *Der politisierende Generalstab. Die friderizianische Kriege in der amtlichen deutschen Militärgeschichtsschreibung, 1890–1914* (Freiburg, 1993); S. Lange, *Hans Delbrück und der 'Strategiestreit'* (Freiburg, 1995). **6.** J. Wintjes, '"Not an ordinary game, but a school of war". Notes on the early history of the Prusso-German Kriegsspiel', *Vulcan*, 4 (2016), 52–75; J. Niemeyer and G. Ortenburg, *Die hannoversche Armee, 1780–1903* (Beckum, 1981), pp. 13–14; P. Schuurman, 'Models of war, 1770–1830: The birth of wargames', *History of European Ideas*, 43 (2017), 442–55, and his 'A game of contexts: Prussian-German professional wargames and leadership concept of mission tactics, 1870–1880', *WiH*, 28 (2021), 504–24. **7.** T. Brechenmacher, 'Eduard von Peucker', in D. Bild et al. (eds.), *Klassiker der Pädagogik im Militär* (Baden-Baden, 1999), pp. 107–30; S.E. Clemente, *For king and Kaiser! The making of the Prussian army officer, 1860–1914* (Westport, CT, 1992). **8.** R. Jaun, *Preussen vor Augen: Das schweizerische Offizierskorps im militärischen und gesellschaftlichen Wandel des Fin de Siècle* (Zurich, 1999), pp. 380, 426–42; G. Rapp and V. Hofer, *Der schweizerische Generalstab*, vol. I (Basel, 1983), pp. 135–49; V. Hofer, *Der schweizerische Generalstab*, vol. II (Basel, 1983), pp. 51, 111–30; G. Gahlen, *Das bayerische Offizierskorps, 1815–1866* (Paderborn, 2010), pp. 345–418. **9.** I. Deák, *Beyond nationalism: A social and political history of the Habsburg officer corps, 1848–1918* (Oxford, 1990), pp. 78–94, 111–12; W. Wagner, 'Die k.(u.)k. Armee: Gliederung und Aufgabenstellung', in A. Wandruszka (ed.), *Die bewaffnete Macht* (Vienna, 1987), pp. 142–633 at 244–61, 494–524. **10.** L. Höbelt, 'Die Marine', in Wandruszka (ed.), *Die bewaffnete*

Macht, pp. 687–763 at 743–4; T.D. Gottschall, *By order of the Kaiser: Otto von Diederichs and the rise of the imperial German navy, 1865–1902* (Annapolis, MD, 2003), pp. 85–7; R. Hobson, *Imperialism at sea: Naval strategic thought, the ideology of sea power and the Tirpitz plan, 1875–1914* (Leiden, 2002), pp. 131–6. **11.** V. Berghahn, *Militarism: The history of an international debate, 1861–1979* (Oxford, 1981), pp. 7–9. **12.** A. Bethen, *Napoleons Königreich Westfalen: Lokale, deutsche und europäische Erinnerungen* (Paderborn, 2012), pp. 45–119. **13.** M. Hewitson, *Absolute war: Violence and mass warfare in the German lands* (Oxford, 2017); K. Hagemann, *Revisiting Prussia's wars against Napoleon* (Cambridge, 2015); L.S. James, *Witnessing the Revolutionary and Napoleonic Wars in German Central Europe* (Basingstoke, 2013). **14.** C.W. v. Faber du Faur, *With Napoleon in Russia* (London, 2001); W. Mähle and N. Bichhoff (eds.), *Armee im Untergang: Württemberg und der Feldzug Napoleons gegen Rußland 1812* (Stuttgart, 2017). **15.** R. Müller and W. Rother, *Die kurfürstlich-sächsische Armee um 1791* (Berlin, 1990); F.L. Sachse, *Das preussische Heer* (Berlin, 1830); H.A. Eckert and D. Monten, *Das deutsche Bundesheer* (Dortmund, 1990). **16.** P. Paret, *Art as history: Episodes in the culture and politics of nineteenth-century Germany* (Princeton, NJ, 1988). Many of Menzel's images are reproduced in K.U. Keubke and H. Schnitter, *Adolph Menzel und das Heer Friedrichs II. von Preußen* (Berlin, 1991). **17.** F. Becker, *Bilder von Krieg und Nation. Die Einigungskriege in der bürgerlichen Öffentlichkeit Deutschlands 1864–1913* (Munich, 2001); T. Rohkrämer, *Der Militärismus der 'kleinen Leute'. Die Kriegerveeine im deutschen Kaiserreich, 1871–1914* (Munich, 1990). **18.** M.S. Coetzee, *The German Army League: Popular nationalism in Wilhelmine Germany* (Oxford, 1990); J. Rüger, *The great naval game: Britain and Germany in the age of empire* (Cambridge, 2007), pp. 95–8; M.N. Vego, *Austro-Hungarian naval policy, 1904–14* (London, 1996), pp. 38, 183, 202. **19.** On this debate, see D. Blackborn and G. Eley, *The peculiarities of German history* (Oxford, 1984). **20.** W. Löschburg, *Ohne Glanz und Gloria. Die Geschichte des Hauptmanns von Köpenick* (Berlin, 1996); B.C. Hett, 'The "Captain of Köpenick" and the transformation of German criminal justice', *CEH*, 36 (2003), 1–43. **21.** D. Schoenbaum, *Zabern: Consensus politics in Imperial Germany* (London, 1982); C.J. Fischer, *Alsace to the Alsatians? Visions and division of Alsatian regionalism, 1870–1939* (New York, 2010), pp. 88–95. **22.** I. Löppenberg, 'Wider Raubstaat, Großkapital und Pickelhaube': Die katholische Militarismuskritik und Militärpolitik des Zentrums 1860 bis 1914* (Frankfurt am Main, 2009); L. Quidde, *Caligula* (Frankfurt/M., 1977); R. Chickering, *Imperial Germany and a world without war: The peace movement and German society, 1892–1914* (Princeton, NJ, 1975); N. Stargardt, *The German idea of militarism: Radical and socialist critics 1866–1914* (Cambridge, 1994); A. Hall, *Scandal, sensation and social democracy: The SPD press and Wilhelmine Germany, 1890–1914* (Cambridge, 1977), pp. 116–42.. **23.** R. Chrastil, *The siege of Strasbourg* (Cambridge, MA, 2014); A. Horne, *The fall of Paris* (London, 1965), pp. 209–13. **24.** D. Porch, *The march to the Marne: The French army, 1871–1914* (Cambridge, 1981), pp. 35–7. See generally D. Showalter, *The wars of German unification* (Harlow, 2004), pp. 313–24; B.M. Scienna, 'A predisposition to brutality? German practices against civilians and francs-tireurs during the Franco-Prussian War, 1870–1871, and their relevance for the German "military Sonderweg" debate', *Small Wars and Insurgencies*, 30 (2019), 968–93. **25.** Quoted in G. Wawro, *The Franco-Prussian War* (Cambridge, 2003), p. 289. The majority of francs-tireurs in fact wore uniforms and all were under military command and regulations within weeks of their being mobilized. Further discussion in M. Hewitson, *The people's wars: Histories of violence on the German lands* (Oxford, 2017), pp. 414–31; F. Kühlich, *Die deutschen Soldaten im Krieg von 1870/71* (Frankfurt am Main, 1995). **26.** S. Förster, 'Facing "people's war": Moltke the Elder and Germany's military options after 1871', *Journal of Strategic Studies*, 10 (1987), 209–30 at 212; ibidem and J. Nägler (eds.), *On the road to total war: The American Civil War and the German Wars of Unification, 1861–1871* (Cambridge, 1997). **27.** R. Buß, *Der Kombattentenstatus. Die kriegsrechtliche Entstehung* *eines Rechtsbegriffs und seine Ausgestaltung in Verträgen des 19. und 20. Jahrhunderts* (Bochum, 1992), pp. 151–79; W. Friedrich, *Die völkerrechtliche Stellung von Söldnertruppen im Kriege* (Bad Honnef, 1978), pp. 14–21; J. Crossland, *War, law and humanity: The campaign to control warfare, 1853–1914* (London, 2018), pp. 115–32, 153–89. **28.** For an overview of campaigns see J. Kraus and T. Müller, *The German colonial troops from 1889 to 1914* (Vienna, 2009), pp. 178–219. **29.** S. Kuß and B. Martin (eds.), *Das Deutsche Reich und der Boxeraufstand* (Munich, 2002). **30.** J. Sarkin-Hughes, *Germany's genocide of the Herero* (Woodbridge, 2011), pp. 94–6. **31.** For the following, S. Kuß, *German colonial wars and the context of military violence* (Cambridge, MA, 2017), pp. 37–75; P.N. Lehmann, 'Between Waterberg and Sandveld: An environmental perspective on the German-Herero War of 1904', *GH*, 32 (2014), 533–58; I.V. Hull, *Absolute destruction: Military culture and the practices of war in Imperial Germany* (Ithaca, NY, 2006), pp. 7–90. **32.** J. Zimmerer, *From Windhoek to Auschwitz? On the relationship between colonialism and the Holocaust* (New York, 2015); B. Madley, 'From Africa to Auschwitz: How German South West Africa included ideas and methods adopted and developed by the Nazis in Eastern Europe', *EHQ*, 35 (2005), 429–64; D. Olusoga and C.W. Erichsen, *The Kaiser's Holocaust: Germany's forgotten genocide and the colonial roots of Nazism* (London, 2011). **33.** J.L. Tone, *War and genocide in Cuba, 1895–1898* (Chapel Hill, NC, 2006); D. Walter, *Colonial violence* (London, 2017), pp. 136–7. **34.** M.B. Nielsen, 'Delegitimating empire: German and British representation of colonial violence, 1918–19', *IHR*, 42 (2020), 833–50; *The Guardian*, 13 August 2020, p. 24; Reuters, 22 September 2021. Two lawsuits filed in the US were rejected in 2004 and 2019. **35.** U. Frevert, *A nation in barracks: Conscription, military service and civil society in modern Germany* (London, 2004), pp. 189–90. For the following, A. Lenherr, *Das schweizerische Militärwesen der Restaurationszeit* (Osnabrück, 1976), pp. 75–157; L. Cole, *Military culture and popular nationalism in late imperial Austria* (Oxford, 2014), pp. 63–107. **36.** D.J. Hughes, *The king's finest: A social and bureaucratic profile of Prussian general officers, 1871–1914* (New York, 1987), pp. 26–7; A. Confino, *The nation as local metaphor: Württemberg, Imperial Germany and national memory, 1871–1918* (Chapel Hill, NC, 1997); O. Zimmer, *Remaking the rhythms of life: German communities in the age of the nation state* (Oxford, 2013). **37.** J. Kraus, *Bayerische Fahnen* (Vienna, 2017); *Die Fahnen und Standarten der Königlich Sächsischen Armee 1806–1918* (issued by the Arbeitskreis Sächsische Militärgeschichte, Dresden, 2000); J. Lucas, *Fighting troops of the Austro-Hungarian army, 1868–1914* (Tunbridge Wells, 1987), pp. 204–9, 218–21. **38.** R. Müller and M. Lachmann, *Spielmann – Trompeter – Hoboist. Aus der Geschichte der deutschen Militärmusiker* (Berlin-DDR, 1988), pp. 26–36. **39.** Frevert, *Nation in barracks*, pp. 159, 164–8, 178. **40.** Deák, *Beyond nationalism*, pp. 114–25; Gahlen, *Das bayerische Offizierskorps*, pp. 133–56; Hughes, *King's finest*, pp. 57–60, 68–74; Jaun, *Preussen vor Augen*, p. 381. **41.** J. Steinauer and R. Syburra-Bertelletto, *Courir l'Europe: Valaisans au service étranger, 1790–1870* (Sion, 2009), pp. 24–118. **42.** H.J. Hansen, *Ships of the German fleets, 1848–1945* (New York, 1975), pp. 72–3; O. Bezzel, *Die königliche bayerische Armee vom 1825–1866* (Munich, 1931), p. 77; G. Ortenburg, *Waffe und Waffengebrauch im Zeitalter der Einigungskriege* (Koblenz, 1990), pp. 190–1; Lucas, *Austro-Hungarian army*, pp. 26–7. **43.** D.E Showalter, 'Army, state and society in Germany, 1871–1914', in J.R. Dukes and J. Remak (eds.), *Another Germany* (London, 1988), pp. 1–18 at 15–16; Wagner, 'Armee', p. 107; *An occupational risk: What every police agency should do to prevent suicide amongst its officers* (Police Executive Research Forum report, 2019). **44.** C. Jahr, *Gewöhnliche Soldaten: Desertion und Deserteure im deutschen und britischen Heer, 1914–1918* (Göttingen, 1998), pp. 47–57, 254. The rate appears to have been even lower in the Habsburg army, which recorded only 388 deserters out of 439,621 men in 1912: Wagner, 'Armee', p. 560. **45.** J.A. Meier (ed.), *Des milices Genevoises* (Zürich, 2008), p. 13. **46.** K.H. Lutz, *Das badische Offizierskorps, 1840–1870/71* (Stuttgart, 1997), pp. 43–8, 88–97, 200–3;

Gahlen, *Das bayerische Offizierskorps*, pp. 265–311. In addition to these two works, the following discussion of officers draws on K. Demeter, *Das deutsche Offizierskorps in Gesellschaft und Staat, 1650–1945*, 4th ed. (Frankfurt am Main, 1965), pp. 37–47; M. Kitchen, *The German officer corps, 1890–1914* (Oxford, 1968); N. v. Preradovich, *Die Führungsschichten in Österreich und Preussen (1804–1918)* (Wiesbaden, 1955), pp. 42–58, 124–53, 173–6; Deák, *Beyond nationalism*, pp. 169–74; Wagner, 'Armee', pp. 265–7, 532–9; H. Meier-Welcker (ed.), *Untersuchungen zur Geschichte des Offizierskorps* (Stuttgart, 1962), pp. 49–57; D.C. Albu-Lisson, *Von der k.u.k. Armee zur Deutschen Wehrmacht. Offiziere und ihr Leben im Wandel politischer Systeme und Armeen* (Frankfurt am Main, 2011), pp. 20–70. **47.** G. Stolz, *Die Schleswig-Holsteinische Erhebung* (Husum, 1996), pp. 59, 197–8. **48.** A. Sked, *The survival of the Habsburg empire: Radetzky, the imperial army and class war 1848* (New York, 1979), pp. 44–8; L. Sondhaus, *In the service of the emperor: Italians in the Austrian armed forces, 1814–1918* (Boulder, CO, 1990). **49.** G.E. Rothenberg, *The Army of Francis Joseph* (West Lafayette, IN, 1976), pp. 61, 108; L. Höbelt, 'Die Marine', in Wandruszka (ed.), *Die bewaffnete Macht*, pp. 687–763 at 742. **50.** Deák, *Beyond nationalism*, pp. 97–108, 147–8; K.U. Keubke and R. Munn, *Mecklenburger Truppen in Schleswig-Holstein, in Baden und bei inneren Unruhen im eigenen Lande, 1848/49* (Schwerin, 2012), pp. 106–7; Jaun, *Preussen vor Augen*, pp. 315–44, 380–1. **51.** H. Herwig, *The German naval officer corps: A social and political history, 1890–1918* (Oxford, 1973), pp. 69–173. **52.** Hofer, *Der schweizerische Generalstab*, pp. 155–68; Jaun, *Preussen vor Augen*, pp. 59–60, 375–7, 388–401, and his *Das Eidgenössisch Generalstabskorps, 1804–1874* (Basel, 1983), p. 235. **53.** R. Chickering, *We men who feel most German: A cultural study of the Pan German League, 1886–1914* (London, 1984). **54.** *Sammlung der Gestze und Verordnungen die Eidgenössische Kriegsverfassung betreffend* (Zürich, 1819), with papers on revisions in AEG F7. **55.** Bezzel, *Bayerische Armee*, pp. 107–8. For this and the following, see also S. Kesper-Biermann, '"Jeder Soldat ist Staatsbürger": Reformen im Militärrecht in Deutschland 1800 bis 1872', in K.H. Lutz et al. (eds.), *Reform, Reorganisation, Transformation* (Munich, 2010), pp. 132–51; Wagner, 'Armee', pp. 268–77, 539–60. **56.** HSAS, A6 Bü.75; A30a Bü.28; A202 Bü.2418; U. Ludwig, *Das Duell im alten Reich* (Berlin, 2016), esp. pp. 128–33; U. Frevert, *Men of honour: A social and cultural history of the duel* (Cambridge, 1995); G. Gahlen, 'Das Duell im bayerischen Offizierskorps im 19. Jahrhundert', in U. Ludwig (ed.), *Das Duell* (Konstanz, 2012), pp. 259–73. **57.** Jaun, *Preussen vor Augen*, pp. 63–6, 374; W.D. Gruner, *Das bayerische Heer, 1824 bis 1864* (Boppard am Rhein, 1972), pp. 51–9, 163, 258–9. **58.** S. Lange, *Der Fahneneid: Die Geschichte der Schwurverpflichtung im deutschen Militär* (Bremen, 2002), pp. 41–81, 292–3; T. Schieder, 'Der Fahneneid als politischea Problem in der deutschen Geschichte', in *Der Fahneneid* (Cologne, 1970), pp. 15–34 at 18–27. **59.** Eckert and Monten, *Bundesheer*, p. 30. **60.** U. Herr and J. Nguyen, *The German infantry from 1871 to 1914*, 2 vols. (Vienna, 2008), esp. I, pp. 30–157. **61.** J.K. Kube, *Militaria: A study of German helmets and uniforms, 1729–1918* (West Chester, PA, 1990); R. v. Ottenfeld and O. Teuber, *Die Österreichische Armee von 1700 bis 1867*, 2 vols. (Vienna, 1895); J. Burlet, *Geschichte der eidgenössischen Militäruniformen 1852 bis 1992* (Egg, 1992); G. Förster et al., *Uniformen europäischer Armeen* (Berlin-DDR, 1978), pp. 220–9. **62.** J.C. Allmayer-Beck, 'Die bewaffnete Macht in Staat und Gesellschaft', in Wandruszka (ed.), *Die bewaffnete Macht*, pp. 1–141 at 113. See generally B. Sicken (ed.), *Stadt und Militär* (Paderborn, 1998). **63.** W. Ribbe (ed.), *Geschichte Berlins*, 2 vols. (Munich, 1988), I, pp. 413. **64.** Albu-Lisson, *Von der k.u.k. Armee*, pp. 219–36; Deák, *Beyond nationalism*, pp. 139–45; Hughes, *King's finest*, pp. 95–102; Lutz, *Das badische Offizierskorps*, pp. 152–64, 188–90; Gahlen, *Das bayerische Offizierskorps*, pp. 437–76. **65.** Frevert, *Nation in barracks*, pp. 171–99. **66.** W. Watts, *The Swedish intelligencer*, 3 parts (London, 1633–4), pt. 2, p. 95a. For similar stories recorded by a female author, see M.A. Junius, 'Bamberg im Schweden-Kriege', *Bericht des Historischen Vereins zu Bamberg*, 52 (1890), 1–168 at 121–2, and 53 (1891),

169–230 at 178. See generally M. Füssel, 'Frauen in der Schlacht? Weibliche Soldaten im 17. und 18. Jahrhundert zwischen Dissimulation und Sensation', in K. Latzel et al. (eds.), *Soldatinnen* (Paderborn, 2011), pp. 159–78. **67.** J. Stüssi-Lauterburg and H. Luginburg, *Vivat das Bernerbiet bis an d'r Welt ihr End! Berns Krieg im Jahre 1798 gegen die Franzosen* (Baden, 2000), pp. 262–7. **68.** K. Hagemann, 'Female patriots: Woman, war and the nation in the period of the Prussian-German anti-Napoleonic Wars', *Gender and History*, 16 (2004), 397–424 at 415. See also Hagemann, *Prussia's wars*, pp. 159–70, 194–207. **69.** Rüger, *Naval game*, pp. 132–5. **70.** D. Ellerbrock, 'Warum Germania bewaffnet war und trotzdem nicht wählen durfte', *Werkstatt Geschichte*, 64 (2013), 31–54; H. Watanebe O'Kelly, *Beauty or beast? The woman warrior in the German imagination from the Renaissance to the present* (Oxford, 2010); Frevert, *Nation in barracks*, pp. 30–40, 75–6, 127–30, 208–12. **71.** J. Remak, *A very civil war: The Swiss Sonderbund War of 1847* (Boulder, CO, 1993), pp. 126, 181; U. Herr, *Das Militär des Herzogtums Sachsen-Coburg und Gotha unter Herzog Ernst II. (1844–1867)* (Berlin, 2018), pp. 95–7; Bezzel, *Bayerische Armee*, pp. 46–7, 101–3. **72.** For the following, see J.F. Hutchinson, *Champions of charity: War and the rise of the Red Cross* (Boulder, CO, 1996); P. Boissier, *History of the International Committee of the Red Cross* (Geneva, 1985); C. Moorehead, *Dunant's dream: War, Switzerland and the history of the Red Cross* (London, 1998); Crossland, *War, law and humanity*, pp. 83–7. **73.** T. Buk-Swienty, *1864: The forgotten war that shaped Europe* (London, 2015), pp. 53–68. Appia accompanied the Prussians, while a Dutch officer, Charles van der Velde, was attached to the Danes. **74.** Wagner, 'Armee', pp. 261–6, 524–32. **75.** Quoted in M. Stein and G. Bauer, *Franco-Prussian War, 1870/71*, vol. I, *Uniforms and equipment of the German armies* (Vienna, 2020), p. 42. see also R.A. Gabriel, *Between flesh and steel: A history of military medicine from the middle ages to the wars in Afghanistan* (Washington, DC, 2013), pp. 105–33. **76.** J.E. Herzenberg, 'Johann Friedrich August von Esmarch', *Iowa Orthopaedic Journal*, 8 (1988), 85–91. **77.** J.S. Haller Jr., *Battlefield medicine: A history of the military ambulance from the Napoleonic Wars through World War I* (Carbondale, IL, 1992), pp. 68–72; J.H. Quataert, *Staging philanthropy: Patriotic women and the national imagination in dynastic Germany, 1813–1916* (Ann Arbor, MI, 2001), pp. 54–89. **78.** Kraus and Müller, *German colonial troops*, p. 175; H. Hartmann, *The body populace: Military statistics and demography in Europe before the First World War* (Cambridge, MA, 2018). **79.** Statistics from B.Z. Urlanis, *Bilanz der Kriege* (Berlin-DDR, 1965), pp. 106, 258. **80.** Haller Jr., *Battlefield medicine*, pp. 96–106. **81.** B. Wunder, *Geschichte der Bürokratie in Deutschland* (Frankfurt am Main, 1986), pp. 58–60; L.S. James, 'The experience of demobilisation: War veterans in the Central European armies and societies after 1815', in A. Forrest et al. (eds.), *War, demobilisation and memory* (Basingstoke, 2010), pp. 68–83. **82.** G. Hollenberg, 'Landstände und Militär in Hessen-Kassel', *HJLG*, 34 (1984), 101–27 at 110–23. **83.** T. Rohrkrämer, 'Heroes and would-be heroes: Veterans' and reservists' associations in Imperial Germany, in M.F. Boemeke et al. (eds.), *Anticipating total war: The German and American experiences, 1871–1914* (Cambridge, 1999), pp. 189–215; Cole, *Military culture*, pp. 126–308. **84.** M. Clodfelter, *Warfare and armed conflicts: A statistical reference to casualty and other figures, 1500–2000* (Jefferson, NC, 2001), pp. 206–7, 210–11; R. Overmans (ed.), *In der Hand des Feindes* (Cologne, 1999), pp. 5–6. The overall death rate among French prisoners was 8.1 per cent, but this included many wounded men who succumbed shortly after capture. **85.** Chapters by S. Neff and I.V. Hull, in S. Scheipers (ed.), *Prisoners in war* (Oxford, 2010). **86.** For this and the following, see Remak, *A very civil war*, p. 157; Urlanis, *Bilanz der Kriege*, pp. 91, 93–7, 103, 117, 256–7, 318–19, 325; Staroste [sic], *Tagebuch über die Ereignisse in der Pfalz und Baden im Jahre 1849* (Potsdam, 1853), pp. 286–7. Around 52,000 of the deaths in the campaign against the Hungarians were due to the cholera epidemic. **87.** S. Chapman, *The rise of merchant banking* (London, 1998), pp. 83–4. See generally, E. Klein, *Geschichte der öffentlichen Finanzen in Deutschland* (Wiesbaden, 1974), pp. 100–25;

Rothenberg, *Army of Francis Joseph*, pp. 10, 41–2, 52, 58. **88.** Gruner, *Das bayerische Heer*, pp. 48–50, 61–8, 105–29, 153–76, 220–54, 333–4. **89.** J. Schlürmann, 'Das Militär der Freien und Hansastadt Lübeck 1623–1867', in E.S. Fiebig and J. Schlürmann (eds.), *Handbuch zur nordelbischen Militärgeschichte* (Husum, 2010), pp. 165–204 at 189; AEG, D28 budgets for 1818 and 1820. **90.** N. Svendson, *The First Schleswig-Holstein War, 1848–50* (Solihull, 2007), p. 131. **91.** W. Treue, 'Die Finanzierung der Kriege 1864–1871 durch die Deutschen Länder', *VSWG*, 75 (1988), 1–14. **92.** For this and the following, L.D. Steefel, 'The Rothschilds and the Austrian loan of 1865', *JMH*, 8 (1935), 27–40; Wagner, 'Armee', pp. 291–302, 587–91; G. Wawro, 'Inside the whale: The tangled finances of the Austrian army 1848–1866', *WiH*, 3 (1996), 42–65. **93.** Deák, *Beyond nationalism*, p. 74. The crown, introduced in 1892, was worth two florins. **94.** H.P. Ullmann, *Der deutsche Steuerstaat: Geschichte der öffentlichen Finanzen vom 18. Jahrhundert bis heute* (Munich, 2005), pp. 36, 64, 100; A. Chowdhury, *The myth of international order: Why weak states persist and alternatives to the state fade away* (Oxford, 2018), pp. 14, 98, 102. **95.** D.E. Showalter, *Railroads and rifles: Soldiers, technology, and the unification of Germany* (Hamden, CT, 1975), pp. 91–2. **96.** W.H.B. Smith, *Mauser rifles and pistols* (Harrisburg, PA, 1946); N. Yorulmaz, *Arming the sultan: German arms trade and personal diplomacy in the Ottoman empire before World War I* (London, 2014), pp. 6, 31–2, 109–32. **97.** W. Manchester, *The arms of Krupp* (London, 1969); H. James, *Krupp: The history of a legendary firm* (Princeton, NJ, 2012). **98.** G. Kronenbitter, Armeerüstung und wirtschaftliche Entwicklung in Österreich(-Ungarn) 1860 bis 1890', in M. Epkenhans and G.P. Groß (eds.), *Das Militär und der Aufbruch in die Moderne 1860 bis 1890* (Munich, 2003), pp. 213–44. **99.** M. Scherrer, *125 Jahre Eidgenössische Konstruktionswerkstätte Thun* (Thun, 1988); A. Vautraves, 'L'armament en Suisse', in R. Jaun and D. Rieder (eds.), *Schweizer Rüstung* (Baden, 2013), pp. 14–29 at 18–20 **100.** S. Fiedler, *Kriegswesen und Kriegführung im Zeitalter der Einigungskriege* (Koblenz, 1991), p. 128; G. Ortenburg, *Waffe und Waffengebrauch im Zeitalter der Millionenheere* (Bonn, 1992), pp. 152–3; Wagner, 'Armee', pp. 283–5, 572–7. **101.** For this and the following, see R.J. Winklareth, *Naval shipbuilders of the world from the age of sail to the present day* (London, 2000), pp. 243–73, and the works by M. Epkenhans, *Die Wilhelmische Flottenrüstung 1908–1914* (Munich, 1991); 'Krupp and the Imperial German Navy, 1898–1914', *JMilH*, 64 (2000), 335–70; 'Military-industrial relations in imperial Germany, 1870–1914', *WiH*, 10 (2003), 1–26. **102.** Vego, *Austro-Hungarian naval policy*, pp. 30–1, 76–7, 182; Höbelt, 'Die Marine', pp. 753–5. The contract for the *Svant István* dreadnought was given to the Hungarian firm Danubius, based in Fiume, in 1912, despite this being much slower to complete ships than STT. **103.** J.D. Scott, *Vickers: A history* (London, 1962), pp. 83–9.

13. Demagogues and Democrats

1. As argued by A. Watson, *Ring of steel: Germany and Austria-Hungary in World War I* (London, 2014), p. 4. **2.** J. Sheehan, *Where have all the soldiers gone? The transformation of modern Europe* (New York, 2009). **3.** S. Broadberry and M. Harrison, *The economics of World War I* (Cambridge, 2005), pp. 7–11. Germany's invasion of neutral Belgium added another 7.5 people to the Allied total, though the majority were in the conquered areas. **4.** J. Verhey, *The spirit of 1914: Militarism, myth, and mobilisation in Germany* (Cambridge, 2000); Watson, *Ring of steel*, pp. 53–73. **5.** Quoted in T. Grady, *A deadly legacy: German Jews and the Great War* (New Haven, CT, 2017), p. 19. Slightly different wording in Verhey, *Spirit*, pp. 65–6. **6.** H. Grebing, *History of the German labour movement* (Leamington Spa, 1985), pp. 97–8. Management of the war economy is discussed below on pp. 739–42. **7.** Quotes from Watson, *Ring of steel*, p. 249, and G. Wawro, *A mad catastrophe: The outbreak of World War I and the collapse of the Habsburg empire* (New York, 2014),

p. 171. For the German mobilization, see D.E. Showalter, *Instrument of war: The German army, 1914–18* (Oxford, 2016), pp. 42–5. **8.** R. Jaun, *Geschichte der Schweizer Armee* (Zürich, 2019), pp. 135–63. **9.** L. Sondhaus, *World War One: The global revolution* (Cambridge, 2011), pp. 99–125; J. Kraus and T. Müller, *The German colonial troops from 1889 to 1914* (Vienna, 2009), pp. 222–47. The naval dimension to the war is covered on pp. 649–54. **10.** H. Strachan, *The First World War in Africa* (Oxford, 2004); E. Paice, *Tip and run: The untold tragedy of the First World War in Africa* (London, 2007). **11.** B. Langenspiepen et al., *Halbmond und Kaiseradler: Breslau und Goeben am Bosporus, 1914–1918* (Hamburg, 1999). See generally R. Johnson, *The Great War in the Middle East* (Oxford, 2016); R. Gingeras, *Fall of the sultanate: The Great War and the end of the Ottoman empire, 1908–1922* (Oxford, 2016). **12.** H.H. Herwig, *The Marne 1914: The opening of World War I and the battle that changed the world* (New York, 2009); D.E. Showalter et al., *The German failure in Belgium, August 1914* (Jefferson, NC, 2019). For Kluck's own account, first published in English in 1923, see *The march on Paris: The memoirs of Alexander von Kluck, 1914* (London, 2012). **13.** H. Afflerbach, *Falkenhayn* (Munich, 1994), esp. pp. 186–9. **14.** Showalter, *Instrument*, p. 36. **15.** R.A. Doughty, *Pyrrhic victory: French strategy and operations in the Great War* (Cambridge, MA, 2005), pp. 46–104. **16.** A. von der Goltz, *Hindenburg: Power, myth, and the rise of the Nazis* (Oxford, 2009). **17.** H.H. Herwig, *The First World War: Germany and Austria-Hungary, 1914–1918* (London, 1997), p. 420. See also the excellent biography by J. Lockenour, *Dragonslayer: The legend of Erich Ludendorff in the Weimar Republic and Third Reich* (Ithaca, NY, 2021). **18.** D.E. Showalter, *Tannenberg: Clash of Empires* (Hamden, CT, 1991). **19.** R. Reese, *The imperial Russian army in peace, war, and revolution, 1856–1917* (Lawrence, KS, 2021); G. Tunstall, *The Austro-Hungarian army and the First World War* (Cambridge, 2021). Good coverage of the opening campaigns from the Habsburg perspective in Wawro, *Mad catastrophe*, pp. 124–339, and of the Eastern Front generally in M.S. Neiberg and D. Jordan, *The history of World War I: The Eastern Front* (London, 2018). **20.** Herwig, *First World War*, p. 139. See also A. Watson, *The fortress: The great siege of Przemysl* (London, 2019). **21.** M. Thompson, *The white war: Life and death on the Italian front, 1915–19* (London, 2009). **22.** I. Deák, *Beyond nationalism: A social and political history of the Habsburg officer corps, 1848–1918* (Oxford, 1990), pp. 192–3; Herwig, *First World War*, pp. 119–20; Wawro, *Mad catastrophe*, pp. 376–80. **23.** The classic study is Fritz Fischer, *Germany's aims in the First World War* (New York, 1967). See also K.H. Janssen, *Macht und Verblendung: Kriegszielpolitik der deutschen Bundesstaaten, 1914–1918* (Göttingen, 1963); Watson, *Ring of steel*, pp. 4–5, 257–76; Herwig, *First World War*, pp. 159–62, 304–5. **24.** Numbers from Herwig, *First World War*, p. 216. **25.** The former is argued by Afflerbach, *Falkenhayn*, pp. 360–75, but contested by P. Jankowski, *Verdun* (Oxford, 2014), pp. 26–46. See also R.T. Foley, *German strategy and the path to Verdun* (Cambridge, 2005). **26.** C. Duffy, *Through German eyes: The British and the Somme 1916* (London, 2006); R. Prior and T. Wilson, *The Somme* (New Haven, CT, 2005). **27.** L. Halewood, 'A matter of opinion: British attempts to assess the attrition of German manpower, 1915–1917', *Intelligence and National Security*, 32 (2017), 335–50. **28.** T.C. Dowling, *The Brusilov offensive* (Bloomington, IN, 2008); Tunstall, *Austro-Hungarian army*, pp. 248–59. **29.** G.E. Torrey, *The Romanian battlefront in World War I* (Lawrence, KS, 2011); M.B. Barrett, *Prelude to Blitzkrieg: The 1916 Austro-German campaign in Romania* (Bloomington, IN, 2013). For Romania's entry into the war, see D. Hamlin, *Germany's empire in the east: Germans and Romanians in an era of globalization and total war* (Cambridge, 2017), pp. 143–71. **30.** M. Kitchen, *The silent dictatorship: The politics of the German High Command under Hindenburg and Ludendorff (*New York, 1978); R.B. Asprey, *The German High Command at war* (New York, 1991). **31.** A.J. May, *The passing of the Hapsburg monarchy, 1914–1918* (Philadelphia, PA, 1966–8), pp. 422–47; W. Dornik, *Des Kaisers Falke: Wirken und*

Nach-Wirken von Franz Conrad von Hötzendorf (Innsbruck, 2013), pp. 166–76. **32.** The view of Watson, *Ring of steel*, p. 416, and L. Sondhaus, *German submarine warfare in World War I: The onset of total war at sea* (New York, 2017), pp. 101–5. The submarine campaign is discussed further on pp. 651–4. **33.** U. Kluge, *Die deutsche Revolution, 1918/1919* (Frankfurt am Main, 1985), p. 48. **34.** G.A. Craig, *The politics of the Prussian army, 1640–1945* (Oxford, 1955), pp. 318–26; Watson, *Ring of steel*, pp. 458–60. **35.** H. Hagenlucke, *Deutsche Vaterlandspartei: Die nationale Rechte am Ende des Kaiserreiches* (Dusseldorf, 1997). **36.** E. Greenhaulgh, *The French army in the First World War* (Cambridge, 2014), pp. 201–19. **37.** Hamlin, *Germany's empire*, pp. 281–314. **38.** W. Dornik, 'Verwaltung der "Beute": Organisatorische Struktur und wirtschaftliche Ausbeutung der Ukraine durch die Mittelmächte 1918', in ibidem et al. (eds.), *Krieg und Wirtschaft* (Innsbruck, 2010), pp. 471–87. **39.** J. Macdonald and Ž. Cimprič, *Caporetto and the Isonzo campaign* (Barnsley, 2021); M.A. Morselli, *Caporetto 1917* (London, 2001); Thompson, *White war*, pp. 294–327. **40.** R.L. Dinardo and D.J. Hughes, 'Germany and coalition warfare in the world wars', *WiH*, 8 (2001), 166–90 at 171–83. **41.** Quoted in D.T. Zabecki (ed.), *Germany at war*, 4 vols. (Santa Barbara, CA, 2014), p. 792. **42.** D.T. Zabecki, *The German 1918 offensives* (London, 2006); M. Middlebrook, *The Kaiser's battle, 21 March 1918* (London, 1978); M. Kitchen, *The German offensives of 1918* (Charleston, SC, 2001); J. Boff, *Haig's enemy: Crown Prince Ruprecht and Germany's war on the Western Front* (Oxford, 2018), pp. 201–32. **43.** Herwig, *First World War*, pp. 367–73; Thompson, *White war*, pp. 344–6. **44.** W. Deist, 'The military collapse of the German empire', *WiH*, 3 (1996), 186–207; B. Ziemann, *Violence and the German soldier in the Great War* (London, 2017), pp. 135–55. **45.** Thompson, *White war*, pp. 356–68; May, *Hapsburg monarchy*, pp. 716–808. **46.** G.D. Feldman, *Army, industry, and labor in Germany 1914–1918* (Princeton, NJ, 1966), pp. 180–94, 253–404. **47.** Lockenour, *Dragonslayer*, pp. 73–109; M. Ludendorff (ed.), *Erich Ludendorff* (Munich, 1939); Goltz, *Hindenburg*, pp. 52–64. **48.** S. Stephenson, *The final battle: Soldiers of the Western Front and the German Revolution of 1918* (Cambridge, 2009), pp. 70–121; I.V. Hull, 'Military culture, Wilhelm II, and the end of the monarchy in the First World War', in A. Mombauer and W. Deist (eds.), *The Kaiser* (Cambridge, 2003), pp. 235–58. **49.** J. Muldoon, *Building power to change the world: The political thought of the German council movement* (Oxford, 2020); D.J. Peukert, *The Weimar Republic* (London, 1993), pp. 22–51; F.L. Carsten, *Revolution in Central Europe, 1918–19* (London, 1972), pp. 55–71; Stephenson, *Final battle*, pp. 121–34. **50.** Quotations from Groener's letter to his wife, 17 November 1918, in R. Gerwarth, *November 1918: The German Revolution* (Oxford, 2020), p. 135; see also Stephenson, *Final battle*, pp. 119–21. **51.** B. Lowry, *Armistice 1918* (Kent, OH, 1996). **52.** Sailor Richard Stumpf's diary entry, 8 November 1918, in D. Horn (ed.), *War, mutiny and revolution in the German navy* (New Brunswick, NJ, 1967), p. 419. **53.** W. Schivelbusch, *The culture of defeat* (New York, 2003); Lockenour, *Dragonslayer*, pp. 10–20. **54.** Dr Bernhard Bardacht's diary entry, 3 November 1918, in B. Bardacht, *Carnage and care on the Eastern Front* (New York, 2018), p. 282. **55.** O. Bartov and E.D. Weitz (eds.), *Shatterzone of empires: Violence and coexistence in the German, Habsburg, Russian and Ottoman borderlands* (Bloomington, IN, 2013); R. Gerwarth, *The vanquished: Why the First World War failed to end, 1917–1923* (London, 2016), and ibidem and J. Horne (eds.), *War in peace: Paramilitary violence in Europe after the Great War* (Oxford, 2012). **56.** L. Jedlicka, 'The Austrian Heimwehr', *JCH*, 1 (1967), 127–44; K. Glabauf, *Die Volkswehr 1918–20 und die Gründung der Republik* (Vienna, 1993); D.C. Albu-Lisson, *Von der K.u.K. Armee zur Deutschen Wehrmacht* (Frankfurt am Main, 2011), pp. 229–38; Carsten, *Revolution*, pp. 78–107. **57.** R. Bessel, *Germany after the First World War* (Oxford, 1993), pp. 49–74. **58.** Prussian Guardsman Albert Quinkert, diary entry 22 November 1918, in K.A. Reinartz and K. Rudolph (eds.), *Das Kriegstagebuch des Albert Quinkert (1914–1919)* (Münster, 2018), p. 664. On demobilization, see R. Blobaum, *A* *minor apocalypse: Warsaw during the First World War* (Ithaca, NY, 2017), pp. 233–4; A.R. Seipp, *The ordeal of peace: Demobilisation and the urban experience in Britain and Germany, 1917–1921* (Aldershot, 2009), pp. 180–3; B. Ziemann, *War experiences in rural Germany, 1914–1923* (Oxford, 2007), pp. 212–16; Stephenson, *Final battle*, pp. 152–92, 207–10. **59.** M. Jones, *Founding Weimar: Violence and the German Revolution of 1918–19* (Cambridge, 2016), pp. 120–6 (quote from p. 121). **60.** E. Meyer, *Solothurnische Geschichte in Einzelbildern* (Olten, 2002), pp. 243–57; Jaun, *Schweizer Armee*, pp. 160–3, 200–2. **61.** Kluge, *Revolution*, pp. 185–6. **62.** S. Haffner, *Der verratene Revolution* (Hamburg, 1969); C. Harman, *The lost revolution* (London, 1982). **63.** D.C. Large, *The politics of law and order: A history of the Bavarian Einwohnerwehr, 1918–21* (Philadelphia, PA, 1980). **64.** Stephenson, *Final battle*, pp. 193–298; S. Miller and H. Potthoff, *A history of German Social Democracy from 1848 to the present* (Leamington Spa, 1986), pp. 65–6. **65.** G. Noske, *Von Kiel bis Kapp* (Berlin, 1920), p. 68. See also W. Wette, *Gustav Noske* (Dusseldorf, 1987). **66.** W. Mulligan, *The creation of the modern German army: General Walther Reinhardt and the Weimar Republic, 1914–1930* (New York, 2005), pp. 44–58; H.H. Herwig, 'The First Congress of Workers' and Soldiers' Councils and the problem of military reform', *CEH*, 1 (1968), 150–65. The relevant cabinet minutes are printed in C.B. Burdick and R.H. Lutz (eds.), *The political institutions of the German Revolution, 1918–1919* (New York, 1966), pp. 167–76. **67.** C. Caballero Jurado, *The German Freikorps, 1918–23* (Oxford, 2001); R.G.L. Waite, *Vanguard of Nazism: The Free Corps movement in post-war Germany, 1918–1923* (Cambridge, MA, 1982); N.H. Jones, *Hitler's heralds: The story of the Freikorps, 1918–1923* (London, 1987). **68.** Jones, *Founding Weimar*, pp. 211–39; Gerwarth, *November 1918*, p. 157. **69.** V. Liulevicius, *War land on the Eastern Front: Culture, national identity, and German occupation in World War I* (Cambridge, 2001); K. Richter, *Fragmentation in East Central Europe: Poland and the Baltics, 1915–1929* (Oxford, 2020), pp. 109–56; J. Böhler, *Civil war in Central Europe, 1918–1921* (Oxford, 2020), pp. 96–115, and ibidem et al. (eds.), *In the shadow of the Great War: Physical violence in East Central Europe, 1917–1923* (Oxford, 2021); H. Schulze, 'Der Oststaat-Plan 1919', *Vierteljahreshefte für Zeitgeschichte*, 18 (1970), 123–63. **70.** M. Strohn, *The German army and the defence of the Reich* (Cambridge, 2011), pp. 69, 96–8. **71.** https://history.state.gov/historicaldocuments/frus1919Parisv03/d3 (accessed 7 November 2021). See also K. Schwabe, *Versailles: Das Wagnis eines demokratischen Friedens, 1919–1923* (Paderborn, 2018); L.V. Smith, *Sovereignty at the Paris Peace Conference of 1919* (Oxford, 2018); M.S. Neiberg, *The Treaty of Versailles* (Oxford, 2017). **72.** A. Kramer, 'The first wave of international war crimes trials: Istanbul and Leipzig', *European Review*, 14 (2006), 441–55. **73.** M.S. Neiberg, *Fighting the Great War* (Cambridge, MA, 2005), pp. 352–3. **74.** L. Martin (ed.), *The treaties of peace, 1919–1923*, 2 vols. (New York, 1924), II, pp. 789–931. **75.** R. Luža, *Austro-German relations in the Anschluß era* (Princeton, NJ, 1975), pp. 3–17. **76.** M. Salewski, *Entwaffnung und Militärkontrolle in Deutschland, 1919–1927* (Munich, 1966), pp. 17, 31–2; P. Towle, *Enforced disarmament from the Napoleonic campaigns to the Gulf War* (Oxford, 1997), pp. 35, 66–73, 89–97. For the Allied politicians' misunderstanding of the Prussian recruitment after 1808, see W.O. Shanahan, *Prussian military reforms, 1786–1813* (New York, 1945), pp. 11–16. **77.** A. Fleury, 'Neutralité Suisse et Société des Nations', in R. Haudenreich (ed.), *Marignano 1515–2015* (Lenzburg, 2014), pp. 295–304. **78.** F.W. Fanning, *Peace and disarmament: Naval rivalry and arms control, 1922–1933* (Lexington, KY, 1995). **79.** Towle, *Enforced disarmament*, pp. 73–87, 97–9. **80.** Strohn, *German army*, pp. 68–82. **81.** See pp. 654–5. **82.** *HDM*, VI, 98–100. **83.** Lockenour, *Dragonslayer*, pp. 84–93; Mulligan, *Reinhardt*, pp. 138–54; *HDM*, VIII, 347–53, 361–4; W. Reininghaus (ed.), *Der Arbeiteraufstand im Ruhrgebiet 1920* (Münster, 2020). **84.** H. Meier-Welcker, *Seeckt* (Frankfurt am Main, 1967); W. Mühlhausen, 'Hans von Seeckt und die Organisation der Reichswehr in der Weimarer Zeit', in K.H. Lutz et al. (eds.),

Reform, Reorganisation und Transformation (Munich, 2010), pp. 245-62. **85.** O. Gessler, *Reichswehrpolitik im Weimarer Zeit* (Stuttgart, 1958), p. 434. **86.** R.M. Citino, *The path to Blitzkrieg: Doctrine and training in the German army, 1920-1939* (Boulder, CO, 1999), pp. 11-34; B. Condell and D.T. Zabecki, *On the German art of war* (Boulder, CO, 2001), pp. 2-3. Further discussion of Blitzkrieg on pp. 639-40, 688-90. **87.** J. Corum, *The roots of Blitzkrieg: Hans von Seeckt and German military reform* (Lawrence, KS, 1992); Strohn, *German army*, pp. 93-102. **88.** H.J. Gordon Jr., *The Reichswehr and the German Republic, 1919-1926* (Princeton, NJ, 1956); R. Bergien, 'Paramilitary volunteers for Weimar Germany's "Wehrhaftmachung"', in C.G. Krüger and S. Levsen (eds.), *War volunteering in modern times* (Basingstoke, 2011), pp. 189-210. **89.** C. Fischer, *The Ruhr crisis, 1923-1924* (Oxford, 2003); M. Pawley, *The watch on the Rhine* (London, 2007), pp. 89-97; Strohn, *German army*, pp. 133-60. **90.** R.J. Evans, *The coming of the Third Reich* (New York, 2004), pp. 184-94; I. Kershaw, *Hitler 1889-1936* (London, 1998), pp. 198-212; Lockenour, *Dragonslayer*, pp. 96-109. **91.** J.V. Herrero Pérez, *The Spanish military and warfare from 1899 to the Civil War* (Basingstoke, 2017), p. 171. **92.** J.P. Fox, 'Max Bauer: Chiang Kai-shek's first German military advisor', *JCH*, 5 (1970), 21-44; W.C. Kirby, *Germany and Republican China* (Stanford, CA, 1984); B.K. Walsh, 'The German military mission to China, 1928-38', *JMH*, 46 (1974), 502-13. **93.** H. Pogge von Strandmann, 'Rapallo: Strategy in preventative diplomacy', in V.R. Berghahn and M. Kitchen (eds.), *Germany in the age of total war* (London, 1981), pp. 123-46; I.O. Johnson, *Faustian bargain: The Soviet-German partnership and the origins of the Second World War* (Oxford, 2021); M. Zeidler, *Reichswehr und Rote Armee, 1920-1933* (Munich, 1993). **94.** K. Bird, *Erich Raeder* (Annapolis, MD, 2006), pp. 68-9, 77-8; *HDM*, VIII, 422-30. **95.** As argued by Citino, *Blitzkrieg*, pp. 152-221, 243-4. For the following, see B. Ziemann, 'The Reichswehr and armament policies', in N. Rossol and B. Ziemann (eds.), *The Oxford handbook of the Weimar Republic* (Oxford, 2022), pp. 218-41; Strohn, *German army*, pp. 160-70, 182-4. **96.** F.L. Carsten, *The Reichswehr and politics 1918 to 1933* (London, 1966), pp. 253-4; J. Hürter, *Wilhelm Groener: Reichswehrminister am Ende der Weimarer Republik* (Munich, 1993). **97.** *GSWW*, I, 392-404. **98.** D. Schumann, *Political violence in the Weimar Republic, 1918-1933* (New York, 2009); K. Rohe, *Das Reichsbanner Schwarz-Rot-Gold* (Dusseldorf, 1966); M. Kitchen, 'Paramilitaries and Social Democracy', in Berghahn and Kitchen (eds.), *Germany*, pp. 170-88. **99.** T. Straumann, *1931: Debt, crisis and the rise of Hitler* (Oxford, 2019); Evans, *Coming*, pp. 232-308. **100.** B.E. Crim, *Antisemitism in the German military community and the Jewish response, 1914-1938* (Lanham, MD, 2014), pp. 135-42. See generally P. Fritzsche, *Hitler's first 100 days* (Oxford, 2021), and Evans, *Coming*, pp. 310-90, and his *The Third Reich in power* (London, 2005). **101.** D. Siemens, *Stormtroopers* (New Haven, CT, 2017), pp. 3-179. **102.** J.-L. Leleu, *La Waffen-SS* (Caen, 2007); G. Stein, *The Waffen SS* (Ithaca, NY, 1966). SS recruitment is covered on pp. 621, 710-11. **103.** Good coverage of rearmament in *GSWW*, I, 405-539. For the high command's enthusiasm: *GSWW*, IX, 500-23, **104.** *GSWW*, I, 615-35. Intervention in Spain is covered on pp. 668-9. **105.** *Documents on German foreign policy, 1918-1945*, Series D, vol. I (Washington, DC, 1949), pp. 29-39. See also *GSWW*, I, 636-9. **106.** Strohn, *German army*, pp. 231-44; K.J. Müller, *Generaloberst Ludwig Beck* (Paderborn, 2008). The high command's relationship to war crimes is discussed on pp. 692-9. **107.** F.L. Carsten, *The First Austrian Republic, 1918-1938* (Aldershot, 1986). **108.** C.E. Edmondson, *The Heimwehr and Austrian politics, 1918-1936* (Athens, GA, 1978). **109.** E.A. Schmidl, *Der 'Anschluß' Österreichs*, 3rd ed. (Bonn, 1994); L. Jedlicka, *Ein Heer im Schatten der Parteien: Die militärpolitische Lage Österreichs 1918-1938* (Graz, 1955), pp. 128-87. **110.** *GSWW*, I, 651-79. **111.** A. Tooze, *The wages of destruction* (London, 2006), pp. 285-325, 661-6; *GSWW*, I, 360-72. **112.** B.H. Shepherd, *Hitler's soldiers: The German army in the Third Reich* (New Haven, CT, 2016), p. 55. **113.** A.B. Rossino, *Hitler strikes Poland* (Lawrence, KS, 2003); *GSWW*, II,

81–140; J. Centek and A. Smolinski, 'Das Polnische Heer in den Jahren 1935–1939', in *Von Söldnerheeren zu UN Truppen* (issued by the Heeresgeschichtliches Museum, Vienna, 2011), pp. 137–60. **114.** M. Olex-Szczytowski, 'The German military occupation and National Socialist crimes, 1939–1944', *WiH*, 28 (2021), pp. 380–404 at 383–9; *GSWW*, V, 41–62, 152–202. **115.** E. Harvey, 'Homelands on the move: Gender, space and dislocation in the Nazi resettlement of German minorities from Eastern and South Eastern Europe', in M. Röger and R. Lewerowitz (eds.), *Women and men at war* (Osnabrück, 2012), pp. 35–57. **116.** P. Longerich, *Holocaust* (Oxford, 2010). For a provocative but interesting comparison, see E.B. Westermann, *Hitler's Ostkrieg and the Indian Wars* (Norman, OK, 2016) **117.** *GSWW*, I, 181–219; IV, 471–89; J. Holland, *The rise of Germany, 1939–1941* (New York, 2015), pp. 178–99; J. Kiszely, *Anatomy of a campaign: The British fiasco in Norway 1940* (Cambridge, 2017). **118.** K.H. Frieser, *The Blitzkrieg legend: The 1940 campaign in the west* (Annapolis, MD, 2005), p. 29. **119.** Citino, *Blitzkrieg*, p. 251. For the campaign, see R.E. Powaski, *Lightning war: Blitzkrieg in the west 1940* (Indianapolis, IN, 2002); Holland, *Rise*, pp. 200–96; *GSWW*, I, 232–316. **120.** H. Senn, *Erhaltung und Verstärkung der Verteidigungsbereitschaft zwischen den beiden Weltkriegen* (Basel, 1991), pp. 80–199; Jaun, *Schweizer Armee*, pp. 168–200. **121.** D.M. Segesser, 'Common doctrine rather than secret conversations: Military cooperation between France and Switzerland in the 1920s and 1930s', *WiH*, 10 (2003), 60–91. **122.** S.P. Holbrook, *Target Switzerland: Swiss armed neutrality in World War II* (Cambridge, MA, 2003); U. Schwarz, *The eye of the hurricane: Switzerland in World War Two* (London, 1980); R. Schürmann, *Helvetische Jäger* (Zurich, 2009), pp. 79–94; Jaun, *Schweizer Armee*, pp. 120–44. **123.** *GSWW*, I, 361–415. The roles of the Luftwaffe and navy are discussed further on p. 670. **124.** The order is printed in M. Carlyle (ed.), *Documents on foreign affairs, 1939–1946*, vol. II (Oxford, 1954), pp. 68–76. For the decision process, see I. Kershaw, *Fateful choices: Ten decisions that changed the world, 1940–1941* (New York, 2007), pp. 54–90; *GSWW*, IV, 18–51. **125.** S.G. Fritz, *The first soldier: Hitler as a military leader* (New Haven, CT, 2018), pp. 123–7; W. Wette, *The Wehrmacht* (Cambridge, MA, 2006), pp. 90–3, 139–56, On the complicity of the Wehrmacht's leadership, see J. Förster, *Die Wehrmacht im NS-Staat* (Munich, 2009); J. Hürter, *Hitlers Heerführer: Die deutschen Oberbefehlshaber im Krieg gegen die Sowjetunion 1941/42* (Munich, 2006). **126.** N. Stargardt, *The German war* (New York, 2015), pp. 183–5. See more generally T. Snyder, *Bloodlands: Europe between Hitler and Stalin* (New York, 2010). **127.** P. Longerich, *Wannsee* (Oxford, 2021); R.J. Evans, *The Third Reich at war* (London, 2008), pp. 217–318; *GSWW*, IV, 47–513. **128.** D. Glantz, *Stumbling colossus: The Red Army on the eve of world war* (Kansas City, 1998); G.F. Krivosheev, *Soviet casualties and combat losses in the twentieth century* (London, 1997), pp. 91, 110–13. For the Wehrmacht's assessment, see *GSWW*, IV, 52–93. Full coverage of operations in the Mediterranean in *GSWW*, III. **129.** R.L. DiNardo, *Germany and the Axis powers* (Lawrence, KS, 2005). For excellent surveys of each ally's contribution, see R.D. Müller, *The unknown Eastern Front* (London, 2014); D. Stahel (ed.), *Joining Hitler's crusade: European nations and the invasion of the Soviet Union, 1941* (Cambridge, 2018). **130.** *GSWW*, IV, 199–224. **131.** C. Goeschel, *Mussolini and Hitler* (New Haven, CT, 2018); M. Knox, *Common destiny: Dictatorship, foreign policy, and war in Fascist Italy and Nazi Germany* (Cambridge, 2000); J.J. Sandovich, 'German military incompetence through Italian eyes', *WiH*, 1 (1994), 39–62. On Italian planning, see J. Gooch, *Mussolini and his generals* (Cambridge, 2007), pp. 384–522. For the war in the Mediterranean, see *GSWW*, III, 5–136, 180–555, 641–53. **132.** G. Wolnik, *Mittelalter und NS-Propaganda* (Münster, 2004), p. 85. **133.** Concise overview by D. Stahel, *Operation Barbarossa* (Cambridge, 2009). The same author provides more detailed discussions of the 1941–2 campaigns in his *Kiev 1941* (Cambridge, 2012); *Operation Typhoon* (Cambridge, 2013); *The battle for Moscow* (Cambridge, 2015); *Retreat from Moscow* (New York, 2019). **134.** *GSWW*, VI, 863–8; C. Bekker, *The Luftwaffe diaries* (New York,

1994), p. 377; D.M. Glantz, *Colossus reborn: The Red Army at war, 1941–1943* (Kansas City, 2005), esp. p. 6.   **135.** R. Overmans, *Deutsche militärische Verluste im Zweiten Weltkrieg*, 3rd ed. (Munich, 2004), p. 283.   **136.** *GSWW*, IV, 39–40.   **137.** *GSWW*, VI, 11–189; VII, 737–47.   **138.** H.J. Krug et al., *Reluctant allies: German-Japanese naval relations in World War II* (Annapolis, MD, 2001); G. Huff, *World War II and Southeast Asia* (Cambridge, 2020); see also A. Buchanan, *World War II in global perspective, 1931–1945* (Oxford, 2019).   **139.** B. Wegner, 'Ein Krieg um die Rohestoffe: Ökonomische Aspekte der deutschen Kriegführung gegen die Sowjetunion', in Dornik (ed.), *Krieg und Wirtschaft*, pp. 499–513.   **140.** A. Beevor, *Stalingrad* (London, 1999); D.M. Glantz and J.M. House, *The Stalingrad trilogy*, 3 vols. (Lawrence, KS, 2009–14); T. Diedrich, *Paulus: Das Trauma von Stalingrad* (Paderborn, 2008), pp. 194–298. For the 1942–3 campaign generally, see *GSWW*, VI, 843–1216.   **141.** M. Kitchen, *Rommel's desert war* (Cambridge, 2009); J.P. Greene and A. Massignani, *Rommel's North African campaign* (Conshohocken, PA, 1994); *GSWW*, III, 654–754; VI, 631–827.   **142.** J. Gooch, '"Neither defeat nor surrender": Italy's change of alliances in 1943', in H. Afflerbach and H. Strachan (eds.), *How fighting ends* (Oxford, 2012), pp. 351–68.   **143.** R.M. Citino, *The Wehrmacht's last stand: The German campaigns of 1944–1945* (Lawrence, KS, 2017), pp. 59–108.   **144.** S. Newton, *Kursk: The German view* (Cambridge, MA, 2002); D.M. Glantz and J. House, *The battle of Kursk* (Lawrence, KS, 1999); N. Zetterling and A. Frankson, *Kursk 1943: A statistical analysis* (Abingdon, 2000).   **145.** D. Glantz, *The siege of Leningrad, 1941–44* (Osceolo, WI, 2001).   **146.** See for example, D. Krüger and K.J. Dogwiler, 'Das württembergische V. Armeekorps im Kampf um die Krim 1944', *ZWLG*, 79 (2020), 331–74, and more generally, Fritz, *First soldier*, pp. 310–13.   **147.** *GSWW*, V, 20–404.   **148.** *GSWW*, VII, 459–697; Citino, *Wehrmacht's last stand*, pp. 157–225; Krivosheev, *Soviet casualties*, pp. 144–6.   **149.** This is discussed further on pp. 694–6.   **150.** Leleu, *Waffen-SS*, pp. 46–53; D.K. Yelton, *Hitler's Volkssturm* (Lawrence, KS, 2002). The weapons programme is discussed on pp. 676–7.   **151.** For this and the following see I. Kershaw, *The end: The defiance and destruction of Hitler's Germany, 1944–1945* (New York, 2011); R. Bessel, *Germany 1945* (London, 2009), pp. 10–66, 93–147; C. Duffy, *Red storm on the Reich: The Soviet march on Germany 1945* (London, 1991).   **152.** C.B. Macdonald, *The last offensive* (New York, 1973).   **153.** A. Beevor, *The fall of Berlin, 1945* (London, 2002); R. Bessel, 'The German surrender of 1945', in Afflerbach and Strachan (eds.), *How fighting ends*, pp. 395–405.   **154.** Bessel, *Germany 1945*, pp. 175–6.   **155.** H.W. Maull, 'Germany and Japan: The new civilian powers', *Foreign Affairs*, 69 (1990), 96–116; S. Harnisch and H.W. Maull (eds.), *Germany as a Civilian Power? The foreign policy of the Berlin Republic* (Manchester, 2001); T.U. Berger, *Cultures of antimilitarism: National security in Germany and Japan* (Baltimore, MD, 1998).   **156.** M. Mareš and R. Stojar, 'Extreme right-wing paramilitary units in Eastern Europe', in A. Mammone et al. (eds.), *Mapping the extreme right in contemporary Europe* (London, 2012), pp. 159–72.   **157.** B. Steil, *The Marshall Plan* (Oxford, 2018), pp. 88–93; J. Reinisch, *The perils of peace: The public health crisis in occupied Germany* (Oxford, 2013), pp. 20–56.   **158.** P.M. Stirk, 'Benign occupations: The Allied occupation of Germany and the international law of occupation', in C. Erlichman and C. Knowles (eds.), *Transforming occupation in the Western zones of Germany* (London, 2018), pp. 43–61. See generally D. Botting, *From the ruins of the Reich: Germany 1945–1949* (New York, 1986); K.-D. Henke, *Die amerikanische Besatzung Deutschlands*, 2nd ed. (Munich, 1996); F. Taylor, *Exorcising Hitler: The occupation and denazification of Germany* (London, 2011). The social impact of occupation is covered on pp. 722–5.   **159.** R. Boehling, 'Transitional justice? Denazification in the US zone of occupied Germany', in Erlichmann and Knowles (eds.), *Transforming occupation*, pp. 63–80; K. Jarausch, *After Hitler: Recivilising Germans, 1945–1995* (Oxford, 2006), pp. 48–55; J. Jones, 'Eradicating Nazism from the British zone of Germany', *GH*, 8 (1990), 145–62; O. v. Wrochem, *Erich von Manstein*, 2nd ed. (Paderborn, 2009), pp. 128–38.   **160.** The numbers incarcerated in the Soviet zone remain a matter of controversy. I have followed the figures given in A.H. Beattie, *Allied internment camps in occupied Germany* (Cambridge, 2019), and B. Greiner, *Suppressed terror: History and perception of Soviet special camps in Germany* (Lanham, MD, 2014), rather than the higher total given in U. Merten, *The Gulag in East Germany: Soviet special camps, 1945–1950* (Amherst, NY, 2018). **161.** A.S. Rosenbaum, *Prosecuting Nazi war criminals* (Boulder, CO, 1993); K. C. Priemel, *The betrayal: The Nuremberg Trials and German divergence* (Oxford, 2016); Wette, *Wehrmacht*, pp. 205–23, 242–50. **162.** A. Eichmüller, *Die SS in der Bundesrepublik* (Berlin, 2018). **163.** For example, O. Bartov, 'The Holocaust', in R. Gellately (ed.), *The Oxford illustrated history of the Third Reich* (Oxford, 2018), pp. 213–41 at 238, and more generally D. Cesarani, *Justice delayed: How Britain became a refuge for Nazi war criminals* (London, 1992). **164.** V.G. Hébert, *Hitler's generals on trial* (Lawrence, KS, 2010), pp. 201–3. Further discussion on pp. 696–700. **165.** R.G. Miller, *To save a city: The Berlin airlift, 1948–1949* (College Station, TX, 2008). **166.** T. Hochscherf et al. (eds.), *Divided but not disconnected: German experiences of the Cold War* (New York, 2010). **167.** D.C. Large, *Germans to the front: West German rearmament in the Adenauer era* (Chapel Hill, NC, 1996), pp. 26–8; C. Madsen, *The Royal Navy and German naval disarmament, 1942–1947* (London, 1998). **168.** F. Hesztera, *Von der 'A-Gendarmerie' zur 'B-Gendarmerie'* (Mattighofen, 1992), and W. Blasi et al. (eds.), *B-Gendarmerie, Waffenlager und Nachrichtendienste* (Vienna, 2004). **169.** A. Fleury, 'Neutralité suisse et Union Européenne dans la Guerre froide', in Haudenreich (ed.), *Marignano*, pp. 305–14; H. de Weck, 'Rupture ou évolution? La neutralité Suisse 1975–2012', in ibid, pp. 315–35. **170.** T. Diedrich et al. (eds.), *Handbuch der bewaffneten Organe der DDR* (Berlin, 1998); T. Diedrich and R. Wenzke, *Die getarnte Armee. Geschichte der Kasernierten Volkspolizei der DDR 1952–1956* (Berlin, 2003). **171.** A. Baring, *Uprising in East Germany: June 17, 1953* (Ithaca, NY, 1972); I.-S. Kowalczuk and S. Wolle, *Roter Stern über Deutschland. Sowjetische Truppen in der DDR*, 2nd ed. (Berlin, 2010), pp. 167–78. **172.** G. Glaser, *Armee gegen das Volk? Zeitgenössische Studie mit Dokumenten zur Einsatzplanung des Militärs im Innern der DDR (1949–1965/66)* (Frankfurt am Main, 2009). **173.** Kowalczuk and Wolle, *Roter Stern*, pp. 182–90 **174.** K. Ruane, *The rise and fall of the European Defense Community: Anglo-American relations and the crisis of European defense, 1950–1955* (New York, 2000); S.A. Goldberg, *From disarmament to rearmament: The reversal of US policy toward West Germany, 1946–1955* (Athens, OH, 2017). **175.** D. Krüger, *Hans Speidel und Ernst Jünger* (Paderborn, 2016); A. Searle, *Wehrmacht Generals, West German Society, and the Debate on Rearmament, 1949–1959* (London, 2003); F. Reichenberger, *Der gedachte Krieg. Vom Wandel der Kriegsbilder in der Bundesrepublik* (Berlin, 2018), pp. 116–30; A. Keßelring and T. Loch, 'Himmerod war nicht der Anfang. Bundesminister Eberhard Wildermuth und die Anfänge westdeutscher Sicherheitspolitik', *MZ*, 74 (2015), 60–96. **176.** The text of the Himmerod Memorandum is printed in H.J. Rautenberg and N. Wiggershaus, 'Die Himmeroder Denkschrift von Oktober 1950', *MGM*, 21 (1977), 135–206. Discussion in T. Vogel, 'The Himmerod Memorandum and the beginning of West German security policy', in J.S. Corum (ed.), *Rearming Germany* (London, 2011), pp. 3–28. For the pan-European dimension, see J. Tattenberg, '"The fatherland perished in the frozen wastes of Russia": West Germans in search of the European soldier, 1940–1967', *History of European Ideas*, 46 (2020), 190–208. **177.** J. Zimmermann, *Ulrich de Maizière* (Munich, 2012), pp. 135–66; Krüger, *Speidel*, pp. 89–101, 129–74; Large, *Germans to the front*, p. 114. **178.** See the chapters by M. Uhl, D.N. Filippovych, and V. Gavrilov in J. Hoffenaar and D. Krüger (eds.), *Blueprints for battle: Planning for war in Central Europe, 1948–1968* (Lexington, KY, 2012). **179.** Reichenberger, *Der gedachte Krieg*, pp. 155–85. **180.** Ibid, pp. 277–368. **181.** R. Wenzke, 'Die Nationale Volksarmee (1956–1990)', in Diedrich et al. (eds.), *Bewaffeten Organe*, pp. 423–535 at 448–51; H. Bröckermann, '"Musterschüler" ohne Ambition? Die NVA und der Wandel von Militärdoktrin und Operationsplannung des

Warschauer Paktes in der 1970er/80er Jahren', in H. Möllers and R.J. Schlaffer (eds.), *Sonderfall Bundeswehr?* (Munich, 2014), pp. 113–27; F. Zilian Jr., *From confrontation to cooperation: The takeover of the National People's (East German) Army by the Bundeswehr* (Westport, CT, 1999), p. 35. **182.** R. Wenzke, *Die NVA und die Prager Frühling 1968* (Berlin, 1995); Kowalczuk and Wolle, *Rote Stern*, pp. 190–201. **183.** D. Krüger et al. (eds.), *Fulda Gap: Battlefield of the Cold War alliances* (Lexington, KY, 2017). **184.** T. Dyson, *The politics of German defence and security: Policy leadership and military reform in the post-Cold War era* (New York, 2007), pp. 25–32. **185.** R. Gutsche, 'Nur ein Erfüllungshilfe? Die SED-Führung und die militärische Option zur Niederschlagung der Opposition in Polen 1980/81', in K. Schroeder (ed.), *Geschichte und Transformation des SED-Staates* (Berlin, 1994), pp. 166–79; Kowalczuk and Wolle, *Rote Stern*, pp. 201–5. For the broader context, see O. Bange, *Sicherheit und Staat. Die Bündnis- und Militärpolitik der DDR im internationalen Kontext, 1969–1990* (Berlin, 2017). **186.** B.M. Linn, *Echo of battle: The army's way of war* (Cambridge, MA, 2007), pp. 173–233; Reichenberger, *Der gedachte Krieg*, pp. 370–419. **187.** G. Digutsch, *Das Ende der Nationalen Volksarmee und der Aufbau der Bundeswehr in den neuen Länder* (Frankfurt am Main, 2004), pp. 46–56; Wenzke, 'Nationale Volksarmee', pp. 511–13; M.E. Sarote, *The collapse: The accidental opening of the Berlin Wall* (New York, 2014). **188.** M.E. Sarote, *1989: The struggle to create post-Cold War Europe* (Princeton, NJ, 2009); K.H. Jarausch, *The rush to German unity* (Oxford, 1994); S.F. Szabo, *The diplomacy of German unification* (New York, 1992), pp. 95–105. **189.** In addition to Zilian, *From confrontation*, and Digutsch, *Das Ende*, see W. v. Scheven, 'Die Bundeswehr und der Aufbau Ost', in K.J. Bremm et al. (eds.), *Entschieden für Frieden: 50 Jahre Bundeswehr* (Freiburg, 2005), pp. 441–55; Schönbohm's own account, *Two armies and one fatherland* (New York, 1996), and the documents in H. Ehlert (ed.), *Armee ohne Zunkunft. Das Ende der NVA und die deutsche Einheit* (Berlin, 2002). **190.** B. Giegerich, 'The North Atlantic Treaty Organisation', in H. Meijer and M. Wyss (eds.), *The handbook of European defence policies and armed forces* (Oxford, 2018), pp. 377–91 at p. 384. **191.** M.E. Sarote, *Not one inch: America, Russia, and the making of post-Cold War stalemate* (New Haven, CT, 2021); M. Kaldor, *New and old wars: Organised violence in a global era* (Cambridge, 2012); S. Böckenförde, 'German security policy', in I. Wiesner (ed.), *German defence politics* (Baden-Baden, 2013), pp. 23–48. **192.** Statistics from P. Fichtenbauer and M.C. Ortner (eds.), *A history of the Austrian army* (Vienna, 2015), p. 293. **193.** T.C.B. Jahn, 'Responding responsibly: West German relations with the *Mujahideen* during the Soviet-Afghan War', *IHR*, 42 (2020), 755–73. **194.** D. Marsh, *The Euro: The politics of the new global currency* (New Haven, CT, 2009). **195.** Quoted in A. Sakaki et al., *Reluctant warriors: Germany, Japan, and their US alliance dilemma* (Washington, DC, 2020), p. 185. **196.** H. Tewes, 'How civilian? How much power? Germany and the eastern enlargement of NATO', in Harnisch and Maull (eds.), *Civilian power*, pp. 10–25; B.C. Rathbun, 'The myth of German pacificism', *German Politics and Society*, 24 (2006), 68–81. **197.** N. Philippi, 'Civilian power and war: The German debate about out-of-area operations, 1990–99', in ibid, pp. 49–67; F.J. Meiers, 'Von der Scheckbuchdiplomatie zur Verteidigung am Hindukusch', *Zeitschrift für Außen- und Sicherheitspolitik*, 3 (2010), 201–22. **198.** P. Driest, 'Die Auslandseinsätze der Bundeswehr zwischen Politik und Verfassungsrecht', in Bremm et al. (eds.), *Entschieden für Frieden*, pp. 507–24. **199.** F. A. Stengel, *The politics of military force: Antimilitarism, ideational change, and post-Cold War German security discourse* (Ann Arbor, MI, 2020). **200.** G. Joetze, *Der letzte Krieg in Europa? Das Kosovo und die deutsche Politik* (Stuttgart, 2001); W. Mirow, *Strategic culture matters: A comparison of German and British military interventions since 1990* (Berlin, 2009), pp. 47–51. **201.** *Deutschland Magazine*, 1/2011, p. 9. See also the list in Bremm et al. (eds.), *Entschieden für Frieden*, pp. 665–9, and I. Kraft, 'Germany', in Meijer and (eds.), *European defence*, pp. 52–70 at 59–60. **202.** P. Eder, 'Stand der Streitkräfte in Ausbildung, Ausrüstung und Konzeption in Österreich', in T. Jäger and R. Thiele (eds.), *Transformation* *der Sicherheitspolitik* (Wiesbaden, 2011), pp. 73–90 at 79, 82. **203.** ISAF's total was then 132,457, including 90,000 US and 9,500 UK personnel. The German contingent represented two-thirds of all overseas deployed personnel. **204.** G. Kümmel and N. Leonhard, 'Casualty shyness and democracy in Germany', *Security and Peace*, 22 (2004), 119–26; R. Glatz, 'ISAF lessons learned: A German perspective', *Prism*, 2 (2011), 169–76; T. Noetzel, 'The German politics of war: Kunduz and the war in Afghanistan', *International Affairs*, 87 (2011), 397–417; Mirow, *Strategic culture*, pp. 66–72. **205.** Interview in *Deutschland Magazine*, 4 (2014), 6–7. **206.** *Deutsche Welle*, 19 August 2021. **207.** H. Kundnani, *The paradox of German power*, 2nd ed. (London, 2016), pp. 56–66; D. Krüger, 'Deutschland und die Gemeinsame Aussen- und Sicherheitspolitik der Europäischen Union', in Bremm et al. (eds), *Entschieden für Frieden*, pp. 525–47; A. Hyde Price, 'The Common Security and Defence Policy', in Meijer and Wyss (eds.), *European defence*, pp. 392–406; Sakaki et al., *Reluctant warriors*, pp. 113–15. **208.** G. Hauser and M. Mantovani, 'Austria and Switzerland', in Meijer and Wyss (eds.), *European defence*, pp. 197–219. **209.** *Deutschland Magazine* (November 2018), 36–9; ibid (April 2019), 18–21; Bundeswehr.de (accessed 15 November 2021). **210.** Kraft, 'Germany', pp. 59–62. **211.** *Deutschland Magazine*, 4 (2015), 22–57; ibid (April 2019); *Deutschland Edition* (July 2020), 44–7. **212.** U. Krotz and K. Wolf, 'Franco-German defence and security cooperation', in Meijer and Wyss (eds.), *European defence*, pp. 440–57 at 454.

14. From Total War to the End of War?

1. G.E. Rothenberg, *The army of Francis Joseph* (West Lafayette, IN, 1976), p. 177. **2.** R.T. Foley, *German strategy and the path to Verdun* (Cambridge, 2004), pp. 109–20; H. Afflerbach, 'Wilhelm as supreme warlord in the First World War', *WiH*, 5 (1998), 427–49. **3.** A.J. May, *The passing of the Hapsburg monarchy, 1914–1918* (Philadelphia, PA, 1966–8), pp. 133–69. **4.** W. Mulligan, *The creation of the modern German army: General Walther Reinhardt and the Weimar Republic 1914–1930* (New York, 2005), pp. 111–36. **5.** G.P. Megargee, 'Triumph of the null: Structure and conflict in the command of German land forces, 1939–1945', *WiH*, 4 (1997) 60–80; R.D. Müller, *Hitler's Wehrmacht, 1935–1945* (Lexington, KY, 2016), p. 68; *GSWW*, I, 508–20. **6.** H.R. Roper (ed.), *Blitzkrieg to defeat: Hitler's war directives* (New York, 1965); G.P. Megargee, *Inside Hitler's high command* (Lawrence, KS, 2000). For a somewhat over-enthusiastic discussion of mission tactics, see J. Wittmann, *Auftragstaktik* (Norderstedt, 2012). **7.** For example, Hans Speidel's critique, which is discussed in D. Krüger, *Hans Speidel und Ernst Jünger* (Paderborn, 2016), pp. 105–17. **8.** S.G. Fritz, *The first soldier: Hitler as a military leader* (New Haven, CT, 2018), pp. 369–71. **9.** T. Diedrich et al. (eds.), *Handbuch der bewaffneten Organe der DDR* (Berlin, 1998), pp. 8–19. **10.** H.R. Rautenberg, 'Streitkräfte und Spitzengliederung – zum Verhältnis von ziviler und bewaffneter Macht bis 1990', in K.J. Bremm et al, (eds.), *Entschieden für Frieden: 50 Jahre Bundeswehr* (Freiburg, 2005), pp. 107–22; M. Rink, *Die Bundeswehr, 1950/55–1989* (Berlin, 2015), pp. 47–52; J. Zimmermann, *Ulrich de Maizière* (Munich, 2012), pp. 326–428. **11.** A. Searle, 'Internecine secret service wars revisited: The intelligence career of Count Gerhard von Schwerin, 1945-1956', *MGM*, 71 (2012), 25–55. **12.** M.J. Lowry, *The forge of West German rearmament: Theodor Blank and the Amt Blank* (New York, 1990); D.C. Large, *Germans to the front: West German rearmament in the Adenauer era* (Chapel Hill, NC, 1996), pp. 56–61, 111–13; Zimmermann, *De Maizière*, pp. 135–46. **13.** D. Heuer, 'The Federal Defence Administration', in I. Wiesner (ed.), *German defence politics* (Baden-Baden, 2013), pp. 193–224; K. Johanny, 'Ein Teil der Bundeswehr wie die Streitkräfte – 50 Jahre Bundeswehrverwaltung', in Bremm et al. (eds.), *Entschieden für Frieden*, pp. 199–214. **14.** M. Pohlmann, 'German intelligence at war, 1914-1918', *Journal of Intelligence History*, 5 (2005), 33–62; L. Sondhaus, *World War*

One (Cambridge, 2011), pp. 237–41. **15.** M. Healy, *Vienna and the fall of the Habsburg empire: Total war and everyday life in World War I* (Cambridge, 2004), pp. 97–107. **16.** K.E. Densford, 'The Wehrmann in Eisen: Nailed statures as barometers of Habsburg social order during the First World War', *ERH*, 24 (2017), 305–24. **17.** I. Kershaw, *Hitler 1889–1936* (London, 1998), pp. 121–6. **18.** Minutes from the naval conference, 8 February 1943, in J.P. Mallmann Showell (ed.), *Fuehrer conferences on naval affairs 1939–1945* (London, 1990), pp. 308–9. **19.** L. Paine, *German military intelligence in World War Two: The Abwehr* (New York, 1984); D. Kahn, *Hitler's spies: German military intelligence in World War II* (New York, 1978). **20.** I. Garden, *Battling with the truth: The contrast in the media reporting of World War II* (Stroud, 2016). **21.** S.P. Holbrook, *Target Switzerland: Swiss armed neutrality in World War II* (Cambridge, MA, 2003), pp. 47–71, 135–7, 165–6, 248–50; U. Schwarz, *The eye of the hurricane: Switzerland in World War Two* (London, 1980), pp. 101–17. **22.** A. Kesselring, *Die Organisation Gehlen und die Neuformierung des Militärs in der Bundesrepublik* (Berlin, 2017). **23.** R. Hutchinson, *German foreign intelligence from Hitler's war to the Cold War* (Lawrence, KS, 2019); T. Wolf, *Die Entstehung des BND* (Berlin, 2018); K.D. Henke, *Geheime Dienste. Die politische Inlandsspionage der Organisation Gehlen, 1946–1953* (Berlin, 2018); Rink, *Bundeswehr*, pp. 81–4. **24.** J. Gieseke, 'Das Ministerium für Staatssicherheit (1950–1990)', in Diedrich et al. (eds.), *Bewaffneten Organe*, pp. 371–422; J. Hoffenaar, 'East German military intelligence for the Warsaw Pact in the Central Sector', in ibidem and D. Krüger (eds.), *Blueprints for battle* (Lexington, KY, 2012), pp. 75–92. **25.** I. Kraft, 'Germany', in H. Meijer and M. Wyss (ed.), *The handbook of European defence policies and armed forces* (Oxford, 2018), pp. 52–70 at 63–4; V. Boulanin, 'Cyber capabilities' in ibid, pp. 760–78 at 765–8. **26.** German and Habsburg totals from H.H. Herwig, *The First World War: Germany and Austria-Hungary, 1914–1918* (London, 1997), pp. 77, 129, 204, 234–5, 360; W. Philpott, *War of attrition* (New York, 2014), pp. 128–9. Slightly different figures in S. Tucker, *The European powers in the First World War* (London, 1999), p. 173. **27.** R. Bessel, *Germany after the First World War* (Oxford, 1993), p. 248. **28.** T. Loch, *Das Gesicht der Bundeswehr: Kommunikationsstrategien in der Freiwilligenwerbung der Bundeswehr 1956 bis 1989* (Munich, 2008), pp. 73–5; *HDM*, VIII, 323, 374. **29.** J. Weitzdörfer-Henk, 'Warum brauchen wir die Wehrpflicht?', in K.H. Lutz et al. (eds.), *Reform, Reorganisation, Transformation* (Munich, 2010), pp. 295–315. **30.** Loch, *Gesicht der Bundeswehr*, pp. 75–85. See generally U. Frevert, *A nation in barracks: Conscription, military service and civil society in modern Germany* (London, 2004), pp. 250–5. **31.** R. Browning, *Ordinary men: Reserve Police Battalion 101 and the Final Solution in Poland* (New York, 1992); E.B. Westermann, *Hitler's Police Battalions: Enforcing racial war in the East* (Kansas City, KS, 2005). **32.** J.-L. Leleu, *La Waffen-SS* (Caen, 2007), pp. 219–31, 252–5, 261–77. The foreigners are discussed on pp. 709–11. **33.** R. Overmans, *Deutsche militärische Verluste im Zweiten Weltkrieg*, 3rd ed. (Munich, 2004), pp. 215, 217; *GSWW*, V, 833–1070; D.K. Yelton, *Hitler's Volkssturm* (Lawrence, KS, 2002), pp. 46–8. **34.** P. Heider, 'Die Gesellschaft für Sport und Technik (1952–1990)', in Diedrich et al. (eds.), *Bewaffneten Organe*, pp. 164–96. **35.** P.J. Lapp, *General bei Hitler und Ulbricht: Vincenz Müller, eine deutsche Karriere* (Berlin, 2003), p. 208. The conscription law was devised prior to Müller's forced retirement in 1958, but implementation was delayed until the Wall had been built. **36.** R. Wenzke, 'Die Nationale Volksarmee (1956–1990)', in Diedrich et al. (eds.), *Bewaffneten Organe*, pp. 423–535 at 433, 443–5, 464. **37.** D.C. Large, *Germans to the front: West German rearmament in the Adenauer era* (Chapel Hill, NC, 1996), pp. 253–7; S. Maninger, 'Soldiers of misfortune: Is the demise of national armed forces a core contributing factor in the rise of private security companies?', in T. Jäger and G. Kümmel (eds.), *Private Military and Security Companies* (Wiesbaden, 2007), pp. 69–85 at 70–1. **38.** A. Müller, 'The Bundeswehr reserve', in Wiesner (ed.), *German defence politics*, pp. 181–91. **39.** Wenzke, 'Nationale Volksarmee', pp. 444–5. **40.** R. Pommerin, 'Die

Wehrpflicht', in Bremm et al. (eds.), *Entschieden für Frieden*, pp. 304–10; P. Klein, 'Die Akzeptanz der Bundeswehr in der deutschen Bevölkerung', in ibid, pp. 471–82; Frevert, *Nation in barracks*, pp. 267–74. **41.** *Deutschland Magazine*, 1/2011, 10–11. **42.** E. Krahman, *States, citizens and the privatisation of security* (Cambridge, 2010), pp. 177–91; S. Collmer, 'Suspending the conscript system', in Wiesner (ed.), *German defence politics*, pp. 333–44; R. Jaun, *Geschichte der Schweizer Armee* (Zürich, 2019), pp. 337–449. **43.** www.bundeswehr.de (accessed 7 October 2021). **44.** K. Hagemann and S.O. Rose, 'War and gender: The age of the world wars', in K. Hagemann et al. (eds.), *Gender, war and the western world since 1600* (Oxford, 2020), pp. 371–409 at 387; R. Chickering, *Imperial Germany and the Great War* (Cambridge, 1998), pp. 114–20 **45.** H. Boack, 'Forgotten female soldiers in an unknown army: German women working behind the lines, 1914–1918', *Women's History Review*, 23 (2014), 577–94; B. Schönberger, 'Motherly heroines and adventurous girls: Red Cross nurses and women army auxiliaries in the First World War', in K. Hagemann and S. Schüler-Springorum (eds.), *Home and front* (New York, 2002), pp. 87–113; H.J. Hansen, *Ships of the German fleets, 1848–1945* (New York, 1975), p. 98. **46.** W. Lower, *Hitler's furies: German women in the Nazi killing fields* (Boston, MA, 2014), pp. 6–7; K. Hagemann, 'History and memory of female military service in the age of world wars', in Hagemann et al. (eds), *Gender, war and the western world*, pp. 470–97 at 480–2; F. Maubach, 'Love, comradeship and power: German auxiliaries and gender relations in the occupied territories', in M. Röger and R. Lieserowitz (eds.), *Women and men at war* (Osnabrück, 2012), pp. 157–77 at 165. **47.** F. Brühöfener, 'Sex and the soldier: The discourse about the moral conduct of Bundeswehr soldiers and officers during the Adenauer era', *CEH*, 48 (2015), 523–40. **48.** Wenzke, 'Nationale Volksarmee', p. 464; C. Heitmann, *Schützen und Helfen? Luftschutz und Zivilverteidigung in der DDR 1955 bis 1989/90* (Berlin, 2006), pp. 274–9. **49.** G. Kümmel 'Freundin oder Feindin? Frauen als Soldatinnen der Bundeswehr', in Bremm et al. (eds.), *Entschieden für Frieden*, pp. 483–505. For the Kreil case, see https://eur-lex.europa.eu/legal-content/EN/TXT/?uri=CELEX%3A61998CJ0285 (accessed 22 November 2021). **50.** http://www/vbs/admin.ch/de/vbs/zahlen-fakten/armee. html (accessed 21 May 2020). **51.** Herwig, *First World War*, p. 421; A. Watson, *Ring of steel* (London, 2014), p. 280; M.E. Haskew, *The Wehrmacht, 1939–1945* (London, 2011), p. 183. **52.** M. Rauchensteiner, *Zwischen den Blöcken. NATO, Warschauer Pakt, und Österreich* (Vienna, 2010); P. Eder, 'Stand der Streitkräfte in Ausbildung, Ausrüstung und Konzeption in Österreich', in in T. Jäger and R. Thiele (eds.), *Transformation der Sicherheitspolitik* (Wiesbaden, 2011), pp. 73–90; G. Hauser and M. Mantovani, 'Austria and Switzerland', in Meijer Wyss (eds.), *European defence*, pp. 197–219 at 205. **53.** Jaun, *Schweizer Armee*, pp. 530–1; http://www/vbs/admin.ch/de/vbs/zahlen-fakten/armee.html (accessed 21 May 2020). **54.** A. Wagner, 'Die Kampfgruppen der Arbeiterklasse (1953–1990)', in Diedrich et al. (eds.), *Bewaffneten Organe*, pp. 280–337. **55.** Wenzke, 'Nationale Volksarmee', pp. 430, 494; Heitmann, *Schützen und Helfen?*, pp. 4–5. **56.** www.bundeswehr.de (accessed 7 October 2021). **57.** H. Wulf, 'Konflikt, Krieg und Kriegsgewinnler. Liberalisierung der Wirtschaft – Reprivatisierung des Militärs', in S. Förster et al. (eds.), *Rückkehr der Condottieri?* (Paderborn, 2010), pp. 311–24 at 314; https://data.worldbank.org/indicator/MS.MIL.TOTL.P1 (accessed 4 January 2022). These totals exclude reservists. **58.** R. Raths, *Vom Massensturm zur Stoßtrupptaktik. Die deutsche Landkriegtaktik im Spiegel von Dienstvorschriften und Publizistik 1906 bis 1918* (Freiburg, 2009); F. Buchholz et al., *The Great War dawning: Germany and its army at the start of World War I* (Vienna, 2013), p. 162; J.A. Dredger, *Tactics and procurement in the Habsburg military, 1866–1918* (Basingstoke, 2017), pp. 235–65, 285. **59.** B. Ziemann, *Violence and the German soldier in the Great War* (London, 2017), p. 21. for the Langemarck myth, see M. Connelly and S. Goebel, *Ypres* (Oxford, 2018), pp. 30–5, 131–2, 137–8, 154, 171–2. **60.** M. Samuels, *Command or control? Command, training, and tactics in the British and German armies, 1888–1918* (London, 1995), pp. 158–97; R.T. Foley, 'The other side of the wire: The

German army in 1917', in P. Dennis and J. Grey (eds.), *1917: Tactics, training and technology* (Canberra, 2007), pp. 155–78; R.T. Foley, 'Learning war's lessons: The German army and the battle of the Somme 1916', *JMilH*, 75 (2011), 471–504; M. Strohn, *The German army and the defence of the Reich* (Cambridge, 2011), pp. 40–62. **61.** P. Strong and S. Marble, *Artillery in the Great War* (Barnsley, 2013); M.C. Ortner, *The Austro-Hungarian artillery from 1867 to 1918* (Vienna, 2007), pp. 356–637. **62.** P. Buttar, *Germany ascendant: The Eastern Front 1915* (Oxford, 2017), pp. 157–235. **63.** R.-D. Müller, 'Total war as the result of new weapons? The use of chemical agents in World War I', in R. Chickering and S. Förster (eds.), *Great war, total war* (Cambridge, 2000), pp. 95–111; H. Harris, '"To serve mankind in peace and the fatherland in war": The case of Fritz Haber', *GH*, 10 (1992), 24–37; S. Bruendel, 'Chemistry as a weapon, biology as an argument: Professional expertise and intellectual intervention of Fritz Haber and Georg Friedrich Nicolai in World War I', in F. Agostini (ed.), *Università e Grande Guerra in Europa* (Milan, 2020), pp. 214–29; L.F. Haber, *The poisonous cloud: Chemical warfare in the First World War* (Oxford, 1986); J.P. Zanders (ed.), *Innocence slaughtered: Gas and the transformation of warfare and society* (London, 2016); I.O. Johnson, *Faustian bargain: The Soviet-German partnership and the origins of the Second World War* (Oxford, 2021), pp. 54–60, 132–4, 139–41. **64.** B.Z. Urlanis, *Bilanz der Kriege* (Berlin-DDR, 1965), pp. 159–60, 272; J.S. Haller Jr, *Battlefield medicine* (Carbondale, IL, 2011), p. 159. **65.** *GSWW*, V, 760–83. **66.** D.T. Zabecki, *Steel wind: Colonel Georg Bruchmüller and the birth of modern artillery* (Westport, CT, 1994). Pulkowski's diary has been published as *Am 10. Dezember in Kiernozia: Kopfschuss* (Norderstedt, 2019). **67.** B.I. Gudmundsson, *Stormtroop tactics: Innovation in the German army, 1914–1918* (Westport, CT, 1989); R. Raths, *Vom Massensturm zur Stoßtrupptaktik: Die deutsche Landkriegtaktik im Spiegel von Dienstvorschriften und Publizistik 1906 bis 1918* (Freiburg, 2009); A. King, *The combat soldier: Infantry tactics and cohesion in the twentieth and twenty-first centuries* (Oxford, 2013), pp. 132–47; W. Mähle, 'Der "alte Alpino": Theodor Sproesser und Erwin Rommel im Feldzug gegen Italien', *ZWLG*, 78 (2019), 259–93; P. Lieb, '"Wüstenfuchs" und "Bluthund" in den Alpen. Erwin Rommel und Ferdinand Schörner in der Schlacht von Karfreit 1917', *MZ*, 77 (2018), 78107. **68.** This is the core argument of R.M. Citino, *The German way of war from the Thirty Years War to the Third Reich* (Lawrence, KS, 2005). See also D.W. Oetting, *Auftragstaktik: Geschichte und Gegenwart einer Führungskonzeption* (Bonn, 1993). **69.** Ziemann, *Violence*, p. 213. **70.** For example, R.M. Citino, *The path to Blitzkrieg: Doctrine and training in the German army, 1920–1939* (Boulder, CO, 1999), pp. 223–9. The TF is printed with commentary in B. Condell and D.T. Zabecki, *On the German art of war: Truppenführung* (Boulder, CO, 2001). Further discussion in Strohn, *German army*, pp. 107–29, 185–202. A revised edition was issued in 1942. **71.** F. Römer, *Comrades: The Wehrmacht from within* (Oxford, 2019), pp. 263–73; N. Stargardt, *The German war: A nation under arms, 1939–1945* (New York, 2015), pp. 197–206; G. Stein, *The Waffen SS* (Ithaca, NY, 1966), pp. 130–2. **72.** A. King, *The combat soldier: Infantry tactics and cohesion in the twentieth and twenty-first centuries* (Oxford, 2013), pp. 112, 122–3, 15–7, 187–98; Leleu, *Waffen-SS*, pp. 341–6, 392–410, 682–9. **73.** Overmans, *Verluste*, pp. 238–9, 250–1, 265–6. **74.** According to G.F. Krivosheev, *Soviet casualties and combat losses in the twentieth century* (London, 1997), pp. 259–60, German 88-mm guns destroyed 47,200 Soviet tanks and self-propelled guns across 1942–3 alone. **75.** D.R. Dorondo, *Riders of the Apocalypse: German cavalry and modern warfare, 1870–1945* (Annapolis, MD, 2012), pp. 39–73; Herwig, *First World War*, p. 129; Rothenberg, *Army*, pp. 194, 205. **76.** W. Wagner, 'Die k.(u.)k. Armee: Gliederung und Aufgabenstellung', in A. Wandruszka (ed.), *Die bewaffnete Macht* (Vienna, 1987), pp. 142–633 at 434–5; Citino, *Blitzkrieg*, pp. 47, 52–3, 145–6. **77.** Dorondo, *Riders*, pp. 124–233. **78.** H. Senn, *Erhaltung und Verstärkung der Verteidigungsbereitschaft zwischen den beiden Weltkriegen* (Basel, 1991), pp. 209–17; Jaun, *Schweizer Armee*, pp. 269, 277, 332. **79.** O. Layriz,

Mechanical traction in war (London, 1900); A. Toprani, *Oil and the great powers: Britain and Germany, 1914–1945* (Oxford, 2019), p. 138; W. Deist, 'The military collapse of the German empire', *WiH*, 3 (1996), 186–207 at 190–1. See also Buchholz et al., *Great War*, pp. 253–75, 290–5, 334–8, 349–52. **80.** *GSWW*, V, 744, 1,035–6; J. Holland, *The rise of Germany 1939–1941* (New York, 2015), pp. 88–93. **81.** I am grateful to Jan Tattenberg for the reference to Halder's 1952 essay in the Bundesarchiv/Militärarchiv, Freiburg im Breisgau, N553/8. **82.** Dredger, *Tactics and procurement*, pp. 204–5, 208. **83.** D.E. Showalter, *Instrument of war: The German army, 1914–18* (Oxford, 2016), p. 194. **84.** J. Sheldon, *The German army at Cambrai* (Barnsley, 2009); B. Cooper, *The ironclads of Cambrai* (London, 2002); A.J. Smithers, *Cambrai: The first great tank battle 1917* (London, 1992). **85.** Hagiography still permeates biographies of Guderian, see K. Macksey, *Guderian: Creator of the Blitzkrieg* (New York, 1976). Further discussion in J. Corum, *The roots of Blitzkrieg: Hans von Seeckt and German military reform* (Lawrence, KS, 1992), pp . 136–43; R. Hart, *Guderian: Panzer pioneer or myth maker?* (Dulles, VA, 2006). **86.** For the different types, see S.W. Mitcham Jr., *The Panzer legions* (Mechanicsburg PA, 2007), pp. 6–25; Haskew, *Wehrmacht*, pp. 58–95. **87.** Leleu, *Waffen SS*, pp. 339–40. **88.** Showalter, *Instrument*, pp. 189–92; Herwig, *First World War*, pp. 250–2. **89.** F.W. Seidler, *Die Organisation Todt: Bauen für Staat und Wirtschaft, 1938–1945* (Koblenz, 1987); K.H. Patel, *Soldiers of labor: Labor service in Nazi Germany and New Deal America, 1933–1945* (New York, 2005). **90.** C.B. MacDonald, *The Siegfried Line campaign* (Washington, DC, 1990 reprint), pp. 30–5; G. Forty, *Fortress Europe: Hitler's Atlantic Wall* (Shepperton, 2002). **91.** U. Schwarz, *The eye of the hurricane: Switzerland in World War Two* (London, 1980), pp. 47–52. **92.** Examples in T. Lindenberger, 'Die Deutsche Volkspolizei (1945–1990)', in Diedrich et al. (eds.), *Bewaffneten Organe*, pp. 97–152 at 110–011, 134–5; Wenzke, 'Nationale Volksarmee', pp. 430–2, 445–7, 466–8. **93.** F. Zilian Jr., *From confrontation to cooperation: The takeover of the National People's (East German) Army by the Bundeswehr* (Westport, CT, 1999), pp. 33–4 **94.** T. Diedrich and R. Wenzke, *Die getarnte Armee: Geschichte der Kasernierten Volkspolizei der DDR, 1952–1956* (Berlin, 2003), pp. 542–6; D. Niemietz, *Das feldgraue Erbe. Die Wehrmachtseinflüsse im Militär der SBZ/DDR* (Berlin, 2006); P. Fichtenbauer and M.C. Ortner (eds.), *A history of the Austrian army from Maria Theresa to the present day* (Vienna, 2015), pp. 257–85, 294–301. **95.** Diedrich and Wenzke, *Die getarnte Armee*, pp. 99–111; Zilian, *From confrontation*, pp. 31–7. **96.** M. Ford and A. Gould, 'Military identities, conventional capability, and the politics of NATO standardisation at the beginning of the Second Cold War, 1970–1980', *IHR* (2019), 775–92 at 783. The citizen-soldier ideal is discussed on pp. 719–22. **97.** Gieseke, 'Staatssicherheit', pp. 379, 387–8, 404–5. **98.** Rink, *Bundeswehr*, pp. 45–77, 147–66; W. Etschmann and H. Spreckner (eds.), *Zum Schutz der Republik Österreich: 50 Jahre Bundesheer* (Vienna, 2005); Eder, 'Stand der Streitkrafte', pp. 73–90; Jaun, *Schweizer Armee*, pp. 245–336. **99.** Jäger and Thiele (eds.), *Transformation*, passim. **100.** Quoted in T. Dyson, *The politics of German defence and security: Policy leadership and military reform in the post-Cold War era* (New York, 2007), p. 122. **101.** Dyson, *German defence*, pp. 89–94, 112–47; G. Digutsch, *Das Ende der Nationalen Volksarmee und der Aufbau der Bundeswehr in den neuen Länder* (Frankfurt am Main, 2004), pp. 397–408; J.P. Weisswange, 'Die Transformation der Bundeswehr', in Lutz et al. (eds.), *Reform*, 435–42.; M. Engelhardt, 'Jointness in the Bundeswehr', in Wiesner (ed.), *German defence politics*, pp. 163–79. **102.** D. Klos et al., 'The military service', in Wiesner (ed.), *German defence politics*, pp. 127–61 at 131–42. **103.** Quoted in H. Kundnani, *The paradox of German power* (London, 2016), p. 68. **104.** King, *Combat soldier*, pp. 278–80. **105.** Kraft, 'Germany', p. 66. **106.** Statistics compiled from A. Sokol, *The imperial and royal Austro-Hungarian navy* (Annapolis, MD, 1968), p. 159; R. Gray (ed.), *Conways all the world's fighting ships, 1906–1921* (London, 1985), p. 136. **107.** M. Cox, *Hunger in war and peace: Women and children in Germany, 1914–1924* (Oxford, 2019), pp. 4–47; H. De Jong, 'Between the devil and the deep blue sea: The Dutch economy in World War I', in S. Broadberry and M. Harrison (eds.), *The economics of World War I* (Cambridge, 2005), pp. 137–68. 108. Toprani, *Oil*, pp. 137–45. 109. M. Epkenhans, *Tirpitz: Architect of the German High Seas Fleet* (Washington, DC, 2008), pp. 59–68. 110. See generally P.G. Halperin, *A naval history of World War I* (London, 1994); N. v. Martiny, *Bilddokumente aus Österreich-Ungarns Seekrieg 1914–18*, 2 vols., 2nd ed. (Graz, 1973). 111. E.P. Hoyt, *Defeat at the Falklands: Germany's East Asia Squadron 1914* (London, 1981). For an account by a German survivor, H. Pochhammer, *Before Jutland: Admiral von Spee's last voyage* (London, 1931). 112. E. Kebbe Chatterton, *The sea raiders* (London, 1931); R.K. Lochner, *The last gentleman of war* (London, 1990); K. Yates, *Graf Spee's raiders* (London, 1995). 113. R. Gardiner (ed.), *Conway's all the world's fighting ships, 1860–1905* (London, 1979), pp. 148–9. 114. E. Rössler, *Die deutschen U-Boote und ihre Werften*, 2 vols. (Bonn, 1979–80), I, pp. 11–73; H. Fock, *Kampfschiffe. Marineschiffbau auf deutschen Werften 1870 bis heute* (Hamburg, 1995), p. 23; L. Sondhaus, *German submarine warfare in World War I: The onset of total war at sea* (New York, 2017), pp. 14–72. 115. N. Steel and P. Hart, *Jutland 1916* (London, 2004). The official German account was written by Rear Admiral Friedrich Lützow, *Der Nordseekrieg: Doggerbank und Skagerrak* (Oldenburg, 1931), pp. 76–156. 116. D. Horn (ed.), *War, mutiny and revolution in the German navy* (New Brunswick, NJ, 1967), pp. 123–97. 117. D.R. Messinger, *Find and destroy: Antisubmarine warfare in World War I* (Annapolis, MD, 2001). 118. H.H. Herwig, 'Total rhetoric, limited war: Germany's U-boat campaign, 1917–1918', in Chickering and Förster (eds.), *Great war, total war*, pp. 189–206; D. Bönker, 'A German way of war? Narratives of German militarism and maritime warfare in World War I', in S.O. Müller and C. Torp (eds.), *Imperial Germany revisited* (Oxford, 2011), pp. 227–38; Gray, *Conway's 1906–1921*, pp. 340–5. 119. K. Scheer, *Germany's High Seas Fleet in the World War* (London, 1920), pp. 355–7; H. v. Waldeyer-Hartz, *Admiral von Hipper* (London, 1933), pp. 250–60. 120. D. Woodward, *The collapse of power: Mutiny in the High Seas Fleet* (London, 1973), pp. 118–68; M. Jones, *Founding Weimar: Violence and the German Revolution of 1918–19* (Cambridge, 2016), pp. 32–48. 121. A. Dodson, *The Kaiser's battlefleet: German capital ships, 1871–1918* (Barnsley, 2016), pp. 144–57; F. Ruge, *Scapa Flow 1919: The end of the German fleet* (London, 1973); D. Van der Vat, *The grand scuttle: The sinking of the German fleet at Scapa Flow in 1919* (Annapolis, MD, 1986). 122. Sondhaus, *Submarine warfare*, pp. 216–18. 123. W. Aichelburg, *Kriegschiffe auf der Donau* (Vienna, 1982), pp. 28–33; G. Pawlik et al., *Die k.u.k Donauflotille 1870–1918* (Graz, 1997), pp. 155–6, 168–71. 124. *HDM*, VIII, 384. 125. W. Schultz, *Linenschiff Schleswig-Holstein* (Herford, 1991), pp. 186–92. 126. G. Schreiber, 'Thesen zur ideologischen Kontinuität in den machtpolitischen Zielsetzungen der deutschen Marineführung 1897 bis 1945', in W. Rahn (ed.), *Deutsche Marinen im Wandel* (Munich, 2005), pp. 427–49; *HDM*, VIII, 383–7, 391–9. 127. K. Bird, *Erich Raeder* (Annapolis, MD, 2006). 128. J. Maiolo, *The Royal Navy and Nazi Germany, 1933–39* (London, 1998). 129. *HDM*, VIII, 479–86; *GSWW*, I, 456–79; II, 60–7; Mallmann Showell (ed.), *Fuehrer conferences*, pp. 29–38. 130. A.K. Muggenthaler, *German raiders of World War II* (Englewood Cliffs, NJ, 1977); *GSWW*, II, 349–58. 131. *GSWW*, IV, 346–85; Bird, *Raeder*, pp. 175–94. 132. Bird, *Raeder*, 195–209. Text in Mallmann Showell (ed.), *Fuehrer conferences*, pp. 306–8. 133. C. Blair, *Hitler's U-boat war*, 2 vols. (London, 1996–8); Römer, *Comrades*, pp. 189–99. 134. R. Bessel, *Germany 1945* (London, 2009), pp. 67–92. 135. D.R. Snyder, 'Arming the Bundesmarine: The United States and the build-up of the German Federal Navy 1950–1960', *JMilH*, 66 (2001), 477–500; Wenzke, 'Nationale Volksarmee', 431–2, 447–8, 474–6; H. Ehlert, 'Die Hauptverwaltung für Ausbildung (1949–1952)', in Diedrich et al. (eds.), *Bewaffneten Organe*, pp. 253–80 at 273–4; Diedrich and Wenzke, *Die getarnte Armee*, pp. 151–68, 394–402, 610–15. 136. Kesselring, *Die Organisation Gehlen*, pp. 71–6; Fock, *Kampfschiffe*, pp. 174–6; Rössler, *U-Boote*, II, 156–7. 137. G. Paloczi-Horvath, *From monitor to missile boat: Coast defence ships and coastal defence since 1860* (London, 1996), pp. 117-24; R. Arendt, 'Die Bundesmarine als Flotte im Bündnis', in Bremm et al. (eds.), *Entschieden für Frieden*, pp. 123–35. **138.** https://www.bundeswehr.de/de/organisation/marine (accessed 27 November 2021). See also Klos et al., 'Military service', 150-7. **139.** R.D. Layman, *Before the aircraft carrier: The development of aviation vessels, 1849–1922* (London, 1989), p. 13. **140.** P. Fritzsche, *A nation of flyers: German aviation and the popular imagination* (Cambridge, MA, 1992), pp. 9–43. **141.** A. Imrie, *Pictorial history of the German Army Air Service 1914–1918* (London, 1971), pp. 17–18. **142.** Wagner, 'Armee', pp. 476–8; Layman, *Before the aircraft carrier*, pp. 21–30; R. Schürmann, *Helvetischer Jäger* (Zurich, 2009), pp. 15–60; J. Morrow, *The Great War in the air: Military aviation from 1909–1921* (Washington, DC, 1993). **143.** See generally, J. Morrow, *German air power in World War I* (Lincoln, NE, 1982). **144.** T. Gallagher, *Outcast Europe: The Balkans, 1789–1989* (London, 2013), p. 73. **145.** Layman, *Before the aircraft carrier*, pp. 31–82; C. Geinitz, 'The first air war against noncombatants: Strategic bombing of German cities in World War I', in Chickering and Förster (eds.), *Great war, total war*, pp. 207–25. **146.** S. Schüler-Springorum, 'Flying and killing: Military masculinity in German pilot literature, 1914–1939', in Hagemann and ibidem (eds), *Home/front*, pp. 205–32. **147.** Fichtenbauer and Ortner, *Austrian army*, p. 204 **148.** Schürmann, *Helvetischer Jäger*, pp. 60–82. **149.** R. Overy, *Goering: Hitler's iron knight* (London, 2012). **150.** J. Buckley, *Air power in the age of total war* (London, 1999), pp. 70–98; J. Corum, *The Luftwaffe: Creating the operational air war, 1918–1940* (Lawrence, KS, 1997), pp. 182–223. For the key figures, see also H. Faber (ed.), *Luftwaffe: An analysis by former Luftwaffe generals* (London, 1995). **151.** R. Proctor, *Hitler's Luftwaffe in the Spanish Civil War* (Westport, CT, 1983); R.H. Wheatley, *Hitler and Spain: The Nazi role in the Spanish Civil War, 1936–1939* (Lexington, KY, 1989); J. Corum, *Legion Condor, 1936–39* (Oxford, 2020). **152.** W. Murray, *The Luftwaffe 1933–1945: Strategy for defeat* (Washington, DC, 1996); W.H. Tantum IV and E.J. Hoffschmidt, *The rise and fall of the German airforce* (Old Greenwich, CT, 1969), esp. pp. 7, 12, 19; *GSWW*, I 480–504. **153.** S. Neitzel, 'Kriegsmarine and Luftwaffe co-operation in the war against Britain, 1939–1945', *WiH* (2003), 448–63; J. Corum, *Luftwaffe*, pp. 83, 109–12. **154.** C. Bekker, *The Luftwaffe diaries: The German air force in World War II* (New York, 1994 reprint), pp. 278–94; H. Faber (ed.), *Luftwaffe: An analysis by former Luftwaffe generals* (London, 1979), pp. 236–44. **155.** J. Sadler, *Operation Mercury: The fall of Crete, 1941* (Barnsley, 2007); *GSWW*, III, 527–55. **156.** Tantum and Hoffschmidt, *German airforce*, pp. 28–33, 204–5, 395; *GSWW*, V, 890–1. **157.** *GSWW*, II, 374–407; IV, 330–1, 371–2; J. Gardiner, *The Blitz: Britain under attack* (London, 2010). **158.** R. Overy, *The bombers and the bombed: Allied air war over Europe, 1940–1945* (London, 2013), pp. 27, 359–428, 433; *GSWW*, , 475–6. Britain's total loss was 65,000 fatalities, while Bomber Command lost 55,500 of its 125,000 personnel. **159.** J. Arnold, *The Allied air war and urban memory* (Cambridge, 2011); B. Niven (ed.), *Germans as victims: Remembering the past in contemporary Germany* (Basingstoke, 2006), particularly the editor's own chapter and that by A. Huyssen. For the Allied bombing campaign see also *GSWW*, VI, 469–597; VII, 7–152. **160.** Overy, *Bombers*, pp. 88–93, 107–230. **161.** Ibid, pp. 272–97; Bessel, *Germany 1945*, pp. 23–5. **162.** Stargardt, *German war*, pp. 345–418; S. Neitzel and H. Welzer, *Soldaten: On fighting, killing and dying* (New York, 2012), pp. 114, 125. **163.** E. Hampe, *Der zivile Luftschutz im Zweiten Weltkrieg* (Frankfurt am Main, 1963). **164.** Overy, *Bombers*, pp. 231–317; J.J. Torrie, 'The home front', in R. Gellately (ed.), *The Oxford illustrated history of the Third Reich* (Oxford, 2018), pp. 275–310 at 300–2, 305–6; *GSWW*, IX, 371–474. **165.** D.L. Caldwell and R. Muller, *The Luftwaffe over Germany: Defense of the Reich* (London, 2007); *GSWW*, VI, 478–91, 521–52, 597–621; VII, 159–356; Tantum and Hoffschmidt, *German airforce*, pp. 274, 298. **166.** Faber, *Luftwaffe*, p. 39. **167.** H. James, *Krupp: The history of a legendary firm* (Princeton, NJ, 2012), p. 136. **168.** M.J.

Neufeld, *The rocket and the Reich* (New York, 1995); B. King and T. Kutta, *Impact: The history of Germany's V-weapons in World War II* (Rockville, NY, 1998); *GSWW*, VII, 420–58. **169**. C. Hall, '"The other end of the trajectory": Operation Backfire and the German origins of Britain's ballistic missile programme', *IHR*, 42 (2020), 1,118–36. **170**. L. Hunt, *Secret agenda: The United States government, Nazi scientists and Project Paperclip, 1945 to 1990* (New York, 1991); Neufeld, *Rocket*, pp. 268–72. **171**. T. Powers, *Heisenberg's war: The secret history of the German bomb* (Cambridge, MA, 2000); *GSWW*, V, 783–801. **172**. F. Reichenberger, *Der gedachte Krieg. Vom Wandel der Kriegsbilder in der Bundesrepublik* (Berlin, 2018), pp. 198–296; U. Kühn, 'Nuclear, chemical and biological weapons', in Meijer and Wyss (eds.), *European defence policies*, pp.727–42 at 739; O. Meier, 'A civilian power caught between the lines: Germany and nuclear non-proliferation', in S. Harnisch and H.W. Maull (eds.), *Germany as a Civilian Power? The foreign policy of the Berlin Republic* (Manchester, 2001), pp. 68–87. **173**. K. Arlt, 'Sowjetische (russische) Truppen in Deutschland (1945–1994)', in Diedrich et al. (eds.), *Bewaffneten Organe*, pp. 593–632 at 607–8. **174**. J. Stüssi-Lauterburg and S. Frey, *Unvollständiges Protokoll eines Krieges, der nicht stattfand* (Lenzburg, 2009); Jaun, *Schweizer Armee*, pp. 259–60, 288–9; Schürmann, *Helvetischer Jäger*, pp. 135–53. **175**. Ibid, pp. 109–229; F. Lombardi, *The Swiss Air Power. Wherefrom? Whereto?* (Zurich, 2009), pp. 61–133; W. Hainzl, *Die Luftstreitkräfte Österreichs1955 bis heute*, 3rd ed. (Graz, 2000). **176**. Diedrich and Wenzke, *Die getarnte Armee*, pp. 134–50, 385–94, 602–10. **177**. J.S. Corum, 'Building a new Luftwaffe: The United States Air Force and Bundeswehr planning for rearmament, 1950–60', *JSS*, 27 (2004), 89–113; W. Schmidt, 'From Befehlsausgabe to "briefing": The Americanisation of the Luftwaffe', in T.W. Maulucci Jr. and D. Junker (eds.), *GIs in Germany* (Cambridge, 2013), pp. 252–70; H. Möllers, '50 Jahre Luftwaffe', in Bremm et al. (eds.), *Entschieden für Frieden*, pp. 155–82. **178**. W. Jahn, 'Der Luftschutz und die Zivilverteidigung der DDR (1955–1990)', in Diedrich et al. (eds.), *Bewaffneten Organe*, pp. 551–76; Heitmann, *Schützen und Helfen?*, passim. **179**. Klos et al., 'Military service', pp. 147–50; Kraft, 'Germany', p. 66.

15. Citizens in Uniform

1. R. Jaun, *Das schweizerische Generalstabskorps, 1875–1945* (Basel, 1991), pp. 420–1. **2**. R.M. Citino, *The path to Blitzkrieg: Doctrine and training in the German army, 1920–1939* (Boulder, CO, 1999), pp. 74–144; J. Corum, *Legion Condor, 1936–39* (Oxford, 2020), pp. 27–8; M. Vego, 'German war gaming', *Naval War College Review*, 65 (2012), 106–47. See generally D. Bald, *Der deutsche Offizier: Sozial- und Bildungsgeschichte des deutschen Offizierskorps im 20. Jahrhundert* (Munich, 1982). **3**. M. Strohn, *The German army and the defence of the Reich* (Cambridge, 2011), pp. 189–90. **4**. R. Wenzke, 'Die Nationale Volksarmee (1956–1990)', in T. Diedrich et al. (eds.), *Handbuch der bewaffneten Organe der DDR* (Berlin, 1998), pp. 423–535 at 436–7, 453, 480–1. **5**. J. Zimmermann, *Ulrich de Maizière* (Munich, 2012), pp. 219–65. **6**. https://www.bundeswehr.de/en/organization/further-fmod-departments/bundeswehr-command-and-staff-college (accessed 29 November 2021). **7**. F. Naumann, *Mitteleuropa* (Berlin, 1915); D. Hamlin, *Germany's empire in the east: Germans and Romanians in an era of globalization and total war* (Cambridge, 2017), pp. 3–20. See also K. Kopp, *Germany's wild east: Constructing Poland as a colonial space* (Ann Arbor, MI, 2012). **8**. D.T. Murphy, *The heroic earth: Geopolitical thought in Weimar Germany* (Kent, OH, 1997). **9**. M. Geyer, 'People's war: The German debate about a levée en masse in October 1918', in D. Moran and A. Waldron (eds.), *The people in arms* (Cambridge, MA, 2003), pp. 124–58. **10**. W. Deist, 'Strategy and unlimited warfare in Germany: Moltke, Falkenhayn and Ludendorff', in R. Chickering and S. Förster (eds.), *Great war, total war* (Cambridge, 2000), pp. 265–79. **11**. E. Ludendorff, *Der totale Krieg*

(Munich, 1935). See the discussion in R. Chickering, 'The sore loser: Ludendorff's total war', in idem and S. Förster (eds.), *The shadows of total war* (Cambridge, 2013), pp. 151–78. **12.** S. Smith, *Russia in revolution* (Oxford, 2016). **13.** R. Bessel, *Nazism and war* (London, 2004). **14.** G.P. Gross, *Mythos und Wirklichkeit. Geschichte des operative Denkens im deutschen Heer von Moltke d.Ä. bis Heusinger* (Paderborn, 2012), pp. 197–202; U. Bitzel, *Die Konzeption des Blitzkrieges bei der deutschen Wehrmacht* (Frankfurt am Main, 1991), pp. 158–67; N. Zetterling, *Blitzkrieg from the ground up* (Oxford, 2017). **15.** E.-J. Howell, *Von den Besiegten lernen? Die kriegsgeschichtliche Kooperation der U.S. Armee und der ehemaligen Wehrmachtselite, 1945–1961* (Berlin, 2015); R. Hutchinson, *German foreign intelligence from Hitler's war to the Cold War* (Lawrence, KS, 2019), pp. 201–32; K. Souter, 'To stem the red tide: The German Report Series and its effects on American defense doctrine, 1948–1954', *JMilH*, 57 (1993), 653–88. **16.** R. Smelser and E.I. Davies II, *The myth of the Eastern Front: The Nazi-Soviet war in American popular culture* (Cambridge, 2008). **17.** H. Möller and U. Wengst (eds.), *50 Jahre Institut für Zeitgeschichte. Eine Bilanz* (Munich, 1999). **18.** A. Kramer, *Dynamic of destruction: Culture and mass killing in the First World War* (Oxford, 2007); J. Horne and A. Kramer, *German atrocities, 1914* (New Haven, CT, 2001), esp. pp.89–174. **19.** D.E. Showalter, *Instrument of war: The German army, 1914–18* (Oxford, 2016), pp. 189–91, 213–14; J.E. Gumz, *The resurrection and collapse of empire in Habsburg Serbia, 1914–1918* (Cambridge, 2009). **20.** R. Blobaum, *A minor apocalypse: Warsaw during the First World War* (Ithaca, NY, 2017), esp. p. 232; S. Kauffmann, *Elusive alliance: The German occupation of Poland in World War I* (Cambridge, MA, 2015); T. Grady, *A deadly legacy: German Jews and the Great War* (New Haven, CT, 2017), pp. 74–97; Hamlin, *Germany's empire*, pp. 180–5. **21.** A. Kramer, 'German war crimes, 1914 and 1941: The question of continuity', in S.O. Müller and C. Torp (eds.), *Imperial Germany revisited* (New York, 2011), pp. 239–50. **22.** J. Crouthamel, *An intimate history of the front: Masculinity, sexuality and German soldiers in the First World war* (Basingstoke, 2014); P. Fox, *The image of the soldier in German culture, 1871–1933* (London, 2018), pp. 108–15. **23.** T. Kühne, *The rise and fall of comradeship: Hitler's soldiers, male bonding, and mass violence in the twentieth century* (Cambridge, 2017), and his *Belonging and genocide: Hitler's community, 1918–1945* (New Haven, CT, 2010); K. Theweleit, *Male fantasies* (Cambridge, 1987). Further discussion of the Freikorps' mentality in M. Fulbrook, *Dissonant lives*, 2 vols. (Oxford, 2018), I, 72–81. **24.** T. Nevin, *Ernst Jünger* (London, 1997); D. Krüger, *Hans Speidel und Ernst Jünger* (Paderborn, 2016), ch. 6; E. Krimmer, *The representation of war in German literature from 1800 to the present* (Cambridge, 2010), pp. 71–88; B. Ziemann, *Violence and the German soldier in the Great War* (London, 2017), pp. 63–90. **25.** S. Kienitz, 'Body damage: War disability and construction of masculinity in Weimar Germany', in K. Hagemann and S Schüler-Springorum (eds.), *Home/front* (New York, 2002), pp. 187–91. **26.** F. Römer, *Comrades: The Wehrmacht from within* (Oxford, 2019), pp. 252–307; J.-L. Leleu, *La Waffen-SS* (Caen, 2007), pp. 564, 568–9, 682–3; S. Neitzel and H. Welzer, *Soldaten: On fighting, killing and dying* (New York, 2012), p. 274. See also the case study presented by F. Schnell, 'Justifying murder: Performativity in the letters of Sergeant Mathias Müller, Police Battalion 309, from 1941/42', *GH*, 38 (2020), 616–37. **27.** E.B. Westermann, *Drunk on genocide: Alcohol and mass murder in Nazi Germany* (Ithaca, NY, 2021). **28.** F. Römer, 'Die Wehrmacht und der Kommissarbefehl', *MZ*, 69 (2010), 243–74; W. Wette, *The Wehrmacht: History, myth, reality* (Cambridge, MA, 2006), pp. 92–8, 112–23; 284; *GSWW*, IV, 99–120, 510–13. **29.** R. Scheck, *Hitler's African victims: The German army massacres of Black French soldiers in 1940* (Cambridge, 2008); T.J. Laub, *After the fall: German policy in occupied France, 1940–1944* (Oxford, 2010); S.B. Farmer, *Martyred village: Commemorating the 1944 massacre of Oradour-sur-Glane* (Berkeley, CA, 1999); Leleu, *La Waffen-SS*, pp. 772–809; B.H. Shepherd, 'Military violence, occupation and the death of the German army, 1944–5: A case study from the Italian front', paper presented to the German History Society conference, 16 April 2018. 30. Lieutenant Johannes Teyssen quoted in Römer, *Comrades*, pp. 213–14. 31. The brutalization thesis is argued by O. Bartov, *The Eastern Front, 1941–45: German troops and the barbarisation of warfare* (London, 1985). 32. B. Sait, *The indoctrination of the Wehrmacht: Nazi ideology and the war crimes of the Germany military* (New York, 2019), esp. p. 85. See generally C. Hartmann et al. (eds.), *Verbrechen der Wehrmacht. Bilanz einer Debatte* (Munich, 2005); *GSWW*, IX, 525–647. 33. P. Blood, *Birds of prey: Hitler's Luftwaffe, ordinary soldiers, and the Holocaust in Poland* (Stuttgart, 2021). 34. B. Shepherd, *War in the wild east: The German army and Soviet partisans* (Cambridge, MA, 2004); C.D. Melson, 'German counterinsurgency revisited', *Journal of Military and Strategic Studies*, 14 (2011), 1–33, and his *Kleinkrieg: The German experience with guerrilla warfare from Clausewitz to Hitler* (Philadelphia, PA, 2016), which prints the 1935 and 1944 manuals. 35. H. Pieper, 'The German approach to counter-insurgency in the Second World War', *IHR*, 37 (2015), 631–42. For an unconvincing attempt to refute this and blame only the Nazi elite, see K.J. Arnold, *Die Wehrmacht und die Besatzungspolitik in der besetzten Gebieten der Sowjetunion* (Berlin, 2005). 36. Römer, *Comrades*, pp. 308–55; Neitzel and Welzer, *Soldaten*, pp. 99–156; Wette, *Wehrmacht*, pp. 90–138. 37. W. Wette, *Retter in Uniform: Handlungsspielräume im Vernichtungskrieg der Wehrmacht* (Frankfurt am Main, 2003); *GSWW*, IX, 906–7. 38. H. Mommsen, *Alternatives to Hitler: German resistance under the Third Reich* (London, 2003), pp. 238–52; Christian Gerlach, 'Männer des 20. Juli und der Krieg gegen die Sowjetunion', in H. Heer and K. Naumann (eds.), *Vernichtungskrieg. Verbrechen der Wehrmacht, 1941–1944* (Hamburg, 1995), pp. 427–46; M. Olex-Szczytowski, 'The German military occupation and National Socialist crimes, 1939–1944', *WiH*, 28 (2021), 380–404; *GSWW*, IX, 771–834. 39. I. Kershaw, *The end* (New York, 2011), pp. 29–53; O. v. Wrochem, *Erich von Manstein*, 2nd ed. (Paderborn, 2009), pp. 98–101; R. Hansen, *Disobeying Hitler: German resistance after Valkyrie* (Oxford, 2014); *GSWW*, IX, 835–925. 40. J.K. Jeffrey, *In the house of the hangman: The agonies of German defeat, 1943–1949* (London, 2005); A. Weinreb, *Modern hungers: Food and power in twentieth-century Germany* (Oxford, 2017), pp. 90–103; B. Blum, ' "My home, your castle": British requisitioning of German homes in Westphalia', in C. Erlichmann and C. Knowles (eds.), *Transforming occupation in the Western zones of Germany* (London, 2018), pp. 115–32; N. Stargardt, *The German war* (New York, 2015), pp. 545–64. 41. D.F. Crew, *Bodies and ruins: Imagining the bombing of Germany, 1945 to the present* (Ann Arbor, MI, 2017); A. Assmann, *Der lange Schatten der Vergangenheit* (Munich, 2006); F. Biess, *Homecomings: Returning prisoners of war and the legacies of defeat in postwar Germany* (Princeton, NJ, 2006), pp. 48–52, 61–3, 69; R.G. Moeller, 'The politics of the past in the 1950s: Rhetorics of victimisation in East and West Germany', in B. Niven (ed.), *Germans as victims* (Basingstoke, 2006), pp. 26–42. 42. *Die Wehrmachtsberichte, 1939–1945*, 3 vols. (Cologne, 1989), III, 568–9. 43. J. Brüggemann, *Männer von Ehre? Die Wehrmachtgeneralität im Nürnberger Prozeß 1945/46* (Paderborn, 2018), esp. pp. 151–61; V.G. Hébert, *Hitler's generals on trial* (Lawrence, KS, 2010). 44. Wrochem, *Manstein*, pp. 138–52. See also K. v. Lingen, *Kesselring's letzte Schlacht: Kriegsverbrecherprozesse, Vergangenheitspolitik und Wiederbewaffnung* (Paderborn, 2004). 45. E. v. Manstein, *Verlorene Siege* (Bonn, 1955; English edn 1958). Further discussion in Gross, *Mythos und Wirklichkeit*, pp. 219–64, 272–4. Rommel was similarly lionized in post-war Anglophone literature: P. Major, ' "Our friend Rommel": The Wehrmacht as "worthy enemy" in post-war British popular culture', *GH*, 26 (2008), 520–35. 46. A. Speer, *Inside the Third Reich* (London, 1970). Critical appraisal in W. Schroeter, *Albert Speer. Aufstieg und Fall eines Mythos* (Paderborn, 2018). 47. J. Westemeier (ed.), *'So war der deutsche Landser … ': Das populäre Bild der Wehrmacht* (Paderborn, 2019). 48. C. Morina, *Legacies of Stalingrad: Remembering the Eastern Front in Germany since 1945* (Cambridge, 2011). 49. G. Ritter, *Staatskunst und Kriegshandwerk* (1954–68), published in English translation as *The sword and the sceptre*,

4 vols. (London, 1972–3). Critical appraisal in C. Cornelissen, *Gerhard Ritter. Geschichtswissenschaft und Politik im 20. Jahrhundert* (Düsseldorf, 2001). See also N. Frei, *Vergangenheitspolitik. Die Anfänge der Bundesrepublik und die NS Vergangenheit* (Munich, 2003); R.G. Moeller, *War stories: The search for a usable past in the Federal Republic of Germany* (Berkeley, CA, 2001). **50.** D.F. Crew, 'Photography and cinema', in R. Gellately (ed.), *The Oxford illustrated history of the Third Reich* (Oxford, 2018), pp. 157–87 at 177–80, 185–7. **51.** G. Hartman (ed.), *Bitburg in moral and political perspective* (Bloomington, IN, 1986). **52.** R. Mitten, *The politics of antisemitic prejudice: The Waldheim phenomenon in Austria* (Boulder, CO, 1992). For a general comparison between the two Germanies and Austria in this respect, see M. Fulbrook, *Reckonings: Legacies of Nazi persecution and the quest for justice* (Oxford, 2018). **53.** H. Heer, '20 Jahre Wehrmachtausstellung', in Westemeier (ed.), *'So war der deutsche Landser . . . '*, pp. 79–100; Wette, *Wehrmacht*, pp. 269–77. **54.** M. Meisner and H. Kleffner (eds.), *Extreme Sicherheit: Rechtsradikale in Polizei, Verfassungsschutz, Bundeswehr und Justiz* (Freiburg, 2019), esp. pp. 260–72; https://taz.de/taz-Recherche-auf-Englisch/!5558072/ (accessed 5 January 2021). **55.** B. Hamann, *Bertha von Suttner* (Syracuse, NY, 1996); A. Eyffinger, *'The stars of eternal truth and right': Bertha von Suttner's campaign for peace, social justice and womanhood* (Oisterwijk, 2013). **56.** B. Ziemann, *War experience in rural Germany, 1914–1923* (Oxford, 2007), p. 245; *GSWW*, I, 69–71. **57.** Krimmer, *War in German literature*, pp. 65–103. See also A. Mombauer, 'The German centenary of the First World War', *War and Society*, 36 (2017), 276–88. **58.** C. Philpott, *Relics of the Reich: The buildings the Nazis left behind* (Barnsley, 2016). **59.** For example, in Switzerland: R. Jaun, *Preussen vor Augen: Das schweizerische Offizierskorps im militärischen und gesellschaftlichen Wandel des Fin de Siècle* (Zurich, 1999), pp. 152, 233–53; R. Schürmann, *Helvetische Jäger* (Zurich, 2009), pp. 57–74. **60.** H. Nehring, *Politics of security: British and West German protest movements and the early Cold War, 1945–1970* (Oxford, 2013), pp. 198–205; B. Ziemann, 'German angst?' Debating Cold War anxieties in West Germany, 1945–90', in M. Grant and B. Ziemann (eds.), *Understanding the imaginary war* (Manchester, 2018), pp. 116–39. **61.** S. Schregel, *Der Atomtod von der Wohnungstür* (Frankfurt am Main, 2011). **62.** For the critical group of serving soldiers, known as the 'Darmstädter Signal', see J. Tattenberg, 'The structural transformation of the military public sphere: War, knowledge, and military elites in West Germany, 1940–1989' (DPhil, University of Oxford, 2021), ch. 4. **63.** T. Diedrich and R. Wenzke, *Die getarnte Armee: Geschichte der Kasernierten Volkspolizei der DDR, 1952–1956* (Berlin, 2003), pp. 241–9; Fulbrook, *Dissonant lives*, II, 106–7. **64.** Biess, *Homecomings*, pp. 126–42. **65.** C. Heitmann, *Schützen und Helfen? Luftschutz und Zivilverteidigung in der DDR 1955 bis 1989/90* (Berlin, 2006), pp. 243–54; A. Saunders, 'Growing up on the front line: Young East Germans and the effects of militarism during the 1980s', *Debatte. Journal of Contemporary Central and Eastern Europe*, 13 (2005), 283–97. **66.** R. Jaun, *Geschichte der Schweizer Armee* (Zürich, 2019), pp. 308–15; Schürmann, *Helvetische Jäger*, pp. 182–242. **67.** W. Mirow, *Strategic culture matters: A comparison of German and British military interventions since 1990* (Berlin, 2009), pp. 18–30; G. Kümmel, 'Between rejection of war and intervention fatigue: The armed forces, the state and society in Germany', in I. Wiesner (ed.), *German defence politics* (Baden-Baden, 2013), pp. 307–31. **68.** A. Watson, 'Voluntary enlistment in the Great War', in C.G. Krüger and S. Levsen (eds.), *War volunteering in modern times* (Basingstoke, 2011), pp. 163–88. **69.** M. Jeismann, *Das Vaterland der Feinde: Studien zum nationalen Feindbegriff und Selbstverständnis in Deutschland und Frankreich, 1792–1918* (Stuttgart, 1992); P. Panayi, *The enemy in our midst: Germans in Britain during the First World War* (Oxford, 1991). **70.** Wenzke, 'Nationale Volksarmee', p. 460; quotation from J. Schönbohm, *Two armies and one fatherland* (New York, 1996), p. 27. **71.** Ideology is stressed by O. Bartov, *Hitler's army: Soldiers, Nazis, and war in the Third Reich* (Oxford, 1992). See also the sources cited in n. 31 above. **72.** S. Neitzel (ed.), *Taping Hitler's generals: Transcripts of secret conversations,*

1942–45 (London, 2013); Neitzel and Welker, *Soldaten*; Römer, *Comrades*; see also S. Fritz, *Frontsoldaten: The German soldier in World War II* (Lexington, KY, 1995). 73. Leleu, *Waffen-SS*, pp. 232–55, 413–538, 719–24, 798–9, 811; D.K. Yelton, *Hitler's Volkssturm* (Lawrence, KS, 2002), pp. 119–49, 160–1. 74. E. Shils and M. Janowitz, 'Cohesion and disintegration in the Wehrmacht in World War II', *Public Opinion Quarterly*, 12 (1948), 280–315. 75. Leleu, *Waffen-SS*, p. 533. 76. Römer, *Comrades*, pp. 199–205; Stargardt, *German war*, pp. 502–5, 546. 77. The otherwise useful study by C. Jahr, *Gewöhnliche Soldaten: Desertion und Deserteure im deutschen und britischen Heer 1914–1918* (Göttingen, 1998), only refers to officially recorded deserters. By November 1918 the total number of deserters probably reached 185,000 with a further 1 million 'shirkers' absent in the rear areas: W. Deist, 'The military collapse of the German empire', *WiH*, 3 (1996), 186–207. 78. M. Messerschmidt, *Die Wehrmachtjustiz, 1933–1945* (Paderborn, 2005); S.R. Welch, '"Harsh but just"? German military justice in the Second World War', *GH*, 19 (1999), 368–99; Stargardt, *German war*, pp. 209–15; J. Zimmermann, 'German soldiers and surrender, 1945', in H. Afflerbach and H. Strachan (eds.), *How fighting ends* (Oxford, 2012), pp. 369–82. 79. C. Madsen, 'Victims of circumstance: The execution of German deserters by surrendered German troops under Canadian control in Amsterdam, May 1945', *Canadian Military History*, 2 (1993), 93–113. 80. Diedrich and Wenzke, *Die getarnte Armee*, pp. 524–42; Wenzke, 'Nationale Volksarmee', pp. 440–1, 459–63; F. Zilian Jr., *From confrontation to cooperation: The takeover of the National People's (East German) Army by the Bundeswehr* (Westport, CT, 1999), p. 39. 81. T. Loch, *Das Gesicht der Bundeswehr: Kommunikationsstrategien in der Freiwilligenwerbung der Bundeswehr 1956 bis 1989* (Munich, 2008), pp. 105–322. 82. Jahr, *Gewöhnliche Soldaten*, p. 64; R. Overmans, *Deutsche militärische Verluste im Zweiten Weltkrieg*, 3rd ed. (Munich, 2004), p. 217; Leleu, *Waffen-SS*, pp. 190–218. Useful case study of the Wehrmacht's 253rd Division in *GSWW*, IX, 689–770. 83. C. Koller and P. Huber, 'Armut, Arbeit, Abenteuer: Sozialprofil und Motivationsstruktur von Schweizer Söldnern in der Moderne', *VWSG*, 102 (2015), 30–51; J. McLellan, *Antifascism and memory in East Germany: Remembering the International Brigades, 1945–1989* (Oxford, 2004), esp. pp. 16–19; G. Tremlett, *The International Brigades* (London, 2020); G. Callejo Leal, 'Brigandistas suizos en la Guerra Civil Española (1936–1938)', in idem (ed.), *La presencía suiza en la milicia Española* (Madrid, 2017), pp. 119–26. 84. S. O'Connor and M. Gutmann, 'Under a foreign flag: Integrating foreign units and personnel in the British and German armed forces, 1940–1945', *Journal of Modern European History*, 14 (2016), 321–41 at 334; D. Stahel (ed.), *Joining Hitler's crusade: European nations and the invasion of the Soviet Union, 1941* (Cambridge, 2018); K.W. Estes, *A European anabasis: Western European volunteers in the German army and SS, 1940–1945* (New York, 2008); Leleu, *Waffen-SS*, p. 188, and his 'From the Nazi Party's shock troops to the "European" mass army: The Waffen-SS volunteers', in Krüger and Levsen (eds.), *War volunteering*, pp. 231–47. 85. *GSWW*, V, 896–8; M. Edele, *Stalin's defectors: How Red Army soldiers became Hitler's collaborators, 1941–1945* (Oxford, 2017), pp. 19–36; S. Kudryashov, 'Ordinary collaborators: The case of the Travniki Guards', in L. Erickson and M. Erickson (eds.), *Russia: War, peace and diplomacy* (London, 2005), pp. 226–39. 86. R.D. Müller, *The unknown Eastern Front: The Wehrmacht and Hitler's foreign soldiers* (London, 2014), pp. 225–32. 87. X. Moreno Juliá, 'Spain', in Stahel (ed.), *Joining Hitler's crusade*, pp. 193–213; X.-M. Núñez Seixas, 'An approach to the social profile and ideological motivations of the Spanish volunteers of the "Blue Division", 1941–44', in Krüger and Levsen (eds.), *War volunteering*, pp. 248–74. 88. Edele, *Stalin's defectors*, pp. 137–46; Müller, *Unknown Eastern Front*, pp. 219–21; Estes, *European anabasis*, pp. 25–6, 33, 102. 89. H. Fry, *Churchill's German army* (London, 2010); P.J. Lapp, *General bei Hitler und Ulbricht: Vincenz Müller, eine deutsche Karriere* (Berlin, 2003), pp. 143–7; T. Diedrich, *Paulus: Das Trauma von Stalingrad* (Paderborn, 2008), pp. 319–64. 90. I. Deák, *Beyond nationalism: A social and political history* of the Habsburg officer corps, 1848–1918 (Oxford, 1990), pp. 195–7; B.E. Crim, *Antisemitism in the German military community and the Jewish response, 1914–1938* (Lanham, MD, 2014), pp. 8–13. **91.** M. Geheran, *Comrades betrayed: Jewish World War I veterans under Hitler* (Ithaca, NY, 2020); T. Grady, *The German-Jewish soldiers of the First World War in history and memory* (Liverpool, 2011), and his *Deadly legacy*. **92.** Wette, *Wehrmacht*, pp. 84–6. **93.** N. v. Preradovich, *Die Führungsschichten in Österreich und Preussen (1804–1918)* (Wiesbaden, 1955), p. 153; M. Funck, 'Ready for war? Conceptions of military manliness in the Prusso-German officer corps before the First World War', in Hagemann and Schüler-Springorum (eds.), *Home/front*, pp. 43–67. **94.** D.C. Albu-Lisson, *Von der K.u.K. Armee zur Deutschen Wehrmacht* (Frankfurt am Main, 2011), pp. 231–71. **95.** *HDM*, VI, 59–66, 95–8; VIII, 365–72, 431–49; S. Malinowksi, *Nazis and nobles: The history of a misalliance* (Oxford, 2020). **96.** *GSWW*, V, 918–42; M. Knox, '1 October 1942: Adolf Hitler, Wehrmacht officer policy and social revolution', *HJ*, 43 (2000), 801–25; G. Stein, *The Waffen SS* (Ithaca, NY, 1966), p. 13. **97.** F. Pauli, *Wehrmachtsoffiziere in der Bundeswehr* (Paderborn, 2010); R. Stumpf, 'Die Wiederverwendung von Generalen und die Neubildung militärischen Eliten in Deutschland und Österreich nach 1945', in K.J. Bremm et al. (eds.), *Enschieden für Frieden: 50 Jahre Bundeswehr* (Freiburg, 2005), pp. 73–96; H.R. Hammerich and R.J. Schlaffer (eds.), *Militärische Aufbaugenerationen der Bundeswehr 1955 bis 1970* (Munich, 2011); B.M. Scianna, 'Rebuilding an Austrian army: The Bundesheer's founding generation and the Wehrmacht past, 1955–1970', *WiH*, 26 (2019), 105–23. **98.** Lapp, *Vincenz Müller*, pp. 151–2; H. Ehlert, 'Die Hauptverwaltung für Ausbildung (1949–1952)', in Diedrich et al. (eds.), *Bewaffneten Organe*, pp. 253–80 at 255–8, 272. **99.** Wenzke, 'Nationale Volksarmee', pp. 435–9, 452–6. **100.** A. Bickford, *Fallen elites: The military other in post-unification Germany* (Stanford, CA, 2011). **101.** H. Boack, 'Forgotten female soldiers in an unknown army: German women working behind the lines, 1914–1918', *Women's History Review*, 23 (2014), 577–94 at 583–8; M. Healy, *Vienna and the fall of the Habsburg empire: Total war and everyday life in World War I* (Cambridge, 2004), pp. 204–9. **102.** L.D.H. Sauerteig, 'Sex, medicine and morality during the First World War', in R. Cooter et al. (eds.), *War, medicine and modernity* (Stroud, 1998), pp. 167–88; Crouthamel, *Intimate history*, pp. 18–63; A. Watson, *Ring of steel* (London, 2014), pp. 290–2. **103.** D. Ellerbrock, 'Warum Germania bewaffnet war und trotzdem nicht wählen dürfte', *Werkstatt Geschichte*, 64 (2013), 31–54 at 50–3; B. Kundrus, 'Gender wars: The First World War and the construction of gender relations in the Weimar Republic', in Hagemann and Schüler-Springorum (eds.), *Home/front*, pp. 159–80. **104.** *GSWW*, V, 945–9, 1003–5; U. Frevert, *Women in German history* (Leamington Spa, 1990), pp. 207ff; C. Koonz, *Mothers in the fatherland* (London, 1986). **105.** R. Mühlhäuser, *Sex and the Nazi soldier: Violent, commercial and consensual contacts during the war in the Soviet Union, 1941–1945* (Edinburgh, 2020); B. Beck, 'Rape: The military trials of sexual crimes committed by soldiers in the Wehrmacht', in Hagemann and Schüler-Springorum (eds.), *Home/front*, pp. 255–73; R. Scheck, 'Collaborators of the heart: The forbidden love affairs of French prisoners of war and German women in Nazi Germany', *JMH*, 90 (2018), 352–82; M. Röger, *Wartime relations: Intimacy, violence, and prostitution in occupied Poland, 1939–1945* (Oxford, 2021), and idem and R. Leiserowitz (eds.), *Women and men at war: A gender perspective on World War II and its aftermath in Central and Eastern Europe* (Osnabrück, 2012). **106.** F. Virgil, *Shorn women: Gender and punishment in Liberation France* (New York, 2002); 'Sexuality, Holocaust, stigma', *GH*, 39, no. 1 (2021), special issue. **107.** Neitzel and Wetzer, *Soldaten*, pp. 171–2; W. Lower, *Hitler's furies: German women in the Nazi killing fields* (Boston, MA, 2014). **108.** L. Treber, *Mythos Trümmerfrauen* (Essen, 2014). **109.** Quoted in S. Stephenson, *The final battle: Soldiers of the Western Front and the German Revolution of 1918* (Cambridge, 2009), p. 95. **110.** S. Lange, *Der Fahneneid. Die Geschichte der Schwurverpflichtung im deutschen Militär* (Bremen, 2002), pp. 87–111; W. Mühlhausen, 'Hans von Seeckt und die Organisation der Reichswehr in der Weimarer

Republik', in K.H. Lutz et al. (eds.), *Reform, Reorganisation, Transformation* (Munich, 2010), pp. 245–62 at 254–6. **111.** Lange, *Fahneneid*, pp. 113–46. **112.** Stein, *Waffen SS*, pp. 20–2, 29–30; Leleu, *Waffen-SS*, pp. 460–70, 570–83. **113.** R. Schlaffer, 'Der Wehrbeauftragte – Kontrolleur der Inneren Führung der Bundeswehr', in Bremm et al. (eds.), *Entschieden für Frieden*, pp. 397–407. **114.** Lange, *Fahneneid*, pp. 147–83, 251–3; S.B. Gareis, 'The making of Germany's security and defence policy', in Wiesner (ed.), *German defence politics*, pp. 49–77. **115.** R.J. Schlaffer and W. Schmidt (eds.), *Wolf Graf von Baudissin, 1907–1993* (Münster, 2007). **116.** M.G. Lux, *Innere Führung: A superior concept of leadership?* (Berlin, 2009); K.U. Bormann, 'Als "Schule der Nation" überfordert. Konzeptionelle Überlegungen zur Erziehung des Soldaten in der Aufbauphase der Bundeswehr', in Lutz et al. (eds.), *Reform, Reorganisation, Transformation*, pp. 345–68; F. Nägler, 'Innere Führung', in Bremm et al. (eds.), *Entschieden für Frieden*, pp. 321–39. **117.** Quoted in D.C. Large, *Germans to the front: West German rearmament in the Adenauer era* (Chapel Hill, NC, 1996), p. 199. **118.** R. Müller and M. Lachmann, *Spielmann – Trompeter – Hoboist: Aus der Geschichte der deutschen Militärmusiker* (Berlin, 1988), pp. 36–7; M.F. Heidler, 'Militärreformen im Spiegel der Militärmusik', in Lutz et al. (eds.), *Reform, Reorganisation, Transformation*, pp. 523–43. **119.** Scianna, 'Rebuilding an Austrian army', passim. **120.** D. Abenheim, *Reforging the iron cross: The search for tradition in the West German armed forces* (Princeton, NJ, 1988); R. Wenzke, 'Die preußischen Heeresreformen als militärhistorische Tradition in der Nationalen Volksarmee', in Lutz et al. (eds.), *Reform, Reorganisation, Transformation* (Munich, 2010), pp. 369–81. **121.** *Verräter? Vorbilder? Kontroverse Deutungen des 20. Juli 1944 seit 1945* (issued by the Haus der Geschichte Baden Württemberg, Berlin, 2016); J. Lockenour, *Soldiers as citizens: Former Wehrmacht officers in the Federal Republic of Germany, 1945–1955* (Lincoln, NE, 2001), pp. 153–88. **122.** P.E. Swett, 'Neither too hard, nor too soft: Hellmuth Heye, the Quick controversy and West Germany's "Citizens in uniform"', *GH*, 37 (2019), 54–76; D. Bald, 'Die Militärreform in der "Ära Brandt"', in Bremm et al. (eds.), *Entschieden für Frieden*, pp. 341–53. **123.** E. Birk et al. (eds.), *Tradition für die Bundeswehr* (Berlin, 2012). The 2018 instructions are available at https://www.bmvg.de/de/aktuelles/der-neue-traditionserlass-23232 (accessed 5 December 2021). **124.** J.E. Edmonds, *The occupation of the Rhineland, 1918–1929* (London, 1944); M. Pawley, *The watch on the Rhine* (London, 2007). **125.** M. Gebhardt, *Crimes unspoken: The rape of German women at the end of the Second World War* (Cambridge, MA, 2015); I.-S. Kowalczuk and S. Wolle, *Roter Stern über Deutschland. Sowjetische Truppen in der DDR*, 2nd ed. (Berlin, 2010), pp. 35–40, 94–7. **126.** C.T. Müller, 'Stationierung und Mobilität ausländischer Truppen in Deutschlands während des "Kalten Krieges"', in C. Rass (ed.), *Militärische Migration vom Altertum bis zur Gegenwart* (Leiden, 2016), pp. 189–202. **127.** A.R. Seipp, "We have to pay the price": German workers and the US Army, 1945–1989', *WiH*, 26 (2019), 563–84. **128.** C. Lusane, *Hitler's Black victims: The historical experiences of Afro-Germans, European Blacks, Africans, and African Americans in the Nazi era* (London, 2003); T.M. Campt, *Other Germans: Black Germans and the politics of race, gender, and memory in the Third Reich* (Ann Arbor, MI, 2004). **129.** T.L. Schroer, *Recasting race after World War II: Germans and African Americans in American-occupied Germany* (Boulder, CO, 2007), p. 185. **130.** Quoted in T.W. Maulucci, Jr. and D. Junkers (eds.), *GIs in Germany: The social, economic, cultural and political history of the American military presence* (Cambridge, 2013), p. 18. **131.** S. Eisenhuth, *Die Schutzmacht: Die Amerikaner in Berlin, 1945–1994* (Göttingen, 2018). **132.** K.-D. Henke, *Die amerikanische Besetzung Deutschlands*, 2nd ed. (Munich, 1996). **133.** K. Arlt, 'Sowjetische (russische) Truppen in Deutschland (1945–1994)', in Diedrich et al. (eds.), *Bewaffneten Organe*, pp. 593–632. **134.** Kowalczuk and Wolle, *Roter Stern*, p. 221. **135.** S. Hahn, 'How varied the image of heart trauma has become: The development of cardiovascular surgery during the First World War', in M. Larner et al. (eds.), *War and medicine* (London, 2008), pp. 46–55. **136.** H.H. Herwig,

The First World War: Germany and Austria-Hungary, 1914–1918 (London, 1997), p. 297. **137.** Ziemann, *Violence and the German soldier*, p. 23; J.S. Haller Jr, *Battlefield medicine* (Carbondale, IL, 2011), pp. 157–8, 184–93. **138.** F. Reid, *Medicine in First World War Europe* (London, 2017), pp. 40, 51; J.H. Quataert, *Staging philanthropy: Patriotic women and the national imagination in dynastic Germany, 1813–1916* (Ann Arbor, MI, 2001), pp. 270–91, and her 'Women's wartime services under the cross: Patriotic communities in Germany, 1912–1918', in R. Chickering and S. Förster (eds.), *Great war, total war* (Cambridge, 2000), pp. 453–83. **139.** H.R. Perry, *Recycling the disabled: Army, medicine and modernity in World War I Germany* (Manchester, 2015). **140.** P. Lerner, *Hysterical men: War, psychiatry, and the politics of trauma in Germany, 1890–1930* (Ithaca, NY, 2003); W.U. Eckart, '"The most extensive experiment that the imagination can conceive": War, emotional stress, and German medicine, 1914–1918', in Chickering and Förster (eds.), *Great war, total war*, pp. 133–49. **141.** K. Hausen, 'The German nation's obligations to the heroes' widows of World War I', in M.R. Higonnet et al. (eds.), *Behind the lines: Gender and the two world wars* (New Haven, CT, 1987), pp. 126–40. **142.** D. Cohen, *The war come home: Disabled veterans in Britain and Germany, 1914–1939* (Berkeley, CA, 2001); Ziemann, *War experience*, pp. 240–52. **143.** *HDM*, VIII, 369. **144.** Lower, *Hitler's furies*, pp. 43–53. **145.** These claims have been made by N. Ohler, *Blitzed: Drugs in Nazi Germany* (London, 2015). **146.** Stargardt, *German war*, p. 192. **147.** J.M. Diehl, *The thanks of the fatherland: German veterans after the Second World War* (Chapel Hill, NC, 1993); Lockenour, *Soldiers as citizens*, pp. 33–63; Kühne, *Comradeship*, pp. 215–38. **148.** https://www.dbwv.de/ (accessed 5 December 2021). **149.** E. Grunwald and R. Vollmuth, 'Der Sanitätsdienst', in Bremm et al. (eds.), *Entschieden für Frieden*, pp. 183–98; Diedrich and Wenzke, *Getarnte Armee*, pp. 548–52; Zilian, *From confrontation to cooperation*, pp. 97–121. **150.** M. Stibbe, *Civilian internment during the First World War* (London, 2019); C. Jahr, 'Zivilisten als Kriegsgefangene. Die Internierung von "Feindstaaten Ausländern" in Deutschland während des Ersten Weltkrieges am Beispiel des "Engländerlagers" in Ruhleben', in R. Overmans (ed.), *In der Hand des Feindes* (Cologne, 1999), pp. 297–322. **151.** F. Bugnion, *Confronting the hell of the trenches* (Geneva, 2018), pp. 27–86. **152.** A.R. Kramer, 'Prisoners in the First World War', in S. Scheipers (ed.), *Prisoners in war* (Oxford, 2010), pp. 75–90. **153.** R.B. Arneson, *Total warfare and compulsory labor: A study of the military-industrial complex in Germany during World War I* (The Hague, 1964); G.D. Feldman, *Army, industry, and labor in Germany, 1914–1918* (Princeton, NJ, 1966), pp. 149–252. **154.** G. Wurzer, 'Das Schicksal der deutschen Kriegsgefangen in Rußland im Ersten Weltkrieg', in Overmans (ed.), *Hand des Feindes*, pp. 362–85; Bugnion, *Confronting*, pp. 86–94. **155.** A. Huber, 'The internment of prisoners of war and civilians in neutral Switzerland, 1916–19', in S. Manz et al. (eds.), *Internment during the First World War* (London, 2019), pp. 252–72; Bugnion, *Confronting*, pp. 75–86. **156.** M. Cox, *Hunger in war and peace: Women and children in Germany, 1914–1924* (Oxford, 2019), pp. 287–96. **157.** B. Cabanes, *The Great War and the origins of humanitarianism, 1918–1924* (Cambridge, 2014); N. Wylie, 'The 1929 Prisoner of War Convention and the building of the interwar prisoner of war regime', in Scheipers (ed.), *Prisoners*, pp. 91–108. **158.** R. Scheck, 'The treatment of Western prisoners of war in Nazi Germany', *WiH*, 28 (2021), 635–55. **159.** R. Overmans, 'The treatment of prisoners of war in the Eastern European theatre of operations, 1941–45', in Scheipers (ed.), *Prisoners*, pp. 127–40. **160.** M. Spoerer and J. Fleischhacker, 'Forced labourers in Nazi Germany', *Journal of Interdisciplinary History*, 33 (2002), 169–204; *GSWW*, V, 858–68, 1003–5. **161.** F. Bugnion, *The International Committee of the Red Cross and the protection of war victims* (Geneva, 2014), pp. 167–243; J.-C. Favez, *The Red Cross and the Holocaust* (Cambridge, 1999); S.P. Holbrook, *Target Switzerland: Swiss armed neutrality in World War II* (Cambridge, MA, 2003), pp. 143–56, 201–30. **162.** F. Théofilakis, *Les prisonniers de la guerre allemands en France, 1944–1949* (Paris, 2014); R. Bessel, *Germany 1945*

(London, 2009), pp. 199–203; Overmans, *Verluste*, pp. 284–92; Biess, *Homecomings*, pp. 45, 179–80, 204. **163.** Useful comparative statistics in R. Chickering, *Imperial Germany and the Great War* (Cambridge, 1998), p. 195, with more detail in *Wirtschaft und Statistik*, 2 (1922), pp. 385–7, 487; Bayerisches Kriegsarchiv, *Die Bayern im Großen Krieg, 1914–1918* (Munich, 1925), p. 595; F. v. Graevenitz, *Die Entwicklung des württembergischen Heerwesens* (Stuttgart, 1921), I, 13; Deák, *Beyond nationalism*, pp. 192–3; Cox, *Hunger*, pp. 85–134, 171–203, 242–3. **164.** Watson, *Ring of steel*, pp. 160–206. **165.** P. Nivet, *Les réfugiés français de la Grande Guerre* (Paris, 2004), pp. 75–6; C.J. Fischer, *Alsace to the Alsatians? Visions and division of Alsatian regionalism, 1870–1939* (New York, 2010), pp. 110–48; S.A. Wempe, *Revenants of the German empire: Colonial Germans, imperialism, and the League of Nations* (New York, 2019). **166.** M. Jones, *Founding Weimar: Violence and the German Revolution of 1918–19* (Cambridge, 2016), p. 211; J. Böhler, *Civil war in Central Europe, 1918–1921* (Oxford, 2020), pp. 102, 113. **167.** J. Corum, *Legion Condor, 1936–39* (Oxford, 2020), pp. 86–7. **168.** M. Clodfelter, *Warfare and armed conflicts: A statistical reference to casualty and other figures, 1500–2000* (Jefferson, NC, 2001), pp. 495–515. **169.** Overmans, *Verlüste*, pp. 212, 255–61. **170.** Ibid, pp. 230; Müller, *Unknown Eastern Front*, pp. 65, 87, 103, 158–83, 252. **171.** Overmans, *Verlüste*, pp. 220–1, 234. **172.** E. Heinemann, *What difference does a husband make? Women and marital status in Nazi and post-war Germany* (Berkeley, CA, 1999); Biess, *Homecomings*, pp. 120–5; Kühne, *Comradeship*, p. 228. **173.** R.M. Douglas, *Orderly and humane: The expulsion of Germans after the Second World War* (London, 2013); D.W. Gerlach, *The economy of ethnic cleansing: The transformation of the German-Czech borderlands after World War II* (Cambridge, 2017); A. Demshuk, *The lost German East: Forced migration and the politics of memory, 1945–1970* (Cambridge, 2014); R. Wittlinger, 'Taboo or tradition? The "Germans as victims" theme in the Federal Republic until the mid–1990s', in Niven (ed.), *Germans as victims*, pp. 62–75. **174.** Diedrich, 'Nationale Volksarmee', p. 350; P. Fichtenbauer and M.C. Ortner (eds.), *A history of the Austrian army from Maria Theresa to the present day* (Vienna, 2015), p. 292; www.bundeswehr.de (accessed 7 October 2021). **175.** H.P. Ullmann, *Der deutsche Steuerstaat: Geschichte der öffentlichen Finanzen vom 18. Jahrhundert bis heute* (Munich, 2005), pp. 90-8; Herwig, *First World War*, pp. 230–1, 257–9; Chickering, *Imperial Germany*, p. 195; O. Longchamp, 'Au service des intérêts financiers. Les débats autour de l'amortissement des dettes fédérales après la Deuxième Guerre Mondiale (1945–1955)', in V. Goebner et al. (eds.), *Kriegswirtschaft und Wirtschaftskriege* (Zurich, 2008), pp. 289–311. **176.** M. Spoerer and M. Hantke, 'The imposed gift of Versailles: The fiscal effects of restricting the size of Germany's armed forces, 1924–1929', *EcHR*, 63 (2010), 849–64. **177.** Ullmann, *Steuerstaat*, pp. 99-131. **178.** A. Tooze, *The wages of destruction* (London, 2006); Ullmann, *Steuerstaat*, pp. 142–78. **179.** *GSWW*, V, 678. **180.** J. Scherner and E.N. White (eds.), *Paying for Hitler's war: The consequences of Nazi hegemony for Europe* (Cambridge, 2016); M. Mazower, *Hitler's empire: Nazi rule in occupied Europe* (London, 2008), pp. 259–93; *GSWW*, V, 298–307. **181.** Kowalczuk and Wolle, *Roter Stern*, pp. 68-75; J. Farquharson, '"A game of cat and mouse"? Dismantling for reparations in the British zone of Germany, 1947–1950', *GH*, 15 (1997), 333–57. **182.** Deutsche Bundestag, *Die Entschädigungszahlungen an jüdische Opfer des Nationalsozialismus* (Berlin, 2007), p. 3. See generally, J. Fisch, *Reparationen nach dem Zweiten Weltkrieg* (Munich, 1992). **183.** T. Vonyó, *The economic consequences of the war: West Germany's growth miracle after 1945* (Cambridge, 2018); Ullmann, *Steuerstaat*, pp. 186–213. **184.** M. Graf, 'Before Strauss: The East German struggle to avoid bankruptcy during the debt crisis revisited', *IHR*, 42 (2020), 737–54. **185.** *SIPRI yearbook 2021* (Oxford, 2021), p. 265; B. Giegerich, 'The North Atlantic Treaty Organisation', in H. Meijer and M. Wyss (eds.), *The handbook of European defence policies and armed forces* (Oxford, 2018), pp. 277–91 at 384–90; G. Hauser and M. Mantovani, 'Austria and Switzerland', in ibid, pp. 197–219 at 201–7; Jaun, *Schweizer Armee*, pp.

532–3. **186.** S. Broadberry and M. Harrison (eds.), *The economics of World War I* (Cambridge, 2005), which also includes good overviews on Germany and Austria-Hungary. **187.** Herwig, *First World War*, pp. 230–44, 272–83, 352–61. **188.** Feldman, *Army, industry, and labor*, pp. 197–249; J.A. Moses, *German trade unionism from Bismarck to Hitler*, 2 vols. (London, 1982), II, pp. 177–212; H. James, *Krupp: The history of a legendary firm* (Princeton, NJ, 2012), pp. 135–9. **189.** Creveld, 'World War I and the revolution in logistics', and A. Offer, 'The blockade of Germany and the strategy of starvation, 1914–1918', both in Chickering and Förster (eds.), *Great war, total war*. **190.** H. Strachan, *The First World War* (Oxford, 2001), pp. 1,027–36. **191.** A. Offer, *The First World War: An agricultural interpretation* (Oxford, 1989); A. Roerkohl, *Hungerblockade und Heimatfront* (Stuttgart, 1991); J. Kocka, *Facing total war: German society 1914–1918* (Ann Arbor, MI, 1984), pp. 121–2; Weinreb, *Modern hungers*, pp. 17–23; N.P. Howard, 'The social and political consequences of the Allied food blockade of Germany, 1918–19', *GH*, 11 (1993), 161–88. **192.** Cox, *Hunger*, pp. 47–59, 202–4, 237–366; Weinreb, *Modern hungers*, pp. 29–39. **193.** G. Aly, *Hitler's beneficiaries* (London, 2007); Weinreb, *Modern hungers*, pp. 39–86; *GSWW*, V, 462–73, 508–36. **194.** Tooze, *Wages of destruction*, p. 673. **195.** A. Toprani, *Oil and the great powers: Britain and Germany, 1914–1945* (Oxford, 2019), pp. 145–252. **196.** For an illuminating case study, see C. Michaelis, *Rüstungsmanagement der Ministerien Todt und Speer. Das Beispiel Panzerentwicklung und Panzerkommission* (Münster, 2020). **197.** *GSWW*, I, 195–315; V, 293–831. **198.** Editors' introduction to Diedrich et al. (eds.), *Bewaffneten Organe*, pp. 20–1. **199.** A.M. Eckert, *West Germany and the Iron Curtain: Environment, economy, and culture in the borderlands* (Oxford, 2019). **200.** D.A. Browder, 'The GI dollar and the Wirtschaftswunder', *Journal of European Economic History*, 22 (1993), 601–11. **201.** Quote from P. Singer, *Corporate warriors: The rise of the privatised military industry* (Ithaca, NY, 2003), p. 54. See also G. Digutsch, *Das Ende der Nationalen Volksarmee und der Aufbau der Bundeswehr in den neuen Länder* (Frankfurt am Main, 2004), pp. 27–80, 342–53; Zilian, *From confrontation to cooperation*, pp. 161–70. **202.** T. Dyson, *The politics of German defence and security: Policy leadership and military reform in the post-Cold War era* (New York, 2007), pp. 77, 107–11, 141. **203.** H. Heumann, 'The armaments acquisition process', in Wiesner (ed.), *German defence politics*, pp. 251–80. **204.** E. Krahman, *States, citizens and the privatisation of security* (Cambridge, 2010), pp. 156–71; G. Richter, 'Privatisation in the German armed forces', T. Jäger and G. Kümmel (eds.), *Private Military and Security Companies* (Wiesbaden, 2007), pp. 165–76, and his 'Modernisation in the Bundeswehr: Privatisation and public-private partnerships', in Wiesner (ed.), *German defence politics*, pp. 281–91. **205.** K. Johanny, 'Ein Teil der Bundeswehr wie die Streitkräfte – 50 Jahre Bundeswehrverwaltung', in Bremm et al. (eds.), *Entschieden für Frieden*, pp. 199–214 at 210–11. **206.** James, *Krupp*, pp. 151–3, 180–204; R.I. Winklareth, *Naval shipbuilding in the world* (London, 2000), pp. 253–73. **207.** Wenzke, 'Nationale Volksarmee', pp. 476–7; H. Fock, *Kampfschiffe. Marineschiffbau auf deutschen Werften 1870 bis heute* (Hamburg, 1995), pp. 178–83. **208.** D.H. Kollmer, 'Die materielle Aufrüstung der Bundeswehr von den Anfängen bis heute', in Bremm et al. (eds.), *Entschieden für Frieden*, pp. 215–30; E. Rössler, *Die deutschen U-Boote und ihre Werften*, 2 vols. (Bonn, 1979–80), II, 155–85; Fock, *Kampfschiffe*, pp. 184–6. **209.** J. Stüssi-Lauterburg and S. Frey, *Unvollständiges Protokoll eines Krieges, der nicht stattfand* (Lenzburg, 2009), pp. 24–68; R. Jaun and D. Rieder (eds.), *Schweizer Rüstung* (Bern, 2010); Schürmann, *Helvetische Jäger*, pp. 101–217. **210.** A. Sakaki et al., *Reluctant warriors: Germany, Japan, and their US alliance dilemma* (Washington, DC, 2020), pp. 135–71. **211.** *Der Spiegel*, 3 December 2012. **212.** *SIPRI yearbook 2021*, pp. 297–8. **213.** R. Evertz, 'Germany', in C. Bakker and M. Sossai (eds.), *Multilevel regulation of military and security companies* (Oxford, 2012), pp. 215–32.

Index